STREE

Lancashire

First published in 1997 by

Philip's, a division of
Octopus Publishing Group Ltd
2-4 Heron Quays, London E14 4JP

Second colour edition 2001
Third impression 2004

ISBN 0-540-07976-6 (pocket)

Printed and bound in Spain
by Cayfosa-Quebecor

Contents

III **Key to map symbols**

IV **Key to map pages**

VI **Route planning**

VIII **Administrative and Postcode boundaries**

1 **Street maps** at 2½ inches to 1 mile

220 **Street maps** at 1¼ inches to 1 mile

237 **Street maps** at 2½ inches to 1 mile

239 **Index** of towns and villages

240 **Index** of streets, hospitals, industrial estates, railway stations, schools, shopping centres and universities

Digital Data

The exceptionally high-quality mapping found in this book is available as digital data in TIFF format, which is easily convertible to other bitmapped (raster) image formats.

The index is also available in digital form as a standard database table. It contains all the details found in the printed index together with the National Grid reference for the map square in which each entry is named.

For further information and to discuss your requirements, please contact Philip's on 020 7644 6932 or james.mann@philips-maps.co.uk

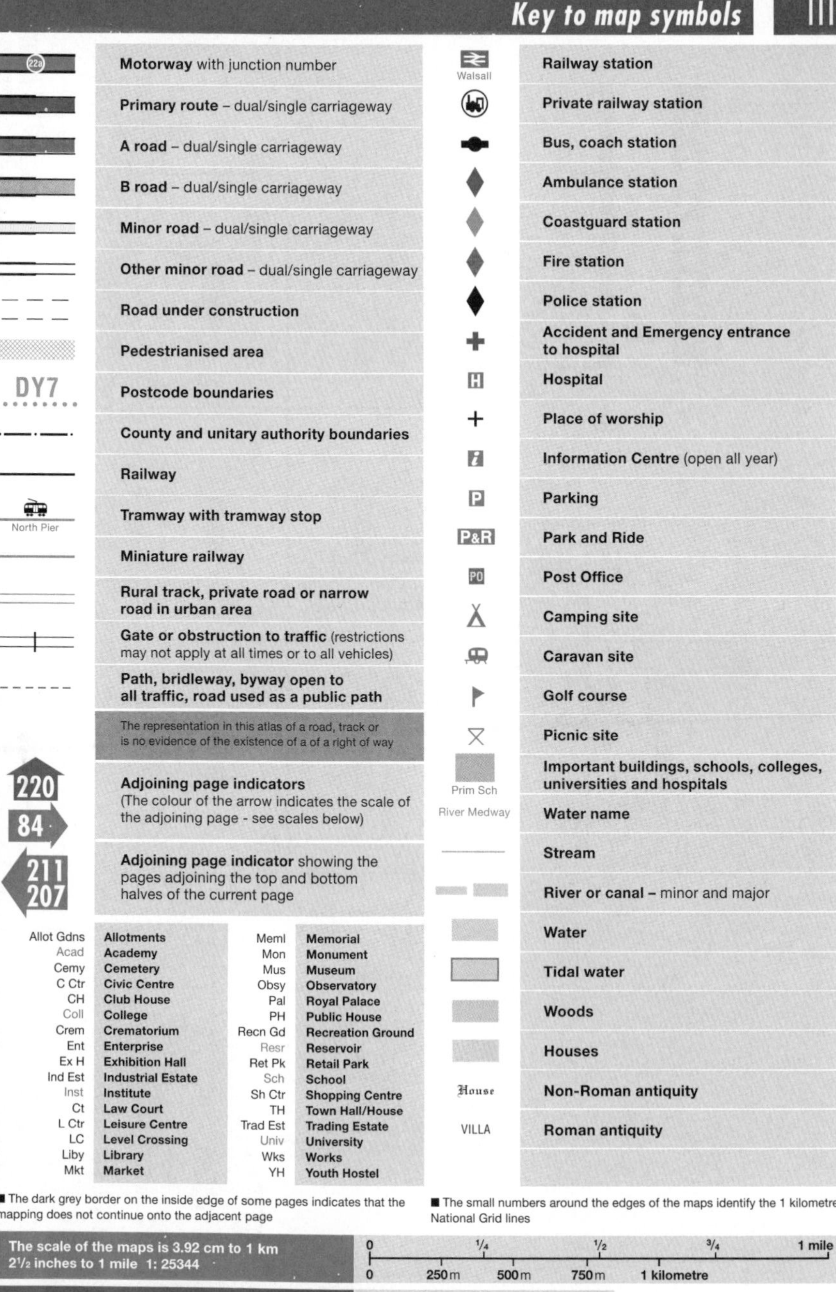
22a
Motorway with junction number
Primary route – dual/single carriageway
A road – dual/single carriageway
B road – dual/single carriageway
Minor road – dual/single carriageway
Other minor road – dual/single carriageway
Road under construction
Pedestrianised area
DY7
Postcode boundaries
County and unitary authority boundaries
Railway
North Pier
Tramway with tramway stop
Miniature railway
Rural track, private road or narrow road in urban area
Gate or obstruction to traffic (restrictions may not apply at all times or to all vehicles)
Path, bridleway, byway open to all traffic, road used as a public path
The representation in this atlas of a road, track or is no evidence of the existence of a of a right of way
220
84
Adjoining page indicators (The colour of the arrow indicates the scale of the adjoining page - see scales below)
211
207
Adjoining page indicator showing the pages adjoining the top and bottom halves of the current page
Allot Gdns Allotments
Acad Academy
Cemy Cemetery
C Ctr Civic Centre
CH Club House
Coll College
Crem Crematorium
Ent Enterprise
Ex H Exhibition Hall
Ind Est Industrial Estate
Inst Institute
Ct Law Court
L Ctr Leisure Centre
LC Level Crossing
Liby Library
Mkt Market
Meml Memorial
Mon Monument
Mus Museum
Obsy Observatory
Pal Royal Palace
PH Public House
Recn Gd Recreation Ground
Resr Reservoir
Ret Pk Retail Park
Sch School
Sh Ctr Shopping Centre
TH Town Hall/House
Trad Est Trading Estate
Univ University
Wks Works
YH Youth Hostel
Walsall
Railway station
Private railway station
Bus, coach station
Ambulance station
Coastguard station
Fire station
Police station
Accident and Emergency entrance to hospital
H
Hospital
Place of worship
i
Information Centre (open all year)
P
Parking
P&R
Park and Ride
PO
Post Office
Camping site
Caravan site
Golf course
Picnic site
Prim Sch
Important buildings, schools, colleges, universities and hospitals
River Medway
Water name
Stream
River or canal – minor and major
Water
Tidal water
Woods
Houses
House
Non-Roman antiquity
VILLA
Roman antiquity
■ The dark grey border on the inside edge of some pages indicates that the mapping does not continue onto the adjacent page
■ The small numbers around the edges of the maps identify the 1 kilometre National Grid lines
The scale of the maps is 3.92 cm to 1 km
2½ inches to 1 mile 1: 25344
0 ¼ ½ ¾ 1 mile
0 250m 500m 750m 1 kilometre

The scale of the maps on pages numbered in green is 1.96 cm to 1 km (1¼ inches to 1 mile) 1: 50688

0 ¼ ½ ¾ 1 mile

0 250m 500m 750m 1 kilometre

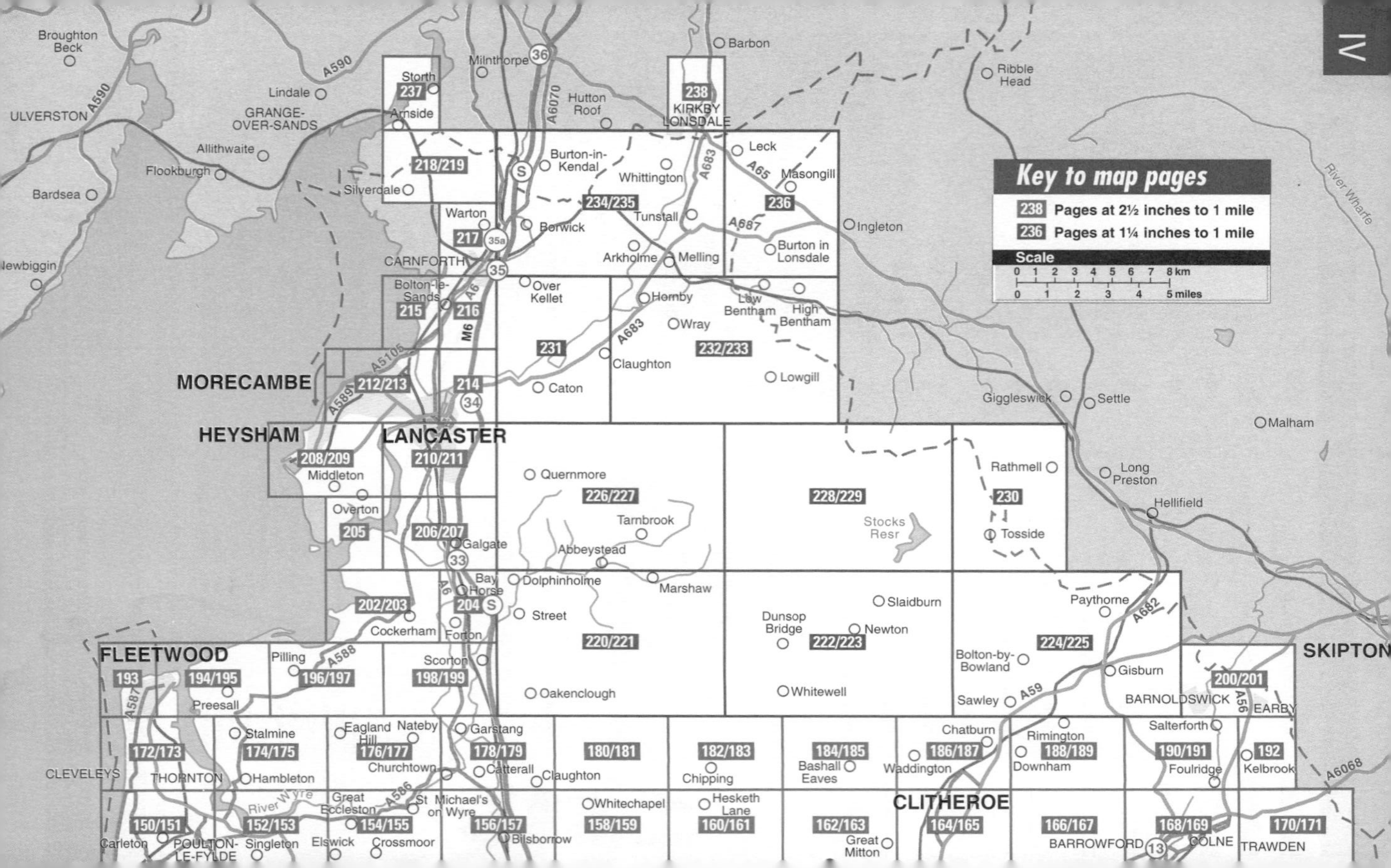
Key to map pages
238 Pages at 2½ inches to 1 mile
236 Pages at 1¼ inches to 1 mile
Scale
0 1 2 3 4 5 6 7 8 km
0 1 2 3 4 5 miles
MORECAMBE
HEYSHAM
LANCASTER
FLEETWOOD
SKIPTON
CLITHEROE
CARNFORTH
ULVERSTON
GRANGE-OVER-SANDS
KIRKBY LONSDALE
CLEVELEYS
THORNTON
POULTON-LE-FYLDE
BARNOLDSWICK
EARBY
BARROWFORD
COLNE
TRAWDEN
237 218/219 217 215 216 214 212/213 208/209 210/211 205 206/207 202/203 204
238 234/235 236 231 232/233 226/227 228/229 230 220/221 222/223 224/225
193 194/195 196/197 198/199 200/201
172/173 174/175 176/177 178/179 180/181 182/183 184/185 186/187 188/189 190/191 192
150/151 152/153 154/155 156/157 158/159 160/161 162/163 164/165 166/167 168/169 170/171
Broughton Beck
Lindale
Allithwaite
Flookburgh
Bardsea
Newbiggin
Storth
Arnside
Silverdale
Milnthorpe
Hutton Roof
Barbon
Ribble Head
Burton-in-Kendal
Whittington
Warton
Borwick
Tunstall
Arkholme
Melling
Leck
Masongill
Burton in Lonsdale
Ingleton
Bolton-le-Sands
Over Kellet
Hornby
Wray
Low Bentham
High Bentham
Claughton
Caton
Lowgill
Giggleswick
Settle
Malham
Middleton
Overton
Quernmore
Tarnbrook
Abbeystead
Galgate
Bay Horse
Dolphinholme
Marshaw
Stocks Resr
Rathmell
Tosside
Long Preston
Hellifield
Cockerham
Forton
Street
Slaidburn
Dunsop Bridge
Newton
Paythorne
Bolton-by-Bowland
Gisburn
Sawley
Pilling
Preesall
Scorton
Oakenclough
Whitewell
Stalmine
Eagland Hill
Nateby
Garstang
Churchtown
Catterall
Claughton
Chipping
Bashall Eaves
Waddington
Chatburn
Rimington
Downham
Salterforth
Foulridge
Kelbrook
Hambleton
River Wyre
Great Eccleston
St Michael's on Wyre
Whitechapel
Hesketh Lane
Carleton
Singleton
Elswick
Crossmoor
Bilsborrow
Great Mitton
River Wharfe
A590
A6070
A683
A65
A687
A6
M6
A5105
A589
A588
A587
A586
A59
A682
A56
A6068
36
35a
35
34
33
13
S

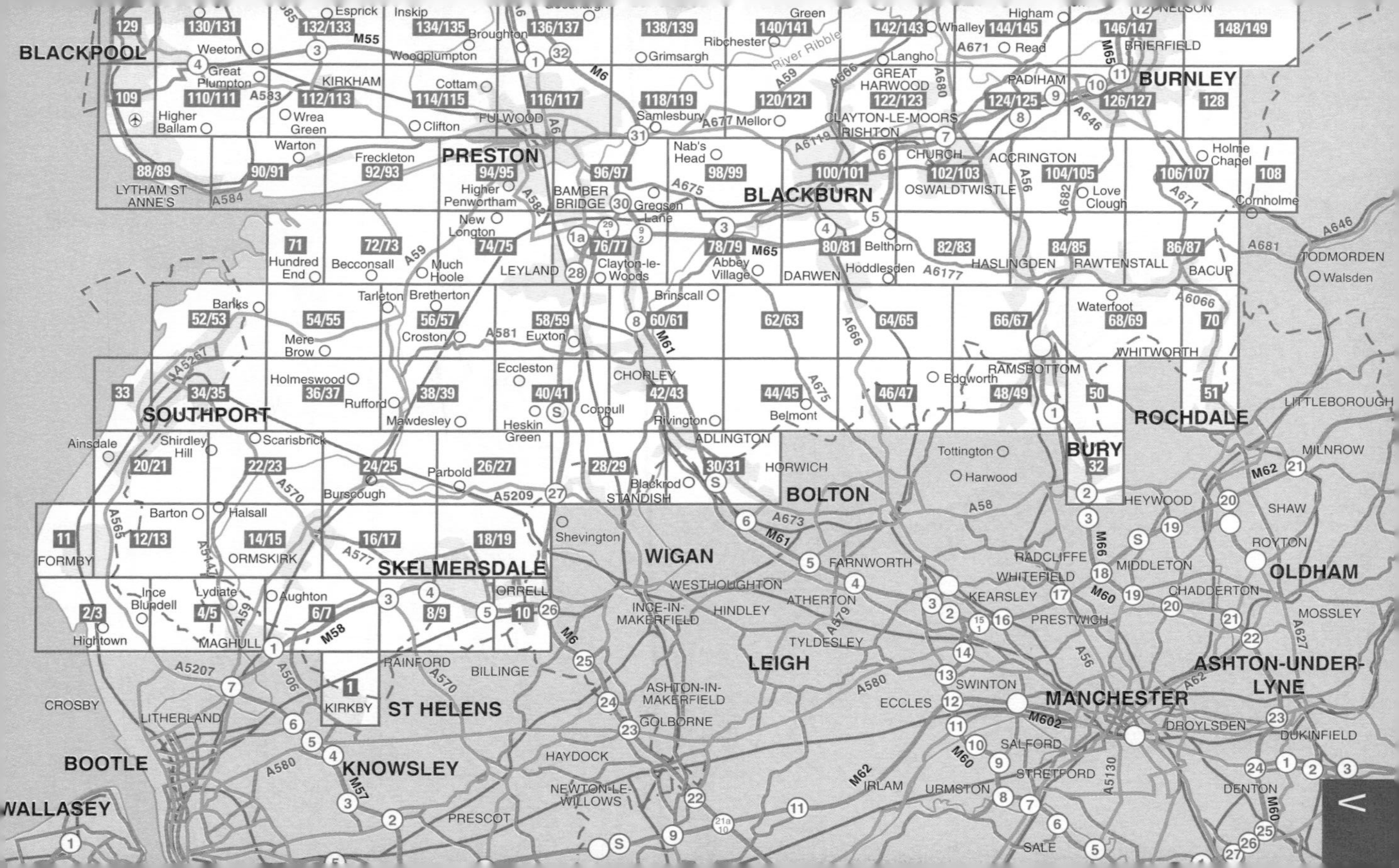
V
BLACKPOOL
PRESTON
BLACKBURN
BURNLEY
SOUTHPORT
SKELMERSDALE
WIGAN
BOLTON
BURY
ROCHDALE
OLDHAM
ASHTON-UNDER-LYNE
MANCHESTER
LEIGH
ST HELENS
KNOWSLEY
BOOTLE
WALLASEY
LYTHAM ST ANNE'S
KIRKHAM
FULWOOD
LEYLAND
CHORLEY
DARWEN
ACCRINGTON
OSWALDTWISTLE
CHURCH
RISHTON
CLAYTON-LE-MOORS
GREAT HARWOOD
PADIHAM
BRIERFIELD
NELSON
HASLINGDEN
RAWTENSTALL
BACUP
TODMORDEN
Walsden
Cornholme
Holme Chapel
WHITWORTH
RAMSBOTTOM
LITTLEBOROUGH
MILNROW
SHAW
ROYTON
HEYWOOD
MIDDLETON
CHADDERTON
MOSSLEY
DUKINFIELD
DROYLSDEN
DENTON
RADCLIFFE
WHITEFIELD
PRESTWICH
KEARSLEY
FARNWORTH
WESTHOUGHTON
ATHERTON
TYLDESLEY
HINDLEY
INCE-IN-MAKERFIELD
ASHTON-IN-MAKERFIELD
GOLBORNE
SWINTON
ECCLES
SALFORD
STRETFORD
URMSTON
IRLAM
SALE
HAYDOCK
NEWTON-LE-WILLOWS
PRESCOT
BILLINGE
RAINFORD
KIRKBY
ORRELL
STANDISH
ADLINGTON
HORWICH
Shevington
FORMBY
ORMSKIRK
MAGHULL
CROSBY
LITHERLAND
Hightown
Ince Blundell
Lydiate
Aughton
Barton
Halsall
Ainsdale
Shirdley Hill
Scarisbrick
Burscough
Parbold
Rufford
Holmeswood
Mawdesley
Heskin Green
Eccleston
Coppull
Blackrod
Rivington
Belmont
Edgworth
Tottington
Harwood
Banks
Mere Brow
Tarleton
Bretherton
Croston
Euxton
Much Hoole
Hundred End
Becconsall
New Longton
Higher Penwortham
BAMBER BRIDGE
Gregson Lane
Clayton-le-Woods
Abbey Village
Brinscall
Hoddlesden
Belthorn
Waterfoot
Love Clough
Nab's Head
Samlesbury
Mellor
Ribchester
Grimsargh
Green
Langho
Whalley
Read
Higham
Broughton
Woodplumpton
Inskip
Esprick
Weeton
Great Plumpton
Wrea Green
Higher Ballam
Warton
Freckleton
Clifton
Cottam
River Ribble
M6
M55
M65
M61
M58
M57
M62
M60
M66
M602
A6
A59
A56
A58
A565
A570
A577
A580
A584
A583
A582
A581
A5209
A5147
A5207
A5267
A506
A573
A579
A673
A675
A666
A677
A6119
A6177
A6066
A680
A682
A671
A671
A681
A646
A627
A62
A5130
129
130/131
132/133
134/135
136/137
138/139
140/141
142/143
144/145
146/147
148/149
109
110/111
112/113
114/115
116/117
118/119
120/121
122/123
124/125
126/127
128
88/89
90/91
92/93
94/95
96/97
98/99
100/101
102/103
104/105
106/107
108
71
72/73
74/75
76/77
78/79
80/81
82/83
84/85
86/87
52/53
54/55
56/57
58/59
60/61
62/63
64/65
66/67
68/69
70
33
34/35
36/37
38/39
40/41
42/43
44/45
46/47
48/49
50
51
20/21
22/23
24/25
26/27
28/29
30/31
32
11
12/13
14/15
16/17
18/19
2/3
4/5
6/7
8/9
10
1

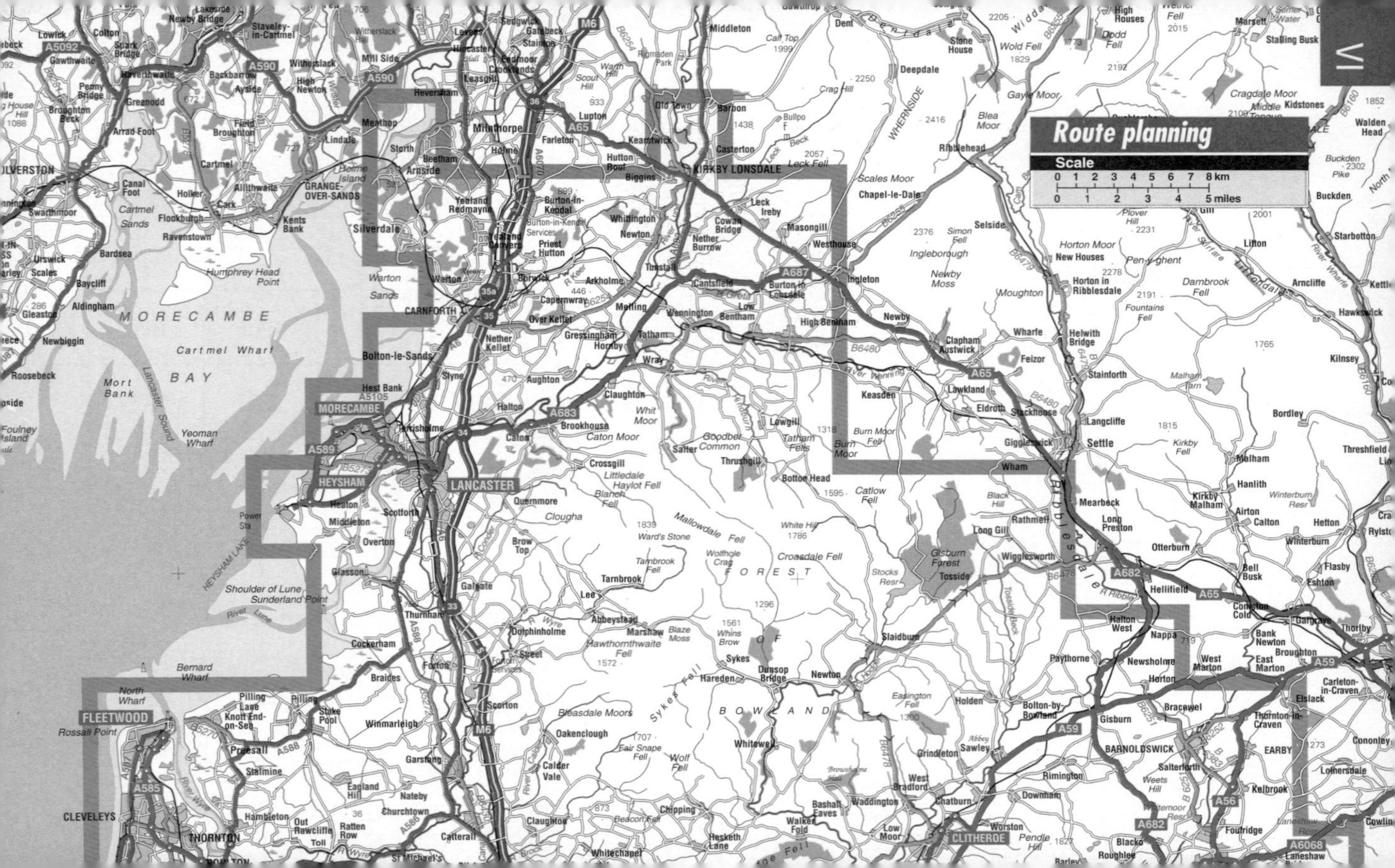
Route planning
Scale
0 1 2 3 4 5 6 7 8 km
0 1 2 3 4 5 miles
LANCASTER
MORECAMBE
HEYSHAM
FLEETWOOD
CLEVELEYS
THORNTON
CARNFORTH
KIRKBY LONSDALE
CLITHEROE
BARNOLDSWICK
GRANGE-OVER-SANDS
MORECAMBE BAY
FOREST OF BOWLAND
Ribblesdale
Settle
Ingleton
Ingleborough
Whernside
Pen-y-ghent
Milnthorpe
Arnside
Silverdale
Garstang
Slaidburn
Gisburn
Hellifield
Malham
Skipton
Ulverston
Cartmel
Kendal
Bentham
Halton
Caton
Galgate
Scorton
Pilling
Preesall
Dunsop Bridge
Newton
Gargrave
Earby
A65
A683
A687
A590
A6
M6
A682
A59
A56
A588

VII
BLACKPOOL
PRESTON
BLACKBURN
BURNLEY
ACCRINGTON
ROCHDALE
BURY
BOLTON
WIGAN
CHORLEY
LEIGH
MANCHESTER
SALFORD
OLDHAM
ASHTON-UNDER-LYNE
ST HELENS
SKELMERSDALE
SOUTHPORT
BOOTLE
LYTHAM ST ANNE'S
FORMBY
CROSBY
ORMSKIRK
LEYLAND
DARWEN
HORWICH
RAWTENSTALL
HASLINGDEN
RAMSBOTTOM
HEYWOOD
MIDDLETON
CHADDERTON
PRESTWICH
RADCLIFFE
FARNWORTH
SWINTON
ECCLES
STRETFORD
URMSTON
DENTON
DROYLSDEN
TODMORDEN
BACUP
NELSON
KIRKBY
PRESCOT
WALLASEY
FULWOOD
KIRKHAM
FRECKLETON
RIVER RIBBLE

Major administrative and
Postcode boundaries
County and unitary authority boundaries
District boundaries
Postcode boundaries
Area covered by this atlas
Scale
0 5 10 15 km
0 5 10 miles
Cumbria
North Yorkshire
Lancashire
Lancaster
Ribble Valley
Wyre
Fylde
Blackpool
Preston
South Ribble
Chorley
West Lancashire
Hyndburn
Burnley
Pendle
Rossendale
Blackburn with Darwen
Calderdale
Rochdale
Bolton
Bury
Wigan
St Helens
Sefton
SD
SJ
LA11
LA7
LA6
LA5
LA4
LA3
LA2
LA1
BD24
BD23
BD23
BB18
BB7
BB9
BB8
BB12
BB10
BB11
BB6
BB1
BB2
BB5
BB3
BB4
OL14
OL13
OL12
HX7
BL0
BL7
BL8
BL6
BL9
FY7
FY6
FY5
FY2
FY3
FY1
FY4
FY8
PR3
PR2
PR1
PR4
PR5
PR6
PR7
PR9
PR8
L40
WN6
WN1
WN8
WN5
WN11
L37
L39
L38
L31
L29
L33
Arnside
Kirkby Lonsdale
Burton-in-Kendal
Silverdale
Burton in Lonsdale
Carnforth
High Bentham
Wray
Halton
Morecambe
Caton
Heysham
Lancaster
Overton
Galgate
Glasson
Dolphinholme
Forton
Rathmell
Slaidburn
Dunsop Bridge
Gisburn
Pilling
Fleetwood
Barnoldswick
Salterforth
Garstang
Bleasdale
West Bradford
Downham
Cleveleys
Hambleton
Chipping
Clitheroe
Great Eccleston
Barley
Colne
Carleton
Trawden
Goosnargh
Longridge
Nelson
Whalley
Blackpool
Catforth
Weeton
Burnley
Kirkham
Great Harwood
Fulwood
Mellor
Holme Chapel
Preston
Lytham St Anne's
Warton
Hoghton
Blackburn
Oswaldtwistle
Belthorn
Walmer Bridge
Haslingden
Leyland
Darwen
Bacup
Shawforth
Banks
Tarleton
Brinscall
Irwell Vale
Southport
Holmeswood
Eccleston
Chorley
Belmont
Ramsbottom
Tonacliffe
Ainsdale
Burscough
Parbold
Standish
Horwich
Bury
Haskayne
Ormskirk
Skelmersdale
Formby
Aughton
Orrell
Hightown
Maghull
30
40
50
60
70
80
90

Brookfield Farm
Voces Farm
Walkden House Farm
Hesketh's Shroggs
Sewage Works
Grayson's Farm
Barrow Nook Hall
Simonswood Brook
New Bridge Farm
L39
High Barn Farm
Abram's Farm
Wood House Farm
STOPGATE LA
Hall's Folly
Timber Yard
Wild Goose Slack
Gate House Bridge
SIMONSWOOD IND PK
Woodwards Plantation
Woods Farm
Bridge Farm
Southead
L33
NORTH PERIMETER RD
Spencer's House Farm
Eccleston House
Simonswood Moss
Ashcroft's Plantation
Acorn Venture Urban Farm
Works
NORTH MERSEY BSNS CTR
Sch
Northwood
KNOWSLEY IND PK
Top House Farm
BOUNDARY LA
KIRKBY
Football Academy
Orchard Works
CAPITOL TRAD EST
Kirkby Moss
Charley Wood
Sports Ctr
L32
COUNTY RD
ENTERPRISE WORKSHOPS

A
B
C
D
E
F
8
7
05
6
5
04
4
3
03
2
1
02
27
28
29
Mount Pleasant
ALEXANDRA RD
ALBERT RD
ELSWORTH CL
STAPLETON RD
Marsh Farm
Range High Sch
L37
ST LUKE'S CHURCH RD
Sewage Works
Works
Raven Meols Hills
Raven Moels Hills Nature Reserve
Sefton Coastal Path
Cambrai Cottage
Grange Farm
Altcar Training Camp
GRANGE RD
LC
DANGER AREA
River Alt
Battery Cottage
Sefton Coastal Path
DANGER AREA
L38
Altcar Rifle Range
DANGER AREA
MARK RD
HESTER CL
LOWER ALT RD
RATHBONE RD
VILLAGE WAY
WIGNALLS MEADOW
DANGER AREA
Formby Bank
Hightown
Liverpool Bay
BRENTWOOD CL
ALTON CL
MAYFAIR CL
Sefton Coastal Path

12
4

A
B
C
D
E
F
Lovelady's Farm
B5424 LIVERPOOL RD
A565
FORMBY BY-PASS
Alt Bridge
NEW CSWY
Long Covert
River Alt
L37
Engine Cotts
ENGINE LA
Main Sluice
ACRES LA
NEW MEADOW LA
MIDDLE WITHINS LA
Tickle's Farm
Top Withins
WITHINS LA
8
7
05
6
5
04
4
3
03
2
1
02
Moss Farm
NORTH END LA
North End
North End Farm
MARSH LA
New Moss Wood
Oliverson's Farm
Whitedge Farm
Riding's Moss Wood
Hamgate Farm
MOSS LA
Orrell Hill Wood
Lady Green Farm
SCAFFOLD LA
Lady Green
Weld Blundell Arms (PH)
Tristram's Farm
Rigmaiden Farm
Carr Houses
ST GEORGE'S RD
ALT RD
ERSLAKE WAY
EMERSON CL
WINDERMERE RD
THIRLMERE RD
Hightown
ORRELL HILL LA
B5193
Pheasant Inn (PH)
Orrell Hill Farm
LADY GREEN LA
CARR HOUSE LA
High Farm
L38
Ince Blundell
1 SANDILANDS GR
2 BLUNDELL AVE
3 BLUNDELL RD
ELMCROFT LA
SANDY LA
THE CROSS
MOOR LA
THE CLOSE
LADY GREEN
VICTORIA RD
BACK O'THE TOWN LA
HALL LA
Waterhen Clump
Sports Gd
Moor Farm
Cemy
PARK WALL RD
Holt's Hey Wood
CROSS BARN LA
Ince Blundell Hall
ELVINGTON RD
Wood Farm
GORSEY LA
Moss Farm
MOSS LA
MOOR LA
West Lodge
Flea Moss Wood
Sniggery Farm
Moss Wood
Woodham Knoll
L23
Sunnyfield Farm
B5193
A565
31
32

4

3
13

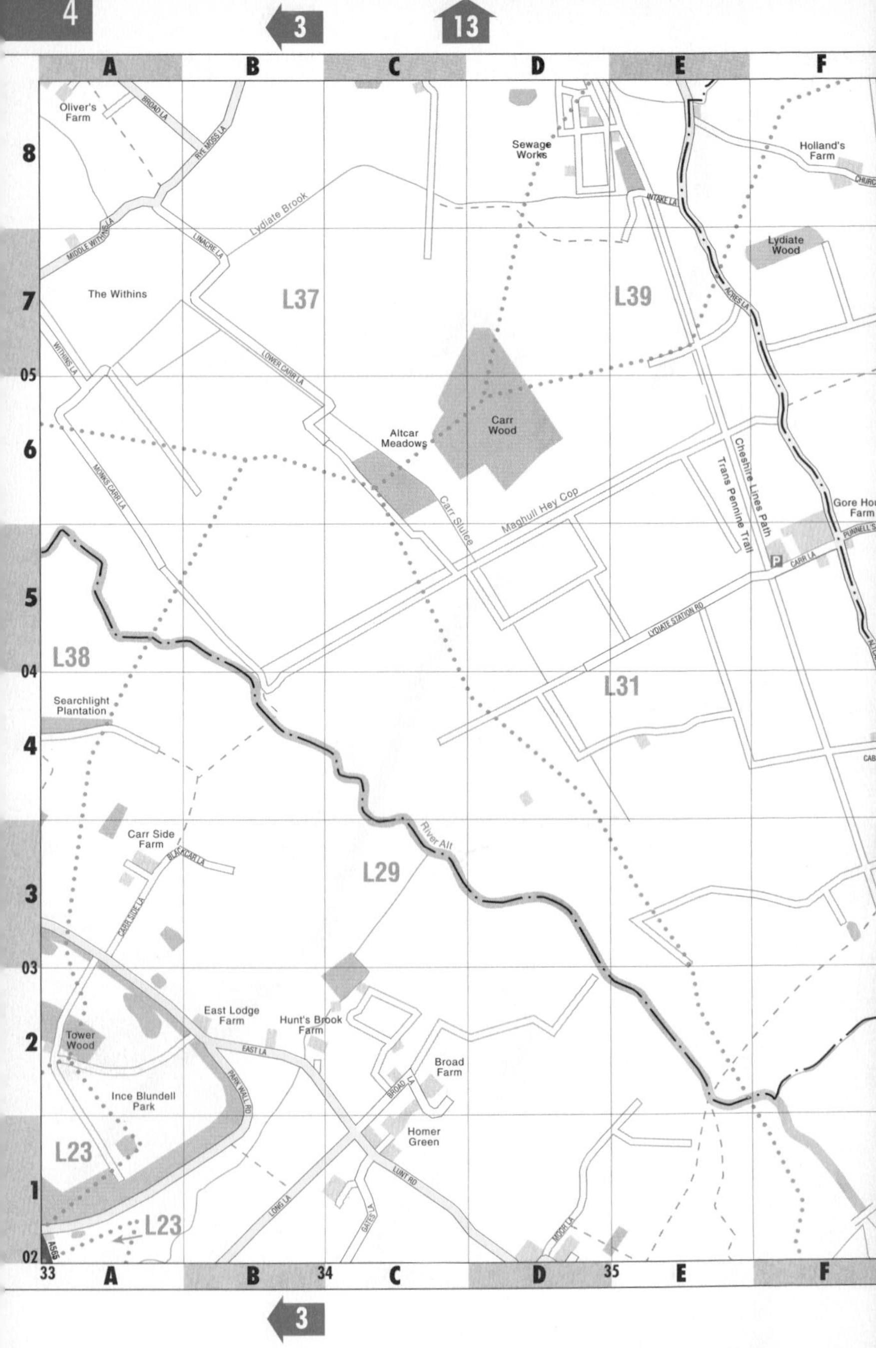
A
B
C
D
E
F
8
7
05
6
5
04
4
3
03
2
1
02
Oliver's Farm
BROAD LA
RYE MOSS LA
MIDDLE WITHINS LA
LINACRE LA
Lydiate Brook
Sewage Works
Holland's Farm
INTAKE LA
Lydiate Wood
The Withins
L37
L39
ACRES LA
WITHINS LA
LOWER CARR LA
Altcar Meadows
Carr Wood
MONKS CARR LA
Carr Sluice
Maghull Hey Cop
Trans Pennine Trail
Cheshire Lines Path
Gore Hou Farm
CARR LA
LYDIATE STATION RD
L38
Searchlight Plantation
L31
Carr Side Farm
BLACKCAR LA
River Alt
L29
CARR SIDE LA
East Lodge Farm
Hunt's Brook Farm
Tower Wood
EAST LA
Broad Farm
Ince Blundell Park
PARK WALL RD
BROAD LA
Homer Green
L23
LUNT RD
LONG LA
GATES LA
MOOR LA
L23
A565
33
34
35

3

14
6
Rimmer's Bridge
Lydiate Brook
Church View Farm
Hollin House Green Farm
Bridgefoot Farm
Hollin House Farm
L39
Lydiate Hall Farm
Jackson's Bridge Farm
Beaconsfield Farm
Hill Top Farm Kennels
Rose Hill Farm
Cherry Tree Farm
Rosemount Nurseries
Northway Nurseries
SOUTHPORT RD
L31
St Gregory's RC Jun & Inf Schs
Windmill
Lydiate
Crisp's Farm
Gore Houses
Lydiate Cty Prim Sch
St Thomas CE Prim Sch
Mill House Farm
Leeds & Liverpool Canal
NORTHWAY
Upper Gore Farm
Maghull Brook
Northway Cty Prim Sch
MAGHULL SMALLHOLDINGS EST
St John Bosco RC Prim Sch
Green Park Cty Prim Sch
Cheshire Lines Path
Peel Farm
Trans Pennine Trail
LIVERPOOL RD N
B5422 WESTWAY
Deyes High Sch
St Andrews Maghull CE Prim Sch
MAGHULL
THE MAGHULL HOMES
Sudell Brook
ROBBIN'S BRIDGE
Hotel
PH
1 EAST RD
2 HOWARD CL
3 LANCASTER CL
4 LABURNUM GR
5 BEECHWOOD CT
6 ORCHARD CT
A B C D E F
8 7 6 5 4 3 2 1
05 04 03 02
36 37 38

5
15

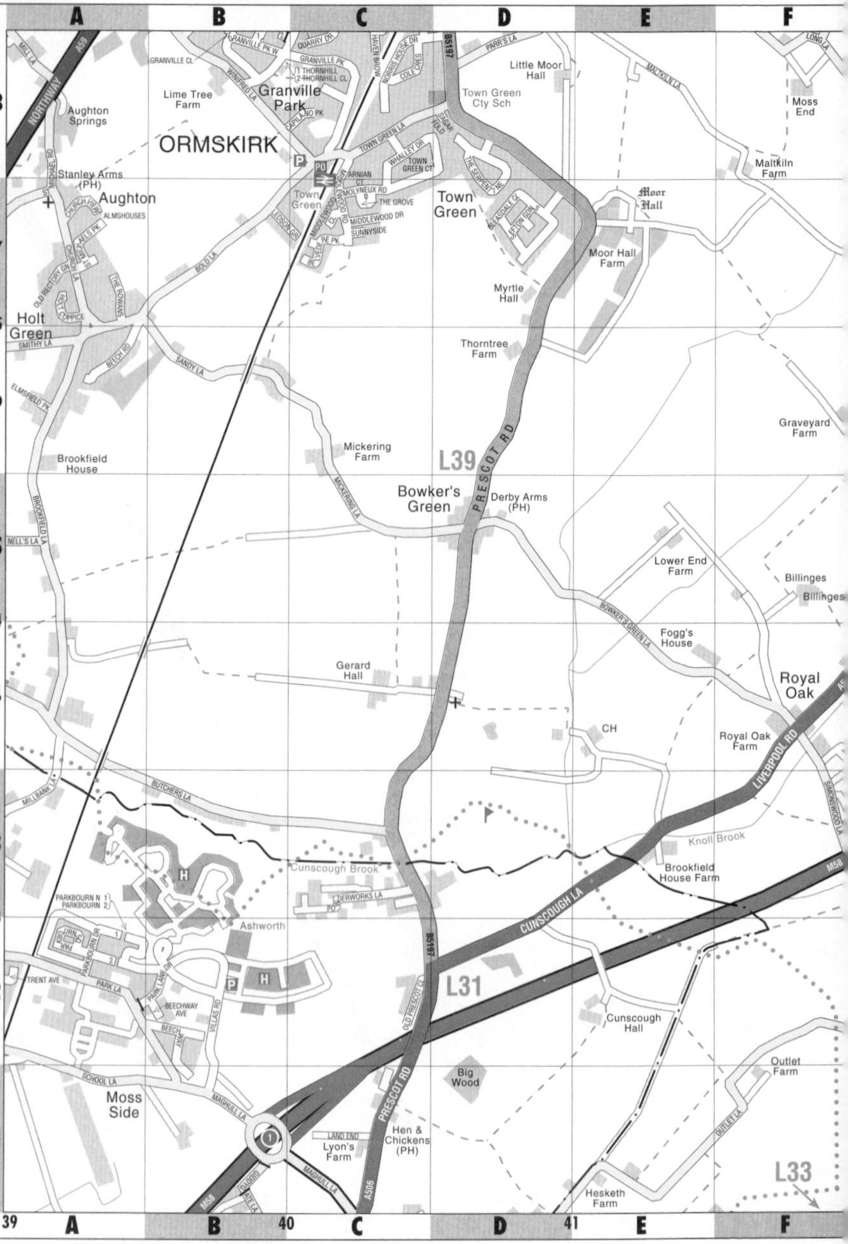
A
B
C
D
E
F
8
7
05
6
5
04
4
3
03
2
1
02
39
40
41
NORTHWAY
A59
MILL LA
GRANVILLE CL
GRANVILLE PK W
QUARRY DR
GRANVILLE PK
1 THORNHILL
2 THORNHILL CL
HAVEN BROW
NORRIS HOUSE DR
COLE CRES
B5197
PARR'S LA
Little Moor Hall
MALTKILN LA
LONG LA
Lime Tree Farm
WINIFRED LA
Granville Park
Town Green Cty Sch
Moss End
Aughton Springs
CAPILANO PK
SAGAR FOLD
ORMSKIRK
TOWN GREEN LA
WHALLEY DR
TOWN GREEN CT
THE SERPENTINE
Maltkiln Farm
P
PO
Stanley Arms (PH)
Aughton
ST MICHAEL RD
CHURCH VIEW
ALMSHOUSES
Town Green
ARNIAN CT
MOLYNEUX RD
THE GROVE
MIDDLEWOOD DR
SUNNYSIDE
LEDSON GR
MIDDLEWOOD CL
BELVEDERE PK
Town Green
BLEASDALE CL
SEFTON GDNS
Moor Hall
Moor Hall Farm
AELS PK
CHURCH LA
OLD RECTORY GN
HOLT COPPICE
THE ROWANS
BOLD LA
Myrtle Hall
Holt Green
SMITHY LA
BEECH RD
Thorntree Farm
SANDY LA
ELMSFIELD PK
Graveyard Farm
Mickering Farm
Brookfield House
L39
PRESCOT RD
Bowker's Green
Derby Arms (PH)
MICKERING LA
BROOKFIELD LA
NELL'S LA
Lower End Farm
Billinges
Billinges
BOWKER'S GREEN LA
Fogg's House
Gerard Hall
Royal Oak
CH
Royal Oak Farm
LIVERPOOL RD
MILLBANK LA
BUTCHERS LA
SIMONSWOOD LA
Knoll Brook
Cunscough Brook
H
Brookfield House Farm
DERWORKS LA
PO
M58
PARKBOURN N 1
PARKBOURN 2
Ashworth
CUNSCOUGH LA
PARKBOURN DR
B5197
TRENT AVE
PARK LA
PARK LANE DR
P
H
L31
BEECHWAY AVE
BEECH WAY
VILLAS RD
OLD PRESCOT CL
Cunscough Hall
SCHOOL LA
Big Wood
Outlet Farm
Moss Side
MAGHULL LA
PRESCOT RD
OUTLET LA
LAND END
Hen & Chickens (PH)
Lyon's Farm
1
MAGHULL LA
A506
L33
M58
Hesketh Farm

5

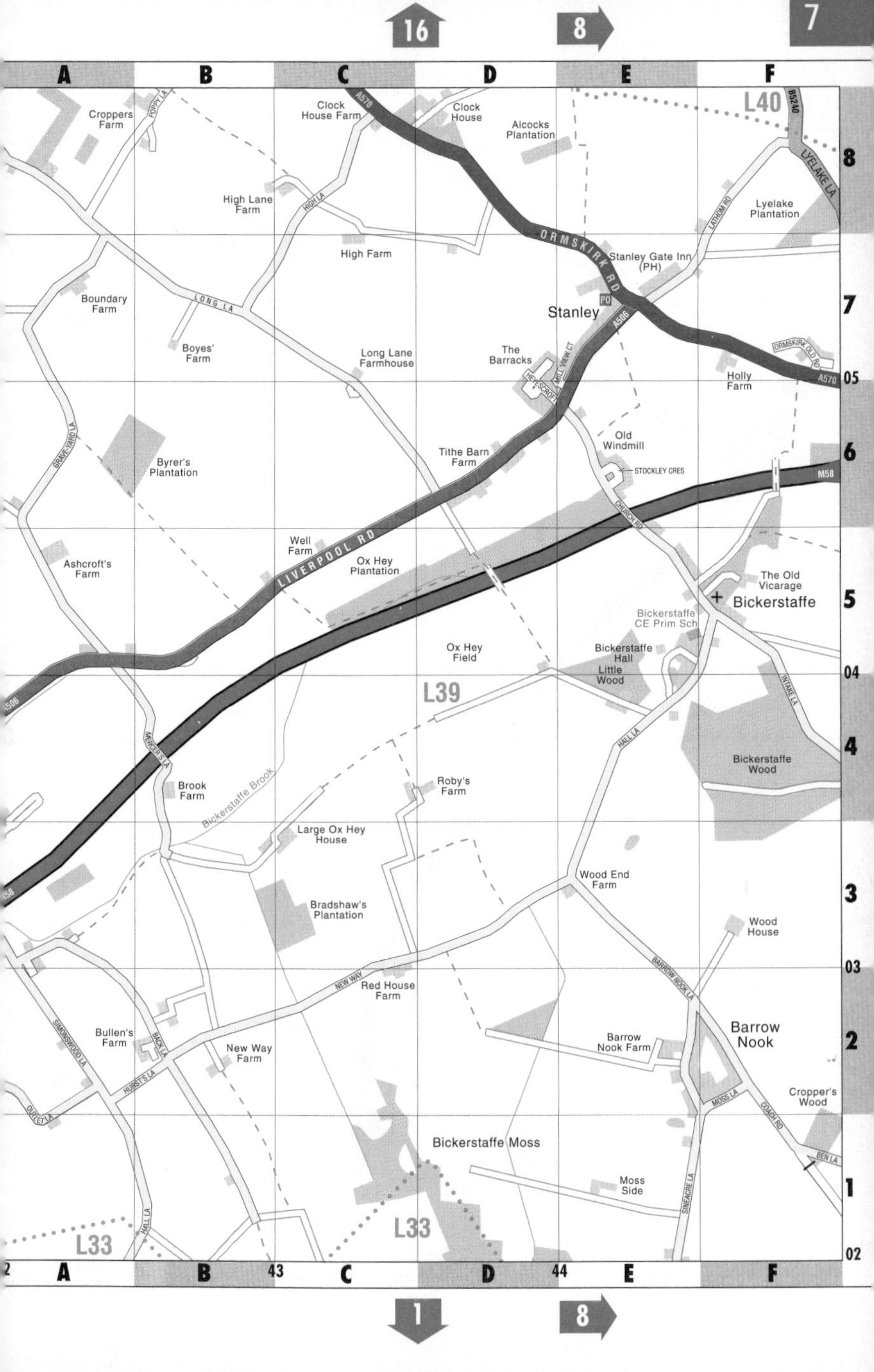

16
8
A
B
C
D
E
F
Croppers Farm
POPPY LA
Clock House Farm
A570
Clock House
Alcocks Plantation
L40
B5240
8
LYELAKE LA
High Lane Farm
HIGH LA
Lyelake Plantation
LATHOM RD
High Farm
ORMSKIRK RD
Stanley Gate Inn (PH)
Boundary Farm
LONG LA
PO
Stanley
7
A506
Boyes' Farm
Long Lane Farmhouse
The Barracks
MILL VIEW CT
HEYESCROFT
ORMSKIRK OLD RD
Holly Farm
A570
05
GRAVE-YARD LA
Old Windmill
Byrer's Plantation
Tithe Barn Farm
STOCKLEY CRES
6
M58
CHURCH RD
Well Farm
LIVERPOOL RD
Ox Hey Plantation
Ashcroft's Farm
The Old Vicarage
Bickerstaffe
5
Bickerstaffe CE Prim Sch
Ox Hey Field
Bickerstaffe Hall
Little Wood
04
A506
L39
INTAKE LA
HALL LA
MERCER'S LA
4
Bickerstaffe Wood
Brook Farm
Roby's Farm
Bickerstaffe Brook
Large Ox Hey House
Wood End Farm
M58
3
Bradshaw's Plantation
Wood House
03
NEW WAY
Red House Farm
BARROW NOOK LA
SIMONSWOOD LA
Barrow Nook
2
Bullen's Farm
BACK LA
New Way Farm
Barrow Nook Farm
HURST'S LA
MOSS LA
COACH RD
Cropper's Wood
OUTLET LA
Bickerstaffe Moss
BEN LA
Moss Side
SINEACRE LA
1
HALL LA
L33
L33
02
42
A
B
43
C
D
44
E
F
1
8

7
17

A B C D E F
L40
8
Blaguegate Moss
Primrose Farm
Lyelake Farm
LYELAKE LA
7
Four Lane Ends
Stanley Farm
SKELMERSDALE RD
LIVERPOOL RD
KERFOOTS LA
B5240
B5312
05
A570
6
3
Wash Farm
RAINFORD RD
Colliery Plantation
Rose Farm
5
Ivy House
Bickerstaffe Moss
Higherend Farm
Hey's Crossing
04
L39
Holly Lane Farm
Brookdale
4
COAL PIT LA
Barker's Brook
HOLLY LA
Long Plantation
Big Ferny Knoll Farm
Ferny Knoll
3
Intake Farm
Holly Fold Farm
WA11
03
Ben Lane Farm
INTAKE LA
BEN LANE CT
2
Park Hill
Lodge Farm
PH
Red Delph Farm
LODGE LA
BEN LA
1
Moss House Farm
Kenyon's Wood
Rigby's Wood
COACH RD
SIDING LA
RED DELPH LA
ORMSKIRK RD
B5203
02
West Gillibrands
WEST GILLIBRANDS IND EST
RAILWAY RD
WN8
Peel Farm
White Moss
WHITE MOSS RD
WHITE MOSS RD S
A5068
GLENBURN RD
M58
4
MOSS LANE VIEW
Nursery
MOSS LA
Moss Lane Farm
HOLLY FOLD LA
FERNY KNOLL RD
BUSHEY LA
KESWICK WAY 1
CONISTON WAY 2
WINDERMERE DR
BUTTERMERE CRES
KENDAL CL
KENDAL DR
SPRINGFIELD
NEWS LA
RAIL CL
Rainford Junction
Bridge Farm
JUNCTION RD
WELBOURNE
WAVERLEY
LIVERPOOL RD
WESTGATE
ASHWALL ST
JUBILEE DR
WALLCROFT ST
WHEATACRE
WALDRON
WHITEHEY
WHITE STOCK
HIGH ST
WOODROW
WOODCROFT
WINSTANLEY RD
WOLVERTON
WIGAN RD
B5312
DERBY RD
VILLAGE WAY
OLD TOWN CL
OLD TOWN WAY
VILLAGE CL
WHITE MOSS RD
GLADDEN PL
GARDINERS PL
GILLIBRANDS RD
GREENHEY PL
GERRARD PL
45 46 47

7

18
10
A
B
C
D
E
F
8
7
05
6
5
04
4
3
03
2
1
02
48
49
50
SKELMERSDALE
Glenburn High Sch
Skelmersdale Coll (Westbank Ctr)
Delphside Prim Sch
Hillside Cty Sch
Tanhouse
St Marks RC Sch
GRIMSHAW RD
East Gillibrands
Tawd Bridge
Skelmersdale Sports Ctr
St Mathew's RC Prim Sch
Holland Moor Cty Prim Sch
Holland Moor
WINDMILL RD
NEWGATE RD
STANNANOUGHT RD
Moorside Prim Sch
Little Digmoor Cty Prim Sch
Bishop Martin CE Prim Sch
Digmoor
Playing Fields
St Luke's RC Prim Sch
DIGMOOR RD
M58
A577
B5312
A5068
Moss Farm
Moss Side Farm
River Tawd
WN8
West Pimbo
East Pimbo
Ind Est
Hotel
Holland Moss
Moor Side Farm
Barton House
Upholland
Lower Balcony Farm
Nursery
LC
Balcarres Farm
Crawford Cty Sch
LONG LA
PIMBO LA
Millets
WA11
Maggots Nook
Red House Farm
Crawford
The Crawford (PH)
Billinge Bounty Farm
Strawberry Cottage
Black Brook
Scythe Stone Delph Farm
Hay's House
Maddocks
LANGWOOD LA
REEDS BROW
MAGGOTS NOOK RD
NEWS LA

10

9
19

A
B
C
D
E
F
ORRELL
Hall Green
Newgate
Up Holland
Orrell Post
Tontine
Far Moor
Higher End
Billinge
Longshaw
Brownlow
Bispham
WN8
WN5
WA11
Upholland Tunnel
Higher Tower Hill Farm
Well Cross Farm
The Lawns Farm
Lower Pimbo
Higher Pimbo Farm
Pimbo Bushes
Mountains Farm
Heaton House
Promised Land Farm
Brownlow Farm
Up Holland High Sch
Orrell Newfold Cty Prim Sch
St James' RC Prim Sch
Holgate Prim Sch
St Peter's RC High Sch
Orrell Water Park
Farrar's Farm
Winstanley Coll
Greenslate Farm
Moss Wood
New House Farm
Longshaw Bottom
ORMSKIRK RD
SCHOOL LA
ORRELL RD
MOOR RD
ST JAMES' RD
GANTLEY RD
UPHOLLAND RD
M58
M6
A577
B5206
51
52
53

9

12
A
B
C
D
E
F
8
7
09
6
5
08
4
3
07
2
1
06
Cloven-le-Dale
LC
Woodvale Airfield
Fisherman's Path
Formby Hills
Freshfield Caravan Pk
Nature Reserve
Clarence House Sch
LITTLE BREWERY LA
BREWERY LA
KENTON CL
ST ANNE'S RD
STANLEY RD
MASSAM'S LA
WEST LA
RIMMER'S AVE
ARGARMEOLS RD
FISHERMANS CL
MONTAGU MEWS 1
LAWSWOOD 2
CH
STANLAWE RD
MERSEY AVE
GREGSON'S AVE
CUMMINS AVE
QUEENS AVE
MAYFIELD CT
RED BARNES
TIMMS LA
CRICKET PATH
WRIGLEYS LA
THE PADDOCK
GOLF RD
VICTORIA WAY
MONTAGU RD
SHIREBURN RD
FAIRWAYS CT
BADGERS RAKE
TOWER END
VICTORIA RD
Freshfield
L37
GRANGE LA
DERBY RD
PIERCEFIELD RD
DEANS CT
BORROWDALE
COLLEGE PATH
HAZELBANK GDNS
VICARAGE CL
LENTON AVE
SQUIRREL GN
BIRCH GN
FIRS CRES
FIRS CL
FIRS LINK
ST PETER'S AVE
HOLMWOOD DR
COLLEGE CL
GORSE WAY
PROCTOR RD
OAKFIELD DR
LARCH WAY
VICARAGE RD
VAUGHAN CL
FRESHFIELD CT
OLD TOWN LA
BREDON CT
RYMERS GN
MANOR LODGE
BYRON CL
GRABURN RD
ST GEORGE'S RD
OLD MILL LA
Formby High Sch
LARKHILL LA
DUNES DR
HARINGTON RD
ST PETER'S CL
BARKFIELD LA
COLLEGE AVE
FRESHFIELD RD
BARKFIELD AVE
LONG LA
Sandfield Farm
Sefton Coastal Path
BLUNDELL AVE
WICKS CRES
WICKS GREEN CL
WARREN GN
BEECH DR
WELD DR
HOLMWOOD GDNS
THE EVERGREENS
HOLMWOOD CL
COPPICE LEYS
FORMBY
LONSDALE RD
CLIFDEN CT
HALSALL LA
Holy Trinity CE Prim Sch
THE GALLERY
PAGE CT
FURNESS AVE
THE CLOISTERS
SCHOOL AVE
SCHOOL LA
CHAPEL ALLEY
ROSEMARY LA
SUNNINGDALE GDNS
ALDERSON CRES
DAVENHAM RD
HARINGTON GN
HARINGTON CL
WICKS LA
WICKS GN
INCE CRES
WICKS GDNS
BUTTERMERE CL
ENNERDALE CL
GRISEDALE CL
HEYWOOD CL
MICHAELS CL
ORMS WAY
BROWS LA
CHAPEL LA
SUMNER RD
CROPTON RD
ELBOW LA
THREE TUNS LA
St Jerome's RC Prim Sch
Woodlands Prim Sch
GREENLOON'S DR
FOXHILL CL
TARN RD
GRASMERE RD
RYDAL AVE
WOODLANDS RD
ESKDALE CL
SPRUCE WAY
HAZLEHURST CL
KIRKLAKE BANK
EDENHURST CL
SPRINGFIELD
DERWENT AVE
CONISTON RD
MERE RD
LANGDALE CL
MARSH BROWS
ASHURST CT
DUKES WAY
DUKE ST
MEADOW CROFT
PHILLIPS CL
Liby
Formby
FORMBY BRIDGE
KIRKLAKE RD
CHURCH GN
CHURCH WAY
ST LUKE DR
BUSHBY'S PK
BROOKS WAY
BROOKS RD
WARD AVE
CHINDIT CL
SEFTON RD
FORMBY ST
KINGS CL
KINGS RD
MEOLS CL
PHILLIP'S LA
RAVENSCROFT
WALKER CL
GLENDALE WAY
TYRERS CL
DICKINSON RD
DICKINSON CL
NORBURN CRES
BIRKEY LA
QUEEN'S RD
BUSHBY'S LA
Eccles Crossing
RAVEN MEOLS LA
LIFEBOAT RD
Shorrocks Hill
ST LUKE'S CHURCH RD
LIME TREE WAY
TOP HILL
PINEWOOD CL
SEALAND CL
SEALAND AVE
FOSTER RD
ANDREWS YORT
St Luke's Sch
MAPLE CL
ELM DR
JUBILEE RD
ELSON RD
GEORGIAN PL
CARR'S CRES
CRESCENT AVE
ROSTRON CRES
BICKERSTAFFE GR
KENSINGTON RD
SANDRINGHAM RD
WINDSOR RD
PARK AVE
PARK WAY
NURSERY DR
HAREBELL CL
THE RAVENS
Bill's La
ASHCROFT RD
KENT RD
BEECHWOOD DR
ASH GR
CEDAR DR
SYCAMORE GR
CHESTNUT WAY
ASPEN GR
MILFORD DR
CAMBRIDGE RD
FUNCHAL AVE
CARR'S CRES W
HAMPTON RD
BALMORAL DR
EDINBURGH RD
CASTLE DR
MARINA RD
MAYFIELD AVE
SANDHURST CL
HEYDON CL
HADSTOCK AVE
STAPLETON RD
ECCLES CL
ANDREWS CL
LANCASTER RD
OSBORNE DR
HOGGS HILL LA
ALTCAR LA
BARTON HEYS RD
SUTTON RD
KEW RD
BURWELL AVE
ORWELL CL
ELSWORTH CL
TADLOW CL
MELDRETH CL
ALEXANDRA RD
ALBERT RD
PARK RD
BELVEDERE DR
Sewage Works
28
29
2
12

11
20
A
B
C
D
E
F
8
7
09
6
5
08
4
3
07
2
1
06
30
31
32
3
Woodvale Airfield
Formby Hall
Formby Hall Farm
Golf Driving Range
Water Meadow Nursery
CH
Rice's Nursery
Formby Moss
BROAD LA
Sandy Brook
SOUTHPORT OLD RD
White Grass
Rain Gauge
Fine Jane's Brook
ALDER LA
Trans Pennine Trail
Cheshire Lines Path
GORSEY LA
NORTH MOSS LA
EIGHT ACRE LA
North Moss Farm
Shalom
Fine Jane's Pumping Sta
Rose Farm
South Moss Farm
Warren Farm
HEATHER CL
Pasture La
L39
THE RYDINGS
HAWKSWORTH DR
HAWKSWORTH CL
LONGTON DR
DEANSGATE LA N
BRACKENWAY
SPYMERS CROFT
GORSEFIELD
HEATHWAYS
HEATHFIELD CL
THE SPINNEY
LINGDALES
PARADISE LA
B5424
SOUTHPORT RD
PRIMROSE CL
LINGFIELD
FORMBY BY-PASS
Downholland Brook
WRIGLEYS LA
THE PADDOCK
St Peter's CE Prim Sch
RYEGROUND LA
CLIFTON RD
NEW RD
DEANSGATE LA
MOUNT HOUSE RD
MOUNT HOUSE CL
MOSS LA
Freshfield Prim Sch
MOSS SIDE
LITTLE HEY LA
L37
DOWNHOLLAND MOSS LA
Thirty Acre La
Downholland Moss
CABLE ST
DOBBS DR
SMITHY CL
SMITHY GN
WATCHYARD LA
Southern Heyes Farm
FORMBY
Altcar La
CHURCH RD
GARDNER RD
MITTEN'S LA
HIGHER MOSS
WHITEHOUSE LA
CATTAN GN
MOSS GN
MAWDSLEY CL
DEVON FARM WAY
NORRIS WAY
CHURCH CL
WHITEHOUSE AVE
CHURCH CLOSE CT
KENYON'S LA
BULL COP
Formby Moss
MIDDLE MOSS LA
Our Lady Of Compassion RC Prim Sch
LOWES GN
BURLINGTON AVE
PRIESTHOUSE LA
FLAXFIELD RD
PRIESTHOUSE CL
CHAPEL HOUSE WALK
GLENMARSH WAY
FORMBY BSNS PK
STEPHENSON WAY
SUTTON'S LA
YORK RD
ROSEBAY CL
CROSS GN
B5195
ALTCAR RD
Formby's Farm
BROAD LA
WHALLEY DR
BOLTON CL
BUCKFAST DR
Rose Nursery
CROSS GREEN CL
HAWTHORNE CRES
DITCHFIELD
BEAUFORT
SEAFIELD
BYLAND CL
CARTMEL DR
LYTLES CL
THE NURSERIES
REDGATE
1 BATTLE WAY
2 CLEVE WAY
3 CROWLAND WAY
4 KIRKSTALL DR
5 FORMBY LA
6 CLOISTER GN
Sutton's Farm
Tyrer's Farm
BROAD LA
LIVESLEY'S LA
CORONATION AVE
FORMBY FIELDS
ABBEY CL
REDGATE DR
FOUNTAINS WAY
FRIARS WALK
ALT RD
TINTERN DR
LORD SEFTON WAY
DOCTOR'S LA
CONIFER CT
RAVEN MEOLS LA
THIRLMERE AVE
Redgate Prim Sch
PRIORY CL
ROYAL CRES
ABBOTS WAY
ABBOTS CL
LIVERPOOL RD
KENT AVE
MAYFLOWER IND EST
GABLE MEWS
SHORT CROFT LA
Altcar Hall
Tatlock's Farm
ASPINALL CRES
BROAD LA
KENT RD
PO
RIVER CL
NEW CSWY
Great Altcar
MARINA RD
MONKS CL
MONKS DR
UNION HOOK
ENGINE LA
ALTCAR LA
THE BARNS
Little Altcar
A565

11
3

21
14
A
B
C
D
E
F
L37
PLEX MOSS LA
Plex Moss House
Carr Moss
Park House Farm
8
HEATHY LA
Barton Grove
Barton Moss
GORSEY LA
Little Wood
7
Gerrard's Hall Farm
STATION RD
Hesketh Farm
09
Barton Brook
SHAW LA
Hook Wood
Barton
Leather Barrow's Ditch
WELL LA
6
Downholland Moss
MOSS LA
Chisnall Brook
Blundell's Farm
5
OLD MOSS LA
JACKSON CL
PO
QUEENS
08
RIDING LA
Rough Brook
L39
SUMNER AVE
PARK CRES
Orritt's Wood
Haskayne
4
NEW LA
P
Sewage Wks
SCHOOL LA
Leeds & Liverpool Canal
Cheshire Lines Brook
Trans Pennine Trail
Shacklady's Heath
Moss Heath
OLD LA
NEW LA
3
Haskayne CE Sch
BACK LA
Thorns Farm
Moss Wood
07
HIGHER MOSS LA
BLACK-A-MOOR LA
Altcar Moss
OWEN'S LA
2
MIDDLE MOSS LA
BURGESS LA
L37
Winter Pasture Plantation
Rabbit Hill
Worrall House Farm
New Hill House
ALTCAR LA
B5195
1
WOOD LA
FLATMAN'S LA
Marl Pit Wood
CAUSEWAY LA
RYE MOSS LA
ACRES LA
Lydiate Brook
Hill House
Hill House Plantation
06
34
35
4
14

13
22

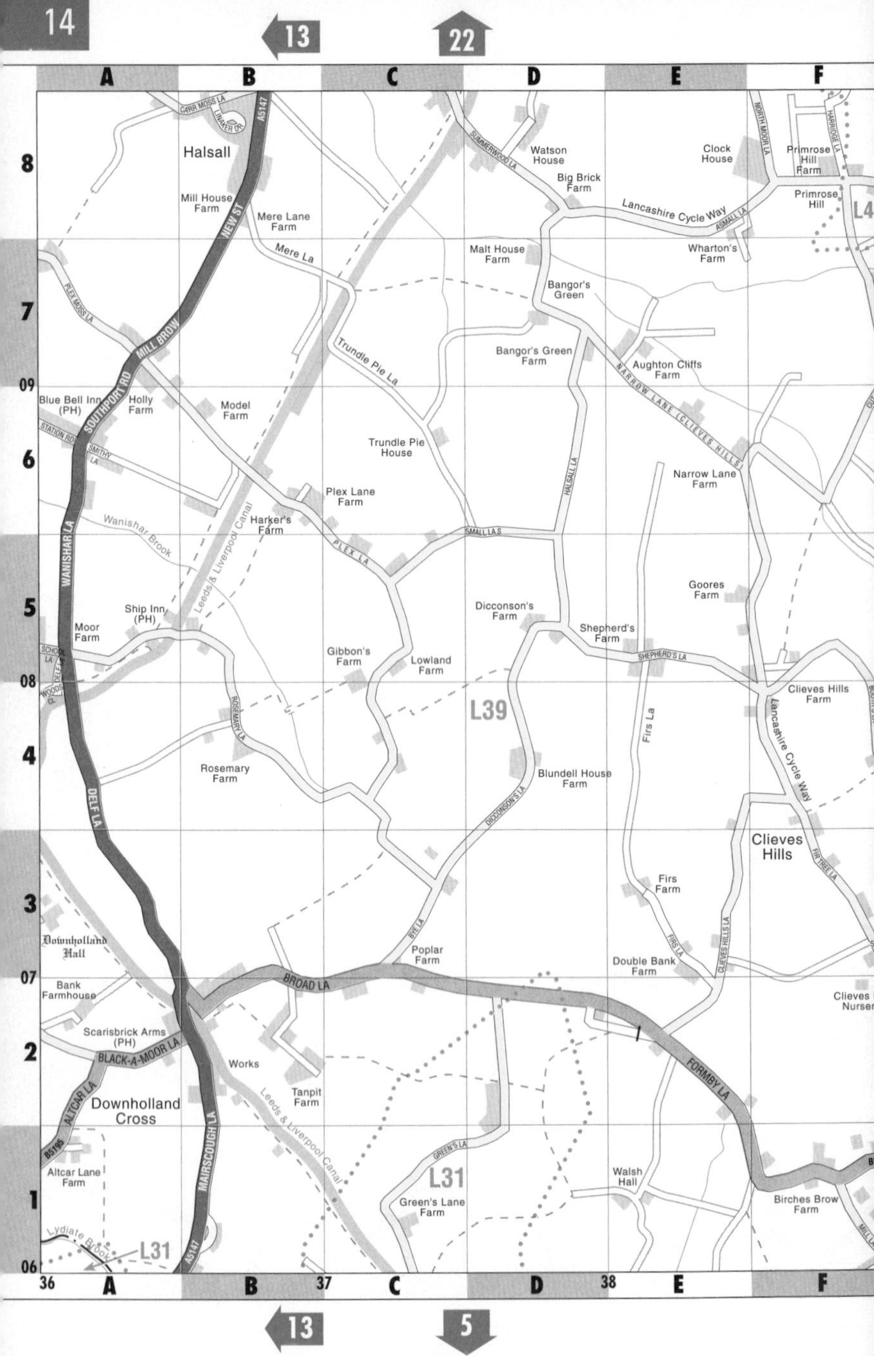
Halsall
Mill House Farm
Mere Lane Farm
Mere La
Watson House
Big Brick Farm
Clock House
Primrose Hill Farm
Primrose Hill
Lancashire Cycle Way
Malt House Farm
Wharton's Farm
Bangor's Green
Bangor's Green Farm
Aughton Cliffs Farm
Trundle Pie La
Blue Bell Inn (PH)
Holly Farm
Model Farm
Trundle Pie House
Narrow Lane Farm
Plex Lane Farm
Harker's Farm
Wanishar Brook
Leeds & Liverpool Canal
Goores Farm
Dicconson's Farm
Shepherd's Farm
Moor Farm
Ship Inn (PH)
Gibbon's Farm
Lowland Farm
Clieves Hills Farm
L39
Rosemary Farm
Blundell House Farm
Firs La
Lancashire Cycle Way
Clieves Hills
Firs Farm
Downholland Hall
Poplar Farm
Double Bank Farm
Bank Farmhouse
Clieves Nurser
Scarisbrick Arms (PH)
Works
Tanpit Farm
Downholland Cross
L31
Altcar Lane Farm
Walsh Hall
Green's Lane Farm
Birches Brow Farm
Lydiate Brook
L31
CARR MOSS LA
LINAKER DR
A5147
NEW ST
MILL BROW
SOUTHPORT RD
PLEX MOSS LA
STATION RD
SMITHY LA
WANISHAR LA
SCHOOL LA
WOODS CL
DELF LA
BLACK-A-MOOR LA
ALTCAR LA
B5195
MAIRSCOUGH LA
SUMMERWOOD LA
NORTH MOOR LA
HARRIDGE LA
ASMALL LA
NARROW LANE (CLIEVES HILLS)
HALSALL LA
SMALL LA S
PLEX LA
ROSEMARY LA
DICCONSON'S LA
SHEPHERD'S LA
BYE LA
BROAD LA
FORMBY LA
FIRS LA
CLIEVES HILLS LA
FIR TREE LA
GREEN'S LA
MILL LA
A B C D E F
8 7 09 6 5 08 4 3 07 2 1 06
36 37 38

13
5

23
16

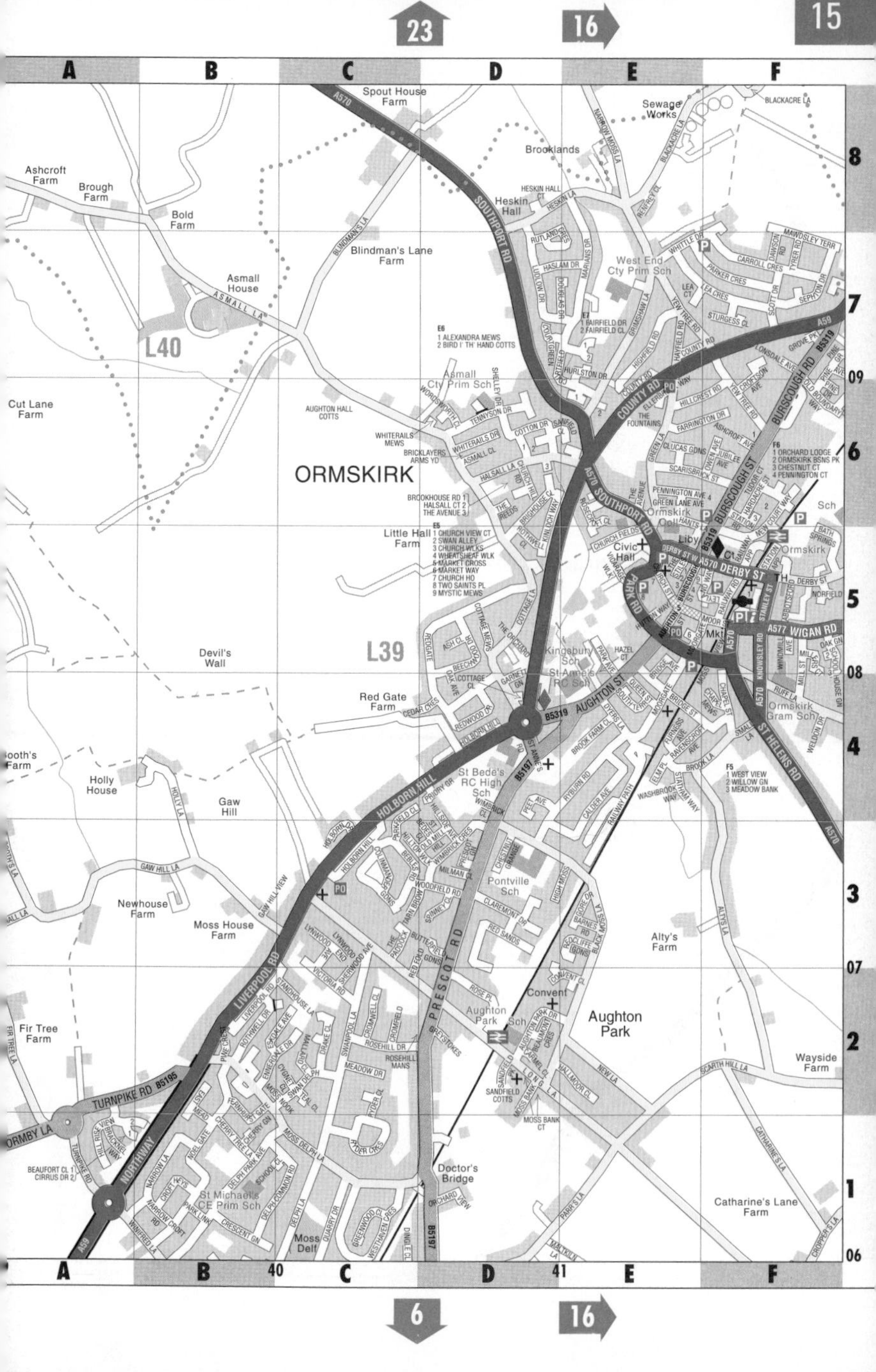
A
B
C
D
E
F
8
7
09
6
5
08
4
3
07
2
1
06
40
41
Spout House Farm
A570
Sewage Works
BLACKACRE LA
NARROW MOSS LA
Brooklands
BLACKACRE LA
Ashcroft Farm
Brough Farm
Bold Farm
HESKIN HALL CT
Heskin Hall
HESKIN LA
RENFREY CL
MAWDSLEY TERR
SOUTHPORT RD
BLINDMAN'S LA
Blindman's Lane Farm
RUTLAND CRES
HASLAM DR
West End Cty Prim Sch
CARROLL CRES
PARKER CRES
Asmall House
ASMALL LA
LUDLOW DR
DOUGLAS DR
GRIMSHAW LA
LEA CT
LEA CRES
YEW TREE RD
STURGESS CL
SCOTT DR
SEPHTON DR
E7
1 FAIRFIELD DR
2 FAIRFIELD CL
E6
1 ALEXANDRA MEWS
2 BIRD I' TH' HAND COTTS
L40
CURZON GREEN
HIGHFIELD RD
HAYFIELD RD
COUNTY RD
A59
GROVE PK
LONSDALE AVE
BURSCOUGH RD
B5319
HURLSTON DR
Asmall Cty Prim Sch
SHELLEY DR
Cut Lane Farm
AUGHTON HALL COTTS
WORDSWORTH CL
TENNYSON DR
COTTON DR
SANDFIELD CL
ELLERBROOK WAY
HILLCREST RD
FARRINGTON DR
ASHCROFT AVE
WHITERAILS MEWS
WHITERAILS DR
THE FOUNTAINS
CLUCAS GDNS
JUBILEE AVE
OWEN AVE
BRICKLAYERS ARMS YD
ASMALL CL
SCARISBRICK ST
F6
1 ORCHARD LODGE
2 ORMSKIRK BSNS PK
3 CHESTNUT CT
4 PENNINGTON CT
ORMSKIRK
HALSALL LA
CHURCH HILL RD
PENNINGTON AVE
GREEN LANE AVE
TUDOR CL
HARDACRE ST
BURSCOUGH ST
BROOKHOUSE RD 1
HALSALL CT 2
THE AVENUE 3
THE REEDS
BRIGHOUSE CL
KINLOCH WAY
A570 SOUTHPORT RD
Ormskirk Coll
NEW COURT WAY
Sch
Little Hall Farm
E5
1 CHURCH VIEW CT
2 SWAN ALLEY
3 CHURCH WLKS
4 WHEATSHEAF WLK
5 MARKET CROSS
6 MARKET WAY
7 CHURCH HO
8 TWO SAINTS PL
9 MYSTIC MEWS
ROTHWELL CL
CHURCH FIELDS
Civic Hall
Liby
DERBY ST W
A570 DERBY ST
BATH SPRINGS
Ormskirk
VICARAGE WLK
PARK RD
RAILWAY RD
TH
DERBY ST
NORFIELD
STANLEY ST
COTTAGE LA
COTTAGE MEWS
AUGHTON ST
MOOR ST
Mkt
A577 WIGAN RD
REDGATE
ASH CL
BEECH
L39
Kingsbury Sch
St Anne's RC Sch
HAZEL CT
PARK AVE
KNOWSLEY RD
MILL ST
OAK GN
Devil's Wall
OAK AVE
COTTAGE CL
GARNETT GN
BRIDGE AVE
QUEEN ST
SOUTH TERR
MOORGATE
BRIDGE ST
CHAPEL ST
CHAPEL MEWS
A570
RUFF LA
Ormskirk Gram Sch
Red Gate Farm
CEDAR CRES
REDWOOD DR
B5319
AUGHTON ST
DYERS LA
FURNESS AVE
RAVENSCROFT AVE
WELDON DR
HOLBORN HILL
ST ANNE'S RD
BROOK FARM CL
BROOK LA
ST HELENS RD
Booth's Farm
Holly House
HOLLY LA
Gaw Hill
St Bede's RC High Sch
PRIORY GR
B5197
RYBURN RD
ELM PL
WASHBROOK WAY
STATHAM WAY
F5
1 WEST VIEW
2 WILLOW GN
3 MEADOW BANK
PEET AVE
WIMBRICK CL
CALDER AVE
RAILWAY PATH
HOLBORN HILL
PARKFIELD CL
HILLSIDE
HILLTOP WLK
OLD MILL AVE
WIMBRICK CRES
CHESTNUT GRANGE
GAW HILL LA
COLLINGWOOD GDNS
BEBLES RD
MILMAN CL
PRESCOT PL
PO
WOODFIELD RD
Pontville Sch
HIGH MOSS
Newhouse Farm
GAW HILL VIEW
TARN BROW
SPINNEY CL
CLAREMONT DR
BARNES RD
RED SANDS
ALTYS LA
Moss House Farm
LYNWOOD AVE
SHERWOOD AVE
THE PADDOCK
BUTTERFIELD GDNS
REDCLIFFE GDNS
BLACK MOSS LA
Alty's Farm
LIVERPOOL RD
PRESCOT RD
VICTORIA RD
CONVENT CL
Convent
ROSE PL
STANDHOUSE LA
Aughton Park Sch
Aughton Park
Fir Tree Farm
FIR TREE LA
PINE CREST
ROTHWELL DR
ESKDALE AVE
SWANPOOL LA
CROMWELL CL
CROMFIELD
GREYSTOKES
ROSEHILL DR
ROSEHILL MANS
MEADOW DR
AUGHTON PARK DR
BEAUMONT CRES
CARMEL CL
HALLMOOR CL
NEW LA
SCARTH HILL LA
Wayside Farm
TURNPIKE RD
B5195
SANDFIELD COTTS
LONG LA
MOSS BANK CT
ORMBY LA
RISE VIEW
HILLTOP
BRACKNEL WAY
CHERRY TREE LA
CHERRY GN
DELPH PARK AVE
MOSS NOOK
MOSS DELPH LA
RYDER CL
RYDER CRES
CATHARINE'S LA
BEAUFORT CL 1
CIRRUS DR 2
NORTHWAY
NARROW LA
CROFT HEYS
SCHOOL CL
St Michael's CE Prim Sch
DELPH COMMON RD
Doctor's Bridge
ORCHARD VIEW
PARK LINK
NARROW CROFT RD
CRESCENT GN
DELPH LA
QUARRY DR
GREENWOOD CL
WESTHAVEN CRES
DINGLE CL
B5197
Moss Delf
PARR'S LA
MALTKILN LA
Catharine's Lane Farm
CROPPER'S LA
WINIFRED LA
A59

6
16

15
24

A
B
C
D
E
F
8
7
09
6
5
08
4
3
07
2
1
06
42
43
44
Abbey Farm
Burscough Priory
Jump's Farm
Bullen's Wood
Heyes Farm
Sycamore House Farm
HIGH LA
A59
ABBEY LA
MILL DAM LA
BLYTHE LA
LADY ALICE'S DR
Needless Inn Farm
Timbobbin Farm
Mains Wood
Grove Farm
Bath Lodge
SANDY LA
Robinsons Farm
CRANES LA
LATHOM LA
CH
Dark Lane Farm
DARK LA
Bath Farm
Leas Farm
New Park Brook
NURSERY AVE
QUARRY MOUNT
Hettings House
Charlesbye Mews
CHARLESBYE AVE
WATERWORKS RD
PENDLE DR
GREETBY HILL
New Park Wood
Leveldale
Halsall's Lodge
LADY'S WLK
Ormskirk CE Prim Sch
ORMSKIRK
CASTLE LA
DERBY HILL
DERBY HILL RD
TOWER HILL
EDGLEY DR
THOMPSON AVE
FIELD WLK
Crosshall High Sch
L40
SUNNYFIELDS
OAKFIELDS
TAYLOR AVE
LATHAM AVE
Otterheads Farm
Cross Hall Farm
A577
WIGAN RD
PO
CROSSHALL BROW
Mawdsley's Farm
Sefton Brook
Birchenholt
H
DICCONSON WAY
Ormskirk & District General
PO
HALTON CHASE
GREENACRE
MEADOWBRIDGE CL
DICK'S LA
MILTON DR
NORMANHURST
BEECH MEADOW
BLAIRGOWRIE GDNS
Westhead
HOLLY CL
FORGE CL
Dingle Heye Farm
Ruff Wood
RUFF LA
WOODLANDS CL
Threlfalls Farm
Lathom St James CE Sch
WIGAN RD
Ruff Farm
Wellfield
L39
BRIGHOUSE GN
B5240
PLOUGH
A570
Edge Hill Univ Coll
VICARAGE CL
ST JAMES CL
BEWCASTLE DR
VARLIAN CL
WELLFIELD LA
VICARAGE LA
SLACK HOUSE COTTS
SCHOOL LA
ST HELENS RD
A577 DICKET
DICKET'S BROW
B5240
Slack House Farm
SCARTH HILL LA
WN8
Westhead Farm
Turner's Farm
Scarth Hill
Wtr Twr
Delph Farm
Fosters Farm
WHITELEYS LA
SCARTH HILL LA
Goose Brook
LYELAKE LA
Brookdale Farm
Stuart's Farm
Scarth Hill Farm
ORMSKIRK RD
Grapel Farm
Wiswall's Farm
POPPY LA
CROPPER'S LA
White House Farm
A570
B5240

15
7

25
18
A B C D E F
8
7
09
6
5
08
4
3
07
2
1
06
46
47
8
18
Ten acre Wood
Box Plantation
Tawd Vale Camp
Five acre Wood
Delf Wood
Tears Farm
Lowes
WN8
Ormskirk Lathom Park CE Prim Sch
Beechlawn
THE ALMONRY
CRANES LA
Cranes Hall Farm
HALL LA
West Wing
Lathom Park
Black Plantation
Research & Development Laboratory
Claytons
River Tawd
Spa Roughs
Damsteads
Nurseries
L40
Lord's Cottage
Stand Farm
SPA FOLD
DICK'S LA
Plough Inn (PH)
Spa Farm
SPA LA
VALE LA
COBB'S CLOUGH RD
COBB'S BROW LA
COBB'S BROW
Rogers Farm
Our Lady Queen of Peace RC High Sch
Websters
Washway Farm
PLOUGH LA
Cock Farm
Works
STANLEY WAY
SEATON PL
Stanley
SEDDON PL
SUMMER ST
GLENBURN RD
Lathom High Sch
F2
1 THORNBER
2 TEMPLEMARTIN
3 THORNBY
4 THORNDALE
MOSS COTTS
STATHAM RD
E2
1 SYCAMORE DR
2 TENBY
3 TEWKESBURY
4 TEVIOT
A577
FIRSWOOD RD
WN8
Slate Farm
SLATE LA
Works
Chapel House
SELBY PL
STANLEY RD
A5068
Fyles' Farm
DICKET'S LA
OLD ENGINE LA
NEVERSTITCH RD
Black Moss Sch
Brookfields Cty Prim Sch
SKELMERSDALE
BLAGUEGATE LA
Blaguegate
ORMSKIRK RD
Halfpenny La
HOLLANDS LA
Holland's Farm
Playing Fields
Works
B5312 RAILWAY RD
St Richards RC Prim Sch
Pennylands
Park Cty Prim Sch
Trinity Prim Sch
St Edmund's RC Prim Sch
Crow Orch Sch
WINDROWS
WINDGATE
HIGH ST
B5240

17
26

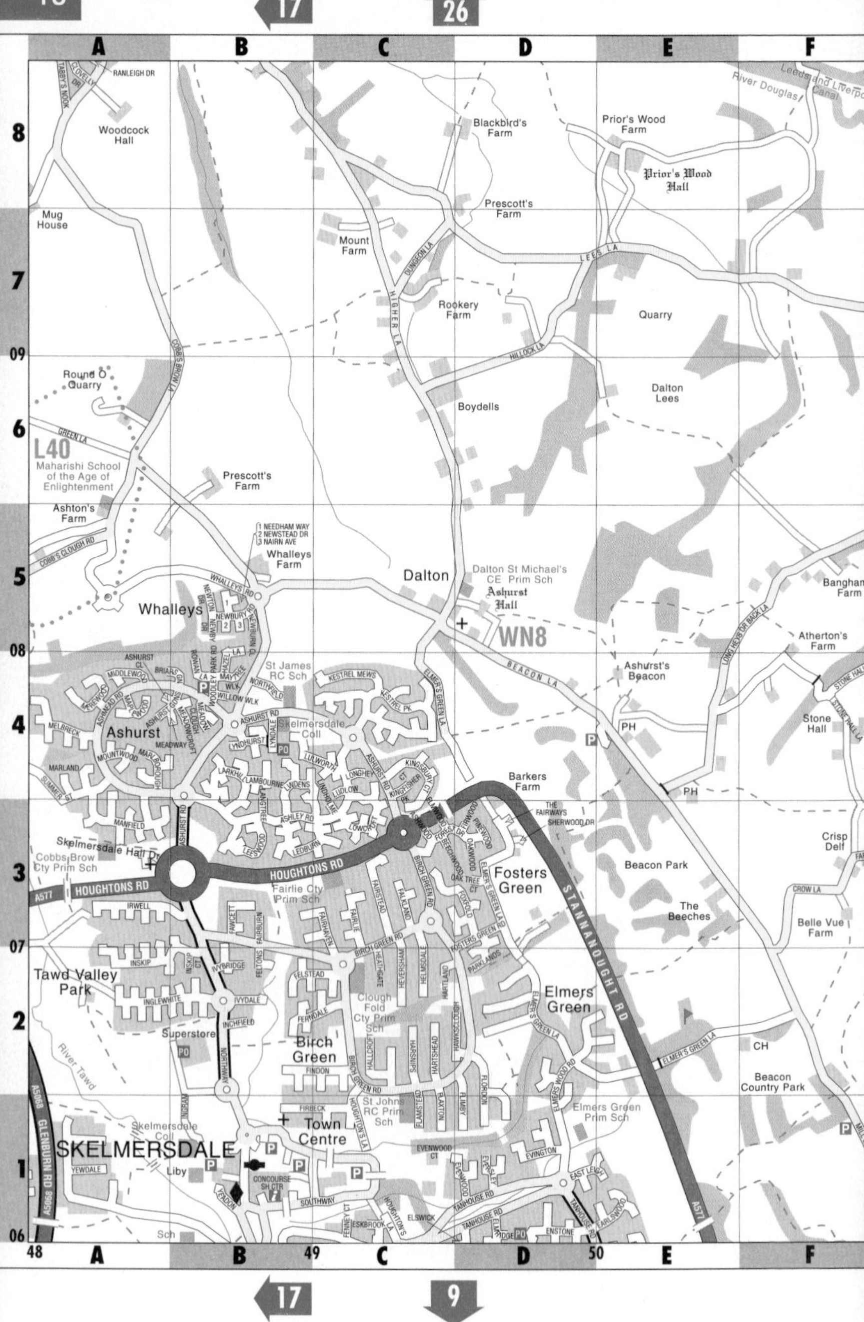

Woodcock Hall
Mug House
Blackbird's Farm
Prior's Wood Farm
Prior's Wood Hall
Prescott's Farm
Mount Farm
Rookery Farm
Quarry
Round O Quarry
Boydells
Dalton Lees
L40
Maharishi School of the Age of Enlightenment
Prescott's Farm
Ashton's Farm
Whalleys Farm
Dalton
Dalton St Michael's CE Prim Sch
Ashurst Hall
Bangham Farm
Whalleys
WN8
Atherton's Farm
Ashurst's Beacon
St James RC Sch
Skelmersdale Coll
Ashurst
Stone Hall
Barkers Farm
Crisp Delf
Cobbs Brow Cty Prim Sch
Fairlie Cty Prim Sch
Fosters Green
Beacon Park
The Beeches
Belle Vue Farm
Tawd Valley Park
Elmers Green
Clough Fold Cty Prim Sch
Superstore
Birch Green
Beacon Country Park
St Johns RC Prim Sch
Elmers Green Prim Sch
Town Centre
SKELMERSDALE
Skelmersdale Coll
Liby
Sch
HOUGHTONS RD
STANNANOUGHT RD
GLENBURN RD
BEACON LA
LEES LA
HIGHER LA
HILLOCK LA
River Douglas
Leeds and Liverpool Canal
River Tawd
1 NEEDHAM WAY
2 NEWSTEAD DR
3 NAIRN AVE
A B C D E F
8 7 6 5 4 3 2 1
09 08 07 06
48 49 50

17
9

27

A
B
C
D
E
F
8
7
09
6
5
08
4
3
07
2
1
06
52
53
BEACON VIEW
SPRING BANK
LOWTHER TERR
ASHFIELD TERR
B5375
SKULL HOUSE LA
THE VALE
GREENSLATE
GLEN DR
AVE
DINGLE AVE
BACK LA
VALE CL
HULLET CL
GREAVES CL
STOCKLEY DR
RUNSHAW AVE
BIRLEY CL
WHITEHALL AVE
MOOR AVE
ROOKERY AVE
WOODNOOK RD
NEWGATE AVE
Refuse Tip
East Quarry
Appley Bridge
APPLEY LA N
BEECH TREE AVE
FINCH MILL AVE
GROVEWOOD DR
PARK HEY DR
HERMITAGE CL
HILL CL
HIGHGATE CRES
Shevington Vale Prim Sch
Hullet Hole Wood
The Railway (PH)
Appley Bridge
MILL LA
MILL BANK
THE DELL
PO
Shevington Vale
CANAL BANK
THE BEACONS
CARWOOD CL
SHELLINGFORD CL
COXFIELD
ASH CL
THE NOOK
Martin's Farm
The Inn Between (PH)
HEYES ST
TILBURY GR
CHISACRE DR
ABBEY DALE
MABERRY CL
BRADHAVEN
MILES LA
SPEAKMANS DR
LEES LA
River Douglas
APPLEY LA S
AYREFIELD GR
Calico Wood Farm
M6
Halliwell Farm
Douglas Bank Farm
Holland Lees
LONG HEYS OR BACK LA
Quarry
Leeds & Liverpool Canal
Broadridings Farm
Shevington Com Prim Sch
HOUGHTON LA
CALICO WOOD AVE
MILES LA
B5375
NEW MILES LA
CH
STONE HALL LA
Forest Fold Farm
WN6
Ayrefield Farm
Coppice Bank Wood
BANK BROW
BANK RD
MAITLAND AVE
BEECHWOOD AVE
NAYLORFARM AVE
DOUGLAS AVE
DR
ST ANNE'S CT
THE OVAL
OAKWOOD
B5206
QUEENSWAY
WOODLANDS DR
PRINCE'S PK
GREENVALE
Lees Wood
Green Alley Wood
WN8
TAN PIT COTTS
Bank Top
AYREFIELD RD
Ayrefield House
Star Inn (PH)
ROBY MILL
Roby Mill
FARLEY LA
Walthew Green
Gathurst
Roby Mill CE Prim Sch
ST GABRIEL CL
Cemy
SCHOOL LA
Walthew Green Farm
B5206
Fox Inn (PH)
PO
WHITLEY RD
Johnson's Farm
Dean Brook
Dean Wood
ACKHURST LA
Convent
The Kingfisher (PH)
Quarry (dis)
Walthew Park
Pearson's Farm
GATHURST RD
Rough Park Wood
St Joseph's Con Ctr
LAFFORD LA
WN5
St John Rigby RC Sixth Form Coll
Jollies i'th Dean
Collage Farm
Orrell House Farm
STONE
BROW
GATHURST RD
St Teresa's RC Prim Sch
COLLEGE RD
HILL LA
HART'S LA
B5206
M6
SPRING RD

10

33

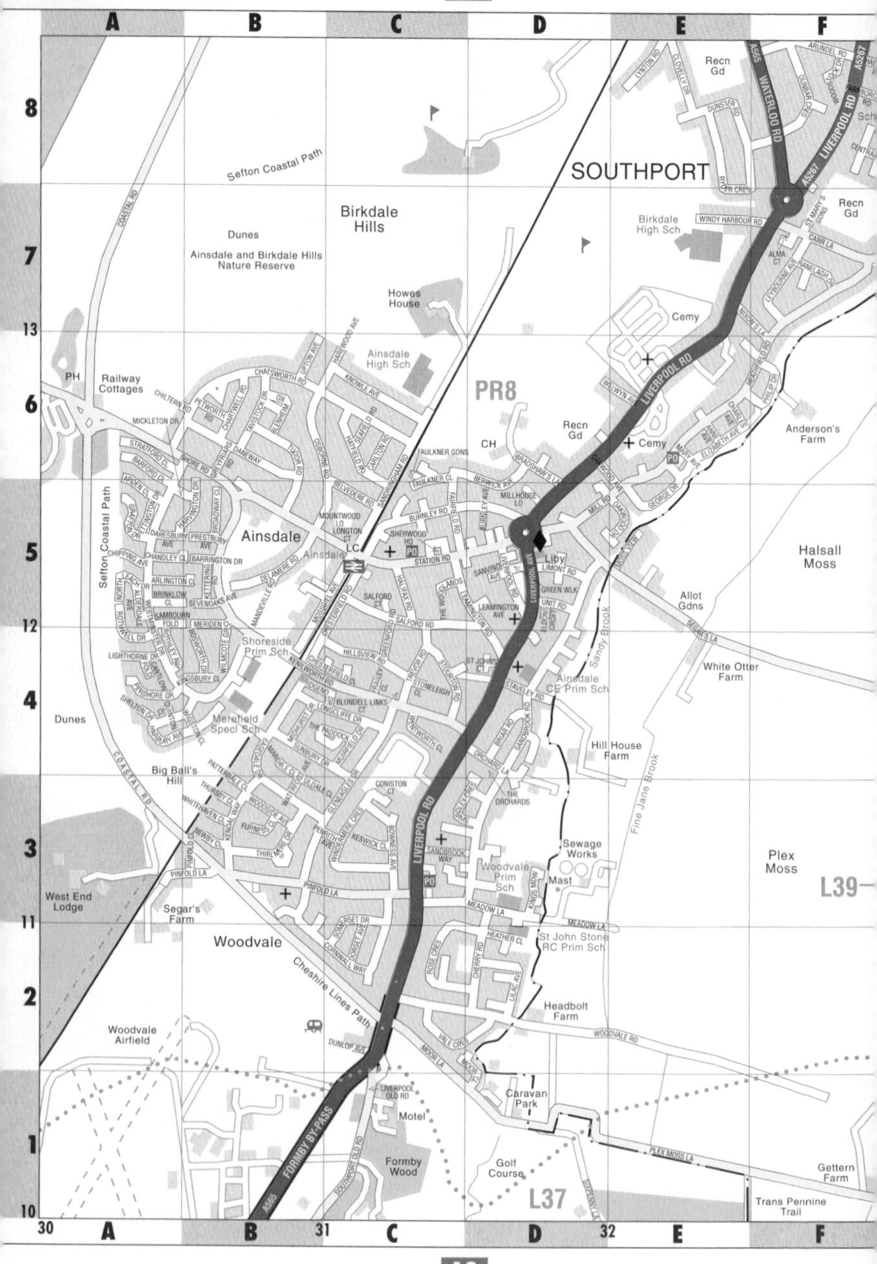
A
B
C
D
E
F
8
7
13
6
5
12
4
3
11
2
1
10
30
31
32
SOUTHPORT
Recn Gd
A565 WATERLOO RD
A5267 LIVERPOOL RD
ARUNDEL RD
LYNTON RD
CLOVELLY DR
DUNSTER RD
DUNBAR CRES
WOODSTOCK DR
Sch
CENTRAL
RYDER CRES
Sefton Coastal Path
Birkdale Hills
Dunes
Ainsdale and Birkdale Hills Nature Reserve
COASTAL RD
Birkdale High Sch
WINDY HARBOUR RD
ST MARY'S GDNS
CARR LA
ALMA CT
LEYBOURNE AVE
RANELAGH DR
Recn Gd
Howes House
Cemy
NIXON'S LA
Ainsdale High Sch
PR8
LIVERPOOL RD
WELWYN AVE
HEATHFIELD RD
PHILIP DR
PH
Railway Cottages
CHILTERN RD
CHATSWORTH RD
UPTON AVE
HAREWOOD AVE
KNOWLE AVE
MICKLETON DR
PETWORTH RD
CHARTWELL RD
TAVISTOCK DR
BLENHEIM RD
SEAFIELD RD
HATFIELD RD
CARLTON RD
CHARLES AVE
ANNE AVE
ELIZABETH AVE
MARY AVE
Anderson's Farm
Recn Gd
CH
Cemy
PO
STRATFORD CL
SHORE RD
GREYFRIARS RD
DANEWAY
TUDOR RD
OSBORNE RD
SANDRINGHAM RD
FAULKNER GDNS
FAULKNER CL
BERWICK AVE
BRADSHAW'S LA
GARTWOOD AVE
BARFORD CL
ARDEN CL
GRAFTON DR
HARVINGTON DR
BROADWAY CL
BELVEDERE RD
MILLHOUSE LO
MILL RD
OAKWOOD RD
GEORGE DR
BURNLEY RD
FAIRFIELD RD
BURNLEY AVE
MOUNTWOOD LO
LONGTON CT
DARESBURY AVE
PRESTBURY AVE
Ainsdale
SHERWOOD HO
LC
Ainsdale
PO
STATION RD
Liby
MOSS VIEW
Halsall Moss
CHIPPING AVE
CHANDLEY CL
BARRINGTON DR
DELAMERE RD
SALFORD CT
HALIFAX RD
THE WOODLANDS
SANVINO AVE
LIVERPOOL RD
LIVERPOOL AVE
LIMONT RD
ARLINGTON CL
KETTERING RD
GREEN WLK
Allot Gdns
BRINKLOW CL
SEVENOAKS AVE
LEAMINGTON RD
LEAMINGTON AVE
UNIT RD
CROFT
ELDONS
SAMBOURN FOLD
MERIDEN CL
MANDEVILLE RD
MOSSGIEL AVE
CHESTERFIELD RD
SALFORD RD
SEGAR'S LA
ROTHWELL DR
WESTMINSTER DR
ROTHLEY AVE
BOSWORTH DR
WILMCOTE GR
Shoreside Prim Sch
Sefton Coastal Path
HILLSVIEW RD
GREENFORD RD
TREVOR RD
STOURTON RD
ST JOHNS CT
Sandy Brook
LIGHTHORNE DR
CANTLOW FOLD
KINGSBURY CL
KENILWORTH RD
CHESTERFIELD CL
FRAILEY CL
STONELEIGH CL
White Otter Farm
Ainsdale CE Prim Sch
STAVELEY RD
BRIDGEND
BLUNDELL LINKS CT
LONGCLIFFE DR
Dunes
PERSHORE GR
SHELTON DR
QUINTON CL
WIGSTON CL
HARBURY AVE
Merefield Specl Sch
MIDHURST DR
THE PADDOCK
MUIRFIELD DR
WENTWORTH CL
BRIAR RD
SANDBROOK RD
Hill House Farm
SUNBURY DR
ORCHARD LA
Big Ball's Hill
COASTAL RD
PATTERDALE CL
THURSBY CL
ESKDALE DR
MARGATE CL
WATERFOOT AVE
ULDALE CL
GLENEAGLES DR
CONISTON CT
THE ORCHARDS
Fine Jane Brook
WHITEHAVEN CL
WOODSIDE AVE
KENDAL WAY
FURNESS CL
PENRITH AVE
WINDERMERE CRES
KESWICK CL
BOWNESS AVE
SANDBROOK WAY
Sewage Works
NEWBY CL
THIRLMERE DR
Plex Moss
PINFOLD CL
PINFOLD LA
Woodvale Prim Sch
Mast
PO
L39
West End Lodge
Segar's Farm
PINFOLD LA
KINGS MDW
MEADOW LA
MEADOW LA
SOMERSET DR
DORSET AVE
HEATHER CL
St John Stone RC Prim Sch
Woodvale
CORNWALL WAY
ROSE CRES
CHERRY RD
LILAC AVE
Cheshire Lines Path
Headbolt Farm
Woodvale Airfield
DUNLOP AVE
VALE CRES
WOODVALE RD
MOOR LA
MOOR CL
LIVERPOOL OLD RD
Caravan Park
Motel
FORMBY BY-PASS
A565
SOUTHPORT OLD RD
Formby Wood
Golf Course
PLEX MOSS LA
L37
Gettern Farm
Trans Pennine Trail

12

34
22
A
B
C
D
E
F
SHAFTESBURY AVE
SUFFOLK RD
ESSEX RD
HALSALL RD
Farnborough Road
Inf & Jun Schs
GUILDFORD RD
NEW CUT CL
CENTRAL AVE
Gorsehill
Farm
Fine Jane's Brook
PR8
Boundary Brook
LONDON LA
BIRKDALE COP
B5243
White Moss
Farm
Hodge's
Farm
8
Renacres
Moss
7
East Crantum
Farm
London
Farm
King's
Covert
The
Willows
Shirdley
Hill
SHAW CL
13
NEW CUT LA
SHAWS GARTH
6
New
Moss
RENACRES LA
Short Ranks
Farm
Halsall
Moss
Old Canal
Manor House
Farm
BARLOW'S LA
CABIN LA
5
Olverston
House
12
L39
HEADBOLT LA
4
SEGAR'S LA
New Cut Brook
Rain
Bag
Barn House
Farm
Front
Covert
SPENCER'S LA
3
MICHAEL'S LA
11
Heather
Farm
Green Kettle
House
2
PR8
PLUMPTON LA
Colonel's
Holt
Gettern Mere
Farm
CARR MOSS LA
Plex
Moss
Holt
Farm
1
L37
Carr
Moss
PLEX MOSS LA
10
33
34
35
13
22

21
35

A
B
C
D
E
F
8
7
13
6
5
12
4
3
11
2
1
10
36
37
38
PR8
L40
L39
A570
B5243
B5242
A5147
SNAPE GN
TURNING LA
Black Brook Bridge
Carr Cross
Cat Tail House
Sandy Brook
JACKSMERE LA
Jack's Mere
St Mark's CE Prim Sch
Scarisbrick
Mount Farm
WOODLAND AVE
HILLCREST DR
CULSHAW WAY
BESCAR BROW LA
EVERARD CL
Chapel School Plantation
CHURCH FIELDS
HEATHEY LA
Jacksmere House
Hooton's Farm
BULLENS LA
SOUTHPORT RD
Eas Brook
PH
SHAW CL
Shirdley Hill
WILLOW BROOK
Bullen's Brook
SHAWS GARTH
Delph Wood
Black Brook
BLACK MOSS LA
Black Moss Farm
Park Plantation
Ellen's Home Farm
Scarisbrick Wood
Lower House Farm
Wharton's Farm
Sutch's Farm
Paddock Wood
Carr Brook
RENACRES LA
Renacres Hall
Brook House Farm
GORSUCH LA
Gorsuch Hall
Scarisbrick Bridge
WHEELWRIGHTS WHARF
Gregory Farm
NEW CUT LA
Pinfold
FOUR LANE ENDS
Model House Farm
Leeds & Liverpool Canal
Marsh Hey Farm
Halsall Moss
MORRIS HEY
PINFOLD LA
Bristow Farm
GREGORY LA
MORRIS LA
White House Farm
SMALL LA
HALSALL RD
High Wood
Gesterfield Farm
Grange Farm
THE BARRACKS
CROSS LA
Halsall House
NORTH MOOR LA
THE RUNNEL
Mill Brook
Halsall
North Moor Pit
North Moor
NEW ST
SUMMERWOOD LA
CHESTNUT CL
Halsall Hall
HALSALL HALL DR
Works
CARR MOSS LA
Carr Moss Farm
HALSALL MANOR CT
St Cuthbert's CE Prim Sch
HARRIDGE LA

21
14

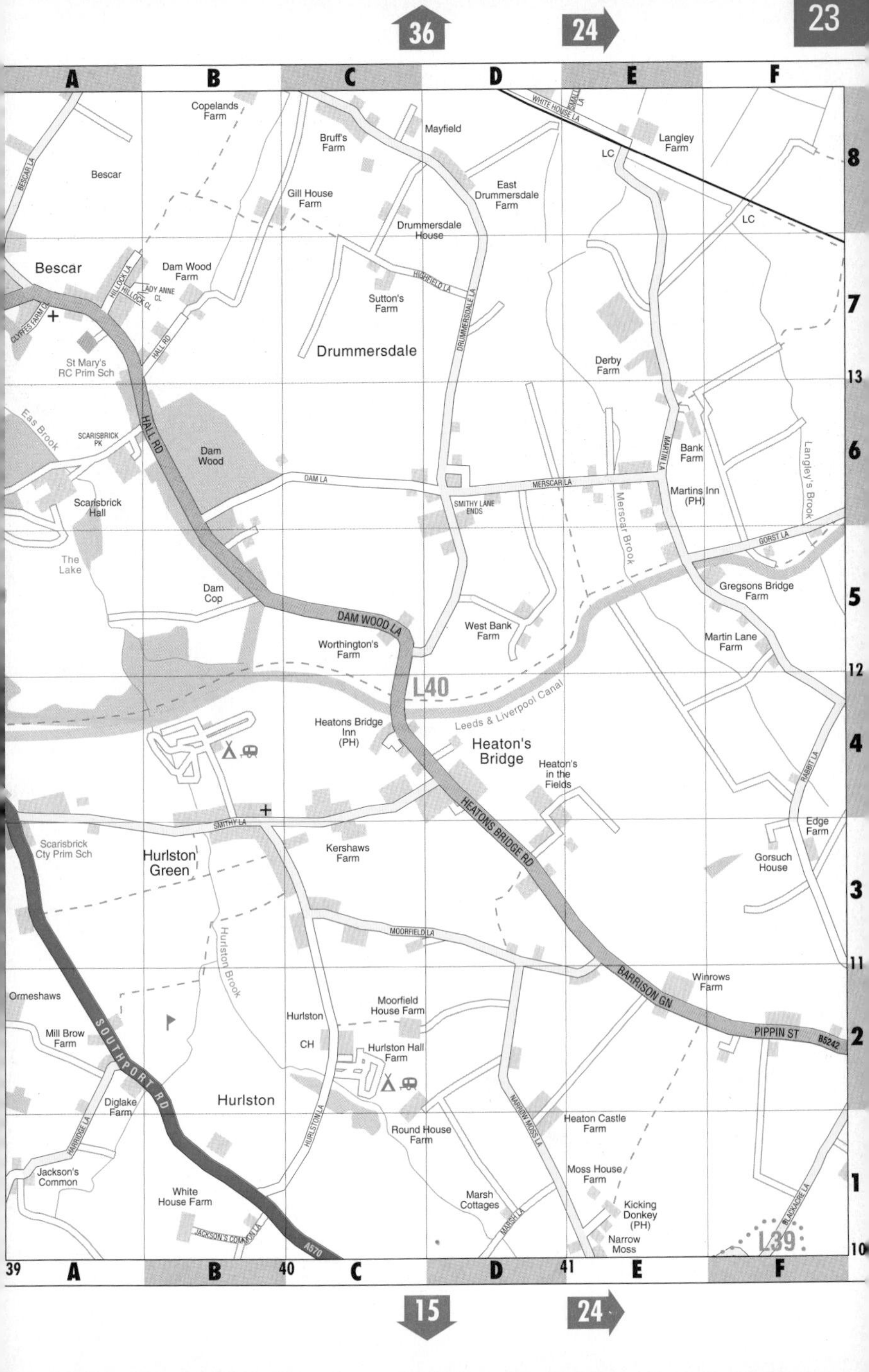
36
24
A
B
C
D
E
F
Copelands Farm
Bruff's Farm
Mayfield
WHITE HOUSE LA
SMALL LA
Langley Farm
LC
8
BESCAR LA
Bescar
Gill House Farm
East Drummersdale Farm
Drummersdale House
LC
Bescar
Dam Wood Farm
HILLOCK LA
LADY ANNE CL
HILLOCK CL
HIGHFIELD LA
Sutton's Farm
7
CLIFFES FARM CL
HALL RD
DRUMMERSDALE LA
Drummersdale
St Mary's RC Prim Sch
Derby Farm
13
Eas Brook
SCARISBRICK PK
HALL RD
Dam Wood
MARTIN LA
Bank Farm
Langley's Brook
6
DAM LA
MERSCAR LA
Martins Inn (PH)
Scarisbrick Hall
SMITHY LANE ENDS
Merscar Brook
GORST LA
The Lake
Dam Cop
Gregsons Bridge Farm
5
DAM WOOD LA
West Bank Farm
Worthington's Farm
Martin Lane Farm
12
L40
Leeds & Liverpool Canal
Heatons Bridge Inn (PH)
Heaton's Bridge
4
Heaton's in the Fields
RABBIT LA
SMITHY LA
HEATONS BRIDGE RD
Edge Farm
Scarisbrick Cty Prim Sch
Hurlston Green
Kershaws Farm
Gorsuch House
3
Hurlston Brook
MOORFIELD LA
11
BARRISON GN
Winrows Farm
Ormeshaws
Moorfield House Farm
SOUTHPORT RD
Hurlston
Mill Brow Farm
PIPPIN ST
B5242
2
CH
Hurlston Hall Farm
Diglake Farm
Hurlston
NARROW MOSS LA
Heaton Castle Farm
HARRIDGE LA
HURLSTON LA
Round House Farm
Jackson's Common
Moss House Farm
1
White House Farm
Marsh Cottages
Kicking Donkey (PH)
BLACKACRE LA
JACKSON'S COMMON LA
MARSH LA
Narrow Moss
L39
A570
10
39
40
41
15
24

23
37

Brandreth Farm
Curlew Farm
Burscough Moss
Moss Farm
New House Farm
Sewage Works
Marsh Moss
Wood End Farm
Marsh Moss House
Monks Farm
Moss Nook
Back Moss Lane Farm
Batloom
New Lane
LC
New Lane
Crabtree Bridge Farm
Crabtree LC
Factory
Burscough Bridge
New Lane Bridge (swing)
Farmers Arms (PH)
Martin Hall Farm
Sports Ctr
St John's CE Prim Sch
Burscough Bridge Meth Prim Sch
Orrell Farm
Latham Slipway (PH)
Crabtree Farm
Wks
Leeds & Liverpool Canal
Langley's Brook
Burscough Cty Prim Sch
Liby
Priory High Sch
L40
Burscough
Burscough Junc
Plantation Cott
Langley's Brook Farm
Burscough Lordsgate Township CE Prim Sch
Yew Tree Farm
Airfield (dis)
Ind Est
Burscough RC Prim Sch
Burscough Hall Farm
Bull and Dog Inn (PH)
Hotel
Merridale Farm
Works
Mill Dam Farm
Abbey Brook
Ellar Brook
Warm Row Farm
Blythe Cotts
Blythe Hall
LIVERPOOL RD N
LIVERPOOL RD S
SQUARE LA
JUNCTION LA
MOSS LA
PIPPIN ST
HIGH LA
1 LABURNUM GR
2 WILLOW CRES
E5
1 STATION APP
2 PALAIS BLDGS
3 SMITHY WLK
1 SCHOOL HOUSE GR
2 KILLINGBECK CL
3 CRABTREE CL
1 BOUNDARY LA
2 WILLOW END
3 CLARKFIELD CL
1 BRETHERTON CT
2 PARDOE CT
3 COACH HO CT
4 THORNABRIDGE AVE
5 PARBOLD CL
6 RICHMOND CT
A B C D E F
8 7 6 5 4 3 2 1
13 12 11 10
42 43 44

23
16

38
26
A
B
C
D
E
F
Springwell Farm
Prescott's Farm
Prescott Bridge
Wham Bridge
Anchor Farm
Saulthouse Farm
Copperwood Inn
Latham's Farm
MOSS LA
A59
MISSION COTTS
LC
Townsend's Farm
RUFFORD RD
B5246
Wham Ditch
Mill Ditch
River Douglas
Warper's Moss
L40
Hoscar Moss
MEADOW LA
MAINS LA
Wanes Blades Bridge
Snipe Hall Farm
WARPERS MOSS LA
Leeds & Liverpool Canal (Rufford Branch)
New Sutch Farm
Eller Brook
Nurseries
Old Sutch House
Bleak Hall Farm
BLEAK LA
WOOD LA
Tryer's Farm
WANES BLADES RD
SUTCH LA
Shaw's LC
Sandyways Farm
SCHOOL LA
Runnel Brow
Four Lane Ends LC
Hoscar
Stocks Farm
DAISY LA
WHEAT LA
PH
CARR LA
Tawdside
Sewage Works
Henry's Farm
HOSCAR MOSS RD
Glovers Bridge
FROG LA
River Tawd
DEANS LA
Carr Lane Farm
MOSS BRIDGE
BRIARS LA
BRIARS BROOK
HOLLOWFORD LA
RING O'BELLS LA
CANAL BANK
THREE OAKS CL
Briars Hall Farm
Ring o'Bells
Moss Bridge
MOSS BRIDGE LA
Leeds & Liverpool Canal
Spencer's Bridge
Rigby's Farm
BACK LA
Duttons Farm
LOWRY HILL LA
B5240
Newburgh
HOBCROSS LA
Lathom
Taylor's Farm
Lowry Hill
COURSE LA
SANDY LA
A5209
HALL LA
Round Thorn
WN8
Nursery
Watkinson's Farm
Lower Park Farm
Lawrensons Farm
TEARS LA
8
7
13
6
5
12
4
3
11
2
1
10
46
47
17
26

25
39

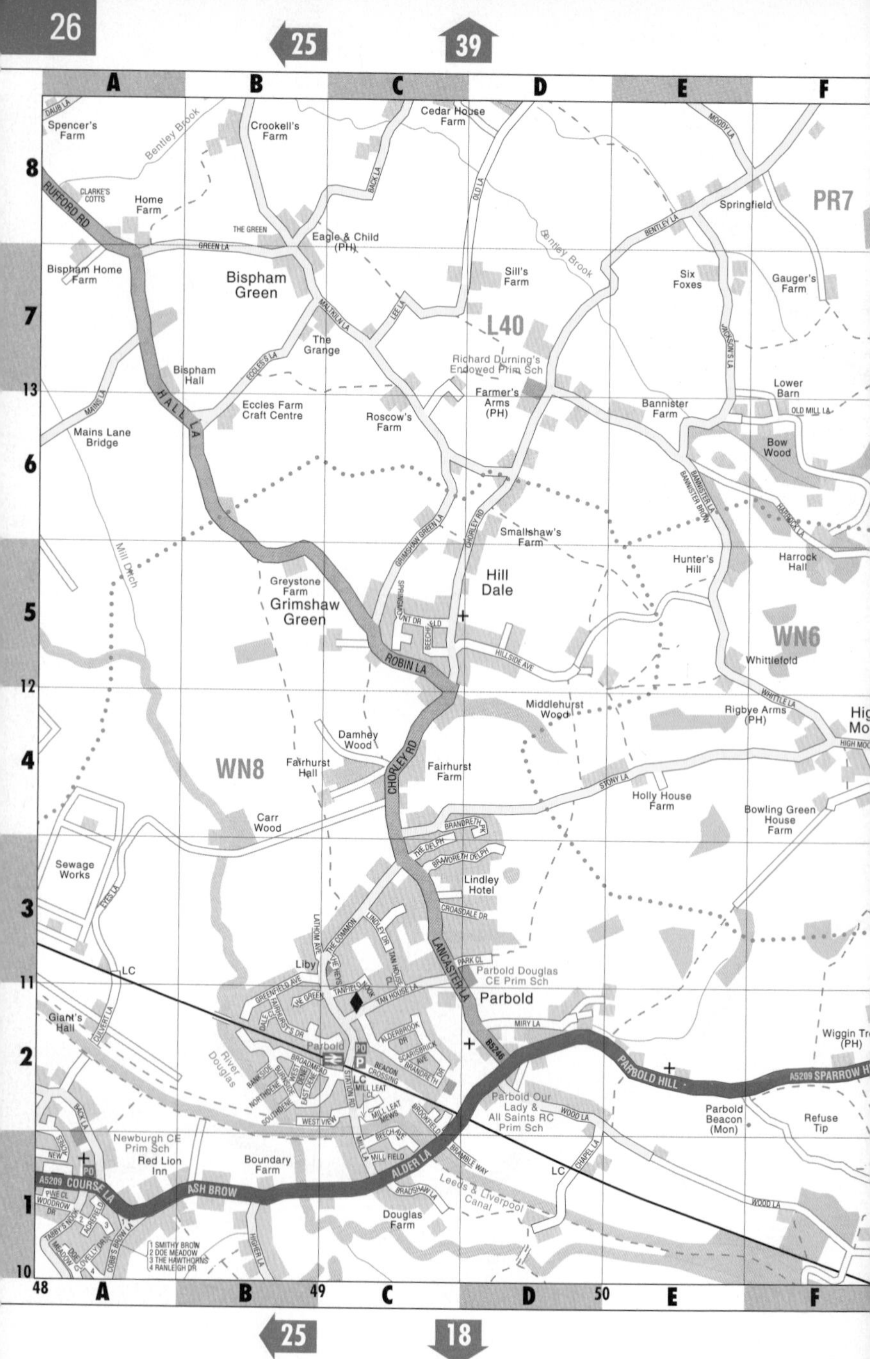
A
B
C
D
E
F
Spencer's Farm
Crookell's Farm
Cedar House Farm
Bentley Brook
RUFFORD RD
CLARKE'S COTTS
Home Farm
THE GREEN
GREEN LA
Eagle & Child (PH)
BACK LA
OLD LA
Springfield
PR7
BENTLEY LA
MOODY LA
Bispham Home Farm
Bispham Green
Sill's Farm
Six Foxes
Gauger's Farm
MALTKILN LA
LEE LA
L40
The Grange
JACKSON'S LA
Richard Durning's Endowed Prim Sch
Bispham Hall
ECCLES'S LA
Farmer's Arms (PH)
Lower Barn
MAINS LA
HALL LA
Eccles Farm Craft Centre
Roscow's Farm
Bannister Farm
OLD MILL LA
Mains Lane Bridge
Bow Wood
BANNISTER LA
BANNISTER BROW
HARROCK LA
Mill Ditch
GRIMSHAW GREEN LA
CHORLEY RD
Smallshaw's Farm
Hunter's Hill
Harrock Hall
Greystone Farm
Hill Dale
Grimshaw Green
BEECHFIELD
HILLSIDE AVE
WN6
Whittlefold
ROBIN LA
WHITTLE LA
Middlehurst Wood
Rigbye Arms (PH)
Damhey Wood
WN8
Fairhurst Hall
Fairhurst Farm
HIGH MOOR
STONY LA
Holly House Farm
Carr Wood
Bowling Green House Farm
BRANDRETH PK
THE DELPH
BRANDRETH DELPH
Sewage Works
Lindley Hotel
EYES LA
CROASDALE DR
LATHOM AVE
THE COMMON
LINDLEY DR
TAN HOUSE CL
LANCASTER LA
Liby
PARK CL
Parbold Douglas CE Prim Sch
LC
GREENFIELD AVE
THE GREEN
TANFIELD NOOK
TAN HOUSE LA
Parbold
Giant's Hall
CULVERT LA
MIRY LA
ALDERBROOK DR
SCARISBRICK AVE
River Douglas
Parbold
BROADMEAD
BEACON CROSSING
BRANDRETH DR
B5246
PARBOLD HILL
A5209 SPARROW H
Wiggin Tree (PH)
STATION RD
MILL LEAT CL
MILL LEAT MEWS
Parbold Our Lady & All Saints RC Prim Sch
WOOD LA
Parbold Beacon (Mon)
Refuse Tip
BACK LA
WEST VIEW
BROOKFIELD
Newburgh CE Prim Sch
Red Lion Inn
Boundary Farm
MILL LA
MILL FIELD
BRAMBLE WAY
CHAPEL LA
A5209 COURSE LA
ASH BROW
ALDER LA
Leeds & Liverpool Canal
BRADSHAW LA
WOOD LA
Douglas Farm
HIGHER LA
1 SMITHY BROW
2 DOE MEADOW
3 THE HAWTHORNS
4 RANLEIGH DR
48
49
50
8
7
13
6
5
12
4
3
11
2
1
10

25
18

40
28

A
B
C
D
E
F
Sanderson House
Charity Farm
PR7
Scarisbrick Arms (PH)
Copyhold Farm
Higher Wrennall
Cowling's Farm
High Hopes
Sandhole Farm
North Tunley
Wrightington Bar
Dwerry House
Toogood Farm
Harrock Hill
PR7
Harrock Old Windmill
Wrights Coverts
L40
Mossy Lea
Mast
Wrightington Mossy Lea Prim Sch
Butteries Wood
Hesketh House
Hill House Fold
Stone Leach
Higher Barn
South Tunley Farm
Hind's Head (PH)
Diglake Farm
Pine Covert
Lathom's Charity Farm
Tunley Brook
Tunley Moss Farm
Lassell House Farm
Robin Hood
WN6
High Moor Farm
Moss House Farm
Hunger Hill
Boggart House
Robin Hood Farm
Boar's Den Farm
Bury Hey Wood
Tunley Moss
Primrose Woods
Wrightington Hotel
Black Field Plantation
Dangerous Corner
Parbold Hall
The Rookery
Wrightington Pond
Wrightington
The Dingle
Delf House
WN8
Big Wood
Delf House Wood
Nursery
All Saints CE Prim Sch
NORTH QUARRY BSNS PK
SPARROW HILL
HALL LA
CROW ORCHARD RD
APPLEY LA N
MOSSY LEA RD
WOOD LA
B5250
B5375
A5209
8
7
13
6
5
12
4
3
11
2
1
10
52
53

19
28

27
41

Coppull
PR7
Elmhurst Farm
Blainscough Hall
Wet Oaks Wood
Vause Farm
Coppull Moor Farm
Alison Arms (PH)
Patrick Farm
St John's CE Prim Sch
Coppull Moor
Chisnall Wood
Moorhouse Farm
The Grange
Bogburn Hall Farm
Stars Brook
Langtree Old Hall Farm
New Seven Stars (PH)
PRESTON RD
Cross Farm
WN1
Chadwick Farm
Lone Farm
WN6
Gorse Hall
St Joseph's Wrightington RC Prim Sch
Potters Farm
Thompson House
Pepper Lane Farm
Langtree Hall
Saddle Hill Farm
Shevington Moor
Standish Com High Sch
St Marie's RC Prim Sch
STANDISH
Hotel
Chamberlain's Farm
Black Horse Farm
ALMOND BROOK RD
CROW ORCHARD RD
RECTORY LA
Lark Hill
Schs
Liby
HIGH ST
SCHOOL LA
Bridge Farm
CHISNALL LA
COPPULL MOOR LA
MOSSY LEA RD
PEPPER LA
LANGTREE LA
SHEVINGTON LA
B5251 SPENDMORE LA
CHAPEL LA

27

42
30
A
B
C
D
E
F
Coppull Old Hall
Coppull Hall Wood
Coppull Hall
COPPULL HALL LA
GREEN LA
Green Lane Farm
Pear Tree Farm
JOLLY TAR LA
PR7
Coppull Brow Farm
WIGAN LA
A5106
Eller Brook
Moss Ditch
Grey Horse (PH)
Holt Farm
Buckow Brook
Mill Bridge Farm
White Cross Hotel (PH)
Talbot House Farm
Refuse Tip
Bores Farm
BORES HILL
Wrennalls Farm
PLATT LA
BRADLEY LA
HUTTON ST
Crown Hotel (PH)
Bradley Brook
CHORLEY RD
BRADLEY HILL TRAD EST
WN6
Rectory Farm
RECTORY LA
Refuse Tip
Worthington Hall
Kilhey Court Hotel
WN1
Worthington Lakes (Resrs)
Works
LAKE SIDE COTTS
MAYFAIR COTTS
BARROWCROFT CL
BROOKSIDE RD
CORNWALL CRES
DORSET RD
WESSEX CL
ESSEX
SUSSEX CL
DEVON DR
CANAL ROW
Arley Wood
CH
ARLEY LA
Crawshaw Hall
Adlington Park
Adlington Hall Farm
River Douglas
Leeds and Liverpool Canal
Aberdeen Bridge
BL6
Aberdeen Farm
Hollins Head
BLUNDELL LA
Worthington Farm
WN2
Pennington Farm
PENNINGTON LA
Sand Pit
Sand Pit
Rigby House Farm
COMMON END
STONEY LA
THE COMMON
CRAWFORD AVE
OLD SCHOOL LA
CASTLE DR
ADLINGTON
SANDRINGHAM CL
LEWIS CL
CASTLE HOUSE LA
BALMORAL
SANDY LA
CARRINGTON RD
PARK RD
ACRESFIELD
WINDSOR AVE
WARWICK ST
GRAFTON ST
CHAPEL ST
SMITH ST
HOLDEN ST
CROOK ST
STONER RD
BONDS LA
THE POPLARS
HATTON ST
Adlington Cty Prim Sch
Rigshaw Bridge
Allanson Hall
PR6
WESTHOUGHTON RD
A6
DANESWAY
CHATSWORTH CT
8
7
13
6
5
12
4
3
11
2
1
10
58
59

30

29

43

ADLINGTON
Anderton
PR6
PR7
BL6
WN1
WN2
Rothwells Farm
Anderton Park
Tan Pits Farm
The Shawes
Roscoe Lowe
Lower Rivington Resr
The Castle
Headley Cross House
Millstone Hotel (PH)
Works
Woodward House Farm
Huyton House
Grimeford Village
Brown House Farm
Anderton Manor Farm
Lakeland Farm
Grimeford Farm
Goodman's Fold Farm
Crow's Nest Farm
White Hill
Great Ryeley
Whitehill Farm
Denton's Farm
Rivington Service Area
Anderton Old Hall Farm
CH
PH
River Douglas
Sewage Works
Crowshaw Farm
Holmes House
New Inn (PH)
Pennington Hill
Little Scotland
Rollinson House Farm
Makinson's Farm
Blackrod
Wood's Barn Farm
Ridgeway Arms Hotel (PH)
Copperas House
Sibbering's Farm
Cemy
Tucker's Hill Farm
Tucker's Hill
Ridgway Bridge
St Paul's CE Prim Sch
St Joseph's RC Prim Sch
Sch
Liby
Adlington
Blackrod
CHORLEY RD
BOLTON RD
BLACKROD BY-PASS RD
CHURCH ST
MANCHESTER RD
STATION RD
RAILWAY RD
M61
A673
B6227
B5408
B5238
A6
1 OLLERTON ST
2 NIGHTINGALE ST
3 CARLISLE PL
4 BROAD OAK CL
1 CONISTON AVE
2 WINDERMERE DR
3 FACTORY LA
4 FIELDING PL
1 GABBOT ST
2 ANDERTON ST
1 STATION RD
2 CEMETERY VIEW
3 WALTON ST
4 CANAL ST
5 GAS ST
6 ATHERTON ST
7 OTTERSIDE ST
VICTORIA ST 1
BIG FOLD 2
RIVINGTON ST 3
HORROBIN LA
GRIMEFORD LA
GREENLAND LA
ANDERTON LA
BLUNDELL LA
COPPERAS LA
DARK LA
LITTLE SCOTLAND
TUCKER'S HILL BROW
CROWN LA
MOSS LA
STAR LA
A B C D E F
8 7 6 5 4 3 2 1
13 12 11 10
60 61 62

29

44

B4
1 DICKINSON CT
2 PETER MARTIN ST
3 WRIGHT ST W
4 JULIA MEWS
5 WHITTON MEWS
6 MOTTRAM MEWS
7 FLOCKTON CT
8 CROXTON WLK
9 BEATRICE MEWS

B4
10 HARCOURT MEWS
11 ABRAHAM ST
12 SPRING GDNS
13 RAWLINSON ST
14 ABBOTT ST
15 ROBINSON ST
16 BACK RAWLINSON ST

E1
1 SYCAMORE WLK
2 ROWAN AVE
3 FIR TREE WAY
4 BIRCH TREE WAY
5 CHERRY TREE WAY
6 ELM GR
7 ARROWSMITH CT
8 ASH GR
9 OAK AVE

50

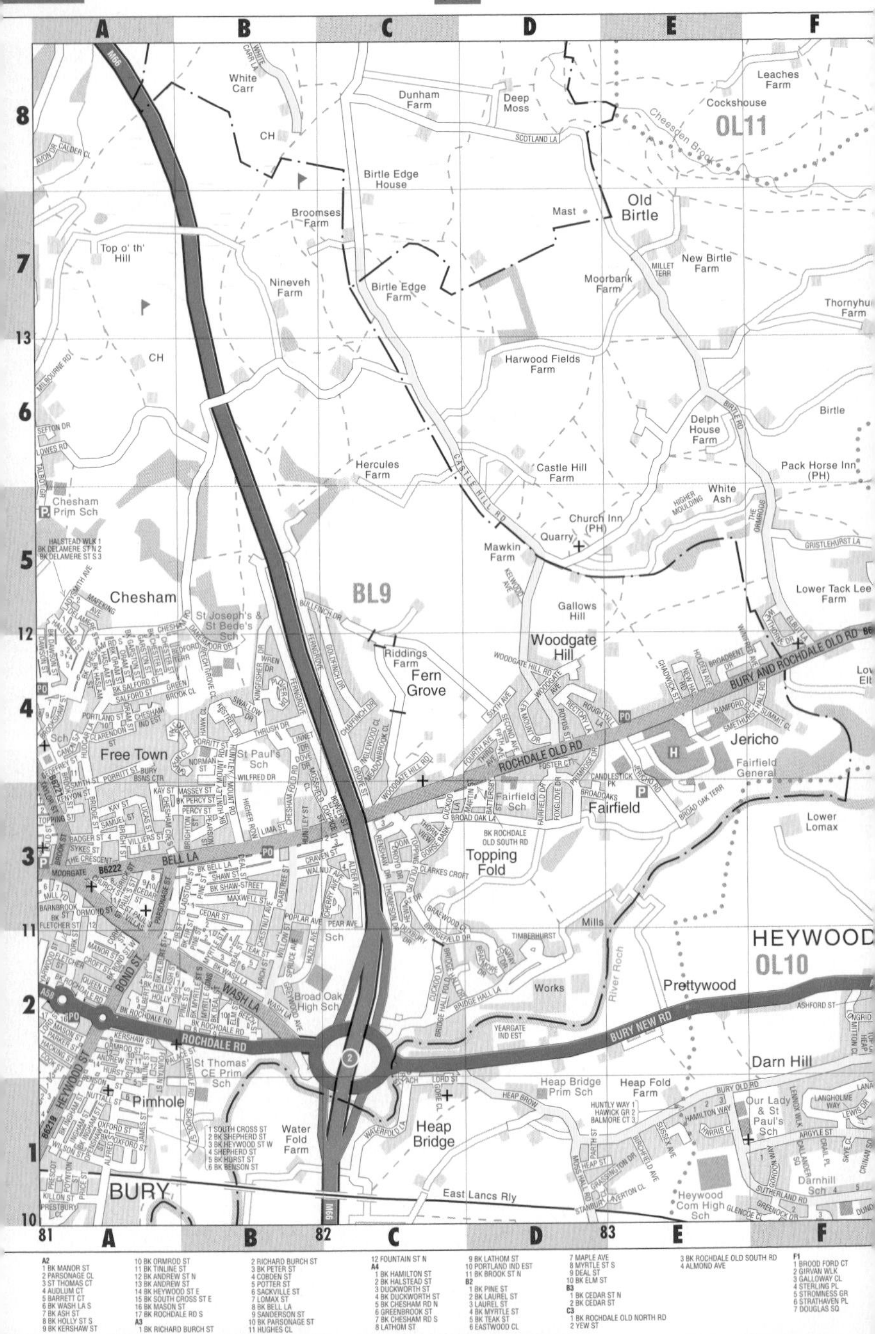

A2
1 BK MANOR ST
2 PARSONAGE CL
3 ST THOMAS CT
4 AUDLUM CT
5 BARRETT CT
6 BK WASH LA S
7 BK ASH ST
8 BK HOLLY ST S
9 BK KERSHAW ST
10 BK ORMROD ST
11 BK TINLINE ST
12 BK ANDREW ST N
13 BK ANDREW ST
14 BK HEYWOOD ST E
15 BK SOUTH CROSS ST E
16 BK MASON ST
17 BK ROCHDALE RD S

A3
1 BK RICHARD BURCH ST
2 RICHARD BURCH ST
3 BK PETER ST
4 COBDEN ST
5 POTTER ST
6 SACKVILLE ST
7 LOMAX ST
8 BK BELL LA
9 SANDERSON ST
10 BK PARSONAGE ST
11 HUGHES CL
12 FOUNTAIN ST N

A4
1 BK HAMILTON ST
2 BK HALSTEAD ST
3 DUCKWORTH ST
4 BK DUCKWORTH ST
5 BK CHESHAM RD N
6 GREENBROOK ST
7 BK CHESHAM RD S
8 LATHOM ST
9 BK LATHOM ST
10 PORTLAND IND EST
11 BK BROOK ST N

B2
1 BK PINE ST
2 BK LAUREL ST
3 LAUREL ST
4 BK MYRTLE ST
5 BK TEAK ST
6 EASTWOOD CL
7 MAPLE AVE
8 MYRTLE ST S
9 DEAL ST
10 BK ELM ST

B3
1 BK CEDAR ST N
2 BK CEDAR ST

C3
1 BK ROCHDALE OLD NORTH RD
2 YEW ST
3 BK ROCHDALE OLD SOUTH RD
4 ALMOND AVE

F1
1 BROOD FORD CT
2 GIRVAN WLK
3 GALLOWAY CL
4 STERLING PL
5 STROMNESS GR
6 STRATHAVEN PL
7 DOUGLAS SQ

34

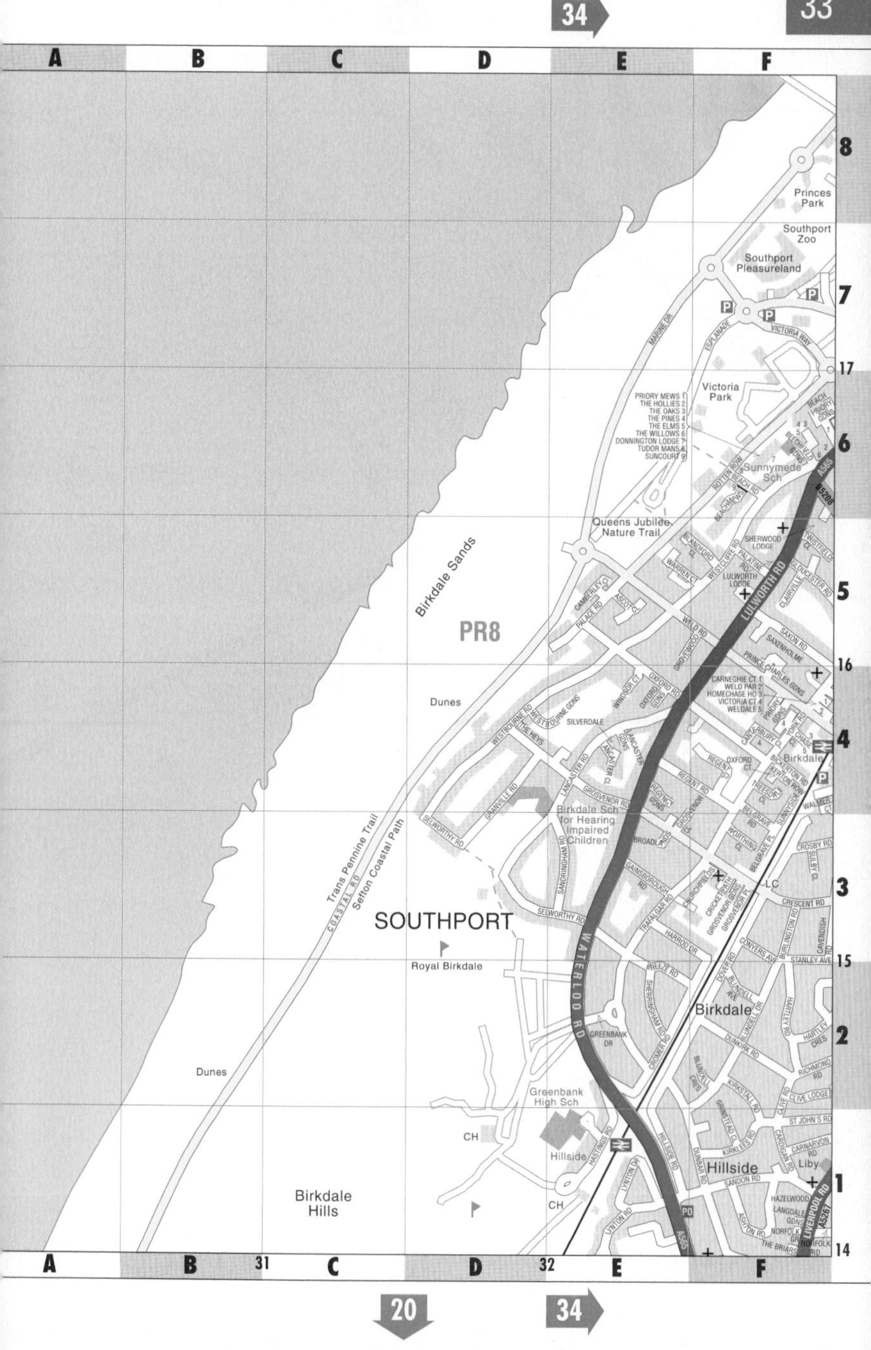

A
B
C
D
E
F
8
7
17
6
5
16
4
3
15
2
1
14
31
32
Princes Park
Southport Zoo
Southport Pleasureland
MARINE DR
ESPLANADE
VICTORIA WAY
Victoria Park
PRIORY MEWS 1
THE HOLLIES 2
THE OAKS 3
THE PINES 4
THE ELMS 5
THE WILLOWS 6
DONNINGTON LODGE 7
TUDOR MANS 8
SUNCOURT 9
Sunnymede Sch
ROTTEN ROW
BEACH RD
BEACHMEWS
Queens Jubilee Nature Trail
Birkdale Sands
PR8
SHERWOOD LODGE
LULWORTH LODGE
LULWORTH RD
A565
B5208
WESTCLIFFE RD
PALATINE RD
WARREN CT
CAMBERLEY CL
PALACE RD
ASCOT CL
WELD RD
GROVEWOOD
SAXON RD
SAXENHOLME
PRINCE CHARLES GDNS
CARNEGHIE CT 1
WELD PAR 2
HOMECHASE HO 3
VICTORIA CT 4
WELDALE 5
OXFORD RD
OXFORD GDNS
WINDSOR CT
Dunes
WESTBOURNE RD
WESTBOURNE GDNS
THE HEYS
SILVERDALE
LANCASTER GDNS
LANCASTER CL
LANCASTER RD
GRANVILLE RD
GROSVENOR RD
REGENCY GDNS
REGENT RD
OXFORD CT
CANTERBURY CL
Birkdale
BICKERTON RD
KERTON ROW
TREESDALE CL
SUNNYSIDE
WALMER CT
SELWORTHY RD
Birkdale Sch for Hearing Impaired Children
BROADLANDS
BELGRAVE RD
WORTHING CL
BELGRAVE PL
CROSBY RD
SULBY CL
Trans Pennine Trail
Sefton Coastal Path
COASTAL RD
SANDRINGHAM RD
GAINSBOROUGH RD
CHURCHFIELDS
CRICKET PATH
GROSVENOR GDNS
GROSVENOR PL
LC
CRESCENT RD
SOUTHPORT
TRAFALGAR RD
HARROD DR
CONVERS AVE
BURLINGTON RD
CAVENDISH
STANLEY AVE
Royal Birkdale
WATERLOO RD
BREEZE RD
SHERRINGHAM RD
DOVER RD
BLUNDELL AVE
BLUNDELL DR
HARTLEY RD
HARTLEY CRES
GREENBANK DR
CROMER RD
DUNKIRK RD
RICHMOND RD
Dunes
BLUNDELL CRES
KIRKSTALL RD
CLIVE RD
CLIVE LODGE
Greenbank High Sch
GRINSTEAD CL
ST JOHN'S RD
CARDIGAN RD
CH
HASTINGS RD
Hillside
HILLSIDE RD
DUNBAR RD
KIRKLEES RD
CARNARVON RD
Liby
Hillside
SANDON RD
LIVERPOOL RD
A5267
LYNTON DR
HAZELWOOD
LANGDALE GDNS
Birkdale Hills
CH
LYNTON RD
PO
ASHTON RD
NORFOLK GR
NORFOLK RD
THE BRIARS

20
34

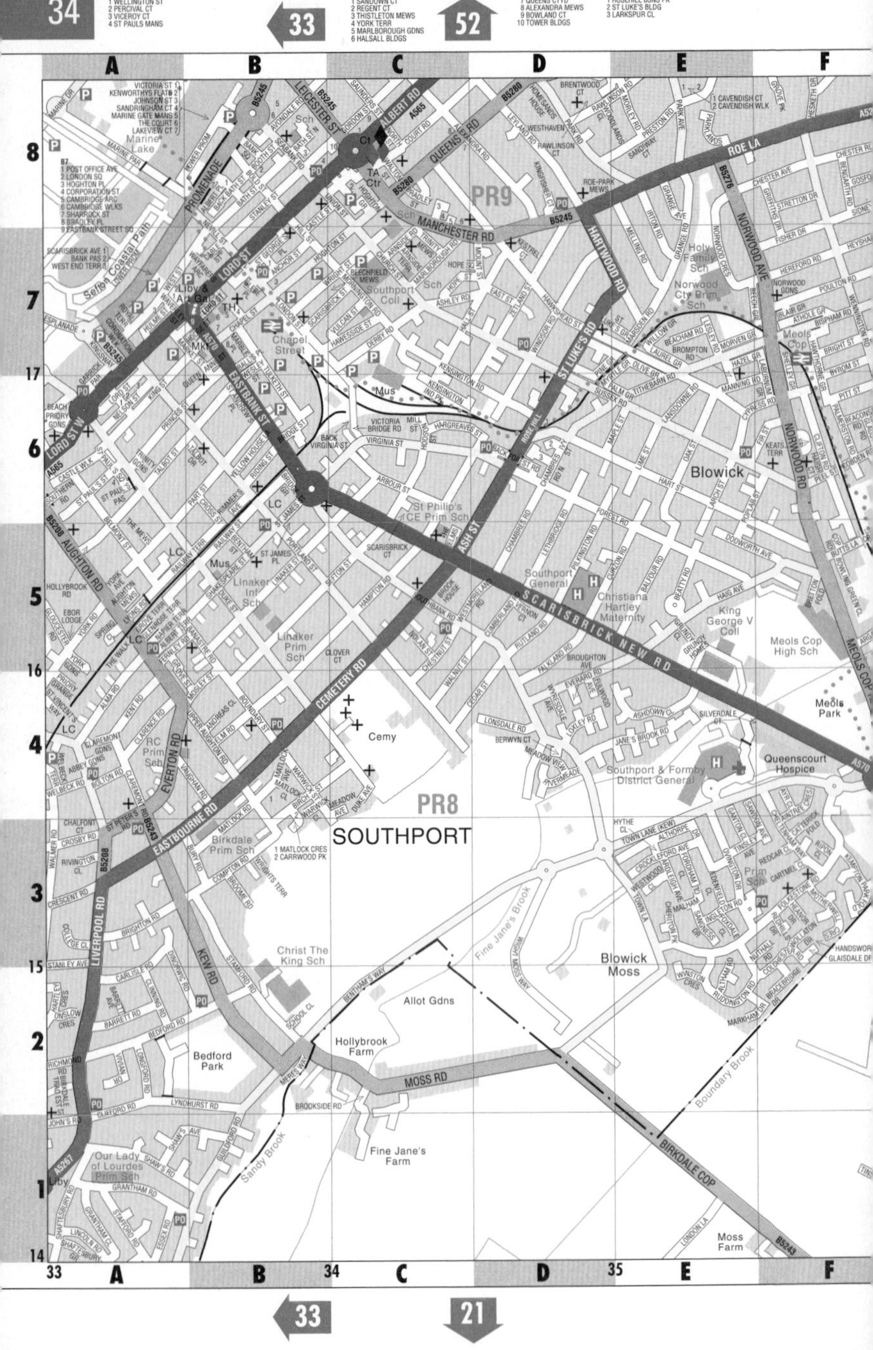

34
A6
1 WELLINGTON ST
2 PERCIVAL CT
3 VICEROY CT
4 ST PAULS MANS
33
C8
1 SANDOWN CT
2 REGENT CT
3 THISTLETON MEWS
4 YORK TERR
5 MARLBOROUGH GDNS
6 HALSALL BLDGS
52
C8
7 QUEENS CTYD
8 ALEXANDRA MEWS
9 BOWLAND CT
10 TOWER BLDGS
D6
1 ROSEHILL BSNS PK
2 ST LUKE'S BLDG
3 LARKSPUR CL
A
B
C
D
E
F
VICTORIA ST 1
KENWORTHYS FLATS 2
JOHNSON ST 3
SANDRINGHAM CT 4
MARINE GATE MANS 5
THE COURT 6
LAKEVIEW CT 7
B7
1 POST OFFICE AVE
2 LONDON SQ
3 HOGHTON PL
4 CORPORATION ST
5 CAMBRIDGE ARC
6 CAMBRIDGE WLKS
7 SHARROCK ST
8 BRADLEY PL
9 EASTBANK STREET SQ
SCARISBRICK AVE 1
BANK PAS 2
WEST END TERR 3
1 CAVENDISH CT
2 CAVENDISH WLK
Marine Lake
Sefton Coastal Path
PROMENADE
LORD ST
LEICESTER ST
ALBERT RD
QUEENS RD
MANCHESTER RD
ROE LA
NORWOOD AVE
HARTWOOD RD
ST LUKE'S RD
EASTBANK ST
Chapel Street
Southport Coll
Liby & Art Gal
TH
Mkt
Mus
PR9
Holy Family Sch
Norwood Cty Prim Sch
Meols Cop
Blowick
St Philip's CE Prim Sch
ASH ST
SCARISBRICK NEW RD
Southport General
Christiana Hartley Maternity
King George V Coll
Meols Cop High Sch
Meols Park
Queenscourt Hospice
Southport & Formby District General
Linaker Inf Sch
Linaker Prim Sch
CEMETERY RD
Cemy
AUGHTON RD
EVERTON RD
RC Prim Sch
EASTBOURNE RD
PR8
SOUTHPORT
Birkdale Prim Sch
1 MATLOCK CRES
2 CARRWOOD PK
LIVERPOOL RD
KEW RD
Christ The King Sch
Fine Jane's Brook
Blowick Moss
Allot Gdns
Hollybrook Farm
MOSS RD
Bedford Park
Boundary Brook
Sandy Brook
Fine Jane's Farm
BIRKDALE COP
Our Lady of Lourdes Prim Sch
Liby
Moss Farm
8
7
17
6
5
16
4
3
15
2
1
14
33
34
35
33
21

A
B
C
D
E
F
High Park
Bishop David Sheppard CE Sch
Pool House Farm
Pitts House Covert
Peet's Farm
Wyke Hey Farm
Hooton's Cottages
Middle Drain
Three Pools Waterway
Recn Gd
Wks
Brook Farm Bridge
PR9
The Old Pool
Wyke House Farm
Big Wood
THE AVENUE
Twist's Covert
Hodge's Farm
Wyke Thorn Farm
Heath Covert
THE MEOLS COP RETAIL PK
Sheepfold Farm
Sandy Brook
New House Farm
Pool Hey Crossing
Shaw's Farm
Scarisbrick Moss
Perch Pool Covert
Pool Hey
Wyke Cop Crossing
Drummersdale Drain
Nursery
PR8
High Brows Covert
Crem
Wyke Road Farm
L40
Brown Edge
SOUTHPORT RD
Black Brook
Sandy Brook Farm
Snape Green
Carr Cross
MOSS LA
STRAIGHT UP LA
DOLLY'S LA
PITTS HOUSE LA
WYKE LA
WYKE WOOD LA
PERCH POOL LA
POOL HEY LA
WYKE COP RD
WOODMOSS LA
HARES LA
NEW HALL DR
TURNING LA
SCARISBRICK NEW RD
NEW FOUL LA
CROWLAND ST
BLOWICK BSNS PK
A570
RIMMER GN
SNAPE GN
CAT TAIL LA
8
7
17
6
5
16
4
3
15
2
1
14
37
38

35
54

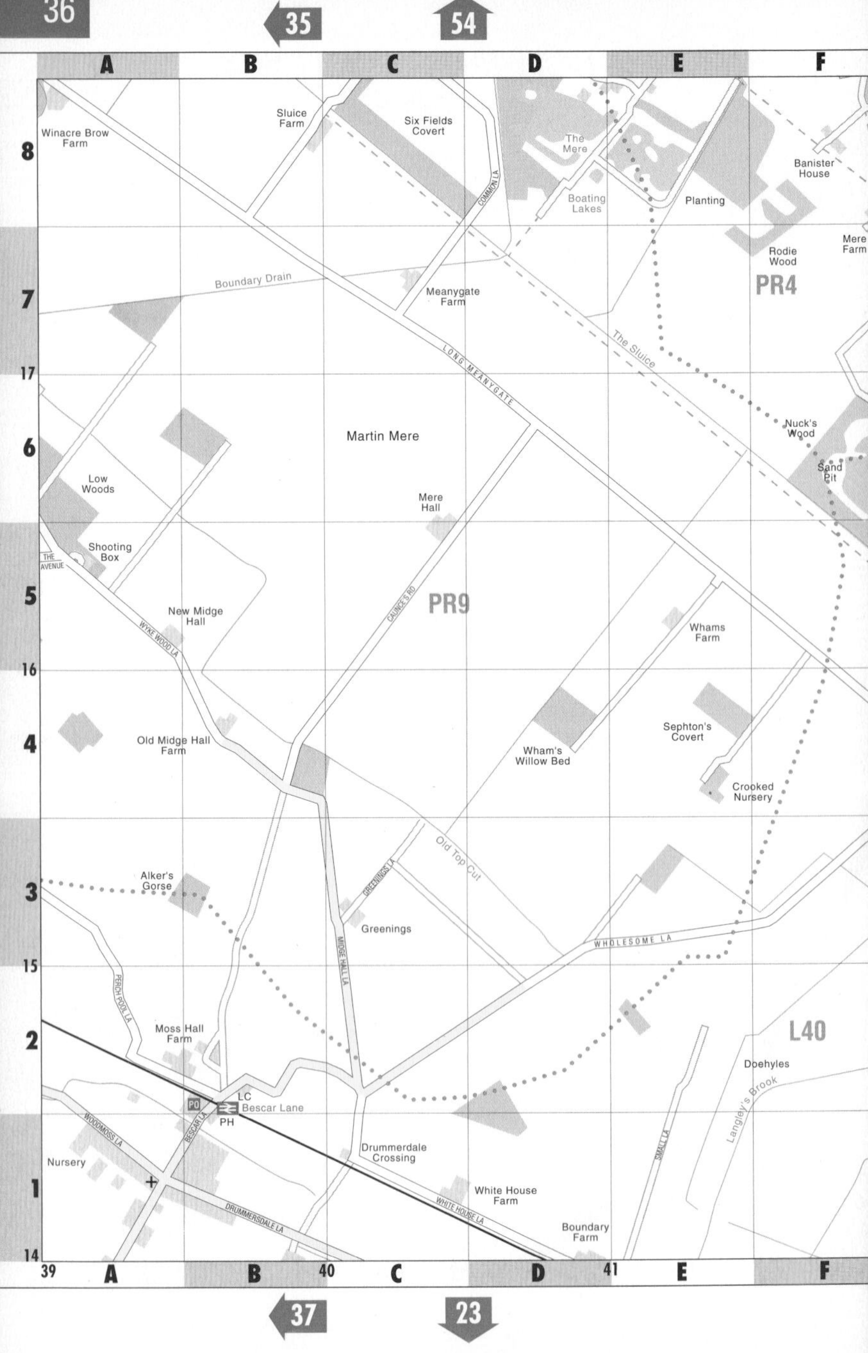
A
B
C
D
E
F
8
7
17
6
5
16
4
3
15
2
1
14
39
40
41
Winacre Brow Farm
Sluice Farm
Six Fields Covert
The Mere
Boating Lakes
Planting
Banister House
Mere Farm
Rodie Wood
PR4
COMMON LA
Boundary Drain
Meanygate Farm
The Sluice
LONG MEANYGATE
Nuck's Wood
Sand Pit
Martin Mere
Low Woods
Mere Hall
Shooting Box
THE AVENUE
PR9
CAUNCE'S RD
New Midge Hall
WYKE WOOD LA
Whams Farm
Sephton's Covert
Old Midge Hall Farm
Wham's Willow Bed
Crooked Nursery
Old Top Cut
Alker's Gorse
GREENINGS LA
Greenings
MIDGE HALL LA
WHOLESOME LA
PERCH POOL LA
Moss Hall Farm
L40
Doehyles
Langley's Brook
PO
LC
Bescar Lane
PH
WOODMOSS LA
BESCAR LA
Drummerdale Crossing
SMALL LA
Nursery
White House Farm
WHITE HOUSE LA
DRUMMERSDALE LA
Boundary Farm

37
23

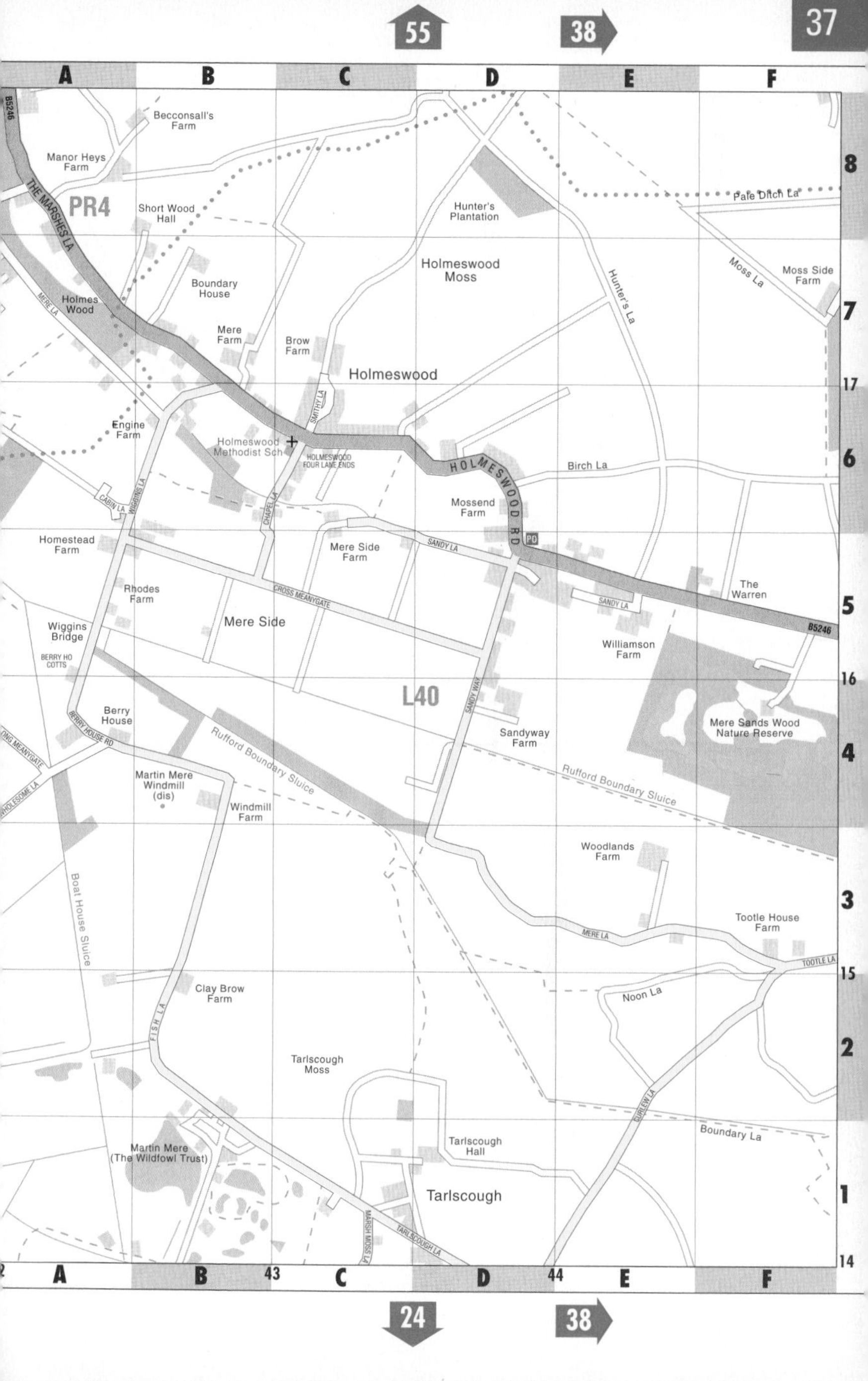
A
B
C
D
E
F
B5246
Becconsall's Farm
Manor Heys Farm
THE MARSHES LA
PR4
Short Wood Hall
Hunter's Plantation
Pale Ditch La
8
Holmeswood Moss
Hunter's La
Moss La
Moss Side Farm
Boundary House
MERE LA
Holmes Wood
7
Mere Farm
Brow Farm
Holmeswood
17
SMITHY LA
Engine Farm
Holmeswood Methodist Sch
HOLMESWOOD FOUR LANE ENDS
HOLMESWOOD RD
Birch La
6
CABIN LA
WIGGINS LA
CHAPEL LA
Mossend Farm
Homestead Farm
Mere Side Farm
SANDY LA
PO
Rhodes Farm
CROSS MEANYGATE
SANDY LA
The Warren
5
Wiggins Bridge
Mere Side
B5246
BERRY HO COTTS
Williamson Farm
16
L40
SANDY WAY
Berry House
Mere Sands Wood Nature Reserve
BERRY HOUSE RD
Rufford Boundary Sluice
Sandyway Farm
4
MEANYGATE
Rufford Boundary Sluice
WHOLESOME LA
Martin Mere Windmill (dis)
Windmill Farm
Woodlands Farm
Boat House Sluice
3
Tootle House Farm
MERE LA
TOOTLE LA
15
Clay Brow Farm
Noon La
FISH LA
2
Tarlscough Moss
CURLEW LA
Boundary La
Martin Mere (The Wildfowl Trust)
Tarlscough Hall
1
Tarlscough
MARSH MOSS LA
TARLSCOUGH LA
14
A
B
43
C
D
44
E
F

37
56

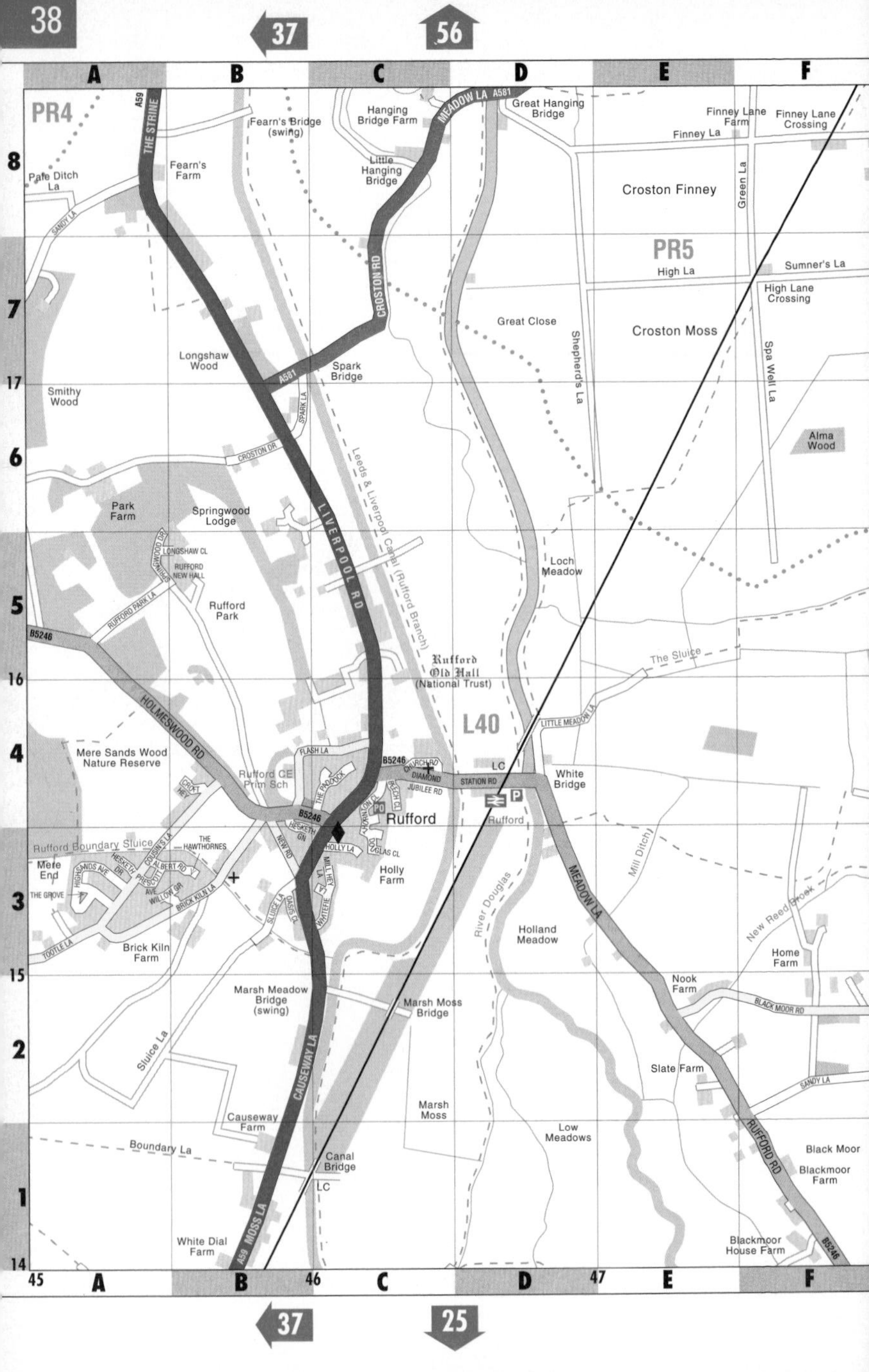
PR4
Pale Ditch La
THE STRINE
A59
Fearn's Farm
Fearn's Bridge (swing)
Hanging Bridge Farm
Little Hanging Bridge
MEADOW LA
A581
Great Hanging Bridge
Finney Lane Farm
Finney Lane Crossing
Finney La
Croston Finney
Green La
PR5
High La
Sumner's La
High Lane Crossing
SANDY LA
CROSTON RD
Great Close
Croston Moss
Shepherd's La
Spa Well La
Longshaw Wood
Spark Bridge
SPARK LA
Smithy Wood
Alma Wood
CROSTON DR
Leeds & Liverpool Canal (Rufford Branch)
LIVERPOOL RD
Park Farm
Springwood Lodge
SPRINGWOOD DR
LONGSHAW CL
RUFFORD NEW HALL
Loch Meadow
Rufford Park
RUFFORD PARK LA
B5246
Rufford Old Hall (National Trust)
The Sluice
HOLMESWOOD RD
L40
LITTLE MEADOW LA
Mere Sands Wood Nature Reserve
FLASH LA
CHURCH RD
DIAMOND
JUBILEE RD
STATION RD
LC
White Bridge
Rufford CE Prim Sch
CROFT HEY
THE PADDOCK
BEECH CL
HORNTON CL
PO
Rufford
HESKETH GN
NEW RD
HOLLY LA
DOUGLAS CL
Rufford Boundary Sluice
THE HAWTHORNES
COUSIN'S LA
HESKETH DR
ALBERT RD
PRESCOTT AVE
WILLOW GR
BRICK KILN LA
Mere End
HIGHLANDS AVE
THE GROVE
MILL HEY LA
WHITEFIE
SLUICE LA
OASIS CL
Holly Farm
Mill Ditch
MEADOW LA
River Douglas
New Reed Brook
Holland Meadow
Home Farm
TOOTLE LA
Brick Kiln Farm
Marsh Meadow Bridge (swing)
Marsh Moss Bridge
Nook Farm
BLACK MOOR RD
Sluice La
CAUSEWAY LA
Slate Farm
Marsh Moss
Causeway Farm
Low Meadows
Boundary La
Canal Bridge
LC
RUFFORD RD
Black Moor
Blackmoor Farm
MOSS LA
White Dial Farm
Blackmoor House Farm
A
B
C
D
E
F
8
7
17
6
5
16
4
3
15
2
1
14
45
46
47

37
25

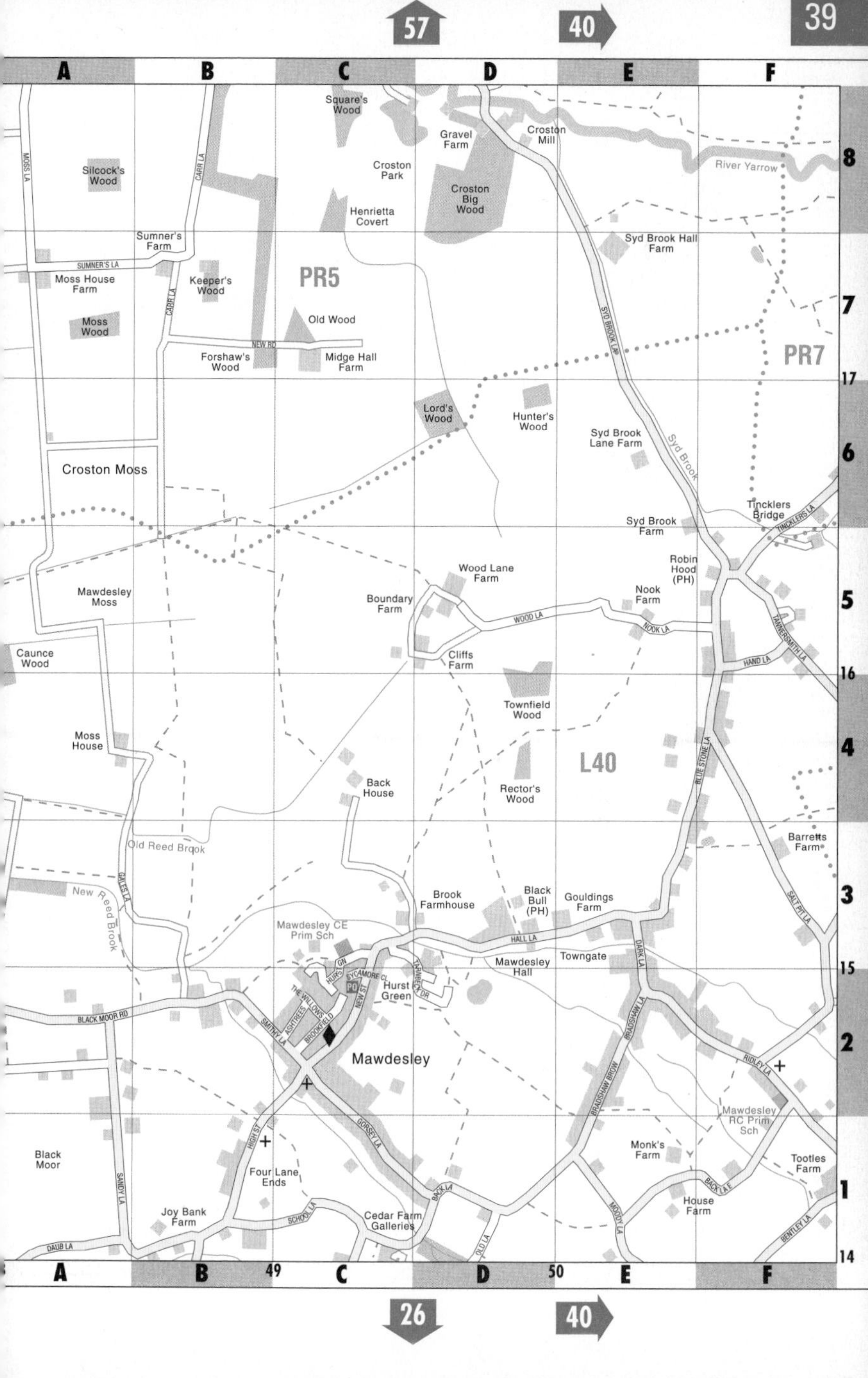
57
40
A
B
C
D
E
F
8
7
17
6
5
16
4
3
15
2
1
14
49
50
26
40
Square's Wood
Gravel Farm
Croston Mill
Croston Park
Croston Big Wood
River Yarrow
Silcock's Wood
MOSS LA
CARR LA
Henrietta Covert
Sumner's Farm
Syd Brook Hall Farm
SUMNER'S LA
Moss House Farm
Keeper's Wood
PR5
Old Wood
Moss Wood
NEW RD
SYD BROOK LA
PR7
Forshaw's Wood
Midge Hall Farm
Lord's Wood
Hunter's Wood
Syd Brook Lane Farm
Syd Brook
Croston Moss
Tincklers Bridge
TINCKLERS LA
Syd Brook Farm
Robin Hood (PH)
Wood Lane Farm
Mawdesley Moss
Boundary Farm
Nook Farm
WOOD LA
NOOK LA
TANNERSMITH LA
Caunce Wood
Cliffs Farm
HAND LA
Townfield Wood
Moss House
BLUE STONE LA
L40
Back House
Rector's Wood
Old Reed Brook
Barretts Farm
GALES LA
New Reed Brook
Brook Farmhouse
Black Bull (PH)
Gouldings Farm
SALT PIT LA
Mawdesley CE Prim Sch
HALL LA
DARK LA
Mawdesley Hall
Towngate
SYCAMORE CL
PO
Hurst Green
NEW ST
TARNBECK DR
BLACK MOOR RD
THE WILLOWS
ASHTREES
BROOKFIELD
SMITHY LA
BRADSHAW LA
Mawdesley
RIDLEY LA
BRADSHAW BROW
Mawdesley RC Prim Sch
GORSEY LA
HIGH ST
Black Moor
Monk's Farm
Tootles Farm
Four Lane Ends
SANDY LA
BACK LA
BACK LA E
House Farm
Joy Bank Farm
SCHOOL LA
Cedar Farm Galleries
MOODY LA
OLD LA
BENTLEY LA
DAUB LA

39 58

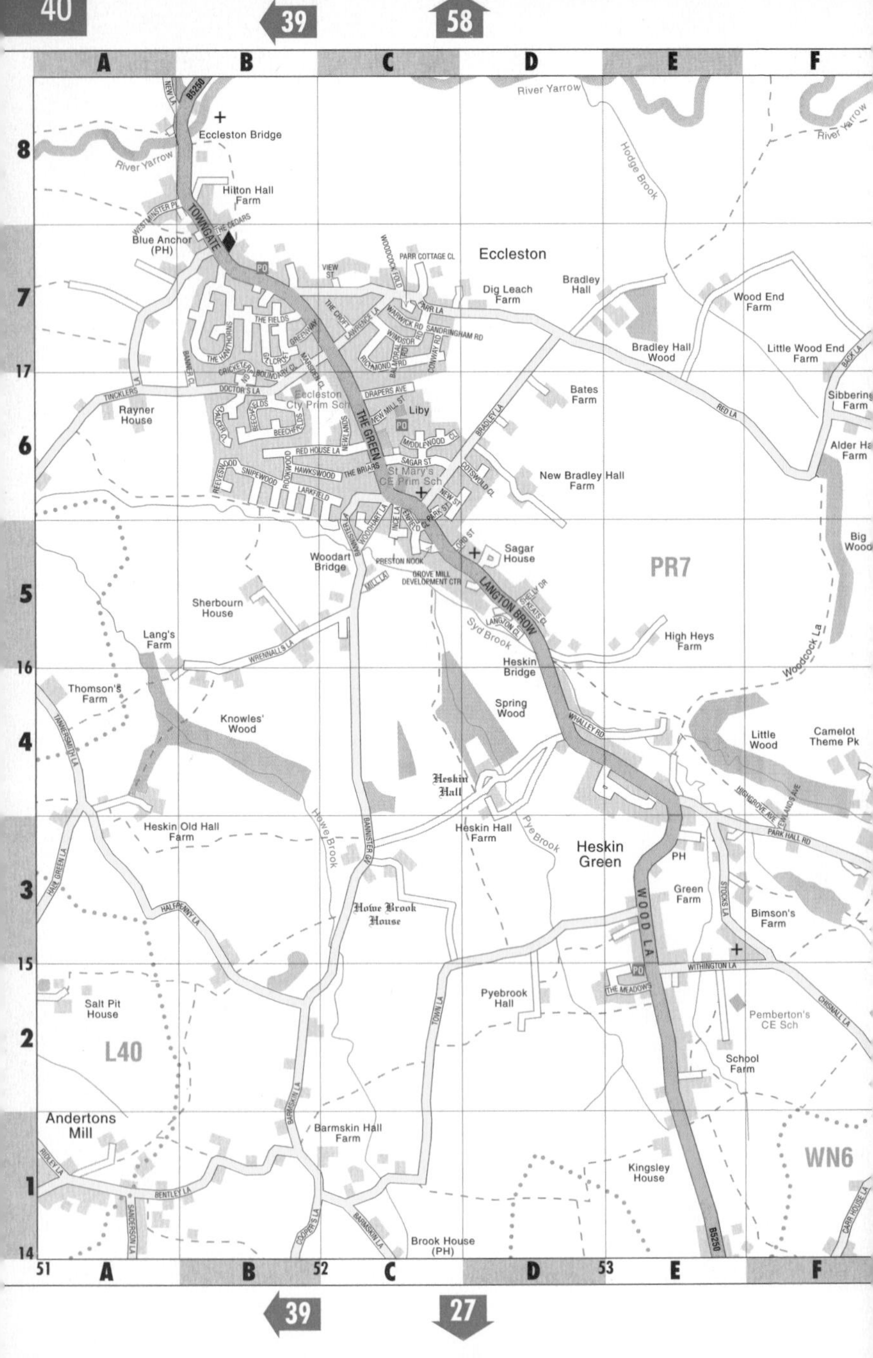

A B C D E F
River Yarrow
Eccleston Bridge
Hilton Hall Farm
Blue Anchor (PH)
Eccleston
Dig Leach Farm
Bradley Hall
Wood End Farm
Bradley Hall Wood
Little Wood End Farm
Rayner House
Bates Farm
Sibbering Farm
Eccleston Cty Prim Sch
Liby
St Mary's CE Prim Sch
New Bradley Hall Farm
Alder Ha Farm
Woodart Bridge
Sagar House
PR7
Big Wood
Sherbourn House
Lang's Farm
High Heys Farm
Heskin Bridge
Thomson's Farm
Knowles' Wood
Spring Wood
Little Wood
Camelot Theme Pk
Heskin Hall
Heskin Old Hall Farm
Heskin Hall Farm
Heskin Green
PH
Green Farm
Bimson's Farm
Howe Brook House
Salt Pit House
Pyebrook Hall
Pemberton's CE Sch
L40
School Farm
Andertons Mill
Barmskin Hall Farm
Kingsley House
WN6
Brook House (PH)
TOWNGATE
THE GREEN
LANGTON BROW
WOOD LA
RED LA
PARR LA
BRADLEY LA
WHALLEY RD
PARK HALL RD
WITHINGTON LA
BANNISTER GV
TOWN LA
BARMSKIN LA
HALFPENNY LA
BENTLEY LA
TINCKLERS LA
DOCTOR'S LA
WRENNALLS LA
Woodcock La
Hodge Brook
Syd Brook
Pye Brook
Howe Brook
8 7 17 6 5 16 4 3 15 2 1 14
51 52 53

39 27

59
42

28
42

E1
1 GERMAN LA
2 CLEVELAND ST
3 SPRINGFIELD RD N
4 MILL ST

C8
1 SPRINGFIELD RD
2 WOODVILLE RD
3 CROWN ST
4 ST THOMAS'S SQ
5 BACK MOUNT
6 MEALHOUSE LA
7 CHORCLIFFE HO
8 KELLETT ST
9 STANLEY PL
10 HIGH ST
11 CANNON ST
12 MARKET PL
13 FAZAKERLEY ST

41

C8
14 BACK FAZAKERLEY ST
15 FOUNDRY ST
16 ST MARY'S WLK
17 DEVONSHIRE CT

60

D8
1 PORTLAND ST
2 BRUNSWICK ST
3 EAST CHORLEY BSNS CTR
4 MACKAY CROFT
5 MACKENZLE CL
6 CAMERON CROFT
7 SANDHAM ST
8 HOUGHTON ST
E8
1 WHIMBERRY CL
2 COLYTON RD E
3 THE CAUSEWAY
4 THE MOORINGS
5 CHATHAM PL
6 HEALD ST
7 BRIGHTON ST
8 TEMPERANCE ST

A5
1 ARNOLD PL
2 JACKSON RD
3 BRANCKER ST
B5
1 TARN HOWS CL
2 BAMBER ST
3 GRAFTON CT
B6
1 VENTNOR RD
2 LETCHWORTH PL
3 ASPEN GDNS
4 BLACK HORSE ST
C6
1 KNOWLES ST
2 COVENTRY ST
3 NORRIS ST
4 GILBERT ST
5 HINDLEY ST
6 CATHERINE ST
C7
1 AVENHAM RD
2 ROBERTS ST
3 LENNON ST
4 PARSON'S BROW
5 WHALLEY ST
6 CHEAPSIDE
7 HALLIWELL CT
8 HALLIWELL PL
9 OXFORD ST

41

C7
10 CAMBRIDGE ST
11 BANNISTER ST
12 RAWCLIFFE RD

29

D6
1 BACK ASHBY ST
2 THE ASTLEY CTR
3 QUEEN ST E
D7
1 ALBERT ST
2 NORTHUMBERLAND ST
3 SALISBURY ST
4 CLARENCE ST
5 SHERBOURNE ST
6 CASTLE ST
7 SUTCLIFFE ST
8 DUXBURY HO
9 PERCY ST
E7
1 CAVENDISH ST
2 STEPHENSON ST
3 LAWSON ST
4 ST ANNES RD
5 WINDERMERE RD
6 THE BROOKES
7 SCHOOL HOUSE MEWS
8 ST JAME'S ST
9 ST JAME'S PL
10 CLARENDON ST

A
B
C
D
E
F
Grey Heights
Grey Heights Wood
Hurst Hill
Siddow Fold
White House
Works
Spen Cob
Manor House
HEAPEY FOLD LA
MOOR RD
Johnson's Farm
Jepson's Gate
High Bullough Resr
Bibbys Farm
Anglezarke Woodland Trail
Fish Barn Farm
Jepson's Farm
Kays Farm
BACK LA
Ainsworths Farm
Anglezarke Resr
imbrick
Stone's House
PH
P
Waring's Farm
Brindles Farm
Parson's Bullough
PARSON'S BULLOUGH RD
HODGE BROW
PR6
Alance Bridge
Hallsworth Fold Farm
OLDE STONEHEATH CT
Holland Fold
Yarrow Resr
Nab's Farm
LANE ENDS
KNOWSLEY LA
LONG LA
HUT LA
BROAD OAK COTTS
River Yarrow
Yew Tree Inn (PH)
NICK HILTON'S LA
THE STREET
CH
Dean Wood House
NICK HILTON'S BROW
Nick Hilton's Bridge
Blindhurst
PR7
BL6
Hall o' th' Hill Farm
Broad Oak Farm
NICKLETON BROW
SLACK'S LA
NICKLETON
Rivington
SHEEP HOUSE LA
Slack's Farm
Cunliffe Farm
Upper Rivington Resr
Bay Horse Hotel (PH)
PO
MILL HILL COTTS
Lonsdale Farm
Shaw Place
BABYLON LA
NEW RD
Rivington Sch
RIVINGTON LA
Croft Bridge
Fairview
New House
HORROBIN LA
MAJOR BOTTOMS
WATERFORD CL
MILLBROOK ROW
STONEGATE FOLD
Springfield Cottages
CHORLEY RD
BROOK ST
OLLERTON ST
DAISY HILL DR
SUTTON LA
WINDERMERE DR
THIRLMERE CL
M61
8
7
17
6
5
16
4
3
15
2
1
14
61
62

43
62

A
B
C
D
E
F
8
7
17
6
5
16
4
3
15
2
1
14
63
64
65
Anglezarke Moor
Devil's Ditch
Black Lower Hill
Counting Hill
Redmond's Edge
High Shores
Rushy Brow
Limestone Clough
Standing Stones Hill
PR6
Limestone Brook
White Ledge Hill
Lead Mines Clough
BL7
Spitlers Edge
Holts Flat
Higher Anshaw
Sam Pasture
Will Narr
Hordern Pasture
River Yorrow
RIVINGTON RD
Hordern Stoops
BL6
DEAN HEAD LA
Wilcock's Farm
Moor Bottom
Sparks Bridge
Moses Cocker's
Bradleys
Shore
SHEEP HOUSE LA
BELMONT RD
Noon Hill Slack
Winte Hill
Masts
Noon Hill
HALL LA
Rivington Hall Barn
Catter Nab
Rivington Moor
Brere's Meadow Pit

43
31

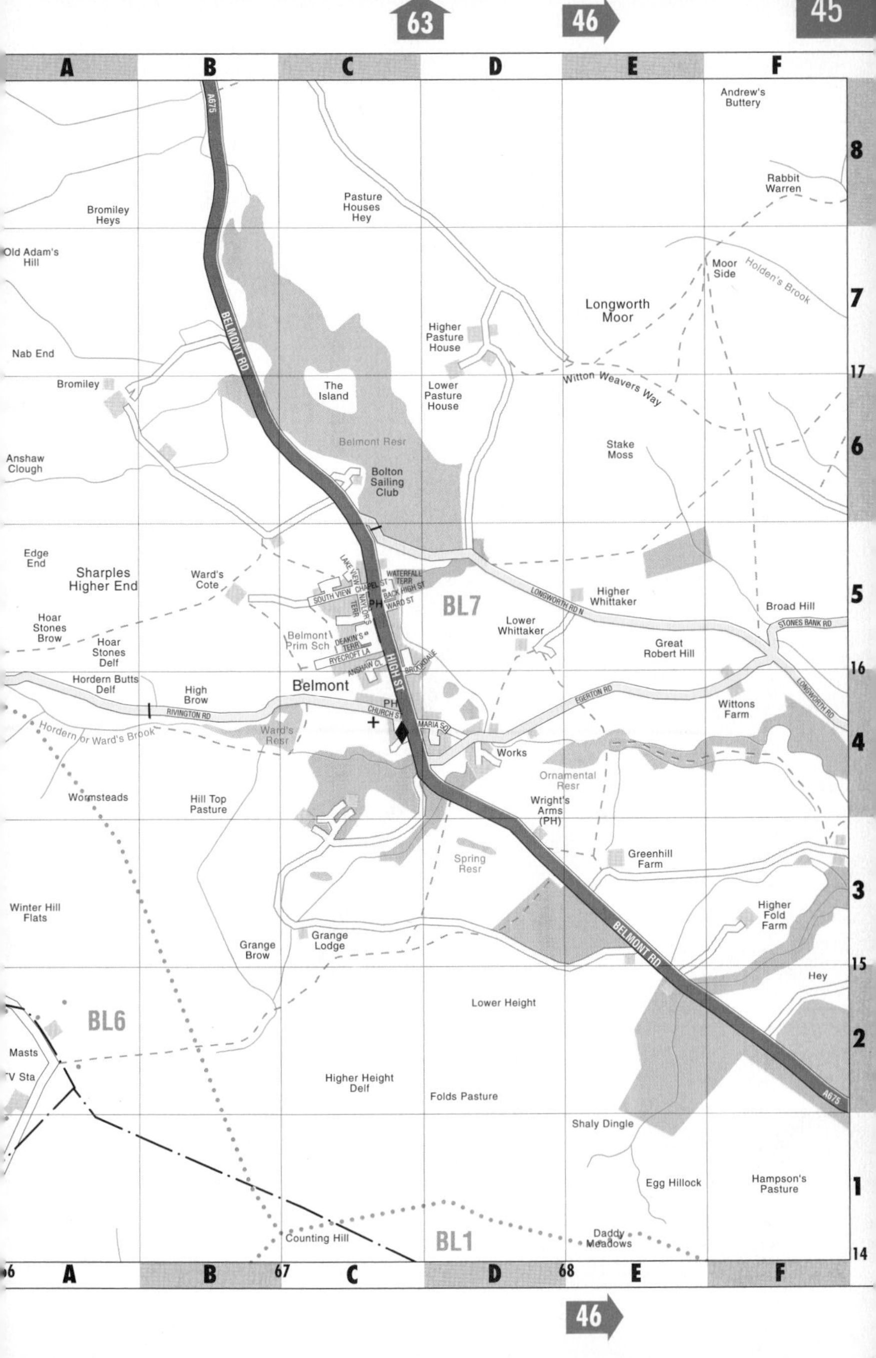

63
46
A
B
C
D
E
F
8
7
17
6
5
16
4
3
15
2
1
14
A675
Andrew's Buttery
Rabbit Warren
Bromiley Heys
Pasture Houses Hey
Old Adam's Hill
Moor Side
Holden's Brook
Longworth Moor
Higher Pasture House
Nab End
Bromiley
The Island
Lower Pasture House
Witton Weavers Way
BELMONT RD
Belmont Resr
Anshaw Clough
Stake Moss
Bolton Sailing Club
Edge End
Sharples Higher End
Ward's Cote
LAKE VIEW
WATERFALL TERR
CHAPEL ST
BACK HIGH ST
SOUTH VIEW
NAYLORS TERR
WARD ST
PH
BL7
LONGWORTH RD N
Higher Whittaker
Broad Hill
STONES BANK RD
Hoar Stones Brow
Hoar Stones Delf
Belmont Prim Sch
DEAKIN'S TERR
RYECROFT LA
ANSHAW CL
HIGH ST
BROOKDALE
Lower Whittaker
Great Robert Hill
Hordern Butts Delf
High Brow
Belmont
EGERTON RD
Wittons Farm
LONGWORTH RD
RIVINGTON RD
CHURCH ST
MARIA SQ
Hordern or Ward's Brook
Ward's Resr
Works
Ornamental Resr
Wormsteads
Hill Top Pasture
Wright's Arms (PH)
Greenhill Farm
Spring Resr
Winter Hill Flats
Higher Fold Farm
Grange Brow
Grange Lodge
Hey
BL6
Lower Height
Masts
TV Sta
Higher Height Delf
Folds Pasture
Shaly Dingle
Egg Hillock
Hampson's Pasture
Counting Hill
BL1
Daddy Meadows
66
67
68

46

45
64

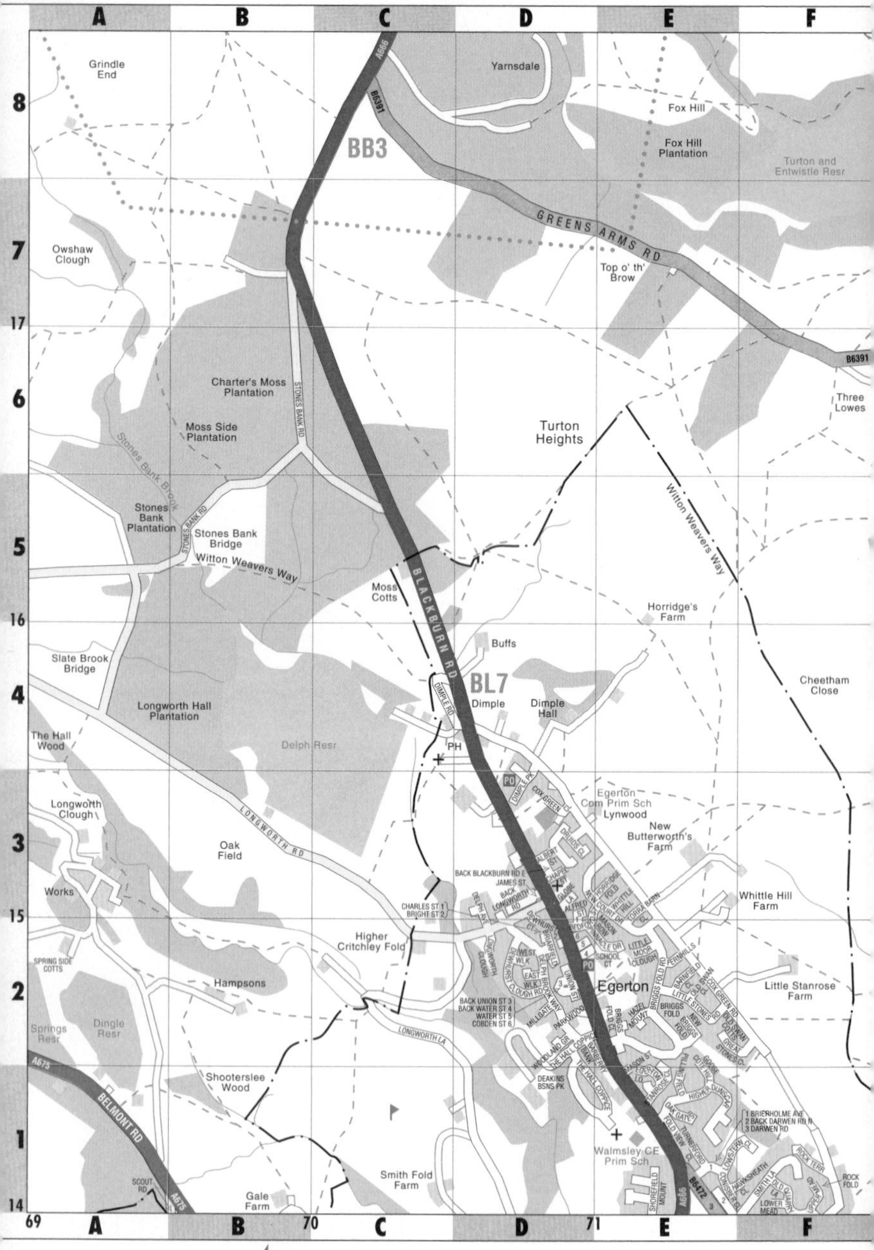

A B C D E F

8
7
17
6
5
16
4
3
15
2
1
14

Grindle End
Yarnsdale
Fox Hill
Fox Hill Plantation
BB3
Turton and Entwistle Resr
GREENS ARMS RD
B6391
A666
Owshaw Clough
Top o' th' Brow
Charter's Moss Plantation
STONES BANK RD
Moss Side Plantation
Turton Heights
Three Lowes
Stones Bank Brook
Stones Bank Plantation
Stones Bank Bridge
Witton Weavers Way
BLACKBURN RD
Moss Cotts
Horridge's Farm
Buffs
Slate Brook Bridge
BL7
Dimple
Dimple Hall
DIMPLE RD
Cheetham Close
Longworth Hall Plantation
The Hall Wood
PH
Delph Resr
Longworth Clough
Egerton Com Prim Sch
Lynwood
New Butterworth's Farm
Oak Field
LONGWORTH RD
Works
BACK BLACKBURN RD E
JAMES ST
CHARLES ST 1
BRIGHT ST 2
Whittle Hill Farm
Higher Critchley Fold
SPRING SIDE COTTS
Hampsons
Egerton
Little Stanrose Farm
BACK UNION ST 3
BACK WATER ST 4
WATER ST 5
COBDEN ST 6
Springs Resr
Dingle Resr
LONGWORTH LA
A675
BELMONT RD
Shooterslee Wood
DEAKINS BSNS PK
1 BRIERHOLME AVE
2 BACK DARWEN RD N
3 DARWEN RD
Walmsley CE Prim Sch
Smith Fold Farm
SCOUT RD
Gale Farm
ROCK FOLD
A666
B6472

69 A B 70 C D 71 E F

45

65
48

A
B
C
D
E
F
8
7
17
6
5
16
4
3
15
2
1
14
Hill Top
Entwistle
EDGE LA
Dingle Farm
Pleasant View
New House Farm
Wheatsheaf Farm
Strawbury Duck (PH)
OVERSHORES RD
RAILWAY TERR
ENTWISTLE HALL LA
SCHOOL VIEW
SCHOOL LA
Hob Lane Farm
HOB LA
BROADHEAD RD
Hazel Clough Farm
PLANTATION RD
Entwistle
CROW TREES LA
Isherwood Fold
BLACKBURN RD
ISHERWOOD FOLD
HOLLY BANK
Witton Weavers Way
Horrocks Fold Farm
Greenthorne
GREENTHORNE CL
FOXDALE CL
PATRIDGE RD
HORROCKS RD
CROWNDALE
AINSDALE AVE
CROWN GDNS
CROWN POINT
GREENACRES
Nabbs Farm
Armsgrove Farm
THOMASON FOLD
MOORFIELD
MEADOWFIELD
HEATHERFIELD
MAY ST
PH
Edgworth
SHARPLES MEADOW
SHARPLES GN
Mill
GREENS ARMS RD
OVER HOUSES
Wayoh Resr
LOWER MEADOW
WAYOH CROFT
MEADOW WAY
MARS ST
BARN MEADOW
HARBOUR LA
MARLED HEY
BENSON ST
BARLOW CT
PARK RD
BRANDWOOD FOLD
Temple Farm
Spring Bank Farm
BL7
Billy Brook
BOLTON RD
HAWORTH ST
Edgworth Prim Sch
BURY RD
Higher Barn Farm
EMBANKMENT RD
MOUNT PLEASANT
BEECH ST
BACK SANDY BANK RD
SANDY BANK RD
Fir Trees
CHAPEL GRN
Chapeltown
Clough House Farm
Chetham Arms Hotel (PH)
TOWER CT
TOWER ST
CHAPEL FIELDS
CHARLOTTE ST
HIGH ST
MARTIN ST
Pallet Farm
KAY ST
STATION RD
Victoria Mill
LC
WELLINGTON RD
YALE ST
Turton Bottoms
BIRCHES RD
KNOTTS BROW
Witton Weavers Way
BACK HIGH ST
Bradshaw Brook
Birches
Quarlton Fold Farm
BURY RD
BOTTOM O' TH' KNOTTS BROW
Turton Tower
Tower Farm
Lithermans Bridge
Jumbles
Walves Resr
BURY RD
Horrobin Lodge
Bull's Head Inn (PH)
RAMSBOTTOM RD
A676
TOTTINGTON RD
B6213
CHAPELTOWN RD
THE COPSE
THE SPINNEY
HORROBIN LA
LEES COTTS
Torra Barn
Jumbles Country Park
Turton Heights (PH)
WATLING ST
Hazelhurst Brook
HORROBIN FOLD
King William Inn (PH)
Jumbles Resr
WALSH FOLD
CH
BL2
BL8
BRADSHAW RD
Lamb Inn (PH)
Toye Farm
Top of Turton
The Last Drop Village
Holts Fold
BROMLEY CROSS
REDHILL WAY
HAYDOCK LA
B6391
HILLSIDE AVE
GRANGE RD
A676
2
73
74

48

47
66

Longshaw Head
CROWTHORN RD
Quarlton Heights
DANGER AREA
Barons Farm
Red Brook
Holcombe Head Farm
Harcles Hill
Harcles Hill Farm
Wickenlow Hill Farm
PLANTATION RD
MOORBOTTOM RD
Holcombe Hey Fold Farm
Red Earth Farm
BL7
Taylor's Farm
Boardman's Farm
Peel Twr
Hawkshaw Farm
Holcombe Rifle Ranges
Top o' th' Moor Farm
HAWKSHAW LA
Simons Farm
BL8
HEY HOUSE MEWS
Peel Wlk
Hey House
Higher House Farm
Range House
Darul-Uloom Islamic Coll
Top of Quarlton
New Hoyles
Dawes Bank Farm
SPENLEACH LA
Lower House
Works
EMERALD COTTS
Redisher Farm
HOLCOMBE OLD RD
Bramley Fold Farm
HOLCOMBE MEWS 1
THE PRECINCT 2
HOLCOMBE CT 3
GLENMORE RD 4
REDISHER LA
REDISHER CROFT
Mast
GREENSIDE CL
MOOR WAY
Loe Bridge
Loe Farm
BLO
BOLTON RD W
QUARLTON DR
Kenyon's Farm
A676 RAMSBOTTOM RD
BOLTON RD
PH
CROICHBANK
TROUTBECK CL
St Mary's CE Prim Sch
Mill
MANDEVILLE TERR
The Knoll
HILLSTONE CL
GREENMOUNT DR
B6215
DUNEDIN RD
JACKDAW RD
COLERIDGE RD
BYRON RD
SWAN RD
KEATS RD
ST AUSTELL DR
B6213
TWO BROOKS LA
Hawkshaw
Sunny Top
CHISHOLME CL
GREENMOUNT CL
REDWING RD
Higher Barn Farm
CROICHLEY FOLD
Holhouse Farm
HOLHOUSE LA
HOLCOMBE RD
Greenmount Prim Sch
KIMBLE CL
TURTON RD
Bradshaw Head
Two Brooks Farm
LOMAX ST
LARKFIELD CL
CH
ORCHARD WAY
WATLING ST
Holly Mount RC Prim Sch
P
Greenmount
HOVE CL
HAYFIELD CL
GREENPARK CL
FELLSIDE CL
BRANDLESHOLME RD
Holly Mount
Holly Mount Farm
OLD GREEN
BROOKSIDE CRES
SHEPHERDS CL
ROYSTON CL
STATION RD
HOLCOMBE RD

47

B5
1 GLENEAGLES WAY
2 BROWN ST
3 AJAX ST
4 CHARLOTTE ST
5 KERENHAPPUCH ST
6 WELL ST W
7 WEST ST
8 WATER ST
9 COLLING ST
10 ALFRED ST
11 BK ALFRED ST
12 FREDERICK ST
13 DOROTHY ST
14 PILKINGTON ST
15 OX ST
16 EDGAR ST
17 EDGAR ST W
18 TIB ST
19 ELLIS ST

B6
1 COULTHURST ST
2 TAPE ST
3 KATE ST
4 DOUGLAS STREET BK
5 TANNERS CROFT
6 VESTA ST
7 BUCHANAN ST
8 CALTHA ST

C6
1 KILLER ST
2 BK BRIDGE ST
3 ROOK ST
4 ST PAUL'S ST
5 CHURCH ST
6 MARKLAND ST
7 SMITHY ST
8 OLD GROUND ST
9 STRANG ST
10 PALATINE ST
11 SCOTLAND PL
12 WOODLANDS VIEW

67
50

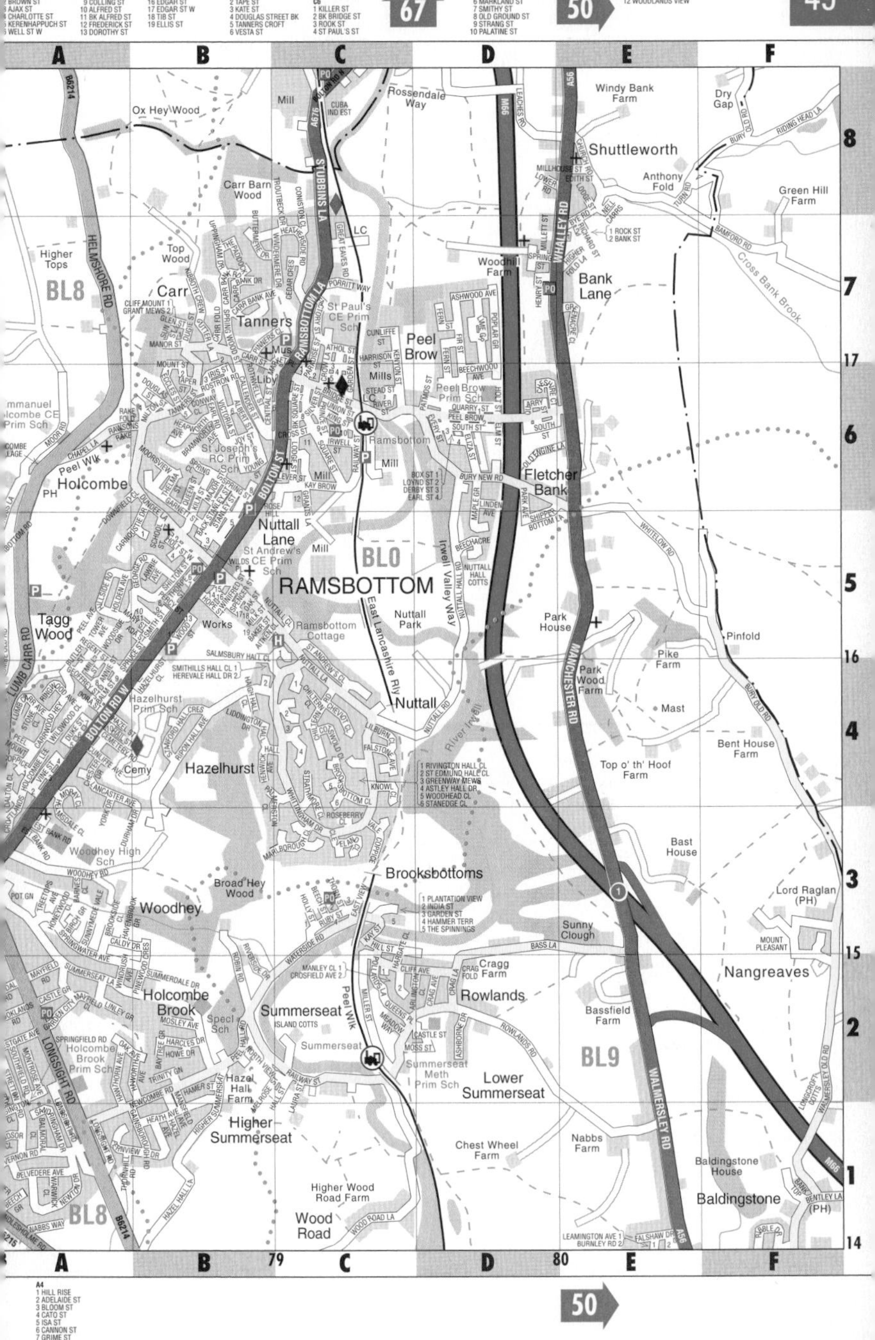

A4
1 HILL RISE
2 ADELAIDE ST
3 BLOOM ST
4 CATO ST
5 ISA ST
6 CANNON ST
7 GRIME ST
8 FLAX ST
9 ZAMA ST
10 ELSIE ST

50

49
68

A
B
C
D
E
F
8
7
17
6
5
16
4
3
15
2
1
14
81
82
83
RIDING HEAD LA
A680
Mill
Smithy Carr Farm
Kay Close Farm
Rossendale Way
COAL RD
Fecit Farm
FECIT LA
Turf Moor
Man Road Ditc
ROCHDALE RD
Rossendale Sch
BL0
BLACK LA
Moor Side Farm
MOOR SIDE LA
Close Nooks Farm
Cheesden Pasture
Cheesden Brook
BAMFORD RD
Gate House
Harden Brook
Tom Hill
OL12
Cheesden Bridge
Cheesden
Wham Hill
Wham Hill Farm
Harden Moor
Lumb Bridge
New Inn (PH)
Owd Betts (PH)
Rochdale Way
EDENFIELD RD
Ashworth Moor
Throstle Hill
Croston Close
Croston Close Bottoms
Ashworth Moor Resr
Mam Hill
Ridshaw Farm
Far Buckhurst Brow
Kirkby's
CROSTON CLOSE RD
Buckhurst Brow
BUCKHURST RD
Rough Lee
Snape Hill
Buckhurst Farm
BL9
Far Croft Head
Closes
SALES'S LA
Sales's Farm
Top o' th' Hill Farm
Whitewall Farm
Deeply Vale
Deeply Hill
Lark Mount
DEEPLY VALE LA
ASHWORTH RD
OL11
Wind Hill
Bird Fields
Stand Lees Farm
Wind Hill Farm
Copped Hill Farm
Cob House Nab
Gindles Farm
Copped Hill
BENTLEY LA
M66
Cob House Farm
WHITE CARR LA
Shephe Hey

49
32

C1
1 GLEN ROYD
2 PRETORIA ST
3 LOWER GN
4 POPLAR AVE
5 BALFOUR RD
6 TENBY GR
7 TRENGROVE ST
8 AIR HILL TERR
9 BENTINCK ST

C1
10 BACK PATIENCE ST
11 PATIENCE ST
12 WOODSTOCK ST
13 BLENHEIM ST
14 MARLBOROUGH ST
15 MEANWOOD BROW
16 PRESTON ST
17 LISBON ST

F1
1 FURTHER HEIGHTS RD
2 LAURIE PL
3 MOORFIELD PL
4 HENDRIFF PL
5 SAWYER ST
6 MILFORD ST
7 DENTON ST
8 INDUSTRY RD
9 HENLEY ST
10 GRASMERE ST
11 DERWENT ST
12 INKERMAN ST
13 ALMA ST
14 PEMBROKE CT
15 DAVID ST N
16 DAVID ST
17 JEPHEYS PL
18 TAYLORS PL
19 WELLINGTON ST
20 FOLLY WLK
21 PARK HILL
22 VICTORIA ST
23 UPPER GEORGE ST
24 BUNYAN ST
25 ALMA IND EST

Marshside Sands
Wks
Marshside Nature Reserve
Marshside Marsh
PR9
Stanley High Sch
Sefton Coastal Path
Marshside
Southport Sands
MARINE DR
Bank Nook
SOUTHPORT
CH
HESKETH RD
COCKLE DICK'S LA
HESKETH LINKS CT
CAMBRIDGE RD
PARK CRES
Hesketh Park
ALBERT RD
PR8
Marine Lake
Sefton Coastal Path
LEICESTER ST
B5245
B5280
A565
FAIRWAY
PROMENADE
LATHOM RD
ALBANY RD
KNOWSLEY RD
AVONDALE RD N
LEYLAND RD
PARK RD W
FLEETWOOD RD
ARGYLE CT
CLIFF RD
HOWARD CT
ALBERT CT
GRANVILLE CT
ARGYLE RD
BROCKLEBANK RD
POPLAR BANK
PARK RD
ALEXANDRA RD
GORDON ST
GORDON AVE
AVONDALE RD
SAUNDERS ST
IRVING ST
PARK AVE
ALLERTON RD
RAWLINSON RD
PRESTON RD
HENLEY CT
HENLEY DR
ROOKERY RD
MAPLEWOOD
CAMBRIDGE CT
GRIFFON HOUSE
FLEETWOOD CL
PAUL'S LA
KNOB HALL LA
KNOB HALL GDNS
THRELFALLS CL
TREETOP VILLAS
WILLOWHEY
ELSWICK RD
MARSHSIDE RD
THE LAWNS
EMMANUEL RD
CAMBRIDGE GDNS
CH
PO
A B C D E F
8 7 21 6 5 20 4 3 19 2 1 18
33 34 35

34

Crossens Marsh
High Brow
Brade's Farm
Goose Dub Farm
Goose Dub Covert
Fiddler's Ferry
Sewage Works
Sefton Coastal Path
Playing Fields
Ppg Sta
Banks
Sandy Bridge
WATER LA
SOUTHPORT NEW RD
A565
St John's CE Prim Sch
PR9
Recn Gd
Three Pools Waterway
Land Houses
The Sluice
Back Drain
PRESTON NEW RD
RUFFORD RD
B5244
Moss Side Farm
Wks
Peterhouse Sch
Pressfield Sch
Larkfield Prim Sch
Moss Cottage
Bankfield Farm
Rye Hey
Middle Drain
Botanic Gardens
Churchtown Prim Sch
Botanic Gardens Mus
BANKFIELD LA
Sutton's Covert
Fish Pond Covert
Churchtown Moss
Ainscough's Covert
Churchtown
New Plantation
Meols Hall
Gore Hey Covert
MILL LA
A5267
BOTANIC RD
MARINE DR
CHARNLEY'S LA
RALPH'S WIFE'S LA
VICARAGE LA
CHURCH RD
STATION RD
NEW LA
BLUNDELL LA
LITTLE LA
DOLLY'S LA
CABIN LA
NORTH RD
FYLDE RD
CAMBRIDGE RD
Liby

53
71

Tinsley's Farm
Boundary Farm
Far Banks
Heath Farm
Brookfield's Farm
Gore Hall Farm
New House Farm
New House Farm
Bank View Farm
Banks Meth Prim Sch
Moss Edge Farm
Nursery
Nursery
Wright's Plantation
Sugar Stubbs Coverts
Holmes Moss
Brand Heald
St Stephens' CE Prim Sch
L Ctr
PR9
Little Runner
Moss Side Farm
Gravel Farm
Sugar Stubbs
Jump's Farm
Hollywood Farm
Woodend Farm
Wright's Farm
DALWEB IND PK
Runner Plantations
SOUTHPORT NEW RD
Tarleton Runner
Long Ditch Bridge
Boundary Farm
Gravel Farm
PR4
Legh House Farm
Ring Ditch
Tarleton Mere Brow CE Prim Sch
THE GRAVEL
Mere Brow
Back Drain
The Sluice
COMMON LA
Mere Meanygate
MARSH RD
RYDING'S LA
NEW LANE PACE
LITTLE LA
GORSEY LA
GEORGE'S LA
CHARNLEY'S LA
BOND'S LA
CHAPEL LA
SQUARE HOUSE LA
BOUNDARY MEANYGATE
CHURCH RD
FLEETWOOD DR
LONG LA
MOSS LA
BOUNDARY LA
HESKETH AVE
AVELING DR
GREAVES CL
STATION RD
GUINEA HALL LA
WOODVALE CT
GREAVES HALL AVE
WESTERDALE DR
AVENHAM CL
BOLTON'S COP
GRAVEL LA
THE CLOSE
OAKFORD CL
GREEN LA
SUGAR STUBBS LA
MOSS SIDE LA
BOBBINERS LA
MERE LA
A565
B5246
LONGFOLD
CINDER LA
TABBY NOOK
A B C D E F
8 7 21 6 5 20 4 3 19 2 1 18
39 40 41

53
36

72
56

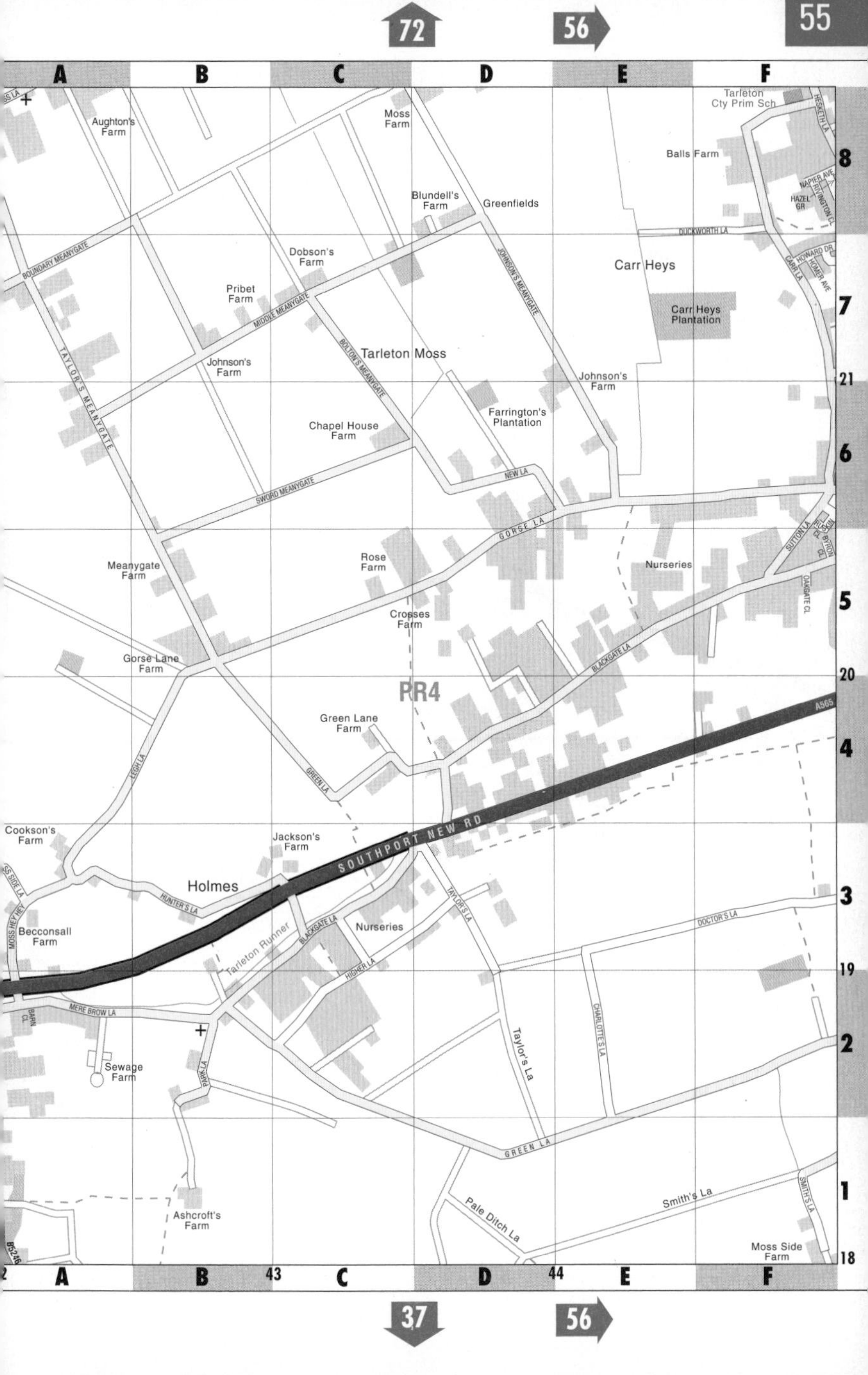
A
B
C
D
E
F
Aughton's Farm
Moss Farm
Tarleton Cty Prim Sch
HESKETH LA
Balls Farm
Blundell's Farm
Greenfields
NAPIER AVE
RIVINGTON CL
HAZEL GR
DUCKWORTH LA
BOUNDARY MEANYGATE
Dobson's Farm
Carr Heys
HOWARD DR
HOMER AVE
CARR LA
Pribet Farm
MIDDLE MEANYGATE
JOHNSON'S MEANYGATE
Carr Heys Plantation
TAYLOR'S MEANYGATE
BOLTON'S MEANYGATE
Tarleton Moss
Johnson's Farm
Johnson's Farm
Farrington's Plantation
Chapel House Farm
NEW LA
SWORD MEANYGATE
GORSE LA
SUTTON LA
BYRON CL
Meanygate Farm
Rose Farm
Nurseries
OAKGATE CL
Crosses Farm
Gorse Lane Farm
BLACKGATE LA
PR4
A565
Green Lane Farm
LEGH LA
GREEN LA
Cookson's Farm
Jackson's Farm
SOUTHPORT NEW RD
Holmes
HUNTER'S LA
TAYLOR'S LA
MOSS HEY HEY
Becconsall Farm
BLACKGATE LA
Nurseries
DOCTOR'S LA
Tarleton Runner
HIGHER LA
MERE BROW LA
BARN CL
CHARLOTTE'S LA
Taylor's La
Sewage Farm
PARK LA
GREEN LA
Pale Ditch La
Smith's La
SMITH'S LA
Ashcroft's Farm
Moss Side Farm
B5246
8
7
21
6
5
20
4
3
19
2
1
18
43
44

37
56

55
73

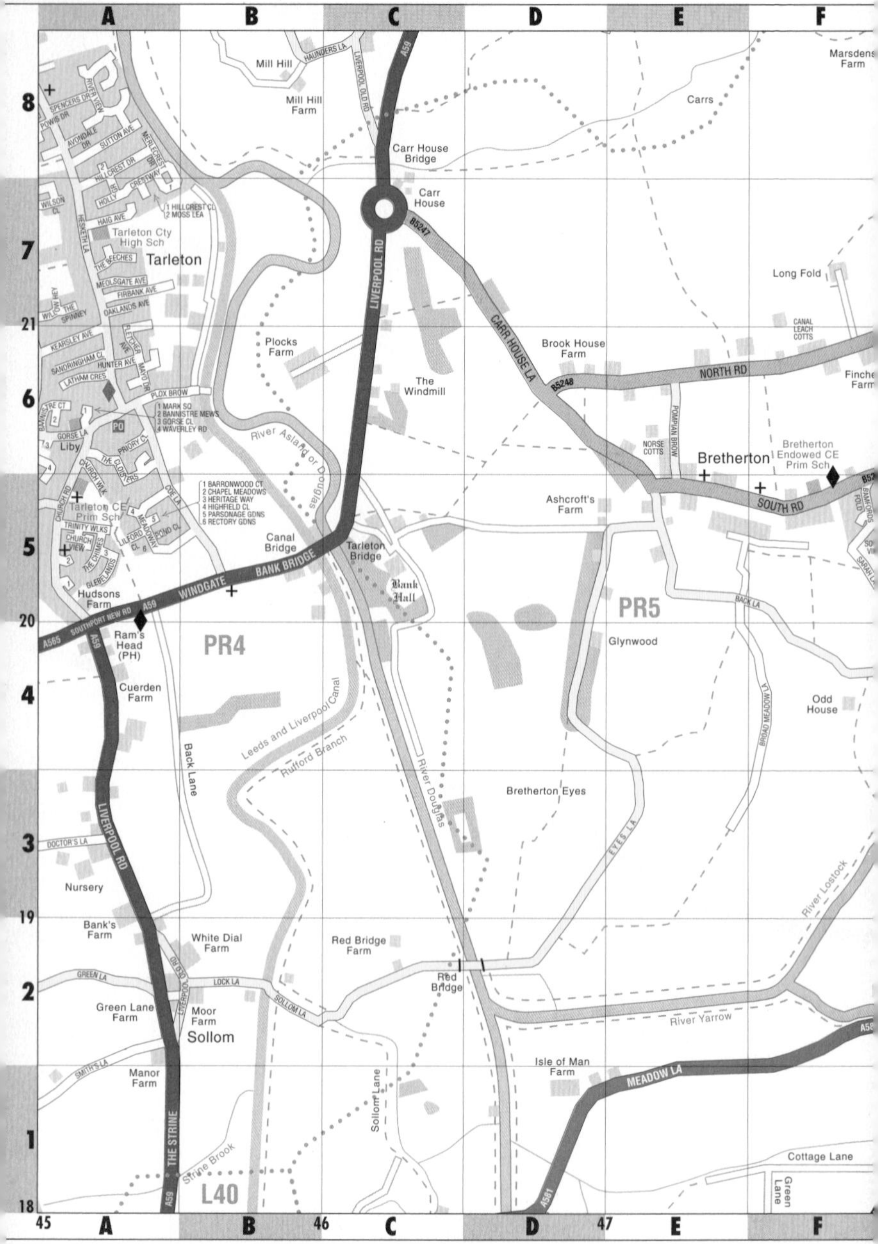

A B C D E F

8
7
21
6
5
20
4
3
19
2
1
18

Mill Hill
HAUNDERS LA
LIVERPOOL OLD RD
A59
Mill Hill Farm
Marsdens Farm
Carrs
Carr House Bridge
Carr House
SPENCERS DR
RIVER VIEW
POWIS DR
AVONDALE DR
SUTTON AVE
MERLECREST DR
HILLCREST DR
HOLLY RD
CRESTWAY
WILSON CL
1 HILLCREST CL
2 MOSS LEA
HAIG AVE
HESKETH LA
Tarleton Cty High Sch
B5247
Tarleton
THE BEECHES
MEOLSGATE AVE
FIRBANK AVE
OAKLANDS AVE
WILLOW HEY
THE SPINNEY
LIVERPOOL RD
Long Fold
CANAL LEACH COTTS
KEARSLEY AVE
SANDRINGHAM CL
FLETCHER AVE
HUNTER AVE
LATHAM CRES
MAYO DR
Plocks Farm
CARR HOUSE LA
Brook House Farm
NORTH RD
Finche Farm
The Windmill
PLOX BROW
B5248
BANNISTRE CT
1 MARK SQ
2 BANNISTRE MEWS
3 GORSE CL
4 WAVERLEY RD
PO
GORSE LA
Liby
PRIORY CL
THE CLOISTERS
CHURCH WALK
River Asland or Douglas
NORSE COTTS
POMPIAN BROW
Bretherton
Bretherton Endowed CE Prim Sch
CHURCH RD
COE LA
1 BARRONWOOD CT
2 CHAPEL MEADOWS
3 HERITAGE WAY
4 HIGHFIELD CL
5 PARSONAGE GDNS
6 RECTORY GDNS
Tarleton CE Prim Sch
Ashcroft's Farm
SOUTH RD
BAMFORDS FOLD
TRINITY WLKS
CHURCH VIEW
THE CHIMES
LILFORD CL
MEADOWAY
POND CL
Canal Bridge
Tarleton Bridge
GLEBELANDS
BANK BRIDGE
WINDGATE
Bank Hall
SARAH LA
Hudsons Farm
PR5
BACK LA
A565
SOUTHPORT NEW RD
A59
Ram's Head (PH)
PR4
Glynwood
Cuerden Farm
Leeds and Liverpool Canal
Rufford Branch
Odd House
BROAD MEADOW LA
Back Lane
River Douglas
Bretherton Eyes
LIVERPOOL RD
DOCTOR'S LA
EYES LA
River Lostock
Nursery
Bank's Farm
White Dial Farm
Red Bridge Farm
GREEN LA
LOCK LA
Red Bridge
LIVERPOOL OLD RD
Green Lane Farm
Moor Farm
SOLLOM LA
Sollom
River Yarrow
A58
SMITH'S LA
Manor Farm
Isle of Man Farm
MEADOW LA
Sollom Lane
THE STRINE
Strine Brook
Cottage Lane
Green Lane
L40
A59
A581

45 A B 46 C D 47 E F

55
38

74
58
A
B
C
D
E
F
PR4
Carr Brook
Holme House Farm
Manor House
Moss La
Cocker Bar Bridge Farm
Boundary Farm
Doles La
Green Lane Farm
Cocker Bar Rd
B5248
Broadfield Farm
Green La
Bretherton Moss
Four Lane Ends
North Rd
Norris's Farm
Highgrove Ct 1
Nixons Ct 2
The Pines
Nixon La
8
7
21
Wade Brook Rd 1
The Causeway 2
Wymott
Pump House La
Wray Cres
Cutt Cl
Glover Cl
Willow Rd
The Maples
6
Marl Cop
HM Prison
HM Prison
Moor Hey Cotts
South Rd
PO
Blue Anchor Inn (PH)
Copeland Farm
Over Hall
Flag La
Stanning's Folly
Brook House
Moss La
5
Wymott Brook
Johnson House Farm
20
PR5
Lostock Bridge Farm
Back La
Littlewood Hall Farm
Lostock Bridge
River Lostock
Littlewood Bridge
Great Nelsons Farm
Holker La
Ulnes Walton La
4
Bretherton Rd
Barber's Moor
Whiteley's Farm
Works
Ridley La
Croston
B5249
Brickcroft La
Peartree Rd
The Orchard
Lostock Rd
Moor Rd
3
The Mill (Hotel)
Lansdale Ave
Lonsdale Dr
Brookfield
Twin Lakes Ind Est
Coniston Way
Wood
Bramble
Station Rd
Gradwells
B5249
19
The Bishop Rawstorne CE High Sch
Rosecrofts Farm
Railway View
Croston
Croston Methodist Prim Sch
Nurseries
Southport Rd
A581
2
Meadowside
St Michael's Terr
LC
Westfields
Pavilion View
B5247
Willowbank Cotts
Trinity & St Michael's CE Prim Sch
Cock Robin
Meadowlane Bridge
Riverside Cres
Westhead Rd
Highfield Rd
Oaklands Farm
Meadow La
Yarrow Cl
Castle Wlks
Tory Cl
Town Rd
Shevington Cswy
Jubilee Ho
Carvers Brow
The Hillocks
Melrose Gdn
Butterfly Hall
Back Drinkhouse La
Drinkhouse Rd
Turflands
Church
PO
Sarscow La
Drink House
Carver's Farm
Sch
North Park
Sarscow Farm
Drinkhouse La
Cemy
1
Drinkhouse Farm
Carr La
River Yarrow
Home Farm
PR7
Moss La
Grape La
18
49
50
39
58

57
75

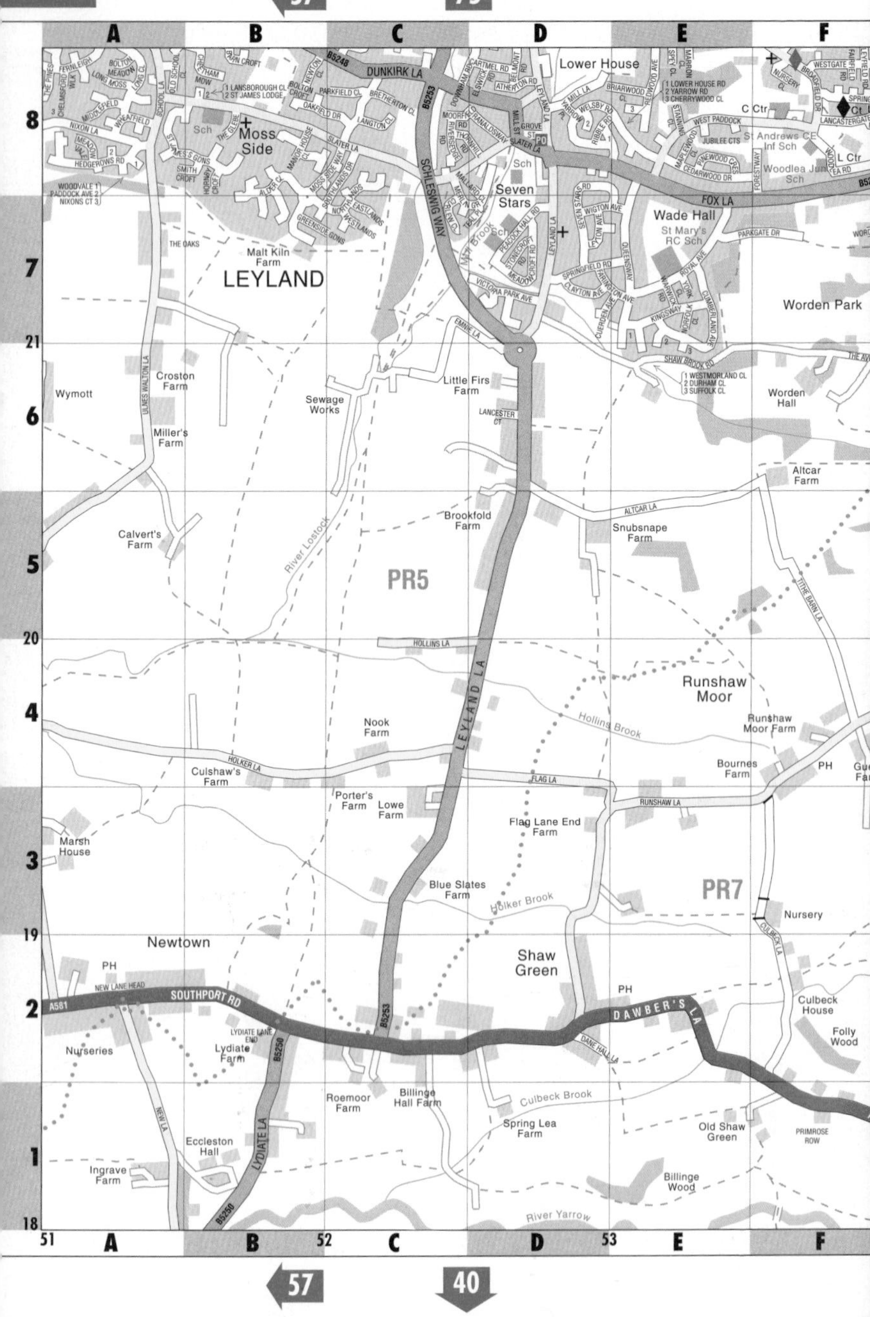
LEYLAND
Moss Side
Seven Stars
Lower House
Wade Hall
Worden Park
Worden Hall
Wymott
Croston Farm
Miller's Farm
Calvert's Farm
Malt Kiln Farm
Sewage Works
Little Firs Farm
Brookfold Farm
Snubsnape Farm
Altcar Farm
PR5
PR7
Runshaw Moor
Runshaw Moor Farm
Bournes Farm
Nook Farm
Culshaw's Farm
Porter's Farm
Lowe Farm
Flag Lane End Farm
Marsh House
Blue Slates Farm
Newtown
Shaw Green
Nursery
Culbeck House
Folly Wood
Nurseries
Lydiate Farm
Roemoor Farm
Billinge Hall Farm
Spring Lea Farm
Old Shaw Green
Billinge Wood
Eccleston Hall
Ingrave Farm
River Lostock
Hollins Brook
Holker Brook
Culbeck Brook
River Yarrow
SCHLESWIG WAY
LEYLAND LA
SOUTHPORT RD
DAWBER'S LA
DUNKIRK LA
FOX LA
HOLKER LA
FLAG LA
RUNSHAW LA
ALTCAR LA
HOLLINS LA
LYDIATE LA
NEW LA
CULBECK LA
TITHE BARN LA
ULNES WALTON LA
EMNIE LA
SHAW BROOK RD
A581
B5253
B5248
B5250

57
40

76
60

41
D1
1 DALE AVE
2 TALBOT ROW
3 AMBLESIDE ROW
60

59 77

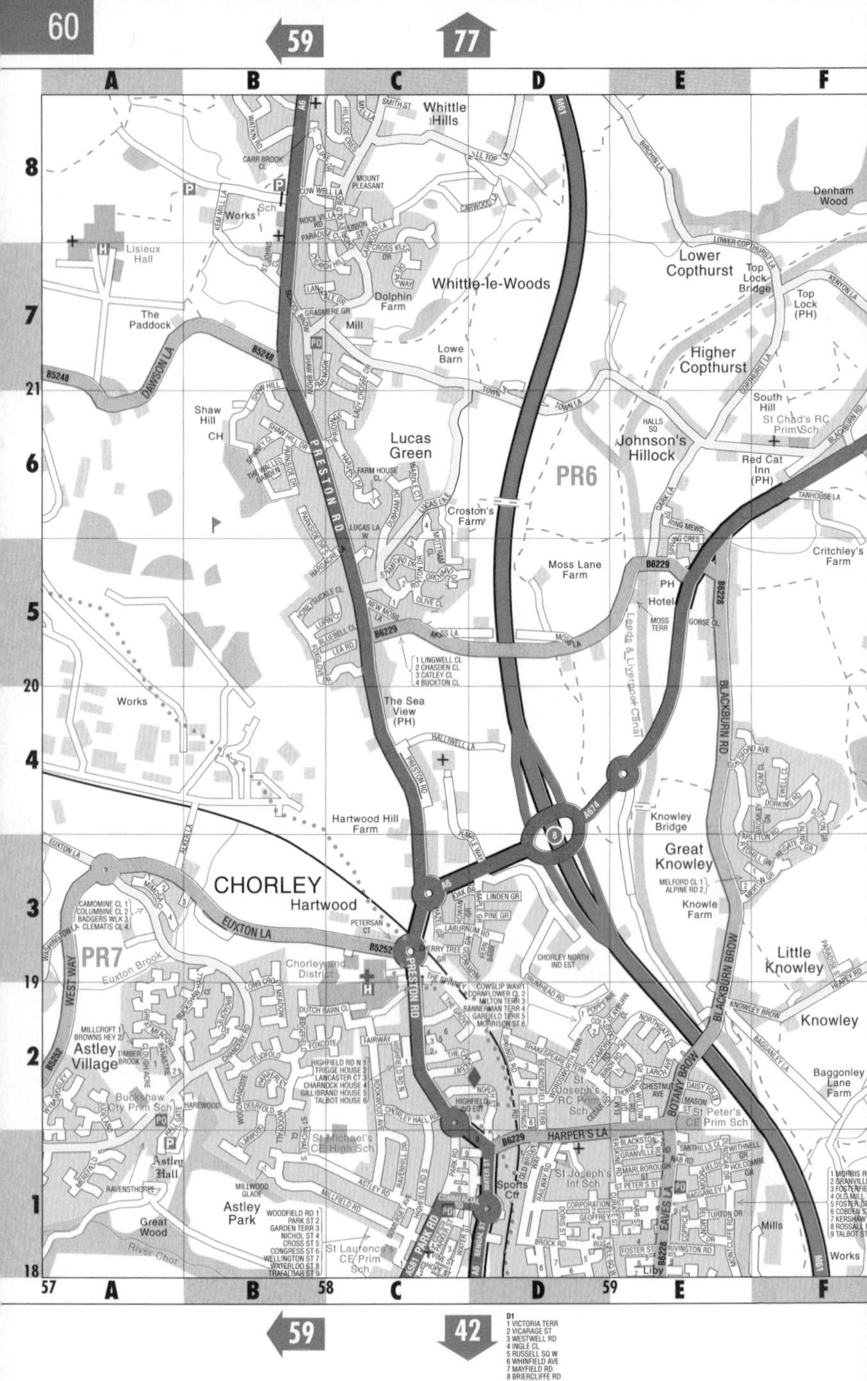

59 42

D1
1 VICTORIA TERR
2 VICARAGE ST
3 WESTWELL RD
4 INGLE CL
5 RUSSELL SQ W
6 WHINFIELD AVE
7 MAYFIELD RD
8 BRIERCLIFFE RD
9 PRESTON ST

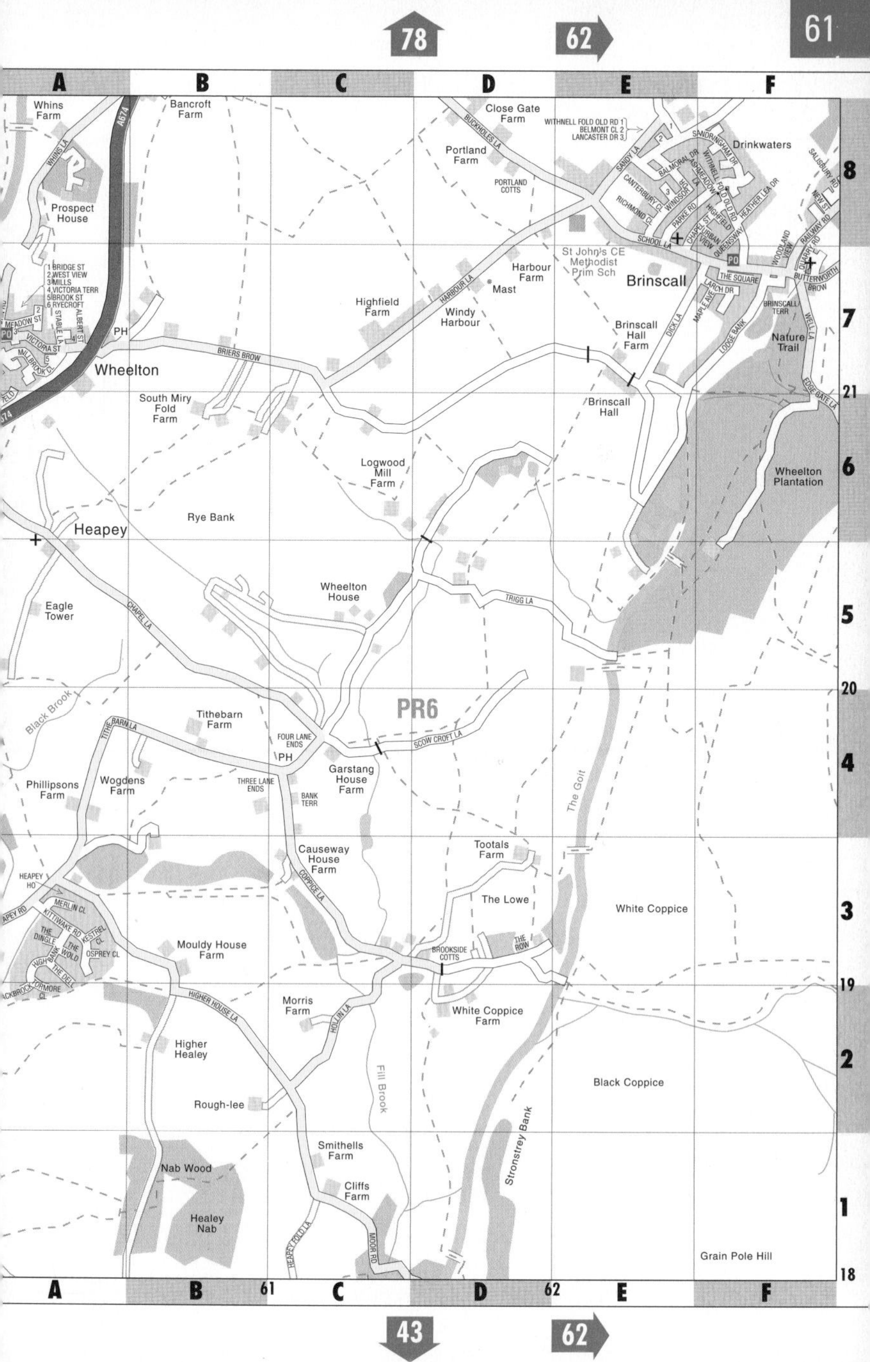
78
62
A B C D E F
Whins Farm
Bancroft Farm
Close Gate Farm
WITHNELL FOLD OLD RD 1
BELMONT CL 2
LANCASTER DR 3
Drinkwaters
Portland Farm
PORTLAND COTTS
Prospect House
St John's CE Methodist Prim Sch
Harbour Farm
Mast
Brinscall
Highfield Farm
Windy Harbour
1 BRIDGE ST
2 WEST VIEW
3 MILLS
4 VICTORIA TERR
5 BROOK ST
6 RYECROFT
Brinscall Hall Farm
Nature Trail
PH
Wheelton
BRIERS BROW
South Miry Fold Farm
Brinscall Hall
Logwood Mill Farm
Wheelton Plantation
Rye Bank
Heapey
Wheelton House
TRIGG LA
Eagle Tower
CHAPEL LA
Black Brook
PR6
Tithebarn Farm
FOUR LANE ENDS
PH
SCOW CROFT LA
Garstang House Farm
Phillipsons Farm
Wogdens Farm
THREE LANE ENDS
BANK TERR
The Goit
Causeway House Farm
Tootals Farm
The Lowe
White Coppice
Mouldy House Farm
BROOKSIDE COTTS
THE ROW
Morris Farm
White Coppice Farm
Higher Healey
Fill Brook
Black Coppice
Rough-lee
Smithells Farm
Stronstrey Bank
Nab Wood
Cliffs Farm
Healey Nab
Grain Pole Hill
8 7 21 6 5 20 4 3 19 2 1 18
A B 61 C D 62 E F
43
62

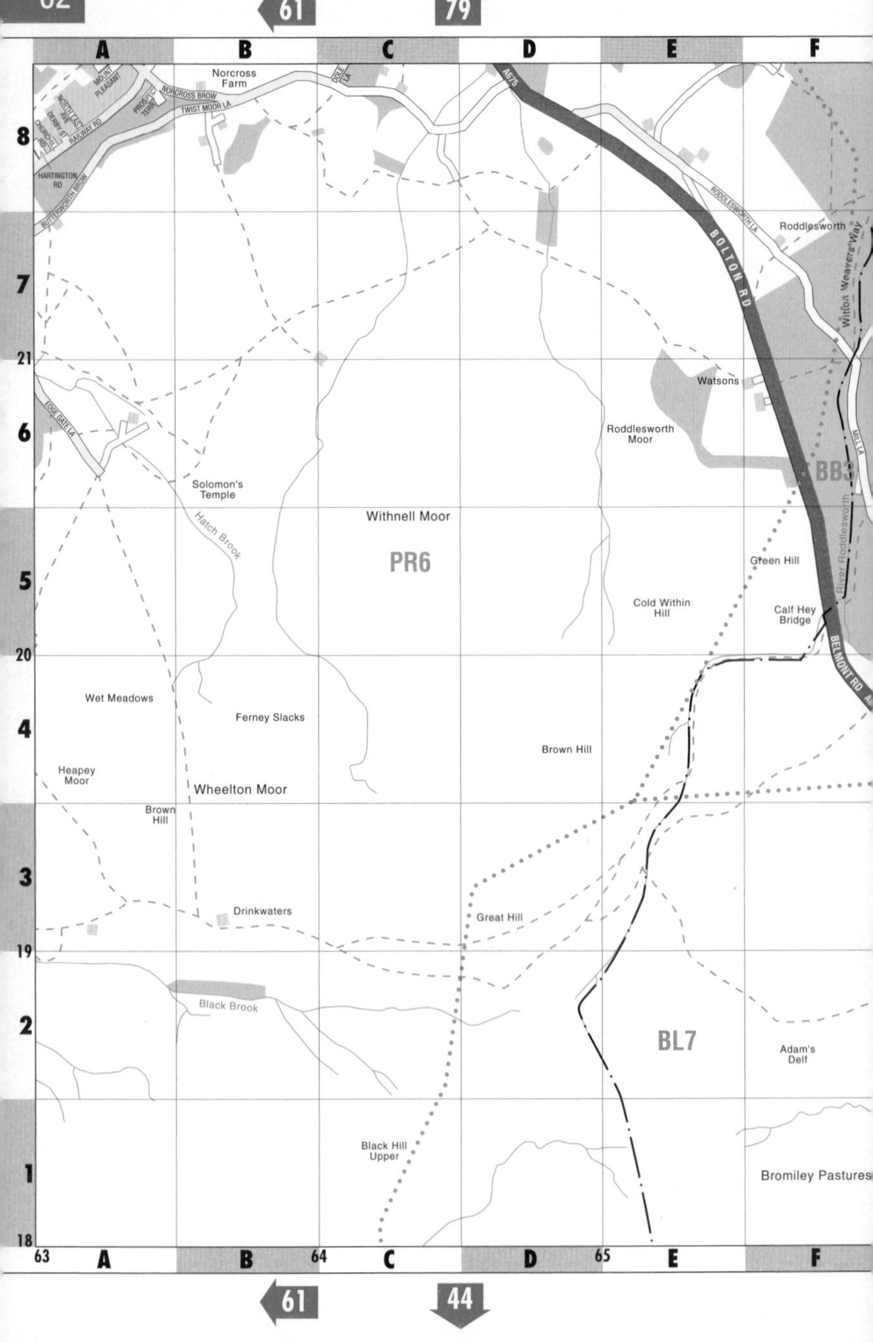
61
79
A
B
C
D
E
F
Norcross Farm
MOUNT PLEASANT
NORTH EAST AVE
DERBY ST
RAILWAY RD
CHURCHILL RD
PROSPECT TERR
NORCROSS BROW
TWIST MOOR LA
DOLE LA
A675
HARTINGTON RD
BUTTERWORTH BROW
RODDLESWORTH LA
Roddlesworth
BOLTON RD
Witton Weavers Way
EDGE GATE LA
Watsons
MILL LA
Roddlesworth Moor
BB3
Solomon's Temple
Hatch Brook
Withnell Moor
PR6
River Roddlesworth
Green Hill
Cold Within Hill
Calf Hey Bridge
BELMONT RD
Wet Meadows
Ferney Slacks
Brown Hill
Heapey Moor
Wheelton Moor
Brown Hill
Drinkwaters
Great Hill
Black Brook
BL7
Adam's Delf
Black Hill Upper
Bromiley Pastures
8
7
21
6
5
20
4
3
19
2
1
18
63
64
65
61
44

80
64

A
B
C
D
E
F
Ryal Farm
Roddlesworth
Nature Trail
Royal Arms
(PH)
Roddlesworth
Vistor Ctr
HOLLINSHEAD TERR
Tockholes
No 2 Plantation
Stepback Brook
Higher
Wenshead
Sunnyhurst Hey
Resr
Jubilee Tower
Darwen
Hill
SNIDDLE HILL LA
Sniddle Hill
Farm
TURN LA
WESTLAND AVE
GRANVILLE RD
MANOR RD
INVERNESS RD
BELGRAVE
EAST PK AVE
RADFIELD RD
ARLINGTON RD 1
LIME AVE 2
Belgrave
Height
Side
New Barn
Tockholes
No 3 Plantation
TOCKHOLES RD
BB3
Green Lowe
Farm House
DUCKSHAW RD
Duckshaw Clough
Darwen Moor
Duckshaw Brook
MILL LA
Slipper
Lowe
Duckshaw
Farm
Thorny Bank
Plantation
ccadilly
Cartridge Hill
Brown Lowe
Whitehall
Farm
Conyries
Plantation
Black Hill
Turn Lowe
CROOKFIELD RD
BELMONT RD
Wilding
Fields
Witton Weavers Way
BL7
Green Lowe
Little Hill
Old Man's
Hill
Hulton Pasture
Lower
Pasture Barn
Turton Moor
Long Lands
A675
8
7
21
6
5
20
4
3
19
2
1
18
67
68

45
64

A8
1 HESSE ST
2 GLENTHORN TERR
3 BUFF ST
4 CLEMENT ST
5 BECKETT ST
6 STANSFIELD ST
7 SPRINGFIELD FLATS
8 ALICE ST
9 JEPSON ST
10 COBDEN ST
11 SPRING GDNS
12 RADFORD BANK GDNS
13 NOBLE ST

63

A8
14 RADFIELD AVE
15 HILLSIDE AVE
16 HILL HOS
17 MILL GAP ST
18 HAMER ST

81

B6
1 SPRINGVALE BSNS PK
2 WATERY LA IND EST
3 RAWLINSON ST
4 ST BARNABAS ST
5 BLACKPOOL ST
6 MORTON WLK
7 SPRINGTHORPE ST
8 WESTCOTE ST
9 MELBOURNE ST

B8
1 PRIMROSE TERR
2 GADFIELD ST
3 RAILWAY VIEW
4 HIGHFIELD ST
5 CROSS BARN WLK
6 MELITA ST
7 ROSE HILL TERR
8 ASHTON RD

C7
1 THE MEWS
2 CAUSEWAY ST
3 PICKUP FOLD
4 CRANBERRY CHASE
5 TUNNEL ST

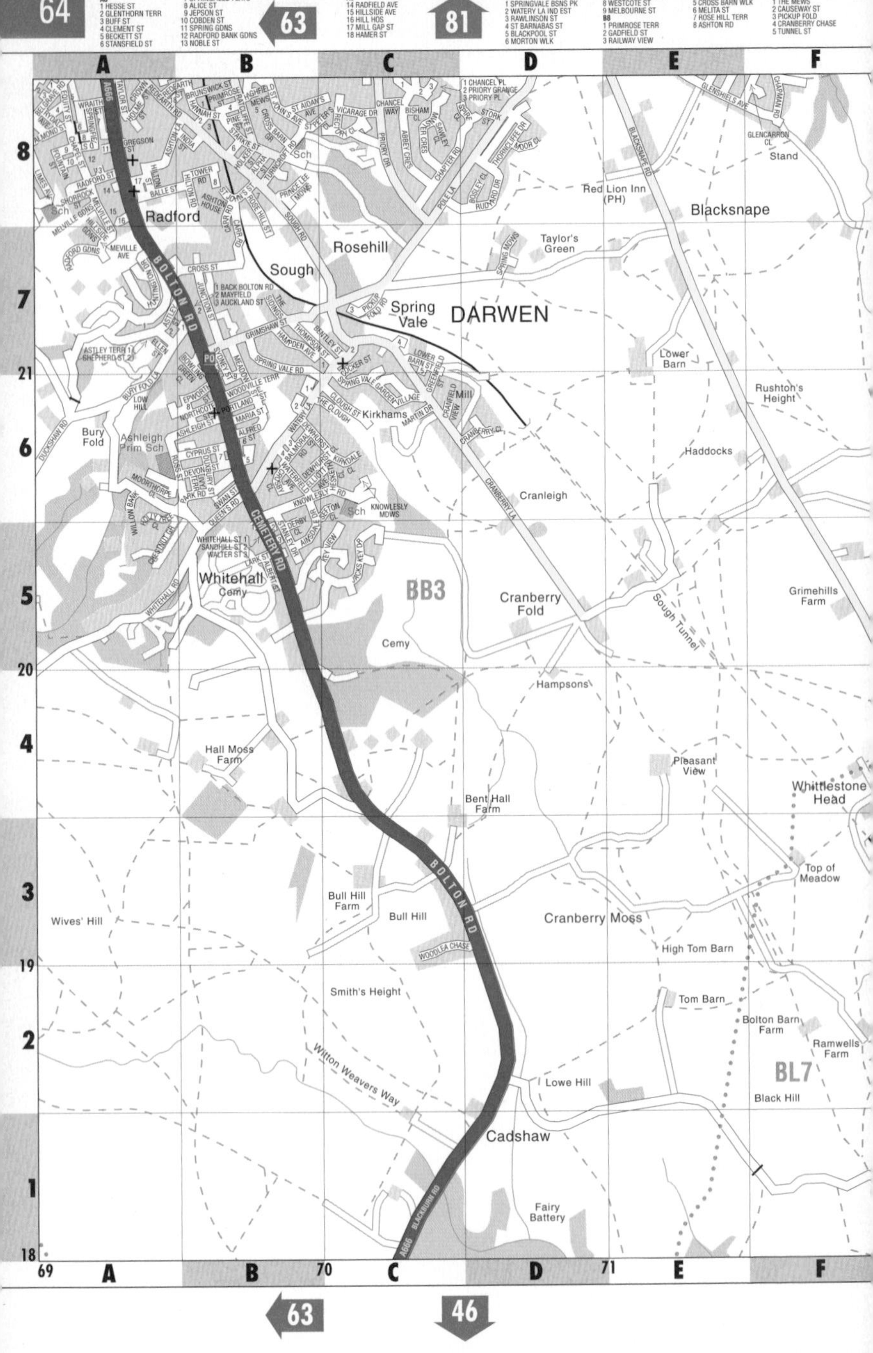

63
46

A
B
C
D
E
F
Lower Pastures
Sunnyfield Farm
Green Hill
Moss Brook
BB4
8
Bentley Moss
Pastures Higher Barn
Hog Low Pike
Whinberry Pasture
BB3
7
Black Height
Pastures
Scotland Resr
Hoddlesden Moss
21
Grey Stone Hill
Clough Head
6
Cuckoldmans
Orrell Moss
Higher Head
Soot Hill
Longshoot Farm
Broadhead
5
Horse Hey
BROADHEAD RD
Whowells
Higher Aushaw
20
Broadmeadow Farm
Lower House
Grimehills
KNOWSLEY LA
4
Grimehills Bridge
Toby Inn (PH)
Aushaw Moss
Steen Hill
Hall Hill Farm
Naze End
Broadhead Brook
BL7
Higher Barn
3
Pike House
Springside Farm
The Naze
ROUND BARN
19
Orrell Cote Farm
Poultry Farm
Little Edge Farm
BLACKBURN RD
LEE LA
Stanley Hill
2
Stanley Farm
Cote Farm
Slacks Farm
Bisley Moor Side Farm
Bank Wood
Wayoh Fold Cottage
Wayoh Farm
Edgworth Moor
MOORSIDE RD
Entwistle
Moor Side Farm
Willows Farm
Wayoh Bridge
Crowthorn Sch
1
Witton Weavers Way
EDGE LA
CROWTHORN RD
Crooked Walls
18
73
74

65
83

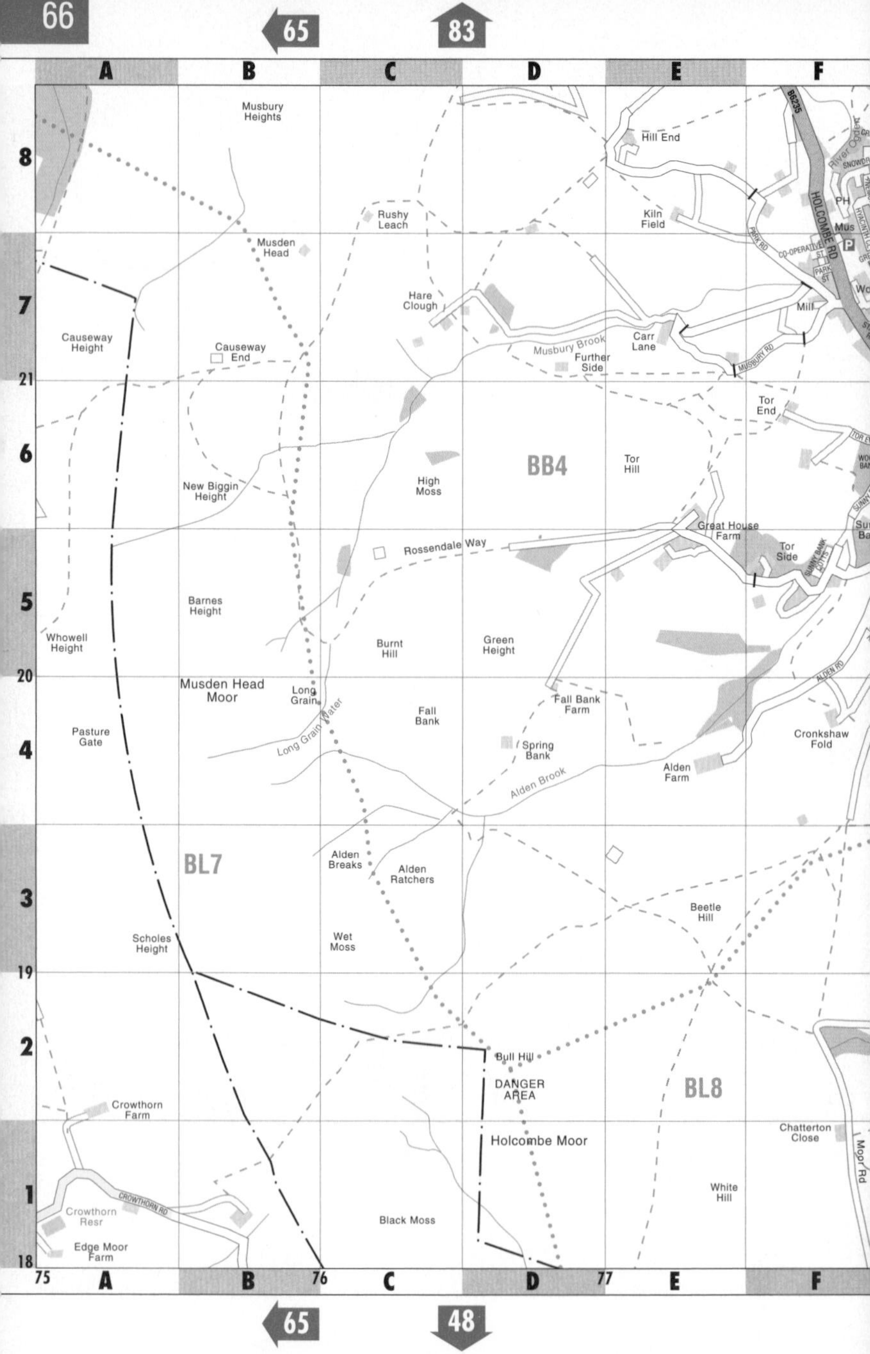
A
B
C
D
E
F
Musbury Heights
Hill End
B6235
River Ogden
Rushy Leach
Kiln Field
HOLCOMBE RD
PH
Mus
Musden Head
PARK RD
CO-OPERATIVE ST
PARK ST
Hare Clough
Mill
Causeway Height
Causeway End
Musbury Brook
Carr Lane
Further Side
MUSBURY RD
Tor End
BB4
Tor Hill
New Biggin Height
High Moss
Great House Farm
Rossendale Way
Tor Side
SUNNY BANK COTTS
Barnes Height
Whowell Height
Burnt Hill
Green Height
ALDEN RD
Musden Head Moor
Long Grain
Fall Bank
Fall Bank Farm
Long Grain Water
Pasture Gate
Spring Bank
Cronkshaw Fold
Alden Farm
Alden Brook
BL7
Alden Breaks
Alden Ratchers
Beetle Hill
Scholes Height
Wet Moss
Bull Hill
DANGER AREA
BL8
Crowthorn Farm
Holcombe Moor
Chatterton Close
Moor Rd
White Hill
CROWTHORN RD
Crowthorn Resr
Black Moss
Edge Moor Farm
8
7
21
6
5
20
4
3
19
2
1
18
75
76
77

65
48

84
68

A B C D E F

8
7
21
6
5
20
4
3
19
2
1
18

A B 79 C D 80 E F

49
68

67
85

F8
1 IVY ST
2 GEORGE'S ROW
3 PILLING ST
4 SPRING GARDENS ST
5 MARKET ST
6 TENTERFIELD ST
7 YARE ST
8 THORNFIELD AVE
9 WOOD LEA BANK
10 INDUSTRIAL COTTS

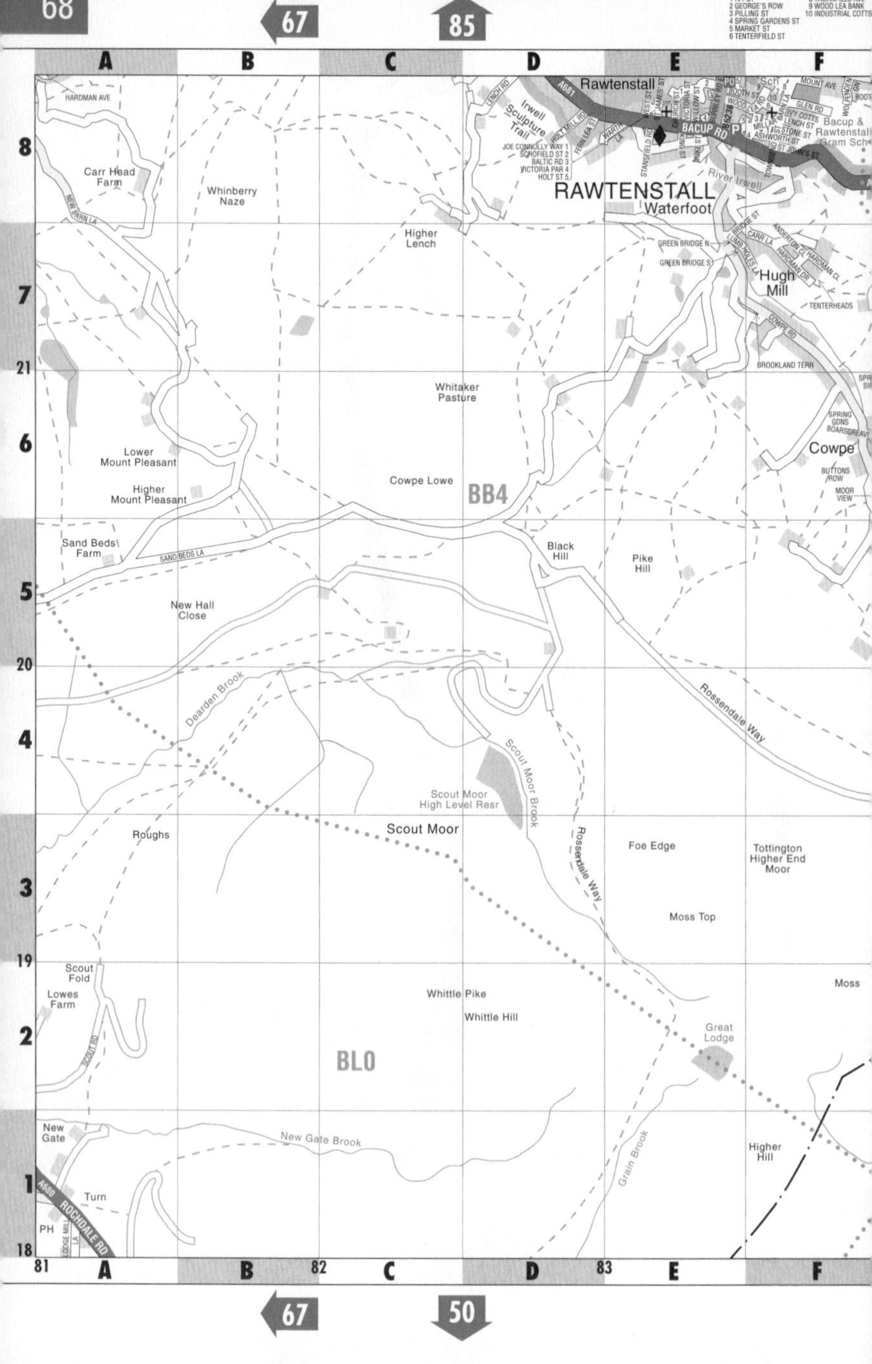

67
50

86
70
A
B
C
D
E
F
Waterbarn
Stackstead
Glen Top
BB4
B3
1 WEST GDNS
2 ASHWORTH TERR
3 TUNSTEAD MILL TERR
4 CROW TREE AVE
BOOTH RD
NEWCHURCH RD
Brandwood
Rake Head
ROYDS RD
MOOR VIEW
BLACKWOOD RD
ATHERTON WAY
TAYLOR HOLME IND EST
BRANDWOOD PK
RAKEHEAD LA
Nun Hills
PLEASANT VIEW
River Irwell
BACUP
Wks
Sch
VICTORIA ST
RUSHWORTH BLDGS
HOLME ST
OLD KILN
WARDLE ST
A681
A6066
NEW LINE
St Saviour's CE Prim Sch
Moorlands Park
Stubbylee Park
STUBBYLEE LA
E8
1 FERNHILL CRES
2 FERNHILL GR
3 QUEEN'S TERR
4 FERNHILL WAY
5 RUSHTON ST
6 BACK RUSHTON ST
Irwell Sculpture Trail
Cemy
LEE RD
Lee Farm
D8
1 BANKFIELD TERR
2 LILAC TERR
3 ASHWORTH ST
4 SPRING TERR
5 KILN TERR
6 FERNVILLE TERR
7 BROOKES ST
8 CLOUGH ST
9 BACK CEMETERY TERR
PROSPECT TERR
UNSWORTH ST
CUTLER LA
Greens
Greens Clough
C8
1 PRIMROSE BANK
2 STANSFIELD ST
3 TURNER ST
4 GEORGE ST
5 QUEEN ST
6 CLEGG ST
7 ALBION ST
8 DALE ST
9 PRIMROSE ST
10 OLIVER ST
11 GARDEN ST
12 OLD SCHOOL MEWS
13 UNION CT
14 CHAPEL ST
15 TRINITY ST
16 MOUNT PLEASANT
17 LUKE ST
Mast
Height
Lower Boarsgreave
ST GEORGE'S TERR
COWPE RD
Higher Boarsgreave
OL13
Lee Moss
Greens Moor
Brandwood Moor
Cowpe Resr
Well Clough
Brandwood Lower End Moor
Jackson's Moor
Cragg High Level Tank
ROOLEY MOOR RD
Top of Leach
Rossendale Way
Old Laurence Top
Whitworth Lower End Moor
BB4
Cowpe Moss
Walstead Clough
Old Sink Slack
Red Pits
Hail Storm Hill
Hamer Hill
OL12
Prickshaw Brook
Withens Hey
Great Ding
Little Ding
Naden Brook
Ding Clough
Clegg Ding
Rooley Moor
8
7
21
6
5
20
4
3
19
2
1
18
85
86
70

69 87

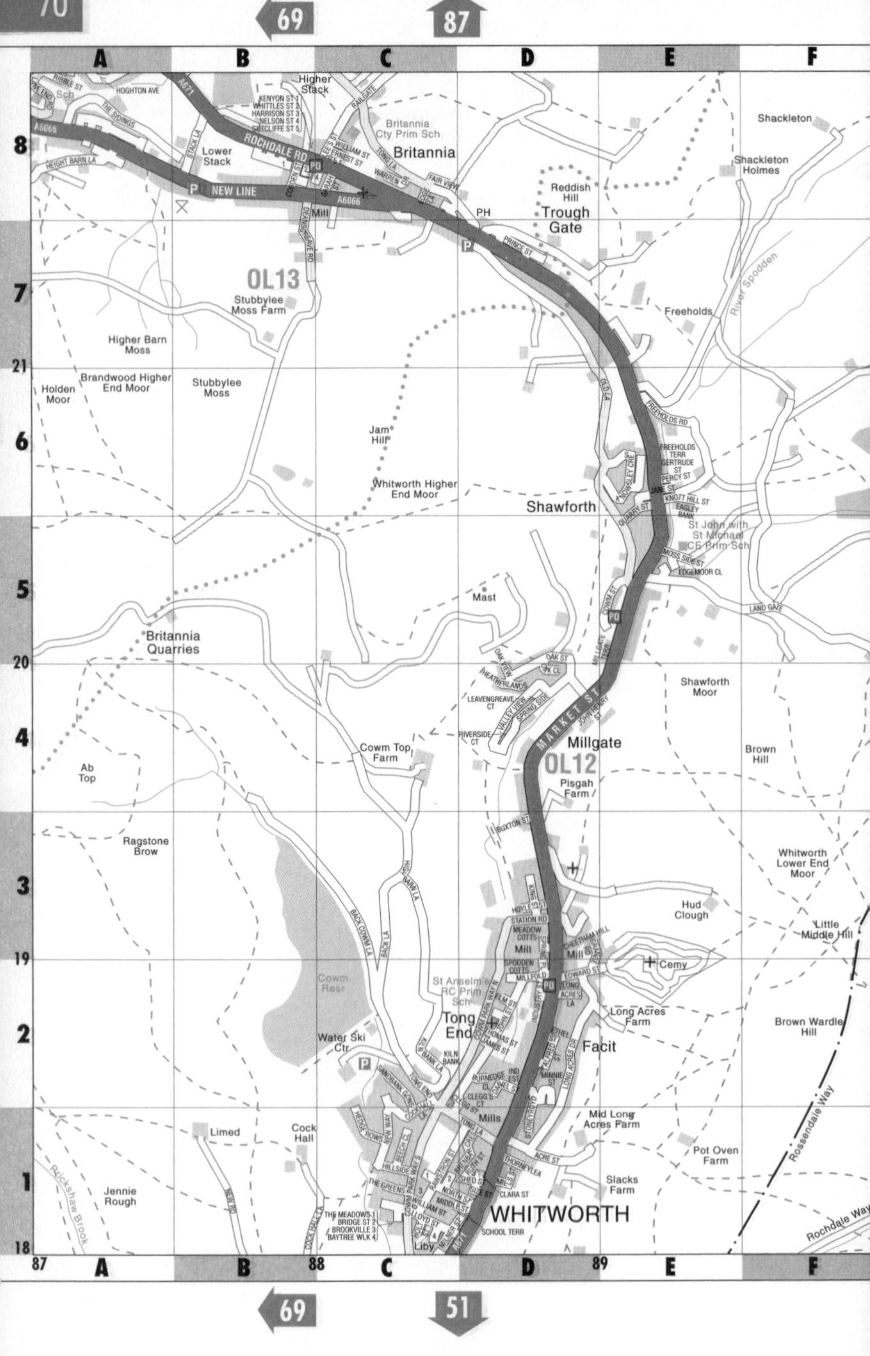
A B C D E F
8 7 21 6 5 20 4 3 19 2 1 18
87 88 89
Higher Stack
Britannia Cty Prim Sch
Britannia
Lower Stack
ROCHDALE RD
NEW LINE
A6066
A671
Shackleton
Shackleton Holmes
Reddish Hill
Trough Gate
PH
Mill
PRINCE ST
OL13
Stubbylee Moss Farm
Freeholds
River Spodden
Higher Barn Moss
Holden Moor
Brandwood Higher End Moor
Stubbylee Moss
Jam Hill
Whitworth Higher End Moor
Shawforth
St John with St Michael CE Prim Sch
FREEHOLDS RD
Mast
LAND GATE
Britannia Quarries
Shawforth Moor
MARKET ST
Millgate
OL12
Pisgah Farm
Cowm Top Farm
Ab Top
Brown Hill
Ragstone Brow
Whitworth Lower End Moor
Hud Clough
Little Middle Hill
Cemy
Cowm Resr
St Anselm's RC Prim Sch
Tong End
Long Acres Farm
Brown Wardle Hill
Water Ski Ctr
Facit
Mills
Mid Long Acres Farm
Limed
Cock Hall
Pot Oven Farm
Rossendale Way
Jennie Rough
Slacks Farm
WHITWORTH
Rochdale Way
Brickshaw Brook
Liby
THE MEADOWS 1
BRIDGE ST 2
BROOKVILLE 3
BAYTREE WLK 4
KENYON ST 1
WHITTLES ST 2
HARRISON ST 3
NELSON ST 4
SUTCLIFFE ST 5

69 51

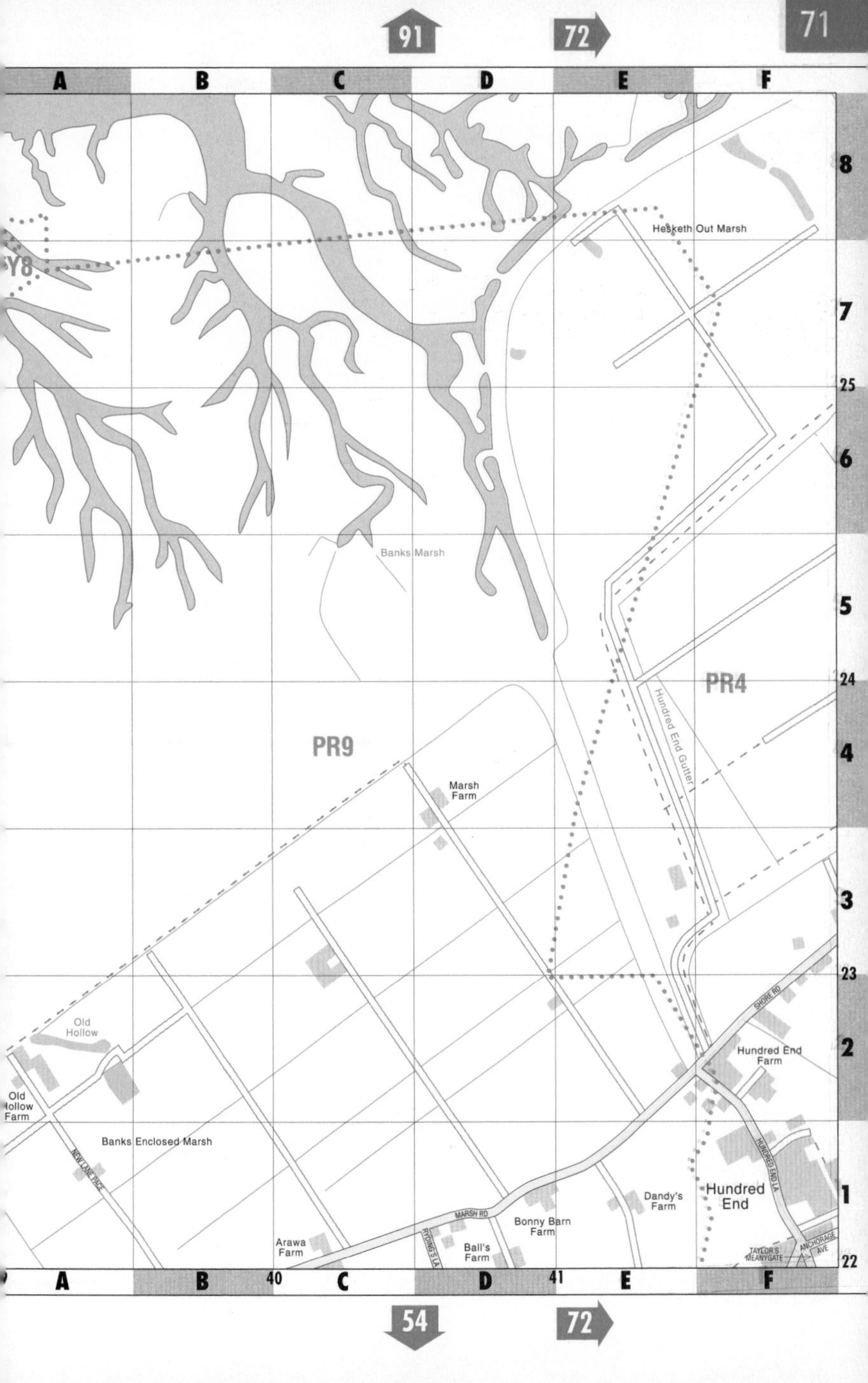
A
B
C
D
E
F
8
Hesketh Out Marsh
7
25
6
Banks Marsh
5
24
PR4
Hundred End Gutter
PR9
4
Marsh
Farm
3
23
SHORE RD
Old
Hollow
2
Hundred End
Farm
Old
Hollow
Farm
Banks Enclosed Marsh
NEW LANE PACE
HUNDRED END LA
1
Dandy's
Farm
Hundred
End
MARSH RD
Bonny Barn
Farm
Arawa
Farm
RYDING'S LA
Ball's
Farm
TAYLOR'S
MEANYGATE
ANCHORAGE
AVE
22
40
41

71
92

Hesketh Out Marsh
Ribble Bank Farm
Westgate Farm
Hesketh New Marsh
Anchorage Farm
Carr Heys Watercourse
Hesketh Old Marsh
Hesketh-with-Becconsall All Saints CE Sch
PR4
Hesketh Bank
Bank Farm
Wright's Farm
New Manor Farm
Ribble View Farm
Hesketh
New Farm
West Lancash Light Rly
Kingsfold Christian Sch
Becconsall
Nurseries
Millers Farm
Hesketh Moss
Pear Tree Farm
River Asland or Douglas
SHORE RD
GUIDE RD
MARSH RD
STATION RD
BECCONSALL LA
NEWARTH LA
MOSS LA
BOUNDARY LA
BOUNDARY MEANYGATE
JOHNSON'S MEANYGATE
FERMOR RD
HESKETH LA
MILL LA
SIDNEY AVE
GRANVILLE AVE
CHAPEL RD
CROPPER GDNS
1 THISTLE CL
2 PRIMROSE CL
3 CORNFLOWER CL
4 BLUEBELL CL
PO
PH

71
55

93
74

A
B
C
D
E
F
Back La
Nurseries
Grange La
Marsh La
Hall Pool Bridge
Hall Pool
Ribble Way
Dolphin Inn (PH)
Tarra Carr Gutter
Marsh Farm
Mast
Sewage Works
Nursery
Hall La
Meadow Head La
Hall Green
Longton Brickcroft Nature Reserve
Highfield Dr
Hall Carr La
Tranmoor
Higher Furlong
Little Hoole Marsh
Odd House
Hall Carr Farm
Fairview Cl
Liverpool New Rd
Liverpool Old Rd
Old Mill Ct
School St
Sea View
Walmer Gn
Walmer Bridge
Marsh House Farm
Lower Marsh House
Station Rd
River Asland or Douglas
Marsh Farm
Sewage Works
PR4
PR4
Lane Ends Farm
Longton By-Pass A59
Knoll La
Balls Farm
Pine Ave
Becconsall Marsh
Ravenskerne
Brook La
Meadow
Long
Marlfield
Oldfield
Birchfield
Thornfield
Rakes Brook
Southfield Gdns
Felton Way
Acre Gr
Westcroft
Copper Beech Cl
Critchley Cl
Becconsall Hall
Becconsall La
Fir Tree Cl
Liverpool Old Rd
Much Hoole
Green Hey
Middle Hey
Great Hey
Swallow Field
Barnfield
Kirk Head
Wingate
Liverpool Rd
Park Ave
Northall
Moss House La
Much Hoole Marsh House
Lane House Farm
Northern Ave
Smithy La
Goose Green
Hunger Hill Farm
Marsh Farm
Haunders La
Rose & Crown (PH)
Hoole CE Prim Sch
Town La
Much Hoole Town
Church Farm
Liverpool Old Rd
Lunds La
Manor House
Carr Brook
Nursery
Dobson's Farm
PR5
A59
Manorcroft 1
Orchard La 2
Brookway 3
Aspendale Cl
Meadoway
Longacre
Park Farm Cl
Sedgefield
Chestnut Cres
Dale Ave
Ash Gr
The Maltings
Birkdale Cl
Birkdale Ave
Tuson Croft
Grove Ave
Brook Hey
Stonefield
Woodlands Way
Formby Cres
Bentley Park Rd
Liverpool Rd
Townfield Cl
Mereside Cl
Drumacre La W
PO
PO
8
7
6
5
4
3
2
1
25
24
23
22
46
47

56
74

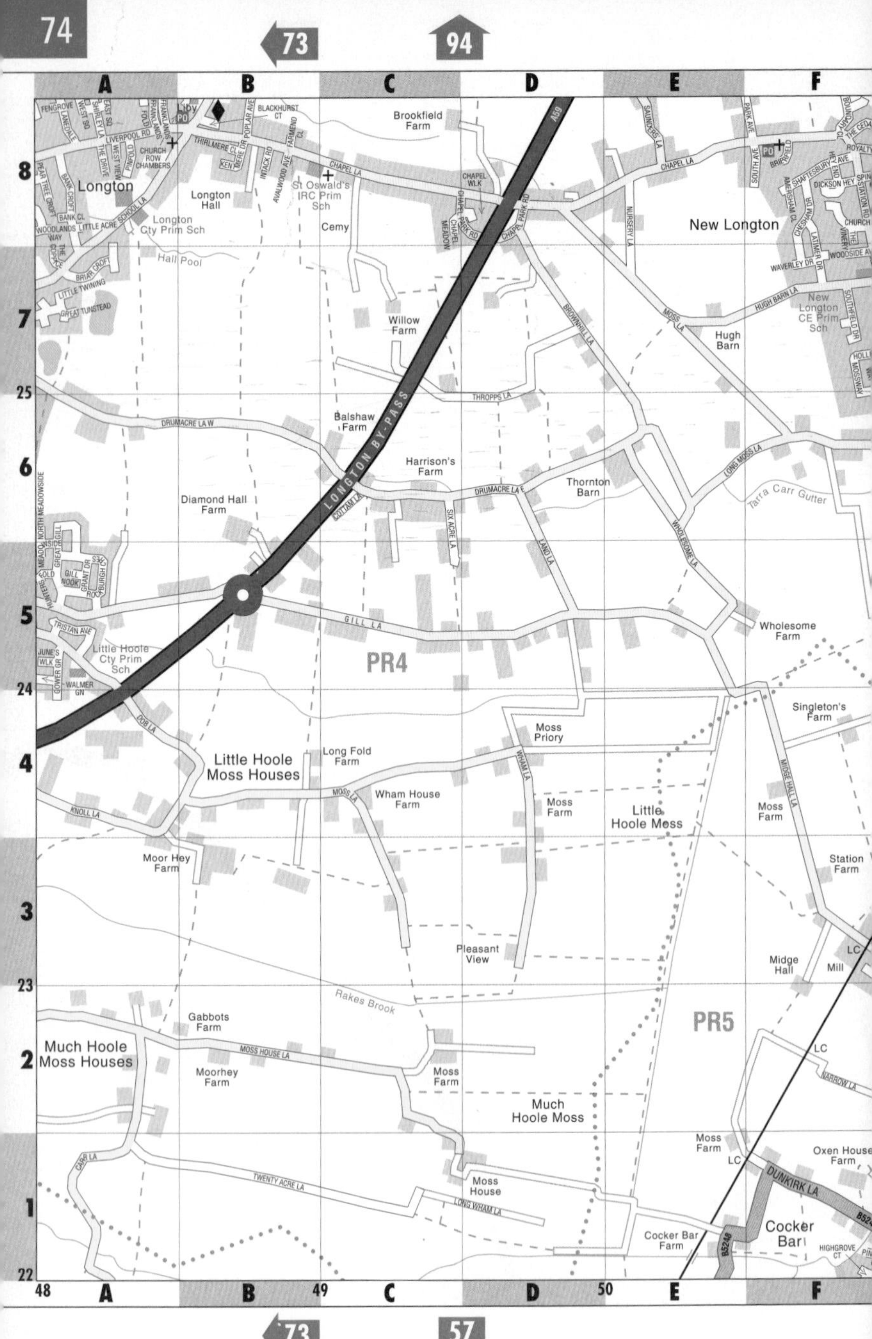
73
94
Longton
Longton Hall
Longton Cty Prim Sch
St Oswald's IRC Prim Sch
Cemy
Brookfield Farm
New Longton
New Longton CE Prim Sch
Hugh Barn
Willow Farm
Balshaw Farm
Harrison's Farm
Thornton Barn
Diamond Hall Farm
LONGTON BY-PASS
A59
CHAPEL LA
DRUMACRE LA W
DRUMACRE LA E
GILL LA
THROPPS LA
LONG MOSS LA
MOSS LA
HUGH BARN LA
Tarra Carr Gutter
Hall Pool
PR4
Little Hoole Cty Prim Sch
Wholesome Farm
Singleton's Farm
Moss Priory
Long Fold Farm
Little Hoole Moss Houses
Wham House Farm
Moss Farm
Little Hoole Moss
Moor Hey Farm
Station Farm
Pleasant View
Midge Hall
Mill
Rakes Brook
PR5
Gabbots Farm
Much Hoole Moss Houses
MOSS HOUSE LA
Moorhey Farm
Much Hoole Moss
Moss House
TWENTY ACRE LA
LONG WHAM LA
Cocker Bar Farm
Cocker Bar
Oxen House Farm
DUNKIRK LA
NARROW LA
B5248
48
49
50
57

95
76

B1
1 BARN CROFT
2 THE MEADOWS
3 HOLMES MEADOW
4 ROSTREVOR CL

D1
1 JACKSON RD
2 MICKLEFIELD CT
3 ORRELL CL
4 HOMESTEAD CL
5 FIELDEN ST
6 LANGHOLM CL

E1
1 ELMWOOD AVE
2 BLEACHERS DR

58
76

76
A8
1 FIR TREES CRES
2 ORCHARD CROFT
3 BRIDGE CT
4 SCHOOL HILLOCKS COTTS
5 LONSDALE MEWS
6 BARNFIELD
7 SEPHTON ST
8 HOGHTON ST
9 JUBILEE RD
10 HOPE TERR
11 WILLIAM ST
12 VICTORIA TERR
75
B8
1 ST JAMES CT
2 FERN CL
3 MAUREEN AVE
4 MARILYN AVE
5 CEDAR AVE
96
C8
1 NORTH GR
2 THE PICKERINGS
3 BRIDGE RD
4 NEW PASTURES
5 CHARTWELL RISE
6 STONEBRIDGE CL
7 FELLWAY CL
8 WOODSTOCK CL
E8
1 CO-OPERATIVE ST
2 SMITHY ST
3 NELSON ST
4 HOPWOOD ST
5 CRANBOURNE ST
6 REGENTSWAY
F8
1 CAM CL
2 BLEASDALE CL
3 DUNSOP CL
4 HAREDEN CL
5 FELL CL
6 HODDER CL
7 MONTGOMERY ST
8 JACKSON ST
9 CAMBRIDGE RD
10 PRINCESS ST
11 SERGEANT ST
12 GROVE ST
13 SMITH ST
Tardy Gate
Lostock Hall
BROWNEDGE RD
LONDON WAY
Ind Est
Bamber Bridge
River Lostock
STATION RD
LOSTOCK LA
BAMBER BRIDGE
FARINGTON RD
Cuerden Green
Banastres at Bank
Stoney Lane House
Fowler Lane Bridge
Rigby's Farm
Works
Oakfield
STANIFIELD LA
Sand Pit
Clock House
Cuerden Hall
Cock Cabin Wood
Bottoms
PR5
LYDIATE LA
WIGAN RD
CENTURION WAY
Farington
Leverhouse Prim Sch
Cuerden Farm
Cuerden Valley Park
Farington Cty Prim Sch
Calderbanks
Clayton Bridge
Golden Hill
GOLDEN HILL LA
St Catherine's Sch
Clayton-le-Woods
TOWN BROW
LANCASTER LA
LEYLAND WAY
Turpin Green
Lancaster Lane Prim Sch
Leyland Meth Jun & Inf Schs
LEYLAND
A
B
C
D
E
F
54
55
56
A1
1 CHATSWORTH RD
2 YEWLANDS DR
3 YEWLANDS AVE
4 MOSLEY ST
5 BELGRAVE RD
6 REGENT RD
7 ARGYLE RD
8 NORTHCOTE ST
9 DOROTHY AVE
A7
1 CHADWICH GDNS
2 SOUTH VIEW
3 EAST VIEW
4 KELLET ACRE
5 BRACKENBURY CL
B1
1 ORCHARD ST
2 HEMSLEY GN
3 WILTON PL
4 BURGHLEY CT
5 STRATFIELD PL
6 SPRING ST
7 CEDAR CT
8 CHARNOCK ST
9 BRETHERTON TERR
10 STANLEY ST
11 SANDFIELD ST
12 STARKIE ST
75
B2
1 THE SQUARE
2 BELVEDERE RD
3 CROSS ST
4 BAKER ST
5 ST AMBROSE TERR
6 FLEETWOOD ST
7 GRUNDY ST
8 HEWITT ST
9 GOLDEN HILL
59
B7
1 GARDEN ST
2 PRINCES ST
3 BIRTWISTLE ST
4 QUEEN ST
5 FAIRFIELD ST
6 KING ST
C1
1 STIRLING CL
C2
1 ST MARGARET'S RD
2 THE CLOISTERS
3 THE CHASE
4 ST CATHERINES CL
C3
1 SPRINGCROFT
2 STEVENSON AVE
3 ST MARLOW AVE
4 ST MICHAEL'S RD

97
78

A
B
C
D
E
F
Walton Summit
Ind Est
Hospital Crossing
Bank Head Farm
Duckworth House
Mill
Gregson Lane Crossing
Jack Green
Jack Green Fold Farm
Haddock Park Wood
Mill Wood
Seed Lee
PR5
M65
Pippin Street Farm
Pippin Street
Brindle
Chesham Farm
PR6
Clayton Brook
Cty Prim Sch
Hawks Clough
Clayton Brook
Slack Farm
Brindle St James' CE Prim Sch
Beech Tree Sch
Westwood Prim Sch
Sports Ctr
Green Wood
Holm Lea
Thorpe Green
High Cop Farm
Highfield
Liby
Hotel
Clayton Green
Works
Holt
Bury Farm
Holt Lane Farm
Top o' th' Lane
Hough Hill
Manor Road Cty Prim Sch
Clayton-le-Woods CE Prim Sch
Denham Hill
Walmsley Fold
Carvers Farm
Denham Hall
Lower Wood End
Huggart's Farm
River Lostock
Hill Top Farm
PRESTON RD
SANDY LA
CLAYTON GREEN RD
WESTWOOD RD
CLAYTON BROOK RD
8
7
25
6
5
24
4
3
23
2
1
22
58
59

60
78

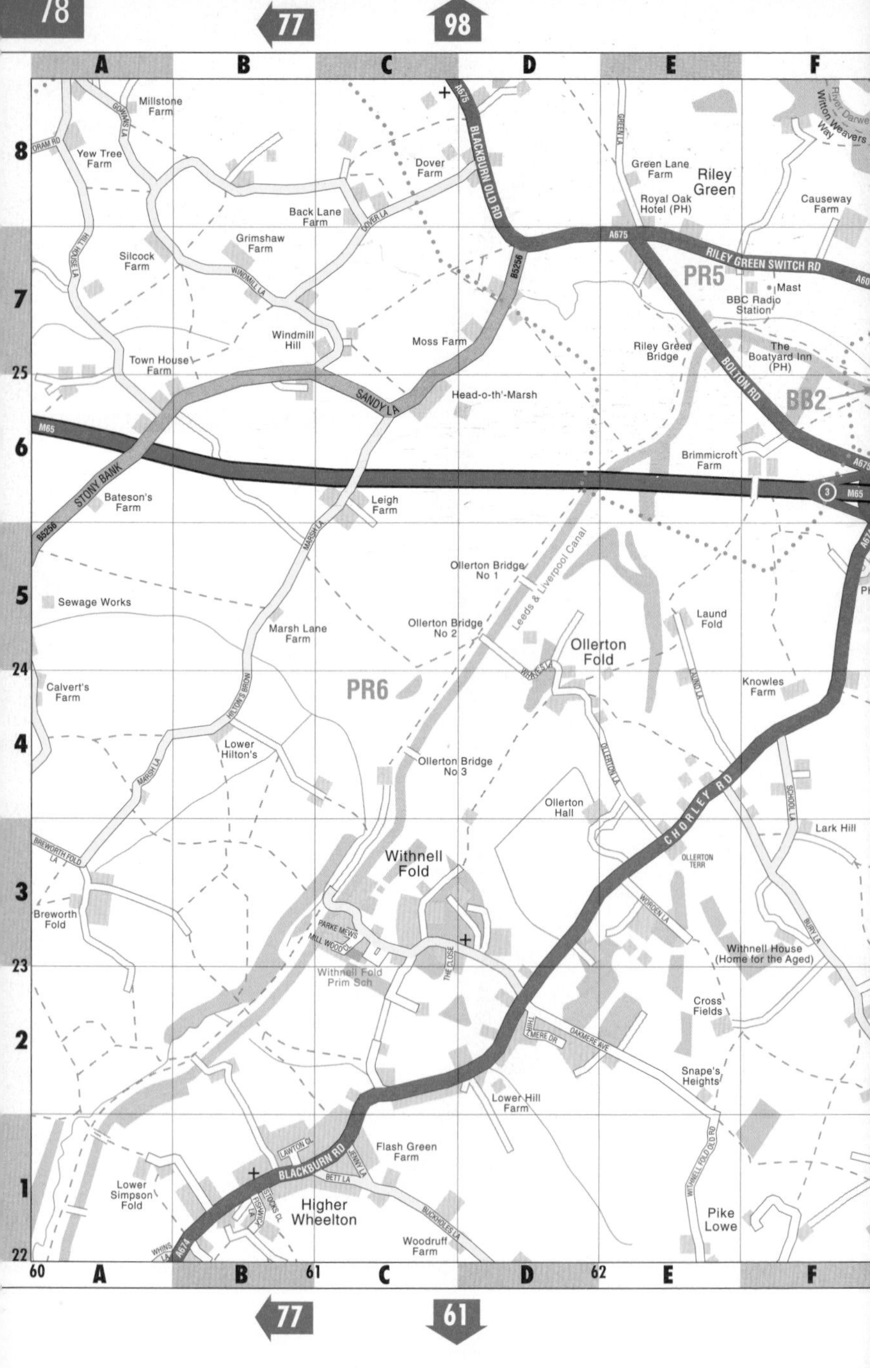
77
98
A
B
C
D
E
F
8
7
25
6
5
24
4
3
23
2
1
22
Millstone Farm
Yew Tree Farm
Dover Farm
Back Lane Farm
Grimshaw Farm
Silcock Farm
Windmill Hill
Town House Farm
Moss Farm
Head-o-th'-Marsh
Green Lane Farm
Riley Green
Royal Oak Hotel (PH)
Causeway Farm
RILEY GREEN SWITCH RD
PR5
Mast
BBC Radio Station
Riley Green Bridge
The Boatyard Inn (PH)
BOLTON RD
BB2
Brimmicroft Farm
River Darwen
Witton Weavers Way
BLACKBURN OLD RD
A675
B5256
SANDY LA
M65
STONY BANK
Bateson's Farm
Leigh Farm
MARSH LA
Ollerton Bridge No 1
Sewage Works
Ollerton Bridge No 2
Leeds & Liverpool Canal
Laund Fold
Marsh Lane Farm
Ollerton Fold
Calvert's Farm
PR6
Knowles Farm
LAUND LA
HILTON'S BROW
Lower Hilton's
Ollerton Bridge No 3
OLLERTON LA
Ollerton Hall
CHORLEY RD
Lark Hill
SCHOOL LA
BREWORTH FOLD LA
Withnell Fold
OLLERTON TERR
Breworth Fold
WORDEN LA
PARKE MEWS
MILL WOOD CL
THE CLOSE
BURY LA
Withnell House (Home for the Aged)
Withnell Fold Prim Sch
Cross Fields
OAKMERE AVE
MERE DR
Snape's Heights
Lower Hill Farm
Flash Green Farm
LAWTON CL
BLACKBURN RD
JENNY LA
BETT LA
WITHNELL FOLD OLD RD
Lower Simpson Fold
Higher Wheelton
STOCKS CL
FISHWICK LA
BUCKHOLES LA
Pike Lowe
Woodruff Farm
A674
WHINS LA
60
61
62
A
B
C
D
E
F
77
61

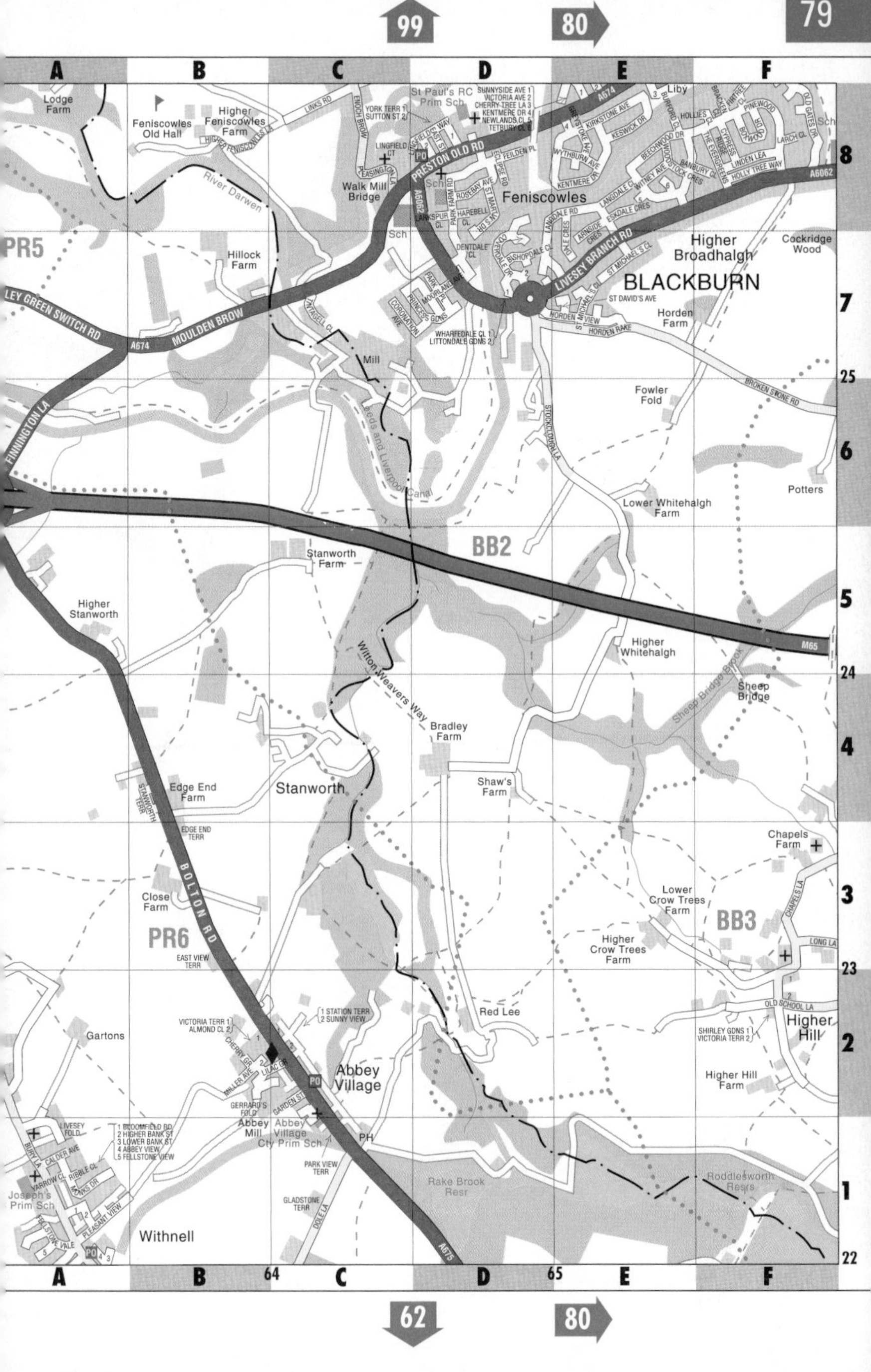
99
80
A
B
C
D
E
F
Lodge Farm
Feniscowles Old Hall
Higher Feniscowles Farm
St Paul's RC Prim Sch
Feniscowles
Walk Mill Bridge
Liby
PRESTON OLD RD
A674
A6062
River Darwen
PR5
Hillock Farm
Higher Broadhalgh
Cockridge Wood
BLACKBURN
LIVESEY BRANCH RD
MOULDEN BROW
LEY GREEN SWITCH RD
Mill
Horden Farm
Fowler Fold
BROKEN STONE RD
FINNINGTON LA
Leeds and Liverpool Canal
STOCKCLOUGH LA
Potters
Lower Whitehalgh Farm
BB2
Stanworth Farm
Higher Stanworth
M65
Higher Whitehalgh
Witton Weavers Way
Sheep Bridge Brook
Sheep Bridge
Bradley Farm
Shaw's Farm
Edge End Farm
Stanworth
Chapels Farm
BOLTON RD
Close Farm
Lower Crow Trees Farm
BB3
PR6
Higher Crow Trees Farm
Red Lee
Gartons
Higher Hill
Abbey Village
Higher Hill Farm
Abbey Mill
Abbey Village Cty Prim Sch
PH
Rake Brook Resr
Roddlesworth Resrs
Joseph's Prim Sch
Withnell
A675
64
65
8
7
25
6
5
24
4
3
23
2
1
22
62
80

79
100

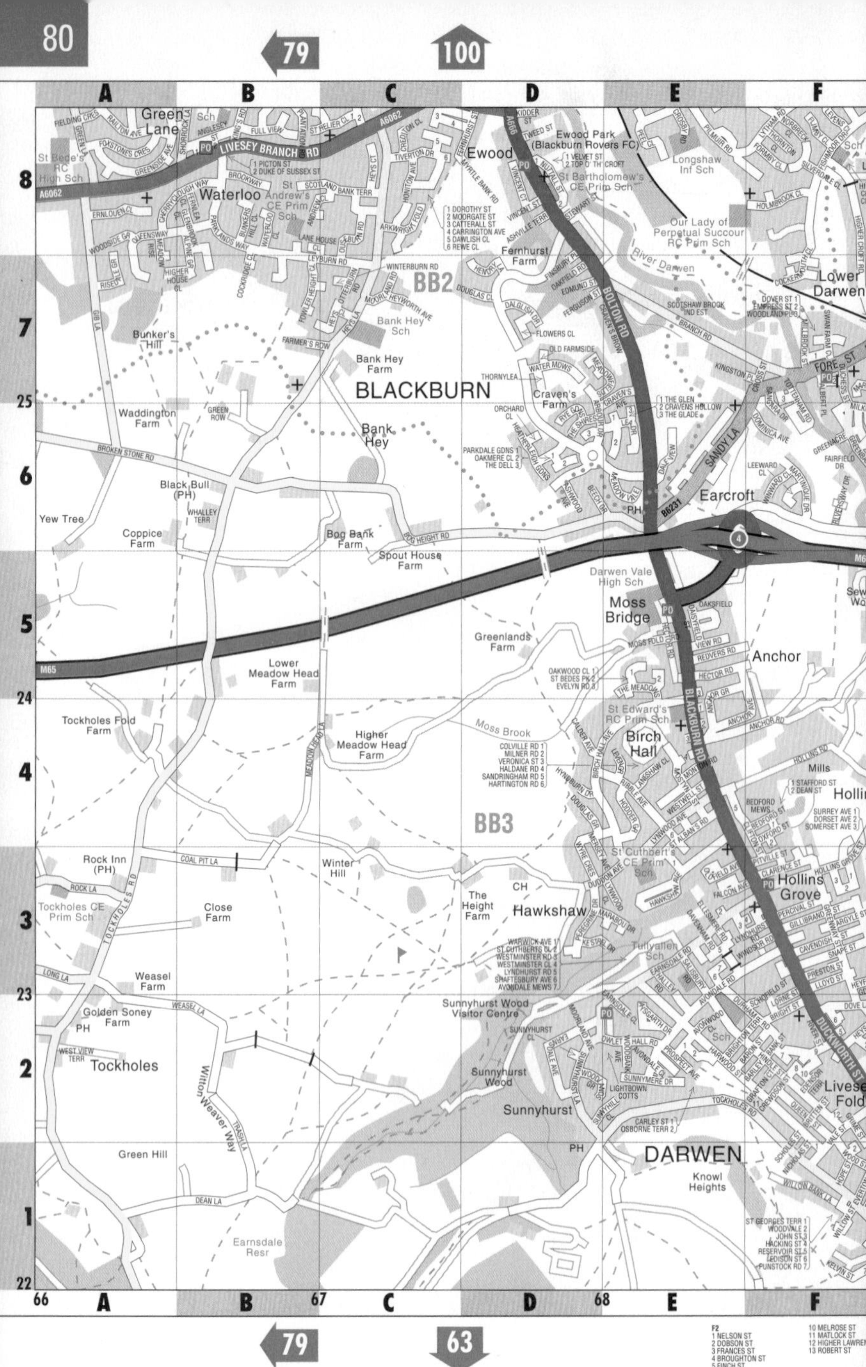

79
63

F2
1 NELSON ST
2 DOBSON ST
3 FRANCES ST
4 BROUGHTON ST
5 FINCH ST
6 DERWENT ST
7 ALEXANDRA VIEW
8 ALEXANDRA RD
9 WOOD STREET LIVESEY FOLD
10 MELROSE ST
11 MATLOCK ST
12 HIGHER LAWREN
13 ROBERT ST

101
82
A
B
C
D
E
F
8
7
25
6
5
24
4
3
23
2
1
22
70
71
1 CHILDREY WLK
2 BISHOPSTONE CL
3 LIDDINGTON CL
4 ASTON WLK
5 EASTCOTT CL
6 STREATLY WLK
7 BEECHWOOD MEWS
Fishmoor Resr
Guide Resr
Guide
COPSTER HILL CL
SCHOOL LA
B6231
A6177
M65
PO
PH
THE OLD SCH HOUSE
HASLINGDEN RD
SPINNING AVE
LOUIS WILLIAM ST
Blackamoor Broadlands & Dame Evelyn Fox Special Schs
NEW MEADOW CL
Higher House Farm
Blackamoor
BLACKAMOOR RD
ROMAN RD
Sough Pits
SOUGH LA
Blackhill Farm
B2
St James CE Prim Sch
AINTREE DR
STOPES BROW
BLACKAMOOR RD
PICKERING FOLD
WALKER RD
BELTHORN RD
GREENFIELD VIEW
ASTER CH
WISTERIA DR
DAHLIA CL
DELPHINIUM WAY
PRIMULA DR
PRUNELLA DR
WALKER PARK IND EST
Aspinall Fold
BB1
Scar Edge
ELTON RD
KINGS WAY
BARONS WAY
MEADOWCROFT
CENTURION WAY
CENTURIAN WAY
NEPTUNE WAY
Ind Est
BRIARCROFT
MOORCROFT
Lower Darwen Prim Sch
KNIGHT CRES
DAVY FIELD RD
DAVY FIELD BROW
Davy Field Bridge
Wood Bank Farm
Pulford Farm
Rann
Syke Mill
BOTTOM OF THE BROW
SUTCLIFFE TERR
PROSPECT TERR
RYDAL MOUNT
JAMES ST
HOLDEN ST
KENDAL ROW
Belthorn
Dog Inn (PH)
CHAPEL ST
Belthorn CE Prim Sch
Davy Field Brook
Woodhead Farm
New Waterside Paper Mill
Bank Fold
NURSERY NOOK
Lower Grimshaw Farm
Higher Grimshaw Farm
ECCLESHILL GDNS
GLOBAL WAY
Works
JOHNSON RD
Waterside Brook
Goose House Bridge
Manor House Farm
Handel's Arms (PH)
Show Fold
GOOSE HOUSE LA
1 QUAKERFIELDS
2 OWEN ST
3 CHAPELS BROW
4 TEMPLETON CL
5 SUMMERTON WLK
6 ALLERTON CL
7 CORNFIELD ST
8 DARWEN ENT CTR
9 HUTCHINSON CT
Darwen Moorland High Sch
BB3
LOWER WATERSIDE FARM COTTS
VICTORIA BLDGS
MILL COTTS
Waterside
WATERSIDE TERR
LEONARD TERR
Works
Chapels
KNOWLE LA
MOOR LA
DANDY ROW
Pot House
Harwood Fold
HOLDEN FOLD
WINDERMERE DR
AMBLESIDE DR
POT HOUSE LA
THIRLMERE DR
CONISTON DR
HAWTHORN AVE
Duke of York Inn (PH)
CLOVER TERR
LIGHTBOWN ST
EXCHANGE ST
NINSON RD
HAZEL AVE
SYCAMORE GR
ASH GR
LAUREL AVE
BEECH AVE
Shorey Bank
Sch
Brocklehead Farm
ST PAUL'S TERR
CLIFTON TERR
JOHNSON NEW RD
ELLISON ST
ST JAMES' CRES
OLIVE LA
WALMSLEY ST
ANYON ST
RICHMOND TERR
NEWTON ST
PERRY ST
PO
1 WORDSWORTH GDNS
2 TWO GATES WLK
3 MEADOW GATE
4 ELIZABETH HO
5 NORRIS ST
6 GARNETT ST
7 WHALLEY CRES
8 HIGHER SOUTH ST
9 HIGHER CHURCH ST
10 BRANDWOOD ST
11 HODGSON ST
Harwood's Farm
ROBIN BANK RD
Darwen
TUDOR CL
LONDON TERR
SANDON ST
TWO GATES DR
BROAD GATE
Marsh House
ELLISON FOLD LA
St Paul's Sch
HODDLESDEN FOLD 1
QUEEN'S SQ 2
SYDNEY ST 3
ALBERT ST 4
GRAHAM ST 5
PLEASANT VIEW
Hoddlesden
P
ATLAS RD
SARAH ST
TYTHEBARN ST
ROSE ST
BURNS WLK
ELSWICK ST
ELLISON FOLD TERR
MILTON CL
SUDELL CL
AVALLON WAY
Mast
HARWOOD'S LA
ALPINE CL
QUEEN ST
Ranken Arms (PH)
MARKET ST
Liby
Mkt
RAILWAY RD
ENTWISTLE ST
VERNON ST
Sch
TOWER VIEW
LISBON DR
ARSHAM GR
HODDLESDEN RD
GLENCOE AVE
LONG HEY LA
CHURCH ST
BANK ST
JOSEPH ST
NANCY ST
SUDELL RD
CAMBRIDGE ST
ELY CL
MARSH HOUSE LA
GLENSHIELS AVE
GLENEAGLES AVE
CARUS AVE
CHAPMAN RD
HARGREAVES ST
BOLTON RD
A666
SUNNYBANK ST
STAR ST
EDMUND ST
LILY ST
BEGONIA ST
CLOISTER DR
PRIORY DR
CHANCEL PL
Marsh House Mill
POLE LA
BLACKSNAPE RD
A
B
C
D
E
F
10 THE CIRCUS
11 WILLIAM ST
12 BK DUCKWORTH ST
13 STUART CL
14 MIDVILLE PL
15 SOUTH ST
16 GREEN ST E
17 CROFT ST
18 PARLIAMENT ST
19 CHURCH BANK ST
20 CHURCH TERR
21 VICTORIA ST
22 FOUNDRY ST
23 HARDMAN WAY
24 COCHRAN ST
25 LOWER CROSS ST
26 FRANKLIN ST
64
82

81
102

A
B
C
D
E
F
8
7
25
6
5
24
4
3
23
2
1
22
72
73
74
Whittaker Hall
Moss Hall
B6236
Bumper Hall
Broad Carr Farm
Broughton Barn
COBBS LA
Red Shell Farm
HASLINGDEN RD
P
Lower Eden
SOUGH LA
RED SHELL LA
Higher Bold Venture
BB5
A6177
PH
Whetstone Edge
Mast
Oswaldtwistle Moor
BELTHORN RD
TOWER VIEW
ELTON RD
Higher Warmwithens
BB1
Dry Hill
Grey Mare Inn (PH)
JACKSON HEIGHTS RD
Jackson Height
Rushy Hill
Pickup Bank Resr
Shooters Hill
Nab Hill
Rough Hill
GRANE RD
BB4
Pike Low
Shorrock Fold
Pickup Bank Height
Rossendale Way
Pickup Bank
Old Rosins Inn (PH)
LONG HEY LA
Haslingden Grane
BB3
Great Hill
BROADHEAD RD
Boardman Close
Lark Hill Farm
Edgerton Moss
BL7

81
65

103
84

A
B
C
D
E
F
Meadow Head Farm
ALMA PL
Works
MANCHESTER RD
A680
BACK LA
BLACKBURN RD
Accrington Moor
Meadow Top Farm
BRIDGE HOUSES
Mattbridge
Red Walls
BROADFIELD
RAMS CLOUGH LA
Trees Farm
Paragon Works
Farther Friar Hill Farm
Coach & Horses Hotel (PH)
Rams Clough
Sandybeds Farm
Lark Hill Farm
HASLINGDEN RD
ROUNDHILL RD
ROUNDHILL LA
BB5
High Cockham
Roundhill
Moor Lane Farm
MOOR LA
B6236
Elm Tree Farm
Thirteen Stone Hill
Rossendale Way
Coldwells
Haslingden Moor
Copy Farm
Higher Swineherd Lowe Farm
Deep Clough
Picker Hill
TODD HALL RD
Rossendale Way
Todd Hall Farm
COB CASTLE RD
UNICORN PK
CARRS IND EST
UNDERBANK RD
Windy Harbour Farm
Quarry (dis)
Clod Farm
BB4
Hutch Bank
HEAP CLOUGH
GRANE RD
Leys End
Haslingden Grane Trail
Cemy
CALF HEY RD
Duke of Wellington (PH)
Hutch Bank
HUTCH BANK RD
Cemy
Rothwell Fold
Ogden Resr
Holden Wood Resr
GREAVES ST
STONE ST
A6177
B6235
PH
QUARRY BANK
GAS ST
HOLDEN R
Calf Hey Resr
HOLCOMBE RD
WARBURTON ST 1
MUSBURY VIEW 2
WARBURTON BLDGS 3
Rossendale Way
Tenements Farm
Holden Wood
HOLDEN WOOD DR
Chy
EDINBURGH RD
8
7
25
6
5
24
4
3
23
2
1
22
76
77

66
84

83
104
A
B
C
D
E
F
Rising Bridge
Stone Fold
Needless
BB5
Goodshaw
1 EAST VIEW
2 HOYLE ST
3 WORSLEY ST
Stonefold CE Prim Sch
Hollin Gate Farm
Sherfin
SHERFIN NOOK
TANNER BARN
SHERFIN SIDE
MANCHALES
Carr Bank Farm
Pinner Clough
PINNER LA
Cribden Moor
Con Ctr
Scar Foot Farm
Carterplace Hall
SHAW ST
EDWARD ST
PILLING ST
TAYLOR ST
MAIDEN ST
TATTERSALL ST
Brow Edge
Hugh Rake Top
HUGH RAKE
POPLAR TERR
GLEBE COTTS
B6236 ROUNDHILL RD
Acre
Hud Hey
HUD HEY RD
HUD HEY IND EST
Crawshaw Hall Wood
CLOUGH END RD
Cribden Side
HOLMES TERR 1
EAST ST 2
WOODCROFT AVE 3
THORN ST 4
WOODCROFT ST 5
THE HOLMES 6
ROSEDALE ST 7
FAIRVIEW 8
OLIVE TERR 9
SUNNY LEA ST 10
Lound Farm
BURNLEY RD
BLACKBURN RD
Martin Croft
MARTIN CROFT RD
OLD CARR MILL ST
1 BROOK ST
2 BACK CARR MILL ST
3 BACK BEEHIVE TERR
Slate Farm
CRIBDEN LA
Reeds Holme
Holden Vale
Cribden Hill
Works
Sunny Field Farm
North Hag
1 BARNES ST
2 VALE ST
3 CROSS ST S
4 DELPH ST
5 RAILWAY RD
6 SMITHY BROW
7 SMITHY BROW CT
8 WILKINSON ST
BB4
Collinge Farm
Laund
Cribden End
CRIBDEN END LA
Top of Slate
HIGHER LA
HUD RAKE
LAUND ST 1
CRIBDEN ST 2
BACK CONSTABLELEE 3
MARGARET ST 4
ALEXANDRIA ST 5
HOBSON ST 6
COMMERCE ST
HASLINGDEN
CRIBDEN END LA
Mast
Cribden Flats
Mast
CARRS IND EST
Longshoot
LAUND LA
KIRK HILL RD
Rawtenstall St Mary's Prim Sch
Well Bank
ROSEWOOD AVE
CEDAR AVE
MAPLE AVE
Height End
Oakenhead Wood
TOP OF BANK
Dry Ski Slope
St James The Lesser RC Prim Sch
OAKENHEAD WOOD OLD RD
HASLINGDEN OLD RD
BARNES AVE
TA Ctr
HURSTWOOD ENT PK
St Mary's RC Prim Sch
Whitaker Park
Ind Est
1 EDALE AVE
2 COWES AVE
Pike Law
LOWER CRIBDEN AVE
Belmont Sch
ST MARY'S CT 1
HENRY ST 2
Mus
Lane Side
Rossendale General
EGYPT MOUNT
MANCHESTER RD
Spring Vale
HASLINGDEN RD
A681
Rawtenstall Sta
New Hey Br
Mill
Cribden House Sch
Countryside Ctr
LC
NEW HALL HEY BSNS PK
New Hall Hey
1 TOR VIEW
2 RAWTENSTALL RD
All Saints RC High Sch
Irwell Valley Way
River Irwell
East Lancashire Rly
Syke Side
HELMSHORE RD
Sports Ctr
Wood Top
KNOWSLEY ROAD IND EST
Helmcroft
A56
A680
A682
CHERRY CRES
78
79
80
8
7
25
6
5
24
4
3
23
2
1
22
A1
1 JUBILEE CT
2 SANDRINGHAM GR
3 HOLDEN WOOD DR
4 CLARENCE AVE
5 HELMCROFT
A3
1 UNICON PK
2 UNDERBANK WAY
3 LINCOLN ST
4 QUEEN ANNE ST
5 THOMAS ST
6 MARSDEN ST
7 SUNNYBANK ST
B1
1 HELMCROFT CT
2 BEAUMARIS CL
3 CRICCIETH CL
B2
1 GREENFIELD GDNS
2 HAZELDENE AVE
3 BANK MILL ST
4 NORTHCOTE ST
5 LANESIDE HO
6 SIZE HOUSE VILLAGE
7 ST PETER'S PL
8 WHITECROFT AVE
B3
1 BACK REGENT ST
2 HARTLEY ST
3 ST JAMES CL
4 DAVITT CL
83
B3
5 RATCLIFFE FOLD
6 BURGESS ST
7 CENTRAL SQ
8 OLD SCHOOL MEWS
9 SMITHY ST
10 RATCLIFFE ST
11 DEARDENGATE CROFT
12 COAL HEY
13 COAL HEY ST
67
B3
14 NEW ST
15 SALISBURY ST
16 BEACONSFIELD ST
17 STORE ST
18 ROCK ST
19 LACY CT
20 SOUTH VIEW
E2
1 OSBORNE TERR
2 AMBLESIDE AVE
3 EGYPT TERR
4 OLD ROW
5 SPRING TERR S
6 GARNALL'S BLDGS
7 ALMSHOUSES
8 FIELDING'S BLDGS
F1
1 SYCAMORE CRES
2 HILL VIEW
3 HARDMAN AVE
4 SHAWFIELD
5 BARLOWS BLDGS
6 DALE VIEW
7 CARR MOUNT

105
86
Crawshawbooth
Crawshawbooth Cty Prim Sch
Bottomley Bank Farm
Crown Farm
Swinshaw Moor
Peersclough Farm
Forest Holme
Bank Top
Height Side Farm
Rake Foot
Rush Bed
Reeds Farm
Higher Bank Top
Hargreaves Arms (PH)
Higher Walls
Lumb
Bonfire Hill
Mast
Salisbury Farm
Wheat Head
Higher Constablelee
Whitewell Bottom
The Height
Top o' th' Height
Works
BB4
Brock Clough Farm
Constable Lee
Chapel Hill Farm
Meadowhead
Alder Grange High Sch
Cemy
Myrtle Earth Farm
Spring Side
Marl Pits Sports Complex
Far Height Side
Scout
Higher Cloughfold
Seat Naze
Piercy
Lower Cloughfold
St Peter's RC Prim Sch
Edgeside
BOCHOLT WAY
BACUP RD
River Irwell
Mill
Cloughfold
Newchurch
Hareholme
Irwell Sculpture Trail
RAWTENSTALL
Swiss Clough
Hall Carr
Newchurch CE Prim Sch
Booth Fold
Staghills
BURNLEY RD E
ST MARY'S WAY
A682
A681
B6238
82
83
68
86

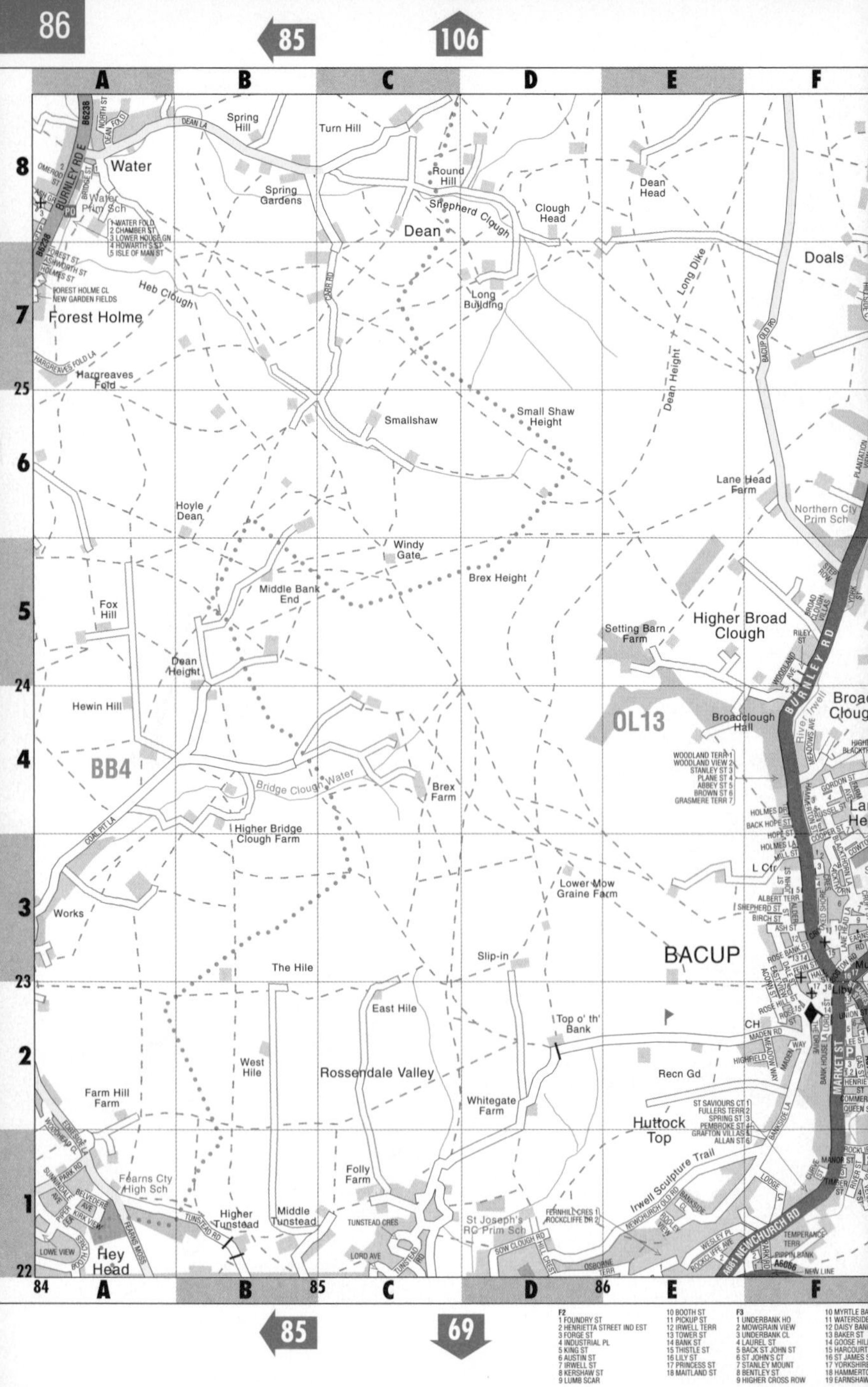

F2
1 FOUNDRY ST
2 HENRIETTA STREET IND EST
3 FORGE ST
4 INDUSTRIAL PL
5 KING ST
6 AUSTIN ST
7 IRWELL ST
8 KERSHAW ST
9 LUMB SCAR
10 BOOTH ST
11 PICKUP ST
12 IRWELL TERR
13 TOWER ST
14 BANK ST
15 THISTLE ST
16 LILY ST
17 PRINCESS ST
18 MAITLAND ST

F3
1 UNDERBANK HO
2 MOWGRAIN VIEW
3 UNDERBANK CL
4 LAUREL ST
5 BACK ST JOHN ST
6 ST JOHN'S CT
7 STANLEY MOUNT
8 BENTLEY ST
9 HIGHER CROSS ROW
10 MYRTLE BA
11 WATERSIDE
12 DAISY BANK
13 BAKER ST
14 GOOSE HILL
15 HARCOURT
16 ST JAMES S
17 YORKSHIRE
18 HAMMERTO
19 EARNSHAW

107

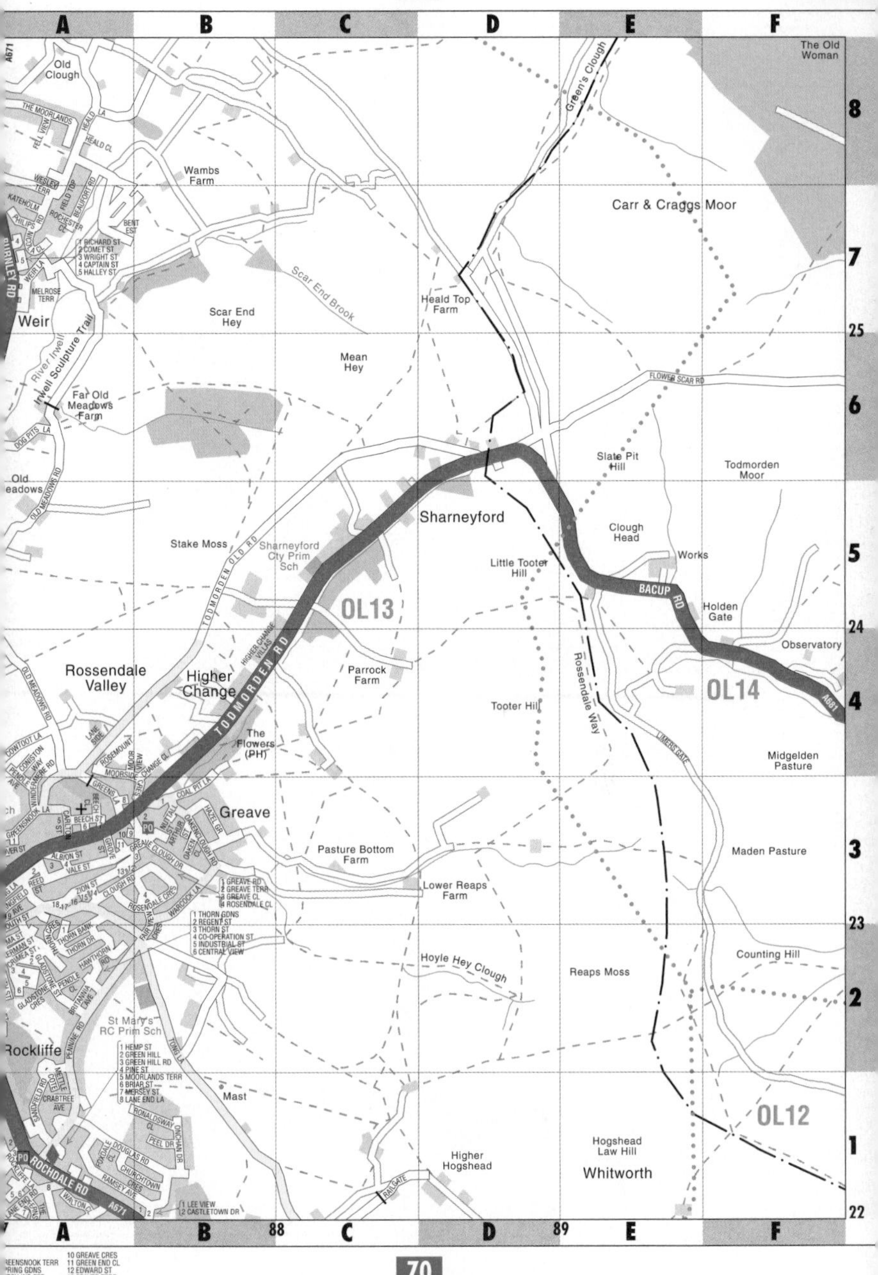

REENSNOOK TERR
PRING GDNS
EECH IND EST
ROSS ST
REENSNOOK MEWS
HRIST CHURCH ST
LM ST
HE COURTYARD
REAVE CLOUGH CL

10 GREAVE CRES
11 GREEN END CL
12 EDWARD ST
13 BEAVER TERR
14 HANNAH ST
15 ASHWORTH ST
16 COWGILL ST
17 WARKWORTH TERR
18 VENTURE ST
19 TONG HO

70

109

A
B
C
D
E
F
8
7
29
6
5
28
4
3
27
2
1
26
30
31
32
St Annes
St Annes's Pier
Lancashire Coastal Way
Pleasure Island
Mayfield Prim Sch
FY8
CLIFTON DR N
CLIFTON DR S
ST ANNE'S RD E
Mus
Mkt
TH
Liby
Coll
Sch
St Anne's
THE BURLINGTON CTR
ASHTON GARDEN CT
1 EATON CT
2 KENILWORTH
3 RUSSELL CT
QUAY WEST 1
VERNON LODGE 2

89
110
90
A8
1 BANNISTRE CL
2 BEVERLEY CT
3 TALBOT CT
4 SILVERBURN
5 FELLBOROUGH LODGE
6 GROSVENOR CT
D6
1 TUXFORD CT
2 KNIGHTSBRIDGE CL
3 BELGRAVE CL
4 TWICKENHAM PL
A
B
C
D
E
F
8
7
29
6
5
28
4
3
27
2
1
26
34
35
B5261
B5233
ST ANNE'S RD E
HEYHOUSES LA
NORTH HOUSES LA
MOSS HALL LA
Govt Bldgs
Hey Houses
Moss Hall Farm
Cemy
Crem
GRAND MANOR DR
CARDINAL GDNS
REGENT AVE
Big Wood
Ansdell
Blackpool & The Fylde Coll Ansdell Campus
Lytham St Anne's High Sch
Royal Lytham St Anne's
LYTHAM ST ANNE'S
BLACKPOOL RD
FY8
Hall Wood
1 FIRSWOOD CL
2 CEDARWOOD CL
3 GREENWOOD CL
4 CHERRYWOOD AVE
5 BIRCHWOOD CL
6 SILVERWOOD CL
7 FERNWOOD CL
8 KINGSWOOD CL
9 NORTHWOOD CL
Lytham Hall
CH
FAIRWAYS 1
SUNNINGDALE CT 2
WENTWORTH MEWS 3
1 PREESALL CL
2 PICKERING CL
WADDINGTON CT
LEVER CT
SINCLAIR CT
Clifton
CLIFTON DR S
Queen Mary Sch
1 BOULEVARD GDNS
2 RAESIDE CT
King Edward VII & Queen Mary Jun Sch
King Edward VII Sch
Ansdell & Fairhaven
Liby
L Ctr
1 ELMSWOOD CL
2 LARCHWOOD CL
3 MAPLEWOOD CL
4 HALL PARK CTR
Hall Park Prim Sch
INNER PROM
CLIFTON DR
Fairhaven
Ribble Discovery Ctr
Fairhaven Lake
GRANNY'S BAY 1
HIGH LEGH 2
LAKE POINT
WATERS REACH
THE COVE
SEVILLE CT
Stanner Bank
Granny's Bay
Lancashire Coastal Way Promenade
THE WILLOWS
ST JOHNS WOOD
1 COURT ROYAL
2 RIVERSLEIGH CT
CHURCH RD
WEST BEACH
A584
THE LEYLANDS
River Ribble
C4
1 WORDSWORTH CT
2 KINGSWAY CT
3 CRYSTAL LODGE
4 ST PAUL'S WLK
D4
1 BELVEDERE CT
2 PRINCES RD
3 WINDSOR LODGE
4 OXFORD CT
5 WOODLANDS CT

89
111
A
B
C
D
E
F
8
7
29
6
5
28
4
3
27
2
1
26
36
37
38
B5259
Brick Hill
Farm
Smeath Hill
Farm
Bulwer's
Wood
Wrea Brook
Moss Side
Villa
PEG'S LA
CARTMELL LA
Bridge Hall
Farm
Manor House
Farm
Little Birks
Farm
PR4
Eastham Hall
Farm
SALTCOTES RD
BALLAM RD
Birks
Farm
Long
Wood
Eastham
Hall
EASTHAM
COTTS
HUCK LA
Birks
Wood
Eastham
Bridge
Carr
Farm
Liggard Brook
Lytham Hall
Park
LABURNUM AVE
LAUREL AVE
LILAC AVE
CH
FY8
Cemy
Saltcotes
LODGE LA
Warton Ha
Farm
Warton Lod
Farm
GREEN DR
NORFOLK RD
St Peter's
RC Prim Sch
1 MENDIP CL
2 CHILTERN CL
BOUNDARY RD
MORNINGTON RD
LYTHAM RD
A5
Watch
Wood
Lytham
CE Prim
Sch
St Bede's RC
High Sch
PRESTON RD
MYTHOP RD
MEADOW
LA
Lytham
Dock
GRAVING DOCK RD
MARINE
IND CTR
DOCK RD
PARK VIEW CT 1
BROOKFIELD TERR 2
PARK VIEW RD
WATERFRONT MARINE
& IND EST
Lytham
Lytham
Liby
STATION RD
EAST BEACH
CENTRAL BEACH
WEST BEACH
A584
Lancashire Coastal Way
Lytham
Lifeboat
Museum
Lytham
Windmill
(Mus)
LB
Sta
Jetty
River Ribble
A3
1 ST CUTHBERT'S CL
2 HORSFALL AVE
3 THE SERPENTINE
4 CECIL CT
5 LOWTHER CT
6 ST CUTHBERT'S CT
7 LOWOOD LODGE
8 ASHTON ST
9 THE HOMESTEAD
10 RIBBLE LODGE
11 LIVESEY ST
B3
1 TALBOT TERR
2 PLEASANT ST
3 CLIFTON PAR
4 CLIFTON SQ
5 DICCONSON TERR
6 CLIFTON WLK
7 SHEPHERD ST
8 SQUIRES CT
9 GEORGE ST
10 BADGERS WLK W
89
C3
1 MILLBROOK MEWS
2 FRECKLETON CT
3 CLIFTON CT
4 ELIM CT
5 BIRCH ST
6 ST JOHN'S CT
7 GLENGARRY
C4
1 MYTHOP CL
2 GILDERDALE CT
3 KIELDER CT
D4
1 LIONS CT
2 BRIDGE CT
3 BRIDGE HO
4 BROWNING AVE
5 WORDSWORTH AVE
6 BEDFORD RD
7 HARBOUR HO
8 HAMILTON CL

112
92

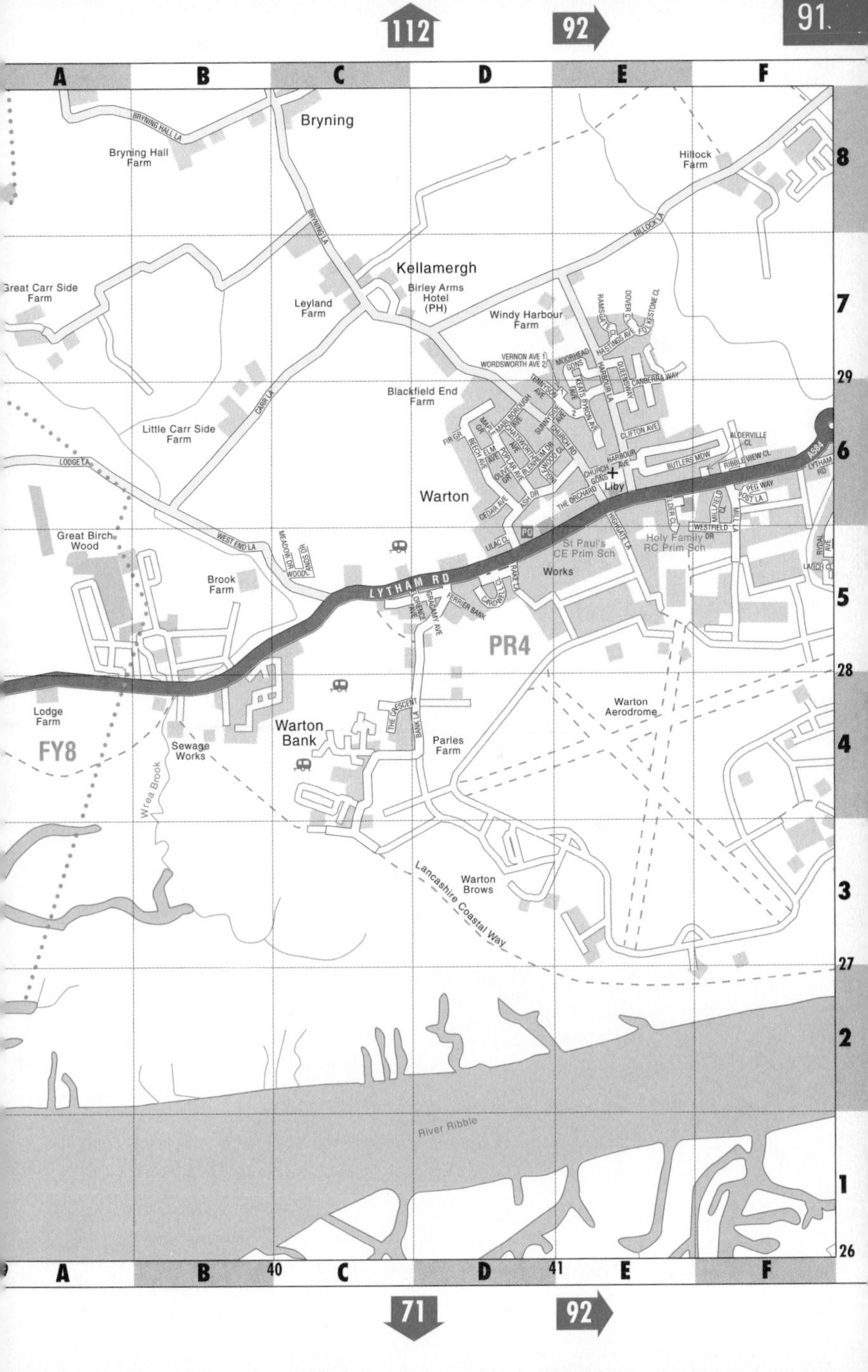
Bryning
Bryning Hall Farm
BRYNING HALL LA
Hillock Farm
BRYNING LA
HILLOCK LA
Kellamergh
Great Carr Side Farm
Leyland Farm
Birley Arms Hotel (PH)
Windy Harbour Farm
Blackfield End Farm
CARR LA
Little Carr Side Farm
LODGE LA
Warton
Liby
WEST END LA
Great Birch Wood
Brook Farm
LYTHAM RD
St Paul's CE Prim Sch
Holy Family RC Prim Sch
Works
PR4
A584
Lodge Farm
FY8
Sewage Works
Warton Bank
Parles Farm
Warton Aerodrome
Wrea Brook
Warton Brows
Lancashire Coastal Way
River Ribble
A
B
C
D
E
F
8
7
29
6
5
28
4
3
27
2
1
26
40
41

71
92

91
113

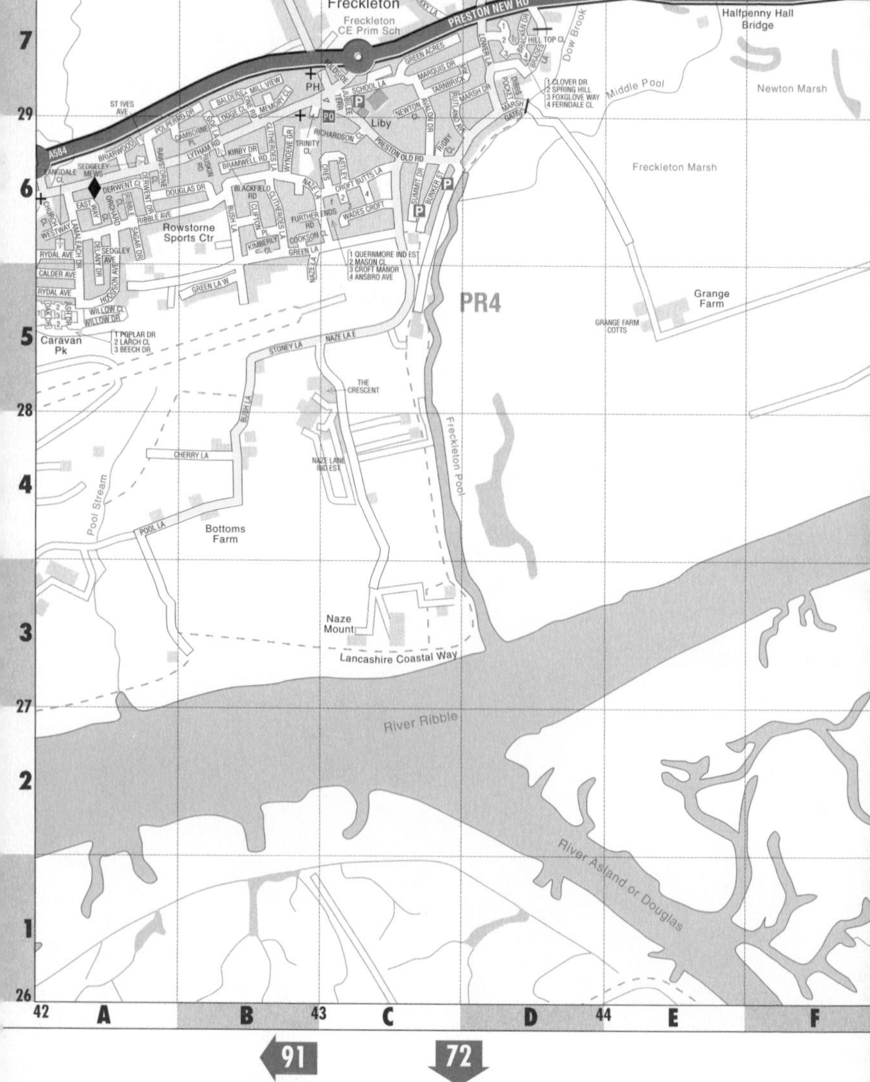
A
B
C
D
E
F
8
7
29
6
5
28
4
3
27
2
1
26
42
43
44
Nurseries
Strike Farm
Strike Lane Cty Prim Sch
Marbank Farm
Lower House Farm
Nursery
Toll House Bridge
Raker House Farm
Freckleton
Freckleton CE Prim Sch
PRESTON NEW RD
Halfpenny Hall Bridge
Dow Brook
Middle Pool
Newton Marsh
PH
Liby
PO
1 CLOVER DR
2 SPRING HILL
3 FOXGLOVE WAY
4 FERNDALE CL
Freckleton Marsh
Rowstorne Sports Ctr
1 QUERNMORE IND EST
2 MASON CL
3 CROFT MANOR
4 ANSBRO AVE
PR4
Grange Farm
GRANGE FARM COTTS
Caravan Pk
1 POPLAR DR
2 LARCH CL
3 BEECH DR
THE CRESCENT
NAZE LANE IND EST
Freckleton Pool
Pool Stream
Bottoms Farm
Naze Mount
Lancashire Coastal Way
River Ribble
River Asland or Douglas

91
72

114
94
A
B
C
D
E
F
Eastwood Plantation
A583
LODGE LA
Deepdale Brook
Savick Bridge
PH
BLACKPOOL RD
A583
A584
Three Nooks
Savick Brook Farm
Savick Brook
PRESTON NEW RD
Clifton Marsh Farm
Clifton Marsh
Sewage Works
River Ribble
PR4
Ribble Way
Farrers Farm
Woodfold Farm
GRANGE LA
Bottom of Hutton
Hutton Marsh
Westlands Farm
Middle Grange
Old Grange
GRANGE LA
Farrer's Wood
Longton Brook
Longton Marsh
Pilot's Cottage
GRANGE LA
SEVEN SANDS
ARKHOLME DR
HAMBLETON CL
TARNDALE
WELLFIELD
GRANGEFIELD
BACK LA
8
7
29
6
5
28
4
3
27
2
1
26
46
47
73
94

93
115

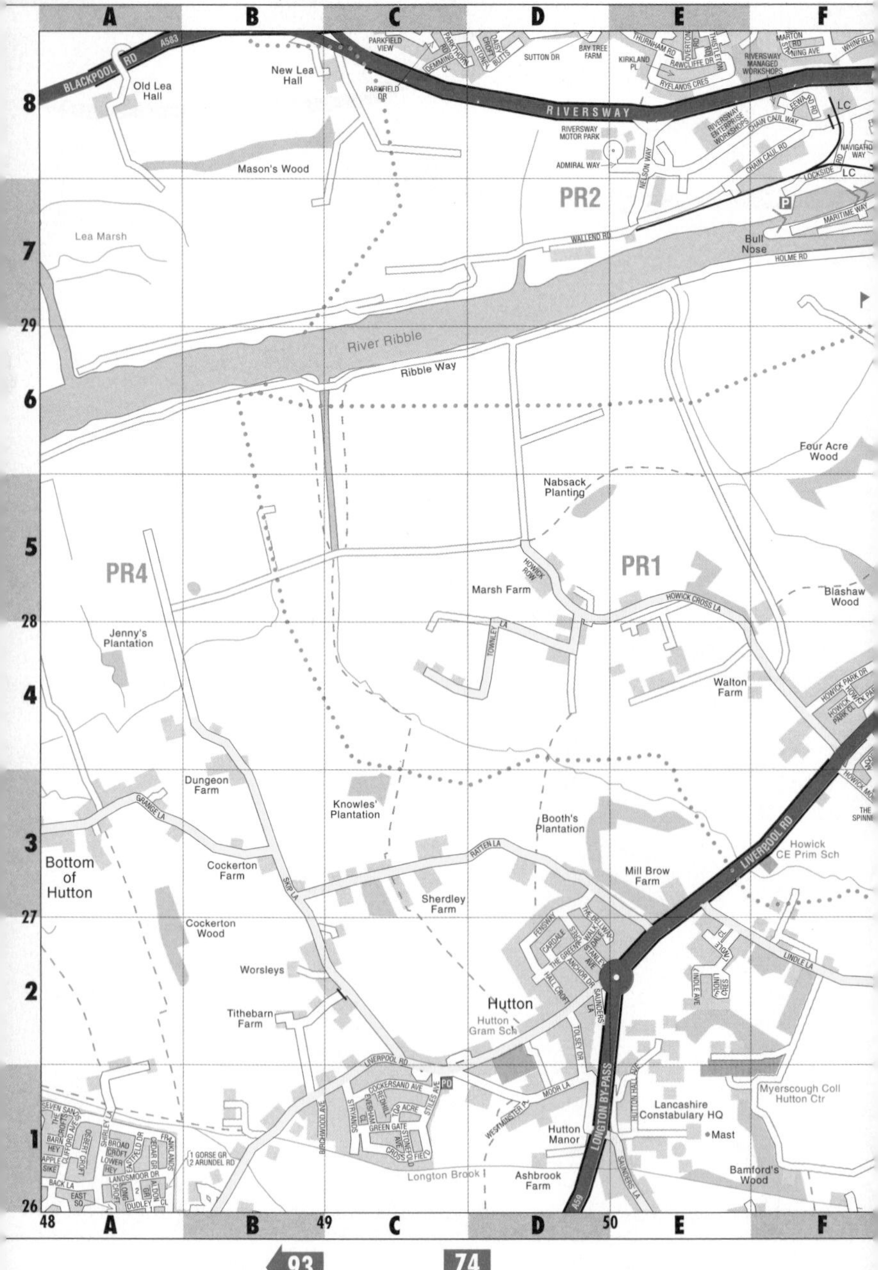
A
B
C
D
E
F
8
7
29
6
5
28
4
3
27
2
1
26
48
49
50
BLACKPOOL RD
A583
Old Lea Hall
New Lea Hall
PARKFIELD VIEW
PARKFIELD DR
DEMMING CL
PARKTHORN RD
DAISY CROFT
STONE
BUTTS
SUTTON DR
BAY TREE FARM
THURNHAM RD
KIRKLAND PL
RAWCLIFFE DR
RYELANDS CRES
RIVERSWAY MANAGED WORKSHOPS
MARTON RD
NING AVE
WHINFIELD
RIVERSWAY
RIVERSWAY MOTOR PARK
ADMIRAL WAY
NELSON WAY
RIVERSWAY ENTERPRISE WORKSHOPS
CHAIN CAUL WAY
CHAIN CAUL RD
LEEWARD RD
LC
NAVIGATION WAY
LOCKSIDE
P
MARITIME WAY
Mason's Wood
PR2
Lea Marsh
WALLEND RD
Bull Nose
HOLME RD
River Ribble
Ribble Way
Four Acre Wood
Nabsack Planting
PR4
PR1
HOWICK ROW
Marsh Farm
HOWICK CROSS LA
Blashaw Wood
TOWNLEY LA
Jenny's Plantation
Walton Farm
HOWICK PARK DR
HOWICK PARK CL
Dungeon Farm
GRANGE LA
Knowles' Plantation
Booth's Plantation
THE SPINNEY
Howick CE Prim Sch
Bottom of Hutton
Cockerton Farm
RATTEN LA
SKIP LA
Mill Brow Farm
LIVERPOOL RD
Sherdley Farm
Cockerton Wood
FENSWAY
CARDALE
THE GREENWAY
THE DELLWAY
STANLEY AVE
ANCHOR DR
HALL CROFT
LINDLE CL
LINDLE LA
LINDLE AVE
LINDLE CRES
Worsleys
Hutton
Hutton Gram Sch
SAUNDERS LA
TOLSEY DR
Tithebarn Farm
LIVERPOOL RD
COCKERSAND AVE
REDHILL
EVESHAM CL
STRYANDS
TOP ACRE
STILES AVE
PO
GREEN GATE
STONEFOLD AVE
CROSS FIELD
MOOR LA
WESTMINSTER PL
HUTTON HALL AVE
Myerscough Coll Hutton Ctr
Lancashire Constabulary HQ
Mast
Hutton Manor
LONGTON BY-PASS
SEVEN SANDS
THE CROFTS
BARN HEY
CLIFFORD AVE
OSBERT CROFT
SHIRLEY LA
BROAD CROFT
LOWER HEY
FAIRFIELD DR
CEDAR GR
FRANKLANDS
APPLE SIKE
LANDSMOOR DR
BACK LA
EAST SQ
LONG CROFT
ALTON GR
DUDLEY CL
1 GORSE GR
2 ARUNDEL RD
BIRCHWOOD AVE
Longton Brook
Ashbrook Farm
A59
Bamford's Wood

93
74

EST VIEW TERR
ADDY ST
A ST
MARK'S PL W
MARK'S PL E
E CLOISTERS
7 ASHTON ST
8 ST WALBURGES GDNS
9 WESTON ST
10 CROFT ST
11 STEWART ST
12 ATHOLL ST
13 COOKWOOD HO
E8
1 GILDOW ST
2 GRADWELL ST
3 BHAILOK ST
4 COLD BATH ST
5 RADNOR ST
6 POLLARD ST
7 STOCKS ST
8 ST PETER'S SQ
F8
1 ST PETER'S CL
2 ST PETER'S ST
3 ADELPHI PL
4 RODNEY ST
5 HOPE ST
6 MARSH LA
7 CHANDLER ST
8 MOUNT PLEASANT
9 BACK SEED ST
10 SIMPSON ST
11 UNION ST
116
F8
12 CLAYTON'S GATE
13 FORESTERS HALL
14 NORTHUMBERLAND HO
15 WESTMORLAND HO
16 CUMBERLAND HO
17 CRAGG'S ROW
96
F8
18 SINGLETON ROW
19 BECKETT CT
20 MELLING ST
21 GARDNER ST
22 MELBOURNE ST
23 TRINITY FOLD
24 BISPHAM ST
25 SIZEHOUSE ST
26 TENTERFIELD ST
27 TRINITY PL
28 LOWTHIAN ST
29 ORCHARD ST
30 BIRLEY ST
A B C D E F
8 7 29 6 5 28 4 3 27 2 1 26
PR2
PRESTON
Riversway Docklands
WATERY LA
RIVERSWAY
WEST STRAND
STRAND RD
GUILD WAY
MARSH LA
RING WAY
CORPORATION ST
FRIARGATE
Univ of Central Lancashire
Works
Ribble Way
Penwortham New Bridge
LIVERPOOL RD
The Holme
River Ribble
St Stephen's CE Prim Sch
PR1
Broadgate
Preston
Fishergate Ctr
Ribble Viaduct
Penwortham Bridge
Lower Penwortham
Penwortham Prim Sch
St Teresa's RC Prim Sch
Penwortham Girls High Sch
Higher Penwortham
Howick Cross
Cemy
Hurst Grange Park
St Mary Magdalen RC Prim Sch
Whitefield Prim Sch
Middleforth CE Prim Sch
Middleforth Green
LEYLAND RD
Upper Farm
All Hallows RC High Sch
GOLDEN WAY
Skew Bridge
Millbrook Wood
Mill Brook
Gables Farm
Penwortham Lane
Nutter's Platt
Kingsfold
PR4
Prior Farm
Crook's Farm
Balshaw Farm
Holme Farm
PR5
BEE LA
FLAG LA
A582
B5254
A B 52 C D 53 E F
3
CROMWELL AVE
WINGATES
BERRY FIELD
2
ROSEMARY CT
SORREL CT
CINNAMON CT
BANNISTER'S BIT
WOODVILLE RD W
D2
1 LOWER CROFT
2 HIGHER CROFT
3 FORSHAW RD
4 CROFTERS WLK
5 OLD HEY CROFT
6 FAIRHAM AVE
7 OLDFIELD
D6
1 BEECH ST
2 RIBBLE CT
3 TAY ST
4 TYNE ST
5 CLIFTON ST
D7
1 PALEY RD
2 HUNT ST
3 CARNARVON RD
E2
1 PETERFIELD RD
2 TUSON HOUSE
3 DICKENSONS FIELD
4 THE PADDOCK
5 STURMINSTER CL
6 HAMBLEDON DR
7 WINSLOW CL
8 STUDHOLME CL
E4
1 SWALLOW AVE
2 DOVE AVE
3 LARK AVE
4 MIDDLEFORTH IND EST
5 MARSHALL'S CL
6 FINCH'S COTTS
7 PROSPECT PL
8 CHURCH BROOK HO
75
E6
1 BEECH TERR
2 WARTON ST
3 RIBBLE CL
4 HIND ST
5 SOUTH CLIFF ST
6 NORTH CLIFF ST
E7
1 KAY ST
2 NUTTER RD
96
E7
3 MARKLAND ST
4 SAVOY ST
5 RED CROSS ST
6 KINGSWOOD ST
7 BURLEIGH RD
8 LADYMAN ST
9 SPRING BANK
10 OSBOURNE ST
11 FISHERGATE CT
F2
1 GILLER FOLD
2 NORTHLEACH AVE
3 SUMPTER CT
4 CHELFORD CL
5 BURWOOD CL
F7
1 CHARNLEY ST
2 ST WILFRED ST
3 FLEET ST
4 CHAPEL WLKS
5 ST GEORGE'S SH CTR
6 FRIARGATE WLK
7 FISHERGATE WLK
8 CHEAPSIDE
9 WINCKLEY ST
10 TEMPLE CT
11 WINCKLEY CT
12 CHADDOCK ST
13 BAIRSTOW ST

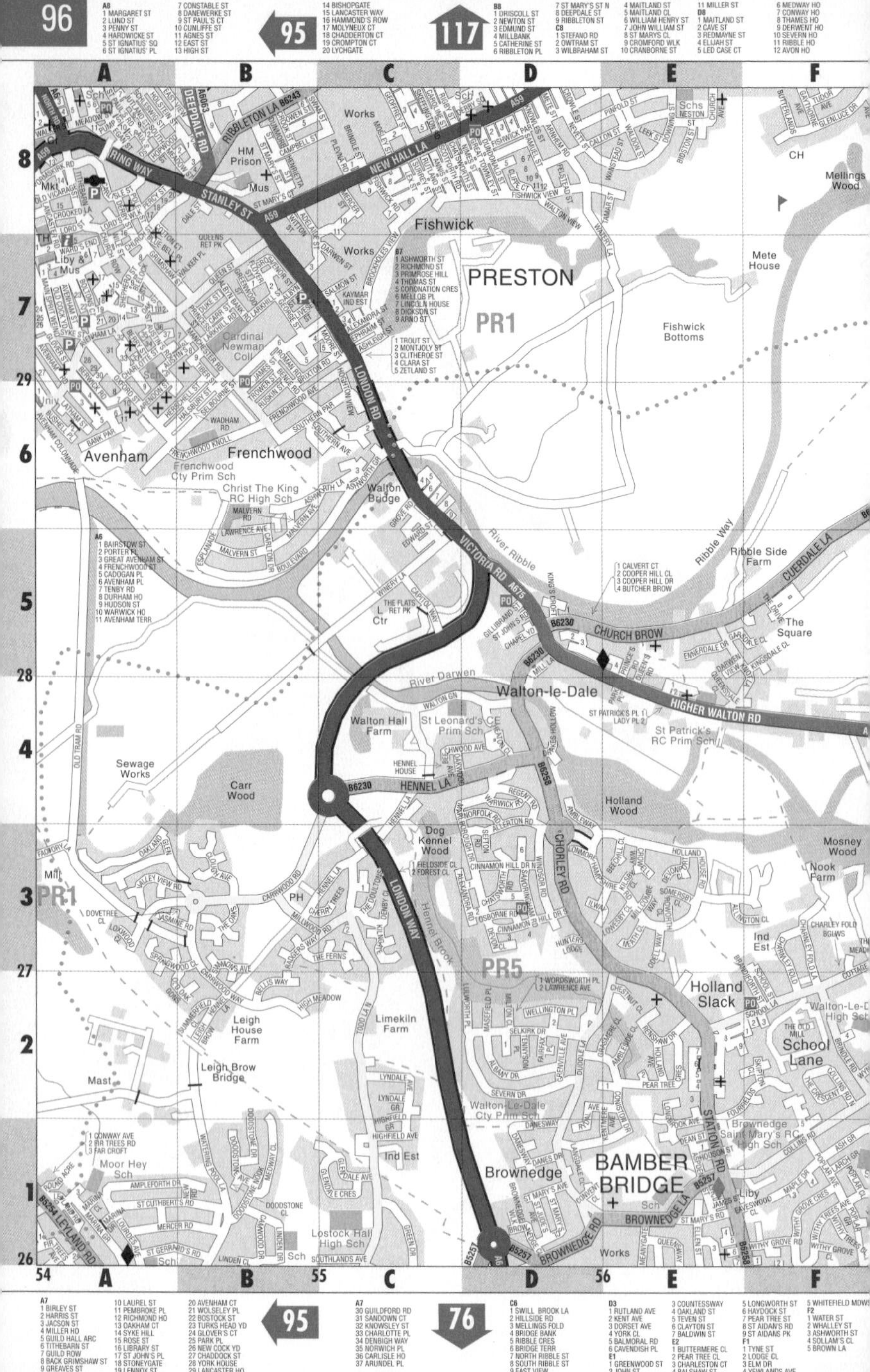
A8
1 MARGARET ST
2 LUND ST
3 PENNY ST
4 HARDWICKE ST
5 ST IGNATIUS' SQ
6 ST IGNATIUS' PL
7 CONSTABLE ST
8 DANEWERKE ST
9 ST PAUL'S CT
10 CUNLIFFE ST
11 AGNES ST
12 EAST ST
13 HIGH ST
95
14 BISHOPGATE
15 LANCASTER WAY
16 HAMMOND'S ROW
17 MOLYNEUX CT
18 CHADDERTON CT
19 CROMPTON CT
20 LYCHGATE
117
B8
1 DRISCOLL ST
2 NEWTON ST
3 EDMUND ST
4 MILLBANK
5 CATHERINE ST
6 RIBBLETON PL
7 ST MARY'S ST N
8 DEEPDALE ST
9 RIBBLETON ST
C8
1 STEFANO RD
2 OWTRAM ST
3 WILBRAHAM ST
4 MAITLAND ST
5 MAITLAND CL
6 WILLIAM HENRY ST
7 JOHN WILLIAM ST
8 ST MARYS CL
9 CROMFORD WLK
10 CRANBORNE ST
11 MILLER ST
D8
1 MAITLAND ST
2 CAVE ST
3 REDMAYNE ST
4 ELIJAH ST
5 LED CASE CT
6 MEDWAY HO
7 CONWAY HO
8 THAMES HO
9 DERWENT HO
10 SEVERN HO
11 RIBBLE HO
12 AVON HO
A B C D E F
8 7 29 6 5 28 4 3 27 2 1 26
54 55 56
PRESTON
PR1
PR5
Fishwick
Avenham
Frenchwood
Walton-le-Dale
BAMBER BRIDGE
Brownedge
Holland Slack
School Lane
HM Prison
Cardinal Newman Coll
Christ The King RC High Sch
Frenchwood Cty Prim Sch
Walton Bridge
Fishwick Bottoms
Mete House
Mellings Wood
Ribble Side Farm
The Square
River Ribble
River Darwen
Walton Hall Farm
St Leonard's CE Prim Sch
St Patrick's RC Prim Sch
Sewage Works
Carr Wood
Holland Wood
Dog Kennel Wood
Mosney Wood
Nook Farm
Hennel Brook
Limekiln Farm
Leigh House Farm
Leigh Brow Bridge
Mast
Moor Hey Sch
Lostock Hall High Sch
Walton-Le-Dale Cty Prim Sch
Brownedge Saint Mary's RC High Sch
RING WAY
STANLEY ST
NEW HALL LA
LONDON RD
VICTORIA RD
CHURCH BROW
HIGHER WALTON RD
CUERDALE LA
HENNEL LA
LONDON WAY
CHORLEY RD
STATION RD
BROWNEDGE RD
BROWNEDGE LA
LEYLAND RD
DEEPDALE RD
RIBBLETON LA
A6
1 BAIRSTOW ST
2 PORTER PL
3 GREAT AVENHAM ST
4 FRENCHWOOD ST
5 CADOGAN PL
6 AVENHAM PL
7 TENBY RD
8 DURHAM HO
9 HUDSON ST
10 WARWICK HO
11 AVENHAM TERR
B7
1 ASHWORTH ST
2 RICHMOND ST
3 PRIMROSE HILL
4 THOMAS ST
5 CORONATION CRES
6 MELLOR PL
7 LINCOLN HOUSE
8 DICKSON ST
9 ARNO ST
1 TROUT ST
2 MONTJOLY ST
3 CLITHEROE ST
4 CLARA ST
5 ZETLAND ST
1 CALVERT CT
2 COOPER HILL CL
3 COOPER HILL DR
4 BUTCHER BROW
1 FIELDSIDE CL
2 FOREST CL
1 WORDSWORTH PL
2 LAWRENCE AVE
1 CONWAY AVE
2 RR TREES RD
3 FAR CROFT
A7
1 BIRLEY ST
2 HARRIS ST
3 JACSON ST
4 MILLER HO
5 GUILD HALL ARC
6 TITHEBARN ST
7 GUILD ROW
8 BACK GRIMSHAW ST
9 GREAVES ST
10 LAUREL ST
11 PEMBROKE PL
12 RICHMOND HO
13 OAKHAM CT
14 SYKE HILL
15 ROSE ST
16 LIBRARY ST
17 ST JOHN'S PL
18 STONEYGATE
19 LENNOX ST
20 AVENHAM CT
21 WOLSELEY PL
22 BOSTOCK ST
23 TURKS HEAD YD
24 GLOVER'S CT
25 PARK PL
26 NEW COCK YD
27 CHADDOCK ST
28 YORK HOUSE
29 LANCASTER HO
95
A7
30 GUILDFORD RD
31 SANDOWN CT
32 KNOWSLEY ST
33 CHARLOTTE PL
34 DENBIGH WAY
35 NORWICH PL
36 CARLISLE HO
37 ARUNDEL PL
76
C6
1 SWILL BROOK LA
2 HILLSIDE RD
3 MELLINGS FOLD
4 BRIDGE BANK
5 RIBBLE CRES
6 BRIDGE TERR
7 NORTH RIBBLE ST
8 SOUTH RIBBLE ST
9 EAST VIEW
D3
1 RUTLAND AVE
2 KENT AVE
3 DORSET AVE
4 YORK CL
5 BALMORAL RD
6 CAVENDISH PL
E1
1 GREENWOOD ST
2 JOHN ST
3 COUNTESSWAY
4 OAKLAND ST
5 TEVEN ST
6 CLAYTON ST
7 BALDWIN ST
E2
1 BUTTERMERE CL
2 PEAR TREE CL
3 CHARLESTON CT
4 BALSHAW ST
5 LONGWORTH ST
6 HAYDOCK ST
7 PEAR TREE ST
8 ST AIDAN'S RD
9 ST AIDANS PK
F1
1 TYNE ST
2 LODGE CL
3 ELM DR
4 YEWLANDS AVE
5 WHITEFIELD MDWS
F2
1 WATER ST
2 WHALLEY ST
3 ASHWORTH ST
4 SOLLAM'S CL
5 BROWN LA

118
98
A
B
C
D
E
F
Eyes Wood
PR2
PR1
Ribble Way
River Ribble
PRESTON NEW RD
A59
M6
31
B6230
8
Works
Cowell's Farm
VICARAGE LA
Cuerdale Hall
New Hall Tavern (PH)
Roacher Hall
7
Walmsley Fold
New Hall Farm
Cuerdale Wood
29
CUERDALE LA
Mill
Roach Bridge
ROACH BRIDGE COTTS
ROACH RD
GREEN LA
6
Woodhouse Farm
Smithy House
Roach Bridge
Potter Lane Farm
Swaines Fold
Darwen Side Farm
Fleetwood Hall
POTTER LA
Sallom House
Cottage Farm
5
Osbaldeston House Wood
PR5
River Darwen
Beeston Wood
28
Higher Walton
Bannister Hall
Carver Fold
Carr Wood
Jolly Fold
Coupe Green
1 ROSSALL CL
2 WINSTER CL
3 SILVERDALE CL
4 METHUEN CL
5 MANSFIELD DR
Beeston Brook
4
HIGHER WALTON RD
Works
Coupe Green Cty Prim Sch
Rass Wood
The Hey
Mills
Swan Inn (PH)
Higher Walton CE Prim Sch
HOGHTON LA
3
Old Oak Inn (PH)
Olive Farm
Prospect Hill
ASHTREE CT
A675
27
Cooper House Farm
GREGSON LA
Tottering Temple Farm
FOUR LANE ENDS
Gregson Lane
2
30
Drum Head Brook
Middle Shuttling Fields
Black Horse (PH)
Frith's Farm
Hewn Gate Farm
Fowler Brook
Brindle Gregson Lane Cty Prim Sch
1
Livesey Green Farm
LC
St Joseph's RC Prim Sch
M6
M61
26
58
59

97
119

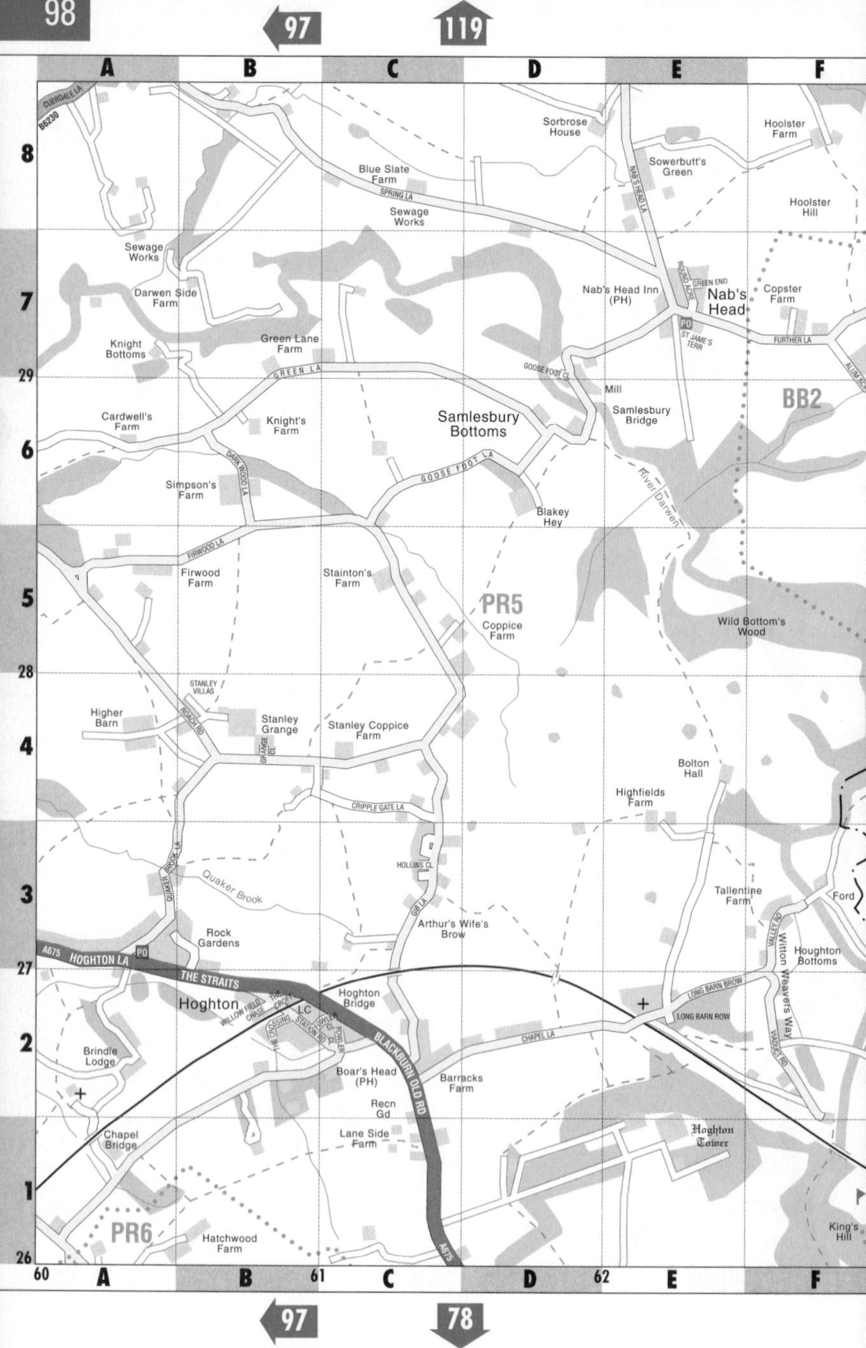
A B C D E F
8 7 6 5 4 3 2 1
29 28 27 26
60 61 62
CUERDALE LA
B6230
Sorbrose House
Hoolster Farm
Blue Slate Farm
SPRING LA
Sowerbutt's Green
NAB'S HEAD LA
Sewage Works
Hoolster Hill
Sewage Works
Darwen Side Farm
Nab's Head Inn (PH)
ROUND ACRE
GREEN END
Nab's Head
Copster Farm
PO
ST JAME'S TERR
FURTHER LA
Knight Bottoms
Green Lane Farm
GREEN LA
GOOSE FOOT CL
Mill
BB2
Cardwell's Farm
Knight's Farm
Samlesbury Bottoms
Samlesbury Bridge
DARK WOOD LA
GOOSE FOOT LA
River Darwen
Simpson's Farm
Blakey Hey
FIRWOOD LA
Firwood Farm
Stainton's Farm
PR5
Coppice Farm
Wild Bottom's Wood
STANLEY VILLAS
ROACH RD
Higher Barn
Stanley Grange
Stanley Coppice Farm
GRANGE CL
Bolton Hall
Highfields Farm
CRIPPLE GATE LA
HOLLINS CL
QUAKER BROOK LA
Quaker Brook
GIB LA
Tallentine Farm
Ford
Arthur's Wife's Brow
VALLEY RD
Rock Gardens
Witton Weavers Way
Houghton Bottoms
A675
HOGHTON LA
PO
THE STRAITS
Hoghton
Hoghton Bridge
LONG BARN BROW
LONG BARN ROW
WILLOW FIELD CHASE
THE CROFT
LC
THE CROSSING
STATION RD
FOWLER CL
FOWLER
BLACKBURN OLD RD
CHAPEL LA
VIADUCT RD
Brindle Lodge
Boar's Head (PH)
Barracks Farm
Recn Gd
Chapel Bridge
Lane Side Farm
Hoghton Tower
PR6
Hatchwood Farm
A675
King's Hill

97
78

120
100
Stanley House
Bolton Fold
Hacking House
Lodge Wood
PRESTON NEW RD
YEW TREE DR
Hotel
Ravenswing Farm
FURTHER LA
Woodfold Park Farm
Arley Brook
Arley Farm
Jeffery Wood
Woodfold Hall
Billinge Scarr
Lower Bencock Farm
SCARR LA
Middle Shorrock Hey Farm
CARR LA
White House Pond
Stock's Farm
Westholme Sch
ALUM SCAR LA
HEATHFIELD PK
Old Woodfold Farm
MEINS RD
WOODGATES RD
PALL MALL
BILLINGE END RD
BILLINGE SIDE
Lower Shorrock Hey Farm
Billinge Hill
Alum House Wood
Clog and Billycock (PH)
KILLIARDS LA
Lee Farm
BB2
UNDER BILLINGE LA
Close Farm
Witton Weavers Way
Billinge Nook
BILLINGE END RD
Butler's Delf
Woodcock Hill
Witton Park Country Park
PR5
Maiden House Farm
Visitors Ctr
Lower Fold
Crem
Cemy
Hunter's Hill
WOODCOCK HILL RD
Pleasington Nature Reserve
CABIN HILL
LONG LA
Pleasington Old Hall
Trout Brook Farm
River Darwen
OLD HALL LA
BILLINGE VIEW
Higher Park Farm
SANDY LA
TOWER RD
HILLCREST RD
PRIORY CT
Witton Weavers Way
TOWER RD
GEDDES ST
Throstle Nest Brow
PH
REGENTS CL
Butler's Bridge
CHERRY LEA
CHERRY TREE TERR 1
HUNTERS LODGE 2
GLADSTONE TERR 3
Cherry Tree
WOOD VIEW
BOWDEN AVE
Tongue Hill
Playing Fields
Brownlands Farm
Pleasington
PRESTON OLD RD
Leeds and Liverpool Canal
Pleasington
Cherry Tree
LIVESEY HALL CL
THE CRESCENT
RANNOCH DR
SOLWAY AVE
St Francis CE Prim Sch
4 MELFORT CL
5 TORRIDON CL
WOODLANDS AVE
VICTORIA AVE
SPRINGFIELD
BROWNLOW TERR
CH
VICTORIA RD
ROSE HILL RD
Liby
A677
A6119
A674
8
7
29
6
5
28
4
3
27
2
1
26
A
B
C
D
E
F
64
65
79
100

E5
1 CALENDAR ST
2 MARKET AVE
3 AINSWORTH MALL
4 COBDEN CT
5 GROSVENOR WAY
6 SPRING HILL
7 VICTORIA CT
8 MARKET WAY
9 STONYBUTTS
10 LORD STREET MALL
11 CORPORATION ST
12 LORD ST W
13 LOWER COCKCROFT

E5
14 HIGHER COCKCROFT
15 NEW MARKET ST
16 TOWN HALL ST
17 RICHMOND TERR
18 EXCHANGE ST
19 MUSEUM ST

E5
20 SUDELL CROSS
21 LIMBRICK
22 MORTON ST
23 RICHMOND HILL
24 BOLTON'S CT
25 VICTORIA ST

E6
1 HODDER ST
2 BROOKFIELD ST
3 HARTLEY ST
4 VICTORIA CROSS
5 WATFORD ST
6 WILLOUGHBY ST
7 WIMBERLEY GDNS
8 WIMBERLEY PL

F6
1 ST MICHAEL'S CT
2 ST ALBAN'S CT
3 TRINITY CT
4 WINDERMERE CL
5 BUTTERMERE CL
6 THIRLMERE CL
7 BOWLAND HO
8 PRIMROSE CT
9 ORIOLE CL
10 BROOKHOUSE BSN
11 WHITEWELL PL
12 BROOKHOUSE GDN
13 WILLIAM HERBERT

99
121

B1
1 CAVE ST
2 HERSCHELL ST
3 CANAL ST
4 KING'S BRIDGE CL
5 BEVERLEY ST
6 BRIDGE HO
7 WHARF HO

E3
1 NEW GARDEN ST
2 HARGREAVES LA
3 LISTER ST
4 HUTCHINSON ST
5 ST ANN'S ST
6 FREDERICK ST
7 ROSE ST

E4
1 PARADISE LA
2 PARADISE TERR
3 HEATON ST
4 OLD BANK ST
5 TATTERSALL ST
6 PILKINGTON ST
7 MARKET STREET LA

F3
1 MERCHANTS QUAY
2 WATERFRONT
3 PIER HO
4 ST FRANCES CL
5 ST ANNES CL

99
80

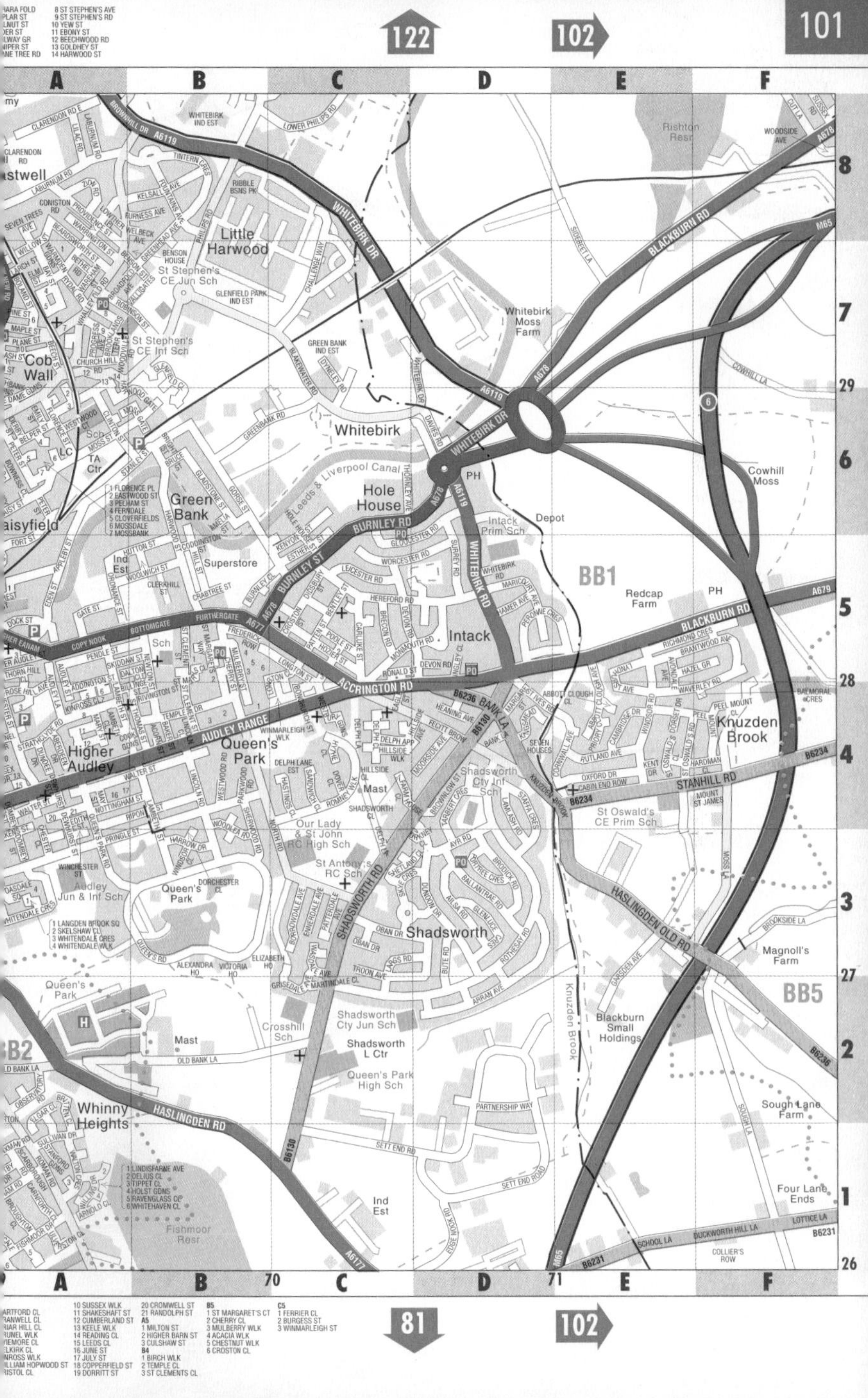

101
122
102
81
102
A
B
C
D
E
F
8
7
29
6
5
28
4
3
27
2
1
26
70
71
8 ST STEPHEN'S AVE
9 ST STEPHEN'S RD
10 YEW ST
11 EBONY ST
12 BEECHWOOD RD
13 GOLDHEY ST
14 HARWOOD ST
Little Harwood
Whitebirk
Whitebirk Moss Farm
Rishton Resr
WHITEBIRK DR
BLACKBURN RD
M65
A678
A6119
A679
St Stephen's CE Jun Sch
St Stephen's CE Inf Sch
GLENFIELD PARK IND EST
GREEN BANK IND EST
WHITEBIRK IND EST
RIBBLE BSNS PK
Cob Wall
Leeds & Liverpool Canal
Hole House
Green Bank
Superstore
Ind Est
BURNLEY RD
BURNLEY ST
Intack Prim Sch
Depot
Cowhill Moss
COWHILL LA
BB1
Redcap Farm
PH
Intack
ACCRINGTON RD
AUDLEY RANGE
Queen's Park
Higher Audley
Knuzden Brook
STANHILL RD
B6234
St Oswald's CE Prim Sch
Shadsworth Cty Inf Sch
Our Lady & St John RC High Sch
St Antony's RC Sch
Mast
Shadsworth
SHADSWORTH RD
HASLINGDEN OLD RD
Magnoll's Farm
BB5
Blackburn Small Holdings
Knuzden Brook
Shadsworth Cty Jun Sch
Shadsworth L Ctr
Queen's Park High Sch
Crosshill Sch
Audley Jun & Inf Sch
BB2
Whinny Heights
HASLINGDEN RD
Fishmoor Resr
Ind Est
SETT END RD
PARTNERSHIP WAY
Sough Lane Farm
Four Lane Ends
DUCKWORTH HILL LA
SCHOOL LA
LOTTICE LA
B6231
B6236
B6130
A6177
1 FLORENCE PL
2 EASTWOOD ST
3 PELHAM ST
4 FERNDALE
5 CLOVERFIELDS
6 MOSSDALE
7 MOSSBANK
1 LANGDEN BROOK SQ
2 SKELSHAW CL
3 WHITENDALE CRES
4 WHITENDALE WLK
1 LINDISFARNE AVE
2 DELIUS CL
3 TIPPET CL
4 HOLST GDNS
5 RAVENGLASS CL
6 WHITEHAVEN CL
10 SUSSEX WLK
11 SHAKESHAFT ST
12 CUMBERLAND ST
13 KEELE WLK
14 READING CL
15 LEEDS CL
16 JUNE ST
17 JULY ST
18 COPPERFIELD ST
19 DORRITT ST
20 CROMWELL ST
21 RANDOLPH ST
A5
1 MILTON ST
2 HIGHER BARN ST
3 CULSHAW ST
B4
1 BIRCH WLK
2 TEMPLE CL
3 ST CLEMENTS CL
B5
1 ST MARGARET'S CT
2 CHERRY CL
3 MULBERRY WLK
4 ACACIA WLK
5 CHESTNUT WLK
6 CROSTON CL
C5
1 FERRIER CL
2 BURGESS ST
3 WINMARLEIGH ST

101
123

D3
1 ST ANDREW'S CT
2 KAY ST
3 BENT ST
4 COOPERS CL
5 PEEL ST
6 THOMAS ST
7 HIGHER PEEL ST
8 SMITHY BRIDGE ST
9 OAK ST

E4
1 BACKHOUSE ST
2 HARTLEY ST
3 HODGSON ST
4 DALE ST
5 SPRING ST
6 MOUNT PLEASANT ST
7 OFF MOUNT PLEASANT ST
8 WATSON ST
9 PADDOCK ST
10 LOCK ST
11 MEADOW CT
12 ST PAUL'S CT
13 WORSLEY CT

F4
1 GAYLE WAY
2 BURNSALL RD
3 REETH WAY
4 BUCKDEN RD

COLN CT
OSEY HOUSE
NBURY CL
RCESTER AVE
SHAM CL
VERN CL
7 STRATFORD WAY
C5
1 CHRIST CHURCH SQ
2 CHRIST CHURCH ST
3 NUTTALL ST MEWS
4 PRIESTLEY NOOK
5 EDMUND ST
6 NAPIER ST
7 WELLINGTON CT
8 SPRING GDNS
9 HARGREAVES ST
10 CHAPEL ST
11 ST LEGER CT
12 MIDLAND ST
13 QUARRY ST
C6
1 MANOR BROOK
2 ARNOLD ST
3 BRADSHAW ST E
4 HOOD ST
5 RAILWAY VIEW
6 KENYON ST
7 MASON ST
8 CORNHILL
9 BURNLEY RD
10 WATER ST
11 BACK WATER ST
12 INFANT ST
124
C6
13 QUEEN ST
14 TASKER ST
15 BRIDGE ST
16 DUTTON ST
104
A
B
C
D
E
F
8
7
29
6
5
28
4
3
27
2
1
26
Dill Hall
Laneside
Playing Fields
Crem
Cemy
Hillock Vale
Moorhead High Sch
St Christopher's CE High Sch
Peel Park
Milnshaw
HYNDBURN RD
WHALLEY RD
QUEEN'S RD
BURNLEY RD
EASTGATE
Lower Fold
ACCRINGTON
Owl Hall
New High Riley
Accrington Sta
Mkt TH
Barnfield
High Riley
Scaitcliffe
Springhill Prim Sch
St Anne's RC Inf Sch
Lower Withams
Oak Hill Park
BB5
Heights Farm
Woodnook Cty Prim Sch
Woodnook
Bullough Park
Playing Field
Laund
Fern Gore
Art Gal
MANCHESTER RD
Meadow Top Farm
Miller Fold
St Peter's CE Prim Sch
St Oswald's RC Prim Sch
Rothwell Heights
The Hollins High Sch
Higher Baxenden
Wooley Lane Farm
Red Lion Inn (PH)
Bedlam
Icconhurst
Gaulkthorn
Green Haworth CE Prim Sch
Baxenden CE Prim Sch
Shoulder of Mutton (PH)
Green Haworth
Friar Hill
Baxenden
Lower Baxenden
Lower Friar Hill Farm
76
77
83
104

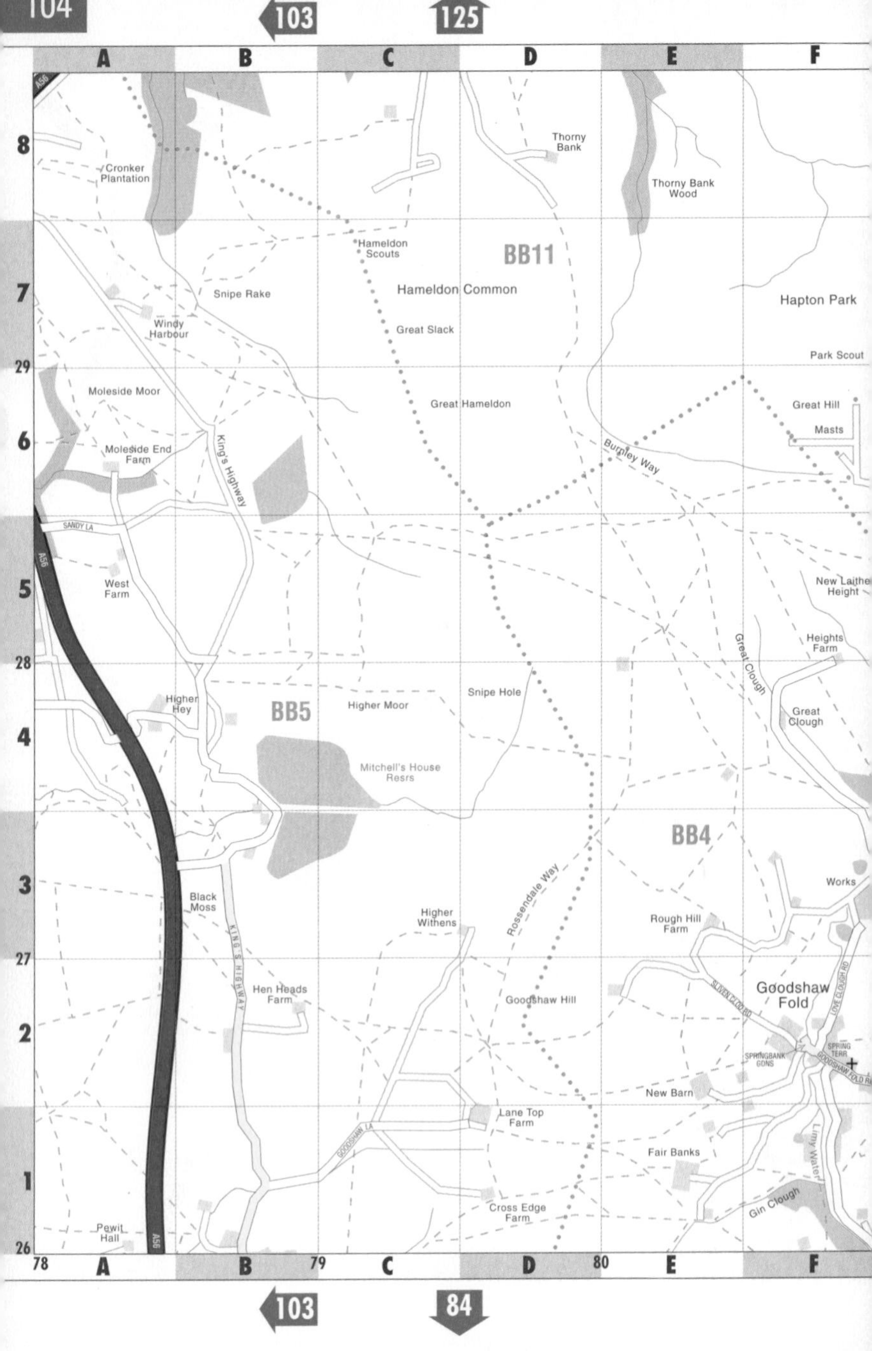
103
125
A
B
C
D
E
F
8
7
29
6
5
28
4
3
27
2
1
26
78
79
80
A56
Cronker Plantation
Thorny Bank
Thorny Bank Wood
Hameldon Scouts
BB11
Snipe Rake
Hameldon Common
Hapton Park
Windy Harbour
Great Slack
Park Scout
Moleside Moor
Great Hameldon
Great Hill
Masts
Moleside End Farm
King's Highway
Burnley Way
SANDY LA
West Farm
New Laithe Height
Heights Farm
Great Clough
Higher Hey
BB5
Higher Moor
Snipe Hole
Great Clough
Mitchell's House Resrs
BB4
Works
Black Moss
Higher Withens
Rossendale Way
Rough Hill Farm
KING'S HIGHWAY
Hen Heads Farm
Goodshaw Hill
Goodshaw Fold
SLIVEN CLOUGH RD
LOVE CLOUGH RD
SPRINGBANK GDNS
SPRING TERR
GOODSHAW FOLD RD
New Barn
Lane Top Farm
GOODSHAW LA
Limy Water
Fair Banks
Gin Clough
Cross Edge Farm
Pewit Hall
103
84

126 106
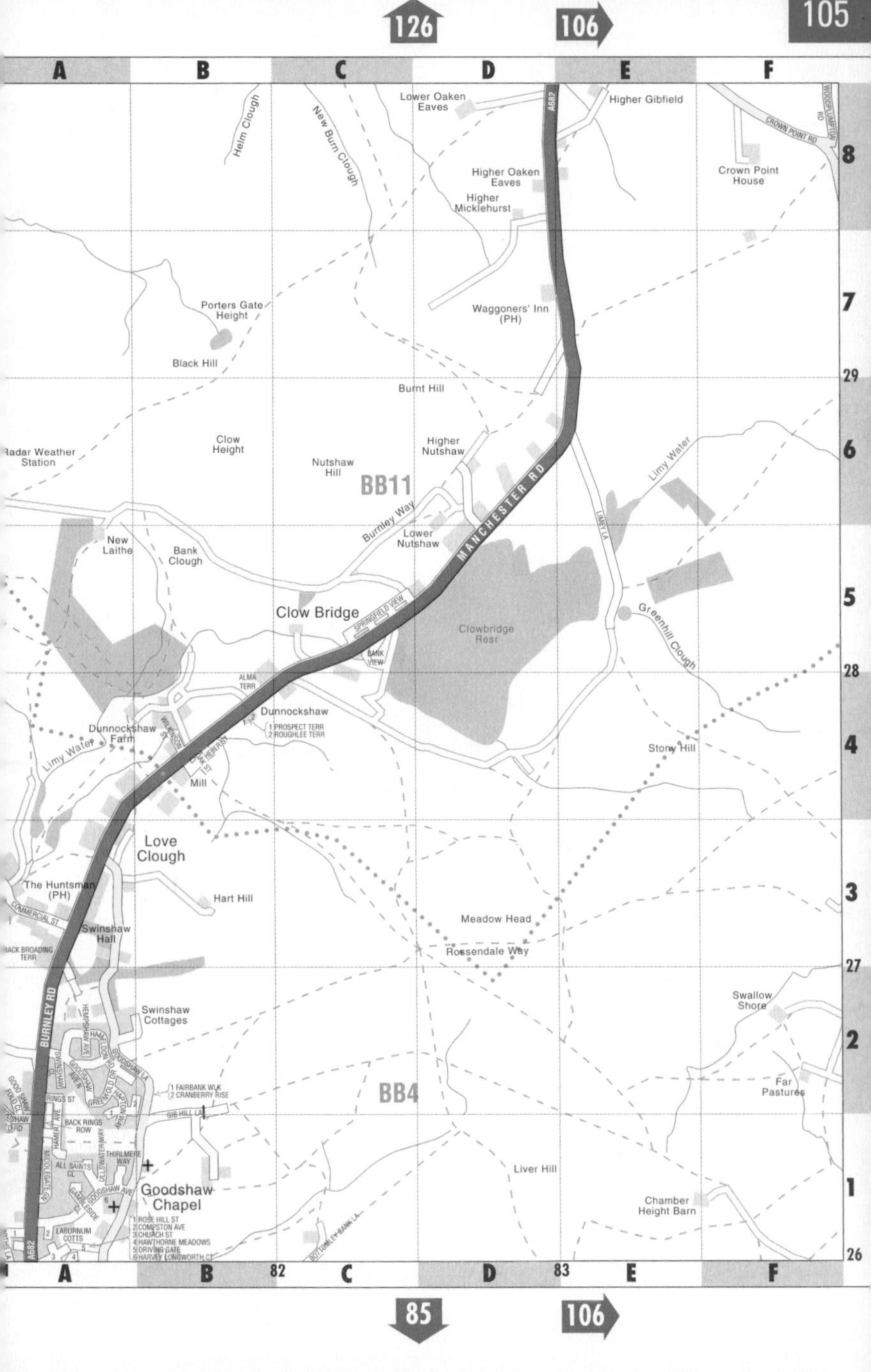

85 106

105
127

105
86

128
108

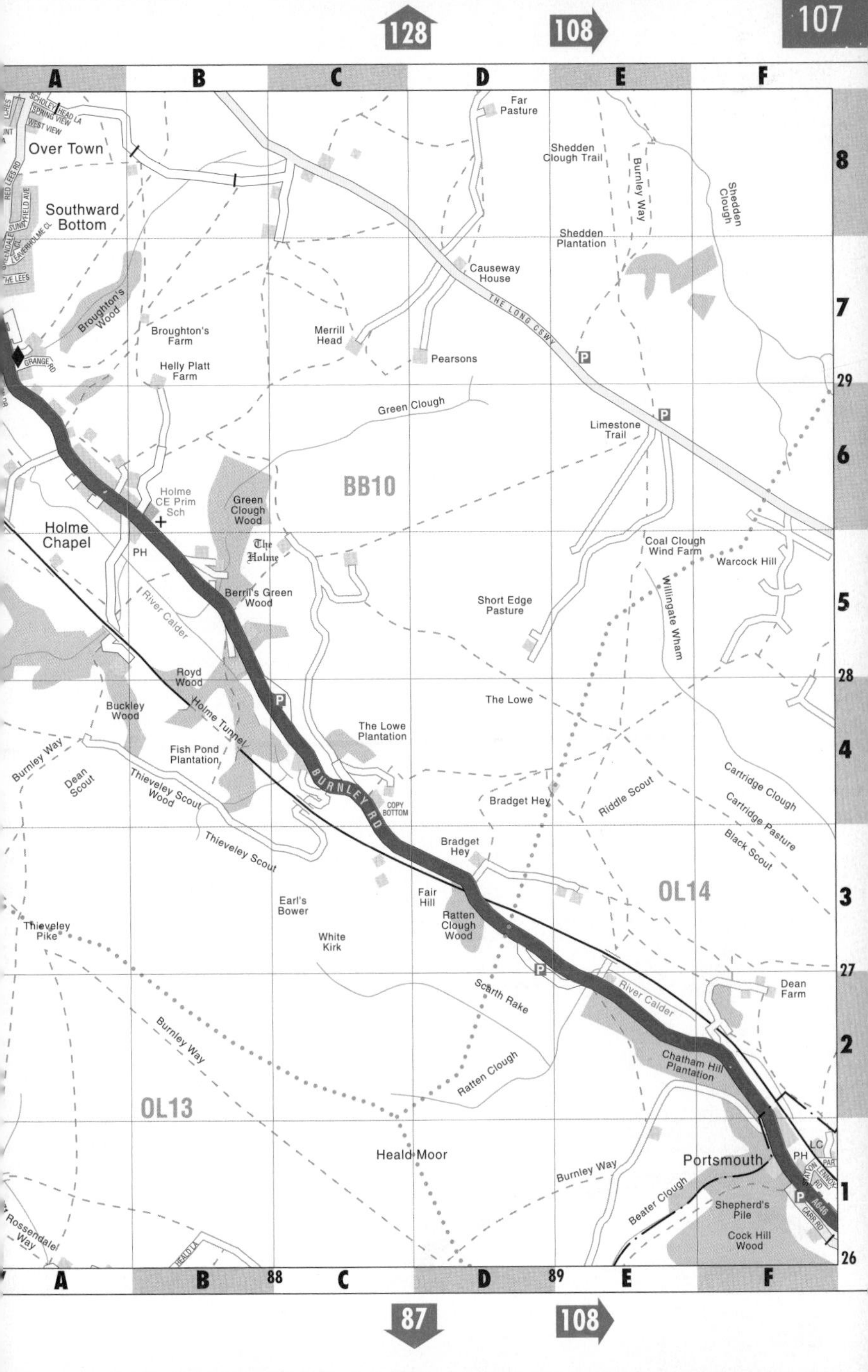

87
108

107

A1
1 DURN ST
2 HOLYOAKE ST
3 GREENFIELD TERR
4 CARRFIELD VILLAS
5 STUBLEY HOLME

B1
1 GLEN VIEW ST
2 GLADSTONE ST
3 SUNNY BANK TERR
4 PALMA ST
5 HARRISON ST
6 HIRST ST
7 SUN TERR
8 OAKLEIGH TERR
9 CORNHOLME TERR

B1
10 ACKROYD ST
11 BOBBIN MILL CL
12 PARKSIDE CL
13 DAISY BANK ST
14 STANSFIELD TERR
15 BROWN BIRKS ST
16 PEAR PL
17 PEAR ST
18 SPRING VILLAS

107

C1
1 SPRING ST
2 THOMAS ST
3 STATION RD
4 BROOKFIELD ST
5 SOUTH VIEW ST
6 HUDSON ST
7 COLLEGE ST
8 GARFIELD ST
9 VICTORIA ST

BLACKPOOL
South Pier
Blackpool South Pier
Sandcastle (L Pool)
Pleasure Beach/ Sandcastle
Monorail
Blackpool Pleasure Beach
Miniature Rly
Pleasure Beach
The Star
Burlington Rd
Tramway
PROMENADE
Harrowside/ Solarium
Harrow Pl/ Carousel
Lancashire Coastal Way
Abercorn Pl
Starr Gate
Squires Gate
Holiday Camp
Dunes
The New Thursby Nursing Home
Starr Hills
Lytham St Annes Local Nature Reserve
CLIFTON DR N
St Cuthbert's RC Prim Sch
Palatine High Sch
South Shore
Thames Prim Sch
Arnold Sch
Arnold Jun Sch
LYTHAM RD
Liby
FY4
Hawes Side Prim Sch
Highfield High Sch
Morton Cty Prim Sch
COMMON EDGE RD
Common Edge
HAWES SIDE LA
YEADON WAY
SQUIRES GATE LA
PROGRESS WAY
A5230
Ind Est
Airport Terminal
Helicopter Terminal
Control Tower
Blackpool Airport
Playing Field
FY8
HIGHBURY RD
B6
1 CLIFTON CT
2 NATEBY CT
3 BRIXHAM PL
4 COLDALE CT
BROADFIELD AVE 1
MYERSCOUGH AVE 2
ELSWICK PL 3
INSKIP PL 4
NEWLYN AVE 5
NEWLYN CT 6
RUTHERFORD PL 1
SANDRIDGE PL 2
LEMON TREE CT 3
LINSAY CT 4
DOWNHAM PL 5
HOWARD CL 1
BLENHEIM PL 2
KIRKSTONE RD 1
LANGDALE RD 2
AMBLESIDE RD 3
WINDERMERE SQ 1
SPRING GDNS 2

109 130

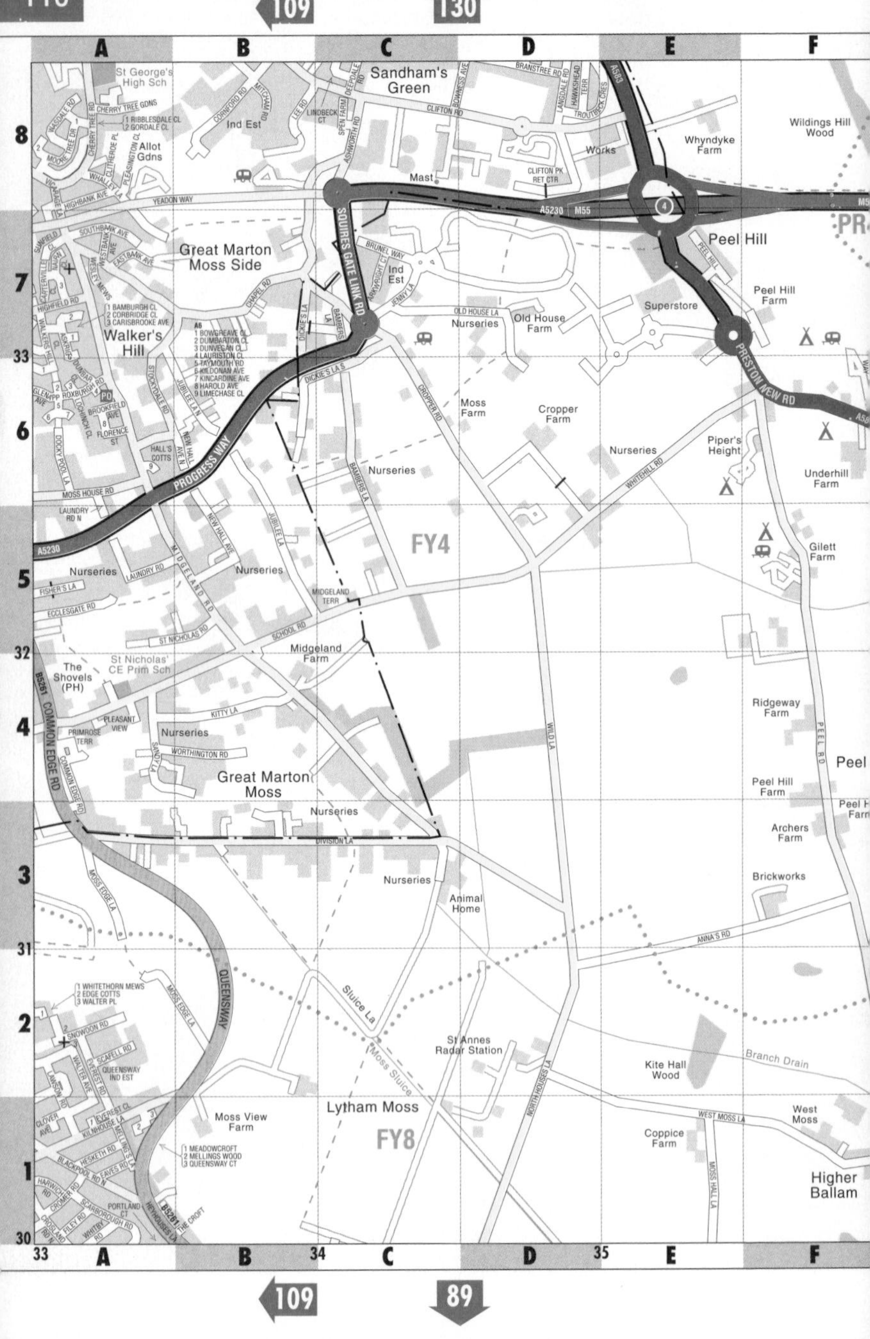

109 89

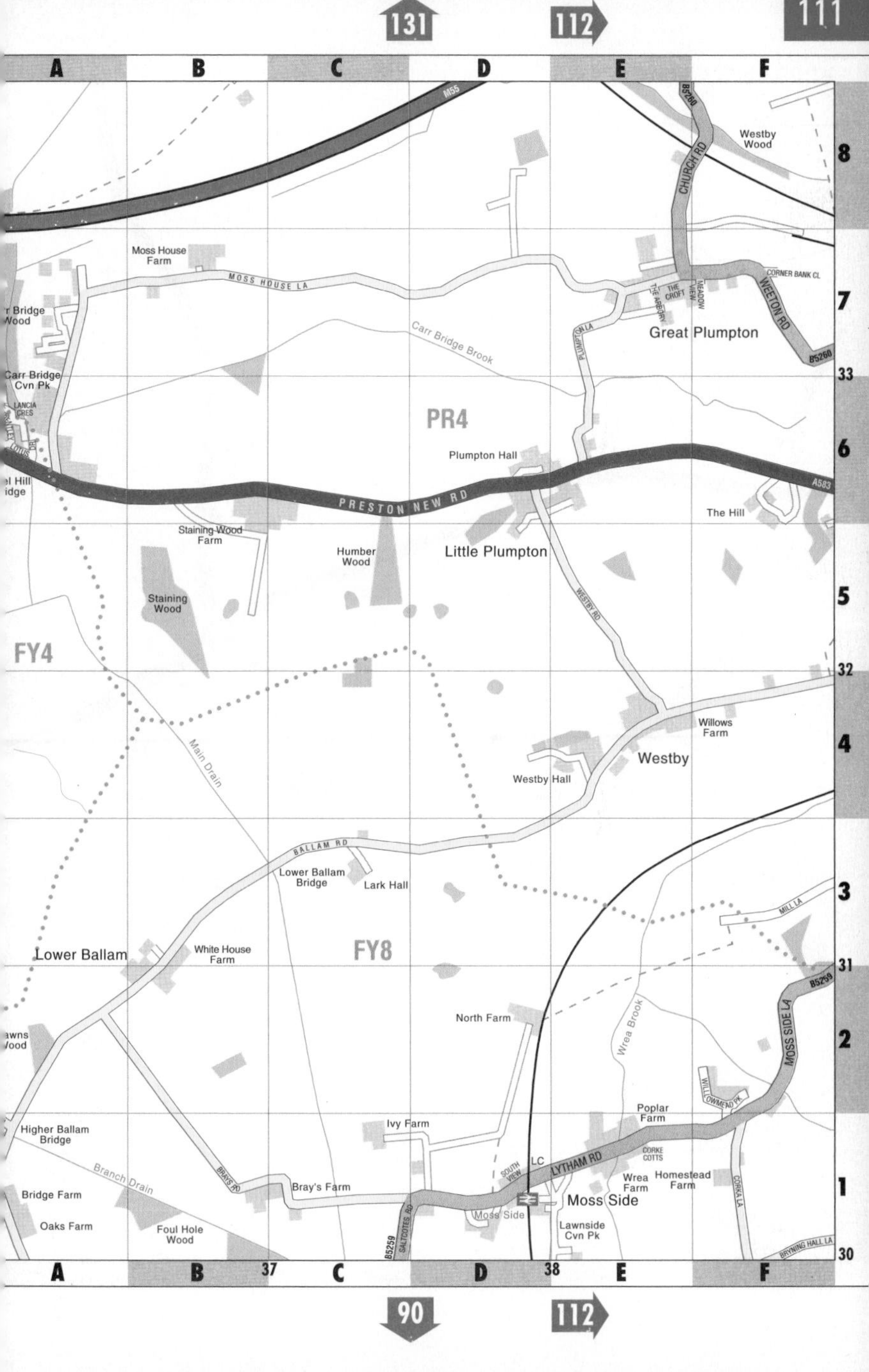
131
112
A
B
C
D
E
F
M55
B5260
Westby Wood
8
CHURCH RD
Moss House Farm
MOSS HOUSE LA
CORNER BANK CL
THE ARBORY
THE CROFT
MEADOW VIEW
WEETON RD
7
r Bridge
Vood
PLUMPTON LA
Great Plumpton
Carr Bridge Brook
B5260
Carr Bridge
Cvn Pk
33
LANCIA CRES
PR4
6
Plumpton Hall
el Hill
idge
A583
PRESTON NEW RD
The Hill
Staining Wood Farm
Humber Wood
Little Plumpton
WESTBY RD
Staining Wood
5
FY4
32
Willows Farm
4
Main Drain
Westby
Westby Hall
BALLAM RD
Lower Ballam Bridge
Lark Hall
3
MILL LA
Lower Ballam
White House Farm
FY8
31
B5259
North Farm
Wrea Brook
MOSS SIDE LA
2
awns
Vood
WILLOWMEAD PK
Poplar Farm
Higher Ballam Bridge
Ivy Farm
CORKE COTTS
LC
LYTHAM RD
Branch Drain
SOUTH VIEW
BRAYS RD
Bray's Farm
Wrea Farm
Homestead Farm
CORKA LA
1
Bridge Farm
Moss Side
Moss Side
SALTCOTES RD
Oaks Farm
Foul Hole Wood
Lawnside Cvn Pk
B5259
BRYNING HALL LA
30
A
B
37
C
D
38
E
F
90
112

111
132

F5
1 THE COURTYARD
2 STATION RD
3 SMITH ST
4 SHERBURNE AVE
5 SUNNY BANK MILL
6 NELSON ST
7 WOODLANDS AVE
8 SANDHURST CL
F6
1 BILLINGTON ST
2 EVEREST CT
3 BILLINGTON ST E
4 PORTER ST E
A
B
C
D
E
F
8
7
33
6
5
32
4
3
31
2
1
30
39
40
41
Stanley House Farm
Slack Wood
Crook't Tree Brow
WEETON RD
Mill Farm
Wesham House
FLEETWOOD RD
A585
Recn Gd
St Joseph's RC Prim Sch
Bradkirk Hall
Wesham Park
GARSTANG RD N
HAWTHORN CL 1
BRAMBLE CL 2
Kirkham Junc
Mill
MARKET ST
WHITWORTH ST
STATION RD
Kirkham & Wesham
Whinbrick
WHINBRICK COTTS
PRESTON NEW RD
A583
BLACKPOOL RD
Wrongway Brook
Brook Wood
Mere Farm
WHINBRICK TERR
FOX LANE ENDS
WEETON RD
B5260
1 SANDOWN CL
2 FIRFIELD CL
The Willows RC Prim Sch
Kirkham Gram Sch
Stable Wood
B5259
RIBBY RD
BALLAM RD
PR4
Ribby Hall
Sports Ctr
Wall Wood
Halls Wood
Kirkham Grammer Jun Sch
KIRKHAM BY-PASS
Ribby
Wrea Brook
STATION RD
BROOK MILL IND EST
RIBBY RD
Brown's Farm
Ribby Hall Leisure Village
Caravan Pk
Shepherd's Farm
Windmill
Blackburn's Farm
1 HEDGE ROW
2 MANOR COTTS
3 SMITH FOLD
4 CHURCH ROW
Wrea Green
Bracken Strip Wood
Kirkham Camp (dis)
MOSS SIDE LA
Hill Farm
BRYNING AVE
Greenways Nurseries
BRYNING LA
Newfold Farm
Lower Wood
FY8
Fairfield Farm
Prospect Farm
New House Farm
BRYNING HALL LA
Green Valley Farm

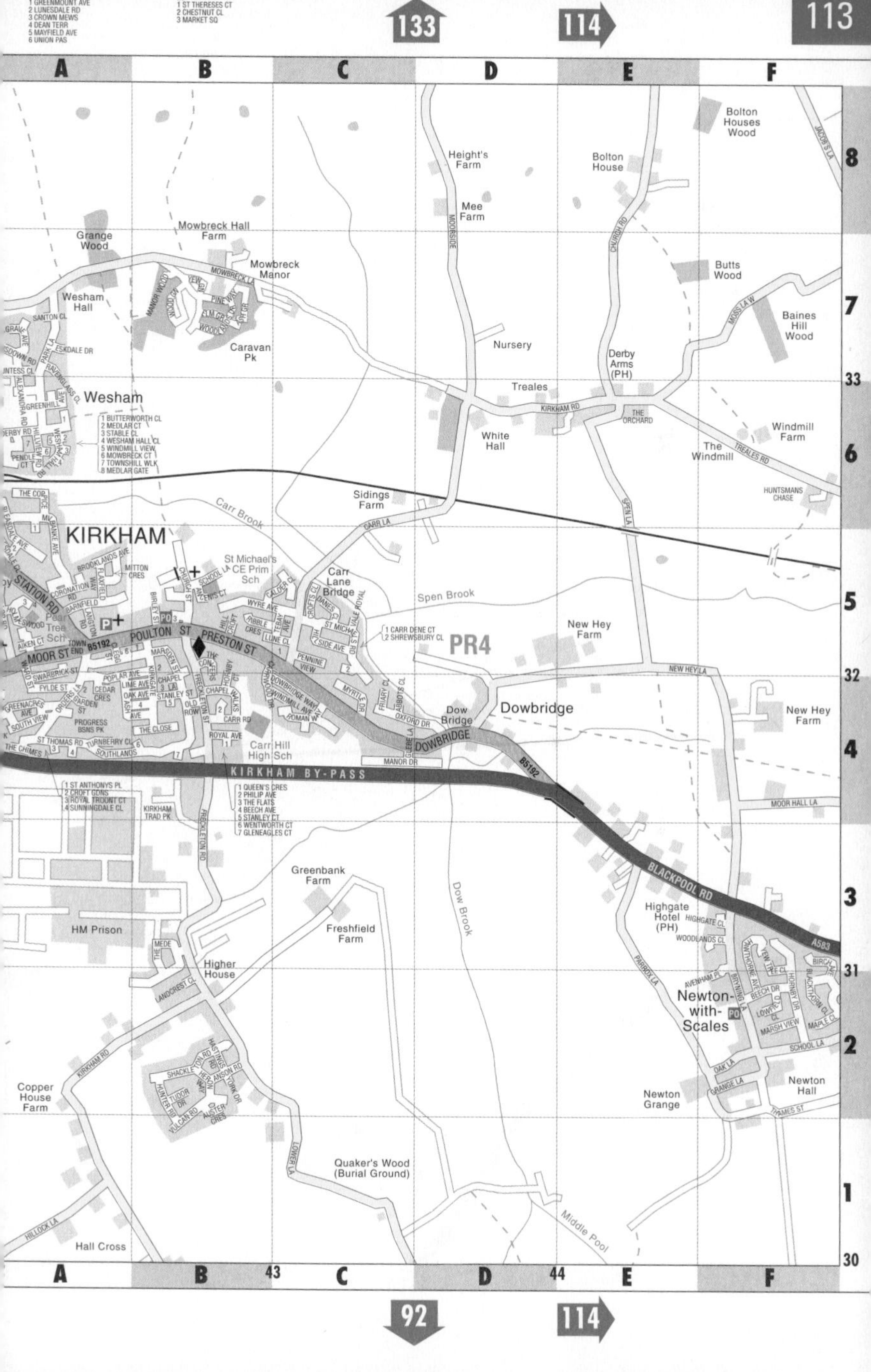
A5
1 GREENMOUNT AVE
2 LUNESDALE RD
3 CROWN MEWS
4 DEAN TERR
5 MAYFIELD AVE
6 UNION PAS
B5
1 ST THERESES CT
2 CHESTNUT CL
3 MARKET SQ
133
114
KIRKHAM
Wesham
Grange Wood
Mowbreck Hall Farm
Mowbreck Manor
Wesham Hall
Caravan Pk
Height's Farm
Mee Farm
Bolton Houses Wood
Bolton House
Butts Wood
Baines Hill Wood
Nursery
Derby Arms (PH)
Treales
White Hall
The Windmill
Windmill Farm
Sidings Farm
Carr Brook
St Michael's CE Prim Sch
Carr Lane Bridge
Spen Brook
New Hey Farm
PR4
Dowbridge
Dow Bridge
New Hey Farm
Carr Hill High Sch
KIRKHAM BY-PASS
1 BUTTERWORTH CL
2 MEDLAR CT
3 STABLE CL
4 WESHAM HALL CL
5 WINDMILL VIEW
6 MOWBRECK CT
7 TOWNSHILL WLK
8 MEDLAR GATE
1 CARR DENE CT
2 SHREWSBURY CL
1 ST ANTHONYS PL
2 CROFT GDNS
3 ROYAL TROONT CT
4 SUNNINGDALE CL
1 QUEEN'S CRES
2 PHILIP AVE
3 THE FLATS
4 BEECH AVE
5 STANLEY CT
6 WENTWORTH CT
7 GLENEAGLES CT
KIRKHAM TRAD PK
HM Prison
Greenbank Farm
Freshfield Farm
Higher House
Dow Brook
Highgate Hotel (PH)
Newton-with-Scales
Newton Hall
Newton Grange
Copper House Farm
Quaker's Wood (Burial Ground)
Middle Pool
Hall Cross
MOOR ST
POULTON ST
PRESTON ST
STATION RD
BLACKPOOL RD
KIRKHAM RD
TREALES RD
MOSS LA W
CHURCH RD
MOORSIDE
SPEN LA
NEW HEY LA
MOOR HALL LA
CARR LA
MOWBRECK LA
FRECKLETON RD
PROGRESS BSNS PK
LOWER LA
PARROX LA
SCHOOL LA
HIGHGATE CL
WOODLANDS CL
HILLOCK LA
43
44
92
114

113
134
A
B
C
D
E
F
8
7
33
6
5
32
4
3
31
2
1
30
45
46
47
Moss House Farm
MOSS LA E
New Bridge
Long Park Wood
Pepper Hill
BLACKLEACH LA
Pinfold Farm
DAGGER RD
MOSS LA W
Moss Side Farm
Six Mile Bridge
JACOB'S LA
Silly Nook Wood
BOLTONS CROFT
Grace Mire House
STORE YARD
PH
Salwick Bridge
Treales Cottage
Livesey Wood
Many Pits Wood
Moorfield
Molly's Plantation
Lancaster Canal
TREALES RD
Fir Tree Farm
Wilson's Bridge
Salwick Hall
Bucks Moss Wood
Harbour Farm
Cookson's Plantation
Ash Plantation
Salwick Bridge
Whinny Turn Wood
Salwick
RAILWAY COTTS
Ward's House Bridge
The Dingle
STATION RD
PR4
Springfields Plantation
Ward's House
MOOR HALL LA
Crook's Plantation
VICARAGE LA
CHURCH LA
PH
Clifton Windmill
Works
LEA LA
Lea Town
Salwick
PH
CHURCH PK
DARKINSON LA
A583
DEEPDALE LA
CEDAR CL
HILL CRES
ALDER CL
SCALE HALL LA
SCHOOL LA
Stanagate Plantation
Pear Tree Farm
PEAR TREE COURTYARD
Deepdale Brook
St Mary's RC Primary Sch
1 BLUECOAT CRES
2 SUNNY BANK AVE
BLACKPOOL RD
Raike's Farm
Newton Bluecoat CE Prim Sch
THAMES ST
CLIFTON LA
MEADOW CL
ASH LA
CLIFTON DR
MEADOW C
ASH CT
Hanging Banks Plantation
FIRST AVE
Clifton
SQUIRRELS CHASE
Clifton Hall
DARKINSON LA
HIGHFIELD CL
PRESTON OLD RD
DIXON'S FARM MEWS
SILVER ST
PO
Clifton Bridge
1 MULBERRY CL
2 JUBILEE TERR
3 STANAGATE
LODGE LA
Savick Brook
A583

135
116
115
A
B
C
D
E
F
M55
B5411
8
School Farm
Houghton House Farm
Lower Bartle
Higher Bartle
TABLEY LA
ROSEMARY LA
BLACKLEACH LA
BARTLE LA
Bartle Hall
Old Vicarage Farm
SANDY LA
7
Nog Tow
1 BROOK MDW
2 DAISYFIELDS
LIGHTFOOT LA
B6241
Maxey House
33
SANDRINGHAM WAY 1
BLENHEIM WAY 2
BIDEFORD WAY 3
BUDE CL 4
BARNSTAPLE WAY 5
ASHFIELD CT 6
Ivy Farm
Sitting Goose Inn (PH)
Moor Hall
Haydock Farm
HONITON WAY
KINGSLEY RD
TANTERTON HALL RD
6
Saddle Inn (PH)
LEA LA
HOYLES LA
PR4
Cottam
MILLER LA
SANDYFIELDS
FLOWERFIELD
COTTAM GN
POPPYFIELD
MEADOWBARN CL
SWALLOWFIELDS
TAG LA
MARKFIELD CL
TAG CROFT
5
WORCHESTER GDNS 1
WILTSHIRE MEWS 2
THE CHASE
THE GRANGE
MERRY TREES LA
PH
Cottam Hall
TOM BENSON WAY
COTTAM HALL LA
TAG FARM CT
HOLLYBANK CL
EASTBOURNE CL
WHITBY AVE
THE WEALD
HEREFORD GR
AVON GDNS
ROSEBERRY AVE
ROSEWOOD AVE
1 CROSIER WLK
2 ROSEDENE CL
Cottam Cty Prim Sch
HAYDOCKS LA
KEATS WAY
VALENTINES MDW
THE GABLES
THE EVERGREENS
MILLERSGATE
32
Moor Hey
Lea Endowed CE Prim Sch
SIDGREAVES LA
COTTAM WAY
COLERIDGE CL
FINCH LA
DUNNOCK LA
HARGREAVES CT 1
WHITBY PL 2
NEWLYN PL 3
REDCAR AVE
DUNDON CL
Holy Family RC Prim Sch
Ingol Prim Sch
4
Bryars Farm
Earl's Farm
Lancaster Canal
Quaker's Bridge
Westleigh
VALENTINES LA
BRIDGEND CT 1
RUTHIN CT 2
NEWPORT CT 3
PENARTH CT 4
MONMOUTH CT 5
PORTHCAWL CT 6
BARDSEA PL 7
COTTAM AVE
Works
CRESWELL AVE
BARRY AVE
DUNBAR RD
RAILWAY COTTS
Cotty Brook (PH)
Preston Sports Arena
3
Halsall's Farm
LEA RD
ALDER COPPICE
WILLOW COPPICE
HAZEL COPPICE
SAVICK WAY
SUMMER TREES AVE
MILLER FIELD
WHITE MDW
B6241
Lady Head Runnel
DARKINSON LA
31
PR2
LIME GR
Leyland Bridge
Savick Cty Prim Sch
LUTON RD
WEST PARK AVE
QUEENSWAY
KINGSWAY
ELM AVE
Brewer House Farm
CH
New House Farm
Savick Brook
ARNSIDE RD
CARTMEL PL
HENDON PL
STAVELEY PL
LYNDHURST DR
LICHFIELD RD
2
Ashton-on-Ribble High Sch
ALDWYCH DR
BROADWAY
HEYWOOD RD
BIRKDALE DR
Liby
A5085
NELSON CRES
NELSON DR
PARKSIDE
Lea
CHARLES WAY
BLACKPOOL RD
BARTLE RD
BALLAM RD
SALWICK PL
MYTHOP PL
SAVICK AVE
NORTH SYKE AVE
HACKLANDS AVE
LINCOLN CHASE
GILHOUSE AVE
GREENSIDE
VICTORIA PARK AVE
NORBRECK RD
NORCROSS PL
Ashton Park
Larches
1
DOONEY DR
PINE WALKS
ALDFIELD AVE
RANGLIT AVE
Sch
THORNTREES AVE
GREAVES TOWN LA
WESTERLONG LA
ELSWICK RD
NATEBY PL
ASTONGATE
LARCHWOOD
1 WESTLEIGH RD
2 STAINING AVE
3 OAKLANDS GR
RIVERSWAY
A5085
BLACKPOOL RD
THE CAMPIONS
HAWTHORN CRES
BLACKTHORN CL
OLD GREAVES TOWN LA
PREESALL RD
LARCHES LA
WESTBY PL
30
49
50
C1
1 FULFORD AVE
2 ROSE BANK
3 MAPLEBANK
4 WHITELENS AVE
5 PARKFIELD CL
6 PARKFIELD CRES
7 HARDWEN AVE
94
D1
1 THE CRESCENT
2 HOLMFIELD CRES
3 THORNPARK DR
4 WHITETHORN SQ
5 DAISY CROFT
116
E1
1 CHARLESWAY CT
2 THE PLOUGHLANDS
3 WHITEHOLME PL
4 WEETON PL
5 ROSEACRE PL
6 THE WOODLANDS
7 ALDCLIFFE RD
8 FORTON RD
9 THURNHAM RD
E2
1 GREENDALE MEWS
2 EXETER PL
3 DOWNHAM PL
4 NEWARK PL

115
136

115
95

C1
1 THRELFALL ST
2 BRAMPTON ST
3 ELTON ST
4 BRUNSWICK PL
5 PECHELL ST
6 BLANCHE ST

E1
1 ADELPHI HO
2 HEYSHAM ST
3 DERWENT HALL
4 DOUGLAS HALL
5 TOWN BROOK HO

F1
1 SHELDON CT
2 PRESTON ENT CTR
3 AUGHTON WLK
4 BECKETT CT
5 HANOVER ST

SHAW ST
TURNER ST
CROMWELL ST
ALICE SQ
ALEXANDRA PAVILION
ROYAL BROOK HO
ELIZABETH SQ
ALBERT TERR
EDWARD SQ

A1
10 STAFFORD RD

B1
1 ISHERWOOD ST
2 STRUTT ST
3 BULLFINCH ST
4 GRAHAM ST
5 DEEPDALE HO

C1
1 ST JOSEPH'S TERR
2 HERMON ST
3 ANSDELL ST
4 POYNTER ST
5 HOLMAN ST
6 GILLETT ST
7 CURWEN ST
8 WIGNALL ST
9 ST LUKE'S PL

C1
10 ALEXANDRA HO

D1
1 ASHELDON ST
2 BRADDON ST
3 BEENLAND ST
4 TUNBRIDGE ST
5 SALISBURY ST
6 CALVERLEY ST
7 TUNBRIDGE PL
8 TRURO PL
9 WELLS ST

D1
10 GRIMSARGH ST
11 CANTERBURY RD
12 LEVENS ST

E1
1 HAWARDEN RD
2 CAVENDISH RD
3 IDDESLEIGH RD
4 MANNING RD

F3
1 AINSCOUGH BROOK HO
2 RIBBLETON HALL CRES

F4
1 LAUDERDALE CRES
2 EDLESTON LODGE
3 LEICESTER LODGE
4 HOLLAND LODGE
5 ROTHWELL LODGE
6 BIRCHALL LODGE
7 ELATON LODGE
8 TRAVERA LODGE
9 SHERBORNE LODGE

117
138

117
97

139
120

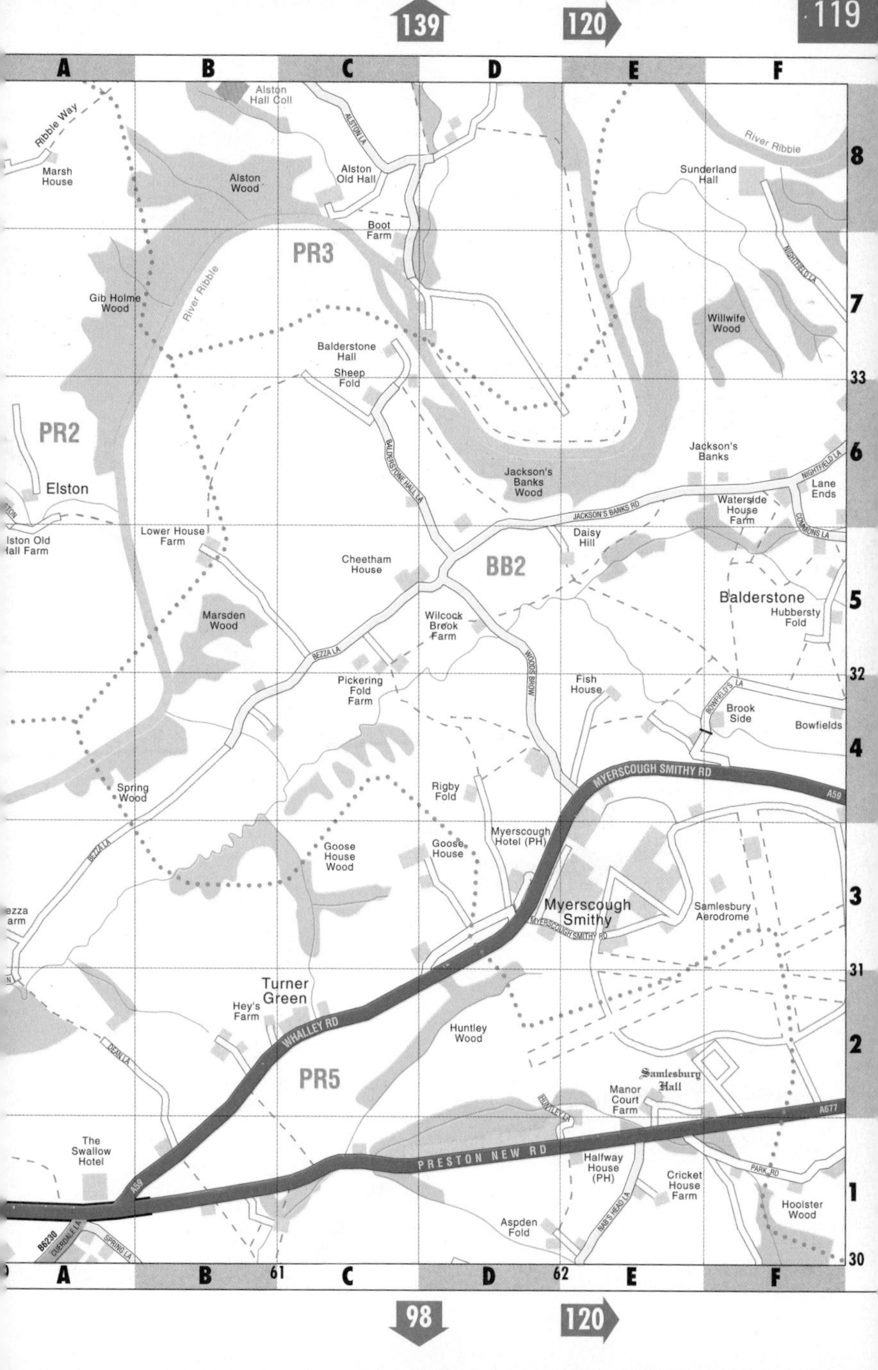

98
120

119
140

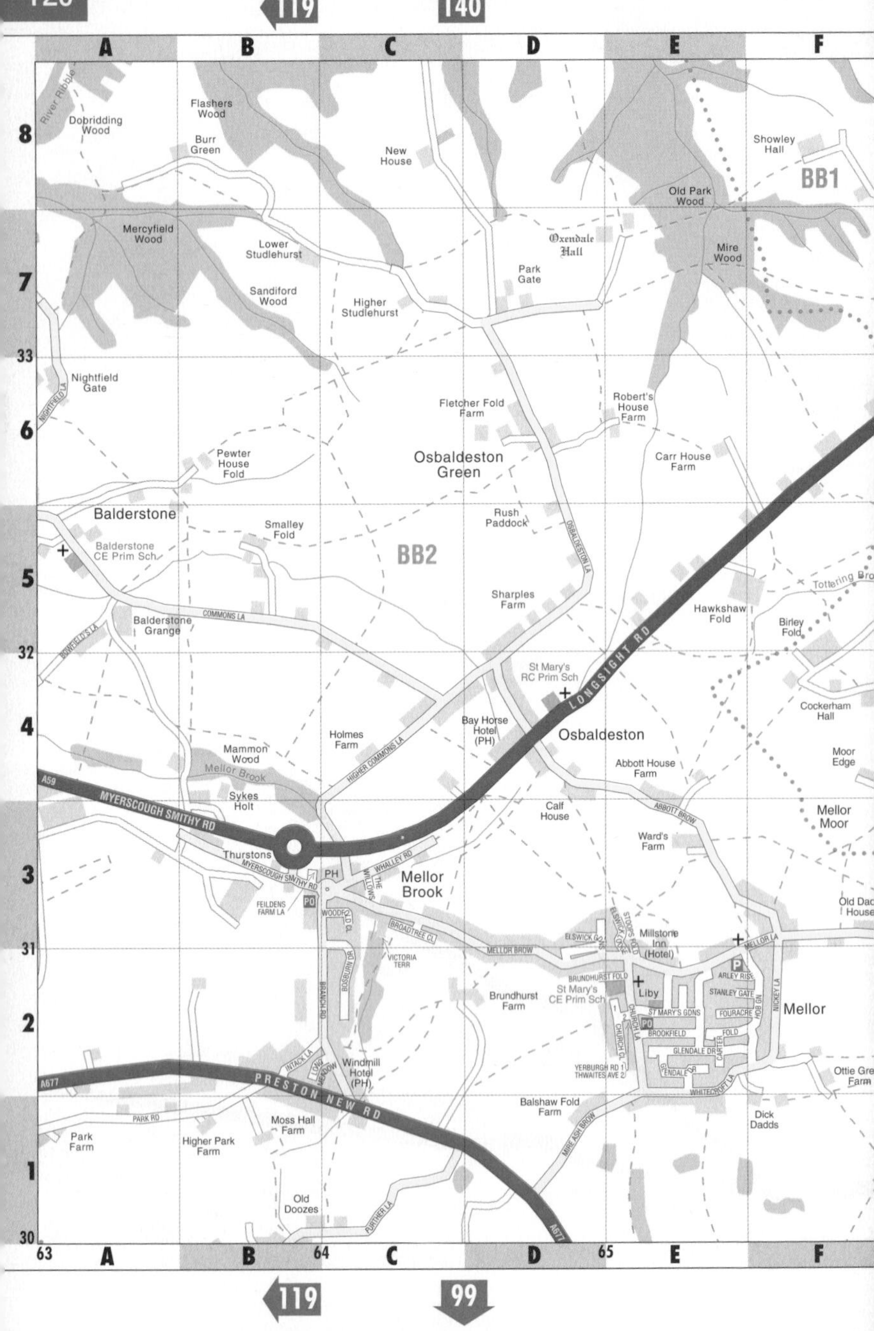

119
99

141
122

100
122

E1
1 BLENHEIM CL
2 OUTRAM LA
3 HAYDOCK ST
4 CHATSWORTH CL
5 THORNWOOD CL
6 PENSHAW CL
7 GOODSHAW CL

121
142

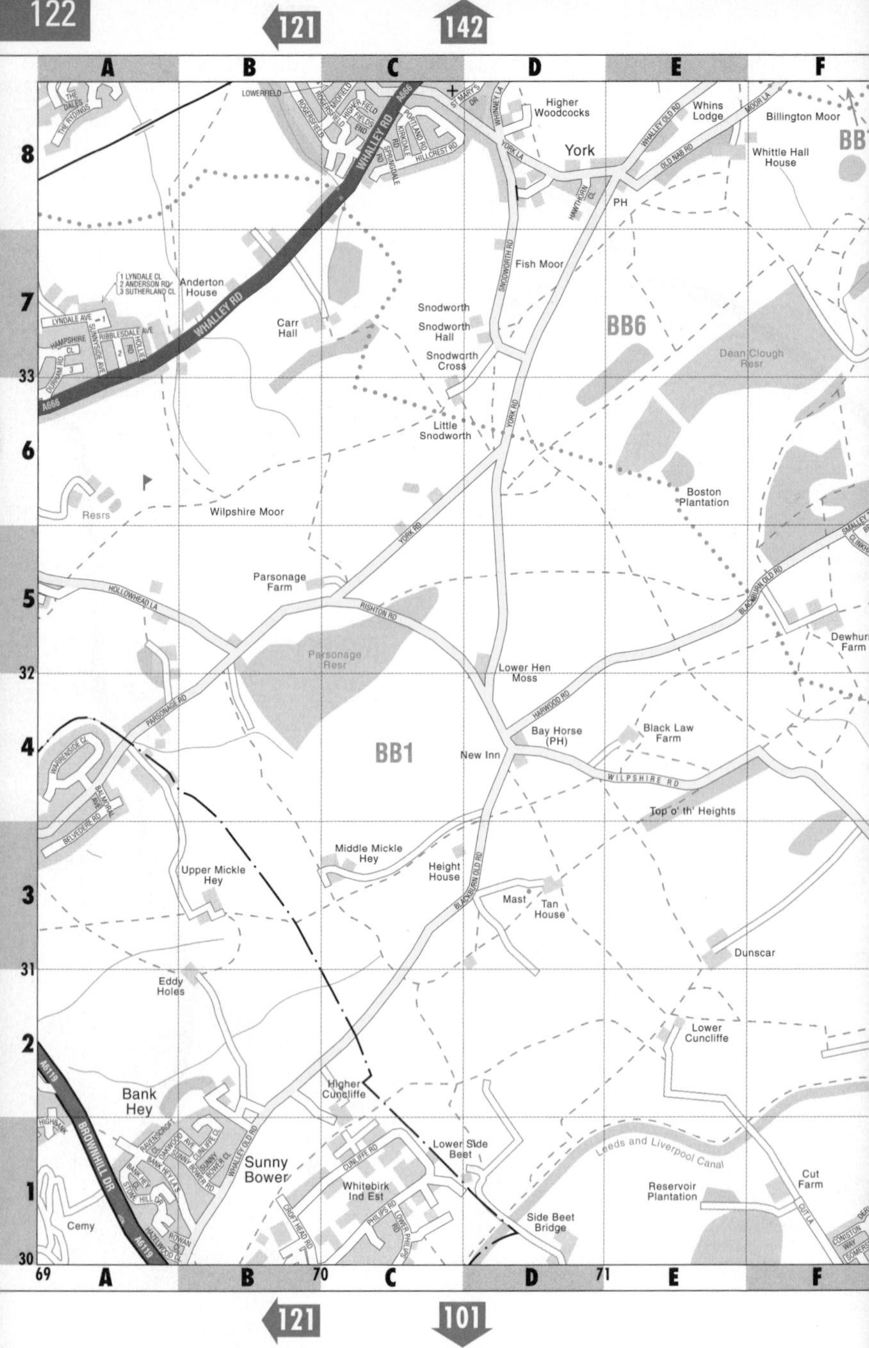

121
101

C5
1 HAYDOCK SQ
2 FRANKLIN AINSWORTH HO
3 DELPH CT
4 SOUTH VIEW
5 BACK CHURCH ST
6 BRIDGE ST
7 EDWARD ST
8 TOWN HALL SQ
9 TOWN HALL ST
10 JOINERS ALLEY
11 LOYND ST
12 COMMERCIAL ST
13 WESTWELL ST
14 KING ST
15 NOWELL ST
16 WALMSLEY ST
17 SEGAR ST

102

124

F2
1 BARNES SQ
2 GRIMSHAW ST
3 TALBOT AVE
4 KING ST

F3
1 STOPFORD CT
2 BRANCH RD
3 FRANCIS ST
4 ANN ST
5 JACKSON ST
6 DRYDEN ST
7 NORFOLK CL
8 GLOUCESTER AVE
9 ALMA ST
10 DANIEL ST
11 FORT ST
12 JAMES ST
13 GEORGE ST
14 NEW CHURCH CL
15 BACK ARTHUR ST
16 MERCER ST

123
144

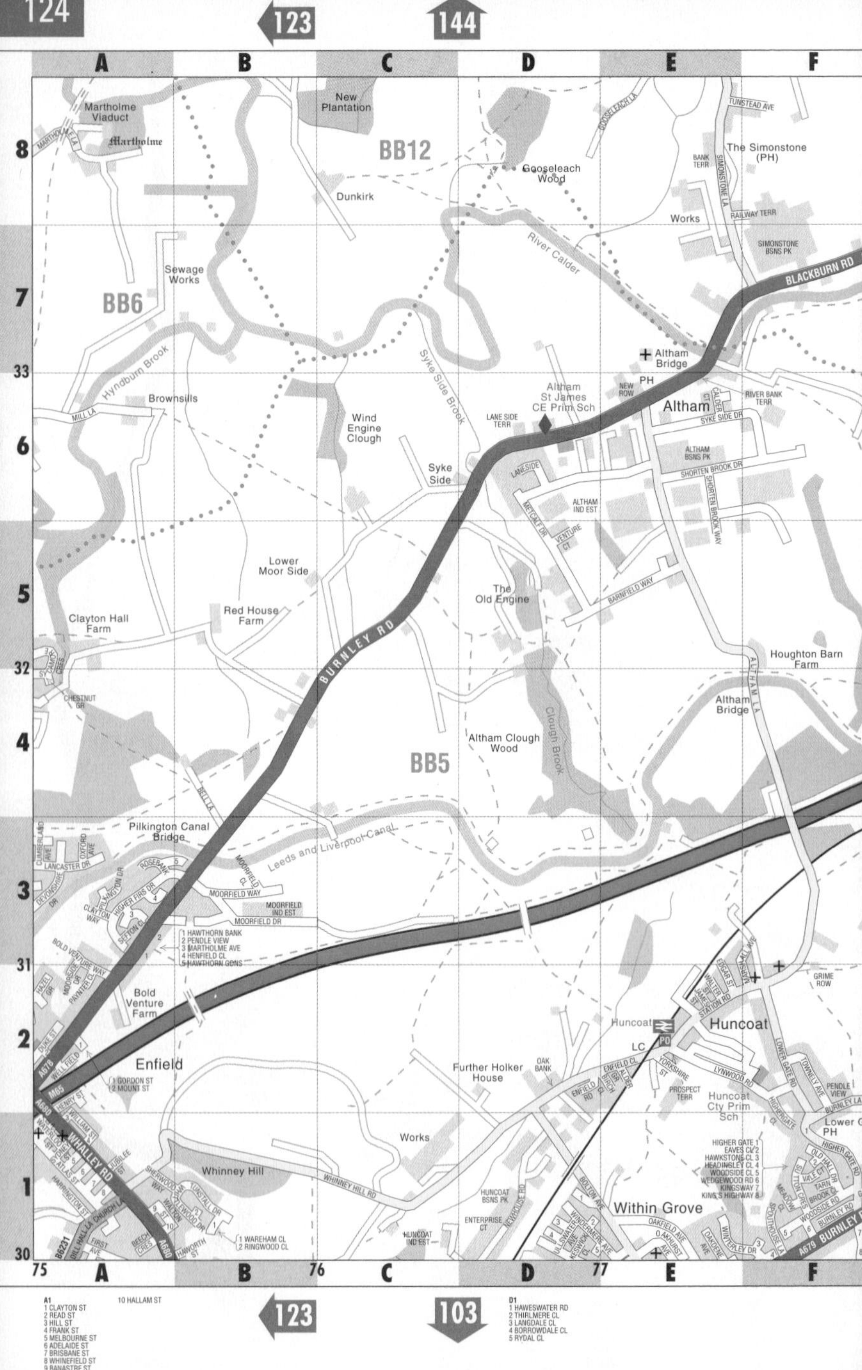

A1
1 CLAYTON ST
2 READ ST
3 HILL ST
4 FRANK ST
5 MELBOURNE ST
6 ADELAIDE ST
7 BRISBANE ST
8 WHINEFIELD ST
9 BANASTRE ST
10 HALLAM ST

D1
1 HAWESWATER RD
2 THIRLMERE CL
3 LANGDALE CL
4 BORROWDALE CL
5 RYDAL CL

123
103

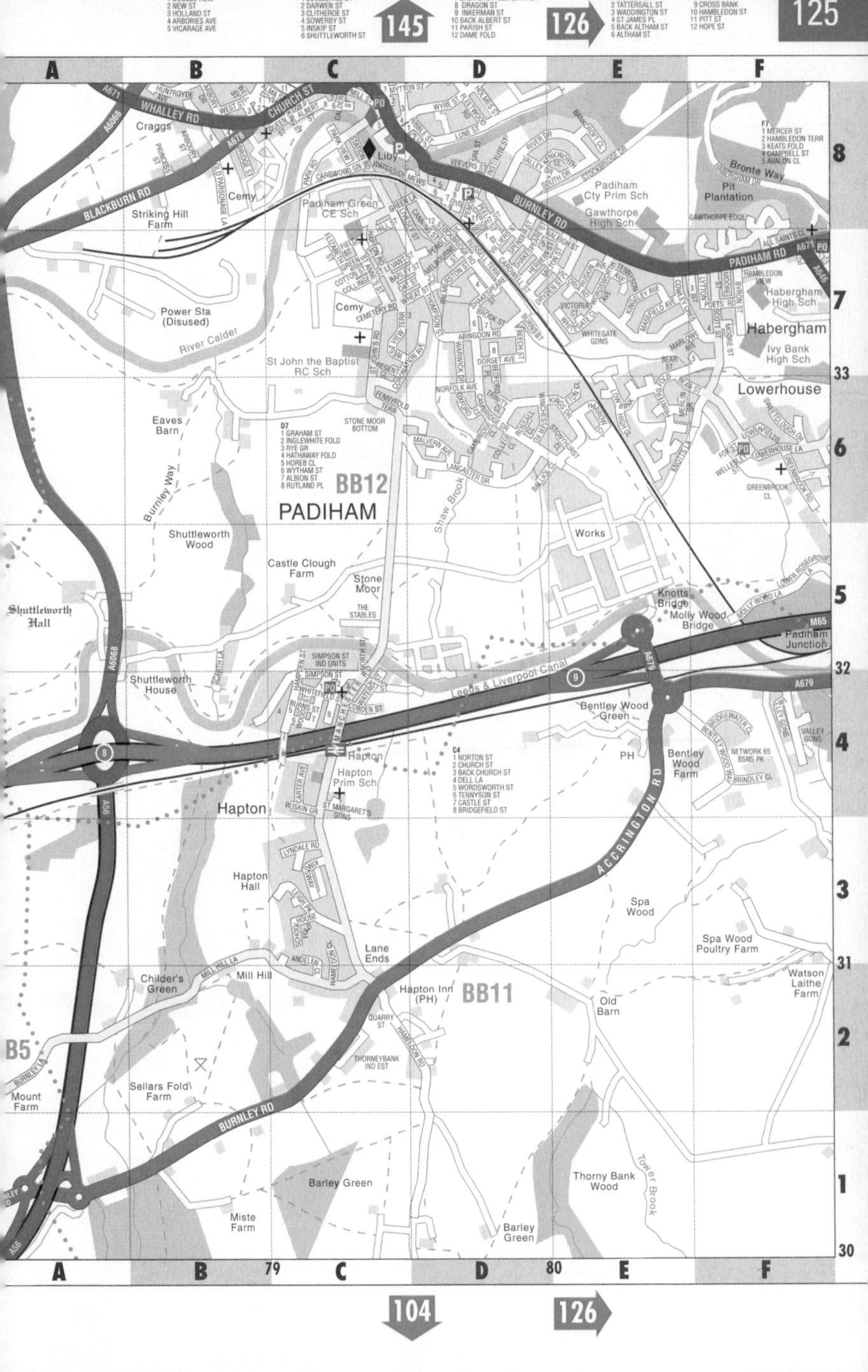
B8
1 DOUBLE ROW
2 NEW ST
3 HOLLAND ST
4 ARBORIES AVE
5 VICARAGE AVE
C8
1 ECCLESHILL ST
2 DARWEN ST
3 CLITHEROE ST
4 SOWERBY ST
5 INSKIP ST
6 SHUTTLEWORTH ST
145
C8
7 BACK SHUTTLEWORTH ST
8 DRAGON ST
9 INKERMAN ST
10 BACK ALBERT ST
11 PARISH ST
12 DAME FOLD
126
D8
1 MORLEY ST
2 TATTERSALL ST
3 WADDINGTON ST
4 ST JAMES PL
5 BACK ALTHAM ST
6 ALTHAM ST
7 HAPTON ST
8 WESLEY ST
9 CROSS BANK
10 HAMBLEDON ST
11 PITT ST
12 HOPE ST
A
B
C
D
E
F
WHALLEY RD
CHURCH ST
BLACKBURN RD
Craggs
Cemy
Striking Hill Farm
Liby
Padiham Green CE Sch
Padiham Cty Prim Sch
Gawthorpe High Sch
BURNLEY RD
PADIHAM RD
Bronte Way
Pit Plantation
F7
1 MERCER ST
2 HAMBLEDON TERR
3 KEATS FOLD
4 CAMPBELL ST
5 AVALON CL
Habergham High Sch
Habergham
Ivy Bank High Sch
Lowerhouse
Power Sta (Disused)
River Calder
St John the Baptist RC Sch
Eaves Barn
D7
1 GRAHAM ST
2 INGLEWHITE FOLD
3 RYE GR
4 HATHAWAY FOLD
5 HOREB CL
6 WYTHAM ST
7 ALBION ST
8 RUTLAND PL
BB12
PADIHAM
Burnley Way
Shuttleworth Wood
Castle Clough Farm
Stone Moor
Works
Shuttleworth Hall
Knotts Bridge
Molly Wood Bridge
M65
Padiham Junction
Shuttleworth House
Leeds & Liverpool Canal
Bentley Wood Green
Bentley Wood Farm
NETWORK 65 BSNS PK
Hapton
Hapton Prim Sch
C4
1 NORTON ST
2 CHURCH ST
3 BACK CHURCH ST
4 DELL LA
5 WORDSWORTH ST
6 TENNYSON ST
7 CASTLE ST
8 BRIDGEFIELD ST
ACCRINGTON RD
Hapton Hall
Spa Wood
Spa Wood Poultry Farm
Lane Ends
Childer's Green
Mill Hill
Hapton Inn (PH)
BB11
Old Barn
Watson Laithe Farm
B5
Sellars Fold Farm
Mount Farm
BURNLEY RD
THORNEYBANK IND EST
Thorny Bank Wood
Tower Brook
Barley Green
Miste Farm
A
B
79
C
D
80
E
F
104
126

C6
1 IVORY ST
2 FRANKLIN ST
3 AINSLIE ST
4 WHITE BULL ST
5 ST JOHN'S RD
6 ST JOHN'S CT
7 COULTATE ST
8 CONISTON ST
C7
1 IGHTENHILL PK MEWS
2 ROMFORD ST
3 QUARRY BANK ST
4 LARK ST
125
D6
1 BROUGHTON ST
2 PLOVER VIEW
3 PADIHAM RD
4 BREAD ST
5 MONMOUTH ST
6 PENISTONE ST
146
D6
7 HORACE ST
8 ADELAIDE ST
9 BERESFORD ST
E6
1 WAVERLEY ST
2 SOUTHEY ST
3 DUCKETT ST
4 BURNHAM TRAD PK
5 CRANMER ST
6 TRINITY TWRS
7 WILFIELD ST
8 BELLE VUE PL
9 HOPWOOD ST
F6
1 SYDNEY ST
2 WESTGATE TRAD CTR
3 FOUNDRY ST
4 ROYLE RD
5 BLACKBURN ST
6 ORCHARD BRIDGE
7 VEEVERS ST
8 GAS ST
9 BRICK ST
10 CURZON ST
11 PARADISE ST
12 COAL ST
13 ST JAMES'S ROW
14 HARGREAV
15 TANNER ST
16 FREE TRADE
17 MEADOW S
18 SUTCLIFFE
19 CANAL ST
A B C D E F
8 7 33 6 5 32 4 3 31 2 1 30
81 82 83
Crow Wood House Farm
Burnley Way
Bullions Close Farm
Wellfield Farm
Park Hill Convent Prep Sch
Lodge Plantation
Bronte Way
D7
1 EDGELEY CT
2 HUNTROYDE CL
3 WHEATLEY CL
4 COVERDALE WAY
5 WESLEY GR
6 GREENGATE CL
Stoneyholme
BB12
PADIHAM RD
KIDDROW LA
PRINCESS WAY
Whittlefield
Habergham High Sch
St Augustine's RC Prim Sch
Lowerhouse Cty Jun Sch
Holyoake Farm
LIVERPOOL RD
Leeds & Liverpool Canal
Mills
Rose Grove
1 SNOWDEN ST
2 WHITE ST
3 OLD SCHOOL ROW
4 THE GROVE
5 ALLENDALE ST
Burnley Barracks
WESTWAY
WESTGATE
TRAFALGAR ST
CAVALRY WAY
ACCRINGTON RD
1 STANSFIELD ST
2 STOCKHOLM ST
M65
Works
Crem
Old Holme Farm
Cemy
Playing Fields
St Hilda's RC Girls' Sch
Scott Park
LANDSDOWNE RD 1
CLEVELANDS MT 2
CLEVELANDS GR 3
MANCHESTER RD
ROSSENDALE RD
Ind Est
TRANS BRITTANIA ENTERPRISE CTR
BB11
Habergham Clough
Habergham Hall Farm
Rosehill Inf Sch
Rosehill Jun Sch
Rose H
GLEN VIEW RD
NEW RD
Iron House
New Barn
New Barn Clough
Further Barn
Long Syke
Broadhead Moor Farm
Hollin Cross Farm
Lower Gibfield
Lower Micklehurst
CROWN POINT RD
A682
125
C5
1 HOMER ST
2 HARTLEY ST
3 WOODPECKER HILL
4 PARTRIDGE WLK
5 GOLDFINCH GN
6 NIGHTINGALE CRES
7 SANDPIPER SQ
8 SWALLOW PL
105
D5
1 HARCOURT ST
2 CAMBRIDGE ST
3 GROVE ST
4 PALM ST
E5
1 ELLIS ST
2 PICCADILLY SQ
3 SEFTON TERR
4 SEFTON AVE
5 AUSTIN ST
6 WILLIS ST
7 WHITEHAVEN ST
8 ALWIN ST
9 ST MATTHEW'S CT
10 ABBEYFIELD HO
11 PRINCE ST
F5
1 VICTORIA ST
2 YORKES ST
3 MOUNT PLEASANT ST
4 PLEASANT PL
5 ST PAUL'S CT
6 STANLEY ST
7 THORNEY BANK ST
8 DENT ROW
9 ESCAR ST
10 SACKVILL

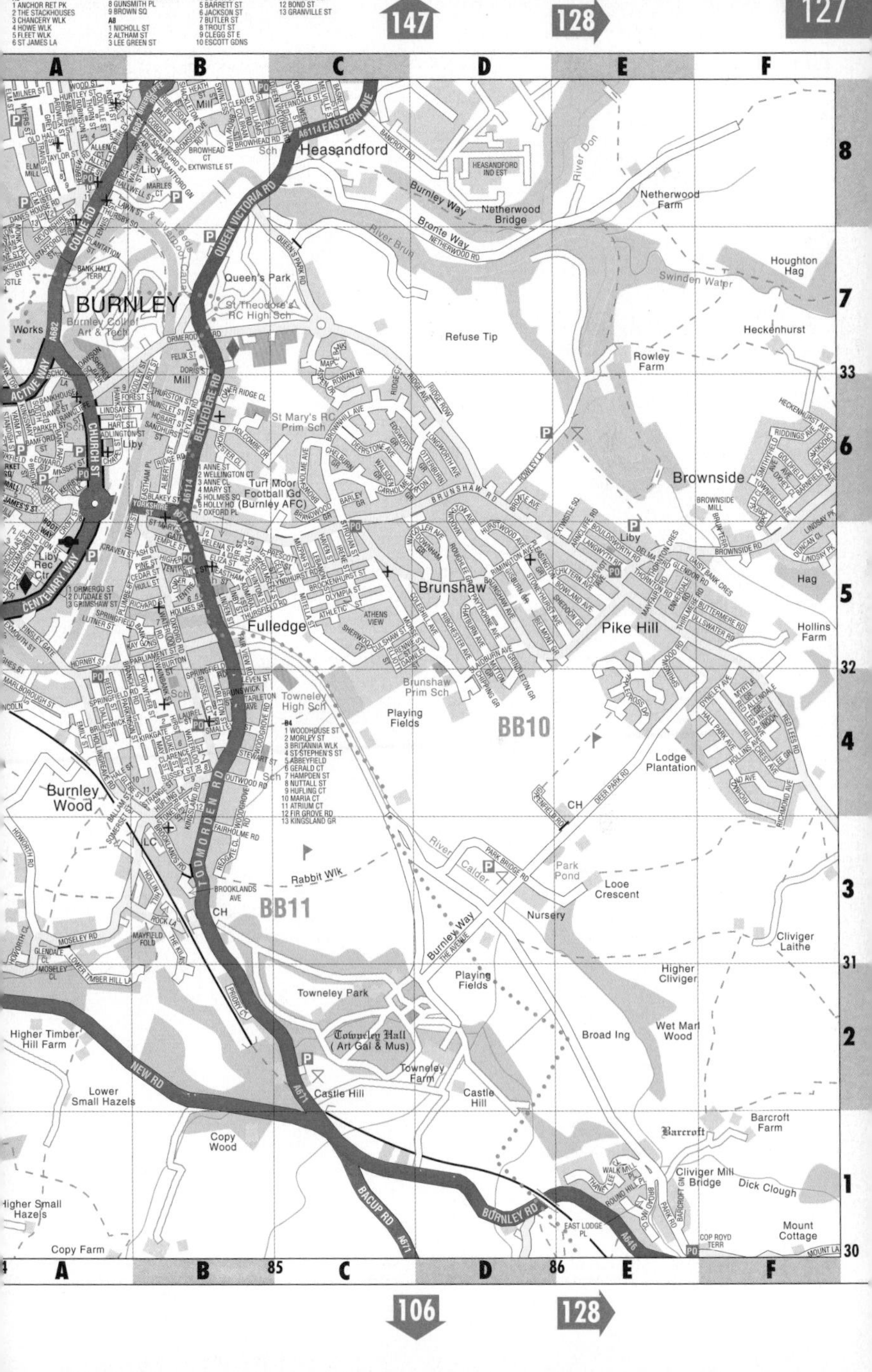

A6
1 ANCHOR RET PK
2 THE STACKHOUSES
3 CHANCERY WLK
4 HOWE WLK
5 FLEET WLK
6 ST JAMES LA
7 BURNLEY BSNS CTR
8 GUNSMITH PL
9 BROWN SQ
A8
1 NICHOLL ST
2 ALTHAM ST
3 LEE GREEN ST
4 BOOTH CT
5 BARRETT ST
6 JACKSON ST
7 BUTLER ST
8 TROUT ST
9 CLEGG ST E
10 ESCOTT GDNS
11 HEBREW SQ
12 BOND ST
13 GRANVILLE ST
147
128
BURNLEY
Heasandford
Netherwood Farm
Netherwood Bridge
Houghton Hag
Swinden Water
Queen's Park
Refuse Tip
Heckenhurst
Rowley Farm
Brownside
Brunshaw
Pike Hill
Fulledge
Turf Moor Football Gd (Burnley AFC)
Hollins Farm
Hag
Towneley High Sch
Playing Fields
BB10
Lodge Plantation
B4
1 WOODHOUSE ST
2 MORLEY ST
3 BRITANIA WLK
4 ST STEPHEN'S ST
5 ABBEYFIELD
6 GERALD CT
7 HAMPDEN ST
8 NUTTALL ST
9 HUFLING CT
10 MARIA CT
11 ATRIUM CT
12 FIR GROVE RD
13 KINGSLAND GR
Burnley Wood
Rabbit Wlk
BB11
Park Pond
Looe Crescent
Nursery
Cliviger Laithe
Towneley Park
Higher Cliviger
Higher Timber Hill Farm
Towneley Hall (Art Gal & Mus)
Broad Ing
Wet Marl Wood
Towneley Farm
Lower Small Hazels
Castle Hill
Barcroft Farm
Copy Wood
Cliviger Mill Bridge
Dick Clough
Higher Small Hazels
Mount Cottage
Copy Farm
106
128

127
148

127
107

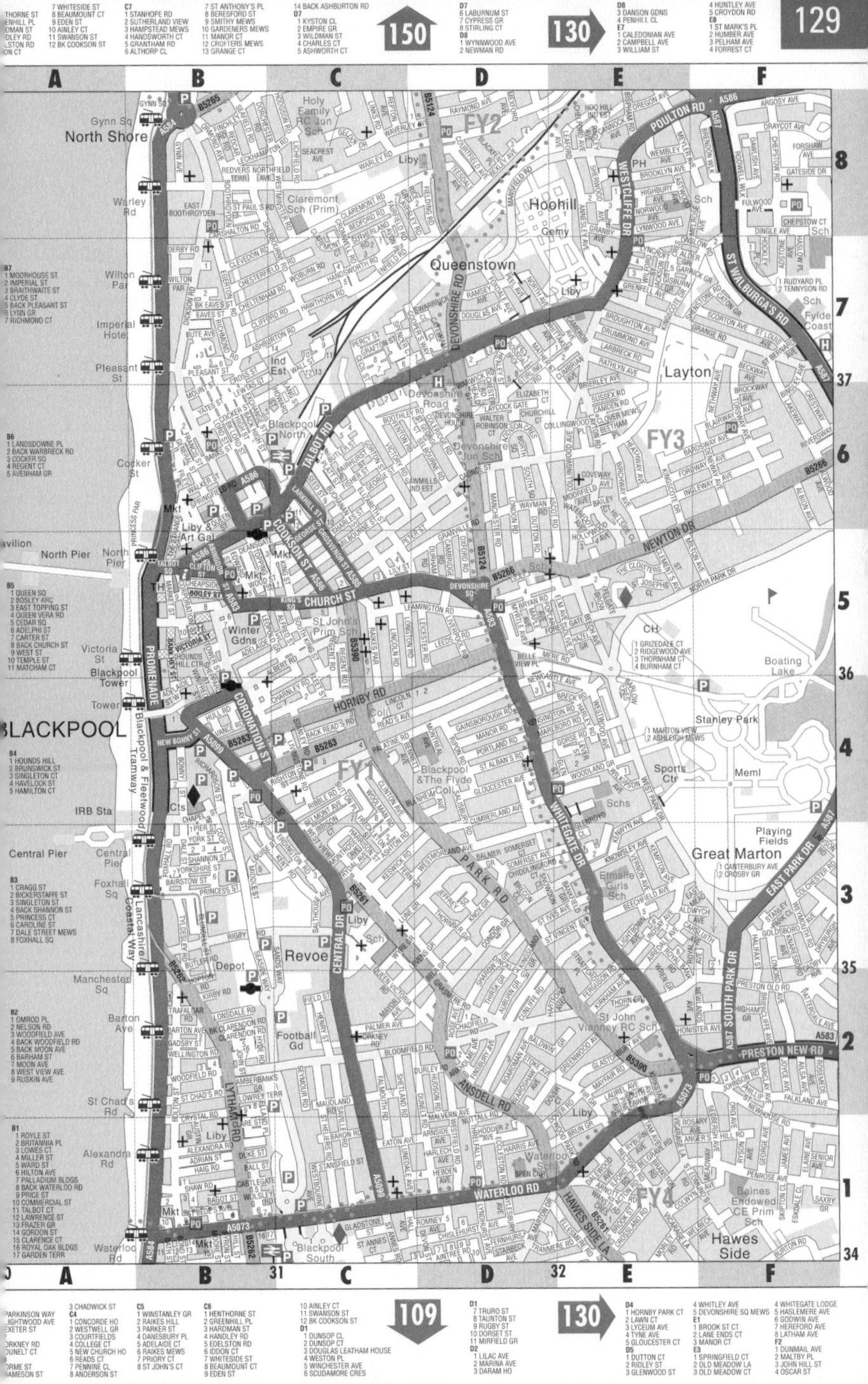
C7
1 STANHOPE RD
2 SUTHERLAND VIEW
3 HAMPSTEAD MEWS
4 HANDSWORTH CT
5 GRANTHAM RD
6 ALTHORP CL
7 WHITESIDE ST
8 BEAUMOUNT CT
9 EDEN ST
10 AINLEY CT
11 SWANSON ST
12 BK COOKSON ST
7 ST ANTHONY'S PL
8 BERESFORD ST
9 SMITHY MEWS
10 GARDENERS MEWS
11 MANOR CT
12 CROFTERS MEWS
13 GRANGE CT
14 BACK ASHBURTON RD
D7
1 KYSTON CL
2 EMPIRE GR
3 WILDMAN ST
4 CHARLES CT
5 ASHWORTH CT
150
130
D7
6 LABURNUM ST
7 CYPRESS GR
8 STIRLING CT
D8
1 WYNNWOOD AVE
2 NEWMAN RD
D8
3 DANSON GDNS
4 PENHILL CL
E7
1 CALEDONIAN AVE
2 CAMPBELL AVE
3 WILLIAM ST
4 HUNTLEY AVE
5 CROYDON RD
E8
1 ST MARK'S PL
2 HUMBER AVE
3 PELHAM AVE
4 FORREST CT
A
B
C
D
E
F
Gynn Sq
North Shore
Warley Rd
Wilton Par
Imperial Hotel
Pleasant St
Cocker St
North Pier
North Pier
Victoria St
Blackpool Tower
Tower
BLACKPOOL
IRB Sta
Central Pier
Central Pier
Foxhall Sq
Manchester Sq
Barton Ave
St Chad's Rd
Alexandra Rd
Waterloo Rd
PROMENADE
Blackpool & Fleetwood Tramway
Lancashire Coastal Way
FY2
FY1
FY3
FY4
Holy Family RC Jun Sch
Claremont Sch (Prim)
Hoohill
Cemy
Queenstown
Layton
Devonshire Road
Devonshire Jun Sch
Blackpool North
Winter Gdns
Liby & Art Gal
Mkt
Ind Est
St John's Prim Sch
Blackpool & The Flyde Coll
Revoe
Depot
Football Gd
Stanley Park
Sports Ctr
Meml
Boating Lake
Playing Fields
Great Marton
Elmslie Girls Sch
St John Vianney RC Sch
Waterloo Sch
Baines Endowed CE Prim Sch
Hawes Side
Blackpool South
DEVONSHIRE RD
WESTCLIFFE DR
POULTON RD
ST WALBURGA'S RD
TALBOT RD
CHURCH ST
NEWTON DR
HORNBY RD
CORONATION ST
CENTRAL DR
PARK RD
WHITEGATE DR
EAST PARK DR
SOUTH PARK DR
PRESTON NEW RD
WATERLOO RD
ANSDELL RD
LYTHAM RD
HAWES SIDE LA
B7
1 MOORHOUSE ST
2 IMPERIAL ST
3 BRAITHWAITE ST
4 CLYDE ST
5 BACK PLEASANT ST
6 LYNN GR
7 RICHMOND CT
B6
1 LANDSDOWNE PL
2 BACK WARBRECK RD
3 COCKER SQ
4 REGENT CT
5 AVENHAM GR
B5
1 QUEEN SQ
2 BOSLEY ARC
3 EAST TOPPING ST
4 QUEEN VERA RD
5 CEDAR SQ
6 ADELPHI ST
7 CARTER ST
8 BACK CHURCH ST
9 WEST ST
10 TEMPLE ST
11 MATCHAM CT
B4
1 HOUNDS HILL
2 BRUNSWICK ST
3 SINGLETON CT
4 HAVELOCK ST
5 HAMILTON CT
B3
1 CRAGG ST
2 BICKERSTAFFE ST
3 SINGLETON ST
4 BACK SHANNON ST
5 PRINCESS CT
6 CAROLINE ST
7 DALE STREET MEWS
8 FOXHALL SQ
B2
1 OMROD PL
2 NELSON RD
3 WOODFIELD AVE
4 BACK WOODFIELD RD
5 BACK MOON AVE
6 BARHAM ST
7 MOON AVE
8 WEST VIEW AVE
9 RUSKIN AVE
B1
1 ROYLE ST
2 BRITANNIA PL
3 LOWES CT
4 MILLER ST
5 WARD ST
6 HILTON AVE
7 PALLADIUM BLDGS
8 BACK WATERLOO RD
9 PRICE ST
10 COMMERCIAL ST
11 TALBOT CT
12 LAWRENCE ST
13 FRAZER GR
14 GORDON ST
15 CLARENCE CT
16 ROYAL OAK BLDGS
17 GARDEN TERR
1 RUDYARD PL
2 TENNYSON RD
1 GRIZEDALE CT
2 RIDGEWOOD AVE
3 THORNHAM CT
4 BURNHAM CT
1 MARTON VIEW
2 ASHLEIGH MEWS
1 CANTERBURY AVE
2 CROSBY GR
8
7
37
6
5
36
4
3
35
2
1
34
31
32
3 CHADWICK ST
C4
1 CONCORDE HO
2 WESTWELL GR
3 COURTFIELDS
4 COLLEGE CT
5 NEW CHURCH HO
6 READS CT
7 PENNINE CL
8 ANDERSON ST
C5
1 WINSTANLEY GR
2 RAIKES HILL
3 PARKER ST
4 DANESBURY PL
5 ADELAIDE CT
6 RAIKES MEWS
7 PRIORY CT
8 ST JOHN'S CT
C6
1 HENTHORNE ST
2 GREENHILL PL
3 HARDMAN ST
4 HANDLEY RD
5 EDELSTON RD
6 IDDON CT
7 WHITESIDE ST
8 BEAUMOUNT CT
9 EDEN ST
10 AINLEY CT
11 SWANSON ST
12 BK COOKSON ST
D1
1 DUNSOP CL
2 DUNSOP CT
3 DOUGLAS LEATHAM HOUSE
4 WESTON PL
5 WINCHESTER AVE
6 SCUDAMORE CRES
109
D1
7 TRURO ST
8 TAUNTON ST
9 RUGBY ST
10 DORSET ST
11 MIRFIELD GR
D2
1 LILAC AVE
2 MARINA AVE
3 DARAM HO
130
D4
1 HORNBY PARK CT
2 LAWN CT
3 LYCEUM AVE
4 TYNE AVE
5 GLOUCESTER CT
D5
1 DUTTON CT
2 RIDLEY ST
3 GLENWOOD ST
4 WHITLEY AVE
5 DEVONSHIRE SQ MEWS
E1
1 BROOK ST CT
2 LANE ENDS CT
3 MANOR CT
E3
1 SPRINGFIELD CT
2 OLD MEADOW LA
3 OLD MEADOW CT
4 WHITEGATE LODGE
5 HASLEMERE AVE
6 GODWIN AVE
7 HEREFORD AVE
8 LATHAM AVE
F2
1 DUNMAIL AVE
2 MALTBY PL
3 JOHN HILL ST
4 OSCAR ST

A8
1 ARGOSY CT
2 GATESIDE CT
3 FURNESS CT
4 CHIPPING CT
5 SLAIDBURN WLK

129
151

C1
1 LANGDALE PL
2 CRUMMOCK PL

129
110

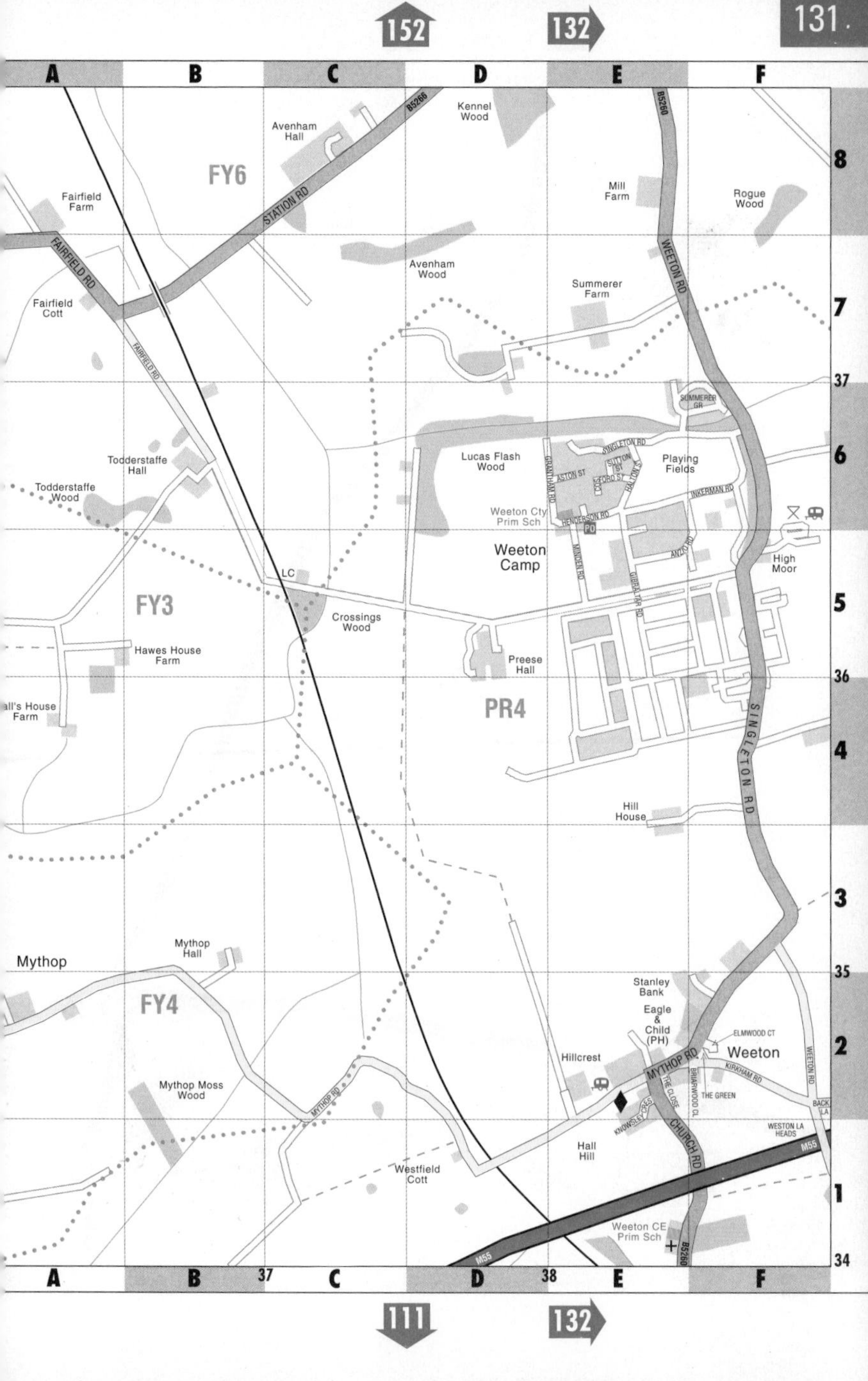
A
B
C
D
E
F
8
7
37
6
5
36
4
3
35
2
1
34
Avenham Hall
Kennel Wood
FY6
B5266
STATION RD
B5260
Fairfield Farm
Mill Farm
Rogue Wood
FAIRFIELD RD
WEETON RD
Avenham Wood
Summerer Farm
Fairfield Cott
FAIRFIELD RD
SUMMERER GR
SINGLETON RD
Lucas Flash Wood
GRANTHAM RD
ASTON ST
SUTTON ST
FORD ST
HALTON ST
Playing Fields
Todderstaffe Hall
Todderstaffe Wood
INKERMAN RD
Weeton Cty Prim Sch
HENDERSON RD
PO
Weeton Camp
MINDEN RD
ANZIO RD
High Moor
LC
GIBRALTAR RD
FY3
Crossings Wood
Hawes House Farm
Preese Hall
all's House Farm
PR4
SINGLETON RD
Hill House
Mythop Hall
Mythop
Stanley Bank
FY4
Eagle & Child (PH)
ELMWOOD CT
Weeton
Hillcrest
MYTHOP RD
THE CLOSE
BRIARWOOD CL
KIRKHAM RD
WEETON RD
THE GREEN
Mythop Moss Wood
MYTHOP RD
KNOWSLEY CRES
BACK LA
WESTON LA HEADS
CHURCH RD
Hall Hill
M55
Westfield Cott
Weeton CE Prim Sch
M55
B5260
37
38

131
153

131
112

A
B
C
D
E
F
Carr Wood
8
Elswick Leys
SASWICK CT
Nigget Wood
7
Stanley Farm
37
ROSEACRE RD
Roseacre Hall
6
Roseacre
Roseacre Wood
PR4
5
Boundary Farm
Carr Wood
North Greenhills
New Hall
36
HAMLET GROVE
Holmes Wood
HOGARTH CRES
INSKIP RD
LILAC CRES
LADIES ROW
4
South Greenhills
Scholar Brook
Wharles
ROSEACRE RD
Eagle and Child (PH)
White Carr Farm
3
Ferdy's Wood
Medlar Woods
MOORSIDE
35
WHITE CARR LA
CHURCH RD
2
Ivy Dene Farm
M55
Pasture Barn
Boggart Pits
Treales CE Prim Sch
West View Farm
Carrot Wood
Moor Side
Cross Hill Farm
1
CROSS LA
BLUE MOOR
JACOB'S LA
34
A
B
43
C
D
44
E
F

133 155

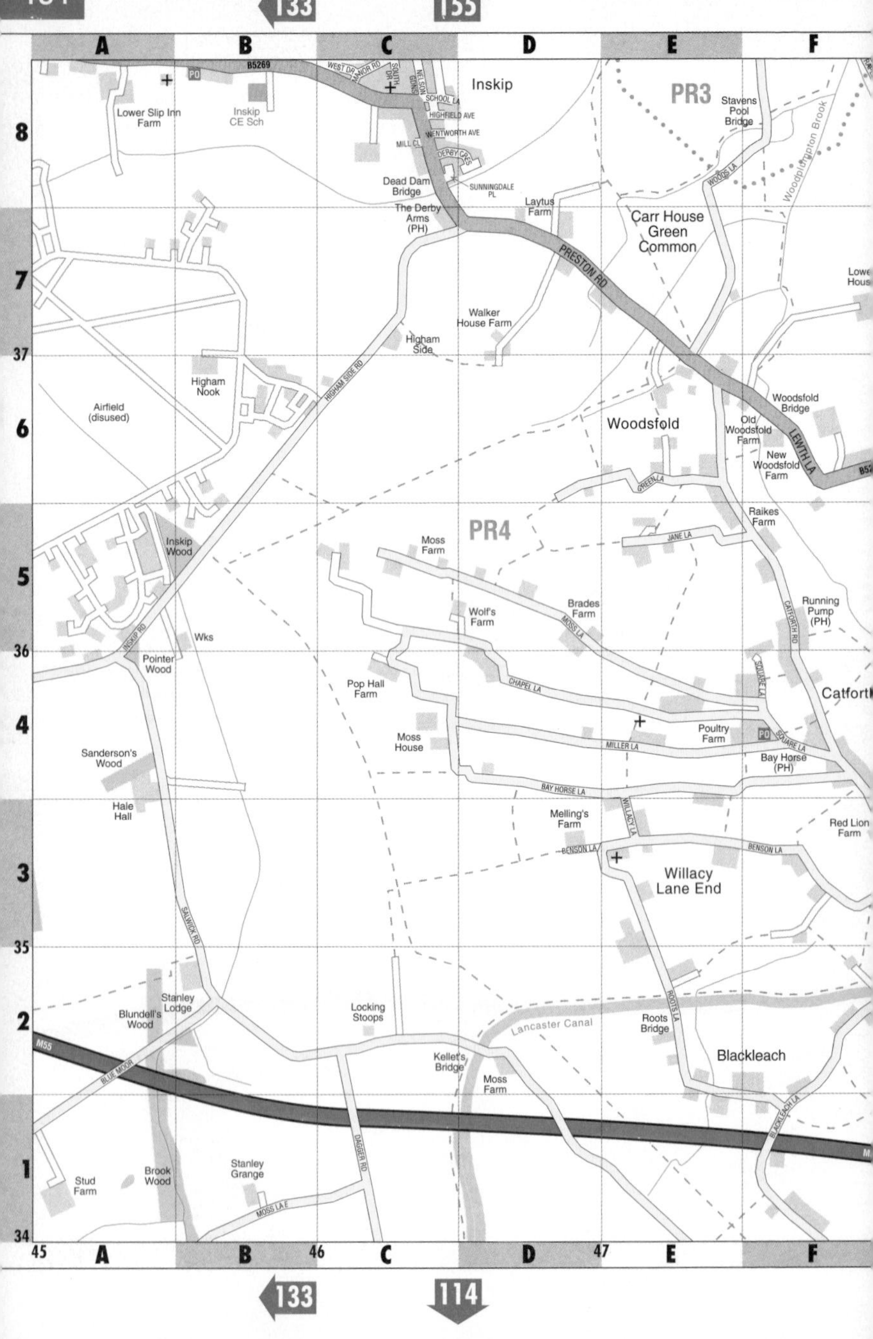

133 114

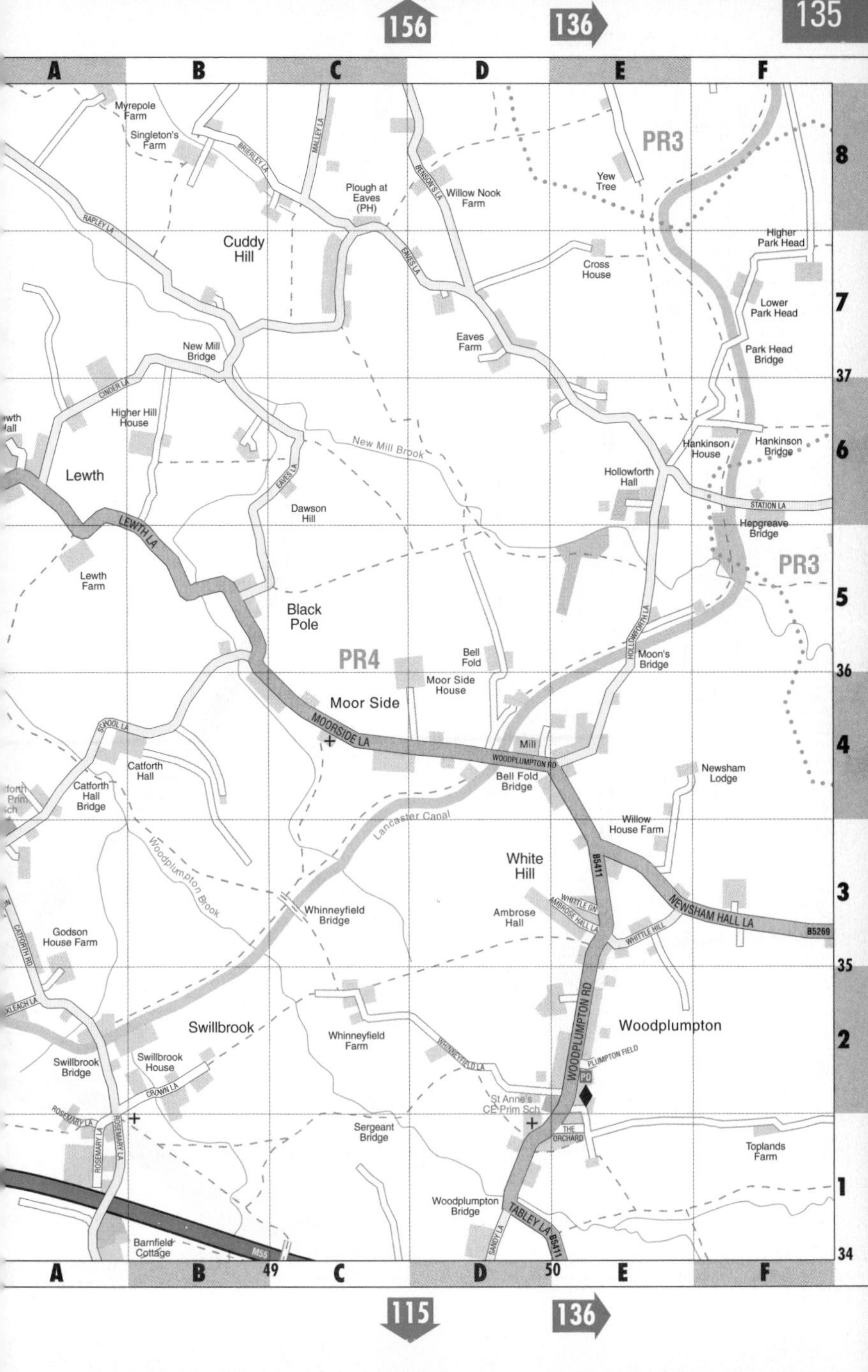
A
B
C
D
E
F
Myrepole Farm
Singleton's Farm
BRIERLEY LA
MALLEY LA
BENSON'S LA
PR3
Yew Tree
Plough at Eaves (PH)
Willow Nook Farm
RAPLEY LA
Cuddy Hill
EAVES LA
Higher Park Head
Cross House
Lower Park Head
Eaves Farm
New Mill Bridge
Park Head Bridge
CINDER LA
Higher Hill House
New Mill Brook
Hankinson House
Hankinson Bridge
Lewth
EAVES LA
Hollowforth Hall
STATION LA
Dawson Hill
LEWTH LA
Hepgreave Bridge
PR3
Lewth Farm
Black Pole
HOLLOWFORTH LA
PR4
Bell Fold
Moon's Bridge
Moor Side House
Moor Side
SCHOOL LA
MOORSIDE LA
Mill
WOODPLUMPTON RD
Catforth Hall
Bell Fold Bridge
Newsham Lodge
Catforth Hall Bridge
Lancaster Canal
Willow House Farm
Woodplumpton Brook
White Hill
B5411
NEWSHAM HALL LA
Whinneyfield Bridge
Ambrose Hall
WHITTLE GN
AMBROSE HALL LA
WHITTLE HILL
B5269
Godson House Farm
CATFORTH RD
WOODPLUMPTON RD
Woodplumpton
Swillbrook
Whinneyfield Farm
PLUMPTON FIELD
Swillbrook Bridge
Swillbrook House
WHINNEYFIELD LA
CROWN LA
PO
St Anne's CE Prim Sch
ROSEMARY LA
ROSEMARY LA
Sergeant Bridge
THE ORCHARD
Toplands Farm
Woodplumpton Bridge
TABLEY LA
SANDY LA
B5411
Barnfield Cottage
M55
8
7
37
6
5
36
4
3
35
2
1
34
49
50

135
157

135
116

158
138
A
B
C
D
E
F
Westfield Brook
Westfield Wood
Rigby Wood
Cross House
Middleton Hall
Eaves Green Hall
Eaves Green
EAVES GREEN LA
8
Little Westfield
MILL LA
7
Field Foot Farm
GOOSNARGH LA
37
Oliverson's CE Prim Sch
Bushell's
MILL LA
OAKLEAF C
WILLOW GR
NOOK FIELD
GREEN ACRE
NORTHGATE
CHURCHGATE
PARKGATE
HIGHGATE
BEACON DR
CHURCH LA
THE CROFT
Bushell's Arms (PH)
CAMFORTH HALL LA
6
Goosnargh
GRINDLESTONE CT
Cumeragh Village
BLEASDALE RD
THE SQUARE
CUMERAGH LA
B5269
PR3
Meadowcroft
Mast
WHITTINGHAM LA
Stags Head (PH)
Cemetery
5
Parkinson's House
Whittingham Hall
Whittingham House
Guild Park
Dean House
36
NOELS VILLA
New Field
Chingle Hall
4
Cowell's Farm
Pudding Pie Nook
Works
3
Blundle Brook
Cockshoot Wood
35
Haighton Manor
New Chingle Hall
Haighton Green
32
PR2
2
HAIGHTON GREEN LA
Boyse's Farm
M55
Sea Mark
D'URTON LA
1
Savick Brook
Haighton Top
FERNYHALGH LA
MIDGERY LA
M6
34
A
B
55
C
D
56
E
F
117
138

137
159

137
118

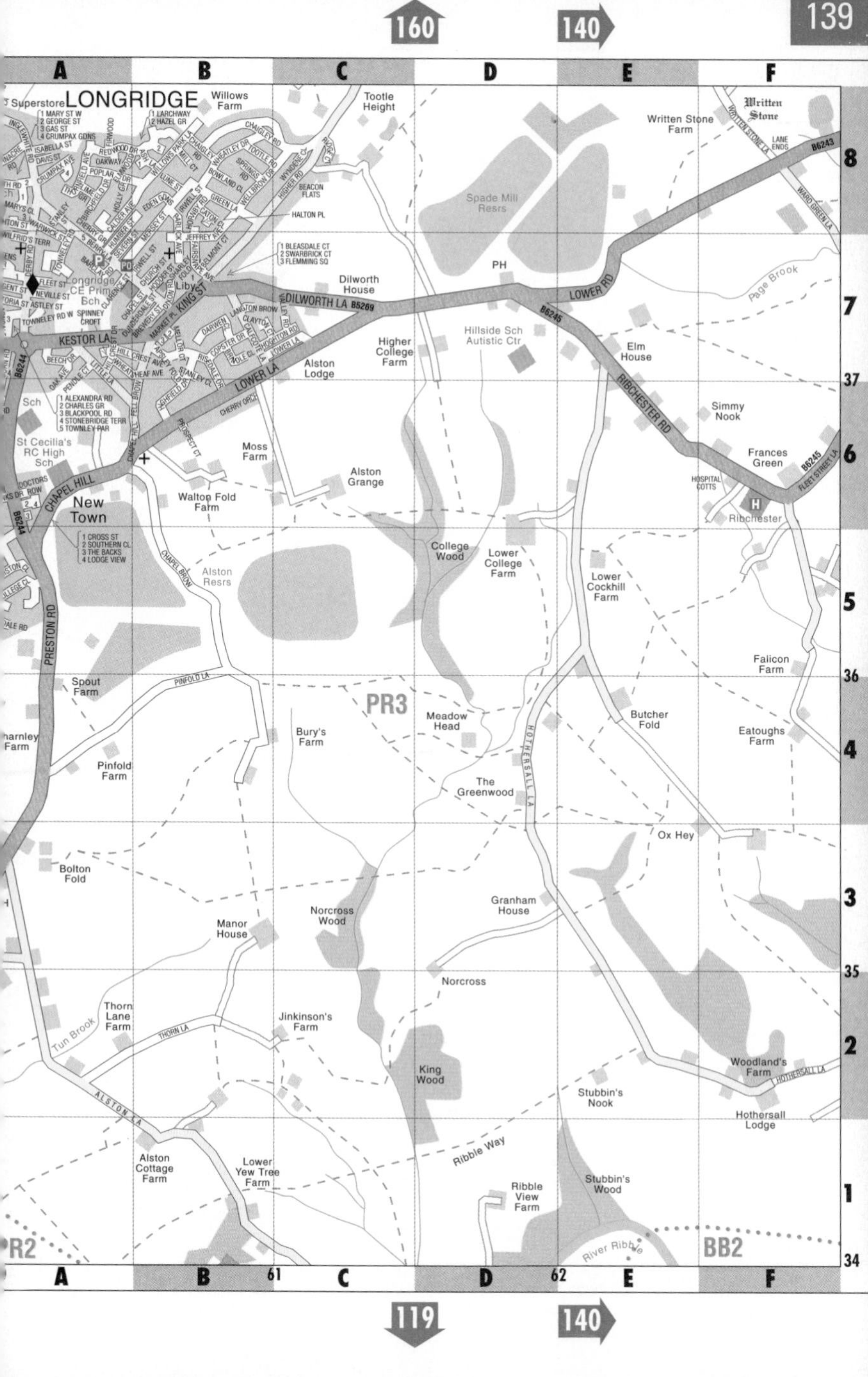
A B C D E F
LONGRIDGE
Superstore
Willows Farm
Tootle Height
Written Stone
Written Stone Farm
Spade Mill Resrs
PH
Dilworth House
DILWORTH LA B5269
LOWER RD
B6245
B6243
KING ST
KESTOR LA
LOWER LA
Higher College Farm
Hillside Sch Autistic Ctr
Alston Lodge
Elm House
RIBCHESTER RD
Simmy Nook
Frances Green
Moss Farm
Alston Grange
CHAPEL HILL
New Town
Walton Fold Farm
St Cecilia's RC High Sch
Ribchester
College Wood
Lower College Farm
Lower Cockhill Farm
Alston Resrs
PRESTON RD
B6244
Falicon Farm
Spout Farm
PINFOLD LA
PR3
Meadow Head
Bury's Farm
Butcher Fold
Eatoughs Farm
Pinfold Farm
The Greenwood
HOTHERSALL LA
Ox Hey
Bolton Fold
Norcross Wood
Granham House
Manor House
Norcross
Thorn Lane Farm
Tun Brook
Jinkinson's Farm
THORN LA
King Wood
Woodland's Farm
Stubbin's Nook
Hothersall Lodge
ALSTON LA
Ribble Way
Alston Cottage Farm
Lower Yew Tree Farm
Ribble View Farm
Stubbin's Wood
River Ribble
PR2
BB2
8 7 6 5 4 3 2 1
37 36 35 34
61 62

139
161

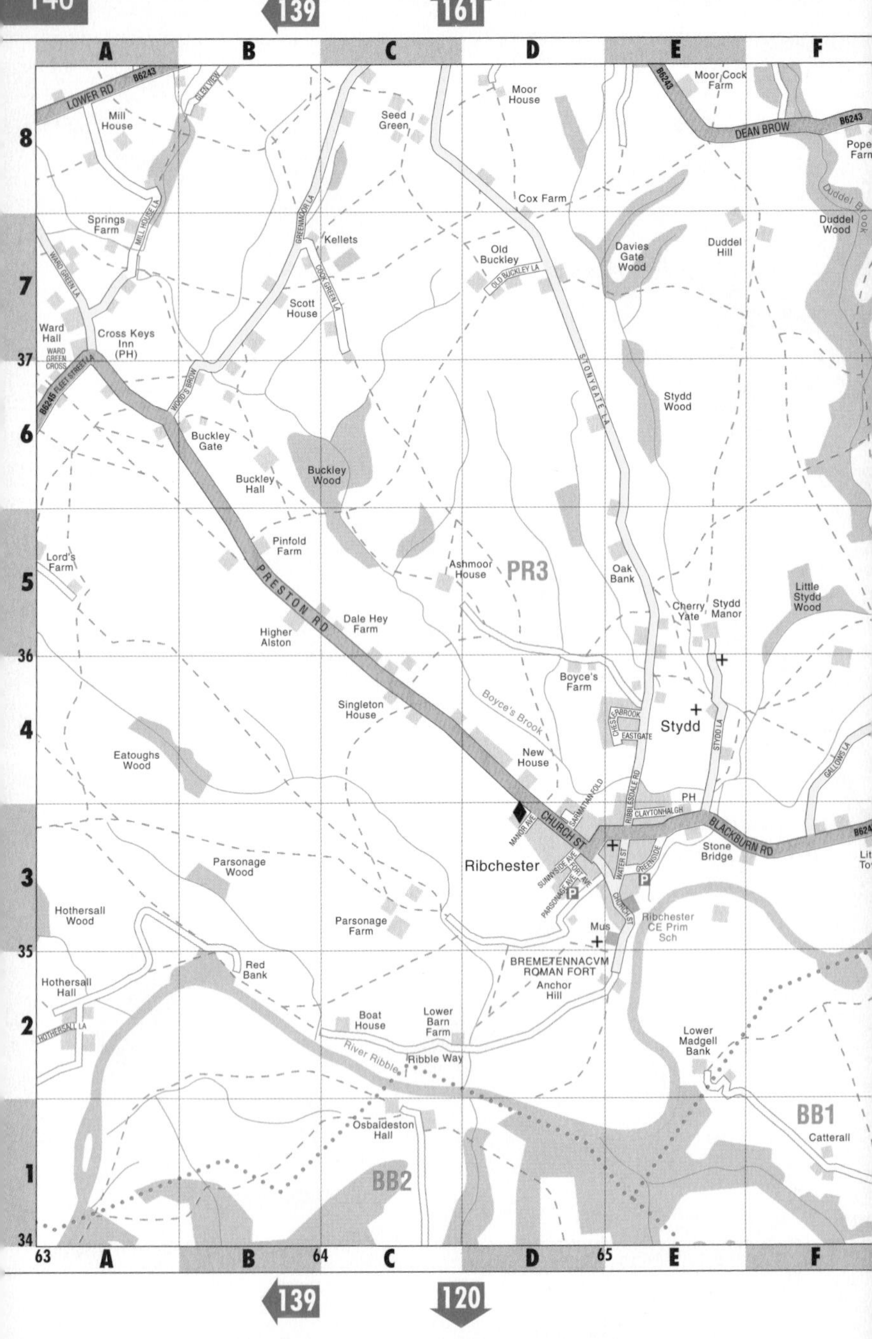

139
120

162
142

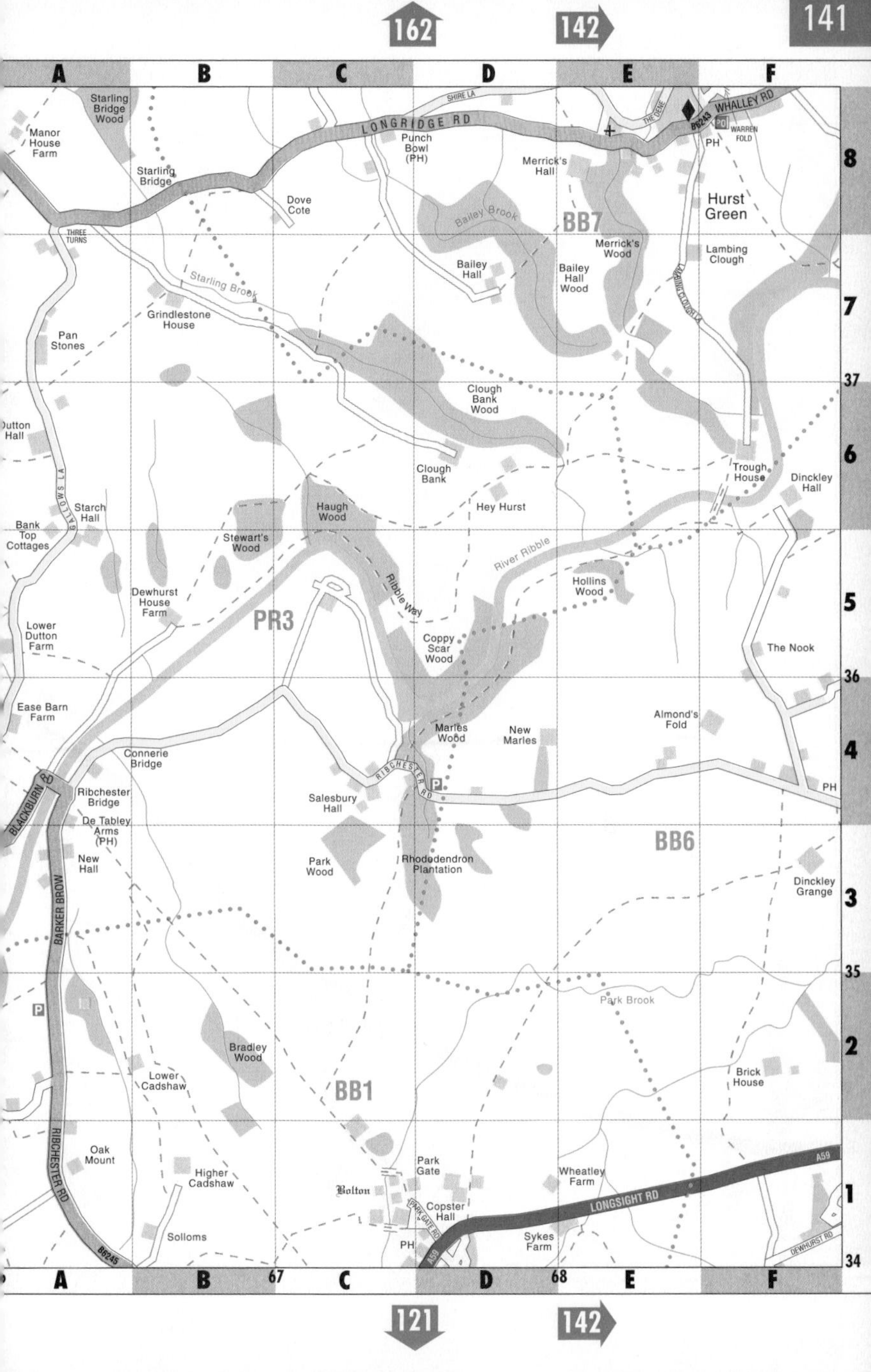

121
142

141
163

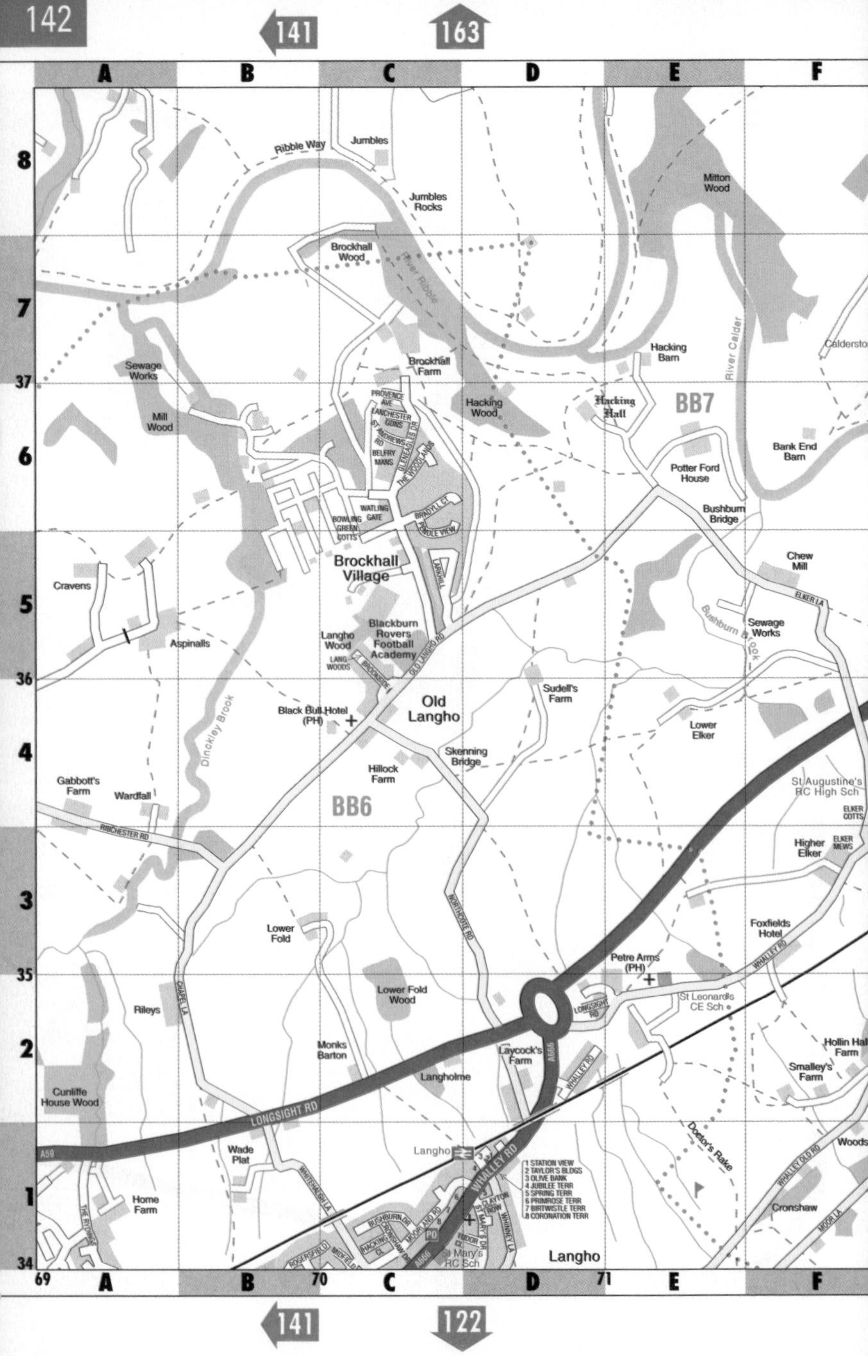

141
122

164
144
A
B
C
D
E
F
8
7
37
6
5
36
4
3
35
2
1
34
73
74
Common Side
Brook House
Cemy
Spread Eagle (PH)
Lamb Roe
Tithe Barn
Wiswell
Sheep Cote Farm
Wiswell Hall Farm
Show House Farm
Calderstones
Oakhill Coll
Deer Park Wood
Nethertown
Whalley
Lawsonsteads
Clerk Hill
Sewage Wks
Spring Wood Nature Trail
Whalley Abbey
Whalley Viaduct
River Calder
Whittam's Farm
Whalley Bridge
Painter Wood
Hole House Farm
BB7
Sir John's Wood
Planes Wood
Portfield
Nab Side Farm
Nab Wood
Turn Hill
Hodge Field
Billington
Mast
Brierley's Farm
Whalley Banks
Hillocks
Horse Bowers
Park Head Farm
Miles Hill
Black Hill
Lower White Carr
Heys Farm
Moreton Hall Farm
Dean Wood
Dionysius Wood
Cock Wood
BB12
BB6
Dean Bridge
Cock Bridge
MITTON RD
ACCRINGTON RD
BURNLEY RD
WHALLEY RD
STATION RD
KING ST
WHALLEY OLD RD
MOOR LA
123
144

143
165
Wiswell Eaves
Wiswell Eaves Farm
Jeppe Knave Grave
Wilkin Heys
Whins Farm
Whins House
Sabden
Sabden Cty Prim Sch
Liby
St Mary's RC Sch
Works
Wiswell Moor Houses
Mast
Bramley Farm
Wiswell Moor Farm
Lower Barn Farm
BB7
WHALLEY RD
CLERK HILL RD
Hillside Farm
Brogden Farm
Cobden Farm
Robinson's Wood
Well Wood
Lane Side Farm
Wiswell Moor Bottom
Lower Clerk Hill
Hollins Farm
Whittaker's Farm
White Hill
Shady Walks
Hodgeon Stone Plantation
BACK LA
Withams Farm
Sabden Brook
Read Heights
TRAPP LA
New Hall Farm
High Lea Barn
Higher Trapp Hotel (PH)
Lower Read Wood Farm
High House Farm
BB12
Lower Trapp Cottage
OLD ROMAN RD
Read Old Bridge
Easterley Farm
Houlker's Farm
Law Farm
Sagar Heys
Coppy Plantation
Read Hall
HAMMOND DR
Read
Top Barn
Read CE Sch
Read Park
Hammond Ground
Front Field
WHALLEY RD
A671
Simonstone
Simonstone CE Prim Sch
Simonstone Hall
Bridge Hey Wood
Scot Ground
Allot Gdns
BB6
SIMONSTONE LA
GOOSELEACH LA
143
124

166
146
A
B
C
D
E
F
8
7
37
6
5
36
4
3
35
2
1
34
79
80
BADGER WELLS COTTS
New York
Heyhouses
Hey Barn Farm
Drivers
Dean Farm
1 SABDEN BROOK CT
2 LITTLEMOOR CL
3 LITTLEMOOR HO
Back o' th' Hill
BB7
Sabden Brook
MOUNT PLEASANT
STUMP HALL RD
Dean Height
Stump Hall
Chew Barn
PADIHAM RD
Dry Corner
The Height
Hill Top
Padiham Heights
BACK LA
Sagar Hill
Copthurst
PENDLE VIEW 1
HAMBLEDON TERR 2
WESLEY PL 3
SLACK
Black Hill
SABDEN RD
Copthurst
Moor Barn
Higham
Acres Brook
Mill
PH
PO
A6068
Cavaliers
BARKERFIELD CL
1 ANDERTON RD
2 NUTTER CRES
3 HOLLINHURST VIEW
4 CHAPEL ST
5 GARDEN ST
6 WILKINSON ST
7 GAWTHORPE VIEW
8 DAME FOLD
Old Jeremy's Farm
Holly Brow
BARROWFORD RD
FIR TREES GR
FIR TREES LA
Foulds House
Northwood
Hencock
West Close
Northwood
Height Side
SABDEN RD
BB12
Priddy Bank Farm
Fir Trees Brook
Northwood Farm
High House
Whittaker Clough
Trap House
WHINS LA
Wall Green
Hollins Farm
Huntroyde
HIGHAM RD
PENNINE GR
High Whittaker Farm
Brookfoot Farm
Hargrove
Higher Slade
SLADE LA
Black Wood
Huntroyde Brook
1 ESKDALE GDNS
2 THIRLMERE AVE
Mona Bents Plantation
Jack Hill
Burnley Way
Lower Slade
GRASMERE AVE
HARGROVE AVE
GROVE LA
Grove Lane Plantation
River Calder
Huntroyde Demesne
FAIRWEATHER CT
Playing Fields
Gawthorpe Hall
WHALLEY RD
A671
Dean Bridge
Mast
WOODLANDS GR
ARBORY DR
PIERCE CL
NORTH ST
EAST ST
BANK ST
RYCLIFFE ST
GUY ST
HIGH ST
HIGHAM ST
COBDEN ST
INGHAM ST
LAWRENCE ST
Works
Home Farm

C1
1 THE MEWS
2 CHAPEL WLK
3 SPRING GARDENS TERR
4 HALL HILL ST
5 CROSSHILLS
6 ST GILES TERR
7 ST GILES ST
8 ST LEONARD'S ST
9 CLAYBANK FOLD
10 CLAYBANK
11 HAVELOCK ST
12 CHURCH LA
13 GAWTHORPE ST
14 BARBON ST
15 JOHN O' GAUNT ST
16 CENTRAL BLDGS
17 FACTORY LA
18 COPTHURST ST
19 HAMBERGHAM ST
20 VICTORIA APARTMENTS
21 CLITHEROE ST
125
D1
1 KAY ST
2 DEAN ST
3 CHIPPING ST
4 PARTRIDGE HILL
5 PARTRIDGE HILL ST
146

145
167

145
126

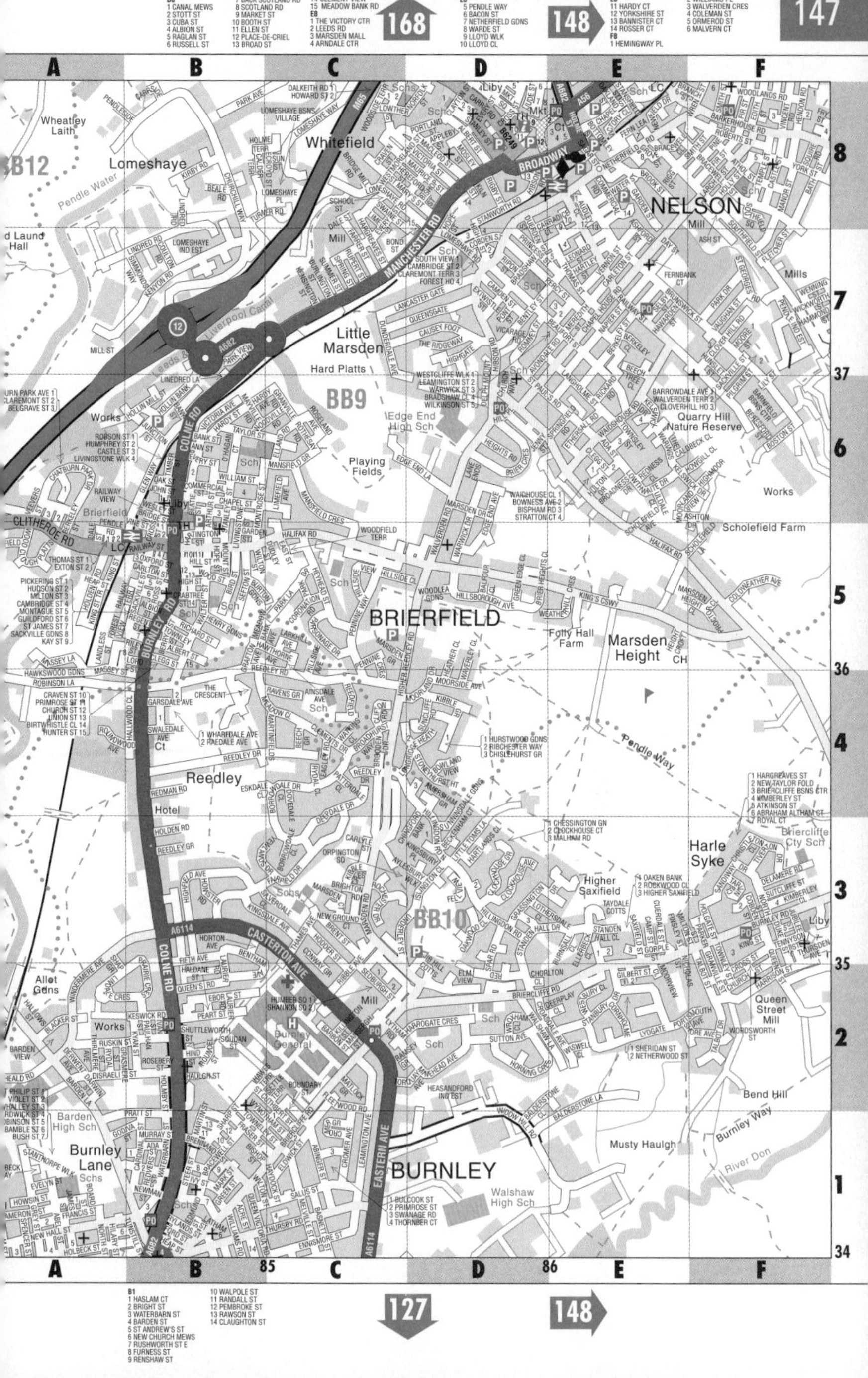
D8
1 CANAL MEWS
2 STOTT ST
3 CUBA ST
4 ALBION ST
5 RAGLAN ST
6 RUSSELL ST
7 BACK SCOTLAND RD
8 SCOTLAND RD
9 MARKET ST
10 BOOTH ST
11 ELLEN ST
12 PLACE-DE-CRIEL
13 BROAD ST
14 CLEMENT VIEW
15 MEADOW BANK RD
E8
1 THE VICTORY CTR
2 LEEDS RD
3 MARSDEN MALL
4 ARNDALE CTR
168
E8
5 PENDLE WAY
6 BACON ST
7 NETHERFIELD GDNS
8 WARDE ST
9 LLOYD WLK
10 LLOYD CL
148
E8
11 HARDY CT
12 YORKSHIRE ST
13 BANNISTER CT
14 ROSSER CT
F8
1 HEMINGWAY PL
2 WILLIAMS PL
3 WALVERDEN CRES
4 COLEMAN ST
5 ORMEROD ST
6 MALVERN CT
A B C D E F
8 7 37 6 5 36 4 3 35 2 1 34
85 86
Wheatley Laith
BB12
Lomeshaye
Pendle Water
Laund Hall
Whitefield
LOMESHAYE IND EST
M65
MANCHESTER RD
BROADWAY
NELSON
Leeds & Liverpool Canal
Little Marsden
Hard Platts
BB9
Edge End High Sch
Playing Fields
Quarry Hill Nature Reserve
Works
Mills
Scholefield Farm
CLITHEROE RD
Brierfield
COLNE RD
BURNLEY RD
HALIFAX RD
BRIERFIELD
Folly Hall Farm
Marsden Height
Pendle Way
Reedley
Hotel
Harle Syke
Briercliffe Cty Sch
Higher Saxifield
BB10
A6114
CASTERTON AVE
Allot Gdns
Burnley General
Queen Street Mill
Bend Hill
Burnley Way
Barden High Sch
Burnley Lane
BURNLEY
Walshaw High Sch
Musty Haugh
River Don
EASTERN AVE
HEASANDFORD IND EST
B1
1 HASLAM CT
2 BRIGHT ST
3 WATERBARN ST
4 BARDEN ST
5 ST ANDREW'S ST
6 NEW CHURCH MEWS
7 RUSHWORTH ST E
8 FURNESS ST
9 RENSHAW ST
10 WALPOLE ST
11 RANDALL ST
12 PEMBROKE ST
13 RAWSON ST
14 CLAUGHTON ST
127
148

147
169

147
128

A
B
C
D
E
F
8
7
37
6
5
36
4
3
35
2
1
34
0
91
92
BURNLEY RD
Mast
Slack Laithe
Meadow
Bottom
Farm
New Laith
Lodge Hill
Naze End
Trowden Brook
Pasture
Springs
Mean Moss
Slitterforth
Farm
Little Moss
Moss Barn
Higher Draught
Gates
Alder Hurst
End
Beaver
PARK
COTTS
Oaken
Bank
Gilford
Clough
Alder Hurst
Alder Hurst
Head
Spoutley Lumb
Boulsworth
Dyke
BB8
Fords
Antley Gate
Ford
Coldwell Inn
Activity Ctr
Deerstone Moor
Round Hole Beck
Bronte Way
Upper
Coldwell
Resr
Round Hole
Pendle Way
Will Moor Clough
BACK LA
Lower
Coldwell Resr
Will Moor
Bedding Hill Moor
Swains Plat Clough
Shuttleworth
Pasture
Lad Law
Red Spa
Mere Clark
Dike Head
Boulsworth Hill
HALIFAX RD
BB10
Red Spa Moor
Broad Bank
House
Braeside
Thursden
New
Bridge
Hey Slacks Clough
MALIFF RD
Robin Hood's
House
Tom Groove
Thursden Valley
New
Plantation
Burnley Way
Cockridge
Copy
Black Clogh
Tom Groove
Hey Slack
HX7
Ell Clough
HALIFAX RD
Rieve
Edge
Tom Groove
Head
White Bent
Rapes Hole
Hanson
Fold
Crown Point Flat

172

F7
1 WHEATFIELD CL
2 CHARDONNAY CRES
3 GARNET CL
4 MARBLE AVE
5 OPAL CL
6 BRIDGEWATER AVE
7 PRENTON GDNS
8 THE SHAY
9 PRIESTIELD
10 BESCOT WAY
11 SIXFIELDS

129

E1
1 BRODERICK AVE
2 FOX IND EST
3 CHELSEA CT
4 CHELSEA MEWS
5 BROMLEY CT
6 PEARL AVE
7 HENLEY CT
8 DELAWARE RD

A B C D E F

8
7
41
6
5
40
4
3
39
2
1
38

Norcross
Norcross Hall
Primrose Bank
Trapp Farm
Willow Farm
Rington
Rington Farm
Ryscar Farm
Carleton
Carleton Sch
Woodhouse Farm
Carleton Crossing
The Blackpool Sixth Form Coll
Highfurlong
Highfurlong Sch
Collegiate High Sch
Millfield High Sch
Tarngate Crossing
FY5
Bay Court
Breedy Butts
Carleton Green Cty Prim Sch
Springfield Farm
FY6
FY3
Cheshire House
Baines Sch
Little Thornton
Thornton Hall Farm
Blackpool & Fleetwood Yacht Club
Thornton Hall
Ashley Hall
Thornton Lodge (PH)
Prospect Farm
Skippool
Skippool Marsh
Skippool Bridge
Bridge House
River Wyre
Wyre Way
Main Dyke
Recn Ctr
CH
Civic Ctr
The Lanterns
The Breck Cty Prim Sch
Brook Field Sch
Poulton RC St John's Prim Sch
Cemy
Ind Est
Little Poulton
Hodgson High Sch
Liby
Teanlowe Ctr
Sch
Carr Head Prim Sch
POULTON-LE-FYLDE
Oldfield Carr Farm
Brockholes Wood
LC

AMOUNDERNESS WAY
FLEETWOOD RD S
FLEETWOOD RD
POULTON RD
TITHEBARN ST
BLACKPOOL RD
GARSTANG RD W
GARSTANG RD E
BRECK RD
STATION RD
SKIPPOOL RD
LAMBS RD
MAINS LA
NORCROSS LA
ANDERSHOLME LA
NEW RD
HARDHORN RD
B5268
B5267
B5412
A585
A586
A588
A587

1 HAWKSTONE CL
2 WENSLEYDALE CL
3 DALESFORD CL
4 RIDGEWAY DR
5 THORNFIELD AVE
6 CHELTENHAM CRES

1 HAWTHORNE LEA
2 DORCHESTER CL

1 CHISWELL GR
2 MILLERSDALE CL
3 ASHCOMBE GATE
4 CRANBOURNE GR
5 BALFOUR CL

PASTURE FIELD 1
PALFREY CL 2
PLECK PL 3

ST MARTINS CL 1
THE ORCHARDS 2
FOUR LANE ENDS 3

1 SHERBOURNE CT
2 SHERBOURNE CL
3 TAYLORS CL
4 THE PADDOCK

WHARFDALE CT 1
ASHLET CT 2

SAWTHORPE WLK 1
WINSCAR WLK 2
DALE DYKE WLK 3

BRENTWOOD AVE 3
GARSTANG CL 4

THE BRAMBLINGS 1
THE LAPWINGS 2
THE FULMARS 3

1 BURNSALL AVE
2 WILLOW GR

1 TYNEDALE PL
2 ST MARY CL
3 ST CATHERINE CL
4 ST THOMAS CL
5 OTTERBURN CL
6 RATHMELL CL
7 SILSDEN CL
8 ELTHAM CT
9 SHIPLEY CL
10 PAYTHORNE CL

A B 34 C D 35 E F

151
174

151
131

175
154

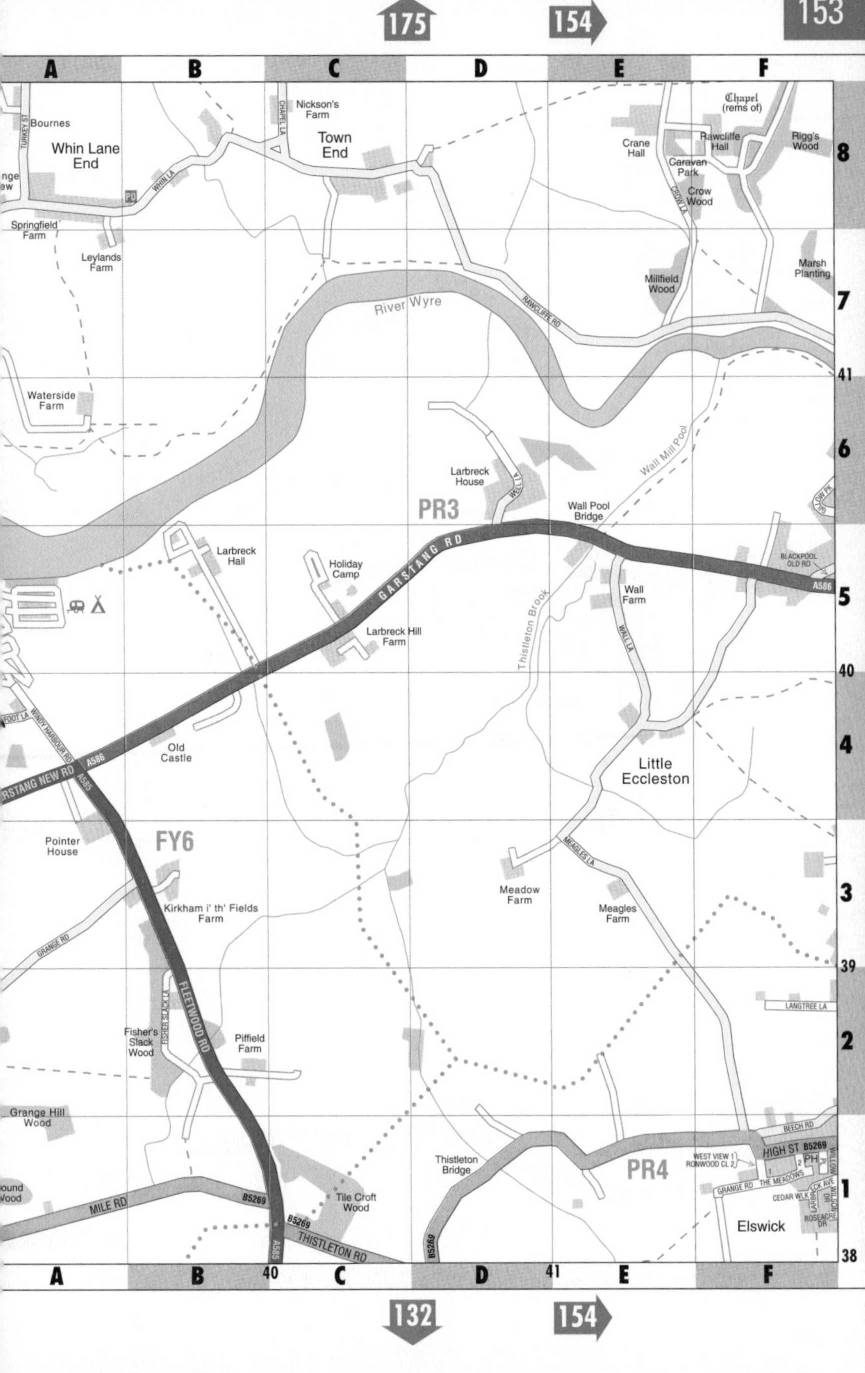

132
154

153
176

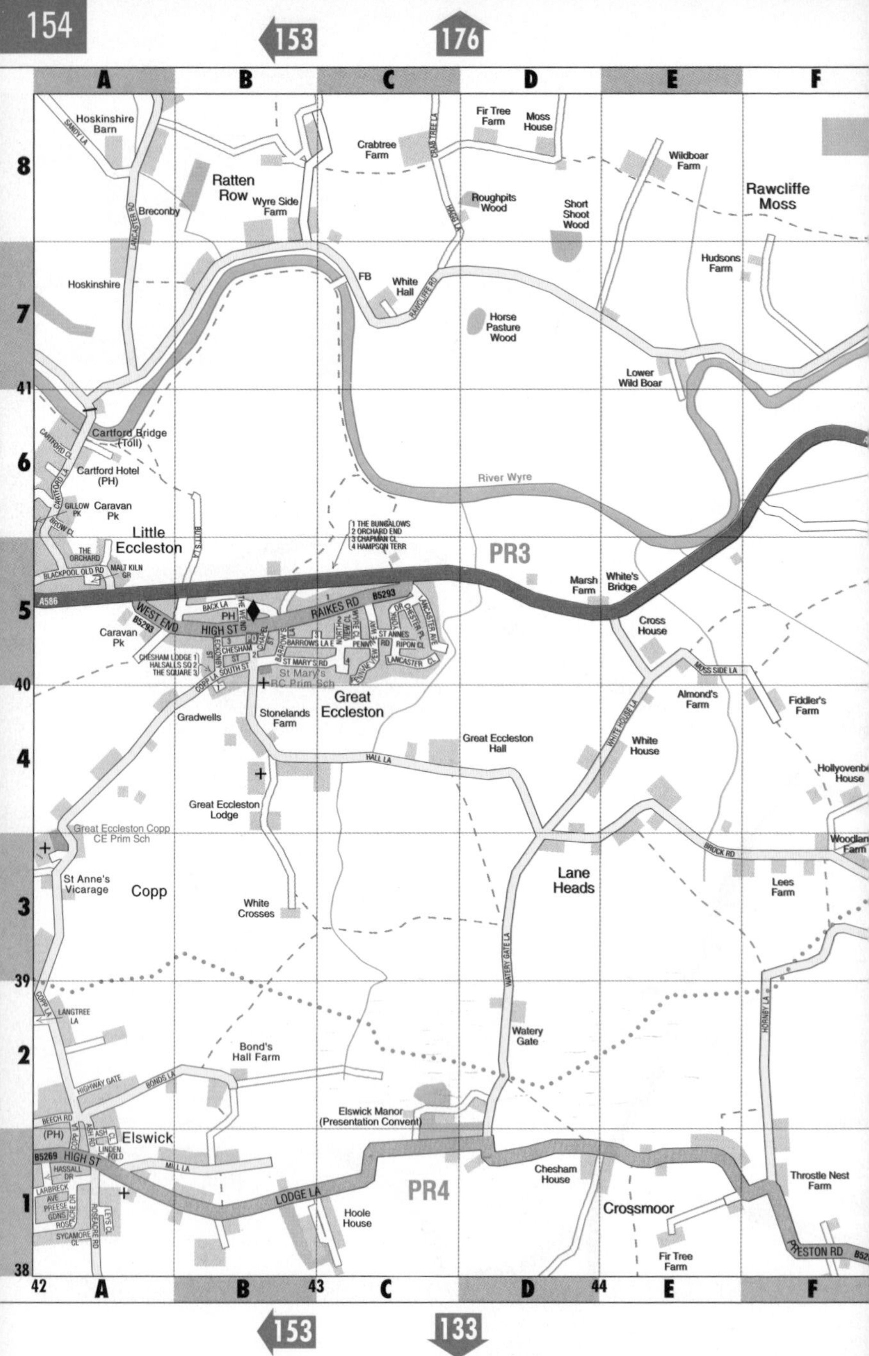

153
133

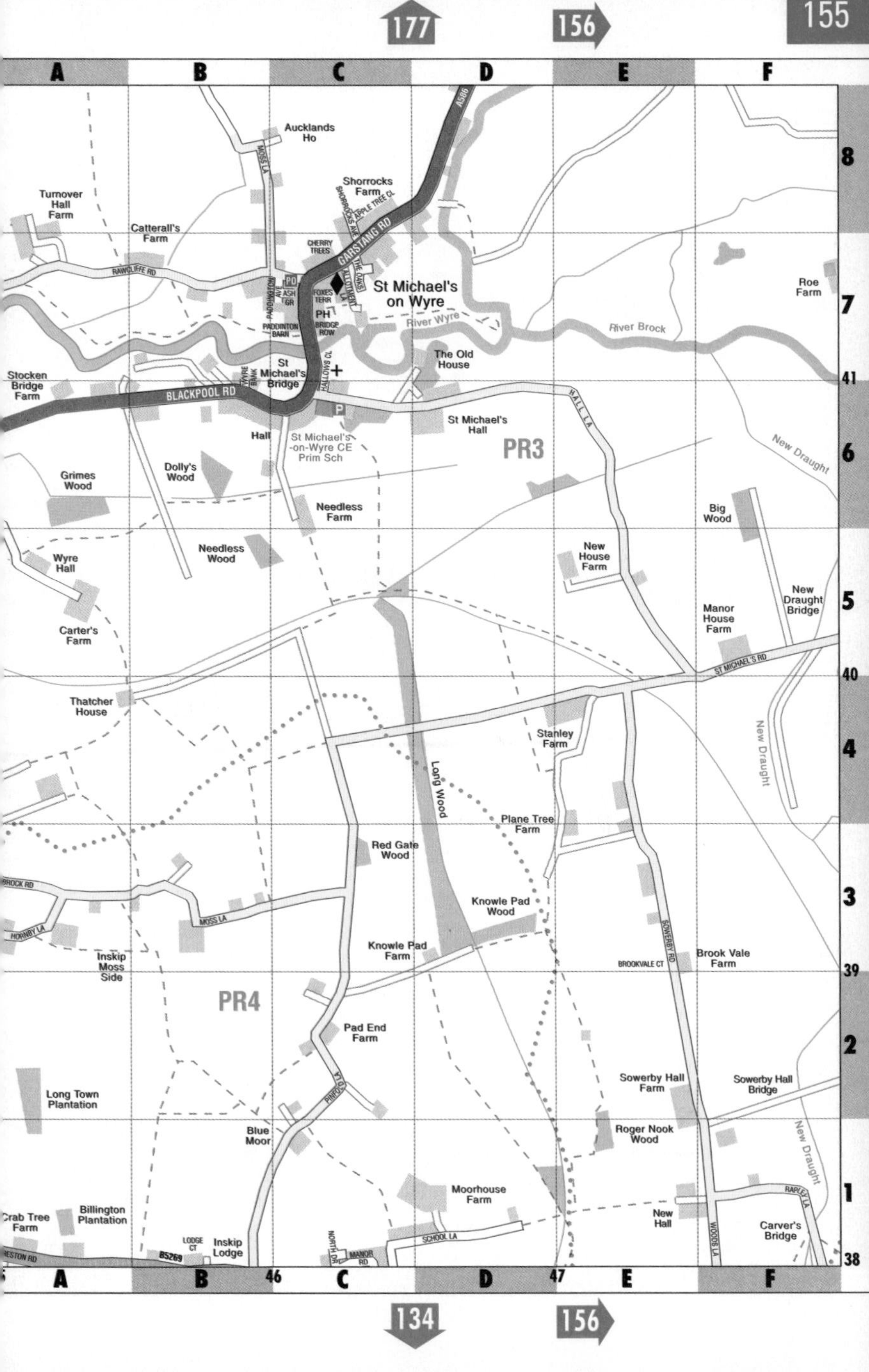
177
156
A
B
C
D
E
F
8
7
41
6
5
40
4
3
39
2
1
38
46
47
134
156
A586
Aucklands Ho
MOSS LA
Shorrocks Farm
SHORROCKS AVE
APPLE TREE CL
Turnover Hall Farm
Catterall's Farm
CHERRY TREES
GARSTANG RD
THE OAKS
RAWCLIFFE RD
PADDINGTON AVE
PO
ASH GR
FOXES TERR
ALLOTMENT LA
St Michael's on Wyre
Roe Farm
PH
PADDINTON BARN
BRIDGE ROW
River Wyre
River Brock
St Michael's Bridge
HALLOWS CL
WYRE BANK
The Old House
Stocken Bridge Farm
BLACKPOOL RD
HALL LA
P
Hall
St Michael's-on-Wyre CE Prim Sch
St Michael's Hall
PR3
New Draught
Grimes Wood
Dolly's Wood
Needless Farm
Big Wood
Wyre Hall
Needless Wood
New House Farm
New Draught Bridge
Manor House Farm
Carter's Farm
ST MICHAEL'S RD
Thatcher House
New Draught
Stanley Farm
Long Wood
Plane Tree Farm
Red Gate Wood
BROCK RD
Knowle Pad Wood
MOSS LA
HORNBY LA
Knowle Pad Farm
SOWERBY RD
Brook Vale Farm
BROOKVALE CT
Inskip Moss Side
PR4
Pad End Farm
Sowerby Hall Farm
Sowerby Hall Bridge
Long Town Plantation
PINFOLD LA
Roger Nook Wood
New Draught
Blue Moor
Moorhouse Farm
RAPLEY LA
Crab Tree Farm
Billington Plantation
New Hall
Carver's Bridge
WOODS LA
LODGE CT
Inskip Lodge
NORTH DR
MANOR RD
SCHOOL LA
B5269
PRESTON RD

155
178

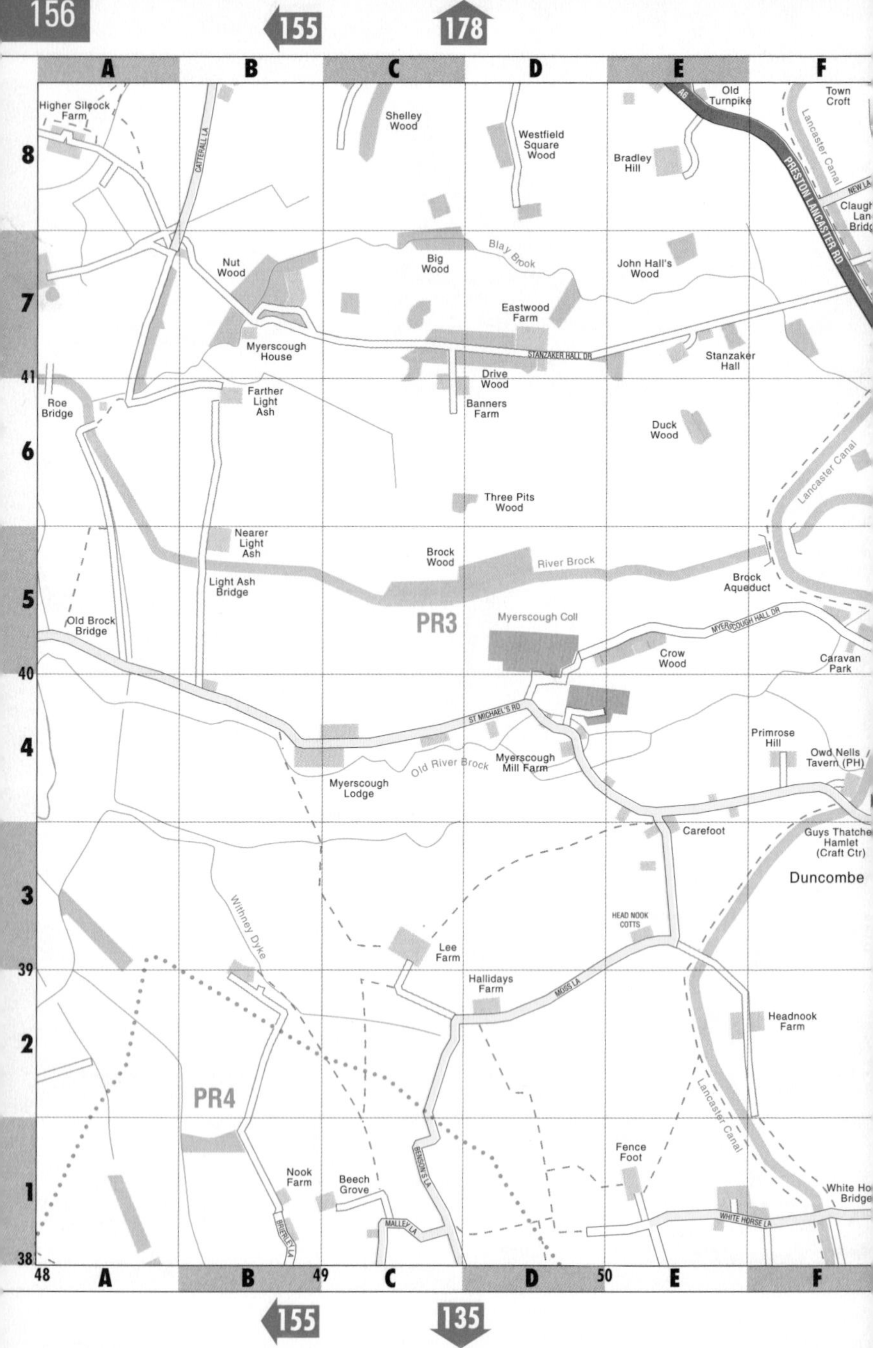

155
135

179 158

136 158

157
180

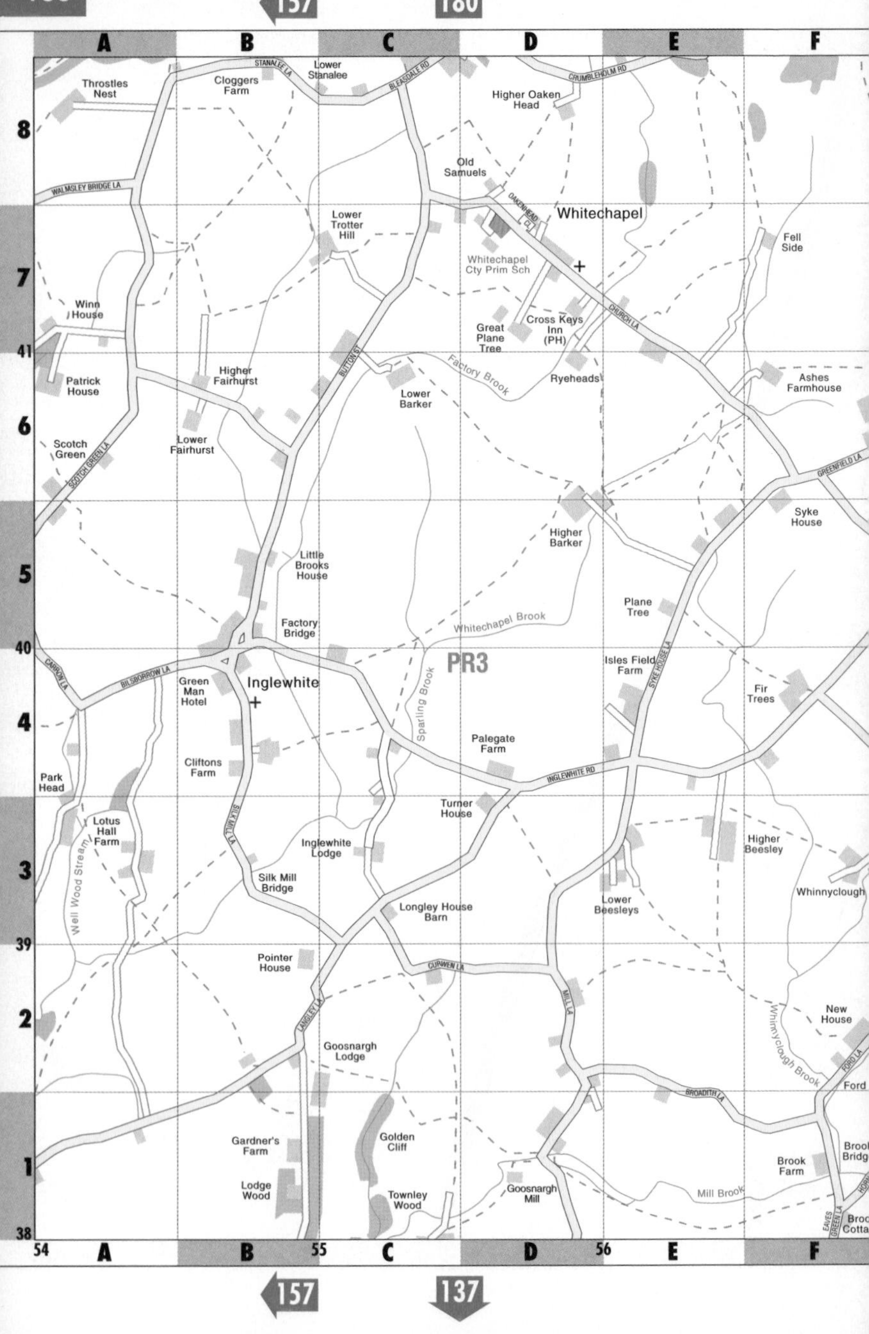

157
137

181
160

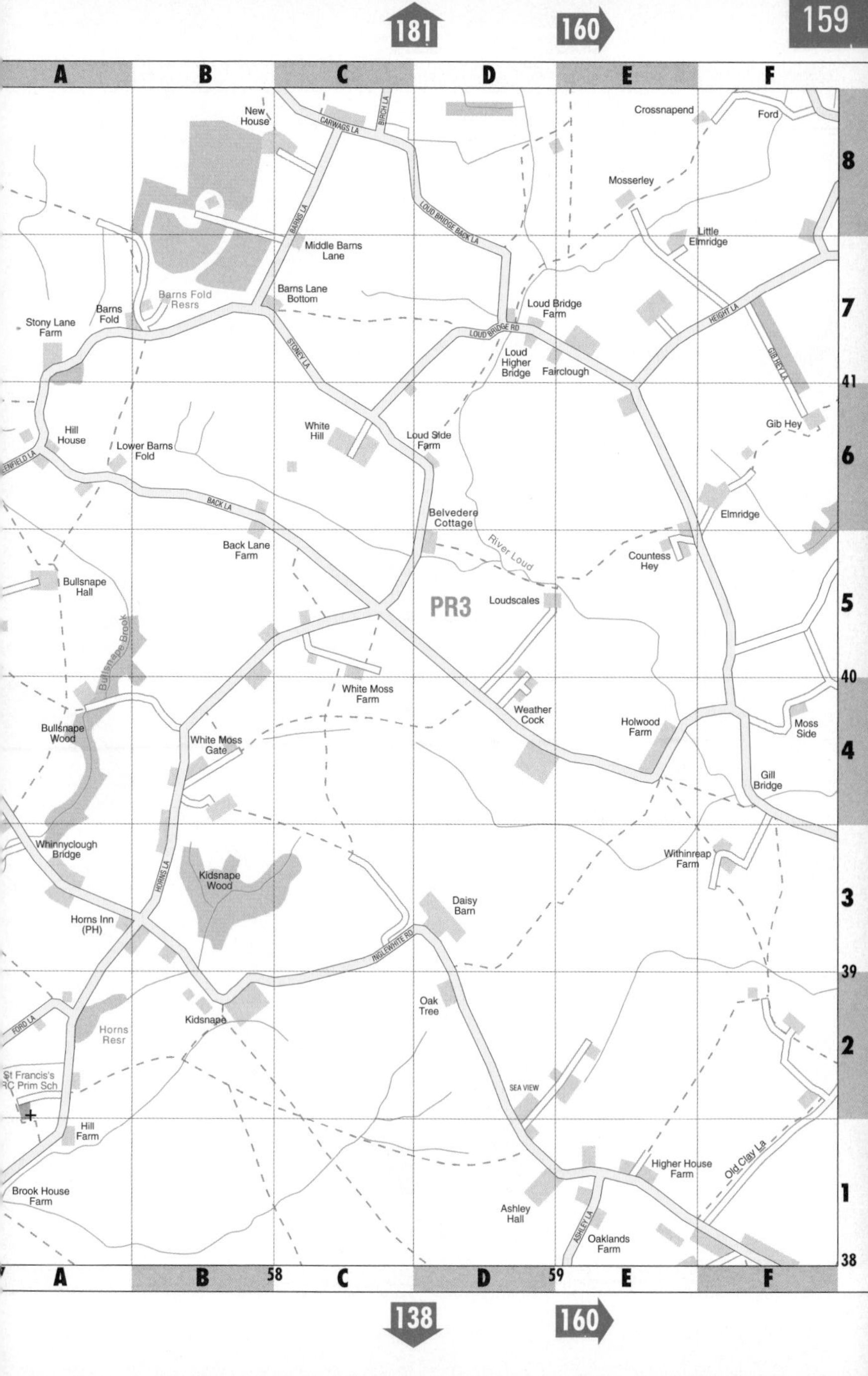

138
160

159
182

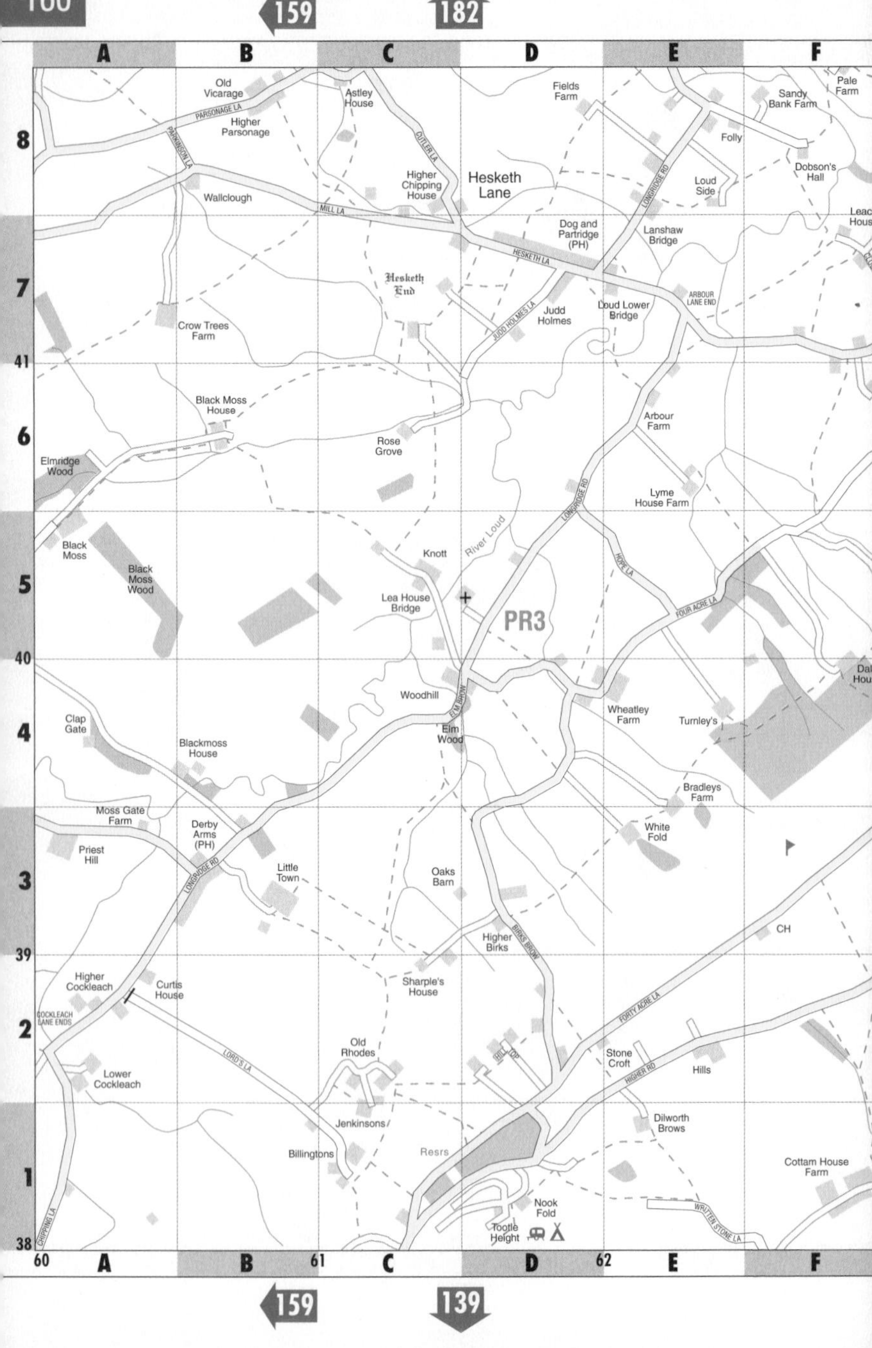

159
139

183
162
A
B
C
D
E
F
River Loud
Park Wood
Mocking Brook Wood
Bradley Hall Plantation
BRADLEY CT
Bradley Hall
Head of Moor
Weed Acre Farm
8
BB7
7
Rams Clough
Rams Clough Wood
Thornley Hall
Spire Hill
ROCK BROW
Woodstraw House
41
FOUR ACRE LA
West House Barn
6
Meg Hall
Thornley Hall Fell
Giles Farm
Moor Game Hall
5
Gannow Fell
FORTY ACRE LA
Cardwell House
Jeffrey Hill
40
Lennox Farm
PR3
Fell House
Plantation Farm
4
Longridge Fell
Myers's Farm
Forty Acre Farm
OLD CLITHEROE RD
Low Hill Wood
Cowley Brook Farm
Hougher Fall Farm
Low Mill House
3
Cuckoo Hall
HUNTINGDON HALL RD
Newdrop Inn (PH)
HIGHER RD
Goodshaw House
39
High House
Cutler's Hill
2
Hoardsell
Dutton Manor
Moor Hey
Lane Ends
Squire House
Knowle Green
Longfield
Hall's Arms (PH)
AIREY HO
NEW ROW COTTS
1
Moss Gate
Moor Nook
B6243
CLITHEROE RD
LOWER RD
GLEN VIEW
GREENMOOR LA
STONYGATE LA
TOP OF FAWNA RD
B6243
38
A
B
64
C
D
65
E
F
140
162

161
184
A
B
C
D
E
F
8
7
41
6
5
40
4
3
39
2
1
38
66
67
68
Bull Hill
Planetree Hall
Chapel House
Craven Heifer (PH)
Walker Fold
Rakefoot
Moss Plantation
Chaigley Hall Wood
Hare Hill
High Beacon
Longridge Fell Forest Wlk
Green Thorn Fell
Longridge Fell
Turner Fold
BIRDY BROW
Green Thorn
Brownslow
Nooks
Chilsey Green
Fell Side Farm House
Morton House
Brook Bottom
Brownslow Brook
BB7
Stock Bridge
Throstle Nest
Holly Hall
Higher Stonyhurst Park
OLD CLITHEROE RD
Intack
PR3
Crowshaw House
Higher Deer House
STOCKBRIDGE COTTS
Lower Deer House
Crowshaw Lodge (Resr)
Deer House Wood
Stonyhurst Park
Dashwood
Coll
Greengore
Dean Brook
Huntingdon Hall
Hudd Lee Wood
HUNTINGDON HALL RD
Hill Farm
Fox Fall Wood
Higher Hudd Lee
Lower Hudd Lee Farm
Mill Wood
SMITHY ROW
SHIREBURN COTTS
Carlinghurst
Shireburn House
New House
Doe Hill
St Joseph RC Prim Sch
Bailey House
THE DENE
AVENUE RD
BILSBERRY COTTS
B6243
WHALLEY
161
141

185
164
A
B
C
D
E
F
Cheetall
Moss Wood
Darwens Farm
Hodder House
8
Manor Farm
Chaigley Manor
CHAIGLEY CT
CHAIGLEY FARM COTTS
BAILEY BANK
Higher Hodder Bridge
7
Withgill Farm
Withgill Knoll
Thirty Acres
HODDER BRIDGE CT
41
Withgill Fold
Sugar's Barn
BIRDY BROW
WITHGILL PIGGETY COTTS
6
NEW LA
B6243
Sugar Fold
Rydding's Farm
Scott House
Cock Meadow Plantation
Kemble End
MILKING LA
Pig Hill Brook
Angerham
5
Scott House Wood
River Hodder
Over Hacking Wood
40
Eastham House Farm
Hodder Place
Over Hacking
HODDER CT
BB7
4
Toot Hill
Malkin La
Moyser Wood
Bankhurst
Mitton Green
JUD FALLS
Bradhurst Barn
WOODFIELDS
Bradhurst Farm
B6246
3
CHURCH LA
Ribble Way
KNOWLES BROW
Lower Hodder Bridge
St Mary's Hall
Gore's Pond
Bridge
Three Fishes (PH)
Stonyhurst Coll
Great Mitton
39
Great Mitton Hall
Spring Wood
Ribble Way
Hall Barns
Loach Field Wood
2
Aspinall Arms (PH)
Cat Scar Wood
Mitton Bridge
New Barn
Winckley Hall
Holden's Breast
Mitton Hall
MITTON RD
Winckley Hall Farm
B6246
River Ribble
Fair Field
WHALLEY RD
1
Little Mitton Farm
B6243
Fox Fields
Cross Gills
38
A
B
70
C
D
71
E
F
142
164

163
186
D7
1 CURZON ST
2 MONK ST
3 BARN CROFT
4 HENTHORN CL
5 DEAN MEADOW
6 VICTOR MEWS
D8
1 CARDIGAN CL
2 ALBERMARLE CT
3 BALDWIN HILL
4 MONTAGUE ST
5 WHALLEY ST
6 CORPORATION ST
7 MOSS ST
8 JOHN WALL CT
E8
1 CHURCH ST
2 HARRIS CT
3 MARKET PL
4 BOWLAND CT
5 SADDLERS MEWS
6 WILKIN SQ
7 THE EMPORIUM
8 OLD STATION CT
9 PARSONAGE COTTS
10 CARDIGAN AVE
F8
1 ALBION ST
2 DUCK ST
3 SHAW BRIDGE ST
4 PENDLE CT
5 BOLLAND CL
6 BROTHERTON MDWS
CLITHEROE
Stephen Bridge
Low Moor
Throstle Nest Farm
Edisford Bridge Inn (PH)
Roefield L Ctr
Clitheroe Castle (rems of)
Mus
Liby
EDISFORD RD
BAWDLANDS
PARSON LA
MOOR LA
WATERLOO RD
Edisford Cty Prim Sch
Edisford Bridge
Edisford Hall
Rose Cottage
WINDERMERE AVE 1
ENNERDALE CL 2
HARGREAVES CT 3
St James's CE Sch
QUEENSWAY
Sch
HENTHORN RD
Siddows Hall
Primrose
Depot
Little Moor
Fulshaw Wood
Lower Standen
Higher Standen
Siddows
River Ribble
Standen Cottage
Sewage Works
Barrow Clough
Standen Hall
Ribble Way
WHALLEY RD
Barraclough House
Oak Wood
Barra Clough Wood
BB7
Limehouse Farm
Fishes and Peggy Hill
Brown Hill Barn
Lower Standen Hey Farm
Shuttleworth Farm
Higher Standen Hey Farm
CH
Barrow Gardens
A671
Park Farm
Barrow Nurseries
Barrow Brook
Barrow (VC) Prim Sch
PH
1 HAYHURST FARM TE
2 MEARLEY BROOK FO
3 STANDEN ROAD BL
1 PAYNTER CL
2 TRAFFORD GDNS
3 CATLOW TERR
4 MILL BROOK PL
5 CHORLTON TERR
6 ABBEY TERR
7 COCKERILL TERR
8 OLD ROW
Barrow
MITTON RD
B6246
B6243
A59
Lane Side
72
73
74
163
143

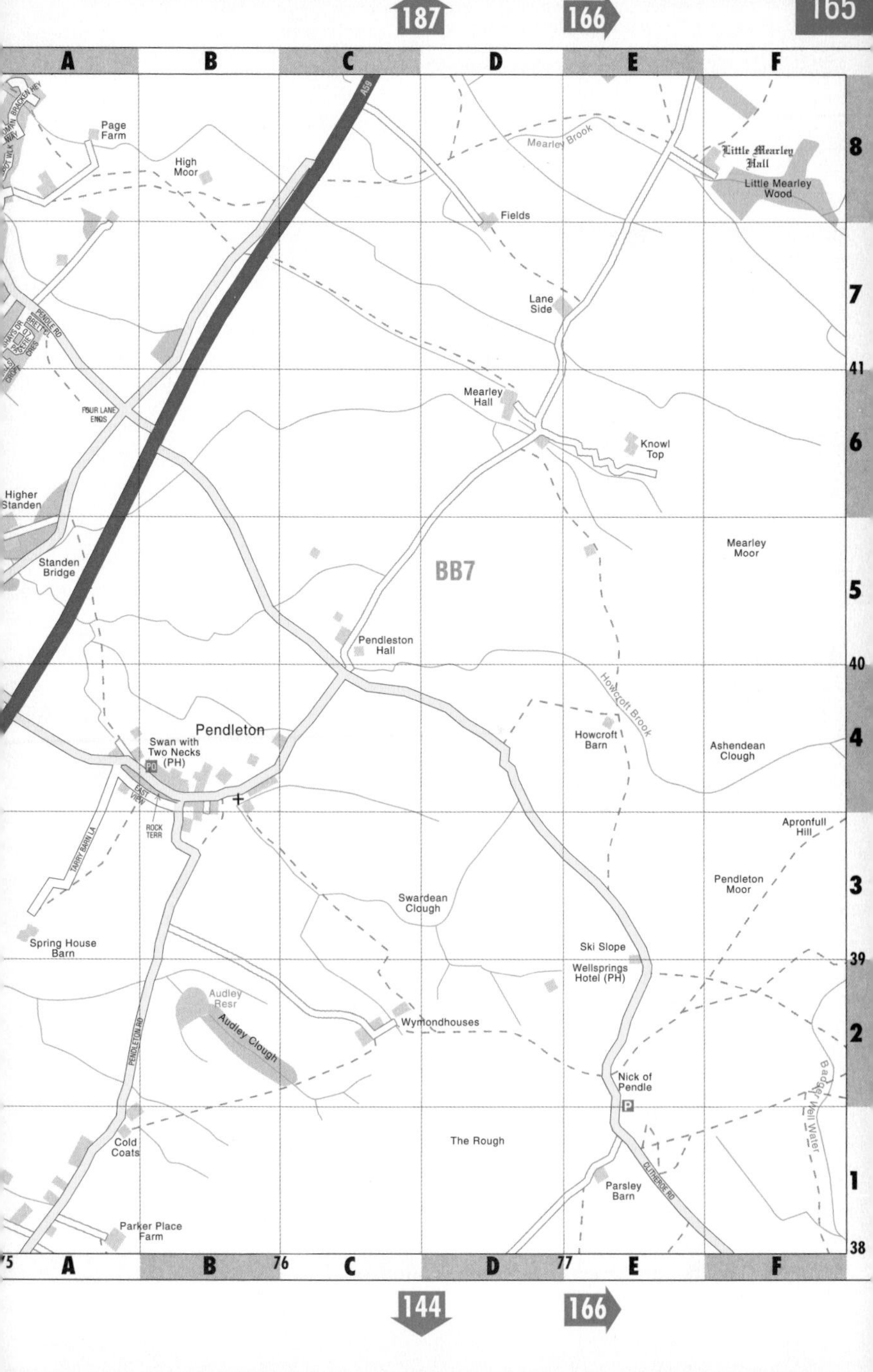
187
166
A
B
C
D
E
F
8
7
41
6
5
40
4
3
39
2
1
38
75
76
77
A59
Page
Farm
High
Moor
Mearley Brook
Little Mearley
Hall
Little Mearley
Wood
Fields
Lane
Side
PENDLE RD
FOUR LANE
ENDS
Mearley
Hall
Knowl
Top
Higher
Standen
Standen
Bridge
BB7
Mearley
Moor
Pendleston
Hall
Howcroft Brook
Pendleton
Swan with
Two Necks
(PH)
PO
EAST
VIEW
ROCK
TERR
Howcroft
Barn
Ashendean
Clough
Apronfull
Hill
TARRY BARN LA
Swardean
Clough
Pendleton
Moor
Spring House
Barn
Ski Slope
Wellsprings
Hotel (PH)
Audley
Resr
Audley Clough
Wymondhouses
PENDLETON RD
Nick of
Pendle
P
Badger Well Water
Cold
Coats
The Rough
CLITHEROE RD
Parsley
Barn
Parker Place
Farm
144
166

165
188

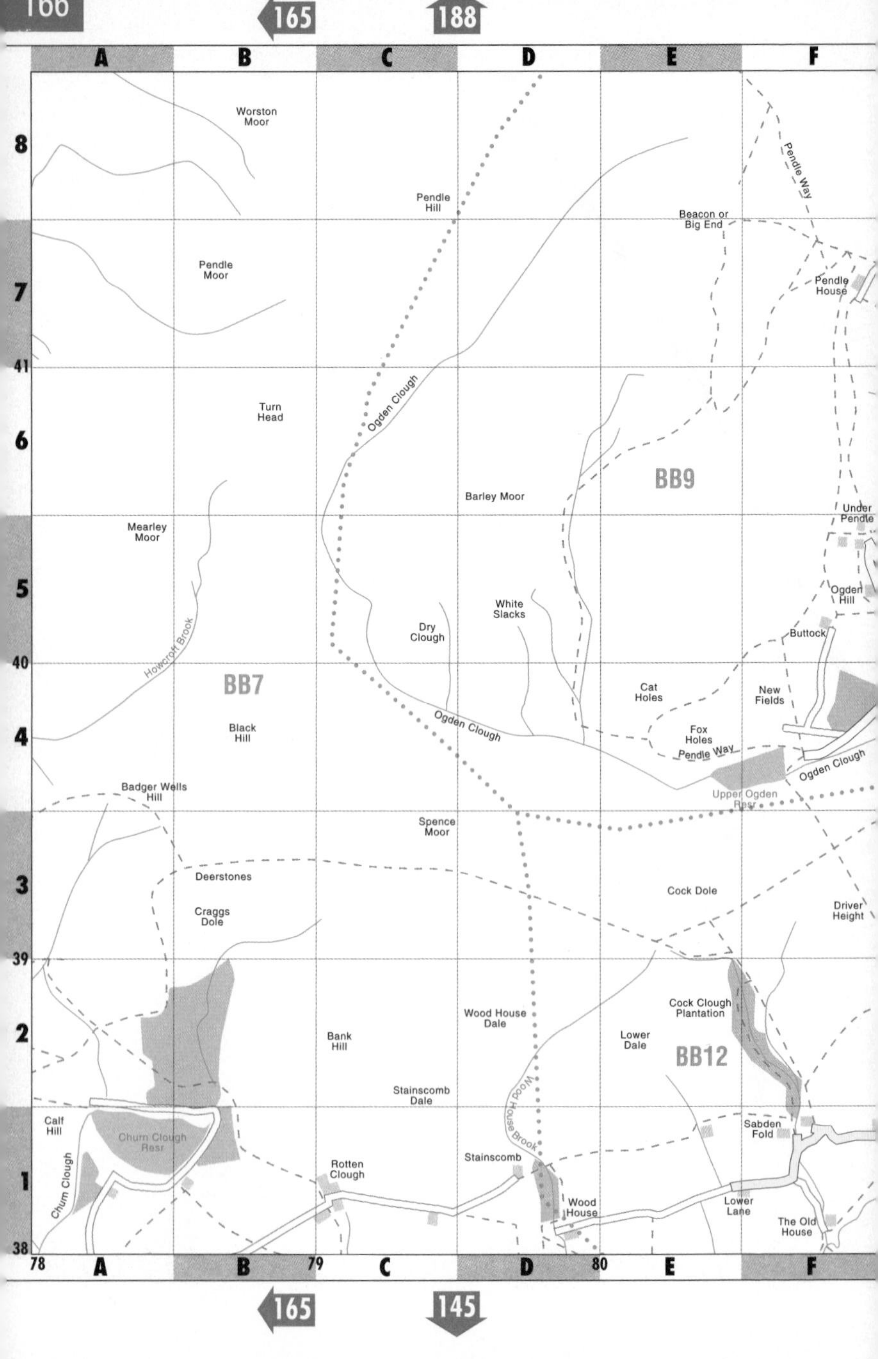

165
145

189
168

146
168

167
190

A B C D E F

Lower Whitehead
Lanefield
Blacko Laithe Farm
Brownley Park Farm
Burnt House Farm
Spout House Farm
Blacko
Blacko Prim Sch
Beverley
New House
Bank Ends
Blacko Water
Blacko Foot
Pendle Way
Cockpit Hill Farm
Great Stonedge Farm
Cross Gaits Inn (PH)
Flax Moor Farm
Hollin Top
Pendle Water
Water Meetings
North Farm
Middlewood
Croft House
Hollin Farm
Old Hall Farm
Higher Ridge Farm
Lower Ridge Farm
Ralph Laithe
Bay Horse Inn (PH)
Pasture House
BB9
Roughlee
Crow Trees
West Pasture
Higherford Old Bridge
Higherford
Barrowford Locks
Barrowford Resr
BB8
Caravan Site
Higher Oaklands Farm
Lower Fulshaw
Fulshaw Head Farm
Fulshaw
Barrowford Bridge
Ridgaling Farm
Oaklands
BARROWFORD
Pendle Heritage Ctr
Park
Cemy
Lowerford
BB12
Works
Colne Water
Playing Fields
Recn Gd
Swing Bridge
Sandy Hall
Cemy
Trough Laithe Farm
Newbridge
Mill
Allot Gdns
Holy Saviour's RC Prim Sch
Laund Farm
Nelson & Colne Coll
Marles Hill
Playing Field
Bradley
Carr Hall
Carr Laund
Higgen Clough
Victoria Park
BB12

D4
1 BACK EAST BANK
2 EAST BANK
3 MILTON ST
4 JAMES ST
5 BALDWIN ST
6 GRIMSHAW ST
7 STANSFIELD CL
8 BACK PETER ST
9 PETER ST
10 PROSPECT TERR
11 DAVID ST

1 PARADISE ST
2 FOLD
3 HOLT SQ
4 BANK HOUSE MEWS
5 WALTON ST
6 BANK HOUSE ST
7 BROOKBANK

BUCKDEN GATE 1
WOODALE LAITHE 2
HETTON LEA 3
CRACOE GILL 4
DEERDALE CT 5
ST CLEMENTS CT 6
WHEATLEY GR 7
KINGSHOTTE GDNS 8

LOWER LEITHE COTTS 1
ST MICHAEL'S CT 2

SANDY LA 1
DUCKWORTH ST 2
MAUD ST 3
KING EDWARD TERR 4

HAWTHORNE CL 1
CHATSWORTH CL 2

C1
1 RONBURY CL
2 DONSHORT MEWS
3 HINDLEY CT
4 SAFFRON CL
5 SANDRINGHAM CL
6 BEDFORD ST
7 BUCCLEUCH RD

84 A B 85 C D 86 E F

D1
1 WESTFIELD
2 HENRY ST
3 BALL ST
4 MERTON ST
5 KENDAL ST
6 BEDDINGTON ST
7 WEST ST
8 GORDON RD
9 BACK CLAYTON ST
10 EAST ST
11 CLAYTON CL
12 NILE ST
13 SEEDHILL TERR
14 NORTH ST
15 SCOTLAND RD
16 WELLINGTON ST
17 NEW BROWN ST
18 CLAYTON ST

D3
1 SHARP ST
2 BUTTERFIELD ST
3 FOUNTAIN SQ
4 LONSDALE GDNS
5 HIGHFIELD CRES
6 CORONATION PL
7 BELMONT TERR
8 HOLMEFIELD CT
9 ALBERT TERR

167

D3
10 CORLASS ST
11 CAMDEN ST
12 CROMWELL TERR
13 MOUNT ST
14 HAWTHORNE GR
15 ASH TREE WLK

147

E1
1 SUSSEX ST
2 OAK ST
3 ELEANOR ST
4 POLLARD ST
5 BRADLEY FOLD
6 CALEB ST
7 THROSTLE ST
8 WALTON ST
9 ELM ST
10 BEECH ST
11 BANK ST
12 BRADLEY VIEW
13 ST PHILIP'S ST
14 HARVEY ST
15 SELDON ST
16 BARKERHOUSE RD
17 WILLIAM ST
18 ARTHUR ST
19 PARROCK ST

F1
1 RUTLAND ST
2 EAGLE ST
3 RAVEN ST
4 VULCAN ST
5 PRIORY ST
6 PLANTATION ST
7 HILDROP RD
8 PERTH ST
9 WICKLIFFE ST
10 CANNON ST
11 EARL ST
12 ROSEHILL AVE

F2
1 LANSBURY PL
2 BENNETT ST
3 HACKING ST
4 SHERIDAN ST
5 MARLIN ST
6 IRVINE ST
7 ALGAR ST
8 ALPHA ST
9 PARKER ST
10 COLBRAN ST
11 THURSBY PL

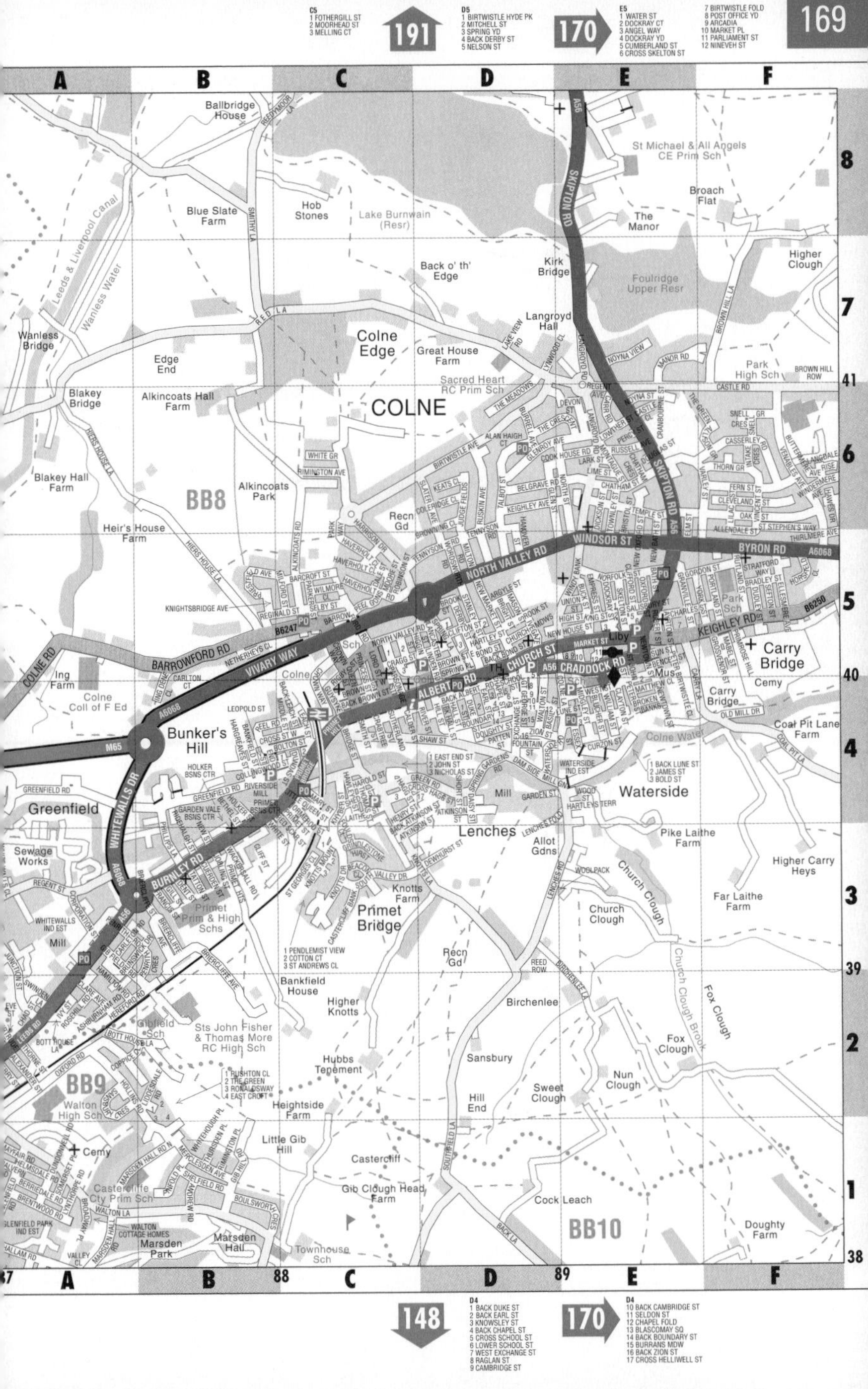
169
C5
1 FOTHERGILL ST
2 MOORHEAD ST
3 MELLING CT
191
D5
1 BIRTWISTLE HYDE PK
2 MITCHELL ST
3 SPRING YD
4 BACK DERBY ST
5 NELSON ST
170
E5
1 WATER ST
2 DOCKRAY CT
3 ANGEL WAY
4 DOCKRAY YD
5 CUMBERLAND ST
6 CROSS SKELTON ST
7 BIRTWISTLE FOLD
8 POST OFFICE YD
9 ARCADIA
10 MARKET PL
11 PARLIAMENT ST
12 NINEVEH ST
Ballbridge House
Blue Slate Farm
Hob Stones
Lake Burnwain (Resr)
St Michael & All Angels CE Prim Sch
Broach Flat
The Manor
SKIPTON RD
Kirk Bridge
Foulridge Upper Resr
Higher Clough
Back o' th' Edge
Leeds & Liverpool Canal
Wanless Water
Wanless Bridge
Edge End
Colne Edge
Great House Farm
Langroyd Hall
Park High Sch
Sacred Heart RC Prim Sch
Blakey Bridge
Alkincoats Hall Farm
COLNE
Blakey Hall Farm
BB8
Alkincoats Park
Recn Gd
Heir's House Farm
WINDSOR ST
BYRON RD
NORTH VALLEY RD
BARROWFORD RD
VIVARY WAY
COLNE RD
Ing Farm
Colne Coll of F Ed
Colne
Liby
Mus
Carry Bridge
Cemy
ALBERT RD
CHURCH ST
CRADDOCK RD
KEIGHLEY RD
Bunker's Hill
Coal Pit Lane Farm
Colne Water
Greenfield
Waterside
Lenches
Mill
Allot Gdns
Pike Laithe Farm
Sewage Works
WHITEWALLS DR
BURNLEY RD
Higher Carry Heys
Knotts Farm
Primet Bridge
Church Clough
Far Laithe Farm
Primet Prim & High Schs
Mill
Recn Gd
1 PENDLEMIST VIEW
2 COTTON CT
3 ST ANDREWS CL
Bankfield House
Birchenlee
Fox Clough
Higher Knotts
Church Clough Brook
Gibfield Sch
Sts John Fisher & Thomas More RC High Sch
Sansbury
BB9
Hubbs Tenement
Nun Clough
Walton High Sch
1 RUSHTON CL
2 THE GREEN
3 RONALDSWAY
4 EAST CROFT
Heightside Farm
Hill End
Sweet Clough
Cemy
Little Gib Hill
Castercliff
Castercliff Cty Prim Sch
Gib Clough Head Farm
Cock Leach
BB10
Doughty Farm
Marsden Park
Marsden Hall
Townhouse Sch
A
B
C
D
E
F
1
2
3
4
5
6
7
8
38
39
40
41
87
88
89
148
D4
1 BACK DUKE ST
2 BACK EARL ST
3 KNOWSLEY ST
4 BACK CHAPEL ST
5 CROSS SCHOOL ST
6 LOWER SCHOOL ST
7 WEST EXCHANGE ST
8 RAGLAN ST
9 CAMBRIDGE ST
170
D4
10 BACK CAMBRIDGE ST
11 SELDON ST
12 CHAPEL FOLD
13 BLASCOMAY SQ
14 BACK BOUNDARY ST
15 BURRANS MDW
16 BACK ZION ST
17 CROSS HELLIWELL ST

169
192

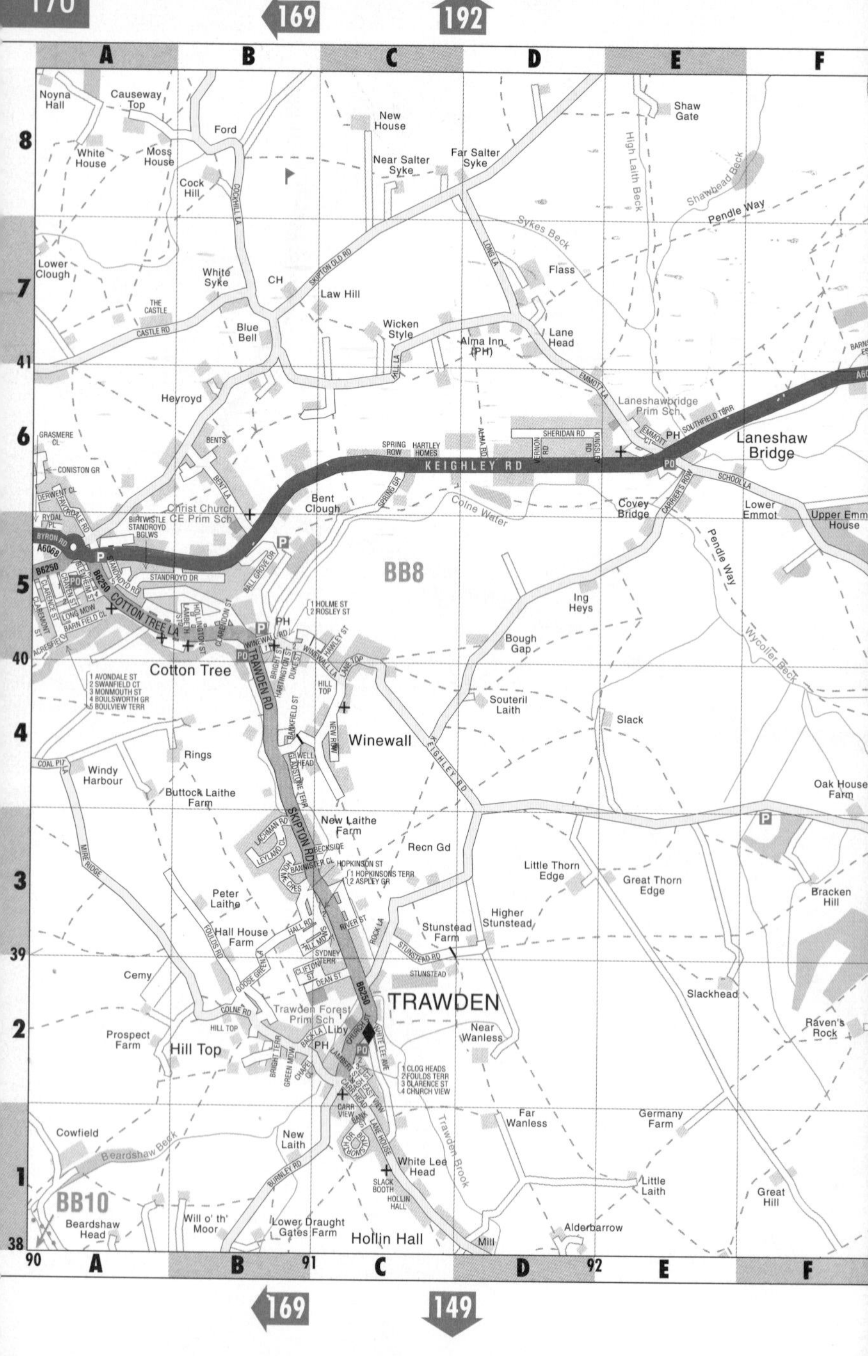

169
149

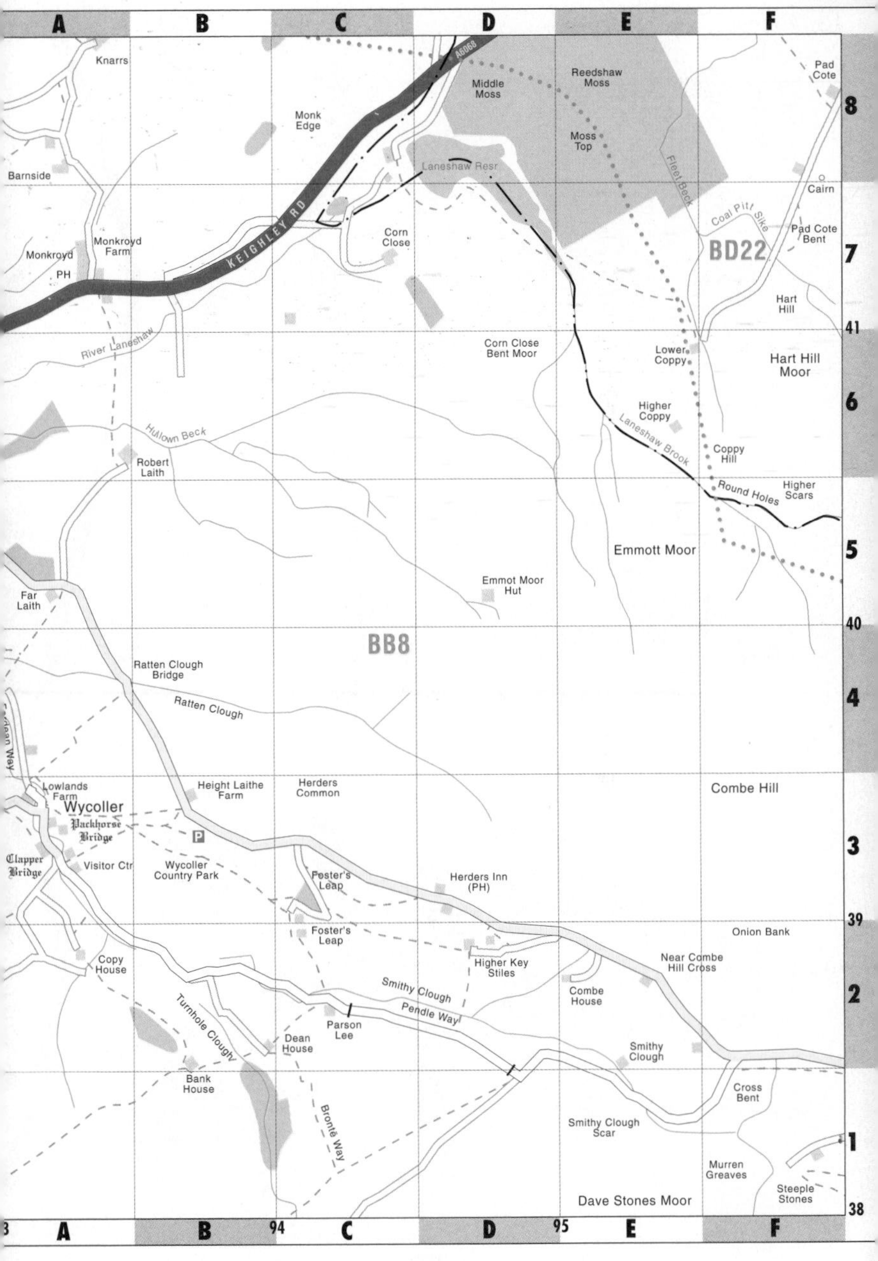

A
B
C
D
E
F
Knarrs
A6068
Middle Moss
Reedshaw Moss
Pad Cote
8
Monk Edge
Moss Top
Barnside
Laneshaw Resr
Fleet Beck
Cairn
KEIGHLEY RD
Coal Pitt Sike
Corn Close
Pad Cote Bent
Monkroyd Farm
Monkroyd
PH
BD22
7
Hart Hill
41
River Laneshaw
Corn Close Bent Moor
Lower Coppy
Hart Hill Moor
6
Higher Coppy
Hullown Beck
Laneshaw Brook
Robert Laith
Coppy Hill
Round Holes
Higher Scars
5
Emmott Moor
Emmot Moor Hut
Far Laith
40
BB8
Ratten Clough Bridge
4
Ratten Clough
Lowlands Farm
Height Laithe Farm
Herders Common
Combe Hill
Wycoller
Packhorse Bridge
P
3
Clapper Bridge
Visitor Ctr
Wycoller Country Park
Foster's Leap
Herders Inn (PH)
39
Onion Bank
Foster's Leap
Copy House
Higher Key Stiles
Near Combe Hill Cross
Smithy Clough
Combe House
2
Pendle Way
Turnhole Clough
Parson Lee
Dean House
Smithy Clough
Bank House
Cross Bent
Brontë Way
Smithy Clough Scar
1
Murren Greaves
Steeple Stones
Dave Stones Moor
38
A
B
94
C
D
95
E
F

193

150

F4
1 REDWING AVE
2 CURLEW CL
3 WHITECREST AVE
4 BARNFIELD CL
5 WIDGEON CL
6 COLCHESTER DR
7 PORTSMOUTH CL

F1
1 TUDOR CL
2 SHERWOOD PL
3 RICHARDS WAY
4 GLADSTONE WAY
5 POCHARD PL
6 DOVE CL
7 INGLENOOK CL
8 HERIOT CL
9 BUNTING PL
10 SANDPIPER PL
11 THROSTLE
12 REDSTART
13 KITTIWAKE
14 MOORHEN

194
174
A
B
C
D
E
F
8
7
6
5
4
3
2
1
45
44
43
42
34
35
Refuse Tip
Refuse Tip
FY7
FY6
FY5
Bank End
AGGLEBYS RD
Barnaby's Sands
Hay Nook
CORCAS LA
The Heads
BROWN'S LA
Wyre Way
Caravan Pk
SPRINGFIELD TERR
VENTURES
ENTERPRISE WAY
Works
Burrow's Marsh
River Wyre
BURROW'S LA
Burrow's Farm
FLEETWOOD RD
1 PLOVER CL
2 FIELDFARE CL
DUNLIN CL
MALLARD CL
BOURNE WAY
BOURNE RD
SALTASH RD
EAGLE BROW
CRYSTAL RD
GAMBLE RD
1 THORNTON PL
2 PARKSIDE VIEW
MALLOWDALE
HONEY MOOR
WEMBLEY
Burn Naze
EDWARD ST
HAPTON ST
ROCK ST
JOHN ST
BUTTS RD
Ind Est
PH
POACHERS WAY
THE MALTINGS
THE CHASE
KILDARE AVE
1 WESTFIELD CT
2 WALKER WAY
3 ORCHARD CL
SPRINGFIELD DR
Trunnah
BUTTS CL
CROFT CT
WEST DR
TAYWOOD
RETA DR
BENNETT RD
FAIRCLOUGH RD
MILDRED CL
COOKSON RD
FLEETWOOD RD N
HEYS ST
MERROD ST
Sch
RED MARSH DR
1 CHESTER CT
2 BROOKSIDE CTR
Works
CRABTREE RD
FAIRHOLMES WAY
HOLMES RD
Sch
Schs
BROOKSIDE
TENNYSON AVE
BARDSWAY
MARSH RD
BYRON AVE
PATTERDALE AVE
WHARFEDALE AVE
DOVEDALE AVE
B5439
TRUNNAH RD
HOLLY RD
HOLLY LA
LONGMEADOW
Wyre Estuary Cty Pk
Kneps Farm
RIVER RD
Wyreside Ecology Ctr
HATFIELD CL
AVONSIDE AVE
WARING DR
SNELL CRES
GORDON AVE
LONGTON CL
LANSDALE CL
Royles Brook Prim Sch
THORNTON
Stanah
STANAH GDNS
1 FERNDALE CL
2 SPRINGBANK AVE
Brook Farm
Hillylaid Crossing
HILLYLAID RD
CATHROW WAY
Stanah House Farm
CHURCH RD
KEELE
SHREWSBURY DR
WELLS CL
CHURCHILL CL
ROYLES CL
GRANGE AVE
GLENMORE AVE
WINDSOR AVE
HARRISON AVE
BANCROFT AVE
LAWSONS RD
HULME AVE
DIANNE RD
FIELDHOUSE AVE
OAKWOOD CL
TREETOWER WAY
CAERNARVON
BRADES AVE
GRAVERS FIELD
STANAH RD
1 ASHDALE GR
2 REDWOOD GDNS
3 HURSTLEIGH HEIGHTS
THE GRANARY
MARSH MILL
PLEASANT GR
BOWNESS AVE
CROWDER AVE
DEVONSHIRE AVE
DEVONSHIRE MEWS
STUART RD
ELMSIDE CL
OXENDALE RD
KELSONS AVE
WOODLEY AVE
WOODFIELD RD
Raikes
SILCOCK'S COTTS
Sports Ctr
CONISTON AVE
RYDAL AVE
ULLSWATER AVE
SANDRINGHAM AVE
ROSSENDALE AVE
HEATHER CL
BRIAR RD
ELMWOOD DR
ALDER CL
TORENTUM
BROOKFIELD RD
BROOKFIELD AVE
HASTINGS RD
HASTINGS CL
ENDERLEY CT
FARNWORTH RD
WHARTON AVE
ST JOHN'S AVE
Aylesbury House
UNDERBANK RD
Nestleton
Liby
VICTORIA RD E
CONISTON CRES
ULLSWATER CRES
LIME GR
ASH DR
STATION RD
WILLOW CL
LAMBS RD
Stanah Cty Jun & Inf Schs
RAIKES RD
SANDOWN RD 1
WOODFIELD CT 2
Marsh Farm
B5268
AINTREE RD
ASCOT RD
PARK RD
B5439
LC
ELLESMERE AVE
AINSDALE AVE
Sch
LOW-DALE
B5412
10 THORNLEIGH CL
11 ROEHAMPTON CL
12 ROEDEAN CL
B2
1 CARLISLE GR
2 CHURCHILL CL
3 COUNSELL CT
4 LINADALE AVE
B3
1 FAIRHOLMES CL
2 CRABTREE ORCH
3 KINGSTON MEWS
4 LOWES CT
5 LOWESWAY
6 HOUGHTON CT
7 GRIZEDALE CT
8 ROYLES BROOK CL
C1
1 BRIAR MEWS
2 BRAY HEYS
3 EDGEWAY PL
4 LAWSONS CT
5 MAYFAIR GDNS
6 LAWSWOOD
7 THORNTON CTR
151
D1
1 ROSEWOOD CL
2 CHATSWORTH CL
3 WILLOW TREE GDNS
4 ACACIA CL
5 FAIRHAVEN CL
6 LAMBS HILL CL
174

173
195

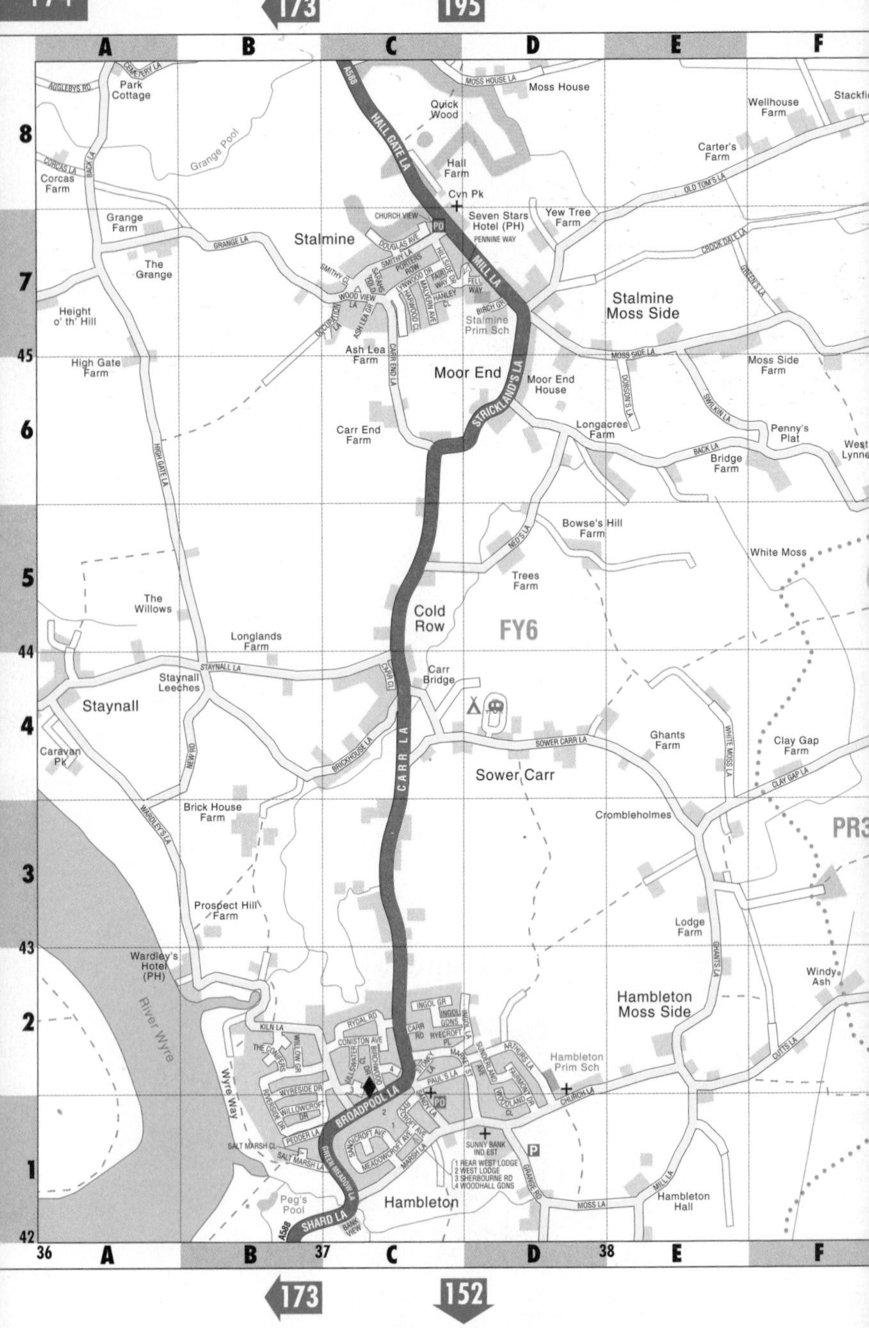

173
152

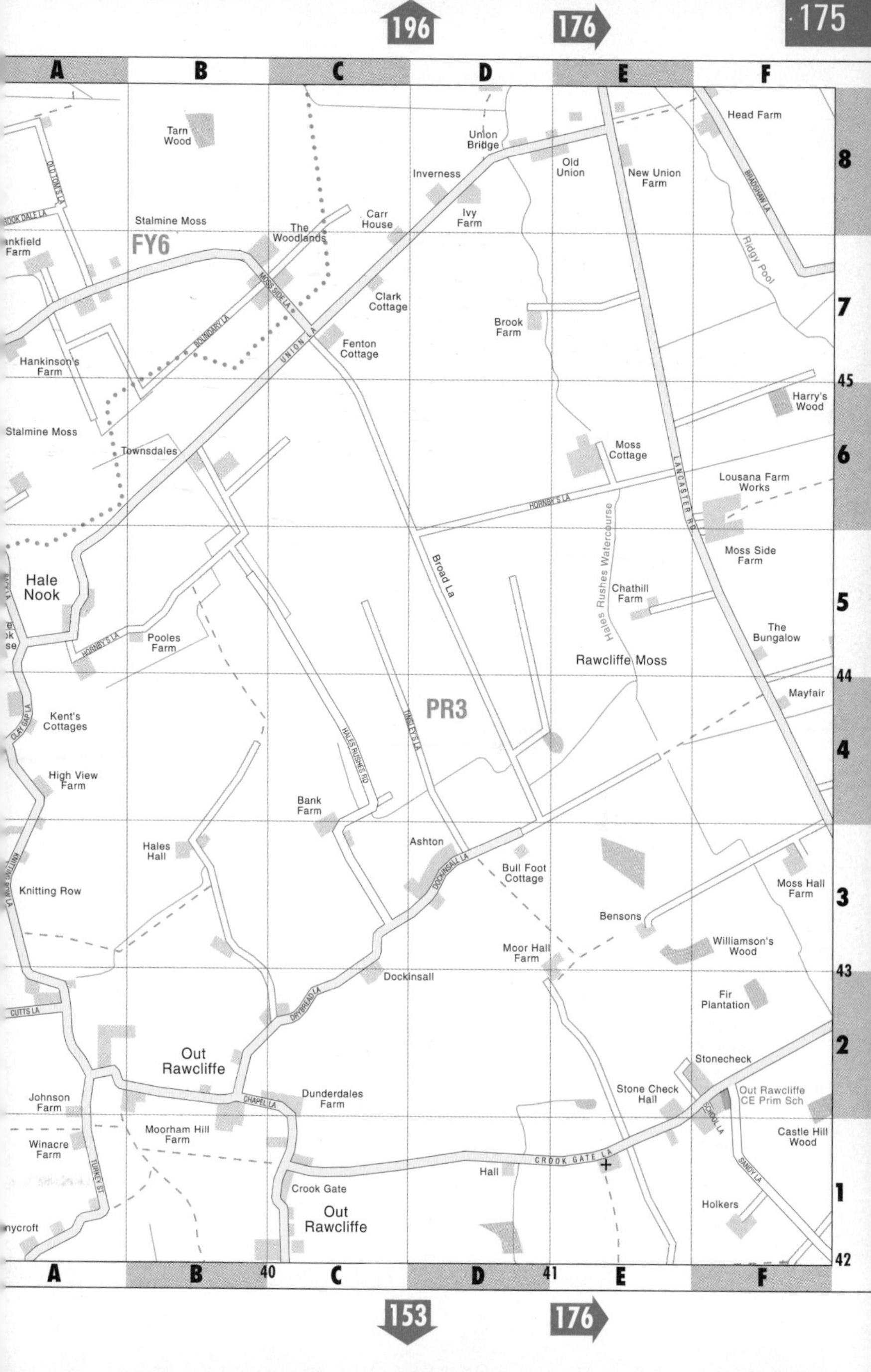
196
176
A
B
C
D
E
F
Tarn Wood
Union Bridge
Old Union
New Union Farm
Head Farm
Inverness
Ivy Farm
Carr House
The Woodlands
Stalmine Moss
FY6
OLD TOM'S LA
BROOK DALE LA
BRADSHAW LA
Ridgy Pool
Clark Cottage
Brook Farm
MOSS SIDE LA
BOUNDARY LA
UNION LA
Fenton Cottage
Hankinson's Farm
Harry's Wood
Stalmine Moss
Townsdales
Moss Cottage
HORNBY'S LA
LANCASTER RD
Lousana Farm Works
Hales Rushes Watercourse
Moss Side Farm
Broad La
Hale Nook
Chathill Farm
The Bungalow
Pooles Farm
Rawcliffe Moss
Kent's Cottages
CLAY GAP LA
Mayfair
PR3
HALES RUSHES RD
TINSLEY'S LA
High View Farm
Bank Farm
Ashton
Hales Hall
DOCKINSALL LA
Bull Foot Cottage
Moss Hall Farm
Knitting Row
KNITTING ROW LA
Bensons
Moor Hall Farm
Williamson's Wood
Dockinsall
Fir Plantation
CUTTS LA
DRYBREAD LA
Out Rawcliffe
Stonecheck
Johnson Farm
CHAPEL LA
Dunderdales Farm
Stone Check Hall
Out Rawcliffe CE Prim Sch
SCHOOL LA
Moorham Hill Farm
Castle Hill Wood
Winacre Farm
CROOK GATE LA
SANDY LA
Hall
TURKEY ST
Crook Gate
Out Rawcliffe
Holkers
8
7
45
6
5
44
4
3
43
2
1
42
40
41
153
176

175
197

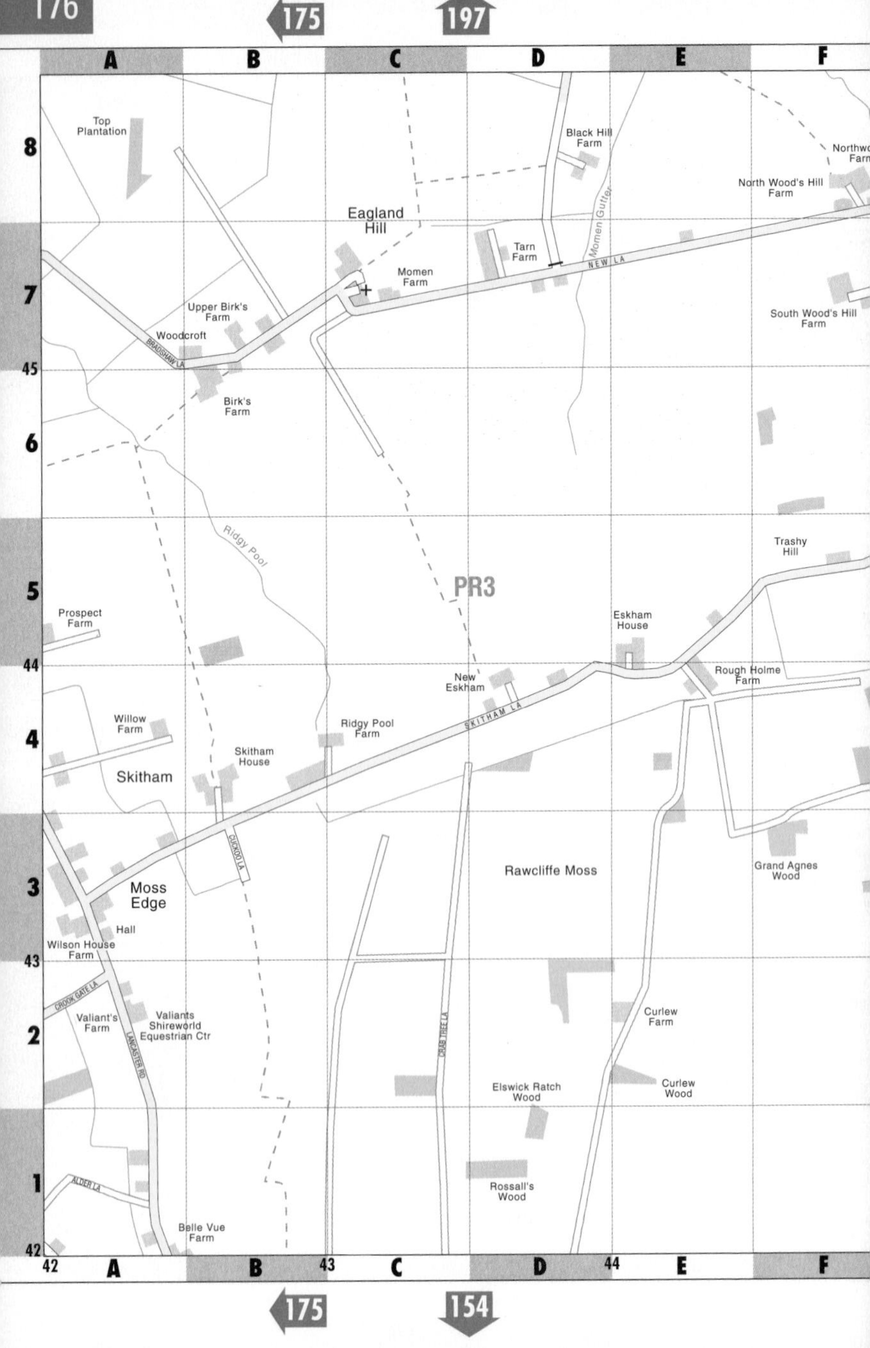

175
154

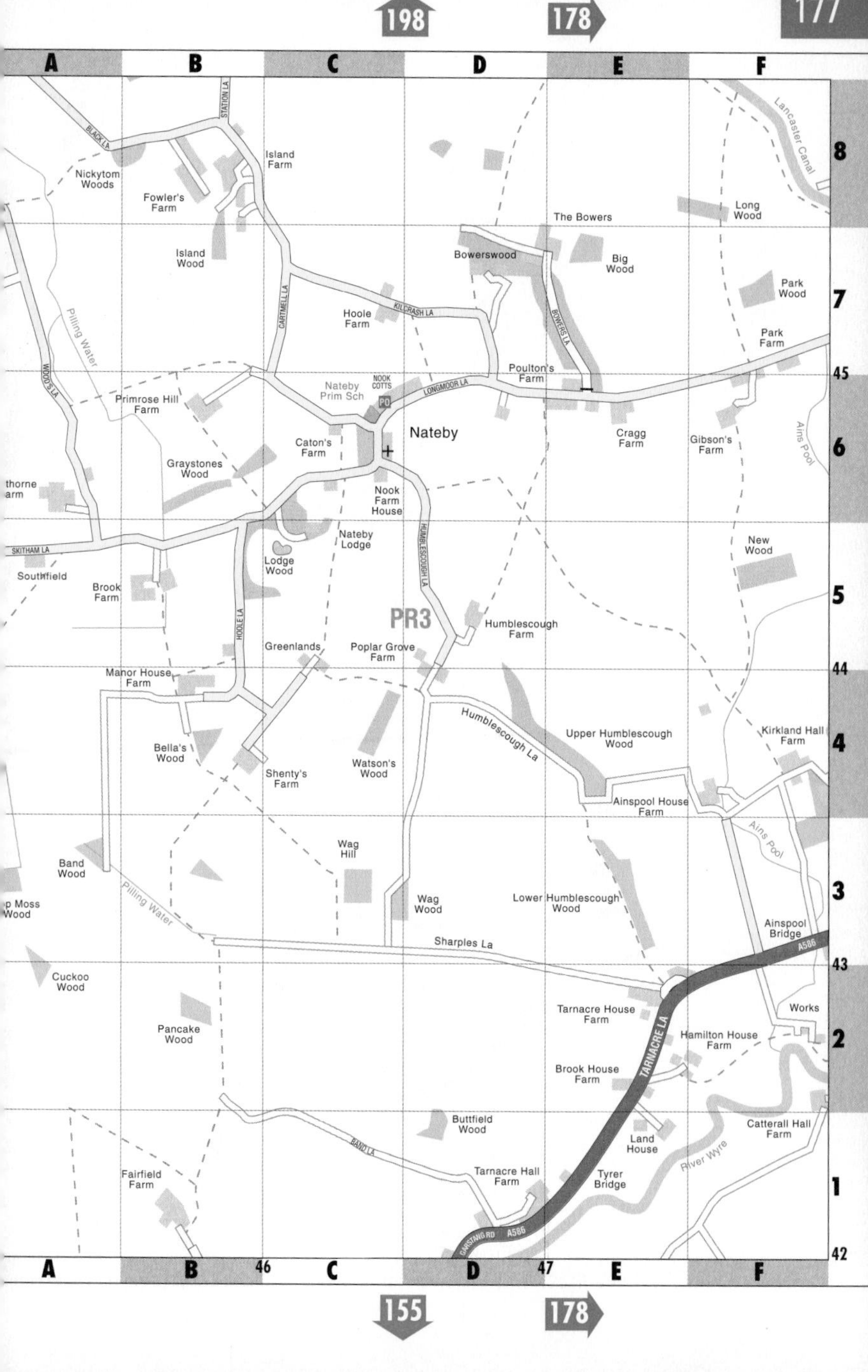
198
178
A
B
C
D
E
F
8
7
45
6
5
44
4
3
43
2
1
42
46
47
155
STATION LA
BLACK LA
Island Farm
Nickytom Woods
Fowler's Farm
Island Wood
Lancaster Canal
Long Wood
The Bowers
Bowerswood
Big Wood
Park Wood
Hoole Farm
KILCRASH LA
CARTMELL LA
BOWERS LA
Park Farm
Pilling Water
WOODS LA
Primrose Hill Farm
Nateby Prim Sch
NOOK COTTS
PO
LONGMOOR LA
Poulton's Farm
Nateby
Caton's Farm
Cragg Farm
Gibson's Farm
Ains Pool
Graystones Wood
thorne
arm
Nook Farm House
SKITHAM LA
Nateby Lodge
Lodge Wood
HUMBLESCOUGH LA
New Wood
Southfield
Brook Farm
HOOLE LA
PR3
Humblescough Farm
Greenlands
Poplar Grove Farm
Manor House Farm
Humblescough La
Upper Humblescough Wood
Kirkland Hall Farm
Bella's Wood
Shenty's Farm
Watson's Wood
Ainspool House Farm
Ains Pool
Wag Hill
Band Wood
Pilling Water
p Moss
Wood
Wag Wood
Lower Humblescough Wood
Ainspool Bridge
Sharples La
A586
Cuckoo Wood
Tarnacre House Farm
Works
Pancake Wood
TARNACRE LA
Hamilton House Farm
Brook House Farm
Buttfield Wood
Land House
Catterall Hall Farm
BAND LA
River Wyre
Fairfield Farm
Tarnacre Hall Farm
Tyrer Bridge
CARSTANG RD
A586
155
178

177
199

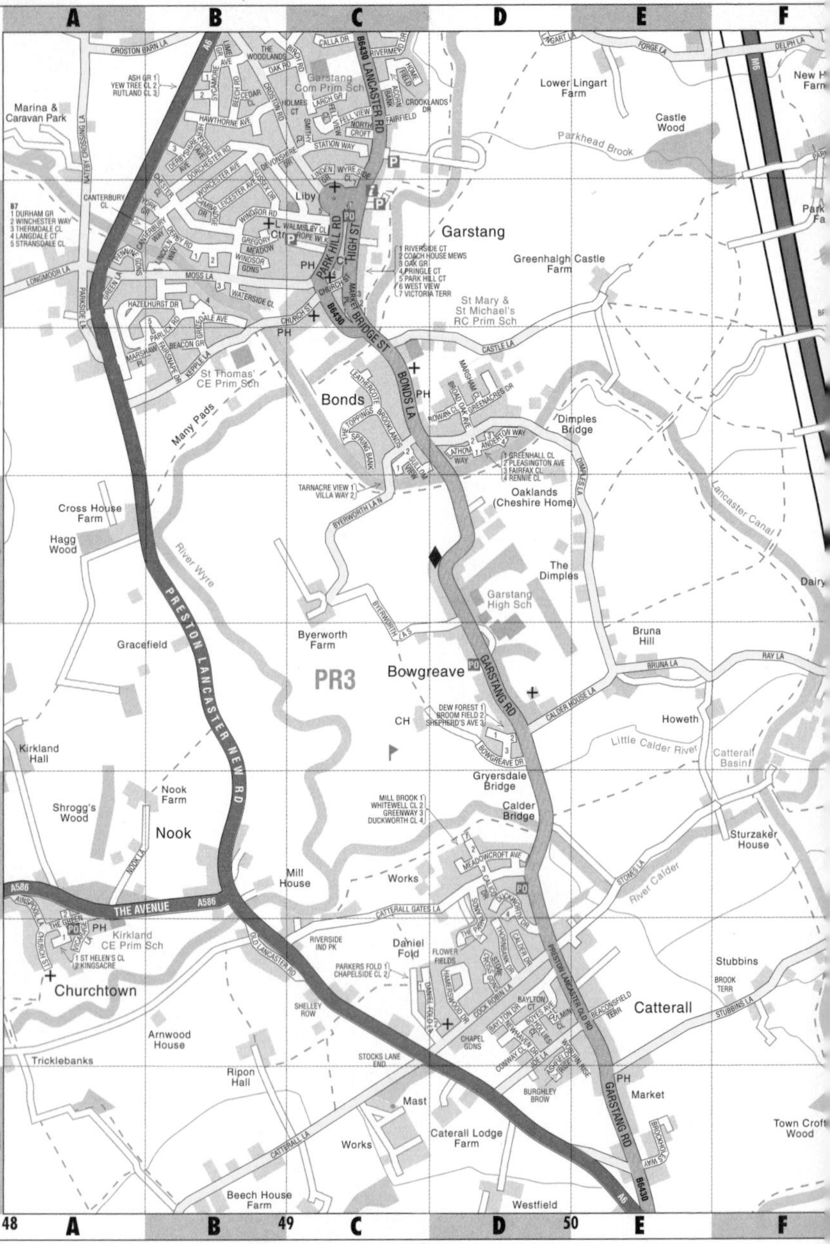

A B C D E F

8 7 6 5 4 3 2 1

Marina & Caravan Park
Lower Lingart Farm
Castle Wood
Garstang Com Prim Sch
Parkhead Brook
Garstang
Greenhalgh Castle Farm
St Mary & St Michael's RC Prim Sch
St Thomas' CE Prim Sch
Bonds
Dimples Bridge
Many Pads
Cross House Farm
Hagg Wood
Oaklands (Cheshire Home)
Lancaster Canal
River Wyre
The Dimples
Garstang High Sch
Gracefield
Byerworth Farm
PR3
Bowgreave
Bruna Hill
Howeth
Kirkland Hall
Little Calder River
Catterall Basin
Gryersdale Bridge
Nook Farm
Shrogg's Wood
Nook
Calder Bridge
Sturzaker House
Mill House
Works
River Calder
Kirkland CE Prim Sch
Daniel Fold
Stubbins
Churchtown
Catterall
Arnwood House
Tricklebanks
Ripon Hall
Mast
Market
Works
Caterall Lodge Farm
Town Croft Wood
Beech House Farm
Westfield

PRESTON LANCASTER NEW RD
GARSTANG RD
THE AVENUE
A6
A586
B6430
M6

B7
1 DURHAM GR
2 WINCHESTER WAY
3 THERMDALE CL
4 LANGDALE CT
5 STRANSDALE CL

1 RIVERSIDE CT
2 COACH HOUSE MEWS
3 OAK GR
4 PRINGLE CT
5 PARK HILL CT
6 WEST VIEW
7 VICTORIA TERR

1 GREENHALL CL
2 PLEASINGTON AVE
3 FAIRFAX CL
4 RENNIE CL

TARNACRE VIEW 1
VILLA WAY 2

DEW FOREST 1
BROOM FIELD 2
SHEPHERD'S AVE 3

MILL BROOK 1
WHITEWELL CL 2
GREENWAY 3
DUCKWORTH CL 4

1 ST HELEN'S CL
2 KINGSACRE

PARKERS FOLD 1
CHAPELSIDE CL 2

ASH GR 1
YEW TREE CL 2
RUTLAND CL 3

48 49 50 42 43 44 45

A
B
C
D
E
F
Heald Wood
Heald Farm
Vale House
VICTORIA TERR
SCHOOL COTTS
ALBERT TERR
PO
BURNSIDE
AVE
VALE TERR
THE HOLME
Mill
LONG ROW
Landskill
PARKHEAD LA
LONG LA
North Toppings Wood
Calder Vale
PRIMROSE COTTS
Calder Vale
Lucas's Farm
Walker House
Dobson's Farm
Janet's Hill Wood
Springs Wood
Lower House
STRICKENS LA
Sullom Side
Whitefield
Sullom High Wood
Tongue Lea Wood
Cobble Hey Wood
Cobble Hey
The Holt
Sullom Holt Farm
SULLOM SIDE LA
Lees Farm
Sullom Hill
Sullom Wood
Infield House
Eccles Farm
Stirzaker House Farm
Ringing Hill
PR3
Butt Hill
Bell Wood
Mill Banks Wood
SANDHOLME LA
HOBBS LA
Woodlands
BELL LA
Sullom End
Carr Wood
River Calder
Curwen Wood
BUTT HILL LA
Dandy Birks
Sandholme Mill
Gonder Lane Wood
Foggs Farm
Sandholme Bridge
GARDNER'S LA
Crabtree Nook
Kay's Wood
Dandy Birks Wood
GONDER LA
Gardner's Wood
Tewit Farm
Cross House
CLECKEN LA
Claughton Smithy
SMITHY LA
Rough Hey Wood
High House
STUBBINS LA
Blindhurst Wood
Mount Pleasant Farm
Claughton
Lower Carr Wood
Claughton Hall
LODGE RD
Clarkson's Farm
Old Lodges
MAY LA
Bowman Wood
St Mary's RC Prim Sch
WALMSLEY BRIDGE LA
OLD LODGE LA
M6
8
7
45
6
5
44
4
3
43
2
1
42
52
53

179
220

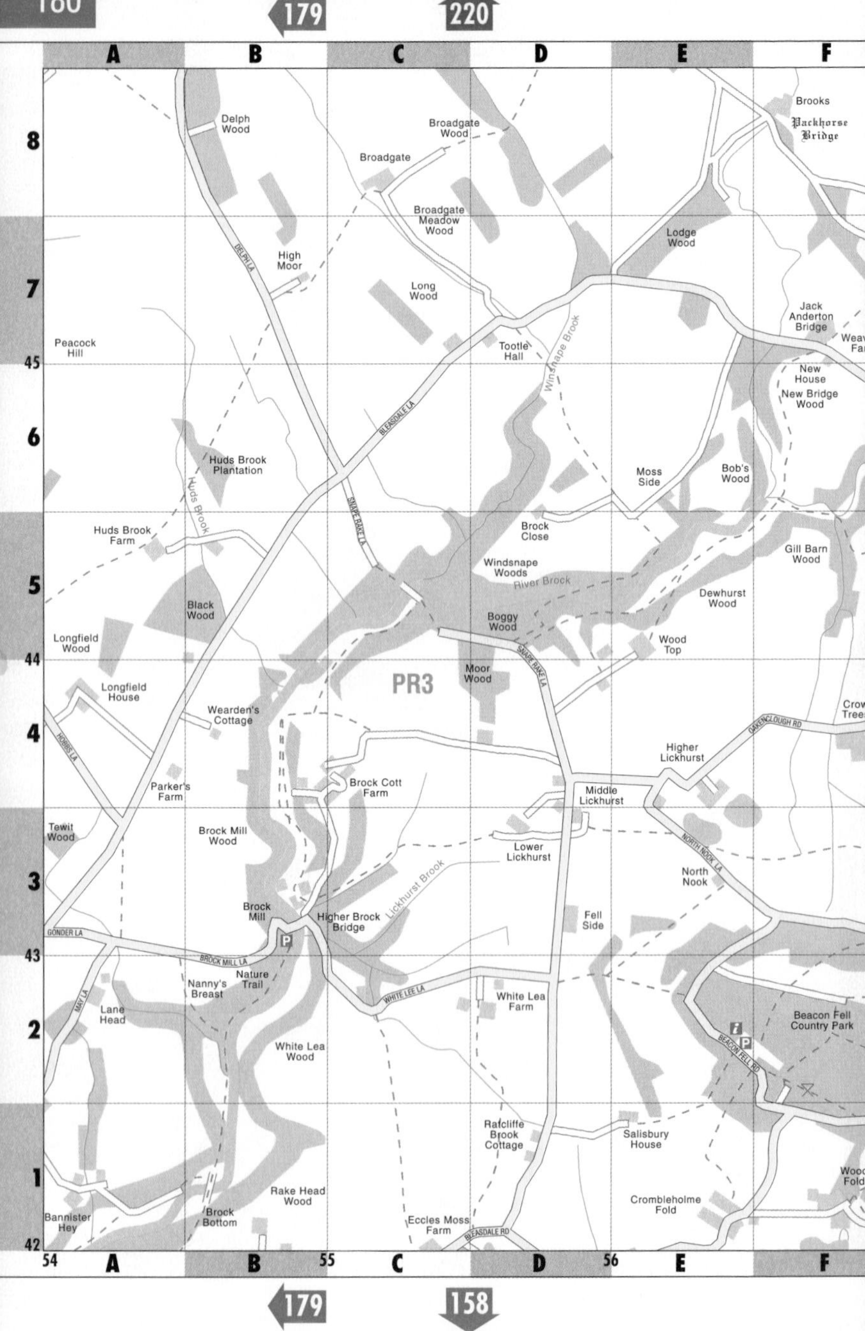

179
158

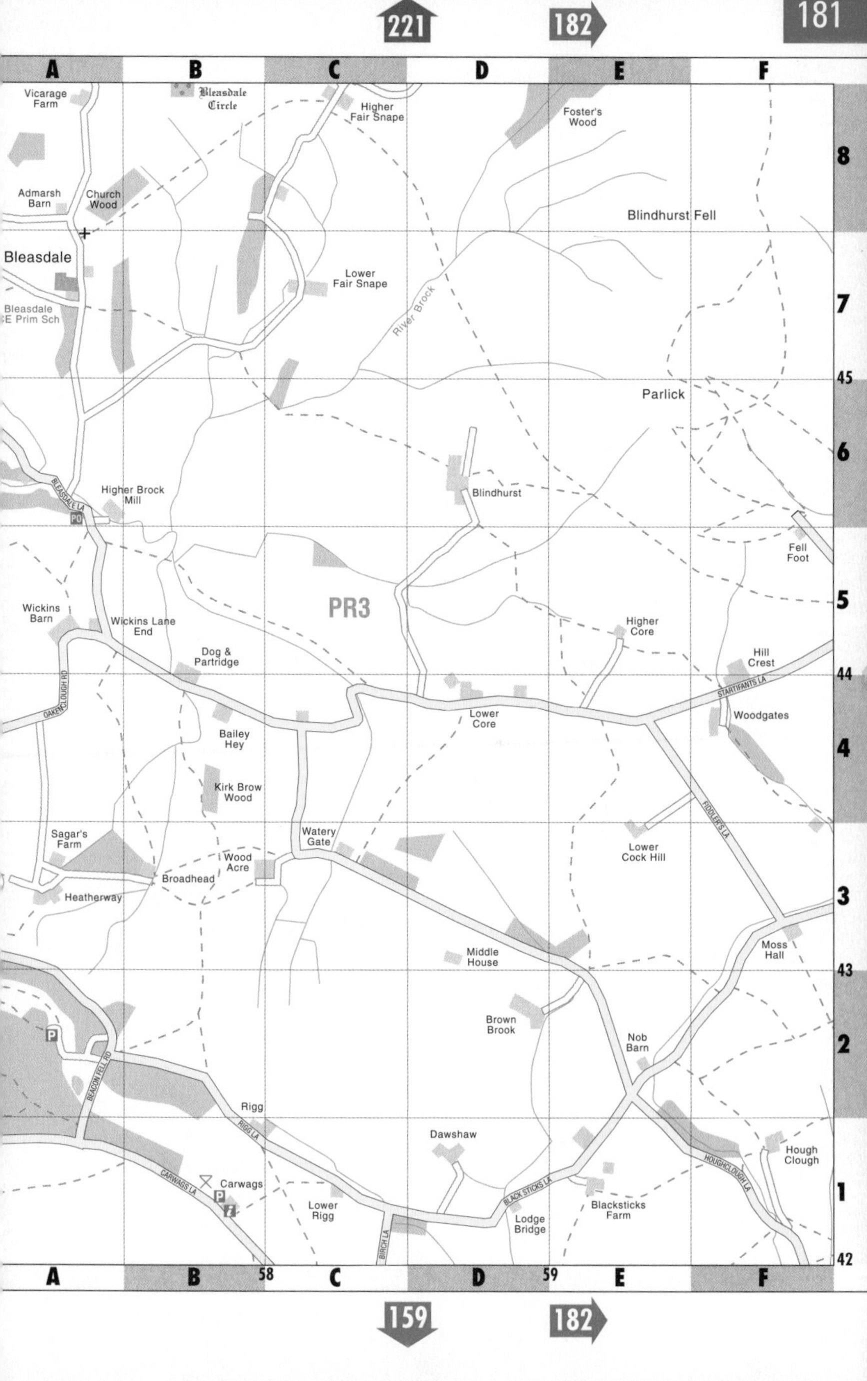
A B C D E F
Vicarage Farm
Bleasdale Circle
Higher Fair Snape
Foster's Wood
8
Admarsh Barn
Church Wood
Blindhurst Fell
Bleasdale
Lower Fair Snape
7
Bleasdale
E Prim Sch
River Brock
45
Parlick
6
BLEASDALE LA
Higher Brock Mill
Blindhurst
Fell Foot
5
Wickins Barn
Wickins Lane End
PR3
Higher Core
Dog & Partridge
Hill Crest
44
OAKENCLOUGH RD
STARTIFANTS LA
Lower Core
Woodgates
Bailey Hey
4
Kirk Brow Wood
FIDDLER'S LA
Sagar's Farm
Watery Gate
Lower Cock Hill
Wood Acre
Broadhead
Heatherway
3
Moss Hall
Middle House
43
Brown Brook
Nob Barn
2
BEACON FELL RD
Rigg
RIGG LA
Dawshaw
Hough Clough
HOUGHCLOUGH LA
Carwags
CARWAGS LA
BLACK STICKS LA
Blacksticks Farm
1
Lower Rigg
Lodge Bridge
BIRCH LA
42
A B 58 C D 59 E F

181
221

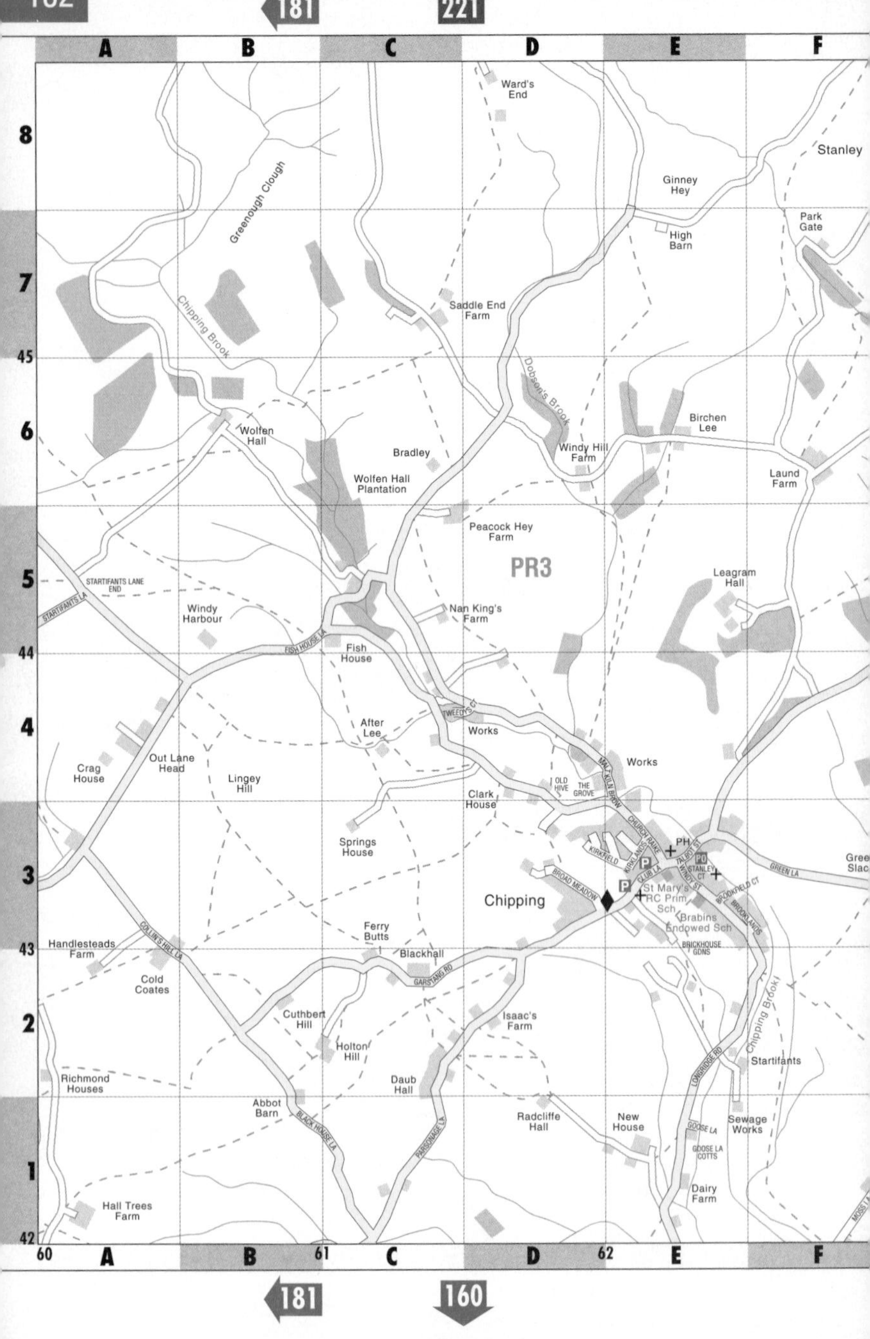

181
160

222
184
A
B
C
D
E
F
8
7
45
6
5
44
4
3
43
2
1
42
64
65
Lickhurst Farm
Higher Greystoneley
Park Style
Breast Wood
Lower Greystoneley
Greystoneley Brook
Buckbanks Wood
Ing Wood
Buckbanks Barn
New Ground Wood
Holme Barn
Knot Barn
Long Plantation
Knot Hill
Far Barn
Pale Wood
Swaney Holme Wood
Leagram Mill
PR3
Lower Lees
BB7
Clough Wood
Throstle Nest
Wardlsey
Hill Clough
River Hodder
Townley House
Dairy Barn
Hodder Hole Wood
Stakes
Leagram Brook
Doe Barn
New Plantation
Townley Moss Wood
Loud Mytham
Doeford Bridge
Loud Mytham Bridge
High Head Wood
Green Lands
High Head
Dusty Clough Wood
Woodtop Wood
Wood Top
Brook Wood
Yew Tree Farm
Bailey Hippings
River Loud
Gibbon Bridge
Cherry Tree House
Moss Side
MOSS LA
Gibbon Bridge Hotel
Elliotts
Loud Carr
Carr Side Farm
161
184

183
222

183
162

223
186
A
B
C
D
E
F
BROWSHOLME RD
Hodgson Moor
Daisy Hill
Sod Kiln Shoot
Elm Clough
Bashall Brook
Buckstall
Hare Clough
Birch Hill
Flatts
Braddup Clough
FREEHOLDS LA
Burbles Hill
Calf House
T Plantation
Blackhill Wood
RABBIT LA
Moor Piece
FREEHOLDS LA
Sandy Ford Brook
WHINNY LA
Braddup Wood
Braddup Farm
Hollins Wood
Gannies Farm
Kitchens
Colthurst Hall
Braddup House
Talbot Bridge
CROSS LA
BB7
Ridge Page Fold
Marsdens
Clough Bottom
Page Fold
Sandy Ford
Lower New House
Coulthurst
Bashall Eaves
PO
Rugglesmire
Bashall Brook
Mason Green
Cow Hey Brook
Red Pump Inn (PH)
Cow Hey
Backridge Plantation
Lower Titherington
Horse Hey
Back-Ridge Farm
Moss Barn
Bashall Hall
Bashall Lodge Plantation
River Hodder
Bashall Town
8
7
45
6
5
44
4
3
43
2
1
42
70
71
163
186

185
223

A B C D E F

8
Mill Farm
Cuttock Clough Farm
Hancocks
Drake House
Drakehouse Brook
Brocklehurst
Whittakers
MILL LA
Leemings
Feazer Wood
B6478
FELL RD
FREEHOLDS LA
7
Thornbers
Bookers
OAK RIDGE
ASH DR
WILLOW GR
FELL VIEW
PENDLE VIEW
MOOR LA
BROOKSIDE CRES
CROSSWAYS
RIBBLE DR
WOODLANDS DR
RODDER DR
FIRST AVE
RIBBLE VIEW
BOWLAND GATE LA
WHITTAKERS LA
Dove Syke
Greg Sike
Feazer Farm
45
Eaves Hall
Halsteads
6
Hospital Wood
Westfield End
EASTFIELD DR
HILLSIDE DR
WESTFIELD DR
GRINDLETON RD
Moor Roads
SLAIDBURN RD
CROSS LA
Linton Croft House
Old Town Head
Pillings
HAZEL DENE
PO
Hollins
Chancery Farm
Meadow Head
WADDINGTON RD
PH
CHAPEL CL
CHAPEL LA
Old Hall
West Bradford
5
King Henry's Grove
Lane Side
MILLS
MILLBROOK CT 1
MEADOW CROFT 2
BROOK VILLAS 3
CLITHEROE RD
Waddington & West Bradford CE Prim Sch
WADDINGTON HOSPL
THE SQUARE
WEST BRADFORD RD
44
Horrocksford Hall
Bradford Bridge
PO
REGENT ST
BRANCH RD
BEECHTHORPE AVE
BELLE VUE LA
Waddington Hall
BB7
Coplow Hill
Waddington
4
Works
Ribble Way
Pinder Hill
WEST VIEW
WADDOW GR
Lillands
Horrocksford
EDISFORD RD
CHURCH CL
PINDER CL
WADDOW VIEW
QUEENSWAY
WEST BRADFORD RD
RIBBLE VIEW
TWITTER LA
Waddington Brook
LC
Cross Hill
CLITHEROE RD
3
Wetters Bridge
Works
Brungerley
Horse Shoe Wood
River Ribble
43
Sewage Works
MOORLAND RD
Moorland Sch
Fields House
Knunck Knowles
Hall Wood
Brungerley Bridge
2
Waddow Hall
HOLME
HIPPINGS WAY
RIBBLESDALE AVE
DUNCROFT CL
PIMLICO RD
WARWICK DR
DORSET DR
SOMERSET AVE
DENBIGH
BRIDGE CT
Pendle Cty Prim Sch
Cemy
Boy Bank Wood
TUCKER HILL
KNUNCK KNOWLES DR
EASTHAM ST
HAWTHORNE PL
PARK AVE
LONGSIGHT AVE
CHATBURN RD
TOWER HILL GROVE
Ribble Way
WADDINGTON RD
FOX ST
PRINCESS AVE
ALLEYS GN
CAUSEWAY CROFT
1
Shireburn
BRUNGERLEY AVE
MILTON AVE
B6478
RADECLYFFE ST
KENDAL ST
LIME ST
SALTHILL RD
CORBRIDGE CT
P
BACK COMMONS
SWAN MDW
KIRKMOOR CL
RAILWAY VIEW RD
RAILWAY VIEW AVE
BRENNAND ST
CHURCH BROW
YORK ST
A671
BROOK ST
WHITTLE CL
SALTHILL VIEW
Sch
Clitheroe
42

72 A B 73 C D 74 E F

185
164

E1
1 COWPER AVE
2 CHESTER AVE
3 ST DENY'S CROFT
4 ST MARY'S ST
5 CHURCH BROW GDNS
6 KIRKMOOR RD
7 BLACK LA CROFT

F1
1 WELL TERR
2 NORTH ST
3 STAMFORD PL

224
188

165
188

187
224

187
166

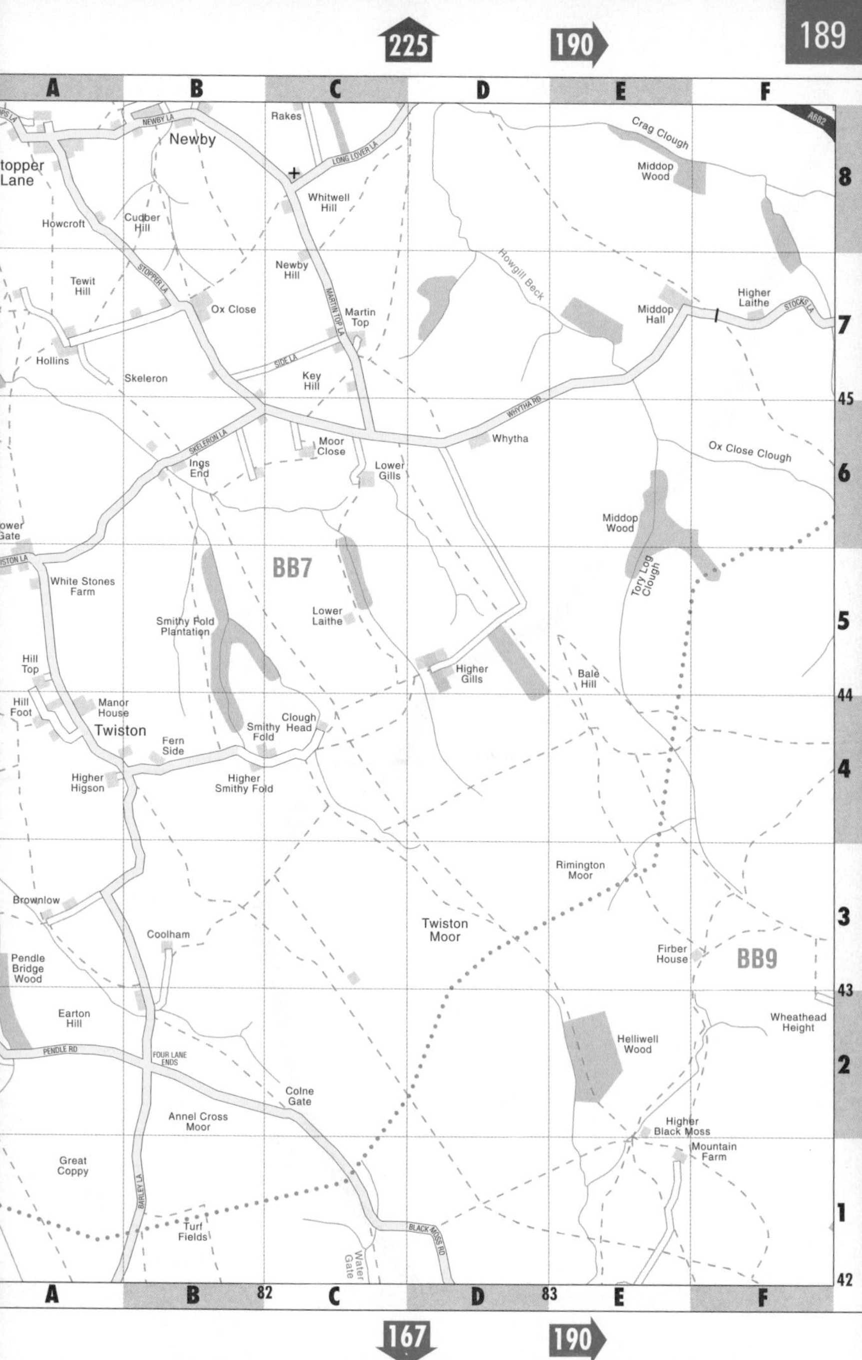
225
190
A
B
C
D
E
F
Newby
NEWBY LA
Rakes
LONG LOVER LA
Stopper Lane
Crag Clough
Middop Wood
Whitwell Hill
Howcroft
Cudber Hill
Tewit Hill
STOPPER LA
Newby Hill
MARTIN TOP LA
Howgill Beck
Ox Close
Martin Top
Middop Hall
Higher Laithe
STOCKS LA
Hollins
SIDE LA
Skeleron
Key Hill
WHYTHA RD
SKELERON LA
Moor Close
Whytha
Ox Close Clough
Ings End
Lower Gills
Middop Wood
BB7
White Stones Farm
Tory Log Clough
Lower Laithe
Smithy Fold Plantation
Hill Top
Higher Gills
Bale Hill
Hill Foot
Manor House
Twiston
Clough Head
Smithy Fold
Fern Side
Higher Higson
Higher Smithy Fold
Rimington Moor
Brownlow
Twiston Moor
Coolham
Firber House
BB9
Pendle Bridge Wood
Earton Hill
Wheathead Height
Helliwell Wood
PENDLE RD
FOUR LANE ENDS
Colne Gate
Annel Cross Moor
Higher Black Moss
Mountain Farm
Great Coppy
BARLEY LA
Turf Fields
BLACK MOSS RD
Water Gate
8
7
45
6
5
44
4
3
43
2
1
42
82
83
167
190

189
225

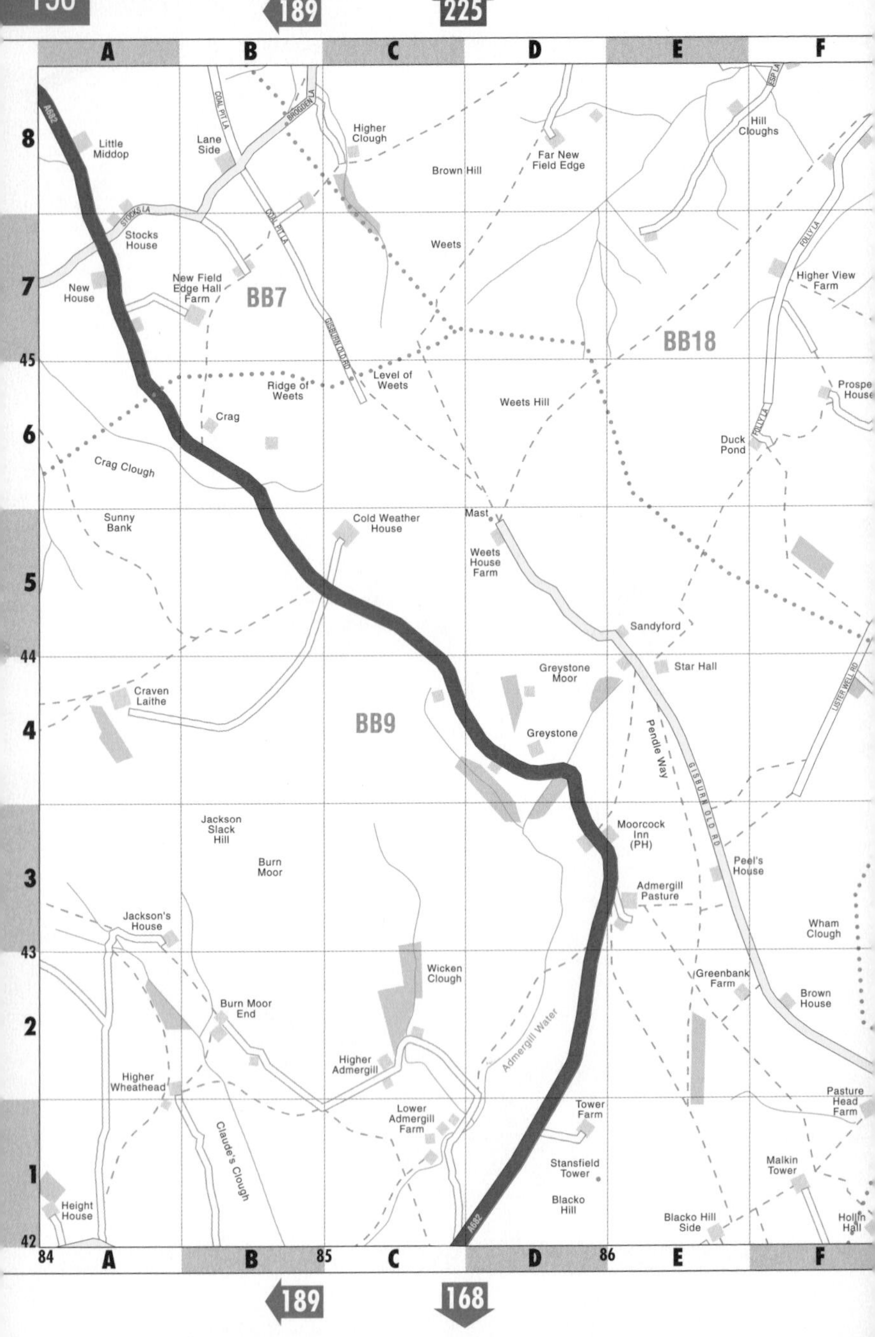

189
168

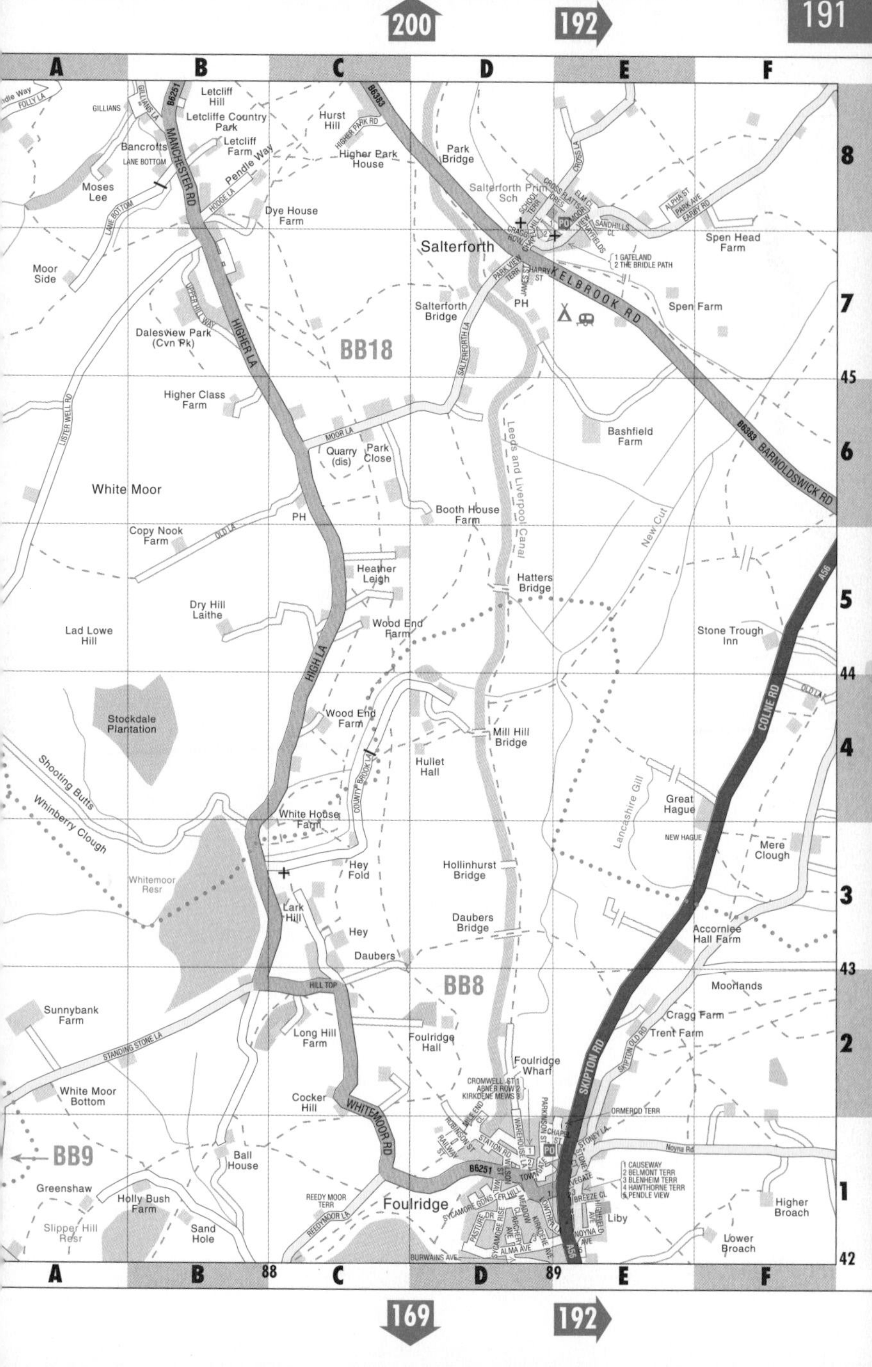

200
192
A
B
C
D
E
F
8
7
6
5
4
3
2
1
45
44
43
42
88
89
Letcliff Hill
Letcliffe Country Park
Hurst Hill
Letcliff Farm
Bancrofts
LANE BOTTOM
Pendle Way
Higher Park House
Park Bridge
GILLIANS
FOLLY LA
GILLIANS LA
B6251
MANCHESTER RD
B6383
HIGHER PARK RD
CROSS LA
Moses Lee
HODGE LA
Dye House Farm
Salterforth Prim Sch
CROSS FLATTS
SCHOOL TERR
ELM CL
ALPHA ST
PARK AVE
EARBY RD
SANDHILLS CL
Salterforth
Spen Head Farm
1 GATELAND
2 THE BRIDLE PATH
KELBROOK RD
PARK VIEW TERR
HARRY ST
JAMES ST
Moor Side
LANE BOTTOM
UPPER HILL WAY
HIGHER LA
Salterforth Bridge
PH
Spen Farm
Dalesview Park (Cvn Pk)
BB18
SALTERFORTH LA
Higher Class Farm
LISTER WELL RD
MOOR LA
Leeds and Liverpool Canal
Bashfield Farm
B6383
BARNOLDSWICK RD
Quarry (dis)
Park Close
White Moor
PH
Booth House Farm
Copy Nook Farm
OLD LA
New Cut
Heather Leigh
Hatters Bridge
A56
Dry Hill Laithe
Lad Lowe Hill
Wood End Farm
Stone Trough Inn
HIGH LA
COLNE RD
OLD LA
Stockdale Plantation
Wood End Farm
Mill Hill Bridge
Hullet Hall
COUNTY BROOK LA
Shooting Butts
Whinberry Clough
White House Farm
Lancashire Gill
Great Hague
NEW HAGUE
Mere Clough
Whitemoor Resr
Hey Fold
Hollinhurst Bridge
Lark Hill
Hey
Daubers Bridge
Accornlee Hall Farm
Daubers
HILL TOP
BB8
Moorlands
Sunnybank Farm
Long Hill Farm
Cragg Farm
Trent Farm
STANDING STONE LA
Foulridge Hall
SKIPTON OLD RD
Foulridge Wharf
White Moor Bottom
CROMWELL ST
ABNER ROW
KIRKDENE MEWS
Cocker Hill
WHITEMOOR RD
SKIPTON RD
ORMEROD TERR
BB9
Ball House
STATION RD
WAREHOUSE LA
PARKINSON ST
CHAPEL ST
STONEY LA
Noyna Rd
B6251
1 CAUSEWAY
2 BELMONT TERR
3 BLENHEIM TERR
4 HAWTHORNE TERR
5 PENDLE VIEW
Greenshaw
Holly Bush Farm
REEDY MOOR TERR
REEDYMOOR LA
Foulridge
SYCAMORE GDNS
PASTURE DR
SYCAMORE RISE
BREEZE CL
Liby
Higher Broach
Slipper Hill Resr
Sand Hole
Lower Broach
ALMA AVE
BURWAINS AVE
NOYNA AVE
A56
A
B
C
D
E
F
169
192

191
201

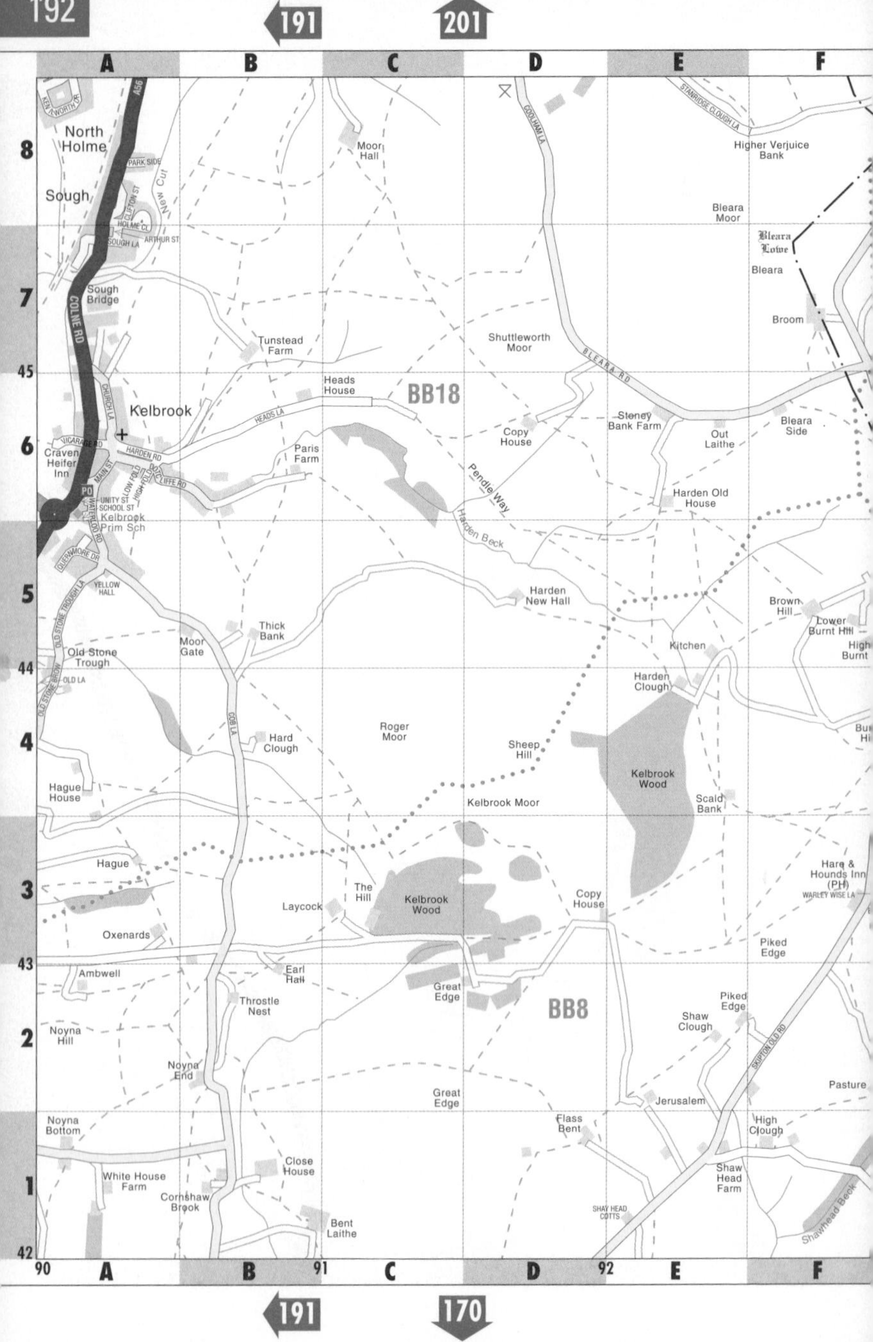

191
170

194

172

E2
1 HATFIELD WLK
2 HATFIELD GDNS
3 LANGDALE CT
E3
1 MASONS CT
2 WESTWOOD AVE
3 LONSDALE CRES

194

E4
1 MOWBRAY PL
2 STRATFORD PL
3 GRASMERE AVE

F2
1 WESTHEAD WLK
2 HATFIELD MEWS
3 GREGSON DR
4 EDMONDSEN PL
5 ARMITSTEAD WAY
6 FORSHAW CL
7 CROOKALL CL
8 ARMITSTEAD CT
9 NOBLETT CT
10 MAYFIELD PL
11 HARBOUR CL
F3
1 WARRENHURST HO
2 EASTWOOD AVE
3 ADDISON RD
F4
1 ROSE CT
2 SEYMOUR ST
3 ALBANY RD

193

A4
1 ST MARGARET'S CT
2 DELTA LA
3 POULTON GR
4 LAWRENCE ROW

193
173

196

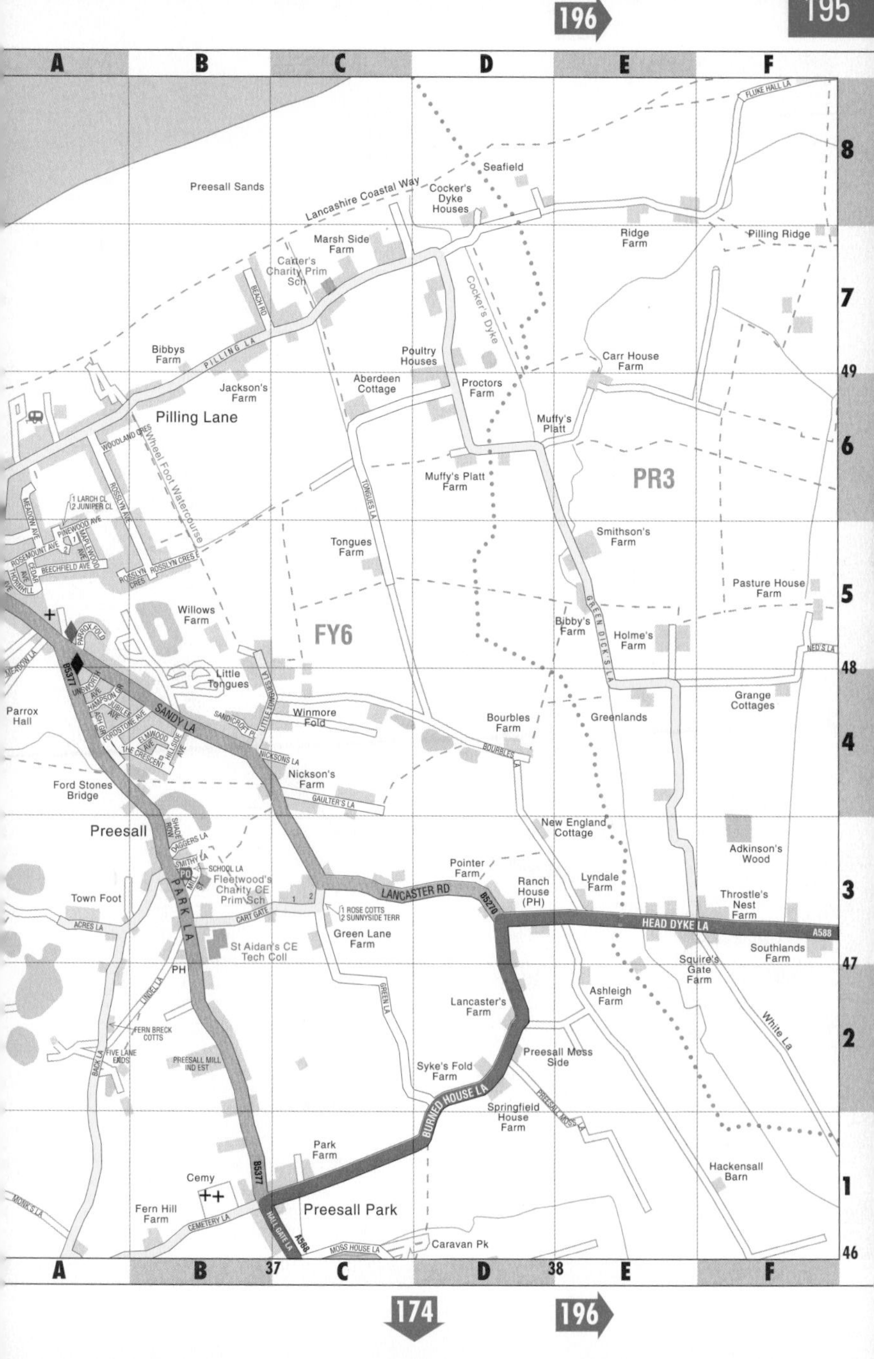
A B C D E F
8 7 49 6 5 48 4 3 47 2 1 46
37 38
Preesall Sands
Lancashire Coastal Way
Seafield
Cocker's Dyke Houses
FLUKE HALL LA
Marsh Side Farm
Carter's Charity Prim Sch
Ridge Farm
Pilling Ridge
BEACH RD
Cocker's Dyke
Bibbys Farm
PILLING LA
Poultry Houses
Carr House Farm
Jackson's Farm
Aberdeen Cottage
Proctors Farm
Pilling Lane
Muffy's Platt
WOODLAND CRES
Wheel Foot Watercourse
ROSSLYN AVE
Muffy's Platt Farm
PR3
1 LARCH CL
2 JUNIPER CL
MEADOW AVE
PINEWOOD AVE
MAPLEWOOD AVE
TONGUES LA
Smithson's Farm
ROSEMOUNT AVE
CEDAR AVE
BEECHFIELD AVE
ROSSLYN CRES
Tongues Farm
THORNHILL AVE
Pasture House Farm
Willows Farm
PARROX FOLD
FY6
GREEN DICK'S LA
Bibby's Farm
Holme's Farm
NED'S LA
MEADOW LA
B5377
Little Tongues
LITTLE TONGUES LA
UNSWORTH AVE
HAMPSON GR
JUBILEE AVE
Grange Cottages
Parrox Hall
SANDY LA
Winmore Fold
Bourbles Farm
Greenlands
SANDICROFT PL
FORDSTONE AVE
ELMWOOD AVE
THE CRESCENT
HILLSIDE AVE
BOURBLES LA
NICKSONS LA
Nickson's Farm
Ford Stones Bridge
GAULTER'S LA
New England Cottage
Preesall
SHADE ROW
DAGGERS LA
SCHOOL LA
SMITHY LA
Adkinson's Wood
PO
Pointer Farm
Ranch House (PH)
Lyndale Farm
Fleetwood's Charity CE Prim Sch
LANCASTER RD
B5270
Throstle's Nest Farm
Town Foot
PARK LA
1 ROSE COTTS
2 SUNNYSIDE TERR
HEAD DYKE LA
A588
ACRES LA
CART GATE
Green Lane Farm
St Aidan's CE Tech Coll
Southlands Farm
Squire's Gate Farm
PH
GREEN LA
Ashleigh Farm
LINDEL LA
Lancaster's Farm
White La
FERN BRECK COTTS
FIVE LANE ENDS
BACK LA
PREESALL MILL IND EST
Preesall Moss Side
Syke's Fold Farm
BURNED HOUSE LA
PREESALL MOSS LA
Springfield House Farm
Park Farm
Hackensall Barn
Cemy
B5377
MONK'S LA
Fern Hill Farm
CEMETERY LA
Preesall Park
HALL GATE LA
A588
MOSS HOUSE LA
Caravan Pk

174

196

195

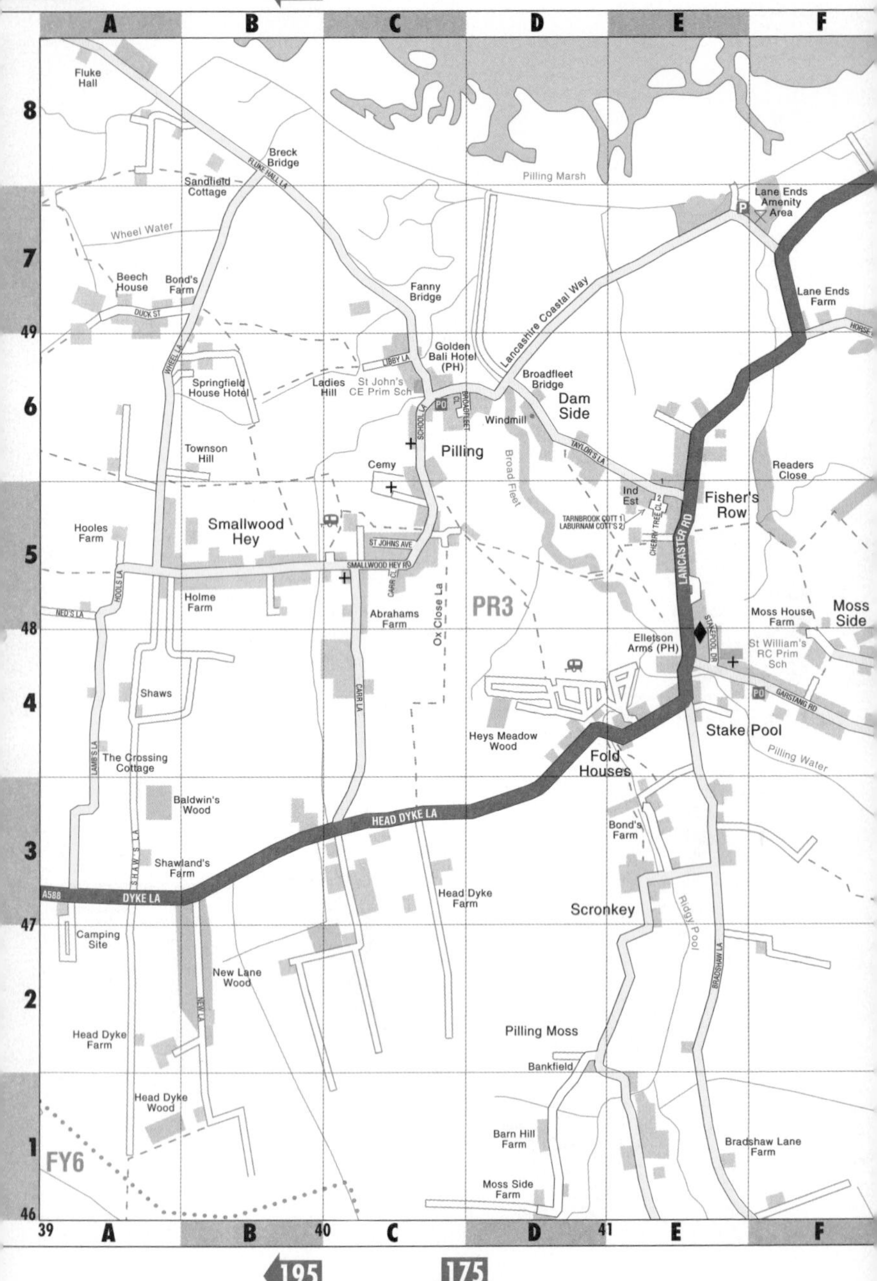

A
B
C
D
E
F
8
7
49
6
5
48
4
3
47
2
1
46
39
40
41
Fluke Hall
Breck Bridge
FLUKE HALL LA
Sandfield Cottage
Pilling Marsh
Lane Ends Amenity Area
Wheel Water
Beech House
Bond's Farm
DUCK ST
Fanny Bridge
Lane Ends Farm
HORSE
Lancashire Coastal Way
WHEEL LA
Golden Bali Hotel (PH)
LIBBY LA
Springfield House Hotel
Ladies Hill
St John's CE Prim Sch
Broadfleet Bridge
Dam Side
SCHOOL LA
BROADFLEET
Windmill
Pilling
Broad Fleet
TAYLOR'S LA
Townson Hill
Cemy
Readers Close
Ind Est
Fisher's Row
Hooles Farm
Smallwood Hey
TARNBROOK COTT 1
LABURNAM COTT'S 2
CHERRY TREE CL
LANCASTER RD
ST JOHNS AVE
SMALLWOOD HEY RD
HOOLS LA
Holme Farm
CARR CL
Ox Close La
PR3
NED'S LA
Abrahams Farm
Moss House Farm
Moss Side
Elletson Arms (PH)
STAKEPOOL DR
St William's RC Prim Sch
Shaws
CARR LA
GARSTANG RD
Stake Pool
Heys Meadow Wood
Pilling Water
LAMB'S LA
The Crossing Cottage
Fold Houses
Baldwin's Wood
HEAD DYKE LA
Bond's Farm
SHAW'S LA
Shawland's Farm
A588
DYKE LA
Head Dyke Farm
Scronkey
Ridgy Pool
Camping Site
New Lane Wood
BRADSHAW LA
NEW LA
Pilling Moss
Head Dyke Farm
Bankfield
Head Dyke Wood
Barn Hill Farm
Bradshaw Lane Farm
FY6
Moss Side Farm

195
175

A
B
C
D
E
F
Wrampool Bridge
A588
Mill House
Gulf Farm
Wrampool House
Birch House Farm
Moss Edge
Lancashire Coastal Way
GULF LA
Near Moss Farm
Moss House Farm
Moss Edge Farm
Tarn Farm
LA2
Pilling Hall
Cockerham Moss
Moss House
Parkfield Farm
Bond's Farm
HORSE PARK LA
Gull Moss
Crawley's Dyke
PEAHALL LA
PR3
Poplar Farm
Winmarleigh Moss
Works
Poplar Grove
Works
Jarvis Carr Farm
GARSTANG RD
Brookfield
Calcald's Farm
Carr Bridge
Stafford's Farm
Crawley's Cross Farm
Crookabreast Farm
Bone Hill Bridge
ISLAND LA
Cumming Carr
Cogie Hill Farm
Pilling Water
BONE HILL LA
Bone Hill Farm
BLACK LA
Rushy Slack Farm
Kentucky Farm
8
7
49
6
5
48
4
3
47
2
1
46
43
44

197
203

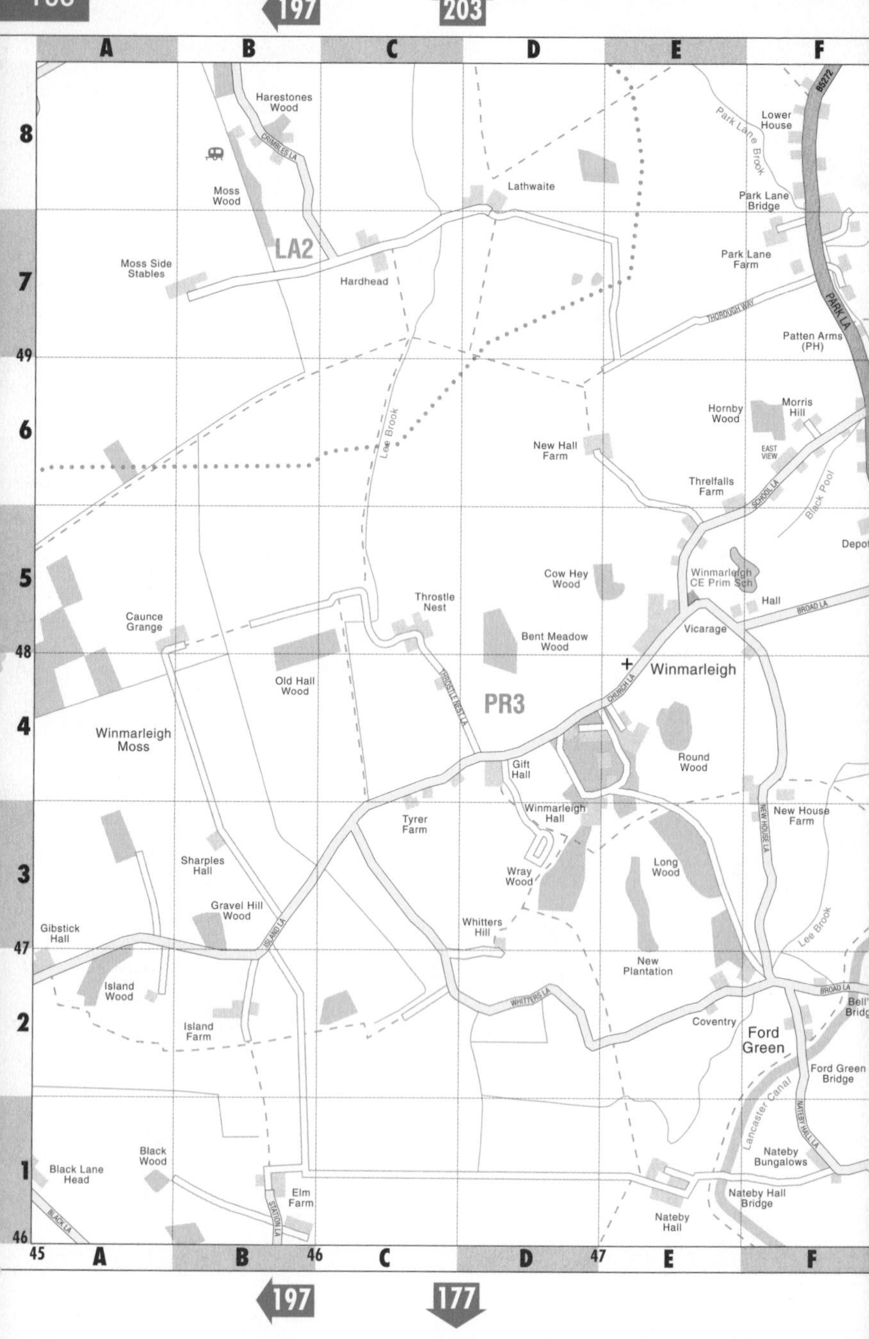

197
177

204
220

178
220

225

B2
1 BACK CHAPEL
2 JEEP HILL
3 BROOK ST
4 ORCHARD ST
5 GARDEN ST
6 MARKET ST
7 BACK SKIPTON RD
8 FORESTER'S BLDGS
9 ST JAMES' RD
10 ST JAMES' SQ
11 GREEN ST
12 BESSIE ST
13 EAST VIEW
14 PLEASANT VIEW
15 FAR EAST VIEW
16 EAST PAR
17 WELL HOUSE SQ
18 EAST HILLS ST
19 CO-OPERATIVE ST
20 RAILWAY ST
21 SUSSEX ST

225

B3
1 HOLINS CT
2 DAM SIDE
3 BAIRSTOW ST
4 BROGDEN ST
5 BRUCE ST
6 CORNMILL TERR
7 NORTH PAR
8 SOUTH PAR
9 MASONS WAY

191

C2
1 MYRTLE GR
2 BEECH GR
3 UNITY ST
4 TURNER ST
5 STUART ST
6 CRAVEN ST

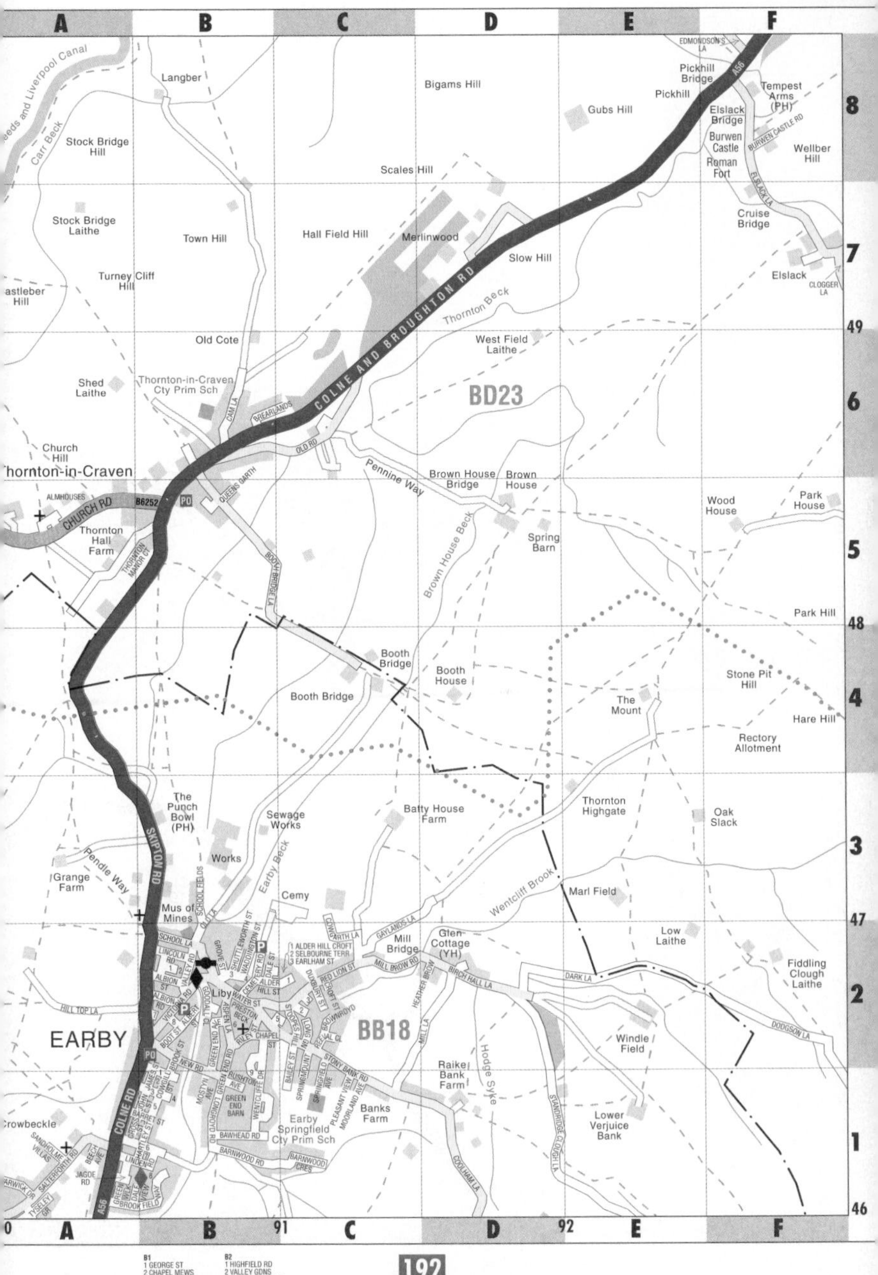

B1
1 GEORGE ST
2 CHAPEL MEWS
3 APPLEGARTH ST
4 RIVERSIDE TERR
5 WILLIAM ST
6 ROSTLE TOP RD
7 LINDEN CT
8 JAGOE MEWS
9 THE BUNGALOWS

B2
1 HIGHFIELD RD
2 VALLEY GDNS
3 LOWER CROFT ST
4 SHAW SQ
5 WELBURY CL
6 WILKINSON MOUNT
7 VICTORIA ST
8 EDWARD ST

192

205

A
B
C
D
E
F
8
7
53
6
5
52
4
3
51
2
50
1
42
43
44
Thursland Hill
Cockersand Abbey (remains of)
Bank Houses
Higher Bank House
Lancashire Coastal Way
Bank End
HILLAM LA
Cockerham Marsh
LA2
Braides
Sand Side
Sand Villa Cottages
Sand Side
Beechfield
Sweetings
Sand Villa
Mill House Bridge
PR3
A588

197

206
204
A
B
C
D
E
F
8
7
53
6
5
52
4
3
51
2
1
50
A588
Launds Farm
The Launds
Cock Hall Woods
Cock Hall
Flat Wood
Home Farm
Norbreck Farm
Broad Gate
Hillam Lane Farm
HILLAM LA
Hasty Beck
Hill House Farm
Berries Head
Hillam Farm
Hillam
Hillam House
Know Hill Wood
LANCASTER RD
Batty Hill
Up Town
Johnny Bees
Centre Wood
Cockerham
WILLY LA
RECTORY GDNS
Manor Inn (PH)
River Cocker
Centre Farm
Green Breck
Pattys
P
PO
B5272
Cockerham Hall
MAIN ST
Cocker House Bridge
COCKERHAM RD
Cockerham Road Bridge
Cockerham Parochial CE Prim Sch
Hillside House
Marsh Houses
MARSH LA
MARSH CL
MARSH HOS
LA2
TANSY LA
Lancaster Canal
Lancashire Coastal Way
Shepherd's Farm
Clifton House Farm
Marsh House
West Lodge
CROOKHEY GDNS
Cocker Bridge
Clifton Hill
Cocker Wood
Cappershead Wood
Crookhey Hall Sch
Breck's Bridge
Stony Lane Bridge
River Cocker
Higher Crookhey Farm
PR3
STONY LA
GARSTANG RD
Goose Green
CRIMBLES LA
Little Crimbles
Crookall Bridge
Crookhey Farm
Weasel Wood
Richmond Grove Farm
Great Crimbles
Raingills Farm
RATCLIFFE WHARF LA
Forton Hall Farm
Middle Crimbles
Burns Bridge
Lee Brook
Patten House Farm
PARK LA
GULF LA
Cockerham Moss
B5272
46
47
198
204

203 207 220

203 199 220

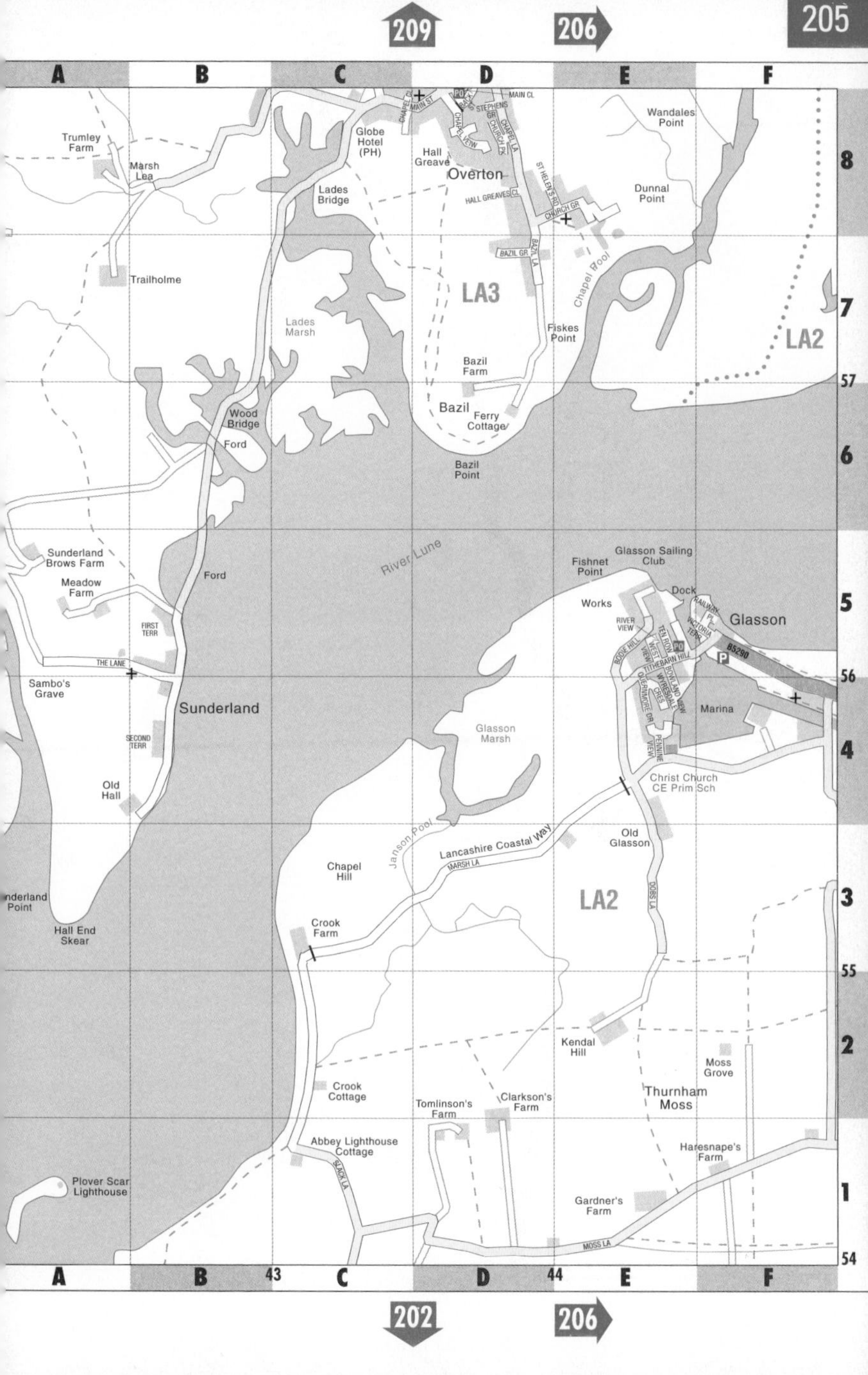
209
206
A
B
C
D
E
F
Trumley Farm
Marsh Lea
Trailholme
Globe Hotel (PH)
Lades Bridge
Hall Greave
Overton
Wandales Point
Dunnal Point
LA3
Lades Marsh
Chapel Pool
Fiskes Point
LA2
Bazil Farm
Bazil
Ferry Cottage
Bazil Point
Wood Bridge
Ford
Sunderland Brows Farm
Meadow Farm
River Lune
Glasson Sailing Club
Fishnet Point
Works
Dock
Glasson
B5290
Marina
Sambo's Grave
Sunderland
Glasson Marsh
Old Hall
Christ Church CE Prim Sch
Old Glasson
Janson Pool
Lancashire Coastal Way
MARSH LA
Chapel Hill
LA2
Crook Farm
Hall End Skear
Kendal Hill
Moss Grove
Thurnham Moss
Crook Cottage
Tomlinson's Farm
Clarkson's Farm
Abbey Lighthouse Cottage
Haresnape's Farm
Plover Scar Lighthouse
Gardner's Farm
MOSS LA
SLACK LA
DOBS LA
THE LANE
FIRST TERR
SECOND TERR
8
7
57
6
5
56
4
3
55
2
1
54
43
44
202
206

205
210

205
203

LA1
LA2
Mast
Met Sta
Dam Head Bridge
Dam Head Farm
Thorn Hill
Cander Bank
Old School House
Long Lane End
Eastrigg
Hazelrigg
Condergarth
CH
Banton House
Lane Side
Thornfield
Univ of Lancaster
Hotel
Brandrigg
Barrow Greaves
River Conder
Higher Kit Brow
Sefton's Farm
Kitchen Grange
Barker House
Ward Farm
Ward Houses
Lower Kit Brow
Higher Knowe Hill
Knowe Hill
Whitley Beck
Langshaw La
Ellel
Lunds Green
Pipe House
School Villas
Damside Cotts
Boldens
Cocker Clough Wood
Galgate Silk Mills Ind Est
1 Airedale
2 Crofters Fold
Cockshades Hill
Crag End
Galgate
St John's CE Prim Sch
Cockshades
Railway Farm
Walker's-i'-th'-Fields
Brunstow
Brunstow Wood
Skew Bridge
Smith Green
Galgate Bridge
Cocker Bridge
Smith Green Farm
School House
Borbles Hall
Ellel Crag
River Cocker
Lane House
Coppy House Barn
Junction Bridge
Double Bridge
Hampson Green
Lancaster Canal
Chatburn House
Newland Home Farm
Newland Hall
Nuthurst Farm
Hampson Cotts
Hampson La
Preston Lancaster Rd
Main Rd
Stoney La
Salford Rd
Chapel St
Chapel La
Swaledale
Wharfdale
Green La
Park La
East La
Barker Sq 1
Middle La 2
Kit Brow La
Bay Horse Rd
Procter Moss Rd
Long La
Hazelrigg La
Scriffen La
Highland Brow
Vernon Cres
A4
1 Meadow Pk
2 Leachfield Cl
3 Vernon Pk
4 Vernon Ct
5 John St
6 Tanhouse
7 Downham Cotts
8 Teesdale
9 East View
10 Mulberry Cotts
11 Makinsons Row
M6
A6
PO
P
33
A B C D E F
8 7 57 6 5 56 4 3 55 2 1 54
49 50

F8
1 STRAWBERRY MEWS
2 BACK KNOWLYS RD
3 KNOWLYS DR
4 KNOWLYS CRES
5 TARNBROOK RD

A B C D E F

HEYSHAM

Lower Heysham

Higher Heysham

Chapel Hill

Heysham Head

Barrows

Half Moon Bay

Near Naze

Mast

North Wharf

Heysham Harbour

South Quay

Fish Quay

North Round Head

South Jetty

Heysham

LA3

Heysham Nuclear Power Sta Nature Reserve

Heysham Nuclear Power Sta Vis Ctr

Nuclear Power Stas

Heysham Banks

St Peter's CE Prim Sch

Trumacar Com Prim Sch

CH

PH

Caravan Pk

WALKERS IND EST

Mast

Whittam Hill

Heysham Bus Park

Ind Est

Greendales Farm

Greendales L Pk

ST MARY'S RD 1
HESKETH RD 2

GLEN VIEW AVE 1
ST MILDRED'S WAY 2
BERKELEY CT 3
CURWEN AVE 4
CHERRY TREE CL 5
HEATHFOOT DR 6
PENHALE CT 7
PENHALE CL 8

F7
1 DOUGLAS AVE
2 MORETON GR
3 HAZEL BANK
4 FARRIERS FOLD

1 SAXON HEIGHTS
2 BRADFORD GR
3 HESSAM HEIGHTS

A589, A683, ROTHESAY RD, TRUMACAR, MIDDLETON WAY, MIDDLETON RD, HEYSHAM RD, PRINCESS ALEXANDRA WAY, MONEY CLOSE LA, SMITHY LA, KNOWLYS RD, LONGLANDS LA, WESLEY DR, BERWICK WAY, KINTYRE WAY, HEYSHAM PK, HEYSHAM HALL GR, HEYSHAM HALL DR, GLEN VIEW DR, CYPRUS RD, ARRAN AVE, ROYAL RD, SHORE RD, FLARE RD, BAY RD, FIELD RD, PORT WAY, PENROD WAY, McDONALD RD, CONNAUGHT RD, LONDONDERRY RD, OAKVILLE RD, WESTMORLAND GR, MELVILLE RD, COMBERMERE GR, BROOKLANDS DR, TOMLINSON RD, BELL-AIRE PARK HOMES, HEYSHAM MOSSGATE RD, DROVERS WLK, SEYMOUR GR, HILLSEA AVE, LISTER GR, HILLMOUNT AVE, GAS FIELD RD, COMPRESSION RD, WORKSHOP RD, STALLS RD, SIDINGS RD, MAIN AVE, CARR LA, PENNINGTON CT, BAY VIEW COTTS, KESWICK GR, WARREN RD, DELAMERE AVE, HEATHFOOT AVE, SYCAMORE GDNS, PENHALE GDNS

8 7 61 6 5 60 4 3 59 2 1 58

212
210
A
B
C
D
E
F
8
7
61
6
5
60
4
3
59
2
1
58
43
44
Oxcliffe Hill Farm
St Patrick's RC Prim Sch
Snatchems
Golden Ball Inn (PH)
Lythe Bridge
North Farm
Downlands Farm
Radio Mast
Oxcliffe Pool
Moss Gate Farm
Moss Side Farm
High Bridge
Peggymarsh Pool
River Lune
Heysham Moss
Riverside Farm
Hillside Farm
Heaton Marsh
Great Swart Hill
Woodhouse Farm
Mast
Heaton
Windmill Hill
Heysham Moss Sidings
Cottam Farm
LA3
Meadup House
Heaton Hall
Wks
Heaton Park House
Wymber Hill Farm
Colloway Pool
Colloway Farm
Works
Downy Field Farm
Colloway Marsh
Colloway Hill
Middleton
Moss La
Westmoor Farm
St Helen's CE Sch
Sewage Works
LA2
A683
CLAY LA
MOSS RD
LANCASTER RD
HEATON BOTTOM RD
DOWNEYFIELD RD
MIDDLETON RD
CROOK NOOK
KEVIN GR
YENHAM LA
PEDDER DR
PEDDER AVE
PEDDER RD
LOW RD
HALL DR
CARR LA
GARDEN TERR
PRIMROSE COTTS
WESTBOURNE RD
MILL HILL GR
HALLAM LA
OLD TRAFFORD PK
CHEDWORTH AVE
GILSTEAD AVE
LITTLEDALE AVE
ROSEDALE AVE
BURFORD DR
1 CHARLBURY GR
2 ABINGDON GR
3 HURSTLEIGH DR
THISTLE BREAK
LONGMEADOW LA
THE SPINNEY
JENNY NOOK
205
210

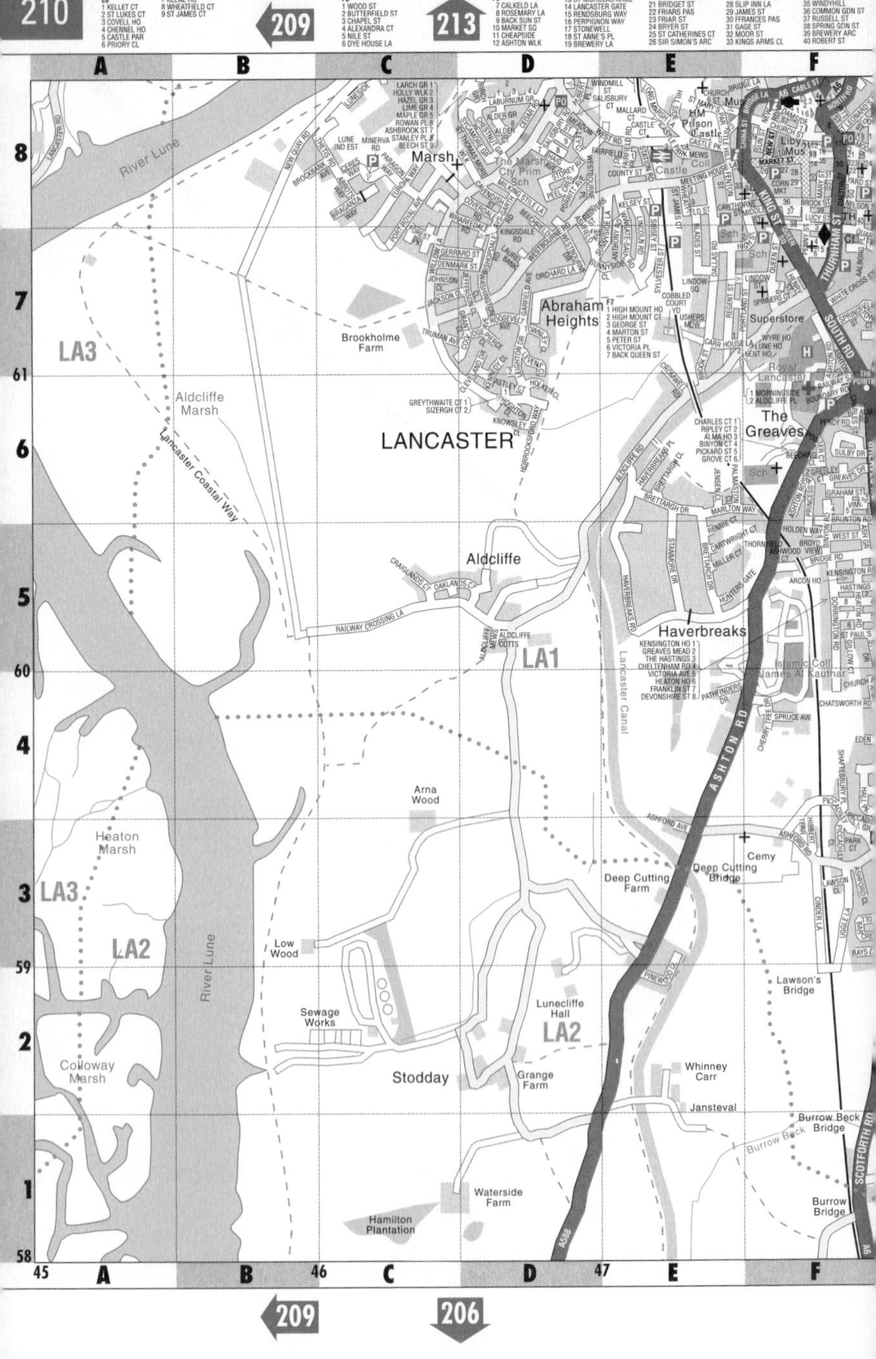
E8
1 KELLET CT
2 ST LUKES CT
3 COVELL HO
4 CHENNEL HO
5 CASTLE PAR
6 PRIORY CL
7 KELNE HO
8 WHEATFIELD CT
9 ST JAMES CT
209
F8
1 WOOD ST
2 BUTTERFIELD ST
3 CHAPEL ST
4 ALEXANDRA CT
5 NILE ST
6 DYE HOUSE LA
213
F8
7 CALKELD LA
8 ROSEMARY LA
9 BACK SUN ST
10 MARKET SQ
11 CHEAPSIDE
12 ASHTON WLK
13 ST NICHOLAS ARCS
14 LANCASTER GATE
15 RENDSBURG WAY
16 PERPIGNON WAY
17 STONEWELL
18 ST ANNE'S PL
19 BREWERY LA
20 GREAT JOHN ST
21 BRIDGET ST
22 FRIARS PAS
23 FRIAR ST
24 BRYER ST
25 ST CATHERINES CT
26 SIR SIMON'S ARC
27 MARKET GATE
28 SLIP INN LA
29 JAMES ST
30 FFRANCES PAS
31 GAGE ST
32 MOOR ST
33 KINGS ARMS CL
34 ALMSHOUSES
35 WINDYHILL
36 COMMON GDN ST
37 RUSSELL ST
38 SPRING GDN ST
39 BREWERY ARC
40 ROBERT ST
A
B
C
D
E
F
8
7
61
6
5
60
4
3
59
2
1
58
45
46
47
River Lune
LANCASTER RD
LUNESIDE
NEW QUAY RD
LARCH GR 1
HOLLY WLK 2
HAZEL GR 3
LIME GR 4
MAPLE GR 5
ROWAN PL 6
ASHBROOK ST 7
STANLEY PL 8
BEECH ST 9
LUNE IND EST
MINERVA RD
PARAGON WAY
EUROPA WAY
BROCKBANK AVE
CERES WAY
BRAGANZA WAY
PORT ROYAL AVE
FOREST PK
Marsh
The Marsh Cty Prim Sch
LABURNUM GR
ALDER GR
CEDAR RD
PO
WINDMILL ST
SALISBURY CT
MALLARD CT
CASTLE CT
LONG MARSH LA
HM Prison
Castle
Mus
Liby
Mus
MARKET ST
KING ST
CHINA ST
BRIDGE LA
CABLE ST
NORTH RD
A6
DAMSIDE
NEW ST
CHURCH ST
CORN MKT
BROCK ST
LUCY ST
THURNHAM ST
DALTON
MOOR
CASTLE PK
PARK MEWS
Coll
MEETING HOUSE LA
WEST RD
COUNTY ST
FAIRFIELD RD
STATION RD
WESTBOURNE PL
STOREY AVE
PEEL CRES
PORRITT AVE
MILKING STILE LA
CAVENDISH ST
COVERDALE RD
WHARFEDALE RD
KINGSDALE RD
WESTBOURNE RD
GERRARD ST
DENMARK ST
JOHNSON CL
JACKSON CL
JEFFERSON CL
WASHINGTON CL
LAUREL BANK
ORCHARD LA
GARFIELD AVE
SUNNYSIDE LA
SUNNYSIDE RD
KELSEY ST
LINCOLN RD
SIBSEY ST
SYLVESTER ST
ST JAMES CT
BLADES ST
DALLAS RD
HIGH ST
QUEEN ST
SPINNERS CT
LINDOW ST
COBBLED COURT YD
USHERS MDW
REGENT ST
PORTLAND ST
Superstore
SOUTH RD
WHITE CROSS
WYRE HO
LUNE HO
KENT HO
CARR HOUSE LA
Sch
Abraham Heights
F7
1 HIGH MOUNT HO
2 HIGH MOUNT CT
3 GEORGE ST
4 MARTON ST
5 PETER ST
6 VICTORIA PL
7 BACK QUEEN ST
Brookholme Farm
ROOSEVELT AVE
TRUMAN AVE
COOLIDGE AVE
PIERCE
TOWNLEY CL
LEVENS CL
LEIGHTON DR
HOLKER CL
ASTLEY CT
KENNEDY CL
CLEVELAND DR
HOGHTON CL
KNOWSLEY CL
HORROCKSFORD WAY
GREYTHWAITE CT 1
SIZERGH CT 2
LANCASTER
Royal Lancaster
H
1 MORNINGSIDE
2 ALDCLIFFE PL
BOUNDARY RD
RAILWAY ST
The Greaves
CROMWELL RD
ALDCLIFFE RD
HAVERBREAKS PL
BRETTARGH CL
BRETTARGH DR
CHARLES CT 1
RIPLEY CT 2
ALMA HO 3
BINYON CT 4
PICKARD ST 5
GROVE CT 6
JENSEN CL
PALMASTON CL
MARLTON WAY
RENNIE CT
CARTWRIGHT CT
MILLER CT
HUNTERS GATE
STANMORE DR
THORNFIELD
ASHWOOD CT
BROYD VIEW
HOLDEN WAY
WEST ST
BRIDGE RD
ARCON HO
KENSINGTON RD
HASTINGS
HEATON RD
DORRINGTON RD
ST PAUL'S
GILLOW CT
CHURCH
CHATSWORTH RD
GRESLEY
GREAVES DR
SULBY DR
GRAHAM ST
PRINCESS
ASHTON RD
BEECHING
LA3
Aldcliffe Marsh
Lancaster Coastal Way
Aldcliffe
CRAIGLANDS CT
OAKLANDS CT
RAILWAY CROSSING LA
ALDCLIFFE MEWS
ALDCLIFFE COTTS
LA1
HAVERBREAKS RD
Haverbreaks
KENSINGTON HO 1
GREAVES MEAD 2
THE HASTINGS 3
CHELTENHAM RD 4
VICTORIA AVE 5
HEATON HO 6
FRANKLIN ST 7
DEVONSHIRE ST 8
PATHFINDERS DR
Islamic Coll
Jamea Al Kauthar
CHERRY TREE DR
SPRUCE AVE
Lancaster Canal
ASHTON RD
SHAFTESBURY PL
PICCADILLY
EDEN
Arna Wood
ASHFORD AVE
ASHFORD RD
HIBBERT TERR
PARK CT
Cemy
Heaton Marsh
LA3
Deep Cutting Farm
Deep Cutting Bridge
LAWSON CL
CINDER LA
UGGLE LA
RAYS
LA2
Low Wood
PINEWOOD CL
River Lune
Lawson's Bridge
Sewage Works
Lunecliffe Hall
LA2
Colloway Marsh
Stodday
Grange Farm
Whinney Carr
Jansteval
Burrow Beck Bridge
Burrow Beck
SCOTFORTH RD
Waterside Farm
Hamilton Plantation
Burrow Bridge
A588
A6
209
206

214
226

207
226

E5
1 BK QUEEN ST
2 BK LINES ST
3 WASHINGTON AVE
4 RABY ST
5 RIBBLESDALE CT
6 PRIMROSE ST
7 WHITMOOR CL

209

G4
1 KENTMERE GR
2 BUTTERMERE AVE
3 BLEA TARN PL
4 WINDERMERE CT
5 LOWESWATER DR

6
HOME BREEZE HO
TUDOR GR
PALMER GR
SEABORN GR
LODGES CT
LAISTER CT

C2
1 KEER BANK
2 GILPIN CL
3 BELA CL
4 CRAKE BANK
5 GREGARETH CL
6 WINDHOLME
7 CROASDALE
8 WHITENDALE
9 BRINDLE CL

D1
1 CHARNLEY ST
2 BRIERY ST
3 FURNESS ST
4 MARSH ST
5 HUTTON WAY
6 BORDER CT
7 RICHARDS WLK
8 COWDREY MEWS

D2
1 BURNFELL RD
2 TARNBROOK RD
3 RAYGILL PL
4 AUSTWICK RD
5 RAWTHEY RD
6 MEARBECK PL
7 CROSSHILL PL
8 BROWGILL PL
9 WHITERAY RD

E1
1 RIVERSIDE LOFTS
2 REYNOLDS ST
3 BRUNTON'S WAREHOUSE
4 VICTORIA WHARF
5 BUOYMASTERS
6 THE REEDS

E2
1 UDALE PL
2 ASHDALE PL
3 CONDER PL
4 FOXDALE PL
5 ROEBURN PL
6 HINDBURN PL

F1
1 CAPTAIN'S ROW
2 PARK HO
3 LORD ST
4 BACK LORD ST
5 PHOENIX ST

F2
1 SKERTON
2 LABURNUM RD
3 KENT ST
4 RIVERSWAY
5 MILLRACE CT
6 SKERTON HO
7 BRIDGE HO

F3
1 BULLER ST
2 RUSKIN RD
3 DAISY ST
4 REGAL TERR
5 ALDEN TERR
6 ASHBOURNE CL
7 LINDETH GDNS
8 RICHMON HO

F4
1 RIPON AVE
2 SELBY AVE
3 FARLETON CT
4 ESKRIDGGE CL

210
214

213 216 231

A1
1 MARDALE RD
2 GREBE WHARF
3 GLADSTONE TERR
4 FACTORY HILL
5 ST LEONARD CT
6 DE VITRE ST
7 SWALLOW WHARF

213 211 231

216

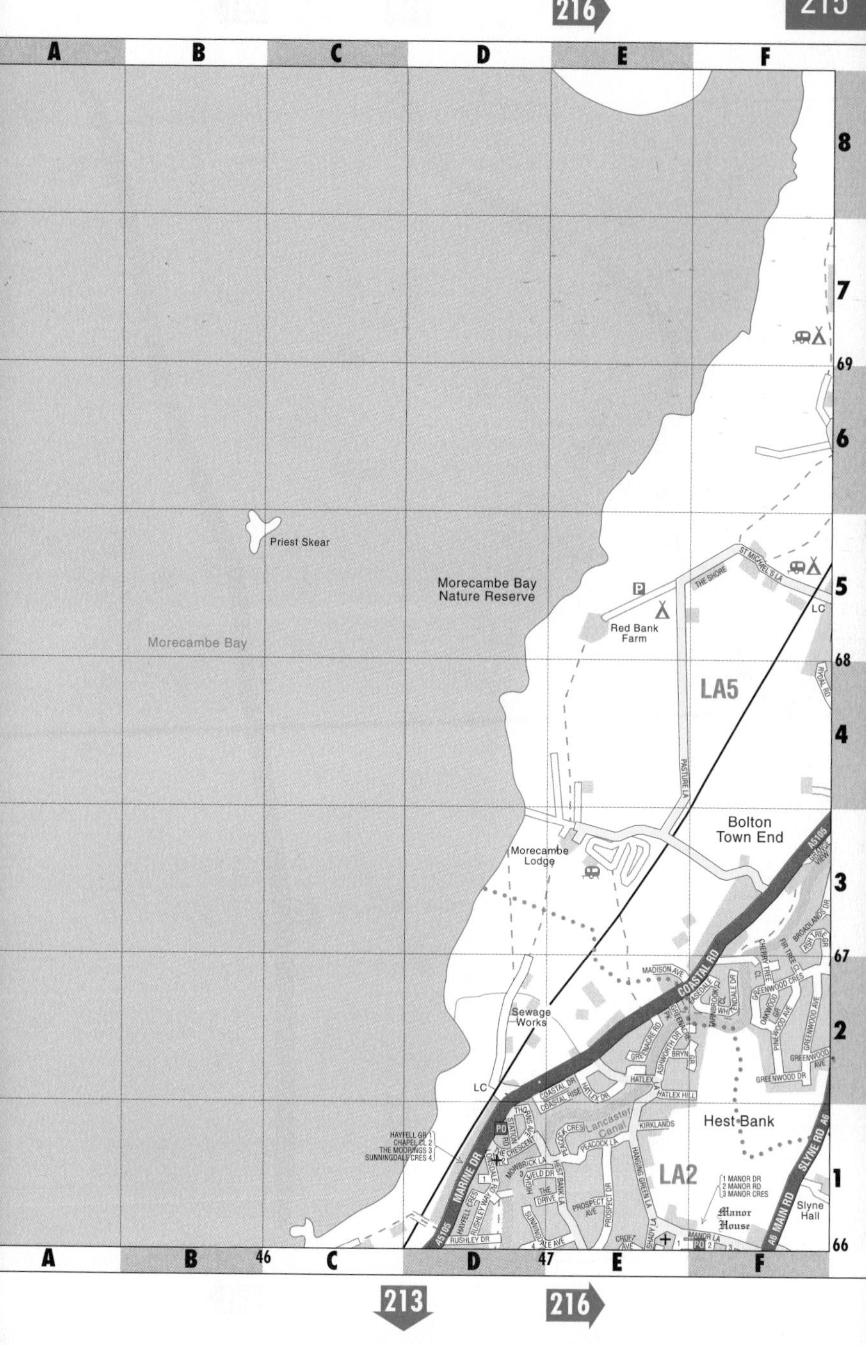
A
B
C
D
E
F
8
7
69
6
5
68
4
3
67
2
1
66
46
47
Priest Skear
Morecambe Bay Nature Reserve
Morecambe Bay
Red Bank Farm
THE SHORE
ST MICHAEL'S LA
LC
LA5
RYDAL RD
PASTURE LA
Bolton Town End
Morecambe Lodge
A5105
GRANGE VIEW
BROADLANDS DR
ASH TREE GR
FIR TREE CL
CHERRY TREE CL
MADISON AVE
COASTAL RD
EASEDALE
GREENWOOD CRES
Sewage Works
GREENACRE RD
ASHWORTH DR
BRYN GR
PINEWOOD AVE
GREENWOOD AVE
GREENWOOD DR
HATLEX
HATLEX HILL
LC
COASTAL DR
COASTAL RISE
HATLEX DR
Lancaster Canal
KIRKLANDS
Hest Bank
HAYFELL GR 1
CHAPEL CL 2
THE MOORINGS 3
SUNNINGDALE CRES 4
STATION RD
THE CRESCENT
PEACOCK CRES
PEACOCK LA
MOWBRICK LA
HANGING GREEN LA
SLYNE RD A6
LA2
1 MANOR DR
2 MANOR RD
3 MANOR CRES
MARINE DR
HIGHFIELD DR
THE DRIVE
HEST BANK LA
PROSPECT AVE
PROSPECT DR
Manor House
Slyne Hall
HAYFELL CRES
RUSHLEY WAY
RUSHLEY DR
SUNNINGDALE AVE
CROFT AVE
SHADY LA
MANOR LA
A6 MAIN RD
A5105

213
216

215 217 231

215 214 231

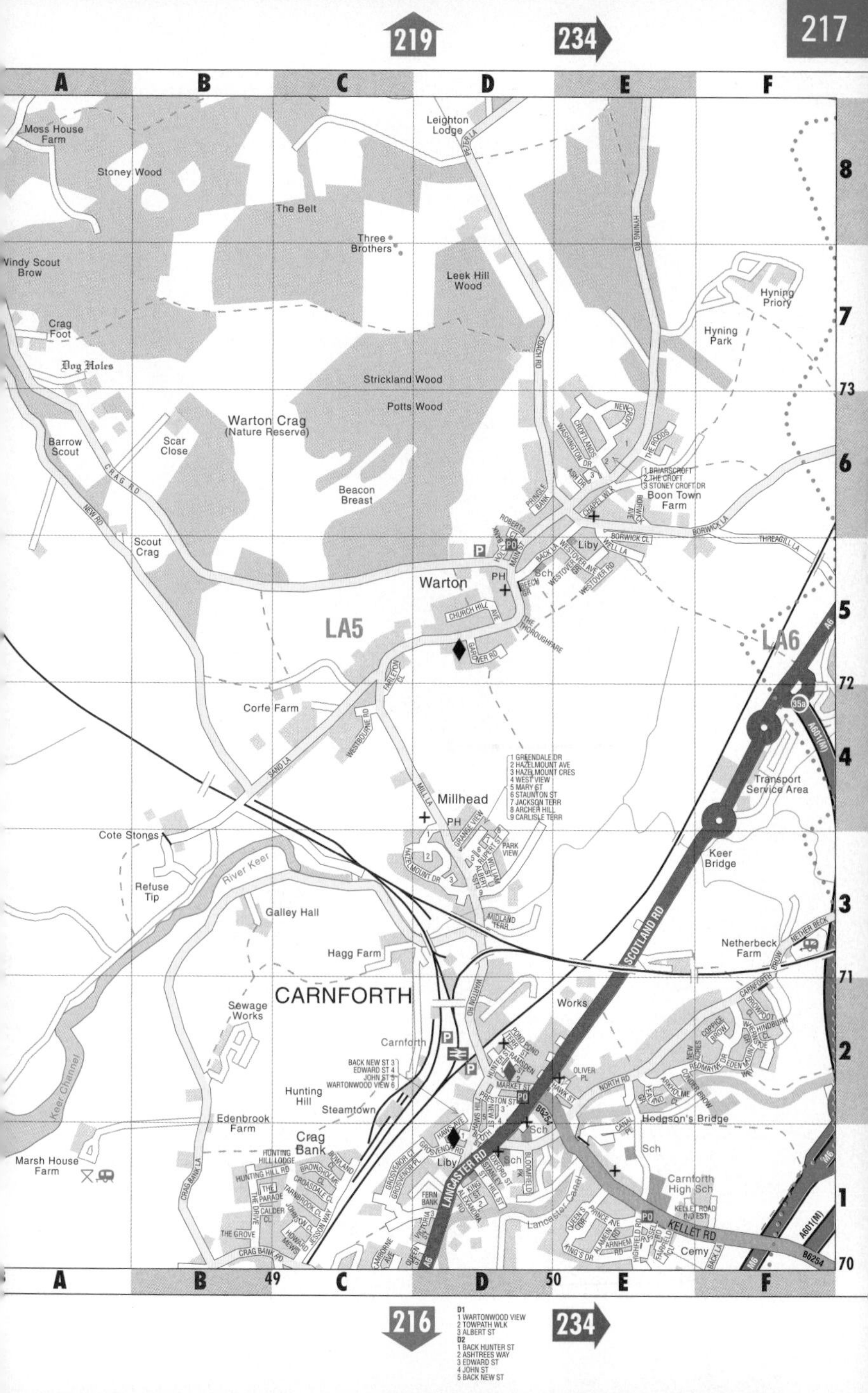

216
234

D1
1 WARTONWOOD VIEW
2 TOWPATH WLK
3 ALBERT ST
D2
1 BACK HUNTER ST
2 ASHTREES WAY
3 EDWARD ST
4 JOHN ST
5 BACK NEW ST

237

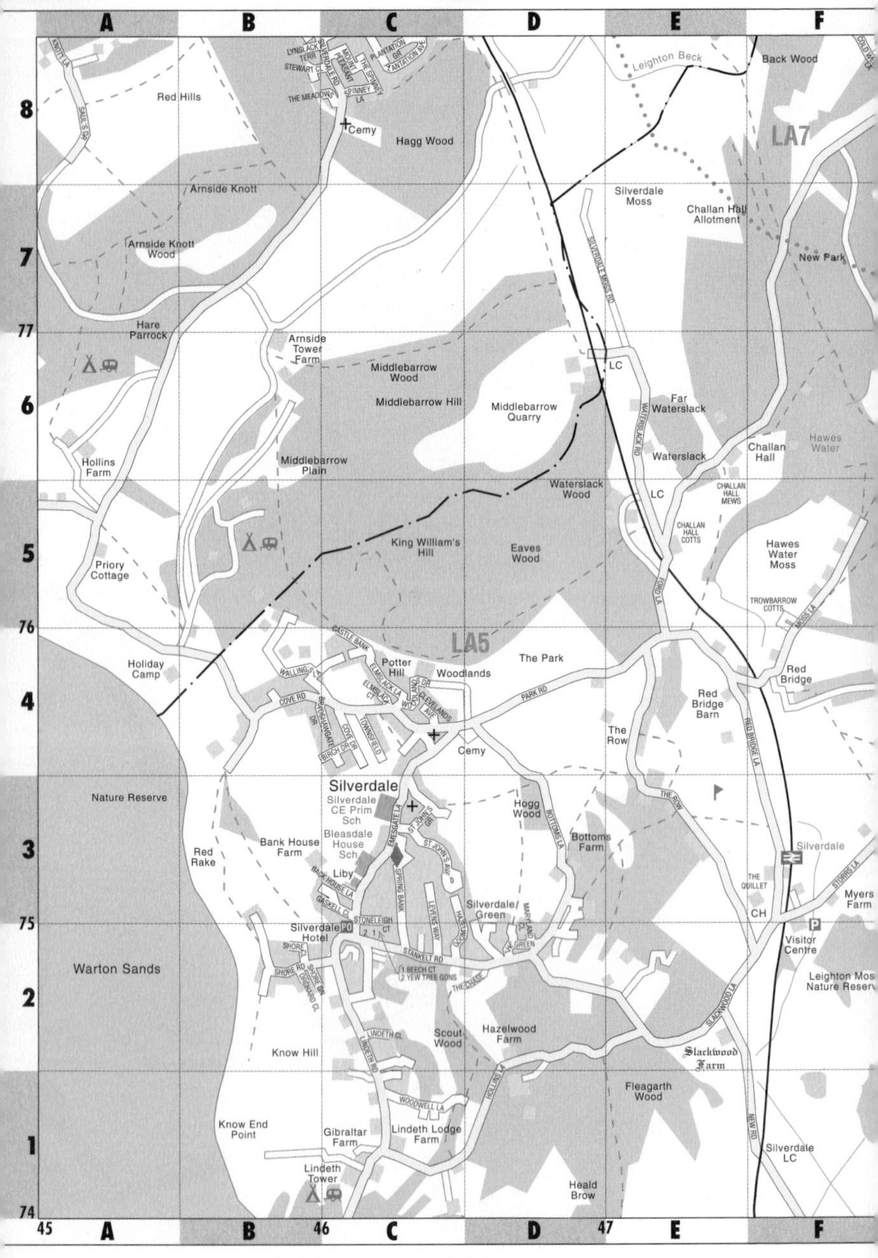

A B C D E F
8 7 77 6 5 76 4 3 75 2 1 74
45 46 47
Red Hills
Cemy
Hagg Wood
Leighton Beck
Back Wood
LA7
Arnside Knott
Silverdale Moss
Challan Hall Allotment
Arnside Knott Wood
New Park
Hare Parrock
Arnside Tower Farm
Middlebarrow Wood
LC
Middlebarrow Hill
Middlebarrow Quarry
Far Waterslack
Hollins Farm
Middlebarrow Plain
Waterslack
Challan Hall
Hawes Water
Waterslack Wood
King William's Hill
Eaves Wood
Hawes Water Moss
Priory Cottage
LA5
Holiday Camp
Potter Hill
Woodlands
The Park
Red Bridge
Red Bridge Barn
The Row
Cemy
Silverdale
Silverdale CE Prim Sch
Nature Reserve
Hogg Wood
Bleasdale House Sch
Bank House Farm
Bottoms Farm
Red Rake
Liby
Silverdale Green
Silverdale Hotel
CH
Myers Farm
Visitor Centre
Warton Sands
Leighton Moss Nature Reserve
Scout Wood
Hazelwood Farm
Know Hill
Slackwood Farm
Fleagarth Wood
Know End Point
Gibraltar Farm
Lindeth Lodge Farm
Silverdale LC
Lindeth Tower
Heald Brow

234

A B C D E F

Leighton House
Leighton Beck Bridge
Beetham Caravan Pk
LA7
Oasis Wildlife Park Visitor Centre
8
A6
Brackenthwaite Rd
Leighton Beck
Gait Barrows (Nature Reserve)
Brackenthwaite Farm
Hale Moss
Hall More Farm
7
East Coppice
Thrang End Wood
Main Drain
77
Thrang End Farm
Hazel Grove
6
Thrang Moss
White Moss
Thrang Brow La
Thrang Coppice
West Coppice
Birch Cottage
Yealand Hall Allotment
Trough Plantation
Yealand Storrs
Moss La
5
Yealand Hall
Silverdale Rd
The Trough
76
Brow Foot Farm
LA5
Eight Acre La
Storrs La
Nineteen Acre La
4
Storrs Moss
Round Top
Yealand Redmayne
Meadows Cl
The Meadows
PO
Well La
Cringlebarrow Wood
Storrs Farm
Footeran La
Leighton Moss (Nature Reserve)
Yealand Conyers CE Prim Sch
3
Flat La
75
Rose Acre La
Old Hall Farm
Grisedale Farm
Deepdale Wood
New Inn (PH)
The Pool
Dykes Farm
A6
2
Yealand Manor
Dykes La
Leighton Hall Home Farm
Yealand Rd
Dykes House
Yealand Conyers
Grisedale Wood
Leighton Hall
Leighton Park
1
Peter La
Hermitage Wood
Hyning Rd
Snape La
74

A B 49 C D 50 E F

217
234

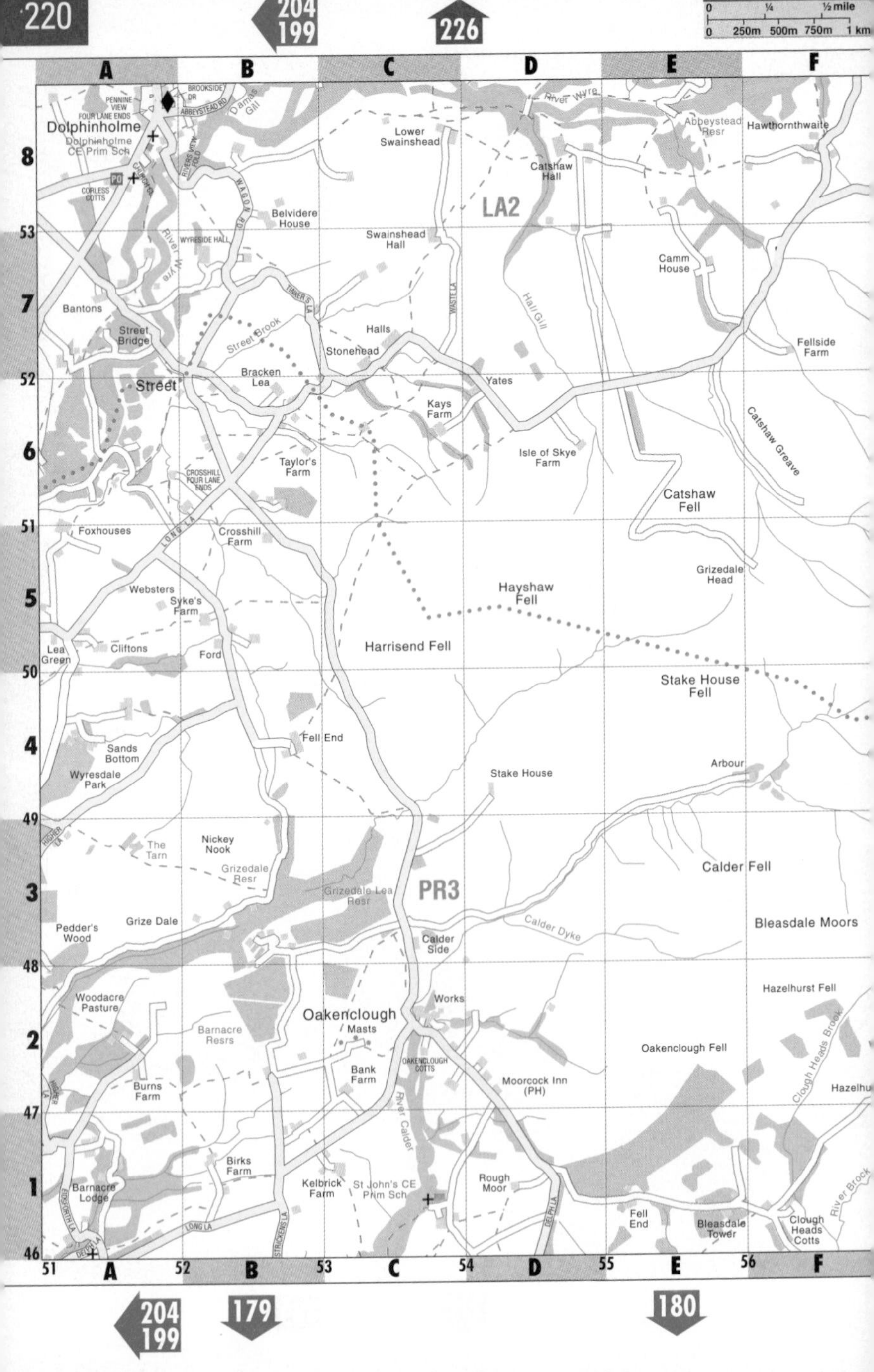
204
199
226
Scale: 1¼ inches to 1 mi
Dolphinholme
Dolphinholme CE Prim Sch
PENNINE VIEW
FOUR LANE ENDS
BROOKSIDE DR
ABBEYSTEAD RD
Damas Gill
RIVERS VIEW FOLD
CORLESS COTTS
WAGON RD
River Wyre
WYRESIDE HALL
Lower Swainshead
Belvidere House
Swainshead Hall
Catshaw Hall
Abbeystead Resr
Hawthornthwaite
LA2
Camm House
Hall Gill
Bantons
Street Bridge
Street
Street Brook
TINKER'S LA
WASTE LA
Halls
Stonehead
Bracken Lea
Yates
Kays Farm
Fellside Farm
Catshaw Greave
Isle of Skye Farm
Taylor's Farm
CROSSHILL FOUR LANE ENDS
Catshaw Fell
Foxhouses
Crosshill Farm
LONG LA
Grizedale Head
Websters
Syke's Farm
Hayshaw Fell
Lea Green
Cliftons
Ford
Harrisend Fell
Stake House Fell
Fell End
Sands Bottom
Wyresdale Park
Stake House
Arbour
HIGHER LA
The Tarn
Nickey Nook
Grizedale Resr
Calder Fell
Grizedale Lea Resr
PR3
Pedder's Wood
Grize Dale
Calder Dyke
Calder Side
Bleasdale Moors
Woodacre Pasture
Works
Hazelhurst Fell
Oakenclough
Masts
Barnacre Resrs
Bank Farm
OAKENCLOUGH COTTS
Oakenclough Fell
Clough Heads Brook
Burns Farm
Moorcock Inn (PH)
River Calder
Hazelhu
Birks Farm
Barnacre Lodge
Kelbrick Farm
St John's CE Prim Sch
Rough Moor
River Brock
EDGEFORTH LA
LONG LA
DELPH LA
STRICKENS LA
Fell End
Bleasdale Tower
Clough Heads Cotts
204
199
179
180

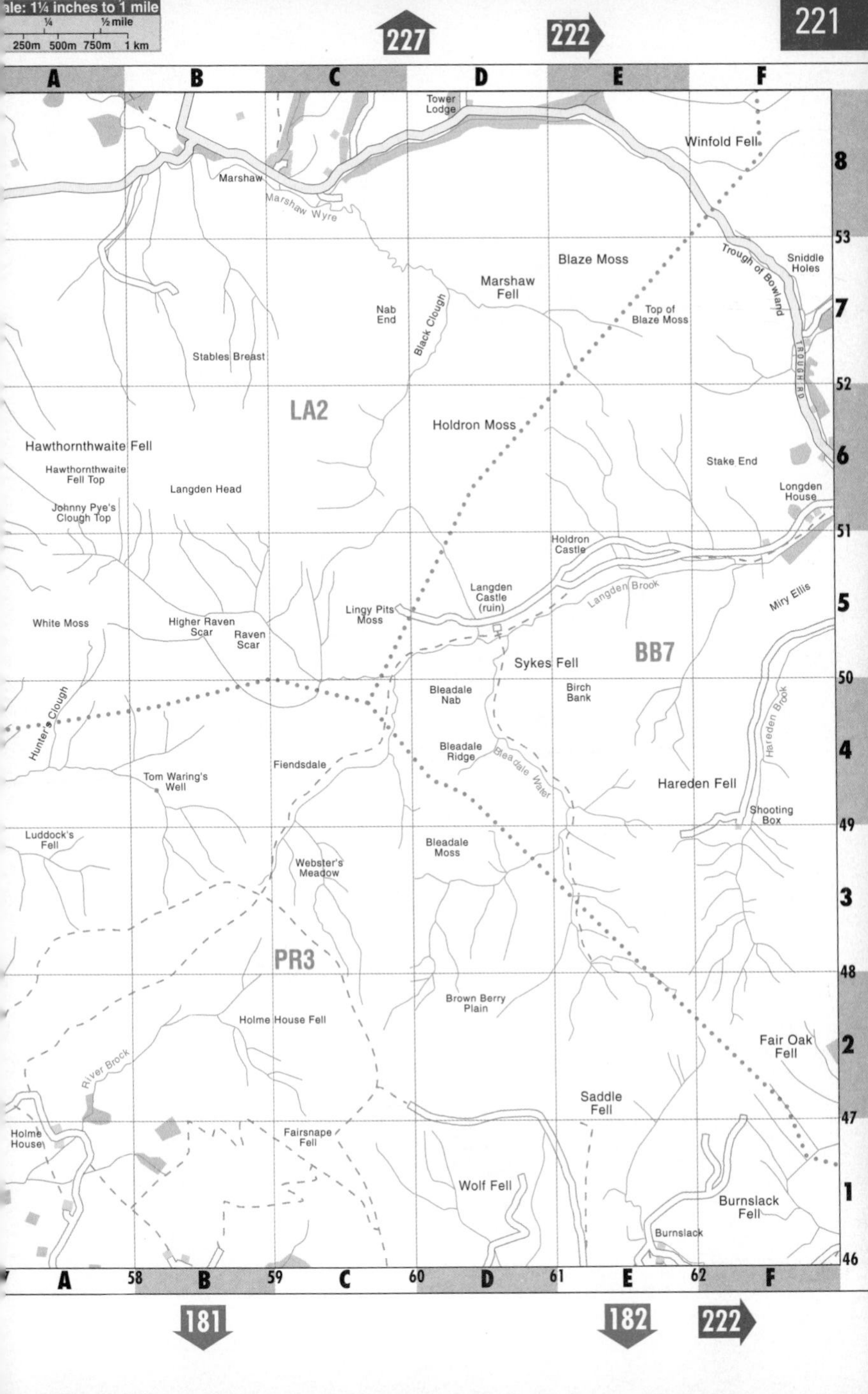
ale: 1¼ inches to 1 mile
¼
½ mile
250m 500m 750m 1 km
227
222
A B C D E F
Tower Lodge
Winfold Fell
Marshaw
Marshaw Wyre
Blaze Moss
Trough of Bowland
Sniddle Holes
Marshaw Fell
Nab End
Black Clough
Top of Blaze Moss
Stables Breast
TROUGH RD
LA2
Holdron Moss
Hawthornthwaite Fell
Hawthornthwaite Fell Top
Langden Head
Stake End
Longden House
Johnny Pye's Clough Top
Holdron Castle
Langden Castle (ruin)
Langden Brook
Miry Ellis
Lingy Pits Moss
White Moss
Higher Raven Scar
Raven Scar
Sykes Fell
BB7
Bleadale Nab
Birch Bank
Hunter's Clough
Hareden Brook
Bleadale Ridge
Bleadale Water
Fiendsdale
Tom Waring's Well
Hareden Fell
Shooting Box
Luddock's Fell
Bleadale Moss
Webster's Meadow
PR3
Brown Berry Plain
Holme House Fell
Fair Oak Fell
River Brock
Saddle Fell
Holme House
Fairsnape Fell
Wolf Fell
Burnslack Fell
Burnslack
8 53 7 52 6 51 5 50 4 49 3 48 2 47 1 46
58 59 60 61 62
181
182
222

221
228

221
183
184

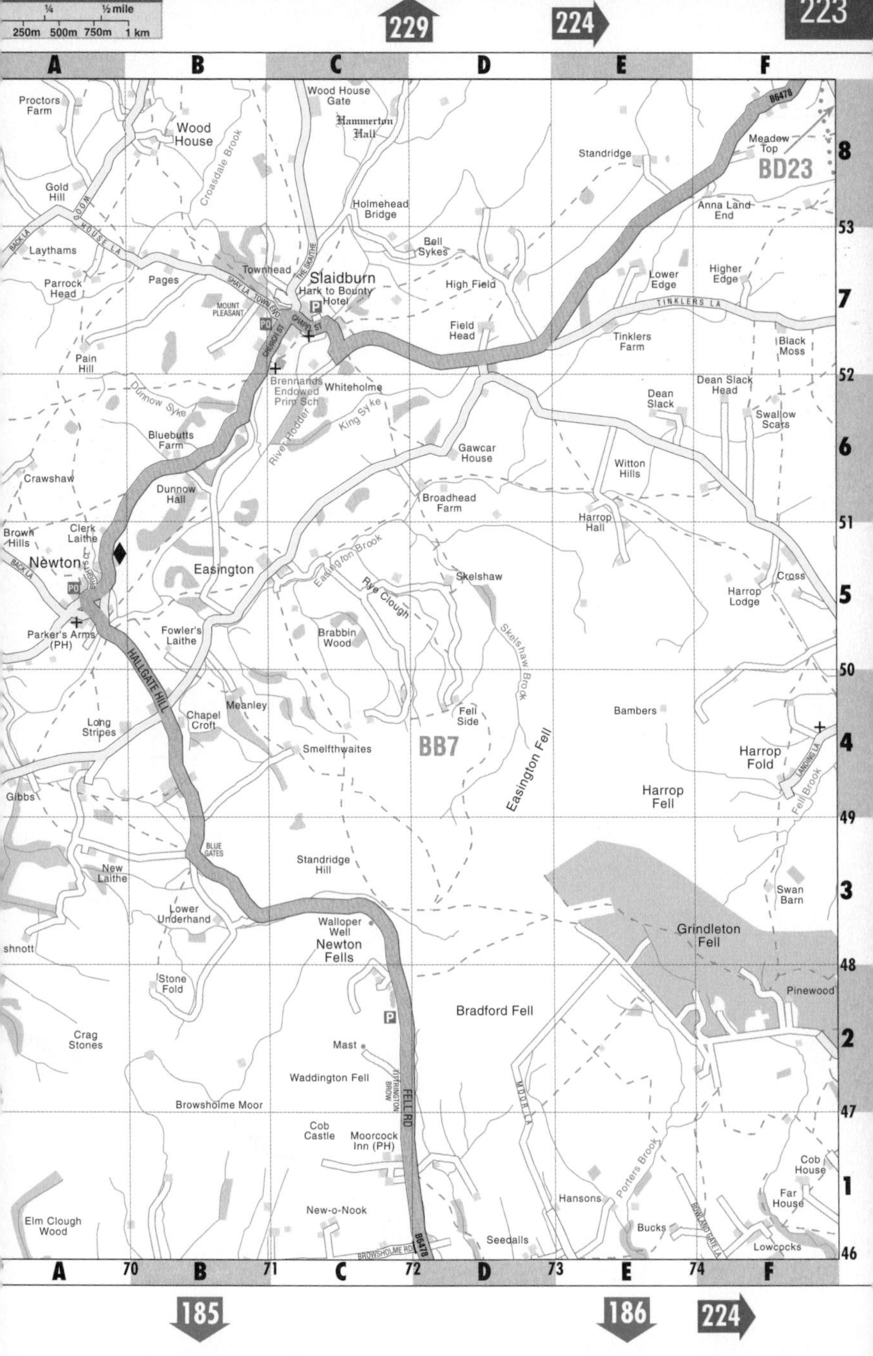
ale: 1¼ inches to 1 mile
¼
½ mile
250m 500m 750m 1 km
229
224
A B C D E F
Proctors Farm
Wood House
Wood House Gate
Hammerton Hall
Croasdale Brook
Gold Hill
Standridge
Meadow Top
BD23
B6478
Holmehead Bridge
Anna Land End
Back La
Wood House La
Laythams
Bell Sykes
Parrock Head
Pages
Townhead
Slaidburn
Hark to Bounty Hotel
High Field
Lower Edge
Higher Edge
Shay La
Town End
The Skaithe
Mount Pleasant
Church St
Chapel St
Tinklers La
Field Head
Tinklers Farm
Black Moss
Pain Hill
Brennands Endowed Prim Sch
Whiteholme
Dean Slack Head
Dean Slack
Swallow Scars
Dunnow Syke
King Syke
River Hodder
Bluebutts Farm
Gawcar House
Witton Hills
Crawshaw
Dunnow Hall
Broadhead Farm
Harrop Hall
Brown Hills
Clerk Laithe
Newton
Easington
Easington Brook
Rye Clough
Skelshaw
Cross
Harrop Lodge
Parker's Arms (PH)
Fowler's Laithe
Brabbin Wood
Skelshaw Brook
Hallgate Hill
Meanley
Fell Side
Bambers
Long Stripes
Chapel Croft
Smelfthwaites
BB7
Easington Fell
Harrop Fold
Landing La
Fell Brook
Gibbs
Harrop Fell
Blue Gates
Standridge Hill
New Laithe
Swan Barn
Lower Underhand
Walloper Well
Newton Fells
Grindleton Fell
shnott
Stone Fold
Pinewood
Bradford Fell
Crag Stones
Mast
Waddington Fell
Twitterington Brow
Fell Rd
Moor La
Browsholme Moor
Cob Castle
Moorcock Inn (PH)
Porters Brook
Cob House
Far House
Hansons
New-o-Nook
Bucks
Bowland Gate La
Seedalls
Elm Clough Wood
Browsholme Rd
Lowcocks
8 53 7 52 6 51 5 50 4 49 3 48 2 47 1 46
A 70 B 71 C 72 D 73 E 74 F
185
186
224

223
230

Scale: 1¼ inches to 1 mile

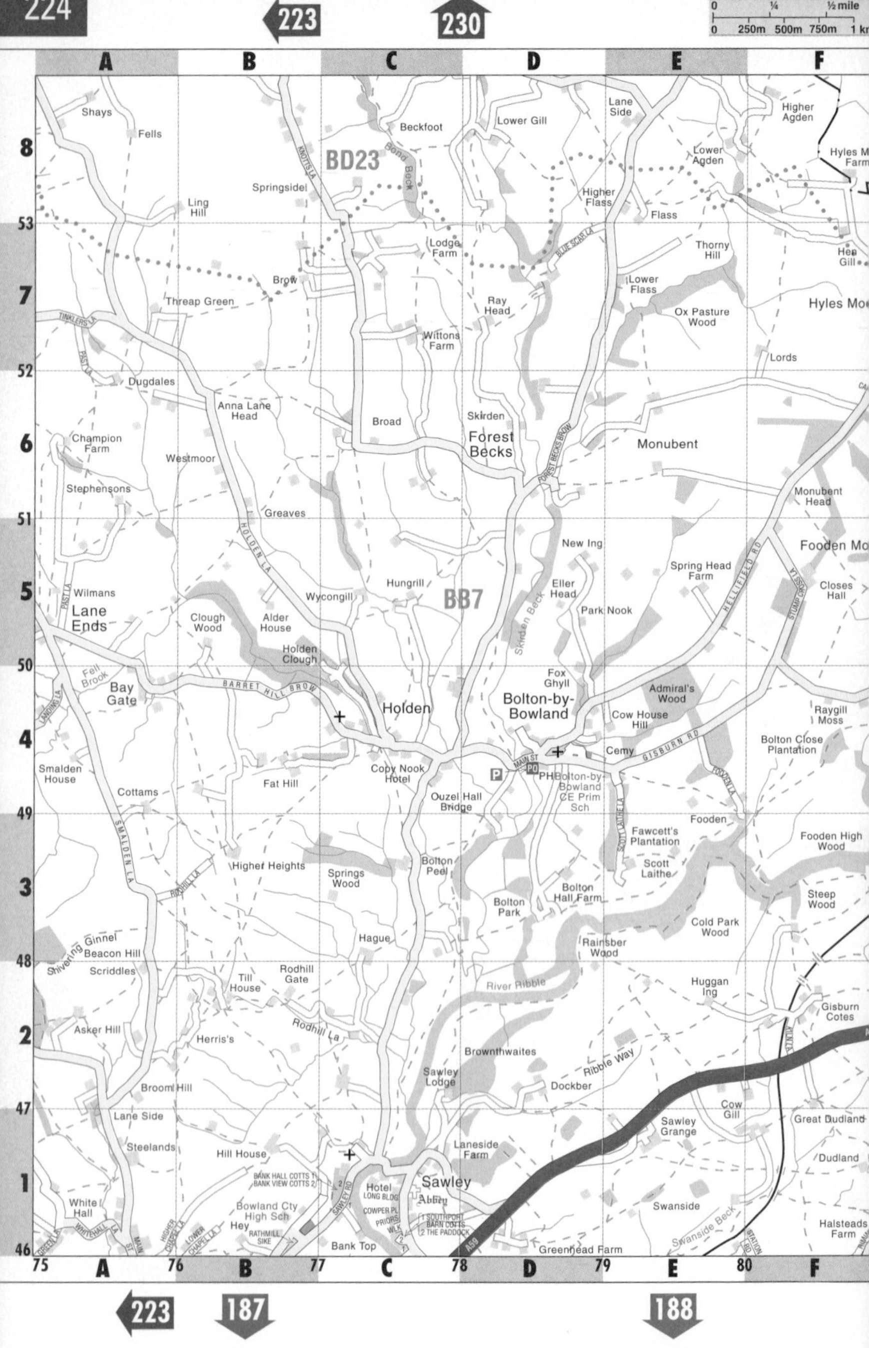

223
187
188

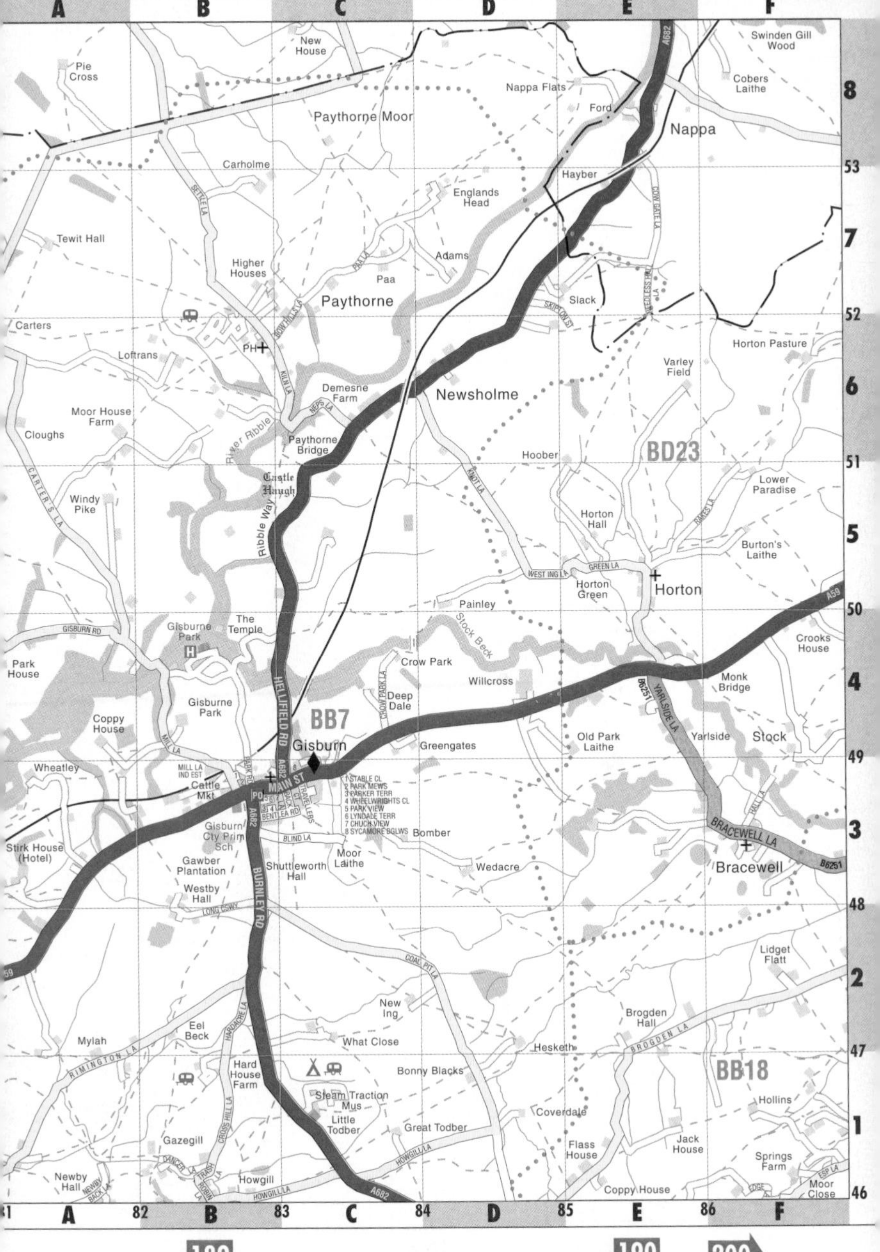
Scale: 1¼ inches to 1 mile
¼
½ mile
250m 500m 750m 1 km
Pie Cross
New House
Paythorne Moor
Nappa Flats
Ford
Nappa
Swinden Gill Wood
Cobers Laithe
Carholme
Hayber
Englands Head
Tewit Hall
Higher Houses
Adams
Paa
Paythorne
Slack
Carters
Loftrans
PH
Horton Pasture
Varley Field
Demesne Farm
Newsholme
Moor House Farm
Cloughs
River Ribble
Paythorne Bridge
Hoober
BD23
Castle Haugh
Windy Pike
Ribble Way
Horton Hall
Lower Paradise
Burton's Laithe
Horton Green
Horton
Painley
Stock Beck
The Temple
Gisburne Park
Crooks House
Park House
Crow Park
Willcross
Monk Bridge
Gisburne Park
Deep Dale
Coppy House
BB7
Gisburn
Greengates
Old Park Laithe
Yarlside
Stock
Wheatley
Cattle Mkt
MAIN ST
HELLIFIELD RD
BURNLEY RD
1 STABLE CL
2 PARK MEWS
3 PARKER TERR
4 WHEELWRIGHTS CL
5 PARK VIEW
6 LYNDALE TERR
7 CHUCH VIEW
8 SYCAMORE BGLWS
Bomber
Gisburn Cty Prim Sch
Stirk House (Hotel)
Gawber Plantation
Shuttleworth Hall
Moor Laithe
Wedacre
Bracewell
Westby Hall
Lidget Flatt
New Ing
Eel Beck
Mylah
What Close
Brogden Hall
Hesketh
Hard House Farm
Bonny Blacks
BB18
Steam Traction Mus
Hollins
Little Todber
Great Todber
Coverdale
Gazegill
Flass House
Jack House
Springs Farm
Newby Hall
Howgill
Coppy House
Moor Close
A B C D E F
8 53 7 52 6 51 5 50 4 49 3 48 2 47 1 46
81 82 83 84 85 86
189
190
200

211
207
231
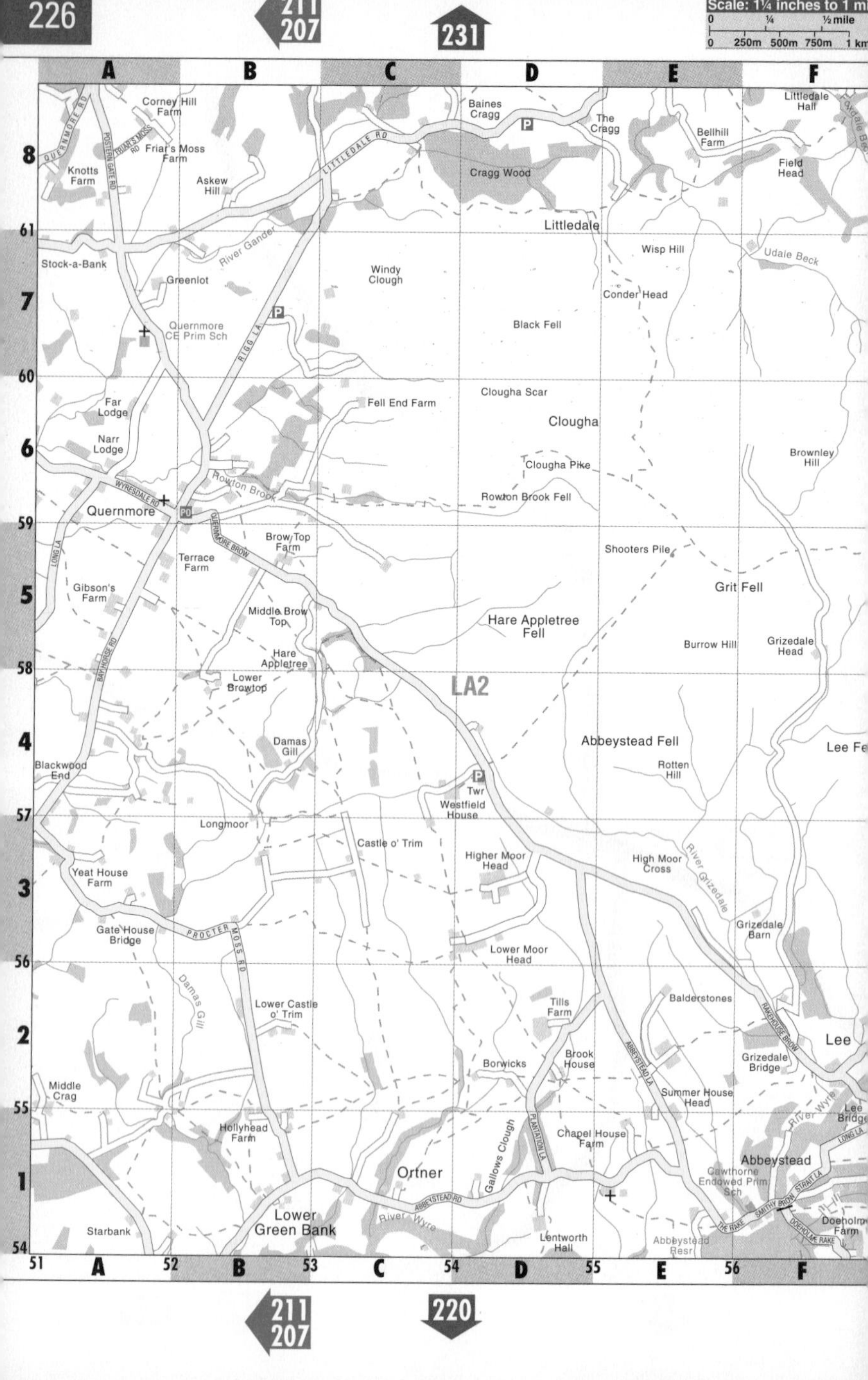

211
207
220

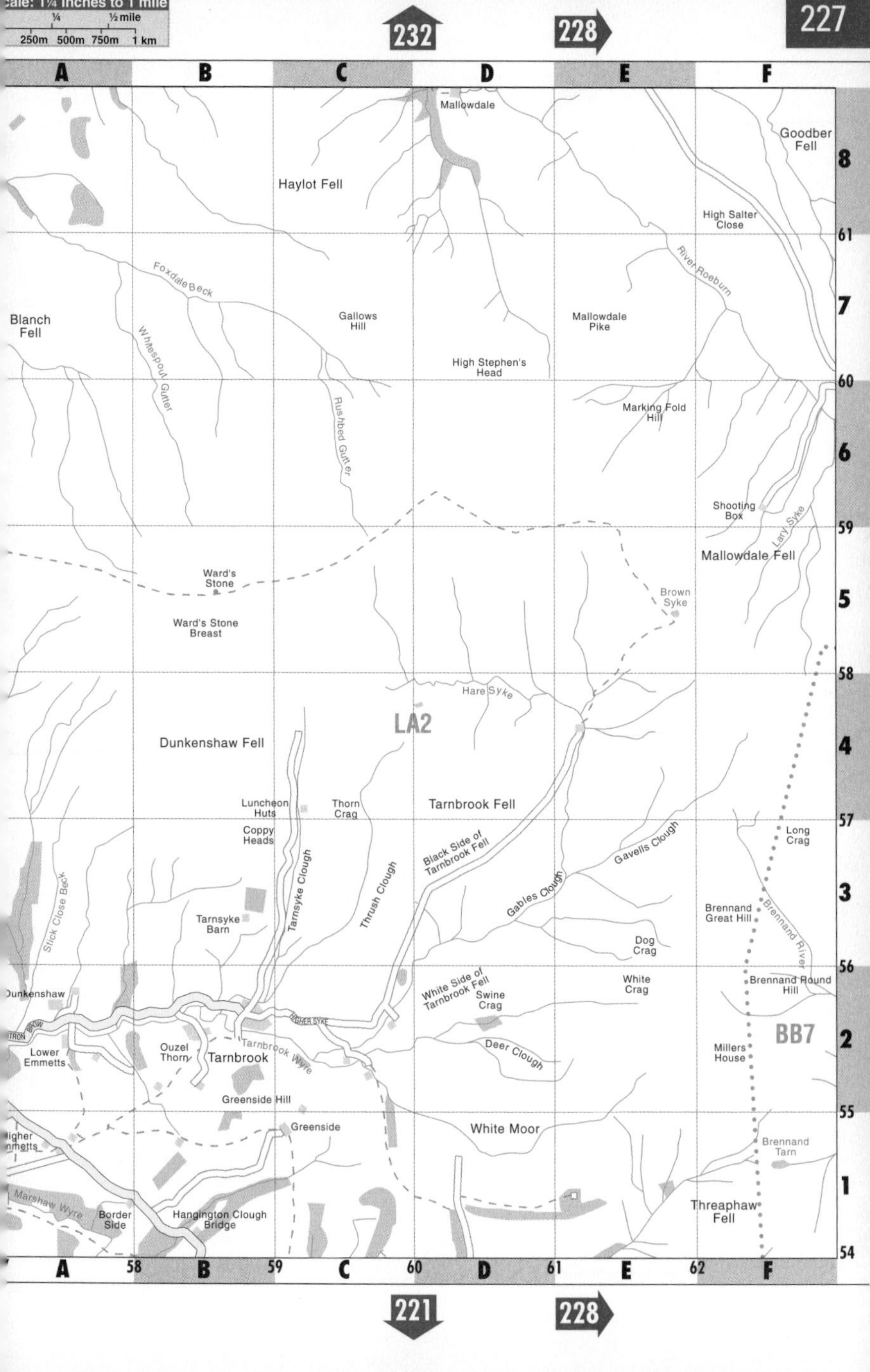
cale: 1¼ inches to 1 mile
¼
½ mile
250m
500m
750m
1 km
232
228
Mallowdale
Goodber Fell
Haylot Fell
High Salter Close
Foxdale Beck
River Roeburn
Blanch Fell
Whitespout Gutter
Gallows Hill
Mallowdale Pike
High Stephen's Head
Rushbed Gutter
Marking Fold Hill
Shooting Box
Lary Syke
Mallowdale Fell
Ward's Stone
Brown Syke
Ward's Stone Breast
Hare Syke
LA2
Dunkenshaw Fell
Luncheon Huts
Thorn Crag
Tarnbrook Fell
Coppy Heads
Long Crag
Black Side of Tarnbrook Fell
Gavells Clough
Tarnsyke Clough
Thrush Clough
Stick Close Beck
Gables Clough
Brennand Great Hill
Brennand River
Tarnsyke Barn
Dog Crag
Dunkenshaw
White Side of Tarnbrook Fell
White Crag
Brennand Round Hill
Swine Crag
HIGHER SYKE
BB7
Lower Emmetts
Ouzel Thorn
Tarnbrook
Tarnbrook Wyre
Deer Clough
Millers House
Greenside Hill
Greenside
White Moor
Brennand Tarn
Marshaw Wyre
Border Side
Hangington Clough Bridge
Threaphaw Fell
A B C D E F
8 61 7 60 6 59 5 58 4 57 3 56 2 55 1 54
58 59 60 61 62
221
228

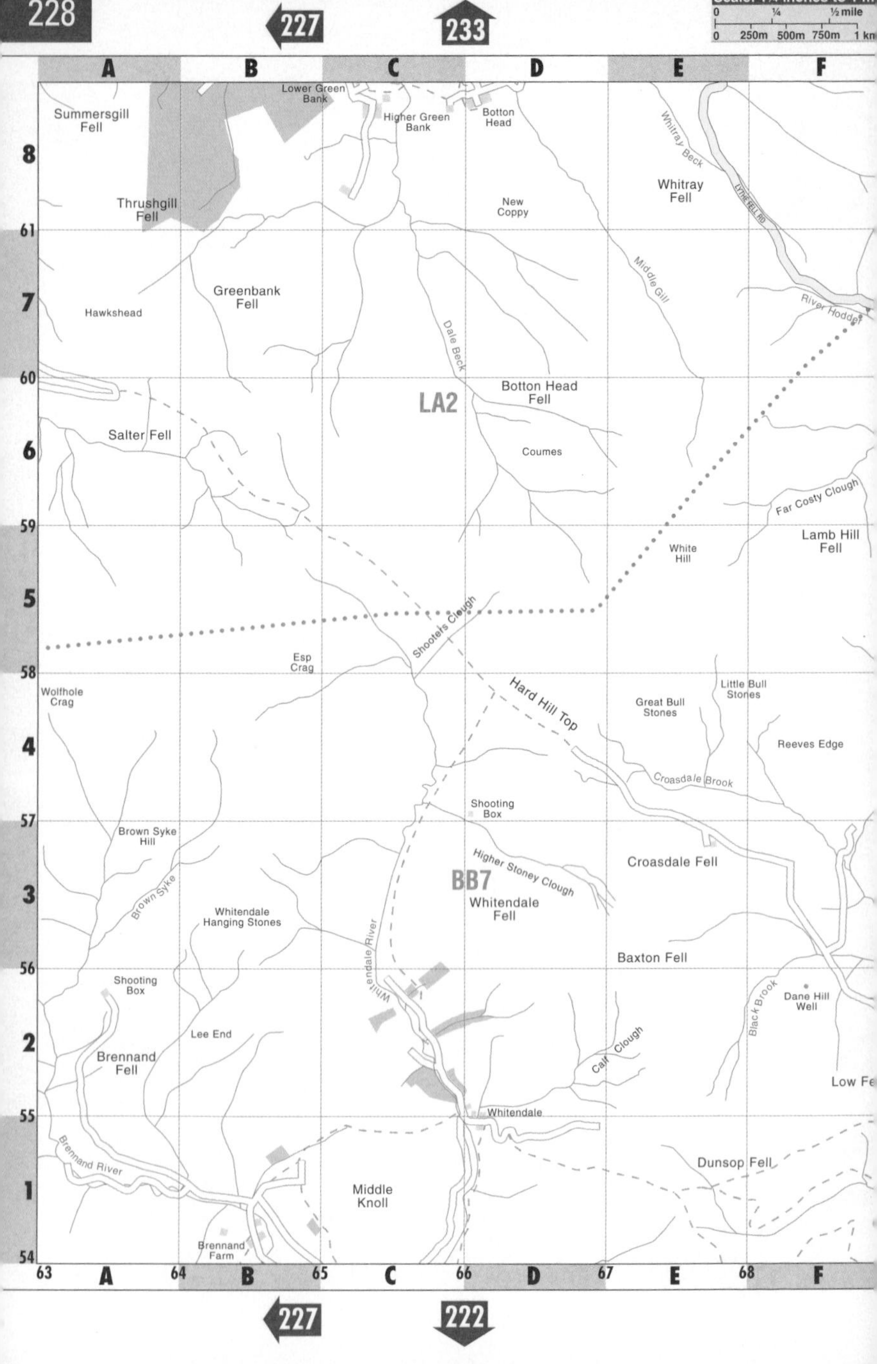
227
233
Scale: 1¼ inches to 1 mile
0
¼
½ mile
0
250m
500m
750m
1 km
A
B
C
D
E
F
8
61
7
60
6
59
5
58
4
57
3
56
2
55
1
54
63
64
65
66
67
68
Summersgill Fell
Lower Green Bank
Higher Green Bank
Botton Head
Whitray Beck
Whitray Fell
LYTHE FELL RD
Thrushgill Fell
New Coppy
Middle Gill
Greenbank Fell
Hawkshead
Dale Beck
River Hodder
Botton Head Fell
LA2
Salter Fell
Coumes
Far Costy Clough
Lamb Hill Fell
White Hill
Shooters Clough
Esp Crag
Wolfhole Crag
Hard Hill Top
Little Bull Stones
Great Bull Stones
Reeves Edge
Croasdale Brook
Shooting Box
Brown Syke Hill
Higher Stoney Clough
Croasdale Fell
BB7
Brown Syke
Whitendale Fell
Whitendale Hanging Stones
Whitendale River
Baxton Fell
Shooting Box
Black Brook
Dane Hill Well
Lee End
Brennand Fell
Calf Clough
Low Fe
Whitendale
Brennand River
Dunsop Fell
Middle Knoll
Brennand Farm
227
222

Scale: 1¼ inches to 1 mile
¼
½ mile
250m 500m 750m 1 km
230
A B C D E F
Austwick Common
Clapham Common
LA2
Keasden Beck
Broad Shaw
Great Harlow
Brown Bank
Cold Stone Plain
Bowland Knotts
Cold Stone
Knotteranum
Fair Hill Coppy
Halstead Fell
Crutchenber Fell
Catlow Fell
Hasgill Fell
Cat Knot
KEASDEN RD
Halsteads Farm
Pike Side
Cross of Greet Bridge
River Hodder
Catlow
Green Pike
Dale House
Old Ing
Low Laithe
Higher Clough
Coat Rakes Bridge
White Syke
Lock Bridge
Cocklick End
Hasgill Beck
Bloe Greet
Costy Clough
New House
Lower Clough
Lamb Hill Farm
BB7
White Hill House
Kenibus
Saddle Hill
Hasgill
BD23
Hare Clough Beck
Collyholme Wood
Bottoms Beck
Brunton Laithe
SCHOOL LA
Fell Side
Merrybent Hill
Walkers
Forest Walks
Gisburn Forest
Stocks Reservoir
Causeway
Stephen Park
Fell End
Clough
Harkers
Moor Syke
HOLE HOUSE LA
Cocklet Hill
Hollins House
Croasdale Brook
Croasdale House
Lower Barn
BROKEN BANK HEAD
Black House
Hammerton Mere
Barn Gill
Brook House Green
DUGDALE LA
Higher Wood House
WOOD HOUSE LA
Phynis
Shay House
Rain Gill
Lower Stony Bank
B6478
Dunsop Farm
Stephen Moor
8
61
7
60
6
59
5
58
4
57
3
56
2
55
1
54
70 71 72 73 74
223
230

229

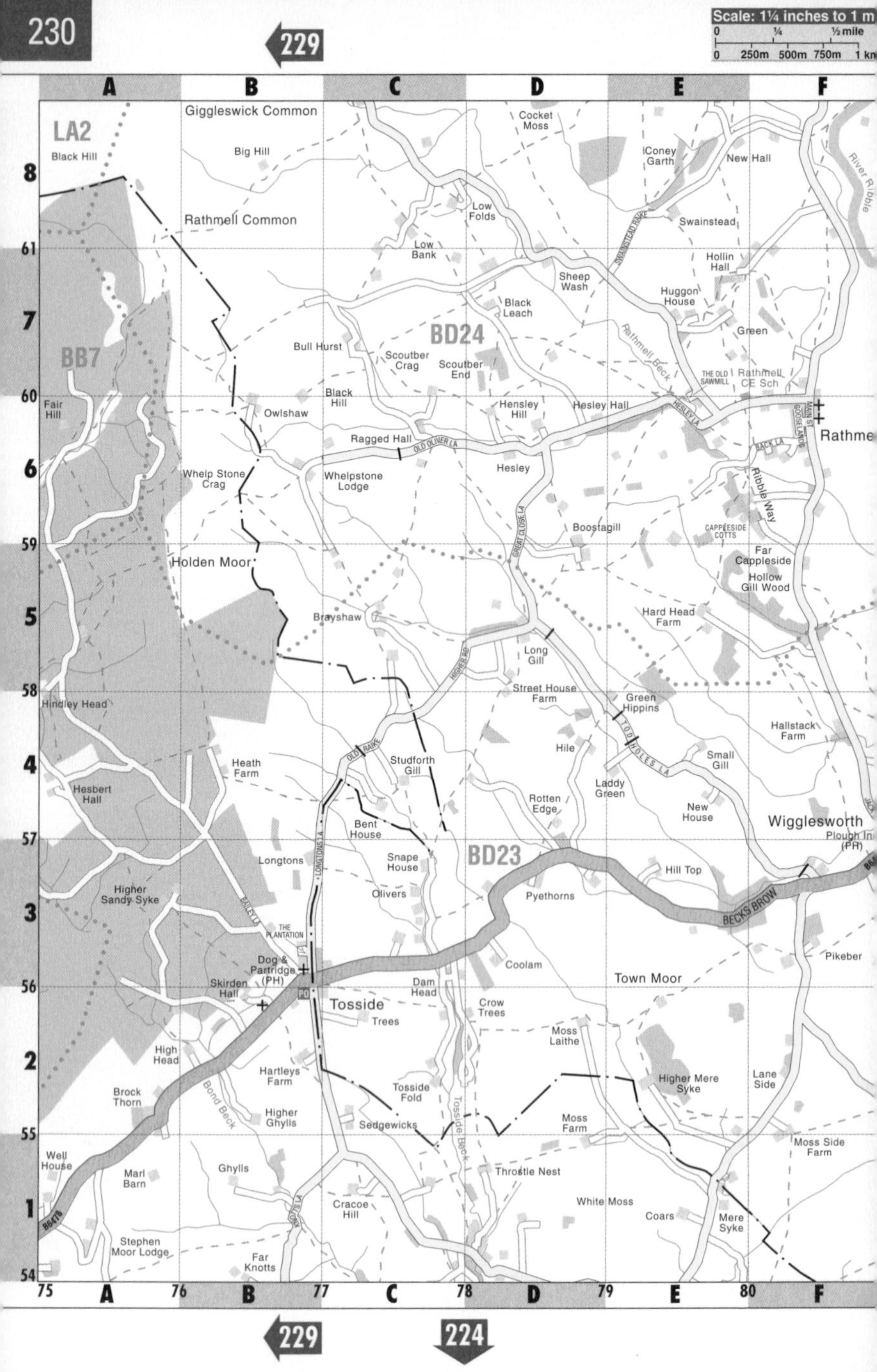
Scale: 1¼ inches to 1 m
Giggleswick Common
LA2
Black Hill
Big Hill
Cocket Moss
Coney Garth
New Hall
River Ribble
Rathmell Common
Low Folds
Swainstead
Low Bank
Hollin Hall
Sheep Wash
Huggon House
Black Leach
BB7
BD24
Green
Bull Hurst
Scoutber Crag
Scoutber End
Rathmell Beck
THE OLD SAWMILL
Rathmell CE Sch
Fair Hill
Black Hill
Owlshaw
Hensley Hill
Hesley Hall
Rathme
Ragged Hall
OLD OLIVER LA
Hesley
Whelp Stone Crag
Whelpstone Lodge
Ribble Way
Boostagill
CAPPLESIDE COTTS
Far Cappleside
Holden Moor
Hollow Gill Wood
Brayshaw
Hard Head Farm
Long Gill
Hindley Head
Street House Farm
Green Hippins
Hallstack Farm
Heath Farm
Studforth Gill
Hile
Small Gill
Hesbert Hall
Laddy Green
Rotten Edge
New House
Wigglesworth
Bent House
Plough Inn (PH)
Longtons
Snape House
BD23
Hill Top
Higher Sandy Syke
Olivers
Pyethorns
BECKS BROW
THE PLANTATION
Dog & Partridge (PH)
Coolam
Pikeber
Skirden Hall
Dam Head
Town Moor
Tosside
Crow Trees
Trees
Moss Laithe
High Head
Hartleys Farm
Higher Mere Syke
Lane Side
Brock Thorn
Bond Beck
Tosside Fold
Higher Ghylls
Sedgewicks
Tosside Beck
Moss Farm
Moss Side Farm
Well House
Marl Barn
Ghylls
Throstle Nest
White Moss
Cracoe Hill
Coars
Mere Syke
Stephen Moor Lodge
Far Knotts
B6478

229
224

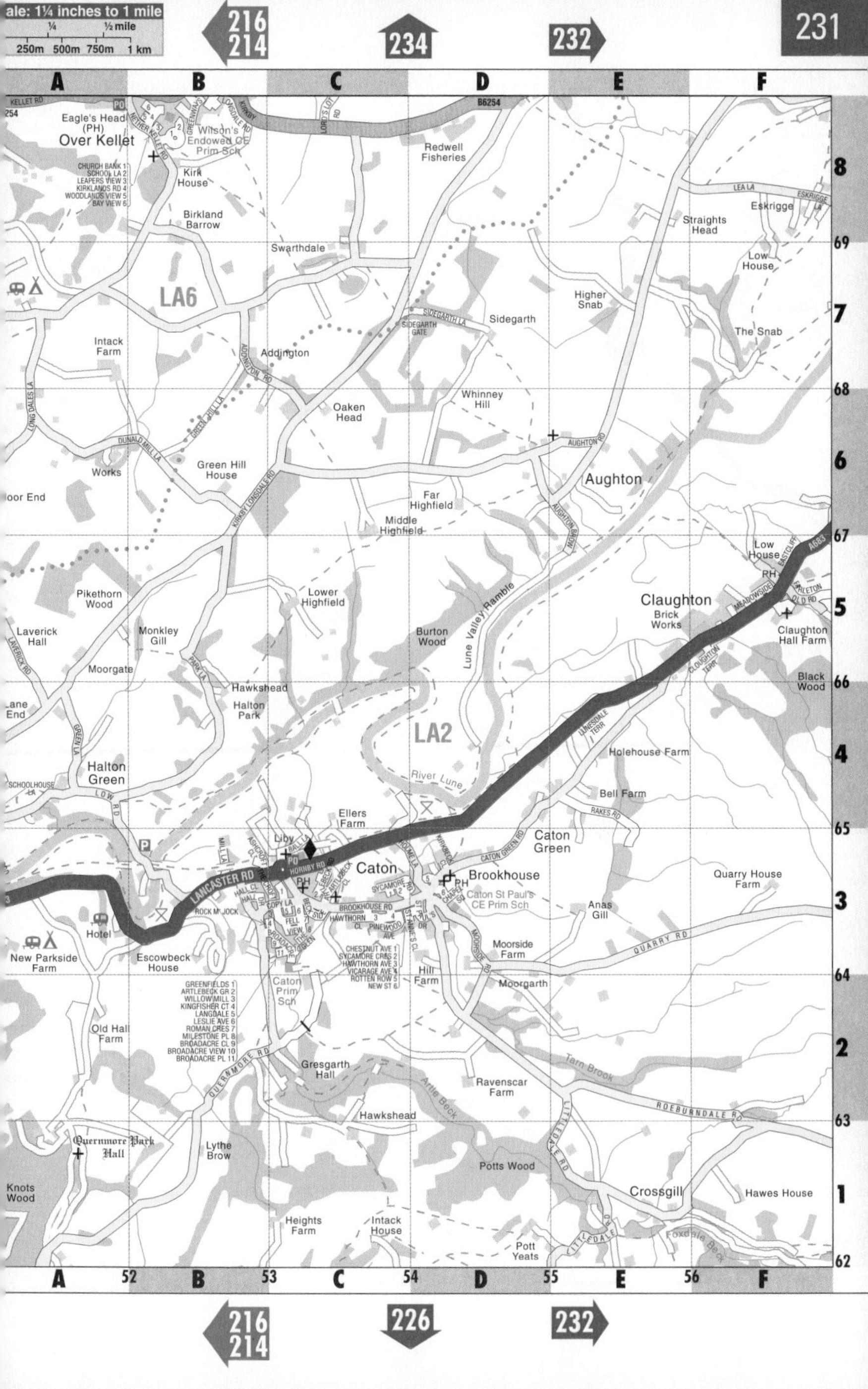
Scale: 1¼ inches to 1 mile
¼
½ mile
250m 500m 750m 1 km
216
214
234
232
A B C D E F
Eagle's Head (PH)
Over Kellet
Wilson's Endowed CE Prim Sch
Kirk House
Birkland Barrow
Redwell Fisheries
Swarthdale
LA6
Intack Farm
Addington
Sidegarth
Oaken Head
Whinney Hill
Straights Head
Eskrigge
Low House
Higher Snab
The Snab
Green Hill House
Works
Moor End
Far Highfield
Middle Highfield
Aughton
Pikethorn Wood
Laverick Hall
Monkley Gill
Moorgate
Lower Highfield
Burton Wood
Lune Valley Ramble
Claughton
Brick Works
Claughton Hall Farm
Low House
Black Wood
Lane End
Hawkshead
Halton Park
LA2
Halton Green
River Lune
Holehouse Farm
Bell Farm
Ellers Farm
Caton Green
Caton
Brookhouse
Caton St Paul's CE Prim Sch
Quarry House Farm
Anas Gill
Hotel
New Parkside Farm
Escowbeck House
Moorside Farm
Hill Farm
Moorgarth
Caton Prim Sch
Old Hall Farm
Gresgarth Hall
Ravenscar Farm
Tarn Brook
Artle Beck
Hawkshead
Quernmore Park Hall
Lythe Brow
Potts Wood
Knots Wood
Crossgill
Hawes House
Heights Farm
Intack House
Pott Yeats
Foxdale Beck
CHURCH BANK 1
SCHOOL LA 2
LEAPERS VIEW 3
KIRKLANDS RD 4
WOODLANDS VIEW 5
BAY VIEW 6
GREENFIELDS 1
ARTLEBECK GR 2
WILLOW MILL 3
KINGFISHER CT 4
LANGDALE 5
LESLIE AVE 6
ROMAN CRES 7
MILESTONE PL 8
BROADACRE CL 9
BROADACRE VIEW 10
BROADACRE PL 11
CHESTNUT AVE 1
SYCAMORE CRES 2
HAWTHORN AVE 3
VICARAGE AVE 4
ROTTEN ROW 5
NEW ST 6
LANCASTER RD
HORNBY RD
QUARRY RD
ROEBURNDALE RD
QUERNMORE RD
LITTLEDALE RD
AUGHTON RD
AUGHTON BROW
KIRKBY LONSDALE RD
ADDINGTON RD
DUNALD MILL LA
GREEN HILL LA
LONG DALES LA
LAVERICK RD
GREEN LA
PARK LA
LOW RD
SCHOOLHOUSE LA
SIDEGARTH LA
LEA LA
LORD'S LOT RD
KELLET RD
NETHER KELLET RD
B6254
A683
CATON GREEN RD
RAKES RD
MOORSIDE RD
LUNESDALE TERR
CLAUGHTON TERR
MEADOWSIDE
OLD RD
BROOKHOUSE RD
ROCK M JOCK
8 69 7 68 6 67 5 66 4 65 3 64 2 63 1 62
52 53 54 55 56
216
214
226
232

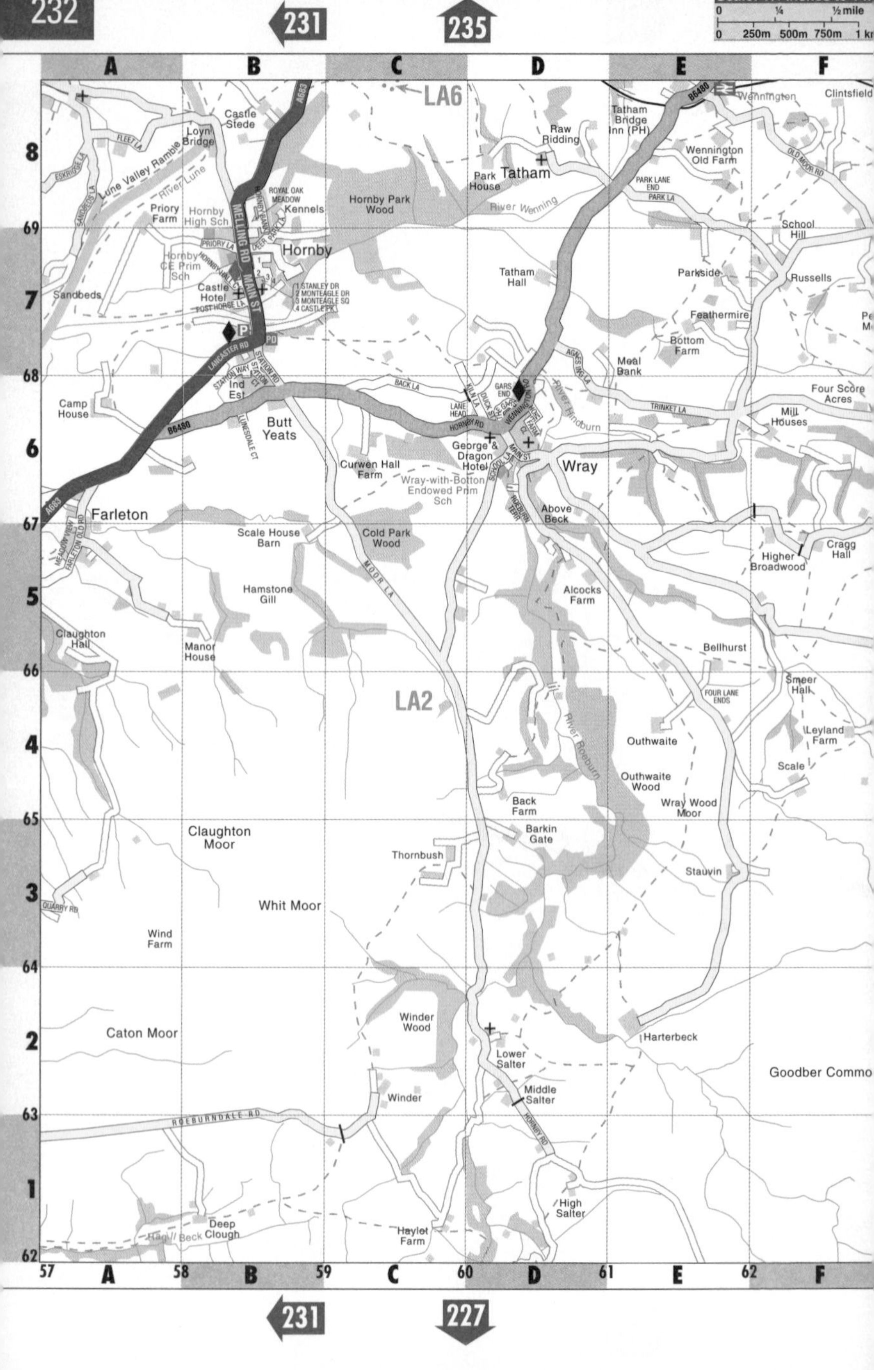
231
235
Scale: 1¼ inches to 1 mile
LA6
Castle Stede
Loyn Bridge
Lune Valley Ramble
River Lune
Priory Farm
Hornby High Sch
Royal Oak Meadow
Kennels
Hornby Park Wood
Hornby
Hornby CE Prim Sch
Castle Hotel
Sandbeds
1 STANLEY DR
2 MONTEAGLE DR
3 MONTEAGLE SQ
4 CASTLE PK
MELLING RD
MAIN ST
LANCASTER RD
STATION RD
Ind Est
Camp House
Butt Yeats
B6480
A683
Farleton
Raw Ridding
Tatham
Park House
River Wenning
Tatham Hall
Tatham Bridge Inn (PH)
Wennington
Wennington Old Farm
Clintsfield
PARK LANE END
PARK LA
OLD MOOR RD
School Hill
Parkside
Russells
Feathermire
Bottom Farm
Meal Bank
Four Score Acres
Mill Houses
TRINKET LA
River Hindburn
BACK LA
HORNBY RD
George & Dragon Hotel
Curwen Hall Farm
Wray-with-Botton Endowed Prim Sch
Wray
Above Beck
Scale House Barn
Cold Park Wood
Higher Broadwood
Cragg Hall
Hamstone Gill
MOOR LA
Alcocks Farm
Claughton Hall
Manor House
Bellhurst
LA2
Smeer Hall
FOUR LANE ENDS
Leyland Farm
River Roeburn
Outhwaite
Outhwaite Wood
Scale
Back Farm
Wray Wood Moor
Claughton Moor
Barkin Gate
Thornbush
Stauvin
Whit Moor
QUARRY RD
Wind Farm
Winder Wood
Caton Moor
Harterbeck
Lower Salter
Goodber Common
Middle Salter
Winder
ROEBURNDALE RD
HORNBY RD
High Salter
Deep Clough
Haylot Farm
231
227

cale: 1¼ inches to 1 mile
¼ ½ mile
250m 500m 750m 1 km

B8
1 CHEAPSIDE
2 BANK COTT
3 CROWTREES
4 BAYNES COTTS
5 GREENFOOT
6 GREEN HEAD COTTS
7 THE TERRACE
8 VICTORIA BLDGS

236

D8
1 PINEWOOD COTTS
2 ASHFIELD COTTS
3 TWEED STREET CT
4 TWEED ST
5 SUNNYSIDE
6 MILL GDNS
7 COLLINGWOOD TERR
8 LAIRGILL ROW
9 GRASMERE CL
10 GRASMERE DR
11 BANKS RISE
12 LAKEBER CL
13 BANKS WAY
14 LAKEBER DR
15 INGLEBOROUGH VIEW
16 GOODENBER CRES

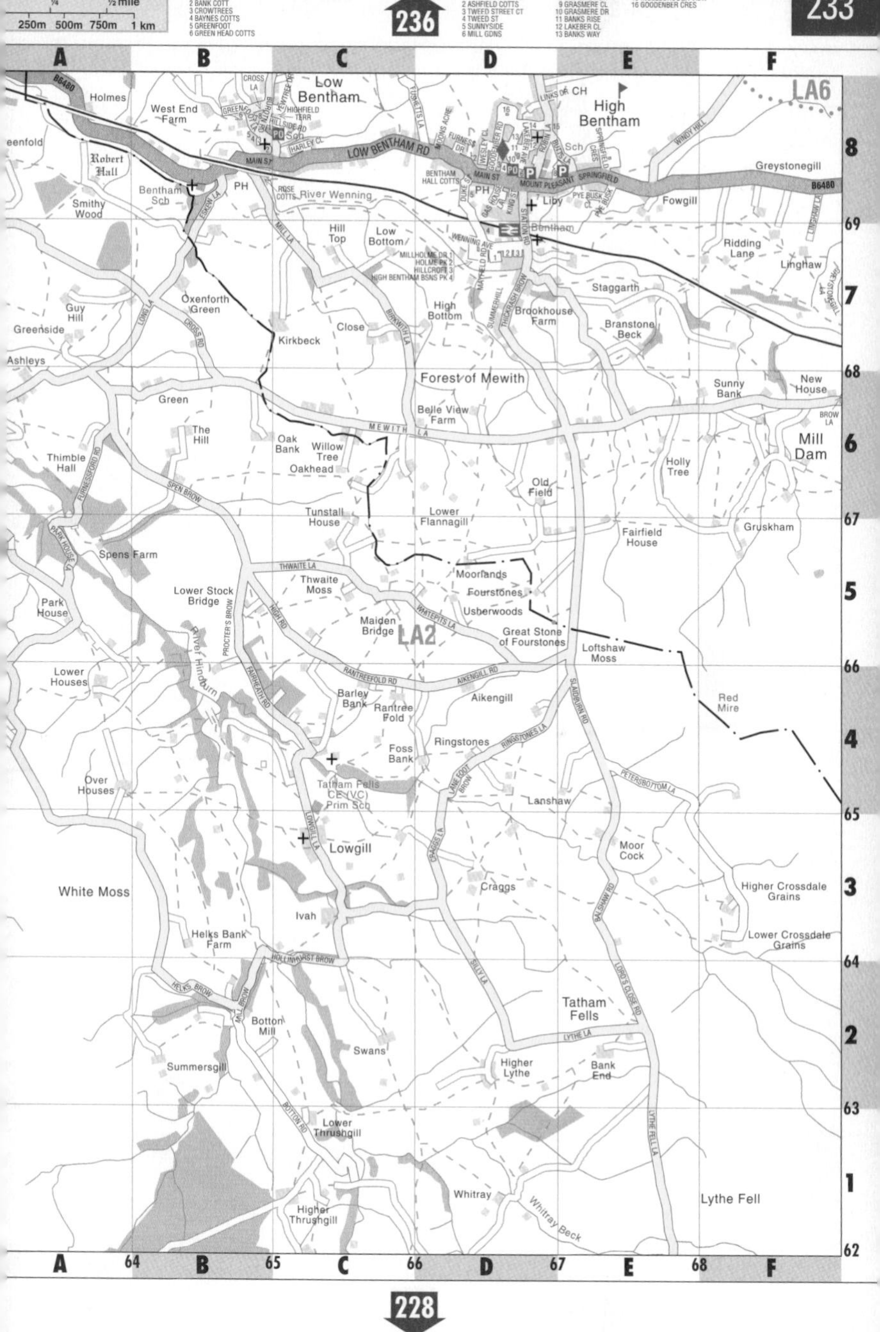

228

219 217

Scale: 1¼ inches to 1 mile

219 217

231

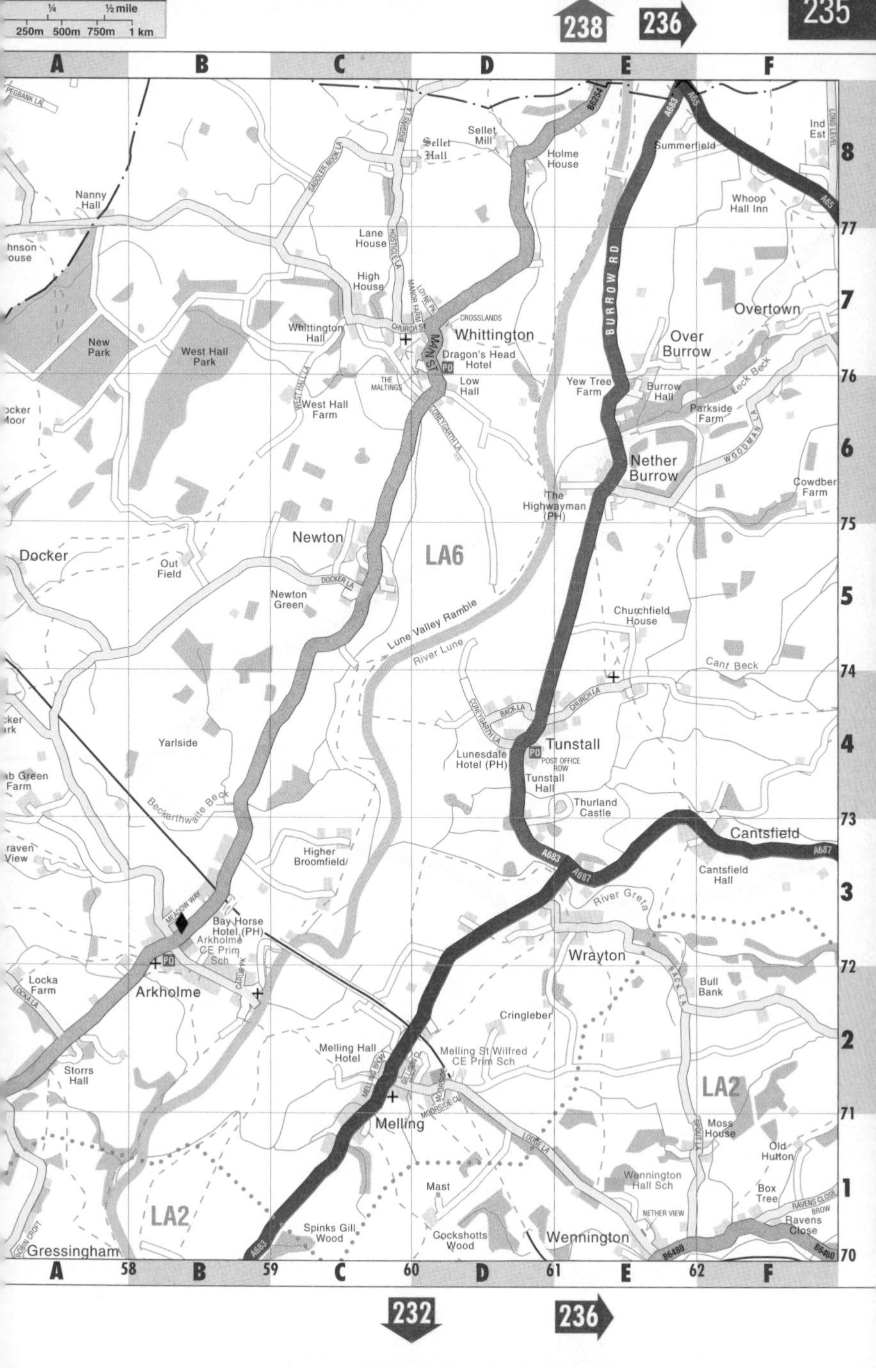
ale: 1¼ inches to 1 mile
¼
½ mile
250m 500m 750m 1 km
238
236
A
B
C
D
E
F
Sellet Hall
Sellet Mill
Holme House
Summerfield
Ind Est
Nanny Hall
Whoop Hall Inn
Lane House
High House
Overtown
New Park
West Hall Park
Whittington Hall
Whittington
Dragon's Head Hotel
Over Burrow
Low Hall
Yew Tree Farm
Burrow Hall
Parkside Farm
West Hall Farm
Nether Burrow
The Highwayman (PH)
Cowdber Farm
Newton
LA6
Docker
Out Field
Newton Green
Lune Valley Ramble
River Lune
Churchfield House
Cant Beck
Yarlside
Tunstall
Lunesdale Hotel (PH)
Tunstall Hall
Thurland Castle
Beckerthwaite Beck
Higher Broomfield
Cantsfield
Cantsfield Hall
River Greta
Bay Horse Hotel (PH)
Arkholme CE Prim Sch
Wrayton
Locka Farm
Arkholme
Bull Bank
Cringleber
Melling Hall Hotel
Melling St Wilfred CE Prim Sch
Storrs Hall
LA2
Melling
Moss House
Old Hutton
Mast
Wennington Hall Sch
Box Tree
Ravens Close
LA2
Spinks Gill Wood
Cockshotts Wood
Wennington
Gressingham
BURROW RD
MAIN ST
A683
A65
A687
B6254
B6480
58
59
60
61
62
70
71
72
73
74
75
76
77
1
2
3
4
5
6
7
8
232
236

235

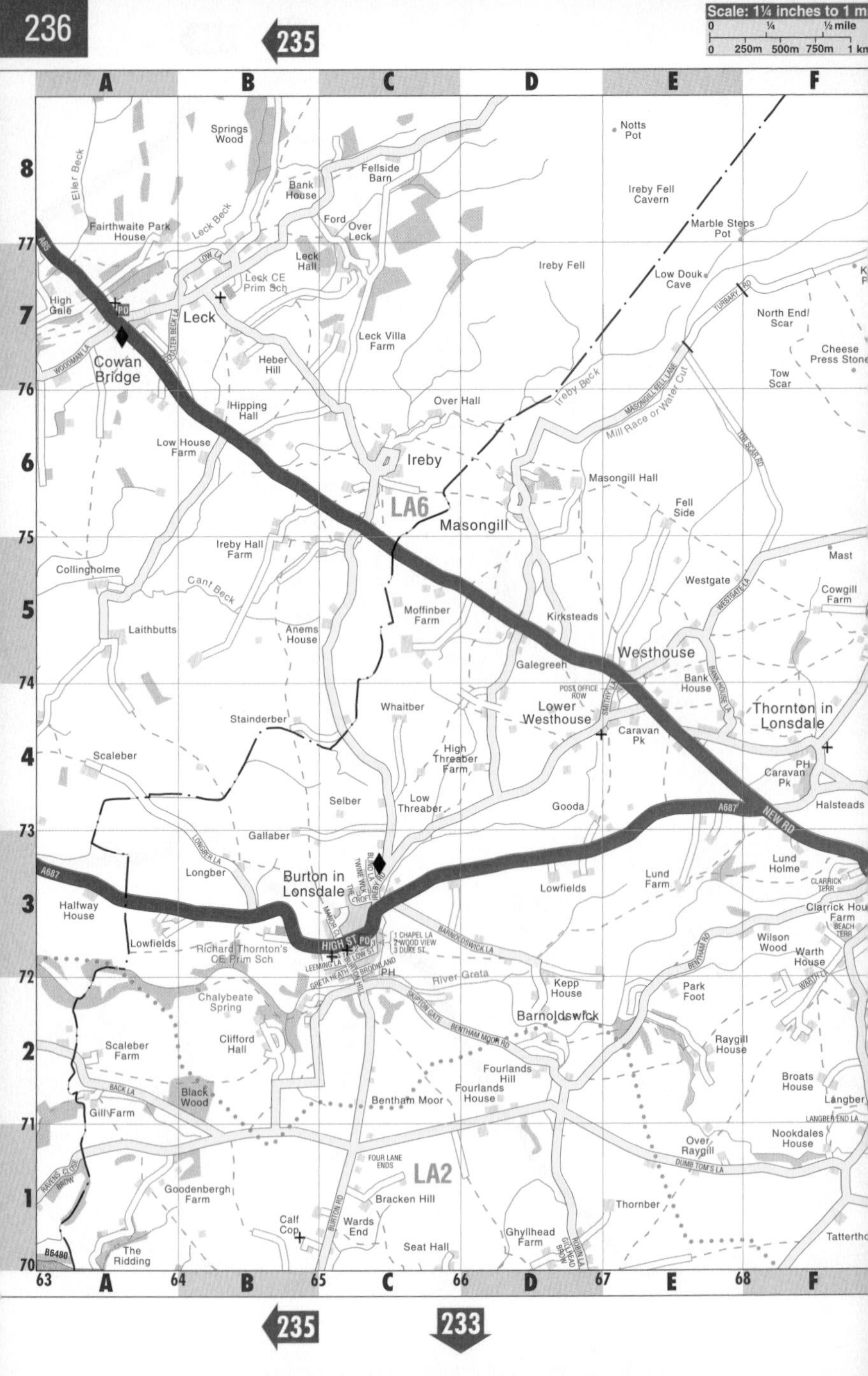
Scale: 1¼ inches to 1 mile
Springs Wood
Notts Pot
Fellside Barn
Bank House
Ireby Fell Cavern
Eller Beck
Leck Beck
Fairthwaite Park House
Ford
Over Leck
Marble Steps Pot
Leck Hall
Ireby Fell
Low Douk Cave
Leck CE Prim Sch
High Gale
Leck
North End Scar
Leck Villa Farm
Cowan Bridge
Heber Hill
Cheese Press Stone
Tow Scar
Ireby Beck
Hipping Hall
Over Hall
Mill Race or Water Cut
Low House Farm
Ireby
Masongill Hall
LA6
Fell Side
Masongill
Ireby Hall Farm
Mast
Collingholme
Westgate
Cant Beck
Cowgill Farm
Moffinber Farm
Laithbutts
Anems House
Kirksteads
Westhouse
Galegreen
Bank House
Lower Westhouse
Whaitber
Thornton in Lonsdale
Stainderber
Caravan Pk
Scaleber
High Threaber Farm
Selber
Low Threaber
Gooda
Halsteads
Gallaber
NEW RD
Lund Holme
Longber
Burton in Lonsdale
Lund Farm
Lowfields
Halfway House
Clarrick House Farm
Lowfields
Richard Thornton's CE Prim Sch
HIGH ST
Wilson Wood
Warth House
River Greta
Kepp House
Park Foot
Chalybeate Spring
Barnoldswick
Scaleber Farm
Clifford Hall
Raygill House
Fourlands Hill
Fourlands House
Broats House
Black Wood
Bentham Moor
Langber
Gill Farm
Nookdales House
Over Raygill
FOUR LANE ENDS
LA2
Goodenbergh Farm
Bracken Hill
Thornber
Calf Cop
Wards End
Ghyllhead Farm
Seat Hall
The Ridding
Tattertho

235
233

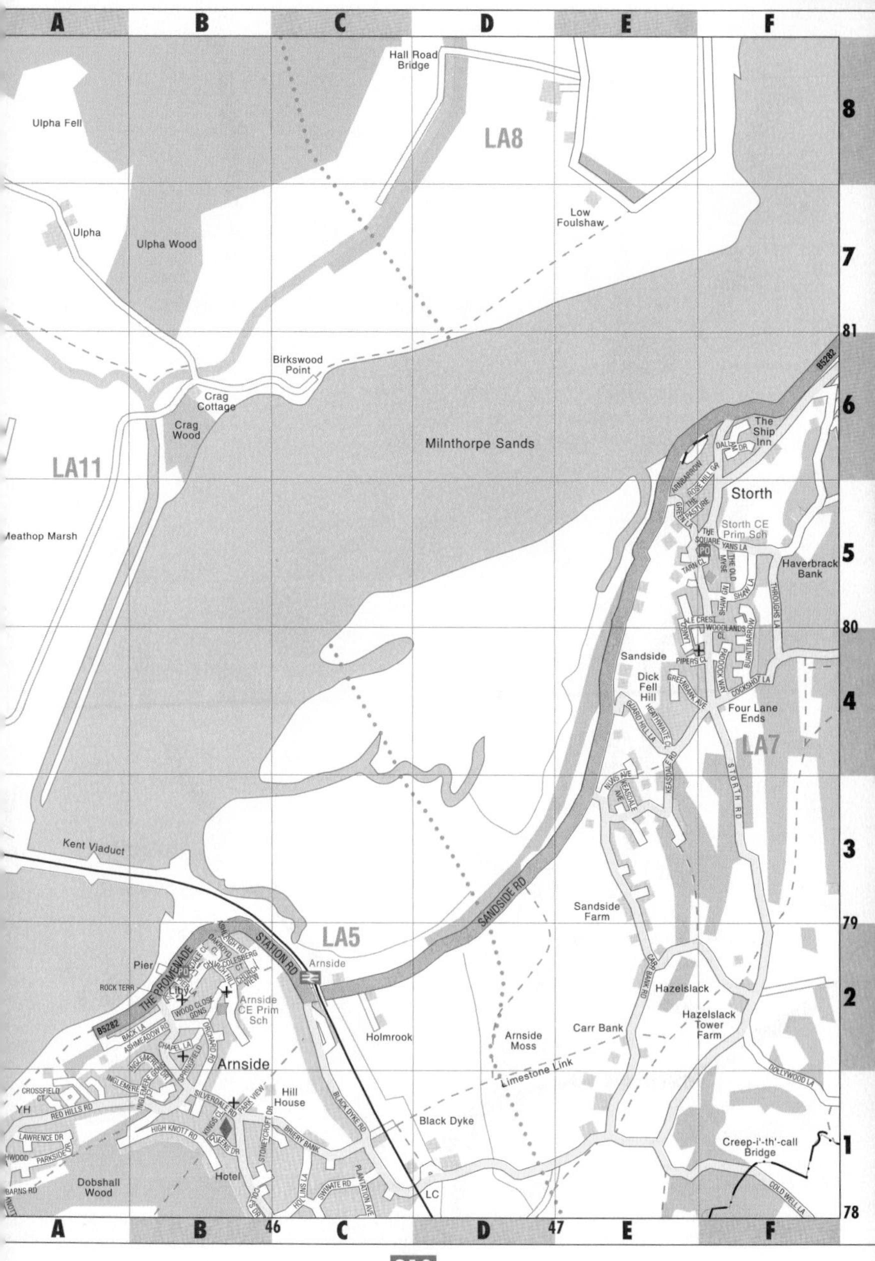

A
B
C
D
E
F
8
7
81
6
5
80
4
3
79
2
1
78
46
47
Hall Road Bridge
LA8
Ulpha Fell
Ulpha
Ulpha Wood
Low Foulshaw
Birkswood Point
Crag Cottage
Crag Wood
Milnthorpe Sands
LA11
Meathop Marsh
B5282
The Ship Inn
Storth
Storth CE Prim Sch
Haverbrack Bank
Sandside
Dick Fell Hill
Four Lane Ends
LA7
Kent Viaduct
SANDSIDE RD
Sandside Farm
LA5
STATION RD
THE PROMENADE
Pier
Arnside
ROCK TERR
Arnside CE Prim Sch
Holmrook
Arnside Moss
Carr Bank
Hazelslack
Hazelslack Tower Farm
Limestone Link
Arnside
Hill House
Black Dyke
YH
Dobshall Wood
Hotel
LC
Creep-i'-th'-call Bridge
STORTH RD
THROUGHS LA
COCKSHOT LA
CARR BANK RD
DOLLYWOOD LA
COLD WELL LA
BLACK DYKE RD
BRIERY BANK
PLANTATION AVE
RED HILLS RD
LAWRENCE DR
PARKSIDE DR
HIGH KNOTT RD
SILVERDALE RD
PARK VIEW
ORCHARD RD
CHAPEL LA
BACK LA
ASHMEADOW RD
INGLEMERE CL
CROSSFIELD CT
STONEYCROFT DR
QUEENS DR
KEASDALE RD
HEATHWAITE CL
GREENBANK AVE
PIPERS CL
PADDOCK WAY
BURNTBARROW
WOODLANDS CL
SHAW LA
YANS LA
THE SQUARE
TARN CL
THE PASTURE
ROSE HILL GR
DALLAM DR
GREEN LA

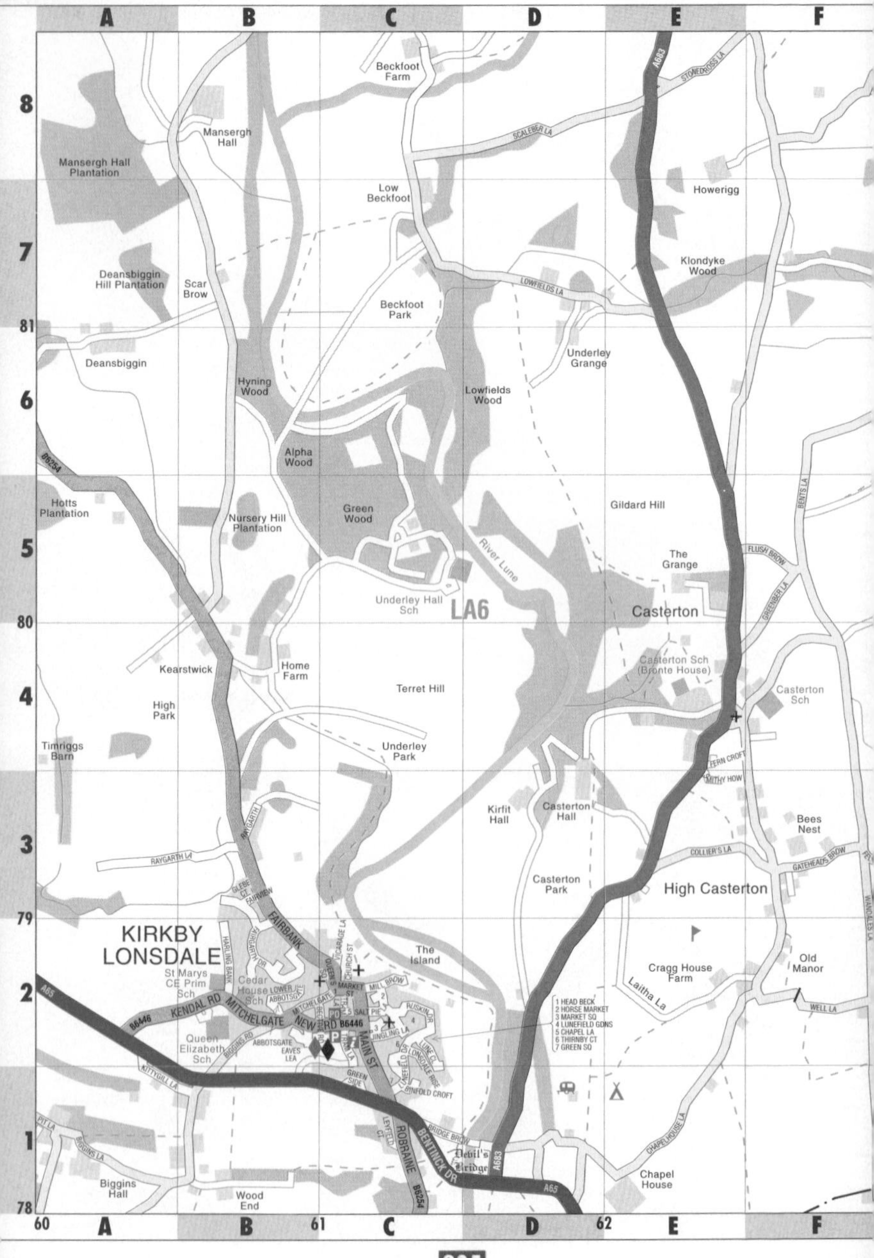
A
B
C
D
E
F
8
7
81
6
5
80
4
3
79
2
1
78
60
61
62
Beckfoot Farm
A683
STONECROSS LA
Mansergh Hall
SCALEBER LA
Mansergh Hall Plantation
Low Beckfoot
Howerigg
Klondyke Wood
Deansbiggin Hill Plantation
Scar Brow
LOWFIELDS LA
Beckfoot Park
Underley Grange
Deansbiggin
Hyning Wood
Lowfields Wood
Alpha Wood
B6254
Hotts Plantation
Nursery Hill Plantation
Green Wood
Gildard Hill
BENTS LA
River Lune
The Grange
FLUSH BROW
Underley Hall Sch
LA6
Casterton
GREENBER LA
Kearstwick
Home Farm
Casterton Sch (Bronte House)
Terret Hill
Casterton Sch
High Park
Timriggs Barn
Underley Park
FERN CROFT
SMITHY HOW
RAYGARTH
Kirfit Hall
Casterton Hall
Bees Nest
RAYGARTH LA
COLLIER'S LA
GATEHEADS BROW
Casterton Park
High Casterton
GLEBE CT
FAIRVIEW
FAIRBANK
KIRKBY LONSDALE
HARLING BANK
VICARAGE LA
CHURCH ST
QUEEN'S SQ
The Island
Cragg House Farm
Old Manor
St Marys CE Prim Sch
Cedar House Sch
LOWER ABBOTSGATE
MARKET ST
MILL BROW
Laitha La
WELL LA
A65
KENDAL RD
MITCHELGATE
NEW RD
B6446
SALT PIE
RUSKIN DR
JINGLING LA
1 HEAD BECK
2 HORSE MARKET
3 MARKET SQ
4 LUNEFIELD GDNS
5 CHAPEL LA
6 THIRNBY CT
7 GREEN SQ
Queen Elizabeth Sch
BIGGINS RD
ABBOTSGATE
EAVES LEA
MAIN ST
LUNE CL
LONSDALE RISE
KITTYGILL LA
GREEN SIDE
BINFOLD CROFT
LEYFIELD CT
BRIDGE BROW
PIT LA
BIGGINS LA
ROBRAINE
BENTINCK DR
Devil's Bridge
CHAPELHOUSE LA
Biggins Hall
Wood End
B6254
Chapel House

235

Street names are listed alphabetically and show the locality, the Postcode District, the page number and a reference to the square in which the name falls on the map page

Roberts St. 7 Rawtenstall BB4..............85 A3

Full street name This may have been abbreviated on the map

Location number If present, this indicates the street's position on a congested area of the map instead of the name

Town, village or locality in which the street falls.

Postcode District for the street name

Page number of the map on which the street name appears

Grid square in which the centre of the street falls

Abbreviations used in the index

App	Approach	Cl	Close	Espl	Esplanade	N	North	S	South
Arc	Arcade	Comm	Common	Est	Estate	Orch	Orchard	Sq	Square
Ave	Avenue	Cnr	Corner	Gdns	Gardens	Par	Parade	Strs	Stairs
Bvd	Boulevard	Cotts	Cottages	Gn	Green	Pk	Park	Stps	Steps
Bldgs	Buildings	Ct	Court	Gr	Grove	Pas	Passage	St	Street, Saint
Bsns Pk	Business Park	Ctyd	Courtyard	Hts	Heights	Pl	Place	Terr	Terrace
Bsns Ctr	Business Centre	Cres	Crescent	Ind Est	Industrial Estate	Prec	Precinct	Trad	Trading Est
Bglws	Bungalows	Dr	Drive	Intc	Interchange	Prom	Promenade	Wlk	Walk
Cswy	Causeway	Dro	Drove	Junc	Junction	Ret Pk	Retail Park	W	West
Ctr	Centre	E	East	La	Lane	Rd	Road	Yd	Yard
Cir	Circus	Emb	Embankment			Rdbt	Roundabout		

Town and village index

Abbey Village . . . 79 C2
Abbeystead . . . 226 F1
Accrington . . . 103 E6
Adlington . . . 30 B7
Altham . . . 124 E6
Andertons Mill . . . 40 A1
Appley Bridge . . . 19 C8
Arkholme . . . 235 B2
Arnside . . . 237 B2
Aughton . . . 231 E6
Bacup . . . 69 E8
Balderstone . . . 120 A5
Baldingstone . . . 49 F1
Bamber Bridge . . . 96 E1
Bank Lane . . . 49 E7
Banks . . . 53 F6
Barber's Moor . . . 57 D3
Barley . . . 167 B5
Barley Green . . . 167 D5
Barnoldswick . . . 200 C1
Barrow . . . 164 D1
Barrowford . . . 168 C4
Barton . . . 136 B7
Becconsall . . . 72 E1
Belmont . . . 45 C4
Belthorn . . . 81 F6
Bescar . . . 23 A7
Beverley . . . 168 E7
Bickerstaffe . . . 7 F5
Billington . . . 143 B3
Bilsborrow . . . 157 A5
Bispham Green . . . 26 B7
Blackburn . . . 100 F1
Blacko . . . 168 D7
Blackpool . . . 129 A4
Blackrod . . . 30 D2
Bolton Green . . . 41 C8
Bolton-by-B . . . 224 D4
Bolton-le-S . . . 216 B5
Bonds . . . 178 C6
Borwick . . . 234 B4
Bowgreave . . . 178 D4
Bracewell . . . 225 F3
Bretherton . . . 56 E6
Brierfield . . . 147 D5
Brindle . . . 77 F5
Brinscall . . . 61 E7
Broadfield . . . 75 E1
Brockhall Village . . . 142 C5
Brookbottoms . . . 49 C3
Broughton . . . 136 D3
Brownside . . . 127 F6
Burnley . . . 127 A7
Burscough . . . 24 D4
Burscough Bridge . . . 24 D5
Burton in L . . . 236 C3
Burton-in-K . . . 234 C7
Bury . . . 32 A1
Butt Yeats . . . 232 B6
Cadshaw . . . 64 D1
Calder Vale . . . 179 E7
Carleton . . . 151 A5
Carnforth . . . 217 C2
Casterton . . . 238 E5
Catforth . . . 134 F4
Caton . . . 231 C3
Catterall . . . 178 E2
Chapeltown . . . 47 C4
Charnock Green . . . 41 C6
Charnock Richard . . . 41 D4
Chatburn . . . 187 D5
Chipping . . . 182 D3
Chorley . . . 42 D6
Church . . . 102 E7
Churchtown . . . 178 A2
Claughton . . . 179 D2
Claughton, Lancaster . . . 231 E5
Clayton Brook . . . 77 A5
Clayton Green . . . 77 A3
Clayton-le-M . . . 123 D2
Clayton-le-W . . . 76 D2
Cleveleys . . . 172 C3
Clifton . . . 114 D1
Clitheroe . . . 164 D8
Clow Bridge . . . 105 C5
Cockden . . . 148 B2
Cockerham . . . 203 C6
Cold Row . . . 174 C5
Colne . . . 169 C6
Coppull . . . 41 E2
Copster Green . . . 121 D8
Corner Row . . . 132 E2
Cornholme . . . 108 B1
Cottam . . . 115 D5
Coupe Green . . . 97 E4
Cow Ark . . . 184 C8
Crossgill . . . 231 E1
Croston . . . 57 B2
Cuddy Hill . . . 135 B7
Cumeragh Village . . . 137 F6
Darwen . . . 80 E1
Dolphinholme . . . 220 A8
Downham . . . 188 B5
Drummersdale . . . 23 C7
Duncombe . . . 156 F3
Dunsop Bridge . . . 222 C5
Eagland Hill . . . 176 C8
Earby . . . 201 A2
Earnshaw Bridge . . . 75 E2
Eccleston . . . 40 D7
Edenfield . . . 67 D3
Edgworth . . . 47 D6
Egerton . . . 46 E2
Ellel . . . 207 B5
Elswick . . . 154 A1
Enfield . . . 124 A2
Esprick . . . 132 D5
Euxton . . . 59 D3
Fairview . . . 43 A1
Farington . . . 75 F6
Farleton . . . 232 A6
Fence . . . 146 E7
Fisher's Row . . . 196 E5
Fleetwood . . . 194 A6
Ford Green . . . 198 F2
Forest Holme . . . 86 A7
Formby . . . 11 E3
Forton . . . 204 B3
Foulridge . . . 191 D1
Freckleton . . . 92 C7
Fulwood . . . 116 D5
Galgate . . . 207 B3
Garstang . . . 178 D7
Gisburn . . . 225 C4
Glasson . . . 205 F5
Goodshaw Chapel . . . 105 B1
Goosnargh . . . 137 C6
Great Altcar . . . 12 E1
Great Eccleston . . . 154 C4
Great Harwood . . . 123 D4
Great Knowley . . . 60 E3
Great Mitton . . . 163 F3
Great Plumpton . . . 111 E7
Greenhalgh . . . 132 C5
Gregson Lane . . . 97 E2
Grimsargh . . . 138 D1
Grindleton . . . 187 B7
Hale Nook . . . 175 A5
Halsall . . . 22 C1
Halton . . . 214 F7
Halton Green . . . 231 A4
Hambleton . . . 174 C1
Hammerton Mere . . . 229 E1
Hampson Green . . . 207 C1
Hapton . . . 125 B4
Haskayne . . . 13 F4
Haslingden . . . 84 B4
Hawkshaw . . . 48 C2
Hesketh Bank . . . 72 D4
Hesketh Lane . . . 160 D8
Heskin Green . . . 40 D3
Hest Bank . . . 215 E1
Heysham . . . 208 D7
Heywood . . . 32 F2
High Bentham . . . 233 E8
High Casterton . . . 238 E3
High Cross . . . 130 C8
Higham . . . 145 E5
Higher Walton . . . 97 B4
Higher Wheelton . . . 78 B1
Higherford . . . 168 E5
Highfurlong . . . 151 A2
Hightown . . . 2 F3
Hill Dale . . . 26 D5
Hoddlesden . . . 81 F1
Hoghton . . . 98 B2
Hollins Lane . . . 204 D2
Holme Chapel . . . 107 A6
Holmes . . . 55 B3
Holmeswood . . . 37 C7
Hornby . . . 232 B7
Horton . . . 225 E5
Horwich . . . 31 D4
Hoscar . . . 25 D4
Huncoat . . . 124 E2
Hurlston . . . 23 B2
Hurlston Green . . . 23 B3
Hurst Green . . . 141 F8
Hutton . . . 94 D2
Ince Blundell . . . 3 E4
Inglewhite . . . 158 B4
Inskip . . . 134 D8
Jack Green . . . 77 F8
Johnson's Hillock . . . 60 E6
Kelbrook . . . 192 A6
Kingsfold . . . 95 D2
Kirkby . . . 1 A2
Kirkby Lonsdale . . . 238 A2
Kirkham . . . 113 A5
Knott End-on-S . . . 194 E5
Knowle Green . . . 161 B1
Knowley . . . 60 F2
Lancaster . . . 210 C6
Lane Bottom . . . 148 B3
Lane Ends . . . 224 A5
Lane Heads . . . 154 D3
Laneshaw Bridge . . . 170 F6
Langho . . . 142 D1
Lea Town . . . 114 F3
Leck . . . 236 B7
Lewth . . . 135 A6
Leyland . . . 76 A1
Limbrick . . . 43 A6
Little Eccleston . . . 154 A5
Little Knowley . . . 60 F3
Little Plumpton . . . 111 D5
Littledale . . . 226 D8
Longridge . . . 139 A8
Longshaw . . . 10 E1
Longton . . . 74 A8
Lostock Hall . . . 76 A7
Low Bentham . . . 233 C8
Lower Ballam . . . 111 A3
Lower Bartle . . . 115 D8
Lower Green Bank . . . 226 B1
Lowgill . . . 233 C3
Lucas Green . . . 60 C6
Lytham . . . 90 B3
Lytham St Anne's . . . 89 C5
Maghull . . . 5 B1
Mawdesley . . . 39 C2
Melling . . . 235 C1
Mellor . . . 120 F2
Mellor Brook . . . 120 C3
Mere Brow . . . 54 E2
Mereclough . . . 128 A1
Mereside . . . 130 B1
Middleton . . . 209 A2
Moor End . . . 174 C6
Moor Side . . . 133 D1
Morecambe . . . 212 B5
Moss Edge . . . 176 A3
Moss Side . . . 75 B1
Much Hoole . . . 73 D3
Nab's Head . . . 98 E7
Nangreaves . . . 49 F2
Nappa . . . 225 E8
Nateby . . . 177 D6
Nelson . . . 147 E8
Nether Kellet . . . 216 F5
New Lane . . . 24 B6
New Longton . . . 74 E8
Newburgh . . . 25 F2
Newchurch . . . 85 F1
Newsham . . . 136 A5
Newsholme . . . 225 D6
Newton . . . 223 A5
Newton-with-S . . . 113 F2
Newtown . . . 58 A2
Norcross . . . 151 A7
Normoss . . . 130 B7
Oakenclough . . . 220 C2
Ollerton Fold . . . 78 D5
Ormskirk . . . 15 C6
Orrell . . . 10 E7
Osbaldeston . . . 120 D4
Oswaldtwistle . . . 102 B3
Out Rawcliffe . . . 175 C1
Over Burrow . . . 235 E7
Over Kellet . . . 231 A8
Over Town . . . 107 A8
Overton . . . 205 D8
Padiham . . . 125 C6
Parbold . . . 26 D2
Paythorne . . . 225 C7
Peel . . . 110 F4
Peel Hill . . . 110 E7
Pendleton . . . 165 B4
Penwortham . . . 95 C5
Pilling . . . 196 C6
Pilling Lane . . . 195 B6
Pinfold . . . 22 F4
Pleasington . . . 99 C1
Potters Brook . . . 204 B5
Poulton-le-F . . . 151 E2
Preesall . . . 195 A3
Preesall Park . . . 195 C1
Preston . . . 95 C8
Quernmore . . . 226 A6
Radford . . . 64 A8
Rainford Junction . . . 8 F2
Rake Foot . . . 85 A7
Ramsbottom . . . 49 C5
Rathmell . . . 230 F6
Ratten Row . . . 154 B8
Rawtenstall . . . 85 B1
Read . . . 144 D2
Red Scar . . . 118 B5
Ribchester . . . 140 D3
Riley Green . . . 78 E8
Rimington . . . 188 F8
Ring o'Bells . . . 25 B2
Rishton . . . 123 C2
Rising Bridge . . . 84 A8
Rivington . . . 43 F2
Rochdale . . . 51 C2
Royal Oak . . . 6 F4
Rufford . . . 38 C4
Runshaw Moor . . . 58 E4
Sabden . . . 144 F8
Salesbury . . . 121 D6
Saltcotes . . . 90 D5
Salterforth . . . 191 D7
Salwick . . . 114 E3
Samlesbury . . . 118 E1
Samlesbury Bottoms . . . 98 D6
Sawley . . . 224 C1
Scarisbrick . . . 22 E7
Scorton . . . 199 E6
Scronkey . . . 196 E3
Sharneyford . . . 87 D5
Sherwood . . . 117 A6
Shevington . . . 19 F5
Shevington Moor . . . 38 A2
Shirdley Hill . . . 22 A6
Shuttleworth . . . 49 E8
Silverdale . . . 218 C3
Simonstone . . . 144 E1
Singleton . . . 152 E1
Skelmersdale . . . 18 A1
Slaidburn . . . 223 C7
Smallwood Hey . . . 196 B5
Sollom . . . 56 B2
Sough . . . 192 A8
Southport . . . 34 C3
Spen Brook . . . 167 D2
Spring Vale . . . 64 C7
St Michael's on W . . . 155 C7
Staining . . . 130 E5
Stake Pool . . . 196 E4
Stalmine . . . 174 C7
Standish . . . 28 F2
Staynall . . . 174 A4
Storth . . . 237 F5
Street . . . 220 A6
Sunny Bower . . . 122 B1
Swillbrook . . . 135 B2
Tardy Gate . . . 76 B8
Tarleton . . . 56 A7
Thistleton . . . 132 C8
Thornton . . . 173 D1
Thornton in L . . . 236 F4
Thornton-in-C . . . 201 A6
Thorpe Green . . . 77 E4
Tockholes . . . 80 A2
Tosside . . . 230 C2
Town End . . . 153 C8
Trawden . . . 170 C2
Tunstall . . . 235 E4
Turner Green . . . 119 C2
Waddington . . . 186 C4
Walk Mill . . . 106 F8
Walmer Bridge . . . 73 F5
Walton Summit . . . 77 B8
Walton-le-D . . . 96 D4
Warton . . . 91 D6
Warton, Carnforth . . . 217 D5
Water . . . 86 A8
Waterside . . . 81 E3
Weeton . . . 131 F2
Weeton Camp . . . 131 D5
Weir . . . 87 A7
Wennington . . . 235 E1
West Bradford . . . 186 F5
Westby . . . 111 E4
Westhead . . . 16 D4
Westhouse . . . 236 E5
Whalley . . . 143 B5
Wharles . . . 133 F4
Wheatley Lane . . . 167 E1
Wheelton . . . 61 A7
White Stake . . . 75 B7
Whitechapel . . . 158 D7
Whitehall . . . 64 B5
Whitewell Bottom . . . 85 F5
Whittington . . . 235 D7
Whittle-le-W . . . 60 C7
Whittlestone Head . . . 64 F4
Whitworth . . . 70 D1
Wilpshire . . . 121 E5
Winewall . . . 170 C4
Winmarleigh . . . 198 E4
Wiswell . . . 143 F7
Within Grove . . . 124 E1
Withnell . . . 79 B1
Withnell Fold . . . 78 C3
Woodplumpton . . . 135 E2
Woodsfold . . . 134 E6
Worsthorne . . . 128 A5
Wray . . . 232 D6
Wrayton . . . 235 E3
Wrea Green . . . 112 B3
Wrightington Bar . . . 27 F7
Wymott . . . 57 F6
Yealand Redmayne . . . 219 E4

A

A K Bsns Pk PR9 35 A6
Aalborg Pl LA1 210 F7
Abbey Cl Formby L37 12 B2
Orrell WN8 10 C7
Abbey Cres BB3 64 C8
Abbey Dale
Appley Bridge WN6 19 D7
Burscough L40 24 F3
Abbey Dr WN5 10 E6
Abbey Farm BB7 143 B6
Abbey Fields BB7 143 C5
Abbey Fold L40 24 D5
Abbey Gdns PR8 34 A4
Abbey Gr PR6 30 B7
Abbey La L40 24 C1
Abbey Mews BB7 143 C5
Abbey Rd Blackpool FY4 109 D5
Whalley BB7 143 C5
Abbey St Accrington BB5 103 C6
Accrington, Scaitcliffe BB5 103 C5
Bacup OL13 86 F4
Preston PR2 95 D8
Abbey Terr BB7 164 D1
Abbey View PR6 79 A1
Abbey Village Cty Prim Sch PR6 79 C1
Abbey Wlk PR1 95 D3
Abbeydale LA3 212 E2
Abbeyfield 5 BB11 127 B4
Abbeyfield Cl LA1 211 A3
Abbeyfield Ho
Barnoldswick BB18 200 A3
10 Burnley BB11 126 E5
Abbeystead WN8 9 C7
Abbeystead Dr LA1 211 A3
Abbeystead Ho 8 LA1 211 A3
Abbeystead La LA2 226 E2
Abbeystead Rd LA2 226 C1
Abbeyville FY4 109 C6
Abbeywood WN8 9 C6
Abbot Meadow PR1 95 D4
Abbot Wlk BB7 165 A8
Abbots Cl Formby L37 12 A1
Kirkham PR4 113 C4
Rawtenstall BB4 85 A4
Abbots Croft BB7 143 C5
Abbots Row FY8 89 D6
Abbots Way Formby L37 12 B1
Lancaster LA1 210 C8
Abbotsford L39 15 F5
Abbotsford Ave BB2 100 D1
Abbotsford Rd FY3 130 A3
Abbotsgate LA6 238 B2
Abbotsway PR1 95 C6
Abbott Brow BB2 120 E3
Abbott Clough Ave BB1 101 E4
Abbott Clough Cl BB1 101 E4
Abbott Croft PR2 116 A7
Abbott St 14 BL6 31 B4
Abbotts Wlk FY7 194 A5
Abel St BB10 127 A8
Abercorn Pl FY4 109 B5
Abercrombie Rd FY3 193 F4
Aberdare Cl BB1 100 E7
Aberdeen Dr BB1 101 A4
Aberdeen Gdns OL12 51 D4
Aberdeen Rd LA1 211 A7
Abernethy St BL6 31 D2
Abingdon Dr PR2 116 B1
Abingdon Gr LA3 209 A7
Abingdon Rd BB12 125 D7
Abingdon St FY1 129 B5
Abinger St BB10 147 C1
Abington Dr PR9 54 A5
Abner Row BB8 191 D1
Abraham Altham Ct BB10 147 F3
Abraham St
Accrington BB5 103 B5
Blackburn BB2 100 E2
11 Horwich BL6 31 B4
Abrams Fold PR9 53 F5
Abrams Gn PR9 53 F5
Acacia Cl 4 FY5 173 D1
Acacia Rd PR2 117 E2
Acacia Wlk 4 BB1 101 B5
Accrington & District Golf Course BB5 102 B6
Accrington & Rossendale Coll BB5 103 D5
Accrington & Rossendale Coll Rawtenstall Ctr BB4 84 F2
Accrington Rd
Blackburn BB1 101 C4
Burnley BB11 126 C5
Hapton BB11 125 E3
Whalley BB6,BB7 143 E4
Accrington Sta BB5 103 B6
Accrington Victoria Hospl BB5 103 B7
Acer Gr PR2 117 F3
Ackhurst La WN5 19 F2
Ackhurst Rd PR7 41 F8
Ackroyd St 10 OL14 108 B1
Acorn Ave BB5 102 F3
Acorn Bank PR3 178 C8
Acorn Bsns Ctr L33 1 B1
Acorn Cl PR5 59 A8
Acorn Mews FY4 130 D1
Acorn St Bacup OL13 86 F2
Blackburn BB1 101 B4
Acornfield Rd L33 1 D2
Acre Ave OL13 69 D8
Acre Cl BL0 67 D3
Acre Gate FY4 109 E7
Acre Gr PR4 73 F3
Acre Mill Rd OL13 69 D8
Acre Moss La LA4 212 D4
Acre St Brierfield BB10 148 A3
Burnley BB10 147 B1
Whitworth OL12 70 D1
Acre View OL13 69 D7
Acrefield Blackburn BB2 100 A7
Clayton Brook PR5 77 C5
Newburgh WN8 26 A1
Padiham BB12 145 C1
Acregate WN8 9 C7
Acregate La PR1 117 D1
Acremount BB12 144 D2
Acres La Great Altcar L37 3 E8
Maghull L31,L39 4 E7
Preesall FY6 195 A3
Acres The BB6 143 E8
Acresbrook Rd BB12 145 F6
Acresfield Adlington PR7 29 F6
Colne BB8 170 A5
Acresfield Cl BL6 30 C3
Acreswood Cl PR7 28 E8
Active Way BB11 127 A6
Acton Rd FY4 129 E1
Ada St Blackburn BB2 100 C5
Burnley BB10 147 B1
Nelson BB9 147 E6
Ramsbottom BL0 49 B5
Adamson St Burnley BB12 126 C6
Padiham BB12 145 C1
Addington Rd LA2,LA6 231 B7
Addington St BB1 101 A4
Addison Cl BB2 100 C5
Addison Cres FY3 129 D6
Addison Ct FY6 194 D5
Addison Rd FY7 194 A3
Addison St BB5 103 C7
Addle St LA1 211 A4
Adelaide Ave FY5 151 C8
Adelaide Ct 5 FY1 129 C5
Adelaide La BB5 103 C5
Adelaide St
Accrington BB5 103 C5
Blackpool FY1 129 B5
8 Burnley BB11 126 D6
6 Enfield BB5 124 A1
Fleetwood FY7 194 B5
Preston PR1 96 B8
2 Ramsbottom BL0 49 A4
Rawtenstall BB4 85 A7
Adelaide St W FY1 129 B4
Adelaide Terr BB2 100 C5
Adelphi Ho 1 PR1 116 E1
Adelphi Pl 3 PR1 95 F8
Adelphi St
6 Blackpool FY1 129 B5
Burnley BB11 127 A7
Lancaster LA1 211 A6
Preston PR1 116 E1
Standish WN6 28 E2
Adlington Ave FY6 151 B3
Adlington Cty Prim Sch PR7 29 F7
Adlington St BB11 127 A6
Adlington Sta PR6 30 A7
Admiral Cl FY8 109 E1
Admiral St BB10 127 B5
Admiral Way PR2 94 D7
Admirals Sound FY5 172 C2
Admiralty Cl L40 24 C2
Adrian St FY1 129 B1
Adstone Ave FY3 129 F7
Agate St BB1 121 F1
Ager St OL13 69 C8
Agglebys Rd FY6 173 F8
Agnes Ing La LA2 232 D7
Agnes St Blackburn BB2 100 C3
11 Preston PR1 96 A8
Agnew Rd FY7 193 F4
Agnew St FY8 90 A3
Aiken Ct PR4 113 A5
Aikengill Rd LA2 233 D4
Ailsa Ave FY4 129 F2
Ailsa Cl PR3 136 B8
Ailsa Rd BB1 101 D3
Ailsa Wlk LA3 208 E7
Ainley Ct 10 FY1 129 C6
Ainscough Brook Ho 1 PR2 117 F3
Ainsdale & Birkdale Hills Nature Reserve PR8 20 B7
Ainsdale Ave
Blackpool FY2 150 E5
Brierfield BB10 147 C5
Edgworth BL7 47 E6
Fleetwood FY7 172 D7
Thornton FY5 173 D1
Ainsdale CE Prim Sch PR8 20 D4
Ainsdale Cl LA1 213 D3
Ainsdale Dr Darwen BB3 64 B5
Preston PR2 115 E2
Whitworth OL12 51 D7
Ainsdale High Sch PR8 20 C6
Ainsdale Sta PR8 20 C5
Ainse Rd BL6 30 B3
Ainslie Cl BB6 123 B5
Ainslie Rd PR2 116 E3
Ainslie St 3 BB12 126 C6
Ainsworth Ave BL6 31 E2
Ainsworth Mall BB1 100 E5
Ainsworth St BB1 100 E5
Aintree Cres PR8 34 F4
Aintree Dr BB3 81 A7
Aintree Rd Blackpool FY4 129 D1
Aintree Rd *continued*
Thornton FY5 151 B8
Air Hill Terr 8 OL12 51 C1
Airdrie Cres BB11 126 D4
Airdrie Pl FY2 150 E6
Aire Cl LA3 213 B3
Airedale LA2 207 B4
Airedale Ave FY3 129 E3
Airedale Ct FY6 151 C4
Airegate L31 5 B2
Airey Ho PR3 161 D1
Airey St BB5 103 D3
Airton Garth BB9 168 C3
Aitken Cl BL0 49 B5
Aitken St Accrington BB5 103 C7
Haslingden BL0 67 C5
Ajax St 3 BL0 49 B5
Alamein Rd LA5 217 E1
Alan Gr LA3 208 F6
Alan Haigh Ct BB8 169 D6
Alan Ramsbottam Way BB6 123 E4
Alandale Cl PR5 59 B7
Alaska St BB2 100 E2
Albany Ave FY4 109 B5
Albany Cl FY6 130 E8
Albany Dr
Bamber Bridge PR5 96 D2
Copster Green BB1 121 C8
Albany High Sch PR7 42 E5
Albany Rd Blackburn BB2 100 B6
3 Fleetwood FY7 193 F4
Lytham St Anne's FY8 89 C5
Morecambe LA4 212 C4
Southport PR9 52 C1
Albatros St PR1 117 B1
Albemarle St BB7 164 D8
Albermarle Ct 2 BB7 164 D8
Albert Ct PR9 52 D1
Albert Ho BB4 85 D1
Albert Pl Blackburn BB3 80 F7
Southport PR8 34 B8
Albert Rd
Barnoldswick BB18 200 B2
Blackpool FY1 129 C5
Colne BB8 169 D4
Formby L37 2 B8
Fulwood PR2 116 F3
Lancaster LA1 213 F1
Leyland PR5 59 C8
Lytham St Anne's FY8 89 A7
Morecambe LA4 212 C4
Preston PR1 116 F2
Rawtenstall BB4 85 A8
Rufford L40 38 A3
Southport PR9 52 D1
Albert Sq 11 FY7 194 B5
Albert St Accrington BB5 103 C5
Blackburn BB2 100 C2
Brierfield BB9 147 B5
Burnley BB11 127 B6
Bury BL9 32 A2
3 Carnforth LA5 217 D1
Carnforth,Millhead LA5 217 D3
1 Chorley PR7 42 D7
2 Church BB5 102 E6
Clayton-le-M BB5 123 F2
Darwen BB3 64 B5
Earby BB18 201 B2
Egerton BL7 46 D3
Fleetwood FY7 194 B4
Great Harwood BB6 123 D4
Hoddlesden BB3 81 F1
Horwich BL6 31 B4
Kirkham PR4 112 F6
Lytham St Anne's FY8 90 C3
Nelson BB9 147 D8
Oswaldtwistle BB5 102 E4
Padiham BB12 125 C8
Ramsbottom BL0 49 B6
Rishton BB1 123 B1
Wheelton PR6 61 A7
Whitewell Bottom BB4 85 E5
Whitworth OL12 51 C8
Albert Terr Bacup OL13 86 F3
9 Barrowford BB9 168 D3
Calder Vale PR3 179 E8
8 Preston PR1 117 A1
Rawtenstall BB4 85 B2
Southport PR8 34 A5
Alberta Cl BB2 100 B8
Albion Ave FY3 129 F6
Albion Ct BB11 126 E4
Albion Mews LA1 214 A1
Albion Rd Blackburn BB2 100 D1
Earby BB18 201 B2
Albion St Accrington BB5 103 B6
Bacup OL13 87 A3
7 Bacup,Stacksteads OL13 69 C8
Blackburn BB2 100 C1
Brierfield BB9 147 B5
Burnley BB11 126 E5
Chorley PR7 42 C7
1 Clitheroe BB7 164 F8
Earby BB18 201 B2
Lancaster LA1 214 A1
4 Nelson BB9 147 D8
7 Padiham BB12 125 D7
Albrighton Cl PR5 76 B7
Albrighton Cres PR5 76 B7
Albrighton Rd PR5 76 C7
Albyn Bank Rd PR1 96 B7
Albyn St E PR1 96 B7
Alcester Ave PR1 95 C5
Alconbury Cres FY5 172 C2
Aldate Gr PR2 116 A2
Aldcliffe Cotts LA1 210 D5
Aldcliffe Ct LA4 212 E3
Aldcliffe Mews LA1 210 D5
Aldcliffe Pl LA1 210 E7
Aldcliffe Rd Lancaster LA1 210 E6
7 Preston PR2 115 E1
Alden Cl BB4 67 A6
Alden Rd BB4,BL8 66 F5
Alden Rise BB4 67 A6
Alder Terr 5 LA1 213 F3
Alder Ave Bury BL9 32 C3
Rawtenstall BB4 85 B2
Alder Bank Blackburn BB2 100 B4
20 Rawtenstall BB4 85 A3
Alder Cl Leyland PR5 58 B8
Newton-with-S PR4 114 A2
Thornton FY5 173 C1
Alder Coppice PR2 115 E3
Alder Ct Fleetwood FY7 193 C2
Lancaster LA1 210 D8
Alder Dr
Charnock Richard PR7 41 D3
Gregson Lane PR5 97 E1
Alder Gr Blackpool FY3 129 E7
Coppull PR7 41 F1
Huncoat BB5 124 E2
Lancaster LA1 210 D8
Lytham St Anne's FY8 90 A4
Poulton-le-F FY6 151 D1
Alder Grange High Sch BB4 85 A4
Alder Hill Croft BB18 201 C2
Alder Hill St BB18 201 B2
Alder La Formby L37,L39 12 E7
Moss Edge PR3 176 A1
Parbold WN8 26 C1
Alder Meadow Cl OL12 51 A1
Alder Rd PR2 118 A4
Alder St Bacup OL13 86 F3
4 Blackburn BB1 101 A7
Burnley BB12 126 C7
Rawtenstall BB4 85 B3
Alderbank BL6 30 F3
Alderbrook Dr WN8 26 C2
Alderdale Ave PR8 20 A5
Alderfield PR1 95 D3
Alderford Cl BB7 164 C7
Alderley WN8 9 C6
Alderley Ave FY4 109 B5
Alderley Hts LA1 213 F3
Alderman Foley Dr OL12 51 A2
Alderney Cl BB2 100 B1
Alders The PR3 199 C1
Aldersleigh Cres PR5 97 D1
Alderson Cres L37 11 F4
Alderville Cl PR4 91 F6
Alderway BL0 67 C1
Alderwood Gr BL0 67 D4
Aldfield Ave PR2 115 C1
Aldingham Ct LA4 212 E3
Aldingham Wlk LA4 212 D5
Aldon Gr PR4 94 A1
Aldon Rd FY6 151 F2
Aldren's La LA1 213 F3
Aldwych Ave FY3 129 E3
Aldwych Dr
Bamber Bridge PR5 76 B7
Preston PR2 116 A2
Aldwych Pl BB1 121 F2
Alert St PR2 116 C1
Alexander Cl
Accrington BB5 103 E1
Burscough L40 24 F3
Alexander Ct FY6 151 D3
Alexander Dr L31 5 D3
Alexander Gr BB12 126 B6
Alexander Pl PR2 138 D1
Alexander St BB9 169 A2
Alexandra Cl BB5 123 E3
Alexandra Ct 4 LA1 210 F8
Alexandra Ho
Blackburn BB1 101 B3
10 Preston PR1 117 C1
Alexandra Mews
1 Ormskirk L39 15 E6
8 Southport PR9 34 C8
Alexandra Pavilion 5 PR1 117 A1
Alexandra Pl BB6 123 D6
Alexandra Rd
Bamber Bridge PR5 96 D3
Blackburn BB2 100 C6
Blackpool FY1 129 B1
Burscough L40 24 D4
Carnforth LA5 217 D1
8 Darwen BB3 80 F2
Formby L37 11 B1
Kirkham PR4 113 A6
Lancaster LA1 213 F3
Longridge PR3 139 A7
Lytham St Anne's FY8 89 A7
Morecambe LA3 212 B3
Southport PR9 34 D8
Thornton FY5 151 C8
Alexandra St
Clayton-le-M BB5 123 E3
Preston PR1 96 C7
Alexandra View 7 BB3 80 F2
Alexandria Dr FY8 88 F5
Alexandria St BB4 84 F4
Alford Fold PR2 116 D7
Alfred St Blackpool FY1 129 C5
Bury BL9 32 A1
Darwen BB3 64 B6
Egerton BL7 46 D3
Lancaster LA1 211 A8
10 Ramsbottom BL0 49 B5
Whitworth OL12 70 D2
Algar St 7 BB9 168 F2
Alice Ave PR5 76 A1
Alice Sq 4 PR1 117 A1
Alice St Accrington BB5 103 D7
Barnoldswick BB18 200 B2
8 Darwen BB3 64 A8
Morecambe LA4 212 F5
Oswaldtwistle BB5 102 E3
Alicia Ct OL12 51 E1
Alicia Dr OL12 51 E1
Alisan Rd FY6 151 B5
Alker La PR7 60 B3
Alker St PR7 42 C7
Alkincoats Rd BB8 169 C5
All Hallows RC High Sch PR1 95 A3
All Hallows Rd FY2 150 D5
All Saint's Cl BB5 102 B4
All Saints CE Prim Sch
Appley Bridge WN6 27 C1
Chorley PR7 42 B5
Clayton-le-M BB5 123 F2
All Saints Cl
Padiham BB12 125 F7
Rawtenstall BB4 105 A1
All Saints RC High Sch BB4 84 D1
All Saints Rd FY2 150 E6
All Saints' Rd FY8 88 E6
Allan Critchlow Way BB1 123 B2
Allan St OL13 86 F1
Allandale FY4 109 C5
Allandale Ave FY5 172 F4
Allen Cl Cleveleys FY5 172 D1
Fleetwood FY7 193 D2
Allen Ct BB10 127 A8
Allen St BB10 127 A8
Allen Way FY7 193 D2
Allenbury Pl FY3 130 A2
Allenby Ave PR2 117 B4
Allenby Rd FY8 88 E8
Allendale Gr BB10 127 F4
Allendale St Burnley BB12 126 B6
Colne BB8 169 F5
Allengate PR2 116 F4
Allerton Cl BB3 81 A2
Allerton Dr BB12 126 D6
Allerton Rd
Bamber Bridge PR5 96 D4
Southport PR9 52 E1
Alleys Gn BB7 186 E1
Alleytroyds BB5 102 E5
Alliance Bsns Pk BB5 103 A5
Alliance St BB5 103 F1
Allington Cl PR5 96 E3
Allison Gr BB8 169 F6
Allonby Ave FY5 172 E4
Allotment La PR3 155 C7
Allsprings Cl BB6 123 D6
Allsprings Dr BB6 123 D6
Alma Ave BB8 191 D1
Alma Cl WN8 10 C7
Alma Ct Orrell WN8 10 C7
Southport PR8 20 F7
Alma Dr PR7 41 E4
Alma Hill WN8 10 C7
Alma Hill Est WN8 10 C7
Alma Ho LA1 210 F6
Alma Ind Est 23 OL12 51 F1
Alma Par WN8 10 C7
Alma Pl Accrington BB5 83 E8
Clitheroe BB7 164 D7
Alma Rd Lancaster LA1 210 F6
Laneshaw Bridge BB8 170 D6
Orrell WN8 10 C7
Southport PR8 34 A4
Alma Row PR5 97 E1
Alma St Bacup OL13 87 A2
Blackburn BB2 100 D5
9 Clayton-le-M BB5 123 F3
Padiham BB12 125 C8
Preston PR1 117 A1
13 Rochdale OL12 51 F1
Alma Terr BB11 105 B4
Almhouses BD23 201 A5
Almond Ave
Burscough Bridge L40 24 E6
4 Bury BL9 32 C3
Almond Brook Rd WN6 28 C1
Almond Cl
Abbey Village PR6 79 B2
Fulwood PR2 117 D6
Penwortham PR1 95 B3
Almond Cres BB4 67 F8
Almond St BB3 64 A8
Almonry The L40 17 B7
Almshouses
34 Lancaster LA1 210 F8
Ormskirk L39 6 A7
7 Rawtenstall BB4 84 E2
Alnwick Cl BB12 126 E7
Alpha St Darwen BB3 64 B8
8 Nelson BB9 168 F2
Salterforth BB18 191 E8
Alpic Dr FY5 150 C7
Alpine Ave
Bamber Bridge PR5 76 B7
Blackpool FY4 109 E5
Alpine Cl
Bamber Bridge PR5 76 B7
Hoddlesden BB3 81 E1
Alpine Gr BB2 80 B8
Alpine Rd PR6 60 E3
Alpine View LA5 216 A6
Alsop St PR1 116 F2
Alston Ave FY5 172 D4
Alston Cl BB7 144 F8
Alston Dr LA4 213 B5
Alston Hall Coll PR3 119 B8
Alston La PR2,PR3 139 A2

Alston Lane RC Prim Sch
PR3 138 F2
Alston Rd FY2 150 E2
Alston St PR1 117 D1
Alt Rd Formby L37 12 B2
Hightown L38 3 A4
Altcar La Formby L37 11 F1
Haskayne L39 14 A2
Maghull L31 4 F5
Runshaw Moor PR5 58 E5
Altcar Rd L37 12 B2
Altham Bsns Pk BB5 124 E6
Altham Ind Est BB5 124 D6
Altham La BB5 124 F4
Altham Rd Morecambe LA4 212 F3
Southport PR8 34 E2
Altham St 2 Burnley BB10 127 A8
6 Padiham BB12 125 D8
Altham St James CE Prim Sch BB5 124 D6
Altham Wlk LA4 212 F3
Althorp Cl 6 FY1 129 C7
Althorpe Dr PR8 34 E3
Altom St BB1 100 E6
Alton Cl L38 2 F2
Altys La L39 15 F3
Alum Scar La BB2 99 A6
Alvern Ave PR2 116 D4
Alvern Cres PR2 116 D4
Alvina La L33 1 A5
Alwin St 8 BB11 126 E5
Alwood Ave FY3 129 F6
Amber Ave BB1 121 F2
Amber Gate PR2 115 F6
Amberbanks Gr FY1 129 B2
Ambergate WN8 9 B7
Amberley St BB2 100 C2
Amberwood PR4 112 F5
Amberwood Dr BB2 100 A1
Ambledene PR5 77 A5
Ambleside Ave
Barnoldswick BB18 200 A3
Euxton PR7 59 D1
Knott End-on-S FY6 194 F6
2 Rawtenstall BB4 84 E2
Ambleside Cl
Bamber Bridge PR5 96 E2
Blackburn BB1 101 A6
Huncoat BB5 103 E8
Ambleside Dr BB3 81 C3
Ambleside Rd
Blackpool FY4 130 D1
Fulwood PR2 117 E5
Lancaster LA1 214 B2
Lytham St Anne's FY8 109 E1
Maghull L31 5 D2
Ambleside Wlk PR2 117 E5
Ambleway PR5 96 C4
Ambrose PR5 76 B2
Ambrose Hall La PR4 135 E3
Amelia St BB1 101 B6
Amersham WN8 9 C7
Amersham Cl PR4 74 F8
Amersham Gr BB10 147 D4
Amethyst St BB1 121 F2
Amounderness Way
Cleveleys FY5 172 F4
Fleetwood FY7 194 A3
Thornton FY5 151 C7
Ampleforth Dr PR5 96 A1
Amy Johnson Way FY4 109 E4
Amy St OL12 51 B1
Ancenis Ct PR4 113 B5
Anchor Ave BB3 80 F4
Anchor Ct PR1 95 F7
Anchor Dr PR4 94 D2
Anchor Gr BB3 80 E5
Anchor Rd BB3 80 F4
Anchor Ret Pk 1 BB11 127 A6
Anchor St PR9 34 B7
Anchor Way FY8 109 E1
Anchorage Ave PR4 71 F1
Anchorage Mews FY7 194 B3
Anchorage Rd FY7 194 B3
Anchorsholme La FY5 150 F8
Anchorsholme La E FY5 172 E1
Anchorsholme La W FY5 172 C1
Anchorsholme Prim Sch
FY5 150 E8
Ancliffe La LA2,LA5 216 B2
Andelen Cl BB11 125 C3
Anders Dr L33 1 A5
Andersholme La FY5 151 A8
Anderson Cl LA1 211 B6
Anderson Rd BB1 122 A7
Anderson St 8 FY1 129 C4
Anderton Cl BB4 68 F7
Anderton La BL6 30 E4
Anderton Prim Sch PR6 30 B8
Anderton Rd Euxton PR7 59 D1
Higham BB12 145 F5
Anderton St Adlington PR7 30 A7
Chorley PR7 42 C7
Anderton Way PR3 178 D6
Andertons Way PR2 117 D5
Andreas Cl PR8 34 B4
Andrew Ave BB4 84 F1
Andrew Cl Blackburn BB2 80 B8
Ramsbottom BL8 48 F1
Andrew Rd BB9 169 B1
Andrew St Bury BL9 32 A2
Preston PR1 117 C1
Andrews Cl L37 11 E1
Andrews La L37 11 E1
Andrews Yort L37 11 E1
Anemone Dr BB4 66 F8
Angel Way 3 BB8 169 E5
Angela St BB2 100 B1
Anger's Hill Rd FY4 129 F1
Angle St BB10 127 A8
Anglesey Ave BB12 126 A7
Anglesey St BB2 80 B8
Anglezarke Rd PR6 30 A7
Anglezarke Woodland Trail PR6 43 D6
Anglian Cl BB5 102 C5
Angus St OL13 69 C8
Aniline St PR6 42 E8
Ann St Barrowford BB9 168 D3
Brierfield BB9 147 B6
4 Clayton-le-M BB5 123 F3
Skelmersdale WN8 8 E8
Anna's Rd FY4 110 E3
Annan Cres FY4 130 C1
Annandale Gdns WN8 10 A7
Annarly Fold BB10 128 A5
Annaside Cl 2 FY4 109 E7
Anne Ave PR8 20 E6
Anne Cl BB10 127 B5
Anne St BB11 127 B5
Annesley Ave FY3 129 E8
Annie St Accrington BB5 103 C7
Ramsbottom BL0 49 A4
5 Rawtenstall BB4 85 A2
Annis St PR1 96 C8
Ansbro Ave PR4 92 C6
Ansdell & Fairhaven Sta FY8 89 D4
Ansdell Cty Prim Sch FY8 89 C5
Ansdell Gr Fulwood PR2 116 C3
Southport PR9 53 A4
Ansdell Rd Blackpool FY1 129 D2
Horwich BL6 31 C4
Ansdell Rd N FY8 89 D4
Ansdell Rd S FY8 89 D3
Ansdell St 3 PR1 117 C1
Ansdell Terr BB2 100 E1
Anselm Ct FY2 150 B3
Anshaw Cl BL7 45 C5
Anson Cl FY8 109 D1
Anson Rd PR4 113 B2
Anstable Rd LA4 213 A5
Anthony Rd LA1 210 E7
Antrim Rd FY2 150 C1
Anvil Cl WN5 10 D5
Anvil St OL13 69 E8
Anyon La LA2 204 E6
Anyon St BB3 81 B2
Anzio Rd PR4 131 E5
Apiary The PR5 57 A6
Appealing La FY8 109 E2
Apple Cl BB2 100 C4
Apple Ct BB2 100 C4
Apple St BB2 100 C4
Apple Tree Cl PR3 155 C8
Apple Tree Way BB5 102 E5
Appleby Cl Accrington BB5 103 D5
Gregson Lane PR5 97 E1
Appleby Dr BB9 168 D4
Appleby Rd FY2 150 D1
Appleby St Blackburn BB1 101 A5
Nelson BB9 147 D8
Preston PR1 116 F1
Applecross Dr BB10 127 E4
Applefields PR5 59 B7
Applegarth
Barnoldswick BB18 200 C3
Barrowford BB9 168 B1
Applegarth Rd LA3 209 A8
Applegarth St 3 BB18 201 B1
Applesike PR4 94 A1
Appleton Cl FY6 151 A2
Appleton Rd WN8 17 F2
Appletree Cl
Lancaster LA1 211 A3
Penwortham PR1 95 C2
Appletree Dr LA1 211 A3
Applewood Cl FY8 89 F3
Appley Bridge Sta WN6 19 C7
Appley Cl WN6 27 C2
Appley La N WN6 27 C1
Appley La S WN6,WN8 19 C6
Approach Way BB11 126 F2
Apsley Brow L31 5 B1
Apsley Fold PR3 139 B6
Aqueduct Rd BB2 100 D1
Aqueduct St PR1 116 E1
Arago St BB5 103 C7
Aragon Cl L31 5 E3
Arbories Ave 4 BB12 125 B8
Arbory Dr BB12 125 B8
Arbory The PR4 111 E7
Arbour Dr BB2 80 D6
Arbour La Kirkby L33 1 B2
Shevington Moor WN6 28 B1
Arbour Lane End PR3 160 E7
Arbour St PR8 34 C6
Arboury St BB12 125 B8
Arcadia 9 BB8 169 E5
Arcadia Ave L31 5 D3
Arch St Burnley BB11 126 F6
4 Darwen BB3 81 A1
Archbishop Hutton's Prim Sch LA5 217 D5
Archbishop Temple Sch
PR2 116 F5
Archer Hill LA5 217 D3
Archery Ave BB8 191 D1
Arches The BB7 143 B6
Arcon Ho LA1 210 F5
Arcon Rd PR7 41 E1
Ardee Rd PR1 95 D6
Arden Cl Hest Bank LA2 213 E8
Southport PR8 20 A5
Arden Gn FY7 193 E4
Ardengate LA1 210 F4
Ardleigh Ave PR8 34 E3
Ardley Rd BL6 31 C4
Ardmore Rd FY2 150 D2
Ardwick St BB10 127 A8
Argameols Cl PR8 34 F5
Argarmeols Gr L37 11 E5
Argarmeols Rd L37 11 E6
Argosy Ave FY3 129 F8
Argosy Ct 1 FY3 130 A8
Argyle Ct PR9 52 D1
Argyle Rd 7 Leyland PR5 76 A1
Poulton-le-F FY6 151 E3
Southport PR9 52 D2
Argyle St Accrington BB5 103 B6
Colne BB8 169 D5
Darwen BB3 80 F3
Heywood OL10 32 F1
3 Lancaster LA1 211 A7
Argyll Ct FY2 150 C1
Argyll Rd Blackpool FY2 150 C1
Preston PR1 117 A1
Ariel Way FY7 193 E4
Arkholme Ave FY1 129 D2
Arkholme CE Prim Sch
LA6 235 B3
Arkholme Cl LA5 217 E2
Arkholme Ct LA4 212 E3
Arkholme Dr PR4 93 F1
Arkwright Ct FY4 110 C7
Arkwright Fold BB2 80 C8
Arkwright Rd PR1 116 F2
Arkwright St
Burnley BB12 126 C7
Horwich BL6 31 C2
Arley Gdns BB12 126 F7
Arley La WN1,WN2 29 D2
Arley Rise BB2 120 E2
Arley St PR6 42 D8
Arlington Ave FY4 109 B7
Arlington Cl
Ramsbottom BL9 49 C2
Southport PR8 20 A5
Arlington Rd BB3 63 F8
Armadale Rd FY2 150 E1
Armitstead Ct 8 FY7 193 F2
Armitstead Way 5 FY7 193 F2
Armstrong St Horwich BL6 31 C2
Preston PR2 116 B2
Arnbarrow LA7 237 E6
Arncliffe Ave BB5 102 F4
Arncliffe Gr BB9 168 C3
Arncliffe Rd Burnley BB10 127 E5
Morecambe LA3 212 A1
Arndale Cl FY7 193 C2
Arndale Ctr 4 BB9 147 E8
Arndale Rd PR3 139 A7
Arnhem Rd Carnforth LA5 217 E1
Preston PR1 96 D8
Arnian Ct L39 6 C7
Arno St 9 PR1 96 B7
Arnold Ave FY4 109 C7
Arnold Cl Blackburn BB2 101 A1
Burnley BB11 126 E2
Fulwood PR2 117 E2
Arnold Jun Sch FY4 109 C6
Arnold Pl 1 PR7 42 A5
Arnold Rd FY8 90 D4
Arnold Sch FY4 109 C7
Arnold St 2 BB5 103 C6
Arnott Rd Blackpool FY4 129 E1
Fulwood PR2 116 C2
Arnside Ave Blackpool FY1 129 D1
Lytham St Anne's FY8 89 C7
Arnside CE Prim Sch
LA5 237 B2
Arnside Cl
Clayton-le-M BB5 123 E2
Coupe Green PR5 97 E4
Lancaster LA1 211 B3
Arnside Cres Blackburn BB2 79 E8
Morecambe LA4 212 F6
Arnside Rd Broughton PR3 136 D2
Preston PR2 115 E2
Southport PR9 34 C7
Arnside Sta LA5 237 C2
Arnside Terr PR9 34 C7
Arran Ave BB1 101 D2
Arran Cl LA3 208 E7
Arran St BB11 126 D5
Arrow La LA2 214 F7
Arrowsmith Cl PR5 97 E2
Arrowsmith Ct 7 BL6 31 E1
Arrowsmith Dr PR5 97 E2
Arrowsmith Gdns FY5 172 E5
Arroyo Way PR2 117 B4
Arthur St Bacup OL13 87 B3
Barnoldswick BB18 200 A3
Blackburn BB2 100 C4
Brierfield BB9 147 B6
Burnley BB11 126 E6
Clayton-le-M BB5 123 F3
6 Fleetwood FY7 194 B5
Great Harwood BB6 123 D6
18 Nelson BB9 168 E1
Preston PR1 95 E7
Sough BB18 192 A7
Arthur St N 5 FY7 194 B5
Arthur Way BB2 100 C4
Arthurs La FY6 174 D2
Artle Pl LA1 213 E2
Artlebeck Cl LA2 231 C3
Artlebeck Gr LA2 231 C3
Artlebeck Rd LA2 231 C3
Arundel Ave FY2 150 B5
Arundel Dr FY6 151 C5
Arundel Pl 37 PR1 96 A7
Arundel Rd Longton PR4 94 A1
Lytham St Anne's FY8 89 C4
Arundel Rd *continued*
Southport PR8 20 F8
Arundel St BB1 123 A2
Arundel Way PR5 59 C8
Ascot Cl Lancaster LA1 211 B4
Southport PR8 33 E5
Ascot Gdns LA2 213 F8
Ascot Rd Blackpool FY3 129 E6
Thornton FY5 151 B8
Ascot Way BB5 103 D5
Ash Ave Galgate LA2 206 F4
Haslingden BB4 84 C3
Kirkham PR4 113 A4
Ash Bank Cl PR3 136 B8
Ash Brow WN8 26 B1
Ash Cl Appley Bridge WN6 19 D7
Barrow BB7 164 D1
Elswick PR4 154 A1
Ormskirk L39 15 D5
Rishton BB1 102 B8
Ash Coppice PR2 115 D2
Ash Ct PR4 114 D2
Ash Dr
Carnforth,Warton LA5 217 E6
Freckleton PR4 92 A5
Freckleton,Warton PR4 91 D6
Poulton-le-F FY6 151 E2
Thornton FY5 173 C1
West Bradford BB7 186 D7
Ash Field PR6 77 C3
Ash Gr Bamber Bridge PR5 96 F1
Barnoldswick BB18 200 B2
Chorley PR7 42 C5
Darwen BB3 81 B2
Formby L37 11 C1
Garstang PR3 178 B8
8 Horwich BL6 31 E1
Kirkham PR4 113 B7
Lancaster LA1 210 F5
Longton PR4 73 F8
New Longton PR4 74 F6
Orrell WN5 10 F6
Preesall FY6 195 A4
Ramsbottom BL0 48 F3
3 Rawtenstall BB4 85 A3
Skelmersdale WN8 17 D1
St Michael's on W PR3 155 C7
Water BB4 86 A8
Wrea Green PR4 112 C3
Ash Holme PR1 117 C3
Ash La Clifton PR4 114 E2
Great Harwood BB6 123 B6
Longridge PR3 139 B8
Ash Lea Gr FY6 174 C7
Ash Mdw PR2 115 E3
Ash Rd Coppull PR7 28 E8
Elswick PR4 154 A1
Ash St Bacup OL13 86 F3
Blackburn BB1 101 A7
Blackpool FY4 109 C6
Burnley BB11 127 B5
Bury BL9 32 A2
Fleetwood FY7 194 A4
Great Harwood BB6 123 C6
Nelson BB9 147 F8
Oswaldtwistle BB5 102 D4
Southport PR8 34 C5
Trawden BB8 170 C2
Ash Tree Gr LA5 215 F3
Ash Tree Wlk 15 BB9 168 D3
Ashborne Dr BL9 49 D2
Ashbourne Cl 6 LA1 213 F3
Ashbourne Cres PR2 116 A5
Ashbourne Dr LA1 213 F3
Ashbourne Gr LA3 212 F2
Ashbourne Rd LA1 213 F3
Ashbrook St LA1 210 D8
Ashburnham Rd BB8 169 A2
Ashburton Rd FY1 129 B7
Ashby St PR7 42 D6
Ashcombe Gate FY5 151 D7
Ashcroft LA3 212 B1
Ashcroft Ave L39 15 F6
Ashcroft Cl LA2 231 B3
Ashcroft Rd Formby L37 11 F1
Kirkby L33 1 C3
Ashdale Cl L37 11 C2
Ashdale Gr FY5 173 E2
Ashdale Pl 2 LA1 213 E2
Ashdene OL12 51 D4
Ashdown Cl Carleton FY6 151 B5
Southport PR8 34 E4
Ashdown Dr PR6 77 C2
Ashdown Mews PR2 117 E6
Asheldon St 1 PR1 117 D1
Ashendean View BB12 145 D1
Ashfield PR2 116 F8
Ashfield Ave
Lancaster LA1 210 D7
Morecambe LA4 213 B6
Ashfield Cl BB9 168 C1
Ashfield Cotts 2 LA2 233 D8
Ashfield Ct Blackpool FY2 150 E6
Fulwood PR2 115 F6
Ashfield Rd Adlington PR6 30 B8
Blackpool FY2,FY5 150 E6
Burnley BB11 126 F6
Chorley PR7 42 B7
Ashfield Rise PR3 178 D2
Ashfield Terr WN6 19 C8
Ashfields PR5 75 B1
Ashford Ave LA1 210 E3
Ashford Cl LA1 210 F3
Ashford Cres PR3 136 C3
Ashford Rd Lancaster LA1 210 F3
Preston PR2 115 E2
Ashford St Heywood OL10 32 F2
Nelson BB9 147 E7
Ashgrove PR1 117 E1
Ashlands Cl BL0 67 D2
Ashleigh Ct PR2 117 A7
Ashleigh Mews FY3 129 E4
Ashleigh Prim Sch BB3 64 A6
Ashleigh Rd LA5 237 B2
Ashleigh St Darwen BB3 64 B6
Preston PR1 96 C7
Ashlet Ct FY6 151 C3
Ashley Cl Blackpool FY2 150 D2
Thornton FY5 151 B7
Ashley La PR3 138 C8
Ashley Rd
Lytham St Anne's FY8 109 F1
Skelmersdale WN8 18 B3
Southport PR9 34 C7
Ashley St BB12 126 F7
Ashmead Rd WN8 18 A4
Ashmeadow Gr LA6 216 F5
Ashmeadow La PR6 61 F8
Ashmeadow Rd
Arnside LA5 237 B2
Nether Kellet LA6 216 F5
Ashmoor St PR1 116 E1
Ashmore Gr FY5 172 D1
Ashmount Dr OL12 51 F2
Ashness Cl Fulwood PR2 116 F8
Horwich BL6 30 F3
Ashton Ave FY6 194 D5
Ashton Cl PR2 95 A8
Ashton Ct Fleetwood FY6 194 D5
Lancaster LA1 210 F7
Ashton Dr Lancaster LA1 213 E2
Nelson BB9 147 E6
Ashton Garden Ct FY8 88 E7
Ashton House BB3 64 B8
Ashton La BB3 64 A8
Ashton Meml LA1 211 B7
Ashton Rd Blackpool FY1 129 C3
8 Darwen BB3 64 B8
Lancaster LA1,LA2 210 E4
Morecambe LA4 212 F5
Southport PR8 33 F1
Ashton St Longridge PR3 139 A8
8 Lytham St Anne's FY8 90 A3
7 Preston PR2 95 D8
Ashton Wlk 12 LA1 210 F8
Ashton-on-Ribble High Sch PR2 115 F2
Ashtongate PR2 115 F1
Ashtree Ct Fulwood PR2 116 A4
Higher Walton PR5 97 C3
Ashtree Gr PR1 95 B4
Ashtrees L40 39 C2
Ashtrees Way 2 LA5 217 D2
Ashurst Cl WN8 18 A4
Ashurst Ct L37 11 E2
Ashurst Gdns WN8 18 B4
Ashurst Rd
Clayton-le-W PR5 76 D1
Shevington Moor WN6 28 B2
Skelmersdale WN8 18 B4
Ashville Terr BB2 80 D8
Ashwall St WN8 8 E8
Ashwell Pl FY5 150 C7
Ashwood WN8 18 C3
Ashwood Ave Darwen BB3 80 D6
Ramsbottom BL0 49 D7
Ashwood Cl FY8 89 E4
Ashwood Ct LA1 210 F5
Ashwood Rd PR2 116 D7
Ashworth Cl BB2 100 C5
Ashworth Ct 5 FY3 129 D7
Ashworth Dr LA2 215 E2
Ashworth Gr PR1 96 C6
Ashworth Hospl L31 6 B2
Ashworth La
Newchurch BB4 85 F3
Preston PR1 96 C6
Ashworth Rd
Blackpool FY4 110 C8
Newchurch BB4 85 F2
Rochdale OL11 50 E2
Ashworth St
Accrington BB5 103 E2
15 Bacup OL13 87 A3
3 Bacup, Stackstead OL13 69 D8
3 Bamber Bridge PR5 96 F2
Forest Holme BB4 86 A7
1 Preston PR1 96 B7
Rawtenstall BB4 68 F8
8 Rishton BB1 123 B1
Ashworth Terr
2 Bacup OL13 69 B8
7 Darwen BB3 81 A1
Askrigg Cl Accrington BB5 103 E5
Blackpool FY4 110 A7
Asland Cl PR5 76 F8
Asland Gdns PR9 53 C4
Asmall Cl L39 15 D6
Asmall Cty Prim Sch L39 15 D6
Asmall La Haskayne L39,L40 14 E8
Ormskirk L39,L40 15 B7
Aspden St PR5 96 E1
Aspels Cres PR1 95 C4
Aspels Nook PR1 95 C4
Aspels The PR1 95 C4
Aspen Dr BB10 127 C7
Aspen Fold BB5 102 B5
Aspen Gdns 3 Chorley PR7 42 B6
Rochdale OL12 51 A1
Aspen Gr L37 11 C1
Aspen La Earby BB18 201 B2
Oswaldtwistle BB5 102 C4
Aspendale Cl PR4 73 F8

Aspinal Cl PR1 95 D2
Aspinall Cres L37 12 F1
Aspinall Rd WN6 28 B1
Aspinall St BL6 31 D1
Aspinall Way BL6 31 C1
Aspley Gr BB8 170 C3
Asshawes The PR6 42 F1
Assheton Pl PR2 117 E4
Assheton Rd BB2 100 A5
Aster Ch BB3 81 A7
Astland Gdns PR4 72 F2
Astland St FY8 88 E6
Astley Cres PR4 92 C6
Astley Ct LA1 210 D6
Astley Ctr The 2 PR7 42 D6
Astley Gate BB2 100 E5
Astley Hall Dr BL0 49 C4
Astley Park Sp Sch PR7 42 B8
Astley Rd PR7 60 C1
Astley St Chorley PR6,PR7 60 C1
Darwen BB3 64 A7
Longridge PR3 139 A7
Astley Terr BB3 64 A7
Aston Ave FY5 173 A2
Aston St PR4 131 E6
Aston Way PR5 75 C2
Aston Wlk BB2 81 A8
Athelstan Fold PR2 116 C3
Athens View BB10 127 C5
Atherton Rd PR5 58 D8
Atherton St Adlington PR7 30 A6
Bacup OL13 69 C8
Atherton Way OL13 69 B8
Athletic St BB10 127 C5
Athlone Ave FY2 150 C2
Athol Gr PR6 42 E6
Athol St Nelson BB9 147 F8
Ramsbottom BL0 49 C7
Athol St N BB11 126 D5
Athol St S BB11 126 D5
Athole Gr PR9 34 F7
Atholl St 12 PR1 95 D8
Atkinson Art Gal PR8 34 B7
Atkinson Liby PR8 34 B7
Atkinson St
Brierfield BB10 147 F3
Colne BB8 169 C3
Colne BB8 169 D4
Atlas Rd BB3 81 B1
Atlas St BB5 124 A1
Atrium Ct 11 BB11 127 B4
Aubigny Dr PR2 116 D4
Auburn Gr FY1 129 D2
Auckland St BB3 64 B7
Audenlea FY5 172 F3
Audenshaw Rd LA4 212 F4
Audley Cl
Lytham St Anne's FY8 89 D5
Nelson BB9 147 E8
Audley Jun & Inf Sch
BB1 101 A3
Audley La BB1 101 A4
Audley Range BB1 101 B4
Audley St BB1 101 A5
Audlum Ct 4 BL9 32 A2
Aughton Brow LA2 231 E6
Aughton Ct LA1 213 F4
Aughton Hall Cotts L39 15 C6
Aughton Mews PR8 34 A5
Aughton Park Dr L39 15 D2
Aughton Park Sta L39 15 D2
Aughton Rd Aughton LA2 231 E6
Southport PR8 34 A5
Aughton St Fleetwood FY7 194 B5
Ormskirk L39 15 E4
Aughton St Michael's
CE Prim Sch L39 15 B1
Aughton Wlk 3 PR1 116 F1
Augusta Cl OL12 51 E2
Augusta St Accrington BB5 103 C4
Rochdale OL12 51 E1
Auster Cres PR4 113 B2
Austin Cres PR2 116 B4
Austin Gr FY1 129 B1
Austin St 6 Bacup OL13 86 F2
5 Burnley BB11 126 E5
Austin Way FY4 111 A7
Austin's La BL6 31 F1
Austins Cl PR5 59 A8
Austwick Rd 4 LA1 213 D2
Austwick Way BB5 103 E5
Avallon Way BB3 81 C1
Avalon Cl BB12 125 F7
Avalon Dr PR4 92 C7
Avalwood Ave PR4 74 B8
Avebury Cl Blackburn BB2 81 A8
Horwich BL6 31 F1
Aveling Dr PR9 54 A6
Avelon Cl L31 5 B5
Avenham Cl PR9 54 B5
Avenham Colonnade PR1 96 A6
Avenham Ct 20 PR1 96 A7
Avenham Gr 5 FY1 129 B6
Avenham La PR1 96 A7
Avenham Pl
Newton-with-S PR4 113 F2
6 Preston PR1 96 A6
Avenham Rd
1 Chorley PR7 42 C7
Preston PR1 96 A7
Avenham Terr 11 PR1 96 A6
Avenue Par BB5 103 D6
Avenue Rd
Hurst Green BB7 162 E1
Normoss FY3 130 B7
Avenue The Adlington PR6 30 A8
Banks PR9 53 F5
Barley BB12 167 C5
Burnley BB10,BB11 127 D3
Carleton FY6 151 C4
Churchtown PR3 178 A3
Fulwood PR2 116 A6
Garstang PR3 199 B1
Leyland PR5 59 A6
Ormskirk L39 15 D6
Ormskirk L39 15 E6
Orrell WN5 10 D3
Penwortham PR1 95 B5
Preston PR2 115 D1
Southport PR8 35 F5
Aviemore Cl 5 BB1 101 A4
Avocet Ct PR5 75 A1
Avon Ave FY7 172 D8
Avon Bridge PR2 116 C8
Avon Cl BB2 100 D3
Avon Ct BB12 126 D7
Avon Dr
Barnoldswick BB18 200 C3
Bury BL9 32 A8
Avon Gdns PR4 115 D5
Avon Gn FY7 193 E4
Avon Ho 12 PR1 96 D8
Avon Pl FY1 129 C8
Avon St FY8 88 E6
Avondale Ave
Blackburn BB1 101 E5
Burnley BB12 126 C7
Avondale Cl BB3 80 E2
Avondale Cres FY4 109 F7
Avondale Dr
Bamber Bridge PR5 76 B8
Ramsbottom BL0 48 F3
Tarleton PR4 56 A8
Avondale Mews BB3 80 E3
Avondale Prim Sch BB3 80 E2
Avondale Rd Chorley PR7 42 C7
Darwen BB3 80 E3
Lancaster LA1 211 A6
Lytham St Anne's FY8 88 C8
Morecambe LA3 212 B3
Nelson BB9 147 D7
Southport PR9 34 B8
Avondale Rd N PR9 52 C1
Avondale St Colne BB8 170 A5
Standish WN6 28 E2
Avonhead Cl BL6 30 F3
Avonside Ave FY5 173 A3
Avonwood Cl BB3 80 E2
Avroe Cres FY4 109 D4
Aylesbury Ave FY4 129 D1
Aylesbury Ho L31 5 B4
Aylesbury Wlk BB10 147 D3
Ayr Cl PR8 34 F4
Ayr Ct FY7 172 E7
Ayr Gr BB11 126 D3
Ayr Rd BB1 101 D3
Ayr St LA1 211 B7
Ayrefield Gr WN6 19 D6
Ayrefield Rd WN8 19 C4
Ayrton Ave FY4 109 D7
Ayrton St BB8 169 E5
Ays-Garth Rd LA1 210 D8
Aysgarth Ave PR2 116 F7
Aysgarth Ct 1 FY4 109 F7
Aysgarth Dr
Accrington BB5 103 D6
Darwen BB3 80 E2
Lancaster LA1 213 F4
Azalea Cl Clayton-le-W PR5 76 E2
Preston PR2 117 C6
Azalea Gr LA4 213 A5
Azalea Rd BB2 100 B6

B

Babbacombe Ave FY4 109 B6
Babylon La PR6 30 B8
Back Albert Rd BB8 169 D4
Back Albert St Bury BL9 32 A2
10 Padiham BB12 125 C8
Back Alfred St 11 BL0 49 B5
Back Altham St 5 BB12 125 D8
Back Andrew St 13 BL9 32 A2
Back Andrew St N 12 BL9 32 A2
Back Arthur St 15 BB5 123 F3
Back Ash St 7 BL9 32 A2
Back Ashburton Rd
14 FY1 129 C7
Back Ashby St 1 PR7 42 D6
Back Atkinson St BB8 169 C4
Back Avondale Rd (E)
LA3 212 B3
Back Avondale Rd (W)
LA3 212 B3
Back Bath St PR8 34 B8
Back Beehive Terr BB4 84 B3
Back Bell La 8 Bury BL9 32 A3
Bury BL9 32 B3
Back Benson St BL9 32 A1
Back Blackburn Rd E BL7 46 D3
Back Bolton Rd BB3 64 B7
Back Bond St BB8 169 D5
Back Bond St W BL9 32 A2
Back Boundary St
14 BB8 169 D4
Back Bourne's Row PR5 97 E1
Back Bridge St 2 BL0 49 C6
Back Broading Terr BB4 105 A3
Back Brook St N 11 BL9 32 A4
Back Brow WN8 10 C7
Back Brown St BB8 169 C4
Back Burnley Rd BB5 103 C6
Back Calton Terr LA4 212 E6
Back Cambridge St
10 BB8 169 D4
Back Canada St BL6 31 B3
Back Carr Mill St BB4 84 B5
Back Cedar St 2 BL9 32 B3
Back Cedar St N 1 BL9 32 B3
Back Cemetery Terr
9 OL13 69 D8
Back Chapel St
1 Barnoldswick BB18 200 B2
4 Colne BB8 169 D4
Horwich BL6 31 C3
Back Chesham Rd N
5 BL9 32 A4
Back Chesham Rd S
7 BL9 32 A4
Back Chester St BL9 32 A4
Back Church St
Barrowford BB9 168 D3
8 Blackpool FY1 129 B5
5 Great Harwood BB6 123 C5
3 Hapton BB12 125 C4
1 Newchurch BB4 85 E1
Back Clarendon Rd FY1 129 B2
Back Clayton St 9 BB9 168 D1
Back Club St PR5 76 E7
Back Colne Rd BB18 200 A1
Back Commons BB7 186 D1
Back Constablelee BB4 84 F4
Back Cookson St 12 FY1 129 C6
Back Cop La FY7 194 B4
Back Cowm La OL12 70 C3
Back Crescent St LA4 212 D5
Back Crown St BL6 31 A4
Back Curzon St FY8 89 A7
Back Darwen Rd N BL7 46 E1
Back Deal St BL9 32 B2
Back Delamere St N BL9 32 A5
Back Delamere St S BL9 32 A5
Back Derby St 4 BB8 169 D5
Back Drinkhouse La PR5 57 B1
Back Duckworth St
4 Bury BL9 32 A4
12 Darwen BB3 81 A1
Back Duke St 1 BB8 169 D4
Back Duncan St BL6 31 C3
Back Earl St 2 BB8 169 D4
Back East Bank 1 BB9 168 D4
Back Eaves St FY1 129 B7
Back Elm St 10 BL9 32 B2
Back Emmett St BL6 31 B3
Back Epsom Rd FY5 150 F8
Back Fazakerley St 14 PR7 42 C8
Back Fir St BL9 32 B2
Back Fletcher St BL9 32 A2
Back Forest Rd PR8 34 D6
Back Garston St BL9 32 A4
Back George St BL6 31 C3
Back Gisburn Rd BB9 168 E7
Back Glen Eldon Rd FY8 88 E7
Back Green St LA4 212 E6
Back Grimshaw St 8 PR1 96 A7
Back Grove Terr LA4 213 B4
Back Hall St BB8 169 D4
Back Halstead St 2 BL9 32 A4
Back Hamilton St 1 BL9 32 A4
Back Harry St BB9 168 D3
Back Haslam St BL9 32 A4
Back Headroomgate Rd
FY8 88 F8
Back Heys BB5 102 E3
Back Heywood St E
14 BL9 32 A2
Back Heywood St W BL9 32 A1
Back High St Belmont BL7 45 C5
Blackpool FY1 129 B6
Edgworth BL7 47 C4
Back Hill St 13 BB4 85 A7
Back Holly St BL9 32 A2
Back Holly St S 8 BL9 32 A2
Back Hope St OL13 86 F4
Back House La LA5 218 C3
Back Hunter St 1 LA5 217 D2
Back Huntley Mount Rd
BL9 32 B3
Back Hurst St BL9 32 A1
Back Ingham St BL9 32 A1
Back Ingham St E BL9 32 A1
Back Kershaw St 9 BL9 32 A2
Back King St BB5 103 B6
Back Knowlys Rd 2 LA3 208 F8
Back La Accrington BB5 103 E1
Appley Bridge WN6 19 E8
Arnside LA5 237 B2
Bolton Green PR7 41 B7
Bretherton PR5 56 E5
Burscough Bridge L40 24 E6
Carnforth LA5,LA6 216 E7
Chorley PR6 43 C6
Clayton Green PR6 77 A2
Clayton Green PR6 77 B1
Cumeragh Village PR3 138 B6
Gisburn BB7 225 C3
Great Eccleston PR3 154 B5
Greenhalgh PR4 132 B4
Grindleton BB7 187 B8
Hale Nook FY6 174 E6
Haskayne L39 13 D3
Higham BB12 145 E6
Leyland PR5 59 C7
Longridge PR3 159 B6
Longton PR4 73 E8
Maghull L39 5 E6
Mawdesley L40 39 D1
Nelson BB10 148 F7
Newburgh L40,WN8 25 E2
Newton BB7 222 F6
Back La *continued*
Preesall FY6 195 A2
Rathmell BD24 230 F6
Rawtenstall BB4 85 A3
Rimington BB7 188 E8
Royal Oak L39 7 B2
Sabden BB12,BB7 145 C6
Skelmersdale, Digmoor WN8 9 D6
Skelmersdale, Holland
Moor WN8 9 E7
Trawden BB8 170 B2
Tunstall LA6 235 D4
Warton, Carnforth LA5 217 D5
Whitworth OL12 70 C3
Wiswell BB7 143 F8
Wray LA2 232 C6
Wrayton LA6 235 E2
Back La E L40 39 F1
Back Lane Side BB4 84 B2
Back Lathom St 9 BL9 32 A4
Back Laurel St 2 BL9 32 B2
Back Leach St BB8 169 C4
Back Lee St BB4 84 B2
Back Lines St 2 LA4 212 E5
Back Longworth Rd BL7 46 D3
Back Lord St
Blackpool FY1 129 B6
4 Lancaster LA1 213 F1
4 Rawtenstall BB4 85 A7
Back Lune St BB8 169 E4
Back Manor St 1 BL9 32 A2
Back Marine Rd LA4 212 C4
Back Marine Rd E LA4 212 G6
Back Mason St 16 BL9 32 A2
Back Moon Ave 5 FY1 129 B2
Back Morecambe St LA4 212 E6
Back Moss La L40 24 F7
Back Mount 5 PR7 42 C8
Back Myrtle St 4 BL9 32 B2
Back Myrtle St S BL9 32 B2
Back Nelson St BL6 31 D3
Back New St 5 LA5 217 D2
Back Nook Terr 2 OL12 51 F3
Back North Cres FY8 88 E6
Back O The Town La L38 3 E3
Back Oddfellows Terr BB4 85 F3
Back Oram St BL9 32 A4
Back Ormrod St 10 BL9 32 A2
Back Owen's Row BL6 31 C3
Back Oxford St BL9 32 A1
Back Parkinson St BB2 100 B2
Back Parsonage St 10 BL9 32 A3
Back Patience St 10 OL12 51 C1
Back Percy St BL9 32 B3
Back Peter St
8 Barrowford BB9 168 D4
3 Bury BL9 32 A3
Back Pine St 1 BL9 32 B2
Back Pleasant St 5 FY1 129 B7
Back Queen St
Great Harwood BB6 123 C5
7 Lancaster LA1 210 F7
1 Morecambe LA4 212 E5
Back Railway View PR7 30 A7
Back Rawlinson St 16 BL6 31 B4
Back Read's Rd FY1 129 C4
Back Regent St 1 BB4 84 B3
Back Rhoden Rd BB5 102 D2
Back Richard Burch St
BL9 32 A3
Back Rings Row BB4 105 A1
Back Rochdale
Old North Rd 1 BL9 32 C3
Back Rochdale Old Rd S
BL9 32 B3
Back Rochdale
Old South Rd 3 Bury BL9 32 C3
Bury, Fairfield BL9 32 D3
Back Rochdale Rd BL9 32 B2
Back Rochdale Rd S
17 BL9 32 A2
Back Rushton St 6 OL13 69 E8
Back Salford St BL9 32 A4
Back Sandy Bank Rd BL7 47 D5
Back School La Orrell WN8 10 C7
Skelmersdale,
Pennylands WN8 17 D2
Back Scotland Rd
7 BB9 147 D8
Back Seed St 9 PR1 95 F8
Back Shannon St 4 FY1 129 B3
Back Shaw-Street BL9 32 B3
Back Shepherd St BL9 32 A1
Back Shuttleworth St
BB12 125 C8
Back Skipton Rd 7 BB18 200 B2
Back South Cross St E
15 BL9 32 A2
Back Spencer St BB4 85 A7
Back Springfield Rd N
FY8 88 E6
Back Square St BL0 49 C6
Back St LA3 205 D8
Back St Anne's Rd W FY8 88 E6
Back St John St 5 OL13 86 F3
Back Stanley St BL0 49 B5
Back Starkie St PR1 95 F6
Back Sun St 9 LA1 210 F8
Back Teak St 5 BL9 32 B2
Back Tinline St 11 BL9 32 A2
Back Union St BL7 46 D2
Back Virginia St PR8 34 B6
Back Warbreck Rd
2 FY1 129 B6
Back Wash La BL9 32 B2
Back Wash La S 6 BL9 32 A2
Back Water St
11 Accrington BB5 103 C6
Back Water St *continued*
Egerton BL7 46 D2
Back Waterloo Rd 8 FY1 129 B1
Back Wellington St BB5 103 C5
Back West Cres FY8 88 E6
Back West End Rd N LA4 212 C4
Back Willow St BB12 126 E6
Back Winterdyne Terr
LA3 212 B4
Back Wood St BL6 31 C3
Back Woodfield Rd
4 FY1 129 B2
Back Wright St BL6 31 B4
Back York St
Clitheroe BB7 164 F8
Rawtenstall BB4 85 A7
Back Zion St 16 BB8 169 D4
Backhouse St 1 BB5 102 E4
Backs The PR3 139 A6
Bacon St 6 BB9 147 E8
Bacup & Rawtenstall
Gram Sch BB4 68 F8
Bacup Golf Course OL13 86 E2
Bacup Old Rd OL13 86 F7
Bacup Rd
Rawtenstall BB4,OL13 68 E8
Rawtenstall, Lower
Cloughfold BB4 85 C2
Sharneyford OL14 87 E5
Walk Mill BB11 106 E6
Baddon Cl LA4 212 F3
Baden Terr BB2 100 D1
Badge Brow BB5 102 E5
Badger Cl BB12 145 D1
Badger Rd PR5 76 A4
Badger St BL9 32 A3
Badger Wells Cotts BB7 145 A8
Badger Wood PR3 157 C7
Badgers Cl BB5 103 E8
Badgers Croft PR2 117 F1
Badgers Rake L37 11 C5
Badgers Way PR5 96 B3
Badgers Wlk PR7 60 A3
Badgers Wlk E FY8 90 C3
Badgers Wlk W 10 FY8 90 B3
Bagganley La PR6 60 F2
Bagnold Rd PR1 117 D1
Bagot St FY1 129 B1
Baildon Rd OL12 51 B1
Bailey Bank BB7 163 A7
Bailey Ct FY3 129 E6
Bailey La Heysham LA3 208 E8
Tosside BD23 230 B3
Bailey St Burnley BB11 126 E5
Earby BB18 201 C2
Bailrigg La LA1 211 A1
Baines Ave FY3 150 F1
Baines Endowed
CE Prim Sch FY4 129 F1
Baines Sch FY6 151 D1
Baines' Endowed
Cty Prim Sch FY5 173 C1
Bairstow St
3 Barnoldswick BB18 200 B3
Blackpool FY1 129 B3
13 Preston PR1 95 F7
Baker St 13 Bacup OL13 86 F3
Blackburn BB1 101 B4
Burnley BB11 126 E5
Lancaster LA1 213 F3
4 Leyland PR5 76 B2
Nelson BB9 168 E1
Ramsbottom BL0 49 B5
Baker's La PR9 52 F3
Bakers Ct FY4 109 F7
Bala Cl BB1 100 E6
Balaclava St BB1 100 E6
Balcarres Cl PR5 76 A1
Balcarres Pl PR5 59 A8
Balcarres Rd Chorley PR7 42 B5
Leyland PR5 59 A8
Preston PR2 116 C2
Balderstone CE Prim Sch
BB2 120 A5
Balderstone Cl BB10 147 D2
Balderstone Hall La BB2 119 C6
Balderstone La BB10 147 E2
Balderstone Rd
Freckleton PR4 92 B7
Preston PR1 95 D5
Baldwin Gr FY1 129 D2
Baldwin Hill 3 BB7 164 D8
Baldwin Rd BB7 164 D8
Baldwin St Bacup OL13 69 B8
7 Bamber Bridge PR5 96 E1
5 Barrowford BB9 168 D4
Blackburn BB2 100 C3
Baldwin's Bldgs 14 BB4 85 A3
Balfour Cl Brierfield BB9 147 D5
Thornton FY5 151 D7
Balfour Ho BB2 100 C4
Balfour Rd Fulwood PR2 116 E3
5 Rochdale OL12 51 C1
Southport PR8 34 E5
Balfour St Blackburn BB2 100 C4
Great Harwood BB6 123 E5
Leyland PR5 76 A1
Balham Ave FY4 109 E5
Ball Grove Dr BB8 170 B5
Ball La LA2 231 C3
Ball St Blackpool FY1 129 B1
3 Nelson BB9 168 D1
Poulton-le-F FY6 151 D3
Ball's Pl PR8 34 B7
Balladen Prim Sch BB4 67 F8
Ballam Rd
Lower Ballam FY8 111 C3
Lytham St Anne's FY8 90 B4

Ballam Rd *continued*
Preston PR2 115 E1
Ballam St BB11 127 A4
Ballantrae Rd BB1 101 D3
Ballater St BB11 126 D3
Balle St BB3 64 A8
Ballet Hill Cres PR3 157 A5
Balliol Cl BB12 125 D6
Balm St BL0 49 A4
Balmer Gr FY1 129 D3
Balmoral PR7 29 E6
Balmoral Ave
Blackburn BB1 122 A4
Clitheroe BB7 164 C6
Leyland PR5 59 C8
Morecambe LA3 212 B3
Balmoral Cl Horwich BL6 31 E2
Ramsbottom BL8 49 A1
Southport PR9 53 B3
Balmoral Cres BB1 101 F4
Balmoral Ct PR7 42 B8
Balmoral Dr Brinscall PR6 61 E8
Formby L37 11 E1
Southport PR9 53 B3
Balmoral Pl FY5 151 C8
Balmoral Rd
Accrington BB5 103 D7
5 Bamber Bridge PR5 96 D3
Blackpool FY4 109 B8
Chorley PR7 42 B8
Darwen BB3 64 B6
Eccleston PR7 40 C7
Haslingden BB4 84 A1
Lancaster LA1 211 A7
Lytham St Anne's FY8 89 A5
Maghull L31 5 C1
Morecambe LA3,LA4 212 C3
New Longton PR4 95 A1
Balmoral Terr FY7 194 B5
Balmore Ct OL10 32 E1
Balniel Cl PR7 42 A7
Balshaw Ave PR7 59 D2
Balshaw Cres PR5 75 F2
Balshaw La PR7 59 D1
Balshaw Lane
Cty Prim Sch PR7 59 E1
Balshaw Rd Leyland PR5 75 F1
Lowgill LA2 233 E3
Balshaw St 4 PR5 96 E2
Balshaw's High Sch PR5 59 B7
Baltic Rd BB4 68 E8
Baltimore Rd FY8 89 B6
Bamber Ave FY2 150 C4
Bamber Bridge
Meth Prim Sch PR5 76 F8
Bamber Bridge Sta PR5 76 E8
Bamber Gdns PR9 35 A8
Bamber St 2 PR7 42 B5
Bamber's Wlk PR4 112 E7
Bambers La Blackpool FY4 110 C6
Blackpool FY4 110 C7
Bamburgh Cl FY4 110 A7
Bamburgh Dr BB12 126 E7
Bamford Cl BL9 32 E4
Bamford Cres BB5 103 D4
Bamford Pl OL12 51 E1
Bamford Rd BL0 50 B6
Bamford St Burnley BB11 127 A6
Nelson BB9 148 A8
Bamfords Fold PR5 56 F5
Bamton Ave FY4 109 C7
Banastre PR7 60 A2
Banastre Rd PR8 34 B5
Banastre St 9 BB5 124 A1
Banbury Ave
Blackpool FY2 150 D1
Oswaldtwistle BB5 102 C4
Banbury Cl
3 Accrington BB5 103 A7
Blackburn BB2 79 F8
Banbury Dr PR2 116 E4
Banbury Rd Longshaw WN5 10 D2
Lytham St Anne's FY8 89 A6
Morecambe LA3 212 F3
Bancroft Ave FY5 173 C2
Bancroft Fold BB18 200 A1
Bancroft Mill (Mus)
BB18 200 B1
Bancroft Rd BB10 127 C8
Bancroft St BB1 100 F5
Band La PR3 177 D1
Bangor Ave FY2 150 D4
Bangor St BB1 100 F7
Bank Ave WN5 10 D5
Bank Bottom BB3 81 A1
Bank Bridge PR4 56 B5
Bank Brow WN8 19 C5
Bank Cl Galgate LA2 206 F3
Longton PR4 74 A8
Bank Cott 2 LA2 233 B8
Bank Cotts BB7 143 B4
Bank Croft PR4 74 A8
Bank Fold BB9 168 E4
Bank Hall Cotts BB7 224 C1
Bank Hall Terr BB10 127 A7
Bank Head La PR5 97 D1
Bank Hey Cl BB1 122 A1
Bank Hey La N BB1 121 F3
Bank Hey La S BB1 122 A1
Bank Hey Sch BB2 80 C7
Bank Hey St FY1 129 B5
Bank House La Bacup OL13 86 F2
Westhouse LA6 236 E4
Bank House St BB9 168 E4
Bank La Blackburn BB1 101 D4
Warton PR4 91 D4
Bank Mdw BL6 31 C4
Bank Mill St 3 BB4 84 B2
Bank Par Burnley BB11 127 A6
Penwortham PR1 95 D3
Preston PR1 96 A6
Bank Pas PR8 34 A7
Bank Pl PR2 116 C1
Bank Rd Appley Bridge WN8 19 D4
Lancaster LA1 213 F3
Bank Sq PR8 34 B8
Bank St Accrington BB5 103 C5
Adlington PR7 30 A7
14 Bacup OL13 86 F2
Bank Lane BL0 49 E7
Barnoldswick BB18 200 C2
Brierfield BB9 147 B6
Chorley PR7 42 C8
9 Church BB5 102 E6
Darwen BB3 81 A1
Edgworth BL7 47 C4
Haslingden BB4 84 B3
11 Nelson BB9 168 E1
Padiham BB12 145 C1
Rawtenstall BB4 85 A2
Trawden BB8 170 C1
Bank Terr Knowley PR6 61 C4
Simonstone BB12 124 E8
Whitworth OL12 51 C8
Bank Top Baldingstone BL9 49 F1
Blackburn BB2 100 C4
Burnley BB11 127 A6
Bank View Hambleton FY6 174 C1
Rawtenstall BB11 105 C5
Bank View Cotts BB7 224 C1
Bankcroft Cl BB12 125 E8
Bankfield Burnley BB11 127 A6
Skelmersdale WN8 9 C7
Bankfield Ct FY5 151 B8
Bankfield Gr FY1 129 E3
Bankfield La PR9 53 B2
Bankfield St Bacup OL13 69 D8
Colne, Bunker's Hill BB8 169 B4
Colne, Winewall BB8 170 B4
Bankfield Terr
1 Bacup OL13 69 D8
Barnoldswick BB18 200 C3
Bankhouse Rd BB9 168 E1
Bankhouse St
Burnley BB11 126 F6
Burnley BB11 127 A6
Banks Bridge Cl BB18 200 C4
Banks Cres LA3 208 F6
Banks Hill BB18 200 A4
Banks Meth Prim Sch PR9 54 B7
Banks Rd Fulwood PR2 116 C3
Southport PR9 53 D6
Banks Rise 11 LA2 233 D8
Banks St Blackpool FY1 129 B6
Lane Bottom BB10 148 B3
Banks Way 13 LA2 233 D8
Banksbarn WN8 9 C7
Banksfield Ave PR2 116 C3
Banksfield Pl PR5 77 A7
Bankside Blackburn BB2 100 E2
Clayton Green PR6 77 B1
Hightown L38 2 F3
Parbold WN8 26 B2
Bankside Cl OL13 86 E1
Bankside La OL13 86 F2
Bankwood WN6 19 E6
Banner Cl PR7 40 B6
Bannerman Terr PR6 60 D2
Bannister Brow L40,WN6 26 E6
Bannister Cl
Higher Walton PR5 97 B4
Trawden BB8 170 B3
Bannister Ct
Blackpool FY2 150 B4
13 Nelson BB9 147 E8
Bannister Dr PR5 75 E1
Bannister Gn PR7 40 C3
Bannister Hall Cres PR5 97 B4
Bannister Hall Dr PR5 97 B4
Bannister Hall La PR5 97 B4
Bannister La Eccleston PR7 40 C5
Hill Dale L40,WN6 26 E6
Leyland PR5 75 E4
Bannister St
11 Chorley PR7 42 C7
Lytham St Anne's FY8 90 B3
Bannister's Bit 4 PR1 95 C2
Bannistre Cl 1 FY8 89 A8
Bannistre Ct PR4 56 A6
Bannistre Mews PR4 56 A6
Bar Cotts BB12 144 E1
Bar St BB10 127 B8
Bar Terr OL12 51 C7
Barbara Castle Way BB1 100 E5
Barberry Bank BL7 46 E2
Barbon Pl LA1 213 E2
Barbon St Burnley BB10 147 C2
14 Padiham BB12 145 C1
Barbrook Cl WN6 28 B2
Barclay Ave Blackpool FY4 129 F2
Burnley BB11 126 C4
Barclay Rd PR3 139 A7
Barcroft Gn BB10 127 E1
Barcroft St BB8 169 C5
Barden Croft BB5 123 F4
Barden Cty Inf Sch BB10 147 A1
Barden High Sch BB10 147 A2
Barden Jun Sch BB10 147 A1
Barden La BB10,BB12 147 A2
Barden Pl PR2 117 D4
Barden Rd BB5 102 F4
Barden St 4 BB10 147 B1
Barden View BB10 147 A2
Bardsea Pl PR2 115 F3
Bardsley Cl WN8 10 A7
Bardsway FY5 173 A3
Bardsway Ave FY3 129 F6
Bare Ave LA4 213 A6
Bare La LA4 213 A5
Bare Lane Sta LA4 213 A6
Barford Cl Orrell WN8 10 A7
Southport PR8 20 A6
Barford Gr BL6 31 F1
Bargee Cl BB1 100 F3
Barham St 6 FY1 129 B2
Barker Brow BB1,PR3 141 A3
Barker Cl LA6 234 B7
Barker La BB2 121 C2
Barker Sq LA2 207 A6
Barkerfield Cl BB12 145 F5
Barkerhouse Rd
Nelson BB10,BB9 148 B8
16 Nelson BB9 168 E1
Barkfield Ave L37 11 E4
Barkfield La L37 11 D4
Barley Bank St BB3 80 F2
Barley Cl BB2 100 D5
Barley Cop La LA1 213 D4
Barley Gr BB10 127 C6
Barley Holme Rd BB4 85 A8
Barley La Barley BB9 167 B7
Blackburn BB2 100 D5
Barley New Rd BB12 167 E5
Barley St BB12 125 C7
Barley Vistors Ctr BB12 167 C5
Barley Way BB2 100 D5
Barleydale Rd BB9 168 E5
Barleyfield PR5 77 C3
Barlow Cres FY3 129 E4
Barlow Ct BL7 47 E5
Barlow St Accrington BB5 103 A6
Bacup OL13 69 B7
Horwich BL6 31 C2
Preston PR1 116 E1
Preston PR1 116 F2
11 Rawtenstall BB4 85 A3
Barlow's La L39 21 D5
Barlows Bldgs 5 BB4 84 F1
Barmouth Ave FY3 130 A3
Barmouth Cres BB1 121 E1
Barmskin La PR7 40 B2
Barn Acre BL6 30 E1
Barn Cl PR4 55 A2
Barn Croft
3 Clitheroe BB7 164 D7
1 Leyland PR5 75 B1
Penwortham PR1 95 B4
Barn Field Cl BB8 170 A5
Barn Gill Cl BB1 100 F3
Barn Hey PR4 94 A1
Barn Hey Rd L33 1 A2
Barn Mdw
Clayton Brook PR5 77 B6
Edgworth BL7 47 D5
Barn Meadow Cres BB1 123 C1
Barnacre Cl Fulwood PR2 117 A8
Lancaster LA1 211 B2
Barnacre Rd PR3 139 A8
Barnard Cl BB5 102 C4
Barnbrook St BL9 32 A3
Barncroft Dr BL6 31 F3
Barnes Ave Cleveleys FY5 172 E5
Rawtenstall BB4 84 F2
Barnes Cl BL0 49 A3
Barnes Dr L31 5 C3
Barnes Rd Morecambe LA3 212 B3
Ormskirk L39 15 E3
Skelmersdale WN8 17 E1
Barnes Sq 1 BB5 123 F2
Barnes St Accrington BB5 103 C6
Burnley BB11 127 A6
Church BB5 102 E6
Clayton-le-M BB5 123 F3
Haslingden BB4 84 B4
Barnfield
6 Bamber Bridge PR5 76 A8
Kirkham PR4 113 A5
Much Hoole PR4 73 E3
Barnfield Ave BB10 127 F6
Barnfield Bsns Ctr BB9 147 F6
Barnfield Cl 4
Cleveleys FY5 172 F4
Egerton BL7 46 E2
Barnfield Dr WN8 9 E7
Barnfield Manor FY6 152 D3
Barnfield St
Accrington BB5 103 D5
Rochdale OL12 51 F2
Barnfield Way BB5 124 E5
Barnmeadow La BB6 123 C5
Barnoldswick
CE Prim Sch BB18 200 B2
Barnoldswick La LA6 236 D3
Barnoldswick Rd
Beverley BB8,BB9 168 F7
Kelbrook BB18 191 F6
Barns La PR3 159 C8
Barns The L37 12 A1
Barnsfold PR2 116 D6
Barnside Euxton PR7 59 C3
Whitworth OL12 51 B8
Barnside Est BB8 170 F7
Barnstaple Way PR4 115 F6
Barnwood Cres BB18 201 C1
Barnwood Rd BB18 201 B1
Baron Rd FY1 129 C1
Baron St Darwen BB3 80 F2
Rawtenstall BB4 85 D1
Barons Cl BB3 81 A7
Barons Way Blackburn BB3 81 A6
Euxton PR7 59 D2
Barracks Rd BB11 126 D6
Barracks The L39 22 C2
Barret Hill Brow BB7 224 B4
Barret St BB18 201 A1
Barrett Ave PR8 34 A2
Barrett Ct 5 BL9 32 A2
Barrett Rd PR8 34 A2
Barrett St 5 BB10 127 A8
Barrington Dr PR8 20 B5
Barrison Gn L40 23 E2
Barritt Rd BB4 84 F2
Barronwood Ct PR4 56 A5
Barrow (VC) Prim Sch
BB7 164 D2
Barrow Nook La L39 7 E2
Barrow's La PR3 154 B5
Barrowcroft Cl WN1 29 B1
Barrowdale Ave BB9 147 F7
Barrowford Rd
Barrowford BB9 168 B1
Colne BB8 169 B5
Fence BB12 146 C7
Barrowford Sch BB9 168 D3
Barrows La LA3 208 E7
Barrows La E PR3 154 B5
Barry Ave PR2 116 A3
Barry Gr LA3 208 F6
Barry St BB12 126 C7
Bartholomew Rd LA4 212 F4
Bartle La PR4 115 C7
Bartle Pl PR2 115 E1
Bartle Rd FY8 89 A8
Bartle St BB11 126 D5
Barton Ave Blackpool FY1 129 B2
Knott End-on-S FY6 194 E5
Barton Ct LA1 211 A4
Barton Gdns LA1 211 B5
Barton Heys Rd L37 11 D1
Barton La PR3 136 E7
Barton Mans FY8 88 C7
Barton Rd Lancaster LA1 211 A4
Lytham St Anne's FY8 88 D8
Barton Row LA6 234 B7
Barton Sq FY6 194 E5
Barton St BB2 100 E5
Barton Streety BB2 100 E5
Bartons Cl PR9 53 D5
Bashall Gr PR5 76 B3
Basil St Colne BB8 169 D4
Preston PR1 117 C2
Basnett St BB10 147 C1
Bass La BL9 49 D3
Bassenthwaite Rd FY3 130 C2
Bassett Way OL12 51 E2
Bastwell Rd BB1 100 F7
Bateman Gr LA4 212 E5
Bateman Rd LA4 212 E5
Bateman St BL6 31 D2
Bates St BB5 123 E3
Bath Mill La LA1 211 A8
Bath Mill Sq 7 LA1 211 A8
Bath Rd FY8 90 B3
Bath Springs L39 15 F5
Bath St Accrington BB5 103 B4
Blackburn BB2 100 C4
Blackpool FY4 129 B1
Colne BB8 169 E5
Lancaster LA1 211 A8
Lytham St Anne's FY8 90 B3
Morecambe LA4 212 D5
Nelson BB9 147 F8
Preston PR2 116 D1
Southport PR8 34 B8
Bath St N PR9 34 B8
Bathurst Ave FY3 130 A7
Bathurst St BB2 100 D5
Batridge Rd BL7 47 A7
Battersby St BL9 32 D3
Battismore Rd LA4 212 E5
Battle Way L37 12 B2
Bawdlands BB7 164 D8
Bawhead Rd BB18 201 B1
Baxenden CE Prim Sch
BB5 103 E1
Baxter St WN6 28 F1
Baxtergate LA4 212 E6
Bay Cl LA3 208 D6
Bay Horse Dr LA1 211 B3
Bay Horse La PR4 134 D4
Bay Horse Rd LA2 207 E4
Bay New Dr LA3 208 F8
Bay Rd Fulwood PR2 117 E2
Heysham LA3 208 D6
Bay St BB1 101 A7
Bay The FY5 172 C5
Bay Tree Farm PR2 94 D8
Bay Tree Rd PR6 77 B3
Bay View LA6 231 B8
Bay View Ave LA2 213 E8
Bay View Cres LA2 213 E8
Bayard St BB12 126 A6
Baycliffe Cres LA4 212 D5
Bayley Fold BB7 164 E8
Bayley St BB5 123 E3
Bayliss Cl PR2 117 F3
Baylton Ct PR3 178 D2
Baylton Dr PR3 178 D2
Baynes Cotts 4 LA2 233 B8
Baynes St BB3 81 F1
Bayside FY7 194 B4
Bayswater FY2 150 C4
Baytree Cl
Bamber Bridge PR5 76 C8
Southport PR9 53 D5
Baytree Gr BL0 49 B2
Baytree Wlk OL12 70 C1
Bayview Cotts LA3 208 E6
Baywood St BB1 100 F7
Bazil Gr LA3 205 D7
Bazil La LA3 205 D7
Bazley Rd FY8 89 D3
Beach Ave Cleveleys FY5 172 D3
Lytham St Anne's FY8 89 C3
Beach Priory Gdns PR8 34 A6
Beach Rd Cleveleys FY5 172 D3
Fleetwood FY7 193 E3
Lytham St Anne's FY8 88 D7
Pilling Lane FY6 195 B7
Southport PR8 33 F6
Beach St
Lytham St Anne's FY8 90 A3
Morecambe LA4 213 A7
Beach Terr LA6 236 F3
Beacham Rd PR8 34 E7
Beachcomber Dr FY5 172 C3
Beachley Rd PR2 116 A4
Beachley Sq BB12 126 D7
Beachmews PR8 33 F6
Beachwood La LA5 237 A1
Beacon Ave PR2 116 D5
Beacon Cl BB8 169 C3
Beacon Crossing WN8 26 C2
Beacon Ctry Pk WN8 18 F2
Beacon Dr PR3 137 D6
Beacon Fell Ctry Pk PR3 180 F2
Beacon Fell Rd PR3 180 E2
Beacon Flats PR3 139 C8
Beacon Gr Fulwood PR2 116 D4
Garstang PR3 178 B6
Beacon Hts WN8 10 A8
Beacon La L40, WN8 18 D4
Beacon Rd
Poulton-le-F FY6 152 A3
Shevington Moor WN6 28 B2
Beacon St PR7 42 D7
Beacon View WN6 19 C8
Beacon View Dr WN8 10 B7
Beacons The WN6 19 D7
Beaconsfield Ave PR1 117 E1
Beaconsfield Rd PR9 34 F6
Beaconsfield St
Accrington BB5 103 D5
Great Harwood BB6 123 C5
10 Haslingden BB4 84 B3
Beaconsfield Terr
Catterall PR3 178 E2
Chorley PR6 60 D2
Beale Rd BB9 147 B8
Beamont Dr PR1 95 D8
Bean Ave FY4 109 E8
Bear St BB12 125 F6
Beardshaw Ave FY1 129 D2
Beardsworth St BB1 101 A7
Beardwood BB2 100 A8
Beardwood Brow BB2 100 B7
Beardwood Dr BB2 100 A7
Beardwood Fold BB2 100 A7
Beardwood High Sch BB2 100 A6
Beardwood Hospital The
BB2 100 A6
Beardwood Mdw BB2 100 A7
Beardwood Pk BB2 100 B7
Bearncroft WN8 9 D6
Bearswood Croft PR6 77 B2
Beatie St BB9 147 B6
Beatrice Ave BB12 126 C7
Beatrice Mews 9 BL6 31 B4
Beatrice Pl BB2 81 A8
Beattock Pl FY2 150 F6
Beatty Ave PR7 42 B6
Beatty Cl FY8 109 D1
Beatty Rd PR8 34 E5
Beauclerk Rd FY8 89 B6
Beaufort L37 12 A2
Beaufort Ave FY2 150 C5
Beaufort Cl Ormskirk L39 15 A1
Simonstone BB12 144 E2
Beaufort Gr LA4 212 G5
Beaufort Rd
Morecambe LA4 213 A5
Weir OL13 87 A7
Beaufort St Nelson BB9 147 E7
Rochdale OL12 51 C1
Beauley Ave BB12 144 E2
Beauly Cl BL0 49 A2
Beaumaris Ave BB2 100 A1
Beaumaris Cl 2 BB4 84 B1
Beaumaris Rd PR5 59 C8
Beaumont Ave BL6 31 C4
Beaumont Coll
(The Spastics Society)
LA1 213 F4
Beaumont Cres L39 15 D2
Beaumont Ct 8 FY1 129 C6
Beaumont Gdns FY6 151 A5
Beaumont Pl LA1 213 F4
Beaumont Rd BL6 31 C4
Beaumont St LA1 213 F4
Beaver Cl BB1 121 F5
Beaver Terr 13 OL13 87 A3
Beavers La WN8 9 D6
Bebles Rd L39 15 C3
Becconsall La PR4 72 F3
Beck Ct FY7 193 D1
Beck Gr FY5 172 E4
Beck Side LA2 231 C3
Beck View 7 LA1 211 A3
Beckdean Ave FY6 151 D2
Beckenham Ct BB10 147 D3
Beckett Ct 19 PR1 95 F8
Beckett St 5 BB3 64 A8
Becks Brow BD23 230 F3
Beckside Barley BB12 167 C5
Trawden BB8 170 C3
Beckside Mews LA6 234 B3
Beckway Ave FY3 129 F7

Bective Rd LA6 238 C2
Bedale Pl FY5 172 E1
Beddington St [6] BB9 168 D1
Bedford Ave FY5 172 D3
Bedford Cl BB5 102 C4
Bedford Mews BB3 80 F4
Bedford Pl Lancaster LA1 211 A4
Padiham BB12 125 D7
Bedford Rd Blackpool FY1 129 C8
Fulwood PR2 117 A4
[6] Lytham St Anne's FY8 90 D4
Southport PR8 34 A2
Bedford St
[6] Barrowford BB9 168 C1
Blackburn BB2 100 C2
Darwen BB3 80 F4
Egerton BL7 46 D2
Bedford Terr Bury BL9 32 A4
Haslingden BB4 67 A8
Bedfordshire Ave BB12 126 B7
Bee La PR1 95 E1
Beech Ave Adlington PR6 30 B8
Bilsborrow PR3 157 A5
Blackpool FY3 129 E5
Darwen BB3 81 B2
Earby BB18 201 A1
Euxton PR7 59 C4
Galgate LA2 206 F4
Horwich BL6 31 E1
Kirkham PR4 113 B4
Leyland PR5 59 A7
Parbold WN8 26 C2
Poulton-le-F FY6 151 D4
Warton PR4 91 D6
Beech Cl Bacup OL13 87 A3
Clitheroe BB7 164 D8
Oswaldtwistle BB5 102 C2
Rishton BB1 102 B8
Rufford L40 38 C4
Skelmersdale WN8 17 E1
Whitworth OL12 70 C1
Wilpshire BB1 121 E6
Beech Cres BB5 124 A1
Beech Ct PR2 116 E7
Beech Dr Formby L37 11 D4
Freckleton PR4 92 A5
Fulwood PR2 116 D8
Haslingden BB4 84 C2
Kirkham PR4 112 E4
Longridge PR3 139 A7
Newton-with-S PR4 113 F2
Poulton-le-F FY6 151 D2
Beech Gdns PR6 77 B1
Beech Gr Accrington BB5 103 A4
[2] Barnoldswick BB18 200 C2
Brierfield BB10 147 C4
Chatburn BB7 187 D5
Darwen BB3 80 D6
Knott End-on-S FY6 194 E6
Lancaster LA2 213 E6
Morecambe LA4 213 A5
Preston PR2 116 B1
Ramsbottom BL8 49 A1
Southport PR9 34 F7
Warton, Carnforth LA5 217 D5
Beech Grove Cl BL9 32 B4
Beech Hill Cl PR5 96 E3
Beech Ind Est [3] OL13 87 A3
Beech Mdw L39 16 A4
Beech Mount BB1 121 F3
Beech Rd Elswick PR4 153 F1
Garstang PR3 178 B8
Halton LA2 214 E7
Leyland PR5 76 A2
Ormskirk L39 6 A6
Beech St Accrington BB5 103 C5
Bacup OL13 87 A3
Barnoldswick BB18 200 B1
Blackburn BB1 101 A7
Bury BL9 32 B2
Clayton-le-M BB5 123 F1
Clitheroe BB7 164 D8
Edgworth BL7 47 D5
Great Harwood BB6 123 C6
Lancaster LA1 210 D8
[10] Nelson BB9 168 E1
Padiham BB12 125 D7
[1] Preston PR1 95 D6
Ramsbottom BL0 49 C3
Rawtenstall BB4 85 A3
Beech St S PR1 95 E6
Beech Terr [1] PR1 95 E6
Beech Tree Ave WN6 19 D8
Beech Tree Cl BB9 147 E7
Beech Tree Sch PR5 77 B4
Beechacre BL0 49 D5
Beecham St LA4 212 E6
Beechcroft Cleveleys FY5 172 C4
Maghull L31 5 D1
Beeches The
Clayton Green PR6 77 C3
Singleton FY6 152 D1
Tarleton PR4 56 A7
Beechfield Hill Dale WN8 26 C5
Lancaster LA1 210 D7
Maghull L31 5 E1
Beechfield Ave
Blackpool FY3 129 E3
Knott End-on-S FY6 195 A5
Wrea Green PR4 112 C4
Beechfield Ct PR5 59 B8
Beechfield Gdns PR8 33 F6
Beechfield Mews PR9 34 C7
Beechfield Rd PR5 59 B8
Beechfields PR7 40 B6
Beeching Cl LA1 210 F6
Beechthorpe Ave BB7 186 B4
Beechtrees WN8 9 D7
Beechway Fulwood PR2 117 A4
Maghull L31 6 B2
Penwortham PR1 95 B3
Beechway Ave L31 6 B2
Beechwood WN8 18 C3
Beechwood Ave
Accrington BB5 103 D3
Bamber Bridge PR5 96 D4
Burnley BB11 126 F3
Clitheroe BB7 164 E6
Fulwood PR2 116 C4
Ramsbottom BL0 49 D6
Shevington WN6 19 F5
Beechwood Cres WN5 10 E6
Beechwood Croft PR6 77 A3
Beechwood Ct
Blackburn BB1 100 F7
Coppull PR7 28 F8
Maghull L31 5 F1
Skelmersdale WN8 9 D6
Beechwood Dr
Blackburn BB2 79 E8
Formby L37 11 C1
Ormskirk L39 15 D5
Thornton FY5 151 B8
Beechwood Gdns LA1 211 A2
Beechwood Gr FY2 150 E4
Beechwood Mews BB1 81 A8
Beechwood Rd
[12] Blackburn BB1 101 A7
Chorley PR7 42 D6
Beenland St [3] PR1 117 D1
Beeston Ave FY6 151 C5
Beetham Ct BB5 123 E2
Beetham Pl FY3 129 E6
Begonia St BB3 81 B1
Beightons Wlk OL12 51 D4
Bela Cl [3] LA1 213 C2
Bela Gr FY1 129 D2
Belfield WN8 9 D6
Belfield Rd BB5 103 C4
Belford Ave FY5 172 F4
Belford St BB12 126 F7
Belfry Cl PR7 59 D4
Belfry Cres WN6 28 F2
Belfry Mans BB6 142 C6
Belfry The FY8 90 D5
Belgarth Rd BB5 103 C7
Belgrave Ave Kirkham PR4 113 A7
Penwortham PR1 95 B3
Belgrave Cl Blackburn BB2 100 B3
[3] Lytham St Anne's FY8 89 D6
Belgrave Cres BL6 31 B3
Belgrave Ct BB12 126 F7
Belgrave Pl
Poulton-le-F FY6 151 B2
Southport PR8 33 F3
Belgrave Rd Blackpool FY4 129 E1
Colne BB8 169 D6
Darwen BB3 64 A8
[5] Leyland PR5 76 A1
Poulton-le-F FY6 151 B3
Southport PR8 33 F3
Belgrave Sq [9] BB3 81 A1
Belgrave St Brierfield BB9 147 A6
Burnley BB12 126 F7
Haslingden BB5 84 A8
Nelson BB9 168 F1
Rochdale OL12 51 D1
Bell La Bury BL9 32 A3
Claughton PR3 179 C4
Clayton-le-M BB5 124 B4
Bell St BB4 84 B3
Bell's Cl L31 5 C4
Bell's La L31 5 B3
Bell-Aire Park Homes
LA3 208 F5
Bellamy Ave LA4 212 D3
Belle Isle Ave OL12 51 C6
Belle View Pl FY3 129 D5
Belle Vue Ave LA1 211 A5
Belle Vue Dr LA1 211 A5
Belle Vue La BB7 186 B4
Belle Vue Pl [8] BB11 126 E6
Belle Vue St
Blackburn BB2 100 C5
Burnley BB11 126 E6
Bellfield Rd LA4 212 F5
Bellingham Rd FY8 90 B4
Bellis Ave PR9 52 F2
Bellis Way PR5 96 B2
Bells La PR5 97 E3
Belmont Ave
Blackpool FY1 129 C4
Fulwood PR2 117 D2
Orrell WN5 10 D3
Poulton-le-F FY6 151 B3
Belmont Cl Brinscall PR6 61 E8
Burscough L40 24 E3
Fulwood PR2 117 D2
Lancaster LA1 213 D3
Belmont Cres PR2 117 D2
Belmont Ct PR3 139 B7
Belmont Dr PR6 60 E1
Belmont Gr BB10 127 D5
Belmont Pl PR7 28 C6
Belmont Rd Adlington PR6 30 B7
Belmont BB3,BL7 63 A2
Fleetwood FY7 194 A3
Fulwood PR2 116 C2
Great Harwood BB6 123 B5
Horwich BL6 31 C7
Leyland PR5 58 D8
Lytham St Anne's FY8 89 C5
Rivington BL6 44 C3
Belmont Sch BB4 84 E2
Belmont St PR8 34 A5
Belmont Terr
[7] Barrowford BB9 168 D3
Foulridge BB8 191 E1
Belmont Way OL12 51 E2
Belper St BB1 101 A6
Belsfield Dr PR4 72 E4
Belshaw Ct BB11 126 A3
Belthorn CE Prim Sch BB1 81 F6
Belthorn Rd BB1 81 E6
Belton Hill PR2 116 D8
Belvedere Ave
Ramsbottom BL8 49 A1
Rawtenstall BB4 86 A1
Belvedere Ct [1] FY8 89 D4
Belvedere Dr Chorley PR7 42 B8
Formby L37 11 F1
Belvedere Pk L39 6 C7
Belvedere Rd Adlington PR6 30 B8
Blackburn BB1 122 A3
Burnley BB10 127 B6
[2] Leyland PR5 76 B2
Southport PR8 20 C5
Thornton FY5 151 C8
Belverdale Gdns FY4 109 F5
Belvere Ave FY4 109 D6
Belvington Cl BB11 126 E5
Belvoir St OL12 51 C1
Ben La Barnoldswick BB18 200 D3
Rainford Junction L39 8 A1
Ben Lane Ct L39 8 B2
Benbow Cl FY8 109 D2
Bence Rd PR1 96 B6
Bence St BB8 169 E5
Bench Carr OL12 51 E1
Benenden Pl [9] FY5 173 A2
Bengal St PR7 60 D1
Bengarth Rd PR9 34 F8
Benjamin Hargreaves
CE Prim Sch BB5 103 D5
Bennett Ave FY1 129 C4
Bennett Dr WN5 10 D4
Bennett Rd FY5 173 A3
Bennett St [2] BB9 168 F2
Bennett's La FY4 109 F6
Bennington St BB1,BB2 100 F3
Benson Ave LA4 212 G4
Benson House BB1 101 C8
Benson La PR4 134 F3
Benson Rd FY3 150 E1
Benson St Blackburn BB1 101 B7
Bury BL9 32 A1
Edgworth BL7 47 E5
Benson's La PR4 156 C1
Bent Est OL13 87 A7
Bent Gap La BB2 100 C4
Bent La Colne BB8 170 B6
Gisburn BB7 225 C3
Leyland PR5 59 C8
Bent St Blackburn BB2 100 D4
Haslingden BB4 67 D8
[3] Oswaldtwistle BB5 102 D3
Bentgate Cl BB4 67 D8
Bentham Ave
Burnley BB10 147 B3
Fleetwood FY7 193 C1
Bentham Cl BB2 100 B1
Bentham Hall Cotts LA2 233 D8
Bentham Moor Rd LA6 236 D2
Bentham Pl WN6 28 F2
Bentham Rd
Barnoldswick LA6 236 E3
Blackburn BB2 100 B1
Lancaster LA1 211 A2
Standish WN6 28 F2
Bentham Sch LA2 233 B8
Bentham St Coppull PR7 41 E1
Southport PR8 34 B5
Bentham Sta LA2 233 D7
Bentham's Way PR8 34 C2
Bentinck Ave FY4 109 B5
Bentinck Rd FY8 88 C8
Bentinck St [9] OL12 51 C1
Bentlea Rd BB7 225 C3
Bentley Dr Kirkham PR4 112 E5
Peel Hill FY4 111 A6
Bentley La
Andertons Mill L40,PR7 40 A1
Bispham Green L40 26 E8
Bury BL9 50 A1
Bentley Park Rd PR4 73 F7
Bentley St [8] Bacup OL13 86 F3
Blackburn BB1 101 C5
Darwen BB3 64 C7
Nelson BB9 147 D7
Rochdale OL12 51 E2
Bentley Wood Way BB11 125 F4
Bentmeadows OL12 51 E1
Benton Rd PR2 117 D4
Bents BB8 170 B6
Bents La LA6 238 F5
Bentwood Rd BB4 84 A3
Beresford Dr PR9 52 F1
Beresford Gdns PR9 52 F2
Beresford Rd BB1 100 D7
Beresford St
[8] Blackpool FY1 129 C7
[9] Burnley BB11 126 D6
Nelson BB9 147 F6
Bergen St BB11 126 B5
Berkeley Cl Chorley PR7 42 D5
Nelson BB9 147 E7
Berkeley Colonnade PR2 117 A4
Berkeley Cres BB12 145 C1
Berkeley Ct LA3 208 E6
Berkeley Dr
Clayton-le-W PR5 76 E4
Berkeley Dr *continued*
Simonstone BB12 144 E2
Berkeley St Brierfield BB9 147 A5
Nelson BB9 147 E7
Preston PR1 116 E1
Berkley Cl PR4 112 E5
Berkshire Ave BB12 126 B7
Berkshire Cl BB1 121 F7
Bernard St OL12 51 E3
Berne Ave BL6 31 A3
Berridge Ave BB12 126 A6
Berriedale Rd BB9 169 A1
Berry Cl WN8 17 F2
Berry Field [3] PR1 95 C3
Berry Ho Cotts L40 37 A5
Berry House Rd L40 37 A4
Berry La PR3 139 A7
Berry St Bamber Bridge PR5 76 A8
Brierfield BB9 147 B5
Burnley BB11 126 F4
Preston PR1 96 A7
Skelmersdale WN8 17 F2
Berry's La FY6 151 C4
Berrys La BB7 143 C2
Bertha St BB5 103 D6
Bertram Ave LA4 212 D4
Bertrand Ave FY3 130 A7
Berwick Ave Cleveleys FY5 172 F4
Southport PR8 20 D5
Berwick Dr Burnley BB12 126 E7
Fulwood PR2 116 D4
Berwick Rd Blackpool FY4 109 C5
Lytham St Anne's FY8 88 F7
Preston PR1 96 A6
Berwick St PR1 117 E1
Berwick Way LA3 208 E7
Berwyn Ave LA4 212 G6
Berwyn Cl BL6 31 C5
Berwyn Ct PR8 34 D4
Beryl Ave Blackburn BB1 121 F2
Cleveleys FY5 172 E1
Bescar Brow La L40 22 F7
Bescar La L40 36 B1
Bescar La Sta L40 36 B2
Bescot Way [10] FY5 150 F7
Bessie St [12] BB18 200 B2
Best St PR4 112 F5
Bethel Ave FY2 150 D4
Bethel Rd BB1 101 A7
Bethel St
Barnoldswick BB18 200 B3
Colne BB8 169 B4
Bethesda Cl BB2 100 D3
Bethesda Rd FY1 129 B3
Bethesda St
Barnoldswick BB18 200 B2
Burnley BB11 126 F6
Betony LA4 213 B6
Betony Cl OL12 51 D3
Bett La PR6 78 C1
Beulah Ave LA4 212 G5
Bevan Pl BB9 168 F2
Beverley Ave
Longshaw WN5 10 E1
Poulton-le-F FY6 130 D8
Beverley Cl Clitheroe BB7 164 E6
Preston PR2 95 C8
Southport PR9 53 C5
Wrea Green PR4 112 A3
Beverley Ct
[2] Lytham St Anne's FY8 89 A8
Morecambe LA4 213 A5
Beverley Dr BB7 164 D6
Beverley Gr FY4 109 C7
Beverley Rd BB9 168 E8
Beverley Rd N FY8 89 A8
Beverley Rd S FY8 89 A8
Beverley St Blackburn BB2 100 B1
Burnley BB11 126 E5
Beverly Cl FY5 151 B8
Bewcastle Dr L40 16 C3
Bexhill Rd PR2 116 A4
Bexley Ave FY2 129 D8
Bexley Pl FY8 89 E5
Bezza La BB2,PR5 119 C5
Bhailok St [3] PR1 95 E8
Bibby Dr FY3 130 E5
Bibby Rd PR9 53 A1
Bibby's La FY2 150 E3
Bickerstaffe CE Prim Sch
L39 7 E5
Bickerstaffe St [2] FY1 129 B3
Bickerton Rd PR8 33 F4
Bicknell St BB1 100 E6
Bideford Ave FY3 130 A6
Bideford Way PR4 115 F6
Bidston St PR1 96 E8
Big Fold BL6 30 D2
Bigdale Dr L33 1 A3
Biggins La LA6 238 A1
Biggins Rd LA6 238 B2
Billinge Ave BB2 100 B5
Billinge Cl BB2 100 B5
Billinge End BB2 100 A6
Billinge End Rd
Blackburn BB2 99 F5
Pleasington BB2 99 B4
Billinge Hospl WN5 10 D2
Billinge Side BB2 99 F5
Billinge St BB1 101 B4
Billinge View BB2 99 F2
Billington Ave BB4 85 A5
Billington Gdns BB7 143 A4
Billington Rd BB11 126 B4
Billington St [1] PR4 112 F6
Billington St E [3] PR4 112 F6
Bilsberry Cotts BB7 162 F1
Bilsborough Hey PR1 95 E2
Bilsborough Mdw PR2 115 E3
Bilsborrow La
Bilsborrow PR3 157 C4
Inglewhite PR3 157 F5
Binbrook Pl PR7 42 A7
Binfold Croft LA6 238 C1
Bingley Ave FY3 129 F6
Bingley Cl PR6 77 C2
Binns St BB4 85 A7
Binyon Ct LA1 210 F6
Binyon Rd LA1 210 F5
Birbeck Rd L33 1 A3
Birbeck Wlk L33 1 A3
Birch Ave Burscough L40 24 E4
Clayton-le-W PR5 76 D3
Cleveleys FY5 172 E2
Euxton PR7 59 C4
Galgate LA2 207 A4
Haslingden BB4 84 C3
Newton-with-S PR4 113 F3
Penwortham PR1 95 A3
Preston PR2 116 A2
Birch Cl Huncoat BB5 124 E2
Maghull L31 5 F1
Whitworth OL12 51 C6
Birch Cres
Gregson Lane PR5 97 E1
Oswaldtwistle BB5 102 F3
Birch Dr LA5 218 C4
Birch Field PR6 77 B3
Birch Gn L37 11 D4
Birch Gr Barrow BB7 164 D1
Lancaster LA1 210 D8
Ramsbottom BL0 49 A3
Stalmine FY6 174 D7
Birch Green Rd WN8 18 C3
Birch Hall Ave BB3 80 D4
Birch Hall La BB18 201 D2
Birch La PR3 181 C1
Birch Rd Chorley PR6 60 E2
Coppull PR7 41 E1
Garstang PR3 178 C8
Birch St Accrington BB5 103 B6
Bacup OL13 86 F3
Fleetwood FY7 194 A4
[5] Lytham St Anne's FY8 90 C3
Skelmersdale WN8 8 E8
Southport PR8 34 B4
Birch Terr BB5 103 D2
Birch Tree Gdns FY3 130 B2
Birch Tree Way [4] BL6 31 E1
Birch View BB7 164 D1
Birch Way FY6 151 C4
Birch Wlk [1] BB1 101 B4
Birchall Lodge [6] PR2 117 F4
Birchbank Gdns BB1 101 A7
Birchenlee La BB8 169 E2
Birches End OL12 51 C5
Birches Rd BL7 47 D4
Birches The L37 11 E5
Birchfield PR4 73 F4
Birchfield Ave OL10 32 E1
Birchfield Dr PR3 139 A8
Birchfield Way L31 5 B5
Birchill Rd L33 1 C2
Birchin La PR6 77 D1
Birchover Cl PR2 116 A5
Birchtree Ave LA3 212 B1
Birchway Ave FY3 129 E6
Birchwood PR5 75 C1
Birchwood Ave PR4 94 B1
Birchwood Cl FY8 89 E4
Birchwood Dr Coppull PR7 41 E2
Fulwood PR2 116 D7
Hambleton FY6 174 C2
Birchwood Way L33 1 A5
Bird i' th' Hand
Cotts [2] L39 15 E6
Bird St Brierfield BB9 147 B5
Preston PR1 95 D6
Birdy Brow BB7 163 A6
Birk St PR1 95 E7
Birkacre Brow PR7 41 F2
Birkacre Rd PR7 41 F4
Birkbeck Pl FY7 193 D2
Birkbeck Way BB10 147 A1
Birkdale Ave
Blackpool FY2 150 E5
Fleetwood FY7 172 E7
Longton PR4 73 F8
Lytham St Anne's FY8 109 F1
Birkdale Cl Lancaster LA1 213 D3
Longton PR4 73 F8
Thornton FY5 151 D8
Birkdale Cop PR8 34 E1
Birkdale Dr PR2 115 E2
Birkdale High Sch PR8 20 E7
Birkdale Prim Sch PR8 34 B3
Birkdale Sch for Hearing
Impaired Children PR8 33 E4
Birkdale Sta PR8 33 F4
Birkdale Trad Est PR8 34 A2
Birkett Dr PR2 118 A3
Birkett Pl PR2 118 A3
Birkett Rd BB5 103 D7
Birkett's Pl LA4 212 F5
Birkey La L37 11 F2
Birklands Ave LA4 212 F4
Birkrig WN8 9 D6
Birks Brow PR3 160 D3
Birkside Way FY4 130 C1
Birkwith La LA2 233 C7
Birley Cl WN6 19 F8
Birley Pl BB10 127 A8
Birley St Blackburn BB1 100 F5
Blackburn BB1 100 F6
Blackpool FY1 129 B5
Kirkham PR4 113 B5

Birley St *continued*
30 Preston PR1 95 F8
1 Preston PR1 96 A7
Birleywood WN8 9 D6
Birnam Gn FY7 193 E4
Birtle Rd BL9 32 E6
Birtwhistle Cl BB9 147 B5
Birtwhistle Fold 7 BB8 169 E5
Birtwistle Ave BB8 169 D6
Birtwistle Ct BB18 200 C1
Birtwistle Hyde Pk 1 BB8 169 D5
Birtwistle St
Accrington BB5 103 C5
3 Bamber Bridge PR5 76 B7
Great Harwood BB6 123 B5
Birtwistle Standroyd Bglws BB8 170 A5
Birtwistle Terr BB6 142 C1
Bisham Cl BB3 64 C8
Bishop David Sheppard CE Sch PR9 35 B7
Bishop Martin CE Prim Sch WN8 9 D6
Bishop Rawstorne CE High Sch The PR5 57 C2
Bishop St Accrington BB5 103 C5
Burnley BB10 147 B1
Nelson BB9 147 D8
Bishopdale Cl
Blackburn BB2 79 D7
Morecambe LA3 213 B3
Bishopdale Rd LA1 210 D7
Bishopgate 14 PR1 96 A8
Bishops Gate FY8 89 D7
Bishopsgate
Highfurlong FY3 151 B1
Lancaster LA1 211 A4
Bishopstone Cl BB2 81 A8
Bishopsway PR1 95 D3
Bison Pl PR5 75 C2
Bispham Ave PR5 75 E4
Bispham Endowed CE Jun Sch FY2 150 D4
Bispham Hall Bsns Pk WN5 10 C2
Bispham Rd Blackpool FY2 150 D3
Blackpool, Carleton FY2 150 F6
Blackpool, Warbreck FY3 129 E8
Carleton FY5,FY6 151 A6
Cleveleys FY5 172 C2
Nelson BB9 147 E6
Southport PR9 34 F7
Bispham St 24 PR1 95 F8
Bittern Cl FY3 130 B6
Bivel St BB12 126 D6
Bk Alfred St BL0 49 B5
Black Abbey St BB5 103 C5
Black Bull La PR2 116 D5
Black Croft PR6 77 B3
Black Dyke Rd LA5 237 C1
Black Horse St
Blackrod BL6 30 C3
4 Chorley PR7 42 B6
Black House La
Chipping PR3 182 B1
Lane Bottom BB10 148 D3
Black La Nateby PR3 177 A8
Ramsbottom BL0 50 B7
Black Lane Croft BB7 186 E1
Black Lane Ends BB8 192 F3
Black Moor Rd L40 39 A2
Black Moss La
Ormskirk L39 15 E3
Scarisbrick L40 22 D6
Black Moss Rd BB9 167 E8
Black Moss Sch WN8 17 D2
Black Sticks La PR3 181 D1
Black-A-Moor La L39 14 A2
Blackacre La L39,L40 15 E8
Blackamoor Broadlands & Dame Evelyn Fox Special Schs BB1 81 B8
Blackamoor Rd BB1 81 C8
Blackberry Hall Cres LA3 209 A8
Blackberry Way PR1 95 B2
Blackbrook PR6 61 A2
Blackburn Brow PR6 60 E3
Blackburn Cath BB1 100 E4
Blackburn Coll BB2 100 D5
Blackburn Old Rd
Blackburn BB1 122 D3
Great Harwood BB1,BB6 122 F5
Hoghton PR5 98 C2
Blackburn Rd
Accrington BB5 103 A6
Accrington BB5 103 C6
Blackburn BB1 101 E8
Clayton-le-M BB5 123 E1
Darwen BB3 80 E4
Edenfield BL0,BB4 67 D5
Egerton BL7 46 C4
Great Harwood BB6 123 C4
Great Knowley PR6 60 E4
Haslingden BB4,BB5 84 B5
Higher Walton PR5 97 B3
Higher Wheelton PR6 78 C1
Oswaldtwistle BB5,BB1 102 C5
Padiham BB12 125 A8
Ribchester PR3 140 E3
Rishton BB1 123 A1
Wheelton PR6 60 F6
Whittlestone Head BB3,BL7 65 B2
Blackburn Royal Infmy BB2 100 D2
Blackburn St
Blackburn BB1 100 E6
Blackburn St *continued*
5 Burnley BB11 126 F6
Chorley PR6 42 E7
Blackburn Sta BB1 100 F4
Blackcar La L29 4 B3
Blacker St BB10 147 A2
Blackfen Pl FY2 129 D8
Blackfield Rd PR4 92 B6
Blackgate La Holmes PR4 55 C3
Tarleton PR4 55 E5
Blackhorse Ave BL6 30 C2
Blackhorse Cl BL6 30 C3
Blackhurst Ct PR4 74 B8
Blackhurst Rd L31 5 C5
Blackleach Ave PR2 138 D1
Blackleach La PR4 134 F1
Blackledge Cl WN5 10 E5
Blackley Gr L33 1 A6
Blacko Bar Rd BB9 168 B7
Blacko Prim Sch BB9 168 D8
Blackpool & Fleetwood Tramway FY2 150 B2
Blackpool & Fleetwood Yacht Club FY5 151 F7
Blackpool & Fylde Coll
Blackpool FY2 150 E6
Fleetwood FY7 194 A4
Blackpool & Fylde Coll of F Ed FY8 88 E5
Blackpool & The Fyde Coll Campus FY6 152 D3
Blackpool & The Fylde Coll Blackpool FY1 129 C4
Blackpool FY1 129 D4
Blackpool & The Fylde Coll (Nautical) FY7 172 E7
Blackpool & The Fylde Coll Ansdell Campus FY8 89 C5
Blackpool Airport FY4 109 D3
Blackpool Central Pier FY1 129 A3
Blackpool North Pier FY1 129 A5
Blackpool North Sta FY1 129 C6
Blackpool Old Rd
Little Eccleston PR3 154 A5
Poulton-le-F FY6 151 B2
Blackpool Pleasure Beach FY4 109 B7
Blackpool Rd
Blackpool FY2 150 D4
Blackpool, Carleton FY6 151 A4
Clifton PR4 93 E8
Longridge PR3 139 A7
Lytham St Anne's FY8 89 D5
Newton-with-S PR4 114 B2
Preston PR1,PR2 116 C2
Preston, Larches PR2 115 E1
St Michael's on W PR3 155 B6
Wrea Green PR4 112 C6
Blackpool Rd N FY8 109 F2
Blackpool Sixth Form Coll The FY3 151 A2
Blackpool South Pier FY4 109 A8
Blackpool South Sta FY4 129 B1
Blackpool St
6 Church BB5 102 E5
5 Darwen BB3 64 B6
Blackpool Tower FY1 129 B5
Blackpool Tramway FY1 129 A4
Blackpool Zoo FY3 130 A4
Blackrod Brow BL6 30 B4
Blackrod By-Pass Rd BL6 30 D2
Blackrod Sta BL6 30 E2
Blacksnape Rd BB3 81 D2
Blackstone Rd PR6 60 E1
Blackthorn Cl
Cleveleys FY5 172 F5
Newton-with-S PR4 113 F2
Preston PR2 115 D1
Rochdale OL12 51 E2
Blackthorn Cres OL13 86 F3
Blackthorn Croft PR6 77 A2
Blackthorn Dr PR1 95 B3
Blackthorn La OL13 86 F3
Blackthorn Mews OL12 51 E2
Blackwood Pl LA1 211 B5
Blackwood Rd OL13 69 B7
Blades St LA1 210 E7
Blaguegate La WN8 17 B2
Blainscough Rd PR7 28 E8
Blair Gr PR9 34 F7
Blair St OL12 51 D1
Blairgowrie Gdns L39 16 A4
Blairway Ave FY3 129 F6
Blake Ave PR5 76 A7
Blake Gdns BB6 123 B4
Blake St BB5 103 B6
Blakehall WN8 9 D7
Blakeley Cres BB18 200 B3
Blakewater Rd BB1 101 C7
Blakey Moor BB2 100 D5
Blakey St BB11 127 B6
Blakiston St FY7 194 A4
Blanche St 6 PR2 116 C1
Blandford Ave FY5 172 C1
Blandford Cl PR8 33 F5
Blandford Rise BL6 31 F1
Blannell St BB11 126 E6
Blascomay Sq 13 BB8 169 D4
Blashaw La PR1 95 A5
Blaydike Moss PR5 75 B1
Blaydon Ave FY5 172 E4
Blaydon Pk WN8 9 D7
Blea Cl BB12 126 B8
Blea Tarn Pl 3 LA4 212 G4
Blea Tarn Rd LA1,LA2 211 C2
Bleachers Dr 2 PR5 75 E1
Bleak La L40 25 D5
Bleakholt Rd BL0 67 F1
Bleara Rd BB18 192 D7
Bleasdale Ave
Cleveleys FY5 150 E8
Clitheroe BB7 164 C7
Kirkham PR4 113 A5
Poulton-le-F FY6 151 C2
Staining FY3 130 E5
Bleasdale CE Prim Sch PR3 181 A7
Bleasdale Cl
2 Bamber Bridge PR5 76 F8
Leyland PR5 59 B7
Ormskirk L39 6 D7
Bleasdale Ct PR3 139 B7
Bleasdale Gr LA3 212 B1
Bleasdale House Sch LA5 218 C3
Bleasdale La PR3 180 C6
Bleasdale Rd
Cumeragh Village PR3 137 F6
Knott End-on-S FY6 194 D5
Lytham St Anne's FY8 90 C4
Whitechapel PR3 158 C8
Bleasdale St E PR1 117 C1
Blelock St PR1 96 A7
Blenheim Ave
Blackpool FY1 129 D4
Kirkham PR4 112 F5
Blenheim Cl
Bamber Bridge PR5 76 C8
Blackburn BB1 121 E1
Blenheim Dr Thornton FY5 173 C2
Warton PR4 91 D6
Blenheim Pl FY8 109 E1
Blenheim Rd PR8 20 B6
Blenheim St Colne BB8 170 A5
13 Rochdale OL12 51 C1
Blenheim Terr BB8 191 E1
Blenheim Way PR4 115 E6
Blessed Sacrament RC Prim Sch PR2 117 F3
Blind La Burton in L LA6 236 C3
Gisburn BB7 225 C3
Higham BB12 146 A6
Blindman's La L39 15 C7
Bloom St 3 BL0 49 A4
Bloomfield Ct PR1 116 E2
Bloomfield Grange PR1 95 C2
Bloomfield Pk LA5 217 D1
Bloomfield Rd
Blackpool FY1 129 C2
Withnell PR6 79 A1
Bloomfield Road Football Gd (Blackpool FC) FY1 129 C2
Blossom Ave FY4 109 F7
Blossoms The PR2 117 C6
Blowick Bsns Pk PR9 35 A6
Blucher St BB8 169 E4
Blue Bell La OL14 108 D2
Blue Bell Pl PR1 96 A7
Blue Gates BB7 223 B3
Blue Moor PR4 134 A2
Blue Scar La BB7 224 D7
Blue Stone La L40 39 F4
Bluebell Ave BB4 67 A8
Bluebell Cl Cleveleys FY5 172 F5
Hesketh Bank PR4 72 E4
Lucas Green PR6 60 C5
Bluebell Gr BB11 126 A5
Bluebell Way PR2 117 F6
Bluebell Wood PR5 75 F3
Bluecoat Cres PR4 114 A2
Bluestone La L31 5 E1
Blundell Ave Formby L37 11 B4
Hightown L38 2 F3
Southport PR8 33 F2
Blundell Cres PR8 33 F2
Blundell Dr PR8 33 F2
Blundell Gr L38 2 F3
Blundell La Blackrod BL6 30 A2
Penwortham PR1 95 B6
Southport PR9 53 C2
Blundell Links Ct PR8 20 C4
Blundell Rd Fulwood PR2 116 E3
Hightown L38 2 F3
Lytham St Anne's FY8 109 F1
Blundell St FY1 129 B3
Blythe Ave FY5 172 E5
Blythe Cotts L40 24 E1
Blythe La L40 24 E1
Blythewood WN8 9 D7
Board St BB10 147 A1
Boarded Barn PR7 59 C3
Boardman Ave FY1 129 D2
Boardman St BL6 30 D2
Boarsgreave La BB4 68 F6
Bobbin Cl BB5 103 A5
Bobbin Mill Cl 11 OL14 108 B1
Bobbin St OL14 108 C1
Bobbiners La PR9 54 A3
Bobby Langton Way L40 24 E5
Bocholt Way BB4 85 A2
Bodiam Rd BL8 48 F2
Bodie Hill LA2 205 E5
Bodkin La PR3 152 F7
Bodmin Ave PR9 53 B5
Bodmin St PR1 117 D1
Boegrave Ave PR5 76 A8
Bog Height Rd BB3 80 C6
Bogburn La PR7 28 D6
Boland St BB1 101 A7
Bold La L39 6 B7
Bold St Accrington BB5 103 D6
Bold St *continued*
Bacup OL13 86 F1
Blackburn BB1 100 E6
Bury BL9 32 A3
Colne BB8 169 E4
Fleetwood FY7 194 B5
Morecambe LA3 212 B4
Preston PR1 116 D1
Southport PR9 34 B8
Bold Venture Way BB5 124 A3
Boleyn Ct FY3 130 A2
Boleyn The L31 5 E3
Bolland Cl 5 BB7 164 F8
Bolland Prospect BB7 164 F7
Bolland St BB18 200 B3
Bolton Ave Accrington BB5 124 D1
Carleton FY6 151 C5
Lancaster LA1 213 F4
Bolton Cl L37 12 A2
Bolton Croft PR5 58 B8
Bolton Gr BB9 168 D3
Bolton La LA5 216 C4
Bolton Rd Abbey Village PR6 79 B3
Adlington BL60,PR6 30 D6
Blackburn BB2 100 D2
Blackburn, Ewood BB2,BB3 80 E7
Cadshaw BB3 64 C3
Chorley PR6 42 E4
Darwen BB3 64 B7
Edgworth BL7 47 D5
Ramsbottom BL8 48 D2
Riley Green PR5,PR6 78 E6
Southport PR8 34 A4
Bolton Rd N BL0 67 D2
Bolton Rd W BL0,BL8 49 A4
Bolton St Blackpool FY1 129 B2
Chorley PR7 42 C7
Colne BB8 169 C4
5 Newchurch BB4 85 E1
Ramsbottom BL0 49 B6
Bolton's Cop PR9 54 D5
Bolton's Ct 24 BB1 100 E5
Bolton's Meanygate PR4 55 C7
Bolton-by-Bowland CE Prim Sch BB7 224 D4
Bolton-le-Sands CE Prim Sch LA5 216 B4
Boltons Croft PR4 114 E7
Boltons Ct PR1 96 A7
Bombay St BB2 100 C3
Bonchurch St BB1 101 C4
Bond Cl BL6 31 C3
Bond St Blackpool FY4 109 B7
12 Burnley BB10 127 A8
Bury BL9 32 A2
Colne BB8 169 D5
Darwen BB3 81 A2
Edenfield BL0 67 E2
Lancaster LA1 211 A8
Nelson BB9 147 D7
Bond's La Adlington PR7 29 F7
Banks PR9 54 A7
Bonds La Bonds PR3 178 C6
Elswick PR4 154 A2
Bone Croft PR6 77 B3
Bone Hill La PR3 197 D1
Bonfire Hill Cl BB4 85 B7
Bonfire Hill Rd BB4 85 A7
Bonney St FY5 173 B3
Bonny Grass Terr BB7 143 A4
Bonny St FY1 129 B4
Bonsall St BB2 100 B2
Boome St FY4 109 C6
Boon Town LA6 234 C7
Boon Wlks LA6 234 C7
Boot St BB18 201 B2
Boot Way BB11 127 A5
Booth Bridge La BD23 201 B5
Booth Cres BB4 86 A1
Booth Ct 4 BB10 127 A8
Booth Rd OL13 69 B8
Booth St Accrington BB5 103 C4
10 Bacup OL13 86 F2
Carnforth LA5 217 D1
Haslingden BB4 84 A4
10 Nelson BB9 147 D8
Rawtenstall BB4 68 E8
Southport PR8 34 B8
Booth's La L39 14 F4
Boothley Rd FY1 129 D6
Boothman Pl BB9 168 E2
Boothman St BB2 100 D2
Boothroyden FY1 129 B8
Bootle St PR1 117 C1
Borage Cl FY5 173 A5
Border Ct 6 LA1 213 D1
Bores Hill WN1 29 C4
Borough Rd BB3 81 A1
Borron La LA6 234 C3
Borrowdale L37 11 F5
Borrowdale Ave
Blackburn BB1 101 C3
Fleetwood FY7 193 E4
Borrowdale Cl
4 Accrington BB5 124 D1
Brierfield BB10 147 C3
Borrowdale Dr BB10 147 C4
Borrowdale Gr LA4 212 G5
Borrowdale Rd
Blackpool FY4 130 B1
Lancaster LA1 211 A8
Leyland PR5 59 B7
Borwick Ave LA5 217 E6
Borwick Cl LA5 217 E6
Borwick Ct Borwick LA6 234 B4
Morecambe LA4 212 E3
Borwick Dr LA1 213 D2
Borwick La LA6 234 B3
Borwick Mews LA6 234 B3
Borwick Rd LA6 234 D3
Bosburn Dr BB2 120 C2
Boscombe Ave LA3 212 B2
Boscombe Rd FY4 109 B6
Bosley Arc 2 FY1 129 B5
Bosley Cl BB3 64 D8
Bostock St 22 PR1 96 A7
Boston Ave FY2 150 D6
Boston Rd Bacup OL13 86 F3
Lytham St Anne's FY8 89 B6
Boston St BB9 147 F6
Bostons BB6 123 B5
Bostonway FY4 109 F8
Bosworth Dr PR8 20 B4
Bosworth Pl FY4 109 B4
Bosworth St BL6 31 B4
Botanic Gardens Mus PR9 53 B2
Botanic Rd PR9 53 B2
Botany Brow PR6 60 E2
Bott House La BB8,BB9 169 A2
Bottom o' th' Knotts Brow BL7 47 E3
Bottom o' th' Rann BB1 81 F6
Bottomdale Rd LA2 214 A8
Bottomgate BB1 101 B5
Bottomley Bank La BB4 85 B8
Bottomley St BB9 147 E8
Bottoms La LA5 218 D3
Botton Rd LA2 233 C1
Boulder St 8 BB4 85 A7
Bouldsworth Rd BB10 127 E5
Boulevard PR1 96 B5
Boulevard Gdns FY8 89 A4
Boulevard The FY8 89 A4
Boulsworth Cres BB9 169 B1
Boulsworth Dr BB8 170 C1
Boulsworth Gr BB8 170 A5
Boulview Terr BB8 170 A5
Boundary Cl Eccleston PR7 40 B6
New Longton PR4 74 F8
Boundary Ct FY3 151 A1
Boundary La
Becconsall PR4 72 E1
Burscough L40 24 F4
Hale Nook FR6,PR3 175 B7
Holmes PR4,PR9 54 E6
Kirkby L33 1 F2
Shevington Moor WN6 28 A3
Boundary Meanygate
Becconsall PR4 72 D1
Holmes PR4 54 F7
Boundary Rd
Accrington BB5 103 D7
Fulwood PR2 116 D3
Lancaster LA1 210 F6
Lytham St Anne's FY8 90 E5
Boundary St
Burnley BB10 147 C2
Colne BB8 169 D4
Leyland PR5 76 B2
Southport PR8 34 B4
Bourbles La FY6 195 D4
Bourne Brow PR3 157 E5
Bourne May Rd FY6 194 D5
Bourne Rd FY5 173 B5
Bourne Way FY5 173 A4
Bourne's Row PR5 97 E1
Bournemouth Rd FY4 109 B6
Bournesfield PR5 97 E1
Bovington Ave FY5 150 F8
Bow Brook Rd PR5 76 C1
Bow Hills La BB7 225 C6
Bow La Leyland PR5 76 B1
Preston PR1 95 E7
Bow St PR5 76 B2
Bowden Ave BB2 99 C1
Bowen St BB2 100 B2
Bower Cl BB2 100 B2
Bower St Blackburn BB2 100 B2
Bury BL9 32 C3
Bowerham Com Prim Sch LA1 211 A6
Bowerham La LA1,LA2 211 B3
Bowerham Rd LA1 211 A5
Bowers La PR3 177 E7
Bowers The PR7 42 D4
Bowes Lyon Pl FY8 89 C7
Bowfell Ave LA4 212 G5
Bowfell Cl FY4 130 D1
Bowfield's La BB2 119 F4
Bowgreave Cl 1 FY4 110 A6
Bowgreave Dr PR3 178 D4
Bowker St BL0 67 C5
Bowker's Green La L39 6 E4
Bowland Ave
Burnley BB10 127 E5
Chorley PR6 42 D8
Fleetwood FY7 172 D8
Bowland Cl Carnforth LA5 217 C1
Longridge PR3 139 B8
Bowland Cres FY3 130 A8
Bowland Ct
4 Clitheroe BB7 164 E8
9 Southport PR9 34 C8
Bowland Cty High Sch BB7 224 B1
Bowland Dr LA1 213 D2
Bowland Gate La BB7 186 E7
Bowland Ho 7 BB1 100 F6
Bowland Pl Fulwood PR2 118 A3
Lytham St Anne's FY8 89 C6
Bowland Rd Fulwood PR2 118 A3
Garstang PR3 199 C1
Heysham LA3 209 A8

Bowland View
Brierfield BB9 147 D4
Garstang PR3 199 C1
Glasson LA2 205 E4
Bowlers Cl PR2 117 C5
Bowlers Wlk OL12 51 F2
Bowling Green Cl
Darwen BB3 64 B7
Southport PR8 34 F5
Bowling Green Cotts BB6 142 C6
Bowlingfield PR2 116 A6
Bowness Ave
Blackpool FY4 130 D1
Lytham St Anne's FY8 109 F2
Nelson BB9 147 E6
Rochdale OL12 51 C1
Southport PR8 20 C3
Thornton FY5 173 B2
Bowness Cl BB1 101 A6
Bowness Pl FY7 193 C1
Bowness Rd Fulwood PR1 118 A1
Lancaster LA1 214 A1
Padiham BB12 145 C2
Bowood Ct FY3 130 B7
Bowran St PR1 95 F8
Box St BL0 49 D6
Boxer Pl PR5 75 C2
Boxwood Dr BB2 79 F8
Boxwood St BB1 100 F8
Boyd Cl WN6 28 F1
Boyes Ave PR3 178 D2
Boyle St BB1 100 F6
Boys La PR2 116 C5
Brabiner La PR2,PR3 138 B4
Brabins Endowed Sch PR3 182 E3
Bracebridge Dr PR8 34 F2
Bracewell Ave FY6 152 A3
Bracewell Cl BB9 147 E8
Bracewell La BB23 225 F3
Bracewell Rd PR2 117 E5
Bracewell St
Barnoldswick BB18 200 B3
Burnley BB10 147 B1
Nelson BB9 147 F8
Bracken Cl Blackburn BB2 79 F8
Chorley PR6 42 E8
Bracken Dr PR4 92 D7
Bracken Gr BB4 67 A8
Bracken Hey BB7 165 A8
Bracken Lea Fold 3 OL12 51 B2
Brackenbury Cl 5 PR5 76 A7
Brackenbury Rd PR1,PR2 116 E3
Brackenbury St PR1 116 F2
Brackenthaite Rd LA5,LA7 219 B7
Brackenway L37 12 A6
Bracknel Way L39 15 A1
Braconash Rd PR5 75 E2
Bradda Rd BB2 100 E1
Braddon St 2 PR1 117 D1
Brade St PR9 53 C4
Brades Ave FY5 173 D2
Brades La PR4 92 D7
Bradford Gr LA3 208 F6
Bradford St BB5 103 D6
Bradkirk La PR5 77 B8
Bradkirk Pl PR5 77 A7
Bradley Ct BB7 161 E8
Bradley Cty Prim Sch BB9 168 E1
Bradley Fold 5 BB9 168 E1
Bradley Gdns BB12 126 B5
Bradley Hall Rd BB9 168 F1
Bradley Hall Trad Est WN6 28 F2
Bradley Hill Trad Est WN6 29 A2
Bradley La Eccleston PR7 40 D6
Standish WN6 28 F2
Bradley Pl 8 PR8 34 B7
Bradley Rd BB9 168 E1
Bradley Rd E BB9 168 E1
Bradley Smithy Cl OL12 51 E2
Bradley St Colne BB8 169 F5
Southport PR9 34 C8
Bradley View 12 BB9 168 E1
Bradman Rd L33 1 D3
Bradshaw Brow L40 39 E2
Bradshaw Cl
Blackburn BB1 100 E8
Nelson BB9 147 E7
Standish WN6 28 D1
Bradshaw La
Corner Row PR4 132 D1
Eagland Hill PR3 176 A7
Mawdesley L40 39 E2
Parbold WN8 26 C1
Scronkey PR3 196 E2
Bradshaw Rd BL7 47 E1
Bradshaw Row BB5 102 F6
Bradshaw St Church BB5 102 F6
7 Lancaster LA1 211 A7
Nelson BB9 147 D7
Bradshaw St E 3 BB5 103 C6
Bradshaw St W BB5 102 F6
Bradshaw's La PR8 20 D6
Bradshawgate Dr LA5 218 C4
Brady St BL6 31 A4
Bradyll Ct BB6 142 C6
Braefield Cres PR2 117 F2
Braemar Ave Southport PR9 52 E2
Thornton FY5 151 C7
Braemar Ct 2 LA4 213 A4
Braemar Wlk FY2 150 F6
Braemore Dr BL9 32 D2
Braeside BB2 100 C6
Braewood Cl BL9 32 D2
Braganza Way LA1 210 C8
Braid Cl PR1 95 D1
Braid's La PR3 179 A7
Braidhaven WN6 19 E7
Braintree Ave PR1 95 E2
Braith Cl FY4 109 F8
Braithwaite St 3 FY1 129 B7
Bramble Cl PR4 112 E6
Bramble Ct
Penwortham PR1 95 E2
1 Thornton FY5 173 A2
Bramble Gdns FY6 151 A2
Bramble St BB10 147 A1
Bramble Way WN8 26 C1
Brambles The
Barrow BB7 164 D1
Blackburn BB2 100 A8
Blackpool FY8 109 B4
Coppull PR7 41 F2
Preston PR2 117 D6
Bramblewood PR5 57 B2
Bramblings The FY6 151 B2
Bramcote Cl L33 1 A4
Bramcote Rd L33 1 A4
Bramhall Rd WN8 17 F2
Bramley Ave Burnley BB12 126 C8
Fleetwood FY7 193 E4
Bramley Cl 8 BB5 102 E5
Bramley View BB7 143 C8
Brampton Ave FY5 172 F4
Brampton Dr LA4 213 B5
Brampton St 2 PR2 116 C1
Bramwell Rd PR4 92 B6
Bramworth Ave BL0 49 B6
Branch Rd
Blackburn BB2,BB3 80 E7
Burnley BB11 127 B4
2 Clayton-le-M BB5 123 F3
Mellor Brook BB2 120 C2
Waddington BB7 186 B4
Branch St Bacup OL13 69 D8
Nelson BB9 147 F8
Brancker St 3 PR7 42 A5
Brandiforth St PR5 96 F2
Brandlesholme Rd BL8 49 A1
Brandon Cl WN8 10 A7
Brandreth Delph WN8 26 C3
Brandreth Dr WN8 26 C2
Brandreth Pk WN8 26 D4
Brandreth Pl WN6 28 F1
Brandwood 6 BB4 85 E1
Brandwood Fold BL7 47 E5
Brandwood Gr BB10 127 C6
Brandwood Pk OL13 69 B8
Brandwood Rd OL13 69 B8
Brandwood St BB3 81 B1
Brandy House Brow BB2 100 F2
Branksome Ave FY5 172 F3
Branksome Dr LA4 212 G4
Branston Rd FY4 129 E1
Branstree Rd FY4 130 C1
Brant Ct FY7 193 C1
Brant Rd PR1 118 A1
Brantfell Dr BB12 126 B8
Brantfell Rd
Blackburn BB1 100 D7
Great Harwood BB6 123 D6
Brantwood BB5 123 E2
Brantwood Ave
Blackburn BB1 101 F5
Morecambe LA4 213 A6
Brantwood Dr
Lancaster LA1 211 A2
Leyland PR5 76 B1
Brassey St BB12 126 C7
Brathay Pl FY7 193 D2
Bray St PR2 116 C1
Brays Heys 2 FY5 173 C1
Brays Rd FY8 111 B1
Brayshaw Pl PR2 117 E4
Brazil Cl LA3 212 D2
Brazley Ave BL6 31 E1
Bread St 4 BB12 126 D6
Bream Wood PR4 112 E4
Brearlands BD23 201 B6
Brearley St OL13 69 D8
Breck Cl FY6 151 E5
Breck Cty Prim Sch The FY6 151 F5
Breck Dr FY6 151 E5
Breck Rd Blackpool FY3 129 E4
Poulton-le-F FY6 151 F6
Breckside Cl FY6 151 E5
Brecon Ave BB5 102 C4
Brecon Cl FY1 129 D3
Brecon Rd BB1 101 C5
Bredon Ave PR7 59 E1
Bredon Cl FY8 90 D5
Bredon Ct L37 11 E4
Breeze Cl Foulridge BB8 191 E1
Thornton FY5 173 A4
Breeze Mount PR5 76 C8
Breeze Rd PR8 33 E2
Brenbar Cres OL12 70 D1
Brendjean Rd LA4 212 F4
Brendon Wlk FY3 129 F8
Brennand Cl
Bamber Bridge PR5 76 F8
Lancaster LA1 213 C2
Brennand St Burnley BB10 147 B1
Clitheroe BB7 186 E1
Brennands Endowed Prim Sch BB7 223 C7
Brent St BB10 147 C3
Brentlea Ave LA3 208 E7
Brentlea Cres LA3 208 E7
Brentwood FY7 193 E2
Brentwood Ave
Burnley BB11 126 E3
Cleveleys FY5 150 D8
Poulton-le-F FY6 151 C3
Brentwood Cl L38 2 F2
Brentwood Ct PR9 52 D1
Brentwood Rd
Adlington PR6 30 B8
Nelson BB9 169 A1
Bretherton Cl PR5 58 C8
Bretherton Ct L40 24 F3
Bretherton Endowed CE Prim Sch PR5 56 F6
Bretherton Rd PR5 57 B4
Bretherton Terr 9 PR5 76 B1
Brett Cl BB7 165 A7
Brettarch Dr LA1 210 E5
Brettargh Cl LA1 210 E6
Brettargh Dr LA1 210 E6
Bretton Fold PR8 34 F5
Brewery Arc 39 LA1 210 F8
Brewery La Formby L37 11 F6
19 Lancaster LA1 210 F8
Brewery St Blackburn BB2 100 D5
Longridge PR3 139 B7
Breworth Fold La PR6 78 A3
Briar Ave PR7 59 C4
Briar Bank Row PR2 117 A8
Briar Cl OL12 51 A1
Briar Croft PR4 74 A7
Briar Field FY2 150 F6
Briar Gr PR2 116 A4
Briar Hill Cl 3 BB1 101 A4
Briar Lea Rd LA6 216 E5
Briar Mews 1 FY5 173 C1
Briar Rd Blackburn BB1 100 F8
Southport PR8 20 D4
Thornton FY5 173 C1
Briar St OL13 87 A1
Briarcroft BB3 81 A6
Briarfield BL7 46 D2
Briarfield Rd FY6 151 B5
Briars Brook L40 25 A2
Briars Gn WN8 18 B4
Briars La Maghull L31 5 E1
Ring o'Bells L40 25 A3
Briars The Eccleston PR7 40 C6
Fulwood PR2 117 D6
Southport PR8 33 F1
Briarscroft LA5 217 E6
Briarwood PR4 92 A6
Briarwood Cl Leyland PR5 58 E8
Weeton PR4 131 F2
Briarwood Ct FY5 151 B7
Briarwood Dr FY2 150 E5
Briary Croft L38 2 F3
Brick Kiln La L40 38 B3
Brick St 9 Burnley BB11 126 F6
Bury BL9 32 A3
Brickcroft La PR5 57 B3
Brickhouse Gdns PR3 182 E3
Brickhouse La FY6 174 C4
Bricklayers Arms Yd L39 15 D6
Bridge Ave L39 15 E5
Bridge Bank 4 PR1 96 C6
Bridge Brow LA6 238 C1
Bridge Cl
Bamber Bridge PR5 76 A8
6 Rawtenstall BB4 85 F1
Bridge Croft
Bolton-le-S LA5 216 A4
Clayton-le-M BB5 123 E4
Bridge Ct
3 Bamber Bridge PR5 76 A8
Clitheroe BB7 186 F2
2 Lytham St Anne's FY8 90 D4
Bridge End
Bamber Bridge PR5 76 C8
Barley BB12 167 C5
Whalley BB7 143 C4
Bridge End Cl BB4 67 A7
Bridge End St OL14 108 C1
Bridge Farm Dr L31 5 F2
Bridge Gr PR8 34 B6
Bridge Hall Dr BL9 32 C2
Bridge Hall Fold BL9 32 C2
Bridge Hall La BL9 32 D2
Bridge Ho Blackburn BB2 100 B1
7 Lancaster LA1 213 F2
3 Saltcotes FY8 90 D4
Bridge House Rd FY4 109 F8
Bridge Hos
Accrington BB5 83 E8
Whitewell Bottom BB4 85 F7
Bridge La LA1 210 F8
Bridge Mill Rd BB9 147 C8
Bridge Rd 3
Bamber Bridge PR5 76 C8
Chatburn BB7 187 D5
Fleetwood FY7 194 B4
Lancaster LA1 210 F5
Lytham St Anne's FY8 89 E4
Morecambe LA4 212 F5
Nether Kellet LA6 216 E4
Preston PR2 116 C2
Bridge Row PR3 155 C7
Bridge St 15
Accrington BB5 103 C6
Bamber Bridge PR5 76 E7
Blackburn BB1 100 E4
Brierfield BB9 147 B5
Burnley BB11 127 A6
Bury BL9 32 A3
Church BB5 102 E6
Colne BB8 169 C4
Darwen BB3 81 A1
Bridge St *continued*
Garstang PR3 178 C6
6 Great Harwood BB6 123 C5
Haslingden BB4 67 C6
Higher Walton PR5 97 B3
Horwich BL6 31 C4
Newchurch BB4 85 F1
Ormskirk L39 15 E4
Padiham BB12 125 B8
Ramsbottom BL0 49 C6
Rawtenstall BB4 68 E7
Rishton BB1 123 B2
Southport PR8 34 B6
Water BB4 86 A8
Wheelton PR6 61 A7
Whitworth OL12 70 C1
Bridge Terr 6 PR1 96 C6
Bridge Wills La PR9 53 C5
Bridgefield Dr BL9 32 D2
Bridgefield St 8 BB12 125 C4
Bridgehall Dr WN8 10 B7
Bridgemill Rd BB1 100 F4
Bridgend Ct PR2 115 F3
Bridgend Dr PR8 20 B4
Bridget St 21 LA1 210 F8
Bridgewater Ave 6 FY5 150 F7
Bridgewater Cl BB11 125 F4
Bridgeway PR5 76 C8
Bridle Path The BB18 191 D7
Bridleway BB4 85 F2
Brief St BB10 127 A8
Brier Cres BB9 147 D6
Brier Dr LA3 208 E7
Brier Heights Cl BB9 147 D5
Briercliffe Ave
Blackpool FY3 129 F2
Nelson BB8 169 B3
Briercliffe Bsns Ctr BB10 147 F3
Briercliffe Cty Sch BB10 147 F3
Briercliffe Rd
Brierfield BB10 147 D2
Burnley BB10 147 C1
8 Chorley PR6 60 D1
Briercliffe St BB8 169 B3
Brierfield New Longton PR4 74 F8
Skelmersdale WN8 9 D6
Brierfield Mansfield High Sch BB9 147 B6
Brierfield Reedley Cty Sch BB10 147 C4
Brierfield Sta BB9 147 B5
Brierholme Ave BL7 46 E1
Brierley Ave FY3 129 E7
Brierley La PR4 135 B8
Brierley Rd PR5 77 A7
Brierley St PR2 116 D1
Briers Brow PR6 61 B7
Briery Bank LA5 237 C1
Briery Cl PR2 117 C4
Briery Hey PR5 77 C6
Briery St 2 LA1 213 D1
Brieryfield Rd PR1 95 D8
Brigg Field BB5 123 F4
Briggs Fold BL7 46 E2
Briggs Fold Cl BL7 46 E2
Briggs Fold Rd BL7 46 E2
Briggs Rd PR2 116 C2
Brighouse Cl L39 15 D6
Brighouse Gn L40 16 F3
Bright St Blackburn BB1 101 B6
Blackpool FY4 109 B8
2 Burnley BB10 147 B1
Bury BL9 32 A3
Clitheroe BB7 164 F8
Colne BB8 169 D5
Colne, Cotton Tree BB8 170 B5
Darwen BB3 80 F2
Egerton BL7 46 D2
Oswaldtwistle BB5 102 D3
Padiham BB12 125 D8
13 Rawtenstall BB4 85 A3
Southport PR9 34 F7
Bright Terr BB8 170 B2
Bright's Cl BB7 223 A5
Brighton Ave
Blackpool FY4 109 B8
Cleveleys FY5 172 D2
Lytham St Anne's FY8 88 F7
Brighton Cres PR2 116 A3
Brighton Rd
Brierfield BB10 147 C3
Southport PR8 34 A3
Brighton St Bury BL9 32 B3
7 Chorley PR6 42 E8
Cornholme OL14 108 C1
Brighton Terr
Blackburn BB2 100 B6
Darwen BB3 80 E2
Brightstone Cl PR9 54 B5
Brigsteer Cl BB5 123 E2
Brindle Cl 9
Lancaster LA1 213 C2
Longridge PR3 139 B7
Walton Summit PR5 77 B8
Brindle Fold PR5 77 C7
Brindle Gregson Lane Cty Prim Sch PR5 97 E1
Brindle Hts PR6 77 F5
Brindle Rd
Bamber Bridge PR5 96 F2
Walton Summit PR5,PR6 77 C7
Brindle St Blackburn BB2 100 C1
Chorley PR7 42 C6
Preston PR1 96 C8
Brindle St James' CE Prim Sch PR6 77 F5
Brindley Cl BB11 125 F4
Brindley St BL6 31 C2
Brink's Row BL6 31 D5
Brinklow Cl PR8 20 A5
Brinscall Terr PR6 61 F7
Brinwell Rd FY4 130 B1
Brisbane Pl FY5 150 F7
Brisbane St 7 BB5 124 A1
Bristol Ave Blackpool FY2 150 E4
Fleetwood FY7 172 C8
Leyland PR5 76 C3
Bristol Cl 9 BB1 101 A4
Bristol St Burnley BB11 126 D3
Colne BB8 169 E5
Morecambe LA4 212 F4
Bristow Ave PR2 116 B2
Britannia Ave OL13 87 A2
Britannia Cotts BB5 102 A1
Britannia Cty Prim Sch OL13 70 C8
Britannia Pl 2 FY1 129 B1
Britannia St BB6 123 C5
Britannia Way BB4 67 A8
Britannia Wlk
3 Burnley BB11 127 B4
Lytham St Anne's FY8 89 C8
British In India Mus BB8 169 E5
British Lawnmower Mus PR8 34 B5
Brittania Dr PR2 95 B7
Brittania Wharf PR2 95 B8
Britten Cl BB2 101 A2
Britten St BB3 80 F2
Britwell Cl BB2 81 A8
Brixey St PR1 95 D6
Brixham Pl 3 FY4 109 B6
Brixton Rd PR1 96 B7
Broad Clough Villas OL13 86 F5
Broad Croft PR4 94 A1
Broad Gate BB3 81 B2
Broad Ing OL12 51 C1
Broad Ing Cl BB10 127 E1
Broad La Ford Green PR3 198 F2
Formby L37 12 E2
Formby L37,L38 4 A8
Haskayne L39 14 B2
Kirkby L32 1 A1
Maghull L29 4 C2
Whalley BB7 143 B5
Winmarleigh PR3 198 F5
Broad Mdw
Bamber Bridge PR5 76 A8
Chipping PR3 182 D3
Broad Meadow La PR5 56 F4
Broad Oak Ave PR3 178 D6
Broad Oak Cl PR6 30 A8
Broad Oak Cotts PR6 43 D3
Broad Oak Gn PR1 95 B3
Broad Oak High Sch BL9 32 B2
Broad Oak La Bury BL9 32 D3
Penwortham PR1 95 B3
Penwortham, Nutter's Platt PR4 95 B2
Staining FY3 130 D5
Broad Oak Rd BB5 103 D5
Broad Oak Terr BL9 32 E3
Broad Sq 9 PR5 59 A8
Broad St 4 Leyland PR5 59 A8
13 Nelson BB9 147 D8
Broadacre Caton LA2 231 C3
Orrell WN8 10 A6
Shevington Moor WN6 28 B2
Broadacre Cl LA2 231 C3
Broadacre Pl LA2 231 C3
Broadacre View LA2 231 C3
Broadbent Dr BL9 32 E4
Broadfield Accrington BB5 83 B8
Broughton PR3 136 B2
Oswaldtwistle BB5 102 F2
Broadfield Ave
Blackpool FY4 109 F5
Poulton-le-F FY6 151 F3
Broadfield Ct FY6 151 F3
Broadfield Dr Leyland PR5 75 E1
Penwortham PR1 95 D2
Broadfield Jun Sch PR5 75 F1
Broadfield Rd BB5 103 A3
Broadfield Sch BB5 102 F2
Broadfield St BB5 102 F3
Broadfields PR7 60 B2
Broadfleet Cl PR3 196 C6
Broadfold Ave BB1 101 B7
Broadgate PR1 95 D6
Broadgreen Cl PR5 75 F1
Broadhead Rd BB3,BL7 65 F5
Broadhurst La WN6 27 F7
Broadhurst Rd FY5 150 E8
Broadhurst Way BB10,BB9 147 C4
Broadith La PR3 158 E1
Broadlands PR8 33 E3
Broadlands Dr LA5 215 F3
Broadlands Pl FY8 89 F4
Broadlea Gr OL12 51 C2
Broadley Fold OL12 51 B6
Broadley St BB4 85 A3
Broadmead WN8 26 B2
Broadness Dr BB9 147 E6
Broadoak Rd L31 5 E1
Broadoaks BL9 32 D3
Broadpool La FY6 174 C1
Broadriding Rd WN6 19 E6
Broadstone Cl OL12 51 A1
Broadtree Cl BB2 120 C3
Broadwater Ave FY7 172 F8
Broadwater Gdns FY7 172 E8
Broadway Accrington BB5 103 B6
Blackburn BB1 121 E2
Blackpool FY4 109 C7
Fleetwood FY7 193 E2

Broadway *continued*
Fulwood PR2 116 D7
Haslingden BB4 67 B8
Horwich BL6 31 D3
Lancaster LA1 213 F2
Leyland PR5 59 B8
Morecambe LA4 212 G5
Nelson BB9 147 D8
Preston PR2 115 F2
Broadway Cl PR8 20 B5
Broadway Cres BB4 67 A8
Broadway Cty Prim Sch BB4 67 C8
Broadway Pl
Barrowford BB9 168 D3
Nelson BB9 169 A1
Broadway St BB2 100 B1
Broadwood Cl PR1 95 B4
Broadwood Dr PR2 116 F7
Broadwood Way FY8 89 E4
Brock Ave FY7 193 D2
Brock Bank BB4 85 F4
Brock Cl LA1 213 E3
Brock Clough Rd BB4 85 F4
Brock Mill La PR3 180 B2
Brock Rd Chorley PR6 60 D1
Lane Heads PR3,PR4 154 E3
Brock Side PR3 157 C6
Brock St LA1 210 F8
Brockbank Ave LA1 210 C8
Brockenhurst St BB10 127 C5
Brockholes Brow PR1,PR2 118 A1
Brockholes Cres FY6 151 E2
Brockholes View PR1 96 C7
Brockholes Way PR3 178 E1
Brockholes Wood Cty Prim Sch PR1 118 A1
Brocklebank Rd PR9 52 E2
Brocklehurst Ave BB5 103 B3
Brocklewood Ave FY6 130 D8
Brockway FY6 151 D2
Brockway Ave FY3 129 F6
Broderick Ave 1 FY2 150 E1
Brodick Rd BB1 101 D3
Brogden La BB18 225 E2
Brogden St 4 BB18 200 B3
Brogden View BB18 200 A4
Broken Bank Head BB7 229 A2
Broken Banks BB8 169 E4
Broken Stone Rd BB2,BB3 80 A6
Bromilow Rd WN8 17 C1
Bromley Cl FY2 150 E1
Bromley Cross BL7 47 B1
Bromley Ct 5 FY2 150 E1
Bromley Gn PR6 60 F4
Bromley Ho BB2 100 C5
Bromley Rd FY8 88 F6
Bromley St Blackburn BB2 100 C5
Preston PR1 95 D8
Brompton Ave L33 1 A5
Brompton Cl FY8 89 D5
Brompton Rd
Poulton-le-F FY6 130 D8
Southport PR8 34 E7
Bromsgrove Ave FY2 150 C4
Bromsgrove Rd BB10 127 B8
Bronte Ave BB10 127 D6
Bronte Cl OL12 51 A1
Brood Ford Ct 1 OL10 32 F1
Brooden Dr BB10 147 C4
Brook Ave Maghull L31 5 E2
Morecambe LA3 212 C3
Scorton PR3 199 E7
Brook Croft PR2 116 B4
Brook Farm Cl L39 15 E4
Brook Field Sch FY6 151 F5
Brook Field Way BB18 201 B1
Brook Gr Cleveleys FY5 172 E4
Morecambe LA3 212 C3
Brook Hey PR4 73 F8
Brook Hey Dr L33 1 A3
Brook Hey Wlk L33 1 A3
Brook Ho PR8 34 C5
Brook La
Charnock Richard PR7 41 C4
Farington PR4,PR5 75 D6
Farington PR4,PR5 75 D7
Much Hoole PR4 73 E3
Ormskirk L39 15 E4
Brook Mdw PR4 115 F7
Brook Mill Ind Est PR4 112 B4
Brook Pl PR2 115 D2
Brook Rd
Lytham St Anne's FY8 90 C3
Morecambe LA3 212 C3
Brook Side L31 5 E1
Brook St Adlington PR6 43 A1
3 Barnoldswick BB18 200 B2
Blackburn BB2 100 B2
Blackpool FY4 129 E1
Bury BL9 32 A3
Clitheroe BB7 186 F1
Colne BB8 169 D5
Earby BB18 201 B2
Fleetwood FY7 172 E8
Haslingden BB4 84 B5
Higher Walton PR5 97 B3
Kirkham PR4 112 F6
Lancaster LA1 210 E7
Nelson BB9 147 E8
Oswaldtwistle BB5 102 E3
Padiham BB12 125 D7
Preston PR1 116 E2
Rishton BB1 123 B1
Southport PR9 53 D4
Wheelton PR6 61 A7
Brook St Ct 1 FY4 129 E1
Brook St N PR2 116 D3
Brook Terr PR3 178 F2
Brook Villas BB7 186 E5
Brookbank BB9 168 E4
Brookdale Adlington PR6 43 A1
Belmont BL7 45 C5
New Longton PR4 75 A6
Rochdale OL12 51 E3
Brookdale Ave FY5 150 E8
Brookdale Cl PR5 59 B6
Brooke Cl Accrington BB5 103 E2
Southport PR9 35 B7
Brooke St PR6 42 E7
Brookes La BB7 143 C5
Brookes St 7 OL13 69 D8
Brookes The 6 PR6 42 E7
Brookfield Croston PR5 57 B3
Mawdesley L40 39 C2
Mellor BB2 120 E2
Parbold WN8 26 C2
Brookfield Ave
Blackpool FY4 110 A6
Fulwood PR2 117 C4
Thornton FY5 173 C1
Brookfield Cl LA5 216 B5
Brookfield Ct PR3 182 E3
Brookfield Dr PR2 116 E8
Brookfield La L39 6 A5
Brookfield Pl PR5 77 A6
Brookfield Prim Sch PR2 117 E5
Brookfield Rd Orrell WN8 10 B7
Shevington Moor WN6 28 B2
Thornton FY5 173 C1
Brookfield St
2 Blackburn BB1 100 E6
4 Cornholme OL14 108 C1
Preston PR1 116 F1
Brookfield Terr
Hampson Green LA2 204 E8
Lytham St Anne's FY8 90 B4
Brookfield View LA5 216 B5
Brookfields Cty Prim Sch WN8 17 D2
Brookford Cl BB12 126 D8
Brookhouse Bsns Ctr 10 BB1 100 F6
Brookhouse Cl
Blackburn BB1 100 F6
Gregson Lane PR5 97 F2
Brookhouse Dr PR5 97 F2
Brookhouse Gdns 12 BB1 100 F6
Brookhouse La BB1 100 F6
Brookhouse Prim Sch BB1 100 F7
Brookhouse Rd Caton LA2 231 C3
Ormskirk L39 15 D6
Brookhouse St PR2 116 D1
Brookland LA6 236 C3
Brookland Cl BB5 123 F4
Brookland St BB4 85 D1
Brookland Terr BB4 68 F7
Brooklands Chipping PR3 182 F3
Horwich BL6 31 C3
Ormskirk L39 16 A6
Preston PR2 116 A1
Brooklands Ave
Burnley BB11 127 B3
Fulwood PR2 116 E7
Haslingden BB4 67 B7
Kirkham PR4 113 A5
Brooklands Ct LA1 211 A4
Brooklands Dr Bonds PR3 178 C6
Heysham LA3 208 F6
Orrell WN5 10 D5
Brooklands Gr L40 24 F3
Brooklands Rd
Burnley BB11 127 B3
Lytham St Anne's FY8 89 C6
Orrell WN8 10 C7
Ramsbottom BL0 49 A2
Brooklands Terr BB1 101 A7
Brooklands The PR4 112 B4
Brooklyn Ave FY3 129 E8
Brooklyn Rd BB1 121 F5
Brooks Rd L37 11 D2
Brooks Way L37 11 D2
Brooksbottom Cl BL0 49 C4
Brookshaw St BL9 32 A4
Brookside
Brockhall Village BB6 142 C5
Coppull PR7 41 F1
Euxton PR7 59 C2
Kirkham PR4 112 F6
Thornton FY5 173 C3
Brookside Cl Leyland PR5 75 E3
Ramsbottom BL0 49 A3
Whalley BB7 143 C5
Brookside Cotts PR7 61 D3
Brookside Cres
Ramsbottom BL8 48 E1
West Bradford BB7 186 D7
Brookside Ctr FY5 173 C3
Brookside Dr LA2 220 A8
Brookside Ind Est BB5 102 C3
Brookside La BB5 102 B3
Brookside Prim Sch BB7 164 F8
Brookside Rd
Fulwood PR2 116 D7
Southport PR8 34 C2
Standish WN1 29 B1
Brookside St BB5 102 C3
Brookside View BB5 102 B4
Brookvale Ct PR3 155 E3
Brookview PR2 117 B5
Brookville OL12 70 C1
Brookway Blackburn BB2 80 B8
Longton PR4 73 F8
Wrea Green PR4 112 A4
Broom Field PR3 178 D4
Broome Rd PR8 34 B3
Broomfield Mill St PR1 116 F1
Broomfield Pl
Blackburn BB2 100 B3
Standish WN6 28 E1
Broomfield Rd
Fleetwood FY7 193 F2
Standish WN6 28 E2
Broomflat Cl WN6 28 E1
Broomholme WN6 19 D7
Brotherod Hall Rd OL12 51 C2
Brothers St BB2 100 A1
Brotherton Mdws 6 BB7 164 F8
Brough Ave FY2 150 F2
Brougham St BB12 126 F7
Broughton Ave
Blackpool FY3 129 E7
Southport PR8 34 D4
Broughton Cl BB2 101 A1
Broughton Gr LA3 212 F3
Broughton High Sch PR3 136 C2
Broughton in Amounderness CE Prim Sch PR3 136 D1
Broughton St
1 Burnley BB12 126 D6
4 Darwen BB3 80 F2
Preston PR1 116 E2
Broughton Tower Way PR2 117 A8
Broughton Way FY6 151 C6
Brow Cl PR3 154 A6
Brow Edge BB4 85 D1
Brow Hey PR5 77 B6
Brow La LA2 233 F6
Brow The PR4 72 E4
Brow View BB10 127 B8
Browfoot Cl LA5 217 F2
Browgate BB7 187 F8
Browgill Pl 8 LA1 213 D2
Browhead Ct BB10 127 B8
Browhead Rd BB10 127 B8
Brown Birks Rd BB5 103 E8
Brown Birks St 15 OL14 108 B1
Brown Edge Cl PR8 35 A2
Brown Hill La BB8 169 F7
Brown Hill Row BB8 169 F7
Brown La
Bamber Bridge PR5 97 A2
Higher Walton PR5 97 A3
Brown Sq 9 BB11 127 A6
Brown St Accrington BB5 103 B5
Bacup OL13 86 F4
Bamber Bridge PR5 76 F8
Blackburn BB1 100 E5
Blackrod BL6 30 D2
Burnley BB11 126 F6
Chorley PR6 42 D8
Clitheroe BB7 164 D7
Fleetwood FY7 194 A3
2 Ramsbottom BL0 49 B5
Thornton FY5 173 B3
Brown St E BB8 169 D5
Brown St W BB8 169 C4
Brown's La Kirkham PR4 112 D3
Thornton FY6 173 E7
Brownedge Cl PR5 96 D1
Brownedge La PR5 96 E1
Brownedge Rd PR5 76 B8
Brownedge Saint Mary's RC High Sch PR5 96 E1
Brownedge Wlk PR5 96 D1
Brownhill Ave BB10 127 C6
Brownhill Dr BB1 122 A1
Brownhill La PR4 74 D7
Brownhill Rd
Blackburn BB1 121 F3
Leyland PR5 75 F1
Brownhill Sch OL12 51 E1
Browning Ave
4 Lytham St Anne's FY8 90 D4
Oswaldtwistle BB5 102 C5
3 Thornton FY5 173 A3
Browning Cl BB8 169 D6
Browning Cres PR1 117 D2
Browning Rd PR1 117 D2
Browning St BB3 81 F1
Brownley St Chorley PR6 42 E7
Clayton Green PR6 77 B1
Brownlow La WN5 10 C1
Brownlow Rd BL6 31 C5
Brownlow St
Blackburn BB1 101 D4
Clitheroe BB7 164 E7
Brownlow Terr BB2 99 C1
Brownroyd BB18 201 C2
Browns Hey PR7 60 A2
Brownside Mill BB10 127 F6
Brownside Rd BB10 127 F5
Brows Cl L37 11 E3
Brows La L37 11 E3
Browsholme LA1 213 C2
Browsholme Ave
Burnley BB10 127 C6
Fulwood PR2 117 F3
Browsholme Cl
Carnforth LA5 217 C1
Normoss FY3 130 B8
Browsholme Hall BB7 184 E7
Browsholme Rd BB7 223 C1
Broxfield Ct FY8 88 D6
Broxton Ave WN5 10 F7
Broyd View LA1 210 F5
Bruce St
5 Barnoldswick BB18 200 B3
Blackburn BB1 101 B6
Burnley BB11 126 D5
Brun Gr FY1 129 E1
Brun St BB11 126 F6
Brun Terr BB10 127 F5
Bruna La PR3 178 E4
Brundhurst Fold BB2 120 E2
Brunel Dr BB1 101 A4
Brunel St Burnley BB12 126 C7
Horwich BL6 31 C2
Brunel Way FY4 110 C7
Brunel Wlk BB1 100 F4
Brungerley Ave BB7 186 E1
Brunshaw Ave BB10 127 D5
Brunshaw Prim Sch BB10 127 D4
Brunshaw Rd BB10 127 D6
Brunswick Ave BL6 31 E2
Brunswick Dr BB8 169 A3
Brunswick Pl 4 PR2 116 C1
Brunswick Rd LA3 212 B3
Brunswick St
Blackburn BB2 100 D4
2 Blackpool FY1 129 B4
Burnley BB11 127 A4
2 Chorley PR6 42 D8
Darwen BB3 64 B8
Nelson BB9 147 E7
Brunswick Terr
Accrington BB5 103 B6
Bacup OL13 69 D8
Brunton Ho LA1 211 A5
Brunton Rd LA1 210 F6
Brunton's Warehouse LA1 213 E1
Brush St BB11 126 C5
Brussels Rd BB3 81 C1
Bryan Rd FY3 129 D5
Bryan St BB2 100 E2
Brydeck Ave PR1 95 E4
Bryer St 24 LA1 210 F8
Bryer's Croft BB1 121 F6
Bryn Gr LA2 215 E2
Bryning & Warton St Paul's CE Prim Sch PR4 91 D6
Bryning Ave Blackpool FY2 150 C4
Wrea Green PR4 112 B3
Bryning Fern La PR4 112 F4
Bryning Hall La
Saltcotes, Moss Side FY8 111 F1
Warton PR4 91 B8
Wrea Green FY8,PR4 112 A1
Bryning La
Newton-with-S PR4 113 F2
Wrea Green PR4 112 B2
Bryony Cl Cleveleys FY5 172 F5
Orrell WN5 10 D5
Bryony Ct LA3 212 E2
Buccleuch Ave BB7 164 D8
Buccleuch Cl BB7 164 D8
Buccleuch Rd 7 BB9 168 C1
Buccleuch St BB11 126 E5
Buchanan St
Blackpool FY1 129 C6
Chorley PR6 42 D7
7 Ramsbottom BL0 49 B6
Buck St Burnley BB11 126 E5
Colne BB8 169 E5
Grindleton BB7 187 B7
Buckden Cl FY5 172 C1
Buckden Gate BB9 168 C3
Buckden Pl LA3 208 F8
Buckden Rd 4 BB5 102 F4
Buckfast Dr L37 12 B2
Buckholes La PR6 78 C1
Buckhurst Rd BL9 50 C3
Buckingham Ave
Horwich BL6 31 E2
Penwortham PR1 95 E2
Buckingham Cl BB4 84 A1
Buckingham Dr BB12 144 D2
Buckingham Gr
Church BB5 102 F7
Formby L37 11 E1
Morecambe LA3 212 C3
Buckingham Pl LA3 212 C3
Buckingham Rd
Lytham St Anne's FY8 89 D4
Maghull L31 5 C1
Morecambe LA3,LA4 212 C3
Buckingham St PR6 42 D7
Buckingham Way FY6 151 C5
Bucklands Ave PR2 116 D2
Buckley Cres FY5 150 D7
Bucknell Pl FY5 150 F7
Buckshaw Cty Prim Sch PR7 60 A2
Buckshaw Hall Cl PR7 60 B2
Buckshaw Terr BB12 144 E2
Buckton Cl PR6 60 C6
Bude Cl PR4 115 F6
Buff St 3 BB3 64 A8
Buffalo Rd PR5 76 A4
Bulcock St BB10 147 C1
Bulk Rd LA1 214 A1
Bulk St LA1 210 F8
Bull Cop L37 12 B3
Bull Park La FY6 152 C8
Bull St BB11 127 A6
Bullens La L40 22 E7
Buller Ave PR1 95 E4
Buller St 1 Lancaster LA1 213 F3
Rawtenstall BB4 85 A2
Bullfinch Dr BL9 32 B5
Bullfinch St 3 PR1 117 B1
Bullion The BB12 167 C5
Bullough Cl BB5 103 A5
Bulmer St PR2 116 C2
Buncer La BB2 100 A4
Bungalows The
Burnley BB11 126 F4
9 Earby BB18 201 B1
Great Eccleston PR3 154 C5
Bunker St PR4 92 C6
Bunkers Hill Cl BB2 80 B8
Bunting Pl 9 FY5 172 F1
Bunyan St 24 OL12 51 F1
Buoymaster 5 LA1 213 E1
Burbank Cl FY4 109 F5
Burdett St BB11 126 D5
Burdock Wlk LA3 212 E2
Burford Cl Blackburn BB2 79 E8
Blackpool FY3 130 A7
Burford Dr LA3 209 A7
Burgate FY4 109 D5
Burgess Ave FY4 109 E7
Burgess Gdns L31 5 C2
Burgess St
2 Blackburn BB1 101 C5
6 Haslingden BB4 84 B3
Burgess' La L37 13 A2
Burgh Hall Rd PR7 42 A3
Burgh La PR7 42 C4
Burgh La S PR7 42 B2
Burgh Mdws PR7 42 C4
Burghley Brow PR3 178 D1
Burghley Cl PR6 77 C2
Burghley Ct 4 PR5 76 B1
Burgundy Cres FY5 150 F7
Burholme Cl PR2 118 A2
Burholme Pl PR2 118 A2
Burholme Rd PR2 118 A2
Burleigh PR1 95 E7
Burleigh Rd 7 PR1 95 E7
Burleigh St BB12 126 F7
Burlington Ave Formby L37 12 B3
Morecambe LA4 212 G5
Burlington Ct FY4 109 B7
Burlington Ctr The FY8 88 E6
Burlington Gdns PR5 59 B8
Burlington Gr LA4 212 G5
Burlington Rd
Blackpool FY4 109 B6
Southport PR8 33 F3
Burlington Rd W FY4 109 A6
Burlington St
Blackburn BB2 100 C5
Chorley PR7 42 D7
Nelson BB9 147 C7
Burn Gr FY5 172 E4
Burn Naze Cty Prim Sch FY5 173 B3
Burnage Gdns FY4 109 D7
Burned House La FY6 195 D2
Burnedge Cl OL12 70 D2
Burneside Cl LA4 212 F4
Burnfell Rd 1 LA1 213 D2
Burnham Cl BB11 126 E5
Burnham Ct Blackpool FY3 129 E5
Morecambe LA3 212 B1
Burnham Gate BB11 126 D5
Burnham Trad Pk 4 BB11 126 E6
Burnley Ave PR8 20 D5
Burnley Barracks Sta BB12 126 E6
Burnley Bsns Ctr 7 BB11 127 A6
Burnley Central Sta BB12 126 F7
Burnley Cl BB1 101 B5
Burnley Coll of Art & Tech BB11 127 A7
Burnley General Hospl BB10 147 C2
Burnley La BB11,BB5 125 A2
Burnley Rd
Accrington, Hillock Vale BB5 103 D8
9 Accrington, Lower Fold BB5 103 C6
Baldingstone BL9 49 E1
Blackburn BB1 101 C6
Brierfield BB10,BB9 147 B5
Brierfield, Harle Syke BB10 147 F3
Burnley BB10,BB11 127 D1
Clayton-le-M BB5 124 C5
Colne BB8,BB9 169 B3
Edenfield BL0 67 D5
Gisburn BB7 225 B3
Hapton BB11 125 B1
Holme Chapel BB10,OL14,BB11,OL13 107 C4
Padiham BB12 125 D8
Rawtenstall, Goodshaw Fold BB4 105 A2
Rawtenstall, Reeds Holme BB4 84 F5
Southport PR8 20 C5
Trawden BB8 170 B1
Weir BB11,BB4 106 C3
Whalley BB6 143 F3
Burnley Rd E
Rawtenstall BB4 68 E8
Water BB4 106 A2
Whitewell Bottom BB4 85 F4
Burnley St BB1 101 C5
Burnley Wood Prim Sch BB11 127 B4
Burns Ave
Lytham St Anne's FY8 90 D4
Oswaldtwistle BB5 102 D5
Thornton FY5 173 A3
Burns Cl WN5 10 D1
Burns Dr BB5 103 E2
Burns Pl FY4 109 F8

Burns Rd FY7 194 A5
Burns St Burnley BB12 126 F7
Hapton BB12 125 C4
Nelson BB9 168 D1
Padiham BB12 125 D7
Preston PR1 117 D2
Burns Way BB6 123 B4
Burns Wlk BB3 81 B1
Burnsall Ave
Blackpool FY3 151 A1
Heysham LA3 208 F8
Burnsall Cl BB10 147 E3
Burnsall Pl
Barrowford BB9 168 C3
Fulwood PR2 117 E4
Burnsall Rd 2 BB5 102 F4
Burnside Edenfield BL0 67 D2
Parbold WN8 26 B2
Burnside Ave
Blackpool FY4 109 E8
Calder Vale PR3 179 E8
Fleetwood FY7 193 C2
Fulwood PR2 117 F3
Burnside Way PR1 95 D3
Burnslack Rd PR2 117 F3
Burntbarrow LA7 237 F4
Burrans Mdw 15 BB8 169 D4
Burrell Ave BB8 169 D6
Burrington Cl PR2 117 D6
Burrow Heights La LA2 206 F8
Burrow Rd
Over Burrow LA6 235 E7
Preston PR1 117 A1
Burrow's La FY6 173 F5
Burscough Bridge Meth Prim Sch L40 24 E5
Burscough Bridge Sta L40 24 E5
Burscough Cty Prim Sch L40 24 F5
Burscough Ind Est L40 24 B5
Burscough Junc Sta L40 24 F4
Burscough Lordsgate Township CE Prim Sch L40 24 E3
Burscough RC Prim Sch L40 24 E2
Burscough Rd L39 15 F7
Burscough St L39 15 F6
Burton Ave LA1 213 C3
Burton Ct FY7 172 C8
Burton Gdns BB9 147 B5
Burton Hill LA6 236 C3
Burton Morewood Prim Sch LA6 234 C7
Burton Pk LA6 234 B7
Burton Rd Blackpool FY4 129 F1
Burton in L LA2 236 C1
Low Bentham LA2 233 B8
Burton St Burnley BB11 127 B5
Rishton BB1 123 C1
Burwains Ave BB8 191 D1
Burwell Ave Coppull PR7 28 D8
Formby L37 11 D1
Burwell Cl Kirkby L33 1 A3
Rochdale OL12 51 D4
Burwen Castle Rd BD23 201 F8
Burwen Cl BB11 126 D3
Burwood Cl 5 PR1 95 F2
Burwood Dr Blackpool FY3 130 A6
Fulwood PR2 117 E3
Bury Bsns Ctr BL9 32 A4
Bury Fold La BB3 64 A6
Bury La PR6 78 F3
Bury New Rd
Heywood BL9,OL10 32 E2
Ramsbottom BL0 49 D6
Bury Old Rd Edenfield BL0 67 F1
Heywood BL9,OL10 32 E1
Nangreaves BL0,BL9 49 F4
Bury Rd Edenfield BL0 67 D3
Edgworth BL7 47 E3
Haslingden BB4 84 B3
Rawtenstall BB4 67 E7
Southport PR8 34 B3
Bury Row BB7 144 F8
Bury St Darwen BB3 81 A1
Oswaldtwistle BB5 102 D3
Buseph Barrow LA4 213 B4
Buseph Ct LA4 213 B4
Buseph Dr LA4 213 B4
Bush La Freckleton PR4 92 B5
Freckleton PR4 92 B6
Bush St BB10 147 B1
Bushburn Dr BB6 142 C1
Bushby's La L37 11 C2
Bushby's Pk L37 11 D2
Bushell Pl PR1 96 A6
Bushell St PR1 116 F1
Bushell's Hosp PR3 137 E6
Bushey La WA11 8 E2
Bussel Rd PR1 95 E2
Butcher Brow PR5 96 E5
Butchers La L39 6 B3
Bute Ave FY1 129 B7
Bute Rd BB1 101 D3
Bute St BB11 126 D3
Butler Pl PR1 116 F2
Butler Rd FY1 129 B3
Butler St Blackpool FY1 129 C6
7 Burnley BB10 127 A8
Preston PR1 95 F7
Ramsbottom BL0 49 A5
Rishton BB1 123 C1
Butlers Mdw PR4 91 E6
Butt Hill La PR3 179 E4
Butt's La PR3 154 B5
Buttercross Cl BB11 126 D2
Butterfield Gdns L39 15 D3
Butterfield St
2 Barrowford BB9 168 D3
2 Lancaster LA1 210 F8
Butterfly Ho LA1 211 B7
Butterlands PR1 96 F8
Buttermere Ave
Chorley PR7 42 B6
Colne BB8 169 F6
Fleetwood FY7 193 C2
2 Morecambe LA4 212 G4
Buttermere Cl
1 Bamber Bridge PR5 96 E2
5 Blackburn BB1 100 F6
Formby L37 11 D3
Fulwood PR2 117 C4
Maghull L31 5 E1
Buttermere Cres WA11 8 F2
Buttermere Ct LA1 214 B1
Buttermere Dr
Knott End-on-S FY6 194 F5
Oswaldtwistle BB5 102 D5
Ramsbottom BL0 49 B7
Buttermere Rd
Burnley BB10 127 F5
Lancaster LA1 214 B1
Longridge PR3 138 F5
Butterworth Brow
Brinscall PR6 62 A7
Chorley PR7 42 A4
Butterworth Cl PR4 113 A6
Buttons Row BB4 68 F6
Butts Barnoldswick BB18 200 B2
Great Harwood BB6 123 B5
Butts Cl FY5 173 C4
Butts Gr BB7 186 E2
Butts La High Bentham LA2 233 E8
Southport PR8 34 F5
Butts Mount BB6 123 C5
Butts Rd FY5 173 C4
Buxton Ave FY2 150 D4
Buxton St Accrington BB5 103 A5
Morecambe LA4 212 F4
Whitworth OL12 70 D3
Bye La L39 14 C3
Bye Rd BL0 49 E8
Bye-Pass Rd LA5 216 A4
Byerworth La N PR3 178 C5
Byerworth La S PR3 178 C4
Byfield Ave FY5 150 E7
Byland Cl Blackpool FY4 109 C5
Formby L37 12 B2
Read BB12 144 D1
Bymbrig Cl PR5 76 E8
Byrom St Blackburn BB2 100 D4
Southport PR9 34 F7
Byron Ave Bolton-le-S LA5 216 A5
Lytham St Anne's FY8 90 D4
Thornton FY5 173 A3
Warton PR4 91 E6
Byron Cl Accrington BB5 103 E2
Formby L37 11 F4
3 Orrell WN5 10 F7
Oswaldtwistle BB5 102 C5
Tarleton PR4 55 F5
Byron Cres PR7 28 F8
Byron Gr BB18 200 A3
Byron Rd Colne BB8 169 F5
Maghull L31 5 D3
Morecambe LA3 212 B3
Ramsbottom BL8 48 F2
Byron Sq BB6 123 B4
Byron St Blackpool FY4 129 B1
Chorley PR6 42 D8
Fleetwood FY7 194 A5
Padiham BB12 125 F7
Byron Terr BB2 100 B3
Byton Wlk L33 1 A4

C

Cabin End Row BB1 101 E4
Cabin Hill BB2 99 B2
Cabin La Holmeswood L40 37 A6
Maghull L31 4 F4
Southport, Churchtown Moss PR9 53 F3
Southport, Halsall Moss L39 21 C5
Cable St Formby L37 12 A4
Lancaster LA1 210 F8
Southport PR8 34 F7
Cabus Cross Roads PR3 199 A5
Cabus Nook La PR3 199 B6
Cadby Ave FY3 129 F3
Cadley Ave PR2 116 B3
Cadley Cswy PR2 116 C4
Cadley Dr PR2 116 B3
Cadogan Pl 5 PR1 96 A6
Cadogan St BB9 168 D2
Cadshaw Cl BB1 100 E8
Cadwell Rd L31 5 B5
Caernarfon Cl FY5 173 D2
Caernarvon Ave BB12 126 A7
Caernarvon Cl BL8 48 F1
Caernarvon Rd BB4 84 A1
Cage La PR4 75 B8
Cairn Ct 5 FY4 109 C5
Cairn Gr FY4 109 C4
Cairndale Dr PR5 59 B6
Cairns Cl BB9 168 C3
Cairnsmore Ave PR1 117 F1
Cairo St BB12 126 D6
Caister Cl WN8 9 E8
Calcott St BB11 126 E2
Caldbeck Cl BB9 147 E6
Caldbeck Rd LA1 214 B1
Calder Ave Billington BB7 143 A4
Chorley PR7 42 B5
Cleveleys FY5 172 F2
Darwen BB3 80 D4
Fleetwood FY7 193 D3
Freckleton PR4 92 A5
Fulwood PR2 116 F6
Longridge PR3 139 A8
Ormskirk L39 15 E4
Whalley BB7 143 A7
Withnell PR6 79 A1
Calder Banks BB1 100 F7
Calder Cl Bury BL9 32 A8
Carnforth LA5 217 B1
Kirkby L33 1 A6
Kirkham PR4 113 C5
Lytham St Anne's FY8 109 F2
Nelson BB9 168 D1
Calder Ct BB5 124 E6
Calder Dr Catterall PR3 178 D2
Lancaster LA3 213 B2
Maghull L31 5 F2
Calder House La PR3 178 D4
Calder Pl BB6 123 E6
Calder Rd Blackpool FY2 150 C1
Rawtenstall BB4 85 A4
Calder St Blackburn BB1 100 F7
Burnley BB11 126 F6
Colne BB8 169 C4
Nelson BB9 168 D1
Padiham BB12 125 C8
Preston PR2 116 C1
Calder Terr BB9 147 B8
Calder Vale
Barrowford BB9 168 D2
Whalley BB7 143 C4
Calder Vale Rd BB12 126 F6
Calder View BB9 168 E5
Calderbank Cl 1 PR5 75 A1
Calderbrook Ave BB11 126 E3
Calderbrook Pl BB11 126 E3
Calderdale Way OL14 108 F1
Caldershaw Ctr The OL12 51 B2
Caldershaw La OL12 51 A2
Caldershaw Prim Sch OL12 51 A1
Caldershaw Rd OL11,OL12 51 A1
Calderstones Hospl BB7 143 A7
Caldervale Ave FY6 151 C3
Calderview Sch BB12 126 F8
Caldew Ct BB5 103 E8
Caldicott Way FY6 151 C6
Caldy Dr BL8 49 A3
Caleb St 6 BB9 168 E1
Caledonian Ave 1 FY3 129 E7
Calendar St 1 BB1 100 E5
Calendine Cl FY5 172 F5
Calf Croft Pl FY8 90 A4
Calf Hall La BB18 200 A2
Calf Hall Rd BB18 200 A2
Calf Hey BB5 123 F4
Calf Hey Rd BB4 83 B2
Calfcote La PR3 139 B7
Calgary Ave BB2 100 B8
Calico Cl BB5 102 B4
Calico Dr PR3 178 D3
Calico St BB2 100 D1
Calico Wood Ave WN6 19 F6
Calkeld La 7 LA1 210 F8
Calla Dr PR3 178 C8
Callander Sq OL10 32 F1
Callender St BL0 49 B6
Callon St PR1 96 E8
Caltha St 8 BL0 49 B6
Calva Cl BB12 126 B8
Calverley St 6 PR1 117 D1
Calverley Way OL12 51 E4
Calvert Ct PR5 96 D5
Calvert Pl FY3 130 A7
Cam Cl 1 PR5 76 F8
Cam La Clayton Green PR6 77 A4
Thornton-in-C BD23 201 B6
Cam St PR1 117 C2
Cam Wood Fold PR6 77 A3
Cambell's Ct FY8 88 E7
Camberley Cl PR8 33 E5
Camborne Ave LA5 216 C8
Camborne Ct FY3 130 B2
Camborne Pl PR4 92 B6
Cambray Rd FY1 150 C1
Cambrian Cl BB1 121 F3
Cambrian Way BB4 84 B1
Cambridge Arc 5 PR8 34 B7
Cambridge Ave
Lancaster LA1 211 B5
Southport PR9 52 F2
Cambridge Cl
Blackburn BB1 100 F4
Padiham BB12 125 D6
Preston PR1 116 E2
Cambridge Ct
Preston PR1 116 F2
Southport PR9 52 F2
Cambridge Dr
Blackburn BB1 101 E4
Garstang PR3 178 B7
Padiham BB12 125 D6
Cambridge Gdns PR9 52 F2
Cambridge Rd
9 Bamber Bridge PR5 76 F8
Blackpool FY1 129 D5
Cleveleys FY5 172 C3
Fleetwood FY7 193 E3
Formby L37 11 D1
Lytham St Anne's FY8 89 E3
Morecambe LA3 212 B3
Orrell WN5 10 F8
Cambridge Rd *continued*
Skelmersdale WN8 17 E1
Southport PR9 52 E2
Cambridge St
Accrington BB5 103 D6
Blackburn BB1 100 F4
Brierfield BB9 147 B5
2 Burnley BB11 126 D5
10 Chorley PR7 42 C7
9 Colne BB8 169 D4
Darwen BB3 81 C1
Great Harwood BB6 123 D5
Haslingden BB4 84 B1
Nelson BB9 147 D7
Preston PR1 116 E2
Cambridge Wlk PR1 116 E2
Cambridge Wlks 6 PR8 34 B7
Camden Pl PR1 95 F6
Camden Rd FY3 129 E6
Camden St 11
Barrowford BB9 168 D3
Nelson BB9 147 D7
Camellia Dr PR5 76 E2
Cameron Ave FY3 129 E7
Cameron Croft 6 PR6 42 D8
Cameron St BB10 147 A1
Camforth Hall La PR3 138 A7
Camms View BB4 67 A8
Camomine Cl PR7 60 A3
Camp St BB10 147 E3
Campbell Ave 2 FY3 129 E7
Campbell St
Blackburn BB1 121 F1
4 Padiham BB12 125 F7
Preston PR1 96 B8
Read BB12 144 D1
Rochdale OL12 51 E2
Campion Cl FY5 172 F5
Campion Ct BB5 102 E4
Campion Dr Haslingden BB4 67 A8
Preston PR2 115 C1
Campion Way
Morecambe LA3 212 E2
Rochdale OL12 51 C3
Campions The PR2 115 C1
Camwood PR5 77 B4
Camwood Dr PR5 96 B1
Canada Cres FY2 150 E3
Canada St BL6 31 B3
Canal Bank
Appley Bridge WN6 19 C7
New Lane L40 24 B6
Ring o'Bells L40 25 C2
Canal Bank Cotts L31 5 C7
Canal Bank Pygons Hill L31 5 C7
Canal Gdns LA5 216 B6
Canal Leach Cotts PR5 56 F6
Canal Mews 1 BB9 147 D8
Canal Pl LA5 217 E1
Canal Row WN2 29 D1
Canal Side BB9 168 D2
Canal St Adlington PR7 30 A6
Blackburn BB2 100 B1
19 Burnley BB11 126 F6
Church BB5 102 E6
Clayton-le-M BB5 123 F2
Canal Wlk PR6 42 F8
Canalside BB1 100 F3
Canberra Cl FY5 150 F7
Canberra Rd PR5 59 B8
Canberraway PR4 91 E7
Candlemakers Ct BB7 164 E8
Candlestick Pk BL9 32 D4
Cann Bridge St PR5 97 B4
Canning Rd PR9 35 A6
Canning St Burnley BB12 126 F7
Padiham BB12 125 D7
Cannock Ave FY3 129 E8
Cannock Gn L31 5 B1
Cannon Hill PR2 116 C1
Cannon St Accrington BB5 103 B5
11 Chorley PR7 42 C8
10 Nelson BB9 168 F1
Preston PR1 95 F7
6 Ramsbottom BL0 49 A4
Canon Cl WN6 28 F2
Canon St BL9 32 A4
Canterbury Ave
Blackpool FY3 129 F3
Lancaster LA1 211 B5
Canterbury Cl Brinscall PR6 61 E8
Carleton FY6 151 C5
Formby L37 11 F5
Garstang PR3 178 A7
Southport PR8 33 F4
Canterbury Rd 11 PR1 117 D1
Canterbury St
Blackburn BB2 100 E4
Chorley PR6 42 E6
Canterbury Way PR3 178 B7
Cantlow Fold PR8 20 A4
Cantsfield Ave PR2 116 B4
Canute St PR1 117 A1
Cape St BB4 85 A2
Capernwray Ct LA6 234 D3
Capernwray Rd LA6 234 B2
Capilano Pk L39 6 C8
Capitol Trad Est L33 1 C2
Capitol Way PR1,PR5 96 C5
Cappleside Cotts BD24 230 E6
Capstan Cl FY8 109 E1
Captain St Horwich BL6 31 B4
Weir OL13 87 A7
Captain's Row 1 LA1 213 F1
Carawood Cl WN6 19 D7
Carcroft Ave FY2 150 D4
Cardale PR4 94 D2
Cardiff St WN8 17 D1
Cardigan Ave
Burnley BB12 126 A7
10 Clitheroe BB7 164 E8
Oswaldtwistle BB5 102 C4
Cardigan Cl 1 BB7 164 D8
Cardigan Pl FY4 109 A5
Cardigan Rd PR8 33 F1
Cardigan St Preston PR2 116 D1
Rochdale OL12 51 E3
Cardinal Allen RC High Sch FY7 172 E8
Cardinal Gdns FY8 89 D6
Cardinal Newman Coll PR1 96 B7
Cardinal Pl FY5 172 E3
Cardinal St BB10 147 B1
Cardwell Cl PR4 91 D5
Cardwell Pl BB2 100 E5
Cardwell St BB12 125 D7
Carfax Fold OL12 51 B2
Carfax Rd L33 1 A4
Carfield WN8 9 E6
Carham Rd BB1 100 E8
Carholme Ave BB10 127 C6
Carisbrooke Ave FY4 110 A7
Carisbrooke Cl FY6 151 C6
Carisbrooke Dr PR9 52 F1
Carl Oway Ave PR2 117 C5
Carl's Way L33 1 A6
Carleton Ave
Blackpool FY3 150 F1
Fulwood PR2 117 D4
Simonstone BB12 144 E2
Carleton Dr PR1 95 A4
Carleton Gate FY6 151 C4
Carleton Gdns FY6 151 B5
Carleton Green Cty Prim Sch FY6 151 C6
Carleton Rd
Great Knowley PR6 60 F3
Nelson BB8 169 A3
Carleton Sch FY6 151 B5
Carleton St
Morecambe LA4 212 D4
Nelson BB9 147 E7
Carleton Way FY6 151 B5
Carley St BB3 80 E2
Carlin Gate FY2 150 B2
Carlinghurst Rd BB2 100 D4
Carlisle Ave
Fleetwood FY7 193 D1
Penwortham PR1 95 A4
Carlisle Gr 1 FY5 173 B2
Carlisle Ho 36 PR1 96 A7
Carlisle Pl PR6 30 A8
Carlisle Rd Accrington BB5 103 D7
Southport PR8 34 A2
Carlisle St Blackburn BB1 100 F4
Preston PR1 96 A8
Rochdale OL12 51 E3
Carlisle Terr LA5 217 D3
Carlton Ave
Clayton Green PR6 77 B2
Orrell WN8 10 A7
Carlton Cl BL6 30 D2
Carlton Ct BB8 169 B5
Carlton Dr PR1 96 B5
Carlton Gdns BB1 100 E6
Carlton Gr Blackpool FY2 150 B4
Horwich BL6 31 D1
Carlton Pl BB7 164 F7
Carlton Rd Blackburn BB1 100 E6
Burnley BB11 126 E5
Leyland PR5 58 F8
Lytham St Anne's FY8 88 F7
Southport PR8 20 C6
Carlton St Bacup OL13 87 A3
Brierfield BB9 147 B5
Preston PR2 95 D8
Carluke St BB1 101 C5
Carlyle Ave FY4 109 B6
Carlyle St BB10 147 C3
Carmel Cl L39 15 D2
Carnarvon Rd
Blackburn BB2 100 B5
3 Preston PR1 95 D7
Southport PR8 33 F1
Carneghie Ct PR8 33 F4
Carnfield Pl PR5 77 B8
Carnforth Ave FY2 150 E5
Carnforth Brow LA5 217 F2
Carnforth Cl BB2 101 A1
Carnforth Dr BL8 49 A2
Carnforth High Sch LA5 217 E1
Carnforth Sta LA5 217 D2
Carnoustie Cl PR2 116 B7
Carnoustie Ct PR1 95 A6
Carnoustie Dr BL0 49 B5
Caroline Cl LA3 208 F8
Caroline Ct BB11 126 B4
Caroline St
6 Blackpool FY1 129 B3
Preston PR1 96 C8
Carr Bank Ave BL0 49 B7
Carr Bank Dr BL0 49 B7
Carr Bank Rd
Ramsbottom BL0 49 B7
Storth LA7 237 E2
Carr Barn Brow PR5 77 C6
Carr Brook Cl PR6 60 B8
Carr Cl Cold Row FY6 174 C4
Poulton-le-F FY6 151 E2
Smallwood Hey PR3 196 C5
Carr Dr PR4 112 E7
Carr End La FY6 174 C6
Carr Field PR5 77 C4
Carr Fold BL0 49 B7
Carr Gate FY5 172 C4

Carr Hall Dr BB9 . . . . .168 C1
Carr Hall Gdns BB9 . . . . . . .168 B1
Carr Hall Rd BB9 . . . . .168 B1
Carr Hall St BB4 . . . . .84 A5
Carr Head BB8 . . . . .170 C2
Carr Head La FY6 . . . . .151 E2
Carr Hey 5 FY5 . . . . .173 A2
Carr Hill High Sch PR4 . . . .113 B4
Carr House La
Bretherton PR5 . . . . .56 D6
Heskin Green WN6 . . . . .40 F1
Ince Blundell L38 . . . . .3 E4
Lancaster LA1 . . . . .210 E7
Carr La Blackburn BB2 . . . . . . .99 F6
Chorley PR7 . . . . .42 D5
Cold Row FY6 . . . . .174 C4
Croston PR5 . . . . .39 B8
Heysham LA3 . . . . .208 E7
Kirkham PR4 . . . . .113 C6
Leyland PR5 . . . . .76 A3
Maghull L31 . . . . .4 F5
Middleton LA3 . . . . .208 F1
Much Hoole PR4 . . . . .74 A1
Rawtenstall, Hall Carr BB4 . . . .85 A1
Rawtenstall, Hugh Mill BB4 . . .68 F7
Ring o'Bells L40 . . . . .25 B3
Singleton FY6 . . . . .152 C1
Smallwood Hey PR3 . . . . .196 C4
Southport PR8 . . . . .20 F7
Tarleton PR4 . . . . .55 F7
Warton PR4 . . . . .91 B6
Carr Mdw PR5 . . . . .77 C6
Carr Mill St BB4 . . . . .84 B5
Carr Moss La Haskayne L39 . .14 B8
Southport L39 . . . . .21 D2
Carr Mount 7 BB4 . . . . .84 F1
Carr Pl PR5 . . . . .77 B7
Carr Rd Barnoldswick BB18 . .200 A3
Blackpool FY5 . . . . .150 D6
Burnley BB11 . . . . .126 E3
Clayton Green PR6 . . . . .77 B2
Colne BB8 . . . . .169 E6
Cornholme OL14 . . . . .107 F1
Darwen BB3 . . . . .64 B8
Fleetwood FY7 . . . . .194 A4
Hambleton FY6 . . . . .174 C2
Horwich BL6 . . . . .31 B5
Kirkham PR4 . . . . .113 B4
Nelson BB9 . . . . .168 C1
Rawtenstall BB4 . . . . .84 F1
Water BB4 . . . . .86 C7
Carr Royd Est FY6 . . . . .152 A3
Carr Side La L29 . . . . .4 A3
Carr St Bamber Bridge PR5 . . .76 E8
Blackburn BB1 . . . . .100 E6
Chorley PR6 . . . . .60 E1
Preston PR1 . . . . .96 B7
Ramsbottom BL0 . . . . .49 B7
Carr View BB8 . . . . .170 C1
Carr's Cres L37 . . . . .11 E1
Carr's Cres W L37 . . . . .11 D1
Carradice Cl BB9 . . . . .147 D8
Carradon Dr WN6 . . . . .28 E1
Carrfield Villas 4 OL14 . . . .108 A1
Carrick Mews FY3 . . . . .130 B2
Carrier's Row BB8 . . . . .170 E6
Carrington Ave BB2 . . . . .80 C8
Carrington Gr LA4 . . . . .213 A5
Carrington Rd
Adlington PR7 . . . . .29 F7
Chorley PR7 . . . . .42 C7
Carrol St PR1 . . . . .117 B1
Carroll Cres L39 . . . . .15 F7
Carron La PR3 . . . . .158 A4
Carrs Croft BB7 . . . . .188 E8
Carrs Ind Est BB4 . . . . .84 A4
Carrs Wood BB2 . . . . .99 F6
Carrside BB9 . . . . .147 B8
Carrwood Dr PR4 . . . . .113 B4
Carrwood Gn BB12 . . . . .125 C8
Carrwood Hey BL0 . . . . .49 A4
Carrwood Pk PR8 . . . . .34 B4
Carrwood Rd PR1,PR5 . . . . . . .96 B3
Carrwood Way PR5 . . . . .96 B2
Carry La BB8 . . . . .169 E4
Carshalton Rd FY1 . . . . .129 B8
Carsluith Ave FY3 . . . . .129 F3
Carson Rd FY4 . . . . .130 A1
Cart Gate FY6 . . . . .195 B3
Carter Ave BB11 . . . . .125 C4
Carter Fold BB2 . . . . .120 E2
Carter St Accrington BB5 . . .103 B4
7 Blackpool FY1 . . . . .129 B5
Burnley BB12 . . . . .126 C7
Carter's Charity Prim Sch
FY6 .195 C7
Carter's La BB7 . . . . .225 A5
Carterville Cl FY4 . . . . .110 A7
Cartford Cl PR3 . . . . .154 A6
Cartford La PR3 . . . . .154 A6
Cartmel Ave
Accrington BB5 . . . . .103 A3
Fleetwood FY7 . . . . .193 D1
Maghull L31 . . . . .5 E2
Cartmel Cl PR8 . . . . .34 F3
Cartmel Dr Burnley BB12 . . .126 B8
Coupe Green PR5 . . . . .97 E4
Formby L37 . . . . .12 B2
Cartmel Pl
Morecambe LA4 . . . . .212 G4
Preston PR2 . . . . .115 E2
Cartmel Rd Blackburn BB2 . .100 A3
Lancaster LA1 . . . . .214 B2
Leyland PR5 . . . . .58 D8
Cartmell La Nateby PR3 . . . .177 C7
Saltcotes, Moss Side FY8 . . . . .90 E8
Cartmell Rd Blackpool FY4 . .130 D1
Lytham St Anne's FY8 . . . . .88 F5
Cartwright Ct LA1 . . . . .210 E5
Carus Ave BB3 . . . . .81 E1
Carus Pk LA6 . . . . .235 B2
Carus St BB3 . . . . .81 F1
Carvers Brow PR5 . . . . .57 B1
Carwags La PR3 . . . . .159 C8
Carwood Gr BL6 . . . . .31 D1
Carwood La PR6 . . . . .60 C8
Caryl Rd FY8 . . . . .88 D8
Caryle Gr LA4 . . . . .213 A6
Casserley Rd BB8 . . . . .169 F6
Casson Gate OL12 . . . . .51 E1
Castercliff Bank BB8 . . . . . .169 C3
Castercliffe Cty Prim Sch
BB9 .169 B1
Castercliffe Rd BB9 . . . . . . .148 B8
Casterton PR7 . . . . .59 C2
Casterton Ave BB10 . . . . . . .147 C3
Casterton Prim Sch
BB10 . . . . .147 C3
Casterton Sch LA6 . . . . .238 F4
Castle Ave FY6 . . . . .151 B6
Castle Bank LA5 . . . . .218 C4
Castle Cl BB8 . . . . .169 E6
Castle Cres BL6 . . . . .31 C5
Castle Ct LA1 . . . . .210 E8
Castle Dr Adlington PR7 . . . . .29 E6
Formby L37 . . . . .11 F1
Castle Fold PR1 . . . . .95 F2
Castle Gate BB7 . . . . .164 E8
Castle Gr BL0 . . . . .49 A2
Castle Hill LA1 . . . . .210 E8
Castle Hill Rd BL9 . . . . .32 D5
Castle House La PR7 . . . . . . .29 E6
Castle La Bonds PR3 . . . . . . .178 D6
Staining FY3 . . . . .130 D5
Westhead L40 . . . . .16 E5
Castle Mount PR2 . . . . .116 F7
Castle Par 5 LA1 . . . . .210 E8
Castle Park Mews LA1 . . . . .210 E8
Castle Pk Hornby LA2 . . . . . .232 B7
Lancaster LA1 . . . . .210 E8
Castle Rd BB8 . . . . .170 A7
Castle St Brierfield BB9 . . . . .147 B6
Burnley BB12 . . . . .126 F7
6 Chorley PR7 . . . . .42 D7
Clitheroe BB7 . . . . .164 E8
7 Hapton BB12 . . . . .125 C4
Nelson BB9 . . . . .147 F8
Preston PR1 . . . . .116 F1
Ramsbottom BL9 . . . . .49 D2
Southport PR9 . . . . .34 B8
Castle Sta LA1 . . . . .210 E8
Castle The BB8 . . . . .170 A7
Castle View
Barnoldswick BB18 . . . . .200 B1
Clitheroe BB7 . . . . .164 E8
Castle Wlk Penwortham PR1 . .95 C7
Southport PR8 . . . . .34 A6
Castle Wlks PR5 . . . . .57 B2
Castlecroft Ave BL6 . . . . .30 D2
Castlegate FY1 . . . . .129 B1
Castlehey WN8 . . . . .9 E6
Castlerigg Dr BB12 . . . . . . .126 B8
Castlerigg Pl FY4 . . . . .130 C1
Castleton Rd PR1 . . . . .117 B1
Castletown Dr OL13 . . . . .87 B1
Cat Tail La PR8 . . . . .35 E1
Catches La OL11 . . . . .51 B1
Catforth Ave FY4 . . . . .130 B1
Catforth Cty Prim Sch
PR4 .135 A4
Catforth Rd Catforth PR4 . . .134 F5
Preston PR2 . . . . .115 E1
Catharine's La L39 . . . . .15 F1
Cathedral Dr LA3 . . . . .212 E2
Cathedral PC Prim Sch
LA1 .211 A7
Catherine Cl PR4 . . . . .112 F7
Catherine St
6 Chorley PR7 . . . . .42 C6
Kirkham PR4 . . . . .112 F6
5 Preston PR1 . . . . .96 B8
Catherine St E BL6 . . . . .31 B4
Catherine St W BL6 . . . . .31 B5
Cathrow Dr PR4 . . . . .75 A7
Catley Cl PR6 . . . . .60 C5
Catlow Hall St BB5 . . . . . . .102 E4
Catlow Terr BB7 . . . . .164 D1
Cato St 4 BL0 . . . . .49 A4
Caton Ave FY7 . . . . .193 D1
Caton Cl Clayton-le-W PR5 . . .76 E2
Longridge PR3 . . . . .139 B8
Southport PR9 . . . . .52 F4
Caton Gr FY3 . . . . .129 F7
Caton Green Rd LA2 . . . . . . .231 D3
Caton Prim Sch LA2 . . . . . . .231 C3
Caton Rd
Lancaster, Bulk LA1 . . . . .214 A1
Lancaster, Newton LA1 . . . . . .214 B4
Caton St Paul's
CE Prim Sch LA2 . . . . .231 D3
Cattan Gn L37 . . . . .12 B3
Catterall Cl FY1 . . . . .129 D7
Catterall Gates La PR3 . . . .178 C3
Catterall La PR3 . . . . .178 C1
Catterall St BB2 . . . . .80 C8
Catterick Fold PR8 . . . . .34 F3
Cattle St BB6 . . . . .123 C5
Caunce Ave PR9 . . . . .54 A6
Caunce St FY1,FY3 . . . . .129 D6
Caunce's Rd PR9 . . . . .36 C5
Causeway Foulridge BB8 . . .191 D1
Great Harwood BB6 . . . . .123 B5
Causeway Ave PR2 . . . . .116 C4
Causeway Croft BB7 . . . . . . .186 F1
Causeway Head BB4 . . . . .67 A8
Causeway La Haskayne L37 . . .13 B1
Causeway La *continued*
Rufford L40 . . . . .38 B2
Causeway St 2 BB3 . . . . .64 C7
Causeway The
3 Chorley PR6 . . . . .42 E8
Southport PR9 . . . . .53 C5
Wymott PR5 . . . . .57 F6
Causey Foot BB9 . . . . .147 D7
Cavalry Way BB11 . . . . .126 D6
Cave St Blackburn BB2 . . . . .100 B1
2 Preston PR1 . . . . .96 D8
Cavendish Cres PR2 . . . . . .117 F3
Cavendish Ct
Bolton-le-S LA5 . . . . .216 A5
Southport PR9 . . . . .34 E8
Cavendish Dr PR2 . . . . .117 F3
Cavendish Pl
6 Bamber Bridge PR5 . . . . . . .96 D3
Blackburn BB2 . . . . .100 B3
Cavendish Rd
Blackpool FY2 . . . . .150 C4
Lytham St Anne's FY8 . . . . .88 D8
Morecambe LA3 . . . . .212 B3
2 Preston PR1 . . . . .117 E1
Southport PR8 . . . . .33 F3
Cavendish St
Barnoldswick BB18 . . . . .200 B1
1 Chorley PR6 . . . . .42 E7
Darwen BB3 . . . . .80 F3
Lancaster LA1 . . . . .210 D8
Cavendish Wlk PR9 . . . . .34 E8
Cavour St BB12 . . . . .126 F7
Cawthorne Endowed
Prim Sch LA2 . . . . .226 F1
Cawthorne St LA1 . . . . .210 E8
Caxton Ave FY2 . . . . .150 C5
Caxton Rd PR2 . . . . .117 B8
Cecil Ct FY8 . . . . .90 A3
Cecil St Barnoldswick BB18 . .200 B3
Blackpool FY1 . . . . .129 C7
4 Lytham St Anne's FY8 . . . . .90 A3
Oswaldtwistle BB5 . . . . .102 E4
Rishton BB1 . . . . .123 C2
Cecilia Rd BB2 . . . . .100 A2
Cecilia St PR1 . . . . .117 D1
Cedar Ave
5 Bamber Bridge PR5 . . . . . . .76 B8
Cleveleys FY5 . . . . .172 E2
Euxton PR7 . . . . .59 C4
Fleetwood FY7 . . . . .172 E8
Haslingden BB4 . . . . .84 C3
Horwich BL6 . . . . .31 E1
Knott End-on-S FY6 . . . . .195 A5
Poulton-le-F FY6 . . . . .130 D8
Preston PR2 . . . . .116 A2
Rawtenstall BB4 . . . . .84 E2
Warton PR4 . . . . .91 D6
Cedar Cl Garstang PR3 . . . . .178 B8
Grimsargh PR2 . . . . .138 D1
Newton-with-S PR4 . . . . .114 A3
Rishton BB1 . . . . .102 B8
Cedar Cres Kirkham PR4 . . . .113 A4
Ormskirk L39 . . . . .15 D4
Ramsbottom BL0 . . . . .49 C7
Cedar Ct Blackburn BB1 . . . . .100 F7
7 Farington PR5 . . . . .76 B1
Cedar Dr L37 . . . . .11 C1
Cedar Farm Galleries L40 . . .39 C1
Cedar Field PR6 . . . . .77 C2
Cedar Gr Longton PR4 . . . . . .94 A1
Orrell WN5 . . . . .10 F6
Skelmersdale WN8 . . . . .17 E1
Cedar House Sch LA6 . . . . .238 B2
Cedar Rd Chorley PR6 . . . . . . .60 D2
Fulwood PR2 . . . . .117 E2
Lancaster LA1 . . . . .210 D8
Cedar Sq 5 FY1 . . . . .129 B5
Cedar St Accrington BB5 . . . .103 D6
Blackburn BB1 . . . . .100 F8
Burnley BB11 . . . . .127 B5
Bury BL9 . . . . .32 A3
Bury BL9 . . . . .32 B3
Morecambe LA4 . . . . .212 C4
Rochdale OL12 . . . . .51 F1
Southport PR8 . . . . .34 D4
Cedar Way PR1 . . . . .95 B3
Cedar Wlk PR4 . . . . .153 F1
Cedars Cl BB18 . . . . .200 A1
Cedars Cty Inf Sch The
BB1 .100 F8
Cedars The Chorley PR7 . . . . .42 B4
Eccleston PR7 . . . . .40 B7
New Longton PR4 . . . . .74 F8
Cedarwood Cl FY8 . . . . .89 E4
Cedarwood Dr PR5 . . . . .58 E8
Cedarwood Pl LA1 . . . . .211 C7
Cedric Pl FY2 . . . . .150 C4
Celia St BB10 . . . . .127 C5
Cemetery La Burnley BB11 . .126 A4
Preesall Park FY6 . . . . .195 B1
Cemetery Rd Earby BB18 . . . .201 B2
Padiham BB12 . . . . .125 C7
Preston PR1 . . . . .117 C1
Ramsbottom BL0 . . . . .49 A4
Southport PR8 . . . . .34 C4
Whitehall BB3 . . . . .64 B5
Cemetery View PR7 . . . . .30 A6
Centenary Way BB11 . . . . . . .127 A5
Central Ave Clitheroe BB7 . . .164 D7
Edenfield BL0 . . . . .67 D2
Gregson Lane PR5 . . . . .97 E2
Kirkham PR4 . . . . .112 F6
Lancaster LA1 . . . . .213 F4
Oswaldtwistle BB5 . . . . .102 C4
Southport PR8 . . . . .20 F8
Central Ave N FY5 . . . . .172 F3
Central Beach FY8 . . . . .90 B3
Central Bldgs 16 BB12 . . . .145 C1
Central Dr Blackpool FY1 . . .129 C3
Lytham St Anne's FY8 . . . . .89 C5
Morecambe LA4 . . . . .212 D5
Penwortham PR1 . . . . .95 A4
Central Lancaster
High Sch LA1 . . . . .214 B1
Central Sq
7 Haslingden BB4 . . . . .84 B3
Maghull L31 . . . . .5 D2
Central St BL0 . . . . .49 C6
Central View OL13 . . . . .87 A2
Centre Dr PR6 . . . . .77 B4
Centurian Way BB1 . . . . .81 B6
Centurion Ct BB1 . . . . .81 B7
Centurion Ind Est PR5 . . . . . .76 B3
Centurion Way PR5 . . . . .76 A4
Ceres Way LA1 . . . . .210 C8
Chad St BB8 . . . . .169 A2
Chadderton Ct 18 PR1 . . . . . .96 A8
Chaddock St 27 PR1 . . . . . . .96 A7
Chadfield Rd FY1 . . . . .129 D2
Chadwich Gdns 1 PR5 . . . . .76 A7
Chadwick St
Blackburn BB2 . . . . .100 D3
3 Blackpool FY1 . . . . .129 C3
Bury BL9 . . . . .32 E4
Chadwick Terr OL12 . . . . .51 D4
Chaffinch Cl FY5 . . . . .172 F5
Chaffinch Ct FY3 . . . . .130 B6
Chaffinch Dr BL9 . . . . .32 C4
Chaigley Ct BB7 . . . . .163 A8
Chaigley Farm Cotts BB7 . .163 A8
Chaigley Rd PR3 . . . . .139 B8
Chain Caul Rd PR2 . . . . .94 F8
Chain Caul Way PR2 . . . . . . .94 F8
Chain House La PR4 . . . . .75 D7
Chain La FY3 . . . . .130 E4
Chalfont Ct PR8 . . . . .34 A3
Chalfont Field PR2 . . . . .116 C5
Challan Hall Cotts LA5 . . . .218 E5
Challan Hall Mews LA5 . . . .218 E5
Challenge Way BB1 . . . . .101 C7
Chamber St BB4 . . . . .86 A8
Chambres Rd PR8 . . . . .34 D5
Chambres Rd N PR8 . . . . .34 D6
Champagne Ave FY5 . . . . . .150 F7
Chancel Pl BB3 . . . . .64 C8
Chancel Way BB3 . . . . .64 C8
Chancery Rd PR7 . . . . .60 B2
Chancery Wlk 3 BB11 . . . . .127 A6
Chandler Bsns Pk PR5 . . . . .75 E2
Chandler St 7 PR1 . . . . .95 F8
Chandlers Croft PR4 . . . . . . .72 E4
Chandlers Rest FY8 . . . . .90 D3
Chandley Cl PR8 . . . . .20 A5
Change Cl OL13 . . . . .87 B4
Changford Gn L33 . . . . .1 A3
Changford Rd L33 . . . . .1 A3
Channel Way PR2 . . . . .95 C8
Channing Rd FY8 . . . . .89 C4
Chapel Alley L37 . . . . .11 F3
Chapel Brow Leyland PR5 . . . .76 B2
Longridge PR3 . . . . .139 B5
Chapel Cl Clitheroe BB7 . . . .164 B8
Hest Bank LA2 . . . . .215 D1
Kirkham PR4 . . . . .112 F7
Overton LA3 . . . . .205 C8
Trawden BB8 . . . . .170 B2
West Bradford BB7 . . . . .186 E5
Whalley BB7 . . . . .143 C5
Chapel Ct BB10 . . . . .148 A3
Chapel Fields BL7 . . . . .47 C4
Chapel Fold 12 Colne BB8 . .169 D4
Wiswell BB7 . . . . .143 F7
Chapel Gdns Catterall PR3 . .178 D2
Hesketh Bank PR4 . . . . .72 E4
Chapel Grange BL7 . . . . .47 C4
Chapel Hill Longridge PR3 . .139 A6
Salterforth BB18 . . . . .191 D7
Chapel Hill La BB4 . . . . .85 B4
Chapel Ho BB11 . . . . .126 C5
Chapel House BB1 . . . . .123 C1
Chapel House Rd BB9 . . . . .147 E7
Chapel La Arnside LA5 . . . . .237 B2
Banks PR9 . . . . .54 B7
Burscough L40 . . . . .24 E2
Burton in L LA6 . . . . .236 C3
Catforth PR4 . . . . .134 D4
Coppull PR7 . . . . .41 F1
Formby L37 . . . . .11 F3
Galgate LA2 . . . . .207 B4
Grindleton BB7 . . . . .187 B8
Hoghton PR5 . . . . .98 D2
Holmeswood L40 . . . . .37 B6
Kirkby Lonsdale LA6 . . . . . . .238 C2
Kirkham PR4 . . . . .113 B4
Langho BB6 . . . . .142 B2
Longton PR4 . . . . .74 C8
New Longton PR4 . . . . .74 E8
Out Rawcliffe PR3 . . . . .175 B2
Overton LA3 . . . . .205 D8
Parbold WN8 . . . . .26 D1
Ramsbottom BL8 . . . . .49 A6
West Bradford BB7 . . . . .186 E5
Wheelton PR6 . . . . .61 B5
Chapel Mdw PR4 . . . . .74 C8
Chapel Mdws PR4 . . . . .56 A5
Chapel Mews
2 Earby BB18 . . . . .201 B1
Ormskirk L39 . . . . .15 F4
Chapel Park Rd PR4 . . . . .74 D8
Chapel Rd Blackpool FY4 . . . .110 B7
Fulwood PR2 . . . . .117 A4
Hesketh Bank PR4 . . . . .72 E4
Chapel Rise BB7 . . . . .143 B4
Chapel Sq LA2 . . . . .231 D3
Chapel St
10 Accrington BB5 . . . . .103 C5
Chapel St *continued*
Adlington PR7 . . . . .29 F6
14 Bacup OL13 . . . . .69 C8
Barnoldswick BB18 . . . . .200 B2
Belmont BL7 . . . . .45 C5
Belthorn BB1 . . . . .81 F6
Blackburn BB2 . . . . .100 D4
Blackpool FY1 . . . . .129 B4
Blackrod BL6 . . . . .30 D2
Brierfield BB9 . . . . .147 B6
Brinscall PR6 . . . . .61 F8
Burnley BB11 . . . . .127 A6
Chorley PR7 . . . . .42 C8
Clayton-le-M BB5 . . . . .123 E3
Colne BB8 . . . . .169 D4
Coppull PR7 . . . . .41 E1
Darwen BB3 . . . . .64 A8
Earby BB18 . . . . .201 B2
Egerton BL7 . . . . .46 D3
Foulridge BB8 . . . . .191 E1
Galgate LA2 . . . . .207 A3
Great Eccleston PR3 . . . . .154 B5
Haslingden BB4 . . . . .84 B3
Higham BB12 . . . . .145 F5
Horwich BL6 . . . . .31 C3
3 Lancaster LA1 . . . . .210 F8
Longridge PR3 . . . . .139 B7
Lytham St Anne's FY8 . . . . .90 A3
Morecambe LA4 . . . . .212 D5
Nelson BB9 . . . . .147 E8
Newchurch BB4 . . . . .85 E1
Ormskirk L39 . . . . .15 F4
Oswaldtwistle BB5 . . . . .102 E4
Poulton-le-F FY6 . . . . .151 D3
Preston PR1 . . . . .95 F7
Rawtenstall BB4 . . . . .85 A8
Rishton BB1 . . . . .123 C1
Slaidburn BB7 . . . . .223 C7
Southport PR8 . . . . .34 B7
Whitworth OL12 . . . . .51 C8
Worsthorne BB10 . . . . .128 A5
Chapel Street Ct 2 FY6 . . . .151 D3
Chapel Street Sta PR8 . . . . . .34 B7
Chapel View LA3 . . . . .205 D8
Chapel Way PR7 . . . . .28 F8
Chapel Wlk Coppull PR7 . . . . .41 E1
Longton PR4 . . . . .74 D8
2 Padiham BB12 . . . . .145 C1
Warton, Carnforth LA5 . . . . . .217 E6
Chapel Wlks Kirkham PR4 . .113 B4
4 Preston PR1 . . . . .95 F7
Chapel Yd PR5 . . . . .96 D5
Chapelhouse La LA6 . . . . . .238 E1
Chapelhouse Wlk L37 . . . . . .12 A3
Chapels BB3 . . . . .81 A3
Chapels Brow BB3 . . . . .81 A3
Chapels La BB3 . . . . .79 F3
Chapelside Cl PR3 . . . . .178 D2
Chapeltown Rd BL7 . . . . .47 C2
Chapman Cl PR3 . . . . .154 C5
Chapman Ct
Barnoldswick BB18 . . . . .200 B3
Fleetwood FY7 . . . . .194 B4
Chapman Rd Fulwood PR2 . .117 A3
Hoddlesden BB3 . . . . .81 F1
Chapter Rd BB3 . . . . .64 C8
Chardonnay Cres 2 FY5 . . . .150 F7
Charlbury Gr LA3 . . . . .209 A7
Charles Ave PR8 . . . . .20 E6
Charles Cl PR4 . . . . .72 E3
Charles Cres PR5 . . . . .97 C3
Charles Ct
4 Blackpool FY3 . . . . .129 D7
Lancaster LA1 . . . . .210 F6
Charles Gr PR3 . . . . .139 A7
Charles La BB4 . . . . .84 A2
Charles Saer
Com Prim Sch FY7 . . . . . .193 D3
Charles St Blackburn BB2 . . .100 D2
Blackpool FY1 . . . . .129 C6
Clayton-le-M BB5 . . . . .123 E2
Colne BB8 . . . . .169 E5
Darwen BB3 . . . . .81 A2
Egerton BL7 . . . . .46 D2
Great Harwood BB6 . . . . .123 C4
Lancaster LA1 . . . . .210 F6
Morecambe LA4 . . . . .212 F5
Nelson BB9 . . . . .168 E2
Newchurch BB4 . . . . .85 F2
Oswaldtwistle BB5 . . . . .102 E3
Charles Way PR2 . . . . .115 E1
Charlesbye Ave L39 . . . . .16 B6
Charlesbye Cl L39 . . . . .16 B6
Charleston Ct 3 PR5 . . . . . . .96 E2
Charlesway Ct 1 PR2 . . . . . .115 E1
Charlesworth Cl L31 . . . . .5 B5
Charley Fold Bglws PR5 . . . . .96 F3
Charley Wood Rd L33 . . . . .1 C1
Charlotte Pl 33 PR1 . . . . .96 A7
Charlotte St
Blackburn BB1 . . . . .100 E6
Burnley BB11 . . . . .126 F5
Edgworth BL7 . . . . .47 C4
Preston PR1 . . . . .96 A7
4 Ramsbottom BL0 . . . . .49 B5
Charlotte's La PR4 . . . . .55 E2
Charnley Cl PR1 . . . . .95 C2
Charnley Fold PR5 . . . . .96 F3
Charnley Fold La PR5 . . . . . . .96 F3
Charnley Rd FY1 . . . . .129 C4
Charnley St Blackburn BB2 . .100 C2
1 Lancaster LA1 . . . . .213 D1
1 Preston PR1 . . . . .95 F7
Charnley's La PR9 . . . . .53 E7
Charnock Ave PR1 . . . . .95 E2

Charnock Brow PR7 41 C7
Charnock Fold PR1 117 A2
Charnock House PR7 60 C2
Charnock Richard CE Prim Sch PR7 41 D4
Charnock St Chorley PR6 42 D7
9 Kirkham PR4 112 F6
8 Leyland PR5 76 B1
Preston PR1 116 F2
Charnwood Ave FY3 130 A7
Charnwood Cl BB2 100 A8
Charter Brook BB6 123 D5
Charter La PR7 41 D3
Charter St BB5 103 A5
Charterhouse Pl BB2 100 B3
Chartwell Cl PR6 77 C2
Chartwell Rd PR8 20 B6
Chartwell Rise 5 PR5 76 C8
Chasden Cl PR6 60 C5
Chase Cl PR8 33 F4
Chase Heys PR9 53 A1
Chase The Burnley BB12 126 D8
Cottam PR4 115 D5
3 Leyland PR5 76 C2
Normoss FY3 130 C7
Silverdale LA5 218 D2
Thornton FY5 173 A4
Chatburn Ave
Burnley BB10 127 D5
Clitheroe BB7 186 F1
Chatburn CE Prim Sch BB7 187 D5
Chatburn Cl
Great Harwood BB6 123 E5
Normoss FY3 130 B8
Rawtenstall BB4 85 A4
Chatburn Gdns OL10 32 F2
Chatburn Old Rd BB7 187 D5
Chatburn Park Ave BB9 147 A6
Chatburn Park Dr
Brierfield BB9 147 A6
Clitheroe BB7 187 A2
Chatburn Rd
Chatburn BB7 187 F5
Clitheroe BB7 187 A3
Fulwood PR2 117 F4
Longridge PR3 139 A7
Chatburn St BB2 100 C5
Chatham Ave FY8 109 E1
Chatham Cres BB8 169 E6
Chatham Pl 5 Chorley PR6 42 E8
Preston PR1 117 B2
Chatham St Colne BB8 169 E6
Nelson BB9 168 D1
Chatsworth Ave
Blackpool FY2 150 C6
Fleetwood FY7 193 D2
Warton PR4 91 D6
Chatsworth Cl
Barrowford BB9 168 B1
Blackburn BB1 121 E1
Chorley PR7 42 B8
2 Thornton FY5 173 D1
Chatsworth Ct PR6 42 F1
Chatsworth Rd
Bamber Bridge PR5 96 D3
Lancaster LA1 210 F4
1 Leyland PR5 76 A1
Lytham St Anne's FY8 88 D7
Morecambe LA4 212 C4
Southport PR8 20 B6
Chatsworth St Preston PR1 96 D8
Rochdale OL12 51 E3
Chatteris Pl FY5 172 C1
Chatterton BL0 67 C2
Chatterton Dr BB5 103 E2
Chatterton Old La BL0 67 C2
Chatterton Rd BL0 67 C1
Chaucer Ave FY5 172 F2
Chaucer Cl PR7 40 B6
Chaucer Gdns BB6 123 B4
Chaucer Prim Sch FY7 194 A4
Chaucer Rd FY7 194 A4
Chaucer St PR1 117 D2
Cheam Ave PR7 42 D6
Cheapside Blackpool FY1 129 B5
6 Chorley PR7 42 C7
Formby L37 12 A2
11 Lancaster LA1 210 F8
1 Low Bentham LA2 233 B8
8 Preston PR1 95 F7
Cheddar Ave FY4 109 D6
Cheddar Dr PR2 117 D6
Chedworth Ave LA3 209 A7
Cheetham Hill OL12 70 D3
Cheetham Meadow PR5 58 B8
Cheetham St BB2 100 C5
Chelburn Gr BB10 127 C6
Chelford Ave FY3 129 E8
Chelford Cl 4 PR1 95 F2
Chelmsford Cl LA1 211 B5
Chelmsford Gr PR7 42 B7
Chelmsford Pl PR7 42 B7
Chelmsford Wlk PR5 58 A8
Chelsea Ave FY2 150 E1
Chelsea Ct 3 FY2 150 E1
Chelsea Mews 4 FY2 150 E1
Chelston Dr BB4 67 A7
Cheltenham Ave BB5 103 C8
Cheltenham Cres
Lytham St Anne's FY8 90 D5
Thornton FY5 151 D8
Cheltenham Dr WN5 10 D2
Cheltenham Rd
Blackburn BB2 100 C5

Cheltenham Rd *continued*
Blackpool FY1 129 B7
Lancaster LA1 210 F5
Cheltenham Way PR8 34 F3
Chennel Ho 4 LA1 210 E8
Chepstow Ct FY3 129 F8
Chepstow Rd FY3 129 F8
Chequer Cl WN8 9 F5
Chequer La WN8 9 F6
Chequers BB5 123 F2
Chequers Ave LA1 211 B4
Cheriton Field PR2 116 C7
Cheriton Gdns BL6 31 B5
Cheriton Pk PR8 34 E3
Cherry Ave BL9 32 C3
Cherry Cl
2 Blackburn BB1 101 B5
Fulwood PR2 117 D6
Kirkham PR4 112 E5
Cherry Cres
Oswaldtwistle BB5 102 D2
Rawtenstall BB4 67 F8
Cherry Gn L39 15 B1
Cherry Gr Abbey Village PR6 79 B2
Burscough Bridge L40 24 E6
Longridge PR3 139 A7
Cherry La PR4 92 B4
Cherry Lea BB2 99 F2
Cherry Orch PR3 139 B6
Cherry Rd PR8 20 D2
Cherry St BB1 101 B5
Cherry Tree Cl
Fisher's Row PR3 196 E5
Hest Bank LA5 215 F2
Heysham LA3 208 E6
Cherry Tree Ct
Blackpool FY4 130 B1
10 Fleetwood FY7 194 B5
Standish WN6 28 D2
Cherry Tree Dr LA1 210 F4
Cherry Tree Gdns FY4 110 A8
Cherry Tree Gr PR6 60 C3
Cherry Tree La
Blackburn BB2 79 E8
Ormskirk L39 15 B1
Rawtenstall BB4 67 F8
Cherry Tree Mews BB11 126 D3
Cherry Tree Rd FY4 130 A1
Cherry Tree Rd N FY4 130 A1
Cherry Tree Sta BB2 99 F1
Cherry Tree Terr BB2 99 F1
Cherry Tree Way
Haslingden BB4 67 B7
5 Horwich BL6 31 E1
Cherry Trees
Bamber Bridge PR5 96 C3
St Michael's on W PR3 155 C7
Cherry Vale PR4 72 F2
Cherry View L33 1 A5
Cherry Wood PR1 95 A3
Cherryclough Way BB2 80 B8
Cherrycroft WN8 9 E6
Cherrydale FY2 150 D5
Cherryfields PR7 59 D4
Cherrywood Ave
Cleveleys FY5 172 C1
Lytham St Anne's FY8 89 E4
Cherrywood Cl PR5 58 E8
Cheryl Dr FY5 151 B8
Chesham Cres BL9 32 A3
Chesham Dr PR4 74 F8
Chesham Fold Rd BL9 32 B4
Chesham Ind Est BL9 32 A4
Chesham Prim Sch BL9 32 A5
Chesham Rd BL9 32 A5
Chesham St PR3 154 B5
Cheshire Ct BL0 49 D6
Cheshire House Cl PR5 75 F7
Chesmere Croft PR1 95 B5
Chesmere Dr PR1 95 B5
Chessington Gn BB10 147 D3
Chester Ave Chorley PR7 42 E4
Cleveleys FY5 172 E2
Clitheroe BB7 186 E1
Poulton-le-F FY6 151 C4
Southport PR9 34 F8
Chester Cl Blackburn BB1 101 A3
Garstang PR3 178 B7
Morecambe LA3 212 E2
Chester Cres BB4 67 B8
Chester Ct FY5 173 C3
Chester Dr BL0 49 A4
Chester Pl Adlington PR6 30 A8
Great Eccleston PR3 154 C5
Lancaster LA1 211 A5
Chester Rd Blackpool FY3 129 D6
Preston PR1 117 C1
Southport PR9 34 F8
Chester St Accrington BB5 103 A5
Blackburn BB1 101 A4
Bury BL9 32 A4
Chesterbrook PR3 140 E4
Chesterfield Cl PR8 20 C4
Chesterfield Rd
Blackpool FY1 129 C7
Southport PR8 20 C5
Chestnut Ave
Blackpool FY4 109 F5
Bolton-le-S LA5 216 A5
Bury BL9 32 B2
Caton LA2 231 C3
Chorley PR6 60 E2
Euxton PR7 59 C4
Penwortham PR1 95 A4
Chestnut Cl
Bamber Bridge PR5 96 E2
Garstang PR3 199 D1
Halsall L39 22 C1

Chestnut Cl *continued*
2 Kirkham PR4 113 B5
Chestnut Cres
Barrow BB7 164 D1
Fulwood PR2 117 E2
Longton PR4 73 F8
Chestnut Ct Leyland PR5 59 A7
3 Ormskirk L39 15 F6
Chestnut Dr
Barnoldswick BB18 200 A1
Fulwood PR2 116 D7
Morecambe LA4 213 B6
Rawtenstall BB4 67 F8
Whalley BB7 143 A7
Chestnut Gdns BB1 100 F7
Chestnut Gr
Accrington BB5 103 A4
Clayton-le-M BB5 124 A4
Darwen BB3 64 A5
Lancaster LA1 210 D8
Chestnut Grange L39 15 D3
Chestnut Rise BB11 126 F4
Chestnut St PR8 34 C5
Chestnut Way L37 11 C1
Chestnut Wlk 5 BB1 101 B5
Chestnuts The PR7 41 F2
Chethams Cl FY5 173 A2
Chevassut Cl BB9 168 C1
Cheviot Ave Burnley BB10 127 E5
Cleveleys FY5 172 F4
Saltcotes FY8 90 E5
Cheviot Cl Horwich BL6 31 C5
Ramsbottom BL0 49 C4
Cheviot St PR1 95 C8
Chew Gdns FY6 151 B3
Chichester Cl
Burnley BB10 127 B6
Thornton FY5 173 A2
Chicken St BB2 100 C4
Chiddlingford Ct FY1 129 D3
Childrey Wlk BB2 81 A8
Chilgrove Ave BL6 30 D1
Chiltern Ave
Blackpool FY4 109 D7
Burnley BB10 127 E5
Euxton PR7 59 D1
Poulton-le-F FY6 151 C3
Chiltern Cl Horwich BL6 31 C5
Lytham St Anne's FY8 90 D5
Ramsbottom BL0 49 C4
Chiltern Mdw PR5 76 D1
Chiltern Rd
Ramsbottom BL0 49 C4
Southport PR8 20 B6
Chilton Cl L31 5 D1
Chilton Mews L31 5 D1
Chimes The Kirkham PR4 113 A4
Tarleton PR4 56 A5
China St Accrington BB5 102 F6
Lancaster LA1 210 F8
Chindit Cl L37 11 D2
Chindits Way PR2 117 B4
Chines The PR2 116 E4
Chingford Bank BB10 147 D3
Chingle Cl PR2 117 E6
Chipping Ave PR8 20 A5
Chipping Ct 4 FY3 130 A8
Chipping Gr Burnley BB10 127 D4
Normoss FY3 130 A8
Chipping La PR3 139 A8
Chipping St 3 BB12 145 D1
Chisacre Dr WN6 19 D7
Chisholm Cl WN6 28 B2
Chisholme Cl BL8 48 F2
Chislehurst Ave FY4 129 D1
Chislehurst Gr BB10 147 D4
Chislehurst Pl FY8 89 E5
Chislett Cl L40 24 D4
Chisnall Ave WN6 27 F6
Chisnall La Coppull PR7 28 C6
Heskin Green PR7 40 F2
Wrightington Bar WN6 28 A5
Chiswell Gr FY5 151 D8
Chiswick Gr FY3 130 B2
Chitheroe Rd PR3 161 C1
Chorcliffe Ho 7 PR7 42 C8
Chorley & District Hospl PR7 60 C2
Chorley Bsns & Tech Ctr PR7 59 E4
Chorley Cl PR9 53 F5
Chorley Golf Course PR6 43 A3
Chorley Hall Rd PR7 60 C2
Chorley Info Ctr PR7 42 C8
Chorley La PR7 41 D3
Chorley New Rd BL6 31 C2
Chorley New Rd Inf Sch BL6 31 D2
Chorley New Rd Prim Sch BL6 31 D2
Chorley North Ind Est PR6 60 D3
Chorley Old Rd
Clayton Green PR6 77 C2
Horwich BL6 31 E3
Chorley Rd Adlington PR6 30 A8
Adlington, Blackrod BL6,PR7 30 B5
Bamber Bridge PR5 96 D3
Blackpool FY3 150 F2
Hill Dale L40,WN8 26 D6
Ollerton Fold BB2,PR6 78 E4
Parbold WN8 26 C4
Standish WN1 29 C3
Chorley St PR6 30 B8
Chorley St James CE Prim Sch PR6 42 E7
Chorley Sta PR6 42 D8
Chorley West Bsns Pk PR7 41 F8
Chorlton Cl BB10 147 D2

Chorlton Gdns BB1 100 F7
Chorlton St BB1 100 F7
Chorlton Terr BB7 164 D1
Christ Church CE Prim Sch Carnforth LA5 217 D1
Glasson LA2 205 E4
Lancaster LA1 211 B8
Christ Church CE Sch LA1 211 A8
Christ Church Prim Sch BB8 170 B5
Christ Church Sq 1 BB5 103 C5
Christ Church St
2 Accrington BB5 103 C5
6 Bacup OL13 87 A3
Preston PR1 95 E7
Christ The King RC High Sch PR1 96 B6
Christ The King RC Prim Sch Blackpool FY3 130 A7
Burnley BB11 126 E3
Christ The King Sch PR8 34 B2
Christian Rd PR1 95 E7
Christiana Hartley Maternity Hospl PR8 34 D5
Christie Ave LA4 212 G4
Christines Cres L40 24 E4
Christleton Cl BB10 147 F3
Church & Oswaldtwistle Sta BB5 102 E5
Church Alley BB5 123 F2
Church Ave
Accrington BB5 103 E2
Lancaster LA1 210 F4
Penwortham PR1 95 C6
Preston PR1 96 E8
Church Bank LA6 231 B8
Church Bank St 19 BB3 81 A1
Church Brook Ho 8 PR1 95 E4
Church Brow
Bolton-le-S LA5 216 A3
Clitheroe BB7 186 E1
Halton LA2 214 E6
Walton-le-D PR5 96 E5
Church Brow Cl LA5 216 A3
Church Brow Gdns BB7 186 E1
Church Cl Clitheroe BB7 186 E1
Dolphinholme LA2 220 A8
Formby L37 12 A3
Freckleton PR4 92 A6
Mellor BB2 120 E2
Ramsbottom BL0 49 B5
Read BB12 144 D2
Southport PR9 35 A8
Waddington BB7 186 B4
Church Close Ct L37 12 A3
Church Ct Bolton-le-S LA5 216 A3
Edenfield BL0 67 D4
Preston PR1 117 C2
Church Dr
Lytham St Anne's FY8 89 F3
Orrell WN5 10 D5
Whalley BB7 143 A7
Church Fields Bescar L40 22 F7
Ormskirk L39 15 E5
Church Fold
Charnock Richard PR7 41 E4
Coppull PR7 28 F8
Church Gdns PR4 91 E6
Church Gn Formby L37 11 C2
Skelmersdale WN8 17 F1
Church Gr LA3 205 E8
Church Hall BB5 102 F7
Church Hill Arnside LA5 237 B2
Nether Kellet LA6 216 F5
Whittle-le-W PR6 60 C7
Church Hill Ave LA5 217 D5
Church Hill Rd
Blackburn BB1 101 A7
Ormskirk L39 15 D6
Church Ho 7 L39 15 E5
Church House Mus PR3 136 D1
Church La Accrington BB5 124 A1
Bilsborrow PR3 157 A4
Broughton PR3 136 D1
Charnock Richard PR7 41 D4
Edenfield BL0 67 D4
Farington PR5 75 F7
Goosnargh PR3 137 D6
Great Harwood BB6 123 C6
Great Mitton BB7 163 E3
Hambleton FY6 174 D1
Kelbrook BB18 192 A6
Maghull L31 5 A8
Mellor BB2 120 E2
Morecambe LA4 212 E6
Newchurch BB4 85 E1
Newton-with-S PR4 114 B3
Ormskirk L39 6 A7
12 Padiham BB12 145 C1
Tunstall LA6 235 E4
Whalley BB7 143 C5
Whitechapel PR3 158 E7
Winmarleigh PR3 198 E4
Wrightington Bar WN6 27 D8
Church Mdws BB8 169 D5
Church Pk Lea Town PR4 114 F3
Overton LA3 205 D8
Church Raike PR3 182 E3
Church Rd
Bamber Bridge PR5 76 E7
Bamber Bridge PR5 76 F6
Banks PR9 54 A6
Bickerstaffe L39 7 E6
Formby L37 12 A5
Kirkham PR4 112 F7
Leyland PR5 59 A8

Church Rd *continued*
Lytham FY8 89 F3
Lytham St Anne's FY8 89 B6
Rufford L40 38 C4
Shuttleworth BL0 49 E8
Singleton FY6 152 F1
Skelmersdale WN8 17 F1
Tarleton PR4 56 A5
Thornton FY5 173 A2
Thornton-in-C BD23 201 A5
Warton PR4 91 D6
Weeton PR4 131 F1
Wharles PR4 133 F2
Church Row Preston PR1 96 A7
Wrea Green PR4 112 B4
Church Row Chambers PR4 74 A8
Church Sq BB10 128 B5
Church St Accrington BB5 103 C5
Adlington PR7 30 A7
Bacup OL13 69 C8
Barnoldswick BB18 200 B2
Barrowford BB9 168 D4
Belmont BL7 45 C4
Blackburn BB1 100 E5
Blackpool FY1 129 C5
Blackrod BL6 30 C2
Brierfield BB9 147 B5
Brierfield, Harle Syke BB10 147 F2
Burnley BB11 127 A6
Bury BL9 32 A3
Chorley PR7 42 C7
Church BB5 102 E6
Churchtown PR3 178 A2
Clayton-le-M BB5 123 F2
1 Clitheroe BB7 164 E8
Colne BB8 169 D5
Croston PR5 57 B1
Darwen BB3 81 A1
Fleetwood FY7 194 B4
Garstang PR3 178 C7
Goodshaw Chapel BB4 105 A1
Great Harwood BB6 123 C5
Halton LA2 214 D6
2 Hapton BB12 125 C4
Haslingden BB4 84 B4
Higher Walton PR5 97 B3
Horwich BL6 31 C3
Kirkby Lonsdale LA6 238 C2
Kirkham PR4 113 B5
Lancaster LA1 210 F8
Leyland PR5 76 B2
Longridge PR3 139 B7
Morecambe LA4 212 E6
Newchurch BB4 85 E1
Ormskirk L39 15 E5
Orrell, Far Moor WN5 10 E5
Orrell, Up Holland WN8 10 C7
Oswaldtwistle BB5 102 D3
Padiham BB12 125 C8
1 Poulton-le-F FY6 151 D3
Preston PR1 96 A7
5 Ramsbottom BL0 49 C6
Rawtenstall BB4 68 E8
Read BB12 144 D2
Rishton BB1 123 A1
Slaidburn BB7 223 C7
Southport PR9 34 C7
Standish WN6 28 E1
Trawden BB8 170 C2
Whittington LA6 235 C7
Whitworth OL12 51 C8
Church Terr 20 BB3 81 A1
Church View Arnside LA5 237 B2
Gisburn BB7 225 B3
Ormskirk L39 6 A7
Salesbury BB1 121 E6
Stalmine FY6 174 C7
Tarleton PR4 56 A5
Trawden BB8 170 C2
Church View Ct 1 L39 15 E5
Church Way Formby L37 11 C2
Nelson BB9 147 D6
Church Wlk Blackburn BB1 121 F3
Euxton PR7 59 C2
Kirkham PR4 112 F7
Preston PR2 117 F5
Tarleton PR4 56 A6
Church Wlks 3 L39 15 E5
Churchfield PR2 116 F6
Churchfields PR8 33 F3
Churchgate
Goosnargh PR3 137 D6
Southport PR9 52 F1
Churchgate Mews PR9 53 A1
Churchill Ave Rishton BB1 102 A8
Southport PR9 52 F2
Churchill Cl 2 FY5 173 B2
Churchill Ct FY3 129 D6
Churchill Dr PR2 117 D4
Churchill Rd
Barrowford BB9 168 B1
Brinscall PR6 62 A8
Fulwood PR2 117 C4
Churchill St OL11,OL12 51 C1
Churchill Way Leyland PR5 76 A2
Nelson BB9 147 B8
Churchlands La WN6 28 F1
Churchside PR4 74 F8
Churchtown Cres OL13 87 B1
Churchtown Ct PR9 53 A2
Churchtown Prim Sch PR9 53 B2
Churchward Sq BL6 31 C2
Churton Gr WN6 28 B2
Cicely Ct BB1 100 F4
Cicely La BB1 100 F5
Cicely St BB1 100 F4

Cinder La Lancaster LA1 210 F3
Lewth PR4 135 A6
Mere Brow PR4 54 F2
Cinderbarrow La LA5,LA6 234 A6
Cinnamon Brow WN8 10 C6
Cinnamon Ct 3 PR1 95 C2
Cinnamon Hill Dr N PR5 96 D3
Cinnamon Hill Dr S PR5 96 D3
Cintra Ave PR2 116 D3
Cintra Terr PR2 116 D3
Circus The 10 BB3 81 A1
Cirrus Dr L39 15 A1
City Hts Cl 21 LA1 211 A8
Clairane Ave PR2 116 E6
Clairville PR8 33 F5
Clancut La PR7 41 F2
Clanfield PR2 116 E7
Clara St Preston PR1 96 C7
Whitworth OL12 70 D1
Clare Ave BB8 169 A2
Clare Rd LA1 213 E2
Clare St Blackpool FY1 129 B1
Burnley BB11 126 D6
Claremont Ave Chorley PR7 42 B7
Clitheroe BB7 164 F7
Claremont Cres LA4 212 C4
Claremont Ct FY1 129 C7
Claremont Dr
Clitheroe BB7 164 F7
Ormskirk L39 15 D3
Claremont Gdns PR8 34 A4
Claremont Pl FY8 88 E8
Claremont Rd
Accrington BB5 103 B8
Blackpool FY1 129 C8
Chorley PR7 42 B5
Morecambe LA4 212 C4
Southport PR8 34 A4
Claremont Sch (Prim)
FY1 129 C8
Claremont St
Brierfield BB9 147 A6
Burnley BB12 126 D6
Colne BB8 170 A5
Claremont Terr BB9 147 D7
Claremount Ave PR5 59 B8
Clarence Ave
Cleveleys FY5 172 D3
4 Haslingden BB4 84 A1
Knott End-on-S FY6 194 E5
Clarence Ct 15 FY4 129 B1
Clarence House Sch L37 11 F6
Clarence Pk BB2 100 B7
Clarence Rd
Accrington BB5 103 A4
Southport PR8 34 A4
Clarence St
Barnoldswick BB18 200 C1
Blackburn BB1 100 D6
Burnley BB11 127 B4
4 Chorley PR7 42 D7
Colne BB8 170 A5
Darwen BB3 80 F3
Lancaster LA1 211 A7
Leyland PR5 76 B2
Morecambe LA4 212 E5
Rawtenstall BB4 85 A7
Rochdale OL12 51 D2
Trawden BB8 170 C2
Clarendon Gr L31 5 C5
Clarendon Rd
Blackburn BB1 100 F8
Blackpool FY1 129 B2
Lancaster LA1 213 F3
Lytham St Anne's FY8 89 A8
Clarendon Rd E
Blackburn BB1 101 A8
Morecambe LA4 212 C4
Clarendon Rd N FY8 88 F8
Clarendon Rd W LA3 212 B4
Clarendon St
Accrington BB5 103 D6
Bury BL9 32 A4
10 Chorley PR6 42 E7
Colne BB8 170 B5
Preston PR1 96 A6
Claret St BB5 103 A5
Clark St LA4 212 E6
Clarke Holme St BB4 85 F2
Clarke St Poulton-le-F FY6 151 F3
6 Rishton BB1 123 B1
Clarke Wood Cl BB7 143 F8
Clarke's Cotts L40 26 A8
Clarke's La OL12 51 E1
Clarkes Croft BL9 32 C3
Clarkfield Cl L40 24 F3
Clarkfield Dr LA4 212 G5
Clarksfield Rd LA5 216 A4
Clarrick Terr LA6 236 F3
Clary St BB12 126 A5
Claughton Ave PR5 76 E1
Claughton Dr LA1 211 A3
Claughton St 14 BB10 147 B1
Clawthorpe Cotts LA6 234 C8
Clay Brow Rd WN8 9 E6
Clay Gap La FY6,PR3 174 F4
Clay La LA3 209 B8
Clay St BB11 126 C5
Claybank 10 BB12 145 C1
Claybank Fold 9 BB12 145 C1
Clayburn Cl PR6 60 E2
Claylands Dr LA5 216 A4
Claypool Prim Sch BL6 31 F1
Claypool Rd BL6 31 E1
Clayton Ave Leyland PR5 58 D7
Rawtenstall BB4 67 E8
Clayton Brook
Cty Prim Sch PR5 77 B5
Clayton Brook Rd PR5 77 C6
Clayton Cl 11 BB9 168 D1
Clayton Cres FY4 109 E6
Clayton Ct PR3 139 B7
Clayton Gdns L40 24 E4
Clayton Gr BB1 121 D6
Clayton Green Rd PR6 77 B3
Clayton Hall Dr BB5 123 F4
Clayton Mews WN8 17 D1
Clayton Row BB6 142 D1
Clayton St
6 Bamber Bridge PR5 96 E1
Barnoldswick BB18 200 C2
Blackburn BB2 100 E4
Colne BB8 169 E4
1 Enfield BB5 124 A1
Great Harwood BB6 123 C5
18 Nelson BB9 168 D1
7 Oswaldtwistle BB5 102 E5
Skelmersdale WN8 17 D1
Clayton Street Ind Units
BB9 168 D1
Clayton Villa Fold PR6 77 A3
Clayton Way BB5 124 A3
Clayton's Gate 12 PR1 95 F8
Clayton-le-Moors
Ind Est BB5 123 E2
Clayton-le-Woods
CE Prim Sch PR6 77 A2
Clayton-le-Woods
Westwood Prim Sch
PR5 77 C4
Claytongate PR7 41 F2
Claytonhalgh PR3 140 E3
Cleator Ave FY2 150 C1
Cleaver St Blackburn BB1 100 F5
Burnley BB10 127 B8
Clecken La PR3 179 D2
Clegg Ave FY5 172 D3
Clegg St 6 Bacup OL13 69 C8
Brierfield BB9 147 B5
Burnley BB10 127 A8
Haslingden BB4 84 B3
Kirkham PR4 113 A5
Nelson BB9 147 E6
Skelmersdale WN8 17 D1
Whitworth OL12 70 C2
Worsthorne BB10 128 A5
Clegg St E 9 BB10 127 A8
Clegg's Ct OL12 70 C2
Clematis Cl PR7 60 A3
Clematis St BB2 100 B6
Clement St Accrington BB5 103 C5
4 Darwen BB3 64 A8
Clement View 14 BB9 147 D8
Clementina St OL12 51 F1
Clements Dr BB10 147 C4
Clengers Brow PR9 53 A3
Clent Ave L31 5 C3
Clent Gdns L31 5 C3
Clent Rd L31 5 C3
Clerk Hill Rd BB7 143 F5
Clerkhill St BB1 101 B5
Cleve Way L37 12 B2
Clevedon Rd
Blackpool FY1 129 B7
Fulwood PR2 116 A4
Cleveland Ave PR2 117 C4
Cleveland Cl BL0 49 C3
Cleveland Dr LA1 210 D7
Cleveland Rd Leyland PR5 75 F2
Lytham St Anne's FY8 90 B3
Cleveland St Chorley PR7 42 C8
Colne BB8 169 F6
2 Coppull PR7 41 E1
Cornholme OL14 108 B1
Clevelands Ave
Morecambe LA3 212 C3
Silverdale LA5 218 C4
Clevelands Gr
Burnley BB11 126 E4
Morecambe LA3 212 C3
Clevelands Mt BB11 126 E4
Clevelands Rd BB11 126 F4
Clevelands Wlk LA3 212 C3
Cleveleys Ave
Cleveleys FY5 172 D3
Fulwood PR2 116 C4
Lancaster LA1 213 C2
Southport PR9 53 A4
Cleveleys Rd
Accrington BB5 103 B8
Blackburn BB2 100 F1
Coupe Green PR5 97 E3
Southport PR9 53 A3
Cleves Ct FY3 130 A2
Cleves The L31 5 E3
Clieves Hills La L39 14 E3
Clifden Ct L37 11 F3
Cliff Ave BL9 49 C2
Cliff Ct FY2 150 B4
Cliff Mount BL0 49 B7
Cliff Pl FY2 150 B4
Cliff Rd PR9 52 D1
Cliff St Colne BB8 169 B3
Padiham BB12 145 D1
Preston PR1 95 E6
Rishton BB1 123 B2
Cliffe Ct PR1 96 D8
Cliffe Dr PR6 60 B8
Cliffe La BB6 123 C6
Cliffe St BB9 168 E1
Clifford Ave Longton PR4 94 A1
Morecambe LA4 212 G6
Clifford Rd Blackpool FY1 129 C7
Southport PR8 34 A2
Clifford St
Barnoldswick BB18 200 C2
Clifford St *continued*
Chorley PR7 42 D8
Colne BB8 169 E5
Cliffs The LA3 212 A2
Clifton Ave Accrington BB5 103 C7
Blackpool FY4 130 C1
Leyland PR5 59 B8
Preston PR2 116 A2
Warton PR4 91 E6
Clifton Cl FY5 173 C1
Clifton Cres Blackpool FY3 130 A2
Fulwood PR1 117 C2
Clifton Ct 1 Blackpool FY4 109 B6
3 Lytham St Anne's FY8 90 C3
Clifton Cty Prim Sch FY8 89 C6
Clifton Dr Blackpool FY4 109 B5
Blackrod BL6 30 C3
Great Harwood BB6 123 C6
Lytham St Anne's FY8 89 D3
Morecambe LA4 213 A5
Penwortham PR1 95 C5
Clifton Dr N FY8 109 B2
Clifton Dr S FY8 88 E5
Clifton Gdns FY8 89 C6
Clifton Gn PR4 114 C2
Clifton Gr Chorley PR7 42 B7
Fulwood PR1 117 C3
Wilpshire BB1 121 F4
Clifton Hospl FY8 89 B5
Clifton La PR4 114 D2
Clifton Lodge FY8 88 E5
Clifton Par 3 FY8 90 B3
Clifton Pk Ret Ctr FY4 110 D8
Clifton Pl Freckleton PR4 92 B6
Fulwood PR2 116 B2
Clifton Rd Blackpool FY4 110 C8
Brierfield BB9 147 C4
Burnley BB12 126 C7
Fleetwood FY7 194 A3
Formby L37 12 A5
Southport PR8 34 F6
Clifton Sq 4 FY8 90 B3
Clifton St Accrington BB5 103 A4
Blackpool FY1 129 B5
Burnley BB12 126 F6
Colne BB8 169 D5
Darwen BB3 80 F4
Lytham St Anne's FY8 90 B3
5 Preston PR1 95 D6
Rishton BB1 123 B1
Sough BB18 192 A8
Trawden BB8 170 C2
Clifton Terr BB3 81 E2
Clifton Wlk 6 FY8 90 B3
Clinkham Rd BB6 123 A5
Clinning Rd PR8 34 A2
Clinton Ave FY1 129 C4
Clinton St BB1 101 A6
Clippers Quay BB1 100 F4
Clitheroe Castle BB7 164 E8
Clitheroe Castle
Mus BB7 164 E8
Clitheroe Hospl BB7 187 A3
Clitheroe Pl FY4 110 A8
Clitheroe Rd
Brierfield BB9 147 A5
Chatburn BB7 187 C3
Lytham St Anne's FY8 89 C6
Sabden BB7 165 E1
Waddington BB7 186 C3
West Bradford BB7 186 F5
Whalley BB7 143 C7
Clitheroe Royal
Gram Sch Clitheroe BB7 186 F1
Clitheroe BB7 187 A2
Clitheroe St
3 Padiham BB12 125 C8
Preston PR1 96 C7
Clitheroe Sta BB7 186 E1
Clitheroes La PR4 92 B6
Clive Ave FY8 109 E1
Clive Lo PR8 33 F2
Clive Rd Penwortham PR1 95 B6
Southport PR8 33 F2
Clive St BB12 126 F8
Clockhouse Ave BB10 147 D3
Clockhouse Ct BB10 147 D3
Clockhouse Gr BB10 147 D3
Clod La BB4 67 C8
Clods Carr La FY6 194 F3
Clog Heads BB8 170 C2
Clogger La BD23 201 F7
Cloister Dr BB3 81 C1
Cloister Gn L37 12 B2
Cloisters LA3 212 F2
Cloisters The
Blackpool FY3 129 E5
Formby L37 11 F3
2 Leyland PR5 76 C2
6 Preston PR2 95 D8
Tarleton PR4 56 A6
Whalley BB7 143 D5
Clorain Cl L33 1 A3
Clorain Rd L33 1 A3
Close The Banks PR9 54 A5
Clayton-le-M BB5 123 F4
Cleveleys FY5 172 D2
Cleveleys, Rossall
Beach FY5 172 D4
Fulwood PR2 117 E6
Garstang PR3 199 B1
Haslingden BB5 84 A8
Ince Blundell L38 3 E3
Kirkham PR4 113 B4
New Longton PR4 75 A7
Weeton PR4 131 E2
Withnell Fold PR6 78 C3
Clough Acre PR7 60 A2
Clough Ave PR1 96 B3
Clough Bank BB7 187 D5
Clough End Rd BB4 84 B5
Clough Fold
Cty Prim Sch WN8 18 C2
Clough Head Visitor Ctr
BB4 83 A3
Clough La
Hesketh Lane PR3 161 A7
Simonstone BB12 144 F1
Clough Rd Bacup OL13 87 A3
Nelson BB9 148 A8
Clough St 8 Bacup OL13 69 D8
Burnley BB11 126 D5
Darwen BB3 64 C6
5 Newchurch BB4 85 F1
Clough Terr BB18 200 B1
Clough The
Clayton Green PR6 77 A3
Darwen BB3 64 C6
Clougha Ave Halton LA2 214 F7
Lancaster LA1 211 B6
Cloughfield PR1 95 D1
Cloughfold Cty Prim Sch
BB4 85 C2
Cloughton Terr LA2 231 F5
Cloughwood Cres WN6 19 D6
Clovelly Ave
Blackpool FY5 150 D6
Fulwood PR2 116 D3
Clovelly Dr Newburgh WN8 26 A1
Penwortham PR1 95 A5
Skelmersdale WN8 18 A8
Southport PR8 20 E8
Clover Ave FY8 110 A1
Clover Crescent BB12 126 D8
Clover Ct Blackpool FY2 150 F6
Southport PR8 34 B5
Clover Dr PR4 92 D7
Clover Field PR6 77 B2
Clover Hill Rd BB9 147 F7
Clover Mews FY3 129 E6
Clover Rd PR7 42 A5
Clover St OL13 87 A3
Clover Terr BB3 81 A3
Cloverfield PR1 95 B4
Cloverfields BB1 101 A6
Cloverhill Ho BB9 147 F7
Club La PR3 182 E3
Club St Bamber Bridge PR5 76 F7
Cornholme OL14 108 B1
Clucas Gdns L39 15 E6
Clyde St Blackburn BB2 100 B3
4 Blackpool FY1 129 B7
Preston PR2 95 C8
Clydesdale Pl PR5 75 C2
Clyffes Farm Cl L40 23 A7
Co-operation St
Bacup OL13 87 A2
Newchurch BB4 85 F2
3 Rake Foot BB4 85 A7
Rawtenstall BB4 85 B2
Co-operative Bldgs BB10 106 F8
Co-operative St
1 Bamber Bridge PR5 76 E8
19 Barnoldswick BB18 200 B2
Haslingden BB4 66 F7
Coach Ho Ct L40 24 E3
Coach Mews LA4 212 C4
Coach Rd Bickerstaffe L39 7 F1
Church BB5 102 E5
Warton, Carnforth LA5 217 D7
Coal Clough Jun & Inf Sch
BB11 126 D5
Coal Clough La BB11 126 E4
Coal Clough Rd OL14 108 B2
Coal Hey 12 BB4 84 B3
Coal Hey St 13 BB4 84 B3
Coal Pit La Accrington BB5 102 F4
Bacup OL13 87 B3
Barnoldswick BB7 190 B7
Colne BB8 169 F4
Darwen BB3 80 B3
Gisburn BB7 225 D2
Rawtenstall BB4 86 A4
Skelmersdale L39 8 D4
Coal Rd BL0 50 C8
Coal St 12 BB11 126 F6
Coastal Dr LA2 215 E2
Coastal Rd
Hest Bank LA2,LA5 215 F2
Morecambe LA4 213 B8
Southport, Birkdale PR8 33 C3
Southport, Woodvale PR8 20 A4
Coastal Rise LA2 215 E2
Coastline Mews PR9 53 A4
Coates Ave BB18 200 C3
Coates Fields BB18 200 C4
Coates La BB18 200 D4
Coates Lane Prim Sch
BB18 200 D3
Cob Castle Rd BB4 83 E3
Cob La BB8,BB18 192 B4
Cob Moor Ave WN5 10 D1
Cob Moor Rd WN5 10 D1
Cobb's Brow L40 17 F5
Cobb's Brow La WN8 18 B6
Cobb's Clough Rd L40 17 F5
Cobbled Court Yd LA1 210 E7
Cobbs Brow Cty Prim Sch
WN8 18 A3
Cobbs La BB5 82 E8
Cobden Ct 3 BB1 100 E5
Cobden Ho BB4 85 D1
Cobden Rd PR9 35 A6
Cobden St Bacup OL13 70 B8
Barnoldswick BB18 200 B1
Brierfield BB10 147 F3
Cobden St *continued*
Burnley BB10 127 B8
4 Bury BL9 32 A3
Chorley PR6 60 E1
10 Darwen BB3 64 A8
Egerton BL7 46 D2
Hapton BB12 125 C4
Nelson BB9 147 D7
Padiham BB12 145 D1
Cobham Ct 2 BB4 85 E1
Cobham Rd BB5 103 D5
Cobourg Cl BB2 100 F2
Cochran St 24 BB3 81 A1
Cock Hall La OL12 51 C8
Cock Robin PR5 57 C2
Cock Robin La PR3 178 D2
Cocker Ave FY6 152 A2
Cocker Bar Rd PR5 57 D8
Cocker La PR5 75 C1
Cocker Rd PR5 77 B7
Cocker Sq 3 FY1 129 B6
Cocker St Blackpool FY1 129 B6
Darwen BB3 64 C7
Cockerham Parochial
CE Prim Sch LA2 203 D4
Cockerham Rd
Garstang PR3 199 B1
Potters Brook LA2,PR3 204 B4
Cockerham Wlk FY3 130 A8
Cockerill St BB4 84 B4
Cockerill Terr BB7 164 D1
Cockermouth Cl BB3 80 F7
Cockersand Ave PR4 94 C1
Cockersand Dr LA1 211 A3
Cockhall La OL12 70 C1
Cockhill La BB8 170 B8
Cocking Yd LA6 234 C7
Cockle Dick's La PR9 52 E2
Cockleach Lane Ends
PR3 160 A2
Cockridge Cl BB2 80 B7
Cockshot La LA7 237 F4
Codale Ave FY2 150 D5
Coddington St BB1 101 B5
Coe La PR4 56 A5
Cog La BB11 126 D4
Cog St BB11 126 D5
Colbran St Burnley BB10 127 B8
10 Nelson BB9 168 F2
Colburne Cl L40 24 F5
Colchester Ave LA1 211 B5
Colchester Dr 6 FY5 172 F4
Colchester Rd
Blackpool FY3 129 F3
Southport PR8 34 F3
Cold Bath St 4 PR1 95 E8
Cold Well La LA7 237 F1
Coldale Ct 4 FY4 109 B6
Coldstream Pl BB2 100 E2
Coldweather Ave BB9 147 F5
Coldwell Inn Activity Ctr
BB10 149 A5
Cole Cres L39 6 C8
Colebatch PR2 116 D5
Coleman St 4 BB9 147 F8
Colenso Rd Blackburn BB1 100 D7
Fulwood PR2 116 C2
Coleridge Ave FY5 173 A3
Coleridge Cl Colne BB8 169 D6
Cottam PR4 115 E4
Coleridge Dr BB5 103 E2
Coleridge Pl BB6 123 B4
Coleridge Rd
Blackpool FY1 129 D6
Longshaw WN5 10 D1
Ramsbottom BL8 48 F2
Coleridge St BB2 100 C3
Coles Dr LA5 237 B1
Colesberg Ct LA5 237 B2
Coleshill Ave BB10 127 D5
Colesville Ave FY5 173 B1
Colin St Barnoldswick BB18 200 B3
Burnley BB11 126 D5
Colinmander Gdns L39 15 C3
Colinton WN8 9 E7
Colldale Terr BB4 84 B2
College Ave Cleveleys FY5 172 C1
Formby L37 11 E4
College Cl Formby L37 11 D4
Longridge PR3 139 A5
Padiham BB12 125 D6
Southport PR8 34 A3
College Ct Accrington BB5 103 A6
4 Blackpool FY1 129 C4
Fulwood PR1 116 F2
College Gate FY5 172 C5
College Path L37 11 D5
College Rd WN8 19 B1
College St Accrington BB5 103 A6
7 Cornholme OL14 108 C1
Collegiate High Sch FY3 151 A1
Collier St BB5 103 E2
Collier's La LA6 238 E3
Collier's Row BB1 101 F1
Colliers St BB5 102 E5
Collin's Hill La PR3 182 A3
Colling St 9 BL0 49 B5
Collinge Fold La BB4 84 F4
Collinge St Padiham BB12 125 C7
Rawtenstall BB4 84 F4
Collingham Pk LA1 211 A2
Collingwood BB5 123 E2
Collingwood Ave
Blackpool FY3 129 E6
Lytham St Anne's FY8 109 E1

Collingwood Pl FY3 129 E6
Collingwood Rd PR7 42 B7
Collingwood St
Colne BB8 169 C4
Standish WN6 28 E1
Collingwood Terr 7 LA2 233 D8
Collins Ave FY2 150 E3
Collins Dr BB5 103 E2
Collins Rd PR5 96 F1
Collins Rd N PR5 96 F2
Collinson St PR1 117 C1
Collisdene Rd WN5 10 E6
Collison Ave PR7 42 C8
Collyhurst Ave FY4 109 E6
Colman Ct PR1 95 D6
Colnbrook WN6 28 B1
Colne & Broughton Rd BD23 201 C6
Colne Coll of F Ed BB8 169 A5
Colne Golf Course BB8 170 B8
Colne La BB8 169 E4
Colne Rd
Barnoldswick BB18 200 A1
Barrowford BB8,BB9 168 F4
Brierfield BB9 147 B6
Burnley BB10,BB11 127 A8
Burnley, Burnley Lane BB10 147 B3
Sough BB18 192 A7
Trawden BB8 170 B2
Colne Sta BB8 169 C4
Colt House Cl PR5 59 A7
Colthirst Dr BB7 187 A2
Coltsfoot Dr PR6 60 D2
Coltsfoot Wlk LA3 212 E2
Columbia Way BB2 100 B8
Columbine Cl Chorley PR7 60 A3
Rochdale OL12 51 C3
Colville Ave 1 FY4 109 C5
Colville Rd BB3 80 E4
Colville St BB10 127 A8
Colwall Cl L33 1 A2
Colwall Rd L33 1 A2
Colwall Wlk L33 1 A2
Colwyn Ave Blackpool FY4 129 E1
Morecambe LA4 212 G6
Colwyn Pl PR2 116 A3
Colyton Cl PR6 42 E8
Colyton Rd PR6 42 E8
Colyton Rd E 2 PR6 42 E8
Combermere Gr LA3 208 E5
Combermere Rd LA3 208 E6
Comer Gdns L31 5 C3
Comet Rd PR5 75 C2
Comet St OL13 87 A7
Commerce St Bacup OL13 86 F2
Haslingden BB4 84 A4
Commercial Rd
Chorley PR7 60 C1
Great Harwood BB6 123 C5
Nelson BB9 147 E8
Commercial St Bacup OL13 69 D8
Barnoldswick BB18 200 B2
10 Blackpool FY1 129 B1
Brierfield BB9 147 B6
7 Church BB5 102 E6
12 Great Harwood BB6 123 C5
Oswaldtwistle BB5 102 D3
Rawtenstall BB4 105 A3
Rishton BB1 123 B1
Common Bank Employment Area PR7 41 F8
Common Bank La PR7 41 F8
Common Edge Rd FY4 109 F6
Common End PR7 29 E5
Common Gdn St 35 LA1 210 F8
Common La PR9 54 C1
Common The Adlington PR7 29 E5
Parbold WN8 26 C3
Commons La BB2 120 B5
Commonside FY8 89 D4
Commonwealth Cl FY8 89 C8
Como Ave BB11 126 C4
Company St 7 BB1 123 B1
Compley Ave FY6 151 C2
Compley Gn FY6 151 C2
Compression Rd LA3 208 E2
Compston Ave BB4 105 A1
Compton Cl FY6 151 C5
Compton Gn PR2 116 D7
Compton Rd PR8 34 B3
Comrie Cres BB11 126 D3
Concorde Ho 1 FY1 129 C4
Concourse Sh Ctr WN8 18 B1
Conder Ave FY5 172 F2
Conder Brow LA5 217 E2
Conder Green Rd LA2 206 F3
Conder Pl 3 LA1 213 E2
Conder Rd PR2 115 E1
Condor Gr Blackpool FY1 129 D3
Lytham St Anne's FY8 88 E8
Conduit St BB9 168 D1
Coneygarth La
Tunstall LA6 235 D4
Whittington LA6 235 D6
Congleton Cl FY4 130 B1
Congress St PR7 60 C1
Conifer Ct L37 12 A2
Conifers The Barton PR3 136 B8
Hambleton FY6 174 B2
Kirkham PR4 113 B5
Maghull L31 5 C3
Conisber Cl BL7 46 E1
Coniston Ave
Accrington BB5 102 F4
Adlington PR6 30 B8
Coniston Ave *continued*
Barnoldswick BB18 200 A3
Carleton FY6 151 B4
Euxton PR7 59 D1
Fleetwood FY7 193 E4
Fulwood PR2 116 D2
Hambleton FY6 174 C2
Knott End-on-S FY6 194 E6
Lytham St Anne's FY8 109 F2
Orrell WN5 10 F7
Padiham BB12 145 C2
Thornton FY5 173 B1
Coniston Cl Longridge PR3 139 A5
Ramsbottom BL0 49 C7
Coniston Cres FY5 173 B1
Coniston Ct
Morecambe LA4 212 F6
Southport PR8 20 C3
Coniston Dr
Bamber Bridge PR5 96 E2
Darwen BB3 81 C2
Coniston Gr BB8 170 A6
Coniston Ho PR1 95 B4
Coniston Rd
Blackburn BB1 101 A8
Blackpool FY4 109 C7
Blackrod BL6 30 D3
Bolton-le-S LA5 216 A4
Carnforth LA5 216 E8
Chorley PR7 42 B6
Formby L37 11 D2
Fulwood PR2 117 C4
Lancaster LA1 214 A2
Maghull L31 5 E2
Morecambe LA4 212 F6
Coniston St 8 BB12 126 C6
Coniston Way Bacup OL13 87 A4
Croston PR5 57 B3
Rainford Junction WA11 8 F2
Rishton BB1 122 F1
Connaught Rd
Heysham LA3 208 D5
Lancaster LA1 211 B5
Preston PR1 95 E5
Consett Ave FY5 172 E5
Constable Ave
Bamber Bridge PR5 76 A7
Burnley BB11 126 F3
Constable Lee Cres BB4 85 A4
Constable Lee St Paul's CE Sch BB4 85 A4
Constable St 7 PR1 96 A8
Convent Cl
Bamber Bridge PR5 96 D1
Leyland PR5 76 C2
Ormskirk L39 15 E2
Convent Cres FY3 130 A8
Conway Ave
Bamber Bridge PR5 96 A1
Blackburn BB1 100 E7
Cleveleys FY5 172 D2
Clitheroe BB7 164 C6
Leyland PR5 59 C8
Normoss FY3 130 B7
Conway Cl Catterall PR3 178 D2
Euxton PR7 59 E1
Haslingden BB4 84 B1
Ramsbottom BL0 49 B6
Conway Cres
Barnoldswick BB18 200 C3
Ramsbottom BL8 48 F2
Conway Ct PR5 97 D2
Conway Dr Bury BL9 32 D2
Fulwood PR2 116 C6
Oswaldtwistle BB5 102 B4
Conway Gr BB10 147 C3
Conway Ho 7 PR1 96 D8
Conway Rd Eccleston PR7 40 C7
Rawtenstall BB4 85 C2
Conyers Ave PR8 33 F3
Cook Gdns BB1 101 B4
Cook Green La PR3 140 C7
Cook House Rd BB8 169 E6
Cook St BL9 32 A2
Cooke St BL6 31 D4
Cookson Cl PR4 92 B6
Cookson Rd FY5 173 B3
Cookson St FY1 129 C5
Cookwood Ho 13 PR1 95 D8
Coolham La BB18 201 D1
Coolidge Ave LA1 210 D7
Coombes The PR2 116 F5
Coop St FY1 129 B3
Cooper Ct FY5 172 D3
Cooper Hill Cl PR5 96 D5
Cooper Hill Dr PR5 96 D5
Cooper Rd PR1 95 D8
Cooper St Bacup OL13 86 F4
Burnley BB11 127 A5
Horwich BL6 31 B4
Nelson BB9 168 E1
Cooper's La PR7 27 B8
Cooper's Way FY1 129 D7
Coopers Cl 4 BB5 102 D3
Coote La PR5 75 F7
Cop La Fleetwood FY7 194 A4
Penwortham PR1 95 C4
Cop Lane CE Prim Sch PR1 95 C3
Cop Rd PR8 34 F5
Cop Royd Terr BB10 127 F1
Cop The FY5 172 D6
Copeland Dr WN6 28 F1
Copeland Pl FY8 90 C4
Copp La PR3,PR4 154 A2
Copper Beech Cl PR4 73 E3
Copperas La BL6 30 B1
Copperfield Cl BB10 127 F6
Copperfield St BB1 100 F3
Copperwood Way PR7 41 F7
Coppice Ave BB5 103 D7
Coppice Brow LA5 217 F2
Coppice Cl Chorley PR6 60 E1
Nelson BB9 169 A2
Coppice Dr Longshaw WN5 10 D2
Whitworth OL12 51 D7
Coppice La PR6,PR7 61 C3
Coppice Leys L37 11 E3
Coppice St BL9 32 C3
Coppice The
Blackburn BB2 100 A7
Clayton-le-M BB5 123 F4
Fulwood PR2 116 B4
Kirkham PR4 113 A6
Longton PR4 74 A7
Morecambe LA4 213 A5
Ramsbottom BL0 49 A4
Coppingford Cl OL12 51 A2
Coppins Gn FY6 151 E1
Coppull & District Cty Prim Sch PR7 41 E1
Coppull Cross Rds PR7 28 F7
Coppull Hall La PR7 42 A1
Coppull Moor La PR7 28 E6
Coppull Parish Church Prim Sch PR7 41 F1
Coppull Rd Chorley PR7 42 A4
Maghull L31 5 C4
Copse Rd FY7 193 F2
Copse The Accrington BB5 102 F5
Chorley PR7 42 B4
Edgworth BL7 47 C2
Copster Dr PR3 139 B7
Copster Hill Cl BB1 81 D8
Copthurst Ave BB12 145 F6
Copthurst La PR6 60 F7
Copthurst St 18 BB12 145 C1
Coptrod Head Cl OL12 51 E4
Copy Bottom BB10 107 C4
Copy La LA2 231 C3
Copy Nook BB1 101 A5
Coral Cl FY4 130 A1
Corbridge Cl
Blackpool FY4 110 A7
Carleton FY6 151 C5
Corbridge Ct BB7 186 E1
Corcas La FY6 173 F8
Cork Rd LA1 211 B5
Cork St BL9 32 A2
Corka La FY8 111 F1
Corke Cotts FY8 111 E1
Corlass St 10 BB9 168 D3
Corless Cotts LA2 220 A8
Corn Mill La FY7 194 B4
Corn Mill Lo L31 5 C2
Corn Mill Yd BB5 123 F2
Cornbrook WN8 9 E7
Corncroft PR1 95 C3
Cornel Gr BB11 126 C4
Cornelian St BB1 121 F2
Corner Bank Cl PR4 111 F7
Corners The FY5 172 C4
Cornfield PR4 115 E6
Cornfield Cl PR4 72 E4
Cornfield Gr BB12 126 A8
Cornfield St BB3 81 B2
Cornflower Cl PR6 60 D2
Cornford Rd FY4 110 B8
Cornhill 8 BB5 103 C6
Cornhill Arc BB5 103 B6
Cornholme BB10 147 E2
Cornholme Jun & Infs Sch OL14 108 A1
Cornholme Terr 9 OL14 108 B1
Cornmill Terr 6 BB18 200 B3
Cornthwaite Rd PR2 116 E3
Cornwall Ave
Blackburn BB1 101 E4
Blackpool FY2 150 C2
Cleveleys FY5 172 F4
Cornwall Cres WN1 29 B1
Cornwall Pl Blackpool FY3 130 B2
Church BB5 102 F7
Cornwall Rd BB1 123 A1
Cornwall Way PR8 20 C2
Corona Ave L31 5 C5
Coronation Ave
Blackburn BB2 79 C7
Formby L37 12 A2
Forton PR3 204 B3
Padiham BB12 125 C7
Coronation Cres 5 PR1 96 B7
Coronation Gr BB4 85 E1
Coronation Pl 6 BB9 168 D3
Coronation Rd
Brierfield BB9 147 C5
Cleveleys FY5 172 C2
Kirkham PR4 113 A5
Lytham St Anne's FY8 89 C4
Maghull L31 5 D3
Coronation St
Barnoldswick BB18 200 C2
Blackpool FY1 129 B4
Great Harwood BB6 123 D6
Coronation Terr BB6 142 C1
Coronation Way LA1 214 A4
Coronation Wlk PR8 34 A7
Corporation St
Accrington BB5 103 A5
10 Blackburn BB2 100 E5
Blackpool FY1 129 B5
Chorley PR6 60 D1
6 Clitheroe BB7 164 D8
Nelson BB8 169 A3
Preston PR1 95 F8
4 Southport PR8 34 B7
Corpus Christi RC High Sch PR2 116 E5
Corranstone Cl BL6 31 B3
Corrib Rd FY2 150 D2
Corringham Rd LA4 212 E5
Corston Gr BL6 30 D1
Corwen Cl BB1 100 E7
Cosford St PR4 131 E6
Cotswold Ave PR7 59 D1
Cotswold Cl Eccleston PR7 40 D6
Ramsbottom BL0 49 C4
Cotswold Dr BL6 31 C5
Cotswold Rd
Blackpool FY2 150 D1
Chorley PR7 42 C6
Lytham St Anne's FY8 90 D5
Cottage Cl L39 15 D4
Cottage Fields PR7 42 B5
Cottage La
Bamber Bridge PR5 96 F3
Ormskirk L39 15 D5
Cottage Mews L39 15 D5
Cottage Wlk OL12 51 C4
Cottam Ave PR2 116 A4
Cottam Cl
Lytham St Anne's FY8 109 F2
Whalley BB7 143 C5
Cottam Ct PR2 116 A2
Cottam Cty Prim Sch PR4 115 D5
Cottam Gn PR4 115 F6
Cottam Hall La PR2 115 F5
Cottam La PR2 116 A2
Cottam Pl FY6 151 C2
Cottam St PR7 42 C6
Cottam Way PR4 115 D4
Cottesloe Pl BB9 168 C3
Cottesmore Pl FY3 130 A6
Cottom Croft BB5 123 F4
Cotton Ct Colne BB8 169 C3
Preston PR1 96 A8
Cotton Dr L39 15 D6
Cotton Hall St BB3 81 A2
Cotton St Accrington BB5 103 B5
Burnley BB12 126 D7
Padiham BB12 125 C7
Cotton Tree La BB8 170 A5
Cottys Brow PR9 52 F3
Coudray Rd PR9 52 E1
Coulston Ave FY2 150 B3
Coulston Rd LA1 211 B6
Coultate St 7 BB12 126 C6
Coulter Beck La LA6 236 A7
Coulthurst St 1 BL0 49 B6
Coulton Rd BB9 147 B7
Counsell Ct 3 FY5 173 B2
Countess Cl PR4 113 A7
Countess Cres FY2 150 C3
Countess Rd BB3 81 A7
Countess St BB5 103 A6
Countess Way PR7 59 D2
Countessway 3 PR5 96 E1
Country Side Ctr BB4 84 E1
County Brook La BB8,BB18 191 C4
County Cl PR5 76 A4
County Rd Kirkby L32 1 A1
Ormskirk L39 15 E6
County St LA1 210 E8
Coupe Gn PR5 97 E4
Coupe Green Cty Prim Sch PR5 97 E4
Coupland St OL12 51 C8
Courage Low La WN6 27 D5
Course La L40,WN8 25 D1
Court Gr BB1 121 E6
Court Hey L31 5 E1
Court Mews PR9 53 A1
Court Rd PR9 34 C8
Court Royal FY8 89 E3
Court The Fulwood PR2 116 C7
Penwortham PR1 95 C4
Southport PR9 34 B8
Courtfield L39 15 D7
Courtfield Ave FY2 129 D8
Courtfields 3 FY1 129 C4
Courtgreen L39 15 D7
Courtyard The
8 Bacup OL13 87 A3
1 Kirkham PR4 112 F5
Courtyard Wks L33 1 C2
Cousin's La L40 38 A3
Cove Dr LA5 218 C4
Cove Rd LA5 218 B4
Cove The Cleveleys FY5 172 C4
Lytham St Anne's FY8 89 D3
Morecambe LA4 213 A7
Covell Ho 3 LA1 210 E8
Coventry St 2 PR7 42 C6
Coverdale Dr BB2 79 D7
Coverdale Rd LA1 210 D8
Coverdale Way BB12 126 D7
Covert The FY5 172 F4
Coveway Ave FY3 129 E6
Cow Gate La BD23 225 E7
Cow Well La PR6 60 B8
Cowan Brae BB1 100 D6
Cowdrey Mews 8 LA1 213 D1
Cowell Way BB2 100 D5
Cowes Ave BB4 84 C2
Cowgarth La BB18 201 C2
Cowgill St 18 Bacup OL13 87 A3
Earby BB18 201 B1
Cowhill La BB1 101 F7
Cowley Cres BB12 125 E7
Cowley Rd Blackpool FY4 109 F8
Fulwood PR2 117 E4
Cowling Brow PR6 42 E7
Cowling Brow Ind Est PR6 42 F6
Cowling La PR5 75 D1
Cowling Rd PR6 42 F6
Cowm Park Way N OL12 70 D2
Cowm Park Way S OL12 70 C1
Cowm St OL12 70 E5
Cowpe Rd BB4 68 F7
Cowper Ave BB7 186 E1
Cowper Pl BB7 224 C1
Cowper St Blackburn BB1 100 F7
Burnley BB11 126 C5
Cowslip Way PR6 60 D2
Cowtoot La OL13 87 A4
Cox Green Cl BL7 46 D3
Cox Green Rd BL7 46 E2
Coxfield WN6 19 D7
Coyford Dr PR9 53 A4
Crab Tree La PR3 176 C2
Crabtree Ave Bacup OL13 87 A1
Newchurch BB4 85 F2
Penwortham PR1 95 A3
Crabtree Bldgs BB4 85 F4
Crabtree Cl L40 24 D4
Crabtree La L40 24 D6
Crabtree Orch 2 FY5 173 B3
Crabtree Rd FY5 173 B3
Crabtree St Blackburn BB1 101 B5
Brierfield BB9 147 B5
Bury BL9 32 B3
Colne BB8 169 C4
Whitewell Bottom BB4 85 F4
Cracoe Gill BB9 168 C3
Craddock Rd BB8 169 E5
Crag Ave BL9 49 D2
Crag Bank Cres LA5 216 C8
Crag Bank La LA5 217 B1
Crag Fold BL9 49 D2
Crag La BL9 49 D2
Crag Rd Lancaster LA1 214 B1
Warton, Carnforth LA5 217 A6
Cragg Row BB18 191 D7
Cragg St 1 Blackpool FY1 129 B3
Colne BB8 169 C5
Cragg's Row 17 PR1 95 F8
Craggs La LA2 233 D3
Craig St LA3 212 A3
Craigflower Ct PR5 77 C7
Craiglands Ave LA3 212 A2
Craiglands Ct LA1 210 C5
Crail Pl OL10 32 F1
Crake Ave FY7 193 C2
Crake Bank 4 LA1 213 D2
Cranberry Chase 4 BB3 64 C7
Cranberry Cl BB3 64 D6
Cranberry La BB3 64 D6
Cranberry Rise BB4 105 A2
Cranborne Cl Horwich BL6 31 F1
Standish WN6 28 D1
Cranborne St
5 Bamber Bridge PR5 76 E8
10 Preston PR1 96 C8
Cranborne Terr BB2 100 C6
Cranbourne Dr Chorley PR6 42 E7
Church BB5 103 A8
Cranbourne Gr FY5 151 E7
Cranbourne St Chorley PR6 42 D7
Colne BB8 169 E6
Cranbrook Ave
Blackpool FY2 150 E5
Oswaldtwistle BB5 102 C4
Cranbrook St BB2 100 D2
Crane St PR7 28 D6
Cranes La L40 16 E7
Cranfield View BB3 64 C6
Crangle Fold BB7 187 A2
Crank Rd WN5 10 D1
Crankshaw St 9 BB4 85 A3
Cranleigh Ave FY2 150 C3
Cranleigh Cl BL6 30 D1
Cranmer St 5 BB11 126 E6
Cranshaw Dr BB1 100 F8
Cranston Rd L33 1 C2
Cranwell Ave LA1 211 B5
Cranwell Cl 2 BB1 101 A4
Cranwell Ct PR4 112 F5
Craven Cl PR2 116 F7
Craven Ct BL6 31 D2
Craven St Accrington BB5 103 A5
6 Barnoldswick BB18 200 C2
Brierfield BB9 147 B5
Burnley BB11 127 A5
Bury BL9 32 C3
Clitheroe BB7 164 E7
Colne BB8 170 A5
Nelson BB9 147 C8
Rawtenstall BB4 84 F2
Craven St E BL6 31 D2
Craven's Ave BB2 80 D6
Craven's Brow BB2 80 E7
Cravendale Ave BB9 168 F3
Cravens Hollow BB2 80 D6
Cravens Hollows BB2 80 E6
Crawford Ave
Adlington PR7 29 E5
Blackpool FY2 150 D5
Chorley PR7 42 B7
Leyland PR5 59 B8
Maghull L31 5 B3
Preston PR1 117 F1
Crawford Cty Sch WN8 9 E3
Crawford Rd WN8 9 D2
Crawford St BB9 168 E1
Crawshaw Dr BB4 85 A6
Crawshaw Grange BB4 85 A7
Crawshaw La BB10 148 D6
Crawshaw St BB5 103 B6
Crawshaw's Bldgs BB4 85 A1

Crawshawbooth
Cty Prim Sch BB4 85 A8
Crediton Ave PR9 53 B5
Crediton Cl BB2 80 C8
Crescent Ave L37 11 E1
Crescent Ct FY4 109 A5
Crescent E FY5 172 D2
Crescent Gn L39 15 B1
Crescent Rd
Poulton-le-F FY6 151 E4
Southport PR8 33 F3
Crescent St PR1 117 C1
Crescent The
Bamber Bridge PR5 96 F2
Blackburn BB2 99 E1
Blackpool FY4 109 B7
Brierfield BB10 147 B4
Carleton FY6 151 C4
Chorley PR7 60 C2
Clitheroe BB7 164 D7
Colne BB8 169 E6
Dunsop Bridge BB7 222 C5
Fleetwood FY7 172 E8
Freckleton PR4 92 C5
Hest Bank LA2 215 D1
Horwich BL6 31 E1
Lostock Hall PR5 76 C8
Lytham St Anne's FY8 88 E6
Preesall FY6 195 B4
Preston, A-on-Ribble PR2 116 B2
1 Preston, Lea PR2 115 D1
Southport PR9 53 C3
Warton PR4 91 C4
Whalley BB7 143 A6
Whitworth OL12 51 C8
Worsthorne BB10 128 A5
Crescent W FY5 172 D2
Cressell Pk WN6 28 B1
Cressingham Wlk LA1 211 B3
Cresswood Ave FY5 172 D1
Crestway Blackpool FY3 129 F6
Tarleton PR4 56 A8
Creswell Ave PR2 115 F3
Creswick Ave BB11 126 F3
Creswick Cl BB11 126 F3
Crewdson St BB3 80 F2
Crewgarth Rd LA3 212 E2
Cribden End La BB4 84 D4
Cribden House Sch BB4 84 E1
Cribden La BB4 84 E5
Cribden St BB4 84 F4
Criccieth Cl 3 BB4 84 B1
Crichton Pl FY4 109 B5
Cricket Path Formby L37 11 F5
Southport PR8 33 F3
Cricketers Gn PR7 40 B6
Crimbles La LA2 203 B2
Crime Well La LA3 208 E7
Crimea St OL13 87 A2
Crinan Sq OL10 32 F1
Cringle Way BB7 187 A2
Cripple Gate WN6 28 A2
Cripple Gate La PR5 98 C4
Critchley Cl PR4 73 F3
Croasdale 7 LA1 213 C2
Croasdale Ave
Brierfield BB10 147 E2
Fulwood PR2 117 E4
Croasdale Cl LA5 217 C1
Croasdale Dr
Cleveleys FY5 172 F4
Clitheroe BB7 164 F7
Parbold WN8 26 C3
Croasdale Sq BB1 101 A3
Croasdale Wlk FY3 130 B8
Crockleford Ave PR8 34 E3
Crocus Cl BB4 66 F8
Crocus Field PR5 59 A7
Croft Acres BL0 67 D2
Croft Ave Burscough L40 24 F3
Hest Bank LA2 213 E8
Orrell WN5 10 D5
Croft Bank PR1 95 C3
Croft Butts La PR4 92 C6
Croft Cl BB4 85 A5
Croft Ct Fleetwood FY7 193 E2
Thornton FY5 173 C3
Croft Field L31 5 E1
Croft Gdns PR4 113 A4
Croft Head Rd BB1 122 B1
Croft Hey L40 38 B4
Croft Heys L39 15 B1
Croft La BB12 145 F6
Croft Manor PR4 92 C6
Croft Mdw PR5 77 C6
Croft Rd PR6 42 E7
Croft St Bacup OL13 86 F3
Burnley BB11 127 A5
Bury BL9 32 A2
Clitheroe BB7 164 E7
17 Darwen BB3 81 A1
Earby BB18 201 C2
Great Harwood BB6 123 C4
Morecambe LA4 212 F5
10 Preston PR1 95 D8
Preston PR1 95 E8
Croft The Blackburn BB1 100 D7
Burton in L LA6 236 C3
Carnforth LA5 217 E6
Caton LA2 231 C3
Cleveleys FY5 172 D2
Eccleston PR7 40 C7
Euxton PR7 59 B3
Fleetwood FY7 193 E2
Garstang PR3 199 B1
Goosnargh PR3 137 D6
Great Plumpton PR4 111 E7
Hoghton PR5 98 B2

Croft The *continued*
Lytham St Anne's FY8 110 B1
Maghull L31 5 B5
Orrell WN5 10 D3
Poulton-le-F FY6 151 D2
Croft Way FY5 151 C8
Crofters Fold Galgate LA2 207 B4
Morecambe LA3 212 B1
Crofters Gn Euxton PR7 59 C3
Preston PR1 116 E2
Crofters La L33 1 A5
Crofters Mews 12 FY1 129 C7
Crofters Wlk 4 PR1 95 D2
Croftgate PR2 116 F5
Croftland Gdns LA5 216 B6
Croftlands Borwick LA6 234 B3
Orrell WN5 10 D4
Ramsbottom BL0 49 A3
Warton, Carnforth LA5 217 E6
Crofton Ave FY2 150 D5
Crofts Cl PR4 113 C5
Crofts The PR4 94 A1
Croftson Ave L39 15 F7
Croftwood Terr BB2 100 A1
Croichbank BL8 48 B2
Croichley Fold BL8 48 D2
Cromarty Sq OL10 32 F1
Crombleholme Rd PR1 117 E1
Cromer Ave BB10 147 C1
Cromer Gr BB10 147 C1
Cromer Pl Blackburn BB1 100 E7
Fulwood PR2 116 A4
Cromer Rd Blackpool FY2 150 E4
Lytham St Anne's FY8 110 A1
Southport PR8 33 E2
Cromfield L39 15 C2
Cromford Wlk 9 PR1 96 C8
Crompton Ave FY4 109 E7
Crompton Ct 10 PR1 96 A8
Crompton Pl BB2 100 C5
Crompton St PR1 117 C1
Cromwell Ave 1 PR1 95 C3
Cromwell Cl L39 15 C2
Cromwell Rd
Blackpool FY1 129 C7
Fulwood PR2 117 D3
Lancaster LA1 210 E6
Penwortham PR1 95 C3
Cromwell St
Accrington BB5 103 B8
20 Blackburn BB1 101 A4
Burnley BB12 126 F8
Foulridge BB8 191 D1
3 Preston PR1 117 A1
Cromwell Terr 12 BB9 168 D3
Cronkeyshaw Rd OL12 51 F1
Cronkshaw St BB10 127 A7
Cronshaw Dr BB6 142 C1
Crook Dale La FY6 174 E7
Crook Gate La PR3 175 E1
Crook Nook LA3 209 B2
Crook St Adlington PR7 29 F7
Chorley PR7 42 B5
Preston PR1 96 B8
Crookall Cl 7 FY7 193 F2
Crooked La PR1 96 A8
Crooked Shore OL13 86 F3
Crookfield Rd BL7 63 B3
Crookhalgh Ave BB10 127 F6
Crookhey Gdns LA2 203 E3
Crookhey Hall Sch LA2 203 E3
Crookings La PR1 95 A6
Crooklands Dr PR3 178 C8
Crookleigh Pl LA3 212 A2
Croos St BB5 103 C5
Cropper Gdns PR4 72 D3
Cropper Rd FY4 110 C6
Cropper's La L39 16 A1
Cropton Rd L37 11 F3
Crosby Cl BB3 64 B6
Crosby Ct FY8 109 F1
Crosby Gr FY3 129 F3
Crosby Pl PR2 116 A4
Crosby Rd Blackburn BB2 100 E1
Lytham St Anne's FY8 109 F1
Southport PR8 34 A3
Crosby St OL12 51 F2
Crosfield Ave BL9 49 C2
Crosier Wlk PR4 115 E5
Crosland Rd L32 1 A1
Crosland Rd N FY8 89 A8
Crosland Rd S FY8 89 A8
Crosley Cl BB5 103 B3
Cross Bank 9 BB12 125 D8
Cross Barn Gr BB3 64 B8
Cross Barn La L38 3 E3
Cross Barn Wlk 5 BB3 64 B8
Cross Brow PR7 41 C8
Cross Edge BB5 103 A1
Cross Field PR4 94 C1
Cross Flatts Cres BB18 191 E8
Cross Fold BB7 187 B8
Cross Gates BB6 123 C5
Cross Gn L37 12 A2
Cross Green Cl L37 12 A2
Cross Green Rd PR2 116 E6
Cross Hagg St BB8 169 C4
Cross Halls PR1 95 C3
Cross Helliwell St 17
BB8 169 D4
Cross Hill Ct LA5 216 A4
Cross Hill Four Lane Ends
PR3 220 B6
Cross Hill La BB7 225 B1
Cross Hos PR7 41 C8
Cross Keys Dr PR6 60 C7
Cross La
Barley Green BB12 167 C4

Cross La *continued*
Halsall L39 22 C1
Low Bentham LA2 233 B8
Moor Side PR4 133 D1
Orrell WN5 10 D3
Ramsbottom BL8 49 A6
Salterforth BB18 191 E8
Waddington BB7 185 E5
Cross Meanygate L40 37 C5
Cross Rd LA2 233 B7
Cross School St 5 BB8 169 D4
Cross Skelton St 6 BB8 169 E5
Cross St 4 Bacup OL13 87 A3
Blackburn BB3 80 F7
Blackpool FY1 129 B7
Brierfield BB9 147 B5
Brierfield, Harle Syke BB10 147 F3
Chorley PR7 60 C1
Clayton-le-M BB5 123 E3
Clitheroe BB7 164 D8
Darwen BB3 64 B7
Earby BB18 201 A1
Fleetwood FY7 194 B5
Great Harwood BB6 123 D5
Higham BB12 145 F6
3 Leyland PR5 76 B2
Longridge PR3 139 A6
Lytham St Anne's FY8 88 D8
Morecambe LA4 212 F5
Nelson BB9 147 D8
Oswaldtwistle BB5 102 D4
Preston PR1 95 F7
Ramsbottom BL0 49 C6
14 Rawtenstall BB4 85 A7
Southport PR8 34 B6
Standish WN6 28 E1
Worsthorne BB10 128 B6
Cross St N BB4 84 B5
Cross St S BB4 84 B4
Cross St W BB8 169 B4
Cross Swords Cl PR7 42 A5
Cross The L38 3 E4
Cross Way FY5 172 D4
Crossdale Ave LA3 212 A2
Crossdale Sq 10 LA1 211 A8
Crosse Hall La PR6 42 F7
Crosse Hall St PR6 42 F7
Crossens Way PR9 53 C6
Crossfield Ct LA5 237 A1
Crossfield Rd WN8 9 C8
Crossfield St BB2 100 F3
Crosshall Brow L40 16 C4
Crosshall High Sch L39 16 B5
Crosshill Pl 7 LA1 213 D2
Crosshill Rd BB2 100 B5
Crosshill Sch BB1 101 C2
Crosshills 5 BB12 145 C1
Crossing The PR5 98 B2
Crossland Rd FY4 129 E1
Crossland St BB5 103 A5
Crosslands LA6 235 D7
Crossley Fold BB11 126 D4
Crossways BB7 186 D7
Croston Ave PR6 30 A8
Croston Barn La PR3 178 A8
Croston Cl 6 BB1 101 B5
Croston Close Rd
BL9,OL12 50 C4
Croston Dr L40 38 B6
Croston La PR7 41 B2
Croston Meth Prim Sch
PR5 57 B2
Croston Rd Croston L40,PR5 38 C7
Farington PR5 75 F6
Garstang PR3 178 B8
Leyland PR5 75 E4
Croston St BB1 101 C5
Croston Sta PR5 57 B3
Croston's Brow PR9 52 F3
Crow Foot Row BB18 200 B1
Crow Hills Rd PR1 95 A6
Crow La Ramsbottom BL0 49 C6
Skelmersdale WN8 18 F3
Town End PR3 153 E8
Crow Orch Cty Prim Sch
WN8 17 F2
Crow Orchard Rd WN6 28 A1
Crow Park La BB7 225 C4
Crow Tree Ave 4 OL13 69 B8
Crow Trees Brow BB7 187 D4
Crow Trees Gdns BB7 187 D5
Crow Trees La BL7 47 C7
Crow Wood Ave BB12 126 D7
Crow Wood Ct BB12 126 E7
Crow Wood Rd BB4 67 D6
Crowborough Cl BL6 31 F1
Crowder Ave FY5 173 B2
Crowell Way PR5 96 E3
Crowland Cl PR9 35 A6
Crowland St PR9 35 A6
Crowland Way L37 12 B2
Crowle St PR1 96 D8
Crown Cl L37 12 A2
Crown Gdns BL7 47 D6
Crown La Fleetwood FY7 194 B4
Horwich BL6 31 A4
Swillbrook PR4 135 B2
Crown Mews 3 PR4 113 A5
Crown Point BL7 47 D6
Crown Point Rd BB11 126 E1
Crown St Accrington BB5 103 B5
3 Chorley PR7 42 C8
Darwen BB3 64 A8
Leyland PR5 76 B3
Preston PR1 95 F8
Crown Way BB8 169 C5
Crowndale BL7 47 D7
Crownest Ind Est BB18 200 B3

Crownest Rd BB18 200 C3
Crownlee PR1 95 A3
Crowshaw Dr OL12 51 E3
Crowther St Burnley BB11 127 B4
Clayton-le-M BB5 123 E3
Crowthorn Rd BL7 66 A1
Crowthorn Sch BL7 65 F1
Crowtrees 3 LA2 233 B8
Crowtrees Gr BB9 167 F5
Crowtrees Rd BB7 144 F8
Croxteth Cl L31 5 E3
Croxton Wlk 8 BL6 31 B4
Croyde Cl PR9 53 B5
Croyde Rd FY8 89 A5
Croydon Rd 5 FY3 129 E7
Croydon St BB2 100 C5
Crumbleholm Rd PR3 180 E1
Crummock Pl 2 FY4 130 C1
Crummock Rd PR1 118 A1
Crumpax Ave PR3 139 A8
Crumpax Gdns PR3 139 A8
Crystal Gr FY8 88 E8
Crystal Lodge 3 FY8 89 C4
Crystal Rd Blackpool FY1 129 B1
Thornton FY5 173 B5
Cub St PR5 76 A4
Cuba Ind Est BL0 49 C8
Cuba St 3 BB9 147 D8
Cuckoo Brow BB1 100 D8
Cuckoo La Bury BL9 32 C2
Bury BL9 32 C3
Moss Edge PR3 176 B3
Cuckstool La BB12 146 E6
Cudworth Rd FY8 109 F1
Cuerdale La PR1,PR5 97 D6
Cuerdale St BB10 147 E3
Cuerden Ave PR5 58 D7
Cuerden Cl PR5 76 E4
Cuerden Rise PR5 76 C7
Cuerden St Chorley PR6 42 E7
Colne BB8 169 B3
Cuerden Valley Pk PR5 76 F3
Cuerden Way PR5 76 D7
Culbeck La PR7 58 F2
Culshaw St
3 Blackburn BB1 101 A5
Burnley BB10 127 C5
Culshaw Way L40 22 F7
Culvert La WN8 26 A2
Cumberland Ave
Blackpool FY1 129 D4
Burnley BB12 126 A6
Clayton-le-M BB5 124 A3
Cleveleys FY5 172 E4
Leyland PR5 58 E7
Cumberland
House 16 PR1 95 F8
Cumberland Rd PR8 34 D5
Cumberland St
12 Blackburn BB1 101 A4
5 Colne BB8 169 E5
Nelson BB9 168 E1
Cumberland View Rd
LA3 212 A3
Cumbrian Ave FY3 129 E7
Cumbrian Way BB12 126 B8
Cumeragh La PR3 138 C6
Cummins Ave L37 11 E5
Cumpstey St BB2 100 E3
Cuncliffe Ct BB5 123 F2
Cunliffe Ave BL0 49 A4
Cunliffe Cl BB1 122 B1
Cunliffe Ho BB4 85 D1
Cunliffe La BB7 143 F8
Cunliffe Rd Blackburn BB1 122 C1
Blackpool FY1 129 D2
Cunliffe St Chorley PR7 42 D7
10 Preston PR1 96 A8
Ramsbottom BL0 49 C7
Cunnery Mdw PR5 76 E1
Cunningham Ave PR7 42 A6
Cunningham Gr BB12 126 B6
Cunscough La L31, L39 6 D3
Curate St Chorley PR6 60 E1
Great Harwood BB6 123 C5
Curlew Cl Blackburn BB1 100 E8
2 Cleveleys FY5 172 F4
Leyland PR5 58 C7
Oswaldtwistle BB5 102 D3
Curlew Gdns BB11 126 C5
Curlew Gr LA3 208 F5
Curlew La L40 37 E2
Curteis St BL6 31 B4
Curtis Dr FY7 193 D3
Curtis St 8 BB4 85 A3
Curve St OL13 86 F1
Curven Edge BB4 67 A7
Curwen Ave LA3 208 E6
Curwen La PR3 158 C2
Curwen St 7 PR1 117 C1
Curzon Pl BB2 100 C3
Curzon Rd
Lytham St Anne's FY8 89 A7
Poulton-le-F FY6 151 E3
Southport PR8 34 E5
Curzon St 10 Burnley BB11 126 F6
1 Clitheroe BB7 164 D7
Colne BB8 169 E4
Cusson Rd L33 1 B1
Custom House La FY7 194 C5
Customs Way PR2 95 C8
Cut La Haskayne L39, L40 14 F6
Rishton BB1 122 F1
Cutgate Rd OL12 51 B1
Cutler Cl BB2 100 C5
Cutler Cres OL13 69 D7
Cutler La Bacup OL13 69 D7
Hesketh Lane PR3 160 C8

Cutt Cl PR5 57 F6
Cutts La FY6 174 F2
Cyclamen Cl PR5 76 E2
Cygnet Cl L39 15 C2
Cygnet Ct L33 1 A2
Cypress Ave FY5 172 E2
Cypress Cl Clayton-le-W PR5 76 E2
Fulwood PR2 118 A4
Cypress Gr
Bamber Bridge PR5 76 B8
7 Blackpool FY3 129 D7
Cypress Rd PR8 34 F6
Cypress Ridge BB2 79 F8
Cyprus Ave FY8 89 B4
Cyprus Rd LA3 208 E7
Cyprus St BB3 64 B6

D

D'urton La PR2,PR3 136 F1
Daffodil Cl Haslingden BB4 67 A8
Rochdale OL12 51 E3
Dagger Rd PR4 114 C8
Daggers Hall La FY4 109 E8
Daggers La FY6 195 B3
Dahlia Cl Blackburn BB3 81 B7
Clayton-le-W PR5 76 E2
Rochdale OL12 51 D3
Dailton Rd WN8 10 A7
Daisy Bank 12 Bacup OL13 86 F3
Lancaster LA1 211 D7
Daisy Bank Cl PR5 75 D1
Daisy Bank Cres BB10 127 E5
Daisy Bank St 13 OL14 108 B1
Daisy Croft PR2 94 D8
Daisy Fold PR6 60 E2
Daisy Hill BB4 85 A3
Daisy Hill Dr PR6 30 A8
Daisy Hill Fold PR7 59 D1
Daisy La Blackburn BB1 100 F6
Fulwood PR1 117 C3
Ring o'Bells L40 25 B4
Daisy Mdw PR5 77 B5
Daisy St Blackburn BB1 101 A6
Colne BB8 169 D4
3 Lancaster LA1 213 F3
Daisyfield Prim Sch BB1 101 A6
Daisyfield St BB3 80 E5
Daisyfields PR4 115 F7
Dalby Cl Cleveleys FY5 150 F7
Fulwood PR1 117 D3
Dalby Cres BB2 100 A1
Dalby La BB2 100 A1
Dale Ave Euxton PR7 59 D1
Hest Bank LA2 213 E8
Longton PR4 73 E8
Dale Cl Burnley BB12 126 D6
Maghull L31 5 C2
Parbold WN8 26 B2
Dale Cres BB2 79 E7
Dale Dyke Wlk FY6 151 B3
Dale La L33 1 B4
Dale St Accrington BB5 103 A6
Bacup OL13 86 F3
8 Bacup, Stacksteads OL13 69 C8
Blackburn BB2 100 D4
Blackpool FY1 129 B3
Brierfield BB9 147 A5
Burnley BB12 126 D6
Colne BB8 169 C5
Earby BB18 201 B2
Haslingden BB4 84 B3
Lancaster LA1 211 A7
Nelson BB9 147 C8
4 Oswaldtwistle BB5 102 E4
Preston PR1 96 B8
Ramsbottom BL0 67 C1
Dale St E BL6 31 D2
Dale St W BL6 31 D2
Dale Street Mews 7 FY1 129 B3
Dale Terr BB7 187 D5
Dale View Billington BB7 143 B4
Chorley PR7 42 C4
Darwen BB2,BB3 80 E6
Earby BB18 201 A1
6 Rawtenstall BB4 84 F1
Dalecrest WN5 10 D1
Dalegarth Cl FY4 130 C1
Dalehead Rd PR5 59 B7
Dales Ct FY4 109 D6
Dales The BB6 122 A8
Dalesford BB4 84 B1
Dalesford Cl FY5 151 C8
Dalesview Cres LA3 208 F7
Dalesview Park (Cvn Pk)
BB18 191 B7
Dalesway BB9 168 C3
Dalewood Ave FY4 129 E1
Dalglish Dr BB2 80 D7
Dalkeith Ave FY3 130 A2
Dalkeith Rd BB9 147 C8
Dall St BB11 127 A4
Dallam Ave LA4 212 F6
Dallam Dr LA7 237 F6
Dallas Ct LA4 213 B4
Dallas Rd Lancaster LA1 210 E7
Morecambe LA4 213 B4
Dallas Road Sch LA1 210 E7
Dallas St PR1 116 E2
Dalmore Rd PR2 116 A3
Dalton Ave FY4 109 D5
Dalton Cl Blackburn BB1 101 B5
Ramsbottom BL0 49 A4
Dalton La LA6 234 C7

Dalton Rd Lancaster LA1 ... 211 A8
Morecambe LA3 ... 212 A3
Dalton Sq LA1 ... 210 F8
Dalton St Burnley BB11 ... 126 D3
Lytham St Anne's FY8 ... 88 D8
Nelson BB9 ... 168 E1
Dalton St Michael's CE Prim Sch WN8 ... 18 D5
Dalweb Ind Pk PR9 ... 54 C3
Dam Head Rd BB18 ... 200 B2
Dam La L40 ... 23 C6
Dam Side
2 Barnoldswick BB18 ... 200 B3
Colne BB8 ... 169 D4
Dam Top BB4 ... 85 B2
Dam Wood La L40 ... 23 C5
Dame Fold Higham BB12 ... 145 F6
12 Padiham BB12 ... 125 C8
Damfield La L31 ... 5 C1
Damside Cotts LA2 ... 207 B5
Damside St LA1 ... 210 F8
Danbers WN8 ... 9 F6
Dancer La BB7 ... 225 B1
Dandy Row BB3 ... 81 C3
Dandy Wlk BB1 ... 100 E4
Dane Hall La PR7 ... 58 D2
Dane St BB10 ... 127 A7
Danes Cl PR4 ... 113 C5
Danes Dr PR5 ... 96 D1
Danes House Rd BB10 ... 127 A8
Danesbury Pl 4 FY1 ... 129 C5
Danesmoor Dr BL9 ... 32 B4
Danesway
Bamber Bridge PR5 ... 96 D1
Chorley PR7 ... 42 F1
Penwortham PR1 ... 95 A4
Daneswood Ave OL12 ... 51 C8
Daneswood Cl OL12 ... 51 C8
Daneway PR8 ... 20 B6
Danewerke St 8 PR1 ... 96 A8
Daniel Fold OL12 ... 51 B2
Daniel Fold La PR3 ... 178 D2
Daniel St 10
Clayton-le-M BB5 ... 123 F3
Whitworth OL12 ... 70 D2
Daniell St BB1 ... 123 A2
Daniels La WN8 ... 9 C7
Danson Gdns 3 FY2 ... 129 D8
Danvers St BB1 ... 123 B2
Daram Ho 3 FY1 ... 129 D2
Darbishire Rd FY7 ... 193 F4
Daresbury Ave PR8 ... 20 A5
Darfield WN8 ... 9 F7
Dark La Blackrod BL6 ... 30 B3
Earby BB18 ... 201 E2
Johnson's Hillock PR6 ... 60 E6
Maghull L31 ... 5 E1
Mawdesley L40 ... 39 E3
Newchurch BB4 ... 85 E1
Ormskirk L40 ... 16 C6
Dark Wood La PR5 ... 98 B6
Darkinson La
Lea Town PR4 ... 114 F1
Preston PR4 ... 115 B2
Darkwood Cres BB7 ... 187 D5
Darley Ave FY4 ... 109 E7
Darley St BL6 ... 31 B5
Darlington St PR7 ... 41 E1
Darmond Rd L33 ... 1 A3
Darnbrook Rd BB18 ... 200 A2
Darnhill Cty Prim Sch OL10 ... 32 F1
Darnley St BB10 ... 127 C5
Dart St PR2 ... 95 C8
Dartford Cl 1 BB1 ... 101 A4
Dartmouth Cl PR4 ... 112 F5
Darul-Uloom Islamic Coll BL8 ... 48 F4
Darwen Cl PR3 ... 139 B7
Darwen Ent Ctr BB3 ... 81 A2
Darwen Golf Course BB3 ... 80 C3
Darwen L Ctr BB3 ... 81 A1
Darwen Moorland High Sch BB3 ... 81 B3
Darwen Rd BL7 ... 46 E1
Darwen St Blackburn BB2 ... 100 E4
Higher Walton PR5 ... 97 B4
2 Padiham BB12 ... 125 C8
Preston PR1 ... 96 C7
Darwen Sta BB3 ... 81 A1
Darwen Vale High Sch BB3 ... 80 E5
Darwen View PR5 ... 96 E5
Darwin St BB10 ... 147 A2
Daub Hall La PR5 ... 97 E3
Daub La L40 ... 39 A1
Dauntesey Ave FY3 ... 130 A6
Davenham Rd Darwen BB3 ... 80 E3
Formby L37 ... 11 F3
Davenport Ave FY2 ... 150 C5
Daventry Ave FY2 ... 150 B4
David St Bacup OL13 ... 69 D8
11 Barrowford BB9 ... 168 D4
Burnley BB11 ... 126 F4
16 Rochdale OL12 ... 51 F1
David St N 15 OL12 ... 51 F1
Davidson St 15 LA1 ... 211 A8
Davies Rd BB1 ... 101 D6
Davis St PR3 ... 139 A8
Davitt Cl 4 BB4 ... 84 B3
Davy Field Brow BB1 ... 81 B6
Davy Field Rd BB1 ... 81 B6
Dawber's La PR7 ... 58 E2
Dawlish Ave FY3 ... 129 F8
Dawlish Cl BB2 ... 80 C8
Dawlish Dr PR9 ... 53 A5
Dawlish Lodge FY8 ... 88 D7
Dawlish Pl PR2 ... 116 A3
Dawnay Rd PR2 ... 117 E3
Dawson Ave
Simonstone BB12 ... 144 E2
Southport PR9 ... 53 C5
Dawson Gdns L31 ... 5 C2
Dawson La PR6,PR7 ... 59 E7
Dawson Pl PR5 ... 77 A7
Dawson Rd
Lytham St Anne's FY8 ... 109 F1
Ormskirk L39 ... 15 F7
Dawson Sq BB11 ... 127 A7
Dawson St BL9 ... 32 A4
Dawson Wlk PR1 ... 116 F1
Day St BB9 ... 147 E7
Daybrook WN8 ... 9 F7
Dayfield WN8 ... 10 B7
Dayton Pl FY4 ... 109 C6
De Lacy Ho BB2 ... 100 C5
De Lacy St Clitheroe BB7 ... 164 D8
Preston PR2 ... 116 D2
De Vitre St 6 LA1 ... 214 A1
Deakin's Terr BL7 ... 45 C5
Deakins Bsns Pk BL7 ... 46 D1
Deal Pl FY8 ... 109 F1
Deal St Blackburn BB1 ... 100 F7
9 Bury BL9 ... 32 B2
Dean Brow PR3 ... 140 F8
Dean Cl Edenfield BL0 ... 67 D3
Orrell WN8 ... 10 C7
Dean Ct FY7 ... 172 D8
Dean Fold BB4 ... 86 A8
Dean Head La BL6 ... 44 A4
Dean La Billington BB6,BB7 ... 143 C1
Darwen BB3 ... 80 B1
Samlesbury PR5 ... 118 F3
Water BB4 ... 86 B8
Dean Mdw 5 BB7 ... 164 D7
Dean Rd BB4 ... 84 B1
Dean St Bamber Bridge PR5 ... 96 E1
Blackpool FY4 ... 109 B8
Burnley BB11 ... 126 F6
Darwen BB3 ... 80 F4
2 Padiham BB12 ... 145 D1
Trawden BB8 ... 170 C2
Dean Terr 4 PR4 ... 113 A5
Dean Wood Ave WN5 ... 10 E8
Deancroft Ave LA3 ... 212 B2
Deanpoint LA3 ... 212 F3
Deans Ct L37 ... 11 F5
Deans La L40,WN8 ... 25 E3
Deansgate Blackpool FY1 ... 129 B5
Morecambe LA4 ... 212 E5
Deansgate La L37 ... 12 B5
Deansgate La N L37 ... 12 A6
Deansgrave BB4 ... 84 B1
Deansgreave Rd OL13 ... 70 B7
Dearden Clough BL0 ... 67 E2
Dearden Fold BL0 ... 67 E2
Dearden Nook BB4 ... 85 A1
Deardengate BB4 ... 84 B3
Deardengate Croft 11 BB4 ... 84 B3
Deben Cl WN6 ... 28 D1
Deborah Ave PR2 ... 117 A7
Dee Rd LA1 ... 213 D2
Dee St FY8 ... 88 E6
Deepdale Ave FY6 ... 151 B5
Deepdale Ct BB9 ... 168 C3
Deepdale Cty Inf Sch PR1 ... 117 B2
Deepdale Cty Jun Sch PR1 ... 117 B2
Deepdale Dr BB10 ... 147 C4
Deepdale Gn BB9 ... 168 C3
Deepdale Ho 5 PR1 ... 117 B1
Deepdale La PR4 ... 114 E3
Deepdale Mill PR1 ... 117 B1
Deepdale Mill St PR1 ... 117 B1
Deepdale Rd
Blackpool FY4 ... 130 C1
Fleetwood FY7 ... 194 A3
Preston PR1 ... 117 B2
Deepdale Sh Pk PR1 ... 117 C3
Deepdale St 8 PR1 ... 96 B8
Deeply Vale La BL9 ... 50 C2
Deer Chace BB12 ... 146 D8
Deer Park La LA2 ... 232 B7
Deer Park Rd BB10 ... 127 E4
Deer Pk BB5 ... 103 E8
Deerfold PR7 ... 60 B2
Deerhurst Rd FY5 ... 150 E7
Deerplay Cl BB10 ... 147 E2
Deerstone Ave BB10 ... 127 C6
Deerstone Rd BB9 ... 148 B8
Deeside FY4 ... 109 E5
Deganwy Ave BB1 ... 100 E7
Deighton Ave 7 PR5 ... 59 A8
Deighton Rd PR7 ... 42 B6
Delamere Ave LA3 ... 208 E6
Delamere Cl BB2 ... 100 B2
Delamere Pl PR6 ... 42 D8
Delamere Rd
Brierfield BB10 ... 147 F3
Skelmersdale WN8 ... 17 F2
Southport PR8 ... 20 B5
Delamere St BL9 ... 32 A5
Delamere Way WN8 ... 10 A7
Delany Dr PR4 ... 92 A6
Delaware Rd 8 FY3 ... 150 E1
Delaware St PR1 ... 117 D1
Delf La Cornholme OL14 ... 108 D3
Haskayne L39 ... 14 A4
Delfby Cres L32 ... 1 A1
Delius Cl BB2 ... 101 A1
Dell Gdns OL12 ... 51 B2
Dell La 4 BB12 ... 125 C4
Dell Mdw OL12 ... 51 C5
Dell Rd OL12 ... 51 B3
Dell Side Way OL12 ... 51 C2
Dell The Appley Bridge WN6 ... 19 D7
Blackburn BB2 ... 80 D6
Fulwood PR2 ... 116 D7
Knowley PR6 ... 61 A3
Orrell WN8 ... 10 B7
Wrea Green PR4 ... 112 B3
Dellar St OL12 ... 51 C1
Dellfield La L31 ... 5 E1
Dellway The PR4 ... 94 D2
Delma Rd BB10 ... 127 E5
Delph App BB1 ... 101 C4
Delph Ave BL7 ... 46 D3
Delph Brook Way BL7 ... 46 D2
Delph Cl BB1 ... 101 C4
Delph Common Rd L39 ... 15 C1
Delph Ct 3 BB6 ... 123 C5
Delph La Blackburn BB1 ... 101 C3
Blackburn BB1 ... 101 C4
Charnock Green PR7 ... 41 D6
Coppull PR7 ... 41 E5
Formby L37 ... 11 C3
Garstang PR3 ... 178 F8
Oakenclough PR3 ... 180 B7
Ormskirk L39 ... 15 C1
Delph Lane Est BB1 ... 101 C4
Delph Mount
Great Harwood BB6 ... 123 B6
Nelson BB9 ... 147 D6
Delph Park Ave L39 ... 15 B1
Delph Rd BB6 ... 123 C5
Delph St Darwen BB3 ... 81 B3
Haslingden BB4 ... 84 B4
Delph The WN8 ... 26 C3
Delph Top L39 ... 16 A6
Delph Way PR6 ... 60 C7
Delphene Ave FY5 ... 150 D6
Delphinium Way BB3 ... 81 A7
Delphside Cl WN5 ... 10 D5
Delphside Prim Sch WN8 ... 9 C8
Delphside Rd WN5 ... 10 D5
Delta La FY7 ... 194 A4
Delta Park Ave PR4 ... 72 E4
Delta Park Dr PR4 ... 72 E4
Deltic Way L33 ... 1 B1
Delves La BB10 ... 148 E7
Demming Cl PR2 ... 94 C8
Denbigh Ave
Cleveleys FY5 ... 172 E1
Southport PR9 ... 52 F3
Denbigh Cl PR5 ... 76 B1
Denbigh Dr BB7 ... 186 F2
Denbigh Gr BB12 ... 126 A7
Denbigh Way 34 PR1 ... 96 A7
Denby Cl PR5 ... 96 C3
Dene Bank Rd BB5 ... 102 E3
Dene The Blackburn BB2 ... 100 B7
Hurst Green BB7 ... 141 E8
Denebank FY2 ... 150 D5
Deneway Ave FY3 ... 129 F6
Denford Ave Leyland PR5 ... 59 B8
Lytham St Anne's FY8 ... 89 A4
Denham La PR6 ... 77 E2
Denham Way FY7 ... 193 F2
Denholme Orrell WN8 ... 10 A7
Skelmersdale WN8 ... 9 F7
Denholme Gr FY2 ... 150 E5
Denis St LA1 ... 211 A8
Denmark Rd
Lytham St Anne's FY8 ... 89 D4
Southport PR9 ... 53 A2
Denmark St LA1 ... 210 D7
Dennis Gr LA4 ... 212 D4
Denny Ave LA1 ... 213 E2
Denny Bank LA2 ... 214 E5
Denny Beck La LA2 ... 214 E5
Denshaw WN8 ... 9 F7
Denstone Ave FY2 ... 150 D4
Dent Row 8 BB11 ... 126 F5
Dent St BB8 ... 169 B3
Denton St
Barnoldswick BB18 ... 200 A3
7 Rochdale OL12 ... 51 F1
Denville Ave FY5 ... 150 F8
Denville Rd Blackburn BB2 ... 100 D5
Preston PR1 ... 117 C1
Denville St BB2 ... 100 D5
Depot Rd Blackpool FY3 ... 150 E1
Kirkby L33 ... 1 D4
Derbe Rd FY8 ... 88 F5
Derby Cl BB3 ... 64 B5
Derby Cres PR4 ... 134 C8
Derby Hill Cres L39 ... 16 A5
Derby Hill Rd L39 ... 16 A5
Derby Pl PR6 ... 30 A8
Derby Rd Blackpool FY1 ... 129 B7
Cleveleys FY5 ... 172 C3
Formby L37 ... 11 E5
Fulwood PR2 ... 116 E3
Garstang PR3 ... 178 B7
Kirkham PR4 ... 113 A6
Lancaster LA1 ... 213 F1
Longridge PR3 ... 139 A7
Lytham St Anne's FY8 ... 89 C5
Poulton-le-F FY6 ... 151 D4
Skelmersdale WN8 ... 8 C8
Southport PR9 ... 34 C7
Derby Sq PR1 ... 96 D8
Derby St Accrington BB5 ... 103 C6
Blackburn BB1 ... 101 A6
Brinscall PR6 ... 62 A8
Burnley BB11 ... 126 E5
Clitheroe BB7 ... 164 F8
Colne BB8 ... 169 D5
Horwich BL6 ... 31 D1
Leyland PR5 ... 76 B2
Derby St *continued*
Morecambe LA4 ... 212 D5
Nelson BB9 ... 168 E1
Ormskirk L39 ... 15 F5
Preston PR1 ... 96 A8
Ramsbottom BL0 ... 49 D6
Rishton BB1 ... 123 C1
Derby St W L39 ... 15 E5
Derbyshire Ave PR3 ... 178 B8
Derek Rd PR6 ... 77 C1
Derham St BB2 ... 100 E3
Derry Rd PR2 ... 117 E3
Dertern La LA5 ... 216 A7
Derwent Ave
Burnley BB10 ... 147 A2
Fleetwood FY7 ... 193 D2
Formby L37 ... 11 D2
Morecambe LA4 ... 212 F5
Padiham BB12 ... 145 C2
Southport PR9 ... 52 F1
Derwent Cl Colne BB8 ... 170 A6
Freckleton PR4 ... 92 A6
Horwich BL6 ... 31 C2
Knott End-on-S FY6 ... 194 F6
Maghull L31 ... 5 F2
Rishton BB1 ... 122 F1
Derwent Cres BB7 ... 164 C7
Derwent Ct LA1 ... 213 C2
Derwent Dr Freckleton PR4 ... 92 A6
Longridge PR3 ... 138 F5
Derwent Hall 3 PR1 ... 116 E1
Derwent Ho 9 PR1 ... 96 D8
Derwent Pl Cleveleys FY5 ... 150 D8
Poulton-le-F FY6 ... 151 D1
Derwent Rd Chorley PR7 ... 42 B5
Lancaster LA1 ... 211 B8
Lytham St Anne's FY8 ... 110 A1
Orrell WN5 ... 10 F8
Derwent St 6 Darwen BB3 ... 80 F2
11 Rochdale OL12 ... 51 F1
Derwentwater Pl PR1 ... 116 F2
Dever Ave PR5 ... 75 D1
Devereux Prep Sch BB9 ... 147 D8
Devon Ave Fleetwood FY7 ... 193 E3
Oswaldtwistle BB5 ... 102 B6
Devon Cl PR5 ... 96 D3
Devon Cres BB4 ... 67 B8
Devon Dr WN1 ... 29 B1
Devon Farm Way L37 ... 12 B3
Devon Gr BB12 ... 126 A7
Devon Pl 2 Church BB5 ... 102 E5
Lancaster LA1 ... 211 A4
Devon Rd BB1 ... 101 C5
Devon St Blackpool FY4 ... 129 D1
Colne BB8 ... 169 E6
Darwen BB3 ... 64 B6
Devona Ave FY4 ... 130 B1
Devonport Cl PR5 ... 96 E3
Devonport Rd BB2 ... 100 C5
Devonport Way PR6 ... 42 E8
Devonshire Ave FY5 ... 173 B2
Devonshire Ct 17 PR7 ... 42 C8
Devonshire Dr
Clayton-le-M BB5 ... 124 A3
Garstang PR3 ... 178 B8
Devonshire Ho FY3 ... 129 D6
Devonshire Jun Sch FY3 ... 129 D6
Devonshire Mews FY5 ... 173 B1
Devonshire Pl PR1 ... 117 E1
Devonshire Rd
Blackpool FY2 ... 150 D2
Burnley BB10 ... 127 A8
Chorley PR7 ... 42 C7
Fulwood PR2 ... 117 A4
Lytham St Anne's FY8 ... 88 D7
Morecambe LA3 ... 212 C3
Rishton BB1 ... 123 A1
Southport PR9 ... 35 A8
Devonshire Road Hospl FY1 ... 129 D7
Devonshire Sq FY3 ... 129 D5
Devonshire Square Mews 5 FY3 ... 129 D5
Devonshire St
Accrington BB5 ... 103 B7
Lancaster LA1 ... 210 F5
Dew Forest PR3 ... 178 D4
Dew Meadow Cl OL12 ... 51 E2
Dewberry Fields WN8 ... 10 B7
Dewhirst Rd OL12 ... 51 F4
Dewhirst Way OL12 ... 51 F4
Dewhurst Ave FY4 ... 109 E8
Dewhurst Cl BB3 ... 64 C6
Dewhurst Clough Rd BL7 ... 46 D2
Dewhurst Ct BL7 ... 46 D3
Dewhurst Rd BB6 ... 141 F1
Dewhurst Row PR5 ... 76 D7
Dewhurst St
Blackburn BB1 ... 101 A4
Colne BB8 ... 169 D3
Darwen BB3 ... 64 B6
Preston PR2 ... 116 D1
Deycroft Ave L33 ... 1 A4
Deycroft Wlk L33 ... 1 A4
Deyes End L31 ... 5 E1
Deyes High Sch L31 ... 5 D1
Deyes La Maghull L31 ... 5 D1
Maghull, Moss Side L31 ... 5 F1
Diamond Jubilee Rd L40 ... 38 C4
Dianne Rd FY5 ... 173 D2
Dib Rd PR4 ... 72 B5
Dibbs Pocket PR4 ... 92 D7
Dicconson Terr 5 FY8 ... 90 B3
Dicconson Way L39 ... 16 A5
Dicconson's La L39 ... 14 D4
Dick La PR6 ... 61 E7
Dick's La L40 ... 16 F4
Dickens Ave BB18 ... 200 A3
Dickens Rd PR7 ... 28 E8
Dickens St BB1 ... 101 A3
Dickensons Field 3 PR1 ... 95 E2
Dicket's Brow L40 ... 16 F3
Dicket's La WN8, L40 ... 17 A2
Dickie's La FY4 ... 110 B7
Dickie's La S FY4 ... 110 C6
Dickinson Cl
Blackburn BB2 ... 100 C3
Formby L37 ... 11 F2
Dickinson Ct 1 BL6 ... 31 B4
Dickinson Rd L37 ... 11 F2
Dickinson St BB2 ... 100 D3
Dickinson St W BL6 ... 31 B4
Dickson Ave PR1 ... 117 D2
Dickson Hey PR4 ... 74 F8
Dickson Rd FY1 ... 129 B7
Dickson St Burnley BB12 ... 126 C6
Colne BB8 ... 169 E6
8 Preston PR1 ... 96 B7
Dickson St W BL6 ... 31 A4
Didsbury St BB1 ... 101 C5
Digham Ave FY5 ... 150 D6
Digmoor Dr WN8 ... 9 C7
Digmoor Rd WN8 ... 9 D6
Dill Hall La BB5 ... 102 F7
Dilworth La PR3 ... 139 C7
Dimmock St BB2 ... 100 C2
Dimple Pk BL7 ... 46 D3
Dimple Rd BL7 ... 46 C4
Dimples La PR3 ... 178 E5
Dinckley Gr FY1 ... 129 D3
Dinckley Sq BB2 ... 100 B6
Dinely St BB5 ... 102 F6
Dingle Ave
Appley Bridge WN6 ... 19 E8
Blackpool FY3 ... 129 F8
Orrell WN8 ... 10 C8
Dingle Cl L39 ... 15 C1
Dingle Rd WN8 ... 10 B7
Dingle The Fulwood PR2 ... 116 D7
Knowley PR6 ... 61 A3
Dinmore Ave FY3 ... 130 A8
Dinmore Pl FY3 ... 130 A7
Dinorwic Rd PR8 ... 34 A2
Dirty Leech OL12 ... 51 F6
Disraeli St BB10 ... 147 A2
Ditchfield L37 ... 12 A2
Division La FY4 ... 110 C3
Dixey St BL6 ... 31 A3
Dixon Rd PR3 ... 139 B7
Dixon St Barrowford BB9 ... 168 C3
Blackburn BB2 ... 100 C4
Horwich BL6 ... 31 B3
Dixon's Farm Mews PR4 ... 114 D1
Dixons La PR2 ... 138 C2
Dob Brow PR7 ... 41 F4
Dob La PR4 ... 74 A4
Dobbin Cl BB4 ... 85 C2
Dobbin La BB4 ... 85 C2
Dobbs Dr L37 ... 12 A4
Dobs La LA2 ... 205 E3
Dobson Ave FY8 ... 88 E8
Dobson Cl WN6 ... 27 E2
Dobson St 2 BB3 ... 80 F2
Dobson's La FY6 ... 174 E6
Dock Ave FY7 ... 194 A2
Dock Rd FY8 ... 90 D4
Dock St Blackburn BB1 ... 101 A5
Fleetwood FY7 ... 194 B4
Docker La LA6 ... 235 C5
Dockinsall La PR3 ... 175 D3
Dockray Ct 2 BB8 ... 169 E5
Dockray St BB8 ... 169 E5
Dockray Yd 4 BB8 ... 169 E5
Docky Pool La FY4 ... 110 A6
Doctor's La Eccleston PR7 ... 40 B6
Great Altcar L37 ... 12 E2
Sollom PR4 ... 55 F3
Doctors Row PR3 ... 139 A6
Dodd Way PR5 ... 77 A6
Dodd's La L31 ... 5 D2
Dodgeons Cl FY6 ... 151 C2
Dodgson La BB18 ... 201 F2
Dodgson Pl PR1 ... 117 C1
Dodgson Rd PR1 ... 117 C1
Dodney Dr PR2 ... 115 C1
Dodson Rd FY3 ... 130 B7
Dodworth Ave PR8 ... 34 E5
Doe Meadow WN8 ... 26 A1
Doeholme Rake LA2 ... 226 F1
Dog Pits La OL13 ... 87 A6
Dole La Abbey Village PR6 ... 79 C1
Chorley PR7 ... 42 C8
Doles La PR5 ... 57 A7
Dolls House & Fleetwood Mus FY7 ... 194 C5
Dolly's La PR9 ... 35 D8
Dollywood La LA7 ... 237 F1
Dolphinholme CE Prim Sch LA2 ... 220 A8
Dombey St Blackburn BB1 ... 101 A3
Blackburn BB1 ... 101 A4
Dominica Ave BB3 ... 80 F6
Dominion Rd BB2 ... 100 C8
Don St FY8 ... 88 E7
Doncaster Rd FY3 ... 130 A3
Donnington Lo PR8 ... 33 F6
Donnington Rd
Carleton FY6 ... 151 C6
Lytham St Anne's FY8 ... 88 F7
Donshort Mews 2 BB9 ... 168 C1
Doodstone Ave PR5 ... 96 B1
Doodstone Cl PR5 ... 96 B1
Doodstone Dr PR5 ... 96 B1
Doodstone Nook PR5 ... 96 B1
Dora St BL0 ... 49 A4
Dorchester Ave BB5 ... 102 C4

Dorchester Cl
Blackburn BB1 101 B3
Thornton FY5 151 C8
Dorchester Dr L33 1 A5
Dorchester Gdns LA3 212 F2
Dorchester Rd
Blackpool FY1 129 B8
Garstang PR3 178 B8
Orrell WN8 10 A7
Doric Gn WN5 10 D3
Doris Henderson Way
LA3 213 B2
Doris St Burnley BB11 127 B7
Chorley PR6 60 D1
Dorking Rd PR6 60 F4
Dorman Rd PR2 117 E3
Dorothy Ave 9 PR5 76 A1
Dorothy St Blackburn BB2 80 C8
13 Ramsbottom BL0 49 B5
Dorrington Rd LA1 210 F5
Dorritt Rd FY4 109 E6
Dorritt St 19 BB1 101 A4
Dorset Ave
3 Bamber Bridge PR5 96 D3
Cleveleys FY5 172 D4
Darwen BB3 80 F3
Padiham BB12 125 D7
Southport PR8 20 C2
Dorset Dr Blackburn BB1 101 E4
Clitheroe BB7 186 F2
Haslingden BB4 67 A8
Dorset Pl BB5 102 F7
Dorset Rd
Lytham St Anne's FY8 88 F8
Preston PR1 117 A1
Rishton BB1 123 A1
Standish WN1 29 B1
Dorset St 10 Blackpool FY4 129 D1
Burnley BB12 126 A6
Dotcliffe Rd BB18 192 A6
Double Row 1 BB12 125 B8
Doughty St BB8 169 D4
Douglas Ave Becconsall PR4 72 F1
Blackpool FY3 129 D7
1 Heysham LA3 208 F7
Horwich BL6 31 C5
Orrell WN8 10 B7
Stalmine FY6 174 C7
Douglas Cl
Bamber Bridge PR5 76 F7
Blackburn BB2 80 D7
Horwich BL6 31 C5
Rufford L40 38 C3
Douglas Ct PR2 116 D3
Douglas Dr Freckleton PR4 92 B6
Heysham LA3 208 F7
Maghull L31 5 F2
Ormskirk L39 15 D7
Orrell WN5 10 F7
Shevington WN6 19 F5
Douglas Gr BB3 80 D4
Douglas Hall 4 PR1 116 E1
Douglas Leatham Ho 3
FY1 129 D1
Douglas Pl Blackburn BB1 121 F1
Fleetwood FY7 193 D3
Douglas Rd Bacup OL13 87 A1
Brierfield BB10 148 A3
Fulwood PR2 116 D3
Shevington Moor WN6 28 B2
Southport PR9 53 C4
Douglas Rd N PR2 116 D3
Douglas Sq 7 OL10 32 F1
Douglas St Colne BB8 169 E6
Lytham St Anne's FY8 88 D6
Preston PR2 95 C8
Ramsbottom BL0 49 B6
Douglas St Back 4 BL0 49 B6
Douglas Way BB10 148 A3
Doultons The PR5 96 C3
Dove Ave 2 PR1 95 E4
Dove Cl 6 FY5 172 F1
Dove Dr BL9 32 B4
Dove La BB3 80 F2
Dove St
Lytham St Anne's FY8 88 D6
Preston PR1 117 B1
Dove Tree Ct FY4 130 B1
Dovecote PR6 77 A3
Dovedale Ave
Blackpool FY3 130 C2
Fulwood PR2 116 A5
Maghull L31 5 C2
Thornton FY5 173 B3
Dovedale Cl
Brierfield BB10 147 C4
Burnley BB12 126 C8
Fulwood PR2 116 A4
Leyland PR5 59 A6
Dovedale Dr WN6 28 E2
Dover Cl Blackburn BB1 101 C4
Ramsbottom BL8 49 A1
Warton PR4 91 E7
Dover Ct FY1 129 D2
Dover Gdns FY6 151 B5
Dover La PR5,PR6 78 C8
Dover Rd Blackpool FY1 129 E2
Lytham St Anne's FY8 88 F8
Southport PR8 33 F2
Dover St Accrington BB5 103 A4
Blackburn BB3 80 F7
Nelson BB9 168 E1
Dovestone Dr FY6 151 B3
Dovetree Cl PR1 96 A3
Dowbridge PR4 113 C4
Dowbridge Way PR4 113 C5
Downes Gr LA4 212 G4
Downeyfield Rd LA3 209 C3
Downfield Cl BL0 49 B6
Downham Ave
Great Harwood BB6 123 F6
Rawtenstall BB4 85 A4
Downham Cotts 7 LA2 207 A4
Downham Dr BB5 103 A3
Downham Gr BB10 127 D5
Downham Pl
Lytham St Anne's FY8 89 C6
3 Preston PR2 115 E2
Downham Rd
Chatburn BB7 187 E5
Leyland PR5 75 D1
Downham St BB2 100 C4
Downham Wlk WN5 10 D1
Downholland Moss La
L37 12 C4
Downing Ct PR3 136 C3
Downing St PR1 96 E8
Downley Cl OL12 51 B2
Downs The FY6 151 D4
Dowry St BB5 103 C6
Dragon St 8 BB12 125 C8
Drake Cl
Lytham St Anne's FY8 109 E1
Ormskirk L39 15 C2
Drakelowe Ave FY4 109 F6
Drakes Croft PR2 116 C3
Drakes Hollow PR5 96 D4
Drammen Ave BB11 126 B5
Draperfield PR7 42 A4
Drapers Ave PR7 40 C6
Draw Well Rd L33 1 D2
Draycombe Ct LA3 212 A2
Draycombe Dr LA3 212 B2
Draycot Ave FY3 129 F8
Drayton Rd LA3 209 A7
Drew St BB11 126 B5
Drewitt Cres PR9 53 D4
Drewton Ave LA3 212 A2
Drinkhouse La PR5 57 A1
Drinkhouse Rd PR5 57 B1
Driscoll St 1 PR1 96 B8
Drive The Bacup OL13 86 F2
Carnforth LA5 217 B1
Edenfield BL0 67 D3
Fulwood PR2 117 B4
Hest Bank LA2 215 E1
Heysham LA3 208 F7
Longton PR4 74 A8
Walton-le-D PR5 96 F5
Driver St 12 BB4 85 A7
Driving Gate BB4 105 A1
Dronsfield Rd FY7 193 F4
Drovers Wlk LA3 208 F7
Druids Cl BL7 46 D3
Drumacre La E PR4 74 D6
Drumacre La W PR4 74 A6
Drumhead Rd PR6 60 D2
Drummersdale La L40 23 D7
Drummond Ave FY3 129 E7
Drybread La PR3 175 C2
Dryburgh Ave FY3 129 F3
Dryden Gr BB6 123 C4
Dryden Rd FY7 194 A4
Dryden St
6 Clayton-le-M BB5 123 F3
Padiham BB12 125 E7
Dryfield La BL6 31 A5
Dubdon Cl LA3 213 B3
Duchess Ct FY2 150 B3
Duchess Dr FY2 150 B3
Duchess St BB3 80 F7
Duchy Ave PR2 117 B4
Ducie Pl PR1 117 F1
Duck St 2 Clitheroe BB7 164 F8
Smallwood Hey PR3 196 A7
Wray LA2 232 D6
Duckett St 3 BB11 126 E6
Ducketts La PR3 157 B8
Duckshaw Rd BB3 63 F6
Duckworth Cl PR3 178 D3
Duckworth Dr PR3 178 D3
Duckworth Hall Brow
BB5 102 A1
Duckworth Hill La BB5 102 B1
Duckworth La
Rawtenstall BB4 67 E8
Tarleton PR4 55 F8
Duckworth St
Barrowford BB9 168 D2
Blackburn BB2 100 D3
3 Bury BL9 32 A4
Church BB5 102 E6
Darwen BB3 80 F2
Duddle La PR5 96 D2
Duddon Ave Darwen BB3 80 E3
Fleetwood FY7 193 D2
Maghull L31 5 F2
Dudley Ave Blackpool FY2 150 D1
Oswaldtwistle BB5 102 C4
Dudley Cl PR4 94 A1
Dudley St Brierfield BB9 147 C5
Colne BB8 169 F5
Morecambe LA4 212 F4
Duerden St BB9 147 D7
Duffins Cl OL12 51 D3
Dugdale Ct FY4 109 F5
Dugdale La BB7 229 F1
Dugdale Rd BB12 126 C7
Dugdale St BB11 127 A5
Dugie St BL0 49 B7
Duke Ave PR8 34 C4
Duke of Sussex St BB2 80 B8
Duke St Bamber Bridge PR5 76 E7
Blackburn BB2 100 D5
Blackpool FY1 129 B1
Brierfield BB10 147 F3
Duke St *continued*
Burnley BB11 127 B4
Burton in L LA6 236 C3
Chorley PR7 42 C6
Clayton-le-M BB5 124 A2
Colne BB8 169 D4
Formby L37 11 F2
Great Harwood BB6 123 B5
Heysham LA3 208 E7
High Bentham LA2 233 D8
Lancaster LA1 213 E1
Oswaldtwistle BB5 102 D3
Preston PR1 96 B7
Ramsbottom BL0 49 A4
Rawtenstall BB4 68 E8
Rochdale OL12 51 F1
Southport PR8 34 B5
Trawden BB8 170 B5
Duke St Cty Prim Sch PR7 42 C6
Duke's Wood La WN8 9 D3
Dukes Brow BB2 100 C6
Dukes Ct BB2 100 B6
Dukes Dr BB3 81 F1
Dukes Mdw PR2 116 A5
Dukes Way L37 11 F2
Dulas Gn L32 1 A1
Dulas Rd L32 1 A1
Dumb Tom's La LA6 236 E1
Dumbarton Cl 2 FY4 110 A6
Dumbarton Rd LA1 211 A7
Dumfries Cl FY2 150 F5
Dunald Mill La LA2,LA6 231 B6
Dunbar Cl FY4 110 A6
Dunbar Cres PR8 20 F8
Dunbar Dr Fulwood PR2 116 D4
2 Heysham LA3 208 E7
Dunbar Rd Fulwood PR2 115 F3
Southport PR8 33 F1
Duncan Ave FY2 150 C6
Duncan Cl Brownside BB10 127 F5
Lytham St Anne's FY8 109 D1
Duncan Pl FY7 193 E4
Duncan St Burnley BB12 126 A5
Horwich BL6 31 C3
Duncroft Cl BB7 186 E2
Dundas St BB8 169 C4
Dundee Cl OL10 32 F1
Dundee Dr BB1 101 A4
Dundee La BL0 49 B6
Dundee St LA1 211 A7
Dunderdale Ave BB9 147 C7
Dunderdale St PR3 139 B7
Dundonald St PR1 96 D8
Dundonnell Rd BB9 169 A1
Dunedin Rd BL8 48 F2
Dunelt Ct 2 FY1 129 C2
Dunelt Rd FY1 129 D2
Dunes Ave FY4 109 B5
Dunes Dr L37 11 C4
Dungeon La WN8 18 C7
Dunham Dr PR6 60 C6
Dunkeld St 5 LA1 211 A7
Dunkenhalgh Way
Church BB5 102 E7
Clayton-le-M BB5 123 E1
Dunkenshaw Cres LA1 211 B2
Dunkirk Ave Carnforth LA5 216 E8
Fulwood PR2 116 C3
Dunkirk La PR5 75 A1
Dunkirk Rd PR8 33 F2
Dunlin Cl FY5 173 A5
Dunlop Ave PR8 20 C2
Dunmail Ave 1 FY3 129 F2
Dunmore St PR1 96 B8
Dunnock La PR4 115 E4
Dunny Shop Ave BB5 103 A4
Dunoon Cl PR2 115 F4
Dunoon Dr BB1 101 D3
Dunoon St BB11 126 D5
Dunrobin Dr PR7 59 D1
Dunscar Dr PR6 60 E1
Dunsop Cl
3 Bamber Bridge PR5 76 F8
1 Blackpool FY1 129 D1
Dunsop Ct 2 FY1 129 D1
Dunsop Rd PR2 117 D4
Dunsop St BB1 100 F7
Dunster Ave BB5 102 C5
Dunster Gr BB7 164 C6
Dunster Rd PR8 20 E8
Dunvegan Cl 3 FY4 110 A6
Durban Gr BB11 126 E4
Durham Ave Burnley BB12 126 B7
Cleveleys FY5 172 E3
Lancaster LA1 211 A4
Lytham St Anne's FY8 88 E7
Durham Cl Blackburn BB1 100 F4
Leyland PR5 58 E6
Morecambe LA3 212 E2
Durham Dr
Oswaldtwistle BB5 102 F3
Ramsbottom BL0 49 B3
Wilpshire BB1 121 F6
Durham Gr PR3 178 B7
Durham Ho 8 PR1 96 A6
Durham Rd Blackpool FY1 129 D5
Darwen BB3 80 F2
Wilpshire BB1 121 F7
Durham St Accrington BB5 103 D7
Skelmersdale WN8 17 D2
Durley Rd FY1 129 D2
Durn St 1 OL14 108 A1
Dutch Barn Cl PR7 60 B2
Dutton Ct 1 FY3 129 D5
Dutton Rd FY3 129 D5
Dutton St 16 BB5 103 C6
Duxbury Cl L31 5 E3
Duxbury Dr BL9 32 C2
Duxbury Hall Rd PR7 42 E3
Duxbury Ho 8 PR6 42 D7
Duxbury Jubilee Pk PR7 42 D3
Duxbury St Darwen BB3 64 B6
Earby BB18 201 C2
Dye House La 6 LA1 210 F8
Dyer St PR4 112 F5
Dyers La L39 15 E4
Dyke La PR3 196 A3
Dyke Nook BB7 164 F6
Dykes La LA5 219 F2
Dymock Rd PR1 117 D1
Dymock Rd N PR1 117 D1
Dyneley Ave BB10 127 F4
Dyneley Rd BB1 101 C7
Dyson St BB2 100 E2

E

Eachill Gdns BB1 102 B8
Eachill Rd 2 BB1 123 B1
Eager La L31 5 B8
Eagle Brow Cl FY5 173 B4
Eagle St Accrington BB5 103 B5
Blackburn BB1 101 C4
2 Nelson BB9 168 F1
Oswaldtwistle BB5 102 C2
Eagles The FY6 151 E5
Eagley Bank OL12 70 E6
Eagley Rd BB10 147 C4
Ealing Gr PR6 60 F3
Eamont Ave PR9 53 B5
Eamont Pl FY7 193 D2
Eanam BB1 100 F5
Eanam Old Rd BB1 100 F5
Earby Rd BB18 191 F8
Earby Springfield
Cty Prim Sch BB18 201 C1
Eardley Rd LA3 208 E8
Earl Rd BL0 49 B6
Earl St
Barnoldswick BB18 200 C2
Blackburn BB1 100 E6
Burnley BB10 127 B8
Clayton-le-M BB5 123 F2
Colne BB8 169 D4
Great Harwood BB6 123 B5
Lancaster LA1 213 F1
11 Nelson BB9 168 F1
Preston PR1 95 F8
Ramsbottom BL0 49 D6
Earlesdon Ave BB18 200 F1
Earlham St BB18 201 C2
Earls Ave PR5 76 E8
Earls Dr BB3 81 E1
Earls Way PR7 59 D2
Earlsway FY3 130 D5
Earlswood WN8 18 E1
Earnsdale Ave BB3 80 D2
Earnsdale Cl BB3 80 E2
Earnsdale Rd BB3 80 E3
Earnshaw Ave OL12 51 E3
Earnshaw Bridge
Cty Infs Sch PR5 75 E2
Earnshaw Dr PR5 75 D1
Earnshaw Rd OL13 86 F3
Earnshaw Row 19 OL13 86 F3
Easby Cl L37 12 A2
Easdale Ave LA4 213 A5
Easedale Cl Burnley BB12 126 B8
Hest Bank LA5 215 F2
Easedale Dr PR8 20 B4
Easington LA1 213 C2
Easington Cres FY3 130 B8
East Ave BB18 200 B2
East Bank
2 Barrowford BB9 168 D4
Water BB4 106 A1
East Bank Ave BB4 84 B2
East Bank Rd FY8 88 E5
East Beach FY8 90 C3
East Boothroyden FY1 129 B8
East Cecil St FY8 90 A3
East Chorley Bsns Ctr 3
PR6 42 D8
East Cliff PR1 95 F6
East Cliff Rd PR1 95 F6
East Cliffe FY8 90 C3
East Cres BB5 103 B8
East Croft BB9 169 B2
East Ct FY5 172 D5
East Dene WN8 26 B2
East End St BB8 169 C4
East Gate BB4 84 B3
East Hills St 18 BB18 200 B2
East Holme FY8 90 C4
East La Ellel LA2 207 B6
Maghull L29 4 B2
East Lancashire Rd BB1 121 F3
East Lancashire Rly
Ramsbottom BL0 49 C5
East Leigh WN8 18 D1
East Lodge Pl BB10 127 E1
East Mead Blackpool FY3 129 F3
Ormskirk L39 15 B2
East Meade L31 5 C2
East Mount WN5 10 F6
East Par 18
Barnoldswick BB18 200 B2
17 Rawtenstall BB4 85 A3
East Park Ave
Blackburn BB1 100 D7
Darwen BB3 63 F8
East Park Dr FY3 130 A5
East Park Rd BB1 100 D6
East Rd Fulwood PR2 117 A3
Lancaster LA1 211 A8
East Rd *continued*
Maghull L31 5 F1
East Sq PR4 94 A1
East St Bamber Bridge PR5 76 E7
Blackburn BB2 100 C3
Blackburn, Feniscowles BB2 79 D8
Brierfield BB9 147 C5
Edenfield BL0 67 D4
Hapton BB12 125 C4
Haslingden BB4 67 A7
Leyland PR5 76 B1
Leyland, Farington PR5 76 B2
Morecambe LA3 212 B4
10 Nelson BB9 168 D1
Padiham BB12 145 C1
12 Preston PR1 96 A8
Rawtenstall BB4 84 F5
Southport PR9 34 D7
East Terr PR7 59 D4
East Topping St 3 FY1 129 B5
East View Bacup OL13 86 F2
13 Barnoldswick BB18 200 B2
9 Galgate LA2 207 A4
Grimsargh PR2 138 B1
Grindleton BB7 187 B7
Haslingden BB5 84 A8
3 Lostock Hall PR5 76 A7
Pendleton BB7 165 B4
Preston PR1 96 A8
Preston, Brookfield PR2 117 F5
9 Preston, Frenchwood PR1 96 C6
Ramsbottom,
Brooksbottoms BL0 49 C3
Ramsbottom, Stubbins BL0 67 C1
Read BB12 144 D2
Trawden BB8 170 C2
Winmarleigh PR3 198 F6
East View Ct LA1 213 D3
East View Terr PR6 79 B3
East Ward Com Prim
Sch BL9 32 B2
East Way PR6 42 D8
East Wlk BL7 46 D2
Eastbank Ave FY4 110 A7
Eastbank St PR8 34 B6
Eastbank Street Sq 9
PR8, PR9 34 B7
Eastbourne Cl PR2 115 F5
Eastbourne Rd
Blackpool FY4 109 B6
Southport PR8 34 A3
Eastcliff LA2 231 F5
Eastcott Cl BB2 81 A8
Eastern Ave BB10 147 C1
Eastfield Dr Longton PR4 94 A1
West Bradford BB7 186 F6
Eastgate Accrington BB5 103 C6
Fulwood PR2 116 E4
Morecambe LA3 213 A2
Ribchester PR3 140 E4
Whitworth OL12 51 C7
Eastham Cotts FY8 90 D6
Eastham Pl BB11 127 B6
Eastham St Burnley BB10 127 B5
Clitheroe BB7 186 E1
Lancaster LA1 211 A7
Preston PR1 116 E1
Eastlands Heysham LA3 209 A7
Leyland PR5 58 C7
Eastmoor Dr BB7 164 F7
Easton Cl PR2 117 D6
Eastpines Dr FY5 150 F8
Eastside FY4 109 F8
Eastway Freckleton PR4 92 A6
Fulwood PR2,PR3 117 B6
Maghull L31 5 E1
Eastway Bsns Village
PR2 117 B8
Eastwood Ave
Blackpool FY3 129 E8
2 Fleetwood FY7 193 F3
Eastwood Cl 6 BL9 32 B2
Eastwood Cres BB4 85 C2
Eastwood Rd PR5 75 F1
Eastwood St
Barnoldswick BB18 200 C3
Blackburn BB1 101 A6
Rawtenstall BB4 85 C2
Eastwood Terr BB18 200 C3
Eaton Ave FY1 129 C1
Eaton Ct FY8 88 F6
Eaton Pl PR4 112 F5
Eaton Way FY6 130 E8
Eaves Ave BB11 126 D2
Eaves Cl BB5 124 F1
Eaves Green La PR3 137 F8
Eaves Green Rd PR7 42 B5
Eaves La Chorley PR6 42 E8
Cuddy Hill PR4 135 D7
Fulwood PR2 116 E3
Eaves Lane Hospl PR6 42 E8
Eaves Lea LA6 238 B2
Eaves Rd FY8 110 A1
Eaves St FY1 129 B7
Eavesdale WN8 9 E8
Eaveswood Cl PR5 96 E1
Ebony St 11 BB1 101 A7
Ebor Lo PR8 34 A5
Ebor St BB10 147 B2
Eccles Rd L37 11 D1
Eccles St Accrington BB5 103 B7
Blackburn BB2 100 E3
Preston PR1 117 C1
Ramsbottom BL0 49 B6
Eccles's La L40 26 B7

Ecclesgate Rd FY4 110 A5
Eccleshill Gdns BB3 81 C4
Eccleshill St 1 BB12 125 C8
Eccleston Cty Prim Sch
PR7 40 B6
Eccleston Rd FY1 129 D1
Eclipse Rd BB2 79 D8
Ecroyd Rd PR2 116 C2
Ecroyd St Leyland PR5 76 A1
Nelson BB9 147 C8
Edale Ave BB4 84 C2
Edale Cl PR5 59 A7
Edale Ct PR1 116 F1
Edale Dr WN6 28 E2
Eddington Rd FY8 89 B4
Eddleston Cl FY3 130 D5
Edelston Rd 5 FY1 129 C6
Eden Ave Edenfield BL0 67 D3
Fleetwood FY7 193 D2
Lytham St Anne's FY8 89 E3
Morecambe LA4 213 B5
Southport PR9 52 F2
Eden Cl BB9 168 D4
Eden Ct BL0 67 D2
Eden Gdns PR3 139 B8
Eden Gr LA5 216 B6
Eden Hall PR1 116 E1
Eden Mount Way LA5 217 F2
Eden Pk Blackburn BB2 99 F8
Lancaster LA1 210 F4
Eden St Accrington BB5 103 A5
Blackburn BB1 101 A5
9 Blackpool FY1 129 C6
Edenfield BL0 67 D1
Leyland PR5 59 A8
Edenfield Ave FY6 151 F2
Edenfield CE Prim Sch
BL0 67 D4
Edenfield Cl PR8 34 E3
Edenfield Rd
Ramsbottom OL11, OL12 50 E4
Rochdale OL11,OL12 51 B1
Edenfield St OL11,OL12 51 C1
Edenhurst Cl L37 11 C2
Edenhurst Dr L37 11 C2
Edensor Terr BB3 80 F2
Edenvale Ave FY2 150 B4
Edenvale Cres LA1 213 E3
Edenvale Rd LA1 213 E3
Edenway PR2 116 D7
Edgar St Accrington BB5 103 B6
Huncoat BB5 124 E2
Nelson BB9 168 F2
16 Ramsbottom BL0 49 B5
Edgar St W 17 BL0 49 B5
Edge Cotts FY8 110 A2
Edge End BB6 123 B5
Edge End Ave BB9 147 D6
Edge End High Sch BB9 147 D6
Edge End La
Brierfield BB9 147 D6
Great Harwood BB6 123 B6
Edge End Rd BB6 123 B5
Edge End Terr BB2 79 B3
Edge Gate La PR6 62 A6
Edge Hall Rd WN5 10 E5
Edge Hill Coll PR7 42 A8
Edge Hill Univ Coll L39 16 A3
Edge La Bacup OL13 70 C8
Barnoldswick BB8 225 F1
Edgworth BL7 47 A8
Rawtenstall BB4 85 D3
Edge Nook Rd BB1 101 D1
Edge Yate La BB4 85 B5
Edgecott Cl LA3 209 A7
Edgefield PR7 60 B2
Edgefield Ct FY3 130 B8
Edgehill Cl PR2 116 D4
Edgehill Cres PR5 75 E2
Edgehill Dr PR2 116 D4
Edgeley Ct BB12 126 D7
Edgemoor Cl OL12 70 E5
Edgeside BB6 123 B5
Edgeside La BB4 85 F2
Edgeware Rd BB2 100 C6
Edgeway Pl 3 FY5 173 C1
Edgeway Rd FY4 109 E5
Edgley Dr L39 16 A5
Edgworth Gr BB10 127 C6
Edgworth Prim Sch BL7 47 D5
Edinburgh Cl PR5 76 C1
Edinburgh Dr BB5 102 F3
Edinburgh Rd Formby L37 11 E1
Haslingden BB4 83 F1
Edisford Cty Prim Sch
BB7 164 C7
Edisford Rd Clitheroe BB7 164 C8
Waddington BB7 186 B4
Edison St BB3 80 F1
Edith St Barnoldswick BB18 200 B3
Blackburn BB1 101 A4
Nelson BB9 147 F8
Shuttleworth BL0 49 E8
Edleston Lodge 2 PR2 117 F4
Edleston St BB5 102 F4
Edmondsen Pl 4 FY7 193 F2
Edmondson St BB18 200 B3
Edmondson's La BD23 201 F8
Edmonton Dr BB2 100 A8
Edmonton Pl FY2 150 F3
Edmund Gennings Ct
BB7 187 D5
Edmund St
5 Accrington BB5 103 C5
Blackburn BB2 80 D7
Edmund St *continued*
Burnley BB10 147 B1
Darwen BB3 81 B1
3 Preston PR1 96 B8
Edmundson St
Blackburn BB2 100 C5
3 Church BB5 102 E6
Edward Ct BB5 102 E6
Edward Sq 9 PR1 117 A1
Edward St Accrington BB5 103 E1
12 Bacup OL13 87 A3
Bamber Bridge PR5 76 E8
Barnoldswick BB18 200 C3
Blackpool FY1 129 B5
Burnley BB11 127 A6
3 Carnforth LA5 217 D2
Chorley PR6 42 D7
8 Church BB5 102 E6
Darwen BB3 81 A2
8 Earby BB18 201 B2
7 Great Harwood BB6 123 C5
Haslingden BB4 84 B6
Horwich BL6 31 A3
Lancaster LA1 211 A8
3 Leyland PR5 59 A8
Lytham St Anne's FY8 88 F7
Morecambe LA4 212 D5
Nelson BB9 168 F2
Preston PR1 95 F8
Rawtenstall BB4 85 A8
4 Rishton BB1 123 B1
Thornton FY5 173 B4
Walton-le-D PR1 96 C5
Whitworth OL12 70 D2
Edward VII Quay PR2 95 B7
Edwell Ave FY4 109 D8
Edwin Waugh Gdns OL12 51 D3
Edwinstowe Rd FY8 89 D6
Egan St PR1 96 A8
Egbert St PR1 117 A1
Egerton WN8 9 D8
Egerton Com Prim Sch
BL7 46 D3
Egerton Gr PR7 42 B6
Egerton Lo BL7 46 E1
Egerton Rd Belmont BL7 45 E4
Blackpool FY1 129 B7
Leyland PR5 75 F2
Preston PR2 116 B1
Egremont Ave FY5 172 D5
Egypt Mount BB4 84 D2
Egypt Terr 3 BB4 84 E2
Eider Cl FY5 172 F5
Eidsforth La PR3 220 A1
Eidsforth Rd LA4 212 E6
Eight Acre Ave BB7 144 F8
Eight Acre La Formby L37 12 B6
Yealand Redmayne LA5 219 E4
Eildon Dr FY6 151 D1
Elaine Ave FY4 129 F1
Elaton Lodge 7 PR2 117 F4
Elbow La L37 11 F3
Elbow St PR7 42 C7
Elbut La BL9 32 F5
Elcho St PR1 117 A2
Elder Cl Clayton Green PR6 77 C2
Fulwood PR2 117 D6
Warton PR4 91 E6
Elder Ct BB5 103 E8
Elder St BB9 168 F2
Elderberry Cl FY5 172 F5
Elderwood Ave FY5 151 B7
Eldon Ct FY8 88 F7
Eldon Cty Prim Sch PR1 116 E2
Eldon Gr LA3 208 F7
Eldon Rd BB1 100 D7
Eldon St Chorley PR6 42 D7
Preston PR1,PR2 116 D2
Eldons Croft PR8 20 D5
Eldwick St BB10 147 C1
Eleanor St Blackburn BB1 100 F5
3 Nelson BB9 168 E1
Electricity St BB5 103 B6
Elgar Cl BB2 101 A2
Elgin Cres BB11 126 D4
Elgin Pl FY3 130 A7
Elgin St 4 Lancaster LA1 211 A7
Preston PR1 117 A2
Elijah St 4 PR1 96 D8
Elim Ct 4 FY8 90 C3
Elim Gdns BB2 100 C1
Elim Pl BB2 100 C1
Eliza St Burnley BB10 127 B5
Ramsbottom BL0 49 D6
Elizabeth Ave PR8 20 E6
Elizabeth Cl FY3 130 D5
Elizabeth Ct Blackpool FY3 129 D6
Edenfield BL0 67 D3
Poulton-le-F FY6 151 D3
Elizabeth Dr BB4 67 A8
Elizabeth Ho
Blackburn BB1 101 B3
Darwen BB3 81 B1
Elizabeth Sq 7 PR1 117 A1
Elizabeth St
Accrington BB5 102 F5
Blackburn BB1 100 F5
Blackpool FY1 129 C6
Burnley BB11 127 A5
Edenfield BL0 67 D3
9 Fleetwood FY7 194 B5
Nelson BB9 168 E1
Padiham BB12 125 C7
Preston PR1 95 F8
Whitewell Bottom BB4 85 F4
Elker Cotts BB7 142 F4
Elker La BB7 142 F5
Elker Mews BB7 142 F3
Elkfield Dr FY3 151 A1
Elkin Rd LA4 212 G5
Elland Pl FY1 129 B1
Elland Rd BB9 147 C6
Ellel Hall Gdns LA2 206 F3
Ellen Ct PR1 116 F2
Ellen St Bamber Bridge PR5 96 E1
Darwen BB3 64 A7
11 Nelson BB9 147 D8
Preston PR1 116 E1
Preston PR1 116 F2
Ellenrod Dr OL12 51 A2
Ellenrod La OL12 51 A2
Ellenshaw Cl Darwen BB3 81 B1
Rochdale OL12 51 A2
Eller Brook Cl PR6 42 F1
Ellerbeck Ave PR2 117 E5
Ellerbeck Cl BB10 147 E3
Ellerbeck Rd BB5 103 B7
Ellerbreck Rd FY5 172 C2
Ellerbrook Dr L40 24 F3
Ellerbrook Rd BB3 81 B1
Ellerbrook Way L39 15 E6
Ellerslie Rd PR2 116 B1
Ellesmere Ave Colne BB8 169 F5
Thornton FY5 173 D1
Ellesmere Gr LA4 212 D3
Ellesmere Rd
Blackpool FY4 129 E1
Darwen BB3 80 E3
Morecambe LA4 212 C4
Elletson St FY6 151 D4
Elliott Ave BB3 64 B6
Elliott Cl PR1 116 E2
Elliott St Burnley BB10 127 C5
Preston PR1 116 E1
Preston PR1 116 E2
Elliott Wlk PR1 116 E2
Ellis Dr LA4 213 A6
Ellis St Barnoldswick BB18 200 B2
1 Burnley BB11 126 E5
19 Ramsbottom BL0 49 B5
Ellisland FY4 130 C1
Ellison Fold BB5 123 E3
Ellison Fold La BB3 81 C1
Ellison Fold Terr BB3 81 B1
Ellison St Accrington BB5 103 B6
Darwen BB3 81 A2
Ellwood Ave
Lancaster LA1 214 A4
Morecambe LA3 212 F2
Ellwood Ct LA3 212 G2
Ellwood Gr LA3 212 F2
Elm Ave Blackpool FY3 129 E5
Galgate LA2 206 F4
Poulton-le-F FY6 151 D3
Preston PR2 116 A2
Warton PR4 91 D6
Elm Brow PR3 160 C4
Elm Cl Barnoldswick BB18 200 A1
Haslingden BB4 84 B3
Rishton BB1 102 B8
Salterforth BB18 191 E8
Elm Ct FY6 151 D3
Elm Dr
3 Bamber Bridge PR5 96 F1
Formby L37 11 D1
Elm Gr Chorley PR6 60 E2
Clayton-le-W PR5 76 D3
Darwen BB3 81 B3
Fulwood PR2 117 E2
6 Horwich BL6 31 E1
Kirkham PR4 113 B7
Morecambe LA4 213 A7
Skelmersdale WN8 17 E1
Elm Mill BB10 127 A8
Elm Pl L39 15 E4
Elm Rd Burscough L40 24 E3
Southport PR8 34 B4
Elm St 7 Bacup OL13 87 A3
Blackburn BB1 101 A7
Burnley BB10 127 A8
Bury BL9 32 B2
Colne BB8 169 E6
Edenfield BL0 67 E3
Fleetwood FY7 194 A4
Great Harwood BB6 123 C4
Haslingden BB4 84 B3
9 Nelson BB9 168 E1
Ramsbottom BL0 49 D6
Rawtenstall BB4 85 A3
Rochdale OL12 51 F1
Whitworth OL12 70 D2
Elm View BB10 147 D2
Elmbank Ave FY5 150 C7
Elmcroft La L38 3 A3
Elmdale Cl L37 11 D2
Elmer's Green La
Skelmersdale, Dalton WN8 18 C4
Skelmersdale, Elmers
Green WN8 18 D2
Elmers Green Prim Sch
WN8 18 D1
Elmers Wood Rd WN8 18 D2
Elmfield Dr PR5 77 C6
Elmfield St BB5 102 F7
Elmhurst Rd FY8 89 B8
Elmpark Gate OL12 51 B3
Elmpark Gr OL12 51 B3
Elmpark Vale OL12 51 B3
Elmpark View OL12 51 B3
Elmpark Way OL12 51 B3
Elmridge WN8 9 D8
Elmridge Cres FY2 150 F3
Elms Ave Cleveleys FY5 172 E2
Lytham St Anne's FY8 89 E3
Elms Ct LA4 213 A7
Elms Dr Morecambe LA4 213 A7
Elms Dr *continued*
Wrea Green PR4 112 B4
Elms Rd LA4 213 A7
Elms Sch PR1 117 A3
Elms The Clayton Green PR6 77 C1
Maghull L31 5 D3
Southport PR8 34 C5
Southport, Birkdale PR8 33 F6
Elmsdale Cl LA1 213 E2
Elmsfield Pk L39 6 A6
Elmside Cl FY5 173 D2
Elmslack Ct LA5 218 C4
Elmslack La LA5 218 C4
Elmsley St PR1 116 E2
Elmslie Girls Sch FY3 129 E3
Elmstead WN8 9 D8
Elmswood Cl FY8 89 F4
Elmwood Chorley PR7 60 B1
Longridge PR3 139 A8
Skelmersdale WN8 18 C3
Elmwood Ave
1 Leyland PR5 75 E1
Preesall FY6 195 B4
Elmwood Cl BB5 103 D6
Elmwood Ct PR4 131 F2
Elmwood Dr
Penwortham PR1 95 B4
Thornton FY5 173 C1
Elmwood Gdns LA1 211 A2
Elmwood St BB11 126 D5
Elsby Ave FY5 151 C8
Elsie St 10 BL0 49 A4
Elsinore Cl FY7 193 F5
Elslack La BD23 201 F7
Elson Rd L37 11 D1
Elston Ave FY3 130 A8
Elston Gn PR2 138 E1
Elston La PR2 118 F7
Elswick WN8 9 C8
Elswick Gdns BB2 120 D3
Elswick Gn PR9 53 A5
Elswick Lodge BB2 120 E3
Elswick Pl Blackpool FY4 109 E5
Lytham St Anne's FY8 89 B8
Elswick Rd Leyland PR5 58 D8
Preston PR2 115 E1
Southport PR9 52 F4
Elswick St BB3 81 B1
Elsworth Cl L37 2 C8
Elterwater FY6 194 E5
Elterwater Pl
Blackpool FY3 130 C2
Lancaster LA1 214 A1
Eltham Ct FY3 151 B1
Elton Rd BB1,BB4 82 B5
Elton St 3 PR2 116 C1
Elvaston Way FY6 151 C6
Elvington Rd L38 3 A2
Ely Cl Darwen BB3 81 C1
Wilpshire BB1 121 F6
Ely Mews PR9 53 A2
Embankment Rd BL7 47 C5
Emerald Ave BB1 121 F2
Emerald Cl FY5 150 F7
Emerald Cotts BL8 48 F3
Emerald St BB1 121 F2
Emerson Ave FY4 109 D7
Emerson Cl L38 3 A4
Emerson Rd PR1 117 D2
Emerson St LA1 211 A4
Emesgate La LA5 218 C3
Emily St Bamber Bridge PR5 76 A8
Blackburn BB1 101 A6
Burnley BB11 127 A4
Emma St BB5 102 F6
Emmanuel Holcombe
CE Prim Sch BL8 49 A6
Emmanuel Rd PR9 52 F2
Emmanuel St PR1,PR2 116 E2
Emmaus Rd LA3 208 F6
Emmerdale Cl BB5 102 D5
Emmett St Horwich BL6 31 B3
Preston PR1 116 F1
Emmott Cl BB8 170 E6
Emmott La BB8 170 D6
Emnie La PR5 58 C7
Empire Gr 2 FY3 129 D7
Empire St BB6 123 D6
Emporium The 7 BB7 164 E8
Empress Ave PR2 116 E4
Empress Cl L31 5 B1
Empress Dr FY2 150 B1
Empress St Accrington BB5 102 F6
Blackburn BB3 80 F7
Colne BB8 169 E5
Empress Way PR7 59 E2
End St BB8 169 B4
Endcliffe Rd LA4 212 F5
Endeavour Cl PR2 95 B7
Enderley Ct FY5 173 C1
Ending Rake OL12 51 C4
Endsleigh Gdns FY4 109 E6
Endsleigh Gr LA1 213 C3
Enfield Cl Eccleston PR7 40 C5
Huncoat BB5 124 E2
Enfield Rd Accrington BB5 124 D2
Blackpool FY1 129 C7
Engine La L37 3 E8
England Ave FY2 150 C4
English Martyrs' Pl PR1 116 F2
English Martyrs' RC
Prim Sch PR1 116 E1
Ennerdale WN8 9 D8
Ennerdale Ave
Blackburn BB1 101 C3
Fleetwood FY7 193 C1
Maghull L31 5 E2
Morecambe LA4 212 G4
Ennerdale Cl
Clitheroe BB7 164 C7
Formby L37 11 D3
Forton PR3 204 B3
Knott End-on-S FY6 194 F6
Lancaster LA1 214 B2
Leyland PR5 59 A7
Ennerdale Dr Ormskirk L39 15 B2
Walton-le-D PR5 96 E5
Ennerdale Rd
Blackpool FY4 130 C1
Burnley BB10 127 E5
Chorley PR7 42 A6
Clitheroe BB7 164 C7
Formby L37 11 E3
Longridge PR3 138 F5
Ennismore St BB10 147 C1
Enoch Brow BB2 79 C8
Enstone WN8 18 D1
Enterprise Ct BB5 124 D1
Enterprise Dr PR5 76 A4
Enterprise Way
Nelson BB8 168 F3
Thornton FY7 173 A6
Enterprise Workshops
Kirkby L33 1 B1
Southport PR9 35 A6
Entwisle Rd BB5 103 B8
Entwistle Hall La BL7 47 B8
Entwistle St BB3 81 A1
Entwistle Sta BL7 47 B8
Ephraim St PR1 96 C7
Epping Cl FY2 150 E5
Epping Pl PR6 42 D8
Epsom Cl PR6 60 F4
Epsom Croft PR6 30 B7
Epsom Gr L33 1 A6
Epsom Rd FY5 150 F8
Epsom Way BB5 103 D5
Epworth St BB3 64 B6
Equity St BB3 64 A8
Erdington Rd FY1 129 C3
Erith Gr FY2 150 C5
Ermine Cl BB2 81 A8
Ermine Pl LA3 213 A3
Ernest St Bacup OL13 70 C8
6 Church BB5 102 E6
Clayton-le-M BB5 123 F1
Cornholme OL14 108 C1
Ernlouen Cl BB2 80 A8
Erskine Rd PR6 60 E1
Escar St 9 BB11 126 F5
Escott Gdns 10 BB10 127 A8
Esher Pond PR2 116 C6
Eshton Terr BB7 164 E7
Esk Ave Edenfield BL0 67 D5
Fleetwood FY7 193 D2
Eskbank WN8 9 C8
Eskbrook WN8 18 C1
Eskdale WN8 9 B8
Eskdale Ave
Fleetwood FY7 193 D1
Ormskirk L39 15 C2
Eskdale Cl Blackpool FY4 129 F1
Brierfield BB10 147 C4
Formby L37 11 D2
Fulwood PR2 116 F8
Eskdale Cres BB2 79 E8
Eskdale Ct FY5 172 D1
Eskdale Dr Formby L37 11 D2
Kirkham PR4 113 A7
Maghull L31 5 E2
Eskdale Gdns BB12 145 C2
Eskdale Gr FY6 194 F6
Eskdale Pl LA4 212 G4
Eskdale Rd Leyland PR5 59 C7
Longridge PR3 138 F6
Eskew La LA2 233 B8
Eskham Cl PR4 112 E6
Eskrigge Cl 4 LA1 213 F4
Eskrigge La LA2 232 A8
Esp La BB8 225 F1
Esplanade
Knott End-on-S FY6 194 D6
Preston PR1 96 B5
Southport PR8 33 F7
Esplanade The
Fleetwood FY7 194 A5
Rishton BB1 102 A8
Essex Ave Burnley BB12 126 B7
Heywood OL10 32 E1
Essex Cl BB2 100 D3
Essex Pl FY2 150 F2
Essex Rd Morecambe LA4 213 B4
4 Rishton BB1 123 A1
Southport PR8 21 A8
Standish WN1 29 B1
Essex St Accrington BB5 103 D6
Barnoldswick BB18 200 B2
Colne BB8 169 E4
Darwen BB3 81 C1
Horwich BL6 31 D1
Nelson BB9 168 E1
Preston PR1 117 A1
Essie Terr BB18 200 B1
Essington Ave LA4 212 D4
Est Bank Rd BL0 49 A3
Esther St BB1 101 C5
Ethel St Barnoldswick BB18 200 C2
Whitworth OL12 70 D2
Ethersall Rd BB9 147 E6
Eton Ave BB5 103 C7
Eton Cl BB12 125 E6
Eton Pk PR2 117 C5
Eton Way WN5 10 F8
Ettington Dr PR8 20 A5
Ettrick Ave FY7 193 D3
Euro Trad Est BB1 100 F7

Europa Dr PR5 76 A4
Europa Way LA1 210 C8
Euston Rd LA4 212 E5
Euston St PR1 95 E7
Euxton CE Sch PR7 59 C2
Euxton Hall Ct PR7 59 C2
Euxton Hall Gdns PR7 59 C1
Euxton Hall Hospl PR7 59 C1
Euxton Hall Mews PR7 59 C2
Euxton La Chorley PR7 60 B3
Euxton PR7 59 E4
Euxton Sta PR7 59 D1
Evans St Burnley BB11 126 F4
Horwich BL6 31 D4
Preston PR2 116 D1
Evanstone Cl BL6 31 B3
Eve St BB9 169 A2
Evelyn Rd BB3 80 E5
Evelyn St BB10 147 A1
Evenwood WN8 18 D1
Evenwood Ct WN8 18 C1
Everard Cl L40 22 F7
Everard Rd PR8 34 D4
Everest Cl FY8 110 A1
Everest Ct 2 PR4 112 F6
Everest Dr FY2 150 C5
Everest Rd FY8 110 A2
Evergreen Ave PR5 59 A7
Evergreen Cl PR7 42 B5
Evergreens The
Blackburn BB2 79 F8
Formby L37 11 D4
Fulwood PR4 115 E4
Eversham Cl PR9 54 A5
Eversholt Cl BB12 146 D7
Eversleigh Ave FY5 173 A3
Eversleigh St PR1 116 E1
Eversley WN8 18 D1
Everton BB2 101 A1
Everton Rd Blackpool FY4 109 C6
Southport PR8 34 A4
Everton St BB3 80 F1
Every St Brierfield BB9 147 B6
Burnley BB11 126 E5
Nelson BB9 147 C8
Nelson BB9 147 D8
Ramsbottom BL0 49 D6
Evesham Ave PR1 95 E2
Evesham Cl
5 Accrington BB5 103 A7
Blackpool FY5 150 E7
Hutton PR4 94 C1
Evesham Rd
Lytham St Anne's FY8 89 A5
Normoss FY3 130 B7
Evington WN8 18 D1
Ewell Cl PR6 60 F4
Ewood BB2 100 D1
Ewood Ct BB2 100 C2
Ewood La BB4 67 C7
Ewood Park (Blackburn Rovers FC) BB2 80 D8
Exchange St
Accrington BB5 102 F5
18 Blackburn BB1 100 E5
Blackpool FY1 129 B6
Colne BB8 169 D4
Darwen BB3 81 A2
Edenfield BL0 67 D3
Exe St PR1 117 B2
Exeter Ave LA1 211 B6
Exeter Dr FY5 173 A2
Exeter Pl 2 PR2 115 E2
Exeter St Blackburn BB2 100 D2
3 Blackpool FY4 129 C1
Exmoor Cl PR9 53 B6
Exmouth St BB11 127 A5
Exton St BB9 147 A5
Extwistle Rd BB10 128 B7
Extwistle Sq BB10 127 E5
Extwistle St Burnley BB10 127 B8
Nelson BB9 147 D7
Eyes La Bretherton PR5 56 E3
Newburgh WN8 26 A3

F

Factory Bank PR1 95 F3
Factory Brow Blackrod BL6 30 D3
Scorton PR3 199 E6
Factory Hill Horwich BL6 31 D4
4 Lancaster LA1 214 A1
Factory La Adlington PR6 30 B8
Barrowford BB9 168 D4
17 Padiham BB12 145 C1
Penwortham PR1 95 F3
Factory St BL0 49 C7
Fair Hill BB4 67 A7
Fair Oak Cl PR2 117 F3
Fair View OL13 70 C8
Fair View Cres OL13 87 B3
Fair View Rd BB11 127 B5
Fair Way FY6 174 C7
Fairacres WN6 28 B1
Fairbairn Ave BB12 126 C8
Fairbairn St BL6 31 B3
Fairbank LA6 238 B2
Fairbank Gr LA4 212 D3
Fairbank Wlk BB4 105 A2
Fairburn WN8 18 B3
Fairclough Rd
Accrington BB5 103 A3
Thornton FY5 173 A3
Fairfax Ave FY2 150 E5
Fairfax Cl PR3 178 D6
Fairfax Pl PR5 96 D2
Fairfax Rd PR2 117 E4
Fairfield PR3 178 C8
Fairfield Ave
Newchurch BB4 85 F2
Normoss FY3 130 B7
Poulton-le-F FY6 151 D3
Fairfield Cl Carnforth LA5 217 E1
Clitheroe BB7 164 C7
Lancaster LA1 210 E8
2 Ormskirk L39 15 E7
Fairfield Ct FY7 193 F2
Fairfield Dr
Brierfield BB10 147 C3
Bury BL9 32 D3
Clitheroe BB7 164 C7
1 Ormskirk L39 15 E7
Preston PR2 116 B2
Fairfield General Hospl BL9 32 E4
Fairfield Gr LA3 212 B2
Fairfield Prim Sch BL9 32 D3
Fairfield Rd Blackpool FY1 129 C8
Fulwood PR2 117 A4
Lancaster LA1 210 E8
Leyland PR5 58 F8
Morecambe LA3 212 B2
Nelson BB9 148 B8
Poulton-le-F FY6 130 F7
Southport PR8 20 C5
Fairfield St Accrington BB5 102 F4
5 Bamber Bridge PR5 76 B7
Fairfields Dr BB3 80 F6
Fairgarth Dr LA6 238 B2
Fairham Ave 6 PR1 95 D2
Fairhaven WN8 18 C3
Fairhaven Ave FY7 172 D7
Fairhaven Cl 5 FY5 173 D1
Fairhaven La FY8 88 E5
Fairhaven Lake FY8 89 C3
Fairhaven Rd
Blackburn BB2 100 F1
Leyland PR5 75 D1
Lytham St Anne's FY8 88 F5
Penwortham PR1 95 E5
Southport PR9 53 B4
Fairhaven Way LA4 212 G5
Fairheath Rd LA2 233 B4
Fairhill Terr BB4 67 A7
Fairholme Rd BB11 127 B3
Fairholmes Cl FY5 173 B3
Fairholmes Way 1 FY5 173 B3
Fairhope Ave
Lancaster LA1 213 E3
Morecambe LA4 213 B6
Fairhope Ct BB2 100 C6
Fairhurst Ave WN6 28 D3
Fairhurst Ct FY5 172 D3
Fairhurst St FY1 129 C6
Fairhurst's Dr WN8 26 B2
Fairlawn Rd FY8 89 F3
Fairlea Ave LA4 213 B6
Fairlie WN8 18 C3
Fairlie Cty Prim Sch WN8 18 C3
Fairmont Dr FY6 174 D2
Fairsnape Ave PR3 139 B7
Fairsnape Dr PR3 178 B6
Fairsnape Rd FY8 90 D4
Fairstead WN8 18 C3
Fairthorn Wlk L33 1 A3
Fairview
Kirkby Lonsdale LA6 238 B3
Rawtenstall BB4 84 F5
Fairview Ave FY8 89 A7
Fairview Cl PR4 73 F5
Fairway Chorley PR7 60 C2
Fleetwood FY7 193 C1
Penwortham PR1 95 B6
Poulton-le-F FY6 151 A2
Southport PR8 52 C2
Whitworth OL12 51 C7
Fairway Gdns FY6 194 D5
Fairway Rd FY4 109 E8
Fairways Fulwood PR2 117 A6
Horwich BL6 31 C3
Lytham St Anne's FY8 89 A6
Fairways Ave PR3 136 C3
Fairways Ct Formby L37 11 C5
Wilpshire BB1 121 F5
Fairways Dr BB11 126 E2
Fairways The WN8 18 D3
Fairweather Ct BB12 145 D1
Fairwinds Ave PR4 72 D4
Falcon Ave BB3 80 E3
Falcon Cl Blackburn BB1 100 D8
Bury BL9 32 B4
Falcon Ct BB5 123 F2
Falcon Dr FY6 151 B2
Falcon St PR1 117 B2
Falinge Fold OL12 51 D1
Falinge Park High Sch OL12 51 D1
Falinge Rd OL12 51 E1
Falkirk Ave FY2 150 C6
Falkland WN8 18 C3
Falkland Ave FY4 129 F2
Falkland Rd PR8 34 D5
Falkland St PR1 95 F7
Fall Barn Rd BB4 85 B2
Fall Kirk LA2 234 F1
Fallbarn Cres BB4 85 A1
Fallbarn Rd BB4 85 B2
Fallowfield Cl PR4 112 E6
Fallowfield Dr
Burnley BB12 126 D8
Rochdale OL12 51 D2
Fallowfield Rd FY8 89 C6
Falmouth Ave
Fleetwood FY7 172 C8
Haslingden BB4 84 C2
Falmouth Rd FY1 129 C2
Falshaw Dr BL9 49 E1
Falstone Ave BL0 49 C4
Far Croft PR5 96 A1
Far East View 15 BB18 200 B2
Far Field PR1 95 D3
Far La PR1 95 C2
Far Moor La LA1 211 C8
Far Nook PR6 60 B7
Faraday Ave BB7 164 D8
Faraday Dr PR2 117 C7
Faraday St BB12 126 D7
Faraday Way FY2 150 F5
Fardes Cl BB2 100 F1
Fareham Cl PR2 117 A4
Fareham Dr PR9 54 A5
Farholme La OL13 69 D8
Faringdon Ave FY4 109 E5
Farington Ave PR5 58 D7
Farington Cty Prim Sch PR5 76 B3
Farington Gate PR5 76 B2
Farington Rd PR5 76 A6
Farington St Paul's CE Prim Sch PR5 75 F7
Farleton Cl LA5 217 C5
Farleton Ct 3 LA1 213 F4
Farleton Old Rd LA2 232 A5
Farley La Orrell WN8 19 A3
Skelmersdale WN8 18 F3
Farm Ave Adlington PR6 30 A8
Bacup OL13 86 F4
Farm Cl Southport PR9 35 A8
Thornton FY5 173 B2
Farm House Cl
Blackburn BB1 101 C4
Lucas Green PR6 60 C6
Farm Meadow Rd WN5 10 E5
Farmdale Dr L31 5 E1
Farmdale Rd LA1 211 B5
Farmend Cl PR4 74 B8
Farmer's Row BB2 80 B7
Farnborough Rd PR8 20 F8
Farnborough Road Inf & Jun Schs PR8 21 A8
Farnell Pl FY4 109 D6
Farnham Way FY6 151 C5
Farnlea Dr LA4 213 A5
Farnworth Rd FY5 173 D1
Farrer St BB9 147 C7
Farrier Rd L33 1 A2
Farriers Fold 4 LA3 208 F7
Farringdon Cl PR1 117 F1
Farringdon Cres PR1 117 F1
Farringdon La PR2 117 F3
Farringdon Pl PR1 117 F1
Farrington Cl BB11 126 C3
Farrington Ct BB11 126 C3
Farrington Dr L39 15 E6
Farrington Pl BB11 126 C3
Farrington Rd BB11 126 B3
Farrington St PR7 42 C8
Farthings The PR7 59 F1
Faulkner Cl PR8 20 C6
Faulkner Gdns PR8 20 C6
Faulkner's La PR3 204 B1
Favordale Rd BB8 170 A5
Fawcett WN8 18 B3
Fawcett Cl BB2 100 D3
Fawcett Rd L31 5 D3
Fayles Gr FY4 130 A1
Fazackerley St PR2 116 C1
Fazakerley St 18 PR7 42 C8
Fearnhead Ave BL6 31 B5
Fearns Cty High Sch OL13 86 A1
Fearns Moss BB4,OL13 86 A1
Fecit La BL0 50 C8
Fecitt Brow BB1 101 D4
Fecitt Rd BB2 100 B6
Federation St BB18 200 A3
Feilden Pl BB2 79 D8
Feilden St BB2 100 D5
Feildens Farm La BB2 120 B3
Felgate Brow FY3 129 E5
Felix St BB11 127 B7
Fell Brow PR3 139 B7
Fell Cl 5 PR5 76 F8
Fell Rd High Casterton LA6 238 F3
Morecambe LA4 213 B4
Waddington BB7 186 A6
Fell View Brierfield BB10 147 D3
Caton LA2 231 C3
Chorley PR6 42 E6
Garstang PR3 178 C8
Grimsargh PR2 138 C2
Weir OL13 87 A7
West Bradford BB7 186 D7
Fell View Cl PR3 178 C8
Fell Way FY6 174 D7
Fellborough Lodge 5 FY8 89 A8
Fellery St PR7 42 C8
Fellgate LA3 213 A2
Fellside Cl BL8 48 F1
Fellside View LA3 208 F7
Fellstone Vale PR6 79 A1
Fellstone View PR6 79 A1
Fellview PR9 53 D6
Fellway Cl 7 PR5 76 C8
Felstead WN8 18 B2
Felstead St PR1 96 D8
Felton Way PR4 73 F3
Feltons WN8 18 B2
Fenber Ave FY4 109 C7
Fencegate BB12 146 C7
Fengrove PR4 74 A8
Fenham Carr La LA1 211 C7
Feniscliffe Dr BB2 100 A2
Feniscowles Cty Jun Sch BB2 79 C7
Feniscowles Prim Sch BB2 79 D8
Fenney Ct WN8 18 C1
Fennyfold Terr BB12 125 C6
Fensway PR4 94 D2
Fenton Ave BB18 200 D3
Fenton Rd Blackpool FY1 129 C6
Fulwood PR2 117 C4
Fenton St LA1 210 E8
Fenwick St BB11 126 D3
Ferguson Gdns OL12 51 F3
Ferguson Rd FY1 129 E2
Ferguson St BB2 80 D7
Fermor Rd Becconsall PR4 72 E1
Preston PR1 117 E1
Fern Ave BB5 102 F3
Fern Bank Carnforth LA5 217 D1
Chorley PR6 60 D3
Lancaster LA1 211 A5
Maghull L31 5 E1
Fern Bank Ave BB18 200 A3
Fern Breck Cotts FY6 195 A2
Fern Cl
2 Bamber Bridge PR5 76 B8
Skelmersdale WN8 17 E1
Fern Croft LA6 238 E4
Fern Ct FY7 193 C1
Fern Dene 2 OL12 51 B2
Fern Gore Ave BB5 103 A3
Fern Gr FY1 129 C3
Fern Hill La OL12 51 A3
Fern Isle Cl OL12 51 B6
Fern Lea BB9 147 E8
Fern Lea St BB4 68 D8
Fern Mdw PR6 77 C2
Fern Rd BB11 126 E4
Fern St Bacup OL13 86 F3
Colne BB8 169 F6
Newchurch BB4 85 F1
Ramsbottom BL0 49 D7
Fern Terr BB4 84 A3
Fernbank Ct BB9 147 E7
Ferncliffe Dr LA3 212 A2
Ferndale Blackburn BB1 101 A6
Skelmersdale WN8 18 C2
Ferndale Ave FY4 109 D7
Ferndale Cl Freckleton PR4 92 D7
Leyland PR5 59 B7
Thornton FY5 173 C2
Ferndale St BB10 127 C8
Ferngrove BL9 32 B5
Fernhill Ave OL13 69 E8
Fernhill Cl OL13 69 E8
Fernhill Cres 1 OL13 69 E8
Fernhill Dr OL13 69 E8
Fernhill Gr 2 OL13 69 E8
Fernhill Pk OL13 69 E8
Fernhill Way 4 OL13 69 E8
Fernhills BL7 46 E2
Fernhurst Ave FY4 129 D1
Fernhurst Gate L39 15 B1
Fernhurst St BB2 80 D8
Fernlea Ave
Barnoldswick BB18 200 B2
Oswaldtwistle BB5 103 A3
Fernlea Cl Blackburn BB2 80 B8
1 Rochdale OL12 51 B2
Fernlea Dr BB5 123 F4
Fernleigh PR5 58 A8
Fernleigh Cl FY2 150 D4
Fernley Rd PR8 34 A5
Ferns The Bacup OL13 87 A1
Bamber Bridge PR5 96 C3
Preston PR2 116 C2
Fernside Way OL12 51 A1
Fernstone Cl BL6 31 A3
Fernview Dr BL0 49 A1
Fernville Terr 6 OL13 69 D8
Fernwood Ave FY5 151 B8
Fernwood Cl FY8 89 E4
Ferny Knoll Rd WA11 8 F4
Fernyhalgh Ct PR2 117 D6
Fernyhalgh Gdns PR2 117 D6
Fernyhalgh La PR2 117 D7
Fernyhalgh Pl PR2 117 D6
Ferrier Bank PR4 91 D5
Ferrier Cl 1 BB1 101 C5
Ferry Rd PR2 94 F8
Ferry Side La PR9 53 C5
Ffrances Pas 30 LA1 210 F8
Fiddler's La Chipping PR3 181 F4
Clayton Green PR6 77 B2
Fidler La PR5 75 F5
Field Cl L40 24 F3
Field Maple Dr PR2 117 F3
Field Rd LA3 208 D6
Field St Blackburn BB2 100 B2
Blackpool FY1 129 C2
Padiham BB12 125 C7
Skelmersdale WN8 17 D2
Field Top OL13 87 A7
Field Wlk L39 16 B5
Fielden St Burnley BB11 126 D5
Chorley PR6 42 E8
5 Leyland PR5 75 D1
Fieldfare Cl
Penwortham PR1 95 E3
Thornton FY5 173 A5
Fieldhouse Ave FY5 173 D2
Fieldhouse Ind Est OL12 51 F2
Fieldhouse Rd OL12 51 F2
Fielding Cres BB2 100 A1
Fielding La
Great Harwood BB6 123 B5
Oswaldtwistle BB5 102 E3
Fielding Pl PR6 30 B8
Fielding Rd FY1 129 D8
Fielding St BB1 123 C1
Fieldings Bldgs 8 BB4 84 E2
Fieldings The L31 5 B4
Fieldlands PR8 35 A2
Fields End BB6 122 C8
Fields Rd BB4 84 C1
Fields The PR7 40 B7
Fieldsend LA3 209 A7
Fieldside Ave PR7 59 C1
Fieldside Cl PR5 96 C3
Fieldview WN8 10 A7
Fieldway FY8 109 E2
Fife Cl PR6 42 E6
Fife St Accrington BB5 103 A4
Barrowford BB9 168 C1
Fifth Ave Blackpool FY4 109 C7
Burnley BB10 147 B3
Bury BL9 32 D4
Filberts Cl PR2 116 C3
Filberts The PR2 116 C3
File St PR7 42 C7
Filey Pl Blackpool FY1 129 B6
Fulwood PR2 116 A4
Filey Rd FY8 110 A1
Filton Gr LA3 213 A3
Finch Cl BB1 100 E6
Finch La Appley Bridge WN6 27 B1
Cottam PR4 115 E4
Finch Mill Ave WN6 19 D7
Finch St 5 BB3 80 F2
Finch's Cotts 6 PR1 95 E4
Finches The FY6 151 B2
Finchley Rd FY1 129 B8
Findon WN8 18 C2
Fine Jane's Way PR9 35 B8
Finnington La BB2 79 A6
Finsbury Ave
Blackpool FY1 129 D2
Lytham St Anne's FY8 89 B4
Finsbury Pl BB2 80 D8
Finsley Gate BB11 127 A5
Finsley St BB10 147 E3
Fir Cl FY7 193 C2
Fir Cotes L31 5 E1
Fir Ct BB5 103 E8
Fir Gr Blackpool FY1 129 E2
Warton PR4 91 D6
Fir Grove Rd 12 BB11 127 B4
Fir St Burnley BB10 127 B5
Bury BL9 32 A2
Haslingden BB4 84 B3
Nelson BB9 147 F8
Ramsbottom BL0 49 D7
Southport PR8 34 F6
Fir Tree Ave PR2 116 B4
Fir Tree Cl Hest Bank LA5 215 F2
Much Hoole PR4 73 E3
Skelmersdale WN8 9 D7
Fir Tree La Haskayne L39 14 F3
Ormskirk L39 15 A2
Fir Tree Pl FY5 150 F8
Fir Tree Way 3 BL6 31 E1
Fir Trees Ave
Bamber Bridge PR5 76 A8
Fulwood PR2 118 A4
Fir Trees Cres 1 PR5 76 A8
Fir Trees Gr BB12 145 E5
Fir Trees La BB12 145 E5
Fir Trees Pl PR2 117 F4
Fir Trees Rd PR5 96 A1
Firbank PR7 59 C2
Firbank Ave PR4 56 A7
Firbank Rd LA1 214 A1
Firbeck WN8 18 C1
Fircroft WN6 28 A2
Firfield Cl PR4 112 E5
Firs Cl L37 11 D5
Firs Cres L37 11 D5
Firs La L39 14 E3
Firs Link L37 11 D4
Firshill Cl FY5 151 B8
First Ave Blackpool FY4 109 C7
Church BB5 103 A8
Clifton PR4 114 C1
Poulton-le-F FY6 151 E3
Preston PR2 116 A2
West Bradford BB7 186 D7
Wrea Green PR4 112 B4
First Terr LA3 205 B5
Firswood Cl FY8 89 E4
Firswood Rd L40, WN8 17 C3
Firtree Cl Blackburn BB2 79 F8
Chorley PR7 42 C3
Firwood Longridge PR3 139 A8
Skelmersdale WN8 18 D3
Firwood La PR5 98 B5
Fish House La PR3 182 B5
Fish La L40 37 B2
Fish Rake La BL0,BB4 67 E6
Fisher Dr Orrell WN5 10 E7
Southport PR9 34 F7
Fisher Slack La FY6 153 B2
Fisher St FY1 129 C6
Fisher's La FY4 110 A5
Fishergate PR1 95 F7
Fishergate Ct 11 PR1 95 E7
Fishergate Ctr PR1 95 F7
Fishergate Hill PR1 95 E6
Fishergate Wlk 7 PR1 95 F7
Fishermans Cl L37 11 E6
Fishermans Reach PR4 112 D4
Fishmoor Dr BB2,BB3 80 F8
Fishwick Cty Prim Sch PR1 117 E1

Fishwick La PR6 78 B1
Fishwick Par PR1 96 D8
Fishwick Rd PR1 96 C8
Fishwick View PR1 96 D8
Fitchfield PR1 95 F2
Fitzgerald St PR1 117 C1
Fitzroy Rd FY2 150 D3
Fitzroy St PR1 95 E7
Five Acres PR5 75 E4
Five Lane Ends
Hampson Green LA2 204 D8
Preesall FY6 195 A2
Singleton FY6 152 D4
Flag La Bamber Bridge PR1 95 F1
Bretherton PR5 57 A5
Limbrick PR6 42 F5
Runshaw Moor PR5,PR7 58 D4
Flag St OL13 69 E8
Flakefleet Ave FY7 193 E1
Flakefleet Prim Sch FY7 193 E2
Flamstead WN8 18 C1
Flare Rd LA3 208 D6
Flash Gate BB1 121 D3
Flash La L40 38 B4
Flat La LA5 219 E3
Flatfield Way L31 5 E1
Flatman's La L39 13 E1
Flats Ret Pk The PR1,PR5 96 C5
Flats The Chorley PR7 42 B6
Kirkham PR4 113 B4
Flax Cl BB4 67 A8
Flax La L40 24 F2
Flax Moss Cl BB4 67 A8
Flax St 8 BL0 49 A4
Flaxfield Rd L37 12 A3
Flaxfield Way PR4 113 A5
Flaxton WN8 18 C1
Fleet La LA2 232 A8
Fleet St Blackpool FY1 129 C4
Chorley PR7 42 C7
Horwich BL6 31 D3
Longridge PR3 139 A7
Lytham St Anne's FY8 88 D8
Nelson BB9 168 E1
3 Preston PR1 95 F7
Fleet Street La PR3 140 A6
Fleet Wlk 5 BB11 127 A6
Fleetgreen LA1 213 E3
Fleetwood Cl
Blackburn BB2 100 F1
Southport PR9 52 F3
Fleetwood Cres PR9 54 A6
Fleetwood Dr PR9 54 A6
Fleetwood High Sch FY7 193 D2
Fleetwood High Sch
Beach Rd Site FY7 193 E3
Fleetwood Hospl FY7 194 B5
Fleetwood Old Rd PR4 132 E3
Fleetwood Rd
Blackpool FY5 150 D7
Burnley BB10 147 C2
Carleton FY6 151 B5
Esprick PR4 132 D5
Fleetwood FY7 193 E1
Kirkham PR4 112 F7
Padiham BB12 125 D8
Southport PR9 52 E3
Thornton FY7 173 A6
Fleetwood Rd N FY5 173 B3
Fleetwood Rd S FY5 151 B7
Fleetwood St
6 Leyland PR5 76 B2
Preston PR2 116 D1
Fleetwood's Charity
Prim CE Sch FY6 195 B3
Fleming Sq BB2 100 E4
Flemming Sq PR3 139 B7
Flensburg Way
Farington PR5 75 E6
Leyland PR5 75 D4
Fletcher Ave PR4 56 A6
Fletcher Rd Preston PR1 117 C1
Rishton BB1 102 A8
Fletcher St Blackburn BB2 100 D3
Bury BL9 32 A2
Nelson BB9 147 F7
Fletcher's Dr L40 24 E4
Flett St PR2 116 C1
Flimby WN8 18 D1
Flimby Cl BB2 80 F8
Flintoff Way PR1 117 B3
Flintron Brow LA2 227 A2
Flip Rd BB4 84 A2
Flockton Ct 7 BL6 31 B4
Flordon WN8 18 D2
Florence Ave
Burnley BB11 126 C4
Warton PR4 91 D5
Florence Pl BB1 101 A6
Florence St Blackburn BB1 101 A6
Blackpool FY4 110 A6
Burnley BB11 126 C5
1 Church BB5 102 E6
Flower Fields PR3 178 D2
Flower Scar Rd OL14 87 E6
Flowerfield PR4 115 E6
Flowers Cl BB2 80 D7
Floyd Rd PR2 117 E3
Floyer St PR1 96 B7
Fluke Hall La PR3 196 B8
Flush Brow LA6 238 F5
Fold BB9 168 E5
Fold Gdns OL12 51 B4
Fold House Caravan Pk
PR3 196 D4
Fold View BL7 46 E1
Folds BL6 30 C3
Folds St BB12 126 F8
Foldside PR4 92 C7
Folkestone Cl
Cleveleys FY5 172 F4
Warton PR4 91 E7
Folkestone Rd
Lytham St Anne's FY8 88 F8
Southport PR8 34 F3
Folly La Barnoldswick BB8 190 F7
Lancaster LA1,LA2 213 D4
Folly Terr BB4 85 B8
Folly Wlk 20 OL12 51 F1
Fontwell Cl WN6 28 F1
Fooden La BB7 224 E4
Foot Mill Cres OL12 51 D2
Foot Wood Cres OL12 51 D2
Football Mus Deedpale
Preston The PR1 117 B2
Footeran La LA5 219 E3
Forbes Ct BB11 126 A3
Ford La Goosnargh PR3 158 F2
Silverdale LA5 218 E5
Ford St Barrowford BB9 168 E4
Burnley BB10 147 B1
Lancaster LA1 213 D1
Fordham Cl PR8 34 E3
Fordside Ave BB5 123 E4
Fordstone Ave FY6 195 A4
Fordway Ave FY3 129 F6
Fore St BB3 80 F7
Foregate PR2 116 E4
Foreside BB9 168 E5
Forest Ave BB12 146 E8
Forest Bank BB4 85 A7
Forest Bank Rd BB4 85 A7
Forest Becks Brow BB7 224 D6
Forest Cl PR5 96 C3
Forest Dr
Lytham St Anne's FY8 89 F4
Shevington Moor WN6 28 A2
Skelmersdale WN8 18 C3
Forest Gate Blackpool FY3 129 E5
Morecambe LA3 213 A2
Forest Gr PR3 136 B8
Forest Ho BB9 147 D7
Forest Holme Cl BB4 86 A7
Forest La BB9 168 B2
Forest Pk LA1 210 C7
Forest Rd PR8 34 D6
Forest St Burnley BB11 127 B6
Forest Holme BB4 86 A7
Nelson BB9 168 D1
Forest View
Barrowford BB9 168 D3
Brierfield BB9 147 A5
Rochdale OL12 51 D2
Forest Way PR2 116 F6
Forester Dr BB12 146 D8
Forester's Bldgs 8 BB18 200 B2
Foresters Hall 13 PR1 95 F8
Forestry Houses BB7 222 C5
Forestway PR5 58 F8
Forfar Gr BB11 126 D3
Forfar St BB11 126 D3
Forge Cl L40 16 E4
Forge La PR3 178 E8
Forge St 3 OL13 86 F2
Forgewood Cl LA2 231 A3
Forgewood Dr LA2 214 F6
Formby Ave FY7 172 D7
Formby Bridge L37 11 E2
Formby Bsns Pk L37 12 B3
Formby By-Pass
Formby L37 12 B5
Hightown L37, L38 3 B8
Formby Cl BB2 80 F8
Formby Cres PR4 73 F8
Formby Fields L37 12 A2
Formby Gdns L37 11 F4
Formby High Sch L37 11 E4
Formby La Formby L37 12 B2
Haskayne L39 14 E2
Formby Pl PR2 115 E2
Formby Rd FY8 109 F1
Formby St L37 11 E2
Formby Sta L37 11 E2
Forrest Ct 4 FY3 129 E8
Forrest St BB1 101 A5
Forrester Cl PR5 75 E1
Forshaw Ave
Blackpool FY3 129 F8
Lytham St Anne's FY8 88 D8
Forshaw Cl 6 FY7 193 F2
Forshaw Rd 3 PR1 95 D2
Fort Ave PR3 140 D3
Fort St Accrington BB5 103 B6
Blackburn BB1 101 A5
11 Clayton-le-M BB5 123 F3
Clitheroe BB7 164 D7
Read BB12 144 D2
Forton Primary Sch PR3 204 B3
Forton Rd 8 PR2 115 E1
Forty Acre La PR3 161 B5
Forward Ind Est PR5 75 E2
Foscote Rd L33 1 A4
Fossdale Moss PR5 75 C1
Fosse Cl BB1,BB2 81 A8
Foster Croft PR1 95 C6
Foster Ct Bury BL9 32 D4
Chorley PR6 60 E1
Foster Rd
Barnoldswick BB18 200 A3
Formby L37 11 D2
Foster St Accrington BB5 103 C7
Chorley PR6 60 E1
Fosterfield Pl PR6 60 E1
Fosters Cl PR9 35 B8
Fosters Green Rd WN8 18 D3
Fothergill St 1 BB8 169 C5
Foul La PR8, PR9 35 A5
Fouldrey Ave FY6 151 F5
Foulds Cl BB8 169 C3
Foulds Rd BB8 170 B3
Foulds Terr BB8 170 C2
Foulridge Wharf BB8 191 D2
Foundry La Halton LA2 214 C7
Halton LA2 214 D6
Foundry St 1 Bacup OL13 86 F2
Blackburn BB2 100 D4
3 Burnley BB11 126 F6
15 Chorley PR7 42 C8
22 Darwen BB3 81 A1
Rawtenstall BB4 84 F1
Fountain Pl BB5 103 B5
Fountain Sq 3 BB9 168 D3
Fountain St
Accrington BB5 103 A5
Barnoldswick BB18 200 C2
Bury BL9 32 A2
Colne BB8 169 D4
Darwen BB3 64 A8
Nelson BB9 168 E1
Fountain St N 12 BL9 32 A3
Fountains Ave
Blackburn BB1 101 B8
Read BB12 144 D1
Fountains Cl PR7 42 D5
Fountains The L39 15 E6
Fountains Way Formby L37 12 B2
Oswaldtwistle BB5 102 B5
Four Acre La PR3 160 E5
Four Lane Ends
Barley BB7 189 B2
Burton in L LA2 236 C1
Carleton FY6 151 B5
Charnock Richard PR7 41 C4
Clitheroe BB7 165 A6
Dolphinholme LA2 220 A8
Gregson Lane PR5 97 D2
Halsall L39 22 D3
Halton LA2 214 B7
Knowley PR6 61 C4
Morecambe LA3 212 A1
Sabden BB12 144 F4
Wray LA2 232 E4
Four Lanes End Rd OL13 69 B8
Four Oaks Rd PR5 77 B7
Fouracre BB2 120 E2
Fourfields PR5 96 E2
Fourth Ave Blackpool FY4 109 C7
Bury BL9 32 D4
Fowler Ave PR5 76 B6
Fowler Cl PR5 98 C2
Fowler Height Cl BB2 80 B7
Fowler Hill La PR3 199 B5
Fowler Ind Pk BL6 31 C2
Fowler La Farington PR5 75 F6
Leyland PR5 76 B5
Fowler St PR2 116 D3
Fox Gr LA3 212 B3
Fox Ind Est 2 FY2 150 E1
Fox La Coupe Green PR5 97 E3
Leyland PR5 58 E7
Fox Lane Ends PR4 112 A5
Fox St Accrington BB5 103 B6
Burnley BB12 125 F6
Clitheroe BB7 186 E1
Horwich BL6 31 C2
Preston PR1 95 F7
Foxcote PR7 60 C2
Foxcroft BB12 126 D8
Foxdale Ave FY3 129 D7
Foxdale Cl Bacup OL13 87 A1
Edgworth BL7 47 E7
Southport PR8 34 E3
Foxdale Gr PR1 117 D3
Foxdale Pl 4 LA1 213 E2
Foxen Dole La BB12 146 A5
Foxes Terr PR3 155 C7
Foxfield Ave LA4 212 F3
Foxfield Cl BB5 102 D4
Foxfold WN8 18 D3
Foxglove Cl
Hesketh Bank PR4 72 E4
Standish WN6 28 D2
Foxglove Ct OL12 51 D3
Foxglove Dr Bury BL9 32 D3
Lucas Green PR6 60 C5
Foxglove Way PR4 92 D7
Foxhall Rd FY1 129 B3
Foxhall Sq 8 FY1 129 B3
Foxhill Bank Brow BB5 102 E5
Foxhill Cl L37 11 C3
Foxhill Dr BB4 85 F4
Foxhole Rd PR7 41 F8
Foxholes Rd Horwich BL6 31 D4
Morecambe LA4 212 G6
Foxhouse La L31 5 F1
Foxhouse St BB2 100 C5
Foxleigh PR5 58 D7
Foxstones Cres BB2 80 A8
Foxstones La BB10 128 B2
Foxwell Cl BB4 84 C2
Foxwood Chase BB5 103 E8
Foxwood Cl WN5 10 E5
Foxwood Dr PR4 112 E5
Foxwood The PR7 41 C1
Frailey Cl PR8 20 C4
France St Blackburn BB2 100 D4
Church BB5 102 E6
Frances St 3 BB3 80 F2
Francis Ave BB9 168 E5
Francis St Blackburn BB2 100 B1
Blackpool FY1 129 B6
Francis St *continued*
Burnley BB10 147 A1
3 Clayton-le-M BB5 123 F3
Colne BB8 169 B3
Preston PR2 116 C1
Frank St
Barnoldswick BB18 200 B2
4 Enfield BB5 124 A1
Preston PR1 116 F1
Franklands PR4 94 A1
Franklands Dr PR2 118 A5
Franklands Fold PR4 74 A8
Franklin Ainsworth Ho
BB6 123 C5
Franklin Rd BB2 100 B3
Franklin St
2 Burnley BB12 126 C6
Clitheroe BB7 164 D7
26 Darwen BB3 81 A1
Lancaster LA1 210 F5
Fraser Ave PR1 95 E5
Fraser St Accrington BB5 103 A4
Burnley BB10 147 B1
Frazer Gr 13 FY4 129 B1
Freckleton CE Prim Sch
PR4 92 C7
Freckleton Ct FY8 90 C3
Freckleton Dr L33 1 A5
Freckleton Rd
Kirkham PR4 113 B3
Southport PR9 52 F4
Freckleton St
Blackburn BB2 100 E4
Blackpool FY1 129 C3
Kirkham PR4 113 B4
2 Lytham St Anne's FY8 90 C3
Frederick Row BB1 101 B5
Frederick St
Accrington BB5 103 A6
Barnoldswick BB18 200 A3
6 Blackburn BB2 100 E3
2 Blackpool FY4 109 D8
Chorley PR6 42 E7
Darwen BB3 81 A2
Oswaldtwistle BB5 102 E4
12 Ramsbottom BL0 49 B5
Fredora Ave FY3 130 A2
Free La BB4 67 A6
Free Trade St 16 BB11 126 F6
Freeholds La
Waddington BB7 185 F6
Waddington BB7 185 F7
Freeholds Rd OL12 70 E6
Freeholds Terr OL12 70 E6
Freeman's La PR7 41 E3
Freemantle Ave FY4 109 B4
Freightway LA3 213 A2
French Cl BB2 100 B4
French Rd BB2 100 B4
Frenchwood Ave
Lytham St Anne's FY8 89 F3
Preston PR1 96 B6
Frenchwood Cty Prim Sch
PR1 96 B6
Frenchwood Knoll PR1 96 B6
Frenchwood St 4 PR1 96 A6
Freshfield Ave BB5 123 E3
Freshfield Ct L37 11 E4
Freshfield Prim Sch L37 12 A4
Freshfield Rd L37 11 E4
Freshfield Sta L37 11 E5
Freshfields PR2 115 D3
Friar St 23 LA1 210 F8
Friar's Moss Rd LA2 226 A8
Friar's Pas 22 LA1 210 F8
Friargate Preston PR1 95 F7
Preston PR1 95 F8
Friargate Wlk 6 PR1 95 F7
Friars The PR2 116 E4
Friars Wlk L37 12 B2
Friary Cl PR4 113 C4
Friday St PR6 42 D8
Frieldhurst Rd OL14 108 C1
Frinton Gr FY2 150 E6
Friths Ave PR5 97 E1
Frobisher Dr FY8 109 D1
Frog La L40 25 D3
Frome St PR1 117 D1
Frontierland Western
Theme Pk LA4 212 C5
Froom St PR6 42 F8
Fry St BB9 147 F8
Fryent Cl BL6 30 D2
Fryer Cl PR1 95 D1
Fulford Ave 1 PR2 115 C1
Fulham St BB9 168 F2
Full View BB2 80 B8
Fullers Terr OL13 86 F1
Fulmar Cres LA3 208 F5
Fulmars The FY6 151 B2
Fulshaw Rd PR2 116 B2
Fulwood & Cadley
Prim Sch PR2 116 D4
Fulwood Ave
Becconsall PR4 72 F1
Blackpool FY3 129 F8
Southport PR8 34 D4
Fulwood Dr LA4 213 B6
Fulwood Hall Hospl PR2 117 C5
Fulwood Hall La PR2 117 B4
Fulwood High Sch PR2 116 D6
Fulwood Hts PR2 117 C5
Fulwood Row PR2 117 E6
Funchal Ave L37 11 D1
Furlong Cres FY3 151 A1
Furlong La FY6 151 D5
Furness Ave
Blackburn BB1 101 B8
Furness Ave *continued*
Fleetwood FY7 193 D1
Formby L37 11 F3
Normoss FY3 130 A8
Ormskirk L39 15 E4
Read BB12 144 D1
Furness Cl Chorley PR7 42 D5
Southport PR8 20 B3
Furness Ct 3 FY3 130 A8
Furness Dr
High Bentham LA2 233 D8
Poulton-le-F FY6 152 A3
Furness Rd LA3 212 A2
Furness St
8 Burnley BB10 147 B1
3 Lancaster LA1 213 D1
Furnessford Rd LA2 233 A6
Furnival Dr L40 24 D4
Further Ends Rd PR4 92 B6
Further Heights Rd 1
OL12 51 F1
Further La BB2,PR5 99 A8
Further Wilworth BB1 121 E2
Furthergate BB1 101 B5
Fushetts La LA2 233 D8
Fylde Ave PR5 75 E4
Fylde Coast Hospl FY3 129 F7
Fylde Ct FY6 194 D5
Fylde Rd
Lytham St Anne's FY8 89 D5
Poulton-le-F FY6 151 E4
Preston PR1,PR2 116 D1
Southport PR9 53 B4
Fylde School Cotts FY3 130 C8
Fylde St Kirkham PR4 113 A4
Preston PR1 95 E8
Fylde View Cl FY6 151 D2

G

Gabbot St PR7 30 A7
Gable Mews L37 12 A1
Gables Pl LA4 212 G5
Gables The PR4 115 E4
Gadfield St 2 BB3 64 B8
Gadsby St FY1 129 B2
Gage St 31 LA1 210 F8
Gaghills Rd BB4 85 F1
Gaghills Terr 3 BB4 85 F1
Gainsborough Ave
Bamber Bridge PR5 76 A7
Blackburn BB2 100 C6
Burnley BB11 126 F3
Morecambe LA4 212 G6
Gainsborough Rd
Blackpool FY1 129 D4
Ramsbottom BL0 49 B1
Southport PR8 33 E3
Gaisgill Ave LA4 212 E3
Gait Barrows
(Nature Reserve) LA7 219 A7
Gale St OL12 51 F3
Gales La L40 39 A3
Galgate Silk Mills
Ind Est LA2 207 B4
Gall La OL14 108 C3
Gallery The L37 11 F3
Galligreaves St BB2 100 D3
Galligreaves Way BB2 100 D3
Galloway Cl 3 OL10 32 F1
Galloway Cres FY2 150 F5
Galloway Rd FY7 193 F5
Gallows La PR3 141 A6
Galway Ave FY2 150 D3
Gamble Rd FY5 173 B4
Gambleside Cl BB4 105 A1
Game St BB6 123 C5
Gamull La PR2 117 F5
Gandy La OL12 51 D4
Gannow La BB12 126 C6
Gantley Ave WN5 10 D3
Gantley Cres WN5 10 D3
Gantley Rd WN5 10 D4
Ganton Cl PR8 34 E3
Ganton Ct PR1 95 A6
Garbett St BB5 103 A4
Garden Ave PR4 112 B4
Garden City BL0 49 A2
Garden Pl LA6 234 C7
Garden Row OL12 51 D2
Garden St Abbey Village PR6 79 C2
Accrington BB5 103 B7
11 Bacup OL13 69 C8
1 Bamber Bridge PR5 76 B7
5 Barnoldswick BB18 200 B2
Blackburn BB2 100 C4
Brierfield BB9 147 B5
Brookbottoms BL0 49 C3
Colne BB8 169 D4
Great Harwood BB6 123 C4
Higham BB12 145 F5
Kirkham PR4 113 A4
Lytham St Anne's FY8 88 E6
Nelson BB9 147 E8
Oswaldtwistle BB5 102 D4
Padiham BB12 145 C1
Preston PR1 95 F7
Rawtenstall BL0 49 C6
Garden Terr
17 Blackpool FY4 129 B1
Chorley PR7 60 C1
Heysham LA3 209 A2
Garden Vale Bsns Ctr
BB8 169 B4
Garden Wlk Cleveleys FY5 172 D5
Preston PR2 116 B1
Gardeners Mews 10 FY1 129 C7

Gardeners Row BB7 144 F7
Gardeners View L33 1 A6
Gardens Gr LA4 212 D4
Gardiners Pl WN8 8 E8
Gardner Arc LA3 212 B4
Gardner Rd Formby L37 12 B4
Lancaster LA1 213 F2
Morecambe LA3 212 B3
Warton, Carnforth LA5 217 D5
Gardner St 21 PR1 95 F8
Gardner's La PR3 179 D3
Garfield Ave LA1 210 D7
Garfield Ct FY3 130 C2
Garfield Dr LA4 213 B4
Garfield St Accrington BB5 103 D5
8 Cornholme OL14 108 C1
Fleetwood FY7 194 B5
Garfield Terr PR6 60 D2
Garland Gr FY7 193 D3
Garnall's Bldgs 6 BB4 84 E2
Garnet Cl 3 FY5 150 F7
Garnet St 8 LA1 211 A8
Garnett Gn L39 15 D4
Garnett Pl WN8 9 A7
Garnett Rd BB7 164 C7
Garnett St Barrowford BB9 168 D2
Darwen BB3 81 B1
Morecambe LA4 212 E6
Ramsbottom BL0 49 B5
Garrick Gr FY3 129 E7
Garrick Par PR8 34 A6
Garrick St BB9 168 F2
Garrison Rd PR2 117 B3
Gars End LA2 232 D6
Gars The LA2 232 D6
Garsdale Ave BB10 147 B4
Garsdale Cl PR5 96 E5
Garsdale Rd PR2 117 E4
Garsden Ave BB1 101 E3
Garstang Cl FY6 151 C3
Garstang Com Prim Sch PR3 178 C8
Garstang High Sch PR3 178 D4
Garstang New Rd FY6 152 E3
Garstang Rd
Bilsborrow PR3 157 A4
Bowgreave PR3 178 D4
Catterall PR3 178 E1
Chipping PR3 182 C2
Cockerham LA2,PR3 203 E2
Fulwood PR1,PR2,PR3 116 E5
Kirkham PR4 112 F6
Little Eccleston PR3,FY6 153 D5
Newsham PR3 136 B4
Singleton FY6 152 C3
Southport PR9 53 A5
St Michael's on W PR3 155 C7
Stake Pool PR3 197 B3
Garstang Rd E FY6 151 E3
Garstang Rd N PR4 112 F7
Garstang Rd S PR4 112 F6
Garstang Rd W FY3,FY6 151 B2
Garstang St BB3 81 A2
Garston St BL9 32 A4
Garstone Croft PR2 116 D6
Garswood Cl
Brierfield BB12 146 F2
Maghull L31 5 E3
Garton Ave FY4 109 D6
Gas Field Rd LA3 208 E2
Gas House La LA2 233 D8
Gas St Adlington PR7 30 A6
Bacup OL13 86 F2
8 Burnley BB11 126 F6
Haslingden BB4 83 F1
Longridge PR3 139 A8
Gas Terr PR5 76 B2
Gaskell Cl LA5 218 C3
Gaskell Cres FY5 173 A2
Gaskell Ho LA1 213 E4
Gaskell Rd PR1 95 E5
Gaskell St PR6 42 E8
Gate Ho PR1 95 E7
Gate St BB1 101 A5
Gategill Gr WN5 10 D3
Gateheads Brow LA6 238 F3
Gateland BB18 191 D8
Gates La L29 4 C1
Gatesgarth Ave PR2 116 F7
Gateside Ct 2 FY3 130 A8
Gateside Dr FY3 129 F8
Gateway Cl FY5 151 D7
Gathurst La WN6 19 F5
Gathurst Rd Fulwood PR2 116 C2
Gathurst WN5 19 F2
Orrell WN5 10 E8
Gaulter's La FY6 195 C4
Gaw Hill La L39 15 B3
Gaw Hill View L39 15 B3
Gawthorpe Edge BB12 125 F8
Gawthorpe Hall BB12 145 F1
Gawthorpe High Sch BB12 125 E8
Gawthorpe Rd BB12 126 D7
Gawthorpe St 13 BB12 145 C1
Gawthorpe View BB12 145 F5
Gaydon Way FY5 150 E7
Gaylands La BB18 201 C2
Gayle Way 1 BB5 102 F4
Gaythorne Ave PR1 96 F8
Geddes St BB2 99 F2
Geldof Dr FY1 129 C8
General St FY1 129 B6
Geneva Rd PR2 117 C4
Genoa St BB11 126 C4
Geoffrey St Bury BL9 32 A4
Chorley PR6 60 E1
Preston PR1 96 C8
Geoffrey St *continued*
Ramsbottom BL0 49 A4
George Ave
Blackpool FY4 129 F1
Great Harwood BB6 123 B4
George Dr PR8 20 E5
George La BB12 144 C2
George Rd BL0 49 B5
George St Accrington BB5 102 F4
4 Bacup OL13 69 C8
Barnoldswick BB18 200 C4
Blackburn BB2 100 E4
Blackpool FY1 129 C5
Blackpool FY1 129 C6
Burnley BB11 126 F5
Chorley PR7 42 C7
13 Clayton-le-M BB5 123 F3
Clitheroe BB7 164 D6
Darwen BB3 81 A2
1 Earby BB18 201 B1
Great Harwood BB6 123 C5
Haslingden BB4 84 B3
Horwich BL6 31 C3
3 Lancaster LA1 210 F7
Leyland PR5 76 B2
Longridge PR3 139 A8
9 Lytham St Anne's FY8 90 B3
Morecambe LA4 212 F5
Oswaldtwistle BB5 102 E5
Preston PR1 96 B7
Rishton BB1 123 B1
Whalley BB7 143 C5
Whitworth OL12 51 C8
George St W BB2 100 D4
George's La Banks PR9 54 A7
Horwich BL6 31 E5
George's Rd PR1 95 F7
George's Row 2 BB4 68 F8
George's Terr WN5 10 D5
Georgian Pl L37 11 E1
Gerald Ct 6 BB11 127 B4
German La
Bolton Green PR7 41 D7
1 Coppull PR7 41 E1
Gerrard Pl WN8 8 F7
Gerrard St Lancaster LA1 210 D7
Preston PR1 95 E7
Gerrard's Fold PR6 79 B2
Gerrard's Terr FY6 151 C4
Gertrude St Nelson BB9 169 A2
Whitworth OL12 70 E6
Ghants La FY6 174 E2
Ghyll La BB18 200 E4
Ghyll Mdws BB18 200 D4
Gib Field Rd BB8 169 A3
Gib Hey La PR3 159 F7
Gib Hill La BB4 105 B2
Gib Hill Rd BB9 169 B1
Gib La Blackburn BB2 80 A7
Hoghton PR5 98 C3
Gibfield Sch BB8 169 B2
Gibraltar Rd PR4 131 E5
Gibraltar St BB2 100 B6
Gibson St BB9 168 F2
Giddygate La L31 6 B1
Gidlow Ave PR6 30 A7
Gilbert Pl L40 24 B4
Gilbert St Brierfield BB10 147 E2
4 Chorley PR7 42 C6
Ramsbottom BL0 67 C1
Rawtenstall BB4 85 D1
Gilbertson Rd PR7 42 E2
Gildabrook Rd FY4 109 D5
Gilderdale Ct 2 FY8 90 C4
Gildow St 1 PR1 95 E8
Giles St Clitheroe BB7 164 E7
Nelson BB9 168 E1
Gilhouse Ave PR2 115 C1
Gill Ct FY4 109 B5
Gill La PR4 74 C5
Gill Nook PR4 74 A5
Gill St Burnley BB12 126 E6
Colne BB8 169 B3
Nelson BB9 168 D1
Gillcroft PR7 40 B7
Giller Cl PR1 95 F2
Giller Dr PR1 95 F2
Giller Fold 1 PR1 95 F2
Gillett St 6 PR1 117 C1
Gillhead Brow LA2 236 D1
Gillians BB18 191 B8
Gillians La BB18 191 B8
Gillibrand Cl PR1 95 C1
Gillibrand Cty Prim Sch PR7 42 B6
Gillibrand Ho PR7 60 C2
Gillibrand St Chorley PR7 42 C7
Darwen BB3 80 F3
Walton-le-D PR1,PR5 96 D5
Gillibrand Wlks PR7 42 C7
Gillibrands Rd WN8 9 A7
Gillies St Accrington BB5 103 C6
Blackburn BB2 100 F3
Gillison Cl LA6 235 C2
Gillow Ct LA1 210 F5
Gillow Pk PR3 153 F6
Gillow Rd PR4 112 F5
Gills Croft BB7 165 A7
Gilpin Ave L31 5 E2
Gilpin Cl 2 LA1 213 C2
Gilsecroft Ave L33 1 A4
Gilstead Ave LA3 209 A8
Gin Bow PR7 42 D6
Gin Croft La BL0 67 E4
Gingham Brow BL6 31 E4
Girvan Gr BB11 126 D5
Girvan Wlk 2 OL10 32 F1
Gisburn Ave FY8 89 C6
Gisburn Cty Prim Sch BB7 225 C3
Gisburn Gr Blackpool FY3 129 E7
Burnley BB10 127 D5
Gisburn Old Rd
Barnoldswick BB7,BB9 190 C7
Foulridge BB9 190 E4
Gisburn Rd
Barnoldswick BB18 200 A3
Barrowford BB9 168 E5
Bolton-by-B BB7 224 E4
Fulwood PR2 117 E4
Gisburn Road Com Prim Sch BB18 200 B3
Gisburn St
Barnoldswick BB18 200 B3
Blackburn BB2 100 C4
Gisburne Park Hospl BB7 225 B4
Gladden Pl WN8 8 E8
Glade The Blackburn BB2 80 D6
Morecambe LA4 213 A5
Glades The FY8 90 C4
Gladeswood Rd L33 1 B1
Gladeway FY5 151 D7
Gladstone Cres OL13 87 A2
Gladstone Rd PR9 34 F6
Gladstone St Bacup OL13 87 A2
Blackburn BB1 101 B6
Blackpool FY4 129 C1
Bury BL9 32 B3
2 Cornholme OL14 108 B1
Great Harwood BB6 123 C5
Gladstone Terr
Abbey Village PR6 79 C1
Barrowford BB9 168 D3
Blackburn BB2 99 F1
Colne BB8 170 B4
3 Lancaster LA1 214 A1
Gladstone Way 4 FY5 172 F1
Glaisdale Dr PR8 34 F3
Glamis Dr Chorley PR7 42 B8
Southport PR9 53 B3
Glamis Rd PR5 59 C8
Glamorgan Gr BB12 126 A7
Glasson Cl BB2 100 F1
Glastonbury Ave FY1 129 E2
Glebe Cl Accrington BB5 103 B5
Burton-in-K LA6 234 C7
Fulwood PR2 116 F4
Maghull L31 5 B1
Standish WN6 28 F1
Glebe Cotts BB4 84 A6
Glebe Ct
Kirkby Lonsdale LA6 238 B3
20 Lancaster LA1 211 A8
Glebe La Banks PR9 54 A7
Kirkham PR4 113 C4
Glebe Pl PR8 34 B7
Glebe Rd Skelmersdale WN8 9 A8
Standish WN6 28 F1
Glebe St Burnley BB11 127 B4
Great Harwood BB6 123 C5
Glebe The PR5 58 B8
Glebelands PR4 56 A5
Gledhill Way BL7 47 A1
Gledstone View BB18 200 A3
Glegside Rd L33 1 A2
Glen Cottage (Youth Hostel) BB18 201 D2
Glen Cres OL13 69 A8
Glen Dr WN6 19 E8
Glen Eldon Rd FY8 88 E7
Glen Garth BB18 200 D3
Glen Gdns OL12 51 F2
Glen Gr PR2 117 F5
Glen Park Dr PR4 72 D4
Glen Rd BB4 68 F8
Glen Royd 1 OL12 51 C1
Glen Sq BB11 126 F2
Glen St Bacup OL13 69 E8
Blackpool FY3 129 E4
Burnley BB11 126 E6
Colne BB8 169 D6
Ramsbottom BL0 49 B7
Glen The Blackburn BB2 80 D6
Caton LA2 231 C3
Fulwood PR2 117 F2
Knott End-on-S FY6 194 E4
Glen View PR3 140 B8
Glen View Ave LA3 208 E6
Glen View Cres LA3 208 E6
Glen View Dr LA3 208 E6
Glen View Rd BB11 126 E2
Glen View St 1 OL14 108 B1
Glen Way BB9 147 B6
Glenapp Ave FY4 110 A6
Glenarden Ave FY5 150 F8
Glenavon Dr OL12 51 D3
Glenborough Ave OL13 69 C8
Glenbrook Cl BB2 80 B8
Glenburn High Sch WN8 9 B8
Glenburn Rd WN8 18 A1
Glencarron Cl BB3 64 F8
Glencoe Ave
Blackpool FY3 151 A1
Hoddlesden BB3 81 E1
Glencoe Cl OL10 32 F1
Glencourse Dr PR2 117 D5
Glencoyne Dr PR9 53 B5
Glencroft PR7 59 C3
Glencross Pl FY4 109 E7
Glendale Ave PR5 96 C1
Glendale Cl Blackpool FY2 150 F5
Burnley BB11 127 A3
Leyland PR5 59 B7
Poulton-le-F FY6 151 C3
Glendale Cres PR5 96 C1
Glendale Dr BB2 120 E2
Glendale Gr Fulwood PR2 117 D2
Kirkby L33 1 A5
Glendale Way L37 11 F2
Glenden Foot OL12 51 D2
Glendene Pk BB1 121 E5
Glendor Rd BB10 127 E5
Gleneagles Ave BB3 81 E1
Gleneagles Ct PR4 113 B4
Gleneagles Dr
Fulwood PR2 116 B7
Morecambe LA4 212 G6
Penwortham PR1 95 A6
Southport PR8 20 C3
Gleneagles Way 1 BL0 49 B5
Glenfield Ave FY2 150 E6
Glenfield Cl BB1 101 B7
Glenfield Park Ind Est
Blackburn BB1 101 B7
Nelson BB9 169 A1
Glenfield Rd BB9 169 A1
Glengarry 7 FY8 90 C3
Glengreave Ave BB1 121 E3
Glenholme Gdns FY6 151 C2
Glenluce Cres BB1 101 D3
Glenluce Dr PR1 96 F8
Glenmarsh Way L37 12 B3
Glenmere Cres FY5 150 C7
Glenmore PR6 77 A3
Glenmore Ave FY5 173 B2
Glenmore Cl BB5 103 E2
Glenmore Rd BL0 48 F2
Glenpark Dr PR9 53 B4
Glenrose Terr PR8 34 A5
Glenroy Ave BB8 169 D6
Glenroyd Cl FY3 129 E3
Glenroyd Dr L40 24 E4
Glenshiels Ave BB3 64 E8
Glenside WN6 27 B2
Glenthorn Terr 2 BB3 64 A8
Glentworth Rd E LA4 212 G3
Glentworth Rd W LA4 212 F3
Glenview Cl PR2 118 A3
Glenview Ct PR2 118 A3
Glenway PR1 95 C4
Glenwood St 3 FY3 129 D5
Global Way BB3 81 A5
Globe La BL7 46 D3
Glossop Cl FY2 150 C6
Gloucester Ave
Accrington BB5 103 A7
Blackpool FY1 129 D4
8 Clayton-le-M BB5 123 F3
Cleveleys FY5 172 D3
Horwich BL6 31 D2
Lancaster LA1 211 A4
Leyland PR5 76 C3
Gloucester Ct
5 Blackpool FY1 129 D4
Horwich BL6 31 D2
Gloucester Dr LA3 212 B3
Gloucester Rd
Blackburn BB1 101 D5
Chorley PR7 42 C6
Lytham St Anne's FY8 89 D4
Rishton BB1 102 A8
Southport PR8 33 F5
Glover Cl PR5 57 F6
Glover St Horwich BL6 31 B4
Preston PR1 96 A7
Glover's Ct 24 PR1 96 A7
Glynn St BB5 102 F7
Godiva St BB10 147 A1
Godley St BB11 127 B6
Godwin Ave 6 FY3 129 E3
Goe La PR4 92 B6
Goit St Blackburn BB2 100 C2
Newchurch BB4 85 F1
Goitside BB9 168 E1
Golbourne St PR1 117 B1
Goldacre La BB6 123 A7
Goldburn Cl PR2 115 F6
Golden Hill 9 PR5 76 B2
Golden Hill La PR5 75 F2
Golden Way
Farington PR1,PR4 75 D7
Penwortham PR1 95 C3
Goldfield Ave BB10 127 F6
Goldfinch Dr BL9 32 C4
Goldfinch Gn 5 BB11 126 C5
Goldfinch St PR1 117 B1
Goldhey St 13 BB1 101 A7
Goldsboro Ave FY3 129 F3
Goldstone Dr FY5 150 F7
Golf Rd L37 11 E5
Golf View PR2 116 A6
Golgotha Rd LA1 211 A6
Gonder La PR3 179 E3
Gooch St BL6 31 C2
Good Shaw Fold Cl BB4 105 A2
Good St PR1 95 E7
Goodall Cl BB18 201 B2
Goodenber Cres 16 LA2 233 D8
Goodenber Rd LA2 233 D8
Goodshaw Ave
Blackburn BB1 121 E1
Rawtenstall BB4 105 A1
Goodshaw Ave N BB4 105 A2
Goodshaw Chapel BB4 105 B1
Goodshaw Cl BB1 100 E8
Goodshaw Fold Rd BB4 104 F2
Goodshaw La
Accrington BB5 104 C1
Rawtenstall BB4 105 B2
Goodwood Ave
Blackpool FY2 150 D1
Fulwood PR2 116 F7
Hest Bank LA2 213 F8
Goodwood Cl LA1 211 B4
Goodwood Rd LA1 211 B4
Goose Cote Hill BL7 46 E1
Goose Foot Cl PR5 98 D7
Goose Foot La PR5 98 C6
Goose Green Ave PR7 41 F1
Goose Green La BB8 170 B2
Goose Hill St 14 OL13 86 F3
Goose House La BB3 81 A3
Goose La PR3 182 E1
Goose La Cotts PR3 182 E1
Goosebutts La BB7 164 F7
Gooselands BD24 230 F6
Gooseleach La BB12 144 E1
Goosnargh La PR3 137 B7
Gordale Cl
Barnoldswick BB18 200 A2
Blackpool FY4 110 A8
Gorden St 11 OL13 69 C8
Gordon Ave
Accrington BB5 103 A4
Maghull L31 5 C3
Southport PR9 52 C1
Thornton FY5 173 B2
Gordon Rd Fleetwood FY7 193 F3
Lytham St Anne's FY8 89 D4
8 Nelson BB9 168 D1
Gordon St Bacup OL13 86 F4
14 Blackpool FY4 129 B1
Burnley BB12 126 F7
Chorley PR6 42 D7
Church BB5 102 E5
Clayton-le-M BB5 124 A2
Colne BB8 169 F5
Darwen BB3 81 A3
Preston PR1 116 E1
Rawtenstall BB4 84 F2
Southport PR9 34 C8
Worsthorne BB10 128 B6
Gordon Way OL10 32 F1
Gordonstoun Cres WN5 10 F7
Gordonstoun Pl
Blackburn BB2 100 C3
8 Thornton FY5 173 A2
Gore Cl BL9 32 C1
Gore Dr L39 15 E3
Gores La L37 11 F5
Gores Rd L33 1 C1
Goring St PR7 42 D7
Gorple Gn BB10 128 B5
Gorple Rd BB10 128 D5
Gorple St BB10 147 E3
Gorrell Cl BB12 167 D2
Gorse Ave FY5 172 F3
Gorse Bank BL9 32 C3
Gorse Cl Great Knowley PR6 60 E5
Tarleton PR4 56 A6
Gorse Gr Fulwood PR2 117 E3
Haslingden BB4 67 A8
Longton PR4 94 A1
Gorse La PR4 55 D5
Gorse Rd Blackburn BB2 100 B5
Blackpool FY3 129 E4
Gorse St BB1 101 B6
Gorse Way L37 11 C4
Gorsefield L37 12 A6
Gorsewood PR5 75 E1
Gorsey La Banks PR9 54 C7
Haskayne L39 13 B7
Hightown L38 3 B2
Mawdesley L40 39 C1
Gorsey Pl WN8 9 B7
Gorst La L40,PR9 24 A6
Gorsuch La L39,L40 22 D4
Gorton Fold BL6 31 C3
Gorton St FY1 129 C6
Gosforth Rd Blackpool FY2 150 C1
Southport PR9 34 F8
Gough La Clayton Brook PR5 77 C5
Walton Summit PR5 77 B6
Goulding Ave PR5 76 B1
Goulding St PR7 42 D6
Gowans La PR6 78 A8
Gower Ct PR5 75 D3
Gower Gdns L40 24 F3
Gower Gr PR4 74 A5
Goyt St FY8 88 F7
Grab La LA1 211 C7
Graburn Rd L37 11 F4
Gracamy Ave PR4 91 D5
Grace St BL6 31 B3
Gradwell St 2 PR1 95 E8
Grafton Ave
Accrington BB5 103 E2
Brierfield BB10 147 B5
Grafton Ct 3 Chorley PR7 42 B5
Darwen BB3 80 F2
Grafton Dr PR8 20 A5
Grafton Pl LA3 212 B3
Grafton Rd Fulwood PR2 117 F4
Morecambe LA3 212 B3
Grafton St Adlington PR7 29 F6
Blackburn BB2 100 D2
Blackpool FY1 129 C7
Clitheroe BB7 164 F8
Nelson BB9 168 F1
Preston PR1 95 E6
Grafton Villas OL13 86 F1
Graham Ave
Appley Bridge WN6 27 C2
Bamber Bridge PR5 76 C8
Graham Rd PR3 199 C2
Graham St Hoddlesden BB3 81 F1
Lancaster LA1 210 F6
Morecambe LA4 212 D5

Graham St *continued*
1 Padiham BB12 125 D7
4 Preston PR1 117 B1
Grampian Way FY8 90 D5
Granary The FY5 173 A2
Granby Ave FY3 129 E8
Granby Cl PR9 52 F3
Granby St BB12 126 D6
Grand Manor Dr FY8 89 D7
Grane Pk BB4 84 A2
Grane Rd BB4 83 C2
Grane St BB4 84 B2
Grange Ave
Barrowford BB9 168 F5
Fulwood PR2 117 F4
Fulwood PR2 118 A4
Great Harwood BB6 123 C6
Rawtenstall BB4 85 B3
Southport PR9 34 E8
Thornton FY5 173 B2
Grange Cl
Great Harwood BB6 123 C6
Hoghton PR5 98 B4
Knott End-on-S FY6 194 F6
Oswaldtwistle BB5 103 A3
Rawtenstall BB4 85 B2
Grange Cres BB4 85 A2
Grange Ct 13 FY1 129 C7
Grange Dr Coupe Green PR5 97 E4
Euxton PR7 59 C4
Grange Farm Cotts PR4 92 E5
Grange Gdns FY6 151 D2
Grange La Accrington BB5 103 C5
Formby L37 11 E5
Longton PR4 93 D3
Newton-with-S PR4 113 F2
Stalmine FY6 174 B7
Grange Park Cl PR1 95 A6
Grange Park Cty Prim Sch
FY3 130 A7
Grange Pl PR2 117 F4
Grange Prim Sch PR2 118 A4
Grange Rd Blackburn BB2 100 B2
Blackpool FY3 129 F7
Edgworth BL7 47 C1
Elswick PR4 153 F1
Fleetwood FY7 193 D3
Fulwood PR2 116 C3
Hambleton FY6 174 D1
Hightown L38 2 E6
Leyland PR5 75 D2
Lytham St Anne's FY8 88 E7
Over Town BB10 107 A7
Rawtenstall BB4 85 B2
Singleton FY6 153 A3
Southport PR9 34 E7
Whitworth OL12 70 D3
Grange St Accrington BB5 103 C5
Barnoldswick BB18 200 A3
Burnley BB11 126 E5
Clayton-le-M BB5 123 E3
Morecambe LA4 213 A6
2 Rawtenstall BB4 85 A2
Grange Terr 19 BB4 85 A3
Grange The Cottam PR4 115 E5
Southport PR9 53 C3
Wilpshire BB1 121 F5
Grange View
Carnforth LA5 217 D3
Hest Bank LA5 215 F3
Grange View Rd LA6 216 F6
Grangefield PR4 93 F1
Granings The PR4 115 D6
Granny's Bay FY8 89 C3
Grant Cl LA1 210 D7
Grant Dr PR4 74 A5
Grant Mews BL0 49 B7
Grant Rd BB2 100 B3
Grant St Accrington BB5 103 A6
Burnley BB11 126 E5
Grantham Cl PR8 34 A1
Grantham Rd
5 Blackpool FY1 129 C7
Southport PR8 34 A1
Grantham St BB2 100 B2
Granton Cl L37 11 E3
Granton Wlk PR2 116 A4
Grants La BL0 49 C6
Granville Ave
Becconsall PR4 72 E2
Maghull L31 5 C2
Granville Cl L39 6 B8
Granville Ct Chorley PR6 60 E1
Southport PR9 52 D1
Granville Gdns BB5 103 D3
Granville Pk L39 6 C8
Granville Pk W L39 6 B8
Granville Rd
Accrington BB5 103 D3
Blackburn BB2 100 B5
Blackpool FY1 129 D5
Brierfield BB9 147 C6
Chorley PR6 60 E1
Darwen BB3 63 F8
Great Harwood BB6 123 D6
Lancaster LA1 213 E3
Morecambe LA3 212 B3
Southport PR8 33 D4
Granville St Adlington PR6 30 A7
Brierfield BB10 147 F2
13 Burnley BB10 127 A8
Colne BB8 169 E5
Haslingden BB4 67 A7
Grape La PR5 57 C1
Grasmere Ave
Blackburn BB1 121 C1
3 Fleetwood FY7 193 E4
Leyland PR5 76 A3
Orrell WN5 10 F8
Orrell, Hall Green WN8 10 B7
Padiham BB12 145 C1
Thornton FY5 173 B2
Grasmere Cl
Accrington BB5 103 D8
Bamber Bridge PR5 96 D2
Colne BB8 170 A5
Euxton PR7 59 E1
Fulwood PR2 117 C4
9 High Bentham LA2 233 D8
Rishton BB1 123 A1
Grasmere Dr 10 LA2 233 D8
Grasmere Gr
Longridge PR3 138 F5
Whittle-le-W PR6 60 B7
Grasmere Rd
Blackpool FY1 129 D2
Formby L37 11 D3
Haslingden BB4 67 C8
Knott End-on-S FY6 194 F6
Lancaster LA1 211 A8
Lytham St Anne's FY8 109 E1
Maghull L31 5 D2
Morecambe LA4 213 A6
Grasmere St Burnley BB10 147 A2
10 Rochdale OL12 51 F1
Grasmere Terr Bacup OL13 86 F4
Chorley PR7 42 B5
Grassington Dr
Brierfield BB10 147 D3
Bury OL10 32 D1
Grassington Pl FY5 150 F8
Grassington Rd FY8 89 C7
Gratton Pl WN8 9 A8
Grave-Yard La L39 7 A6
Gravel Cl PR9 53 F5
Gravel La Banks PR9 53 F5
Banks PR9 54 B3
Gravel The PR4 54 F2
Graver Weir Terr BB4 106 A1
Graving Dock Rd FY8 90 D4
Gravners Field FY5 173 D2
Grayrigg Dr LA4 212 E3
Grays Pl LA3 212 B2
Great Arley Sp Sch FY5 173 B3
Great Avenham St 3 PR1 96 A6
Great Bolton St BB2 100 E3
Great Close La
BD23,BD24 230 D6
Great Croft Cl BB18 200 A3
Great Eaves Rd BL0 49 C7
Great Eccleston Copp
CE Prim Sch PR3 154 A3
Great Flatt OL12 51 B1
Great George St
Colne BB8 169 D5
Preston PR1 117 A1
Great Gill PR4 74 A5
Great Greens La PR5 77 C5
Great Hanover St PR1 117 A1
Great Harwood
Golf Course BB6 123 F7
Great Harwood Prim Sch
BB6 123 B5
Great Hey PR4 73 D3
Great John St 20 LA1 210 F8
Great Lee OL12 51 D3
Great Lee Wlk OL12 51 D2
Great Mdw
Bamber Bridge PR5 76 A8
Chorley PR7 60 A2
Great Shaw St PR1 95 F8
Great Stone of
Fourstones LA2 233 D5
Great Stones Cl BL7 46 E2
Great Townley St PR1 96 D8
Great Tunstead PR4 74 A7
Great Wood Cty Prim Sch
LA4 213 A5
Greave Cl Bacup OL13 87 B3
Rawtenstall BB4 85 A4
Greave Clough Cl 9 OL13 87 A3
Greave Clough Dr OL13 87 B3
Greave Cres 10 OL13 87 A3
Greave Rd OL13 87 B3
Greave Terr OL13 87 B3
Greaves Cl Banks PR9 54 A6
Shevington Vale WN6 19 F8
Greaves Dr LA1 210 F6
Greaves Hall Ave PR9 54 A5
Greaves Mead LA1 210 F5
Greaves Mdw PR1 95 E2
Greaves Rd LA1 210 F6
Greaves St
Great Harwood BB6 123 C4
Haslingden BB4 83 F2
9 Preston PR1 96 A7
Greaves-Town La PR2 115 E1
Grebe Cl FY3 130 B7
Grebe Wharf 2 LA1 214 A1
Green Acre PR3 137 D6
Green Acres PR4 92 C7
Green Ave FY4 109 C6
Green Bank Bacup OL13 69 D8
Barnoldswick BB18 200 D4
Green Bank Ind Est BB1 101 C7
Green Bridge N BB4 68 E7
Green Bridge S BB4 68 E7
Green Brook Cl BL9 32 A4
Green Cl BB11 126 E2
Green Close Pk BB2 100 C2
Green Dick's La PR3 195 E5
Green Dr
Bamber Bridge PR5 96 C1
Barton PR3 136 B8
Cleveleys FY5 172 C5
Clitheroe BB7 187 A2
Fulwood PR2 116 E7
Lytham St Anne's FY8 89 F5
Penwortham PR1 95 B5
Poulton-le-F FY6 130 E8
Saltcotes FY8 90 C5
Green Edge Cl BB9 147 D5
Green End PR5 98 E7
Green End Ave BB18 201 B2
Green End Barn BB18 201 B1
Green End Cl 11 OL13 87 A3
Green End Rd BB18 201 B1
Green Gate Fulwood PR2 116 C3
Hutton PR4 94 C1
Green Haworth
CE Prim Sch BB5 103 B1
Green Haworth
Golf Course BB5 103 B1
Green Head Cotts 6 LA2 233 B8
Green Hey
Lytham St Anne's FY8 90 D4
Much Hoole PR4 73 E3
Green Heys Dr L31 5 F1
Green Hill OL13 87 A1
Green Hill La LA2,LA6 231 B6
Green Hill Rd OL13 87 A1
Green Howarth View
BB5 103 A3
Green La Banks PR9 54 C4
Bilsborrow PR3 157 B2
Bispham Green L40 26 B7
Blackburn BB2 100 A1
Bretherton PR5 57 C7
Chipping PR3 182 F3
Coppull PR7 29 A8
Downham BB7 188 B6
Ellel LA1,LA2 207 B6
Farington PR5 75 E7
Formby L37 11 F5
Freckleton PR4 92 C6
Garstang PR3 178 A7
Grindleton BB7 187 A7
Halton Green LA2 231 A4
Holmes PR4 55 C4
Horton BD23 225 E5
Horwich BL6 31 B5
Lancaster LA1,LA2 214 A6
Longridge PR3 139 B8
Maghull L31 5 A2
Maghull L31 5 C1
Morecambe LA3 212 E2
Ormskirk L39 15 E6
Orrell WN5 10 D3
Padiham BB12 125 C8
Penwortham PR4 95 C1
Preesall FY6 195 C2
Riley Green PR5 78 E8
Samlesbury Bottoms PR5 98 B7
Skelmersdale L40 18 A6
Sollom PR4 55 D1
Standish WN6 28 D1
Storth LA7 237 E5
Woodsfold PR4 134 E6
Green La E PR3 199 C2
Green La The L40 24 F4
Green La W Freckleton PR4 92 B5
Garstang PR3 199 B1
Green Lane Ave L39 15 E6
Green Link L31 5 B2
Green Mdw BB8 170 B2
Green Meadow La FY6 174 C1
Green Mount BB6 143 D8
Green Nook La PR3 138 F6
Green Oak Pl FY5 151 A8
Green Park Cty Prim Sch
L31 5 B2
Green Park Dr L31 5 B1
Green Pk BB7 143 C5
Green Pl PR5 77 A6
Green Rd BB8 169 D4
Green Row BB3 80 B6
Green Side
Kirkby Lonsdale LA6 238 C1
Wrea Green PR4 112 B3
Green Sq LA6 238 C1
Green St Adlington PR6 30 B8
11 Barnoldswick BB18 200 B2
Burnley BB10 147 B1
Chorley PR7 42 A5
Darwen BB3 81 A1
Edenfield BL0 67 E3
Great Harwood BB6 123 B5
Lancaster LA1 214 A1
Lytham St Anne's FY8 90 A3
Morecambe LA4 212 E6
Oswaldtwistle BB5 102 C2
Padiham BB12 125 C7
Rawtenstall BB4 85 A3
Green St E 16 BB3 81 A1
Green The Adlington PR6 42 F2
Bispham Green L40 26 B8
Bolton-le-S LA5 216 B5
Churchtown PR3 178 A2
Colne BB8 169 F6
5 Darwen BB3 81 A1
Eccleston PR7 40 C6
Fulwood PR2 117 F2
Hesketh Bank PR4 72 E3
Nelson BB9 169 B2
Parbold WN8 26 B2
Ramsbottom BL8 48 F1
Silverdale LA5 218 D2
Weeton PR4 131 F2
Green Way 4 FY4 109 F7
Green Wlk Earby BB18 201 A1
Southport PR8 20 D5
Green's La Haskayne L31 14 C1
Stalmine FY6 174 F7
Greenacre Blackburn BB3 80 F6
Westhead L40 16 E4
Greenacre Cl BL0 49 E7
Greenacre Ct LA1 211 B3
Greenacre Pk LA2 215 E2
Greenacre Rd LA2 215 E2
Greenacre St BB7 164 E7
Greenacres Chorley PR7 42 C5
Edgworth BL7 47 E6
Fulwood PR2 116 B7
Read BB12 144 D2
Greenacres Ave PR4 113 A4
Greenacres Dr PR3 178 D6
Greenacres The PR4 94 D2
Greenbank Horwich BL6 31 D1
Poulton-le-F FY6 151 E3
Whitworth OL12 51 C5
Greenbank Ave Maghull L31 5 C3
Orrell WN5 10 D3
Preston PR1 116 D2
Storth LA7 237 E4
Greenbank Dr Fence BB12 146 E8
Southport PR8 33 E2
Greenbank High Sch PR8 33 E1
Greenbank Pk BB4 85 B2
Greenbank Pl PR1 116 E1
Greenbank Rd
Blackburn BB1 101 B6
Penwortham PR1 95 E4
Rochdale OL12 51 F2
Greenbank Sch OL12 51 F1
Greenbank St
Preston PR1 116 D2
Preston PR1 116 E1
Rawtenstall BB4 85 B2
Greenbank Terr BB3 80 F6
Greenbanks FY2 150 F3
Greenbarn Way BL6 30 D1
Greenber La LA6 238 F5
Greenberfield La BB18 200 C4
Greenbriar Cl FY3 150 F1
Greenbrook Cl BB12 125 F6
Greenbrook Rd BB12 125 F6
Greenbrook St 6 BL9 32 A4
Greencliffe La BB10 128 A1
Greencroft PR1 95 D3
Greendale Ave BB4 85 E2
Greendale Cl
Fleetwood FY7 193 C2
Over Town BB10 107 A7
Greendale Dr LA5 217 D3
Greendale Mews 1 PR2 115 E2
Greendale View BB7 187 B8
Greenfield PR4 72 D4
Greenfield Ave
Chatburn BB7 187 D5
Clitheroe BB7 164 C8
Parbold WN8 26 B2
Greenfield Cl PR9 53 A3
Greenfield Ct 2 LA1 211 A7
Greenfield Dr PR5 76 A8
Greenfield Gdns 1 BB4 84 B2
Greenfield Ho 18 LA1 211 A8
Greenfield La PR3 159 A6
Greenfield Rd
Adlington PR6 30 A8
Burnley BB10 127 D4
Chorley PR6 42 E8
Cleveleys FY5 150 E8
Colne BB8 169 B4
Fleetwood FY7 193 F2
Nelson BB8 169 A4
Southport PR8 35 C1
Greenfield St Darwen BB3 64 C6
Haslingden BB4 84 B3
12 Lancaster LA1 211 A8
Rawtenstall BB4 85 A3
Greenfield Terr
3 Cornholme OL14 108 A1
Oswaldtwistle BB5 102 A1
Greenfield View BB3 81 A7
Greenfield Way PR2 116 B5
Greenfields LA2 231 C3
Greenfields Cres PR4 112 E6
Greenfinch Ct FY3 130 B6
Greenfold Dr BB4 105 A2
Greenfoot 5 LA2 233 B8
Greenfoot La LA2 233 B8
Greenford Cl WN5 10 D6
Greenford Rd PR8 20 C4
Greengate Cl BB12 126 D7
Greengate La LA5 216 C8
Greenhalgh La
Adlington PR6 30 B8
Greenhalgh PR4 132 D4
Greenhall Cl PR3 178 D6
Greenham Ave L33 1 A6
Greenhaven WN8 10 B7
Greenhead Ave BB1 101 B7
Greenhead La BB12 146 D5
Greenhey Pl WN8 8 F8
Greenheys Ave FY6 151 B4
Greenheys Cres BL8 48 F1
Greenhill BB6 123 B5
Greenhill Ave PR4 113 A6
Greenhill Pl 2 FY1 129 C6
Greenholme Ave LA4 212 E3
Greenhurst Cl BB2 100 D4
Greenings La PR9 36 C3
Greenland Ave WN6 28 E1
Greenland La PR6 30 D5
Greenlands Cres PR2 117 E3
Greenlands Cty Prim Sch
PR2 117 E3
Greenlands High Sch
FY2 150 E2
Greenlea Cl WN5 10 D5
Greenlea Dr LA4 212 G5
Greenloon's Dr L37 11 C3
Greenloon's Wlk L37 11 C2
Greenmead Cl PR4 115 E5
Greenmoor La PR3 140 B7
Greenmount Ave
1 Kirkham PR4 113 A5
1 Thornton FY5 173 A3
Greenmount Cl BL8 48 F2
Greenmount Dr BL8 48 F2
Greenmount Prim Sch
BL8 48 F2
Greenock Cl BB11 126 D4
Greenock Dr OL10 32 F1
Greenock St BB11 126 D4
Greenpark Cl BL8 48 F1
Greens Arms Rd BB3,BL7 46 E7
Greens La
Bacup, Lane Head OL13 87 A5
Bacup, Nun Hills OL13 69 D7
Haslingden BB4 67 C7
Greens The OL12 70 C1
Greenset Cl LA1 213 E4
Greenside Euxton PR7 59 C3
Fulwood PR4 115 D4
Ribchester PR3 140 E3
Greenside Ave
Blackburn BB2 80 A8
Preston PR2 115 C1
Greenside Cl Kirkby L33 1 A6
Ramsbottom BL8 48 B3
Greenside Dr BL8 48 F1
Greenside Gdns PR5 58 B7
Greenslate Ave WN6 19 E8
Greenslate Ct WN5 10 E3
Greenslate Rd WN5 10 E3
Greensnook La OL13 87 A3
Greensnook Mews 5
OL13 87 A3
Greensnook Terr 1 OL13 87 A3
Greenstone Ave BL6 31 B3
Greensward Cl WN6 28 B1
Greensway PR3 136 C3
Greenthorn Cres PR2 118 A2
Greenthorne Cl BL7 47 E7
Greenvale WN6 19 F4
Greenville Dr L31 5 C1
Greenway Catterall PR3 178 D3
Eccleston PR7 40 B7
Fulwood PR2 116 D7
Horwich BL6 31 F3
Penwortham PR1 95 B4
Greenway Ave WN8 9 B8
Greenway Cl WN8 17 E2
Greenway Ho FY6 151 E3
Greenway Mews BL0 49 C4
Greenway St BB3 80 F3
Greenways Becconsall PR4 72 F1
Lytham St Anne's FY8 89 B6
Orrell WN5 10 D3
Over Kellet LA6 231 B8
Greenwich Dr FY8 89 D5
Greenwood PR5 77 B4
Greenwood Ave
Blackpool FY1 129 E2
Hest Bank LA5 215 F2
Horwich BL6 31 D1
Greenwood Cl
Lytham St Anne's FY8 89 E4
Ormskirk L39 15 C1
Greenwood Cres LA5 215 F2
Greenwood Dr LA5 215 F2
Greenwood La BL6 31 E1
Greenwood Rd WN6 28 E2
Greenwood St
1 Bamber Bridge PR5 96 E1
Preston PR1 96 B7
Greetby Hill L39, L40 16 A6
Greetby Pl WN8 9 A8
Gregareth Cl 5 LA1 213 C2
Gregory Ave FY2 150 C5
Gregory Fold BB4 67 A7
Gregory La L39 22 B3
Gregory Meadow PR3 178 B7
Gregory Pl FY8 90 A3
Gregory's Ct LA1 211 A4
Gregson Cl 5 FY4 109 F7
Gregson Dr 3 FY7 193 F2
Gregson La Blackburn BB2 100 D5
Gregson Lane PR5 97 E1
Higher Walton PR5 97 C2
Gregson Rd LA1 211 A7
Gregson St Darwen BB3 64 A8
Lytham St Anne's FY8 90 A3
Gregson Way PR2 117 B5
Gregson's Ave L37 11 E5
Grenfell Ave FY3 129 E7
Grenville Ave
Bamber Bridge PR5 96 D2
Lytham St Anne's FY8 109 E1
Gresham Rd FY5 172 D1
Gresham St BB4 85 F1
Gresley Ave BL6 31 B3
Gresley Ct LA1 210 F6
Gresley Pl FY2 150 E2
Gressingham Dr LA1 211 A4
Gressingham Ho 3 LA1 211 A3
Greta Heath LA6 236 C3
Greta Pl Fleetwood FY7 193 D3
Lancaster LA1 213 E2
Gretdale Ave FY8 88 E8
Gretna Cres FY5 150 D8
Gretna Rd BB1 121 F1
Grey Heights View PR6 42 E8
Grey St Barrowford BB9 168 D3

Grey St *continued*
Burnley BB10 127 A8
Greyfriars Ave PR2 116 D5
Greyfriars Cres PR2 116 D5
Greyfriars Dr PR1 95 C5
Greyfriars Rd PR8 20 B6
Greyhound Bridge Rd LA1 213 F1
Greystock Ave PR2 116 E6
Greystock Cl PR5 77 B8
Greystock Pl PR2 116 E6
Greystoke Ave BB2 79 E8
Greystoke Pl FY4 109 B5
Greystokes L39 15 D2
Greystokes Ct FY4 109 B5
Greystonegill La LA2 233 F7
Greystones PR5 75 B1
Greystones Dr BB12 146 E8
Greythwaite Ct LA1 210 D6
Greywood Ave BL9 32 B2
Griffin Cl Accrington BB5 124 F1
Burnley BB11 126 B5
Bury BL9 32 B4
Griffin Ct BB2 100 C2
Griffin Park Prim Sch BB2 100 B3
Griffin St BB2 100 B3
Griffiths Dr PR9 34 F8
Griffon Ho PR9 52 F2
Grime Row BB5 124 F2
Grime St Chorley PR7 42 D6
Darwen BB3 80 F2
7 Ramsbottom BL0 49 A4
Grimeford La BL6,PR6 30 C5
Grimeshaw La LA1 214 D3
Grimrod Pl WN8 9 A7
Grimsargh St 10 PR1 117 D1
Grimsargh St Michaels CE Sch PR2 138 C1
Grimshaw Green La L40,WN8 26 C6
Grimshaw La L39 15 E7
Grimshaw Pk BB2 100 F3
Grimshaw Rd WN8 9 D8
Grimshaw St
Accrington BB5 103 A5
6 Barrowford BB9 168 D4
Burnley BB11 127 A5
5 Church BB5 102 E6
2 Clayton-le-M BB5 123 F2
Darwen BB3 64 B7
Great Harwood BB6 123 C5
Preston PR1 96 A7
Grindlestone Ct PR3 137 E6
Grindlestone Hirst BB8 169 C3
Grindleton Brow BB7 187 B7
Grindleton CE Prim Sch BB7 187 C8
Grindleton Cl FY3 130 B8
Grindleton Gr BB10 127 D5
Grindleton Rd
Blackburn BB2 100 C4
Grindleton BB7 187 B7
West Bradford BB7 186 F6
Gringley Rd LA4 212 F3
Grinstead Cl PR8 33 F1
Grisedale Ave BB1 101 C2
Grisedale Cl L37 11 E3
Grisedale Dr BB12 126 B8
Grisedale Pl PR7 42 B5
Grizedale Ave
Garstang PR3 178 B7
Poulton-le-F FY6 151 C3
Grizedale Cl
Clayton-le-M BB5 123 E2
Fulwood PR2 117 F2
Grizedale Cres PR2 118 A2
Grizedale Ct Blackpool FY3 129 E5
7 Thornton FY5 173 B3
Grizedale Pl Fulwood PR2 117 F2
Morecambe LA3 212 B1
Grizedale Rd
Blackpool FY4 130 C1
Lancaster LA1 214 B2
Grosvenor Cl PR8 33 E3
Grosvenor Ct
Carnforth LA5 217 C1
Cleveleys FY5 172 C2
6 Lytham St Anne's FY8 89 A8
Grosvenor Gdns PR8 33 F3
Grosvenor Lodge BB1 121 F6
Grosvenor Park Cty Prim Sch LA3 213 B2
Grosvenor Pl
Carnforth LA5 217 C1
Preston PR2 116 B2
Southport PR8 33 F3
Grosvenor Rd
Carnforth LA5 217 D1
Chorley PR7 42 B6
Morecambe LA3 212 A3
Southport PR8 33 E4
Grosvenor St
Blackpool FY1 129 C5
Burnley BB12 126 F7
Colne BB8 169 F5
Lytham St Anne's FY8 90 C3
Preston PR1 96 B7
Grosvenor Way
4 Blackburn BB1 100 E5
Horwich BL6 31 C3
Grouse St OL12 51 F1
Grove Ave Adlington PR6 30 A7
Longton PR4 73 F8
Grove Cres PR6 30 A7
Grove Ct Lancaster LA1 210 F6
Oswaldtwistle BB5 102 C3
Grove La BB12 145 E1
Grove Mead L31 5 F1
Grove Mill Development Ctr PR7 40 C5
Grove Pk Ormskirk L39 15 F7
Southport PR9 34 F8
Grove Rd Orrell WN8 10 C8
Preston PR1 96 C6
Grove St Accrington BB5 103 A6
Bacup OL13 87 A3
12 Bamber Bridge PR5 76 F8
Barrowford BB9 168 D3
Blackburn BB2 100 E2
3 Burnley BB11 126 D5
Bury BL9 32 C3
Earby BB18 201 B2
Leyland PR5 58 D8
Lytham St Anne's FY8 88 F7
Morecambe LA4 212 C4
Nelson BB9 147 E8
Oswaldtwistle BB5 102 D3
Southport PR8 34 A4
Grove Terr PR8 34 A5
Grove The
Appley Bridge WN6 27 C2
Bilsborrow PR3 157 A5
Burnley BB12 126 B6
Carnforth LA5 217 B1
Chipping PR3 182 D4
Chorley PR7 60 C2
Cleveleys FY5 172 E3
Clitheroe BB7 186 F1
Lancaster LA1 211 A7
Ormskirk L39 6 C7
Penwortham PR1 95 B4
Preston PR2 116 B1
Rufford L40 38 A3
Whalley BB7 143 C5
Grovewood PR8 33 E5
Grovewood Dr WN6 19 E8
Grundy Cl PR8 34 E5
Grundy Homes PR8 34 E5
Grundy Mews FY4 109 C7
Grundy St 7 PR5 76 B2
Grundy's La PR7 42 D1
Guard Hill La LA7 237 E4
Gubberford La PR3 199 D4
Guernsey Ave BB2 100 F1
Guide La BB12 146 A7
Guide Rd PR4 72 E6
Guide Sq BB1 81 B8
Guild Hall Arc 5 PR1 96 A7
Guild Park Hosp PR3 137 F5
Guild Row 7 PR1 96 A7
Guild Way PR1 95 D7
Guildford Ave
Blackpool FY2 150 D6
Great Knowley PR6 60 E4
Guildford Rd
30 Preston PR1 96 A7
Southport PR8 34 B2
Guildford Way FY6 151 C6
Guildhall St PR1 95 F7
Guilford St BB9 147 B5
Guinea Hall La PR9 54 A5
Gulf La LA2,PR3 197 D7
Gummers Howe Wlk LA5 216 E8
Gunsmith Pl 8 BB11 127 A6
Gurney St BB2 100 B3
Gutter La BL0 49 B7
Guy St BB12 145 C1
Guys Thatched Hamlet (Craft Ctr) PR3 156 F3
Guysyke BB8 169 C4
Gynn Ave FY1 129 B8
Gynn Sq FY1 129 B8

H

Habergham Dr BB12 125 F8
Habergham High Sch BB12 126 A7
Habergham High Sch & Sixth Form Ctr BB12 125 F7
Habergham St 19 BB12 145 C1
Hackensall Rd FY6 194 E5
Hacking Cl BB6 142 C1
Hacking Dr PR3 138 F5
Hacking St Bury BL9 32 A2
Darwen BB3 80 F1
3 Nelson BB9 168 F2
Hacklands Ave PR2 115 C1
Haddings La BB12 146 A8
Haddon Ct FY2 150 C5
Haddon Pl PR2 116 D3
Haddon Rd FY2 150 C5
Hadlee Terr LA1 213 D1
Hadleigh Rd FY6 151 C6
Hadrian Rd LA3 213 B3
Hadstock Ave L37 11 D1
Hagg La PR3 154 C8
Hagg St BB8 169 C4
Haig Ave Lancaster LA1 210 D8
Leyland PR5 75 F1
Preston PR2 116 D2
Southport PR8 34 E5
Tarleton PR4 56 A7
Haig Rd FY1 129 B1
Haigh Cl PR7 42 A7
Haigh Cres Chorley PR7 42 B7
Maghull L31 5 C4
Haigh Ct PR8 34 F6
Haigh Hall Cl BL0 49 B4
Haighton Ct PR2 117 A7
Haighton Dr PR2 117 E6
Haighton Green La PR2 137 E2
Hail St BL0 49 A4
Hala Cres LA1 211 A3
Hala Gr LA1 211 A3
Hala Hill LA1,LA2 211 B3
Hala Rd LA1 211 A3
Hala Sq LA1 211 A3
Halcyon Cl 6 OL12 51 B2
Haldane Rd BB3 80 E4
Haldane St BB10 147 B2
Halden Rd LA3 212 B3
Hale Carr Gr LA3 212 B1
Hale Carr La LA3 212 B1
Hale St BB11 127 A4
Hales Rushes Rd PR3 175 C4
Half Acre PR5 76 A8
Half Acre La BL6 30 C2
Halford Pl FY5 150 E7
Halfpenny La
Andertons Mill PR7 40 B3
Longridge PR3 138 F8
Halifax Rd Brierfield BB9 147 C5
Lane Bottom BB10 148 D3
Lane Bottom BB10 149 B1
Nelson BB10,BB9 147 E5
Southport PR8 20 C5
Halifax St FY3 129 F3
Hall Ave FY4 129 C1
Hall Brow Cl L39 16 B4
Hall Carr La PR4 73 D6
Hall Carr Mill Cotts BB4 85 B2
Hall Carr Rd BB4 85 A1
Hall Cl Caton LA2 231 B3
Rawtenstall BB4 85 A6
Hall Coppice The BL7 46 E1
Hall Croft PR4 94 D2
Hall Dr Caton LA2 231 B3
Heysham LA3 209 A2
Morecambe LA4 213 A4
Hall Fold OL12 51 C8
Hall Garth Cl LA6 234 A1
Hall Garth Gdns LA6 234 B1
Hall Gate PR7 60 A2
Hall Gate La FY6 174 C8
Hall Gdns OL12 51 C2
Hall Gn WN8 10 B7
Hall Gr LA3 209 A2
Hall Greaves Cl LA3 205 D8
Hall Green Cl WN8 10 B7
Hall Green La L40,PR7 40 A3
Hall Hill BB7 222 D1
Hall Hill St 4 BB12 145 C1
Hall La Appley Bridge WN6 27 D2
Bickerstaffe L39 7 E4
Bispham Green L40,WN8 26 A6
Bracewell BD23 225 F3
Great Eccleston PR3 154 C4
Ince Blundell L38 3 F3
Kirkby L33 1 A8
Leyland PR5 75 F2
Longton PR4 73 E7
Maghull L31 5 B7
Mawdesley L40 39 D3
Orrell WN5 10 F4
Rivington BL6 44 A2
Royal Oak L39 7 B1
Skelmersdale L40 17 A6
St Michael's on W PR3 155 E6
Hall Mdws BB8 170 C3
Hall Park Ave BB10 127 F4
Hall Park Ctr FY8 89 F4
Hall Park Dr FY8 89 E6
Hall Park Prim Sch FY8 89 F3
Hall Pk LA1 210 F4
Hall Rd Bescar L40 23 B6
Fulwood PR2 116 E5
Penwortham PR1 95 E3
Trawden BB8 170 B3
Hall St Bacup OL13 86 F3
Blackburn BB2 100 E2
Burnley BB11 127 A6
Clitheroe BB7 164 E7
Colne BB8 169 D4
Haslingden BB4 84 B2
Morecambe LA4 212 E6
Preston PR2 116 C1
Ramsbottom BL0 49 C2
12 Rawtenstall BB4 85 A3
Southport PR9 34 C7
Whitworth OL12 51 B8
Whitworth OL12 51 C8
Worsthorne BB10 128 A5
Hall's Cotts FY4 110 A6
Hallam Cres BB9 148 A8
Hallam La LA3 209 A2
Hallam Rd BB9 148 A8
Hallam St 10 BB5 124 A1
Hallbridge Gdns WN8 10 B8
Hallcroft WN8 18 C2
Halley Rd BB3 80 E3
Halley St OL13 87 A7
Hallfield Rd BB6 123 D6
Hallgate Hill BB7 223 B4
Halliwell Ct 7 PR7 42 C7
Halliwell La PR6 60 C4
Halliwell Pl 8 PR7 42 C7
Halliwell St
Accrington BB5 103 E2
Chorley PR7 42 C7
Hallmoor Cl L39 15 E2
Hallows Cl PR3 155 C6
Hallows Farm Ave OL12 51 D2
Hallows St BB10 147 A2
Halls Sq PR6 60 E3
Halsall Dr LA4 213 B6
Hallsalls Sq PR3 154 B5
Hallwell St BB10 127 A8
Hallwood Cl BB10 147 B4
Hallwood Rd PR7 42 A5
Halmot Ct 3 BB4 85 E1
Halmote Ave BB12 145 F5
Halsall Bldgs 6 PR9 34 C8
Halsall Ct L39 15 D6
Halsall Hall Dr L39 22 B1
Halsall La Formby L37 11 F3
Haskayne L39 14 D6
Ormskirk L39 15 D6
Halsall Manor Ct L39 22 B1
Halsall Rd Halsall L39 22 C2
Southport PR8 21 A8
Halsbury St PR1 96 B6
Halstead Cl BB9 168 D4
Halstead La BB9 168 D4
Halstead Rd PR2 117 E5
Halstead St Burnley BB11 126 F5
Bury BL9 32 A4
Worsthorne BB10 128 A6
Halstead Wlk BL9 32 A5
Halton Ave
Clayton-le-W PR5 76 D1
Cleveleys FY5 172 E4
Halton Chase L40 16 E4
Halton Ct LA4 212 E3
Halton Gdns Blackpool FY4 109 F8
Cleveleys FY5 172 F4
Halton Pl Fulwood PR2 117 F4
Longridge PR3 139 B8
Halton Rd Lancaster LA1 214 A4
Maghull L31 5 D3
Nether Kellet LA6 216 E5
Halton St PR4 131 E6
Hambledon Dr 6 PR1 95 E2
Hambledon St 10 BB12 125 D8
Hambledon Terr
Higham BB12 145 F6
2 Padiham BB12 125 F7
Hambledon View
Padiham BB12 125 F7
Read BB12 144 D1
Hambleton Cl PR4 93 F1
Hambleton Prim Sch FY6 174 D2
Hameldon App BB11 126 D5
Hameldon Ave BB5 103 E2
Hameldon Cl BB11 125 C2
Hameldon Rd
Hapton BB11 125 D2
Rawtenstall BB4 105 A2
Hameldon View BB6 123 D5
Hamer Ave Blackburn BB1 101 D5
Rawtenstall BB4 105 A1
Hamer Rd PR2 116 D3
Hamer St 18 Darwen BB3 64 A8
Ramsbottom BL0 49 B2
Rawtenstall BB4 85 A2
Hamerswood Dr PR3 178 D2
Hamilton Ct
6 Blackpool FY1 129 B4
8 Saltcotes FY8 90 D4
Hamilton Dr LA1 213 C3
Hamilton Gr PR2 117 E3
Hamilton Rd
Barrowford BB9 168 C1
Chorley PR7 42 C7
Fulwood PR2 117 D4
Morecambe LA4 213 C6
Nelson BB8 169 A2
Hamilton St BB2 100 D2
Hamilton Way OL10 32 E1
Hamlet Cl BB2 100 C3
Hamlet Gr PR4 133 F4
Hamlet Rd FY7 193 F4
Hamlet The Chorley PR7 42 F1
Lytham St Anne's FY8 109 F2
Hammer Terr BL0 49 C3
Hammerton Gn 18 OL13 86 F3
Hammerton Hall Cl LA1 213 E4
Hammerton Hall La LA1 213 E4
Hammerton Pl FY3 130 A8
Hammerton St Bacup OL13 86 F4
Burnley BB11 126 F5
Hammond Ave OL13 69 D8
Hammond Ct PR1 116 E1
Hammond Dr BB12 144 C2
Hammond Rd L33 1 C3
Hammond St Nelson BB9 147 F7
Preston PR1 116 E1
Preston PR1 116 E2
Preston PR1 116 F2
Hammond's Row 16 PR1 96 A8
Hampden Ave BB3 64 B7
Hampden Rd PR5 76 A2
Hampden St
7 Burnley BB11 127 B4
Hapton BB12 125 C4
Hampsfell Dr LA4 212 E3
Hampshire Cl BB1 122 A7
Hampshire Pl FY4 109 F6
Hampshire Rd
Bamber Bridge PR5 96 D3
Rishton BB1 123 A1
Hampson Ave PR5 76 D1
Hampson Cotts LA2 207 B1
Hampson Gr FY6 195 A4
Hampson La LA2 207 C1
Hampson St BL6 31 B4
Hampson Terr PR3 154 C5
Hampstead Cl FY8 89 E6
Hampstead Mews 3 FY1 129 C7
Hampstead Rd
Fulwood PR2 117 D2
Standish WN6 28 D1
Hampton Cl PR7 42 B8
Hampton Ct FY8 89 C8
Hampton Pl FY5 172 E3
Hampton Rd
Blackpool FY4 109 C8
Formby L37 11 E1
Morecambe LA3 212 B3
Hampton Rd *continued*
Southport PR8 34 C5
Hampton St PR2 116 C2
Hanbury St PR2 116 C1
Hancock St BB2 100 C3
Hand La L40 39 F5
Handbridge The PR2 116 E5
Handel St OL12 51 B8
Handley Rd 4 FY1 129 C6
Handsworth Ct 4 FY1 129 C7
Handsworth Rd FY1 129 C7
Handsworth Wlk PR8 34 F3
Hanging Green La LA2 215 E1
Hanley Cl FY6 174 C7
Hannah St Accrington BB5 103 B5
14 Bacup OL13 87 A3
Darwen BB3 64 B8
Hanover Cres FY2 150 C5
Hanover St Colne BB8 169 D5
Morecambe LA4 212 E5
5 Preston PR1 116 F1
Hanson St
Great Harwood BB6 123 C4
Rishton BB1 123 C1
Hanstock Cl WN5 10 E5
Hants La L39 15 E6
Happy Mount Ct LA4 213 B7
Happy Mount Dr LA4 213 A7
Hapton CE Meth Prim Sch BB11 125 C4
Hapton Rd BB12 125 C7
Hapton St
7 Padiham BB12 125 D8
Thornton FY5 173 B4
Hapton Sta BB11 125 C4
Hapton Way BB4 105 A2
Harbour Ave PR4 91 E6
Harbour Cl 11 FY7 193 F2
Harbour Ho 7 FY8 90 D4
Harbour La Brinscall PR6 61 D7
Edgworth BL7 47 D5
Warton PR4 91 E6
Harbour Way FY7 194 B3
Harbury Ave PR8 20 A4
Harcles Dr BL0 49 B2
Harcourt Mews 10 BL6 31 B4
Harcourt Rd
Accrington BB5 103 D3
Blackburn BB2 100 C6
Blackpool FY4 109 D8
Lancaster LA1 213 E3
Harcourt St 15 Bacup OL13 86 F3
1 Burnley BB11 126 D5
Preston PR1 116 E1
Hard Knott Rise LA5 216 E8
Hardacre La
Lucas Green PR6 60 C5
Rimington BB7 225 B2
Hardacre St L39 15 F6
Hardcastle Rd PR2 116 E3
Harden Rd BB18 192 A6
Hardhorn Ct FY6 151 D3
Hardhorn Rd FY6 151 D2
Hardhorn Way FY6 151 D2
Harding Rd L40 24 D4
Harding St PR6 30 B8
Hardlands Ave LA4 213 B4
Hardman Ave
Rawtenstall BB4 85 A1
Rawtenstall,Hugh Mill BB4 68 A8
Hardman Cl Blackburn BB1 101 F4
Rawtenstall BB4 68 F7
Hardman Dr BB4 68 F7
Hardman St
Blackburn BB2 100 C3
3 Blackpool FY1 129 C6
Hardman Terr OL13 69 D8
Hardman Way 23 BB3 81 A1
Hardsough La BL0 67 D5
Hardwen Ave 7 PR2 115 C1
Hardwicke St 4 PR1 96 A8
Hardy Ave
Barnoldswick BB18 200 A3
Brierfield BB9 147 B6
Hardy Ct 11 BB9 147 E8
Hardy Dr PR7 42 A7
Hardy St Blackburn BB1 121 F1
Brierfield BB9 147 B6
Hare Clough Cl BB2 100 F3
Hare Runs Ho LA1 213 F3
Harebell Cl Blackburn BB2 79 D8
Formby L37 11 F1
Rochdale OL12 51 D3
Hareden Brook Cl BB1 100 F3
Hareden Cl 4 PR5 76 F8
Hareden Rd PR2 117 F2
Harefield Rise BB12 126 D7
Hareholme La BB4 85 D2
Hares La PR8 35 D1
Harestone Ave PR7 42 A5
Harewood PR7 60 B2
Harewood Ave
Blackpool FY3 151 A1
Lancaster LA1 211 A3
Morecambe LA3 212 B2
Simonstone BB12 144 E2
Southport PR8 20 C6
Harewood Cl FY6 151 C5
Harewood Rd PR1 117 C2
Hargate Ave OL12 51 A2
Hargate Cl BL9 49 C2
Hargate Rd FY5 173 C2
Hargher Clough Jun Sch BB11 126 D5
Hargher St BB11 126 D5

Hargreaves Ave PR5 59 B8
Hargreaves Ct
Clitheroe BB7 164 C7
Fulwood PR2 115 F4
Whitewell Bottom BB4 85 F6
Hargreaves Dr BB4 84 F2
Hargreaves Fold La BB4 86 A7
Hargreaves La 2 BB2 100 E3
Hargreaves Rd BB5 102 C4
Hargreaves St
9 Accrington BB5 103 C5
Brierfield BB10 147 F3
14 Burnley BB11 126 F6
Colne BB8 169 B4
Haslingden BB4 84 B3
Hoddlesden BB3 81 F1
Nelson BB9 147 C7
Southport PR8 34 C6
Thornton FY5 173 B3
Whitewell Bottom BB4 85 E5
Hargrove Ave
Burnley BB12 126 D7
Padiham BB12 145 C1
Hargrove Rd BB12 126 D8
Harington Cl L37 11 D3
Harington Gn L37 11 D3
Harington Rd L37 11 D4
Harland St PR2 116 D3
Harland Way OL12 51 B2
Harlech Ave FY1 129 D1
Harlech Cl BB4 84 B1
Harlech Dr Leyland PR5 76 C1
Oswaldtwistle BB5 102 C4
Harleston Rd L33 1 A3
Harleston Wlk L33 1 A3
Harley Cl LA2 233 C8
Harley Rd FY3 129 E4
Harley St BB12 126 C6
Harling Bank LA6 238 B2
Harling Rd PR1 117 D1
Harling St BB12 126 B6
Harold Ave
8 Blackpool FY4 110 A6
Burnley BB11 126 C4
Harold St Burnley BB11 126 D5
Colne BB8 169 C4
Harold Terr PR5 76 A8
Harper St BB18 200 A3
Harper's La PR6 60 D1
Harperley PR7 60 B2
Harpers La BB12 146 D8
Harridge Ave OL12 51 C3
Harridge La L39,L40 23 A1
Harridge St OL12 51 C3
Harridge The OL12 51 C3
Harrier Dr BB1 100 D8
Harriet St BB11 126 E5
Harrington Ave FY4 109 B5
Harrington Rd Chorley PR7 42 B8
Morecambe LA3 212 B3
Harrington St
Accrington BB5 124 A1
Preston PR1 116 F1
Harris Ave FY1 129 D1
Harris Cl OL10 32 E1
Harris Ct 2 BB7 164 E8
Harris Ctr PR2 116 E5
Harris Cty Prim Sch PR2 116 B7
Harris Mus PR5 96 A7
Harris Rd WN6 28 B3
Harris St Fleetwood FY7 194 A4
2 Preston PR1 96 A7
Harrison Ave FY5 173 B2
Harrison Cres Blackrod BL6 30 C3
Morecambe LA3 212 A1
Harrison Dr BB8 169 C6
Harrison La PR4 95 B2
Harrison Rd Adlington PR7 30 A6
Chorley PR7 42 C6
Fulwood PR2 116 E6
Harrison St Bacup OL13 70 B8
Barnoldswick BB18 200 C1
Blackburn BB2 100 D4
Blackpool FY1 129 C3
Brierfield BB10 147 F2
5 Cornholme OL14 108 B1
Horwich BL6 31 B4
Ramsbottom BL0 49 C7
Harrison Terr BB7 187 B8
Harrock La L40,WN6 26 F6
Harrock Rd PR5 76 D1
Harrod Dr PR8 33 E3
Harrogate Cres BB10 147 D2
Harrogate Rd FY8 89 C7
Harrogate Way PR9 53 C6
Harrop Pl PR2 117 E4
Harrow Ave
Accrington BB5 103 C7
Fleetwood FY7 193 F3
Harrow Cl Orrell WN5 10 F8
Padiham BB12 125 E6
Harrow Dr BB1 101 B3
Harrow Gr LA4 213 B4
Harrow Pl Blackpool FY4 109 A5
Lytham St Anne's FY8 89 E5
Harrow St BB5 102 E4
Harrow Stiles La OL13 106 E1
Harrowdale Pk LA2 214 F7
Harrowside FY4 109 B6
Harrowside W FY4 109 A5
Harry St Barrowford BB9 168 D3
Salterforth BB18 191 D7
Harsnips WN8 18 C2
Hart St Blackburn BB1 100 F4
Burnley BB11 127 A6
Hart St *continued*
Southport PR8 34 E6
Hart's Hos BL6 31 D5
Hart's La WN8 9 F8
Hartford Ave FY1 129 D2
Hartington Rd
Brinscall PR6 62 A8
Darwen BB3 80 E4
Preston PR1 95 D7
Hartington St
Brierfield BB9 147 B5
Colne BB8 170 B5
Lancaster LA1 211 B8
Rishton BB1 123 A1
Hartland WN8 18 C2
Hartland Ave PR9 53 B5
Hartlands Cl BB10 147 D3
Hartley Ave BB5 103 A3
Hartley Cres PR8 33 F2
Hartley Homes BB8 170 C6
Hartley Rd PR8 33 F2
Hartley St
3 Blackburn BB1 100 E6
2 Burnley BB11 126 C5
Colne BB8 169 D5
Earby BB18 201 B1
Great Harwood BB6 123 D5
2 Haslingden BB4 84 B3
Horwich BL6 31 B3
Nelson BB9 147 E7
2 Oswaldtwistle BB5 102 E4
Rochdale OL12 51 B1
Hartleys Terr BB8 169 E4
Hartmann St BB5 103 A6
Hartshead WN8 18 C2
Hartwood Gn PR6 60 C3
Hartwood Rd PR9 34 D7
Harvest Dr PR6 60 C6
Harvey Longworth Ct
BB4 105 A1
Harvey St 14 Nelson BB9 168 E1
Oswaldtwistle BB5 102 D4
Harvington Dr PR8 20 B5
Harwich Rd FY8 110 A1
Harwin Cl OL12 51 D3
Harwood Ave FY8 88 E8
Harwood Cl FY6 174 C7
Harwood Gate BB1 101 B6
Harwood La BB6 123 E6
Harwood New Rd BB6 123 E6
Harwood Rd Rishton BB1 123 A2
Wilpshire BB1 122 D4
Harwood St
14 Blackburn, Cob Wall BB1 101 A7
Blackburn, Green Bank BB1 101 B6
Darwen BB3 80 E2
Harwood's La BB3 81 E1
Hasgill Ct LA1 213 E1
Haskayne CE Sch L39 13 E3
Haskoll St BL6 31 D1
Haslam Ct 1 BB10 147 B1
Haslam Dr L39 15 D7
Haslam St BL9 32 A4
Haslemere Ave 5 FY3 129 E3
Haslemere Ind Est PR5 75 F3
Haslingden Grane Trail
BB4 83 A2
Haslingden High Sch BB4 67 B8
Haslingden Old Rd
Blackburn BB1,BB5 101 E3
Haslingden BB4 84 E2
Haslingden Prim Sch BB4 84 B2
Haslingden Rd
Blackburn BB1,BB2 101 B2
Oswaldtwistle BB5 82 D7
Rawtenstall BB4 84 E2
Haslingden St James
CE Prim Sch BB4 84 B3
Haslow Pl FY3 129 F7
Hassall Dr PR4 154 A1
Hassett Cl PR1 95 E6
Hastings Ave
Blackpool FY2 150 E5
Warton PR4 91 E7
Hastings Cl Blackburn BB1 101 C4
Thornton FY5 173 C1
Hastings Pl FY8 90 A3
Hastings Rd Kirkham PR4 113 B2
Lancaster LA1 210 F5
Leyland PR5 76 B2
Preston PR2 116 B1
Southport PR8 33 E1
Thornton FY5 173 C1
Hastings The LA1 210 F5
Haston Lee Ave BB1 121 F3
Hasty Brow Rd LA2 213 D6
Hatfield Ave
Fleetwood FY7 193 F3
Morecambe LA4 213 B6
Hatfield Cl FY5 173 C2
Hatfield Ct LA4 213 B6
Hatfield Gdns 2 FY7 193 E2
Hatfield Mews 2 FY7 193 F2
Hatfield Rd
Accrington BB5 103 D7
Fulwood PR2 117 E3
Southport PR8 20 C6
Hatfield Wlk 1 FY7 193 E2
Hathaway FY4 109 E8
Hathaway Fold 4 BB12 125 D7
Hathaway Rd
Fleetwood FY7 193 E4
Lancaster LA1 213 E3
Hatlex Dr LA2 215 E2
Hatlex Hill LA2 215 E2
Hatlex La LA2 215 E2
Hattersley St BB11 126 E6
Hatton St PR7 29 F6
Haugh Ave BB12 144 E2
Haulgh St BB10 147 B2
Haunders La PR4 73 B1
Havelock Cl BB2 100 D3
Havelock Rd
Bamber Bridge PR5 76 E7
Penwortham PR1 95 E5
Havelock St
Blackburn BB2 100 C2
4 Blackpool FY1 129 B4
Burnley BB12 126 B6
Lancaster LA1 211 A6
Oswaldtwistle BB5 102 D3
11 Padiham BB12 145 C1
Preston PR1 116 D2
Preston PR1 116 E2
Preston PR1 116 F2
Haven Brow L39 6 C8
Haven Rd FY8 90 C3
Haven St BB10 127 C5
Haven Wlk L31 5 C4
Havenbrook Gr BL0 49 A3
Haverbreaks Pl LA1 210 E6
Haverbreaks Rd LA1 210 E5
Haverholt Cl BB8 169 C5
Haverholt Rd BB8 169 C5
Haverthwaite Ave LA3 208 F7
Havre Pk BB18 200 C2
Hawarden Ave LA4 212 F5
Hawarden Rd 1 PR1 117 E1
Hawarden St BB9 147 E7
Hawes Dr BB8 169 F6
Hawes Side La FY4 109 E8
Hawes Side Prim Sch
FY4 109 E7
Hawes Terr BB10 147 B2
Hawesside St PR9 34 C7
Haweswater Ave PR7 42 B6
Haweswater Gr L31 5 F2
Haweswater Pl 3 LA4 213 A4
Haweswater Rd 1 BB5 124 D1
Hawick Gr OL10 32 E1
Hawk Cl BL9 32 B4
Hawk St Burnley BB11 127 A6
Carnforth LA5 217 E2
Hawkeshead Cl BB2 100 B4
Hawkhurst Ave PR2 116 D6
Hawkhurst Cres PR2 116 D6
Hawkhurst Rd
Penwortham PR1 95 E5
Preston PR1 117 B1
Hawkins Cl PR1 116 E1
Hawkins Pl FY2 150 F5
Hawkins St Blackburn BB2 100 B2
Preston PR1 116 E1
Hawks Gr BB4 85 A1
Hawksbury Dr PR1 95 D2
Hawksclough WN8 18 D2
Hawkshaw Ave BB3 80 E3
Hawkshaw Bank Rd BB1 100 D8
Hawkshaw La BL8 48 B5
Hawkshaw St BL6 31 B3
Hawkshead PR1 95 E3
Hawkshead Ave PR7 59 D1
Hawkshead Cl L31 5 E2
Hawkshead Dr LA4 212 F3
Hawkshead Rd
Fulwood PR2 117 E5
Knott End-on-S FY6 194 F6
Hawkshead St
Blackburn BB2 100 B4
Southport PR8, PR9 34 D7
Hawkshead Terr FY4 110 D8
Hawksheath Cl BL7 46 E1
Hawksley St BL6 31 D2
Hawkstone Cl
Accrington BB5 124 F1
Thornton FY5 151 D8
Hawkstone Ct LA4 213 B6
Hawkswood PR7 40 B6
Hawkswood Gdns BB9 147 A4
Hawksworth Ave LA3 212 B2
Hawksworth Cl L37 12 A6
Hawksworth Dr L37 12 A6
Hawksworth Gr LA3 212 A2
Hawksworth Rd BB5 103 B8
Hawley Gn OL12 51 D2
Hawley St Colne BB8 169 C4
Winewall BB8 170 C5
Haworth Ave
Accrington BB5 103 D3
Ramsbottom BL0 49 A2
Rawtenstall BB4 84 F2
Haworth Dr OL13 69 C8
Haworth St
Accrington BB5 124 B1
Edgworth BL7 47 D5
Oswaldtwistle BB5 102 E4
Rishton BB1 123 B1
Haws Ave LA5 217 D1
Haws Hill LA5 217 D1
Hawthorn Ave Caton LA2 231 C3
Darwen BB3 81 C2
Edenfield BL0 67 D2
Fleetwood FY7 172 E8
Orrell WN5 10 F6
Oswaldtwistle BB5 102 F3
Ramsbottom BL0 49 A2
Hawthorn Bank BB5 124 A3
Hawthorn Cl Caton LA2 231 C3
Kirkham PR4 112 E6
Langho BB6 122 D8
Leyland PR5 75 D2
New Longton PR4 75 A7
Hawthorn Cres
Preston PR2 115 D1
Skelmersdale WN8 17 E1
Hawthorn Dr BB1 102 B8
Hawthorn Gdns BB5 124 A3
Hawthorn Rd Bacup OL13 87 A2
Blackpool FY1 129 C7
Bolton-le-S LA5 216 A6
Fulwood PR2 117 E2
Morecambe LA4 213 B4
Hawthorn St BB1 100 F8
Hawthorne Ave
Brierfield BB10 147 C5
Garstang PR3 178 B8
Higher Walton PR5 97 C3
Horwich BL6 31 E1
Newton-with-S PR4 113 F3
Hawthorne Cl
Barrowford BB9 168 B1
Clayton Green PR6 77 B3
Nelson BB9 148 B8
Hawthorne Cres L37 12 A2
Hawthorne Dr BB18 200 C4
Hawthorne Gr
14 Barrowford BB9 168 D3
Carleton FY6 151 B5
Southport PR9 34 F7
Hawthorne Ind Pk BB7 187 A1
Hawthorne Lea FY5 151 C8
Hawthorne Mdws BB4 105 A1
Hawthorne Pl BB7 186 E1
Hawthorne Rd
Burnley BB11 126 F4
Thornton FY5 151 C8
Hawthorne Terr BB8 191 E1
Hawthornes Cty Jun Sch
BB1 100 F8
Hawthornes The L40 38 B3
Hawthorns The
Bilsborrow PR3 157 A5
Eccleston PR7 40 B7
Fulwood PR2 116 F6
Lancaster LA1 211 A2
Newburgh WN8 26 A1
1 Newchurch BB4 85 F1
Wilpshire BB1 121 F6
Haworth Art Gall
BB5 103 D3
Haydock Ave PR5 59 A8
Haydock Gr LA3 212 A1
Haydock La BL7 47 B1
Haydock Rd LA1 211 B3
Haydock Sq 1 BB6 123 C5
Haydock St
6 Bamber Bridge PR5 96 E2
Blackburn BB1 121 E1
Burnley BB10 147 C1
Haydocks La PR4 115 D5
Haydon Ave PR5 76 A7
Hayfell Ave LA4 212 F3
Hayfell Cres LA2 215 D1
Hayfell Gr LA2 215 D1
Hayfield BB2 100 A7
Hayfield Ave
Blackpool FY2 150 E2
Gregson Lane PR5 97 E1
Poulton-le-F FY6 151 E3
Hayfield Cl
Gregson Lane PR5 97 E1
Ramsbottom BL8 48 F1
Hayfield Rd L39 15 E7
Hayfields BB18 191 E8
Hayhurst Cl BB7 143 C6
Hayhurst Farm Terr BB7 164 F7
Hayhurst Rd BB7 143 C6
Hayhurst St BB7 164 F7
Hayling Pl PR2 116 A4
Haylot Dr LA2 214 F7
Haylot Sq 9 LA1 211 A8
Haymans Gn L31 5 E1
Haymarket FY8 89 B6
Haysworth St PR1 116 F2
Haywood Cl
Accrington BB5 103 B8
Sherwood PR2 117 A8
Haywood Rd BB5 103 B8
Hazekbank Gdns L37 11 E5
Hazel Ave
Bamber Bridge PR5 97 A1
Bury BL9 32 B3
Clayton-le-M BB5 123 F2
Darwen BB3 81 B2
Fleetwood FY7 172 F8
Ramsbottom BL0 49 B1
Hazel Bank 3 LA3 208 F7
Hazel Cl
Bamber Bridge PR5 96 F1
Blackburn BB2 100 C4
Penwortham PR1 95 B3
Hazel Coppice PR2 115 E3
Hazel Ct Fulwood PR2 116 E7
Ormskirk L39 15 E5
Hazel Dene BB7 186 E6
Hazel Gr Bacup OL13 87 B3
Bamber Bridge PR5 97 A1
Blackburn BB1 101 F5
Blackpool FY3 129 E5
Chorley PR6 60 C3
Clayton-le-M BB5 124 A2
Clitheroe BB7 164 C7
Fulwood PR2 118 A4
Lancaster LA1 210 D8
Longridge PR3 139 B8
Rawtenstall BB4 84 F4
Southport PR8 34 E7
Tarleton PR4 55 F8
Hazel Hall La BL0 49 B1
Hazel La WN8 18 B4
Hazel Mount BL7 46 E2
Hazel St Haslingden BB5 84 A8
Ramsbottom BL0 49 A4
Hazeldene Ave 2 BB4 84 B2
Hazeldene Rd FY7 193 F2
Hazelhead La PR3 199 E2
Hazelhurst Cl BL0 49 B4
Hazelhurst Dr PR3 178 A7
Hazelhurst Prim Sch BL0 49 A4
Hazelhurst Rd PR2 118 A2
Hazelmere Cty F HQ PR2 116 D8
Hazelmere Rd
Fulwood PR2 116 D8
Preston PR2 116 A1
Hazelmoor BB1 121 E6
Hazelmount Ave LA5 217 D3
Hazelmount Cres LA5 217 D3
Hazelmount Dr LA5 217 C3
Hazelrigg La LA2 207 C7
Hazels The Coppull PR7 41 E1
Wilpshire BB1 121 E6
Hazelwood Silverdale LA5 218 C2
Southport PR8 33 F1
Hazelwood Ave L40 24 E4
Hazelwood Cl
Blackburn BB1 122 A1
Leyland PR5 75 E1
Hazelwood Dr
Hesketh Bank PR4 72 E4
Morecambe LA4 213 B6
Hazelwood Gdns LA1 211 A2
Hazelwood Rd BB9 148 A8
Hazlehurst Cl L37 11 C2
Hazlewood Cl FY5 173 A2
Head Beck LA6 238 C2
Head Dyke La PR3 196 C3
Head Nook Cotts PR3 156 E3
Headbolt La Kirkby L33 1 A5
Southport PR8 21 A4
Headfort Cl FY2 150 D2
Headingley Cl BB5 124 F1
Headlands St OL12 51 E1
Headley Rd PR5 75 E1
Headroomgate Rd FY8 88 F8
Heads La BB18 192 B6
Heald Brow BB18 200 A4
Heald Cl Rochdale OL12 51 C3
Weir OL13 87 A8
Heald Dr OL12 51 C3
Heald House Rd PR5 59 C7
Heald La OL13 87 A8
Heald Rd BB10,BB12 147 A2
Heald St Blackpool FY3 129 D6
6 Chorley PR6 42 E8
Healdwood Cl BB12 146 F3
Healdwood Dr BB12 146 F3
Healey Ave OL12 51 D4
Healey Ct BB11 126 F5
Healey Dell Cotts OL12 51 B4
Healey Dell
Nature Reserve OL12 51 B6
Healey Gr OL12 51 C5
Healey Hall Farm OL12 51 C4
Healey Hall Mews OL12 51 C4
Healey La OL12 51 E3
Healey Mount BB11 126 F4
Healey Prim Sch OL12 51 E3
Healey Row BB11 126 F5
Healey St FY3 129 D7
Healey Stones OL12 51 E4
Healey Wood Cty Inf Sch
BB11 126 F4
Healey Wood Rd BB11 126 F4
Heaning Ave
Accrington BB5 103 D8
Blackburn BB1 101 D4
Heanor Dr PR8 34 F3
Heap Bridge Cty Prim Sch
BL9 32 D1
Heap Brow BL9 32 D1
Heap Clough BB4 83 C3
Heap St Briefield BB9 147 A5
Burnley BB10 147 B1
Bury BL9,OL10 32 D1
Rawtenstall BB4 85 A8
Worsthorne BB10 128 B6
Heapey Fold La PR6 43 C7
Heapey Ho PR6 61 A3
Heapey Rd PR6 60 F2
Heapfold 4 OL12 51 B2
Heaplands BL8 48 F1
Heapworth Ave BL0 49 B6
Heartwood Cl BB2 100 A8
Heasandford Cty Prim Sch
BB10 127 B8
Heasandford Ind Est
Burnley BB10 127 D8
Burnley BB10 147 D2
Heath Ave BL0 49 B1
Heath Gr LA3 208 E6
Heath Hill Dr OL13 69 C8
Heath St BB10 127 B8
Heathbourne Rd OL13 69 C8
Heather Bank
Burnley BB11 126 C4
Rawtenstall BB4 67 F8
Heather Brow BB18 201 D2
Heather Cl Brierfield BB9 147 D4
Burscough L40 24 E4
Chorley PR6 42 E8
Formby L37 12 B5
Haslingden BB4 67 A8
Horwich BL6 31 B4
Southport PR8 20 D2
Thornton FY5 173 B1
Heather Gr PR2 117 E3
Heather Lea Dr PR6 61 F8
Heatherfield BL7 47 E6
Heatherlands OL12 70 D4
Heatherlea Cl WN8 10 C7
Heatherlea Rd BB12 146 D7
Heatherleigh Gdns BB2 80 D6

Heathers The PR5 77 C4
Heatherside Rd BL0 49 C7
Heatherway PR2 117 E6
Heatherways L37 12 A6
Heathey La L39,PR8 22 A7
Heathfield PR6 42 F1
Heathfield Ave OL13 69 C8
Heathfield Cl L37 12 A6
Heathfield Dr PR2 117 E4
Heathfield Pk BB2 99 F6
Heathfield Rd Bacup OL13 69 C8
Fleetwood FY7 193 E2
Southport PR8 20 F6
Heathfoot Ave LA3 208 E6
Heathfoot Dr LA3 208 E6
Heathgate Fence BB12 146 D8
Skelmersdale WN8 18 C2
Heathrow Pl PR7 42 A7
Heathwaite Cl LA7 237 E4
Heathway PR2 116 F5
Heathway Ave FY3 129 E6
Heathy La L39 13 B8
Heatley Cl BB2 100 D3
Heatley St PR1 95 F8
Heaton Bottom Rd LA3 209 E5
Heaton Cl
Bamber Bridge PR5 96 D4
Burscough L40 24 D4
Carleton FY6 151 C5
Morecambe LA3 213 A3
Orrell WN8 10 A7
Thornton FY5 151 C8
Heaton Ho LA1 210 F5
Heaton Mount Ave PR2 116 F7
Heaton Pl PR1 117 E1
Heaton Rd Lancaster LA1 210 F5
Lytham St Anne's FY8 89 A8
Heaton St
3 Blackburn BB2 100 E4
Leyland PR5 75 E2
Standish WN6 28 E1
Heatons Bridge Rd L40 23 D3
Heaviley Gr BL6 31 A5
Hebden Ave FY1 129 D1
Heber St BB11 105 B4
Hebrew Rd BB10 127 A8
Hebrew Sq 11 BB10 127 A8
Heckenhurst Ave BB10 128 A6
Hector Rd BB3 80 E5
Hedge Row PR4 112 B3
Hedge Rows OL12 70 C1
Hedgerow The BB2 100 A8
Hedgerows PR5 58 A8
Heeley Rd FY8 88 E8
Height Barn La OL13 70 A8
Height Croft BB9 147 E5
Height La PR3 159 F7
Height Side La BB4 85 B7
Heights Ave OL12 51 E2
Heights Cl OL12 51 E2
Heights Cotts BB5 103 F4
Heights La OL12 51 E1
Heights Rd BB9 147 D6
Heights The BL6 31 D1
Heightside Ave BB4 85 E2
Heightside Mews BB4 85 E2
Helen's Cl FY4 109 E6
Helena St BB10 127 B5
Helks Brow LA2 233 B2
Hellifield PR2 116 F7
Hellifield Rd
Bolton-by-B BB7 224 F5
Gisburn BB7 225 C4
Helm Cl BB11 126 D2
Helmcroft 5 BB4 84 A1
Helmcroft Ct 1 BB4 84 B1
Helmn Way BB9 168 F2
Helmsdale WN8 18 C2
Helmsdale Cl BL0 49 A4
Helmsdale Rd
Blackpool FY4 109 F7
Nelson BB9 169 A1
Helmshore Prim Sch BB4 67 A7
Helmshore Rd
Haslingden BB4 67 A7
Ramsbottom BL0,BL8,BB4 67 A3
Helmshore Textile
Mus BB4 66 F8
Helmside Ave LA4 212 F3
Helmsley Gn 2 PR5 76 B1
Helston Cl Burnley BB11 126 B4
Southport PR9 53 B5
Helton Cl BB9 168 D4
Helvellyn Dr BB12 126 C8
Hemingway FY4 109 D8
Hemingway Pl 1 BB9 147 F8
Hemp St OL13 87 A1
Hempshaw Ave BB4 105 A2
Henderson Rd
Fleetwood FY7 193 F2
Weeton Camp PR4 131 E6
Henderson St PR1 116 E2
Hendon Pl PR2 115 E2
Hendon Rd BB9 147 F8
Hendriff Pl 4 OL12 51 F1
Hendry La BB2 80 D7
Henfield Cl BB5 124 A3
Henley Ave FY5 172 D2
Henley Ct
7 Blackpool FY2 150 E1
Southport PR9 52 E1
Henley Dr PR9 52 F1
Henley Mews LA3 212 B3
Henley St 9 OL12 51 F1
Hennel House PR5 96 C4
Hennel La
Bamber Bridge PR5 96 B2
Bamber Bridge PR5 96 C3
Hennel La *continued*
Bamber Bridge PR5 96 C4
Henrietta St Bacup OL13 86 F2
Blackburn BB2 100 C5
Preston PR1 96 B8
Henrietta Street Ind Est
OL13 86 F2
Henry Gdns BB9 147 B5
Henry St Accrington BB5 103 D3
Bank Lane BL0 49 D7
Blackpool FY1 129 C2
Church BB5 102 F6
Colne BB8 169 C4
Enfield BB5 124 A2
Lancaster LA1 210 F7
Lytham St Anne's FY8 90 A3
2 Nelson BB9 168 D1
Rawtenstall BB4 84 F2
Rishton BB1 123 B1
Henry Whalley St BB2 100 A2
Henson Ave FY4 109 E6
Henthorn Cl 4 BB7 164 D7
Henthorn Rd BB7 164 C6
Henthorne St 1 FY1 129 C6
Henwick Hall Ave BL0 49 B4
Herbert St Bacup OL13 69 D8
Blackburn BB2 100 D2
Burnley BB11 126 E5
Horwich BL6 31 B4
Leyland PR5 76 A1
Padiham BB12 125 D7
Preston PR1 117 B1
Hereford Ave
7 Blackpool FY3 129 E3
Burnley BB12 126 B7
Garstang PR3 178 B8
Hereford Cl BB5 103 B7
Hereford Dr BB7 164 F7
Hereford Gr PR4 115 D5
Hereford Rd
Blackburn BB1 101 C5
Nelson BB8,BB9 169 A2
Southport PR9 34 F7
Hereford St BB9 147 C8
Herevale Hall Dr BL0 49 B4
Heriot Cl 8 FY5 172 F1
Heritage Way
Cleveleys FY5 172 F1
Tarleton PR4 56 A5
Herkomer Ave BB11 126 E2
Herlebeck Rise LA1 214 B2
Hermitage Cl WN6 19 E7
Hermitage St BB1,BB5 123 C1
Hermitage The FY5 172 F2
Hermitage Way FY8 89 D6
Hermon Rd FY5 172 E1
Hermon St
2 Preston PR1 117 C1
Preston PR1 117 D1
Hern Ave PR5 76 A8
Heron Cl Blackburn BB1 100 D8
Cleveleys FY5 172 F5
Heron Ct BB11 126 C5
Heron Dr LA4 212 F3
Heron Way Blackpool FY3 130 B6
Kirkham PR4 113 B2
Oswaldtwistle BB5 102 E3
Herons Ct L31 5 B4
Heronsyke LA1 213 F4
Herring Arm Rd FY7 194 A2
Herschel Ave BB12 126 C8
Herschell St
Blackburn BB2 100 B1
Preston PR1 96 B6
Hertford St BB2 100 C2
Hesketh Ave Banks PR9 54 A6
Blackpool FY2 150 B4
Hesketh Cl Darwen BB3 64 C6
Preston PR2 117 E1
Hesketh Ct Blackpool FY2 150 B4
Great Harwood BB6 123 E6
Hesketh Dr Maghull L31 5 F1
Rufford L40 38 A3
Shevington Moor WN6 28 A2
Southport PR9 52 F1
Hesketh Gn L40 38 B4
Hesketh La Becconsall PR4 72 F1
Hesketh Lane PR3 160 D7
Tarleton PR4 56 A7
Hesketh Links Ct PR9 52 E2
Hesketh Pl FY7 194 B5
Hesketh Rd
Burscough L40 24 D4
Fulwood PR2 117 E1
Heysham LA3 208 E8
Longridge PR3 139 A8
Lytham St Anne's FY8 110 A1
Southport PR9 52 D2
Hesketh St
Great Harwood BB6 123 C5
Preston PR2 116 C1
Hesketh-with-Becconsall
All Saints CE Sch PR4 72 E4
Heskin Cl L31 5 D4
Heskin Hall Ct L39 15 D8
Heskin La L39 15 D8
Hesley La BD24 230 E6
Hessam Hts LA3 208 F5
Hesse St 1 BB3 64 A8
Hest Bank La LA2 213 E7
Hest Bank Rd LA4 213 A6
Hester Cl L38 2 F4
Hestham Ave LA4 212 E4
Hestham Cres LA4 212 E4
Hestham Dr LA4 212 E4
Hestham Par LA4 212 E4
Hetherington Pl FY2 150 E2
Hetton Lea BB9 168 C3
Heversham WN8 18 C2
Heversham Ave PR2 116 F7
Heversham Cl
Lancaster LA1 211 B3
Morecambe LA4 212 F3
Hewart Dr BL9 32 C3
Hewart St BB12 126 A7
Hewitt Bsns Pk WN5 10 E4
Hewitt St 8 PR5 76 B2
Hewlett Ave PR7 41 D1
Hewlett St PR7 41 D1
Hewngate PR5 97 E1
Hexam Cl BB5 103 E3
Hexham Ave FY5 172 E4
Hexham Rd LA4 213 B5
Hey Bottom La OL12 51 F6
Hey End PR4 74 F8
Hey Head Ave BB4 69 A8
Hey House Mews BL8 48 F4
Hey St BB9 168 E1
Heycrofts View BL0 67 E3
Heydon Cl L37 11 D1
Heyes Rd WN5 10 E6
Heyes St WN6 19 C7
Heyes The PR6 77 B2
Heyescroft L39 7 D6
Heyfold Gdns BB3 80 F3
Heyhead St BB9 147 C5
Heyhouses Ct FY8 89 B8
Heyhouses Endowed
CE Inf Sch FY8 88 F7
Heyhouses Endowed
CE Jun Sch FY8 88 F8
Heyhouses La FY8 89 C7
Heyhurst Rd BB2 100 D5
Heymoor Ave BB6 123 D6
Heys BB5 102 D3
Heys Cl Blackburn BB2 80 C7
Rawtenstall BB4 85 C1
Heys Ct BB2 80 C8
Heys La Barley Green BB12 167 D5
Blackburn BB2,BB3 80 C7
Darwen BB3 80 F2
Great Harwood BB6 123 E5
Heys St Bacup OL13 86 F1
Haslingden BB4 84 A3
Rawtenstall BB4 85 C1
Thornton FY5 173 B3
Heys The Coppull PR7 41 F2
Parbold WN8 26 C3
Southport PR8 33 D4
Heysham Ave LA3 208 F8
Heysham Cres BB2 100 F1
Heysham Cty High Sch
LA3 212 C3
Heysham Hall Dr LA3 208 E6
Heysham Hall Gr LA3 208 E7
Heysham Mossgate Rd
LA3 208 F7
Heysham Nuclear
Power Sta Nature Reserve
LA3 208 D4
Heysham Nuclear
Power Sta Vis Ctr LA3 208 C4
Heysham Pk LA3 208 E7
Heysham Rd
4 Heysham LA3 208 E7
Morecambe LA3 212 A2
Southport PR9 34 F7
Heysham St 2 PR1 116 E1
Heysham Sta LA3 208 C5
Heywood Cl L37 11 E3
Heywood Com High Sch
OL10 32 E1
Heywood Rd PR2 115 E2
Heywood St Bury BL9 32 A1
Great Harwood BB6 123 C4
Heyworth Ave BB2 80 C7
Hibbert Terr LA1 210 F3
Hibson Rd Nelson BB9 147 D8
Nelson, Little Marsden BB9 147 D7
Hic Bibi La PR7 28 E6
Hick's Terr 5 BB1 123 B1
Hickory St BB1 100 F7
Hickson Ave L31 5 C3
Hidings Court La LA4 212 E4
Hiers House La BB8 169 B5
Higgin St Burnley BB10 127 B5
Colne BB8 169 D5
Worsthorne BB10 128 B5
Higgin's La L40 24 C4
High Bank PR6 61 A3
High Banks L31 5 C3
High Barn La OL12 70 C3
High Bentham Bsns Pk
LA2 233 D7
High Bentham Prim Sch
LA2 233 D8
High Cl BB12 125 E6
High Cop PR6 77 F4
High Ct LA4 213 B5
High Fold BB18 192 A6
High Gate FY7 193 D3
High Gate La FY6 174 A6
High Gn PR5 75 F1
High Knott Rd LA5 237 B1
High La Bickerstaffe L39 7 C8
Ormskirk L39, L40 16 A8
Salterforth BB18 191 C5
High Legh FY8 89 C3
High Mdw PR5 96 B2
High Moor La WN6 27 B4
High Moss L39 15 E3
High Mount Ct 2 LA1 210 F7
High Mount Ho 1 LA1 210 F7
High Park Pl PR9 35 A8
High Park Rd PR9 35 A8
High Peak Rd OL12 51 C6
High Rd Halton LA2 214 E7
Knowle Green PR3 161 B3
Lowgill LA2 233 C5
High St Belmont BL7 45 C4
Blackburn BB1 100 E5
Blackpool FY1 129 B6
Brierfield BB9 147 B5
10 Chorley PR7 42 C8
Clitheroe BB7 164 B8
Colne BB8 169 E5
Darwen BB3 81 A1
Edgworth BL7 47 C4
Elswick PR4 153 F1
Fleetwood FY7 194 B4
Garstang PR3 178 C7
Great Eccleston PR3 154 B5
Haslingden BB4 84 B4
Horwich BL6 31 B4
Lancaster LA1 210 F7
Mawdesley L40 39 B1
Nelson BB9 147 D7
Oswaldtwistle BB5 102 F3
Padiham BB12 145 D1
13 Preston PR1 96 A8
Rishton BB1 123 B1
Skelmersdale WN8 17 E1
Standish WN6 28 E1
Higham Gr FY3 129 F2
Higham Hall Rd BB12 145 F5
Higham Rd BB12 145 C3
Higham Side Rd PR4 134 C6
Higham St BB12 145 D1
Highbank BB1 121 F1
Highbank Ave FY4 110 A8
Highbury Ave
Blackpool FY3 129 E8
Fleetwood FY7 193 F3
Highbury Rd FY8 109 E1
Highbury Rd E FY8 109 E1
Highbury Rd W FY8 109 D1
Highcroft Ave FY2 150 E5
Highcroft Way OL12 51 F4
Highcross Ave FY6 130 D8
Highcross Hill FY6 130 D8
Highcross Rd FY6 151 D1
Higher Antley St BB5 103 B5
Higher Audley St BB1 100 F4
Higher Bank Rd PR2 116 F3
Higher Bank St
Blackburn BB2 100 B6
Withnell PR6 79 A1
Higher Barn BL6 31 F3
Higher Barn St 2 BB1 101 A5
Higher Blackthorn OL13 86 F4
Higher Booths La BB4 105 A1
Higher Change
Villas OL13 87 B4
Higher Chapel La BB7 224 A1
Higher Church St BB3 81 B1
Higher Cockcroft 13 BB1 100 E5
Higher Commons La
BB2 120 C4
Higher Croft Kingsfold PR1 95 C2
2 Kingsfold PR1 95 D2
Higher Croft Cotts BB3 80 F8
Higher Croft Rd BB2,BB3 80 F8
Higher Cross Row 9 OL13 86 F3
Higher Cswy BB9 168 D3
Higher Dunscar BL7 46 E1
Higher Eanam BB1 101 A5
Higher Feniscowles La
BB2 79 B8
Higher Field BB6 122 C8
Higher Firs Dr BB5 124 A3
Higher Fold La BL0 49 E7
Higher Furlong PR4 73 F6
Higher Gate BB5 124 F1
Higher Gate Rd BB5 124 F1
Higher Gn FY6 151 E3
Higher Greenfield PR2 116 B5
Higher Heys BB5 102 E3
Higher House Cl BB2 80 A7
Higher House La PR6,PR7 61 B2
Higher La
Barnoldswick BB18 191 B7
Haslingden BB4 84 B4
Holmes PR4 55 C3
Orrell WN8 10 C7
Scorton PR3 199 F4
Skelmersdale WN8 18 C7
Higher Lawrence St 12
BB3 80 F2
Higher London Terr BB3 81 B2
Higher Mdw PR5 76 E1
Higher Mill St BB4 85 A3
Higher Moor Cotts FY2 150 F2
Higher Moor Rd FY3 151 A2
Higher Moss La L37 13 A2
Higher Moulding BL9 32 E5
Higher Park Rd BB18 191 C8
Higher Peel St 7 BB5 102 D3
Higher Perry St BB3 81 B2
Higher Ramsgreave Rd
BB1 121 C3
Higher Rd Longridge PR3 160 E2
Tosside BD23 230 C5
Higher Reedley
Rd BB10,BB9 147 D5
Higher Row BL9 32 B3
Higher Saxifield BB10 147 E3
Higher South St BB3 81 A1
Higher Summerseat BL0 49 B2
Higher Syke LA2 227 C2
Higher Tentre BB11 127 B5
Higher Walton CE Prim Sch
PR5 97 C3
Higher Walton Rd PR5 96 E4
Higher Witton Rd BB2 100 B4
Highergate Cl BB5 124 F2
Highfield Bacup OL13 86 F2
Brinscall PR6 61 F8
Great Harwood BB6 123 B5
Rawtenstall BB4 85 A7
Highfield Ave
Bamber Bridge PR5 96 C1
Brierfield BB10 147 B3
Foulridge BB8 191 E1
Fulwood PR2 117 C4
Inskip PR4 134 C8
Leyland PR5 76 C3
Highfield Cl Adlington PR6 30 A7
Clifton PR4 114 C1
Oswaldtwistle BB5 102 F3
Tarleton PR4 56 A5
Highfield Cres
5 Barrowford BB9 168 D3
Morecambe LA4 212 C4
Nelson BB9 168 E3
Highfield Ct BB4 84 A2
Highfield Dr Fulwood PR2 116 E8
Hest Bank LA2 215 D1
Longridge PR3 139 B6
Longton PR4 73 F6
Penwortham PR1 95 D2
Highfield Gdns BB2 100 E2
Highfield Gr PR5 96 C2
Highfield High Sch FY4 109 E6
Highfield Ind Est PR7 60 D2
Highfield La L40 23 D7
Highfield Mews BB3 64 B8
Highfield Pk
Haslingden BB4 84 A1
Maghull L31 5 F1
Highfield Prim Sch PR6 42 E8
Highfield Priory Sch PR2 117 F5
Highfield Rd Adlington PR6 30 A7
Blackburn BB2 100 E3
Blackpool FY4 109 E6
Blackrod BL6 30 E1
Carnforth LA5 216 E8
Clitheroe BB7 164 F7
Croston PR5 57 D2
Darwen BB3 81 B1
1 Earby BB18 201 B2
Edenfield BL0 67 D3
Ormskirk L39 15 E7
Rawtenstall BB4 85 D1
5 Rishton BB1 123 A1
Southport PR9 53 B3
Highfield Rd N
Adlington PR6 30 A8
Chorley PR7 60 C2
Highfield Rd S PR7 60 C1
Highfield St 4 Darwen BB3 64 B8
Haslingden BB4 84 A2
Highfield Terr LA2 233 C8
Highfurlong Sch FY3 151 A2
Highgale Gdns PR5 76 C7
Highgate Blackpool FY4 109 D5
Goosnargh PR3 137 D6
Nelson BB9 147 D7
Penwortham PR1 95 B5
Highgate Ave PR2 116 E4
Highgate Cl Fulwood PR2 116 F4
Newton-with-S PR4 113 F3
Highgate Cres WN6 19 E7
Highgate La Warton PR4 91 E6
Whitworth OL12 51 C5
Highgate Pl FY8 89 D6
Highgate Rd Maghull L31 5 D3
Orrell WN8 10 B7
Highgrove Ave PR7 40 F3
Highgrove Cl LA4 212 D4
Highgrove Ct PR5 57 F8
Highland Ave PR1 95 B4
Highland Brow LA2 207 A4
Highland Lo WN6 28 D1
Highland Rd BL6 31 E1
Highmeadow WN8 10 A6
Highmoor BB9 147 F6
Highmoor Pk BB7 164 F8
Highrigg Dr PR3 136 F1
Highsands Ave L40 38 A3
Hightown BB4 85 E4
Hightown Rd BB4 85 F4
Hightown Sta L38 3 A4
Highway Gate PR4 154 A2
Highways Ave PR7 59 D1
Higson St BB2 100 D5
Hilary Ave FY2 150 C5
Hilary St BB10 147 A1
Hilbre Cl PR9 52 F1
Hilbre Dr PR9 52 F1
Hilderstone La LA5 234 A7
Hildrop Rd 7 BB9 168 F1
Hill Cl WN6 19 E8
Hill Cres PR4 114 A2
Hill Crest OL13 86 D1
Hill Crest Ave
Burnley BB10 127 F4
Fulwood PR2 116 E8
Longridge PR3 139 A7
Hill Croft PR4 113 B5
Hill End La BB4 85 C1
Hill Hos 16 BB3 64 A8
Hill House Fold La WN6 27 C5
Hill House La
Appley Bridge WN6 27 C5
Jack Green PR6 78 A7
Hill La Blackrod BL6 30 C2
Colne BB8 170 C7
Nether Kellet LA6 216 F4
Hill Pl BB9 147 D6

Hill Rd Lancaster LA1 213 F3
Leyland PR5 76 C1
Penwortham PR1 95 D4
Hill Rd S PR1 95 D3
Hill Rise Haslingden BB4 84 C1
1 Ramsbottom BL0 49 A4
Hill Rise View L39 15 A1
Hill Side LA1 210 E8
Hill St Accrington BB5 103 C5
Barnoldswick BB18 200 C2
Blackburn BB1 101 B5
Blackpool FY4 129 B1
Brierfield BB9 147 B5
Brierfield, Fence BB9 146 F6
Carnforth LA5 217 D1
Colne BB8 169 D4
3 Enfield BB5 124 A1
Oswaldtwistle BB5 102 D5
Padiham BB12 125 C8
Preston PR1 95 F8
Ramsbottom BL9 49 C3
Rawtenstall BB4 85 A7
Southport PR9 34 B7
Hill Top Barrowford BB9 168 D4
Colne BB8 170 C4
Foulridge BB8 191 C2
Longridge PR3 160 D2
New Longton PR4 75 A6
Trawden BB8 170 B2
Hill Top Cl PR4 92 D7
Hill Top La Earby BB18 201 A2
Whittle-le-W PR6 60 D8
Hill View Blackburn BB1 121 E1
2 Rawtenstall BB4 84 F1
Hill View Dr PR7 28 D8
Hill View Rd PR3 199 C1
Hill Wlk PR5 76 A2
Hillam La LA2 203 B7
Hillary Cres L31 5 D1
Hillbrook Rd PR5 75 F2
Hillcrest Maghull L31 5 F1
Skelmersdale WN8 9 B8
Hillcrest Ave
Bolton-le-S LA5 216 A5
Fulwood PR2 116 A4
Hillcrest Cl PR4 56 A8
Hillcrest Dr Bescar L40 22 F7
Longridge PR3 139 A7
Tarleton PR4 56 A8
Hillcrest Rd Blackburn BB2 99 F2
Blackpool FY4 109 B4
Langho BB6 122 C8
Ormskirk L39 15 E6
Hillcroft Fulwood PR2 116 C7
High Bentham LA2 233 D7
Hilldean WN8 10 C8
Hillingdon Rd BB10 147 D3
Hillingdon Rd N BB10 147 D3
Hillkirk Dr OL12 51 C3
Hillmount Ave LA3 208 F8
Hillock Cl L40 23 A7
Hillock La Bescar L40 23 A7
Skelmersdale WN8 18 D7
Warton PR4 91 E7
Hillocks The PR5 57 B1
Hillpark Ave Fulwood PR2 116 D4
Gregson Lane PR5 97 D1
Hills Ct LA1 213 F1
Hills The PR2 118 C7
Hillsborough Ave BB9 147 D5
Hillsea Ave LA3 208 F8
Hillside BB11 126 D3
Hillside Ave
Blackburn BB1 101 C4
Blackrod BL6 30 E1
Brierfield BB10 147 C5
15 Darwen BB3 64 A8
Edgworth BL7 47 B1
Farington PR5 75 F7
Fulwood PR2 116 D4
Hill Dale WN8 26 D5
Horwich BL6 31 C4
Kirkham PR4 113 C5
Ormskirk L39 15 D3
Preesall FY6 195 B4
Hillside Cl Blackburn BB1 101 C4
Blackpool FY3 129 E6
Brierfield BB9 147 C5
Burnley BB11 126 D2
Clitheroe BB7 164 E6
Euxton PR7 59 C1
Great Harwood BB6 123 C6
Thornton FY5 151 D8
Hillside Cres Horwich BL6 31 C4
Weir OL13 86 F7
Whittle-le-W PR6 60 C8
Hillside Cty Sch WN8 9 D8
Hillside Dr Newchurch BB4 85 E2
Stalmine FY6 174 C7
West Bradford BB7 186 F6
Hillside Gdns BB3 64 A7
Hillside Rd Haslingden BB4 84 C3
Low Bentham LA2 233 C8
2 Preston PR1 96 C6
Ramsbottom BL0 49 A5
Southport PR8 33 E1
Hillside Sch Autistic Ctr
PR3 139 D7
Hillside Sta PR8 33 E1
Hillside View BB9 147 C5
Hillside Way OL12 70 C1
Hillside Wlk
Blackburn BB1 101 C4
Rochdale OL12 51 D4
Hillstone Ave OL12 51 D4
Hillstone Cl BL8 48 F2
Hillsview Rd PR8 20 C4
Hilltop OL12 51 C5
Hilltop Dr BB4 67 C7
Hilltop Wlk L39 15 C3
Hillview Rd PR4 113 A6
Hillylaid Rd FY5 173 D2
Hilmont Terr BB1 100 F7
Hilmore Rd LA4 212 D5
Hilstone La FY2 150 D1
Hilton Ave
6 Blackpool FY1 129 B1
Horwich BL6 31 A3
Lytham St Anne's FY8 89 C6
Hilton Ct FY8 88 E5
Hilton Rd BB3 64 B8
Hilton St BB3 64 A8
Hilton's Brow PR6 78 B4
Hinchley Gn L31 5 B1
Hind St Burnley BB10 147 B2
4 Preston PR1 95 E6
Hind's Head Ave WN6 27 F6
Hindburn Ave L31 5 F2
Hindburn Cl LA5 217 F2
Hindburn Pl 6 LA1 213 E2
Hinde St LA1 214 A1
Hindle Fold La BB6 123 C6
Hindle St Accrington BB5 103 B6
Bacup OL13 69 D8
Darwen BB3 80 F2
Haslingden BB4 84 B3
Hindley Beech 1 L31 5 C2
Hindley Cl PR2 117 C7
Hindley Ct 3 BB9 168 C1
Hindley St 5 PR7 42 C6
Hinton St BB10 127 B5
Hippings Meth Prim Sch
BB5 102 E3
Hippings Vale BB5 102 D4
Hippings Way BB7 186 E2
Hirst St Burnley BB11 127 B4
6 Cornholme OL14 108 B1
Padiham BB12 145 C1
Hoarstones Ave BB12 146 D7
Hob Gn BB2 120 F2
Hob La BL7 47 C7
Hobart Pl FY5 150 F8
Hobart St BB11 127 B6
Hobbs La PR3 180 A4
Hobcross La L40 25 A2
Hobson St BB4 84 F4
Hobson's La LA6 234 C2
Hockley Pl FY3 129 F7
Hodder Ave Blackpool FY1 129 D1
Chorley PR7 42 B5
Fleetwood FY7 193 D2
Maghull L31 5 F2
Morecambe LA3 213 B3
Hodder Bridge Ct BB7 163 B7
Hodder Brook PR2 118 A3
Hodder Cl
6 Bamber Bridge PR5 76 F8
Fleetwood FY7 193 C2
Hodder Ct BB7 163 C4
Hodder Dr BB7 186 D7
Hodder Gr Clitheroe BB7 164 C7
Darwen BB3 80 E4
Hodder Pl Blackburn BB1 100 F6
Lancaster LA1 211 B5
Lytham St Anne's FY8 89 C7
Hodder St Accrington BB5 103 D6
1 Blackburn BB1 100 E6
Brierfield BB10 147 C3
Longridge PR3 139 B7
Hodder Way FY6 151 D2
Hoddlesden Fold BB3 81 F1
Hoddlesden Rd BB3 81 E1
Hodge Bank Bsn Pk BB9 168 D2
Hodge Brow BL6 43 F4
Hodge La BB18 191 B8
Hodge St PR8 34 B7
Hodgson Ave PR4 92 A5
Hodgson High Sch FY6 151 F3
Hodgson Pl FY6 151 D2
Hodgson Rd FY1 129 C8
Hodgson St Darwen BB3 81 B1
3 Oswaldtwistle BB5 102 E4
Hodson St
Bamber Bridge PR5 96 E1
Southport PR8 34 C6
Hogarth Ave BB11 126 F3
Hogarth Cres PR4 133 F4
Hogg's La PR7 42 E5
Hoggs Hill La L37 11 F1
Hoghton Ave OL13 70 A8
Hoghton Cl Lancaster LA1 210 D6
Lytham St Anne's FY8 109 F2
Hoghton Gr PR9 34 C8
Hoghton La PR5 97 D3
Hoghton Pl 3 PR9 34 B7
Hoghton Rd Leyland PR5 75 D1
Longridge PR3 139 C7
Hoghton St 8
Bamber Bridge PR5 76 A8
Southport PR9 34 C7
Hoghton Twr PR5 98 E1
Hoghton View PR1 96 C6
Holbeck Ave
Blackpool FY4 109 F8
Morecambe LA4 213 B4
Rochdale OL12 51 D4
Holbeck St BB10 147 A1
Holborn Dr L39 15 C3
Holborn Hill L39 15 C4
Holcombe Brook Prim Sch
BL0 49 A2
Holcombe Ct BL0 48 F2
Holcombe Dr BB10 127 B6
Holcombe Gr PR6 60 E1
Holcombe Lee BL0 49 A4
Holcombe Mews BL0 48 F3
Holcombe Old Rd BL8,BL0 49 A5
Holcombe Rd
Blackpool FY2 150 E1
Haslingden BB4 66 F8
Ramsbottom BL8 48 F2
Holcombe Village BL8 49 A6
Holcroft Pl FY8 89 F4
Holden Ave Bury BL9 32 E4
Ramsbottom BL0 49 A5
Holden Cl BB9 168 C1
Holden Fold BB3 81 B3
Holden La BB7 224 B5
Holden Pl BB4 83 F1
Holden Rd Brierfield BB9 147 A5
Brierfield, Reedley BB10 147 B3
Holden St Accrington BB5 103 B5
Adlington PR7 29 F7
Belthorn BB1 81 F6
Blackburn BB2 100 C4
Burnley BB11 126 F5
Clitheroe BB7 164 F8
Holden Way LA1 210 F5
Holden Wood Dr BB4 83 F1
Hole House La BB7 229 E2
Hole House St BB1 101 C5
Holgate FY4 109 F6
Holgate Dr WN5 10 E6
Holgate Prim Sch WN5 10 E5
Holgate St Brierfield BB10 147 F3
Great Harwood BB6 123 C5
Holhouse La BL8 48 F2
Holker Bsns Ctr BB8 169 B4
Holker Cl Coupe Green PR5 97 E3
Lancaster LA1 210 D6
Holker La PR5 58 B4
Holker St Colne BB8 169 B4
Darwen BB3 64 B8
Holland Ave
Bamber Bridge PR5 96 E2
Rawtenstall BB4 84 F3
Holland Ct WN8 9 D2
Holland House Rd PR5 96 E3
Holland Lodge 4 PR2 117 F4
Holland Moor Cty Prim Sch
WN8 9 E7
Holland Moss WN8 9 A5
Holland Pl BB9 168 E2
Holland Rd PR2 116 C1
Holland St Accrington BB5 102 F6
Blackburn BB1 100 D6
3 Padiham BB12 125 B8
Holland's La WN8 17 A1
Holliers Cl L31 5 E1
Hollies Cl Blackburn BB2 79 F8
Catterall PR3 178 D2
Hollies Rd BB1 122 A7
Hollies The PR8 33 F6
Hollin Bank BB9 147 B6
Hollin Bridge St BB2 100 D2
Hollin Hall BB8 170 C1
Hollin Hill BB11 127 B3
Hollin La Knowley PR7 61 C2
Rawtenstall BB4 85 A4
Hollin Mill St BB9 147 B6
Hollin St BB2 100 C2
Hollin Way Rawtenstall,
Constable Lee BB4 85 A4
Rawtenstall, Rush Bed BB4 85 A6
Hollingreave Rd BB11 127 A4
Hollings PR4 74 F7
Hollington St BB8 170 B5
Hollinhead Cres PR2 116 B4
Hollinhurst Ave PR1 95 C6
Hollinhurst Brow LA2 233 C2
Hollinhurst View BB12 145 F5
Hollins Ave BB10 127 F4
Hollins Cl Accrington BB5 103 C4
Hoghton PR5 98 C3
Hollins Ct 1 BB18 200 B3
Hollins Gr PR2 116 B3
Hollins Grove St BB3 80 F3
Hollins High Sch The
BB5 103 D2
Hollins Hill PR3 204 C2
Hollins La Accrington BB5 103 D3
Arnside LA5 237 C1
Edenfield BL0 67 E2
Hollins Lane PR3 204 C2
Runshaw Moor PR5 58 C4
Hollins Rd
Barnoldswick BB18 200 A2
Darwen BB3 80 F4
Nelson BB9 169 A2
Preston PR1 117 B2
Hollinshead St PR7 42 C8
Hollinshead St Sch PR7 42 C8
Hollinshead Terr BB3 63 B7
Hollinwood Dr BB4 85 A5
Hollowbrook Way 4 OL12 51 D2
Hollowell La BL6 31 D1
Hollowford La L40 25 D2
Hollowforth La PR4 135 E5
Hollowhead Ave BB1 121 F5
Hollowhead Cl BB1 121 F5
Hollowhead La BB1 122 A5
Hollowrane LA6 234 C7
Holly Ave BB4 84 C1
Holly Bank Accrington BB5 103 C4
Edgworth BL7 47 B7
Fulwood PR2 116 C5
Warton, Carnforth LA5 217 D5
Holly Cl Clayton Green PR6 77 B2
Skelmersdale WN8 17 E1
Thornton FY5 173 C3
Westhead L40 16 E4
Holly Cres PR7 41 E2
Holly Fold La L39, WA11 8 E3
Holly Gr Longridge PR3 139 A8
Tarleton PR4 56 A7
Holly Ho BB11 127 B5
Holly La Ormskirk L39 15 B4
Rufford L40 38 C3
Skelmersdale L39, WA11 8 E4
Holly Mews FY8 109 F2
Holly Mount BB4 67 A7
Holly Mount RC Prim Sch
BL8 48 D1
Holly Pl PR5 77 B6
Holly Rd Blackpool FY1 150 C1
Thornton FY5 173 B3
Holly St Blackburn BB1 100 F7
Burnley BB10 127 B5
Bury BL9 32 A2
Nelson BB9 147 F8
Oswaldtwistle BB5 102 D4
Ramsbottom BL0 49 C3
Holly Terr BB1 100 F8
Holly Tree Cl BB3 64 A6
Holly Tree Way BB2 79 F8
Holly Wlk LA1 210 D8
Hollybank Cl PR2 115 F5
Hollybrook Rd PR8 34 A5
Hollywood Ave
Blackpool FY3 129 E5
Penwortham PR1 95 C3
Hollywood Gr FY7 193 F4
Holman St 5 PR1 117 C1
Holmbrook Cl BB2 80 F8
Holmby St BB10 147 B2
Holmdale Ave PR9 53 C4
Holme Ave FY7 172 D8
Holme Bank BB4 84 F1
Holme CE Prim Sch
BB10 107 B6
Holme Cl BB18 192 A7
Holme Cres BB8 170 B3
Holme End BB12 146 F4
Holme Head Cotts BB7 222 C5
Holme Hill BB7 186 E2
Holme House Rd OL14 108 C1
Holme La Caton LA2 231 C3
Haslingden BB4 67 D8
Rawtenstall BB4 67 E8
Holme Lea BB5 123 F4
Holme Mills Ind Est LA6 234 B8
Holme Pk LA2 233 D7
Holme Rd
Bamber Bridge PR5 76 E8
Burnley BB12 126 E7
Clayton-le-M BB5 123 E4
Penwortham PR1,PR2 95 C7
Holme Slack La PR1 117 C3
Holme Slack Prim Sch
PR1 117 C3
Holme St Accrington BB5 103 C6
Bacup OL13 69 D8
Barrowford BB9 168 D2
Colne BB8 170 B5
Darwen BB3 64 A8
Nelson BB9 147 E8
Holme Terr Nelson BB9 147 C8
Rawtenstall BB4 67 D8
Holme The PR3 179 E7
Holme Vale BB4 67 A6
Holmefield Ave FY5 172 E2
Holmefield Cl FY5 172 E2
Holmefield Ct 8 BB9 168 D3
Holmefield Gr L31 5 C1
Holmefield Rd
Knott End-on-S FY6 194 E5
Lytham St Anne's FY8 89 A7
Holmes Ct Fulwood PR1 116 E3
Garstang PR3 178 C8
Holmes Dr OL13 86 F4
Holmes La OL13 86 F3
Holmes Mdws 3 PR5 75 B1
Holmes Rd FY5 173 B3
Holmes Sq BB10 127 B5
Holmes St Burnley BB11 127 B5
Forest Holme BB4 86 A7
Padiham BB12 125 D8
Rawtenstall BB4 85 B3
Holmes Terr BB4 84 F5
Holmes The BB4 84 F5
Holmestrand Ave BB11 126 B4
Holmeswood PR4 113 A5
Holmeswood Cres PR3 136 B8
Holmeswood Four Lane Ends
L40 37 C6
Holmeswood Meth Sch
L40 37 C6
Holmeswood Pk BB4 67 E8
Holmeswood Rd L40 37 D6
Holmfield Cres 2 PR2 115 D1
Holmfield Pk L37 11 D4
Holmfield Rd
Blackpool FY2 150 B2
Fulwood PR2 117 A4
Holmrook Rd PR1 117 B1
Holmsley St BB10 127 B5
Holmwood Cl L37 11 D3
Holmwood Gdns L37 11 D4
Holsands Cl PR2 117 E6
Holst Gdns BB2 101 A1
Holstein Ave OL12 51 D4
Holstein St PR1 96 A8
Holt Ave PR7 41 F2
Holt Brow PR5 59 A6
Holt Coppice L39 6 A7
Holt La PR6 77 E3
Holt Mill Rd BB4 68 D8
Holt Sq BB9 168 E5
Holt St Orrell WN5 10 D5
Holt St *continued*
Ramsbottom BL0 49 D6
Rawtenstall BB4 68 E8
Rishton BB1 123 C1
Whitworth OL12 70 C1
Holt St W BL0 49 B5
Holt's Terr OL12 51 E2
Holts La FY6 151 F2
Holy Cross RC High Sch
PR7 42 C4
Holy Family RC Jun Sch
FY1 129 C8
Holy Family RC Prim Sch
Fulwood PR2 115 F4
Southport PR9 34 E7
Warton PR4 91 E6
Holy Saviour's RC Prim Sch
BB9 168 E2
Holy Souls RC Prim Sch
BB1 121 E1
Holy Trinity CE Prim Sch
Burnley BB11 126 E5
Darwen BB3 81 A1
Formby L37 11 F3
Southport PR9 34 C8
Holy Trinity RC Prim Sch
BB9 147 C5
Holy Trinity RC Sch BB9 147 B5
Holy Trinity Stackstead
CE Prim Sch OL13 69 C8
Holyoake Ave FY2 150 E1
Holyoake St Burnley BB12 126 A6
2 Cornholme OL14 108 A1
Home Breeze Ho 1
LA4 213 A6
Home Farm Cl LA2 232 D6
Home Field PR3 178 C8
Homecare Ave BB7 144 F8
Homechase Ho PR8 33 F4
Homer Ave PR4 55 F7
Homer St 1 BB11 126 C5
Homesands Ho PR9 34 D8
Homestead PR5 77 B4
Homestead Cl 4 PR5 75 D1
Homestead Dr FY7 193 E1
Homestead The 9 FY8 90 A3
Homestead Way FY7 193 E1
Homewood Ave LA4 213 B6
Homfray Ave LA3 213 A3
Homfray Gr LA3 213 A3
Honey Hole BB2 100 E2
Honey Holme La BB10 106 F7
Honey Moor Dr FY5 173 B4
Honeypot La FY6 152 D4
Honeysuckle Cl PR6 60 B5
Honeysuckle Pl FY2 150 F6
Honeysuckle Row PR2 117 E2
Honeysuckle Way OL12 51 D3
Honeywood Cl BL0 49 A3
Honister Ave FY3 129 F2
Honister Cl FY7 193 D3
Honister Rd
Brierfield BB10 147 B3
Lancaster LA1 214 B2
Honister Sq FY8 109 F2
Honiton Ave BB2 80 C8
Honiton Way PR4 115 F6
Hoo Hill Ind Est FY3 129 E8
Hood House St BB11 126 E4
Hood St 4 BB5 103 C6
Hoole CE Prim Sch PR4 73 C1
Hoole La Banks PR9 54 A6
Nateby PR3 177 B5
Hools La PR3 196 A5
Hope Cl FY5 173 B4
Hope La PR3 160 E5
Hope Sq PR9 34 D7
Hope St Accrington BB5 103 B5
Adlington PR6 30 B8
Bacup OL13 86 F4
Blackburn BB2 100 D5
Brierfield BB9 147 B5
Chorley PR7 60 C1
Darwen BB3 80 F1
Great Harwood BB6 123 C4
Haslingden BB4 84 B2
Horwich BL6 31 B4
Lancaster LA1 211 A7
Lytham St Anne's FY8 89 A7
Morecambe LA4 212 F4
Nelson BB9 147 D8
12 Padiham BB12 125 D8
5 Preston PR1 95 F8
Ramsbottom BL0 49 B5
Rawtenstall BB4 85 C1
Southport PR9 34 C7
Worsthorne BB10 128 B6
Hope St N BL6 31 B5
Hope Terr 10
Bamber Bridge PR5 76 A8
Blackburn BB2 100 C6
Hopkinson St BB8 170 B3
Hopkinsons Terr BB8 170 C3
Hopton Rd FY1 129 B2
Hopwood Ave BL6 31 C4
Hopwood St
Accrington BB5 103 B4
4 Bamber Bridge PR5 76 E8
Bamber Bridge PR5 76 F7
Blackburn BB2 100 E3
9 Burnley BB11 126 E6
Preston PR1 96 A8
Horace St 7 BB12 126 D6
Horden Rake BB2 79 E7
Horden View BB2 79 E7
Hordley St BB12 126 A6
Horeb Cl 5 BB12 125 D7
Hornbeam Cl PR1 95 B3

Hornby Ave
Fleetwood FY7 .172 D8
Fulwood PR2 .117 E4
Hornby Bank Hornby LA2 .232 B8
Nether Kellet LA6 .216 F5
Hornby CE Prim Sch LA2 .232 B7
Hornby Croft PR5 .58 B8
Hornby Ct Blackburn BB2 .100 C4
Kirkham PR4 .113 B4
Lancaster LA1 .213 E4
Hornby Dr Lancaster LA1 .211 A4
Newton-with-S PR4 .113 F2
Hornby Hall Cl LA2 .232 B7
Hornby High Sch LA2 .232 B7
Hornby La PR4 .154 F2
Hornby Park Ct 1 FY3 .129 D4
Hornby Rd Blackpool FY1 .129 C4
Caton LA2 .231 C3
Chorley PR6 .42 E6
Longridge PR3 .139 B8
Lytham St Anne's FY8 .88 E5
Southport PR9 .53 A4
Wray LA2 .232 D1
Wray LA2 .232 D6
Hornby St Burnley BB11 .127 A5
Oswaldtwistle BB5 .102 E3
Hornby Terr LA4 .212 F6
Hornby's La
Hale Nook PR3 .175 A5
Moss Edge PR3 .175 D6
Hornchurch Dr PR7 .42 A7
Horncliffe Cl BB4 .67 E8
Horncliffe Rd FY4 .109 B6
Horncliffe View BB4 .67 B8
Horne St BB5 .103 C7
Horning Cres BB10 .147 D2
Horns La PR3 .159 B3
Hornsea Cl PR2 .116 A4
Hornsey Ave FY8 .109 B4
Horridge Fold BL7 .46 E3
Horrobin Fold BL7 .47 C2
Horrobin La Adlington PR6 .30 C8
Edgworth BL7 .47 C2
Rivington PR6,BL6 .43 E1
Horrocks Rd BL7 .47 D6
Horrocksford Way LA1 .210 D6
Horse Mkt LA6 .238 C2
Horse Park La PR3 .197 A5
Horsebridge Rd FY3 .130 B8
Horsefield Ave OL12 .51 C6
Horsfall Ave 2 FY8 .90 A3
Horsfall Cl BB5 .103 B7
Horsfield Cl BB8 .169 F5
Horton Ave BB10 .147 B3
Horwich Bsns Pk BL6 .31 B2
Horwich L Ctr BL6 .31 C3
Horwich Parish
CE Prim Sch BL6 .31 C4
Hoscar Moss Rd L40 .25 D3
Hoscar Sta L40 .25 D4
Hospital Cotts PR3 .139 F6
Hosticle La LA6 .235 C7
Hothersall La PR3 .139 D4
Hough La PR5 .76 A1
Houghclough La PR3 .181 F1
Houghton Ave 5 FY4 .109 D8
Houghton Cl PR1 .95 C3
Houghton Cres 1 FY4 .109 E8
Houghton Ct Halton LA2 .214 E7
6 Thornton FY5 .173 B3
Houghton La WN6 .19 F6
Houghton Rd PR1 .95 C3
Houghton St 8 PR6 .42 D8
Houghton's La WN8 .18 C1
Houghtons Rd WN8 .18 B3
Houldsworth Rd PR2 .116 E3
Hounds Hill 1 FY1 .129 B4
Hounds Hill Ctr FY1 .129 B5
Houseman Pl FY4 .109 E7
Hove Ave FY7 .172 C8
Hove Cl BL8 .48 F1
Hove Rd FY8 .88 F6
Howard Cl Accrington BB5 .102 F5
Lytham St Anne's FY8 .109 E1
Maghull L31 .5 F1
Howard Ct PR9 .52 D1
Howard Dr PR4 .55 F7
Howard Mews LA5 .217 C1
Howard Rd PR7 .42 C5
Howard St Blackpool FY1 .129 C6
Burnley BB11 .126 D5
Nelson BB9 .147 C8
Rishton BB1 .123 A1
Rochdale OL12 .51 F1
Howards La WN5 .10 F7
Howarth Ave BB5 .102 F7
Howarth Cres FY6 .151 E3
Howarth Rd PR2 .116 D3
Howarth's St BB4 .86 A8
Howden Hts FY6 .151 B3
Howe Ave FY4 .109 E8
Howe Croft BB7 .164 F8
Howe Dr BL0 .49 B2
Howe Gr PR7 .42 A7
Howe Wlk 4 BB11 .127 A6
Howells Cl L31 .5 D2
Howgill Ave LA1 .214 A4
Howgill Cl BB9 .147 F6
Howgill La BB7 .225 C1
Howgill Way FY8 .90 D5
Howgills The PR2 .117 A7
Howick CE Prim Sch PR1 .94 F3
Howick Cross La PR1 .94 E5
Howick Moor La PR1 .95 A3
Howick Park Ave PR1 .94 F4
Howick Park Cl PR1 .94 F4
Howick Park Dr PR1 .94 F4
Howick Row PR2 .94 D5
Howorth Cl BB11 .127 A3
Howorth Rd BB11 .127 A3
Howsin St BB10 .147 A1
Hoylake Cl PR2 .116 B6
Hoyle Ave FY8 .109 F2
Hoyle St Bacup OL13 .69 E8
Haslingden BB5 .84 A8
Whitworth OL12 .70 D3
Hoyles La PR4 .115 D6
Hozier St BB1 .101 C5
Hubert Pl LA1 .210 D8
Hubie St BB12 .126 F7
Huck La FY8 .90 E7
Hud Hey Ind Est BB4 .84 B5
Hud Hey Rd BB4 .84 B5
Hud Rake BB4 .84 B4
Hudcar La BL9 .32 A4
Hudson Ct PR5 .77 C8
Hudson Pl BB2 .100 B8
Hudson Rd FY1 .129 D2
Hudson St Accrington BB5 .103 C4
Brierfield BB9 .147 B5
Burnley BB11 .126 D5
6 Cornholme OL14 .108 C1
9 Preston PR1 .96 A6
Hufling Ct 9 BB11 .127 B4
Hufling La BB11 .127 B4
Hugh Barn La PR4 .74 F7
Hugh La PR5 .75 D3
Hugh Rake BB4 .84 F6
Hughes Ave BL6 .31 A4
Hughes Cl 11 BL9 .32 A3
Hughes Gr FY2 .150 E1
Hughes St BB11 .127 A5
Hull Rd FY1 .129 B4
Hull St Burnley BB11 .127 B5
Preston PR2 .95 C8
Hullet Cl WN6 .19 E8
Hulme Ave FY5 .173 C2
Hulme St PR8 .34 A7
Hulton Dr BB9 .147 E6
Humber Ave 2 FY3 .129 E8
Humber Sq BB10 .147 C2
Humber St PR3 .139 A7
Humblescough La PR3 .177 D5
Humphrey St BB9 .147 B6
Huncoat Bsns Pk BB5 .124 D1
Huncoat Cty Prim Sch
BB5 .124 F2
Huncoat Ind Est BB5 .103 D8
Huncoat Sta BB5 .124 E2
Hundred End La PR4,PR9 .71 F1
Hungerford Rd FY8 .88 F5
Hunslet St Burnley BB11 .127 B6
Nelson BB9 .147 F7
Hunt Fold Dr BL8 .48 F1
Hunt Rd L31 .5 D1
Hunt St 2 PR1 .95 D7
Hunter Ave PR4 .56 A6
Hunter Rd PR4 .113 B2
Hunter St
Brierfield BB10,BB9 .147 B5
Carnforth LA5 .217 D2
Hunter's La PR4 .55 B3
Hunters Chase WN5 .10 E1
Hunters Dr BB12 .126 D8
Hunters Fold PR4 .74 A5
Hunters Gn BL0 .48 F3
Hunters Lodge BB2 .99 F1
Hunters Rd PR5 .76 D1
Hunting Hill Lodge LA5 .217 C1
Hunting Hill Rd LA5 .217 B1
Huntingdon Gr L31 .5 C4
Huntingdon Hall Rd PR3 .162 A2
Huntingdon Rd FY5 .172 C1
Huntington Dr BB3 .64 A7
Huntley Ave 4 FY3 .129 E7
Huntley Cl LA4 .213 A5
Huntley La PR5 .119 E1
Huntley Mount Rd BL9 .32 B3
Huntley St BL9 .32 B3
Huntly Way OL10 .32 E1
Huntroyde Ave BB12 .125 B8
Huntroyde Cl BB12 .126 D7
Hunts Field PR6 .77 C2
Huntsmans Chase PR4 .113 F6
Hurlston Ave WN8 .9 C8
Hurlston Dr L39 .15 E7
Hurlston La L40 .23 C1
Hurn Gr PR7 .42 A7
Hurst Brook PR7 .41 F1
Hurst Cres BB4 .85 B3
Hurst Gn L40 .39 C2
Hurst La BB4 .85 B3
Hurst Pk PR1 .95 C4
Hurst St BL9 .32 A2
Hurst's La L39 .7 B2
Hurstead St BB5 .103 E1
Hurstleigh Dr LA3 .209 A7
Hurstleigh Hts FY5 .173 E2
Hurstmere Ave FY4 .109 E8
Hurstway PR2 .116 D7
Hurstway Cl PR2 .116 D7
Hurstwood Ave
Blackburn BB2 .100 A1
Burnley BB10 .127 D5
Hurstwood Ent Pk BB4 .84 A2
Hurstwood Gdns BB9 .147 D4
Hurstwood La BB10 .128 B4
Hurtley St BB10 .127 A8
Hut La PR6 .43 B3
Hutch Bank Rd BB4 .83 F2
Hutchinson Ct BB3 .81 A2
Hutchinson St 4 BB2 .100 E3
Huttock End La OL13 .69 D8
Hutton Cl LA6 .234 C7
Hutton Cres LA4 .212 D4
Hutton Ct WN8 .17 D1
Hutton Dr BB12 .126 E7
Hutton Gr LA4 .212 D4
Hutton Gram Sch PR4 .94 D2
Hutton Hall Ave PR4 .94 E1
Hutton Rd WN8 .17 D1
Hutton St Blackburn BB1 .101 B5
Standish WN1 .29 A3
Hutton Way
5 Lancaster LA1 .213 D1
Ormskirk L39 .15 E5
Huyton Rd PR6,PR7 .30 A6
Huyton Terr PR6 .30 B6
Hyacinth Cl BB4 .66 F8
Hyatt Cres WN6 .28 C3
Hyde Rd Blackpool FY1 .129 B2
Morecambe LA4 .213 B4
Hygiene BB5 .123 E2
Hynd Brook Ho BB5 .103 A5
Hyndburn Bridge BB5 .123 F5
Hyndburn Cl LA3 .213 B3
Hyndburn Dr BB3 .80 D4
Hyndburn Park
Cty Prim Sch BB5 .103 A6
Hyndburn Rd
Accrington BB5 .103 A6
Church BB5 .102 F6
Great Harwood BB6 .123 F5
Hyndburn St BB5 .102 F6
Hyning Rd LA5 .217 E8
Hynings The BB6 .123 B6
Hythe Cl Blackburn BB1 .101 C4
Southport PR8 .34 E3

I

Ibbison Ct FY1 .129 C3
Icconhurst Cl BB5 .103 E2
Ice St BB1 .100 E7
Iddesleigh Rd 3 PR1 .117 E1
Iddon Ct 6 FY1 .129 C6
Idlewood Pl FY5 .150 F8
Idstone Cl BB2 .81 A8
Ightenhill Jun Sch BB12 .126 C6
Ightenhill Park La
Burnley BB12 .126 C8
Padiham BB12 .146 C2
Ightenhill Pk
Mews 1 BB12 .126 C7
Ightenhill Prim Inf Sch
BB12 .126 C6
Ightenhill St BB12 .145 C1
Ilford Rd FY4 .129 E1
Ilkley Ave
Lytham St Anne's FY8 .89 C6
Southport PR9 .53 C6
Ilkley Gr FY5 .150 E8
Illawalla The FY5 .151 E6
Illingworth Rd PR1 .117 E1
Ilway PR5 .96 E3
Imperial Gdns BB9 .168 D1
Imperial St 2 FY1 .129 B7
Ince Cres L37 .11 D3
Ince La PR7 .40 C6
Inch Field BB10 .128 B6
Inchfield WN8 .18 B2
India St Accrington BB5 .102 F6
Darwen BB3 .64 B8
Ramsbottom BL0 .49 C3
Industrial Cotts 10 BB4 .68 F8
Industrial Pl 4 OL13 .86 F2
Industrial St Bacup OL13 .87 A2
Ramsbottom BL0 .67 C1
Industrial Terr BB7 .143 A4
Industry Rd 8 OL12 .51 F1
Industry St Darwen BB3 .81 B2
Whitworth OL12 .70 D2
Infant St 12 BB5 .103 C6
Infirmary Rd BB2 .100 D2
Infirmary Cl BB2 .100 D4
Infirmary St BB2 .100 E2
Ing Dene Cl BB8 .169 B4
Ingersol Rd BL6 .31 E1
Ingfield Terr OL14 .108 C1
Ingham Brow BL6 .31 F4
Ingham St Barrowford BB9 .168 D3
Bury BL9 .32 A1
Padiham BB12 .145 D1
Inglby Cl BB1 .101 D5
Ingle Cl 4 PR6 .60 D1
Ingle Head PR2 .116 D6
Ingle Nook BB10 .127 F4
Ingleborough Dr BB18 .200 A2
Ingleborough Rd LA1 .213 D3
Ingleborough View
Carnforth LA5 .216 E8
15 High Bentham LA2 .233 D8
Ingleborough Way PR5 .76 C2
Ingleby Cl Cleveleys FY5 .172 F5
Standish WN6 .28 D2
Inglehurst Rd BB11 .126 B5
Inglemere Cl LA5 .237 B1
Inglemere Dr LA5 .237 B2
Inglemere Gdns LA5 .237 B1
Inglenook Cl 7 FY5 .172 F1
Ingleton Ave FY2 .150 F4
Ingleton Cl BB5 .103 D5
Ingleton Dr LA1 .211 A4
Ingleton Ho 2 LA1 .211 A3
Ingleton Rd Fulwood PR2 .117 E4
Southport PR8 .34 E3
Ingleway FY5 .172 F3
Ingleway Ave FY3 .129 F6
Inglewhite WN8 .18 A2
Inglewhite Fold 2 BB12 .125 D7
Inglewhite Rd PR3 .159 C3
Inglewood Cl Bury BL9 .32 C4
Fleetwood FY7 .193 C1
Inglewood Cl *continued*
Warton PR4 .91 D6
Inglewood Gr FY2 .150 E5
Ingol Gdns FY6 .174 C2
Ingol Gr FY6 .174 C2
Ingol La FY6 .174 D2
Ingol Prim Sch PR2 .115 F4
Ingot St PR1 .95 D8
Ingram WN8 .18 B1
Ings Ave
Barnoldswick BB18 .200 B3
Rochdale OL12 .51 B2
Ings La OL12 .51 C2
Ingthorpe Ave FY2 .150 D5
Inkerman Rd PR4 .131 F6
Inkerman St Bacup OL13 .87 A2
Blackburn BB1 .100 E6
9 Padiham BB12 .125 C8
Preston PR2 .116 D2
12 Rochdale OL12 .51 F1
Inner Prom FY8 .89 B3
Innes Sch OL12 .51 C1
Inskip WN8 .18 A2
Inskip Ct WN8 .18 B2
Inskip Pl Blackpool FY4 .109 E5
Lytham St Anne's FY8 .89 A8
Inskip Rd Leyland PR5 .75 D2
Preston PR2 .115 E1
Southport PR9 .53 A4
Wharles PR4 .134 A5
Inskip St 5 BB12 .125 C8
Institute St BB12 .125 D8
Intack La BB2 .120 B2
Intack Prim Sch BB1 .101 D5
Intack Rd PR4 .74 B8
Intake Cres BB8 .169 F6
Intake La Maghull L39 .4 E8
Skelmersdale L39 .8 B2
Inver Rd FY2 .150 D3
Inverness Rd BB3 .63 F8
Ipswich Pl FY5 .172 C2
Ipswich Rd PR2 .117 D2
Ireby Rd LA6 .236 C3
Irene Pl BB2 .100 B5
Irene St BB10 .127 C5
Iris St BL0 .49 B6
Iron St Blackburn BB2 .100 E3
Horwich BL6 .31 C2
Irongate PR5 .76 C8
Ironside Cl PR2 .117 B4
Irton Rd PR9 .34 E8
Irvin Ave PR9 .53 C5
Irvin St PR1 .117 B1
Irvine Cl FY2 .150 F5
Irvine St 6 BB9 .168 F2
Irving Pl BB2 .100 B5
Irving St PR9 .52 B1
Irwell WN8 .18 A3
Irwell Rd WN5 .10 F7
Irwell St 7 Bacup OL13 .86 F2
Burnley BB12 .126 A6
Longridge PR3 .139 B7
Longridge PR3 .139 B8
Lytham St Anne's FY8 .88 F7
Ramsbottom BL0 .49 C6
Irwell Terr 12 OL13 .86 F2
Irwell Vale Rd BB4 .67 C6
Irwell Vale Sta BL0 .67 C5
Isa St 5 BL0 .49 A4
Isabella St Longridge PR3 .139 A8
Rochdale OL12 .51 F2
Isherwood Fold BL7 .47 D7
Isherwood St
Blackburn BB2 .100 D1
1 Preston PR1 .117 B1
Preston PR1 .117 C1
Islamic Coll Jamea Al
Kauthar LA1 .210 F5
Island Cotts BL9 .49 C2
Island La PR3 .198 B3
Islay Rd FY8 .89 E6
Isle of Man BB1 .121 E4
Isle of Man St BB4 .86 A7
Isleworth Dr PR7 .42 B7
Islington BB2 .100 E3
Islington Cl BB10 .147 D3
Ivan St BB10 .147 B2
Ivegate Colne BB8 .169 D5
Foulridge BB8 .191 E1
Ivinson Rd BB3 .81 B3
Ivory St 1 BB12 .126 C6
Ivy Ave Blackpool FY4 .109 E5
Haslingden BB4 .84 C3
Ivy Bank PR2 .117 D6
Ivy Bank High Sch BB12 .125 F7
Ivy Cl PR5 .76 E2
Ivy Cotts BB4 .68 F8
Ivy Gr 2 BB4 .85 A3
Ivy St Blackburn BB2 .100 E2
Burnley BB10 .147 B1
Nelson BB8 .169 A2
1 Rawtenstall BB4 .68 F8
Southport PR8 .34 D6
Ivy Terr BB3 .64 B6
Ivybridge WN8 .18 B2
Ivydale WN8 .18 B2

J

Jack La BD23 .230 F4
Jackdaw Rd BL8 .48 F2
Jacks Key Dr BB3 .64 C5
Jacksmere La L40,PR8 .22 B8
Jackson Cl Haskayne L39 .13 F5
Lancaster LA1 .210 C7
Jackson Heights Rd BB1 .82 B4
Jackson Rd 2 Chorley PR7 .42 A5
Jackson Rd *continued*
1 Leyland PR5 .75 D1
Jackson St
8 Bamber Bridge PR5 .76 F8
Blackpool FY3 .129 E7
6 Burnley BB10 .127 A8
Chorley PR7 .42 D6
1 Church BB5 .102 E5
5 Clayton-le-M BB5 .123 F3
Jackson Terr LA5 .217 D3
Jackson's Banks Rd BB2 .119 E6
Jackson's Common La
L40 .23 B1
Jackson's La L40 .26 E7
Jacob St BB5 .103 C5
Jacob's La PR4 .114 A7
Jacson St 3 PR1 .96 A7
Jade Cl L33 .1 A3
Jagoe Mews 8 BB18 .201 B1
Jagoe Rd BB18 .201 A1
James Ave Blackpool FY4 .129 F1
Great Harwood BB6 .123 B5
James Pl Coppull PR7 .28 E8
Standish WN6 .28 D2
James Sq WN6 .28 D2
James St Bacup OL13 .69 B7
Bamber Bridge PR5 .96 E1
Barnoldswick BB18 .200 B1
4 Barrowford BB9 .168 D4
Belthorn BB1 .81 F6
Blackburn BB1 .100 E5
Burnley BB10 .147 A1
Bury BL9 .32 A1
12 Clayton-le-M BB5 .123 F3
Colne BB8 .169 E4
1 Darwen BB3 .81 A1
Earby BB18 .201 B1
Egerton BL7 .46 D3
Great Harwood BB6 .123 B5
Haslingden BB4 .84 A2
Horwich BL6 .30 F3
Huncoat BB5 .124 E2
23 Lancaster LA1 .210 F8
Morecambe LA4 .212 F5
Oswaldtwistle BB5 .102 D3
Preston PR1 .96 B7
Rawtenstall BB4 .85 A2
Rishton BB1 .123 C1
Salterforth BB18 .191 D7
Whitworth OL12 .70 D2
James St W 6 BB3 .81 A1
Jameson Rd FY7 .194 A1
Jameson St 2 FY1 .129 C3
Jane La Catforth PR4 .134 E5
Leyland PR5 .75 A3
Jane St OL12 .70 E6
Jane's Brook Rd PR8 .34 E4
Janice Dr PR2 .116 D7
Janine Cl LA4 .212 D4
Jannat Cl BB5 .103 B5
Jarrett Rd L33 .1 A4
Jarrett Wlk L33 .1 A4
Jarvis St OL12 .51 F1
Jasmine Rd PR1 .96 A3
Jasper St BB1 .121 F1
Jefferson Cl LA1 .210 D7
Jefferson Way OL12 .51 F3
Jeffrey Ave PR3 .139 B7
Jeffrey Hill Cl PR2 .118 C7
Jeffrey Sq FY1 .129 D3
Jellicoe Cl FY8 .109 E1
Jem Gate FY5 .150 D8
Jemmett St PR1 .116 E2
Jenny La Blackpool FY4 .110 C7
Higher Wheelton PR6 .78 C1
Jenny Nook LA3 .209 A7
Jenny St BB9 .147 D6
Jensen Cl LA1 .210 E6
Jensen Dr FY4 .111 A6
Jepheys Pl 17 OL12 .51 F1
Jepheys St OL12 .51 F1
Jepp Hill 2 BB18 .200 B2
Jepps Ave PR3 .136 B7
Jepps La PR3 .136 B8
Jepson St 9 BB3 .64 A8
Jepson Way FY4 .109 F4
Jericho Rd BL9 .32 E4
Jersey Ave FY2 .150 E2
Jersey St BB2 .100 B1
Jervis Cl FY8 .109 D1
Jesmond Ave FY4 .109 B7
Jesmond Gr LA4 .212 G3
Jessel St BB2 .100 B2
Jesson Way LA5 .217 C1
Jevington Way LA3 .209 A7
Jib Hill Cotts BB10 .147 D2
Jingling La LA6 .238 C2
Jinny La BB12 .167 E4
Jobling St BB8 .169 B3
Jockey St BB11 .126 C5
Joe Connolly Way BB4 .68 E8
Joe La PR3 .178 D2
John Cross CE Prim Sch
PR3 .157 A4
John Henry St OL12 .70 D4
John Hill St 3 FY4 .129 F2
John Kay Ct LA1 .213 D3
John o' Gaunt St 15
BB12 .145 C1
John St
2 Bamber Bridge PR5 .96 E1
Barnoldswick BB18 .200 B1
Barrowford BB9 .168 E4
Blackpool FY1 .129 B2
Brierfield BB9 .147 B6

John St *continued*
4 Carnforth LA5 .217 D2
Church BB5 .102 E7
Clayton-le-M BB5 .123 F3
Colne BB8 .169 C4
Coppull PR7 .41 E1
Darwen BB3 .80 F2
Earby BB18 .201 B1
5 Galgate LA2 .207 A4
Haslingden BB4 .84 B3
Leyland PR5 .76 A1
Newchurch BB4 .85 F1
Oswaldtwistle BB5 .102 D3
Thornton FY5 .173 B4
Whitworth OL12 .70 D2
John Wall Ct 8 BB7 .164 D8
John William St 7 PR1 .96 C8
Johnny Barn Cl BB4 .85 D2
Johnny Barn Cotts BB4 .85 D2
Johnson Cl Carnforth LA5 .217 C1
Lancaster LA1 .210 C7
Johnson New Rd BB3 .81 E2
Johnson Rd Blackpool FY4 .129 F2
Waterside BB3 .81 D4
Johnson St PR9 .34 B8
Johnson's Meanygate PR4 .55 D7
Johnspool PR2 .116 C6
Johnston Cl BB2 .100 C5
Johnston St BB2 .100 C5
Johnsville Ave FY4 .109 E7
Joiner's Row BB2 .100 E3
Joiners Alley 10 BB6 .123 C5
Jolly Tar La PR7 .29 B7
Jonathan Cl BB4 .67 A8
Jones St BL6 .31 B4
Jones' Gr FY7 .194 B5
Jones's Yd LA6 .234 B7
Joseph St Barrowford BB9 .168 D2
Darwen BB3 .81 B1
3 Rochdale OL12 .51 D2
Joy Pl OL12 .51 F2
Joy St Ramsbottom BL0 .49 B6
Rochdale OL12 .51 F2
Joyce Ave FY4 .129 F2
Jubilee Ave Ormskirk L39 .15 F6
Orrell WN5 .10 D4
Preesall FY6 .195 A4
Preston PR2 .115 D1
Jubilee Cl BB4 .84 A1
Jubilee Ct 1 BB4 .84 A1
Jubilee Cts PR5 .58 E8
Jubilee Dr Cleveleys FY5 .172 C4
Skelmersdale WN8 .8 E8
Jubilee Ho PR5 .57 B1
Jubilee La FY4 .110 B5
Jubilee La N FY4 .110 B6
Jubilee Rd
9 Bamber Bridge PR5 .76 A8
Church BB5 .102 F7
Formby L37 .11 D1
Haslingden BB4 .84 A1
Jubilee St Blackburn BB1 .100 E4
Brierfield BB10 .147 F3
Darwen BB3 .81 A1
Enfield BB5 .124 A1
Oswaldtwistle BB5 .102 E4
Read BB12 .144 D2
Jubilee Terr Clifton PR4 .114 C1
Freckleton PR4 .92 C7
Langho BB6 .142 D1
Jubilee Trad Est PR1 .116 E1
Jubilee Way FY8 .89 C8
Jud Falls BB7 .163 A3
Judd Holmes La PR3 .160 D7
Jude St BB9 .147 D8
Judeland PR7 .60 A2
Judge Fields BB8 .169 D6
Judith St OL12 .51 C3
Julia Mews 4 BL6 .31 B4
Julia St BL6 .31 B4
July St 17 BB1 .101 A4
Jumbles Ctry Pk BL7 .47 D2
Jumps La OL14 .108 E1
Junction La L40 .24 E3
Junction Rd Preston PR2 .95 D7
Rainford Junction WA11 .8 F1
Junction St Brierfield BB9 .147 B6
Burnley BB12 .126 E6
Burnley, Whittlefield BB12 .126 E7
Darwen BB3 .64 B7
Nelson BB8 .169 A3
June Ave FY4 .130 A1
June St 16 BB1 .101 A4
June's Wlk PR4 .74 A5
Juniper Cl FY6 .195 A5
Juniper Croft PR6 .77 A1
Juniper Ct BB5 .103 E8
Juniper St 6 BB1 .101 A7
Juno St BB9 .168 F2
Jutland St PR1 .96 A8

K

Kairnryan Cl FY2 .150 F5
Kale Gr L33 .1 A5
Kaley La BB7 .187 E5
Kane St PR2 .116 C1
Kate St 3 BL0 .49 B6
Kateholm OL13 .87 A7
Kay Brow BL0 .49 C6
Kay Gdns BB11 .127 B5
Kay St Blackburn BB2 .100 E3
Blackpool FY1 .129 B4
Kay St *continued*
Brierfield BB9 .147 B5
Bury BL9 .32 A3
Clitheroe BB7 .164 D6
Darwen BB3 .81 B1
Edgworth BL7 .47 C4
2 Oswaldtwistle BB5 .102 D4
1 Padiham BB12 .145 D1
1 Preston PR1 .95 E7
Ramsbottom BL0,BL9 .49 C3
Rawtenstall BB4 .85 A2
Kaymar Ind Est PR1 .96 C7
Kayswell Rd LA4 .213 B5
Kearsley Ave PR4 .56 A6
Keasdale Ave LA7 .237 E3
Keasdale Rd LA7 .237 E3
Keasden Ave FY4 .109 D7
Keasden Rd BB7 .229 E6
Keating Ct FY7 .194 A3
Keats Ave Bolton-le-S LA5 .216 A5
Longshaw WN5 .10 D1
Rochdale OL12 .51 A1
Warton PR4 .91 E6
Keats Cl Accrington BB5 .103 E2
Colne BB8 .169 D6
Eccleston PR7 .40 D5
Thornton FY5 .173 A2
Keats Fold 3 BB12 .125 F7
Keats Rd BL8 .48 F2
Keats Terr PR8 .34 F6
Keats Way PR4 .115 D4
Kebs Rd OL14 .108 E3
Keele Cl FY5 .173 A2
Keele Wlk BB1 .100 F4
Keeper's Hey FY5 .173 A4
Keeper's La PR3 .199 F1
Keer Bank 1 LA1 .213 C2
Keer Holme La LA6 .234 E4
Keighley Ave BB8 .169 D6
Keighley Rd Colne BB8 .169 F5
Laneshaw Bridge BB8 .170 D6
Trawden BB8 .170 C4
Keirby Wlk BB11 .127 A6
Keith Gr FY5 .172 D1
Keith St BB12 .126 C6
Kelbrook Dr BB11 .126 E3
Kelbrook Prim Sch BB18 .192 A6
Kelbrook Rd BB18 .191 E7
Kelkbeck Cl L31 .5 F2
Kellet Acre 4 PR5 .76 A7
Kellet Ave PR5 .76 D1
Kellet Ct 1 LA1 .210 E8
Kellet La
Bolton-le-S LA5,LA2 .216 C3
Borwick LA6 .234 B3
Walton Summit PR5 .77 B7
Kellet Rd Carnforth LA5 .217 E1
Over Kellet LA6 .234 A1
Kellet Road Ind Est LA5 .217 F1
Kellett St 8 PR7 .42 C8
Kelmarsh Cl FY3 .130 B2
Kelne Ho 7 LA1 .210 E8
Kelsall Ave BB1 .101 B8
Kelsey St LA1 .210 E8
Kelso Ave FY5 .172 D1
Kelsons Ave FY5 .173 C2
Kelswick Dr BB9 .147 E6
Kelverdale Rd FY5 .150 F8
Kelvin Rd FY5 .150 D6
Kelvin St BB3 .80 F1
Kelwood Ave BL9 .32 D5
Kem Mill La PR6 .60 B8
Kemble Cl BL6 .31 B5
Kemp Ct BB1 .121 F3
Kemp St FY7 .194 B4
Kemple View BB7 .164 D6
Kempton Ave FY3 .129 E3
Kempton Park Fold PR8 .34 F3
Kempton Rd LA1 .211 B4
Kempton Rise BB1 .100 F3
Kenbury Cl L33 .1 A4
Kenbury Rd L33 .1 A4
Kendal Ave
Barrowford BB9 .168 D4
Blackpool FY3 .151 A1
Cleveleys FY5 .172 D4
Kendal Cl WA11 .8 F2
Kendal Dr Maghull L31 .5 E2
Morecambe LA4 .213 B4
Rainford Junction WA11 .8 F2
Kendal Rd
Kirkby Lonsdale LA6 .238 B2
Lytham St Anne's FY8 .109 D1
Ramsbottom BL0 .49 A2
Kendal Rd W BL0 .48 F2
Kendal Row BB1 .81 F6
Kendal St Blackburn BB1 .100 E6
Clitheroe BB7 .186 F1
5 Nelson BB9 .168 D1
Preston PR1 .95 E8
Kendal Way PR8 .20 B3
Kenilworth Ave FY7 .193 E3
Kenilworth Cl BB12 .125 E8
Kenilworth Ct FY8 .88 F6
Kenilworth Dr
Clitheroe BB7 .164 C6
Earby BB18 .192 A8
Kenilworth Gdns FY4 .109 B7
Kenilworth Pl
Fleetwood FY7 .193 E3
Lancaster LA1 .211 A5
Kenilworth Rd
Lytham St Anne's FY8 .88 F6
Morecambe LA3 .212 F3
Southport PR8 .20 B4
Kenlis Rd PR3 .178 F4
Kenmay Way L33 .1 A3
Kenmure Pl PR1 .116 F2
Kennedy Cl LA1 .210 D6
Kennet Dr PR2 .116 F8
Kennett Dr PR5 .76 B2
Kennington Cty Prim Sch PR2 .117 A4
Kennington Rd PR2 .117 A4
Kensington Ave PR1 .95 B6
Kensington Cl BL8 .49 A1
Kensington Ct LA4 .213 A6
Kensington Dr BL6 .31 D3
Kensington Ho LA1 .210 F5
Kensington Ind Pk PR9 .34 C6
Kensington Pl BB11 .126 D4
Kensington Rd
Blackpool FY3 .129 E4
Chorley PR7 .42 B7
Cleveleys FY5 .172 C3
Formby L37 .11 E1
Lancaster LA1 .210 F5
Lytham St Anne's FY8 .89 D4
Morecambe LA4 .212 E5
Southport PR9 .34 C6
Kensington St BB9 .147 C7
Kent Ave 2
Bamber Bridge PR5 .96 D3
Cleveleys FY5 .172 E4
Formby L37 .12 A1
Kent Ct BB9 .168 D4
Kent Dr Blackburn BB1 .101 E4
Clayton-le-W PR5 .76 D1
Kent Ho LA1 .210 F7
Kent Rd Blackpool FY1 .129 C3
Formby L37 .12 A1
Southport PR8 .34 A4
Kent St Blackburn BB1 .100 F4
Burnley BB12 .126 F7
Fleetwood FY7 .194 B5
3 Lancaster LA1 .213 F2
Preston PR1 .116 F2
Kent Way LA3 .213 B3
Kent Wlk BB4 .67 A8
Kent's Cl PR4 .112 E7
Kentmere Ave
Bamber Bridge PR5 .96 E1
Leyland PR5 .76 A3
Kentmere Cl Burnley BB12 .126 B8
Fleetwood FY7 .193 D3
Kentmere Dr Blackburn BB2 .79 E8
Blackpool FY4 .130 C1
Longton PR4 .74 B8
Kentmere Gr 1 LA4 .212 G4
Kentmere Rd LA1 .214 A1
Kenton Cl L37 .11 F6
Kenwood Ave LA4 .212 D4
Kenworthys Flats PR8 .34 B8
Kenwyn Ave FY3 .129 E3
Kenyon La PR6 .60 F7
Kenyon Rd
Morecambe LA4 .213 B5
Nelson BB9 .147 B7
Standish WN6 .28 D2
Kenyon St
6 Accrington BB5 .103 C6
Bacup OL13 .70 B8
Blackburn BB1 .101 C6
Bury BL9 .32 A3
Ramsbottom BL0 .49 C6
Rawtenstall BB4 .85 A3
Kenyon's La L37 .12 A3
Kenyons La L31 .5 E3
Keppel Pl BB11 .126 E6
Kepple La PR3 .178 B6
Kerenhappuch St 5 BL0 .49 B5
Kerfoot's La WN8 .8 C8
Kerr Pl PR1 .95 D8
Kershaw Cl 6 BB4 .85 A7
Kershaw St 8 Bacup OL13 .86 F2
Bury BL9 .32 A2
Chorley PR6 .60 E1
Church BB5 .102 E7
Kerslake Way L38 .3 A4
Kerslea Ave FY3 .130 D8
Kerton Row PR8 .33 F4
Keston Gr FY4 .109 C5
Kestor La PR3 .139 A7
Kestrel Cl Blackburn BB1 .100 D8
Cleveleys FY5 .172 F5
Knowley PR6 .61 A3
Kestrel Ct PR9 .34 D7
Kestrel Dr Bury BL9 .32 B4
Darwen BB3 .80 D3
Kestrel Mews WN8 .18 C4
Kestrel Pk WN8 .18 C4
Keswick Cl Accrington BB5 .124 D1
Maghull L31 .5 E2
Southport PR8 .20 C3
Keswick Ct LA1 .214 B1
Keswick Dr BB2 .79 E8
Keswick Gr Heysham LA3 .208 E5
Knott End-on-S FY6 .194 F5
Keswick Rd Blackpool FY1 .129 C3
Burnley BB10 .147 B2
Lancaster LA1 .214 B1
Lytham St Anne's FY8 .88 E8
Keswick Way WA11 .8 F2
Keswick Wlk LA1 .214 B1
Kettering Rd PR8 .20 B5
Kevin Ave FY6 .151 F5
Kevin Gr LA3 .209 D1
Kew Gdns Leyland PR5 .76 B3
Penwortham PR1 .95 B5
Kew Gr FY5 .172 D1
Kew Rd Formby L37 .11 D1
Nelson BB9 .168 F2
Southport PR8 .34 B3
Kew Woods Prim Sch PR8 .34 F3
Key View BB3 .64 C5
Keynsham Gr BB12 .126 D7
Khyber St BB8 .169 C4
Kibble Cres BB10 .147 C3
Kibble Gr BB9 .147 D4
Kibboth Crew BL0 .49 B7
Kidbrooke Ave FY4 .109 B4
Kidder St BB2 .80 D8
Kiddlington Cl PR5 .76 D8
Kiddrow La BB12 .126 A7
Kidsgrove PR2 .115 F5
Kielder Ct 3 FY8 .90 C4
Kielder Dr BB12 .126 E7
Kilbane St FY7 .193 F1
Kilburn Rd WN5 .10 C5
Kilcrash La PR3 .177 D7
Kildale Cl L31 .5 C2
Kildare Ave FY5 .173 A4
Kildare Rd FY2 .150 D3
Kilgrimol Gdns FY8 .109 C1
Kilkerran Cl PR6 .42 D8
Killer St 1 BL0 .49 C6
Killiard La BB2 .99 E5
Killingbeck Cl L40 .24 D4
Killington St BB10 .147 C2
Killingworth Mews BL6 .31 D1
Killon St BL9 .32 A1
Kilmory Pl FY2 .150 F5
Kilmuir Cl PR2 .117 C5
Kiln Bank OL12 .70 C2
Kiln Bank La OL12 .70 C2
Kiln Cl BB7 .187 A2
Kiln Croft PR6 .77 B3
Kiln Hill BB12 .145 F6
Kiln House Way BB5 .103 A3
Kiln La Hambleton FY6 .174 B2
Paythorne BB7 .225 C6
Rimington BB7 .224 F2
Skelmersdale WN8 .17 E1
Wray LA2 .232 D6
Kiln St Nelson BB9 .147 D8
Ramsbottom BL0 .49 B5
Kiln Terr 5 OL13 .69 D8
Kiln Wlk OL12 .51 E2
Kilnbank Ave LA4 .212 D5
Kilngate PR5 .96 C3
Kilnhouse La FY8 .110 A1
Kilns The BB11 .127 B3
Kilruddery Rd PR1 .95 E5
Kilsby Cl PR5 .96 E3
Kilworth Ht PR2 .116 C5
Kimberley Ave FY4 .109 D5
Kimberley Cl BB10 .147 F3
Kimberley Rd PR2 .116 C2
Kimberley St Bacup OL13 .69 A7
Brierfield BB10 .147 F3
Coppull PR7 .41 E1
Kimberly Cl PR4 .92 B6
Kimble Cl BL8 .48 F2
Kime St BB12 .126 C6
Kincardine Ave 7 FY4 .110 A6
Kincraig Pl FY2 .150 F6
Kincraig Prim Sch FY2 .150 F6
Kincraig Rd FY2 .150 F5
Kindonan Ave 6 FY4 .110 A6
King Edward Ave
Blackpool FY2 .150 B1
Lytham St Anne's FY8 .89 A4
King Edward St BB5 .102 C3
King Edward Terr BB9 .168 D2
King Edward VII & Queen Mary Jun Sch FY8 .89 A4
King Edward VII Sch FY8 .89 B4
King George Ave FY2 .150 B1
King George V Coll PR8 .34 E5
King La BB7 .164 E8
King St Accrington BB5 .103 B6
5 Bacup OL13 .86 F2
6 Bamber Bridge PR5 .76 B7
Barnoldswick BB18 .200 B2
Blackburn BB2 .100 D4
Blackpool FY1 .129 C5
Brierfield BB9 .147 A5
Brierfield, Harle Syke BB10 .147 F3
Carnforth LA5 .217 D1
Chorley PR7 .42 D6
4 Clayton-le-M BB5 .123 F2
Clitheroe BB7 .164 E8
Colne BB8 .169 E5
Fleetwood FY7 .194 A4
14 Great Harwood BB6 .123 C5
Haslingden BB4 .84 B4
High Bentham LA2 .233 D8
Horwich BL6 .31 A4
Lancaster LA1 .210 F8
Leyland PR5 .76 A1
Longridge PR3 .139 B7
Morecambe LA4 .212 E5
Padiham BB12 .125 C8
Ramsbottom BL0 .49 C6
Rawtenstall BB4 .68 E8
Southport PR8 .34 A6
Whalley BB7 .143 C5
Whitworth OL12 .70 D3
King Street Terr BB9 .147 A5
King William St BB1 .100 E5
King's Bridge Cl BB2 .100 B1
King's Bridge St BB2 .100 B1
King's Cl FY6 .151 E3
King's Cres LA3 .212 B3
King's Croft PR5 .96 D5
King's Cswy BB9 .147 E5
King's Dr LA5 .217 E1
King's Highway
Accrington BB5 .104 B2
Huncoat BB5 .103 F8
King's Rd Accrington BB5 .103 B7
Blackburn BB2 .100 B1
Lytham St Anne's FY8 .88 E5
King's Sq FY1 .129 C5
King's Wlk FY5 .172 D5
Kingfisher Bank BB11 .126 C4
Kingfisher Cl BB1 .100 E8
Kingfisher Ct Maghull L31 .5 B4
Oswaldtwistle BB5 .102 E3
Southport PR9 .34 D8
Kingfisher Dr Bury BL9 .32 B4
Poulton-le-F FY6 .151 B2
Kingfisher Mews FY6 .151 B2
Kingfisher Pk WN8 .18 C4
Kingfisher St PR1 .117 B1
Kings Arms Cl 33 LA1 .210 F8
Kings Ave BB4 .85 A1
Kings Cl Arnside LA5 .237 B1
Formby L37 .11 E2
Kings Cres PR5 .76 A1
Kings Ct PR5 .76 A1
Kings Dr Fulwood PR2 .116 D5
Hoddlesden BB3 .81 F1
Padiham BB12 .125 E6
Kings Hey Dr PR9 .52 F1
Kings Mdw PR8 .20 D3
Kings Rd Cleveleys FY5 .172 C2
Formby L37 .11 E2
Kingsacre PR3 .178 A3
Kingsbridge Cl PR1 .95 E2
Kingsbridge Wharfe BB2 .100 B1
Kingsbury Cl PR8 .20 B4
Kingsbury Ct WN8 .18 C4
Kingsbury Pl BB10 .147 D3
Kingsbury Sch L39 .15 E5
Kingscote Dr FY3 .129 E7
Kingsdale Ave
Brierfield BB10 .147 C3
Fulwood PR2 .117 D5
Morecambe LA3 .212 B1
Kingsdale Cl Leyland PR5 .59 B6
Walton-le-D PR5 .96 F5
Kingsdale Rd LA1 .210 D7
Kingsfold Christian Sch PR4 .72 F2
Kingsfold Dr PR1 .95 D2
Kingsfold Prim Sch PR1 .95 D2
Kingshaven Dr PR1 .95 E2
Kingshotte Gdns BB9 .168 C3
Kingsland Gr
Blackpool FY1 .129 D3
13 Burnley BB11 .127 B4
Kingsland Rd BB11 .127 B4
Kingslea PR7 .29 F8
Kingsley Ave BB12 .125 E7
Kingsley Cl Church BB5 .102 F7
Maghull L31 .5 C5
Thornton FY5 .173 A3
Kingsley Dr PR7 .42 A5
Kingsley Rd Blackpool FY3 .130 B2
Cottam PR4 .115 F6
Kingsley St BB9 .168 F2
Kingsmead Blackburn BB1 .101 D4
Chorley PR7 .42 C5
Kingsmede FY4 .109 E6
Kingsmere Ave FY8 .109 F1
Kingsmill Ave BB7 .143 A8
Kingsmuir Ave PR2 .117 D4
Kingsmuir Cl LA3 .208 E7
Kingston Ave
Accrington BB5 .103 A4
Blackpool FY4 .109 C5
Kingston Cl FY6 .194 F6
Kingston Cres
Haslingden BB4 .67 A7
Southport PR9 .53 C5
Kingston Dr FY8 .89 D6
Kingston Mews 3 FY5 .173 B3
Kingston Pl BB3 .80 F7
Kingsway Accrington BB5 .103 A8
Bamber Bridge PR5 .76 E8
Blackburn BB3 .81 A7
Blackpool FY4 .109 C7
Burnley BB11 .127 A6
Cleveleys FY5 .172 C2
Euxton PR7 .59 E2
Great Harwood BB6 .123 F6
Hapton BB11 .125 C3
Heysham LA3 .209 A8
Huncoat BB5 .124 F1
Lancaster LA1 .214 A1
Leyland PR5 .58 E7
2 Lytham St Anne's FY8 .89 C4
Penwortham PR1 .95 B6
Preston PR2 .115 F2
Southport PR8 .34 A7
Kingsway Ave PR3 .136 C3
Kingsway Ct
Broughton PR3 .136 C3
Lytham St Anne's FY8 .89 C4
Morecambe LA3 .212 B1
Kingsway Sports Ctr LA1 .214 A1
Kingsway W PR1 .95 B6
Kingswood Cl FY8 .89 E4
Kingswood Rd PR5 .76 A2
Kingswood St 6 PR1 .95 E7
Kinloch Way L39 .15 D6
Kinnerton Pl FY5 .150 F8
Kinross Cl BB1 .101 A4
Kinross Cres FY4 .130 A1
Kinross St BB11 .126 D4
Kinross Wlk 7 BB1 .101 A4
Kintbury Rd FY8 .88 F4
Kintour Rd FY8 .89 E6
Kintyre Cl FY4 .109 F7
Kintyre Way LA3 .208 E7
Kipling Dr FY3 .130 B2
Kipling Pl BB6 .123 B4
Kirby Dr PR4 .92 B6
Kirby Rd Blackburn BB2 .100 D1
Blackpool FY1 .129 B2
Nelson BB9 .147 B8

Kirk Ave BB7 164 C8
Kirk Head PR4 73 E2
Kirk Hill Rd BB4 84 C3
Kirk House BB5 102 E6
Kirk Rd BB5 102 E7
Kirk View BB4 86 A1
Kirkbeck Cl LA2 231 D3
Kirkby Ave
Clayton-le-W PR5 76 E1
Cleveleys FY5 172 E4
Kirkby Bank Rd L33 1 C2
Kirkby Lonsdale Rd LA2 214 F7
Kirkby Lonsdale Rd
Caton LA2,LA6 231 B6
Over Kellet LA6 234 B1
Kirkdale Ave
Lytham St Anne's FY8 88 F7
Newchurch BB4 85 E1
Kirkdale Cl BB3 64 C6
Kirkdale Gdns WN8 10 A7
Kirkdale Rd BB6 122 C8
Kirkdene Ave BB8 191 D1
Kirkdene Mews BB8 191 D1
Kirkes Rd LA1 211 A7
Kirkfell Dr BB12 126 C8
Kirkfield PR3 182 D3
Kirkgate Burnley BB11 127 B4
Kirkham PR4 113 B4
Kirkgate La LA6 234 B4
Kirkham & Wesham Cty Prim Sch PR4 112 F5
Kirkham & Wesham Sta PR4 112 F6
Kirkham Ave FY1 129 E2
Kirkham By-Pass PR4 113 B4
Kirkham Cl PR5 75 D1
Kirkham Gram Jun Sch PR4 112 F4
Kirkham Gram Sch PR4 112 F5
Kirkham Rd Freckleton PR4 92 B8
Kirkham PR4 113 E6
Kirkham, Freckleton PR4 113 A2
Southport PR9 53 A4
Weeton PR4 131 F2
Kirkham St PR1 95 E8
Kirkham Trad Pk PR4 113 B4
Kirkhill Ave BB4 84 C3
Kirklake Bank L37 11 C2
Kirklake Rd L37 11 D2
Kirkland & Catterall St Helen's CE Prim Sch PR3 178 A2
Kirkland Pl PR2 94 E8
Kirklands Chipping PR3 182 E3
Hest Bank LA2 215 E1
Kirklands Rd LA6 231 B8
Kirklees Rd PR8 33 F1
Kirkmoor Cl BB7 186 D1
Kirkmoor Rd BB7 164 E8
Kirkstall Ave
Blackpool FY1 129 E2
Read BB12 144 D1
Kirkstall Cl PR7 42 D5
Kirkstall Dr
Barnoldswick BB18 200 D3
Chorley PR7 42 D5
Formby L37 12 B2
Kirkstall Rd Chorley PR7 42 D5
Southport PR8 33 F2
Kirkstone Ave
Blackburn BB2 79 E8
Fleetwood FY7 193 D1
Kirkstone Dr
Blackpool FY5 150 C7
Morecambe LA4 212 G5
Kirkstone Rd FY8 109 D1
Kirton Cres FY8 89 C6
Kirton Pl FY5 172 E1
Kit Brow La LA2 207 D6
Kittiwake Cl 13 FY5 172 F1
Kittiwake Rd PR6 61 A3
Kittlingborne Brow PR5 97 A3
Kitty La FY4 110 B4
Kittygill La LA6 238 A1
Knacks La OL12 51 A5
Knaresboro Ave FY3 129 F3
Knaresborough Cl FY6 151 D5
Knebworth Cl PR6 77 C2
Knight Cres BB3 81 A6
Knighton Ave BB2 100 C8
Knights Cl FY5 172 F1
Knightsbrdige Cl PR4 112 E6
Knightsbridge Ave
Blackpool FY4 109 D6
Colne BB8 169 B5
Knightsbridge Cl
Kirkham PR4 112 E6
2 Lytham St Anne's FY8 89 D6
Knightscliffe Cres WN6 19 D6
Knitting Row La PR3 175 A3
Knob Hall Gdns PR9 52 F3
Knob Hall La PR9 52 F3
Knoll La PR4 74 A4
Knoll The LA2 213 E8
Knot Acre PR4 75 A8
Knot La
Newsholme BB7,BD23 225 D5
Walton-le-D PR5 96 F5
Knott Hill St OL12 70 E6
Knott La LA5 218 A8
Knott St BB3 81 A1
Knotts Brow BL7 47 F4
Knotts Dr BB8 169 C3
Knotts La
Bolton-by-B BB7,BD23 224 B8
Colne BB8 169 D3
Padiham BB12 125 E6
Knotts Mount BB8 169 C3
Knowe Hill Cres LA1 211 B3
Knowl Cl BL0 49 C4
Knowl Gap Ave BB4 84 A1
Knowl Mdw BB4 67 A6
Knowle Ave Blackpool FY2 150 C1
Cleveleys FY5 172 E2
Southport PR8 20 C6
Knowle La BB3 81 A3
Knowle The FY2 150 C2
Knowles Brow BB7 163 B3
Knowles Rd FY8 88 E7
Knowles St 1 Chorley PR7 42 C6
Preston PR1 96 D8
Rishton BB1 123 B1
Knowlesly Mdws BB3 64 C6
Knowlesly Rd BB3 64 B6
Knowley Brow PR6 60 E2
Knowlmere St BB5 103 B7
Knowlys Ave LA3 208 F8
Knowlys Cres 4 LA3 208 F8
Knowlys Dr 3 LA3 208 F8
Knowlys Gr LA3 208 F8
Knowlys Rd LA3 208 E8
Knowsley Ave
Blackpool FY3 129 E3
Leyland PR5 76 C4
Knowsley Cl
Gregson Lane PR5 97 F2
Lancaster LA1 210 D6
Knowsley Cres
Thornton FY5 173 C2
Weeton PR4 131 E2
Whitworth OL12 70 E6
Knowsley Dr PR5 97 F2
Knowsley Gate FY7 193 D4
Knowsley Gr BL6 31 D1
Knowsley Ind Pk L33 1 C2
Knowsley La Edgworth BL7 65 E4
Rivington PR6 43 E4
Knowsley Park Way BB4 67 B8
Knowsley Rd
Haslingden BB4 67 B8
Leyland PR5 59 C8
Ormskirk L39 15 F5
Southport PR9 52 C1
Wilpshire BB1 121 F5
Knowsley Rd Ind Est BB4 67 B8
Knowsley Rd W BB1 121 E5
Knowsley Road Ind Est BB4 84 B1
Knowsley St 3 Colne BB8 169 D4
32 Preston PR1 96 A7
Knox Gr FY1 129 D3
Knunk Knowles Dr BB7 186 E1
Knutsford Rd FY3 130 B2
Knutsford Wlk L31 5 D4
Knuzden Brook BB1 101 D4
Korea Rd PR2 117 B4
Kumara Cres FY4 130 B1
Kyan St BB10 147 B2
Kylemore Ave FY2 150 D3
Kyston Cl 1 FY1 129 D7

L

Laburnam Cotts PR3 196 E5
Laburnum Ave
Bamber Bridge PR5 76 B8
Lytham St Anne's FY8 90 B5
Laburnum Cl
Burnley BB11 126 D3
Fulwood PR1 117 C3
Laburnum Dr
Fulwood PR2 116 D8
Oswaldtwistle BB5 102 F3
Skelmersdale WN8 17 D1
Laburnum Gr
Burscough Bridge L40 24 E6
Horwich BL6 31 E1
Lancaster LA1 210 D8
Maghull L31 5 F1
Southport PR8 34 F7
Laburnum Pk LA5 216 C8
Laburnum Rd
Blackburn BB1 101 A8
Chorley PR6 60 D3
Haslingden BB4 67 A7
2 Lancaster LA1 213 F2
Laburnum St
6 Blackpool FY3 129 D7
Haslingden BB4 84 A3
Lacey Ct 19 BB4 84 B3
Lachman Rd BB8 170 B3
Lacy Ave PR1 95 E2
Ladbrooke Gr BB11 126 E2
Ladbury Ave FY8 89 B5
Lade End LA3 208 E8
Ladies Row PR4 133 F4
Ladies Wlk LA1 214 A2
Lady Alice's Dr L40 16 E8
Lady Anne Cl L40 23 B7
Lady Crosse Dr PR6 60 C7
Lady Green Cl L38 3 E3
Lady Green La L38 3 D4
Lady Hey Cres PR2 115 C1
Lady Pl PR5 96 E4
Lady St PR1 95 F8
Lady Well Dr PR2 117 C7
Lady's Wlk L40 16 C6
Ladybower La FY6 151 B3
Ladyman St 8 PR1 95 E7
Ladysmith Ave BL9 32 A5
Ladysmith Rd PR2 116 C2
Ladywell St PR1 95 E8
Lafford La WN8 19 C2
Lagonda Dr FY4 110 F6
Lagonda Way FY4 110 F6
Laidley's Wlk FY7 193 E5
Lairgill Row 8 LA2 233 D8
Laister Ct 6 LA4 213 A6
Laithbutts La LA6 216 F5
Laithe St Burnley BB11 126 F4
Colne BB8 169 C4
Lake Ave LA4 212 C4
Lake Gr LA4 212 C4
Lake Point FY8 89 D3
Lake Rd
Lytham St Anne's FY8 89 C4
Morecambe LA3 212 C3
Lake Rd N FY8 89 C4
Lake Side Cotts WN1 29 C1
Lake View BL7 45 C5
Lake View Rd BB8 169 D7
Lakeber Ave LA2 233 D8
Lakeber Cl 12 LA2 233 D8
Lakeber Dr 11 LA2 233 D8
Lakeland Cl Billington BB7 143 A3
Forton PR3 204 B3
Lakeland Gdns PR7 42 A5
Lakeland Way BB12 126 B8
Lakes Dr WN5 10 E6
Lakeside Ave WN5 10 E3
Lakeview Ct PR9 34 B8
Lakeway FY3 129 F6
Lakewood Ave FY5 172 D1
Lamaleach Dr PR4 92 A6
Lamb Row BB7 144 E7
Lamb's La PR3 196 A4
Lambert Cl PR2 117 E3
Lambert Rd Fulwood PR2 117 E3
Lancaster LA1 213 E3
Lambert St BB8 170 C2
Lambeth Cl Blackburn BB1 101 A4
Horwich BL6 31 D3
Lambeth Ct PR2 116 E5
Lambeth St Blackburn BB1 101 A4
Blackburn BB1 101 B4
Colne BB8 170 B5
Lambing Clough La BB7 141 E7
Lambourne WN8 18 B4
Lambridge Cl LA4 212 E3
Lambs Hill Cl 6 FY5 173 D1
Lambs Rd FY5 151 D8
Lambshear La L31 5 C4
Lambton Gates BB4 85 C2
Lamlash Rd BB1 101 D4
Lammack Prim Sch BB1 121 C1
Lammack Rd
Blackburn BB1 100 C8
Blackburn BB1 100 D8
Lamour Pl FY7 193 D3
Lanark Ave FY2 150 C6
Lanark Cl OL10 32 F1
Lanark St BB11 126 D4
Lancambe Ct LA1 213 C2
Lancashire Coll PR7 42 A8
Lancashire Constabulary HQ PR4 94 E1
Lancashire Rd PR5 76 A4
Lancashire St LA4 212 B4
Lancaster & Lakeland Nuffield Hospl The LA1 211 A7
Lancaster & Morecambe Coll LA1 213 B3
Lancaster & Morecambe Coll (Annexe) LA4 212 E5
Lancaster Ave
Accrington BB5 103 B7
Clayton-le-W PR5 76 E1
Great Eccleston PR3 154 C5
Haslingden BB4 67 B8
Horwich BL6 31 D2
Lytham St Anne's FY8 88 F4
Ramsbottom BL0 49 A4
Thornton FY5 173 C2
Lancaster Castle LA1 210 E8
Lancaster Cl Adlington PR6 30 B7
Great Eccleston PR3 154 C5
Knott End-on-S FY6 194 F5
Maghull L31 5 F1
Southport PR8 33 E4
Lancaster Cres WN8 17 E1
Lancaster Ct PR7 60 C2
Lancaster Dr Banks PR9 53 F5
Brinscall PR6 61 E8
Clayton-le-M BB5 124 A3
Clitheroe BB7 164 C7
Padiham BB12 125 D6
Lancaster Gate Banks PR9 53 F5
Fleetwood FY7 193 D4
14 Lancaster LA1 210 F8
Nelson BB9 147 D7
Lancaster Gdns PR8 33 E4
Lancaster Girls' Gram Sch LA1 210 E7
Lancaster Ho 23 PR1 96 A7
Lancaster L Pk LA1 211 B6
Lancaster La
Clayton-le-W PR5 76 E2
Parbold WN8 26 C3
Lancaster Lane Prim Sch PR5 76 D1
Lancaster Maritime Mus LA1 213 E1
Lancaster Moor Hospl LA1 211 D8
Lancaster Pl Adlington PR6 30 A8
Blackburn BB2 100 B5
Lancaster Rd
Blackpool FY3 130 A3
Carnforth LA5 216 B7
Caton LA2 231 B3
Cockerham LA2 203 C6
Fisher's Row PR3 196 E5
Lancaster Rd continued
Formby L37 11 E1
Garstang PR3 199 C1
Hornby LA2 232 B7
Knott End-on-S FY6 194 F5
Lancaster LA3 209 D3
Lancaster, Slyne LA2 213 F6
Morecambe LA4 212 F5
Morecambe, Torrisholme LA4 213 B4
Moss Edge PR3 175 E6
Preesall FY6 195 C3
Preston PR1 95 F8
Preston PR1 96 A8
Ratten Row PR3 154 A8
Southport PR8 33 E4
Lancaster Rd N PR1 116 F1
Lancaster Road Prim Sch LA4 212 G4
Lancaster Royal Gram Sch LA1 211 A8
Lancaster Royal Gram Sch LA1 211 B7
Lancaster St
Blackburn BB2 100 C4
Colne BB8 169 D5
Coppull PR7 41 F1
Oswaldtwistle BB5 102 C3
Lancaster Way 15 PR1 96 A8
Lancastergate PR5 58 F8
Lancester Ct PR5 58 D6
Lanchester Gdns BB6 142 C6
Lancia Cres FY4 111 A6
Lancing Pl BB2 100 C3
Land End L31 6 C1
Land Gate OL12 70 F5
Land La New Longton PR4 74 D5
Southport PR9 53 D4
Landcrest Cl PR4 113 B2
Landing La BB7 223 F4
Landless St BB9 147 A5
Landseer Ave FY2 150 C4
Landseer Cl BB11 126 E3
Landseer St PR1 117 C1
Landsmoor Dr PR4 94 A1
Lane Bottom BB18 191 B8
Lane End La OL13 87 A1
Lane End Rd OL13 70 A8
Lane Ends Brierfield BB9 147 D6
Dunsop Bridge BB7 222 C5
Longridge PR3 139 F8
Rivington PR6 43 D4
Lane Ends Ct 2 FY4 129 E1
Lane Foot Brow LA2 233 D4
Lane Head LA2 232 D6
Lane Head La OL13 86 F3
Lane House BB8 170 C1
Lane House Cl BB2 80 B8
Lane Side OL13 87 A4
Lane The LA3 205 A5
Lane Top Colne BB8 170 C5
Fence BB12 146 D7
Lanedale PR4 74 A8
Lanefield Dr FY5 172 C4
Laneshaw Cl BB3 80 E4
Laneshawbridge Prim Sch BB8 170 E6
Laneside Altham BB5 124 D6
Great Harwood BB6 123 A6
Laneside Ave
Accrington BB5 103 B8
Higham BB12 145 F6
Laneside Ho 5 BB4 84 B2
Laneside Rd BB4 84 C1
Lang St Accrington BB5 103 A6
Blackpool FY1 129 C6
Lang Woods BB6 142 C5
Langber End La LA6 236 F1
Langcliffe Rd PR2 117 E4
Langdale LA2 231 C3
Langdale Ave
Clitheroe BB7 164 C7
Croston PR5 57 B3
Formby L37 11 D2
Hesketh Bank PR4 72 D4
Rawtenstall BB4 84 E2
Langdale Cl
3 Accrington BB5 124 D1
Bamber Bridge PR5 96 D1
Blackburn BB2 79 E8
Formby L37 11 D2
Freckleton PR4 92 A6
Thornton FY5 173 B2
Langdale Cres PR2 117 E3
Langdale Crest LA7 237 E5
Langdale Ct
3 Fleetwood FY7 193 E2
Garstang PR3 178 B7
Penwortham PR1 95 C4
Langdale Dr Burscough L40 24 E4
Maghull L31 5 E2
Langdale Gdns PR8 33 F1
Langdale Gr PR6 60 B7
Langdale Pl 1
Blackpool FY4 130 C1
Lancaster LA1 214 A2
Langdale Rd
Blackburn BB2 79 E8
Blackpool FY4 130 C1
Carnforth LA5 216 E8
Fulwood PR2 117 E3
Lancaster LA1 214 A2
Leyland PR5 59 B6
Longridge PR3 138 F5
Lytham St Anne's FY8 109 D1
Morecambe LA4 212 G5
Padiham BB12 145 C2
Langdale Rise BB8 169 F6
Langden Brook Mews LA3 213 B2
Langden Brook Sq BB1 101 A3
Langden Cres PR5 76 F8
Langden Dr PR2 118 A3
Langden Fold PR2 138 D1
Langdon Way FY2 150 E2
Langfield BB10 128 B6
Langfield Ave FY4 109 C5
Langfield Cl PR2 116 F8
Langford St BB5 103 E1
Langham Ave BB5 103 B8
Langham Rd
Blackburn BB1 100 D7
Standish WN6 28 D1
Langham St BB12 126 B6
Langho St BB2 100 C1
Langho Sta BB6 142 C1
Langholm Cl 6 PR5 75 D1
Langholme Cl BB9 168 C1
Langholme Rd PR1 95 B4
Langholme St BB9 147 E6
Langholme Way OL10 32 F1
Langley Cl Hightown L38 2 F2
Standish WN6 28 E2
Langley Ct L40 24 B5
Langley La Goosnargh PR3 136 F6
Inglewhite PR3 158 B2
Langley Pl L40 24 B4
Langley Rd Burscough L40 24 B4
Lancaster LA1 211 A7
Langport Cl PR2 116 F8
Langridge Way LA4 212 E3
Langroyd Rd BB8 169 E6
Langsford Cl BB18 200 C2
Langshaw Dr BB7 164 F6
Langshaw La LA2 207 D5
Langstone Cl BL6 31 B3
Langthwaite Rd LA1,LA2 211 E5
Langton Ave WN6 28 E1
Langton Brow
Eccleston PR7 40 D5
Longridge PR3 139 B7
Langton Cl Eccleston PR7 40 D5
Lancaster LA1 214 A4
Leyland PR5 58 C8
Langton Pl WN6 28 E1
Langton Rd PR4 113 A5
Langton St PR1 95 D7
Langtree WN8 18 B3
Langtree La Elswick PR4 153 F2
Standish WN6 28 D3
Langwood FY7 193 E2
Langwood La WA11 9 C1
Langwyth Rd BB10 127 E5
Lansborough Cl PR5 58 B8
Lansbury Pl 1 BB9 168 F2
Lansdown Hill PR2 116 C7
Lansdown Rd PR4 113 A7
Lansdowne Cl BB11 126 F4
Lansdowne Gr LA4 213 A7
Lansdowne Pl 1 FY1 129 B6
Lansdowne Rd
Burnley BB11 126 E4
Lytham St Anne's FY8 89 D5
Morecambe LA4 213 A7
Southport PR8 34 E6
Lansdowne St BB2 100 B3
Lansil Ind Est LA1 214 A3
Lansil Way LA1 214 A3
Lanterns The FY6 151 D4
Lapford Cres L33 1 A4
Lapford Wlk L33 1 A4
Lappet Gr PR4 115 E5
Lapwings The FY6 151 B2
Larbreck Ave PR4 154 A1
Larbreck Rd FY3 129 E7
Larch Ave Chorley PR6 60 E2
Oswaldtwistle BB5 102 F3
Larch Cl Blackburn BB2 79 F8
Freckleton PR4 92 A5
Knott End-on-S FY6 195 A5
Rawtenstall BB4 67 F8
Skelmersdale WN8 17 E1
Larch Dr PR6 61 F7
Larch Gate PR5 97 E2
Larch Gr Bamber Bridge PR5 96 F1
Garstang PR3 178 C8
Lancaster LA1 210 D8
Larch St Blackburn BB1 101 A7
Burnley BB12 126 C7
Bury BL9 32 B2
Nelson BB9 147 F8
Southport PR8 34 E6
Larch Way L37 11 D4
Larches Ave PR2 115 F1
Larches La PR2 115 E1
Larches The BB1 100 F7
Larchgate PR2 117 C7
Larchway PR3 139 B8
Larchwood Lancaster LA1 211 B4
Penwortham PR1 95 B4
Preston PR2 115 E1
Larchwood Cl FY8 89 F4
Larchwood Cres PR5 75 E1
Largs Rd BB1 101 C3
Lark Ave 3 PR1 95 E4
Lark Ct FY7 193 D1
Lark Hill Blackburn BB1 100 F6
Higher Walton PR5 97 B3
Rawtenstall BB4 85 A3
Lark Hill Pl OL12 51 E1
Lark St 4 Burnley BB12 126 C7
Colne BB8 169 E6
Darwen BB3 64 B5

Larkfield PR7 40 B6
Larkfield Cl BL8 48 F1
Larkfield Ct PR9 53 A3
Larkfield La PR9 53 A3
Larkfield Prim Sch PR9 53 A3
Larkhill
Brockhall Village BB6 142 C5
Skelmersdale WN8 18 B4
Larkhill Ave BB10 147 C5
Larkhill Gr L38 2 F3
Larkhill La L37 11 C4
Larkhill Rd PR1 96 B7
Larkhill St Blackpool FY1 129 C6
Preston PR1 96 B7
Larkholme Ave FY7 193 E1
Larkholme Cty Prim Sch
FY7 172 D8
Larkholme La FY7 193 E1
Larkholme Par FY7 193 D1
Larkspur Cl Blackburn BB2 79 D8
3 Southport PR8 34 D6
Last Drop Village The BL7 47 A1
Latham Ave
8 Blackpool FY3 129 E3
Ormskirk L39 16 A5
Latham Cres PR4 56 A6
Latham Rd BL6 30 C3
Latham St Burnley BB10 147 B1
Preston PR1 96 A6
Lathom Ave
Morecambe LA4 212 G4
Parbold WN8 26 B3
Lathom Cl L40 24 E4
Lathom Dr L31 5 E3
Lathom Gr LA4 212 G4
Lathom High Sch WN8 17 F3
Lathom La L40 16 C7
Lathom Rd Bickerstaffe L39 7 F8
Southport PR9 52 C1
Lathom St 8 BL9 32 A4
Lathom St James CE Sch
L40 16 E4
Lathom Way PR3 178 D6
Latimer Cl 2 WN5 10 F7
Latimer Dr PR4 74 F7
Lauderdale Ave FY5 172 D1
Lauderdale Cres 1 PR2 117 F4
Lauderdale Rd PR2 117 F4
Lauderdale St PR1 95 E6
Laund Gate BB12 146 D8
Laund Gr BB5 103 D3
Laund Hey View BB4 84 B1
Laund La Haslingden BB4 84 C3
Ollerton Fold PR6 78 E4
Laund Rd BB5 103 D3
Laund St BB4 84 F4
Laund The PR5 75 A1
Laundry Rd N FY4 110 A5
Laura St BL0 49 C2
Laurel Ave Blackpool FY1 129 E2
Burscough Bridge L40 24 E6
Darwen BB3 81 B2
Euxton PR7 59 B3
Fleetwood FY7 172 F8
Lytham St Anne's FY8 90 B5
Laurel Bank LA1 210 D7
Laurel Bank Ave PR2 116 C3
Laurel Dr
Skelmersdale WN8 17 E2
Thornton FY5 151 B8
Laurel Gr PR8 34 E7
Laurel St 4 Bacup OL13 86 F3
Burnley BB11 127 B4
3 Bury BL9 32 B2
10 Preston PR1 96 A7
Laurels The PR7 41 F3
Laureston Ave LA3 208 F6
Laurie Pl 2 OL12 51 F1
Laurier Ave 3 FY4 109 C6
Laurier Rd BB10 147 B2
Lauriston Cl 4 FY4 110 A6
Lavender Cl PR2 117 C6
Lavender Gr PR7 42 C5
Lavender Hill BB4 67 F8
Laverick Rd LA2 231 A5
Laverton Cl OL10 32 E1
Laverton Rd FY8 89 A4
Law St Cornholme OL14 108 B1
Newchurch BB4 85 F1
Lawley Rd BB2 100 A5
Lawn Ct 2 FY1 129 D4
Lawn St BB10 127 A8
Lawn Tennis Ct FY4 109 D5
Lawns Ave WN5 10 C5
Lawns The PR9 52 F2
Lawnswood Ave
Lancaster LA1 211 A3
Poulton-le-F FY6 151 C2
Lawnswood Cres FY3 130 C2
Lawnswood Dr LA3 212 F2
Lawnwood Ave PR7 42 A5
Lawrence Ave
Bamber Bridge PR5 96 D2
Burnley BB11 126 C4
Burnley BB11 126 C5
Lytham St Anne's FY8 89 A6
Preston PR1 96 B5
Simonstone BB12 144 E2
Lawrence Cl OL12 51 A1
Lawrence Dr LA5 237 A1
Lawrence La PR7 40 C7
Lawrence Rd
Chorley PR7 42 B7
Penwortham PR1 95 B5
Lawrence Row FY7 194 A4
Lawrence St
Blackburn BB2 100 C4
12 Blackpool FY4 129 B1
Fulwood PR2 116 D3
Padiham BB12 145 D1
Whitewell Bottom BB4 85 F4
Lawrie Ave BL0 49 B5
Lawson Cl LA1 210 F3
Lawson Gdns LA2 213 E8
Lawson Pl LA2 213 E8
Lawson Rd Blackpool FY3 130 A3
Horwich BL6 31 C4
Lytham St Anne's FY8 110 A2
Lawson St 3 Chorley PR6 42 E7
Preston PR1 95 F8
Rawtenstall BB4 85 A8
Southport PR9 35 A7
Lawsons Ct 4 FY5 173 C1
Lawsons Rd FY5 173 C2
Lawswood Formby L37 11 E5
6 Thornton FY5 173 C1
Lawton Cl PR6 78 B1
Laxey Gr PR1 117 D3
Laxey Rd BB2 100 E1
Laycock Gate FY3 129 D6
Layton Cty Prim Sch FY3 129 E8
Layton Rd Blackpool FY3 129 E6
Preston PR2 115 E1
Layton Sta FY2 150 E1
Lazenby Ave FY7 193 C2
Lea Bank BB4 85 D2
Lea Cres L39 15 F7
Lea Ct L39 15 E7
Lea Cty Prim Sch PR2 115 D1
Lea Dr BB2 80 E6
Lea Endowed CE Prim Sch
PR4 115 C4
Lea La
Claughton, Lancaster LA2 231 F8
Heysham LA3 208 E6
Lea Town PR4 115 B5
Lea Mount Dr BL9 32 D4
Lea Rd Lucas Green PR6 60 C5
Preston PR2,PR4 115 D3
Lea Way Cl FY5 151 D7
Leach Cres FY8 109 F2
Leach La FY8 109 E1
Leach Pl PR5 77 B8
Leach St Blackburn BB2 100 E2
Colne BB8 169 C4
Leaches Rd BL0 49 D8
Leachfield Cl 2 LA2 207 A4
Leachfield Ind Est PR3 199 B1
Leachfield Rd LA2 206 F4
Leacroft BB3 81 A6
Lead Mines Clough PR6 44 A7
Leadale PR2 115 D2
Leadale Cl WN6 28 D1
Leadale Gn PR5 75 E1
Leadale Rd PR5 75 E1
Leaford Ave FY3 129 E8
Leafy Cl PR5 59 B7
Leagram Cres PR2 118 A3
Leamington Ave
Baldingstone BL9 49 E1
Burnley BB10 147 C1
Southport PR8 20 D5
Leamington Rd
Blackburn BB2 100 B6
Blackpool FY1 129 D5
Lytham St Anne's FY8 88 F6
Morecambe LA4 212 G3
Southport PR8 20 D5
Leamington St BB9 147 E7
Leander Ave FY6 151 D2
Leapers View LA6 231 B8
Leaside Cl OL12 51 D2
Leathercote PR3 178 C6
Leathwood L31 5 E1
Leavengreave Ct OL12 70 D4
Leaver St BB12 126 A5
Leaverholme Cl BB10 107 A7
Leavesley Rd FY1 129 D8
Lebanon St BB10 127 C5
Leck CE Prim Sch LA6 236 B7
Leck Ho 11 LA1 211 A3
Leckhampton Rd FY1 129 B8
Leckonby St PR3 154 B5
Led Case Ct 5 PR5 96 D8
Ledburn WN8 18 B3
Ledbury Rd FY3 130 B7
Ledson Gr L39 6 B7
Lee Brook Cl BB4 85 A4
Lee Gr BB10 127 F4
Lee Green St 3 BB10 127 A8
Lee La Bispham Green L40 26 C7
Great Harwood BB1 123 B3
Horwich BL6 31 B4
Whittlestone Head BL7 65 B2
Lee Rd Bacup OL13 69 E8
Blackpool FY4 110 B8
Nelson BB9 168 F2
Lee St Accrington BB5 103 C6
Bacup OL13 86 F2
Barrowford BB9 168 D3
Longridge PR3 139 A7
Rawtenstall BB4 85 A4
Lee View OL13 87 B1
Lee's St OL13 70 C8
Leebrook Rd BB4 84 F4
Leeds Cl 15 BB1 101 A4
Leeds Rd Blackpool FY1 129 D5
2 Nelson BB9 147 E8
Nelson BB9 168 F1
Leehouse Dr FY6 130 D8
Leek St PR1 96 E8
Leeming La LA6 236 C3
Lees Cotts BL7 47 C2
Lees Ct LA3 208 E7
Lees La WN8 18 E7
Lees Rd Adlington PR6 30 B8
Kirkby L33 1 B2
Lees The BB10 107 A7
Leesands Cl PR2 117 E5
Leeson Ave PR7 41 D4
Leeswood WN8 18 B3
Leet Rd BB12 145 F5
Leeward Cl BB3 80 F6
Leeward Rd PR2 94 F8
Legh La PR4 55 B4
Leicester Ave
Cleveleys FY5 172 E3
Garstang PR3 178 B7
Horwich BL6 31 A3
Leicester Gate FY5 172 E3
Leicester Lodge 3 PR2 117 F4
Leicester Rd
Blackburn BB1 101 C5
Blackpool FY1 129 D5
Preston PR1 117 A1
Leicester St PR9 34 B8
Leigh Brow PR1 96 B2
Leigh Pk BB11 125 C3
Leigh Row PR7 42 C7
Leigh St PR7 42 C7
Leighton Ave
Fleetwood FY7 193 D3
Maghull L31 5 D2
Leighton Ct LA4 212 D3
Leighton Dr LA1 210 D7
Leighton Hall LA5 219 C1
Leighton Moss
(Nature Reserve) LA5 219 A3
Leighton St PR1 95 E8
Leinster Rd LA1 211 A5
Leith Ave FY5 172 D2
Lemon Tree Ct FY8 109 B4
Lemonius St BB5 103 C4
Lench Rd BB4 68 D8
Lench St BB4 68 F8
Lenches Fold BB8 169 D4
Lenches Rd BB8 169 D3
Lendel Cl L37 11 E3
Lennon St 3 PR7 42 C7
Lennox Ct FY4 109 D6
Lennox Gate FY4 109 D7
Lennox Rd OL14 108 A1
Lennox St
19 Preston PR1 96 A7
Worsthorne BB10 128 A6
Lennox Wlk OL10 32 F1
Lenton Ave L37 11 D4
Lentworth Ave FY2 150 D5
Lentworth Dr LA1 211 A4
Lentworth Ho 5 LA1 211 A3
Leonard St
Barnoldswick BB18 200 B2
Nelson BB9 147 E7
Leonard Terr BB3 81 E3
Leopold Gr FY1 129 B5
Leopold Rd BB2 100 B6
Leopold St BB8 169 B4
Leopold Way BB2 81 A8
Lesley Rd PR8 34 E7
Leslie Ave Caton LA2 231 C3
Thornton FY5 173 C2
Letchworth Dr PR7 42 B6
Letchworth Pl 2 PR7 42 B6
Letcliffe Ctry Pk BB18 191 B8
Lethbridge Rd PR8 34 D5
Letitia St BL6 31 A3
Levant St BB12 125 C7
Leven Ave FY7 193 D3
Leven Gr BB3 80 E4
Leven St BB11 127 B4
Levens Cl Banks PR9 54 A5
Blackburn BB2 80 F8
Lancaster LA1 210 D7
Poulton-le-F FY6 130 E8
Levens Ct LA3 212 B2
Levens Dr Clayton-le-W PR5 76 D2
Morecambe LA3 212 B2
Poulton-le-F FY6 151 D1
Levens Gr FY1 129 D3
Levens St 12 PR1 117 D1
Levens Way LA5 218 C3
Levensgarth Ave PR2 116 F8
Lever House La PR5 76 C2
Lever Park Ave BL6 31 B5
Lever Park Sch BL6 31 C3
Lever St Blackpool FY3 129 E4
Ramsbottom BL0 49 C6
Rawtenstall BB4 85 B2
Leverhouse Prim Sch PR5 76 C3
Levine Ave FY4 130 A1
Lewis Cl PR7 29 E6
Lewis Dr OL10 32 F1
Lewis St BB6 123 D5
Lewis Textile Mus BB1 100 E5
Lewtas St FY1 129 B6
Lewth La PR4 135 B5
Lex St PR1 96 C8
Lexton Dr PR9 53 B3
Ley Ct LA1 210 D8
Ley St BB5 103 E2
Leybourne Ave PR8 20 F2
Leyburn Ave
Blackpool FY2 150 C5
Fleetwood FY7 193 E2
Leyburn Cl Accrington BB5 103 E5
Fulwood PR2 117 E5
Leyburn Rd
Blackburn BB2 80 C7
Lancaster LA1 213 F3
Leycester Dr LA1 213 C3
Leyfield PR1 95 E2
Leyfield Cl FY3 151 A1
Leyfield Ct LA6 238 C1
Leyfield Rd PR5 58 F8
Leyland Cl Southport PR9 53 E5
Trawden BB8 170 B3
Leyland Golf Course PR5 59 D8
Leyland La Leyland PR5 58 D7
Leyland PR5 75 D2
Runshaw Moor PR5,PR7 58 D4
Leyland Meth Inf Sch PR5 76 B1
Leyland Meth Jun Sch
PR5 76 B1
Leyland Rd Burnley BB11 127 B6
Penwortham PR1 95 E3
Southport PR9 52 C1
Leyland St BB5 102 F5
Leyland Sta PR5 76 B2
Leyland Warden High Sch
PR5 75 E1
Leyland Way Leyland PR5 76 C1
Ormskirk L39 15 F5
Leylands The FY8 89 F2
Leys Cl Elswick PR4 154 A1
Wiswell BB7 143 F8
Leys Rd FY2 150 D1
Leyster St LA4 212 F5
Leyton Ave PR5 58 D7
Leyton St OL12 51 F2
Libby La PR3 196 C6
Library Mews FY4 109 E7
Library Rd PR6 77 B4
Library St Chorley PR7 42 C7
Church BB5 102 E6
16 Preston PR1 96 A7
Lichen Cl PR7 41 D4
Lichfield Ave LA4 212 G6
Lichfield Rd Blackpool FY1 129 C8
Chorley PR7 42 C6
Preston PR2 115 F2
Liddesdale Rd BB9 169 B2
Liddington Cl BB2 81 A8
Liddington Hall Dr BL0 49 B4
Lidget Ave PR2 115 C1
Lidum Park Ind Est FY8 90 E5
Liege Rd 5 PR5 59 A8
Lifeboat Pl 13 FY7 194 B5
Lifeboat Rd L37 11 B1
Lifton Rd L33 1 A2
Lightbown Ave FY3 129 E3
Lightbown Cotts BB3 80 E2
Lightbown St BB3 81 A3
Lightburne Ave FY8 88 F5
Lightfoot Cl PR2 116 D8
Lightfoot Green La PR4 116 B8
Lightfoot La PR2,PR4 116 B7
Lighthorne Dr PR8 20 A4
Lighthouse Cl 4 FY7 194 B5
Lighthurst Ave PR7 42 C6
Lighthurst La PR7 42 D5
Lightwood Ave
2 Blackpool FY4 129 C1
Lytham St Anne's FY8 89 D3
Lilac Ave 1 Blackpool FY1 129 D2
Haslingden BB4 84 B3
Lytham St Anne's FY8 90 B5
Penwortham PR1 95 F2
Southport PR8 20 D2
Lilac Cl PR4 91 D5
Lilac Cres PR4 133 F4
Lilac Gr Abbey Village PR6 79 C2
Clitheroe BB7 164 C7
Darwen BB3 81 B3
Fulwood PR1 117 C3
Skelmersdale WN8 17 E1
Lilac Rd BB1 101 A8
Lilac St BB8 169 F6
Lilac Terr 2 OL13 69 D8
Lilburn Cl BL0 49 C4
Lilford Cl PR4 56 A5
Lilford Rd BB1 100 D6
Lily Gr Fulwood PR1 117 C3
Lancaster LA1 211 A5
Lily St 16 Bacup OL13 86 F2
Blackpool FY1 129 C5
Darwen BB3 81 B1
Nelson BB9 147 F6
Lima Rd FY8 89 B6
Lima St BL9 32 B3
Limbrick 21 Blackburn BB1 100 E5
Blackburn BB1 100 E6
Limbrick Rd PR6 42 E7
Lime Ave Galgate LA2 207 A4
Kirkham PR4 113 B4
Oswaldtwistle BB5 102 D2
Lime Chase PR2 116 C8
Lime Cl PR1 95 B4
Lime Ct WN8 17 E1
Lime Gr Blackpool FY2 150 E2
Chorley PR7 42 C5
Garstang PR3 178 B8
Lancaster LA1 210 D8
Longridge PR3 139 A8
Lytham St Anne's FY8 88 D8
Poulton-le-F FY6 151 E2
Preston PR2 115 F2
Ramsbottom BL0 49 D7
Skelmersdale WN8 17 E1
Thornton FY5 173 C1
Lime Rd Accrington BB5 103 C7
Haslingden BB4 84 C3
Lime St Blackburn BB1 100 E6
Clitheroe BB7 186 F1
Colne BB8 169 E6
Great Harwood BB6 123 C6
Nelson BB9 147 C8
Southport PR8 34 E6
Lime Tree Gr BB4 85 A4
Lime Tree Way L37 11 C2
Limebrest Ave FY5 151 D8
Limechase Cl 9 FY4 110 A6
Limefield Ave
Brierfield BB9 147 C6
Whalley BB7 143 C6
Limefield Ct BB2 100 B5
Limefield Dr WN8 9 E7
Limefield St BB5 103 D5
Limerick Rd FY2 150 D3
Limers Gate Rochdale OL12 51 F5
Sharneyford OL14 87 E4
Limers La BB6 123 A6
Limes Ave Darwen BB3 64 A8
Euxton PR7 59 C4
Morecambe LA3 212 B3
Limestone Trail BB10 107 E6
Limewood Cl BB5 103 D6
Limey La BB11 105 E6
Limont Rd PR8 20 D5
Lina St BB5 102 F6
Linacre La L37 4 B7
Linadale Ave 4 FY5 173 B2
Linaker Dr L39 14 B8
Linaker Inf Sch PR8 34 B5
Linaker Prim Sch PR8 34 B5
Linaker St PR8 34 B5
Linby St BB10 127 B5
Lincoln Ave Cleveleys FY5 172 E3
Fleetwood FY7 193 E3
Lincoln Chase PR2 115 C1
Lincoln Cl Blackburn BB1 101 B4
Morecambe LA4 212 G3
Lincoln Ct Blackpool FY1 129 C4
1 Church BB5 103 A7
Lincoln Ho 7 PR1 96 B7
Lincoln Pk BB7 187 A1
Lincoln Pl BB4 84 A3
Lincoln Rd Blackburn BB1 101 B4
Blackpool FY1 129 C5
Earby BB18 201 B2
Lancaster LA1 210 E7
Southport PR8 34 A1
Lincoln St Burnley BB11 127 A4
Cornholme OL14 108 B1
3 Haslingden BB4 84 A3
Preston PR1 117 B1
Lincoln Way Clitheroe BB7 187 A2
Garstang PR3 178 B7
Lincoln Wlk PR1 117 B1
Lindadale Ave BB5 103 A3
Lindadale Cl BB5 103 A3
Lindale Ave PR2 138 E1
Lindale Cl LA5 237 B2
Lindale Cres BB10 147 A2
Lindale Gdns FY4 109 E6
Lindale Rd Fulwood PR2 117 A4
Longridge PR3 138 F5
Lindbeck Ct FY4 110 C8
Lindbeck Rd FY4 130 C1
Lindel La FY6 195 B2
Lindel Rd FY7 193 F2
Linden Ave Blackburn BB1 100 D6
Cleveleys FY5 172 F3
Orrell WN5 10 E6
Ramsbottom BL0 49 D6
Linden Cl
Bamber Bridge PR5 96 B1
Barrowford BB9 168 B1
Cleveleys FY5 172 F2
Edenfield BL0 67 D2
Linden Cres BB3 81 C2
Linden Ct 7 Earby BB18 201 B1
Orrell WN5 10 E6
Linden Dr
Bamber Bridge PR5 96 B1
Clitheroe BB7 164 F7
Linden Fold PR4 154 A1
Linden Gn FY5 172 F2
Linden Gr Chorley PR6 60 D3
Fulwood PR2 117 E3
Garstang PR3 178 C8
Orrell WN5 10 E6
Linden Lea Blackburn BB2 79 F8
Rawtenstall BB4 67 F8
Linden Mews FY8 109 F2
Linden Pl FY2 150 E3
Linden Rd Colne BB8 169 D5
Earby BB18 201 B1
Linden St BB10 127 B5
Linden Wlk WN5 10 E6
Lindens WN8 18 B4
Lindeth Cl
Nether Kellet LA6 216 F6
Silverdale LA5 218 C2
Lindeth Gdns 7 LA1 213 F3
Lindeth Rd LA5 218 C2
Lindholme WN8 18 C3
Lindisfarne Ave BB2 100 F1
Lindisfarne Cl BB12 126 E7
Lindle Ave PR4 94 E2
Lindle Cl PR4 94 E2
Lindle Cres PR4 94 E2
Lindle La PR4 95 A2
Lindley Ave WN5 10 C5
Lindley Dr WN8 26 C3
Lindley St
Bamber Bridge PR5 76 B8
Blackburn BB2 100 B2
Lindon Park Rd BB4 67 C7
Lindow Sq LA1 210 E7
Lindow St LA1 210 F7
Lindred Rd BB9 147 B7
Lindsay Ave Blackpool FY3 129 E3
Leyland PR5 76 B1
Lytham St Anne's FY8 89 B6
Poulton-le-F FY6 151 D2
Lindsay Ct Blackpool FY8 109 B4
Morecambe LA3 212 F2

Lindsay Dr PR7 42 A7
Lindsay Pk BB10 127 F5
Lindsay St Burnley BB11 127 A6
Horwich BL6 31 D1
Lindsey Ho 2 BB5 103 A7
Linedred La BB9 147 B7
Lines St LA4 212 E5
Linfield Terr FY4 109 E6
Lingart La PR3 199 D1
Lingdales L37 12 B5
Lingfield Ave BB7 164 E6
Lingfield Cl LA1 211 B3
Lingfield Ct BB2 79 C8
Lingfield Rd FY7 193 F2
Lingfield Way BB2 79 D8
Linghaw La LA2 233 F8
Lingmoor Dr BB12 126 A8
Lingmoor Rd LA1 214 B1
Lingwell Cl PR6 60 C5
Links Ave PR9 52 F3
Links Dr LA2 233 D8
Links Field PR2 116 C3
Links Gate Fulwood PR2 116 C3
Lytham St Anne's FY8 89 A6
Thornton FY5 151 D7
Links Lodge FY8 89 A6
Links Rd Blackburn BB2 79 C8
Blackpool FY1 129 C8
Kirkby L32 1 A1
Knott End-on-S FY6 194 D5
Lytham St Anne's FY8 88 E5
Penwortham PR1 95 B6
Links The FY5 172 C4
Links View FY8 89 C5
Linkside Ave BB9 148 B8
Linley Gr BL0 49 A2
Linnet Cl FY3 130 B6
Linnet Dr BL9 32 B4
Linnet La FY8 89 E7
Linnet St PR1 117 B2
Linton Ave LA3 212 A1
Linton Dr BB11 126 D3
Linton Gdns BB9 168 C3
Linton Gr PR1 95 B5
Linton St PR2 116 D3
Lion Ct 10 BB5 102 E6
Lion La BL6 30 C2
Lion St BB5 102 E6
Lionel St BB12 126 C6
Lions Ct 1 FY8 90 D4
Liptrott Rd PR7 42 A5
Lisbon Dr Burnley BB11 126 E5
Darwen BB3 81 C1
Lisbon St 17 OL12 51 C1
Lisieux Hall Hospl PR6 60 A7
Lister Gr LA3 208 F8
Lister St Accrington BB5 103 A6
3 Blackburn BB2 100 E3
Lister Well Rd BB18 191 A6
Little Acre Longton PR4 74 A8
Thornton FY5 151 D8
Little Banks Cl PR5 77 B6
Little Brewery La L37 11 F6
Little Carr La PR7 42 D5
Little Cl PR1 95 C3
Little Digmoor
Cty Prim Sch WN8 9 B6
Little Fell La LA2 211 E3
Little Fell Rd LA1,LA2 211 F6
Little Flatt OL12 51 B1
Little Hey La L37 12 B4
Little Hoole Cty Prim Sch
PR4 74 A5
Little La Banks PR9 54 B7
Longridge PR3 139 A7
Southport PR9 53 B1
Little Meadow La L40 38 D4
Little Moor BB7 164 E6
Little Moor Clough BL7 46 E2
Little Moor View BB7 164 E6
Little Peel St BB2 100 D5
Little Poulton La FY6 151 F4
Little Queen St BB8 169 C4
Little Scotland BL6 30 B2
Little St BB5 103 A6
Little Stones Rd BL7 46 E2
Little Toms La BB10 147 D3
Little Tongues La FY6 195 B4
Little Twining PR4 74 A7
Little Wood FY7 193 E3
Littledale Ave LA3 209 A8
Littledale Mews LA2 214 B6
Littledale Rd Crossgill LA2 231 E1
Littledale LA2 226 C8
Littlemoor Cl BB7 145 A8
Littlemoor Ho BB7 145 A7
Littlemoor Rd BB7 164 E7
Littleton Gr WN6 28 E2
Littondale Gdns BB2 79 D7
Liverpool Ave PR8 20 D5
Liverpool New Rd PR4 73 F5
Liverpool Old Rd
Much Hoole PR4 73 C1
Much Hoole PR4 73 E3
Sollom PR4 56 B2
Southport PR8 20 C1
Walmer Bridge PR4 73 F5
Liverpool Rd Bickerstaffe L39 7 C5
Blackpool FY1 129 D5
Burnley BB12 126 A6
Formby L37 12 A1
Hightown L37 3 A8
Hutton PR1,PR4 94 F3
Longton PR4 73 F7
Maghull L31 5 D4
Much Hoole PR4 73 D2
Ormskirk L39 15 B2
Penwortham PR1 95 B5
Liverpool Rd *continued*
Preston PR1 95 D6
Royal Oak L39 6 F4
Rufford L40 38 C5
Skelmersdale WN8 8 C8
Sollom PR4 56 A3
Southport PR8 20 F8
Liverpool Rd N
Burscough Bridge L40 24 E5
Maghull L31 5 C2
Liverpool Rd S
Burscough L40 24 D2
Maghull L31 5 C1
Livesey Branch Rd BB2 80 D8
Livesey Ct BB2 100 C2
Livesey Fold PR6 79 A1
Livesey Hall Cl BB2 99 E1
Livesey St
11 Lytham St Anne's FY8 90 A3
Padiham BB12 125 C8
Preston PR1 96 B7
Rishton BB1 123 B2
Livesley's La
Great Altcar L37 12 F2
Haskayne L37 13 A2
Livet Ave FY4 109 D7
Livingstone Rd
Accrington BB5 103 B8
Blackburn BB2 100 B4
Blackpool FY1 129 C4
Livingstone St BB9 147 B5
Livingstone Wlk BB9 147 B6
Lloyd Cl Lancaster LA1 213 D1
10 Nelson BB9 147 E8
Lloyd St Darwen BB3 80 F3
Whitworth OL12 70 C1
Lloyd Wlk 9 BB9 147 E8
Lloyd's Ave LA4 212 D4
Lobden Cres OL12 51 D8
Lochinch Cl FY4 110 A6
Lock Gate BB4 84 C1
Lock La PR4 56 B2
Lock St 10 BB5 102 E4
Locka La Arkholme LA6 234 F3
Lancaster LA1 213 F4
Locke Ind Est BL6 31 B3
Lockerbie Ave FY5 150 D8
Lockfield Dr BB18 200 C4
Lockhart Rd PR1 116 F2
Lockhurst Ave FY5 150 F8
Lockside BB2 100 D2
Lockside Rd PR2 94 F8
Lockwood Ave FY6 151 D4
Lockyer Ave BB12 126 B7
Locomotion Ind Est BL6 31 B2
Lodge Bank PR6,PR7 61 F7
Lodge Cl
2 Bamber Bridge PR5 96 F1
Blackpool FY5 150 C7
Freckleton PR4 92 B7
Lodge Ct Blackpool FY5 150 C7
Inskip PR4 155 B1
Staining FY3 130 D5
Lodge La Bacup OL13 86 F1
Clifton PR4 114 D1
Elswick PR4 154 B1
Farington PR5 75 E6
Melling LA2 235 D1
Rainford Junction L39, WA11 8 D1
Singleton FY6 152 D2
Warton FY8 90 F5
Lodge Mill La BL0 68 A1
Lodge Rd Catterall PR3 179 A1
Orrell WN5 10 E4
Lodge St Accrington BB5 103 C7
Lancaster LA1 210 F8
Preston PR1 95 E8
Ramsbottom BL0 49 C6
Shuttleworth BL0 49 E8
Lodge View Farington PR5 75 E7
Longridge PR3 139 A6
Penwortham PR1 95 F3
Lodges Gr 5 LA4 213 A6
Lodgeside BB5 123 F3
Lodgings The PR2 117 C5
Lodore Rd FY4 109 C6
Lofthouse Way FY7 194 A4
Loftos Ave FY4 109 D8
Logwood St BB1 100 F7
Lois Pl BB2 100 C5
Lomas La BB4 67 F8
Lomax St 7 Bury BL9 32 A3
Great Harwood BB6 123 C5
Ramsbottom BL8 48 F1
Rochdale OL12 51 F1
Lomeshaye Bsns Village
BB9 147 C8
Lomeshaye Cty Jun Sch
BB9 147 C8
Lomeshaye Ind Est BB9 147 B7
Lomeshaye Pl BB9 147 C8
Lomeshaye Rd BB9 147 D7
Lomeshaye Way BB9 147 C8
Lomond Ave Blackpool FY3 129 F2
Lytham St Anne's FY8 89 B5
London La PR8 21 D8
London Rd Blackburn BB1 100 E6
Blackpool FY3 129 D6
Preston PR1 96 C6
London Sq 2 PR8 34 B7
London St Fleetwood FY7 194 B4
Southport PR8, PR9 34 B7
London Terr BB3 81 B2
London Way PR1,PR5 96 C3
London Wlk BB1 100 E6
Londonderry Rd LA3 208 E5
Long Acre PR5 77 C5
Long Acre Cl LA5 216 C8
Long Acre Pl FY8 90 A4
Long Acres Dr OL12 70 D2
Long Barn Brow PR5 98 E2
Long Barn Row PR5 98 E2
Long Bldg BB7 224 A1
Long Butts PR1 95 D2
Long Cl Clitheroe BB7 187 A2
Leyland PR5 58 A8
Long Copse PR7 59 F1
Long Croft Barton PR3 136 B8
Longton PR4 94 A1
Long Croft Mdw PR7 60 B2
Long Cswy BB7 225 B2
Long Cswy The BB10 107 D7
Long Dales La LA6 231 A6
Long Gn BB18 201 C2
Long Hey La BB1,BB3 82 A2
Long Heys or Back
La WN8 18 F5
Long Ing La BB18 200 C2
Long La Abbeystead LA2 226 F1
Banks PR9 54 B6
Bickerstaffe L39 7 B7
Darwen BB3 80 A3
Formby L37 11 E4
Laneshaw Bridge BB8 170 D7
Limbrick PR6 43 B4
Low Bentham LA2 233 B7
Maghull L29 4 B1
Oakenclough PR3 220 B1
Ormskirk L39 6 F8
Pleasington BB2 99 B2
Quernmore LA2 226 A5
Skelmersdale WN8 9 E3
Street PR3 220 B5
Long Lane End LA2 207 E7
Long Level LA6 235 F8
Long Lover La BB7 189 C8
Long Marsh La LA1 213 D1
Long Mdw Chorley PR7 42 A5
Colne BB8 170 A5
Kirkham PR4 112 E5
Mellor Brook BB2 120 B2
Much Hoole PR4 73 F4
Long Meanygate PR9 36 C7
Long Moss PR5 58 A8
Long Moss La PR4 75 A6
Long Row Blackburn BB2 121 B2
Calder Vale PR3 179 E8
Long Wham La PR4 74 D1
Longacre Longton PR4 73 F8
Southport PR9 52 F3
Longacres La OL12 70 D2
Longber La LA6 236 B3
Longbrook Ave PR5 96 E1
Longcliffe Dr PR8 20 C4
Longcroft Cotts BL9 49 F1
Longfield Formby L37 12 B5
Fulwood PR2 116 F8
Penwortham PR1 95 B4
Longfield Ave Coppull PR7 41 E2
Poulton-le-F FY6 151 D4
Longfield Ct BB18 200 B1
Longfield Dr LA5 216 C8
Longfield Manor PR7 42 A5
Longfield Pl FY6 151 D4
Longfield Terr BB10 106 E8
Longfold Maghull L31 5 E1
Mere Brow PR4 54 F2
Longford Ave FY2 150 E5
Longford Rd PR8 34 A2
Longhey WN8 18 C4
Longholme Rd 9 BB4 85 A2
Longhouse La FY6 130 D8
Longlands Ave LA3 208 E8
Longlands Cres LA3 208 F8
Longlands La LA3 208 E7
Longlands Rd LA1 213 E3
Longley Cl PR2 116 F8
Longmeadow La
Heysham LA3 209 A7
Thornton FY5 173 C3
Longmeanygate Leyland,
Earnshaw Bridge PR5 75 D2
Leyland, Midge Hall PR5 75 A2
Longmere Cres LA5 216 C8
Longmire Way LA4 212 D5
Longmoor La PR3 177 E6
Longridge Ave FY4 109 E5
Longridge CE Prim Sch
PR3 139 A7
Longridge Cty Prim Sch
PR3 138 F8
Longridge Dr OL10 32 F2
Longridge Fell Forest Wlk
PR3 162 C7
Longridge Golf Course
PR3 160 F3
Longridge Heath
BB10,BB9 147 D4
Longridge High Sch PR3 139 A6
Longridge Rd
Fulwood PR2 118 B6
Hurst Green BB7,PR3 141 D8
Longridge PR3 160 C4
Longroyd Rd BB18 201 B1
Longsands Cty Prim Sch
PR2 117 D5
Longsands La PR2 117 E6
Longshaw Ave WN5 10 E1
Longshaw Cl
Longshaw WN5 10 E1
Rufford L40 38 A5
Longshaw Comm WN5 10 E1
Longshaw Inf Sch BB2 80 E8
Longshaw Jun Sch BB2 100 E1
Longshaw La BB2 100 D2
Longshaw Old Rd WN5 10 E1
Longshaw St BB2 100 D1
Longsight Ave
Clitheroe BB7 186 F1
Huncoat BB5 103 E8
Longsight Rd Langho BB6 142 B2
Langho BB6 142 D2
Osbaldeston BB1,BB2 120 E4
Ramsbottom BL0 49 A2
Longton Ave FY5 173 B2
Longton Brickcroft
Nature Reserve PR4 73 F7
Longton By-Pass PR4 74 C6
Longton Cl BB1 101 C5
Longton Ct PR8 20 C5
Longton Cty Prim Sch
PR4 74 A8
Longton Dr Formby L37 12 A6
Morecambe LA4 213 A4
Longton Rd Blackpool FY1 129 C5
Burnley BB12 126 E8
Longton St Blackburn BB1 101 C5
Chorley PR6 42 E8
Longton's Cotts LA6 234 B1
Longtons La BD23 230 B3
Longway FY4 109 F8
Longwood Cl FY8 89 E4
Longworth Ave
Blackrod BL6 30 C3
Burnley BB10 127 D6
Coppull PR7 41 F2
Longworth Clough BL7 46 D2
Longworth La BL7 46 C2
Longworth Rd
Billington BB7 143 B4
Egerton BL7 46 B3
Horwich BL6 31 C4
Longworth Rd N BL7 45 D5
Longworth St
5 Bamber Bridge PR5 96 E2
Chorley PR7 42 B6
Preston PR1 117 C1
Lonmore PR5 96 D3
Lonsdale Ave
Fleetwood FY7 193 E3
Morecambe LA4 213 A4
Ormskirk L39 15 F7
Lonsdale Cl PR5 59 A6
Lonsdale Cres 3 FY7 193 E3
Lonsdale Dr PR5 57 B3
Lonsdale Gdns 4 BB9 168 D3
Lonsdale Gr LA4 213 A4
Lonsdale Mews 5 PR5 76 A8
Lonsdale Pl LA1 211 A5
Lonsdale Rd Blackpool FY1 129 B2
Formby L37 11 F3
Hest Bank LA2 215 D1
Morecambe LA4 213 A4
Preston PR1 117 C1
Southport PR8 34 D4
Lonsdale Rise LA6 238 C2
Lonsdale St
Accrington BB5 102 F5
Burnley BB12 126 C7
Nelson BB9 168 F1
Lord Ave OL13 86 C1
Lord Nelson Wharf PR2 95 B8
Lord Sefton Way L37 12 E2
Lord Sq BB1 100 E5
Lord St Accrington BB5 103 B6
Bacup OL13 86 F2
Blackburn BB2 100 E5
Blackpool FY1 129 B6
Brierfield BB9 147 B5
Burscough Bridge L40 24 E5
Bury BL9 32 C1
Chorley PR6 42 D7
Clayton Green PR6 77 C1
Colne BB8 169 C5
Darwen BB3 81 A2
Eccleston PR7 40 C5
Fleetwood FY7 194 B4
Great Harwood BB6 123 C4
Horwich BL6 31 B4
3 Lancaster LA1 213 F1
Lytham St Anne's FY8 88 E7
Morecambe LA4 212 E6
Oswaldtwistle BB5 102 E4
Preston PR1 96 A8
Rawtenstall BB4 85 A2
Rawtenstall, Rake Foot BB4 85 A7
Rishton BB1 123 B1
Southport PR8, PR9 34 B7
Lord St W
11 Blackburn BB2 100 E5
Southport PR8 34 A6
Lord Street Cty Prim Sch
BB8 169 C5
Lord Street Mall 9 BB1 100 E5
Lord Street Prim Sch BL6 31 B4
Lord's Ave PR5 76 B7
Lord's Close Rd LA2 233 E2
Lord's La
Bamber Bridge PR1 95 E1
Longridge PR3 160 B2
Lord's Lot Rd
Over Kellet LA6 234 C1
Over Kellet LA6 234 D1
Lord's Wlk PR1 96 A8
Lords Croft PR6 77 A2
Lordsgate Dr L40 24 E3
Lordsgate La L40 24 C2
Lordsome Rd LA3 212 B2
Lorne Rd FY2 150 D2
Lorne St Chorley PR7 42 C7
Darwen BB3 80 F2
Lytham St Anne's FY8 90 D4
Lorne Way OL10 32 F1
Lorraine Ave PR2 116 E3
Lorton Cl Burnley BB12 126 B8
Fulwood PR2 116 F6
Lostock Gdns FY4 109 E6
Lostock Hall
Cty Prim Sch PR5 96 B1
Lostock Hall High Sch
PR5 96 C1
Lostock Hall Sta PR5 76 B8
Lostock La PR5 76 D7
Lostock Mdw PR6 77 A1
Lostock Rd PR5 57 C3
Lostock Sq PR5 76 B7
Lostock View PR5 76 B7
Lothersdale Cl BB10 147 D3
Lothian Ave FY7 193 D3
Lothian Pl FY2 150 E5
Lottice La BB5,BB1 102 A1
Lotus Dr FY4 111 A6
Loud Bridge Back La
PR3 159 D8
Loud Bridge Rd PR3 159 D7
Loughlin Dr L33 1 A5
Loughrigg Cl BB12 126 B7
Loughrigg Terr FY4 130 C1
Louie Pollard Cres BB6 123 D6
Louis St BL0 67 D5
Louis William St BB1 81 D8
Louise St FY1 129 B3
Loupsfell Dr LA4 212 F4
Lourdes Ave PR5 96 A1
Louvain St BB18 200 A3
Lovat Rd PR1 116 F2
Love Clough Rd BB4 104 F2
Love La BL0 67 E1
Lovely Hall La BB1 121 D7
Low Bank BB12 125 E6
Low Bentham Prim Sch
LA2 233 B8
Low Bentham Rd LA2 233 C8
Low Croft PR3 136 B2
Low Fold BB18 192 A6
Low Gn PR5 75 F1
Low Hill BB3 64 A6
Low La Leck LA6 236 B7
Morecambe LA4 213 B5
Low Moor La BB18 200 B1
Low Moor Rd FY2 150 E3
Low Rd Halton Green LA2 231 A4
Heysham LA3 209 A2
Low St LA6 236 C3
Lowcroft WN8 18 C3
Lowcross Rd FY6 151 E2
Lowe View BB4 86 A1
Lowe's La WN8 17 F8
Lower Abbotsgate LA6 238 B2
Lower Alt Rd L38 2 F4
Lower Antley St BB5 102 F5
Lower Ashworth Cl BB2 100 C4
Lower Audley St BB1,BB2 100 F4
Lower Bank Rd PR2 116 F3
Lower Bank St PR6 79 A1
Lower Barn St BB3 64 C7
Lower Barnes St BB5 123 E4
Lower Burgh Way PR7 42 B4
Lower Carr La L37 4 B7
Lower Chapel La BB7 187 B8
Lower Clough St BB9 168 D2
Lower Clowes BB4 67 E8
Lower Clowes Rd BB4 67 E8
Lower Cockcroft 12 BB2 100 E5
Lower Copthurst La PR6 60 E7
Lower Cribden Ave BB4 84 D2
Lower Croft 1 PR1 95 D2
Lower Croft St 3 BB18 201 B2
Lower Cross St 25 BB3 81 A1
Lower Darwen Prim Sch
BB3 81 A6
Lower East Ave BB18 200 B3
Lower Eccleshill Rd BB3 81 A5
Lower Field PR5 75 F6
Lower Gate Rd BB5 124 F2
Lower Gn Poulton-le-F FY6 151 E3
3 Rochdale OL12 51 C1
Lower Greenfield PR2 116 B5
Lower Hazel Cl BB2 100 C4
Lower Hey PR4 94 A1
Lower Hill Dr PR6 43 A1
Lower Hollin Bank St
BB2 100 D2
Lower House Gn BB4 86 A8
Lower House Rd PR5 58 E8
Lower La Freckleton PR4 92 D7
Haslingden BB4 84 B4
Kirkham PR4 113 C1
Longridge PR3 139 B7
Lower Laithe Dr BB9 168 C3
Lower Leithe Cotts BB9 168 C2
Lower Lune St 7 FY7 194 B5
Lower Makinson Fold BL6 31 D1
Lower Manor La BB12 146 F2
Lower Mdw BL7 47 D6
Lower Mead BL7 46 F1
Lower Mead Dr BB12 146 F2
Lower North Ave BB18 200 B2
Lower Park St BB18 200 C2
Lower Parrock Rd BB9 168 C1
Lower Philips Rd BB1 101 C8
Lower Prom Southport PR8 34 A7
Southport PR8 34 B8
Lower Rd Longridge PR3 139 E7
Ramsbottom BL0 49 E8
Lower Ridge Cl BB10 127 B6
Lower Rook St BB18 200 C2
Lower Rosegrove La
BB12 126 A5

Lower School St 6 BB8 .. 169 D4
Lower Tentre BB11 .... 127 B5
Lower Timber Hill
La BB11 .... 127 A2
Lower Waterside Farm Cotts
BB3 .... 81 E3
Lower West Ave BB18 .... 200 B2
Lower Wilworth BB1 .... 121 E1
Lower Wlk FY2 .... 150 C7
Lowerfield BB6 .... 122 C8
Lowerfields BB12 .... 125 F6
Lowerfold BB6 .... 123 C6
Lowerfold Cl OL12 .... 51 C4
Lowerfold Cres OL12 .... 51 C4
Lowerfold Dr OL12 .... 51 C4
Lowerfold Rd BB6 .... 123 C6
Lowerfold Way OL12 .... 51 C4
Lowergate BB7 .... 164 E8
Lowerhouse Cres BB12 .... 126 A6
Lowerhouse Cty Jun Sch
BB12 .... 126 A6
Lowerhouse Fold BB12 .... 126 A6
Lowerhouse La
Burnley, Lowerhouse BB12 .... 125 F6
Burnley, Rose Grove BB12 .... 126 B6
Lowes Ct 3 Blackpool FY1 .. 129 B1
4 Thornton FY5 .... 173 B3
Lowes Gn L37 .... 12 B3
Lowes Park Golf Course
BL9 .... 32 A7
Lowes Rd BL9 .... 32 A6
Lowesby Cl PR5 .... 96 E3
Loweswater Cl BB5 .... 103 F8
Loweswater Cres BB12 .... 126 B8
Loweswater Dr 5 LA4 .... 212 G4
Lowesway Blackpool FY4 .... 109 F8
5 Thornton FY5 .... 173 B3
Lowfield Cl PR4 .... 113 F2
Lowfield Rd FY4 .... 109 F7
Lowfields La LA6 .... 238 D7
Lowgill La LA2 .... 233 C3
Lowick Cl PR5 .... 97 E4
Lowick Dr FY6 .... 151 D1
Lowland Way FY2 .... 150 F6
Lowlands Rd
Bolton-le-S LA5 .... 216 A5
Morecambe LA4 .... 212 F4
Lowndes St PR1 .... 116 E2
Lowood Gr PR2 .... 115 D1
Lowood Lodge 7 FY8 .... 90 A3
Lowood Pl BB2 .... 100 A6
Lowrey Terr FY1 .... 129 B2
Lowry Cl PR5 .... 76 A7
Lowry Hill La L40 .... 25 B2
Lowstead Pl FY4 .... 109 E6
Lowstern Cl BL7 .... 46 E1
Lowther Ave
Blackpool FY2 .... 150 B2
Maghull L31 .... 5 F2
Morecambe LA3 .... 213 A3
Lowther Cres PR5 .... 75 D2
Lowther Ct Blackpool FY2 .... 150 B2
5 Lytham St Anne's FY8 .... 90 A3
Lowther Dr PR5 .... 75 D3
Lowther La BB8 .... 191 D1
Lowther Pl BB1 .... 101 A8
Lowther Rd Fleetwood FY7 .. 193 F4
Lancaster LA1 .... 214 B1
Lowther St Colne BB8 .... 169 E6
Nelson BB9 .... 147 C8
Preston PR2 .... 116 C1
Lowther Terr
Appley Bridge WN6 .... 19 C8
Lytham St Anne's FY8 .... 90 A3
Lowthian St 23 PR1 .... 95 F8
Lowthorpe Cres PR1 .... 117 B2
Lowthorpe Pl PR1 .... 117 B2
Lowthorpe Rd PR1 .... 117 B2
Lowthwaite Dr BB9 .... 147 E6
Lowton Rd FY8 .... 89 A8
Loxham Gdns FY4 .... 109 D6
Loxley Gn PR2 .... 117 C6
Loxley Pl FY5 .... 150 E7
Loxley Pl E FY5 .... 150 F7
Loxley Rd PR8 .... 34 D4
Loxwood Cl PR5 .... 96 A3
Loynd St
11 Great Harwood BB6 .... 123 C5
Ramsbottom BL0 .... 49 D6
Loyne Pk LA6 .... 235 D7
Loyne Sch The LA1 .... 213 D2
Lubbock St BB12 .... 126 C6
Lucas Ave PR7 .... 41 D8
Lucas La E PR6 .... 60 C6
Lucas La W PR6 .... 60 C5
Lucas St BL9 .... 32 A3
Lucerne Cl PR2 .... 117 C4
Lucerne Rd PR2 .... 117 C4
Lucy St Barrowford BB9 .... 168 D3
Lancaster LA1 .... 210 F8
Morecambe LA4 .... 212 E6
Ludlow WN8 .... 18 C4
Ludlow Dr L39 .... 15 D7
Ludlow Gr FY2 .... 150 F2
Ludlow St WN6 .... 28 D3
Luke St 17 OL13 .... 69 C8
Lulworth WN8 .... 18 C4
Lulworth Ave
Blackpool FY3 .... 130 A3
Preston PR2 .... 116 D2
Lulworth Lo PR8 .... 33 F5
Lulworth Pl PR5 .... 96 D2
Lulworth Rd Fulwood PR2 .. 117 A4
Southport PR8 .... 33 F5
Lumb Carr Ave BL0,BL8 .... 49 A4
Lumb Carr Rd BL0,BL8 .... 49 A4
Lumb Cotts BL0 .... 67 B4
Lumb Flats BL0 .... 67 B4
Lumb Holes La BB4 .... 68 E7
Lumb La BB4 .... 85 F4
Lumb Scar 9 OL13 .... 86 F2
Lund St Blackburn BB2 .... 100 C4
2 Preston PR1 .... 96 A8
Lunds La PR4 .... 73 D1
Lune Ave L31 .... 5 E2
Lune Cl
Kirkby Lonsdale LA6 .... 238 C2
Kirkham PR4 .... 113 C5
Lune Dr Clayton-le-W PR5 .... 76 E2
Morecambe LA3 .... 213 B3
Lune Gr FY1 .... 129 C3
Lune Ho LA1 .... 210 F7
Lune Ind Est LA1 .... 210 C8
Lune Rd Fleetwood FY7 .... 193 F4
Lancaster LA1 .... 213 D1
Lune St Colne BB8 .... 169 E4
Lancaster LA1 .... 213 F1
Longridge PR3 .... 139 B8
Padiham BB12 .... 125 D8
Preston PR1 .... 95 F7
Lune Terr LA1 .... 213 F1
Lune View FY6 .... 194 E6
Lunedale Ave FY1 .... 129 C1
Lunefield Dr LA6 .... 238 C1
Lunefield Gdns LA6 .... 238 C2
Lunesdale Cl FY8 .... 89 C7
Lunesdale Ct
Butt Yeats LA2 .... 232 B6
Lancaster LA1 .... 214 B1
Lunesdale Dr PR3 .... 204 B3
Lunesdale Rd 2 PR4 .... 113 A5
Lunesdale Terr LA2 .... 231 E4
Lunesdale View LA2 .... 214 F7
Luneside LA1 .... 210 C8
Lunt Rd L29 .... 4 C1
Lupin Cl Accrington BB5 .... 103 A7
Lucas Green PR6 .... 60 B5
Lupin Rd BB5 .... 103 B7
Lupton Dr BB9 .... 168 D4
Lupton Pl LA1 .... 213 D3
Lupton St PR7 .... 42 C6
Lutner St BB11 .... 127 A5
Luton Rd Cleveleys FY5 .... 172 E1
Preston PR2 .... 115 F2
Lutwidge Ave PR1 .... 117 C1
Lyceum Ave 3 FY3 .... 129 D4
Lychfield Dr PR5 .... 76 E7
Lychgate 20 PR1 .... 96 A8
Lydd Gr PR7 .... 42 A7
Lyddesdale Ave FY5 .... 150 D8
Lydgate Brierfield BB10 .... 147 E2
Chorley PR7 .... 42 A5
Lydia St BB5 .... 103 B4
Lydiate Cty Prim Sch L31 .... 5 C4
Lydiate La Bilsborrow PR3 .. 157 C6
Leyland PR5 .... 76 C4
Newtown PR7 .... 58 B1
Lydiate Lane End PR7 .... 58 B2
Lydiate Station Rd L31 .... 4 E5
Lydric Ave PR5 .... 97 E2
Lyelake La L40 .... 16 F2
Lymbridge Dr BL6 .... 30 D1
Lyme Gr FY6 .... 194 E5
Lymm Ave LA1 .... 213 C3
Lyncroft Cres FY3 .... 129 E7
Lyndale WN8 .... 18 B4
Lyndale Ave
Bamber Bridge PR5 .... 96 C2
Haslingden BB4 .... 84 B2
Wilpshire BB1 .... 122 A7
Lyndale Cl Leyland PR5 .... 59 B6
Rawtenstall BB4 .... 85 A7
Wilpshire BB1 .... 122 A7
Lyndale Ct FY7 .... 194 B5
Lyndale Gr PR5 .... 96 C2
Lyndale Rd BB11 .... 125 C3
Lyndale Terr BB7 .... 225 B3
Lynden Ave LA4 .... 213 A5
Lyndeth Cl PR2 .... 117 E6
Lyndhurst Maghull L31 .... 5 D1
Skelmersdale WN8 .... 18 B4
Lyndhurst Ave
Blackburn BB1 .... 101 E5
Blackpool FY4 .... 129 D1
Lyndhurst Dr PR2 .... 115 E2
Lyndhurst Gr BB6 .... 123 E6
Lyndhurst Rd
Blackburn BB2 .... 100 E2
Burnley BB10 .... 127 C5
Darwen BB3 .... 80 E3
Darwen BB3 .... 80 F3
Southport PR8 .... 34 B2
Lyndon Ave BB6 .... 123 E6
Lyndon Ct BB6 .... 123 E6
Lynfield Rd BB6 .... 123 E6
Lynn Gr 6 FY1 .... 129 B7
Lynn Pl PR2 .... 117 D2
Lynslack Terr LA5 .... 218 B8
Lynthorpe Rd
Blackburn BB2 .... 100 E2
Nelson BB9 .... 169 A1
Lynton Ave Blackpool FY4 .. 109 D8
Leyland PR5 .... 59 C8
Lynton Ct FY7 .... 172 C8
Lynton Dr PR8 .... 33 E1
Lynton Rd Accrington BB5 .. 102 F4
Southport PR8 .... 33 E1
Lynwood Ave
Blackpool FY3 .... 129 E8
Clayton-le-M BB5 .... 123 F4
Darwen BB3 .... 80 E4
Grimsargh PR2 .... 138 C2
Ormskirk L39 .... 15 C3
Lynwood Cl
Clayton-le-M BB5 .... 123 F4
Colne BB8 .... 169 D7
Darwen BB3 .... 80 E3
Skelmersdale WN8 .... 9 D7
Lynwood Dr FY6 .... 174 C7
Lynwood End L39 .... 15 C3
Lynwood Rd
Blackburn BB2 .... 100 B6
Huncoat BB5 .... 124 E2
Lyons La S PR7 .... 42 D7
Lyons Rd PR8 .... 34 A5
Lystra Ct FY8 .... 88 F5
Lyth Rd LA1 .... 214 B2
Lythall Ave FY8 .... 90 D4
Lytham CE Prim Sch FY8 .... 90 B4
Lytham Cl PR2 .... 116 D3
Lytham Hall FY8 .... 89 F4
Lytham Lifeboat Mus FY8 .. 90 C3
Lytham Rd Blackburn BB2 .. 100 F1
Blackpool FY1,FY4 .... 109 C6
Brierfield BB10 .... 147 C2
Freckleton PR4 .... 92 B6
Fulwood PR2 .... 116 D3
Saltcotes, Moss Side FY8 .... 111 E1
Southport PR9 .... 53 A4
Warton FY8,PR4 .... 91 D5
Lytham St Chorley PR6 .... 42 E7
Rochdale OL12 .... 51 E3
Lytham St Anne's High Sch
FY8 .... 89 C5
Lytham St Anne's Local
Nature Reserve FY8 .... 109 B1
Lytham St Annes L Ctr
FY8 .... 89 D5
Lytham Sta FY8 .... 90 A3
Lytham Windmill (Mus)
FY8 .... 90 C3
Lythcoe Ave PR2 .... 116 C4
Lythe Fell Ave LA2 .... 214 F7
Lythe Fell Rd LA2 .... 228 F8
Lythe La LA2 .... 233 E2
Lytles Cl L37 .... 12 A2
Lytton St BB12 .... 125 F7

M

Mabel St Colne BB8 .... 169 F5
2 Rochdale OL12 .... 51 D2
Maberry Cl WN6 .... 19 D7
Macaulay St BB11 .... 126 C5
Macauley Ave FY4 .... 109 F8
Macbeth Rd FY7 .... 193 E4
Mackay Croft 4 PR6 .... 42 D8
Mackenzie Cl 5 PR6 .... 42 D8
Maclaren Cl FY3 .... 130 D5
Macleod St BB9 .... 147 D8
Maddy St 2 PR1 .... 95 D8
Madeley Gdns OL12 .... 51 C1
Maden Rd OL13 .... 86 F2
Maden St BB5 .... 102 E6
Maden Way OL13 .... 86 F2
Madison Ave
Blackpool FY2 .... 150 B5
Hest Bank LA5 .... 215 E2
Madryn Ave L33 .... 1 A2
Maesbrook Cl PR9 .... 54 B5
Mafeking Ave BL9 .... 32 A5
Mafeking Rd PR2 .... 116 C2
Magdalen Ave FY5 .... 172 D1
Maggots Nook Rd WA11 .... 9 A1
Maghull Homes The L31 .... 5 B1
Maghull La L31 .... 6 B1
Maghull Smallholdings Est
L31 .... 5 F3
Magnolia Cl PR2 .... 117 C6
Magnolia Dr PR5 .... 76 E2
Magnolia Rd PR1 .... 95 B3
Magpie Cl BB11 .... 126 C5
Maharishi School
of the Age of
Enlightenment L40 .... 18 A5
Maida Vale FY5 .... 150 D8
Maiden St BB4 .... 84 B6
Main Ave LA3 .... 208 F3
Main Cl LA3 .... 205 D8
Main Dr FY6 .... 151 E2
Main Rd Bolton-le-S LA5 .... 216 B5
Galgate LA2 .... 207 A3
Hest Bank LA2 .... 215 F1
Nether Kellet LA6 .... 216 F5
Main Sprit Weind PR1 .... 96 A7
Main St Bolton-by-B BB7 .... 224 D4
Burton-in-K LA6 .... 234 B7
Cockerham LA2 .... 203 D4
Gisburn BB7 .... 225 C3
Grindleton BB7 .... 187 B8
Heysham LA3 .... 208 E8
High Bentham LA2 .... 233 D8
Hornby LA2 .... 232 B7
Kelbrook BB18 .... 192 A6
Kirkby Lonsdale LA6 .... 238 C2
Lancaster LA1 .... 213 F2
Low Bentham LA2 .... 233 B8
Overton LA3 .... 205 D8
Rathmell BD24 .... 230 F6
Warton, Carnforth LA5 .... 217 D5
Whittington LA6 .... 235 D7
Wray LA2 .... 232 D6
Mains La Bispham Green L40 .. 26 A6
Poulton-le-F FY6 .... 152 B4
Mainway LA1 .... 213 F2
Mairscough La L39 .... 14 B1
Maitland Ave FY5 .... 172 D1
Maitland Cl 5 PR1 .... 96 C8
Maitland Pl BB4 .... 85 A1
Maitland St 18 Bacup OL13 .. 86 F2
Maitland St *continued*
4 Preston PR1 .... 96 C8
1 Preston PR5 .... 96 D8
Majestic The FY8 .... 88 D6
Major St Accrington BB5 .... 103 B4
Ramsbottom BL0 .... 49 B6
Rawtenstall BB4 .... 85 A7
Makinson Ave BL6 .... 31 E1
Makinson La BL6 .... 31 F4
Makinsons Row 11 LA2 .... 207 A4
Malcolm Pl FY7 .... 193 E4
Malcolm St PR1 .... 117 D1
Malden St PR5 .... 76 A1
Maldern Ave FY6 .... 151 C5
Maldon Pl PR2 .... 117 D2
Malham Ave
Accrington BB5 .... 102 F4
Blackpool FY4 .... 109 D8
Malham Cl Lancaster LA1 .. 213 D3
Southport PR8 .... 34 E3
Malham Gdns BB1 .... 100 F3
Malham Pl PR2 .... 117 E4
Malham Rd BB10 .... 147 D3
Malham Wend BB9 .... 168 C3
Maliff Rd BB10 .... 149 B2
Malkin Cl BB9 .... 168 E8
Malkin La BB7 .... 163 F6
Mall The Burnley BB11 .... 127 A6
Fulwood PR2 .... 117 E2
Lytham St Anne's FY8 .... 89 C7
Mallard Cl Leyland PR5 .... 58 D8
Ormskirk L39 .... 15 C2
Thornton FY5 .... 173 A4
Mallard Ct Blackpool FY3 .. 130 B6
Lancaster LA1 .... 210 E8
Mallard Dr BL6 .... 31 A3
Mallard Ho L31 .... 5 B4
Mallard Pl BB5 .... 102 D3
Mallards Wlk PR5 .... 77 A5
Mallee Ave PR9 .... 53 A3
Mallee Cres PR9 .... 53 A3
Malley La PR4 .... 135 C8
Mallom Ave PR7 .... 59 E1
Mallory Ave L31 .... 5 B4
Mallow Wlk LA3 .... 212 E2
Mallowdale FY5 .... 173 A4
Mallowdale Ave LA3 .... 209 A8
Mallowdale Rd LA1 .... 213 D2
Malt Kiln Brow PR3 .... 182 E4
Malt Kiln Gr PR3 .... 154 A5
Malt St BB5 .... 103 B7
Maltby Pl 2 FY4 .... 129 F2
Malthouse Ct PR2 .... 116 D1
Malthouse The PR2 .... 116 D1
Malthouse Way PR1 .... 95 D3
Maltings The Longton PR4 .. 73 F8
Thornton FY5 .... 173 A4
Whittington LA6 .... 235 D7
Maltkiln La
Bispham Green L40,WN8 .... 26 C7
Ormskirk L39 .... 6 E8
Malton Dr PR5 .... 76 A7
Malvern Ave
Blackburn BB2 .... 100 D1
Blackpool FY1 .... 129 D2
Lancaster LA1 .... 211 A6
Oswaldtwistle BB5 .... 102 E3
Padiham BB12 .... 125 D6
Preston PR1 .... 96 B6
Stalmine FY6 .... 174 C7
Malvern Cl
6 Accrington BB5 .... 103 A7
Bamber Bridge PR5 .... 76 C8
Horwich BL6 .... 31 C5
Malvern Ct 6 BB9 .... 147 F8
Malvern Rd
Lytham St Anne's FY8 .... 89 D5
Nelson BB9 .... 169 A1
Preston PR1 .... 96 B6
Malvern St Preston PR1 .... 96 B5
Standish WN6 .... 28 D3
Malvern Way BB4 .... 67 A7
Manby Cl PR5 .... 97 E3
Manchester Rd
Accrington BB5 .... 103 D3
Barnoldswick BB18 .... 200 B1
Blackpool FY3 .... 129 D6
Blackrod BL6 .... 30 E1
Burnley BB11 .... 126 E4
Clow Bridge BB11 .... 105 D6
Hapton BB11,BB12 .... 125 C4
Haslingden, Ewood
Bridge BB4 .... 67 D7
Haslingden, Lane Side BB4 .... 84 B2
Nelson BB9 .... 147 D7
Preston PR1 .... 96 B7
Ramsbottom BL0,BL9 .... 49 E4
Southport PR9 .... 34 C7
Manchester Road Sta
BB11 .... 126 F5
Mancknols St BB9 .... 148 A7
Mancknols Walton
Cottage Homes BB9 .... 148 B8
Mandella Ct BB1 .... 100 E6
Mandeville Rd PR8 .... 20 B5
Mandeville Terr BL8 .... 48 B2
Manfield WN8 .... 18 A3
Manghales BB4 .... 84 B7
Manion Ave L31 .... 5 B5
Manion Cl L31 .... 5 B5
Manitoba Cl BB2 .... 100 B8
Manley Cl BL9 .... 49 C2
Manner Sutton St BB1 .... 100 F5
Manning Rd
4 Preston PR1 .... 117 E1
Southport PR8 .... 34 E6
Manor Ave Burscough L40 .. 24 D2
Fulwood PR2 .... 117 B4
Manor Ave *continued*
Hest Bank LA2 .... 213 E8
Penwortham PR1 .... 95 B4
Ribchester PR3 .... 140 D3
Manor Beach Cty Prim Sch
FY5 .... 172 D3
Manor Brook 1 BB5 .... 103 C6
Manor Cl Burton in L LA6 .. 236 C3
Coupe Green PR5 .... 97 F3
Hest Bank LA2 .... 213 E8
Manor Cotts PR4 .... 112 B3
Manor Cres Burscough L40 .. 24 D2
Hest Bank LA2 .... 213 F8
Manor Ct 11 Blackpool FY1 .. 129 C7
3 Blackpool, Hawes
Side FY4 .... 129 E1
Fulwood PR2 .... 116 B7
Manor Ctyd LA3 .... 208 E8
Manor Dr Burscough L40 .... 24 D2
Cleveleys FY5 .... 172 D3
Hest Bank LA2 .... 213 E8
Kirkham PR4 .... 113 C4
Manor Farm LA6 .... 235 D7
Manor Fields BB7 .... 143 C5
Manor Gdns L40 .... 24 D2
Manor Gr Morecambe LA3 .. 212 C2
Penwortham PR1 .... 95 A4
Skelmersdale WN8 .... 17 F1
Manor House Cl
Leyland PR5 .... 58 B8
Maghull L31 .... 5 C1
Manor House Cres PR1 .... 117 B3
Manor House Dr WN8 .... 9 E3
Manor House La PR1 .... 117 C3
Manor House Park
Flats FY5 .... 172 C3
Manor La Hest Bank LA2 .... 215 F1
Penwortham PR1 .... 95 B4
Manor Lo L37 .... 11 E4
Manor Pk PR2 .... 117 C4
Manor Pl BB5 .... 102 F7
Manor Rd Blackburn BB2 .... 100 B5
Blackpool FY1 .... 129 D4
Burnley BB12 .... 126 B7
Burscough L40 .... 24 D2
Clayton Green PR6 .... 77 B3
Clitheroe BB7 .... 164 D7
Colne BB8 .... 169 E7
Darwen BB3 .... 63 F8
Fleetwood FY7 .... 193 E4
Garstang PR3 .... 199 C1
Hest Bank LA2 .... 213 F8
Horwich BL6 .... 31 D4
Inskip PR4 .... 134 C8
Southport PR9 .... 53 A2
Whalley BB7 .... 143 C5
Wrea Green PR4 .... 112 B4
Manor Road Cty Prim Sch
PR6 .... 77 B2
Manor St Accrington BB5 .. 103 D7
Bacup OL13 .... 86 F1
Bury BL9 .... 32 A2
Nelson BB9 .... 147 F8
Ramsbottom BL0 .... 49 B7
Manor Steet BB9 .... 147 F8
Manor Way PR4 .... 112 B3
Manor Wood
Fleetwood FY7 .... 193 E4
Kirkham PR4 .... 113 B7
Manorcroft PR4 .... 73 F8
Manse Ave WN6 .... 27 F5
Mansell Way BL6 .... 31 D1
Mansergh St BB10 .... 147 C2
Mansfield Ave BL0 .... 49 B2
Mansfield Cres BB9 .... 147 C6
Mansfield Dr PR5 .... 97 E3
Mansfield Gr BB9 .... 147 C6
Mansfield Rd FY3 .... 129 D8
Mansion House Bldgs 2
BB4 .... 85 A7
Mansion St S BB5 .... 103 D6
Manston Gr PR7 .... 42 A7
Manx Jane's La PR9 .... 53 A4
Manxman Rd BB2 .... 100 F1
Maple Ave Blackpool FY3 .. 129 D5
Brinscall PR6 .... 61 F7
Burscough L40 .... 24 E4
7 Bury BL9 .... 32 B2
Fleetwood FY7 .... 172 F8
Haslingden BB4 .... 84 C3
Horwich BL6 .... 31 E1
Morecambe LA3 .... 212 B2
Thornton FY5 .... 151 C8
Maple Bank BB10 .... 127 C7
Maple Cl Formby L37 .... 11 C1
Newton-with-S PR4 .... 113 F2
Whalley BB7 .... 143 D6
Wilpshire BB1 .... 121 E6
Maple Cres BB1 .... 102 B8
Maple Ct Farington PR5 .... 76 D3
Garstang PR3 .... 199 C1
Maple Dr
Bamber Bridge PR5 .... 96 F1
Oswaldtwistle BB5 .... 102 F3
Poulton-le-F FY6 .... 151 E2
Maple Gr Chorley PR6 .... 60 D3
Fulwood PR2 .... 118 A4
Grimsargh PR2 .... 138 D1
Lancaster LA1 .... 210 D8
Penwortham PR1 .... 95 B4
Ramsbottom BL0 .... 49 D6
Warton PR4 .... 91 D6
Maple Rd PR3 .... 199 C1
Maple St Blackburn BB1 .... 101 A7
Clayton-le-M BB5 .... 123 F1
Great Harwood BB6 .... 123 D6
3 Rishton BB1 .... 123 B1
Southport PR8 .... 34 E6

Maplebank 3 PR2 115 C1
Maples The PR5 57 F6
Maplewood
Skelmersdale WN8 18 A4
Southport PR9 52 F2
Maplewood Ave FY6 195 A5
Maplewood Cl Leyland PR5 58 E8
Lytham St Anne's FY8 89 F4
Maplewood Dr FY5 150 C8
Maplewood Gdns LA1 211 A2
Marabou Dr BB3 80 E3
Marathon Pl PR5 75 C3
Marble Ave 4 FY5 150 F7
Marble Pl PR8 34 B7
Marble St BB5 102 E4
March St BB12 126 F8
Marchbank Rd WN8 17 D1
Marchwood Rd FY3 130 B8
Marcroft Ave FY4 109 E7
Mardale Ave
Blackpool FY4 130 C1
Morecambe LA4 212 G5
Mardale Cl PR8 20 B4
Mardale Cres PR5 59 B7
Mardale Rd Fulwood PR1 118 A1
1 Lancaster LA1 214 A1
Longridge PR3 138 F5
Maresfield Rd PR1 95 E5
Margaret Rd PR1 95 E4
Margaret St
Blackburn BB1 101 D4
Oswaldtwistle BB5 102 C2
1 Preston PR1 96 A8
Rawtenstall BB4 84 F4
Margate Ave FY4 109 E6
Margate Rd Fulwood PR2 116 A4
Lytham St Anne's FY8 88 F8
Maria Ct 10 BB11 127 B4
Maria Sq BL7 45 D4
Maria St BB3 64 B6
Marians Dr L39 15 E7
Maricourt Ave BB1 101 D5
Marilyn Ave 4 PR5 76 B8
Marina Ave
2 Blackpool FY1 129 D2
Poulton-le-F FY3 130 D8
Marina Cl PR5 96 A1
Marina Dr
Bamber Bridge PR5 96 A1
Fulwood PR2 116 E7
Marina Gr PR5 96 A1
Marina Mews FY7 194 B3
Marina Rd L37 11 F1
Marina Way BB18 200 D1
Marine Ave BB11 126 C4
Marine Dr Hest Bank LA2 215 D1
Lytham St Anne's FY8 89 D3
Southport PR8 33 E7
Southport, Marshside
PR8, PR9 52 D4
Marine Gate Mans PR9 34 B8
Marine Ind Ctr FY8 90 D4
Marine Par Fleetwood FY7 193 C1
Southport PR8 34 A8
Marine Rd E LA4 212 F6
Marine Rd W LA3,LA4 212 C4
Marine Road Central
LA4 212 D5
Mariners Cl FY7 193 E1
Mariners Way PR2 95 B8
Marino Cl FY5 151 D8
Maritime St FY7 193 F2
Maritime Way PR2 94 F7
Mark Cl PR1 95 F1
Mark Rd L38 2 F4
Mark Sq PR4 56 A6
Mark St Bacup OL13 69 C8
Burnley BB10 147 B1
Mark's Ave PR5 75 E5
Market Ave 2 BB1 100 E5
Market Cross 5 L39 15 E5
Market Gate 27 LA1 210 F8
Market Pl Adlington PR7 30 A7
12 Chorley PR7 42 C8
3 Clitheroe BB7 164 E8
10 Colne BB8 169 E5
Edenfield BL0 67 D3
Garstang PR3 178 C7
1 Leyland PR5 59 A8
Longridge PR3 139 B7
3 Poulton-le-F FY6 151 D3
Ramsbottom BL0 49 C7
Standish WN6 28 E1
Market Sq Burnley BB11 127 A6
Kirkby Lonsdale LA6 238 C2
3 Kirkham PR4 113 B5
10 Lancaster LA1 210 F8
Lytham St Anne's FY8 90 A3
Nelson BB9 147 D8
Market St Adlington PR7 30 A6
Bacup OL13 86 F2
6 Barnoldswick BB18 200 B2
Blackpool FY1 129 B5
Carnforth LA5 217 D2
Chorley PR7 42 C7
Church BB5 102 E5
Colne BB8 169 E5
Darwen BB3 81 A1
Edenfield BL0 67 D4
Hambleton FY6 174 C2
Kirkby Lonsdale LA6 238 C2
Kirkham PR4 112 F6
Lancaster LA1 210 F8
Morecambe LA4 212 D5
9 Nelson BB9 147 D8
Preston PR1 95 F8
5 Rawtenstall BB4 68 F8
Southport PR8 34 B7
Market St *continued*
Standish WN6 28 E1
Whitworth OL12,OL13 70 D4
Market St W PR1 95 F8
Market Street La 7 BB2 100 E4
Market Way
7 Blackburn BB1 100 E5
6 Ormskirk L39 15 E5
Market Wlk PR7 42 C8
Markham Dr PR8 34 E2
Markham Rd BB2 100 B3
Markham St PR2 116 C1
Markland St
3 Preston PR1 95 E7
6 Ramsbottom BL0 49 C6
Marklands Rd BL6 31 E5
Markross St BB4 85 A2
Marl Ave PR1 95 B4
Marl Cop PR5 57 A6
Marl Croft PR1 95 D2
Marl Gr WN5 10 D4
Marl Hill Cres PR2 118 A2
Marl Pits BB4 85 B3
Marl Pits Sports Complex
BB4 85 C3
Marl Rd L33 1 C3
Marland WN8 18 A4
Marlboro Rd FY3 129 E4
Marlborough WN8 18 A4
Marlborough Ave
Cleveleys FY5 172 D5
Maghull L31 5 D3
Warton PR4 91 D6
Marlborough Cl
Ramsbottom BL0 49 C3
Whitworth OL12 51 C7
Marlborough Dr
Bamber Bridge PR5 96 D3
Fulwood PR2 116 D7
Marlborough Gdns 5 PR9 34 C8
Marlborough Rd
Accrington BB5 103 C7
Lytham St Anne's FY8 109 E1
Morecambe LA3 212 B3
Southport PR9 34 C7
Marlborough St
Burnley BB11 127 A4
Chorley PR6 60 E1
14 Rochdale OL12 51 C1
Marled Hey BL7 47 D5
Marles Ct BB10 127 B8
Marlfield PR4 73 F4
Marlfield Cl PR2 115 F5
Marlhill Rd FY3 130 B8
Marlin St 5 BB9 168 F2
Marlowe Ave
Accrington BB5 103 E2
Padiham BB12 125 F7
Marlowe Cres BB6 123 B4
Marlton Rd BB2 100 D1
Marlton Way LA1 210 E6
Marple Cl WN6 28 B2
Marquis Cl BB3 80 F7
Marquis Dr PR4 92 C7
Marquis St PR4 112 F5
Marron Cl PR5 58 E8
Mars St BL7 47 E6
Marsden Cl PR7 40 B7
Marsden Cres BB9 148 A8
Marsden Ct BB10 147 C3
Marsden Dr BB9 147 D6
Marsden Gr BB9 147 C5
Marsden Hall Rd BB9 148 A8
Marsden Hall Rd N BB9 169 B1
Marsden Hall Road S
BB9 148 A8
Marsden Height Cl BB9 147 F5
Marsden Mall 3 BB9 147 E8
Marsden Park
Golf Course BB9 148 C8
Marsden Prim Sch BB9 147 D7
Marsden Rd Blackpool FY4 109 D8
Brierfield BB10 147 C3
Southport PR9 34 E7
Marsden St
Accrington BB5 103 B4
Blackburn BB2 100 B2
6 Haslingden BB4 84 A3
Kirkham PR4 113 B5
Marsett Cl OL12 51 A1
Marsett Pl PR2 117 E5
Marsh Brows L37 11 E2
Marsh Cl LA2 203 B4
Marsh Cres LA4 213 B4
Marsh Ct 2 FY5 173 A2
Marsh Cty Prim Sch The
LA1 210 D8
Marsh Dr PR4 92 D7
Marsh Gates PR4 92 D7
Marsh Hos LA2 203 B4
Marsh House La BB3 81 C1
Marsh La Brindle PR6 78 B5
Cockerham LA2 203 B4
Glasson LA2 205 D3
Hambleton FY6 174 C1
Hightown L37, L38 3 E6
Longton PR4 73 D8
Ormskirk L40 23 D1
Preston PR1 95 E7
6 Preston PR1 95 F8
Marsh Mill FY5 173 B2
Marsh Moss La L40 24 C7
Marsh Rd Banks PR9 71 D1
Hesketh Bank PR4 72 F4
Thornton FY5 173 A2
Marsh St Blackburn BB1 100 E6
Horwich BL6 31 A4
4 Lancaster LA1 213 D1
Marsh Terr BB3 81 A2
Marsh View PR4 113 F2
Marsh Way PR1 95 C2
Marshall Ave BB5 124 F2
Marshall Gr PR2 116 A4
Marshall's Brow PR1 95 E3
Marshall's Cl Maghull L31 5 C4
5 Penwortham PR1 95 E4
Marshallsay L37 12 A2
Marsham Cl PR3 178 D6
Marsham Gr BB3 81 C1
Marshaw Pl PR3 178 A6
Marshaw Rd LA1 213 D2
Marshdale Rd FY4 109 F7
Marshes La The PR4 37 A8
Marshside Nature Reserve
PR9 52 E5
Marshside Prim Sch PR9 53 A5
Marshside Rd PR9 52 F4
Marston Cl PR2 116 C7
Marston Cres L38 3 A2
Marston Moor PR2 116 C7
Mart La L40 24 E5
Martholme Ave BB5 124 A3
Martholme Cl BB6 123 D6
Martholme La BB6 123 F8
Martin Ave FY8 109 C4
Martin Croft Rd BB4 84 A5
Martin Dr BB3 64 C6
Martin Field Rd PR1 95 E2
Martin La
Drummersdale L40 23 E6
Rochdale OL12 51 B1
Martin Mere
(The Wildfowl Trust) L40 37 B1
Martin St Burnley BB10 147 B1
Bury BL9 32 D3
Edgworth BL7 47 D4
Martin Top La BB7 189 C7
Martindale Cl BB1 101 C2
Martindales The PR6 77 B3
Martinfield PR2 116 F8
Martinfields BB10 147 C4
Martinique Dr BB3 80 F6
Martins Ave PR7 42 E2
Martins La WN8 9 D7
Martland Ave WN6 19 F5
Marton Dr Blackpool FY4 109 D8
Burnley BB11 126 E3
Morecambe LA4 213 B6
Marton Pl LA4 213 B6
Marton Rd PR2 94 F8
Marton St 4 LA1 210 F7
Marton View FY3 129 E4
Marwick Cl WN6 28 D2
Mary Ave PR8 20 E6
Mary Brown Cotts BB7 187 C8
Mary St Blackburn BB1 101 A4
Burnley BB10 127 B5
Carnforth LA5 217 D3
Colne BB8 169 C4
Lancaster LA1 210 F8
Ramsbottom BL0 49 B5
Rishton BB1 123 B1
Mary St E BL6 31 B4
Mary St W Horwich BL6 31 A4
Longridge PR3 139 A8
Marybank Cl PR2 117 C5
Maryland Cl LA5 218 D2
Masefield Ave
Padiham BB12 125 E7
Thornton FY5 173 A3
Masefield Cl BB6 123 B4
Masefield Pl PR5 96 D2
Mason Cl PR4 92 C6
Mason Hill View PR2 117 A4
Mason House Cres PR2 116 A5
Mason Row BL7 46 E2
Mason St 7
Accrington BB5 103 C6
Bury BL9 32 A2
Chorley PR6 60 E2
Colne BB8 169 D5
Egerton BL7 46 E1
Horwich BL6 31 B3
Oswaldtwistle BB5 102 D3
Masonfield PR5 77 B5
Masongill Fell Lane LA6 236 E7
Masons Ct 1 FY7 193 E3
Masons Way 9 BB18 200 B3
Masonwood PR2 117 A6
Massam's La L37 11 F6
Massey Croft OL12 51 C8
Massey La BB9 147 A5
Massey St Brierfield BB9 147 A4
Burnley BB11 127 A6
Bury BL9 32 B3
Masterson Ave BB12 144 D2
Matcham Ct 11 FY1 129 B5
Matchmoor La BL6 31 F4
Mather Ave BB5 103 B8
Mather St FY3 129 D7
Mathias Ct LA4 212 E6
Matlock Ave PR8 34 B4
Matlock Cl PR8 34 B4
Matlock Cres PR8 34 B4
Matlock Gr BB10 147 C2
Matlock Pl PR2 116 A5
Matlock Rd PR8 34 B4
Matlock St 11 BB3 80 F2
Matterdale Rd PR5 59 B7
Matthew Cl BB8 169 E4
Matthew St BB2 100 B2
Matthews Ct FY4 109 D7
Matthias St LA4 212 E6
Mattock Cres LA4 213 B5
Maud St Barrowford BB9 168 D2
Chorley PR7 42 B6
Maudland Bank PR1 95 E8
Maudland Rd
Blackpool FY1 129 C2
Preston PR1 95 E8
Maudsley St
Accrington BB5 103 C6
Blackburn BB1 100 F5
Maureen Ave 3 PR5 76 B8
Maurice Gr FY2 150 E1
Maurice St BB9 147 D8
Mavis Dr PR7 41 E2
Mavis Rd BB2 100 A5
Mawdesley CE Prim Sch
L40 39 C3
Mawdesley RC Prim Sch
L40 39 F2
Mawdsley Cl L37 12 B3
Mawdsley Terr L39 15 F7
Maxwell Gr FY2 150 E2
Maxwell St BL9 32 B3
May Bell Ave FY5 172 F3
May La Bilsborrow PR3 157 C8
Claughton PR3 179 E1
May St Barrowford BB9 168 D2
Blackburn BB1 101 A4
Burnley BB11 127 B4
Edgworth BL7 47 E6
Nelson BB9 168 F2
May Terr BB7 143 A4
Maybank Cl PR9 53 A1
Maybury Ave BB12 126 B7
Maycroft Ave FY6 151 B5
Mayfair BL6 31 D3
Mayfair Cl Haslingden BB4 67 A7
Hightown L38 2 F2
Lytham St Anne's FY8 89 D6
Mayfair Cotts WN1 29 C1
Mayfair Cres BB1 121 F5
Mayfair Dr FY5 151 C8
Mayfair Gdns 5 FY5 173 C1
Mayfair Rd Blackpool FY1 129 E2
Burnley BB10 127 E5
Nelson BB9 169 A1
Mayfayre Ave L31 5 B5
Mayfield BB3 64 B7
Mayfield Ave Adlington PR6 30 A7
Bamber Bridge PR5 76 C8
Blackpool FY4 109 C5
Clitheroe BB7 164 F7
Formby L37 11 C1
Fulwood PR2 116 A5
Fulwood PR2 116 B4
Haslingden BB4 84 A1
5 Kirkham PR4 113 A5
Lancaster LA1 213 E3
Oswaldtwistle BB5 102 F4
Thornton FY5 173 A4
Mayfield Cl BL0 49 A2
Mayfield Ct L37 11 F5
Mayfield Dr LA4 213 A6
Mayfield Fold BB11 127 B3
Mayfield Gdns BB5 102 F4
Mayfield Pl 10 FY7 193 F2
Mayfield Prim Sch FY8 88 E8
Mayfield Rd
Blackburn BB1 121 E3
7 Chorley PR6 60 D1
High Bentham LA2 233 D7
Leyland PR5 59 A7
Lytham St Anne's FY8 88 E8
Orrell WN8 10 B7
Preston PR2 116 B1
Ramsbottom BL0 49 A2
Mayfield Sch PR7 42 C6
Mayfield St BB2 100 E3
Mayflower Ave PR1 95 A3
Mayflower Ind Est L37 12 A1
Mayflower St BB2 100 B2
Maylands Pl BB9 168 C3
Maylands Sq LA4 212 F4
Maynard St PR1,PR2 116 D2
Mayo Dr PR4 56 A6
Mayor Ave FY1 129 C2
Maypark PR5 77 A5
Mayson St BB1 100 E4
Maytree Wlk WN8 18 B4
Mayville Rd BB9 147 B6
McCall Cl PR4 112 A3
McDonald Rd LA3 208 D5
McKenzie St PR5 76 F8
Mead Ave PR5 59 B8
Meadow Ave
Fleetwood FY7 193 E1
Knott End-on-S FY6 195 A6
Southport PR8 34 C4
Meadow Bank Maghull L31 5 B2
3 Ormskirk L39 15 F5
Penwortham PR1 95 C3
Meadow Bank Ave BB10 147 B5
Meadow Bank Rd 15 BB9 147 D8
Meadow Bolton PR5 58 A8
Meadow Brow PR9 53 D5
Meadow Cl Accrington BB5 124 F1
Billington BB7 143 A3
Brierfield BB10 147 C4
Clifton PR4 114 D2
Foulridge BB8 191 D1
Skelmersdale WN8 9 D7
Westhead L40 16 E4
Wrea Green PR4 112 B3
Meadow Clough WN8 18 B4
Meadow Cotts OL12 70 D3
Meadow Court Rd LA4 212 F3
Meadow Cr PR4 112 F6
Meadow Cres FY6 151 A3
Meadow Croft
Nether Kellet LA6 216 F4
West Bradford BB7 186 E5
Meadow Ct 11
Oswaldtwistle BB5 102 E4
Preston PR1 95 E6
Meadow Dr
Bolton-le-S LA5 216 A5
Ormskirk L39 15 C2
Warton PR4 91 C5
Meadow Field PR1 95 E2
Meadow Gate BB3 81 B2
Meadow Gdns BB1 123 B1
Meadow Head Ave OL12 51 D6
Meadow Head Cl BB2 100 A1
Meadow Head La
Darwen BB3 80 B4
Longton PR4 73 F7
Meadow La
Clayton Brook PR5 77 B4
Croston PR5 56 E1
Hesketh Bank PR4 72 F4
Hoscar L40 25 C6
Knott End-on-S FY6 194 F4
Lytham St Anne's FY8 90 E4
Maghull L31 5 F1
Rufford L40 38 D3
Southport PR8 20 D3
Meadow Pk Galgate LA2 206 F4
Garstang PR3 199 C1
Haslingden BL0 67 C4
Kirkham PR4 112 E6
Staining FY3 130 D5
Meadow Reach PR1 95 B2
Meadow Rise BB2 80 A8
Meadow St
Accrington BB5 103 C6
Adlington PR7 30 A6
Barnoldswick BB18 200 A4
17 Burnley BB11 126 F6
Darwen BB3 64 B6
Great Harwood BB6 123 C4
Lancaster LA1 210 D8
Leyland PR5 76 A1
Padiham BB12 145 C1
Preston PR1 96 A8
Wheelton PR6 61 A7
Meadow Vale PR5 58 A8
Meadow View
Clitheroe BB7 164 C8
Farleton LA2 232 A6
Great Plumpton PR4 111 F7
Lancaster LA1 213 D3
Rochdale OL12 51 A1
Southport PR8 34 D4
Meadow Way
Arkholme LA6 235 B3
Bacup OL13 86 F2
Barnoldswick BB18 200 D4
Blackrod BL6 30 E1
Coppull PR7 28 D8
Edgworth BL7 47 E6
Garstang PR3 199 C2
Ramsbottom BL9 49 C2
Meadoway Church BB5 103 A7
Longton PR4 73 F8
Tarleton PR4 56 A5
Meadowbarn Cl PR4 115 E5
Meadowbridge Cl L40 16 E4
Meadowbrook
Blackpool FY3 130 C2
Burscough L40 24 D2
Meadowbrook Cl BL9 32 C4
Meadowcroft
Blackburn BB3 81 A6
Euxton PR7 59 B3
Formby L37 11 F2
Lytham St Anne's FY8 110 A1
Skelmersdale WN8 18 B4
Meadowcroft Ave
Catterall PR3 178 D3
Cleveleys FY5 172 E2
Hambleton FY6 174 C1
Meadowcroft Bsns Pk
PR4 95 B1
Meadowcroft Cl BB4 85 A5
Meadowcroft Gr LA3 212 B1
Meadowcroft Rd PR5 58 D7
Meadowfield Fulwood PR2 116 F8
Halton LA2 214 E7
Orrell WN8 10 A7
Meadowfield Cl LA2 214 E7
Meadowfields BB2 80 D7
Meadowhead Cty Inf Sch
BB2 100 B1
Meadowhead Jun Sch
BB2 80 B8
Meadowlands
Charnock Richard PR7 41 D4
Clitheroe BB7 164 C8
Meadows Ave Bacup OL13 86 F4
Cleveleys FY5 172 F2
Haslingden BB4 84 C2
Meadows Cl LA5 219 E4
Meadows The
Arnside LA5 218 C8
Bamber Bridge PR5 96 F3
Billington BB7 143 A4
Burnley BB12 126 D8
Cleveleys FY5 172 F2
Colne BB8 169 D6
Darwen BB3 80 E5
Elswick PR4 153 F1
Heskin Green PR7 40 E2
2 Leyland PR5 75 B1
Oswaldtwistle BB5 102 F3
Whitworth OL12 70 C1
Yealand Redmayne LA5 219 E3

Meadowside
Claughton, Lancaster LA2 ... 231 F5
Croston PR5 ... 57 A2
Grindleton BB7 ... 187 C8
Lancaster LA1 ... 210 F7
Walmer Bridge PR4 ... 74 A5
Meadowside Ave BB5 ... 123 E3
Meadowside Dr PR5 ... 97 E1
Meadowside Rd LA4 ... 212 E3
Meads Rd PR2 ... 116 B1
Meadup Ct LA3 ... 212 D2
Meadway Becconsall PR4 ... 72 F2
Blackpool FY4 ... 129 F1
Clayton Green PR6 ... 77 B3
Penwortham PR1 ... 95 A5
Ramsbottom BL0 ... 67 C1
Skelmersdale WN8 ... 18 A4
Meadway Cl BL6 ... 31 D3
Meagles La PR3,PR4 ... 153 E3
Mealhouse La 6 PR7 ... 42 C8
Mealrigg La LA6 ... 235 A7
Meanwood Ave FY4 ... 109 F7
Meanwood Brow 15 OL12 ... 51 C1
Meanwood Prim Sch OL12 ... 51 C1
Meanygate PR5 ... 96 E1
Mearbeck Pl 6 LA1 ... 213 D2
Mearley Brook Fold BB7 ... 164 F7
Mearley Rd PR2 ... 117 E4
Mearley St BB7 ... 164 E7
Mearley Syke BB7 ... 164 F8
Meath Rd PR1 ... 95 D6
Mede The PR4 ... 113 B3
Medina Cl BB5 ... 103 B5
Medlar Cl PR4 ... 112 E6
Medlar Ct PR4 ... 113 A6
Medlar Gate PR4 ... 113 A6
Medlar La PR4 ... 132 E4
Medley St OL12 ... 51 F1
Medlock Ave FY7 ... 193 D2
Medlock Pl FY7 ... 193 D2
Medway PR2 ... 116 F6
Medway Ave FY7 ... 172 D8
Medway Cl PR5 ... 96 B1
Medway Dr BL6 ... 31 D3
Medway Ho 6 PR1 ... 96 D8
Meeting House La LA1 ... 210 E8
Meins Croft BB2 ... 100 A6
Meins Rd BB2 ... 99 F6
Melba Rd PR2 ... 117 E3
Melbert Ave PR2 ... 116 C3
Melbourne Ave
Cleveleys FY5 ... 150 F7
Fleetwood FY7 ... 172 E8
Melbourne Cl BL6 ... 31 C3
Melbourne Ct FY5 ... 150 E8
Melbourne Gr BL6 ... 31 C3
Melbourne Rd 11 LA1 ... 211 A8
Melbourne St Darwen BB3 ... 64 B6
5 Enfield BB5 ... 124 A1
2 Newchurch BB4 ... 85 F1
Oswaldtwistle BB5 ... 102 D3
Padiham BB12 ... 125 D7
22 Preston PR1 ... 95 F8
9 Whitehall BB3 ... 64 B6
Melbreck WN8 ... 18 A4
Melbury Dr BL6 ... 31 F1
Meldon Grange LA3 ... 209 A8
Meldon Rd Heysham LA3 ... 209 A7
Heysham LA3 ... 209 A8
Meldreth Cl L37 ... 11 C1
Melford Cl PR6 ... 60 F3
Melford Dr WN5 ... 10 D3
Melfort Cl BB2 ... 99 F1
Melia Cl BB4 ... 84 F2
Melita St 6 BB3 ... 64 B8
Melling Brow LA6 ... 235 C2
Melling Ct 3 Colne BB8 ... 169 C5
Morecambe LA4 ... 212 D3
Melling Ho 4 LA1 ... 211 A3
Melling Rd Hornby LA2 ... 232 B7
Southport PR9 ... 34 E7
Melling St 20 PR1 ... 95 F8
Melling St Wilfred CE Prim Sch LA6 ... 235 D2
Melling's La FY8 ... 110 A1
Mellings PR1 ... 96 C6
Mellings Ave WN5 ... 10 E1
Mellings Fold 3 PR1 ... 96 C6
Mellings Wood FY8 ... 110 A1
Mellishaw La LA3 ... 212 G1
Mellor Brow BB2 ... 120 D2
Mellor Cl Burnley BB11 ... 126 D3
Standish WN6 ... 28 E2
Mellor Ct PR3 ... 139 B7
Mellor La BB2 ... 120 F3
Mellor Pl 6 PR1 ... 96 B7
Mellor Rd Kirkham PR4 ... 113 A5
Leyland PR5 ... 75 D2
Mellowfield Sch PR9 ... 34 C7
Mellwood Ave FY3 ... 150 F1
Melrose Ave
Blackpool FY3 ... 129 E8
Burnley BB11 ... 126 D4
Fulwood PR2 ... 117 C5
Morecambe LA4 ... 212 F5
Oswaldtwistle BB5 ... 102 F3
Southport PR9 ... 53 B5
Melrose Gdn PR5 ... 57 C2
Melrose St 10 Darwen BB3 ... 80 F2
Lancaster LA1 ... 211 A7
Ramsbottom BL0 ... 49 B2
Melrose Terr OL13 ... 87 A7
Melrose Way PR7 ... 42 D5
Melton Gr FY8 ... 89 E3
Melton Pl Cleveleys FY5 ... 150 C8
Leyland PR5 ... 76 B1
Melville Ave BB18 ... 200 A3
Melville Dr BB2 ... 100 D5
Melville Gdns BB3 ... 64 A8
Melville Rd Blackpool FY2 ... 150 C4
Heysham LA3 ... 208 E5
Melville St Burnley BB10 ... 147 C1
Darwen BB3 ... 64 A8
Memorial Gdns PR3 ... 157 A4
Memory Cl PR4 ... 92 B7
Menai Dr PR2 ... 116 D7
Mendip Cl Horwich BL6 ... 31 C5
Saltcotes FY8 ... 90 E5
Mendip Rd PR5 ... 76 D1
Menivale Cl PR9 ... 53 B5
Meols Cl L37 ... 11 E2
Meols Cop High Sch PR8 ... 34 F5
Meols Cop Rd PR8, PR9 ... 34 F4
Meols Cop Retail Pk The PR9 ... 35 A4
Meols Cop Sta PR9 ... 34 F7
Meols Ct PR9 ... 54 A6
Meolsgate Ave PR4 ... 56 A7
Mercer Cres BB4 ... 67 A8
Mercer Ct PR7 ... 42 F1
Mercer Dr BB6 ... 123 E6
Mercer Rd PR5 ... 96 A1
Mercer St 1 Burnley BB12 ... 125 F7
16 Clayton-le-M BB5 ... 123 F3
Great Harwood BB6 ... 123 D5
Preston PR1 ... 96 C8
Mercer's La L39 ... 7 B4
Merchants Landing BB1 ... 100 F3
Merchants Quay 1 BB1 ... 100 F3
Merclesden Ave BB9 ... 169 B1
Mere Ave
Burscough Bridge L40 ... 24 E6
Fleetwood FY7 ... 193 D1
Mere Brook FY3 ... 130 E5
Mere Brow La PR4 ... 55 A2
Mere Cl Broughton PR3 ... 136 C3
Skelmersdale WN8 ... 17 F2
Mere Ct Burnley BB11 ... 126 B4
Burscough Bridge L40 ... 24 E5
Mere Fold PR7 ... 41 D3
Mere La Banks PR9 ... 54 A2
Holmeswood PR4 ... 37 A7
Rufford L40 ... 37 E3
Mere Park Ct FY3 ... 130 A2
Mere Rd Blackpool FY3 ... 129 D5
Formby L37 ... 11 D2
Mere Sands Wood Nature Reserve L40 ... 37 F4
Meredith St BB9 ... 147 E7
Merefell Rd LA5 ... 216 A6
Merefield PR7 ... 60 A1
Merefield Specl Sch PR8 ... 20 B4
Merefold BL6 ... 30 F3
Mereland Cl WN5 ... 10 E6
Mereland Rd FY3 ... 130 A2
Merepark Dr PR9 ... 53 B4
Meres Way PR8 ... 34 B2
Mereside Cl PR4 ... 73 F7
Mereside Inf Sch FY4 ... 130 B1
Merewood WN8 ... 18 A4
Meriden Cl PR8 ... 20 B5
Merlecrest Dr PR4 ... 56 A8
Merlewood BL0 ... 67 E3
Merlewood Ave PR9 ... 53 B3
Merlin Cl PR6 ... 61 A3
Merlin Dr BB5 ... 102 D3
Merlin Gr Leyland PR5 ... 58 C8
Padiham BB12 ... 125 E6
Merlin Rd BB2 ... 100 B6
Merlyn Rd FY5 ... 172 E1
Merrick Ave PR1 ... 96 F8
Merrilox Ave L31 ... 5 D3
Merry Trees La PR2,PR4 ... 115 E5
Merryburn Cl PR2 ... 117 A4
Merscar La L40 ... 23 D6
Mersey Ave Darwen BB3 ... 80 D3
Formby L37 ... 11 E6
Maghull L31 ... 5 F2
Mersey Rd Blackpool FY4 ... 109 B8
Fleetwood FY7 ... 193 F4
Orrell WN5 ... 10 F7
Mersey St Bacup OL13 ... 87 A1
Burnley BB12 ... 126 A6
Longridge PR3 ... 139 B8
Preston PR2 ... 95 C8
Merton Ave PR2 ... 116 F6
Merton Gr PR6 ... 60 F3
Merton St Burnley BB12 ... 126 F7
4 Nelson BB9 ... 168 D1
Messenger St BB9 ... 148 A7
Meta St BB2 ... 100 E2
Metcalf Dr BB5 ... 124 D6
Metcalfe St BB12 ... 126 B5
Mete St PR1 ... 96 D8
Methuen Ave
Coupe Green PR5 ... 97 E3
Fulwood PR2 ... 116 E6
Methuen Cl PR5 ... 97 E3
Methuen Dr PR5 ... 97 F3
Metropolitan Bsns Pk FY3 ... 130 B2
Metropolitan Dr FY3 ... 130 B2
Mettle Cote OL13 ... 87 A1
Meville Ave BB3 ... 64 A7
Mewith La LA2 ... 233 C6
Mews The Morecambe LA4 ... 213 A5
1 Padiham BB12 ... 145 C1
1 Radford BB3 ... 64 C7
Southport PR8 ... 34 A5
Mexford Ave FY2 ... 129 D8
Meyler Ave FY3 ... 129 E8
Michael Pl LA4 ... 212 G5
Michael Wife La
Edenfield BL0 ... 67 F2
Edenfield BL0 ... 67 F3
Michael's La L39 ... 21 C3
Michaels Cl L37 ... 11 E3
Michaelson Ave LA4 ... 213 A4
Mickering La L39 ... 6 C5
Mickleden Ave PR2 ... 116 F7
Mickleden Rd FY4 ... 130 C1
Micklefield Ct 2 PR5 ... 75 D1
Micklegate FY5 ... 150 C7
Micklehurst Cres BB11 ... 126 D2
Mickleton Dr PR8 ... 20 A5
Middle Hey PR4 ... 73 E3
Middle Hill OL12 ... 51 F4
Middle Holly Rd PR3 ... 199 C8
Middle La LA2 ... 207 A6
Middle Meanygate PR4 ... 55 C7
Middle Moss La
Great Altcar L37 ... 12 F3
Haskayne L37 ... 13 A2
Middle St Blackpool FY1 ... 129 B3
Colne BB8 ... 169 C4
Lancaster LA1 ... 210 F8
Whitworth OL12 ... 70 D1
Middle Withins La L37, L38 ... 4 A7
Middlefield PR5 ... 58 A8
Middleforth CE Prim Sch PR1 ... 95 D3
Middleforth Gn PR1 ... 95 E4
Middleforth Ind Est 4 PR1 ... 95 E4
Middlegate LA3 ... 213 A2
Middlegate Gn BB4 ... 105 A1
Middlesex Ave BB12 ... 126 B7
Middleton Ave FY7 ... 193 D1
Middleton Dr BB9 ... 168 E6
Middleton Rd
Heysham LA3 ... 208 E5
Heysham, Middleton LA3 ... 209 B2
Middleton Tower Holiday Ctr LA3 ... 208 E1
Middleton Way LA3 ... 208 F6
Middlewood WN8 ... 18 A4
Middlewood Cl
Eccleston PR7 ... 40 C6
Ormskirk L39 ... 6 C7
Middlewood Dr L39 ... 6 C7
Middlewood Rd L39 ... 6 C7
Midfield BB6 ... 122 C8
Midge Hall La
Drummersdale PR9 ... 36 C3
Leyland PR4,PR5 ... 74 F4
Midgeland Rd FY4 ... 110 B5
Midgeland Terr FY4 ... 110 C5
Midgery La Fulwood PR2 ... 117 B7
Fulwood PR2 ... 117 C6
Fulwood PR2,PR3 ... 117 A8
Midgley St BB8 ... 169 E4
Midhurst Dr PR8 ... 20 B4
Midland St
12 Accrington BB5 ... 103 C5
Nelson BB9 ... 168 E1
Midland Terr LA5 ... 217 D3
Midsummer St BB2 ... 100 C5
Midville Pl 14 BB3 ... 81 A1
Milbanke Ave PR4 ... 113 A5
Milbeck Cl PR3 ... 138 F5
Milbourne Rd BL9 ... 32 A6
Milbourne St FY1 ... 129 C5
Milbrook Cl BB11 ... 126 B5
Milburn Ave FY5 ... 172 F5
Mildred Cl FY5 ... 173 A3
Mile End Cl BB8 ... 191 D1
Mile End Row BB2 ... 100 B6
Mile Rd FY5 ... 153 A1
Mile Stone Mdw PR7 ... 59 D4
Miles Ave OL13 ... 69 D8
Miles La WN6 ... 19 E6
Miles St PR1 ... 116 F2
Miles Wlk PR1 ... 116 E2
Milestone Mdw PR7 ... 59 D4
Milestone Pl LA2 ... 231 C3
Miletas Pl FY8 ... 89 C4
Milford Ave FY2 ... 150 D1
Milford Cl L37 ... 11 C1
Milford St Colne BB8 ... 169 C5
6 Rochdale OL12 ... 51 F1
Milk St BL0 ... 49 B5
Milking La BB3 ... 81 A6
Milking Stile La LA1 ... 210 D8
Mill Bank WN6 ... 19 D7
Mill Brook PR3 ... 178 D3
Mill Brook Pl BB7 ... 164 D1
Mill Brow Haskayne L39 ... 14 A7
Kirkby Lonsdale LA6 ... 238 C2
Lowgill LA2 ... 233 B2
Mill Brow Rd BB18 ... 201 C2
Mill Cl PR4 ... 134 C8
Mill Cotts BB3 ... 81 F3
Mill Ct PR3 ... 139 B8
Mill Dam Cl L40 ... 24 C2
Mill Dam La L40 ... 16 D8
Mill Entrance BB5 ... 123 F2
Mill Field Clayton-le-M BB5 ... 123 F4
Parbold WN8 ... 26 C1
Mill Gap St 17 BB3 ... 64 A8
Mill Gate Fulwood PR2 ... 116 D3
15 Rawtenstall BB4 ... 85 A3
Mill Gdns 6 LA2 ... 233 D8
Mill Gn BB8 ... 169 D4
Mill Haven PR2 ... 116 D3
Mill Hey Ave FY6 ... 151 E1
Mill Hey La L40 ... 38 C3
Mill Hill Oswaldtwistle BB5 ... 102 E4
Preston PR1 ... 95 E8
Mill Hill Bridge St BB2 ... 100 B2
Mill Hill Cotts BL6 ... 43 F1
Mill Hill Gr LA3 ... 209 A2
Mill Hill La BB11 ... 125 B3
Mill Hill St BB2 ... 100 B2
Mill Hill Sta BB2 ... 100 B2
Mill Ho 19 LA1 ... 211 A8
Mill Ho Mews 17 LA1 ... 211 A8
Mill House La
Clayton Brook PR6 ... 77 F8
Longridge PR3 ... 140 A8
Mill House View WN8 ... 10 C7
Mill La Appley Bridge WN6 ... 19 D7
Becconsall PR4 ... 72 F2
Blackburn BB2 ... 100 E4
Bolton Green PR7 ... 41 A8
Bolton Green PR7 ... 59 A1
Bolton-le-S LA5 ... 216 A6
Burscough L40 ... 24 E4
Carnforth LA5 ... 217 D4
Caton LA2 ... 231 B3
Clayton Green PR6 ... 77 C1
Coppull PR7 ... 41 E2
Darwen BB3 ... 63 A5
Earby BB18 ... 201 D2
Eccleston PR7 ... 40 C5
Elswick PR4 ... 154 B1
Fleetwood FY7 ... 194 B4
Fulwood PR2 ... 116 C4
Gisburn BB7 ... 225 B4
Goosnargh PR3 ... 137 E6
Great Harwood BB6 ... 124 A6
Halton LA2 ... 214 F6
Hambleton FY6 ... 174 E1
Haskayne L39 ... 14 F1
Hesketh Lane PR3 ... 160 C8
Heskin Green PR7 ... 41 A2
Horwich BL6 ... 31 D4
Leyland PR5 ... 58 D8
Leyland PR5 ... 75 E3
Low Bentham LA2 ... 233 C7
Orrell WN8 ... 10 A8
Parbold WN8 ... 26 C1
Skelmersdale, Pennylands WN8 ... 17 F2
Southport PR9 ... 53 A1
Staining FY3 ... 130 D5
Stalmine FY6 ... 174 D7
Waddington BB7 ... 186 A8
Walton-le-D PR5 ... 96 D5
Warton PR4 ... 91 F6
Wrea Green PR4 ... 112 A3
Mill La Ind Est BB7 ... 225 B3
Mill Lane Cres PR9 ... 53 A1
Mill Leat Cl WN8 ... 26 C2
Mill Leat Mews WN8 ... 26 C2
Mill Rd Orrell WN5 ... 10 D5
Southport PR8 ... 20 D5
Mill Row BB4 ... 84 F5
Mill St Accrington BB5 ... 103 F1
Adlington PR6 ... 30 B8
Bacup OL13 ... 86 F3
Barnoldswick BB18 ... 200 A2
Barrowford BB9 ... 168 D4
Church BB5 ... 102 F6
Clayton-le-M BB5 ... 123 F2
4 Coppull PR7 ... 41 E1
Great Harwood BB6 ... 123 C5
Haslingden BB4 ... 84 B5
Kirkham PR4 ... 113 A5
Lancaster LA1 ... 211 A8
Leyland, Farington PR5 ... 76 B3
Leyland, Seven Stars PR5 ... 58 D8
Ormskirk L39 ... 15 F5
Oswaldtwistle BB5 ... 102 D3
Padiham BB12 ... 125 C8
Preesall FY6 ... 195 B3
Preston PR1 ... 95 D8
Ramsbottom BL0 ... 49 A4
Southport PR8 ... 34 C6
West Bradford BB7 ... 186 E5
Mill The PR1 ... 95 F8
Mill View PR4 ... 92 B7
Mill View Ct L39 ... 7 E6
Mill Wood Cl PR6 ... 78 C3
Mill Yd BL9 ... 32 A3
Millar Barn La BB4 ... 68 F8
Millar's Pace PR9 ... 53 B5
Millard Cl LA3 ... 208 F5
Millbank Fulwood PR2 ... 116 C3
4 Preston PR1 ... 96 B8
Millbank Brow L40 ... 24 F3
Millbank La L31, L39 ... 5 F3
Millbrook BB12 ... 146 E8
Millbrook Cl
Skelmersdale WN8 ... 17 E2
Wheelton PR6 ... 61 A7
Millbrook Ct BB7 ... 186 E5
Millbrook Mews 1 FY8 ... 90 C3
Millbrook Row PR6 ... 43 B1
Millbrook St BB3 ... 80 F7
Millbrook Way PR1 ... 95 C3
Millcombe Way PR5 ... 96 E3
Millcroft Chorley PR7 ... 60 A2
Fulwood PR2 ... 116 D4
Millcroft Ave WN5 ... 10 D5
Milldyke Cl FY4 ... 109 F6
Miller Ave PR6 ... 79 B2
Miller Cl BB5 ... 102 C5
Miller Cres FY6 ... 152 E1
Miller Ct LA1 ... 210 E5
Miller Field PR2 ... 115 E3
Miller Fold Ave BB5 ... 103 B3
Miller Ho 4 PR1 ... 96 A7
Miller La Catforth PR4 ... 134 E4
Fulwood PR4 ... 115 E5
Miller Rd PR1,PR2 ... 117 E2
Miller St 4 Blackpool FY1 ... 129 B1
11 Preston PR1 ... 96 C8
Ramsbottom BL9 ... 49 C2
Miller's Brow PR3 ... 204 E3
Millers Ct L39 ... 15 F5
Millersdale Cl FY5 ... 151 E7
Millersgate PR4 ... 115 E4
Millet Terr BL9 ... 32 E7
Millett St BL0 ... 49 D7
Millfield Cl PR4 ... 91 F6
Millfield High Sch FY5 ... 151 C8
Millfield Rd Blackpool FY4 ... 109 F6
Chorley PR7 ... 60 C1
Millfold OL12 ... 70 D2
Millgate BL7 ... 46 D2
Millgate Rd 18 BB4 ... 85 A3
Millgate Terr OL12 ... 70 E5
Millham St BB1 ... 100 E6
Millholme Dr LA2 ... 233 D7
Millhouse Lo PR8 ... 20 D5
Millhouse St BL0 ... 49 E8
Millington Ave FY4 ... 109 E8
Millom Ave FY2 ... 150 D4
Millom Cl FY7 ... 172 C8
Millrace Ct 5 LA1 ... 213 F2
Millrose Cl WN8 ... 17 F2
Mills PR6 ... 61 A7
Mills St OL12 ... 70 D1
Millstone Cl PR7 ... 41 F1
Millthorne Ave BB7 ... 164 D7
Millwood Cl BB2 ... 100 A1
Millwood Glade PR7 ... 60 B1
Millwood Rd PR1,PR5 ... 96 B3
Milman Cl L39 ... 15 D3
Milne St BL0 ... 67 C5
Milner Rd Darwen BB3 ... 80 E4
Lytham St Anne's FY8 ... 89 E4
Milner St Burnley BB10 ... 127 A8
Preston PR1 ... 117 A2
Whitworth OL12 ... 51 C8
Whitworth OL12 ... 70 C1
Milnshaw Gdns BB5 ... 103 B7
Milnshaw La BB5 ... 103 B6
Milnthorpe Ave FY5 ... 172 D5
Milton Ave Blackpool FY3 ... 129 F5
Clitheroe BB7 ... 186 E1
2 Thornton FY5 ... 173 A3
Milton Cl
Bamber Bridge PR5 ... 96 D2
Darwen BB3 ... 81 C1
Great Harwood BB6 ... 123 B4
Haslingden BB4 ... 67 A7
Milton Cres FY6 ... 130 D8
Milton Ct PR7 ... 41 E1
Milton Dr L39 ... 16 A4
Milton Gr
Barnoldswick BB18 ... 200 A3
Longshaw WN5 ... 10 D1
Orrell WN5 ... 10 F6
Milton Rd Colne BB8 ... 169 D5
Coppull PR7 ... 28 E8
Milton St
3 Barrowford BB9 ... 168 D4
1 Blackburn BB1 ... 101 A5
Brierfield BB9 ... 147 B5
Brierfield, Harle Syke BB10 ... 147 F3
Clayton-le-M BB5 ... 123 F3
Fleetwood FY7 ... 194 A4
Nelson BB9 ... 168 D1
Oswaldtwistle BB5 ... 102 E4
Padiham BB12 ... 125 E7
Ramsbottom BL0 ... 49 B6
Southport PR9 ... 35 A7
Milton Terr PR6 ... 60 D2
Milton Way L31 ... 5 B1
Mimosa Cl PR7 ... 60 A3
Mimosa Rd PR2 ... 117 E2
Mincing La BB2 ... 100 E4
Minden Rd PR4 ... 131 E5
Minehead Ave BB10 ... 147 D2
Minerva Rd LA1 ... 210 C8
Minnie St OL12 ... 70 D2
Minnie Terr BB2 ... 100 C6
Minor St 11 BB4 ... 85 A7
Minstead Ave L33 ... 1 A2
Minster Cres BB3 ... 64 C8
Minster Dr LA3 ... 212 E2
Minster Pk PR4 ... 115 E5
Minstrel Wlk FY6 ... 151 D4
Mint Ave BB9 ... 168 D4
Mint St BL0 ... 67 C2
Mintholme Ave PR5 ... 97 E2
Mintor Rd L33 ... 1 A2
Mire Ash Brow BB2 ... 120 D1
Mire Ridge BB8 ... 170 A3
Mirfield Gr 11 FY4 ... 129 D1
Miry La WN8 ... 26 D2
Mission Cotts L40 ... 25 B8
Mitcham Rd FY4 ... 110 B8
Mitchelgate LA6 ... 238 B2
Mitchell St Burnley BB12 ... 126 C6
Clitheroe BB7 ... 164 D7
2 Colne BB8 ... 169 D5
Mitella St BB10 ... 127 C5
Mitre St BB11 ... 126 E6
Mitten's La L37 ... 12 B3
Mitton Ave
Barrowford BB9 ... 168 F6
Rawtenstall BB4 ... 85 A4
Mitton Cl OL10 ... 32 F2
Mitton Cres PR4 ... 113 A5
Mitton Dr PR2 ... 118 A3
Mitton Gr BB10 ... 127 D5
Mitton Hos BB9 ... 168 F6
Mitton Rd
Great Mitton BB7 ... 163 F2
Whalley BB7 ... 143 B7
Mitton St BB1 ... 100 F7
Mizpah St BB10 ... 127 C5
Mizzy Rd OL12 ... 51 F1
Moira Cres PR2 ... 117 F4

Moleside Cl BB5 103 D6
Mollington Rd BB2 100 B7
Molly Wood La BB11 125 F5
Molyneux Ct 17 PR1 96 A8
Molyneux Dr FY4 109 D7
Molyneux Pl FY8 90 A4
Molyneux Rd L39 6 C7
Mona Pl PR1 95 E8
Mona Rd BB2 100 E1
Monarch Cres FY8 89 B8
Monarch St BB5 102 E4
Money Close La LA3 208 D4
Moneyclose Gr LA3 208 D5
Monk Hall St BB10 127 A7
Monk St Accrington BB5 103 A6
2 Clitheroe BB7 164 D7
Monk's La FY6 195 A1
Monkroyd Ave BB18 200 A2
Monks Carr La L37, L38 4 A6
Monks Cl L37 12 A1
Monks Dr Formby L37 12 A1
Longridge PR3 139 A6
Withnell PR6 79 A1
Monks Gate FY8 89 D7
Monks La L40 24 D7
Monks Wlk PR1 95 C6
Monkswell Ave LA5 216 A5
Monkswell Dr LA5 216 A6
Monkswood Ave LA4 213 A5
Monmouth Ct PR2 115 F3
Monmouth Rd BB1 101 C5
Monmouth St 5
Burnley BB12 126 D6
Colne BB8 170 A5
Monroe Dr FY7 193 D3
Montagu Mews L37 11 E5
Montagu Rd L37 11 E5
Montague Cl BB2 100 D4
Montague Rd BB11 126 E5
Montague St
Blackburn BB2 100 D5
Blackpool FY4 109 B8
Brierfield BB9 147 B5
4 Clitheroe BB7 164 D8
Colne BB8 169 E6
Montcliffe Rd PR6 60 E1
Monteagle Dr LA2 232 B7
Monteagle Sq LA2 232 B7
Montford Ct BB12 146 F6
Montford Rd BB9 146 F6
Montgomery Ave PR9 35 B6
Montgomery Cl BB5 103 E2
Montgomery Gr BB12 126 C7
Montgomery High Sch
FY2 150 D5
Montgomery St 7 PR5 76 F8
Monthall Rise LA1 214 B1
Montjoly St PR1 96 C7
Monton Rd BB3 80 E4
Montpelier Ave FY2 150 C5
Montreal Ave FY1 129 D4
Montreal Rd BB2 100 C8
Montrose Ave
Blackpool FY1 129 C3
Ramsbottom BL0 49 A2
Montrose Cl PR6 42 E6
Montrose Cres LA3 208 E7
Montrose Dr PR9 52 F1
Montrose St
Blackburn BB2 100 C3
Brierfield BB9 147 B6
Burnley BB11 126 F4
Moody La L40 39 E1
Moody St WN6 28 E1
Moon Ave 7 FY1 129 B2
Moon St PR5 76 E8
Moons Acre LA2 233 D8
Moor Ave
Appley Bridge WN6 19 E8
Penwortham PR1 95 A4
Moor Cl Darwen BB3 64 D8
Lancaster LA1 211 A8
Southport PR8 20 D2
Moor Close La LA6 234 B1
Moor Dr WN8 9 D7
Moor Edge BB7 143 B6
Moor End Cty Prim Sch
BB5 102 D4
Moor Field
New Longton PR4 75 A7
Whalley BB7 143 B6
Moor Gate 14 LA1 211 A8
Moor Hall La PR4 113 F4
Moor Hall St PR1 116 E2
Moor Hey Cotts PR5 57 A6
Moor Hey Sch PR5 96 A1
Moor La Billington BB6,BB7 143 B2
Butt Yeats LA2 232 C5
Clitheroe BB7 164 E8
Darwen BB3 81 B3
Haslingden BB4 83 F6
Hutton PR4 94 D1
Ince Blundell L38, L23 3 E2
Lancaster LA1 211 A8
Langho BB6 122 E8
Maghull L29 4 D1
Padiham BB12 145 C1
Preston PR1 116 F1
Salterforth BB18 191 C6
Southport PR8 20 C2
Waddington BB7 223 D2
West Bradford BB7 186 D7
Whalley BB7 143 B6
Wiswell BB7 143 F7
Moor Nook Cty Prim Sch
PR2 118 A3
Moor Park Ave
Blackpool FY2 150 E4
Moor Park Ave *continued*
Preston PR1 117 A2
Moor Park High Sch PR1 117 A2
Moor Park Inf & Jun Sch
FY2 150 E3
Moor Platt Cl BL6 31 F3
Moor Rd Barber's Moor PR5 57 D3
Chorley PR7 42 B5
Haslingden BB4 66 F5
Orrell WN5 10 E6
Ramsbottom BL8 49 A6
Rivington PR6 43 E7
Moor Side La
Ramsbottom BL0 50 A7
Wiswell BB7 143 F7
Moor St Clayton-le-M BB5 123 F3
Kirkham PR4 113 A5
32 Lancaster LA1 210 F8
Ormskirk L39 15 F5
Moor View Bacup OL13 87 A4
Bacup, Brandwood OL13 69 B7
Rawtenstall BB4 68 F6
Salterforth BB18 191 E8
Moor Way BL8 48 C3
Moorbottom Rd BL8 48 E5
Moorbrook Sch PR2 116 E3
Moorbrook St PR1 116 E1
Moorcroft Blackburn BB3 81 A6
Broughton PR3 136 B2
Edenfield BL0 67 D2
Moorcroft Cres PR2 117 D3
Moore Dr BB12 145 F5
Moore St Blackpool FY4 129 B1
Colne BB8 169 C5
Nelson BB9 147 F7
Padiham BB12 125 F7
Preston PR1 96 C7
Moore Tree Dr FY4 110 A8
Moorend BB7 164 F7
Moores La WN6 28 D2
Moorfield BL7 47 D6
Moorfield Ave
Blackburn BB1 121 E3
Blackpool FY3 129 E6
Carleton FY6 151 B4
Huncoat BB5 103 F8
Moorfield Cl
Clayton-le-M BB5 124 B3
Fulwood PR2 116 E8
Preston PR1 95 A2
Moorfield Dr
Clayton-le-M BB5 124 B3
Fulwood PR2 117 E3
Lytham St Anne's FY8 90 A4
Moorfield Ind Est BB5 124 B3
Moorfield La L40 23 C3
Moorfield Pl 3 OL12 51 F1
Moorfield Rd
Clayton-le-M BB5 124 B3
Leyland PR5 58 C8
Moorfield Sch PR1 117 A3
Moorfield Way BB5 124 B3
Moorfields Blackpool FY2 150 F4
Chorley PR6 60 E1
Moorfields Ave PR2 116 E8
Moorgate Accrington BB5 103 B2
Blackpool FY4 109 F6
Bury BL9 32 A3
Fulwood PR2 116 F5
Ormskirk L39 15 E4
Moorgate Gdns BB2 100 C1
Moorgate Rd BB18 200 A1
Moorgate St BB2 100 C1
Moorhead Gdns PR4 91 E7
Moorhead High Sch BB5 103 A7
Moorhead St 2 BB8 169 C5
Moorhen Pl 14 FY5 172 F1
Moorhey Cres
Penwortham PR1 95 B5
Walton Summit PR5 77 A8
Moorhey Dr PR1 95 B5
Moorhouse Ave BB5 103 A4
Moorhouse Cl BB5 103 A4
Moorhouse St
Accrington BB5 103 A4
1 Blackpool FY1 129 B7
Burnley BB11 126 C5
Moorhouses L38 2 F3
Mooring The 4 PR6 42 E8
Moorings The
Burnley BB12 126 E7
Hest Bank LA2 215 D1
Maghull L31 5 B4
Moorland Ave
Blackburn BB2 79 D7
Clitheroe BB7 186 F3
Darwen BB3 80 D2
Earby BB18 201 C1
Fulwood PR2 117 D4
Poulton-le-F FY6 151 E4
Whitworth OL12 51 C7
Moorland Cl BB9 168 F6
Moorland Cres
Clitheroe BB7 186 F2
Fulwood PR2 117 D4
Whitworth OL12 51 C7
Moorland Dr
Brierfield BB9 147 D4
Horwich BL6 31 F3
Moorland Gate PR6 42 F6
Moorland Gdns FY6 151 E4
Moorland Rd
Blackburn BB2 80 C7
Burnley BB11 126 F3
Clitheroe BB7 186 F2
Langho BB6 142 C1
Lytham St Anne's FY8 89 A7
Poulton-le-F FY6 151 F4
Moorland Rise BB4 84 C2
Moorland Sch BB7 186 E2
Moorland St OL12 51 E1
Moorland Terr OL12 51 A1
Moorland View BB9 147 E6
Moorlands PR1 116 E3
Moorlands Gr LA3 212 B3
Moorlands Terr OL13 87 A1
Moorlands The OL13 87 A8
Moorlands View BL0 67 D5
Moorside Melling LA6 235 D2
Moor Side PR4 133 D3
Moorside Ave
Blackburn BB1 101 D4
Brierfield BB9 147 D4
Fulwood PR2 117 F3
Horwich BL6 31 C4
Moorside Cl LA6 235 D2
Moorside Cres OL13 87 A4
Moorside Cty Prim Sch
LA1 211 B4
Moorside Dr Enfield BB5 124 A2
Preston PR1 95 B2
Moorside La PR4 135 C4
Moorside Prim Sch WN8 9 E7
Moorside Rd Caton LA2 231 D3
Edgworth BL7 65 E1
Moorsview BL0 49 B6
Moorthorpe Cl BB3 64 A6
Moorview Cl BB10 147 E2
Moorview Ct 2 FY4 109 F7
Moorway FY6 151 F4
Moray Cl BL0 49 A4
Morecambe Bay
Com Prim Sch LA4 212 E5
Morecambe Bay
Nature Reserve LA5 215 D5
Morecambe High Sch
LA4 212 F6
Morecambe L Pk LA4 212 C5
Morecambe Rd
Blackburn BB2 100 F1
Lancaster LA3,LA1 213 C2
Morecambe Rd Sch LA3 213 B3
Morecambe St E LA4 212 E6
Morecambe St W LA4 212 E6
Morecambe Sta LA4 212 D5
Moresby Ave FY3 130 B7
Moreton Dr
Poulton-le-F FY6 151 D2
Staining FY3 130 D5
Moreton Gn 2 LA3 208 F7
Moreton St BB5 103 B6
Morewood Dr LA6 234 C7
Morland Ave
Bamber Bridge PR5 76 A7
Kirkham PR4 112 F7
Morley Ave BB2 100 A1
Morley Cl LA1 213 E3
Morley Rd Blackpool FY4 129 E1
Lancaster LA1 213 E3
Southport PR9 34 E8
Morley St 2 Burnley BB11 127 B4
1 Padiham BB12 125 D8
Morningside LA1 210 E7
Mornington Rd
Adlington PR6 30 B8
Lytham St Anne's FY8 90 E4
Penwortham PR1 95 B5
Preston PR1 117 F1
Southport PR9 34 C7
Morris Cl PR5 59 A8
Morris Cres PR2 117 D2
Morris Ct PR2 117 D2
Morris Hey L39 22 D3
Morris La L39,L40 22 E3
Morris Rd Chorley PR6 60 E1
Fulwood PR2 117 D2
Orrell WN8 10 A7
Morrison St PR6 60 D2
Morse St BB10 127 D5
Morston Ave FY2 150 E1
Mort St BL6 31 B4
Mortimer Gr LA3 209 A8
Morton Cty Prim Sch
FY4 109 F7
Morton St 22 BB1 100 E5
Morton Wlk 6 BB3 64 B6
Morven Gr PR8 34 E7
Moscow Mill St BB5 102 E5
Mosedale Dr BB12 126 B8
Moseley Ave BB18 200 F1
Moseley Cl BB11 127 A2
Moseley Rd BB11 127 A3
Mosley Ave BL0 49 B2
Mosley St
Barnoldswick BB18 200 B2
Blackburn BB2 100 E2
4 Leyland PR5 76 A1
Nelson BB9 147 D8
Preston PR1 96 C8
Southport PR8 34 B4
Mosman Pl BB9 168 C3
Moss Acre Rd PR1 95 E2
Moss Ave Orrell WN5 10 D3
Preston PR2 116 A2
Moss Bank Coppull PR7 41 E1
Ormskirk L39 15 D2
Moss Bank Ct L39 15 D2
Moss Bank Pl FY4 109 F8
Moss Bridge L40 25 C3
Moss Bridge La L40 25 C2
Moss Bridge Pk PR5 76 C8
Moss Cl Chorley PR6 42 E8
Haslingden BB4 67 A8
Moss Cotts L40 17 A3
Moss Delph La L39 15 C1
Moss Dr BL6 31 F3
Moss Edge La
Blackpool FY4 110 A3
Lytham St Anne's FY8 110 B2
Moss End Way L33 1 D3
Moss Fold Rd BB3 80 E5
Moss Gate BB1 101 B6
Moss Gn L37 12 B4
Moss Hall La FY8 89 E7
Moss Hall Rd BB5 103 C8
Moss Hey Hey PR4 55 A3
Moss House La
Great Plumpton PR4 111 C7
Much Hoole PR4 74 B2
Stalmine FY6 174 D8
Moss House Rd
Blackpool FY4 110 A6
Broughton PR4 136 B2
Moss La Appley Bridge WN6 27 E3
Bamber Bridge PR5 76 B8
Banks PR9 54 D6
Becconsall PR4 72 C1
Bickerstaffe L39 7 F2
Blackburn BB1,BB5 101 F3
Blackrod BL6 30 F2
Bretherton PR5 57 C8
Burscough L40 25 A7
Burton-in-K LA5 234 A8
Catforth PR4 134 D5
Chipping PR3 183 A1
Clayton-le-W PR5 76 D2
Coppull PR7 41 E1
Croston PR5 39 A8
Duncombe PR3 156 D2
Farington PR5 75 D5
Formby L37, L39 12 E5
Garstang PR3 178 B7
Glasson LA2 205 E1
Hambleton FY6 174 D1
Hightown L38, L23 3 C2
Inskip PR4 155 B3
Kingsfold PR1 95 E1
Kirkby, Northwood L33 1 B3
Leyland PR5 76 C2
Lucas Green PR6 60 D5
Maghull L31 5 E2
Maghull, Lydiate L31 5 D5
New Longton PR4 74 E7
Silverdale LA5 218 F5
Skelmersdale WN8 8 F6
Southport PR9 35 B8
St Michael's on W PR3 155 B8
Walmer Bridge PR4 74 C4
Wymott PR5 57 F5
Moss La E PR4 114 A8
Moss La W PR4 113 F7
Moss Lane View WN8 8 F6
Moss Lea PR4 56 A7
Moss Nook
Burscough Bridge L40 24 E6
Ormskirk L39 15 C2
Moss Pl LA1 214 A4
Moss Rd Lancaster LA3 209 D7
Orrell WN5 10 D3
Southport PR8 34 C2
Moss Side
Barnoldswick BB18 200 C2
Formby L37 12 B4
Moss Side Cty Prim Sch
PR5 75 B1
Moss Side La
Hale Nook FR6,PR3 175 C7
Lane Heads PR3 154 E5
Mere Brow PR4 54 F4
Stalmine FY6 174 E7
Wrea Green PR4 112 A3
Moss Side St OL12 70 E5
Moss Side Sta FY8 111 D1
Moss Side Way PR5 58 C8
Moss St Bamber Bridge PR5 76 B8
Blackburn BB1 101 A6
7 Clitheroe BB7 164 D8
Great Harwood BB6 123 C4
Preston PR1 95 E8
Ramsbottom BL9 49 D2
Moss Terr PR6 60 E5
Moss View Maghull L31 5 F1
Ormskirk L39 15 E4
Southport PR8 20 E5
Moss Way 3 FY4 109 F7
Mossbank BB1 101 A6
Mossbourne Rd FY6 151 C2
Mossbrook Dr PR4 115 F5
Mossdale BB1 101 A6
Mossdale Ave PR2 117 D4
Mossfield Cl
Bamber Bridge PR5 76 B8
Bury BL9 32 B4
Mossfield Rd PR6 42 E8
Mossgate Cty Prim Sch
Heysham LA3 208 F8
Morecambe LA3 212 B1
Mossgiel Ave PR8 20 B5
Mosshill Cl L31 5 C3
Mosslands PR5 75 D1
Mosslawn Rd L32 1 A1
Mosslea Dr PR3 136 B8
Mossom La FY5 150 D7
Mossway PR4 74 F7
Mossy Lea Fold WN6 28 A3
Mossy Lea Rd WN6 27 F5
Mostyn St BB3 80 E4
Motherwell Cres PR8 34 F3
Mottram Cl PR6 60 C5
Mottram Mews 6 BL6 31 B4
Mottram St BL6 31 B4
Moulden Brow BB2 79 B7
Moulding Cl BB2 100 B4
Mounsey Rd PR5 76 F8
Mount Ave Lancaster LA1 213 F3
Morecambe LA4 213 B7
Rawtenstall BB4 68 F8
Mount Carmel Prep Sch
L39 15 D2
Mount Carmel RC High Sch
BB5 103 A4
Mount Cres Orrell WN5 10 F6
Over Town BB10 107 A8
Mount Gdns LA4 213 A7
Mount House Cl L37 12 B5
Mount House Rd L37 12 B5
Mount La Burnley BB10 127 F1
Cornholme OL14 108 C3
Over Town BB10 107 A8
Mount Pleasant
Adlington PR6 30 A8
Arnside LA5 218 C8
16 Bacup OL13 69 C8
Blackburn BB1 100 F5
Brinscall PR6 62 A8
Chatburn BB7 187 D5
Edgworth BL7 47 D5
High Bentham LA2 233 D8
Nangreaves BL9 49 F3
8 Preston PR1 95 F8
Rawtenstall BB4 84 E2
Sabden BB7 145 A7
Slaidburn BB7 223 B7
Whittle-le-W PR6 60 C8
Mount Pleasant La LA5 216 B5
Mount Pleasant Prim Sch
BB5 123 F2
Mount Pleasant St
3 Burnley BB11 126 F5
Cornholme OL14 108 A1
Horwich BL6 31 D1
6 Oswaldtwistle BB5 102 E4
Mount Rd Burnley BB11 126 F4
Fleetwood FY7 194 A5
Mount St Accrington BB5 103 B4
13 Barrowford BB9 168 D3
Blackpool FY1 129 B6
Brierfield BB9 147 B5
Clayton-le-M BB5 124 A2
Fleetwood FY7 194 A4
Great Harwood BB6 123 C6
Horwich BL6 31 D2
Preston PR1 95 F7
Ramsbottom BL0 49 B6
Rawtenstall BB4 84 E2
Southport PR9 34 D7
Mount St James BB1 101 F4
Mount Terr BB4 85 A2
Mount The Blackburn BB2 100 C6
Fleetwood FY7 194 A5
Skelmersdale WN8 9 B8
Mount Zion Ct OL14 108 A1
Mountain Ash OL12 51 B3
Mountain Ash Cl OL12 51 B3
Mountain La BB5 103 C4
Mountain Rd PR7 28 E8
Mountbatten Cl PR2 95 B7
Mountbatten Rd PR7 42 B6
Mountfield Ct WN5 10 F7
Mountside Cl OL12 51 F2
Mountwood WN8 18 A4
Mountwood Lo PR8 20 C5
Mowbray Ave BB2 100 F2
Mowbray Dr Blackpool FY3 150 F1
Burton-in-K LA6 234 C7
Mowbray Pl 1 FY7 193 E4
Mowbray Rd FY7 193 E4
Mowbreck Ct PR4 113 A6
Mowbreck La PR4 113 B7
Mowbrick La LA2 215 D1
Mowgrain View 2 OL13 86 F3
Muirfield PR1 95 A6
Muirfield Cl PR2 116 B6
Muirfield Dr PR8 20 C4
Mulberry Ave PR1 95 A3
Mulberry Cl PR4 114 C1
Mulberry Cotts 10 LA2 207 A4
Mulberry La LA1 211 A2
Mulberry Mews FY2 150 F6
Mulberry St BB1 101 B5
Mulberry Wlk 3 BB1 101 B5
Mulgrave Ave PR2 116 A1
Mullion Cl PR9 53 B5
Muncaster Rd PR1 116 F2
Munro Ave WN5 10 E6
Munro Cres PR2 117 E3
Munster Ave FY2 150 D3
Murchison Gr FY5 172 E1
Murdock Ave PR2 116 D2
Murdock St BB2 100 B4
Murray Ave PR5 75 E5
Murray St Burnley BB10 147 B1
Leyland PR5 76 B1
Preston PR1 116 E1
Musbury Cres BB4 85 A1
Musbury Rd BB4 66 F7
Musbury View BB4 83 F1
Musden Ave BB4 67 A7
Museum of Mines BB18 201 B2
Museum St 19 BB1 100 E5
Myers St
Barnoldswick BB18 200 B1
Burnley BB10 127 A8
Myerscough Ave
Blackpool FY4 109 F5
Lytham St Anne's FY8 88 D8
Myerscough Coll PR3 156 D5
Myerscough Coll -
Hutton Ctr PR4 94 F1

Myerscough Hall Dr PR3 156 E5
Myerscough Planks PR3 157 A2
Myerscough Smithy Rd BB2 119 E4
Myndon St LA1 213 F3
Myra Ave LA4 212 F4
Myra Rd FY8 89 B4
Myrtle Ave Blackpool FY3 129 D5
Burnley BB11 126 D4
Cleveleys FY5 172 F5
Poulton-le-F FY6 151 E5
Myrtle Bank Inf Sch BB11 126 D4
Myrtle Bank Rd
10 Bacup OL13 86 F3
Blackburn BB2 80 C8
Myrtle Dr PR4 113 C4
Myrtle Gdns BL9 32 B2
Myrtle Gr
1 Barnoldswick BB18 200 C2
Burnley BB10 127 F4
Haslingden BB4 84 A1
Morecambe LA3 212 C3
Southport PR9 34 E7
Myrtle St N BL9 32 B2
Myrtle St S 8 BL9 32 B2
Mystic Mews 9 L39 15 E5
Mythop Ave FY8 90 C4
Mythop Cl 1 FY8 90 C4
Mythop Pl PR2 115 F1
Mythop Rd
Lytham St Anne's FY8 90 C4
Weeton FY4,PR4 131 C2
Mythop Village FY4 130 F2
Mytton St BB12 125 D8
Mytton View BB7 164 D7

N

Naarian Ct BB1 100 F7
Nab La Blackburn BB2 100 D5
Oswaldtwistle BB5 102 B4
Nab Rd PR6 60 E1
Nab's Head La PR5 98 E8
Nabbs Fold BL8 48 F3
Nabbs Way BL8 49 A1
Nairn Ave WN8 18 B5
Nairn Cl Blackpool FY4 110 A7
Standish WN6 28 D1
Nairne St BB11 126 D5
Nancy St BB3 81 B1
Nansen Rd Blackburn BB2 100 B3
Fleetwood FY7 194 A3
Nantwich Ave OL12 51 F3
Napier Ave Blackpool FY4 109 B6
Tarleton PR4 55 F8
Napier Cl FY8 109 E1
Napier St
6 Accrington BB5 103 C5
Nelson BB9 147 E7
Napier Terr PR8 34 A5
Naples Ave BB11 126 D4
Naples Rd BB3 81 C1
Naptha La PR4 75 C6
Narcissus Ave BB4 67 A8
Nares Rd BB2 100 B3
Nares St PR2 116 C1
Narrow Croft Rd L39 15 B1
Narrow Gates BB12 167 C5
Narrow La Leyland PR5 74 F2
Ormskirk L39 15 B1
Narrow Lane (Clieves Hills) L39 14 E6
Narrow Moss La L39, L40 15 E8
Narvik Ave BB11 126 B4
Nasmyth St BL6 31 C3
Nateby Ave FY4 109 E5
Nateby Cl Longridge PR3 138 F8
Lytham St Anne's FY8 89 B7
Nateby Crossing La PR3 178 A8
Nateby Ct 2 FY4 109 B6
Nateby Hall La PR3 198 F1
Nateby Pl PR2 115 F1
Nateby Prim Sch PR3 177 C6
Nature Trail PR6 61 F7
Nave Cl BB3 81 C1
Navena Ave FY7 193 E2
Navigation Bsns Village PR2 95 A8
Navigation Way
Blackburn BB1 100 F3
Preston PR2 95 A7
Naylor's Terr BL7 45 C5
Naylorfarm Ave WN6 19 F5
Naze Ct 4 BB4 85 E1
Naze La PR4 92 B6
Naze La E PR4 92 C5
Naze Lane Ind Est PR4 92 C4
Naze Rd BB4 85 E1
Naze View Ave BB4 85 F2
Nealet Fold PR9 53 D5
Near Mdw PR6 77 C3
Neargates PR7 41 D3
Neath Cl Bamber Bridge PR5 96 E3
Blackburn BB1 100 E7
Ned's La Cold Row FY6 174 D5
Smallwood Hey PR3 196 A5
Neddy Hill LA6 234 B7
Neddy La BB7 143 A4
Nedens Gr L31 5 C3
Nedens La L31 5 C3
Needham Ave LA4 212 D3
Needham Rise LA4 212 D3
Needham Way WN8 18 B5
Needless Hall La BD23 225 E7
Nell Carrs BL0 49 E8
Nell La PR5 76 E4
Nell's La L39 5 F5
Nelson & Colne Coll BB9 168 D2
Nelson & Colne FE Coll BB8 169 D5
Nelson Ave PR5 76 B1
Nelson Cres PR2 115 D2
Nelson Ct FY7 193 F3
Nelson Dr PR2 115 D2
Nelson Gdns PR4 134 C8
Nelson Golf Course BB9 147 E4
Nelson Rd
2 Blackpool FY1 129 B2
Brierfield BB10 148 A4
Chorley PR7 42 C7
Fleetwood FY7 193 F3
Nelson Sq BB11 126 F5
Nelson St Accrington BB5 103 C5
Bacup OL13 70 C8
3 Bamber Bridge PR5 76 E8
Clitheroe BB7 164 B8
5 Colne BB8 169 D5
1 Darwen BB3 80 F2
Great Harwood BB6 123 D6
Horwich BL6 31 D3
6 Kirkham PR4 112 F5
Lancaster LA1 210 F8
Lytham St Anne's FY8 90 D3
Morecambe LA4 212 D5
Southport PR8 34 A6
Nelson Sta BB9 147 E8
Nelson Terr PR1 95 D8
Nelson Way PR2 94 E8
Nene Cl PR5 59 B7
Neps La BB7 225 C6
Neptune St BB11 126 F6
Neptune Way BB3 81 B6
Nesswood Ave FY4 109 E6
Neston St PR1 96 E8
Nether Beck LA6 234 A2
Nether Kellet Prim Sch LA6 216 E4
Nether Kellet Rd LA6 231 B8
Nether View LA2 235 E1
Netherby St BB11 126 E4
Netherfield Cl BB12 126 D7
Netherfield Gdns 7 BB9 147 E8
Netherfield Rd BB9 147 E8
Netherheys Cl BB8 169 B5
Netherlands Rd LA4 212 F4
Netherley Rd PR7 28 E8
Nethertown Cl BB7 143 B6
Netherwood Rd BB10 127 D7
Netherwood St BB10 147 E2
Nethway Ave FY3 129 F6
Netley Ave OL12 51 F3
Network 65 Bsns Pk BB11 125 F4
Neverstitch Cl WN8 17 F2
Neverstitch Rd WN8 17 D2
Nevett St PR1 96 D8
Nevill St PR8 34 B7
Neville Ave FY5 172 E1
Neville Dr FY5 151 B8
Neville St PR3 139 A7
Nevy Fold Ave BL6 31 F3
New Acres Carnforth LA5 217 F2
Newburgh WN8 26 A1
New Bank Rd BB2 100 B6
New Barn BB4 67 B6
New Barn La BB4 68 A8
New Barns Rd LA5 237 A1
New Bath St BB8 169 E6
New Bonny St FY1 129 B4
New Briggs Fold BL7 46 E2
New Brown St 17 BB9 168 D1
New Brunswick St BL6 31 B3
New Bury Cl BB5 102 C3
New Chapel La BL6 31 F2
New Chapel St BB2 100 B2
New Church Cl 14 BB5 123 F3
New Church Ho 5 FY1 129 C4
New Church Mews 6 BB10 147 B1
New Cock Yd 26 PR1 96 A7
New Court Dr BL7 46 E3
New Court Way L39 15 F5
New Cswy L37, L38 3 B8
New Cut Cl PR8 21 A8
New Cut La L39, PR8 21 D6
New Fold WN5 10 C4
New Foul La PR8 35 A4
New Garden Fields BB4 86 A7
New Garden St 1 BB2 100 E3
New Ground Ct BB10 147 C3
New Hague BB18 191 F3
New Hall Ave FY4 110 B5
New Hall Ave N FY4 110 B6
New Hall Dr PR8 35 C1
New Hall Hey Bsns Pk BB4 84 F1
New Hall Hey Rd BB4 84 F1
New Hall La PR1 96 C8
New Hall Rd BL9 32 E4
New Hall St BB10,BB12 147 A1
New Hey La PR4 113 E5
New House La PR3 198 F4
New House St BB8 169 E5
New La Burton-in-K LA6 234 B7
Duncombe PR3 156 F8
Eagland Hill PR3 176 D7
Great Mitton BB7 163 E6
Haskayne L39 13 E3
New Lane L40 24 B6
Newtown PR7 58 A1
Ormskirk L39 15 E2
New La *continued*
Oswaldtwistle BB5 102 C2
Penwortham PR1 95 E3
Smallwood Hey PR3 196 B2
Southport PR9 53 E3
Tarleton PR4 55 D6
New Lane Head PR5 58 A2
New Lane Pace PR9 54 B8
New Lane Sta L40 24 B7
New Line OL13 70 B8
New Links Ave PR2 116 A6
New Longton CE Prim Sch PR4 74 F7
New Market St
15 Blackburn BB1 100 E5
Chorley PR7 42 C8
Clitheroe BB7 164 E8
Colne BB8 169 D5
New Meadow Cl BB1 81 A8
New Meadow La L37 3 F8
New Miles La WN6 19 F5
New Mill St Blackburn BB1 100 F6
Eccleston PR7 40 C6
New Moss La PR6 60 C5
New Oxford St BB8 169 E6
New Park St BB2 100 D5
New Pastures 4 PR5 76 C8
New Quay Rd LA1 210 B8
New Rd Adlington PR6 30 D8
Bamber Bridge PR5 96 B1
Blackpool FY8 109 B4
Burnley BB11 127 B2
Coppull PR7 41 F3
Cornholme OL14 108 C4
Croston PR5 39 B7
Earby BB18 201 B2
Formby L37 12 A5
Kirkby Lonsdale LA6 238 C2
Lancaster LA1 210 F8
Newchurch BB4 85 F2
Rufford L40 38 B3
Silverdale LA5 218 F1
Staynall FY6 174 B4
Thornton FY5 151 C7
Thornton in L LA6 236 F4
Warton, Carnforth LA5 217 A6
Whitworth OL12 70 B1
New Rough Hey PR2 115 F6
New Row Altham BB5 124 E6
Colne BB8 170 C4
New Row Cotts PR3 161 D1
New Scotland Rd BB9 168 E1
New St Blackrod BL6 30 D2
Brinscall PR6,PR7 61 F8
Carnforth LA5 217 D2
Caton LA2 231 D3
Colne BB8 169 B3
Eccleston PR7 40 C6
Halton LA2 214 E6
Haskayne L39 14 B8
14 Haslingden BB4 84 B3
Lancaster LA1 210 F8
Mawdesley L40 39 C2
Morecambe LA4 212 D5
Nelson BB9 168 F1
2 Padiham BB12 125 B8
Rochdale OL12 51 E2
New Summerseat House Specl Sch BL0 49 B2
New Taylor Fold BB10 147 F3
New Way Royal Oak L39 7 C2
Whitworth OL12 70 C1
New Wellington Cl BB2 100 C1
New Wellington Gdns BB2 100 C1
New Wellington St BB2 100 C1
Newark Pl Fulwood PR2 116 D8
4 Preston PR2 115 E2
Newark Rd OL12 51 F3
Newark Sq OL12 51 F3
Newark St BB5 102 F5
Newarth La PR4 72 E3
Newbigging Ave BB4 85 F2
Newburgh CE Prim Sch WN8 26 A1
Newburn Cl WN8 18 B5
Newbury Ave 3 FY4 109 D8
Newbury Cl PR2 116 C8
Newbury Gn PR2 116 C8
Newbury Rd
Lytham St Anne's FY8 89 A4
Skelmersdale WN8 18 B5
Newby Ave Fleetwood FY7 193 D1
Poulton-le-F FY6 151 D1
Newby Back La BB7 225 A1
Newby Cl Burnley BB11 126 E2
Southport PR8 20 B3
Newby Dr Clayton-le-W PR5 76 E2
Lancaster LA1 213 F3
Skelmersdale WN8 18 B5
Newby La BB7 189 B8
Newby Pl Blackpool FY4 130 B1
Fulwood PR2 117 D4
Newcastle Ave
Blackpool FY3 129 D4
Cleveleys FY5 172 F4
Newcastle St BB2 100 C3
Newchurch CE Prim Sch BB4 85 E1
Newchurch Cl BB2 100 F2
Newchurch Old Rd OL13 86 E1
Newchurch Rd Bacup OL13 69 C8
Rawtenstall BB4 85 C2
Newcombe Rd BL0 49 B2
Newcroft LA5 217 E6
Newfield Dr
Blackburn BB1,BB2 81 A8
Nelson BB9 147 E8
Newfield Rd PR5 77 A7
Newgate Fulwood PR2 116 E4
Morecambe LA3 213 A2
Newgate Ave WN6 19 E8
Newgate La PR4 75 C8
Newgate Rd WN8 9 F7
Newhaven Dr PR3 178 D2
Newhouse Rd
Accrington BB5 124 D1
Blackpool FY4 129 F2
Newington Ave BB1 121 F3
Newlands PR7 40 C6
Newlands Ave
Blackpool FY3 129 F2
Burscough L40 24 F4
Clitheroe BB7 164 C7
Lancaster LA1 211 B5
Penwortham PR1 95 B5
Rochdale OL12 51 F3
Newlands Cl Blackburn BB2 79 E8
Rochdale OL12 51 F3
Newlands Rd
Lancaster LA1 211 E6
Lancaster, Newlands LA1 211 C5
Lytham St Anne's FY8 89 C5
Morecambe LA4 212 F4
Newlands Way FY6 151 C1
Newlyn Ave Blackpool FY4 109 E5
Maghull L31 5 E1
Newlyn Ct FY4 109 E5
Newlyn Dr WN8 9 D7
Newlyn Pl PR2 115 F5
Newman Gr FY5 172 E5
Newman Rd 2 FY1 129 D8
Newman St BB10 147 B1
Newmarket Ave LA1 211 B3
Newmarket St LA4 213 A7
Newport Ct PR2 115 F3
Newport St BB9 168 E1
News La WA11 8 F2
Newsham Hall La PR4 135 F3
Newsham Pl LA1 211 A5
Newsham Rd LA1 211 A5
Newsham St PR2 116 D1
Newsome St PR5 76 A1
Newstead Dr WN8 18 B5
Newstet Rd L33 1 C2
Newthorn BB5 103 A1
Newton Ave
Poulton-le-F FY6 151 C2
Preston PR1 97 A8
Newton Bluecoat CE Prim Sch PR4 114 A2
Newton Cl Freckleton PR4 92 C7
Leyland PR5 58 B8
Newton Ct PR2 116 B1
Newton Dr Accrington BB5 103 D3
Blackpool FY3 129 E5
Over Town BB10 107 A7
Ramsbottom BL8 49 A1
Skelmersdale WN8 18 B5
Newton Dr E FY3 130 B7
Newton Gr FY5 151 D7
Newton Pl FY3 130 A7
Newton Rd
Lytham St Anne's FY8 89 A7
Preston PR2 116 B2
Newton St Blackburn BB1 101 B5
Burnley BB12 126 C7
Clitheroe BB7 164 D7
Darwen BB3 81 B2
Oswaldtwistle BB5 102 C5
2 Preston PR1 96 B8
Southport PR9 35 A7
Newton Terr LA1 214 A3
Newtown BB18 200 B2
Newtown St BB8 169 E5
Nib La PR1 75 E8
Nichol St PR7 60 C1
Nicholas St
Brierfield BB10 147 E3
Burnley BB11 127 A5
Colne BB8 169 C4
Darwen BB3 80 F1
Nicholl St 1 BB10 127 A8
Nicholson Cres LA4 212 G5
Nick Hilton's La PR6 43 D3
Nickey La BB2 120 F2
Nickleton Brow PR6 43 C2
Nicksons La FY6 195 B4
Nicola Cl OL13 87 A7
Nightfield La BB2 119 F6
Nightingale Cres 6 BB11 126 C5
Nightingale Dr FY6 151 B2
Nightingale Rd BL6 30 C3
Nightingale St PR6 30 A8
Nile St 5 Lancaster LA1 210 F8
12 Nelson BB9 168 D1
Preston PR1 96 A7
Nimes St PR1 96 D8
Nine Elms PR2 116 C6
Nineteen Acre La LA5 219 F4
Nineveh St 12 BB8 169 E5
Nipe La WN8 9 B5
Nithside FY4 130 C1
Niton Cl BB4 84 C1
Nixon La PR5 58 A8
Nixon's La PR8 20 E7
Nixons Ct PR5 57 F8
Nixons La WN8 9 D7
Noble St 13 Darwen BB3 64 A8
Great Harwood BB6 123 C4
Rishton BB1 123 B1
Noblett Ct 8 FY7 193 F2
Noblett St BB1 100 F5
Noel Gate L39 15 B1
Noel Jones Ct FY8 88 E7
Noel Rd LA1 213 E3
Noel Sq PR2 117 E1
Noels Villa PR3 137 E4
Noggarth Rd BB12 167 F2
Nolan St PR8 34 C5
Nook Cotts PR3 177 C6
Nook Cres PR2 138 C1
Nook Farm Ave OL12 51 F3
Nook Field PR3 137 D6
Nook Glade PR2 138 C1
Nook La Bamber Bridge PR5 76 D6
Blackburn BB2 99 F1
Churchtown PR3 178 A3
Mawdesley L40 39 E5
Oswaldtwistle BB5 102 B2
Nook Terr Blackburn BB2 100 A1
1 Rochdale OL12 51 F3
Nook The
Appley Bridge WN6 19 E7
Bolton-le-S LA5 216 A4
Staining FY3 130 D5
Nookfield PR5 75 A1
Nookfield Cl FY8 90 A4
Nooklands PR2 116 E4
Noon Sun St OL12 51 F1
Noor St PR1 117 A1
Nora St BB9 168 D3
Norbreck Cl BB2 80 F8
Norbreck Ct FY5 150 C6
Norbreck Dr PR2 115 E1
Norbreck Prim Sch FY5 150 D8
Norbreck Rd FY5 150 C7
Norburn Cres L37 11 F2
Norbury Cl PR9 53 C5
Norcliffe Rd FY2 150 C5
Norcross Brow PR6 62 B8
Norcross La FY5 151 A7
Norcross Pl PR2 115 F1
Norden Ct
Great Harwood BB6 123 E5
1 Rishton BB1 123 B1
Norden Cty High Sch BB1 123 A2
Norfield L39 15 F5
Norfolk Ave Blackpool FY2 150 B3
Burnley BB12 126 B7
Cleveleys FY5 172 E3
Morecambe LA3 212 B2
Padiham BB12 125 D6
Norfolk Cl
7 Clayton-le-M BB5 123 F3
Leyland PR5 58 E7
Norfolk Gr Church BB5 103 A7
Southport PR8 33 F1
Norfolk Rd
Bamber Bridge PR5 96 D4
Blackpool FY3 130 A2
Longshaw WN5 10 E1
Lytham St Anne's FY8 90 C5
Preston PR1 117 A1
Southport PR8 33 F1
Norfolk St Accrington BB5 103 D7
Blackburn BB2 100 C2
Colne BB8 169 E5
Darwen BB3 81 B1
Lancaster LA1 213 F2
Nelson BB9 168 D1
Rishton BB1 123 A1
Norham Cl BB12 126 E7
Norkeed Rd FY5 150 C7
Norland Dr LA3 208 F8
Norman Cl FY5 172 F1
Norman Rd BB5 102 C5
Norman St Blackburn BB2 100 C3
Burnley BB10 127 A7
Bury BL9 32 B4
Normandie Ave FY2 150 D3
Normandy Rd PR4 136 B3
Normanhurst L39 16 A4
Normington Cl L31 5 C4
Normoss Ave FY3 130 A7
Normoss Rd FY3 130 C7
Norris House Dr L39 6 C8
Norris St 3 Chorley PR7 42 C6
Darwen BB3 81 B1
Fulwood PR2 116 D3
Preston PR1 116 E2
Norris Way L37 12 B3
Norse Cotts PR6 56 E6
North Albert St 12 FY7 194 B5
North Albion St FY7 194 A4
North Ave
Barnoldswick BB18 200 B2
Blackpool FY3 129 D7
Ramsbottom BL8 48 F1
North Bank Ave BB1 121 E1
North Church St FY7 194 B5
North Cliff St 6 PR1 95 E6
North Cliffe Sch BB6 123 B6
North Clifton St FY8 90 B3
North Cres FY8 88 E6
North Croft PR3 178 C8
North Ct Blackpool FY5 150 E8
Cleveleys FY5 172 D5
North Dr Appley Bridge WN6 27 C2
Blackpool FY5 150 D6
Cleveleys FY5 172 E2
Inskip PR4 155 C1
Kirkham PR4 112 F6
Whalley BB7 143 B7
North East Ave PR6 62 A8
North End Football Gd (Preston North End FC) PR1 117 B2
North End La L38 3 A6
North Gr 1 PR5 76 C8
North Highfield PR2 117 E6
North Houses La FY8 110 D1

North Leach Dr PR8 20 A5
North Meade L31 5 C2
North Meadowside PR4 74 A6
North Mersey Bsns Ctr L33 1 D4
North Moor La L39 22 E2
North Moss La L37 12 D7
North Nook La PR3 180 E3
North Par 7 BB18 200 B3
North Park Ave BB9 168 C1
North Park Dr FY3 129 F5
North Perimeter Rd L33 1 D4
North Prom FY8 88 D7
North Quarry Bsns Pk WN6 27 D2
North Rd Blackburn BB1 101 C3
Bretherton PR5 57 B7
Carnforth LA5 217 E2
Lancaster LA1 210 F8
Preston PR1 116 F1
Rawtenstall BB4 85 C2
Southport PR9 53 C4
North Ribble St 7 PR1 96 C6
North Road Sch LA5 217 D1
North Shore Golf Course FY2 150 C3
North Sq Blackpool FY3 129 D6
Cleveleys FY5 172 D5
North St
Barnoldswick BB18 200 B1
Brierfield BB10 147 F3
Burnley BB10 147 A1
Chorley PR7 60 D2
Clitheroe BB7 186 F1
Colne BB8 169 E6
Fleetwood FY7 194 B5
Hapton BB12 125 C5
Haslingden BB4 84 C1
Morecambe LA4 212 E5
14 Nelson BB9 168 D1
Newchurch BB4 85 E1
Padiham BB12 145 C1
Preston PR1 95 F8
Ramsbottom BL0 67 C2
Rawtenstall BB4 85 A2
Southport PR9 34 C8
Water BB4 86 A8
Whitworth OL12 70 C1
North Syke Ave PR2 115 C1
North Vale PR6 42 F1
North Valley Rd BB8 169 D5
North View Kirkham PR4 112 F5
Leyland PR5 58 F8
Ramsbottom, Higher Summerseat BL0 49 B2
Ramsbottom, Strongstry BL0 67 C2
Rawtenstall BB4 85 A8
North View Cl PR3 154 C5
North Warton St FY8 90 C3
Northall PR4 73 E2
Northam Cl PR9 53 A5
Northbrook Gdns PR5 75 E1
Northbrook Rd PR5 75 F1
Northcliffe BB6 123 B6
Northcote Rd Langho BB6 142 C3
Preston PR1 95 D7
Northcote St Darwen BB3 64 B6
4 Haslingden BB4 84 B2
8 Leyland PR5 76 A1
Northdene WN8 26 B2
Northdunes L38 2 F4
Northenden Rd PR7 41 E1
Northern Ave PR4 73 E2
Northern Cty Prim Sch OL13 86 F6
Northfield WN8 18 B4
Northfield Ave FY1 129 B8
Northfield Cl L33 1 A4
Northfield Rd
Blackburn BB1 100 E7
Haslingden BB5 84 A8
Northfleet Ave FY7 193 E2
Northfold Cty Prim Sch FY5 172 E4
Northgate
14 Blackburn BB2 100 E5
Blackpool FY2 150 C4
Goosnargh PR3 137 D6
Leyland PR5 76 B2
Lytham St Anne's FY8 88 D6
Morecambe LA3 213 A2
Whitworth OL12 51 C7
Northgate Dr PR6 60 E2
Northlands Fulwood PR2 116 E6
Leyland PR5 58 C7
Northleach Ave 2 PR1 95 F2
Northside PR7 59 C3
Northumberland Ave
Blackpool FY2 150 B1
Cleveleys FY5 172 F5
Northumberland House PR1 95 F8
Northumberland St
2 Chorley PR7 42 D7
Morecambe LA4 212 D5
Northway Broughton PR3 136 C3
Fleetwood FY7 193 D1
Fulwood PR2 116 D7
Maghull L31, L39 5 E4
Ormskirk L39 15 A1
Skelmersdale WN8 18 B2
Northway Cty Prim Sch L31 5 E3
Northways WN6 28 D2
Northwood Cl
Burnley BB12 126 D7
Lytham St Anne's FY8 89 E4
Northwood Way FY6 151 D2
Norton Ave LA3 212 A3
Norton Dr LA3 212 B2
Norton Gr LA3 212 A2
Norton Pl LA3 212 A2
Norton Rd Garstang PR3 199 C2
Morecambe LA3 212 A2
Rochdale OL12 51 F3
Norton St 1 BB12 125 C4
Norwich Pl Blackpool FY2 150 D5
35 Preston PR1 96 A7
Norwich St BB1 100 F8
Norwood Ave
Becconsall PR4 72 F2
Blackburn BB2 100 E2
Blackpool FY3 129 E8
Nelson BB9 168 F2
Southport PR9 34 E7
Norwood Cl PR6 30 A8
Norwood Cres PR9 34 E7
Norwood Ct 13 LA1 211 A8
Norwood Cty Prim Sch PR9 34 E7
Norwood Dr LA4 213 B3
Norwood Gdns PR9 34 F7
Norwood Rd
Lytham St Anne's FY8 88 C8
Southport PR8, PR9 34 F6
Notre Dame Gdns BB1 101 A6
Nottingham Rd PR1 117 A1
Nottingham St BB1 101 A4
Novak Pl LA4 213 B4
Nowell Gr BB12 144 D2
Nowell St 15 BB6 123 C5
Noyna Ave BB8 191 E1
Noyna Rd BB8 191 E1
Noyna St BB8 169 E6
Noyna View BB8 169 E7
Nun's St LA1 211 A8
Nuns Ave LA7 237 E3
Nurseries The L37 12 A2
Nursery Ave L39 16 A6
Nursery Cl Coppull PR7 41 E4
Leyland PR5 58 F8
Nursery Dr Becconsall PR4 72 F1
Formby L37 11 F2
Nursery La PR4 74 E8
Nursery Nook BB3 81 D5
Nursery Rd L31 5 C4
Nuthall Rd PR8 34 F3
Nuttall Ave
Great Harwood BB6 123 C4
Horwich BL6 31 A3
Nuttall Cl BL0 49 C5
Nuttall Hall Cotts
Ramsbottom BL0 49 D5
Nuttall Hall Rd BL0 49 D5
Nuttall La BL0 49 C4
Nuttall Rd Blackpool FY1 129 D2
Ramsbottom BL0 49 D4
Nuttall St
Accrington BB5 103 C5
Bacup OL13 87 B3
Blackburn, Ewood BB2 80 D8
Blackburn, Longshaw BB2 100 D1
8 Burnley BB11 127 B4
Bury BL9 32 A1
Rawtenstall BB4 85 B3
Nuttall St Mews 3 BB5 103 C5
Nutter Cres BB12 145 F5
Nutter Rd Accrington BB5 103 C7
Cleveleys FY5 172 D3
2 Preston PR1 95 E7

O

O'Hagan Ct BB9 147 B6
Oak Ave Blackpool FY4 109 D8
Euxton PR7 59 D3
Galgate LA2 206 F4
Haslingden BB5 84 A8
9 Horwich BL6 31 E1
Kirkham PR4 113 B4
Longridge PR3 139 A7
Morecambe LA4 213 B6
Ormskirk L39 15 D4
Penwortham PR1 95 B3
Ramsbottom BL0 49 A2
Thornton FY5 151 C8
Oak Bank Accrington BB5 124 D2
Gregson Lane PR5 97 E1
Oak Cl Barrow BB7 164 D1
Rishton BB1 102 B8
Whitworth OL12 70 D4
Oak Cres WN8 17 D1
Oak Croft PR6 77 B2
Oak Dr Chorley PR6 60 C3
Freckleton PR4 92 A5
Halton LA2 214 F7
Oak Gates BL7 46 E1
Oak Gn L39 15 F5
Oak Gr Darwen BB3 81 B2
Garstang PR3 178 C7
New Longton PR4 75 A6
Oak Hill Cl BB5 103 C4
Oak La Accrington BB5 103 D5
Newton-with-S PR4 113 F2
Oak Rd PR3 178 B8
Oak Ridge BB7 186 D7
Oak St Accrington BB5 103 C5
Blackburn BB1 100 F7
Brierfield BB9 147 B6
Burnley BB12 126 C6
Clayton-le-M BB5 123 F1
Colne BB8 169 F6
Fleetwood FY7 194 A4
Great Harwood BB6 123 C6
2 Nelson BB9 168 E1
9 Oswaldtwistle BB5 102 D3
Preston PR1 96 A7
Oak St *continued*
Ramsbottom BL0 49 B5
Rawtenstall BB11 105 B4
Southport PR8 34 E6
Whitworth OL12 70 D5
Oak Terr BB18 200 C3
Oak Tree Ct WN8 18 D3
Oak Tree Dr PR4 112 E4
Oak View Leyland PR5 75 E2
Whitworth OL12 70 D4
Oakdene Ave BB5 124 E1
Oaken Bank BB10 147 E3
Oaken Cl OL13 87 B3
Oakenclough Cotts PR3 220 C2
Oakenclough Rd
Bacup OL13 87 B3
Chipping PR3 180 E4
Oakeneaves Ave BB11 126 D2
Oakengate PR2 117 C7
Oakengates WN6 28 F1
Oakenhead Ct PR3 158 D7
Oakenhead St PR1 117 E1
Oakenhead Wood Old Rd BB4 84 E3
Oakenhurst Rd BB2 100 D4
Oakenshaw Ave OL12 51 C6
Oakenshaw View OL12 51 C6
Oakfield Fulwood PR2 116 F7
Preston PR2 116 B1
Oakfield Ave
Accrington BB5 124 E1
Barnoldswick BB18 200 A3
Clayton-le-M BB5 123 E3
Oakfield Cl BL6 31 F2
Oakfield Cres BB5 102 F4
Oakfield Dr Formby L37 11 D4
Leyland PR5 58 B8
Oakfield Rd Blackburn BB2 80 D7
Hightown L38 2 F2
Oakfields L39 16 A5
Oakford Cl PR9 54 B5
Oakgate Cl PR4 55 F5
Oakgrove FY4 109 D6
Oakham Ct 18 PR1 96 A7
Oakhill Cl L31 5 D2
Oakhill Coll BB7 143 D6
Oakhill Cottage La L31 5 D4
Oakhill Dr L31 5 D4
Oakhill Rd L31 5 D3
Oakhurst Ave BB5 124 E1
Oakland Ave FY5 150 D6
Oakland Glen PR1 96 A3
Oakland St
4 Bamber Bridge PR5 96 E1
Nelson BB9 147 E8
Oaklands Ave
Barrowford BB9 168 D3
Tarleton PR4 56 A7
Oaklands Ct LA1 210 C5
Oaklands Dr
Penwortham PR1 95 A4
Rawtenstall BB4 84 E2
Oaklands Gr PR2 115 F1
Oaklands Rd BL0 67 D2
Oaklands Terr BB1 100 F7
Oaklea WN6 28 A2
Oakleaf Cl PR3 137 C6
Oakleaf Ct FY5 172 D4
Oakleaf Way FY4 130 D1
Oaklee Gr L33 1 A4
Oakleigh WN8 9 D2
Oakleigh Terr 8 OL14 108 B1
Oakley Rd Morecambe LA3 212 A2
Rawtenstall BB4 84 F2
Oakley St BB4 84 E2
Oakmere PR6 77 C3
Oakmere Ave PR6 78 D2
Oakmere Cl BB2 80 D6
Oakmoor Ave FY2 150 E4
Oakridge Cl PR2 116 F7
Oakroyd Cl LA5 237 B2
Oaks Bar BB1 121 C8
Oaks Brow BB1 121 C7
Oaks The
Bamber Bridge PR1 96 B3
Chorley PR7 42 B4
Leyland PR5 58 A7
Poulton-le-F FY6 151 D4
Southport PR8 33 F6
St Michael's on W PR3 155 C7
Oaksfield BB3 80 E5
Oakshaw Dr OL12 51 A1
Oakshott Pl PR5 77 B7
Oaktree Ave
Clayton-le-W PR5 76 D4
Fulwood PR2 116 A4
Oaktree Cl PR2 116 A4
Oakville Rd LA3 208 E5
Oakway PR3 139 A8
Oakwood WN8 18 D3
Oakwood Ave
Bamber Bridge PR5 96 C4
Blackburn BB1 122 B1
Lytham St Anne's FY8 89 E4
Shevington WN6 19 F5
Southport PR8 20 D6
Oakwood Cl Blackpool FY4 109 F4
Brierfield BB10 147 D3
Darwen BB3 80 E5
Thornton FY5 173 D2
Oakwood Dr Fulwood PR2 116 D8
Southport PR8 20 E5
Oakwood Gdns LA1 211 A2
Oakwood Gr LA5 215 F2
Oakwood Rd
Accrington BB5 103 D3
Chorley PR7 42 B6
Coppull PR7 41 F2
Oakwood View PR7 42 B4
Oakworth Ave PR2 117 F5
Oasis Cl L40 38 B3
Oasis Wildlife Park Visitor Ctr LA7 219 F8
Oat St BB12 125 D7
Oban Cres PR1 117 D3
Oban Ct PR2 138 D1
Oban Dr BB1 101 C3
Oban Pl FY2 150 E6
Oban St BB10 127 C8
Observatory Rd BB2 101 A2
Occupation La
Moor End FY6 174 C7
Singleton FY6 152 D4
Ocean Bvd FY4 109 A7
Ocean Ct FY6 194 D5
Ocean Way FY5 172 C3
Odell Way PR5 96 E3
Off Botanic Rd PR9 53 A1
Off Mount Pleasant St BB5 102 E4
Offerton St BL6 31 A3
Ogden Cl BB4 67 A7
Ogden Dr BB4 67 A7
Old Acre L38 2 F3
Old Back La BB7 143 F7
Old Bank La
Blackburn BB1,BB2 101 B2
Blackburn BB2 101 A2
Old Bank St 4 BB2 100 E4
Old Boundary Way L39 15 F6
Old Bridge La FY6 152 B7
Old Bridge Way PR6 60 D1
Old Buckley La PR3 140 D7
Old Carr Mill St BB4 84 B5
Old Clitheroe Rd PR3 161 E3
Old Cock Yd PR1 96 A7
Old Croft PR2 116 D8
Old Dawber's La PR7 59 B1
Old Engine La
Ramsbottom BL0 49 D6
Skelmersdale WN8 17 C2
Old Farmside BB2 80 D7
Old Gates Dr BB2 79 F8
Old Greaves-Town La PR2 115 E1
Old Green BL8 48 F1
Old Greenwood La BL6 31 D1
Old Ground St 8 BL0 49 C6
Old Hall Bsns Pk PR9 35 A5
Old Hall Cl
Bamber Bridge PR5 76 E8
Morecambe LA4 213 B4
Roughlee BB9 168 B5
Old Hall Dr Accrington BB5 124 F1
Bamber Bridge PR5 76 E8
Old Hall La
Charnock Green PR7 41 B6
Pleasington BB2 99 C2
Old Hall Sq BB10 128 A5
Old Hall St BB10 127 A8
Old Hey Croft 5 PR1 95 D2
Old Hive PR3 182 D4
Old House La FY4 110 D7
Old Kiln OL13 69 D8
Old La Bispham Green L40 26 D8
Earby BB18 201 B2
Formby L37 11 F6
Haskayne L39 13 E3
Horwich BL6 31 F2
Kelbrook BB18 191 F4
Maghull L31 5 E4
Salterforth BB18 191 B5
Whitworth OL12,OL13 70 E6
Old Lancaster La PR2 116 D1
Old Lancaster Rd PR3 178 B2
Old Langho Rd BB6 142 C5
Old Laund St BB12 146 E8
Old Links Cl PR9 35 B8
Old Lodge La PR3 157 A8
Old Lord's Cres BL6 31 B5
Old Lostock La PR5 76 E7
Old Mains La FY6 151 F6
Old Market Ct LA4 212 E6
Old Meadow Ct 3 FY3 129 E3
Old Meadow La 2 FY3 129 E3
Old Meadows Rd OL13 87 A5
Old Mill Ct PR4 73 F5
Old Mill Dr BB8 169 F4
Old Mill Hill L39 15 D3
Old Mill La Formby L37 11 F4
Hill Dale L40 26 F6
Old Mill St BB1 100 F6
Old Mill Terr PR6 60 E1
Old Mill The PR5 96 F2
Old Millstones PR1 95 D7
Old Moor Rd LA2 232 F8
Old Moss La L39 13 C5
Old Myse The LA7 237 F5
Old Nab Rd BB6 122 E8
Old Oak Gdns PR1 96 A2
Old Oliver La BD24 230 C6
Old Orchard PR2 116 D5
Old Park La PR9 35 A8
Old Parsonage La BB12 125 B8
Old Pepper La WN6 28 B2
Old Pope La PR4 75 B8
Old Prescot Cl L31 6 C2
Old Quarry La BL7 46 F1
Old Raike BD23 230 C4
Old Rake BL6 31 E5
Old Rd BD23 201 C6
Old Rectory Gn L39 6 A7
Old Roman Rd BB12,BB7 144 A3
Old Row Barrow BB7 164 D1
Kirkham PR4 113 B4
4 Rawtenstall BB4 84 E2
Old Sawmill The BD24 230 E7
Old Sch Mews 8 BB4 84 B3
Old School Cl PR5 58 A8
Old School Ho The PR5 97 B3
Old School La
Adlington PR7 29 E5
Bamber Bridge PR5 76 C6
Euxton PR7 59 D3
Tockholes BB3 79 F2
Old School Mews 12 OL13 69 C8
Old School Row BB12 126 B6
Old School The LA2 214 E6
Old St BB4 85 F1
Old Station Cl PR2 138 D1
Old Station Ct 8 BB7 164 E8
Old Stone Brow BB18 192 A4
Old Stone Trough La BB18 192 A5
Old Swan Cl BL7 46 E2
Old Swan Cotts BL7 46 E2
Old Tom's La FY6 174 E8
Old Town Cl WN8 8 D8
Old Town La L37 11 E4
Old Town Way WN8 8 D8
Old Trafford Pk LA3 209 A4
Old Tram Rd
Bamber Bridge PR5 76 F7
Preston PR1 96 A4
Old Vicarage PR1 96 A8
Old Vicarage Rd BL6 31 F3
Old Will's La BL6 31 B6
Oldbury Pl FY5 150 F8
Olde Stoneheath Ct PR6 43 B4
Oldfield Much Hoole PR4 73 F4
7 Penwortham PR1 95 D2
Oldfield Ave
Blackpool FY2 150 C4
Darwen BB3 80 E3
Oldfield Carr La FY6 151 E1
Oldfield Cl FY6 151 E1
Oldfield Cres FY6 151 E3
Oldfield Rd PR5 77 A7
Oldham St Burnley BB11 126 F4
Morecambe LA4 212 E6
Olivant St BB12 126 C7
Olive Bank BB6 142 D1
Olive Cl PR6 60 C5
Olive Gr Blackpool FY3 129 E5
Skelmersdale WN8 17 E1
Southport PR8 34 E7
Warton PR4 91 D6
Olive La BB3 81 B2
Olive Rd LA1 213 F2
Olive St OL13 69 E8
Olive Terr BB4 84 F5
Oliver Pl LA5 217 E2
Oliver St 10 OL13 69 C8
Oliver's Pl PR2 117 B8
Olivers Pl PR2 117 A8
Oliverson's Ce Prim Sch PR3 137 D6
Ollerton La PR6 78 E4
Ollerton Rd FY8 89 D5
Ollerton St PR6 43 A1
Ollerton Terr PR6 78 E3
Olympia St BB10 127 C5
Omerod St BB4 86 A8
Omrod Pl 1 FY1 129 B2
Onchan Dr OL13 87 B1
Onchan Rd BB2 100 E1
One Ash Cl OL12 51 F2
Onslow Cres PR8 34 A2
Onslow Rd FY3 129 F7
Ontario Cl BB2 100 A8
Oozebooth Terr BB1 100 E7
Oozehead La BB2 100 B5
Opal Cl 5 FY5 150 F7
Opal St BB1 121 F2
Openshaw Dr BB1 100 E8
Openshaw St BL9 32 A1
Oporto Cl BB11 126 E5
Oram Rd PR5 77 F8
Oram St BL9 32 A4
Orange St BB5 103 B8
Orchard Ave
Blackpool FY4 109 C6
Bolton-le-S LA5 216 A6
New Longton PR4 75 A7
Poulton-le-F FY6 151 E1
Orchard Bridge 6 BB11 126 F6
Orchard Cl Becconsall PR4 72 F3
Blackburn BB2 80 D6
Euxton PR7 59 D3
Freckleton PR4 92 A6
Fulwood PR2 116 A5
Hest Bank LA2 213 F8
Silverdale LA5 218 B2
Thornton FY5 173 B4
Wrea Green PR4 112 B3
Orchard Croft 2 PR5 76 A8
Orchard Ct L31 5 F1
Orchard Dr Fleetwood FY7 193 E1
Lucas Green PR6 60 C5
Oswaldtwistle BB5 102 F5
Orchard End PR3 154 C5
Orchard Grange PR1 95 A5
Orchard La Lancaster LA1 210 D7
Longton PR4 73 F8
Southport PR8 20 D4
Orchard Lo 1 L39 15 F6
Orchard Rd Arnside LA5 237 B2
Lytham St Anne's FY8 88 E6
Orchard St 4
Barnoldswick BB18 200 B2
Great Harwood BB6 123 C4

Orchard St *continued*
1 Leyland PR5 76 B1
29 Preston PR1 95 F8
Orchard The Burnley BB11 126 C4
Croston PR5 57 C3
Kirkham PR4 113 E6
Little Eccleston PR3 154 A5
Ormskirk L39 15 D5
Warton PR4 91 E6
Woodplumpton PR4 135 E1
Orchard View L39 15 D1
Orchard Way BL8 48 F1
Orchard Wlk PR2 138 C2
Orchards The
Barnoldswick BB18 200 C3
Carleton FY6 151 B5
Southport PR8 20 D4
Orchid Cl WN8 10 B6
Orchid Way OL12 51 D3
Ord Ave FY4 129 F1
Ord Rd PR2 116 C2
Orders La PR4 113 A4
Ordnance St BB1 101 A5
Oregon Ave FY3 129 E8
Oriole Cl 9 BB1 100 F6
Orkney Cl BB1 101 D3
Orkney Rd 1 FY1 129 C2
Orme Ho L39 16 A5
Orme St 1 FY1 129 C3
Ormerod Rd BB10,BB11 127 B7
Ormerod St
Accrington BB5 103 B5
Burnley BB11 127 A5
Colne BB8 169 C4
Haslingden BB4,BB5 84 B7
5 Nelson BB9 147 F8
Rawtenstall BB4 85 A2
Thornton FY5 173 B4
Worsthorne BB10 128 A5
Ormerod Terr
Barrow BB6 143 D8
Foulridge BB8 191 E1
Ormond Ave
Blackpool FY1 129 B8
Westhead L40 16 E4
Ormond St BL9 32 A3
Ormonde Cres L33 1 A2
Ormont Ave FY5 172 E2
Ormrod St BL9 32 A2
Ormrods The BL9 32 F5
Orms Way L37 11 E3
Ormsby Cl WN6 28 E2
Ormskirk & District General Hospl L39 16 A4
Ormskirk Bsns Pk 2 L39 15 F6
Ormskirk CE Prim Sch L39 16 A6
Ormskirk Coll L39 15 E5
Ormskirk Gram Sch L39 15 F4
Ormskirk Lathom Park CE Prim Sch L40 17 A8
Ormskirk Old Rd L39 7 F7
Ormskirk Rd Bickerstaffe L39 7 E7
Orrell WN8 10 A7
Preston PR1 96 A8
Rainford Junction WA11 8 D1
Skelmersdale, Blaguegate WN8 17 C1
Skelmersdale, Tanhouse WN8 9 D7
Ormskirk Sta L39 15 F5
Ormskirk Tourist Information Ctr L39 15 F5
Ormston Ave BL6 31 C5
Orpen Ave BB11 126 F3
Orpington Sq BB10 147 C3
Orrell Cl 3 PR5 75 D1
Orrell Gdns WN5 10 F6
Orrell Hill La L38 3 C4
Orrell La L40 24 D5
Orrell Newfold Cty Prim Sch WN5 10 D4
Orrell Rd WN5 10 E7
Orrell Sta WN5 10 E4
Orrell Water Pk WN5 10 E4
Orrest Rd PR1 118 A1
Orton Ct BB9 168 D4
Orwell Cl L37 11 D1
Osbaldeston La BB2 120 D5
Osbert Croft PR4 94 A1
Osborne Ave FY5 172 F1
Osborne Cres LA3 212 C3
Osborne Dr PR6 77 C2
Osborne Gr Cleveleys FY5 172 D5
Morecambe LA4 212 D3
Osborne Rd
Bamber Bridge PR5 96 D3
Blackburn BB2 100 B6
Cleveleys FY5 172 D5
Formby L37 11 E1
Lytham St Anne's FY8 88 F5
Morecambe LA3,LA4 212 C3
Southport PR8 20 B6
Osborne St 10 PR1 95 E7
Osborne Terr Bacup OL13 69 D8
Darwen BB3 80 E2
1 Rawtenstall BB4 84 E2
Spen Brook BB12 167 D2
Whitewell Bottom BB4 85 F4
Osborne Way BB4 84 A1
Osbourne Rd FY4 109 B8
Osbourne Way PR1 117 A1
Oscar St 4 FY4 129 F2
Oslo Rd BB11 126 B5
Osprey Cl Blackburn BB1 100 D8
Knowley PR6 61 A3
Oswald Rd
Lytham St Anne's FY8 90 D4
Preston PR2 116 C1
Oswald St Accrington BB5 103 D6
Blackburn BB1 100 E6
Burnley BB12 126 F8
Oswaldtwistle BB5 102 D3
Rishton BB1 123 C2
Oswaldtwistle Mill BB5 102 E4
Otley Rd FY8 89 B7
Ottawa Cl BB2 100 A8
Otterburn Cl FY3 151 B1
Otterburn Gr BB10 127 D6
Otterburn Rd BB2 80 C7
Otters Cl PR2 117 F2
Ottershaw Gdns BB1 100 E8
Ottery Cl PR9 53 A5
Otway St PR1 116 E2
Oulton Cl L31 5 B4
Our Lady & St Edward's RC Prim Sch PR2 116 D8
Our Lady & St Gerard's RC Prim Sch PR5 76 A8
Our Lady & St John RC High Sch BB1 101 C3
Our Lady & St Paul's RC Prim Sch OL10 32 F1
Our Lady Of Compassion RC Prim Sch L37 12 A3
Our Lady of Lourdes RC Prim Sch Carnforth LA5 217 E1
Southport PR8 34 A1
Our Lady of Perpetual Succour RC Prim Sch BB2 80 E8
Our Lady of the Assumption RC Prim Sch FY4 109 F5
Our Lady Queen of Peace RC High Sch WN8 17 F4
Our Lady Star of the Sea RC Prim Sch FY8 88 F6
Our Lady's RC High Sch
Fulwood PR2 116 C4
Lancaster LA1 213 F1
Ousby Ave LA3 212 E2
Ousby Rd LA3 212 E2
Ouseburn Rd BB2 80 C8
Out La PR5 57 C2
Out Moss La LA4 212 E4
Out Rawcliffe CE Prim Sch PR3 175 F2
Outer Prom FY7 193 E5
Outlet La L31, L39 6 F1
Outram La BB1 121 E1
Outram Way PR5 76 E8
Outterside St PR7 30 A6
Outwood Rd BB11 127 B4
Ouzle Rock BB12 167 E2
Oval The WN6 19 F5
Ovangle Rd LA3 213 B2
Over Hos BL7 47 B6
Over Town BB10 128 A1
Overdale Gr FY3 130 A8
Overdell Dr OL12 51 C4
Overfield Way OL12 51 F2
Overshores Rd BL7 47 B8
Overton Rd PR2 94 E8
Ovington Dr PR8 34 E3
Owen Ave L39 15 F6
Owen Ct BB5 123 F3
Owen Rd LA1 213 F2
Owen St Accrington BB5 103 C7
Burnley BB12 126 A5
Darwen BB3 81 A3
Preston PR1 96 B8
Owen's La L39 13 E2
Owen's Row BL6 31 C3
Owens St PR5 42 E7
Owlet Hall Rd BB3 80 E2
Owtram St 2 PR1 96 C8
Ox Hey BB5 123 A2
Ox Hey Ave PR2 115 C1
Ox St 15 BL0 49 B5
Oxcliffe Ave LA3 212 A1
Oxcliffe Gr LA3 212 A1
Oxcliffe Rd LA3 212 C2
Oxendale Rd FY5 173 D2
Oxenholme Ave FY5 172 D4
Oxenhurst Rd FY3 130 A8
Oxford Ave BB5 124 A3
Oxford Cl Blackburn BB1 100 F4
Padiham BB12 125 D6
Oxford Ct
4 Lytham St Anne's FY8 89 D4
Southport PR8 33 F4
Oxford Dr Blackburn BB1 101 E4
Kirkham PR4 113 C4
Oxford Gdns PR8 33 E4
Oxford Pl Burnley BB10 127 B5
Lancaster LA1 213 E3
Oxford Rd
Bamber Bridge PR5 76 F8
Blackpool FY1 129 D5
Burnley BB11 127 B5
Cleveleys FY5 172 D3
Fleetwood FY7 193 E3
Fulwood PR2 116 D4
Lytham St Anne's FY8 88 E8
Lytham St Anne's, Ansdell FY8 89 D4
Nelson BB9 169 A2
Orrell WN5 10 F8
Skelmersdale WN8 17 E1
Southport PR8 33 E4
Oxford St Accrington BB5 103 B6
Adlington PR7 30 A6
Brierfield BB9 147 B5
Oxford St *continued*
Bury BL9 32 A1
Carnforth LA5 217 D1
9 Chorley PR7 42 C7
Colne BB8 169 E5
Darwen BB3 80 F4
Lancaster LA1 213 F3
Morecambe LA4 212 E6
Preston PR1 96 A6
Oxford Way Fleetwood FY7 193 E3
Rochdale OL12 51 E2
Oxhey Cl BB10 127 F6
Oxheys Ind Est PR1 116 D2
Oxheys St PR1 116 D2
Oxhill Pl FY5 150 F7
Oxhouse Rd WN5 10 D4
Oxley Cl PR4 112 F5
Oxley Rd PR1 117 D1
Oxley Rd N PR1 117 D1

P

Paa La BB7 225 C7
Packet La LA5 216 A4
Paddington Ave PR3 155 C7
Paddington Barn PR3 155 C7
Paddock Ave PR5 58 A8
Paddock Dr FY3 130 C2
Paddock Rd WN8 9 C5
Paddock St 9 BB5 102 E4
Paddock The
Blackburn BB2 100 A8
Carleton FY6 151 C5
Formby L37 12 A5
Fulwood PR2 117 A6
Ormskirk L39 15 C3
Oswaldtwistle BB5 102 E4
4 Penwortham PR1 95 E2
Ramsbottom BL0 49 B7
Rufford L40 38 C4
Sawley BB7 224 C1
Southport PR8 20 C4
Thornton FY5 151 B8
Paddock Way LA7 237 F4
Padgate Pl BB11 126 B4
Padiham Green CE Sch BB12 125 C8
Padiham Rd Burnley BB12 126 E6
Burnley, Whittlefield BB12 126 C7
3 Burnley, Whittlefield BB12 126 D6
Padiham BB12 125 F7
Sabden BB7 145 A7
Padstow Cl PR9 53 A5
Padway PR1 95 D2
Page Ct L37 11 F3
Pagefield Cres BB7 165 A7
Pages Ct PR5 76 B7
Paignton Rd BB1 100 D7
Painley Cl FY8 90 A4
Paisley St BB11 126 D5
Palace Ct LA3 212 B4
Palace Gdns BB12 126 B7
Palace Rd PR8 33 E5
Palace St Burnley BB12 126 C7
Bury BL9 32 A2
Palais Bldgs 2 L40 24 E5
Palatine Ave LA1 211 A5
Palatine Cl FY3 130 C6
Palatine High Sch FY4 109 C8
Palatine Rd Blackburn BB2 100 C5
Blackpool FY1 129 C4
Cleveleys FY5 172 D4
Southport PR8 33 F5
Palatine Sq BB11 126 E5
Palatine St 10 BL0 49 C6
Paley Rd 1 PR1 95 D7
Palfrey Cl FY6 151 B6
Pall Mall Blackburn BB2 99 E5
Chorley PR7 42 C6
Palladium Bldgs 7 FY1 129 B1
Palm Ct WN8 17 E2
Palm Dr FY6 151 B6
Palm Gr PR8 34 E6
Palm St Blackburn BB1 101 A7
4 Burnley BB11 126 D5
Palma St 4 OL14 108 B1
Palmaston Cl LA1 210 E6
Palmer Ave FY1 129 C2
Palmer Gr 3 LA4 213 A6
Palmer St BB1 100 D6
Palmerston Cl BL0 49 C4
Palmerston Rd PR9 34 F6
Palmerston St BB12 125 D7
Pansy St N BB5 103 B7
Pansy St S BB5 103 B7
Panton St BL6 31 D1
Parade The LA5 217 B1
Paradise Cl PR6 60 C8
Paradise La
1 Blackburn BB2 100 E4
Formby L37 12 A6
Leyland PR5 75 B1
Paradise St
Accrington BB5 103 B5
Barrowford BB9 168 E5
Blackburn BB2 100 D4
11 Burnley BB11 126 F6
Little Knowley PR6 60 F3
Newchurch BB4 85 F2
Ramsbottom BL0 49 C7
Paradise Terr 2 BB2 100 E4
Paragon Way LA1 210 C8
Parbold Cl Blackpool FY3 150 F1
Burscough L40 24 E3
Parbold Douglas CE Prim Sch WN8 26 D3
Parbold Hill WN8 26 E2
Parbold Our Lady & All Saints RC Prim Sch WN8 26 C2
Parbold Sta WN8 26 C2
Pardoe Cl PR4 72 E3
Pardoe Ct L40 24 F3
Paris BB1 121 E4
Parish St 11 BB12 125 C8
Park Ave
Barnoldswick BB18 200 B1
Barrowford BB9 168 C1
Blackburn BB1 100 D6
Burnley BB11 126 E4
Chatburn BB7 187 D5
Clitheroe BB7 186 E1
Euxton PR7 59 D2
Fleetwood FY7 193 F3
Formby L37 11 F1
Great Harwood BB6 123 D6
Haslingden BB4 84 B1
Lancaster LA1 211 B7
Longshaw WN5 10 E1
Lytham St Anne's FY8 89 E3
Maghull L31 5 D3
Much Hoole PR4 73 E2
New Longton PR4 74 F8
Ormskirk L39 15 E5
Preston PR1 117 B2
Ramsbottom BL0 49 D6
Salterforth BB18 191 E8
Southport PR9 34 E8
Park Bridge Rd BB10 127 D3
Park Cl Hightown L37 2 E8
Parbold WN8 26 D3
Penwortham PR1 95 D4
Park Cotts BB8 149 D7
Park Cres Accrington BB5 103 A4
Bacup OL13 69 F8
Blackburn BB2 100 C6
Haskayne L39 13 F4
Haslingden BB4 84 C1
Morecambe LA4 213 A7
Southport PR9 52 D1
Park Ct LA1 210 F3
Park Cty Prim Sch
Colne BB8 169 F5
Skelmersdale WN8 17 E1
Park Dr Brierfield BB9 147 C5
Nelson BB9 147 F7
Preston PR2 115 D1
Park Farm Cl PR4 73 F8
Park Farm Rd BB2 79 D8
Park Gate Rd BB1 141 D1
Park Hall L Ctr PR7 41 A4
Park Hall Rd PR7 40 F3
Park Hey Dr WN6 19 E7
Park High Sch BB8 169 F6
Park Hill
Barnoldswick BB18 200 C1
21 Rochdale OL12 51 F1
Park Hill Convent Prep Sch BB12 126 A8
Park Hill Ct PR3 178 C7
Park Hill Rd PR3 178 C7
Park Ho 2 LA1 213 F1
Park House La LA2 233 A5
Park La
Brierfield BB10,BB9 147 C5
Caton LA2 231 B5
Ellel LA2 207 A6
Garstang PR3 199 A4
Great Harwood BB6 123 D6
Holmes PR4 55 B2
Horwich BL6 31 D3
Kirkham PR4 113 A7
Maghull L31 5 F3
Oswaldtwistle BB5 102 E3
Penwortham PR1 95 E3
Preesall FY6 195 B3
Wennington LA2 232 E8
Park Lane Dr L31 6 B2
Park Lane End LA2 232 E8
Park Lee Hospl BB2 100 E2
Park Lee Rd BB2 100 E2
Park Link L39 15 B1
Park Mews BB7 225 B3
Park Mill Pl PR1 117 A1
Park Pl
Blackburn, Feniscowles BB2 79 D7
Blackburn, Wilton BB2 100 B3
25 Preston PR1 96 A7
Walton-le-D PR5 96 E4
Park Rd Accrington BB5 103 A6
Adlington PR7 29 F6
Bacup OL13 86 F1
Barnoldswick BB18 200 B1
Blackburn BB2 100 E3
Blackpool FY1 129 D3
Burnley BB10 127 E1
Chorley PR7 42 C8
Coppull PR7 41 E1
Darwen BB3 64 B6
Edgworth BL7 47 E5
Formby L37 11 E1
Fulwood PR2 117 A4
Gisburn BB7 225 B3
Great Harwood BB6 123 D5
Haslingden BB4 66 F7
Kirkham PR4 112 F4
Lancaster LA1 211 A8
Leyland PR5 59 A7
Longshaw WN5 10 F1
Lytham St Anne's FY8 88 E6
Mellor Brook BB2,PR5 120 A1
Morecambe LA4 213 A6
Newchurch BB4 85 F1
Ormskirk L39 15 E5
Park Rd *continued*
Padiham BB12 125 C8
Penwortham PR1 95 D4
Poulton-le-F FY6 151 E4
Ramsbottom BL0 48 F3
Rishton BB1 123 C1
Silverdale LA5 218 D4
Southport PR9 34 D8
Thornton FY5 173 B1
Park Rd W PR9 52 C1
Park Sch FY3 129 E4
Park Side BB18 192 A8
Park Sq LA1 211 A8
Park Sreet E BB9 168 E4
Park St Accrington BB5 103 C6
Barnoldswick BB18 200 B1
Barrowford BB9 168 D4
Chorley PR7 60 C1
Clitheroe BB7 164 E7
Eccleston PR7 40 C6
Great Harwood BB6 123 D5
Haslingden BB4 84 B3
Haslingden, Bridge End BB4 66 F7
Lytham St Anne's FY8 90 B3
Park Stone Rd PR3 136 C3
Park Terr Blackburn BB1 100 D7
Great Harwood BB6 123 D6
Wrea Green PR4 112 B3
Park View Arnside LA5 237 B1
Carnforth LA5 217 D3
Gisburn BB7 225 B3
Newchurch BB4 85 F1
Padiham BB12 125 C8
Penwortham PR1 95 D4
Park View Ave PR2 116 B2
Park View Cl BB9 147 B7
Park View Cotts FY8 90 B4
Park View Ct 2 FY4 109 C6
Park View Rd FY8 90 B4
Park View Terr
Abbey Village PR6 79 C1
Salterforth BB18 191 D7
Park Wall Rd L29, L38 4 B2
Park Way Colne BB8 169 C6
Formby L37 11 F1
Penwortham PR1 95 D4
Park Wlk PR2 117 A4
Park Wood Dr BB4 84 E2
Parkbourn L31 6 A2
Parkbourn Dr L31 6 A2
Parkbourn N L31 6 A2
Parkbourn Sq L31 6 A2
Parkdale Gdns BB2 80 D6
Parke Mews PR6 78 C3
Parke Rd PR6 61 E8
Parker Ave BB7 164 E6
Parker Cres L39 15 F7
Parker La Burnley BB11 127 A5
New Longton PR4 75 C6
Parker St Accrington, Higher Baxenden BB5 103 E2
Accrington, Hillock Vale BB5 103 E8
Barnoldswick BB18 200 A3
3 Blackpool FY1 129 C5
Brierfield BB10 147 B3
Burnley BB11 127 A6
Bury BL9 32 A2
Chorley PR7 60 C1
Colne BB8 169 C5
Lancaster LA1 211 A8
9 Nelson BB9 168 F2
Preston PR2 116 D2
Rishton BB1 123 C2
Parker Terr BB7 225 B3
Parkers Fold PR3 178 C2
Parkfield Ave PR2 116 B2
Parkfield Cl Leyland PR5 58 C8
Ormskirk L39 15 C4
5 Preston PR2 115 C1
Parkfield Cres 6 PR2 115 C1
Parkfield Dr
Lancaster LA1 211 A6
Preston PR2 94 C8
Parkfield Gr L31 5 C1
Parkfield View PR2 94 C8
Parkgate PR3 137 D5
Parkgate Dr
Lancaster LA1 211 C7
Leyland PR5 58 F7
Parkhead La PR3 179 A8
Parkinson La PR3 160 B8
Parkinson St
Blackburn BB2 100 C2
Burnley BB11 127 A4
Foulridge BB8 191 D1
Haslingden BB4 84 A3
Parkinson Way 1 FY4 129 C1
Parkland Cl FY5 172 C1
Parkland Gr LA3 212 B2
Parkland View BB11 126 E2
Parklands
Skelmersdale WN8 18 D2
Southport PR9 34 E8
Parklands Ave PR1 95 A4
Parklands Cl PR1 95 A4
Parklands Dr PR2 116 E8
Parklands Gr PR2 116 E8
Parklands High Sch
Chorley PR7 42 A8
Preston PR1 116 F2
Parklands The PR3 178 D3
Parklands Way BB2 80 B8
Parks The LA4 213 A7
Parkside Fulwood PR1 117 B3
Morecambe LA4 212 F3
Preston PR2 115 D2
Parkside Ave PR7 42 C8
Parkside Cl 12 OL14 108 B1

Parkside Cres WN5 10 F6
Parkside Ct LA4 212 F3
Parkside Dr Arnside LA5 237 A1
Lucas Green PR6 60 B6
Parkside Dr S PR6 60 B6
Parkside La PR3 178 A7
Parkside Rd
Cornholme OL14 108 B1
Lytham St Anne's FY8 89 A7
Nelson BB9 148 B8
Parkside View FY5 173 A4
Parkstone Ave
Carleton FY6 151 B5
Thornton FY5 151 D8
Parksway FY6 194 D5
Parkthorn Rd PR2 94 C8
Parkview Cl LA4 212 E3
Parkway Blackpool FY3 130 A6
Shevington Moor WN6 28 A2
Parkwood BL7 46 D2
Parkwood Ave BB12 126 D7
Parkwood Rd BB1 101 B4
Parliament St
Burnley BB11 127 B5
11 Colne BB8 169 E5
18 Darwen BB3 81 A1
Lancaster LA1 213 F1
Morecambe LA3 212 B4
Orrell WN8 10 C7
Parlick Ave PR3 139 B7
Parlick Rd Fulwood PR2 118 A2
Garstang PR3 178 B6
Parr Cottage Cl PR7 40 C7
Parr La PR7 40 C7
Parr's La L39 15 D1
Parramatta St 8 BB4 85 A2
Parrock Cl PR1 95 E3
Parrock Par BB4 85 A7
Parrock Rd BB9 168 C2
Parrock St
Barnoldswick BB18 200 B2
19 Nelson BB9 168 E1
7 Rawtenstall BB4 85 A7
Parrox Fold FY6 195 A5
Parrox La PR4 113 E2
Parson La BB7 164 E8
Parson's Brow 4 PR7 42 C7
Parson's Bullough Rd
PR6,BL6 43 E5
Parsonage Ave PR3 140 D3
Parsonage Brow WN8 10 A8
Parsonage Cl 2 Bury BL9 32 A2
Morecambe LA3 212 F2
Orrell WN8 10 A7
Parsonage Cotts 9 BB7 164 E8
Parsonage Dr BB10,BB9 147 C5
Parsonage Gdns PR4 56 A5
Parsonage La PR3 182 C1
Parsonage Rd BB1 122 A4
Parsonage St Bury BL9 32 A3
3 Church BB5 102 E5
Colne BB8 169 C4
Part St PR8 34 B6
Parth St OL10 32 D1
Partnership Way BB1 101 D2
Partridge Ave FY5 173 A4
Partridge Dr BB5 103 F1
Partridge Hill 4 BB12 145 D1
Partridge Hill St 5 BB12 145 D1
Partridge Wlk 4 BB11 126 C5
Passmonds Cres
OL11,OL12 51 B1
Past La Lane Ends BB7 224 A5
Lane Ends BB7 224 A7
Pasture Cl
Barnoldswick BB18 200 C4
Burnley BB11 126 E3
Pasture Dr BB8 191 D1
Pasture Field FY6 151 B6
Pasture Field Cl PR5 75 C1
Pasture La
Barrowford BB9 168 C5
Hest Bank LA5 215 E4
Pasture The LA7 237 E5
Pasturegate BB11 126 E3
Pasturegate Ave BB11 126 E4
Pasturelands Dr BB7 143 A3
Pastures The
Blackburn BB2 100 A8
Grimsargh PR2 138 D1
Southport PR9 53 D5
Paterson St BB2 100 E3
Pathfinders Dr LA1 210 E4
Patience St 11 OL12 51 C1
Patmos St BL0 49 D6
Paton St OL12 51 D3
Patrick Ave BB12 144 D2
Patrick Cres BB4 85 C2
Patten St Blackburn BB1 101 C5
Colne BB8 169 D4
Preston PR1 95 F8
Patterdale Ave
Blackburn BB1 101 C3
Blackpool FY3 129 F2
Fleetwood FY7 193 D1
Oswaldtwistle BB5 102 D5
Thornton FY5 173 B3
Patterdale Cl
Brierfield BB10 147 C4
Southport PR8 20 B3
Patterdale Cres L31 5 E2
Patterdale Rd LA1 214 B1
Pattison Cl OL12 51 D3
Paul's La Hambleton FY6 174 C2
Southport PR9 52 F3
Paulhan St BB10 147 B2
Pavey Cl FY4 109 F8
Pavilion Cl OL12 51 F2
Pavilion View PR5 57 B2
Pavilions The PR2 95 C7
Paxton Pl WN8 9 C4
Paxton St BB5 103 B6
Paynter Cl Barrow BB7 164 D1
Enfield BB5 124 A2
Paythorne Ave BB10 127 D5
Paythorne Cl FY3 151 B1
Peabody St BB3 81 A2
Peace St BB11 126 D5
Peacehaven WN8 17 E1
Peachtree Cl PR2 117 D6
Peacock Cres LA2 215 E1
Peacock Dr PR3 199 D1
Peacock Hall Rd PR5 58 D7
Peacock Hill Cl PR2 118 C7
Peacock La LA2 215 E1
Peahall La PR3 197 A4
Pear Ave BL9 32 C3
Pear Pl 16 OL14 108 B1
Pear St 17 OL14 108 B1
Pear Tree Ave PR7 41 F3
Pear Tree Cl 2 PR5 96 E2
Pear Tree Cres PR5 96 E2
Pear Tree Croft PR4 74 A8
Pear Tree Ctyd PR4 114 E2
Pear Tree La PR7 59 E3
Pear Tree Rd PR6 77 B3
Pear Tree Sch PR4 113 A5
Pear Tree St 7 PR5 96 E2
Pearfield PR5 76 A2
Pearl Ave 6 FY2 150 E1
Pearl Brook Ind Est BL6 31 B3
Pearl St Accrington BB5 102 F5
Blackburn BB1 121 F1
Pearson St Blackburn BB2 100 D4
Bury BL9 32 B3
Peart St BB10 147 B2
Peartree Rd PR5 57 B3
Pebble Ct FY5 172 C3
Pechell St 5 PR2 116 C1
Pedder Ave LA3 209 C1
Pedder Dr LA3 209 D1
Pedder Gr LA3 209 D1
Pedder La FY6 174 B1
Pedder Rd LA3 209 C1
Pedder St Morecambe LA4 212 D5
Preston PR2 95 E8
Pedder's La Blackpool FY4 109 D7
Preston PR2 116 A1
Pedders Gr PR2 95 A8
Pedders La PR2 95 A8
Pedders Way PR2 95 A8
Peebles Gr BB11 126 D3
Peel Ave Blackpool FY3 129 D7
Heysham LA3 208 E6
Lancaster LA1 213 F2
Ramsbottom BL0 49 A5
Peel Bank Rd BB5 102 B4
Peel Brow BL0 49 D6
Peel Brow Prim Sch BL0 49 D6
Peel Cl BB2 80 E8
Peel Cres LA1 210 D8
Peel Dr OL13 87 B1
Peel Gdns BB8 169 C5
Peel Hall Rd BL0 49 B2
Peel Hall St PR1 117 B1
Peel Hill FY4 110 E7
Peel Mount Blackburn BB1 101 F4
Ramsbottom BL0 49 A4
Peel Mount Cl BB1 101 F4
Peel Park Ave
Accrington BB5 103 D7
Clitheroe BB7 164 F7
Peel Park Cl
Accrington BB5 103 D7
Clitheroe BB7 164 F7
Peel Park Cty Prim Sch
BB5 103 D7
Peel Pl BB9 168 F6
Peel Rd Colne BB8 169 B4
Fleetwood FY7 193 F3
Peel FY4 110 F4
Skelmersdale WN8 9 E5
Peel St Accrington BB5 103 C6
Adlington PR6 30 B8
Blackburn BB2 100 C2
Chorley PR7 42 C7
Clitheroe BB7 164 E8
Haslingden BB4 84 A3
5 Oswaldtwistle BB5 102 D3
Padiham BB12 125 D8
Preston PR2 95 E8
Rawtenstall BB4 85 C2
Southport PR8 34 F6
Peel Twr BL8 48 F5
Peel Wlk L31 5 B2
Peers Clough Rd BB4 85 F7
Peet Ave L39 15 D4
Peet's La PR9 53 A1
Peg Way PR4 91 F6
Peg's La FY8 90 B8
Pegbank La LA6 235 A8
Pelham Ave 3 FY3 129 E8
Pelham St BB1 101 A6
Pemberton Dr LA4 213 B5
Pemberton Pl LA4 213 B5
Pemberton St BB1 121 E1
Pemberton's CE Sch PR7 40 E2
Pembroke Ave
Blackpool FY2 150 B3
Morecambe LA4 212 G6
Pembroke Cl BL6 31 A4
Pembroke Ct
Blackpool FY2 150 B3
14 Rochdale OL12 51 F1
Pembroke Pl Chorley PR7 42 B6
Leyland PR5 59 A8
Pembroke Pl *continued*
11 Preston PR1 96 A7
Pembroke Rd FY8 89 D4
Pembroke St
Accrington BB5 103 D6
Bacup OL13 86 F1
Blackburn BB2 100 E3
12 Burnley BB10 147 B1
Pembury Ave PR1 95 F3
Pen-y-ghent Way BB18 200 A2
Penarth Ct PR2 115 F3
Pendle Ave Bacup OL13 87 A3
Chatburn BB7 187 E5
Clayton-le-M BB5 123 F4
Pendle Bridge BB12 146 F3
Pendle Cl Bacup OL13 87 A2
Blackpool FY3 150 F1
Pendle Comm Hospl BB9 168 E1
Pendle Ct
Barnoldswick BB18 200 C3
4 Clitheroe BB7 164 F8
Kirkham PR4 113 A6
Longridge PR3 139 A7
Pendle Cty Prim Sch BB7 186 F1
Pendle Dr Blackburn BB2 100 F2
Horwich BL6 31 C5
Ormskirk L39 16 A6
Whalley BB7 143 A7
Pendle Fields BB12 146 D7
Pendle Heritage Ctr BB9 168 E4
Pendle Hill Cl PR2 118 C7
Pendle House BB1 100 F5
Pendle Ind Est BB9 147 F7
Pendle Pl
Lytham St Anne's FY8 90 C4
Skelmersdale WN8 9 D4
Pendle Rd Brierfield BB9 147 A5
Clayton-le-W PR5 76 D1
Clitheroe BB7 165 A7
Downham BB7 188 D3
Great Harwood BB6 123 F6
Lancaster LA1 213 D3
Pendle Row BB12 167 C5
Pendle St Accrington BB5 103 A5
Barrowford BB9 168 C3
Blackburn BB1 101 A5
Nelson BB9 168 D1
Padiham BB12 125 D8
Pendle St E BB7 144 F7
Pendle St W BB7 144 F7
Pendle Terr BB7 188 E8
Pendle Trad Est BB7 187 C4
Pendle View Barley BB12 167 C6
Brockhall Village BB6 142 C6
Clayton-le-M BB5 124 A3
Foulridge BB8 191 E1
Grindleton BB7 187 B7
Higham BB12 145 F6
Huncoat BB5 124 F2
West Bradford BB7 186 D7
Pendle Way Burnley BB12 126 E6
5 Nelson BB9 147 E8
Pendlehurst St BB11 126 E4
Pendlemist View BB8 169 C3
Pendleside BB9 147 B8
Pendleside Cl BB7 144 F7
Pendleton Ave
Accrington BB5 102 F4
Rawtenstall BB4 85 A4
Pendleton Rd
Pendleton BB7 165 A2
Wiswell BB7 143 F8
Penfold L31 5 E1
Pengarth Rd BL6 31 C4
Penguin St PR1 117 B2
Penhale Cl LA3 208 E6
Penhale Ct LA3 208 E6
Penhale Gdns LA3 208 E6
Penhill Cl 4 FY2 129 D8
Penistone St 6 BB12 126 D6
Penketh Pl WN8 9 C5
Penn St BL6 31 C3
Pennine Ave PR7 59 D1
Pennine Cl
7 Blackpool FY1 129 C4
Horwich BL6 31 C5
Pennine Cres BB9 147 C5
Pennine Gdns PR3 178 A7
Pennine Gr BB12 145 C2
Pennine Pl WN8 9 B6
Pennine Rd Bacup OL13 87 A2
Chorley PR6 42 E8
Horwich BL6 31 C5
Pennine View
Dolphinholme LA2 220 A8
Glasson LA2 205 E4
Great Eccleston PR3 154 C5
Kirkham PR4 113 C5
Morecambe LA4 212 E4
Pennine Way
Barnoldswick BB18 200 A2
Brierfield BB9 147 C5
Great Eccleston PR3 154 C5
Stalmine FY6 174 D7
Pennines The PR2 117 A7
Pennington Ave L39 15 E6
Pennington Ct
Heysham LA3 208 E6
4 Ormskirk L39 15 F6
Pennington La WN2 29 E1
Penny House La BB5 103 C7
Penny St Blackburn BB1 100 F5
Lancaster LA1 210 F7
3 Preston PR1 96 A8
Penny Stone Rd LA2 214 E7
Pennyfarthing La 7 FY5 173 A2
Pennystone Rd FY2 150 B4
Penrhos Ave FY7 193 E1
Penrhyn Rd LA1 213 C2
Penrith Ave Cleveleys FY5 172 D4
Heysham LA3 208 F8
Southport PR8 20 C3
Penrith Cres Maghull L31 5 E2
Nelson BB8 169 B3
Penrith Rd BB8 169 A3
Penrod Way LA3 208 D5
Penrose Ave FY4 129 F1
Penrose Pl WN8 9 E4
Penshaw Cl BB1 121 E1
Penswick Ave FY5 172 E1
Pentland Rd L33 1 A4
Penwortham Broad Oak
Cty Prim Sch PR1 95 C2
Penwortham Ct PR1 95 D4
Penwortham Girls High Sch
PR1 95 C5
Penwortham Hall Gdns
PR1 95 E3
Penwortham Prim Sch
PR1 95 A5
Penwortham Priory
High Sch PR1 95 A5
Penzance St BB2 100 B2
Peplow Rd LA3 209 A8
Pepper La WN6 28 B3
Perch Pool La PR9 35 F4
Percival Ct 2 PR8 34 A6
Percival St Accrington BB5 102 F5
Blackburn BB1 100 F7
Darwen BB3 80 F3
Percy Rd LA1 210 F6
Percy St Accrington BB5 103 D6
Blackburn BB2 100 B2
Blackpool FY1 129 C7
Bury BL9 32 B3
9 Chorley PR7 42 D7
Colne BB8 169 E6
Fleetwood FY7 193 F4
Nelson BB9 147 E7
Oswaldtwistle BB5 102 B5
Preston PR1 96 A8
Ramsbottom BL0 49 B5
Whitworth OL12 70 E6
Peregrine Dr BB3 80 D3
Peregrine Pl PR5 75 D2
Peridot Cl BB1 121 F2
Perimeter Rd L33 1 E2
Peronne Cres BB1 101 D5
Perpignon Way 16 LA1 210 F8
Perry St BB3 81 B2
Perryn Pl WN6 28 F1
Pershore Gdns FY3 130 B8
Pershore Gr PR8 20 A4
Pershore Rd FY8 89 B5
Persia St BB5 102 F6
Perth Cl FY5 150 F7
Perth St Accrington BB5 103 A5
Blackburn BB2 100 C3
Burnley BB11 126 D5
Lancaster LA1 211 A7
8 Nelson BB9 168 F1
Peter Birtwistle Cl BB8 169 E5
Peter La LA5 219 E1
Peter Martin St 2 BL6 31 B4
Peter St
9 Barrowford BB9 168 D4
Blackburn BB1 101 A6
Blackpool FY1 129 D5
Chorley PR7 42 C8
Colne BB8 169 E4
5 Lancaster LA1 210 F7
Rawtenstall BB4 85 A2
Peterfield Rd 1 PR1 95 E2
Peterhouse Sch PR9 53 B3
Peters Ave L40 24 E4
Petersan Ct PR7 60 C3
Petersbottom La LA2 233 E4
Petre Cres BB1 102 B8
Petre Rd BB5 123 F2
Petrel Cl BB1 100 D8
Petunia Cl PR5 76 E2
Petworth Rd PR8 20 B6
Pharos Ct 8 FY7 194 B5
Pharos Gr 2 FY7 194 B5
Pharos Pl FY7 194 B5
Pharos St FY7 194 B5
Pheasant Wood Dr FY5 172 F5
Pheasantford Gn BB10 127 B8
Pheasantford St BB10 127 B8
Philip Ave PR4 113 B4
Philip Dr PR8 20 F6
Philip St
Barnoldswick BB18 200 B2
Darwen BB3 81 B1
Philips Rd Blackburn BB1 101 B8
Weir OL13 87 A7
Phillip St FY4 129 F2
Phillip's Cl L37 11 F2
Phillip's La L37 11 F2
Phillips La BB8 169 B3
Phillipstown BB4 85 E4
Phoenix St 5
Lancaster LA1 213 F1
Rochdale OL12 51 C1
Phoenix Way BB11 126 C5
Phyllis St OL12 51 B1
Piazza The LA1 211 C7
Piccadilly LA1 210 F3
Piccadilly Cl LA1 210 F3
Piccadilly Gr LA1 210 F3
Piccadilly Rd BB11 126 E5
Piccadilly Sq 2 BB11 126 E5
Piccadilly St BB4 84 B3
Pickard Cl BB18 200 D4
Pickard St LA1 210 F6
Pickering Cl FY8 89 B7
Pickering Fold BB1 81 B7
Pickering St BB9 147 B5
Pickerings The 2 PR5 76 C8
Pickles Dr L40 24 D4
Pickles St BB12 126 D7
Pickmere Ave FY4 109 E8
Pickmere Cl FY5 173 A4
Pickthorn Cl LA1 213 D4
Pickup Fold 3 BB3 64 C7
Pickup Fold Rd BB3 64 C7
Pickup Rd BB1 102 A8
Pickup St Accrington BB5 102 F5
11 Bacup OL13 86 F2
Blackburn BB1 101 A5
Clayton-le-M BB5 123 F3
Picton St BB2 80 B8
Pier Ho 3 BB1 100 F3
Pier La LA5 237 B2
Pier St FY1 129 B3
Pierce Cl Lancaster LA1 210 D7
Padiham BB12 145 C1
Piercefield Rd L37 11 F5
Piercy Mdw BB4 85 F3
Piercy Mount BB4 85 F3
Piercy Rd BB4 85 F3
Piercy Terr BB4 85 F3
Pierston Ave FY2 150 C1
Pike Ct FY7 193 C2
Pike View BL6 31 D4
Pikelaw Pl WN8 9 C5
Pilgrim St BB9 147 F6
Pilkington Dr BB5 124 A3
Pilkington Rd PR8 34 D5
Pilkington St
6 Blackburn BB1 100 E4
14 Ramsbottom BL0 49 B5
Pilling Ave Accrington BB5 103 E2
Lytham St Anne's FY8 89 C7
Pilling Cl Chorley PR7 42 D6
Southport PR9 52 F5
Pilling Cres FY3 130 A8
Pilling Field BL7 46 E1
Pilling La Chorley PR7 42 D6
Maghull L31 5 A5
Pilling Lane FY6 195 B7
Pilling Pl WN8 9 C5
Pilling St Haslingden BB4 84 B6
3 Rawtenstall BB4 68 F8
Pilmuir Rd BB2 100 E1
Pilot St BB5 103 B7
Pimbo La Orrell WN8 10 A4
Skelmersdale WN8 9 F3
Pimbo Rd WN8 9 C5
Pimhole Rd BL9 32 B2
Pimlico BB7 186 F3
Pimlico Link Rd BB7 187 C2
Pimlico Rd BB7 186 F2
Pinch Clough Rd BB4 85 F5
Pincock Brow PR7 41 C8
Pincock St PR7 41 C8
Pinder Cl BB7 186 B4
Pinder St BB9 168 F2
Pine Ave Blackpool FY1 129 E2
Much Hoole PR4 73 D4
Ormskirk L39 15 F7
Pine Cl Fulwood PR2 117 F4
Halton LA2 214 E6
Newburgh WN8 26 A1
Rishton BB1 102 B8
Skelmersdale WN8 17 F1
Pine Cres
Oswaldtwistle BB5 102 F3
Poulton-le-F FY6 151 E2
Pine Crest L39 15 B2
Pine Dr L39 15 F6
Pine Gr Chorley PR6 60 D3
Clitheroe BB7 164 D7
Garstang PR3 199 C1
Ormskirk L39 15 F7
Southport PR9 34 D7
Pine Lake LA6 234 A3
Pine St Bacup OL13 87 A1
Blackburn BB1 101 A7
Burnley BB11 127 B5
Bury BL9 32 B2
Bury BL9 32 B3
Darwen BB3 64 B8
Haslingden BB4 84 C3
Lancaster LA1 213 E1
Morecambe LA4 212 F4
Nelson BB9 147 F8
Pine St S BL9 32 B2
Pine Way PR4 113 B7
Pine Wlks PR2 115 C1
Pines Cl PR5 77 C4
Pines The Leyland PR5 58 A8
Southport PR8 33 F6
Pineway PR2 116 C4
Pinewood Blackburn BB2 79 F8
Skelmersdale WN8 18 D3
Pinewood Ave
Blackpool FY2 150 E4
Broughton PR3 136 C3
Caton LA2 231 C3
Formby L37 11 D1
Hest Bank LA5 215 F2
Knott End-on-S FY6 195 A5
Morecambe LA4 213 B6
Thornton FY5 151 B7
Pinewood Cl Formby L37 11 D2
Lancaster LA2 210 E2
Southport PR8 35 C1
Pinewood Cotts 1 LA2 233 D8
Pinewood Cres
Leyland PR5 58 E8

Pinewood Cres *continued*
Lytham St Anne's FY8 89 D4
Orrell WN5 10 E6
Ramsbottom BL0 49 B2
Pinewood Dr BB5 103 E6
Pinfold Barrowford BB9 168 E5
Longton PR4 74 A8
Pinfold Cl Preston PR2 117 E5
Southport PR8 20 B3
Pinfold Ct LA3 213 B2
Pinfold La Inskip PR4 155 C2
Lancaster LA1 213 F2
Longridge PR3 139 B4
Pinfold L40 22 F3
Southport PR8 20 B3
Pinfold Pl Nelson BB9 169 B1
Skelmersdale WN8 9 D4
Pinfold St PR1 96 E8
Pingle Croft PR6 77 A2
Pingwood La L33 1 A5
Pink Pl BB2 100 B3
Pink St BB12 126 C6
Pinnacle Dr BL7 46 E2
Pinner La BB4 84 F7
Pinners Cl BL0 49 B7
Pintail Cl Moss Side PR5 75 A1
5 Rochdale OL12 51 B2
Pioneer St BL6 31 C4
Piper Cotts LA4 212 F3
Piper Lea BB4 86 A1
Piper's La LA6 234 C8
Pipers Cl LA7 237 E4
Pippin Bank OL13 86 F1
Pippin St Ormskirk L40 24 A2
Thorpe Green PR6 77 E5
Pit Hey Pl WN8 9 C5
Pitt St Lancaster LA1 210 F8
11 Padiham BB12 125 D8
Preston PR1 95 E7
Southport PR9 34 F6
Pittman Ct PR2 117 B8
Pittman Way PR2,PR3 117 C7
Pitts House La PR9 35 B8
Pittsdale Ave FY3 130 A2
Pitville St BB3 80 F3
Place-de-Criel 12 BB9 147 D8
Plain Pl BB2 100 E3
Plainmoor Dr FY5 150 F7
Plane St Bacup OL13 86 F4
Blackburn BB1 101 A7
Plane Tree Cl BB11 126 D3
Plane Tree Rd 7 BB1 101 A7
Planet Earth OL14 87 F4
Plant St Oswaldtwistle BB5 102 D3
Preston PR2 116 C1
Plantain Wlk LA3 212 E2
Plantation Ave
Arnside LA5 218 C8
Knott End-on-S FY6 194 E5
Plantation Gr LA5 218 C8
Plantation La LA2 226 D1
Plantation Rd
Accrington BB5 103 E6
Blackburn BB2 100 B1
Burscough L40 24 B4
Edgworth BL7 47 F7
Plantation Sq BB5 103 D6
Plantation St
Accrington BB5 103 D6
Bacup OL13 69 C8
Burnley BB10 127 A7
6 Nelson BB9 168 F1
Rawtenstall BB4 85 B2
Plantation The BD23 230 B3
Plantation View
Bacup OL13 86 F6
Ramsbottom BL0 49 C3
Platt Cl BB5 103 A5
Platt La WN1 29 B3
Platt St FY1 129 C6
Platten Gr LA4 212 F5
Platts La L40 24 D2
Pleasant Gr FY5 173 B2
Pleasant Pl 4 BB11 126 F5
Pleasant St Blackpool FY1 129 B7
Haslingden BB4 84 B3
2 Lytham St Anne's FY8 90 B3
Pleasant View Bacup OL13 69 C7
14 Barnoldswick BB18 200 B2
Blackpool FY4 110 A4
Coppull PR7 41 F2
Earby BB18 201 C1
Hoddlesden BB3 81 F1
Leyland PR5 75 C3
Newchurch BB4 85 F1
Withnell PR6 79 A1
Pleasington Ave PR3 178 D6
Pleasington Cl
Blackburn BB2 100 B4
Blackpool FY4 110 A8
Pleasington Gr BB10 127 D5
Pleasington La BB2 79 C8
Pleasington Nature Reserve
BB2 99 D3
Pleasington Rd BB2 99 C1
Pleasington St BB2 100 B4
Pleasington Sta BB2 99 C1
Pleasure Beach Sta FY4 109 B6
Pleck Farm Ave BB1 100 E8
Pleck Pl FY6 151 B6
Pleck Rd BB5 103 C6
Pleckgate Fold BB1 121 E1
Pleckgate High Sch BB1 121 D1
Pleckgate Rd BB1 121 E1
Plevna Rd PR1 96 C8
Plex La L39 14 C5
Plex Moss La L39 13 D8
Plock Gn PR7 42 C5
Plough La L40, WN8 17 A4
Plough Yd BB6 123 D5
Ploughlands The 2 PR2 115 E1
Plover Cl FY5 173 A5
Plover Dr Bury BL9 32 B4
Heysham LA3 208 F5
Plover St Burnley BB12 126 D6
Preston PR1 117 B1
Plover View 2 BB12 126 D6
Plovers Way FY3 130 B6
Plox Brow PR4 56 A6
Plumbe St BB11 127 A5
Plumpton Ave FY4 109 F5
Plumpton Field PR4 135 E2
Plumpton La
Great Plumpton PR4 111 E7
Shirdley Hill L39 21 E2
Plumpton Rd PR2 116 C2
Plumtree Cl PR2 117 C6
Plunge Rd BL0 67 E3
Plungington Rd PR1,PR2 116 E2
Plymouth Ave FY7 172 C8
Plymouth Gr PR6 42 E8
Plymouth Rd FY2,FY3 150 E1
Poachers Way FY5 173 A4
Pochard Pl 5 FY5 172 F1
Pocklington St BB5 103 D2
Podiham Cty Prim Sch
BB12 125 E8
Poets' Rd BB12 125 F7
Pointer Ct LA1 210 F6
Pointer Gr LA2 214 F7
Pointer The LA1 210 F6
Poland St BB5 102 F6
Pole La BB3 64 C8
Pole St Preston PR1 96 A8
Standish WN6 28 E1
Polefield PR2 116 E7
Police St BB3 81 A1
Pollard Pl LA1 214 A4
Pollard Row BB12 167 F1
Pollard St Accrington BB5 103 C7
Burnley BB11 126 D5
4 Nelson BB9 168 E1
6 Preston PR1 95 E8
Pollards La BL9 49 C2
Pollux Gate FY8 89 C4
Polly Gn OL12 51 F3
Polperro Dr PR4 92 A6
Pomfret St Blackburn BB2 100 D3
Burnley BB11 126 E6
Pompian Brow PR5 56 E6
Pond Cl PR4 56 A5
Pond Gdns FY6 151 B6
Pond St LA5 217 D2
Pond Terr LA5 217 D2
Pont St BB9 147 D7
Pontville Sch L39 15 D3
Pool Ct FY7 193 D1
Pool Foot La FY6 152 E4
Pool Hey La PR8, PR9 35 B3
Pool House Ct PR2 116 A6
Pool House Cty Prim Sch
PR2 116 A6
Pool House La PR2 116 A5
Pool La PR4 92 A4
Pool St PR9 53 D5
Poole Rd PR2 117 A4
Poole St BB1 101 C5
Poolhill Cl FY5 150 E7
Poolside Wlk PR9 53 C4
Poot Hall OL12 51 F3
Pope La Fulwood PR2 118 A3
Penwortham PR1 95 C2
Pope Wlk PR1 95 D3
Poplar Ave
Bamber Bridge PR5 96 F1
Blackpool FY3 129 D5
Bury BL9 32 B3
Euxton PR7 59 C4
Great Harwood BB6 123 D6
Horwich BL6 31 E1
Kirkham PR4 113 A4
Longton PR4 74 B8
Poulton-le-F FY6 151 E2
4 Rochdale OL12 51 C1
Warton PR4 91 D6
Poplar Bank PR9 52 D1
Poplar Cl
Bamber Bridge PR5 96 F1
Oswaldtwistle BB5 102 F3
Rishton BB1 102 B8
Poplar Dr Freckleton PR4 92 A5
Longridge PR3 139 A8
Penwortham PR1 95 C5
Skelmersdale WN8 17 F1
Poplar Gr
Bamber Bridge PR5 96 F1
Fulwood PR2 118 A4
Ramsbottom BL0 49 D7
Poplar St Blackburn BB1 100 F7
2 Blackburn BB1 101 A7
Chorley PR7 42 D6
Haslingden BB4 84 B3
Nelson BB9 168 F1
Southport PR8 34 E6
Poplar Terr BB4 84 F6
Poplars The PR7 29 F6
Poppy Ave PR6 60 D2
Poppy La L39 16 B1
Poppyfield PR4 115 F6
Poppyfields PR4 72 E4
Porritt Ave LA1 210 D8
Porritt St Bury BL9 32 A4
Bury BL9 32 B4
Porritt Way BL0 49 C7
Port Royal Ave LA1 210 C8
Port Way Heysham LA3 208 D5
Preston PR2 95 C7
Portal Gr BB12 126 B6
Porter Pl 2 PR1 96 A6
Porter St Accrington BB5 102 F5
Preston PR1 117 B1
Porter St E 4 PR4 112 F6
Porters Row FY6 174 C7
Portfield La BB6 143 F3
Portfield Rd BB7 143 E4
Porthcawl Ct PR2 115 F3
Portland Cotts PR6 61 D8
Portland Ct FY4 110 A1
Portland Dr LA3 212 E2
Portland Ind Est 10 BL9 32 A4
Portland Rd Blackpool FY1 129 D4
Langho BB6 122 C8
Portland St
Accrington BB5 103 A6
Barrowford BB9 168 D3
Blackburn BB2 100 C3
Bury BL9 32 A4
1 Chorley PR6 42 D8
Colne BB8 169 F5
Darwen BB3 64 B6
Lancaster LA1 210 F7
Nelson BB9 147 D8
Preston PR1 95 D7
Southport PR8 34 B5
Portman St PR1 117 B1
Portree Cl PR2 117 C5
Portree Cres BB1 101 D3
Portree Rd FY2 150 E5
Portsmouth Ave BB10 147 E2
Portsmouth Cl 7 FY5 172 F4
Portsmouth Dr PR6 42 E8
Portway FY2 150 E6
Post Horse La LA2 232 B7
Post La PR4 91 F6
Post Office Ave 1 PR9 34 B7
Post Office Row
Tunstall LA6 235 D4
Westhouse LA6 236 E4
Post Office Yd 8 BB8 169 E5
Postern Gate Rd LA2 226 A8
Pot Gn BL0 49 A3
Pot House La Darwen BB3 81 C3
Oswaldtwistle BB5 102 F2
Potter La Coupe Green PR5 97 D5
Samlesbury PR5 118 E2
Potter Pl WN8 9 D5
Potter St 5 BL9 32 A3
Poulton Ave
Accrington BB5 103 A8
Lytham St Anne's FY8 89 B8
Poulton Cres PR5 97 D3
Poulton Gr FY7 194 A4
Poulton Old Rd FY3 150 F1
Poulton RC St John's
Prim Sch FY6 151 E4
Poulton Rd Blackpool FY3 129 E8
Carleton FY6 151 C5
Fleetwood FY7 193 F4
Morecambe LA4 212 E5
Southport PR9 34 F7
Poulton Sq LA4 212 E6
Poulton St Fleetwood FY7 194 A4
Kirkham PR4 113 B5
Preston PR2 116 C1
Poulton-le-Fylde
CE Prim Sch FY6 151 D3
Poulton-le-Fylde Sta
FY6 151 D4
Poulton-le-Sands
CE Prim Sch LA4 212 E6
Powder House La
LA1,LA4 213 C4
Powderworks La L31 6 C3
Powell Ave FY4 109 D8
Powell St
Barnoldswick BB18 200 B3
Burnley BB11 126 E4
Darwen BB3 81 A2
Powis Dr PR4 56 A8
Powis Rd PR2 95 B8
Powys Cl BB4 84 B1
Poynter St 4 PR1 117 C1
Poynton St BL9 32 A1
Prairie Cres BB10 147 B2
Pratt St BB10 147 B1
Precinct The BL0 48 F3
Preesall Cl
Lytham St Anne's FY8 89 B7
Preston PR2 115 E1
Southport PR9 52 F4
Preesall Mill Ind Est FY6 195 B2
Preesall Moss La FY6 195 D2
Preesall Rd PR2 115 E1
Preese Gdns PR4 154 A1
Premier Way FY6 151 F3
Prenton Gdns 7
Blackpool FY5 150 F7
Norcross FY5 151 A7
Prescot Cl BL9 32 A1
Prescot Gn L39 15 D3
Prescot Pl Blackpool FY3 130 A2
Thornton FY5 173 C2
Prescot Rd L31, L39 6 D6
Prescott Ave L40 38 A3
Prescott Rd WN8 9 F4
Prescott St BB10 127 C5
Press Rd FY8 88 D8
Pressfield Sch PR9 53 A3
Prestbury Ave
Blackpool FY4 109 C5
Southport PR8 20 B5
Prestbury Cl BL9 32 A1
Prestbury Dr LA3 212 E2
Preston Beck BB18 201 B2
Preston Coll PR2 116 F5
Preston Coll Trinity Bldg
PR1 95 F8
Preston Coll Winkley Bldg
PR1 95 F7
Preston Ent Ctr 2 PR1 116 F1
Preston Golf Course PR2 117 A6
Preston Lancaster New Rd
PR3 178 B4
Preston Lancaster Old Rd
PR3 178 D2
Preston Lancaster Rd
Bilsborrow PR3 157 A6
Cabus PR3 199 C5
Galgate LA2 207 A5
Potters Brook LA2,PR3 204 C5
Preston New Rd
Blackburn BB2 100 B5
Blackpool FY1,FY3 130 C2
Clifton PR4 93 C7
Freckleton PR4 92 D7
Little Plumpton PR4 111 C6
Mellor Brook BB2, PR5 119 D1
Peel Hill FY4 110 E7
Samlesbury PR2,PR5 118 E1
Southport PR9 53 B4
Preston Nook PR7 40 C5
Preston Old Rd
Blackburn BB2 79 D8
Blackpool FY3 130 A2
Clifton PR4 114 C1
Freckleton PR4 92 C6
Preston Rd
Charnock Richard PR7 41 C4
Chorley PR6,PR7 60 C2
Clayton Brook PR5,PR6,PR7 77 B4
Grimsargh PR2,PR3 138 E2
Inskip PR4 134 D7
Leyland PR5 76 B2
Longridge PR3 139 A5
Lucas Green PR6 60 C4
Lytham St Anne's FY8 90 D4
Ribchester PR3 140 B5
Southport PR9 34 E8
Standish PR7,WN6 28 D5
Preston St Carnforth LA5 217 D2
9 Chorley PR6 60 D1
Darwen BB3 80 F3
Fleetwood FY7 194 B4
Kirkham PR4 113 B5
16 Rochdale OL12 51 C1
Preston Sta PR1 95 E7
Prestwich St BB11 126 E5
Prestwood Pl WN8 9 F4
Pretoria St 2 OL12 51 C1
Price Cl LA1 213 E3
Price St 9 Blackpool FY1 129 B1
Bury BL9 32 A1
Prickshaw OL12 51 B6
Prickshaw La OL12 51 B6
Priestfield Ave BB8 169 B5
Priesthouse Cl L37 12 A3
Priesthouse La L37 12 A3
Priestield 9 Blackpool FY5 150 F7
Norcross FY5 151 A7
Priestley Nook 4 BB5 103 C5
Primet Bridge BB8 169 C4
Primet Bsns Ctr BB8 169 B4
Primet High Sch BB8 169 B3
Primet Hill BB8 169 C4
Primet Hts BB9 169 B3
Primet Prim Sch BB8 169 B3
Primet St BB8 169 C4
Primrose Ave FY4 109 D6
Primrose Bank
1 Bacup OL13 69 C8
Blackburn BB1 100 F6
Blackpool FY2 150 F6
Primrose Cl
Blackburn BB2 100 B2
Formby L37 12 B5
Hesketh Bank PR4 72 E4
Southport PR9 53 C6
Primrose Cotts
Calder Vale PR3 179 E7
Middleton LA3 209 A2
Primrose Ct
8 Blackburn BB1 100 F6
6 Lancaster LA1 211 A7
Morecambe LA4 212 E5
Primrose Dr
Blackburn BB1 100 F5
Bury BL9 32 D4
Primrose Gr PR1 117 C3
Primrose Hill Colne BB8 169 F5
Mellor BB2 121 A3
3 Preston PR1 96 B7
Primrose Hill Prim Sch
PR7 59 B4
Primrose Hill Rd PR7 59 B4
Primrose Hill Sch BB10 147 D2
Primrose La Fulwood PR1 117 C3
Standish WN6 28 D2
Primrose Rd
Clitheroe BB7 164 D6
Fulwood PR1 117 C3
Primrose Row PR7 58 F1
Primrose St
Accrington BB5 103 A4
9 Bacup OL13 69 C8
Brierfield BB9 147 B5
Burnley BB10 147 C1
Chorley PR6 42 D8
Clitheroe BB7 164 D7
Darwen BB3 64 B8
Primrose St *continued*
Lancaster LA1 211 A7
6 Morecambe LA4 212 E5
Primrose Terr
Blackburn BB2 100 B2
Blackpool FY4 110 A4
Langho BB6 142 C1
1 Radford BB3 64 B8
Primrose Way
Carleton FY6 151 B6
Church BB5 102 E7
Primula Dr BB3 81 A7
Prince Ave LA5 217 E1
Prince Charles Gdns PR8 33 F4
Prince Lee Mdws BB3 64 B8
Prince St Bacup OL13 70 D7
11 Burnley BB11 126 E5
Darwen BB3 80 F1
Ramsbottom BL0 49 C6
Prince's Pk WN6 19 F4
Prince's Rd PR5 96 E5
Prince's St BB2 100 D4
Princes Cres LA4 213 A7
Princes Ct PR1 95 B6
Princes Dr PR2 116 E6
Princes Rd 2
Lytham St Anne's FY8 89 D4
Penwortham PR1 95 B6
Princes Reach PR2 95 A7
Princes St Rishton BB1 123 B1
Southport PR8 34 A6
Princes Way
Cleveleys FY5 172 C1
Fleetwood FY7 193 D3
Princess Alexandra Way
LA3 208 D5
Princess Ave
Clitheroe BB7 186 F1
Kirkham PR4 112 F6
Lancaster LA1 210 F6
Poulton-le-F FY6 151 D3
Princess Ct 5 FY1 129 B3
Princess Gdns
Blackburn BB2 79 C7
Morecambe LA4 213 A5
Princess Par FY1 129 B6
Princess Rd Adlington PR6 30 B8
Cleveleys FY5 172 C2
Princess St Accrington BB5 102 F6
17 Bacup OL13 86 F2
10 Bamber Bridge PR5 76 F8
2 Bamber Bridge, Lostock Hall
PR5 76 B7
Blackburn BB2 100 C2
Blackpool FY1 129 B3
Chorley PR7 42 D6
4 Church BB5 102 E6
Colne BB8 169 C4
Great Harwood BB6 123 D5
Haslingden BB4 84 B2
Leyland PR5 76 B1
Nelson BB9 147 D7
Padiham BB12 125 B8
Preston PR1 96 B7
Rochdale OL12 51 F1
Whalley BB7 143 C5
Whitworth OL12 51 C8
Princess Way
Burnley BB12 126 F7
Euxton PR7 59 E2
Princeway FY4 109 C7
Pringle Bank LA5 217 D6
Pringle Ct PR3 178 C7
Pringle St BB1 101 A3
Pringle Wood PR3 136 C2
Prinny Hill Rd BB4 84 A3
Printers Fold BB12 125 E6
Prior's Cl BB2 100 A6
Priors Wlk BB7 224 C1
Priorsgate LA3 212 F2
Priorswood Pl WN8 9 F4
Priory Cl Blackburn BB1 101 E4
Burscough L40 24 D5
Formby L37 12 B2
6 Lancaster LA1 210 E8
Leyland PR5 76 C2
Morecambe LA3 212 F2
Newchurch BB4 85 E2
Penwortham PR1 95 C6
Tarleton PR4 56 A6
Priory Cres PR1 95 C6
Priory Ct 7 Blackpool FY1 129 C5
Burnley BB11 127 B2
Pleasington BB2 99 C2
Priory Dr BB3 64 C8
Priory Gate FY4 109 C5
Priory Gdns PR8 33 F4
Priory Gr L39 15 D4
Priory Grange Darwen BB3 64 C8
Southport PR8 34 A4
Priory High Sch L40 24 E5
Priory La Hornby LA2 232 B7
Penwortham PR1 95 C6
Priory Mews
Lytham St Anne's FY8 89 D7
Southport PR8 33 F6
Priory Nook WN8 10 C7
Priory Oak Cotts PR1 95 C6
Priory Pl BB3 64 C8
Priory Rd WN8 10 C7
Priory St 5 Nelson BB9 168 F1
Preston PR2 95 D8
Priory Way BB18 200 A2
Priory Wlk 6 LA1 211 A8
Pritchard St
Blackburn BB2 100 E2
Burnley BB11 126 E5
Private La BB4 67 C8

Procter Moss Rd
Lancaster LA2 ... 211 D1
Lower Green Bank LA2 ... 226 B3
Procter St BB2 ... 100 F3
Procter's Brow LA2 ... 233 B5
Proctor Cl BB9 ... 147 F5
Proctor Rd L37 ... 11 C4
Progress Ave BB1 ... 101 A7
Progress Bsns Pk PR4 ... 113 A4
Progress Ct FY3 ... 130 B8
Progress Rd BB9 ... 168 F3
Progress St Chorley PR6 ... 42 E8
Darwen BB3 ... 81 B1
Progress Way FY4 ... 110 B6
Promenade Blackpool FY1 ... 129 B5
Blackpool, Bispham FY2 ... 150 B6
Blackpool, South Shore FY4 ... 109 A6
Cleveleys FY5 ... 172 C5
Southport PR8,PR9 ... 34 B8
Promenade N FY5 ... 172 C3
Promenade Rd FY7 ... 194 A5
Promenade S FY5 ... 172 C2
Promenade The LA5 ... 237 B2
Prospect Ave
Bamber Bridge PR5 ... 76 B8
Darwen BB3 ... 80 E2
Hest Bank LA2 ... 215 E1
Prospect Ct PR3 ... 139 B6
Prospect Dr LA2 ... 215 E1
Prospect Gr LA4 ... 212 F4
Prospect Hill
Haslingden BB4 ... 84 A2
4 Rawtenstall BB4 ... 85 A3
Prospect Pl
7 Penwortham PR1 ... 95 E4
Preston PR2 ... 116 B1
Skelmersdale WN8 ... 9 F5
Prospect Rd BB4 ... 85 A3
Prospect St
Great Harwood BB6 ... 123 D5
Lancaster LA1 ... 211 A7
Newchurch BB4 ... 85 F1
Prospect Terr Bacup OL13 ... 69 E7
10 Barrowford BB9 ... 168 D4
Belthorn BB1 ... 81 F6
Brinscall PR6 ... 62 A8
Huncoat BB5 ... 124 E2
Newchurch BB4 ... 85 F1
Rawtenstall BB1 ... 105 B4
Provence Ave BB6 ... 142 C6
Providence St BB1 ... 101 A8
Prudy Hill FY6 ... 151 D4
Prunella Dr BB3 ... 81 A7
Pudding La OL14 ... 108 C2
Pudding Pie Nook La
PR3 ... 136 F4
Puddle House La FY6 ... 130 F8
Pudsey Rd OL14 ... 108 B2
Pump House La PR5 ... 57 F6
Pump St Blackburn BB2 ... 100 D4
Burnley BB11 ... 126 E6
Clitheroe BB7 ... 164 D8
Preston PR1 ... 96 A8
Punnell's La L31 ... 4 F5
Punstock Rd BB3 ... 80 F1
Purbeck Dr BL6 ... 31 F1
Pye Busk LA2 ... 233 E8
Pye Busk Cl LA2 ... 233 E8
Pye's Cotts L39 ... 5 E7
Pygon's Hill La L31 ... 5 D6

Q

Quaile Holme Rd FY6 ... 194 E5
Quaker Brook La PR5 ... 98 A3
Quaker La BB3 ... 81 A2
Quakerfields BB3 ... 81 A2
Quakers Terr WN6 ... 28 D3
Quakers' Pl WN6 ... 28 E1
Quarlton Dr BL8 ... 48 B3
Quarry Bank BB4 ... 83 F1
Quarry Bank St 3 BB12 ... 126 C7
Quarry Dr L39 ... 15 C1
Quarry Farm Ct BB7 ... 187 D5
Quarry Hill OL12 ... 51 E3
Quarry Hill Nature Reserve
BB9 ... 147 F6
Quarry Mount L39 ... 16 A6
Quarry Mount Mews LA1 ... 211 A7
Quarry Rd Brinscall PR7 ... 61 F7
Caton LA2 ... 231 E3
Chorley PR6 ... 42 E6
Halton LA2 ... 214 E6
Lancaster LA1 ... 211 A7
Quarry St
18 Accrington BB5 ... 103 C5
Bacup OL13 ... 87 A2
Blackburn BB1 ... 100 F5
Hapton BB11 ... 125 C2
Padiham BB12 ... 145 D1
Ramsbottom BL0 ... 49 D6
Rochdale OL12 ... 51 E1
Whitworth OL12 ... 70 E6
Quarrybank FY5 ... 150 F8
Quarryside Dr L33 ... 1 A3
Quay West FY8 ... 88 E5
Quayle Ave FY4 ... 109 E8
Quayside FY7 ... 194 B3
Quebec Ave FY2 ... 150 E3
Quebec Rd BB2 ... 100 B8
Queen Anne St
4 Haslingden BB4 ... 84 A3
Southport PR8 ... 34 B7
Queen Elizabeth Cres
BB5 ... 103 D5
Queen Elizabeth Ct LA4 ... 212 D5
Queen Elizabeth Sch LA6 ... 238 B2
Queen Elizabeth's Gram Sch
BB2 ... 100 C6
Queen Elizabeth's
Gram Sch (Annexe) BB2 ... 100 D6
Queen Ho BB4 ... 85 D1
Queen Mary Ave FY8 ... 89 A5
Queen Mary Sch FY8 ... 89 A4
Queen Sq
1 Blackpool FY1 ... 129 B5
Lancaster LA1 ... 210 F7
Queen St
18 Accrington BB5 ... 103 C6
Bacup OL13 ... 86 F2
5 Bacup, Stacksteads OL13 ... 69 C8
4 Bamber Bridge PR5 ... 76 B7
Barnoldswick BB18 ... 200 B1
Barrowford BB9 ... 168 D4
Blackpool FY1 ... 129 B6
Brierfield BB10 ... 147 F2
Burnley BB11 ... 126 F5
Bury BL9 ... 32 A2
Carnforth LA5 ... 217 D1
Clayton-le-M BB5 ... 123 F3
Clitheroe BB7 ... 164 C8
Colne BB8 ... 169 C4
Darwen BB3 ... 80 F2
Fleetwood FY7 ... 194 A4
Great Harwood BB6 ... 123 D5
Hoddlesden BB3 ... 81 F1
Horwich BL6 ... 31 B3
Lancaster LA1 ... 210 F7
Lytham St Anne's FY8 ... 90 A3
Morecambe LA4 ... 212 E5
Nelson BB9 ... 168 E1
Ormskirk L39 ... 15 E4
Oswaldtwistle BB5 ... 102 E4
Padiham BB12 ... 125 C8
Preston PR1 ... 96 B7
Ramsbottom BL0 ... 49 B6
Rawtenstall BB4 ... 85 A2
Whalley BB7 ... 143 C5
Queen St E 3 PR7 ... 42 D6
Queen Street Mill BB10 ... 147 F2
Queen Vera Rd 4 FY1 ... 129 B5
Queen Victoria Hospl
LA4 ... 212 E5
Queen Victoria Rd
Blackpool FY1 ... 129 C2
Burnley BB10 ... 127 B8
Burnley BB10 ... 147 B1
Queen Victoria St BB2 ... 100 B2
Queen's Cl Clitheroe BB7 ... 164 E7
Poulton-le-F FY6 ... 151 E3
Queen's Cres PR4 ... 113 B4
Queen's Ct FY2 ... 150 B2
Queen's Dr Carnforth LA5 ... 217 E1
Oswaldtwistle BB5 ... 102 F3
Queen's Gr PR7 ... 42 C8
Queen's Lancashire
Way BB11 ... 126 F6
Queen's Park High
Sch BB1 ... 101 C2
Queen's Park Hospl BB2 ... 101 A2
Queen's Park Rd
Blackburn BB1 ... 101 A3
Burnley BB10 ... 127 C7
Queen's Prom FY2 ... 150 B5
Queen's Rd
Accrington BB5 ... 103 C7
Blackburn BB1 ... 101 B3
Burnley BB10 ... 147 B2
Chorley PR7 ... 42 C8
Darwen BB3 ... 64 B6
Formby L37 ... 11 D2
Fulwood PR2 ... 116 E3
Lytham St Anne's FY8 ... 88 F5
Walton-le-D PR5 ... 96 E4
Queen's Sq Hoddlesden BB3 ... 81 F1
Kirkby Lonsdale LA6 ... 238 C2
Poulton-le-F FY6 ... 151 D3
7 Rawtenstall BB4 ... 85 A2
Queen's Terr
3 Bacup OL13 ... 69 E8
Blackburn BB2 ... 100 B1
Fleetwood FY7 ... 194 C5
Queens Ave L37 ... 11 E5
Queens Croft L37 ... 11 D2
Queens Ct PR2 ... 116 E3
Queens Ctyd 7 PR9 ... 34 C8
Queens Dr Arnside LA5 ... 237 B1
Fulwood PR2 ... 116 D6
Longridge PR3 ... 139 A7
Morecambe LA4 ... 213 A6
Staining FY3 ... 130 E5
Queens Drive Prim Sch
PR2 ... 116 D5
Queens Garth BD23 ... 201 B5
Queens Gn L39 ... 13 F5
Queens Jubilee
Nature Trail PR8 ... 33 E5
Queens Pl Kirkham PR4 ... 112 F7
Ramsbottom BL9 ... 49 C2
Queens Rd Clitheroe BB7 ... 164 E7
Orrell WN5 ... 10 C5
Southport PR9 ... 34 C8
Queens Rd W BB5 ... 103 A7
Queens Ret Pk PR1 ... 96 B7
Queens Wlk FY5 ... 172 D4
Queensberry Rd BB11 ... 126 E5
Queensborough Rd BB5 ... 103 B7
Queensbury Rd FY5 ... 172 C2
Queenscourt Ave PR1 ... 95 E2
Queenscourt Hospice PR8 ... 34 F4
Queensdale Cl PR5 ... 96 E4
Queensgate Chorley PR7 ... 42 B7
Nelson BB9 ... 147 D7
Queensway
Bamber Bridge PR5 ... 96 E1
Queensway *continued*
Blackburn BB2 ... 80 A8
Blackpool FY4 ... 109 C7
Brinscall PR6 ... 61 F8
Church BB5 ... 102 F7
Clitheroe BB7 ... 164 E7
Euxton PR7 ... 59 E2
Leyland PR5 ... 58 E7
Lytham St Anne's FY4,FY8 ... 110 B2
Newchurch BB4 ... 85 E1
Penwortham PR1 ... 95 B6
Poulton-le-F FY6 ... 151 D3
Preston PR2 ... 115 F2
Shevington WN6 ... 19 F4
Waddington BB7 ... 186 B4
Warton PR4 ... 91 E7
Queensway Cl PR1 ... 95 B6
Queensway Ct FY8 ... 110 A1
Queensway Ind Est FY8 ... 110 A2
Quernmore Ave FY3 ... 130 A3
Quernmore Brow LA2 ... 226 B5
Quernmore CE Prim Sch
LA2 ... 226 A7
Quernmore Dr
Glasson LA2 ... 205 E4
Kelbrook BB18 ... 192 A5
Quernmore Ind Est PR4 ... 92 C6
Quernmore Rd Caton LA2 ... 231 B2
Kirkby L33 ... 1 A3
Lancaster LA1,LA2 ... 211 D7
Quernmore Wlk L33 ... 1 A3
Quillet The LA5 ... 218 F3
Quin St PR5 ... 76 A1
Quinton Cl PR8 ... 20 A4

R

Rabbit La Burscough L40 ... 23 F4
Cow Ark BB7 ... 184 F6
Raby Sq LA4 ... 212 E6
Raby St 4 Morecambe LA4 ... 212 E5
1 Rawtenstall BB4 ... 85 A2
Radburn Brow PR6 ... 77 B3
Radburn Cl PR6 ... 77 B3
Radcliffe Rd FY7 ... 193 F2
Radeclyffe St BB7 ... 186 E1
Radfield Ave 14 BB3 ... 64 A8
Radfield Rd BB3 ... 63 F8
Radford Bank Gdns 12
BB3 ... 64 A8
Radford Gdns BB3 ... 64 A7
Radford St BB3 ... 64 A8
Radley Ave FY3 ... 129 E8
Radnor Ave Burnley BB12 ... 126 A7
Cleveleys FY5 ... 172 F1
Radnor Cl BB5 ... 102 C4
Radnor Dr PR9 ... 52 F3
Radnor St Accrington BB5 ... 103 B7
5 Preston PR1 ... 95 E8
Radway Cl FY5 ... 150 F7
Radworth Cres FY4 ... 130 B1
Raeburn Ave BB11 ... 126 E3
Raedale Ave BB10 ... 147 B4
Raeside Ct FY8 ... 89 A4
Raglan Rd Burnley BB11 ... 126 E5
Morecambe LA3 ... 212 B3
Raglan St 8 Colne BB8 ... 169 D4
5 Nelson BB9 ... 147 D8
Preston PR2 ... 116 D2
Raikes Hill 2 FY1 ... 129 C5
Raikes Hill Dr LA2 ... 213 E8
Raikes Mews 6 FY1 ... 129 C5
Raikes Par FY1 ... 129 C5
Raikes Rd
Great Eccleston PR3 ... 154 C5
Preston PR1 ... 117 C1
Thornton FY5 ... 151 E8
Rail Cl WA11 ... 8 F2
Railgate OL13 ... 70 C8
Railton Ave BB2 ... 80 A8
Railway App L39 ... 15 F5
Railway Ave PR9 ... 53 F5
Railway Cotts Coppull PR7 ... 41 F1
Preston PR4 ... 115 C3
Salwick PR4 ... 114 C4
Railway Crossing La LA1 ... 210 C5
Railway Gr 5 BB1 ... 101 A7
Railway Path L39 ... 15 E4
Railway Pl LA2 ... 205 F5
Railway Rd
Adlington PR6,PR7 ... 30 A7
Blackburn BB1 ... 100 E5
Brinscall PR6 ... 62 A8
Chorley PR6 ... 60 D1
Darwen BB3 ... 81 A1
Haslingden BB4 ... 84 B4
Ormskirk L39 ... 15 F5
Skelmersdale WN8 ... 8 E8
Railway St Bacup OL13 ... 69 B8
20 Barnoldswick BB18 ... 200 B2
Brierfield BB9 ... 147 B5
Burnley BB11 ... 126 F7
Chorley PR7 ... 42 D7
Foulridge BB8 ... 191 D1
Lancaster LA1 ... 210 F6
Leyland PR5 ... 76 B2
Nelson BB9 ... 147 E7
Ramsbottom BL0 ... 49 C6
Ramsbottom,
Summerseat BL0,BL9 ... 49 C2
Southport PR8 ... 34 B5
Railway Terr
Brierfield BB9 ... 147 B5
Edgworth BL7 ... 47 B8
Great Harwood BB6 ... 123 C4
10 Kirkham PR4 ... 112 F6
Rawtenstall BB4 ... 84 F1
Railway Terr *continued*
Simonstone BB12 ... 124 E8
Southport PR8 ... 34 A5
Railway View
5 Accrington BB5 ... 103 C6
Billington BB7 ... 143 B4
Blackburn BB2 ... 100 B2
Brierfield BB9 ... 147 B6
Croston PR5 ... 57 A2
8 Radford BB3 ... 64 B8
Railway View Ave BB7 ... 186 E1
Railway View Rd BB7 ... 186 E1
Rainford By-pass WA11 ... 8 D1
Rainford Junc WA11 ... 8 F2
Rainford Rd L39,WA11 ... 8 C4
Rainhall Cres BB18 ... 200 D3
Rainhall Rd BB18 ... 200 B2
Rainhall Rd Com Prim Sch
BB18 ... 200 B2
Rake Fold BL0 ... 49 A6
Rake Foot BB4 ... 84 B3
Rake La PR4 ... 91 D5
Rake The LA2 ... 226 E1
Rake Top Ave BB12 ... 145 F6
Rakehead La OL13 ... 69 B8
Rakehouse Brow LA2 ... 226 F2
Rakes Bridge BB3 ... 81 A7
Rakes House Rd BB9 ... 168 F2
Rakes La BD23 ... 225 F5
Rakes Rd LA2 ... 231 E4
Raleigh Ave FY4 ... 109 B5
Raleigh Cl FY8 ... 109 D1
Raleigh Rd PR2 ... 116 E6
Raleigh St BB12 ... 125 E7
Ralph St BB5 ... 103 C8
Ralph's Wife's La PR9 ... 53 E6
Ramparts The LA1 ... 214 A2
Ramper Gate FY5 ... 172 D2
Rams Clough La BB5 ... 83 A8
Ramsay Ct FY6 ... 194 D5
Ramsbottom Cottage Hospl
BL0 ... 49 C5
Ramsbottom Heritage
Ctr Mus BL0 ... 49 C7
Ramsbottom La BL0 ... 49 C7
Ramsbottom Rd
Horwich BL6 ... 31 C3
Ramsbottom BL8,BL7 ... 48 A3
Ramsbottom St BB5 ... 103 B7
Ramsbottom Sta BL0 ... 49 C6
Ramsden St LA5 ... 217 D2
Ramsey Ave Bacup OL13 ... 87 A1
Blackpool FY3 ... 129 D7
Fulwood PR1 ... 117 D3
Ramsey Cl FY8 ... 109 D1
Ramsey Gr BB10 ... 147 C2
Ramsey Rd BB2 ... 100 D1
Ramsgate Cl PR4 ... 91 E7
Ramsgate Rd FY8 ... 89 A8
Ramsgreave &
Wilpshire Sta BB1 ... 121 F4
Ramsgreave Ave BB1 ... 121 D2
Ramsgreave Dr BB1 ... 121 D1
Ramsgreave Rd BB1 ... 121 E4
Ramshill Ave FY6 ... 151 B5
Ramson Ct LA3 ... 212 E2
Ranaldsway PR5 ... 58 D8
Randal St BB1 ... 100 E6
Randall St 11 BB10 ... 147 B1
Randolph St 21 BB1 ... 101 A4
Ranelagh Dr PR8 ... 20 F7
Range High Sch L37 ... 2 C8
Ranger St BB5 ... 103 B5
Rangeway Ave FY4 ... 109 C7
Ranglet Rd PR5 ... 77 B7
Rangletts Ave PR7 ... 42 C6
Ranglit Ave PR2 ... 115 C1
Rankin Cl BB18 ... 200 C2
Rankin Dr BB3 ... 81 E1
Ranlea Ave LA4 ... 213 C6
Ranleigh Dr
Newburgh WN8 ... 26 A1
Skelmersdale WN8 ... 18 A8
Rannoch Dr BB2 ... 99 F1
Rantreefold Rd LA2 ... 233 C4
Rapley La PR4 ... 135 A8
Ratcliffe Fold 5 BB4 ... 84 B3
Ratcliffe St Darwen BB3 ... 64 B8
10 Haslingden BB4 ... 84 B3
Ratcliffe Wharf La PR3 ... 204 A1
Rathbone Rd L38 ... 2 F4
Rathlyn Ave FY3 ... 129 E7
Rathmell CE Sch BD24 ... 230 E7
Rathmell Cl FY3 ... 151 B1
Rathmill Sike BB7 ... 224 B1
Rathmore Cres PR9 ... 53 B3
Ratten La PR4 ... 94 D3
Raven Ave BB4 ... 67 A7
Raven Croft BB4 ... 67 B8
Raven Meols La L37 ... 11 F2
Raven Meols Hills
Nature Reserve L37 ... 2 B7
Raven Oak La BB10 ... 128 B5
Raven Pk BB4 ... 67 B8
Raven Rd BB2 ... 100 B5
Raven St 3 Nelson BB9 ... 168 F1
Preston PR1 ... 117 C2
Raven's Cl FY3 ... 130 B7
Ravendale Cl OL12 ... 51 A1
Ravenglass Ave L31 ... 5 D2
Ravenglass Cl
Blackburn BB2 ... 101 A1
Blackpool FY4 ... 109 E7
Kirkham PR4 ... 113 A7
Ravenhead Dr WN8 ... 10 A7
Ravenhead Way WN8 ... 9 F6
Ravenhill Dr PR7 ... 60 C1
Ravens Cl LA1 ... 213 E3
Ravens Close Brow LA2 ... 235 F1
Ravens Gr BB10 ... 147 C4
Ravens The L37 ... 11 F2
Ravens Wood BB2 ... 100 B5
Ravenscroft L37 ... 11 F2
Ravenscroft Ave L39 ... 15 E4
Ravenscroft Cl BB1 ... 122 A1
Ravenscroft Way BB18 ... 200 C3
Ravensthorpe PR7 ... 60 A1
Ravenswing Ave BB2 ... 100 B7
Ravenswood Fulwood PR2 ... 117 E2
Great Harwood BB6 ... 123 B6
Ravenswood Ave FY3 ... 130 B7
Ravenwood Ave FY4 ... 109 D5
Rawcliffe Dr PR2 ... 94 E8
Rawcliffe Rd
12 Chorley PR7 ... 42 C7
Ratten Row PR3 ... 154 C7
Rawcliffe St Blackpool FY4 ... 109 B8
Burnley BB11 ... 127 A6
Rawlinson Ct PR9 ... 34 D8
Rawlinson Gr PR9 ... 52 F1
Rawlinson La PR6 ... 42 E1
Rawlinson Rd PR9 ... 52 E1
Rawlinson St
3 Darwen BB3 ... 64 B6
13 Horwich BL6 ... 31 B4
5 Kirkham PR4 ... 112 F6
Raws St BB11 ... 127 A6
Rawson Ave BB5 ... 103 A4
Rawson St 13 BB10 ... 147 B1
Rawsons Rake BL0,BL8 ... 49 A6
Rawsthorne Ave
Edenfield BL0 ... 67 D2
Haslingden BB4 ... 84 B2
Rawstorne Cl PR4 ... 92 A6
Rawstorne Rd PR1 ... 95 B5
Rawstorne St BB2 ... 100 C4
Rawstron St OL12 ... 70 C1
Rawtenstall Rd BB4 ... 84 C1
Rawtenstall St Mary's
CE Prim Sch BB4 ... 84 F3
Rawtenstall Sta BB4 ... 84 F1
Rawthey Rd 5 LA1 ... 213 D2
Ray La PR3 ... 178 F4
Raybourne Ave FY6 ... 151 C3
Raygarth LA6 ... 238 B3
Raygarth La LA6 ... 238 A3
Raygill Ave BB11 ... 126 D3
Raygill Pl 3 LA1 ... 213 D2
Raymond Ave FY2 ... 129 D8
Raynor St BB2 ... 100 D5
Rays Dr LA1 ... 210 F3
Read CE Sch BB12 ... 144 D2
Read St 2 BB5 ... 124 A1
Read's Ave FY1 ... 129 C4
Reading Cl 14 BB1 ... 101 A4
Reads Ct 6 FY1 ... 129 C4
Reaney Ave 3 FY4 ... 109 E7
Rear West Lodge FY6 ... 174 C1
Record St BB18 ... 200 B1
Rectory Cl Chorley PR7 ... 42 C8
Croston PR5 ... 57 C2
Darwen BB3 ... 64 C8
Newchurch BB4 ... 85 E1
Rectory Gdns
Cockerham LA2 ... 203 C5
Tarleton PR4 ... 56 A5
Rectory La Bury BL9 ... 32 D4
Standish WN1,WN6 ... 29 A1
Rectory Paddock LA2 ... 214 E6
Rectory Rd Blackpool FY4 ... 129 E1
Burnley BB12 ... 126 F7
Southport PR9 ... 53 A1
Red Bank Rd FY2 ... 150 C4
Red Barnes L37 ... 11 F5
Red Bridge La LA5 ... 218 F4
Red Cat La L40 ... 24 E7
Red Cross St 5 PR1 ... 95 E7
Red Delph La WA11 ... 8 E1
Red Fold L39 ... 15 C2
Red Hills Rd LA5 ... 237 A1
Red House La PR7 ... 40 B6
Red La Colne BB8 ... 169 B7
Eccleston PR7 ... 40 E6
Red Lees Ave BB10 ... 127 F4
Red Lees Rd BB10 ... 128 A2
Red Lion Cl L31 ... 5 C1
Red Lion Shopping Ctr L31 ... 5 C1
Red Lion St Burnley BB11 ... 127 A5
Earby BB18 ... 201 C2
Red Marsh Dr FY5 ... 173 C3
Red Marsh Sp Sch FY5 ... 173 B3
Red Rake BB1 ... 100 C7
Red Sands L39 ... 15 D3
Red Scar Ind Est PR2 ... 118 B5
Red Scar St BB8 ... 169 C4
Red Shell La BB1,BB5 ... 82 B7
Red Spar Rd BB10 ... 147 D3
Redcar Ave Cleveleys FY5 ... 172 F5
Fulwood PR2 ... 116 A4
Redcar Cl PR8 ... 34 F3
Redcar Rd Blackpool FY1 ... 129 B8
Lancaster LA1 ... 211 B3
Redcliffe Gdns L39 ... 15 E3
Redcross St OL12 ... 51 F1
Redcross St N OL12 ... 51 F1
Rede Ave FY7 ... 193 C2
Redearth Rd BB3 ... 64 A8
Redearth St BB3 ... 64 A8
Redeswood Ave FY5 ... 150 E8
Redfearn Wood OL12 ... 51 B2
Redgate Formby L37 ... 12 A2
Ormskirk L39 ... 15 D5
Redgate Cl BB11 ... 127 B3

Redgate Dr L37 12 B2
Redgate Prim Sch L37 12 A2
Redhill PR4 94 C1
Redhill Gn PR6 60 E3
Redhills Dr PR8 34 F3
Redisher Cl BL0 48 F3
Redisher Croft BL0 48 F3
Redisher La BL8 48 E3
Redlam BB2 100 B3
Redlam Brow BB2 100 C3
Redman Rd BB10 147 B4
Redmayne Dr LA5 217 F2
Redmayne St 3 PR1 96 D8
Redness Cl BB9 147 E6
Redruth St BB12 126 D6
Redsands Dr PR2 117 D5
Redstart Pl 12 FY5 172 F1
Redvers Rd BB3 80 E5
Redvers St Burnley BB10 147 B1
Lancaster LA1 210 D8
Redvers Terr FY1 129 B8
Redwing Ave 1 FY5 172 F4
Redwing Rd BL8 48 F2
Redwood Ave Leyland PR5 58 E8
Maghull L31 5 C3
Redwood Chase PR4 112 E4
Redwood Cl Blackpool FY4 109 C4
Rochdale OL12 51 B3
Redwood Dr
Longridge PR3 139 A8
Morecambe LA4 213 A5
Ormskirk L39 15 D4
Rawtenstall BB4 67 F8
Redwood Gdns FY5 173 E2
Redwood Hts LA1 211 C7
Reed Row BB8 169 D3
Reed St Bacup OL13 87 A3
Burnley BB11 127 A4
Reedfield Brierfield BB10 147 C4
Clayton Brook PR5 77 C4
Reedfield Pl PR5 77 A6
Reedley Dr Brierfield BB10 147 B4
Brierfield BB10 147 C4
Reedley Gr BB10 147 B3
Reedley Rd BB10,BB9 147 C5
Reedmace Wlk LA3 212 E2
Reeds Brow WA11 9 C1
Reeds Cl BB4 85 A6
Reeds La BB4 85 A6
Reeds The
6 Lancaster LA1 213 E1
Ormskirk L39 15 D6
Reedsholme Cl BB4 85 A6
Reedy Acre Pl FY8 89 F4
Reedy Moor Terr BB8 191 C1
Reedyford Rd BB9 168 E2
Reedymoor La BB8 191 C1
Reeford Gr BB7 164 D7
Rees Pk L40 24 F3
Reeth Way 3 BB5 102 F4
Reeval Cl BB18 201 C2
Reeveswood PR7 40 B6
Reform St OL12 51 F1
Regal Ave FY4 109 E6
Regal Terr 4 LA1 213 F3
Regency Ave PR5 76 D8
Regency Cl PR4 112 E5
Regency Gdns PR8 33 E4
Regent Ave Colne BB8 169 E6
Lytham St Anne's FY8 89 D6
Regent Cl Padiham BB12 125 C7
Southport PR8 33 F4
Regent Ct
4 Blackpool FY1 129 B6
Fulwood PR2 116 E5
Lytham St Anne's FY8 88 D8
2 Southport PR9 34 C8
Regent Dr PR2 116 D4
Regent Gr PR2 116 E5
Regent Park Ave LA3,LA4 212 C3
Regent Park Gr LA4 212 D4
Regent Pk PR2 116 E5
Regent Pl BB9 168 E2
Regent Rd
Bamber Bridge PR5 96 D4
Blackpool FY1 129 C5
Chorley PR7 42 C7
Church BB5 102 F7
6 Leyland PR5 76 A1
Morecambe LA4 212 C3
Southport PR8 33 F4
Regent Rd E FY1 129 C5
Regent St Bacup OL13 87 A2
Blackburn BB1 100 E5
Brierfield BB9 147 B5
Coppull PR7 41 E1
Haslingden BB4 84 B3
Lancaster LA1 210 E7
Longridge PR3 139 A7
Nelson BB9 168 F2
Preston PR1 95 F6
Ramsbottom BL0 49 A4
Rochdale OL12 51 F1
Waddington BB7 186 B4
Regents Cl BB2 99 C2
Regents Terr FY6 151 E3
Regents View BB1 121 E1
Regents Way PR7 59 D2
Regentsway 6 PR5 76 E8
Reginald St BB8 169 C5
Reigate PR6 60 F3
Reiver Rd PR5 75 C3
Renacres Hall L39 22 B5
Renacres La L39 22 B5
Rendel St BB12 126 C7
Rendsburg Way 15 LA1 210 F8
Renfrey Cl L39 15 E8
Rennie Cl PR3 178 D6
Rennie Ct LA1 210 E5
Rennie St BB10 127 C5
Renshaw Dr
Bamber Bridge PR5 96 E2
Bury BL9 32 C3
Renshaw St 9 BB10 147 B1
Renwick Ave FY4 109 D8
Repton Ave Blackpool FY1 129 C8
Morecambe LA4 213 B4
Reservoir St Burnley BB11 126 F4
Darwen BB3 80 F1
Reta Dr FY5 173 A3
Retford Rd L33 1 A2
Revidge Rd BB1,BB2 100 C7
Revoe Sch (Jun & Inf)
FY1 129 C3
Rewe Cl BB2 80 C8
Rexington Bldgs BB11 126 C4
Reynolds St Burnley BB11 126 E3
2 Lancaster LA1 213 E1
Rhoda St BB9 168 F1
Rhoden Rd Leyland PR5 75 C1
Oswaldtwistle BB5 102 D2
Rhodes Ave
Blackburn BB1 100 D8
Haslingden BB4 67 A7
Rhodesway PR5 97 E2
Rhuddlan Cl BB4 84 B1
Rhyddings Cty High Sch
BB5 102 E4
Rhyddings St BB5 102 E4
Rhyl Ave BB1 100 E7
Rhyl St FY7 194 B5
Ribble Ave Brierfield BB10 147 C2
Darwen BB3 80 E4
Freckleton PR4 92 A6
Great Harwood BB6 123 E6
Grindleton BB7 187 B7
Maghull L31 5 E2
Southport PR9 53 C4
Whalley BB7 143 A7
Ribble Bank PR1 95 B6
Ribble Bank St PR1 95 E7
Ribble Brook Ho PR1 116 F1
Ribble Bsns Pk BB1 101 B8
Ribble Cl Freckleton PR4 92 A6
Penwortham PR1 95 E4
3 Preston PR1 95 E6
Withnell PR6 79 A1
Ribble Cres Kirkham PR4 113 B5
5 Preston PR1 96 C6
Ribble Ct 2 PR1 95 D6
Ribble Discovery Ctr FY8 89 C3
Ribble Dr Baldingstone BL9 49 F1
Hesketh Bank PR4 72 E4
West Bradford BB7 186 D7
Ribble Hall PR1 116 F1
Ribble Ho Blackburn BB1 100 F5
11 Preston PR1 96 D8
Ribble La BB7 187 D6
Ribble Lodge 10 FY8 90 A3
Ribble Rd Blackpool FY1 129 C4
Fleetwood FY7 193 F4
Leyland PR5 58 D8
Shevington Moor WN6 28 B2
Ribble St Bacup OL13 70 A8
Blackburn BB1 100 E6
Lytham St Anne's FY8 88 D6
Padiham BB12 125 D8
Preston PR1 95 E7
Ribble View BB7 186 F4
Ribble View Cl PR4 91 F6
Ribble Way BB7 164 C8
Ribblesdale Ave
Accrington BB5 103 B8
Clitheroe BB7 186 E2
Wilpshire BB1 122 A7
Ribblesdale Cl
Blackpool FY4 110 A8
Kirkham PR4 113 A5
Ribblesdale Ct 5 LA4 212 E5
Ribblesdale Cty High Sch
BB7 164 E7
Ribblesdale Dr
Forton PR3 204 B3
Grimsargh PR2 138 C1
Ribblesdale Pl
Barrowford BB9 168 E6
Blackburn BB2 100 C5
Chorley PR7 42 B7
Preston PR1 95 F6
Ribblesdale Rd PR3 140 E3
Ribblesdale St BB10 127 B8
Ribblesdale View BB7 187 E5
Ribbleton Ave PR2 117 E2
Ribbleton Avenue
Cty Inf Sch PR1 117 D2
Ribbleton Avenue
Meth Jun Sch PR1 117 D2
Ribbleton Dr BB5 103 C8
Ribbleton Hall
Cres 2 PR2 117 F3
Ribbleton Hall Dr PR2 117 F3
Ribbleton Hall High Sch
PR2 117 F3
Ribbleton Hospl PR2 117 F2
Ribbleton La PR1 117 C1
Ribbleton Pl 6 PR1 96 B8
Ribbleton St 9 PR1 96 B8
Ribby Ave Kirkham PR4 112 F5
Wrea Green PR4 112 C4
Ribby Pl Blackpool FY4 130 B1
Preston PR2 115 F1
Ribby Rd Kirkham PR4 112 F4
Wrea Green PR4 112 C4
Ribby-with-Wrea
Endowed CE Prim Sch
PR4 112 B4
Ribchester Ave
Blackpool FY4 130 B1
Burnley BB10 127 D5
Ribchester CE Prim Sch
PR3 140 E3
Ribchester Hospl PR3 139 F6
Ribchester Rd
Copster Green BB1 141 A1
Longridge PR3 139 E6
Lytham St Anne's FY8 90 D4
Ribchester BB6,PR3 141 C4
Wilpshire BB1 121 E6
Ribchester Way BB9 147 C4
Rice Gr FY1 129 D8
Richard Burch St 2 BL9 32 A3
Richard Durning's
Endowed Prim Sch L40 26 D7
Richard St Blackburn BB2 100 D4
Brierfield BB9 147 B5
Burnley BB11 127 B5
Shuttleworth BL0 49 E7
Weir OL13 87 A7
Richard Thornton's
CE Prim Sch LA6 236 B3
Richard's St 7 PR4 112 F6
Richard's Way FY8 109 E2
Richards Rd WN6 28 B3
Richards Way 3 FY5 172 F1
Richards Wlk 7 LA1 213 D1
Richardson Cl PR4 92 C6
Richardson St FY1 129 B4
Richmond Ave
Accrington BB5 103 B5
Barnoldswick BB18 200 A3
Burnley BB10 127 F4
Burscough L40 24 E3
Cleveleys FY5 172 E2
Haslingden BB4 84 C2
Lancaster LA1 213 F4
Morecambe LA4 212 G4
Wrea Green PR4 112 B3
Richmond Cl Brinscall PR6 61 E8
Hightown L38 2 F2
Richmond Cres BB1 101 E5
Richmond Ct
7 Blackpool FY1 129 B7
Burscough L40 24 E3
Chorley PR7 42 C6
Leyland PR5 75 B1
Richmond Gr L31 5 E3
Richmond Hill 28 BB1 100 E5
Richmond Hill La PR3 204 D2
Richmond Hill St BB5 103 B5
Richmond Ho
Lancaster LA1 213 F3
12 Preston PR1 96 A7
Richmond Ind Est BB5 103 A5
Richmond Mews L40 24 E3
Richmond Pk BB3 81 A2
Richmond Rd
Accrington BB5 103 A4
Barnoldswick BB18 200 A3
Barrowford BB9 168 C1
Blackpool FY1 129 B7
Chorley PR6 42 E6
Eccleston PR7 40 C7
Lytham St Anne's FY8 88 E6
Southport PR8 33 F2
Richmond St
Accrington BB5 103 A5
Accrington BB5 103 B5
Burnley BB11 126 E5
Horwich BL6 31 B3
2 Preston PR1 96 B7
Richmond Terr
17 Blackburn BB1 100 E5
Clitheroe BB7 164 D7
Darwen BB3 81 A2
Rickard Rd BB9 147 E6
Ridding La BB7 143 B5
Riddings Ave BB10 127 F6
Riddings La BB7 143 C6
Ridehalgh La BB10 148 F2
Ridehalgh St BB8 169 B3
Ridge Ave BB10 127 D6
Ridge Cl PR9 53 C5
Ridge Ct Burnley BB10 127 C7
Longridge PR3 139 C8
Ridge Gr LA3 208 F8
Ridge La
Lancaster, Bulk LA1 214 A1
Lancaster, Ridge LA1 214 C2
Roughlee BB12 167 F4
Ridge Prim Sch The LA1 214 B1
Ridge Rd Burnley BB11 127 B6
Chorley PR6 42 E7
Ridge Row BB10 127 D6
Ridge Sq LA1 214 B1
Ridge St
Barnoldswick BB18 200 B2
Lancaster LA1 214 A1
Ridge Way PR1 95 E4
Ridgeford Gdns PR2 116 D5
Ridgemont PR2 116 C6
Ridgeway Barrowford BB9 168 C3
Barrowford BB9 168 D3
Great Harwood BB6 123 B6
Ridgeway Ave BB2 81 A8
Ridgeway Dr Maghull L31 5 E3
Thornton FY5 151 D8
Ridgeway The
Fleetwood FY7 193 D3
Nelson BB9 147 D7
Ridgeways BB4 84 C2
Ridgmont Cl BL6 31 F3
Ridgmont Dr BL6 31 F3
Ridgway BL6 30 C2
Ridgway Ct FY8 89 A7
Ridgwood Ave FY3 129 E5
Riding Barn St BB5 102 F7
Riding Cl BB18 200 C2
Riding Head La BL0 49 F8
Riding La L39 13 E4
Riding St Burnley BB11 126 E5
Preston PR1 116 F1
Southport PR8 34 B6
Ridings The Burnley BB12 126 D8
Lucas Green PR6 60 C6
Southport PR9 53 A3
Ridley La Barber's Moor PR5 57 D3
Maghull L31 5 D1
Mawdesley L40 39 F2
Ridley Rd PR2 116 C2
Ridley St 2 FY3 129 D5
Rifle St BB4 84 B2
Rigby Ave BL6 30 C4
Rigby Cl PR4 92 C6
Rigby Rd Blackpool FY1 129 B3
Maghull L31 5 B3
Rigby St Colne BB8 169 C5
Nelson BB9 147 D8
Preston PR1 96 C8
Rigg La Chipping PR3 181 B1
Quernmore LA2 226 B7
Rigg St BB9 147 E8
Riley Ave FY8 88 F5
Riley Cl PR5 59 A8
Riley Ct FY8 88 F4
Riley Green Switch Rd
BB2,PR5 78 F7
Riley St Accrington BB5 103 B4
Bacup OL13 86 F5
Brierfield BB9 147 B5
Burnley BB11 127 B4
Earby BB18 201 B2
Rimington Ave
Accrington BB5 103 A3
Burnley BB10 127 D5
Colne BB8 169 C6
Rimington Cl BB2 100 F2
Rimington La BB7 188 D7
Rimington Pl
Lytham St Anne's FY8 89 B6
Nelson BB9 169 B1
Rimmer Gn PR8 35 D1
Rimmer's Ave Formby L37 11 E6
Southport PR8 34 B6
Ring Dyke Way FY8 90 A4
Ring Lows La OL12 51 F4
Ring O'Bells La L40 25 B2
Ring Way PR1 95 F7
Rings St BB4 105 A2
Ringstone Cres BB9 148 B8
Ringstones La LA2 233 D4
Ringtail Ct L40 24 B4
Ringtail Pl L40 24 B4
Ringtail Rd L40 24 B4
Rington Ave FY6 151 B6
Ringway Chorley PR7 42 A7
Cleveleys FY5 172 E4
Ringwood Ave BL0 49 A4
Ringwood Cl Enfield BB5 124 B1
Lytham St Anne's FY8 89 F3
Ringwood Rd PR1 117 C2
Ripley Cl L31 5 E1
Ripley Ct LA1 210 F6
Ripley Dr FY8 89 B6
Ripley St Thomas'
CE Sec Sch LA1 210 F6
Ripon Ave 1 LA1 213 F4
Ripon Cl Cleveleys FY5 172 E5
Great Eccleston PR3 154 C5
Southport PR8 34 F3
Ripon Hall Ave BL0 49 B4
Ripon Pl LA3 208 E6
Ripon Rd Blackpool FY1 129 D4
Lytham St Anne's FY8 89 D5
Oswaldtwistle BB5 102 C5
Ripon St Blackburn BB1 101 B4
Nelson BB9 147 D7
Preston PR1 116 E2
Ripon Terr PR1 117 F1
Rise The LA5 216 B6
Risedale Dr PR3 139 B7
Risedale Gr BB2 80 A7
Rishton Meth Sch BB1 123 B1
Rishton Rd
Clayton-le-M BB5 123 E3
Wilpshire BB1 122 C5
Rishton St FY1 129 C4
Rishton Sta BB1 102 A8
Rising Bridge Rd BB4,BB5 84 A7
Ritherham Ave FY5 172 D3
River Bank Terr BB5 124 E6
River Cl L37 12 B1
River Dr BB12 125 D8
River Hts PR5 76 C8
River Lea Gdns BB7 164 F8
River Par PR1 95 D6
River Rd FY5 173 E3
River St Bacup OL13 86 F1
Blackburn BB1 100 F4
Colne BB8 169 D4
Darwen BB3 80 F2
Lancaster LA1 213 E1
Preston PR1 95 E7
Ramsbottom BL0 49 C6
Trawden BB8 170 C3
River View Glasson LA2 205 E5
Tarleton PR4 56 A8
River Way BB9 168 D4
Rivermead Ct PR3 199 C1
Rivermead Dr PR3 178 C8
Rivermeade PR8 34 D4
Rivers St WN5 10 E6
Rivers View Fold LA2 220 A8
Riversedge Rd PR5 58 C8
Riversgate FY7 193 F4
Riverside
Bamber Bridge PR5 76 E7
Clitheroe BB7 164 B8
Hightown L38 2 F4
Penwortham PR1 95 E5
Preston PR1 95 E5
Riverside Ave PR5 75 E4
Riverside Cl Halton LA2 214 E6
Leyland PR5 75 E4
Riverside Cres PR5 57 A2
Riverside Ct Garstang PR3 178 C7
Whitworth OL12 70 D4
Riverside Dr
Hambleton FY6 174 B1
Ramsbottom BL0 49 B2
Riverside Fold BB12 167 E5
Riverside Ind Pk PR3 178 C2
Riverside Lofts 1 LA1 213 E1
Riverside Mill BB8 169 B4
Riverside Park Ind Est
LA1 214 B4
Riverside Rd PR1 95 E5
Riverside Terr 4 BB18 201 B1
Riverside Wlk BB4 67 A7
Riversleigh Ave
Blackpool FY1 150 C1
Lytham St Anne's FY8 89 E3
Riversleigh Ct FY8 89 E3
Riversway Blackpool FY3 129 F6
4 Lancaster LA1 213 F2
Poulton-le-FY6 151 F5
Preston PR2,PR4 94 D8
Riversway Bsns Village
PR2 95 A8
Riversway Enterprise
Workshops PR2 94 E8
Riversway Managed
Workshops PR2 94 F8
Riversway Motor Pk PR2 94 D7
Riverview Ct LA4 212 E3
Riverway Cl PR5 76 D8
Rivington & Blackrod
Coll Horwich Campus
BL6 31 D2
Rivington & Blackrod
High Sch BL6 31 B6
Rivington & Blackrod
High Sch (Annexe) BL6 31 B4
Rivington Ave
Adlington PR6 30 B7
Blackpool FY2 150 D5
Rivington Cl
Poulton-le-F FY6 151 D3
Southport PR8 34 A3
Tarleton PR4 55 F8
Rivington Ctry Pk BL6 31 A8
Rivington Dr Burscough L40 24 E3
Orrell WN8 10 C7
Rivington Hall Cl BL0 49 C4
Rivington La Adlington PR6 30 D6
Horwich BL6 31 A7
Rivington BL6 43 F1
Rivington Pl PR7 28 D6
Rivington Rd
Belmont BL6,BL7 45 B4
Chorley PR6 60 E1
Rivington St
Blackburn BB1 101 B4
Blackrod BL6 30 D2
Rochdale OL12 51 F1
Rivsersway Dr BB3 80 F6
Roach Bridge Cotts PR5 97 E6
Roach Rd PR5 98 B4
Roach St BL9 32 C2
Road La OL12 51 D4
Robbin's Bridge L31 5 E5
Robert St Accrington BB5 103 C7
Barnoldswick BB18 200 B2
Blackburn BB2 100 E3
Colne BB8 169 E5
13 Darwen BB3 80 F2
Great Harwood BB6 123 D5
10 Lancaster LA1 210 F8
Newchurch BB4 85 F2
Oswaldtwistle BB5 102 D3
Ramsbottom BL0 67 C1
Roberts Ct LA5 217 D6
Roberts St 2 Chorley PR7 42 C7
Nelson BB9 147 F8
7 Rawtenstall BB4 85 A3
Robertson Ct FY7 193 F1
Robin Bank Rd BB3 81 A2
Robin Cl PR7 41 D3
Robin Croft LA2 235 A1
Robin Hey PR5 75 B1
Robin Hill Dr WN6 28 B2
Robin Hill La WN6 28 C3
Robin Hood La WN6 27 B3
Robin House La BB10 148 C4
Robin La
High Bentham LA2 233 D8
Hill Dale WN8 26 C5
Rimington BB7 225 B1
Robin Rd BL0 49 B2
Robin St PR1,PR2 117 D1
Robins Cl FY6 151 A4
Robins La Blackpool FY6 151 A4
Carleton FY6 151 A6
Robinson La
BB10,BB12,BB9 147 A4
Robinson St
Blackburn BB1 101 B7
Burnley BB10 127 A8

Robinson St *continued*
Chatburn BB7 187 E5
Colne BB8 169 C5
Foulridge BB8 191 D1
Fulwood PR2 116 D3
15 Horwich BL6 31 B4
Robraine LA6 238 C1
Robson St BB9 147 B6
Robson Way FY3 151 A2
Roby Mill WN8 19 B3
Roby Mill CE Prim Sch WN8 19 B3
Rochdale Infmy OL12 51 F1
Rochdale Old Rd BL9 32 D4
Rochdale Rd Bacup OL13 87 A1
Bury BL9 32 B2
Edenfield BL0 67 F2
Ramsbottom BL0,BL9 50 B7
Rochester Ave
Cleveleys FY5 172 F4
Morecambe LA4 212 G3
Rochester Cl OL13 87 A7
Rochester Dr BB10 147 C3
Rochford Ave FY5 172 E1
Rock Bridge Fold BB4 85 E5
Rock Brow PR3 161 B7
Rock Fold BL7 46 F1
Rock Hall Rd BB4 84 B3
Rock La Burnley BB11 127 B3
Darwen BB3 80 A3
Trawden BB8 170 C3
Rock m' Jock LA2 231 B3
Rock St Accrington BB5 103 E2
Clitheroe BB7 164 E8
18 Haslingden BB4 84 B3
Horwich BL6 31 B3
Shuttleworth BL0 49 E7
Thornton FY5 173 B4
Rock Terr Arnside LA5 237 B2
Egerton BL7 46 F1
Pendleton BB7 165 B4
9 Rawtenstall BB4 85 A7
Rock Villa Rd PR6 60 C8
Rock Water (Bird Conservation Ctre) BB10 128 C2
Rockburgh Cres PR4 74 A5
Rockcliffe Ave OL13 86 E1
Rockcliffe Dr OL13 86 E1
Rockcliffe Rd OL13 86 F1
Rockcliffe St BB2 100 E2
Rockcliffe Villas OL13 69 E8
Rockfield Gdns 2 L31 5 C2
Rockfield Rd BB5 103 D6
Rockfield St BB2 100 E3
Rockhaven Ave BL6 31 C4
Rockingham Rd FY2 150 D3
Rockliffe La OL13 87 A1
Rockliffe Rd OL13 86 F1
Rockliffe St 5 BB4 85 A3
Rockville BB9 168 E5
Rockville Ave FY5 150 F8
Rockwood Cl BB10 147 E3
Roddlesworth La PR6 62 E8
Roddlesworth Nature Trail BB3 63 B8
Roddlesworth Vistor Ctr BB3 63 B8
Rodhill La BB7 224 B3
Rodney Ave FY8 109 E1
Rodney St Blackburn BB2 100 C3
4 Preston PR1 95 F8
Rodwell Wlk FY3 129 F8
Roe Greave Rd BB5 102 D3
Roe Hey Dr PR7 41 F2
Roe La PR9 34 E8
Roe Lee Park Prim Sch BB1 121 F2
Roe Lee Pk BB1 121 F2
Roe St OL12 51 C1
Roe-Park Mews PR9 34 E8
Roebuck Cl BB2 100 D3
Roebuck Cty Prim Sch PR2 116 D2
Roebuck St PR2 116 C2
Roeburn Dr LA3 213 B2
Roeburn Pl 5 LA1 213 E2
Roeburn Terr LA2 232 D6
Roeburndale Cres LA3 209 A8
Roedean Ave LA4 213 B4
Roedean Cl Maghull L31 5 D2
12 Thornton FY5 173 A2
Roefield L Ctr BB7 164 B8
Rogerley Cl FY8 90 A4
Rogersfield BB6 122 B8
Rolleston Rd BB2 100 B4
Roman Cres LA2 231 C3
Roman Mus PR3 140 E3
Roman Rd
Blackburn BB1,BB2 81 B8
Preston PR1 96 B7
Whittlestone Head BB3 65 A4
Roman Road Prim Sch BB2 80 F8
Roman Way Cleveleys FY5 172 F1
Clitheroe BB7 165 A8
Kirkham PR4 113 C4
Red Scar PR2 118 C6
Roman Way Ind Est PR2 118 C6
Rome Ave BB11 126 C4
Romford Rd PR1 117 C2
Romford St 2 BB12 126 C7
Romiley Dr WN8 17 F2
Romney Ave
Barrowford BB9 168 D3
Blackpool FY4 129 D1
Burnley BB11 126 E3
Fleetwood FY7 193 E3
Romney St BB9 147 D7
Romney Wlk BB1 101 C4
Romsey Ave L37 12 B2
Ronald St Blackburn BB1 101 C5
Burnley BB12 126 A5
Ronaldsway Fulwood PR1 117 D3
Nelson BB9 169 B2
Ronaldsway Cl OL13 87 B1
Ronbury Cl 1 BB9 168 C1
Roney St BB2 100 C5
Ronwood Cl PR4 153 F1
Ronwood Ct PR2 95 B8
Roocroft Sq BL6 30 C2
Roods The LA5 217 E6
Rook St Barnoldswick BB18 200 B2
Colne BB8 169 D5
Nelson BB9 168 E1
Preston PR1 117 B1
3 Ramsbottom BL0 49 C2
Rookery Ave WN6 19 E8
Rookery Cl Chorley PR7 42 A6
Penwortham PR1 95 F2
Rookery Dr PR1 95 F2
Rookery Rd
Barnoldswick BB18 200 C3
Southport PR9 52 F1
Rookwood PR7 40 B6
Rookwood Ave Chorley PR7 60 C2
Cleveleys FY5 172 D1
Rooley Moor Rd
Bacup OL12,OL13 69 C4
Rochdale OL12 51 A3
Rochdale, Spotland Fold OL12 51 C1
Rooley St OL11,OL12 51 C1
Rooley View OL13 86 E1
Roosevelt Ave LA1 210 D7
Roots La PR4 134 E2
Rope Wlk PR3 178 C7
Ropefield Way OL12 51 E3
Rosary Ave FY4 129 E1
Roscoe Lowe Brow PR6 30 D7
Rose Acre La LA5 219 F2
Rose Ave Blackpool FY1 129 D2
Burnley BB11 126 E4
Fulwood PR2 116 C3
Rose Bank Lancaster LA1 211 A5
Rawtenstall BB4 85 A3
Rose Bank St OL13 86 F3
Rose Cl PR5 76 E2
Rose Cotts
Low Bentham LA2 233 B8
Preesall FY6 195 C3
Rose Cres
Skelmersdale WN8 17 E1
Southport PR8 20 C2
Rose Ct 1 FY7 193 F4
Rose Fold PR1 95 D4
Rose Fold Cotts PR1 95 D4
Rose Gdns PR4 72 E4
Rose Gr LA2 206 F4
Rose Grove Sta BB11 126 B5
Rose Hill Euxton PR7 59 C4
Ramsbottom BL0 49 B6
Southport PR8, PR9 34 D6
Rose Hill Ave BB1 101 A4
Rose Hill Gr LA7 237 F6
Rose Hill Rd BB2 99 C1
Rose Hill St Bacup OL13 86 F2
Darwen BB3 64 B8
Rawtenstall BB4 105 A1
Rose Hill Terr 7 BB3 64 B8
Rose La PR1 117 C3
Rose Lea PR2 117 D6
Rose Mt BB4 85 F1
Rose Pl L39 15 D2
Rose St Accrington BB5 103 B4
Bacup OL13 86 F2
7 Blackburn BB2 100 E3
Darwen BB3 81 B1
Leyland PR5 76 B3
Morecambe LA4 212 E6
Newchurch BB4 85 E2
15 Preston PR1 96 A7
Rose Terr PR2 116 B2
Rose Vale St BB4 85 B2
Roseacre FY4 109 C5
Roseacre Dr PR4 154 A1
Roseacre Pl
Lytham St Anne's FY8 89 B8
5 Preston PR2 115 E1
Roseacre Rd PR4 133 D6
Rosebank Edenfield BL0 67 D1
Enfield BB5 124 A3
2 Preston PR2 115 C1
Rosebank Ave 3 FY4 109 C5
Rosebay Ave BB2 79 D8
Rosebay Cl L37 12 A3
Roseberry Ave PR4 115 E5
Roseberry Cl BL0 49 C3
Roseberry St OL14 108 B1
Rosebery Ave
Blackpool FY4 109 B6
Lancaster LA1 211 A5
Lytham St Anne's FY8 89 B4
Morecambe LA4 212 F4
Rosebery St Burnley BB10 147 B2
Southport PR9 35 A6
Rosecroft Cl L39 15 E6
Rosedale Ave
Blackpool FY4 130 A2
Heysham LA3 209 A8
Rosedale St BB4 84 F5
Rosedene LA2 213 F7
Rosedene Cl PR4 115 E5
Rosegarth LA2 213 F7
Rosegrove La BB11 126 B5
Rosegrove Prim Sch BB12 126 A6
Rosehill Ave Burnley BB11 126 E4
12 Nelson BB9 168 F1
Rosehill Bsns Pk 1 PR9 34 D6
Rosehill Dr L39 15 C2
Rosehill Inf Sch BB11 126 F3
Rosehill Jun Sch BB11 126 E3
Rosehill Mans L39 15 C2
Rosehill Rd Burnley BB11 126 F3
Nelson BB8 169 A2
Roseland Ave BB9 147 C6
Roseland Cl L31 5 B4
Roselea Dr PR9 53 C4
Roselyn Ave FY4 109 C5
Rosemary Ave
Blackpool FY4 109 C5
Cleveleys FY5 172 F3
Rosemary Ct 1 PR1 95 C2
Rosemary La Formby L37 11 F3
Haskayne L39 14 B4
8 Lancaster LA1 210 F8
Swillbrook PR4 135 A1
Rosemeade Ave PR5 76 B8
Rosemede Ave FY4 129 F2
Rosemount OL13 87 A4
Rosemount Ave
Barnoldswick BB18 200 A3
Burnley BB11 126 E4
Knott End-on-S FY6 195 A5
Rosendale Cl OL13 87 B3
Rosendale Cres OL13 87 B3
Roseway Blackpool FY4 109 C5
Lytham St Anne's FY8 89 B6
Poulton-le-F FY6 151 C3
Preston PR2 116 A1
Rosewood PR4 115 E5
Rosewood Ave
Blackburn BB1 100 F8
Burnley BB11 126 E3
Haslingden BB4 84 C3
Higher Walton PR5 97 C3
Rosewood Cl
Lytham St Anne's FY8 89 E4
1 Thornton FY5 173 D1
Rosewood Dr PR5 97 B3
Roshaw PR2 138 C1
Rosklyn Rd PR6 42 E7
Rosley St BB8 170 B5
Ross St Brierfield BB9 147 B5
Darwen BB3 64 A6
Rossall Cl Coupe Green PR5 97 E3
Fleetwood FY7 172 D8
Padiham BB12 125 D6
Rossall Ct FY7 193 E3
Rossall Dr PR2 116 C4
Rossall Gate FY7 172 C8
Rossall Gdns FY5 172 D4
Rossall Grange La FY7 193 D3
Rossall Hospl FY7 172 C8
Rossall La FY7 172 E7
Rossall Rd Blackpool FY3 129 D7
Chorley PR6 60 E1
Cleveleys FY5 172 D3
Fulwood PR2 116 C4
Lancaster LA1 213 C2
Lytham St Anne's FY8 89 D4
Rossall Sch FY7 172 C6
Rossall St PR2 116 C1
Rossall Terr BB2 100 E1
Rossendale Ave
Burnley BB11 126 E2
Morecambe LA4 212 F6
Rossendale Ave N FY5 173 B2
Rossendale Ave S FY5 173 B1
Rossendale General Hospl BB4 84 D2
Rossendale Mus BB4 84 E2
Rossendale Rd
Burnley BB11 126 C3
Lytham St Anne's FY8 89 A7
Rossendale Sch BL0 50 A7
Rossendale Ski Ctr BB4 84 E3
Rosser Ct 14 BB9 147 E8
Rossett Ave FY4 130 C1
Rossetti Ave BB11 126 F3
Rossington Ave FY2 150 E5
Rosslyn Ave FY6 195 A6
Rosslyn Cres FY6 195 B5
Rosslyn Cres E FY6 195 B5
Rossmoyne Rd LA1 211 A4
Rostle Top Rd 6 BB18 201 B1
Rostrevor Cl 4 PR5 75 B1
Rostron Cres L37 11 E1
Rostron Rd BL0 49 B6
Rostron's Bldgs BB4 85 D1
Rothay Ave FY7 193 D2
Rothbury Pl FY8 90 C4
Rotherhead Cl BL6 30 F2
Rotherwick Ave PR7 42 B7
Rothesay Cres LA3 208 D5
Rothesay Rd
Blackburn BB1 101 D3
Brierfield BB9 147 C6
Heysham LA3 208 D5
Rothley Ave PR8 20 A4
Rothsay Rd LA3 208 E5
Rothwell Ave BB5 103 C4
Rothwell Cl L39 15 D5
Rothwell Cres PR2 117 F4
Rothwell Ct PR5 76 A2
Rothwell Dr
Fleetwood FY7 193 D3
Ormskirk L39 15 B2
Southport PR8 20 A4
Rothwell Lodge 5 PR2 117 F4
Rothwell Rd PR6 30 B7
Rothwell St BL0 49 B6
Rotten Row Caton LA2 231 D3
Southport PR8 33 F6
Rough Hey Pl PR2 118 B7
Rough Hey Rd PR2 118 B7
Rough Heys BB5 103 A2
Rough Heys La FY4 109 E7
Rough Hill La BL9 32 E4
Rough Lea Rd FY5 172 D2
Rough Lee Rd BB5 103 C4
Roughlee CE Prim Sch BB12 167 F4
Roughlee Gr BB10 127 D5
Roughlee St BB9 168 D2
Roughlee Terr BB11 105 B4
Roughwood Dr L33 1 A4
Round Acre
Bamber Bridge PR5 96 A1
Nab's Head PR5 98 E7
Round Barn BL7 65 B3
Round Hill Pl BB10 127 E1
Round Mdws PR5 75 C1
Round Meade The L31 5 C2
Round Wood PR1 95 C7
Roundel St BB10 147 B2
Roundell Rd BB18 200 C3
Roundhay FY4 109 F8
Roundhill La BB4 84 A7
Roundhill Rd BB4,BB5 83 E6
Roundhill View BB5 84 A8
Roundway FY7 172 C8
Roundway Down PR2 116 C7
Roundway The L38 2 F3
Roundwood Ave BB10 147 A4
Row The Knowley PR7 61 D3
Silverdale LA5 218 E3
Rowan Ave Fulwood PR2 118 A4
2 Horwich BL6 31 E1
Oswaldtwistle BB5 102 D2
Rowan Bank LA2 214 E7
Rowan Cl Blackburn BB1 122 B1
Bonds PR3 178 D6
Burscough Bridge L40 24 F6
Penwortham PR1 95 B3
Rochdale OL12 51 B3
Rowan Croft PR6 77 B1
Rowan Gr Burnley BB10 127 C6
Chorley PR6 60 C3
Rowan La WN8 18 B4
Rowan Tree Cl BB5 103 D7
Rowangate PR2 117 C7
Rowans The Ormskirk L39 6 A7
Poulton-le-F FY6 151 A2
Rowberrow Cl PR2 117 D6
Rowen Pk BB2 100 B8
Rowhampton Cl 11 FY5 173 A2
Rowland Ave BB9 148 A8
Rowland Cl FY5 172 F2
Rowland La FY5 172 F2
Rowland St BB5 103 A5
Rowlands Rd BL9 49 D2
Rowley La BB10 127 D6
Rowntree Ave FY7 193 F3
Roworth Cl PR5 96 E3
Rowsley Rd FY8 88 D7
Rowstorne Sports Ctr PR4 92 B6
Rowton Heath PR2 116 C7
Roxburgh Rd FY4 110 A6
Roxton Cl BL6 31 B5
Roy St OL14 108 A1
Royal Ave Blackpool FY3 129 F3
Fulwood PR2 116 E6
Kirkham PR4 113 B4
Leyland PR5 58 E7
Royal Bank Rd FY3 129 E3
Royal Beach Ct FY8 88 D7
Royal Birkdale Golf Links PR8 33 D3
Royal Brook Ho 6 PR1 117 A1
Royal Cl L37 12 A1
Royal Cres L37 12 A1
Royal Cross Prim Sch PR2 115 E1
Royal Cross Sch for the Deaf PR1 118 A1
Royal Ct BB10 147 F3
Royal Fold LA3 208 E8
Royal Lancaster Infmy LA1 210 F7
Royal Lytham St Anne's Golf Course FY8 89 B5
Royal Oak Ave BB1 121 E1
Royal Oak Bldgs 16 FY4 129 B1
Royal Oak Cotts BB9 168 B4
Royal Oak Meadow LA2 232 B8
Royal Pl FY8 89 C8
Royal Preston Hospl The PR2 116 F6
Royal Rd LA4 212 F6
Royal Terr PR8 34 A7
Royal Troon Ct PR4 113 A4
Royalty Ave PR4 95 A1
Royalty Gdns PR4 75 A8
Royalty La PR4 75 A8
Royalty Mall LA4 212 D5
Royds Ave Accrington BB5 103 C3
Morecambe LA3 212 A2
Royds Gr LA3 212 A1
Royds Rd OL13 69 A7
Royds St Accrington BB5 103 C4
Bury BL9 32 D4
Lytham St Anne's FY8 88 E5
Royle Rd 4 Burnley BB12 126 F6
Burnley BB12 126 F7
Chorley PR7 42 C8
Royle St 1 FY1 129 B1
Roylen Ave FY6 151 B5
Royles Brook Cl 8 FY5 173 B3
Royles Brook Prim Sch FY5 173 A2
Royles Ct FY5 173 B2
Roynton Rd BL6 31 B7
Royshaw Ave BB1 100 E8
Royshaw Cl BB1 100 E8
Royston Cl BL8 48 F1
Royston Rd FY6 151 F5
Royton Dr PR6 60 C5
Ruby St Blackburn BB1 121 F2
Ramsbottom BL0,BL9 49 C3
Rudd St BB4 84 A3
Ruddington Rd PR8 34 E2
Rudman St OL12 51 E2
Rudyard Ave WN6 28 E2
Rudyard Dr BB3 64 D8
Rudyard Pl Blackpool FY3 129 F7
Lytham St Anne's FY8 88 E8
Ruff La L39, L40 16 B4
Rufford Ave L31 5 E3
Rufford CE Prim Sch L40 38 B4
Rufford Dr PR9 53 F5
Rufford New Hall L40 38 B5
Rufford Park La L40 38 A5
Rufford Rd
Bispham Green L40 38 F1
Lytham St Anne's FY8 89 D5
Southport PR9 53 C4
Rufford Sta L40 38 D4
Rufus St PR1 117 C2
Rugby Ave BB5 103 C7
Rugby Dr WN5 10 F8
Rugby St 9 FY4 129 D1
Rumley's Fold BB11 126 E2
Runcorn Ave FY2 150 F2
Rundle Rd PR2 116 D3
Runnel The L39 22 B1
Runnymede Ave FY5 172 D2
Runshaw Ave WN6 19 E8
Runshaw Coll PR5 59 B6
Runshaw La Euxton PR7 59 B3
Runshaw Moor PR7 58 E3
Rupert St Carnforth LA5 217 D3
Nelson BB9 147 C7
Rochdale OL12 51 C1
Rush Hey Bank BB11 106 D8
Rushbed Cotts BB4 85 A6
Rushbed Dr BB4 85 A6
Rushden Rd L32 1 A1
Rushes Farm Cl BB5 102 C4
Rushey Cl BB4 85 A6
Rushley Dr LA2 215 D1
Rushley Way LA2 215 D1
Rushton Ave BB18 201 B1
Rushton Cl BB9 169 B2
Rushton St 5 Bacup OL13 69 E8
Barrowford BB9 168 D3
Great Harwood BB6 123 B4
Rushworth Bldgs OL13 69 C8
Rushworth St E 7 BB10 147 B1
Rushy Field BB5 123 F5
Rushy Hey PR5 76 A7
Rushy Hill View OL12 51 C1
Ruskin Ave
9 Blackpool FY1 129 B2
Colne BB8 169 D6
Leyland PR5 76 A1
Oswaldtwistle BB5 102 C5
Padiham BB12 125 E7
Thornton FY5 173 A3
Ruskin Cl PR4 55 F6
Ruskin Dr
Kirkby Lonsdale LA6 238 C2
Morecambe LA4 213 A6
Ruskin Gr Bolton-le-S LA5 216 A5
Hapton BB11 125 C4
Ruskin Ho LA1 213 E4
Ruskin Rd Freckleton PR4 92 B6
2 Lancaster LA1 213 F3
Ruskin St Burnley BB10 147 A2
Preston PR1 96 B6
Rusland Ave FY4 130 D1
Rusland Dr PR5 97 E4
Ruslands Gdns LA4 212 F4
Russall Ct FY5 172 C5
Russel St OL13 86 F4
Russell Ave Cleveleys FY5 150 D8
Colne BB8 169 E6
Leyland PR5 59 C8
Preston PR1 97 A8
Southport PR9 35 A7
Russell Ct Burnley BB11 127 B4
Lytham St Anne's FY8 88 F6
Southport PR9 53 B4
Russell Dr LA4 213 C4
Russell Pl BB6 123 B5
Russell Rd Carnforth LA5 217 E1
Southport PR9 35 A6
Russell Sq PR6 60 D1
Russell Sq W 5 PR6 60 D1
Russell St Accrington BB5 103 C5
Bacup OL13 86 F4
Blackburn BB2 100 E3
37 Lancaster LA1 210 F8
6 Nelson BB9 147 D8
Russell Terr BB12 125 D7
Russia St BB5 102 F6
Ruth St Edenfield BL0 67 D2
Whitworth OL12 70 D1
Rutherford Pl FY8 109 B4
Ruthin Cl BB1 100 E7
Ruthin Ct PR2 115 F3
Rutland Ave
1 Bamber Bridge PR5 96 D3
Blackburn BB1 101 E4
Burnley BB12 126 A6
Cleveleys FY5 172 E3
Fleetwood FY7 193 F3

Rutland Ave *continued*
Freckleton PR4 .... 92 C7
Lancaster LA1 .... 211 A5
Poulton-le-F FY6 .... 151 C3
Rutland Cl
Clayton-le-M BB5 .... 123 F3
Garstang PR3 .... 178 B8
Rutland Cres L39 .... 15 E7
Rutland Ct FY8 .... 89 D5
Rutland Pl 8 BB12 .... 125 D7
Rutland Rd
Lytham St Anne's FY8 .... 89 D5
Southport PR8 .... 34 D5
Rutland St Accrington BB5 .. 102 F5
Blackburn BB2 .... 100 B3
Colne BB8 .... 169 F5
1 Nelson BB9 .... 168 F1
Preston PR1 .... 96 C8
Rutland Wlk BB4 .... 67 A8
Ryan Cl PR5 .... 75 E1
Ryburn Ave Blackburn BB2 .. 100 B6
Blackpool FY4 .... 129 E1
Ryburn Rd L39 .... 15 E4
Rycliffe St BB12 .... 145 C1
Rydal Ave
Bamber Bridge PR5 .... 96 D2
Blackpool FY1 .... 129 C3
Darwen BB3 .... 64 A8
Fleetwood FY7 .... 193 E4
Formby L37 .... 11 D3
Freckleton PR4 .... 92 A5
Freckleton PR4 .... 92 A6
Orrell WN5 .... 10 F7
Penwortham PR1 .... 95 C3
Poulton-le-F FY6 .... 151 D3
Thornton FY5 .... 173 B1
Rydal Cl 5 Accrington BB5 .124 D1
Blackrod BL6 .... 30 C3
Brierfield BB10 .... 147 C4
Fulwood PR2 .... 117 C4
Padiham BB12 .... 145 C1
Rydal Gr
Knott End-on-S FY6 .... 194 F6
Morecambe LA3 .... 212 A2
Rydal Mount BB1 .... 81 F6
Rydal Pl Chatburn BB7 .... 187 C3
Chorley PR7 .... 42 C6
Colne BB8 .... 170 A5
Rydal Rd Blackburn BB1 .... 101 A7
Hambleton FY6 .... 174 C2
Haslingden BB4 .... 67 C8
Hest Bank LA5 .... 215 F4
Lancaster LA1 .... 211 A8
Lytham St Anne's FY8 .... 88 E8
Morecambe LA3 .... 212 A2
Preston PR1 .... 117 D2
Rydal St BB10 .... 147 A2
Ryddingwood PR1 .... 95 B6
Ryde Cl BB4 .... 84 C1
Ryden Ave Cleveleys FY5 ... 172 D3
Leyland PR5 .... 76 C1
Ryden Rd BB1 .... 121 D6
Ryder Cl L39 .... 15 C2
Ryder Cres Ormskirk L39 .... 15 C1
Southport PR8 .... 20 E7
Ryding's La PR9 .... 54 D8
Rydinge The L37 .... 12 A6
Rydings The BB6 .... 142 A1
Rye Gdns BB2 .... 80 D6
Rye Gr 3 BB12 .... 125 D7
Rye Moss La L37 .... 4 B8
Rye St PR1 .... 117 A1
Ryecroft PR6 .... 61 A7
Ryecroft Ave FY6 .... 174 C1
Ryecroft La BL7 .... 45 C5
Ryecroft Pl FY6 .... 174 C2
Ryefield PR6 .... 61 A7
Ryefield Ave
Haslingden BB4 .... 84 B2
Penwortham PR1 .... 95 D2
Ryefield Ave W BB4 .... 84 B2
Ryefield Pl BB4 .... 84 B2
Ryeground La L37 .... 12 A5
Ryeheys Rd FY8 .... 88 E8
Ryelands Cres PR2 .... 94 E8
Ryelands Cty Prim Sch
LA1 .... 213 D2
Ryelands Rd LA1 .... 213 E2
Ryknild Way LA3 .... 213 B3
Ryland Ave FY6 .... 151 C3
Rylands Rd PR7 .... 42 B7
Rylands St BB10 .... 147 B1
Ryldon Pl FY4 .... 130 A2
Rylstone Dr
Barnoldswick BB18 .... 200 A2
Morecambe LA3 .... 212 A1
Rymers Gn L37 .... 11 E4
Rysdale Cres LA4 .... 212 F4
Ryson Ave FY4 .... 129 F1

S

Sabden Brook Ct BB7 .... 145 A8
Sabden Cty Prim Sch
BB7 .... 144 F8
Sabden Pl FY8 .... 89 C7
Sabden Rd Higham BB12 ... 145 F6
Sabden BB12 .... 145 B4
Whalley BB7 .... 144 A4
Sabden Wlk BB2 .... 100 F2
Saccary La BB1 .... 121 A4
Sackville Gdns BB9 .... 147 A5
Sackville St
Barnoldswick BB18 .... 200 B1
Sackville St *continued*
Blackpool FY4 .... 109 C6
Brierfield BB9 .... 147 B5
10 Burnley BB11 .... 126 F5
6 Bury BL9 .... 32 A3
Chorley PR6 .... 42 E7
Nelson BB9 .... 147 F7
Sacred Heart RC Prim Sch
Blackburn BB2 .... 100 B6
Chorley PR6 .... 42 E7
Church BB5 .... 102 F6
Colne BB8 .... 169 D7
Preston PR2 .... 116 C1
Thornton FY5 .... 173 B3
Saddler Nook La LA6 .... 235 C8
Saddlers Mews 5 BB7 .... 164 E8
Sadler St 4 BB5 .... 102 E5
Saer Cl FY7 .... 193 D3
Saffron Cl 4 BB9 .... 168 C1
Sagar Dr PR4 .... 92 A6
Sagar Fold L39 .... 6 D8
Sagar Holme Terr BB4 .... 85 E5
Sagar La OL14 .... 108 D3
Sagar St Eccleston PR7 .... 40 C6
Nelson BB9 .... 147 E8
Sage Ct PR1 .... 95 C2
Sage La PR1 .... 117 B3
Sahara Fold 1 BB1 .... 101 A7
Sailsbury Cl LA3 .... 212 E2
St Aidan's Ave
Blackburn BB2 .... 100 D2
Darwen BB3 .... 64 B8
St Aidan's CE Prim Sch
Bamber Bridge PR5 .... 96 F1
Blackburn BB2 .... 100 C2
St Aidan's CE Tech Coll
FY6 .... 195 B3
St Aidan's Cl BB2 .... 100 C1
St Aidan's Rd 8 PR5 .... 96 E2
St Aidans Pk 9 PR5 .... 96 E2
St Alban's Ct 2 BB1 .... 100 F6
St Alban's Pl PR7 .... 42 D5
St Alban's RC Prim Sch
BB1 .... 100 F6
St Alban's Rd
Blackpool FY1 .... 129 D4
Darwen BB3 .... 80 E4
Lytham St Anne's FY8 .... 88 F7
St Albans Rd
Morecambe LA4 .... 213 B6
Rishton BB1 .... 102 A8
St Ambrose Terr 5 PR5 .... 76 B2
St Andrew's Ave
Cleveleys FY5 .... 172 D2
Preston PR2 .... 116 B2
St Andrew's CE Prim Sch
Blackburn BB2 .... 80 B8
Leyland PR5 .... 58 F8
Oswaldtwistle BB5 .... 102 D4
Preston PR2 .... 116 B1
Ramsbottom BL0 .... 49 B5
Ramsbottom BL0 .... 49 B5
St Andrew's Cl Leyland PR5 .. 59 A7
Oswaldtwistle BB5 .... 102 D4
Ramsbottom BL0 .... 49 C4
St Andrew's Ct 1 BB5 .... 102 D3
St Andrew's Pl
Blackburn BB1 .... 100 D6
Southport PR8 .... 34 B6
St Andrew's Rd PR1 .... 117 A2
St Andrew's Rd N FY8 .... 88 E7
St Andrew's Rd S FY8 .... 88 F6
St Andrew's St
Blackburn BB1 .... 100 D6
5 Burnley BB10 .... 147 B1
St Andrews Cl Colne BB8 .. 169 C3
Euxton PR7 .... 59 D4
St Andrews Gr LA4 .... 212 G6
St Andrews Maghull
CE Prim Sch L31 .... 5 D1
St Andrews Rd BB6 .... 142 C6
St Andrews Way PR5 .... 59 A8
St Ann's Sq BB7 .... 164 C8
St Ann's St 5 BB2 .... 100 E3
St Anne Edgeside CE
Church & Day Sch BB4 .... 85 F3
St Anne's Ave LA4 .... 213 B5
St Anne's CE Prim Sch
PR4 .... 135 D2
St Anne's Cl Caton LA2 .... 231 C3
Formby L37 .... 11 F6
St Anne's Coll Jun Sch
FY8 .... 88 E5
St Anne's Cres BB4 .... 85 F3
St Anne's Ct WN6 .... 19 F5
St Anne's Dr BB12 .... 146 D7
St Anne's Old Links
Golf Course FY8 .... 109 D2
St Anne's Path L37 .... 11 F6
St Anne's Pl 18 LA1 .... 210 F8
St Anne's Pleasure
Island Family Fun Pk
FY8 .... 88 E5
St Anne's RC Inf Sch
BB5 .... 103 D5
St Anne's RC Prim Sch
Blackburn BB2 .... 100 D4
Leyland PR5 .... 58 D8
St Anne's RC Sch L39 .... 15 E4
St Anne's Rd Formby L37 .... 11 F6
Leyland PR5 .... 76 C3
Ormskirk L39 .... 15 D4
St Anne's Rd E FY8 .... 88 F7
St Anne's Rd W FY8 .... 88 E6
St Anne's St
Padiham BB12 .... 125 C7
Preston PR1 .... 117 A2
St Anne's Sta FY8 .... 88 E7
St Anne's Way BB12 .... 146 D7
St Annes Cl
5 Blackburn BB1 .... 100 F3
5 Church BB5 .... 102 E5
St Annes Ct FY4 .... 129 C1
St Annes Rd
Blackpool FY4 .... 109 D7
4 Chorley PR6 .... 42 E7
Great Eccleston PR3 .... 154 C5
Horwich BL6 .... 31 C4
Southport PR9 .... 52 F4
St Anselm's RC Prim Sch
OL12 .... 70 D2
St Anthony's Cl PR2 .... 116 C4
St Anthony's Cres PR2 .... 116 C4
St Anthony's Dr PR2 .... 116 C4
St Anthony's Pl 7 FY1 .... 129 C7
St Anthony's RC Prim Sch
PR2 .... 116 C4
St Anthony's Rd PR1 .... 117 A2
St Anthonys Pl PR4 .... 113 A4
St Antony's RC Sch BB1 .... 101 C3
St Augustine's RC High Sch
BB7 .... 143 A4
St Augustine's RC Prim Sch
Burnley BB12 .... 126 B6
Preston PR1 .... 96 A7
St Austell Dr BL8 .... 48 F2
St Austell Pl LA5 .... 216 C8
St Austin's Pl PR1 .... 96 A7
St Austin's Rd PR1 .... 96 A7
St Barnabas CE Prim Sch
BB3 .... 64 C6
St Barnabas St
Blackburn BB2 .... 100 C5
4 Darwen BB3 .... 64 B6
St Barnabas' & St Paul's
CE Prim Sch
BB2 .... 100 D5
St Barnabas' Pl PR1 .... 117 A1
St Bartholomew Parish
CE Sch BB6 .... 123 C6
St Bartholomew's
CE Prim Sch Blackburn BB2 80 D8
Whitworth OL12 .... 51 C8
St Bede's Ave FY1 .... 129 B1
St Bede's RC High Sch
Blackburn BB2 .... 80 A8
Lytham St Anne's FY8 .... 90 C4
Ormskirk L39 .... 15 D4
St Bedes Cl L39 .... 15 D3
St Bee's Cl BB2 .... 100 F1
St Bernadette's
RC Prim Sch FY2 .... 150 D5
St Bernadettes
RC Prim Sch LA1 .... 211 B4
St Bernard Ave FY3 .... 129 F7
St Bernard's RC Prim Sch
PR2 .... 115 C1
St Bernard's Rd FY6 .... 194 E6
St Brides Cl BL6 .... 31 A4
St Catherine Cl FY3 .... 151 B1
St Catherine's CE Prim Sch
BL6 .... 31 B3
St Catherine's Dr PR2 .... 116 C4
St Catherine's RC Prim Sch
PR5 .... 76 C2
St Catherines Cl 4 PR5 .... 76 C2
St Catherines Ct 25 LA1 .... 210 F8
St Catherines Way PR5 .... 76 C7
St Cecilia St BB6 .... 123 D5
St Cecilia's RC High Sch
PR3 .... 139 A6
St Celia's Way LA4 .... 213 A6
St Chad's Ave BB7 .... 187 D5
St Chad's Dr LA1 .... 213 D3
St Chad's RC Prim Sch
PR6 .... 60 F6
St Chad's Rd
Blackpool FY1 .... 129 B2
Preston PR1 .... 117 C1
St Chads Cl FY6 .... 151 D2
St Charles' RC Prim Sch
BB1 .... 123 B1
St Charles' Rd BB1 .... 123 B1
St Christines Ave PR5 .... 76 C4
St Christopher's
CE High Sch BB5 .... 103 A7
St Christopher's Rd PR1 .. 117 A2
St Christopher's
Way LA4 .... 212 G6
St Clair Dr PR9 .... 53 A1
St Clair Rd BL8 .... 48 F3
St Clare's RC Prim Sch
PR2 .... 116 F7
St Clares Ave PR2 .... 117 A6
St Clement St
Blackburn BB1 .... 101 B4
Blackburn BB1 .... 101 B5
St Clement's Ave FY3 .... 129 E5
St Clements Ave PR5 .... 76 C3
St Clements Cl 3 BB1 .... 101 B4
St Clements Ct BB9 .... 168 C3
St Crispin Way BB4 .... 84 A2
St Cuthbert St BB10 .... 147 C2
St Cuthbert's CE Prim Sch
Darwen BB3 .... 80 E3
Halsall L39 .... 22 B1
St Cuthbert's Cl
Fulwood PR2 .... 116 D3
1 Lytham St Anne's FY8 .... 90 A3
Southport PR9 .... 53 A2
St Cuthbert's RC Prim
Sch FY4 .... 109 C8
St Cuthbert's Rd
Bamber Bridge PR5 .... 96 A1
Preston PR1 .... 117 A2
Southport PR9 .... 53 A2
St Cuthberts Cl BB3 .... 80 E3
St Cutherbert's Ct 6 FY8 .. 90 A3
St David's Ave
Blackburn BB2 .... 79 E7
Cleveleys FY5 .... 172 D2
St David's Gr FY8 .... 88 D8
St David's Rd Leyland PR5 ... 76 C2
Preston PR1 .... 117 A2
St David's Rd N FY8 .... 88 D8
St David's Rd S FY8 .... 88 F6
St David's Wood BB5 .... 103 D7
St Deny's Croft BB7 .... 186 E1
St Edmund Hall Cl BL0 .... 49 C4
St Edmund's RC Prim Sch
Fleetwood FY7 .... 172 E8
Skelmersdale WN8 .... 17 F1
St Edmund's Rd FY4 .... 129 E1
St Edmund's St BB6 .... 123 D5
St Edward's RC Prim Sch
BB3 .... 80 E4
St Frances Cl 4 BB1 .... 100 F3
St Francis CE Prim Sch
BB2 .... 99 F1
St Francis Cl PR2 .... 117 A7
St Francis' Rd BB2 .... 100 A2
St Francis's RC Prim Sch
PR3 .... 159 A2
St Gabriel Cl WN8 .... 19 C3
St Gabriel's Ave BB1 .... 121 F3
St Gabriel's CE Prim Sch
BB1 .... 121 E2
St George Ct FY1 .... 129 D6
St George's Ave
Blackburn BB2 .... 100 B1
Cleveleys FY5 .... 172 D2
Lytham St Anne's FY8 .... 88 E7
St George's CE Prim Sch
PR7 .... 42 E5
St George's High Sch
FY4 .... 110 A8
St George's La
Cleveleys FY5 .... 172 D2
Lytham St Anne's FY8 .... 88 E6
St George's Pl PR9 .... 34 B7
St George's Quay LA1 .... 213 E1
St George's Rd
Blackpool FY4 .... 109 C6
Formby L37 .... 11 E4
Hightown L38 .... 2 F5
Lytham St Anne's FY8 .... 88 E6
Preston PR1 .... 117 A2
St George's Sh Ctr 5 PR1 .. 95 F7
St George's Sq FY8 .... 88 D7
St George's St PR7 .... 42 C7
St George's Terr BB4 .... 69 A6
St Georges Cl BB8 .... 169 C3
St Georges Rd BB9 .... 147 F7
St Georges Terr BB3 .... 80 F1
St Gerrard's Rd PR5 .... 96 A1
St Giles St 7 BB12 .... 145 C1
St Giles Terr 6 BB12 .... 145 C1
St Gregory Rd PR1 .... 117 B2
St Gregory's Pl PR7 .... 42 C5
St Gregory's RC Inf Sch
L31 .... 5 C4
St Gregory's RC Jun Sch
L31 .... 5 C4
St Gregory's RC Prim Sch
Chorley PR7 .... 42 C5
Fulwood PR1 .... 117 B3
St Helen's CE Sch LA3 .... 209 D1
St Helen's Cl PR3 .... 178 A2
St Helen's Rd
Clayton Green PR6 .... 77 C1
Overton LA3 .... 205 E8
St Helens Cl BB5 .... 102 F3
St Helens Rd L39 .... 16 A2
St Helier Cl BB2 .... 80 C8
St Helier's Pl PR3 .... 136 A7
St Heliers Rd FY1 .... 129 C1
St Hilda's Cl PR7 .... 42 C4
St Hilda's RC Girls' Sch BB11
126 C3
St Hilda's Rd FY8 .... 88 D8
St Hubert's Rd BB6 .... 123 C4
St Hubert's St BB6 .... 123 D5
St Huberts RC Prim Sch
BB6 .... 123 E6
St Ignatius' Pl 6 PR1 .... 96 A8
St Ignatius' RC Prim Sch
PR1 .... 96 A8
St Ignatius' Sq 5 PR1 .... 96 A8
St Ives Ave Blackpool FY1 .. 129 E3
Freckleton PR4 .... 92 A6
St Ives Cres PR2 .... 116 A4
St Ives Rd BB1 .... 101 D4
St Jame's CE Prim Sch
BB3 .... 81 B2
St Jame's Terr PR5 .... 98 E7
St James CE Prim Sch
Blackburn BB3 .... 81 A7
Leyland PR5 .... 58 B8
St James Cl
Bamber Bridge PR5 .... 76 B8
Church BB5 .... 102 E7
3 Haslingden BB4 .... 84 B3
Ormskirk L40 .... 16 C3
St James Ct
Blackburn BB1 .... 100 E7
Heysham LA3 .... 208 E7
9 Lancaster LA1 .... 210 E8
Standish WN6 .... 28 D2
1 Tardy Gate PR5 .... 76 B8
St James La 6 BB11 .... 127 A6
St James Lodge PR5 .... 58 B8
St James Mews
Church BB5 .... 102 E7
Lancaster LA1 .... 213 F1
St James Pl
4 Padiham BB12 .... 125 D8
Southport PR8 .... 34 B5
St James RC Sch WN8 .... 18 B4
St James Rd
Blackpool FY4 .... 109 C6
Church BB5 .... 102 E7
St James Row BB4 .... 85 A3
St James Sq 18 OL13 .... 86 F3
St James St Bacup OL13 .... 86 F2
1 Rawtenstall BB4 .... 85 A3
Southport PR8 .... 34 B6
St James The Lesser
RC Prim Sch BB4 .... 84 F3
St James' Cres BB3 .... 81 B2
St James' Lanehead
CE Prim Sch BB10 .... 147 D2
St James' RC Prim Sch
WN5 .... 10 D4
St James' Rd
9 Barnoldswick BB18 .... 200 B2
Orrell WN5 .... 10 D4
St James' Sq 10 BB18 .... 200 B2
St James' St
Accrington BB5 .... 103 B5
Blackburn BB2 .... 100 C1
Rawtenstall, Waterfoot BB4 ... 68 E8
St James's CE Sch BB7 ... 164 E7
St James's Dr LA6 .... 234 B7
St James's Gdns PR5 .... 58 B8
St James's Pl
Blackburn BB1 .... 100 E7
9 Chorley PR6 .... 42 E7
St James's Rd
Blackburn BB1 .... 100 E7
Preston PR1 .... 116 F2
St James's Row 13 BB11 .. 126 F6
St James's St
Brierfield BB9 .... 147 B5
8 Chorley PR6 .... 42 E7
Clitheroe BB7 .... 164 E7
St Jerome's RC Prim Sch
L37 .... 11 C3
St John Ave FY7 .... 193 D2
St John Bosco RC
Prim Sch L31 .... 5 B2
St John RC Jun Sch
BB10 .... 147 C3
St John Rigby RC
Sixth Form Coll WN5 .... 19 F2
St John Southworth
RC Prim Sch BB9 .... 147 D7
St John St Bacup OL13 .... 86 F3
Colne BB8 .... 169 E5
Horwich BL6 .... 31 B3
St John Stone RC
Prim Sch PR8 .... 20 B2
St John the Baptist
RC Sch BB12 .... 125 C7
St John Vianney RC Sch
FY1 .... 129 E2
St John with St Michael
CE Prim Sch OL12 .... 70 E5
St John's Ave Darwen BB3 .. 64 B8
Morecambe LA3 .... 212 B2
Poulton-le-F FY6 .... 151 E5
Silverdale LA5 .... 218 C3
Thornton FY5 .... 173 D1
St John's CE Meth
Prim Sch PR6 .... 61 E7
St John's CE Prim Sch
Accrington BB5 .... 103 C7
Burscough Bridge L40 .... 24 F5
Coppull PR7 .... 28 D6
Galgate LA2 .... 207 A3
Garstang PR3 .... 220 C1
Nelson BB9 .... 148 A8
Pilling PR3 .... 196 C6
Southport PR9 .... 53 C5
St John's Cl
Accrington BB5 .... 103 E2
5 Rawtenstall BB4 .... 85 A7
Read BB12 .... 144 D2
St John's Ct 6 Bacup OL13 .. 86 F3
6 Blackpool FY1 .... 129 C5
8 Burnley BB12 .... 126 C6
6 Lytham St Anne's FY8 .... 90 C3
St John's Gn PR5 .... 75 E1
St John's Gr
Morecambe LA3 .... 212 B2
Silverdale LA5 .... 218 C3
St John's Mkt FY1 .... 129 C5
St John's Pl Nelson BB9 ... 148 A8
17 Preston PR1 .... 96 A7
St John's Prim Sch
Blackpool FY1 .... 129 C5
Great Harwood BB6 .... 123 C4
Higham BB12 .... 146 A6
St John's RC Inf Sch
BB10 .... 147 B1
St John's Rd 5
Burnley BB12 .... 126 C6
Morecambe LA3 .... 212 A2
Padiham BB12 .... 125 C7
Southport PR8 .... 33 F1
Walton-le-D PR5 .... 96 D5
St John's St Darwen BB3 .... 64 B8
Great Harwood BB6 .... 123 C4
Lytham St Anne's FY8 .... 90 C3
Rawtenstall BB4 .... 68 F8
St John's Terr LA3 .... 212 F2
St Johns Ave Kirkham PR4 .. 112 F4
Smallwood Hey PR3 .... 196 C5
St Johns Cl PR6 .... 60 B7
St Johns Ct PR8 .... 20 B4
St Johns RC Prim Sch
WN8 .... 18 C1
St Johns Wood FY8 .... 89 E3

St Johns' CE Prim Sch
BB1 .... 100 E7
St Joseph & St Bede RC Prim Sch BL9 .... 32 B4
St Joseph's Con Ctr WN8 .. 19 B2
St Joseph's Inf Sch PR6 .... 60 D1
St Joseph's RC Prim Sch
Adlington PR6 .... 30 B8
Bacup OL13 .... 69 D8
Bacup OL13 .... 86 D1
Barnoldswick BB18 .... 200 B3
Chorley PR6 .... 60 D2
Darwen BB3 .... 64 A8
Gregson Lane PR5 .... 97 E1
Hurst Green BB7 .... 162 F1
Kirkham PR4 .... 112 F7
Lancaster LA1 .... 213 F3
Preston PR1 .... 117 C1
Ramsbottom BL0 .... 49 B6
Withnell PR6 .... 79 A1
St Joseph's RC Sch BL6 .... 31 E1
St Joseph's Terr 1 PR1 ... 117 C1
St Joseph's Wrightington RC Prim Sch WN6 .... 28 A3
St Josephs Cl FY3 .... 129 E5
St Jude's Ave PR5 .... 96 D1
St Judes Ave PR5 .... 76 C4
St Katherines Dr BL6 .... 30 C3
St Kentigern's Sch FY3 ... 129 D5
St Lames Lodge FY8 .... 89 A5
St Laurence's CE Prim Sch
PR7 .... 60 C1
St Lawrence Ave BB2 .... 100 B8
St Lawrence CE Prim Sch
PR3 .... 136 B7
St Lawrence St BB6 .... 123 C5
St Lawrence's Ave PR3 .... 136 B8
St Leger Ct 11 BB5 .... 103 C5
St Leonard Ct 5 LA1 .... 214 A1
St Leonard's Ave BL6 .... 31 F1
St Leonard's CE Cty Prim Sch BB12 .... 145 C1
St Leonard's CE Prim Sch
PR5 .... 96 C4
St Leonard's CE Sch BB6 .. 142 E2
St Leonard's Cl PR2 .... 116 A3
St Leonard's Ct FY8 .... 88 D8
St Leonard's Gate LA1 .... 210 F8
St Leonard's Rd FY3 .... 130 A3
St Leonard's Rd E FY8 .... 88 E8
St Leonard's Rd W FY8 .... 88 D8
St Leonard's St 8 BB12 ... 145 C1
St Louis Ave FY3 .... 129 F7
St Luke & St Philip's CE Prim Sch BB2 .... 100 D3
St Luke's Bldg 2 PR8 .... 34 D6
St Luke's CE Prim Sch
Formby L37 .... 11 D1
Lancaster LA1 .... 213 F3
St Luke's CE Sch LA2 .... 213 E8
St Luke's Church Rd
L37, L38 .... 2 C8
St Luke's Ct 1 FY4 .... 109 C6
St Luke's Dr Formby L37 .... 11 C2
Orrell WN5 .... 10 E4
St Luke's Gr PR9 .... 34 E7
St Luke's Pl 9 PR1 .... 117 C1
St Luke's RC Prim Sch
WN8 .... 9 E6
St Luke's Rd
Blackpool FY4 .... 109 C6
Southport PR9 .... 34 D7
St Lukes Ct 2 LA1 .... 210 E8
St Margaret's Ct
1 Blackburn BB1 .... 101 B5
Fleetwood FY7 .... 194 A4
St Margaret's Gdns BB11 .. 125 C4
St Margaret's Rd
Bolton-le-S LA5 .... 216 B6
1 Leyland PR5 .... 76 C2
Morecambe LA4 .... 212 G6
St Margarets Cl PR2 .... 116 A4
St Margarets Way BB1 .... 101 B5
St Maria Goretti RC Prim Sch PR2 .... 117 F5
St Marie's RC Prim Sch
Kirkby L33 .... 1 A3
Southport PR8 .... 34 B8
St Maries RC Prim Sch
WN6 .... 28 E2
St Mark's CE Prim Sch
Bury BL9 .... 32 A4
Scarisbrick L40 .... 22 D7
St Mark's Pl
Blackburn BB2 .... 100 B4
1 Blackpool FY3 .... 129 E8
St Mark's Pl E 5 PR1 .... 95 D8
St Mark's Pl W 4 PR1 .... 95 D8
St Mark's Rd
Blackburn BB2 .... 100 B4
Preston PR1 .... 95 D8
St Marks RC Sch WN8 .... 9 E8
St Marlow Ave 3 PR5 .... 76 C3
St Martin's Coll LA1 .... 211 B6
St Martin's Ct FY5 .... 172 F2
St Martin's Dr BB2 .... 79 D8
St Martin's Rd
Blackpool FY4 .... 109 C6
Lancaster LA1 .... 211 A7
Preston PR1 .... 117 A2
St Martins Cl FY6 .... 151 B5
St Mary & St Michael's RC Prim Sch PR3 .... 178 C6
St Mary Cl FY3 .... 151 B1
St Mary Magdalen RC Prim Sch PR1 .... 95 E4
St Mary Magdalen's CE Prim Sch BB5 .... 103 B7
St Mary Magdalene's RC Prim Sch BB12 .... 126 D8
St Mary's & St Andrews RC Prim Sch PR3 .... 136 A5
St Mary's & St Benedicts RC Prim Sch PR5 .... 96 E1
St Mary's & St Joseph's RC Prim Sch BB1 .... 100 F3
St Mary's Ave
Bamber Bridge PR5 .... 96 D1
Barnoldswick BB18 .... 200 D3
St Mary's CE Prim Sch
Eccleston PR7 .... 40 C6
Mellor BB2 .... 120 D2
Ramsbottom BL8 .... 48 C2
Spen Brook BB12 .... 167 C3
St Mary's Cl PR5 .... 96 D1
St Mary's Ct
Clayton-le-M BB5 .... 123 F2
Preston PR1 .... 96 B8
St Mary's Dr BB6 .... 142 D1
St Mary's Gate
Burnley BB11 .... 127 B5
Euxton PR7 .... 59 C3
St Mary's Gdns
Mellor BB2 .... 120 E2
Southport PR8 .... 20 F7
St Mary's Par LA1 .... 210 E8
St Mary's Pl BB4 .... 84 F2
St Mary's RC High Sch
FY3 .... 129 F7
St Mary's RC Prim Sch
Accrington BB5 .... 102 F4
Bacup OL13 .... 87 B2
Bescar L40 .... 23 A7
Burnley BB10 .... 127 B6
Chipping PR3 .... 182 E3
Chorley PR7 .... 42 A7
Claughton PR3 .... 179 D1
Clayton-le-M BB5 .... 123 F3
Euxton PR7 .... 59 C3
Fleetwood FY7 .... 194 A5
Great Eccleston PR3 .... 154 B5
Haslingden BB4 .... 84 C2
Horwich BL6 .... 31 B4
Horwich BL6 .... 31 D2
Leyland PR5 .... 75 F1
Morecambe LA4 .... 212 F6
Osbaldeston BB2 .... 120 D4
St Mary's RC Primary Sch
PR4 .... 114 F2
St Mary's RC Sch
Langho BB6 .... 142 C1
Leyland PR5 .... 58 E7
Sabden BB7 .... 144 F7
St Mary's Rd
Bamber Bridge PR5 .... 96 E1
Great Eccleston PR3 .... 154 B5
Heysham LA3 .... 208 E8
St Mary's Sixth Form Coll
BB1 .... 100 E7
St Mary's St Clitheroe BB7 .. 186 E1
Nelson BB9 .... 147 C8
Preston PR1 .... 96 B8
St Mary's St N 7 PR1 .... 96 B8
St Mary's Terr 6 BB4 .... 85 A2
St Mary's Way BB4 .... 85 A2
St Mary's Wlk 16 PR7 .... 42 C8
St Marys CE Prim Sch
LA6 .... 238 B2
St Marys Cl Blackburn BB1 .. 101 B5
Longridge PR3 .... 139 A8
8 Preston PR1 .... 96 C8
St Marys Wharfe BB1 .... 100 F3
St Mathew's RC Prim Sch
WN8 .... 9 D7
St Matthew St BB11 .... 126 E5
St Matthew's CE Prim Sch
BB1 .... 100 F4
St Matthew's CE Sch PR1 .. 96 D8
St Matthew's Ct 9 BB11 .. 126 E5
St Michael & All Angels CE Prim Sch BB8 .... 169 E8
St Michael & St John's RC Prim Sch BB7 .... 164 E8
St Michael Rd L39 .... 5 F7
St Michael with St John CE Prim Sch BB1 .... 100 E6
St Michael's CE High Sch
PR7 .... 60 C1
St Michael's CE Prim Sch
Kirkham PR4 .... 113 B5
Ormskirk L39 .... 15 B1
St Michael's Cl
Blackburn BB2 .... 79 E7
Bolton-le-S LA5 .... 216 A4
Chorley PR7 .... 60 B1
Southport PR9 .... 52 F3
St Michael's Cres LA5 .... 216 A4
St Michael's Ct
Barrowford BB9 .... 168 C2
1 Blackburn BB1 .... 100 F6
St Michael's Gr
Bolton-le-S LA5 .... 216 A4
Morecambe LA4 .... 212 F4
St Michael's La LA5 .... 216 A4
St Michael's Pl
Bolton-le-S LA5 .... 216 A4
Newsham PR3 .... 136 B5
St Michael's Rd
Duncombe PR3 .... 156 D4
4 Leyland PR5 .... 76 C3
Preston PR1 .... 117 A2
St Michael's St BB1 .... 100 F7
St Michael's Terr PR5 .... 57 B2
St Michael's-on-Wyre CE Prim Sch PR3 .... 155 C6
St Michaels Pk L39 .... 6 A7
St Michaels Rd
Blackpool FY2 .... 150 D3
Kirkham PR4 .... 113 C5
St Mildred's Way LA3 .... 208 E6
St Monica's Way FY4 .... 130 D1
St Nicholas Arcs 13 LA1 ... 210 F8
St Nicholas Cres LA5 .... 216 B6
St Nicholas Gr PR4 .... 112 B4
St Nicholas La LA5 .... 216 A6
St Nicholas Rd
Blackpool FY4 .... 110 B5
Church BB5 .... 102 F7
St Nicholas' Ave BB7 .... 144 F8
St Nicholas' CE Prim Sch
Blackpool FY4 .... 110 A4
Church BB5 .... 102 F7
St Ogg's Rd LA4 .... 212 F3
St Oswald St LA1 .... 211 A6
St Oswald's CE Prim Sch
BB1 .... 101 E4
St Oswald's Cl
Blackburn BB1 .... 101 E4
Preston PR1 .... 117 C2
St Oswald's RC Prim Sch
Accrington BB5 .... 103 A3
Coppull PR7 .... 28 D8
Longton PR4 .... 74 B8
St Oswald's Rd BB1 .... 101 E4
St Patrick's Pl PR5 .... 96 E4
St Patrick's RC Prim Sch
Heysham LA3 .... 209 A8
Southport PR9 .... 53 A2
Walton-le-D PR5 .... 96 E4
St Patrick's Rd N FY8 .... 88 E7
St Patrick's Rd S FY8 .... 88 F6
St Patrick's Wlk LA3 .... 208 E7
St Paul's Ave
Blackburn BB2 .... 100 D5
Lytham St Anne's FY8 .... 89 B4
Preston PR1 .... 117 A1
St Paul's CE Prim Sch
Adlington PR6 .... 30 A7
Bury BL9 .... 32 B4
Hoddlesden BB3 .... 81 F1
Nelson BB9 .... 147 D6
Oswaldtwistle BB5 .... 102 E4
Ramsbottom BL0 .... 49 C6
St Paul's Cl Adlington PR6 ... 30 A8
Clitheroe BB7 .... 164 C8
St Paul's Ct
5 Burnley BB11 .... 126 F5
12 Oswaldtwistle BB5 .... 102 E4
9 Preston PR1 .... 96 A8
St Paul's Dr Caton LA2 .... 231 D3
Lancaster LA1 .... 210 F5
St Paul's Pas PR8 .... 34 A6
St Paul's RC Prim Sch
BB2 .... 79 D8
St Paul's Rd Blackpool FY1 . 129 B8
Lancaster LA1 .... 210 F5
Nelson BB9 .... 147 E6
Preston PR1 .... 117 A1
1 Rishton BB1 .... 123 A1
St Paul's Sq Preston PR1 .... 96 A8
Southport PR8 .... 34 A6
St Paul's St Blackburn BB2 . 100 D5
Bury BL9 .... 32 A3
Clitheroe BB7 .... 164 C8
Oswaldtwistle BB5 .... 102 E4
4 Ramsbottom BL0 .... 49 C6
Southport PR8 .... 34 A6
St Paul's Terr
Clitheroe BB7 .... 164 C8
Hoddlesden BB3 .... 81 E2
St Paul's Villas BL9 .... 32 A3
St Paul's Wlk 4 FY8 .... 89 C4
St Pauls Cl PR5 .... 75 F7
St Pauls Mans 4 PR8 .... 34 A6
St Peter St Blackburn BB2 .. 100 E4
2 Rishton BB1 .... 123 A1
St Peter's & St Paul's CE Prim Sch BB1 .... 123 A2
St Peter's Ave Formby L37 .... 11 D4
Haslingden BB4 .... 84 B2
St Peter's CE Prim Sch
Accrington BB5 .... 103 A2
Burnley BB11 .... 127 A6
Chorley PR6 .... 60 E2
Darwen BB3 .... 64 B8
Formby L37 .... 12 A5
Fulwood PR2 .... 116 F7
Heysham LA3 .... 208 E7
St Peter's Cl Darwen BB3 .... 64 B8
Formby L37 .... 11 D4
1 Preston PR1 .... 95 F8
Salesbury BB1 .... 121 D6
St Peter's Pl
Fleetwood FY7 .... 194 B4
7 Haslingden BB4 .... 84 B2
St Peter's RC Cath LA1 .... 211 A8
St Peter's RC High Sch
WN5 .... 10 F7
St Peter's RC Inf Sch
BB2 .... 100 B2
St Peter's RC Jun Sch
BB2 .... 100 B2
St Peter's RC Prim Sch
Lytham St Anne's FY8 .... 90 C5
Newchurch BB4 .... 85 E2
St Peter's Rd
Lancaster LA1 .... 211 A8
Newchurch BB4 .... 85 E2
Southport PR8 .... 34 A3
St Peter's Sq 8 PR1 .... 95 E8
St Peter's St Chorley PR6 .... 60 E1
2 Preston PR1 .... 95 F8
St Peters Mews 16 LA1 .... 211 A8
St Philip St BB10 .... 147 A1
St Philip's CE Prim Sch
Nelson BB9 .... 147 E8
Southport PR8 .... 34 C5
St Philip's Rd PR1 .... 117 A2
St Philip's St
Blackburn BB2 .... 100 B3
18 Nelson BB9 .... 168 E1
St Pius X Prep Sch PR2 .... 116 E4
St Richards RC Prim Sch
WN8 .... 17 D1
St Saviour's CE Prim Sch
PR5 .... 76 F7
St Saviour's Cl PR5 .... 76 F7
St Saviour's Com Prim Sch
OL13 .... 70 A8
St Saviour's Cty Prim Sch
OL13 .... 69 F8
St Saviours Ct OL13 .... 86 F1
St Silas's CE Jun Sch
BB2 .... 100 B6
St Silas's Rd BB2 .... 100 B6
St Stephen's Ave 8
Blackburn BB1 .... 101 A7
Blackpool FY2 .... 150 B2
St Stephen's CE Inf Sch
BB1 .... 101 B7
St Stephen's CE Jun Sch BB1 .... 101 B7
St Stephen's CE Prim Sch
Burnley BB11 .... 127 B4
Preston PR1 .... 95 E6
St Stephen's Rd
9 Blackburn BB1 .... 101 A7
Hightown L38 .... 2 F4
Preston PR1 .... 117 A2
Preston PR1 .... 117 B2
Standish WN6 .... 28 C1
St Stephen's St 4 BB11 .... 127 B4
St Stephen's Way BB8 .... 169 F6
St Stephens Rd PR4 .... 112 F4
St Stephens' CE Prim Sch
PR9 .... 54 A5
St Teresa's Ave FY5 .... 172 D1
St Teresa's RC Prim Sch
Cleveleys FY5 .... 172 D1
Orrell WN8 .... 19 B1
Penwortham PR1 .... 95 A5
Preston PR1 .... 117 E1
Southport PR8 .... 34 A4
St Theodore's RC High Sch
BB10 .... 127 B7
St Theresa's Dr PR2 .... 116 C4
St Thereses Ct 1 PR4 .... 113 B5
St Thomas CE Prim BB1 .. 101 B5
St Thomas CE Prim Sch
L31 .... 5 D4
St Thomas Cl
Haslingden BB4 .... 67 A7
Highfurlong FY3 .... 151 B1
St Thomas Ct 3 BL9 .... 32 A2
St Thomas More Wlk
LA1 .... 210 D8
St Thomas Rd PR4 .... 113 A4
St Thomas St BB1 .... 101 B4
St Thomas the Martyr CE Prim Sch WN8 .... 10 B7
St Thomas' CE Prim Sch
Bury BL9 .... 32 B1
Garstang PR3 .... 178 B6
Lytham St Anne's FY8 .... 88 F6
St Thomas' Pl PR1 .... 116 F1
St Thomas' Rd
Lytham St Anne's FY8 .... 88 F6
Preston PR1 .... 117 A2
St Thomas' St PR1 .... 116 F1
St Thomas's Ct WN8 .... 10 C7
St Thomas's Prim Sch
BB9 .... 168 D3
St Thomas's Rd
Chorley PR7 .... 42 C8
Rawtenstall BB4 .... 85 A7
St Thomas's Sq 4 PR7 .... 42 C8
St Veronica's RC Prim Sch
BB4 .... 67 B7
St Vincent Ave FY1 .... 129 E3
St Vincent's RC Prim Sch
OL12 .... 51 A1
St Vincent's Way PR8 .... 34 A4
St Vincents Rd PR2 .... 116 F5
St Walburga's Rd FY3 .... 129 F7
St Walburge Ave PR2 .... 95 E8
St Walburges Gdns 8
PR2 .... 95 D8
St Wilfrid's CE Inf & Jun Sch
FY4 .... 130 C1
St Wilfred's CE Jun & Inf Schs WN6 .... 28 F1
St Wilfred's Dr OL12 .... 51 D4
St Wilfred's RC Sch PR1 .... 95 F7
St Wilfrid St 2 PR1 .... 95 F7
St Wilfrid's CE (Lower) Sch
BB2 .... 100 D4
St Wilfrid's CE (Upper) Sch
BB2 .... 100 D3
St Wilfrid's CE Prim Sch
LA2 .... 214 E7
St Wilfrid's Pk LA2 .... 214 E7
St Wilfrid's RC Prim Sch
PR3 .... 139 A8
St Wilfrid's Rd WN6 .... 28 F1
St Wilfrid's Terr PR3 .... 139 A7
St Wilfrid's Way WN6 .... 28 E1
St Williams RC Prim Sch
PR3 .... 196 E4
St Wulstan's RC Prim Sch
FY7 .... 193 E3
St Wulston's Prim Sch
BB6 .... 123 C5
Salcombe Ave FY2 .... 150 F2
Salcombe Dr PR9 .... 53 A5
Salcombe Rd FY8 .... 109 C1
Salem Mews LA3 .... 208 E8
Salem St BB4 .... 84 B3
Salerno St BB11 .... 126 C4
Sales's La BL9 .... 50 B3
Salesbury CE Prim Sch
BB1 .... 121 D7
Salesbury View BB1 .... 121 F4
Salford BB1 .... 100 E5
Salford Ct PR8 .... 20 C5
Salford Rd Galgate LA2 .... 207 A3
Southport PR8 .... 20 C5
Salford St BL9 .... 32 A4
Salisbury Ave FY6 .... 194 E5
Salisbury Ct
Knott End-on-S FY6 .... 194 E5
Lancaster LA1 .... 210 D8
Salisbury Rd
Blackpool FY1 .... 129 D4
Brinscall PR6,PR7 .... 61 F8
Darwen BB3 .... 80 E3
Horwich BL6 .... 31 F1
Lancaster LA1 .... 210 D8
Preston PR1 .... 95 D7
Salisbury St 3 Chorley PR7 . 42 D7
Colne BB8 .... 169 E5
Great Harwood BB6 .... 123 E6
15 Haslingden BB4 .... 84 B3
5 Preston PR1 .... 117 D1
Southport PR9 .... 35 A6
Sallowfields WN5 .... 10 D5
Sally's La PR9 .... 53 B2
Salmesbury Ave FY2 .... 150 E2
Salmon St PR1 .... 96 C7
Salmsbury Hall Cl BL0 .... 49 C4
Salop Ave FY2 .... 150 C4
Salt Aire Sports Ctr LA1 ... 213 C1
Salt Ayre La
Lancaster LA1 .... 213 D1
Morecambe LA1 .... 213 B2
Salt Marsh Cl FY6 .... 174 B1
Salt Marsh La FY6 .... 174 B1
Salt Pie La LA6 .... 238 C2
Salt Pit La L40 .... 39 F3
Saltash Rd FY5 .... 173 B5
Saltburn St BB12 .... 126 B6
Saltcotes Pl FY8 .... 90 D4
Saltcotes Rd FY8 .... 90 D7
Salter Fell Rd LA1 .... 213 D2
Salter St PR1 .... 116 F1
Salterford La BB10 .... 128 A4
Salterforth La
Barnoldswick BB18 .... 200 E2
Salterforth BB18 .... 191 D7
Salterforth Prim Sch
BB18 .... 191 D8
Salterforth Rd BB18 .... 201 A1
Salthill Ind Est BB7 .... 187 A2
Salthill Rd BB7 .... 186 F1
Salthill View BB7 .... 186 F1
Salthouse Ave FY1 .... 129 C3
Saltpit La L31 .... 5 E1
Salus St BB10 .... 147 C1
Salwick Ave FY2 .... 150 D5
Salwick Cl PR9 .... 52 F5
Salwick Pl
Lytham St Anne's FY8 .... 89 A8
Preston PR2 .... 115 E1
Salwick Rd PR4 .... 134 B3
Salwick Sta PR4 .... 114 C5
Sambourn Fold PR8 .... 20 A5
Samlesbury Aerodrome BB2,PR5 .... 119 F3
Samlesbury CE Prim Sch
PR5 .... 118 D1
Samuel St Bury BL9 .... 32 A3
Preston PR1 .... 96 D8
Sand Beds La BL0,BB4 .... 68 B5
Sand La LA5 .... 217 C4
Sandbank Gdns OL12 .... 70 C2
Sandbeds La LA2 .... 232 A8
Sandbrook Gdns WN5 .... 10 D5
Sandbrook Rd Orrell WN5 .... 10 C5
Southport PR8 .... 20 D4
Sandbrook Way PR8 .... 20 C3
Sandcastle (L Pool) FY4 .... 109 A8
Sanderling Cl FY5 .... 150 F8
Sanderling Rd L33 .... 1 A3
Sanders Gr LA4 .... 212 D4
Sanderson La PR7 .... 27 A8
Sanderson St 9 BL9 .... 32 A3
Sandersons Way FY4 .... 109 F8
Sandfield 4 FY5 .... 173 A2
Sandfield Cotts L39 .... 15 D2
Sandfield Ho 6 LA1 .... 211 A3
Sandfield Pk L39 .... 15 D2
Sandfield Rd OL13 .... 87 A1
Sandfield St 11 PR5 .... 76 B1
Sandford Dr L31 .... 5 D2
Sandford Rd WN5 .... 10 C5
Sandgate Blackpool FY4 .... 109 D5
Chorley PR7 .... 42 D5
Lytham St Anne's FY8 .... 88 C7
Sandham St 7 PR6 .... 42 D8
Sandheys Dr PR9 .... 52 F1
Sandhill St BB3 .... 64 B5
Sandhills L38 .... 2 F3
Sandhills Ave FY4 .... 109 B5
Sandhills Cl BB18 .... 191 E8
Sandholme La PR3 .... 179 A4
Sandholme Villas BB18 .... 201 A1
Sandhurst Ave
Blackpool FY2 .... 150 C5

Sandhurst Ave continued
Lytham St Anne's FY8 88 E7
Sandhurst Cl Formby L37 11 C1
8 Kirkham PR4 112 F5
Sandhurst Ct FY8 88 D6
Sandhurst Grange FY8 88 E7
Sandhurst St BB11 127 B6
Sandhurst Way L31 5 B5
Sandicroft Ave FY6 174 C1
Sandicroft Pl FY6 195 B4
Sandicroft Rd FY1 150 C1
Sandilands Gr L38 2 F3
Sandiway Ct PR9 34 E8
Sandiway Dr BB10 147 F3
Sandiways L31 5 E1
Sandiways Cl FY5 151 C8
Sandon Pl FY4 109 C4
Sandon Rd PR8 33 F1
Sandon St Blackburn BB2 100 C3
Darwen BB3 81 B2
Sandon Terr BB2 100 C3
Sandown Cl PR4 112 E5
Sandown Ct
31 Preston PR1 96 A7
1 Southport PR9 34 C8
Sandown Rd
Haslingden BB4 84 C2
Lancaster LA1 211 B3
Thornton FY5 173 B1
Sandpiper Cl
Blackburn BB1 100 F6
Normoss FY3 130 B6
Sandpiper Ct FY5 172 C2
Sandpiper Pl 10 FY5 172 F1
Sandpiper Sq 7 BB11 126 C5
Sandridge Ave PR7 42 B7
Sandridge Pl FY4 109 B4
Sandringham Ave
Leyland PR5 76 C1
Thornton FY5 173 B1
Sandringham Cl
Adlington PR7 29 E6
5 Barrowford BB9 168 C1
Blackburn BB1 121 E1
Tarleton PR4 56 A6
Sandringham Ct
Lytham St Anne's FY8 89 D4
Morecambe LA4 212 D4
Southport PR8 34 B8
Sandringham Dr
Brinscall PR6 61 F8
Ramsbottom BL8 49 A1
Sandringham Gr 2 BB4 84 A1
Sandringham Park Dr
PR4 75 A8
Sandringham Rd
Bamber Bridge PR5 96 D3
Chorley PR7 42 B8
Darwen BB3 80 E4
Eccleston PR7 40 C7
Formby L37 11 E1
Horwich BL6 31 E2
Lytham St Anne's FY8 89 A5
Morecambe LA4 212 D4
Southport PR8 33 E3
Southport, Ainsdale PR8 20 C5
Sandringham Way PR4 115 E6
Sands Cl BB1 123 B2
Sands Rd BB1 123 B2
Sands The BB7 143 C5
Sands Way FY1 129 C3
Sandsdale Ave PR2 117 C5
Sandside Dr LA4 212 F3
Sandside Rd LA5,LA7 237 D3
Sandwich Cl BB1 101 C4
Sandwick Cl PR2 116 E7
Sandy Bank Rd BL7 47 D5
Sandy Cl FY5 172 C3
Sandy Gate La PR4 136 B2
Sandy La Accrington BB5 103 E5
Adlington PR7 29 F6
Barrowford BB9 168 D2
Bispham Green L40 38 F2
Blackpool FY4 110 A4
Brindle PR5,PR6 78 C6
Brinscall PR6 61 E8
Clayton Green PR6 77 C3
Darwen BB3 80 E6
Fleetwood FY7 172 D7
Hambleton FY6 174 C1
Hightown L38 3 A3
Holmeswood L40 37 D5
Holmeswood L40 37 E5
Leyland PR5 59 A8
Lower Bartle PR4 115 D7
Maghull, Holt Green L39 6 B6
Maghull, Lydiate L31 5 C5
Mawdesley L40 39 A1
Newburgh WN8 25 F1
Ormskirk L40 16 D7
Orrell WN5 10 D4
Out Rawcliffe PR3 175 F1
Pleasington BB2 99 C2
Preesall FY6 195 B4
Skelmersdale WN8 17 D1
Sollom L40 38 A8
Thorpe Green PR6 77 E4
Sandy La Ctr WN8 17 D1
Sandy Pl 8 PR5 59 A8
Sandy Way L40 37 D4
Sandybeds Cl BB5 103 D2
Sandybrook Cl PR2 117 E5
Sandycroft PR2 117 F2
Sandyfields PR4 115 E6
Sandyforth Ave FY5 173 B3
Sandyforth La PR4 116 A8
Sandygate BB11 126 F6
Sandyhall La BB9 168 A2
Sandylands Arc LA3 212 A3
Sandylands Com Prim Sch
LA3 212 B3
Sandylands Ct LA3 212 B4
Sandylands Prom LA3 212 A3
Sanfield Cl L39 15 E6
Sangara Dr BB3 80 F7
Sangness Dr PR8 34 E3
Sansbury Cres BB9 169 A2
Santon Cl PR4 113 A7
Sanvino Ave PR8 20 D5
Sapphire St BB1 121 F1
Sarah La PR5 56 F5
Sarah St Bacup OL13 70 C8
Darwen BB3 81 B1
Edenfield BL0 67 E3
Sarahs Fold FY6 174 C7
Sarmatian Fold PR3 140 D3
Sarscow La PR5 57 E2
Saswick Ct PR4 133 B7
Saul St PR1 95 F8
Saul's Dr LA5 218 A8
Saunder Bank BB11 127 A5
Saunder Height La BB4 85 E3
Saunders Cl BB4 85 A7
Saunders Mews PR7 42 C3
Saunders Rd BB2 100 C5
Saunders St PR9 52 C1
Saunders' La Hutton PR4 94 D2
Hutton PR4 94 E1
Savick Ave PR2 115 D1
Savick Cl PR5 76 F8
Savick Ct PR2 116 D4
Savick Cty Prim Sch PR2 115 E2
Savick Rd PR2 116 D4
Savick Way PR2 115 E3
Saville Ave FY6 151 B6
Saville Rd Blackpool FY1 129 C1
Maghull L31 5 C3
Saville St PR7 42 C5
Savon Hook L37 12 B1
Savoy Ave LA3 212 F3
Savoy St Accrington BB5 102 F5
4 Preston PR1 95 E7
Sawdon Ave PR8 34 E3
Sawley Abbey BB7 224 C1
Sawley Ave
Accrington BB5 103 D7
Blackpool FY4 109 D5
Lytham St Anne's FY8 89 C6
Read BB12 144 D1
Sawley Cl BB3 64 C8
Sawley Cres PR2 117 F2
Sawley Dr BB6 123 F5
Sawley Rd Chatburn BB7 187 E6
Grindleton BB7 187 C8
Sawley BB7 224 C1
Sawmills Ind Est FY1 129 D6
Sawrey Ct BB5 123 E2
Sawthorpe Wlk FY6 151 B3
Sawyer St 5 OL12 51 F1
Saxby Gr FY4 129 F1
Saxenholme PR8 33 F5
Saxifield St BB10 147 E3
Saxon Cl
Oswaldtwistle BB5 102 C5
Thornton FY5 151 C8
Saxon Hey PR2 116 C3
Saxon Hts LA3 208 F5
Saxon Rd PR8 33 F5
Saxon St BB10 127 A7
Scafell Ave LA4 212 G5
Scafell Cl BB12 126 C8
Scafell Rd Lancaster LA1 214 A2
Lytham St Anne's FY8 110 A2
Scaffold La L38 3 D4
Scaitcliffe St BB5 103 B5
Scale Farm Rd LA1 213 C2
Scale Hall La
Lancaster LA1 213 D2
Newton-with-S PR4 114 A2
Scaleber La LA6 238 D8
Scar St BB2 100 B3
Scarborough Rd
Blackburn BB2 101 A1
Lytham St Anne's FY8 110 A1
Scargill Rd LA5,LA6 216 F1
Scarisbrick Ave
Parbold WN8 26 C2
Southport PR8 34 A7
Scarisbrick Cl L31 5 E3
Scarisbrick Ct PR8 34 C6
Scarisbrick Cty Prim Sch
L40 23 A3
Scarisbrick New Rd PR8 34 D5
Scarisbrick Pk L40 23 A6
Scarisbrick St Ormskirk L39 15 E6
Southport PR9 34 B7
Scarlet St PR6 42 E7
Scarlett St BB11 126 E5
Scarr Dr OL12 51 F3
Scarr La BB2 100 A6
Scarsdale Ave FY4 109 C5
Scarth Hill La L39,L40 16 A2
Scarth La BB12 125 B5
Scarth Pk WN8 9 C7
Scawfell Rd PR7 42 B5
Sceptre Way PR5 77 B6
Schleswig St PR1 96 A8
Schleswig Way PR5 75 C1
Schofield Ave FY3 130 B7
Schofield Cl BB4 84 F2
Schofield Rd BB4 84 F2
Schofield St Darwen BB3 80 F2
Haslingden BB4 67 A6
Schofield St continued
Rawtenstall BB4 68 E8
Schola Green La
Morecambe LA4 212 E4
Morecambe LA4 212 E5
Scholars Gn PR2 115 C1
Scholefield Ave BB9 147 E5
Scholefield La BB9 147 F5
Scholes Bank BL6 31 A5
Scholes St BB3 80 F2
Scholey Head La BB10 107 A8
School Ave L37 11 F3
School Brow PR6 60 B7
School Cl Ormskirk L39 15 C1
Southport PR8 34 B2
School Cotts PR3 179 E8
School Ct Egerton BL7 46 E2
Ramsbottom BL0 67 D2
School Field PR5 77 B5
School Fields BB18 201 B3
School Hillocks Cotts 4
PR5 76 A8
School House Gn L39 15 F5
School House Gr L40 24 D5
School House La BB5 103 B1
School House Mews 7
PR6 42 E7
School La
Bamber Bridge PR5 96 F2
Blackburn BB1 81 D8
Brinscall PR6,PR7 61 E8
Burnley BB11 127 A7
Burscough Bridge L40 24 F5
Catforth PR4 135 A4
Earby BB18 201 B2
Edgworth BL7 47 D8
Euxton PR7 59 D3
Farington PR5 75 F7
Formby L37 11 F3
Forton LA2,PR3 204 B3
Freckleton PR4 92 C7
Hammerton Mere BB7 229 E3
Haskayne L39 13 F4
Inskip PR4 155 D1
Kirkham PR4 113 B5
Laneshaw Bridge BB8 170 E6
Leyland PR5 76 A1
Leyland, Moss Side PR5 58 A8
Longton PR4 74 A8
Lytham St Anne's FY8 90 A3
Maghull L31 6 A1
Mawdesley L40 39 C1
Mereclough BB10 128 A1
Newton-with-S PR4 114 A2
Ollerton Fold PR6 78 F4
Orrell, Roby Mill WN8 19 B3
Orrell, Up Holland WN5,WN8 10 C7
Out Rawcliffe PR3 175 F2
Pilling PR3 196 C6
Preesall FY6 195 B3
Simonstone BB12 144 F1
Skelmersdale,
Pennylands WN8 17 E1
Standish WN6 28 D1
Westhead L40 16 E3
Winmarleigh PR3 198 F6
Wray LA2 232 D6
School Rd Blackpool FY4 110 B5
Heysham LA3 208 E7
Hightown L38 2 F4
Thornton FY5 151 C8
School St Accrington BB5 103 B6
Bacup OL13 69 B8
Bamber Bridge PR5 96 F2
Bury BL9 32 B1
Colne BB8 169 D4
Darwen BB3 81 A1
Great Harwood BB6 123 C4
Horwich BL6 31 C3
Kelbrook BB18 192 A6
Leyland PR5 76 B2
Nelson BB9 147 C8
Preston PR1 95 E7
Ramsbottom BL0 49 B5
Rawtenstall BB4 85 A8
Rishton BB1 123 B1
Walmer Bridge PR4 73 F5
Whitewell Bottom BB4 85 F4
School Terr
Salterforth BB18 191 D8
Whitworth OL12 70 D1
School View BL7 47 D8
School Villas LA2 207 B5
Schoolfold PR4 72 E4
Schoolhouse Fold BB11 125 C3
Schoolhouse La LA2 214 F7
Schwartzman Dr PR9 54 A6
Scorton Ave FY3 129 F7
Scorton Hall Pk PR3 199 E6
Scotch Green La PR3 158 A6
Scotforth CE Prim Sch
LA1 211 A4
Scotforth Ct 1 LA1 211 A3
Scotforth Rd
Lancaster LA1 211 A4
Preston PR1 96 C8
Scotland Bank Terr BB2 80 C8
Scotland La BL9 32 D8
Scotland Pl 11 BL0 49 C6
Scotland Rd Carnforth LA5 217 E3
8 Nelson BB9 147 D8
15 Nelson BB9 168 D1
Scotshaw Brook Ind
Est BB2 80 E7
Scotswood Ave FY4 109 D6
Scott Ave Accrington BB5 103 E2
Morecambe LA4 212 C3
Simonstone BB12 144 E2
Scott Cl Blackpool FY4 109 F8
Maghull L31 5 D1
Oswaldtwistle BB5 102 D5
Scott Dr L39 15 F7
Scott Gr LA4 212 D4
Scott Laithe La BB7 224 E3
Scott Mews FY4 109 F8
Scott Park Rd BB11 126 E4
Scott Rd LA3 212 C3
Scott St Clayton-le-M BB5 123 F3
Nelson BB9 168 D1
Padiham BB12 125 F7
Southport PR9 35 A7
Scott's Terr BB11 126 D6
Scott's Wood PR2 116 D7
Scout Rd Edenfield BL0 68 A2
Egerton BL7 46 B1
Newchurch BB4 85 F3
Scow Croft La PR6,PR7 61 D4
Scowcroft Dr LA4 213 A5
Scriffen La LA2 207 D3
Scudamore Cres 6 FY4 129 D1
Sea View Lancaster LA1 211 A5
Longridge PR3 159 D2
Walmer Bridge PR4 73 F5
Sea View Cl LA2 213 D8
Sea View Dr LA2 213 D8
Sea Wall FY7 193 C3
Seabank Rd
Fleetwood FY7 194 A5
Southport PR9 34 B8
Seaborn Gr LA4 212 G6
Seaborn Rd LA4 212 G6
Seabourne Ave FY4 109 B7
Seabrook Dr FY5 150 E8
Seacrest Ave FY1 129 C8
Seacroft Cres PR9 53 B5
Seafield L37 12 A2
Seafield Rd Blackpool FY1 129 B8
Lytham St Anne's FY8 89 F3
Southport PR8 20 C6
Seafore Cl L31 5 B4
Sealand Ave L37 11 E2
Sealand Cl L37 11 D2
Seascale Cl BB2 101 A1
Seaside Way FY1 129 B3
Seathwaite Ave
Blackpool FY4 130 C1
Morecambe LA3 212 B2
Seathwaite Way BB5 103 E8
Seaton Ave FY5 172 E4
Seaton Pl WN8 17 E3
Seaton Way PR9 53 A5
Seattle Ave FY2 150 E2
Seaview Way FY7 194 B3
Seawell Ave LA3 212 A2
Second Ave Blackpool FY4 109 C7
Bury BL9 32 D4
Church BB5 103 A8
Second Terr LA3 205 B4
Sedberg St PR2 116 D3
Sedbergh Ave FY4 129 F1
Sedbergh Cl BB5 103 D5
Sedburgh St BB10 147 C2
Seddon Pl WN8 17 E3
Sedge Ct LA3 212 E2
Sedgefield PR4 73 E8
Sedgeley Mews PR4 92 A6
Sedgfield Cl FY4 109 F6
Sedgley Ave PR4 92 A6
Sedgwick St PR1 117 A1
Sedwell Cl FY8 89 F4
Seed St Blackpool FY1 129 C6
Preston PR1 95 F8
Seedall Ave BB7 164 D7
Seedhill Terr 13 BB9 168 D1
Seedlee Rd PR5 77 A6
Sefton Ave
4 Burnley BB11 126 E5
Orrell WN5 10 D5
Poulton-le-F FY6 151 D1
Sefton Cl Darwen BB3 64 C6
Enfield BB5 124 A3
Orrell WN5 10 D5
Sefton Ct FY8 88 D7
Sefton Dr Bury BL9 32 A6
Lancaster LA1 213 D2
Sefton Gdns L39 6 D7
Sefton La BL6 31 D1
Sefton Rd
Bamber Bridge PR5 96 D3
Formby L37 11 E2
Lytham St Anne's FY8 88 F7
Morecambe LA3 212 B3
Orrell WN5 10 D5
Sefton St Brierfield BB9 147 B5
Colne BB8 169 F5
Southport PR8 34 C5
Sefton Terr 3 BB11 126 E5
Sefton View WN5 10 D5
Segar St
17 Great Harwood BB6 123 C5
Kirkham PR4 112 F6
Segar's La PR8, L39 20 E4
Selborne Mews BB2 100 B3
Selborne St Blackburn BB2 100 B3
Preston PR1 96 B6
Selbourne BB18 201 C2
Selbourne Rd FY1 129 D6
Selby Ave Blackpool FY4 109 D5
Cleveleys FY5 172 F4
2 Lancaster LA1 213 F4
Selby Cl BB5 103 E3
Selby Dr L37 12 B2
Selby Pl WN8 17 D2
Selby Rd PR4 112 F5
Selby St Colne BB8 169 C5
Nelson BB9 147 E7
Selby St continued
Preston PR1 116 D1
Seldon St 11 Colne BB8 169 D4
15 Nelson BB9 168 E1
Selkirk Cl 6 BB1 101 A4
Selkirk Dr PR5 96 D2
Selkirk St BB11 126 D4
Sellers St PR1 117 C1
Selous Rd BB2 100 B3
Selside Dr LA4 212 E3
Selworthy Rd
Southport PR8 33 D3
Southport PR8 33 E3
Senior Ave FY4 129 F1
Seniors Dr FY5 172 F3
Sephton Dr L39 15 F7
Sephton St 7 PR5 76 A8
Sergeant St 11 PR5 76 F8
Serpentine Rd BB11 126 F4
Serpentine The
8 Lytham St Anne's FY8 90 A3
Ormskirk L39 6 D8
Sett End Rd BB1 101 C1
Settle La BB7 225 B7
Settle Pl FY8 89 C7
Settle Terr BB10 147 C2
Seven Acres PR5 77 C5
Seven Hos BB1 101 D4
Seven Sands PR4 94 A1
Seven Stars Prim Sch
PR5 58 D7
Seven Stars Rd PR5 58 D7
Seven Trees Ave BB1 101 A8
Sevenoaks PR7 42 C4
Sevenoaks Ave PR8 20 B5
Sevenoaks Dr FY5 150 F8
Seventh Ave FY4 109 C6
Severn Ave FY7 172 D8
Severn Dr PR5 96 D2
Severn Hill PR2 116 C8
Severn Ho 10 PR1 96 D8
Severn Rd FY4 109 B7
Severn St PR3 139 A7
Seville Ct FY8 89 D3
Seymour Ave LA3 208 F7
Seymour Ct PR1 116 D2
Seymour Dr L31 5 E3
Seymour Gr LA3 208 F7
Seymour Rd
Blackpool FY1 129 C2
Fulwood PR2 116 C3
Lytham St Anne's FY8 89 D4
Seymour St Chorley PR6 42 E8
2 Fleetwood FY7 193 F4
5 Lancaster LA1 211 A8
Shacklady Rd L33 1 A4
Shackleton Rd PR4 113 B2
Shackleton St
Burnley BB10 127 B8
Cornholme OL14 108 C1
Shade Row FY6 195 B3
Shadsworth Cl BB1 101 C4
Shadsworth Cty Inf Sch
BB1 101 D4
Shadsworth Cty Jun Sch
BB1 101 C2
Shadsworth Rd BB1 101 C3
Shady La Clayton-le-W PR5 76 E3
Hest Bank LA2 213 E8
Shaftesbury Ave
Blackpool FY2 150 C2
Burnley BB11 126 F3
Cleveleys FY5 172 D5
Darwen BB3 80 E3
Great Harwood BB6 123 E6
New Longton PR4 74 F8
Normoss FY3 130 B6
Penwortham PR1 95 B6
Southport PR8 21 A8
Shaftesbury Cl FY8 89 D5
Shaftesbury Ct FY2 150 C2
Shaftesbury Gr PR8 34 A1
Shaftesbury Pl Chorley PR7 42 B8
Lancaster LA1 210 F4
Shaftesbury Rd PR8 34 A1
Shakeshaft St 11 BB1 101 A4
Shakespeare Ave BB6 123 B4
Shakespeare Prim Sch
FY7 193 E4
Shakespeare Rd
Fleetwood FY7 193 E4
Lancaster LA1 213 E4
Preston PR1 117 D1
Shakespeare St
Padiham BB12 125 D7
Southport PR8 34 B5
Shakespeare Terr PR6 60 D2
Shakespeare Way BB2 100 C3
Shalbourn Rd FY8 89 A4
Shale St BB12 126 D6
Shalgrove Field PR2 116 C7
Shannon Sq BB10 147 C2
Shannon St FY1 129 B3
Shap Cl Accrington BB5 103 E3
Barrowford BB9 168 D4
Shap Ct FY7 193 D1
Shap Gr BB10 147 A3
Shard La FY6 152 B8
Shard Rd FY6 152 B6
Sharley Fold PR3 139 B7
Sharman Rd FY8 109 F1
Sharneyford Cty Prim Sch
OL13 87 C5
Sharoe Bay Ct PR2 116 F6
Sharoe Green Hospl PR2 116 F4
Sharoe Green La PR2 116 F7
Sharoe Green Pk PR2 117 A5
Sharoe Mount Ave PR2 116 F7

Sharow Gr FY1 129 D3
Sharp St
1 Barrowford BB9 168 D3
Burnley BB10 147 B1
Sharpe's Ave LA1 211 A5
Sharpes Mill LA1 210 F7
Sharples Gn BL7 47 D6
Sharples Mdw BL7 47 D6
Sharples St
Accrington BB5 102 F5
Blackburn BB2 100 D3
Sharrats Path PR7 41 F4
Sharrock St 7 PR8 34 B7
Shaw Bridge St 3 BB7 164 F8
Shaw Brook Cl BB1 102 A8
Shaw Brook Rd PR5 58 E6
Shaw Brow PR6 60 B7
Shaw Cl Blackburn BB2 100 D5
Shirdley Hill L39 22 A6
Shaw Clough Rd BB4 85 F3
Shaw Clough St BB4 85 F3
Shaw Cres L37 12 B3
Shaw Gn LA7 237 F5
Shaw Hill PR6 60 B7
Shaw Hill Dr PR6 60 B6
Shaw Hill Golf Course
PR6 60 B6
Shaw Hill St PR7 42 C7
Shaw La Cornholme OL14 108 C3
Haskayne L39 13 E6
Nether Kellet LA6 216 F4
Storth LA7 237 F5
Shaw Rd Blackpool FY1 129 B1
Horwich BL6 31 B5
Shaw Sq 4 BB18 201 B2
Shaw St Blackburn BB2 100 D5
Bury BL9 32 B3
Colne BB8 169 D4
Haslingden BB4 84 B6
2 Lancaster LA1 211 A8
1 Preston PR1 117 A1
Shaw's Ave PR8 34 A1
Shaw's La PR3 196 A3
Shaw's Rd PR8 34 A1
Shawbridge Ct BB7 164 F8
Shawbrook Cl PR7 59 C5
Shawbury Cl BL6 30 D1
Shawcliffe La BB6,BB7 143 B2
Shawclough Cl OL12 51 D3
Shawclough Com Prim Sch
OL12 51 E3
Shawclough Dr OL12 51 D3
Shawclough Rd OL12 51 C3
Shawclough Way OL12 51 D3
Shawes Dr PR6 30 C7
Shawfield 4 BB4 84 F1
Shawfield La OL12 51 A2
Shaws Garth L39 22 A6
Shay Head Cotts BB8 192 E1
Shay La Longridge PR3 138 F6
Slaidburn BB7 223 B7
Shay The 8 FY5 150 F7
Shays Dr BB7 165 A7
Shear Bank Cl BB1 100 D6
Shear Bank Gdns BB1 100 D6
Shear Bank Rd BB1 100 D6
Shear Brow BB1 100 D7
Shearwater Dr BB1 100 F6
Shed St Colne BB8 169 C4
Oswaldtwistle BB5 102 D3
Whitworth OL12 70 D1
Sheddon Gr BB10 127 E5
Sheep Gap OL12 51 B1
Sheep Gn BB4 84 B3
Sheep Hill Brow PR6 77 A3
Sheep Hill La
Clayton Green PR6 77 A3
Clayton Green PR6 77 B3
Clayton-le-W PR5 76 F2
Sheep House La BL6 44 A3
Sheephill La PR4 75 A7
Sheffield Dr PR2 115 D1
Sheldon Ave WN6 28 E2
Sheldon Ct 1 PR1 116 F1
Shelfield La BB10 148 F7
Shelfield Rd BB9 169 B1
Shelley Cl Bolton-le-S LA5 216 A5
Coppull PR7 28 F8
Shelley Dr Accrington BB5 103 E2
Ormskirk L39 15 D6
Shelley Gdns BB6 123 B4
Shelley Gr Cleveleys FY5 150 D8
Darwen BB3 81 C1
Southport PR8 34 F6
Shelley Mews PR2 116 D1
Shelley Rd PR2 116 C2
Shelley Row PR3 178 C2
Shellfield Rd PR9 53 A4
Shellingford Cl WN6 19 D7
Shelly Dr PR7 40 D5
Shelton Dr PR8 20 A4
Shenley Way PR9 53 D5
Shenstone Rd FY3 129 F7
Shepherd Rd FY8 89 A7
Shepherd Rd N FY8 89 A8
Shepherd St Bacup OL13 86 F3
Bury BL9 32 A1
Darwen BB3 64 A7
7 Lytham St Anne's FY8 90 B3
Preston PR1 96 A7
Shepherd's Ave PR3 178 D4
Shepherd's La L39 14 E5
Shepherds Cl Blackrod BL6 30 C3
Ramsbottom BL8 48 F1
Shepherds Way PR6 42 D8
Sheppard St FY1 129 B4
Sheraton Pk PR2 116 A6
Sherborne Lodge 9 PR2 117 F4
Sherbourne Cl FY6 151 C5
Sherbourne Cres PR1 117 B3
Sherbourne Ct FY6 151 C5
Sherbourne Rd
Accrington BB5 103 E3
Blackpool FY1 129 C7
Hambleton FY6 174 C2
Sherbourne St 5 PR6 42 D7
Sherburn Rd PR1 95 E3
Sherburn Sch PR1 117 A3
Sherburne Ave 4 PR4 112 F5
Sherdley Rd PR5 76 B7
Sherfin Nook BB5 84 B7
Sherfin Side BB5 84 B7
Sheridan Rd BB8 170 D6
Sheridan St Burnley BB10 147 E2
4 Nelson BB9 168 F2
Sheriff St OL12 51 E1
Sheringham Ave FY5 150 D7
Sheringham Way FY6 151 E3
Sherrat St WN8 17 D1
Sherringham Rd PR8 33 E2
Sherwood Ave
Blackpool FY3 129 E8
Ormskirk L39 15 C2
Sherwood Ct BB10 127 C5
Sherwood Cty Prim Sch
PR2 117 A7
Sherwood Dr WN8 18 D3
Sherwood Ho PR8 20 C5
Sherwood Lo PR8 33 F5
Sherwood Pl Chorley PR6 42 D8
2 Cleveleys FY5 172 F1
Sherwood Rd
Blackburn BB1 101 B3
Lytham St Anne's FY8 89 C6
Sherwood Way
Enfield BB5 124 A1
Fulwood PR2 117 A7
Shetland Cl Blackburn BB1 101 C3
Wilpshire BB1 121 F7
Shetland Rd FY1 129 C2
Shevington Com Prim Sch
WN6 19 F6
Shevington Cswy PR5 57 B2
Shevington La WN6 28 B1
Shevington Moor WN6 28 A2
Shevington Vale Prim Sch
WN6 19 E8
Shilton St BL0 49 B5
Shipley Cl FY3 151 B1
Shipley Rd FY8 89 B7
Shipper Bottom La BL0 49 D5
Shirdley Cres PR8 20 C3
Shire Bank Cres PR2 116 E5
Shire La BB7 141 D8
Shireburn Ave BB7 164 C7
Shireburn Cotts BB7 162 E1
Shireburn Rd L37 11 D5
Shireshead Cres LA1 211 A2
Shirley Cres FY2 150 D6
Shirley Gdns BB3 79 F2
Shirley Hts FY6 151 D4
Shirley La PR4 94 A1
Shop La Accrington BB5 103 D5
Higher Walton PR5 97 B4
Maghull L31 5 C1
Shore Ave BB10 147 F2
Shore Cl LA5 218 B2
Shore Gn Cleveleys FY5 172 F3
Cornholme OL14 108 C2
Silverdale LA5 218 B2
Shore New Rd OL14 108 B1
Shore Rd Cleveleys FY5 150 C8
Hesketh Bank PR4 72 C4
Heysham LA3 208 D6
Silverdale LA5 218 B2
Southport PR8 20 B6
Shore The LA5 215 F5
Shorefield Mount BL7 46 E1
Shoreside Prim Sch PR8 20 B4
Shorey Bank BB11 127 A6
Shorrock La BB2 100 B1
Shorrock St BB3 64 A8
Shorrocks Ave PR3 155 C8
Short Clough Cl BB4 85 A6
Short Clough La BB4 85 A6
Short Croft La L37 12 D1
Short St Bacup OL13 69 B8
Colne BB8 169 D4
Shorten Brook Dr BB5 124 E6
Shorten Brook Way BB5 124 E6
Shortlands Dr LA3 208 E7
Shortlands The BB12 145 C2
Shortridge Rd FY4 109 F8
Showfield BB10 128 B6
Showley Brook Cl BB1 121 F4
Showley Ct BB1 121 E6
Showley Rd BB1 121 A6
Shrewsbury Cl PR4 113 C5
Shrewsbury Dr
Lancaster LA1 211 B5
Thornton FY5 173 A2
Shropshire Dr BB1 121 F6
Shuttle Cl BB5 103 A6
Shuttleworth Rd PR1 116 F2
Shuttleworth St
Burnley BB10 147 B2
Earby BB18 201 B2
6 Padiham BB12 125 C8
Rishton BB1 123 B2
Shuttling Fields La PR5 97 B2
Sibbering Brow Preston Rd
PR7 41 C7
Sibsey St LA1 210 E7
Siddow's Ave BB7 164 D7
Side La BB7 189 C7
Sidebeet La BB1 101 E7
Sidegarth Gate LA2 231 C7
Sidegarth La LA2 231 D7
Sidgreaves La PR4 115 B4
Siding La Kirkby L33 1 C7
Rainford Junction WA11 8 C1
Siding Rd FY7 194 A3
Siding St OL13 69 C8
Sidings Rd LA3 208 F2
Sidings The Bacup OL13 70 A8
Spring Vale BB3 64 B7
Whalley BB7 143 C6
Sidmouth Ave BB4 84 C2
Sidmouth Rd FY8 109 C1
Sidney Ave Becconsall PR4 72 F3
Blackpool FY2 150 E2
Sidney Rd PR9 34 F8
Sidney Terr 4 LA1 211 A8
Siemens St BL6 31 C2
Silbury Cl BB2 81 A8
Silcock's Cotts FY5 173 F1
Silk Mill La PR3 158 B3
Silloth Cl BB2 100 F1
Silly La LA2 233 D2
Silsden Ave PR2 117 D5
Silsden Cl FY3 151 B1
Silver Birch Way L31 5 B5
Silver St Clifton PR4 114 D1
Ramsbottom BL0 49 C6
Silverburn 4 FY8 89 A8
Silverdale Becconsall PR4 72 F3
Blackpool FY2 150 E6
Southport PR8 33 E4
Silverdale Ave
Fleetwood FY7 193 D1
Heysham LA3 208 F7
Silverdale CE Prim Sch
LA5 218 C3
Silverdale Cl Blackburn BB2 80 F8
Brierfield BB10 147 B3
Clayton-le-M BB5 123 E2
Coupe Green PR5 97 E4
Leyland PR5 59 B6
Silverdale Ct PR8 34 E4
Silverdale Dr PR2 117 E5
Silverdale Moss Rd LA5 218 D7
Silverdale Rd Arnside LA5 237 B1
Chorley PR6 42 E7
Lytham St Anne's FY8 89 C7
Yealand Redmayne LA5 219 E4
Silverdale Sta LA5 218 F3
Silverstone Gr L31 5 B4
Silverthorne Dr PR9 52 F1
Silverwell St BL6 31 B4
Silverwood Ave FY4 109 D8
Silverwood Cl FY8 89 E4
Silverwood Ct 1 FY4 109 D8
Silvester Rd PR7 42 C6
Silvester St BL6 30 D2
Silvia Way FY7 193 E4
Simfield Cl WN6 28 D1
Simmonds Way BB9 147 B7
Simmons Ave PR1 96 B3
Simmons' St BB2 100 D5
Simonstone Bsns Pk
BB12 124 F8
Simonstone CE Prim Sch
BB12 144 F1
Simonstone La BB12 124 E8
Simonstone Rd BB12,BB7 144 F6
Simonswood Ind Pk L33 1 B6
Simonswood La Kirkby L33 1 A2
Royal Oak L39 6 F3
Simonswood Prim Sch L33 1 A2
Simonswood Wlk L33 1 A2
Simpson Cl BB18 200 D3
Simpson St Blackpool FY4 109 B8
Hapton BB12 125 C4
Oswaldtwistle BB5 102 D3
10 Preston PR1 95 F8
Sinclair Ct FY8 89 B7
Sineacre La Bickerstaffe L39 7 E1
Kirkby L33, L39 1 E8
Singleton Ave Horwich BL6 31 C5
Lytham St Anne's FY8 89 B8
Read BB12 144 D2
Singleton CE Prim Sch
FY6 152 E1
Singleton Cl PR2 116 F7
Singleton Ct 3 FY1 129 B4
Singleton Rd Weeton PR4 131 F4
Weeton Camp PR4 131 E6
Singleton Row 18 PR1 95 F8
Singleton St 3 FY1 129 B3
Singleton Way PR2 116 F7
Sion Cl PR2 117 F4
Sion Hill PR2 117 F4
Sir Simon's Arc 20 LA1 210 F8
Sir Tom Finney Way
PR1,PR2 117 B3
Six Acre La PR4 74 C6
Sixfields 11 FY5 150 F7
Sixpenny La PR8 20 D1
Sixth Ave Blackpool FY4 109 C7
Bury BL9 32 D4
Size House Village 6
BB4 84 B2
Size St OL12 70 D1
Sizehouse St 25 PR1 95 F8
Sizer St PR1 116 F1
Sizergh Ct LA1 210 D7
Sizergh Rd LA4 213 A5
Skaithe The BB7 223 C7
Skeffington Rd PR1 117 C1
Skeleron La BB7 189 B6
Skelmersdale Coll WN8 18 B4
Skelmersdale Coll
(Westbank Campus)
WN8 18 B1
Skelmersdale Coll
(Westbank Ctr) WN8 9 B8
Skelmersdale Rd L39, WN8 8 B7
Skelmersdale Sports Ctr
WN8 9 C7
Skelmersdale Tourist
Information Ctr WN8 18 B1
Skelshaw Cl BB1 101 A3
Skelton St BB8 169 E5
Skelwith Rd FY3 130 B2
Skerton 1 LA1 213 F2
Skerton Ct LA1 213 F2
Skerton High Sch LA1 213 F2
Skerton Ho 6 LA1 213 F2
Skerton Prim Sch LA1 213 F2
Skiddaw Cl BB12 146 C1
Skiddaw Rd Blackpool FY4 109 F8
Lancaster LA1 214 A2
Skiddaw St BB1 101 A5
Skip La PR4 94 B3
Skippool Ave FY6 151 E5
Skippool Rd FY5 151 E7
Skipton Ave Carleton FY6 151 C5
Southport PR9 53 C6
Skipton Cl
Bamber Bridge PR5 96 F2
Blackpool FY4 129 F1
Skipton Cres PR2 117 E5
Skipton Gate LA6 236 C2
Skipton Old Rd Colne BB8 170 C7
Foulridge BB8 191 E2
Skipton Rd
Barnoldswick BB18 200 B2
Barnoldswick, Coates BB18 200 D4
Colne BB8 169 E6
Earby BB18 201 B3
Foulridge BB8 191 E2
Lytham St Anne's FY8 89 B6
Trawden BB8 170 B3
Skipton Rd Bsns Ctr
BB18 200 C3
Skipton St
Morecambe LA4 212 D5
Nappa BB7 225 E7
Skitham La PR3 176 D4
Skull House La WN6 19 D8
Skye Cl OL10 32 F1
Skye Cres BB1 101 C3
Slack BB12 145 F6
Slack Booth BB8 170 C1
Slack Gate OL12 51 F8
Slack House Cotts L39 16 A3
Slack La LA2 205 C1
Slack's La PR6 43 B2
Slackey La PR9 53 C4
Slackwood La LA5 218 E2
Slade La Padiham BB12 145 C1
Padiham BB12 145 C2
Slade St PR1 95 E7
Sladen St OL12 51 F1
Slaidburn Ave
Burnley BB10 127 D5
Rawtenstall BB4 85 A4
Slaidburn Cres PR9 53 B5
Slaidburn Dr
Accrington BB5 103 A4
Lancaster LA1 211 A3
Slaidburn Pl PR2 118 A2
Slaidburn Rd
Fulwood PR2 118 A2
Lowgill LA2 233 E4
Waddington BB7 186 A5
Slaidburn Wlk 5 FY3 130 A8
Slape La LA6 234 C8
Slate La WN8 17 C2
Slater Ave Colne BB8 169 D6
Horwich BL6 31 C4
Slater La
Leyland, Moss Side PR5 58 C8
Leyland, Seven Stars PR5 58 D8
Slater Rd FY5 172 C2
Slater St BB2 100 C1
Slinger Rd FY5 172 C3
Slip Inn La 28 LA1 210 F8
Sliven Clod Rd BB4 104 E2
Sluice La L40 38 B3
Slyne Hall Hts LA2 216 A1
Slyne Rd
Bolton-le-S LA2,LA5 216 A2
Lancaster LA1 213 F3
Morecambe LA4 213 C4
Smalden La BB7 224 A3
Small La Drummersdale L40 23 E8
Ormskirk L39 15 F4
Ormskirk, Clieves Hills L39 15 A3
Small La N L39 22 E2
Small La S L39 14 D6
Smalley Croft PR1 95 F3
Smalley St Burnley BB11 127 B4
Standish WN6 28 E1
Smalley Thorn Brow BB6 122 F6
Smalley Way BB2 100 E2
Smallshaw Ind Est BB11 126 C4
Smallshaw La
Burnley BB11 126 B5
Burnley BB12 126 B6
Smallshaw Rd OL12 51 A4
Smallwood Hey Rd PR3 196 C5
Smeaton St BL6 31 C2
Smethurst Hall Pk WN5 10 C2
Smethurst Hall Rd BL9 32 F4
Smethurst Rd WN5 10 C2
Smirthwaite St BB11 126 D5
Smith Ave PR4 72 F1
Smith Brow BL6 30 C3
Smith Cl PR2 138 C1
Smith Croft PR5 58 B8
Smith La BL7 46 F1
Smith Rd FY5 172 D2
Smith St Adlington PR7 29 F6
13 Bamber Bridge PR5 76 F8
Barnoldswick BB18 200 A1
Burnley BB12 126 E6
Bury BL9 32 A3
Chorley PR7 42 D6
Colne BB8 169 C4
3 Kirkham PR4 112 F5
Nelson BB9 147 F8
Ramsbottom BL0 49 B5
Skelmersdale WN8 17 D1
Whittle-le-W PR6 60 C8
Worsthorne BB10 128 B5
Smith's La PR4 56 A1
Smithills Cl PR6 60 E1
Smithills Hall Cl BL0 49 C5
Smithy Bridge St 8 BB5 102 D3
Smithy Brow
Abbeystead LA2 226 F1
Andertons Mill WN6 27 C8
Haslingden BB4 84 B4
Newburgh WN8 26 A1
Smithy Brow Ct BB4 84 B4
Smithy Cl Brindle PR6 77 F5
Formby L37 12 B4
Garstang PR3 178 C8
Stalmine FY6 174 C7
Smithy Croft FY8 89 C6
Smithy Fold Rochdale OL12 51 C1
Wrea Green PR4 112 B4
Smithy Gn L37 12 B4
Smithy How LA6 238 E3
Smithy La Brindle PR6 77 F6
Claughton PR3 179 B2
Colne BB8 169 B8
Haskayne L39 14 A6
Heysham LA3 208 E6
Holmeswood L40 37 C6
Hurlston Green L40 23 B3
Lytham St Anne's FY8 89 C6
Mawdesley L40 39 C2
Much Hoole PR4 73 E2
Ormskirk L39 6 A6
Preesall FY6 195 B3
Staining FY3 130 E6
Stalmine FY6 174 C7
Westhouse LA6 236 E4
Smithy Lane Ends L40 23 D6
Smithy Mews 9 FY1 129 C7
Smithy Row BB7 162 E1
Smithy St
2 Bamber Bridge PR5 76 E8
9 Haslingden BB4 84 B3
7 Ramsbottom BL0 49 C6
Smithy Wlk 3 L40 24 E5
Smithyfield Ave BB10 127 F6
Snaefell Rd BB2 100 E1
Snape Gn Carr Cross PR8 22 D8
Southport PR8 35 E1
Snape La LA5 219 F1
Snape Rake La PR3 180 D4
Snape St BB3 80 F3
Snapewood La PR3 199 B3
Snell Cres BB8 169 F6
Snell Gr BB8 169 F6
Sniddle Hill La BB3 63 E8
Snipe Cl Blackpool FY3 130 B6
Cleveleys FY5 172 F5
Snipewood PR7 40 B6
Snodworth Rd BB6 122 D7
Snow Hill PR1 95 F8
Snow St BB1 100 F6
Snowden Ave
Blackburn BB1 100 E7
Morecambe LA3 212 A3
Snowden St BB12 126 B6
Snowdon Cl FY1 129 D3
Snowdon Dr BL6 31 C5
Snowdon Rd FY8 110 A2
Snowdrop Cl
Clayton-le-W PR5 76 E2
Haslingden BB4 66 F8
Snowhill La PR3 199 F6
Snowshill Cres FY5 150 F7
Sod Hall La PR4 75 A5
Sollam's Cl 4 PR5 96 F2
Sollom La PR4 56 B2
Solway Ave BB2 99 F1
Solway Cl Blackpool FY2 150 C6
Penwortham PR1 95 E3
Somerby Rd LA4 212 F4
Somerford Cl BB12 126 D7
Somersby Cl PR5 96 E3
Somerset Ave
Blackpool FY1 129 D3
Chorley PR7 60 C1
Clitheroe BB7 186 F2
Darwen BB3 80 F3
Lancaster LA1 211 A6
Wilpshire BB1 121 F6
Somerset Cl BB5 102 F3
Somerset Ct FY1 129 D3
Somerset Dr PR8 20 C3
Somerset Gr BB5 102 F7
Somerset Pk PR2 116 B7
Somerset Pl BB9 169 A1
Somerset Rd Leyland PR5 76 B2
Preston PR1 117 A1
Rishton BB1 123 A1
Somerset St BB11 127 A4
Somerset Wlk BB4 67 B8
Sorrel Cl FY5 172 F5
Sorrel Ct 2 PR1 95 C2
Soudan St BB10 147 B2

Sough La Belthorn BB1 ... 82 A7
Blackburn BB1,BB5 ... 101 F2
Sough BB18 ... 192 A7
Sough Rd BB3 ... 64 B7
South Ave
Barnoldswick BB18 ... 200 B3
Chorley PR7 ... 42 D6
Cleveleys FY5 ... 172 C4
Morecambe LA4 ... 212 F5
New Longton PR4 ... 74 F8
South Cliff St 5 PR1 ... 95 E6
South Clifton St FY8 ... 90 B3
South Cross St BL9 ... 32 A1
South Dr Appley Bridge WN6 ... 27 C2
Fulwood PR2 ... 116 E7
Inskip PR4 ... 134 C8
Padiham BB12 ... 125 E8
South End PR1 ... 95 E5
South Gr Barton PR3 ... 136 B8
Fulwood PR2 ... 116 E8
Morecambe LA4 ... 212 F5
South Hey FY8 ... 89 C6
South Holme FY8 ... 90 B4
South King St FY1 ... 129 C5
South Lawn FY1 ... 129 E2
South Meade L31 ... 5 B1
South Meadow La PR1 ... 95 E6
South Meadow St PR1 ... 96 A8
South Moss Rd FY8 ... 89 C7
South Par
8 Barnoldswick BB18 ... 200 B3
Cleveleys FY5 ... 172 E1
South Park Dr FY3 ... 129 F2
South Pine St BL9 ... 32 B2
South Pk FY8 ... 90 A4
South Prom FY8 ... 88 E5
South Rd Bretherton PR5 ... 56 F5
Coppull PR7 ... 41 E1
Lancaster LA1 ... 210 F7
Morecambe LA4 ... 212 G5
South Ribble Mus PR5 ... 59 A8
South Ribble St 8 PR1 ... 96 C6
South Shore Hospl FY4 ... 109 C5
South Shore St
Church BB5 ... 102 E5
Haslingden BB4 ... 84 A3
South Sq Blackpool FY3 ... 129 D6
Cleveleys FY5 ... 172 D5
South St Accrington BB5 ... 103 C5
Accrington, Hillock Vale BB5 ... 103 E8
Bacup OL13 ... 87 A2
Burnley BB11 ... 127 A6
15 Darwen BB3 ... 81 A1
Great Eccleston PR3 ... 154 B5
Haslingden BB4 ... 84 C1
Lytham St Anne's FY8 ... 90 D4
Newchurch BB4 ... 85 E1
Ramsbottom BL0 ... 49 D6
16 Rawtenstall BB4 ... 85 A3
South Strand FY7 ... 172 E7
South Terr Ormskirk L39 ... 15 E4
Ramsbottom BL0 ... 67 C2
South Valley Dr BB8 ... 169 C3
South View
Bamber Bridge PR5 ... 76 B7
Belmont BL7 ... 45 C5
Bretherton PR5 ... 56 F5
4 Great Harwood BB6 ... 123 C5
20 Haslingden BB4 ... 84 B3
Kirkham PR4 ... 113 A4
2 Lostock Hall PR5 ... 76 A7
Nelson BB9 ... 147 D7
Saltcotes, Moss Side FY8 ... 111 D1
Simonstone BB12 ... 144 E3
South View St 5 OL14 ... 108 C1
South View Terr 2 PR5 ... 59 A8
South Warton St FY8 ... 90 C3
South Westby St FY8 ... 90 B3
Southbank Ave FY4 ... 110 A7
Southbank Rd PR8 ... 34 C5
Southbourne Ave FY6 ... 151 C2
Southbourne Rd FY3 ... 130 A2
Southbrook Rd PR5 ... 75 F1
Southcliffe BB6 ... 123 B6
Southcliffe Ave BB12 ... 126 C7
Southdene WN8 ... 26 B2
Southdown Dr FY5 ... 151 D8
Southdowns Rd PR7 ... 42 D6
Southern Ave
Burnley BB12 ... 126 C7
Preston PR1 ... 96 C6
Southern Cl PR3 ... 139 A6
Southern Par PR1 ... 96 B6
Southern Rd PR8 ... 34 A6
Southey Cl PR2 ... 116 F7
Southey St 2 BB11 ... 126 E6
Southfield PR4 ... 73 E3
Southfield Dr
New Longton PR4 ... 74 F7
Poulton-le-F FY3 ... 130 C8
West Bradford BB7 ... 186 F5
Southfield Gdns PR4 ... 73 E3
Southfield La BB10,BB8 ... 148 C7
Southfield Rd BL0 ... 49 A2
Southfield Sq BB9 ... 147 F8
Southfield St BB9 ... 147 F7
Southfield Terr BB8 ... 170 E6
Southfleet Ave FY7 ... 193 E1
Southfleet Pl FY7 ... 193 E1
Southfold Pl FY8 ... 90 A4
Southgate Fleetwood FY7 ... 172 D8
Fulwood PR2 ... 116 D5
Morecambe LA3 ... 213 A2
Preston PR1 ... 116 F1
Whitworth OL12 ... 51 C7
Southgates PR7 ... 41 D3
Southlands PR4 ... 113 A4
Southlands Ave PR5 ... 96 C1
Southlands Dr PR5 ... 58 C8
Southlands High Sch PR7 ... 42 A5
Southport & Formby District General Hospl PR8 ... 34 E4
Southport Barn Cotts BB7 ... 224 C1
Southport Coll PR9 ... 34 C7
Southport General Infmy PR8 ... 34 D5
Southport New Rd
Banks PR4,PR9 ... 54 D3
Holmes PR4 ... 55 D3
Southport Old Rd L37 ... 12 B7
Southport Pleasureland PR8 ... 33 F7
Southport Rd Chorley PR7 ... 42 A8
Formby L37 ... 12 A5
Haskayne L39 ... 14 A6
Hurlston L40 ... 23 A2
Maghull L31, L39 ... 5 B5
Newtown PR7 ... 58 B2
Ormskirk L39, L40 ... 15 D8
Scarisbrick L40,PR8 ... 22 E7
Southport PR8 ... 35 B2
Southport Terr PR6 ... 42 E7
Southport Zoo PR8 ... 33 F7
Southside PR7 ... 59 C3
Southway Fleetwood FY7 ... 193 D1
Skelmersdale WN8 ... 18 B1
Southwood Ave FY7 ... 193 F3
Southwood Cl FY8 ... 89 E4
Southwood Dr BB5 ... 103 E3
Southworth Ave FY4 ... 109 E7
Southworth St BB2 ... 100 D2
Southworth Way FY5 ... 172 E5
Sovereign Gate FY4 ... 109 F5
Sow Clough Rd OL13 ... 86 D1
Sower Carr La FY6 ... 174 D4
Sowerby Ave FY4 ... 109 D8
Sowerby Rd PR3 ... 155 E3
Sowerby St 4 BB12 ... 125 C8
Spa Fold L40 ... 17 A4
Spa Garth BB7 ... 164 F8
Spa La L40, WN8 ... 17 C4
Spa Rd PR1 ... 95 D7
Spa St Burnley BB12 ... 126 F7
Padiham BB12 ... 125 D8
3 Preston PR1 ... 95 D8
Spark La L40 ... 38 B6
Sparrow Hill WN6,WN8 ... 27 A2
Sparth Ave BB5 ... 123 F3
Sparth Rd BB5 ... 123 F3
Speakmans Dr WN6 ... 19 C6
Speedwell Cl FY5 ... 172 F5
Speedwell St BB2 ... 100 B2
Speke St BB2 ... 100 B2
Spen Brook Cotts BB12 ... 167 C2
Spen Brow LA2 ... 233 B6
Spen Cnr FY4 ... 129 D1
Spen Farm FY4 ... 110 C8
Spen La PR4 ... 113 E6
Spen Pl FY4 ... 109 F8
Spenbrook Rd BB12 ... 167 C3
Spencer Ct FY1 ... 129 C7
Spencer Gr BB6 ... 123 B5
Spencer St Accrington BB5 ... 103 D6
Burnley BB10 ... 147 A1
Ramsbottom BL0 ... 49 B5
10 Rawtenstall BB4 ... 85 A7
Spencer's La Orrell WN5 ... 10 D7
Southport L39 ... 21 B3
Spencers Dr PR4 ... 56 A8
Spencers Fold BB12 ... 167 F1
Spencers La WN8 ... 9 B7
Spendmore La PR7 ... 41 E1
Spenleach La BL8 ... 48 D3
Spenser Cl BB10 ... 128 C4
Spenser St BB12 ... 125 D7
Spey Cl Leyland PR5 ... 58 E8
Standish WN6 ... 28 D1
Speyside FY4 ... 109 D7
Spindle Berry Ct BB5 ... 103 C4
Spinners Ct LA1 ... 210 F7
Spinners Gn OL12 ... 51 F2
Spinners Sq PR5 ... 76 E7
Spinney Brow PR2 ... 117 D4
Spinney Cl Lucas Green PR6 ... 60 B6
New Longton PR4 ... 74 F8
Ormskirk L39 ... 15 D3
Spinney Croft PR3 ... 139 A7
Spinney La LA5 ... 218 C8
Spinney The Arnside LA5 ... 218 C8
Blackburn BB2 ... 100 A8
Burnley BB12 ... 126 D8
Chorley PR6 ... 60 C3
Cleveleys FY5 ... 150 F7
Edgworth BL7 ... 47 C2
Formby L37 ... 12 A5
Grindleton BB7 ... 187 B7
Heysham LA3 ... 209 A7
Lancaster LA1 ... 211 B5
Penwortham PR1 ... 94 F3
Poulton-le-F FY6 ... 151 E4
Rochdale OL12 ... 51 D3
Tarleton PR4 ... 56 A7
Spinning Ave BB1 ... 81 D8
Spinnings The BL0 ... 49 C3
Spire Cl BB3 ... 64 D8
Spiredale Dr WN6 ... 28 F2
Spires Gr PR4 ... 115 E5
Spod Rd OL12 ... 51 D1
Spodden Cotts OL12 ... 70 D2
Spodden Fold OL12 ... 51 C8
Spotland Tops OL12 ... 51 B1
Spout La LA2 ... 235 F1
Spouthouse La BB5 ... 124 F1
Spread Eagle St BB5 ... 102 C5
Spring Ave BB6 ... 123 C6
Spring Bank
Appley Bridge WN6 ... 19 C8
Garstang PR3 ... 178 C6
9 Preston PR1 ... 95 E7
Rochdale OL12 ... 51 D4
Silverdale LA5 ... 218 C3
Spring Bank Terr BB2 ... 100 C2
Spring Brook Ho BB5 ... 123 F2
Spring Cl Kirkby L33 ... 1 A5
Ramsbottom BL0 ... 49 B6
Southport PR8 ... 34 A5
Spring Cres PR6 ... 60 E5
Spring Field WA11 ... 8 E2
Spring Gardens Rd BB8 ... 169 D4
Spring Gardens St 4 BB4 ... 68 F8
Spring Gardens Terr 3 BB12 ... 145 C1
Spring Gdn St 38 LA1 ... 210 F8
Spring Gdns
8 Accrington BB5 ... 103 C5
2 Bacup OL13 ... 87 A3
11 Darwen BB3 ... 64 A8
Freckleton PR4 ... 92 B8
12 Horwich BL6 ... 31 B4
Leyland PR5 ... 58 F8
Lytham St Anne's FY8 ... 109 F1
Penwortham PR1 ... 95 F2
Rawtenstall BB4 ... 68 F6
Spring Gr BB8 ... 170 C6
Spring Hall BB5 ... 123 F5
Spring Hill
5 Blackburn BB1 ... 100 E5
Freckleton PR4 ... 92 D7
Spring Hill Cty Prim Sch BB5 ... 103 B5
Spring Hill Rd
Accrington BB5 ... 102 F4
Burnley BB11 ... 126 F4
Spring La Blackburn BB2 ... 100 B3
Colne BB8 ... 169 D5
Haslingden BB4 ... 84 B4
Nab's Head PR5 ... 98 C8
Spring Mdws BB3 ... 64 D7
Spring Mdw PR5 ... 76 E1
Spring Mews PR6 ... 60 E6
Spring Pl Colne BB8 ... 169 D5
Whitworth OL12 ... 70 D3
Spring Rd WN5 ... 10 F8
Spring Row BB8 ... 170 C6
Spring Side
Rawtenstall BB4 ... 68 F6
Whitworth OL12 ... 70 D4
Spring Side Cotts BL7 ... 46 A2
Spring St Accrington BB5 ... 102 F4
Bacup OL13 ... 86 F1
Bank Lane BL0 ... 49 D7
1 Cornholme OL14 ... 108 C1
Horwich BL6 ... 31 B4
6 Leyland PR5 ... 76 B1
Nelson BB9 ... 147 C7
5 Oswaldtwistle BB5 ... 102 E4
Ramsbottom BL0 ... 49 B6
Rawtenstall BB4 ... 85 A8
Rishton BB1 ... 123 B2
Spring Terr
Accrington BB4 ... 104 F2
4 Bacup OL13 ... 69 D8
Langho BB6 ... 142 D1
Oswaldtwistle BB5 ... 102 D4
Rochdale OL11 ... 51 A1
Spring Terr S 5 BB4 ... 84 E2
Spring Vale PR3 ... 204 B3
Spring Vale Garden Village BB3 ... 64 C6
Spring Vale Rd BB3 ... 64 B7
Spring View
Blackburn BB2 ... 100 C5
Over Town BB10 ... 107 A8
Spring Villas 18 OL14 ... 108 B1
Spring Wood Nature Trail BB7 ... 143 E5
Spring Wood St BL0 ... 49 B7
Spring Yd 3 BB8 ... 169 D5
Springbank BB9 ... 168 E5
Springbank Ave FY5 ... 173 C2
Springbank Gdns BB4 ... 104 F2
Springbrook Ave FY5 ... 150 F8
Springcroft 1 PR5 ... 76 C3
Springdale Rd BB6 ... 122 C8
Springfield Arnside LA5 ... 237 B2
Blacko BB9 ... 168 D8
High Bentham LA2 ... 233 E8
Springfield Ave
Accrington BB5 ... 102 F4
Bacup OL13 ... 87 A3
Blackburn BB2 ... 99 E1
Earby BB18 ... 201 C1
Kirkham PR4 ... 112 E5
Springfield Bank BB11 ... 127 B5
Springfield Cl
Burscough L40 ... 24 D2
Formby L37 ... 11 C2
Whalley BB7 ... 143 D6
Springfield Cres LA2 ... 233 E8
Springfield Ct 1 FY3 ... 129 E3
Springfield Dr
Newchurch BB4 ... 85 E1
Thornton FY5 ... 173 B4
Springfield Flats 7 BB3 ... 64 A8
Springfield Gdns
Bolton-le-S LA6 ... 216 F5
Scorton PR3 ... 199 E6
Springfield Rd
Adlington PR6 ... 30 A8
Springfield Rd *continued*
Blackpool FY1 ... 129 B6
Burnley BB11 ... 127 A4
Burnley BB11 ... 127 B5
1 Chorley PR7 ... 42 C8
Coppull PR7 ... 28 E8
Great Harwood BB6 ... 123 B4
Horwich BL6 ... 31 D1
Leyland PR5 ... 58 D7
Lytham St Anne's FY8 ... 88 E6
Maghull L39 ... 5 F6
Nelson BB9 ... 147 E6
Ramsbottom BL0 ... 49 A2
Rawtenstall BB4 ... 85 B3
Springfield Rd N PR7 ... 28 E8
Springfield St
Blackburn BB2 ... 100 B3
Darwen BB3 ... 64 A8
Lancaster LA1 ... 210 F7
Morecambe LA4 ... 212 C4
Oswaldtwistle BB5 ... 102 D4
Preston PR1 ... 116 E1
Springfield Terr
Blackburn BB2 ... 100 A1
Thornton FY7 ... 173 A6
Springfield View BB11 ... 105 C5
Springhill Ave OL13 ... 69 D8
Springhill Prim Sch BB5 ... 103 A4
Springhill Villas OL13 ... 69 D8
Springmount BB18 ... 201 C2
Springmount Dr WN8 ... 26 C5
Springs Brow PR7 ... 28 D5
Springs Rd Chorley PR6 ... 60 D2
Longridge PR3 ... 139 B8
Springsands Cl PR2 ... 117 E5
Springthorpe St 7 BB3 ... 64 B6
Springvale BB5 ... 102 F4
Springvale Bsns Pk 1 BB3 ... 64 B6
Springwater Ave BL0 ... 49 A3
Springwood Cl PR1 ... 96 A3
Springwood Dr
Chorley PR7 ... 42 E5
Rufford L40 ... 38 A5
Springwood Rd BB10 ... 127 E5
Sprodley Dr WN6 ... 27 B2
Spruce Ave Bury BL9 ... 32 B2
Lancaster LA1 ... 210 F4
Spruce Cl PR2 ... 117 C7
Spruce Ct BB5 ... 103 E8
Spruce St BL0 ... 49 B5
Spruce Way L37 ... 11 C3
Sprucewood Cl BB5 ... 103 D6
Spurrier St PR5 ... 76 A4
Spymers Croft L37 ... 12 A6
Square House La PR9 ... 54 C6
Square La Burscough L40 ... 24 E3
Catforth PR4 ... 134 F4
Square St BL0 ... 49 C6
Square The Blackpool FY3 ... 130 A2
Brinscall PR6 ... 61 F7
Burton-in-K LA6 ... 234 B7
Cleveleys FY5 ... 172 D5
Cumeragh Village PR3 ... 137 F5
Great Eccleston PR3 ... 154 B5
1 Leyland PR5 ... 76 B2
Scorton PR3 ... 199 E6
Storth LA7 ... 237 F5
Waddington BB7 ... 186 B4
Squire Rd BB9 ... 147 F8
Squire's Gate Rd PR2 ... 116 C3
Squires Cl PR5 ... 97 E2
Squires Ct 6
Blackpool FY4 ... 109 C5
8 Lytham St Anne's FY8 ... 90 B3
Squires Gate La FY4 ... 109 D5
Squires Gate Link Rd FY4 ... 110 C7
Squires Rd PR1 ... 95 C6
Squires Wood PR2 ... 117 D6
Squirrel Fold PR2 ... 117 F2
Squirrel Gn L37 ... 11 C5
Squirrel La BL6 ... 31 A4
Squirrel's Chase PR5 ... 76 A7
Squirrels Cl BB5 ... 103 E8
Stable Cl Gisburn BB7 ... 225 B3
Kirkham PR4 ... 113 A6
Stable La PR6 ... 61 A7
Stables Cl BB4 ... 85 A6
Stack Croft PR6 ... 77 A2
Stack La OL13 ... 70 B8
Stackhouses The 2 BB11 ... 127 A6
Stadium Ave FY4 ... 109 E5
Staffa Cres BB1 ... 101 D4
Stafford Ave FY6 ... 151 D1
Stafford Moreton Way L31 ... 5 D1
Stafford Rd
10 Preston PR1 ... 117 A1
Southport PR8 ... 34 A1
Stafford St Burnley BB10 ... 127 A7
Darwen BB3 ... 80 F4
Nelson BB9 ... 148 A8
Skelmersdale WN8 ... 17 D1
Staghills Rd BB4 ... 85 D1
Stainburn Cl WN6 ... 19 E6
Stainforth Ave FY2 ... 150 E5
Staining Ave PR2 ... 94 F8
Staining CE Sch FY3 ... 130 D5
Staining Old Rd FY3 ... 130 D7
Staining Rd FY3 ... 130 C6
Staining Rise FY3 ... 130 E5
Stainning Rd W FY3 ... 130 D5
Stainton Dr BB12 ... 126 E8
Stainton Gr 1 LA4 ... 213 A4
Stakepool Dr PR3 ... 196 E4
Stakes Hall Pl BB2 ... 100 C2
Stalls Rd LA3 ... 208 F2
Stalmine Prim Sch FY6 ... 174 D7
Stamford Ave FY4 ... 109 D7
Stamford Ct FY8 ... 88 D8
Stamford Dr PR6 ... 60 C5
Stamford Pl BB7 ... 186 F1
Stamford Rd
Skelmersdale WN8 ... 17 D2
Southport PR8 ... 34 B2
Stanagate PR4 ... 114 C1
Stanah Cty Inf Sch FY5 ... 173 D1
Stanah Cty Jun Sch FY5 ... 173 D1
Stanah Gdns FY5 ... 173 E2
Stanah Rd FY5 ... 173 E2
Stanalee La PR3 ... 158 B8
Stanbury Cl OL10 ... 32 D1
Stanbury Dr BB10 ... 147 E2
Stancliffe St BB2 ... 100 C3
Standen Hall Cl BB10 ... 147 E3
Standen Hall Dr BB10 ... 147 D3
Standen Rd BB7 ... 164 F7
Standen Road Bglws BB7 ... 164 F7
Standhouse La L39 ... 15 C2
Standing Stone La BB8,BB9 ... 191 A2
Standish Com High Sch WN6 ... 28 C2
Standish St Burnley BB11 ... 127 A6
Chorley PR7 ... 42 D7
Standridge Clough La BB18 ... 201 D1
Standroyd Dr BB8 ... 170 A5
Standroyd Rd BB8 ... 170 A5
Stanedge Cl BL0 ... 49 C4
Stanford Gdns BB2 ... 101 A1
Stanford Hall Cres BL0 ... 49 B4
Stang Top Rd BB9 ... 167 F6
Stangate L31 ... 5 B2
Stanhill La BB5 ... 102 C4
Stanhill Rd BB1,BB5 ... 101 F4
Stanhope Ave LA3 ... 213 A3
Stanhope Ct LA3 ... 213 B3
Stanhope Rd 1 FY1 ... 129 C7
Stanhope St Burnley BB12 ... 126 F7
Darwen BB3 ... 81 A2
Preston PR1 ... 116 E2
Stanier Pl BL6 ... 31 C2
Stanifield Cl PR5 ... 76 B3
Stanifield La PR5 ... 76 C5
Stankelt Rd LA5 ... 218 C2
Stanlawe Rd L37 ... 11 E6
Stanley Ave Cleveleys FY5 ... 172 E2
Hutton PR4 ... 94 D2
Leyland PR5 ... 76 C4
Penwortham PR1 ... 95 E5
Poulton-le-F FY6 ... 151 D3
Southport PR8 ... 33 F3
Stanley Cl PR3 ... 139 B7
Stanley Croft PR4 ... 136 B3
Stanley Ct Accrington BB5 ... 103 D7
Burscough Bridge L40 ... 24 E5
Chipping PR3 ... 182 E3
Kirkham PR4 ... 113 B4
Stanley Dr Darwen BB3 ... 64 B5
Hornby LA2 ... 232 B7
Stanley Fold PR5 ... 75 F8
Stanley Gate
Fleetwood FY7 ... 193 D3
Mellor BB2 ... 120 E2
Stanley Gr Fleetwood FY7 ... 193 D2
Horwich BL6 ... 31 D1
Penwortham PR1 ... 95 A5
Stanley High Sch PR9 ... 52 F4
Stanley Mount 7 OL13 ... 86 F3
Stanley Park Cl FY3 ... 129 F3
Stanley Pl 9 Chorley PR7 ... 42 C8
Lancaster LA1 ... 210 D8
Preston PR1 ... 95 E7
Stanley Prim & Inf Sch FY3 ... 130 B2
Stanley Range BB2 ... 100 B1
Stanley Rd Blackpool FY1 ... 129 C4
Fleetwood FY7 ... 193 F3
Formby L37 ... 11 E6
Kirkham PR4 ... 112 F7
Leyland PR5 ... 76 C4
Lytham St Anne's FY8 ... 89 D3
Morecambe LA3 ... 212 B3
Orrell WN8 ... 10 B7
Stanley St Accrington BB5 ... 103 D6
Bacup OL13 ... 86 F4
Blackburn BB1 ... 101 B6
Brierfield BB9 ... 147 B6
6 Burnley BB11 ... 126 F5
Carnforth LA5 ... 217 D1
Colne BB8 ... 169 D5
Kirkham PR4 ... 113 B4
10 Leyland PR5 ... 76 B1
Longridge PR3 ... 139 A8
Morecambe LA4 ... 212 E6
Nelson BB9 ... 147 D8
Ormskirk L39 ... 15 F5
Oswaldtwistle BB5 ... 102 D3
Preston PR1 ... 96 B8
Ramsbottom BL0 ... 49 B5
Rochdale OL12 ... 51 E1
Southport PR9 ... 34 B8
Stanley Terr PR1 ... 95 E7
Stanley Villas PR5 ... 98 B4
Stanley Way WN8 ... 17 E3
Stanleyfield Cl PR1 ... 117 A1
Stanleyfield Rd PR1 ... 117 A1
Stanmore Ave FY4 ... 109 F6
Stanmore Dr LA1 ... 210 E5
Stannanought Rd WN8 ... 18 E2
Stanning Cl PR5 ... 58 E8
Stanning St PR5 ... 59 A8
Stanrose Cl BL7 ... 46 E1

Stansfeld St BB2 ... 100 C3
Stansfield Ave L31 ... 5 F1
Stansfield Cl 7 BB9 ... 168 D4
Stansfield Rd BB4 ... 68 E8
Stansfield St
2 Bacup OL13 ... 69 C8
Blackpool FY1 ... 129 C1
Burnley BB11 ... 126 B5
6 Darwen BB3 ... 64 A8
Nelson BB9 ... 147 E8
Stansfield Terr 14 OL14 ... 108 B1
Stansford Ct PR1 ... 95 D4
Stansted Rd PR7 ... 42 A7
Stansy Ave LA3 ... 212 B1
Stanthorpe Wlk BB10 ... 147 A1
Stanworth Rd BB9 ... 147 D8
Stanworth St BB10 ... 128 B5
Stanworth Terr PR6 ... 79 B4
Stanzaker Hall Dr PR3 ... 156 D7
Stapleton Rd L37 ... 11 D1
Star Bank OL13 ... 69 D7
Star La BL6 ... 30 F3
Star St Accrington BB5 ... 102 F5
Darwen BB3 ... 81 B1
Starbeck Ave FY4 ... 129 D1
Starfield Cl FY8 ... 90 A4
Starkie St Blackburn BB1 ... 100 F5
Burnley BB11 ... 126 E5
Darwen BB3 ... 64 B8
12 Leyland PR5 ... 76 B1
Preston PR1 ... 95 F6
Starr Gate FY4 ... 109 B4
Starrgate Dr PR2 ... 115 E1
Startifants La PR3 ... 181 F4
Startifants Lane End PR3 ... 182 A5
Startley Nook PR4 ... 75 B6
States Rd FY8 ... 89 B6
Statham Rd WN8 ... 17 E3
Statham Way L39 ... 15 E4
Station App 1
Burscough Bridge L40 ... 24 E5
Ormskirk L39 ... 15 F5
Station Ave WN5 ... 10 D5
Station Brow PR5 ... 76 B2
Station Cl Rishton BB1 ... 102 A8
Wilpshire BB1 ... 121 F4
Station Ct LA2 ... 232 B7
Station La Burton-in-K LA6 ... 234 B7
Nateby PR3 ... 198 B1
Newsham PR3 ... 136 A5
Scorton PR3 ... 199 D7
Station Par OL14 ... 107 F1
Station Rd Adlington PR7 ... 30 A6
Arnside LA5 ... 237 C2
Bamber Bridge PR5 ... 76 E8
Banks PR9 ... 53 F5
Barnoldswick BB18 ... 200 B2
Blackpool FY4 ... 109 B8
Blackrod BL6 ... 30 E1
Burton-in-K LA6 ... 234 B8
Clitheroe BB7 ... 164 E8
Coppull PR7 ... 41 F1
3 Cornholme OL14 ... 108 C1
Croston PR5 ... 57 B3
Edgworth BL7 ... 47 C4
Fleetwood FY7 ... 194 A4
Foulridge BB8 ... 191 D1
Great Harwood BB6 ... 123 D5
Haskayne L39 ... 13 E7
Haslingden BB4 ... 84 B4
Haslingden, Bridge End BB4 ... 67 A7
Hesketh Bank PR4 ... 72 F3
Hest Bank LA2 ... 215 D1
High Bentham LA2 ... 233 D7
Hoghton PR5 ... 98 B2
Hornby LA2 ... 232 B7
Huncoat BB5 ... 124 E2
2 Kirkham PR4 ... 112 F5
Lancaster LA1 ... 210 E8
Lytham St Anne's FY8 ... 90 B3
Maghull L31 ... 5 A6
Morecambe LA4 ... 212 E5
New Longton PR4 ... 74 F8
Ormskirk L39 ... 15 F6
Padiham BB12 ... 125 C8
Parbold WN8 ... 26 C2
Poulton-le-F FY6 ... 151 E4
Ramsbottom BL8 ... 48 F1
Rimington BB7 ... 188 E8
Rishton BB1 ... 123 A1
Rufford L40 ... 38 D4
Salwick PR4 ... 114 C4
Singleton FY6 ... 152 E1
Southport PR8 ... 20 C5
Thornton FY5 ... 173 D1
Walmer Bridge PR4 ... 73 D4
Whalley BB7 ... 143 C5
Whitworth OL12 ... 70 D3
Whitworth, Broadley OL12 ... 51 C5
Wrea Green PR4 ... 112 B4
Station Sq FY8 ... 90 A3
Station Terr
Abbey Village PR6 ... 79 C2
Blackpool FY4 ... 109 B8
Station View BB6 ... 142 D1
Station Way Garstang PR3 ... 178 C8
Hornby LA2 ... 232 B7
Staunton St LA5 ... 217 D3
Staveley Ave L40 ... 24 E4
Staveley Pl PR2 ... 115 E2
Staveley Rd
Skelmersdale WN8 ... 17 E3
Southport PR8 ... 20 D4
Staynall La FY6 ... 174 B4
Stead St BL0 ... 49 C6
Steam Traction Mus BB7 ... 225 C1
Sted Terr BB1 ... 100 E6
Steeley La PR6 ... 42 D7
Steeple View PR2 ... 95 D8
Steer St BB10 ... 147 B1
Steeton Rd FY3 ... 151 B1
Stefano Rd 1 PR1 ... 96 C8
Steiner St BB5 ... 103 A6
Steiner's La BB5 ... 102 E7
Stella Maris High Sch
FY7 ... 194 A5
Step Row OL13 ... 86 F5
Stephen St Blackburn BB2 ... 100 B2
Lytham St Anne's FY8 ... 88 E7
Stephendale Ave PR5 ... 77 B8
Stephens Gr LA3 ... 205 D8
Stephenson Dr BB12 ... 126 C7
Stephenson St
2 Chorley PR6 ... 42 E7
Horwich BL6 ... 31 B2
Stephenson Way L37 ... 12 C3
Sterling Pl 4 OL10 ... 32 F1
Sterndale Ave WN6 ... 28 E2
Stevenson Ave 2 PR5 ... 76 C3
Stevenson St E BB5 ... 103 A5
Stevenson St W BB5 ... 102 F5
Steward Ave LA1 ... 211 B5
Stewart Cl LA5 ... 218 B8
Stewart St Blackburn BB2 ... 80 D8
Burnley BB11 ... 127 B4
11 Preston PR1 ... 95 D8
Stiles Ave PR4 ... 94 C1
Stiles The L39 ... 15 E5
Stirling Cl Chorley PR6 ... 42 E7
Clitheroe BB7 ... 164 C6
1 Leyland PR5 ... 76 C1
Stirling Ct
8 Blackpool FY1 ... 129 D7
Lane Bottom BB10 ... 148 B4
Southport PR9 ... 53 A2
Stirling Dr BB1 ... 100 F4
Stirling Rd Blackpool FY3 ... 129 D7
Lancaster LA1 ... 211 A7
Stirling St BB2 ... 100 B1
Stockbridge Cotts BB7 ... 162 E3
Stockbridge Dr BB12 ... 125 E8
Stockbridge Rd BB12 ... 125 D7
Stockclough La BB2 ... 79 D6
Stockdale Cres PR5 ... 76 F8
Stockdove Way FY5 ... 172 E3
Stockdove Wood FY5 ... 172 E3
Stockholm St BB11 ... 126 B5
Stockley Cres L39 ... 7 E6
Stockley Dr WN6 ... 19 E8
Stockpit Rd L33 ... 1 D2
Stocks Cl PR6 ... 78 B1
Stocks Ct 4 FY6 ... 151 D3
Stocks La
Barnoldswick BB7 ... 190 A7
Blackpool FY6 ... 151 A3
Heskin Green PR7 ... 40 E3
Stocks Lane End PR3 ... 178 C2
Stocks Park Dr BL6 ... 31 C3
Stocks Rd PR2 ... 116 C2
Stocks St 7 PR1 ... 95 E8
Stocksgate OL12 ... 51 B2
Stockwood Cl BB2 ... 100 A8
Stockydale Rd FY4 ... 110 A6
Stoke Ave FY1 ... 129 D2
Stokes Hall Ave PR5 ... 59 A8
Stone Bridge La BB5 ... 102 E3
Stone Cl BL0 ... 49 A4
Stone Croft PR1 ... 95 D2
Stone Cross Gdns PR3 ... 178 D2
Stone Edge Rd BB9 ... 168 E6
Stone Edge View BB9 ... 168 E6
Stone Hall La WN8 ... 19 A5
Stone Hill Dr BB1 ... 122 A1
Stone Hill La OL12 ... 51 A2
Stone Holme Terr BB4 ... 85 A8
Stone House Fold BB11 ... 106 E6
Stone Moor Bottom
BB12 ... 125 C6
Stone Pits BL0 ... 67 E3
Stone Row Head LA1 ... 211 C8
Stone St Haslingden BB4 ... 83 F2
Rawtenstall BB4 ... 68 F8
Stonebarn Dr L31 ... 5 C3
Stonebridge Cl 6 PR5 ... 76 C8
Stonebridge Terr PR3 ... 139 A7
Stonechat Cl FY3 ... 130 B6
Stonecroft BB9 ... 168 E6
Stonecroft Rd PR5 ... 58 D7
Stonecrop WN6 ... 27 D2
Stonedross La LA6 ... 238 E8
Stonefield Longton PR4 ... 73 F8
Penwortham PR1 ... 95 E4
Stonefold Ave PR4 ... 94 C1
Stonefold CE Prim Sch
BB5 ... 84 A7
Stonegate Fold PR6 ... 43 B1
Stonehill Cres OL12 ... 51 A3
Stonehill Dr OL12 ... 51 B3
Stonehill Rd OL12 ... 51 B3
Stoneholme Ind Est BB4 ... 85 A8
Stoneholme Rd BB4 ... 85 A8
Stonehouse Gn PR6 ... 77 B3
Stoneleigh Cl PR8 ... 20 C4
Stoneleigh Ct LA5 ... 218 C3
Stoner Rd PR7 ... 29 F7
Stones Bank Rd BL7 ... 46 B5
Stones La PR3 ... 178 E3
Stoneway Rd FY5 ... 172 E1
Stonewell 17 LA1 ... 210 F8
Stoney Brow WN8 ... 19 B1
Stoney Butts PR2 ... 94 D8
Stoney Croft Dr LA5 ... 217 E6
Stoney Ct BB8 ... 191 E1
Stoney Holt PR5 ... 76 E1
Stoney La Adlington PR7 ... 29 E4
Bamber Bridge PR5 ... 76 C6
Stoney La *continued*
Foulridge BB8 ... 191 E1
Freckleton PR4 ... 92 B5
Galgate LA2 ... 207 B3
Hambleton FY6 ... 174 C2
Longridge PR3 ... 159 C7
Stoney St BB11 ... 127 B4
Stoneybutts 8 BB1 ... 100 E5
Stoneycroft BB10 ... 128 A5
Stoneycroft Ave BL6 ... 31 D4
Stoneycroft Cl BL6 ... 31 D5
Stoneycroft Dr LA5 ... 237 B1
Stoneygate Cleveleys FY5 ... 172 F1
18 Preston PR1 ... 96 A7
Stoneygate La WN6 ... 27 B2
Stoneyholme Prim Sch
BB12 ... 126 F8
Stoneyhurst Ave
Burnley BB10 ... 127 D5
Thornton FY5 ... 151 D8
Stoneyhurst Ht BB9 ... 147 D4
Stoneyroyd OL12 ... 70 D1
Stony Bank PR6 ... 78 A6
Stony Bank Rd BB18 ... 201 C2
Stony Croft Pl 2 FY4 ... 109 C5
Stony Hill Ave FY4 ... 109 C5
Stony La Cockerham PR3 ... 203 F2
Cornholme OL14 ... 108 E2
Hollins Lane PR3 ... 204 D3
Parbold WN6,WN8 ... 26 E4
Stonycroft Ave FY4 ... 109 C5
Stonygate La PR3 ... 140 D6
Stonyhurst PR7 ... 42 C4
Stonyhurst Cl
Blackburn BB2 ... 100 D4
Padiham BB12 ... 125 E6
Stonyhurst Coll BB7 ... 163 A3
Stonyhurst Rd BB2 ... 100 D4
Stoop St BB11 ... 126 C5
Stoopes Hill BB18 ... 201 C2
Stoops Fold BB2 ... 120 E2
Stoops La BB7 ... 188 F8
Stopes Brow BB1,BB3 ... 81 A7
Stopford Ave FY2 ... 150 E2
Stopford Ct 1 BB5 ... 123 F3
Stopgate La L33 ... 1 C7
Stopper La BB7 ... 189 B7
Store St Blackburn BB3 ... 81 A7
17 Haslingden BB4 ... 84 B3
Horwich BL6 ... 31 C4
Store Yard PR4 ... 114 E7
Storey Ave LA1 ... 210 D8
Storey Inst (Coll of F Ed)
LA1 ... 210 E8
Stork Cl FY5 ... 172 F1
Stork St BB3 ... 64 D8
Storrs La LA5 ... 219 B4
Storth CE Prim Sch LA7 ... 237 F5
Storth Rd LA7 ... 237 F3
Stott St 2 Nelson BB9 ... 147 D8
Rochdale OL12 ... 51 F1
Stour Lodge PR2 ... 116 C6
Stourton Rd PR8 ... 20 C4
Stourton St BB1 ... 123 A2
Stout St BB2 ... 100 D4
Straight Up La PR9 ... 35 D8
Strait La LA2 ... 226 F1
Straits BB5 ... 102 E4
Straits La BB12 ... 144 D2
Straits The PR5 ... 98 B2
Strand Rd PR1 ... 95 D7
Strand St W PR2 ... 95 C8
Strand The Blackpool FY1 ... 129 B6
Fleetwood FY7 ... 172 D8
Horwich BL6 ... 31 D3
Strang St 9 BL0 ... 49 C6
Strange St BB11 ... 127 B4
Stransdale Cl PR3 ... 178 B7
Stratfield Pl 5 PR5 ... 76 B1
Stratford Cl Lancaster LA1 ... 213 E3
Southport PR8 ... 20 A6
Stratford Dr PR2 ... 116 D4
Stratford Pl Blackpool FY1 ... 129 E2
2 Fleetwood FY7 ... 193 E4
Stratford Rd Chorley PR6 ... 42 D8
Lytham St Anne's FY8 ... 89 B7
Stratford Way
7 Accrington BB5 ... 103 A7
Colne BB8 ... 169 F5
Strathaven Pl 6 OL10 ... 32 F1
Strathclyde Rd BB1 ... 101 A4
Strathdale FY4 ... 109 F7
Strathmore Cl BL0 ... 49 C4
Strathmore Gr PR7 ... 42 B7
Strathmore Rd PR2 ... 116 E3
Strathyre Cl FY2 ... 150 F5
Stratton Ct BB9 ... 147 E6
Stratton Gr BL6 ... 31 B5
Strawberry Bank BB1 ... 100 D5
Strawberry Mews 1 LA3 ... 208 F8
Streatly Wlk BB2 ... 81 A8
Street The PR6 ... 43 E3
Strellas La LA5 ... 216 C1
Stretton Ave FY4 ... 109 E8
Stretton Dr PR9 ... 34 F8
Stretton Rd BL0 ... 49 A2
Strickens La PR3 ... 179 C6
Strickland Dr LA4 ... 213 A5
Strickland's La FY6 ... 174 D6
Stricklands La PR1 ... 95 E4
Strike La PR4 ... 92 B8
Strike Lane Cty Prim Sch
PR4 ... 92 B8
Strine The L40,PR4 ... 56 A1
Stromness Gr 5 OL10 ... 32 F1
Strongstry Rd BL0 ... 67 C2
Stronsay Pl FY2 ... 150 F6
Stroyan St BB10 ... 127 C5
Strutt St 2 PR1 ... 117 B1
Stryands PR4 ... 94 C1
Sts John Fisher &
Thomas More RC High Sch
BB8 ... 169 B2
Stuart Ave Bacup OL13 ... 69 D8
Morecambe LA4 ... 212 G6
Stuart Cl 13 Darwen BB3 ... 81 A1
Fulwood PR2 ... 117 E3
Stuart Rd Fulwood PR2 ... 117 E3
Thornton FY5 ... 173 C2
Stuart St Accrington BB5 ... 103 B7
5 Barnoldswick BB18 ... 200 C2
Stub La L40 ... 24 A2
Stubbins La Catterall PR3 ... 178 F2
Ramsbottom BL0 ... 49 C8
Sabden BB7 ... 145 A7
Stubbins Prim Sch BL0 ... 67 D1
Stubbins St BL0 ... 67 C1
Stubbins Vale Rd BL0 ... 67 C1
Stubbins Vale Terr BL0 ... 67 B1
Stubbylee La OL13 ... 69 F8
Stubley Holme 5 OL14 ... 108 A1
Stubley La OL14 ... 108 B1
Studfold PR7 ... 60 B2
Studholme Ave PR1 ... 95 E2
Studholme Cl 8 PR1 ... 95 E2
Studholme Cres PR1 ... 95 E2
Stump Cross La BB7 ... 224 F5
Stump Hall Rd BB12 ... 145 F7
Stump La PR6 ... 42 D8
Stunstead BB8 ... 170 C2
Stunstead Rd BB8 ... 170 C3
Sturgess Cl L39 ... 15 F7
Sturminster Cl 5 PR1 ... 95 E2
Styan St FY7 ... 194 A4
Stydd La PR3 ... 140 E4
Sudell Ave L31 ... 5 F2
Sudell Cl BB3 ... 81 C1
Sudell Cross 20 BB1 ... 100 E5
Sudell La L31, L39 ... 5 E6
Sudell Prim Sch BB3 ... 81 B1
Sudell Rd BB3 ... 81 B1
Sudellside St BB3 ... 81 B1
Suffolk Ave BB12 ... 126 A6
Suffolk Cl PR5 ... 58 E6
Suffolk Rd Blackpool FY3 ... 130 A2
Preston PR1 ... 117 A1
Southport PR8 ... 21 A8
Suffolk St BB2 ... 100 C2
Sugar Stubbs La PR9 ... 54 C4
Sugham La LA3 ... 208 F8
Sulby Cl PR8 ... 33 F3
Sulby Dr Fulwood PR2 ... 117 F5
Lancaster LA1 ... 210 F6
Sulby Gr Fulwood PR2 ... 118 A5
Morecambe LA4 ... 213 A6
Sulby Rd BB2 ... 100 E1
Sullivan Dr BB2 ... 101 A1
Sullom Side La PR3 ... 179 C5
Sullom View PR3 ... 178 C6
Sultan St BB5 ... 103 D7
Sulyard St LA1 ... 210 F8
Summer St Horwich BL6 ... 31 B4
Nelson BB9 ... 147 C7
Skelmersdale WN8 ... 18 A4
Summer Trees Ave PR2 ... 115 D3
Summerdale Dr BL0 ... 49 B2
Summerer Rd PR4 ... 131 F6
Summerfield PR5 ... 75 F3
Summerfield Cl PR5 ... 96 B2
Summerfield Dr LA2 ... 213 E7
Summerfields Coppull PR7 ... 28 F7
Lytham St Anne's FY8 ... 88 C8
Summerhill LA2 ... 233 D7
Summerseat La BL0 ... 49 A2
Summerseat Meth Prim
Sch BL9 ... 49 D2
Summerseat Sta BL9 ... 49 C2
Summersgill Rd LA1 ... 213 D2
Summerton Wlk BB3 ... 81 A2
Summerville 4 FY4 ... 109 C6
Summerville Ave FY3 ... 130 E5
Summerville Wlk BB2 ... 100 D5
Summerwood Cl FY2 ... 150 D1
Summerwood La
Halsall L39 ... 22 C1
Haskayne L39 ... 14 D8
Summit Cl BL9 ... 32 F4
Summit Dr PR4 ... 92 C6
Summit St OL10 ... 32 F3
Summit Works BB11 ... 126 E2
Sumner Ave L39 ... 13 F4
Sumner Rd L37 ... 11 F3
Sumner St Blackburn BB2 ... 100 E3
Leyland PR5 ... 76 A1
Sumner's La PR5 ... 39 A7
Sumners Barn PR2 ... 117 E6
Sumpter Croft PR1 ... 95 E2
Sumpter Ct 3 PR1 ... 95 F2
Sun St Colne BB8 ... 169 E5
Lancaster LA1 ... 210 F8
Nelson BB9 ... 147 C8
Ramsbottom BL0 ... 49 B7
Sun Terr 7 OL14 ... 108 B1
Sunacre Ct LA3 ... 212 B3
Sunbank Cl OL12 ... 51 D2
Sunbury Ave PR1 ... 95 D3
Sunbury Dr PR8 ... 20 B4
Suncliffe Rd BB9 ... 147 D4
Suncourt PR8 ... 33 F6
Sunderland Ave
Cleveleys FY5 ... 172 F4
Hambleton FY6 ... 174 D2
Sunderland Dr LA3 ... 212 D2
Sunderland St BB12 ... 126 B6
Sunfield Cl FY4 ... 110 A7
Sunnindale Ave BB4 ... 86 A1
Sunningdale PR4 ... 136 B3
Sunningdale Ave
Blackpool FY4 ... 130 A2
Fleetwood FY7 ... 172 D7
Hest Bank LA2 ... 215 D1
Sunningdale Cl PR4 ... 113 A4
Sunningdale Cres LA2 ... 215 D1
Sunningdale Ct FY8 ... 89 A6
Sunningdale Dr FY5 ... 151 D8
Sunningdale Gdns
Brierfield BB10 ... 147 D3
Formby L37 ... 11 E3
Sunningdale Pl PR4 ... 134 C8
Sunny Bank Kirkham PR4 ... 112 F5
Penwortham PR1 ... 95 F3
Sunny Bank Ave
Blackpool FY2 ... 150 C4
Newton-with-S PR4 ... 114 A2
Sunny Bank Cl BB4 ... 67 A6
Sunny Bank Cotts BB4 ... 66 F5
Sunny Bank Mill 5 PR4 ... 112 F5
Sunny Bank Rd
Blackburn BB2 ... 100 E1
Haslingden BB4 ... 66 F6
Sunny Bank Terr 3 OL14 ... 108 B1
Sunny Bower Cl BB1 ... 122 B1
Sunny Bower Rd BB1 ... 122 B1
Sunny Brow PR7 ... 42 A2
Sunny Dr WN5 ... 10 F6
Sunny Lea St BB4 ... 84 F5
Sunny Rd PR9 ... 53 A2
Sunny View PR6 ... 79 C2
Sunnybank Dr BB5 ... 102 C2
Sunnybank Rd LA5 ... 216 A5
Sunnybank St Darwen BB3 ... 81 A1
7 Haslingden BB4 ... 84 A3
Sunnycliff Ret Pk LA3 ... 212 G1
Sunnyfield Ave
Morecambe LA4 ... 213 A6
Over Town BB10 ... 107 A8
Sunnyfield La BB3 ... 65 A8
Sunnyfields L39 ... 16 A5
Sunnyhill PR2 ... 117 C5
Sunnyhill Cl BB3 ... 80 D2
Sunnyhurst Ave FY4 ... 109 D6
Sunnyhurst Cl BB3 ... 80 D2
Sunnyhurst La BB3 ... 80 D2
Sunnyhurst Rd
Blackburn BB2 ... 100 C5
Blackburn BB2 ... 100 D4
Sunnyhurst Wood
Visitor Ctr BB3 ... 80 D2
Sunnymede Dr L31 ... 5 D3
Sunnymede Sch PR8 ... 33 F6
Sunnymede Vale BL0 ... 49 A3
Sunnymere Dr BB3 ... 80 E2
Sunnyside
5 High Bentham LA2 ... 233 D8
Ormskirk L39 ... 6 C7
Southport PR8 ... 33 F3
Sunnyside Ave
Billington BB7 ... 143 B4
Blackburn BB2 ... 79 E8
Ribchester PR3 ... 140 D3
Warton PR4 ... 91 E6
Wilpshire BB1 ... 122 A7
Sunnyside Cl
Freckleton PR4 ... 92 B7
Lancaster LA1 ... 210 E7
Rawtenstall BB4 ... 85 A6
Sunnyside La LA1 ... 210 E7
Sunnyside Terr FY6 ... 195 C3
Sunset Cl L33 ... 1 A5
Super St BB5 ... 123 E4
Surgeon's Ct PR1 ... 95 F7
Surrey Ave Burnley BB12 ... 126 B7
Darwen BB3 ... 80 F3
Surrey Cl PR9 ... 53 C5
Surrey Rd Barrowford BB9 ... 168 D2
Blackburn BB1 ... 101 D5
Surrey St Accrington BB5 ... 103 D6
Preston PR1 ... 96 C8
Sussex Ave OL10 ... 32 E1
Sussex Cl Church BB5 ... 102 F7
Standish WN1 ... 29 B1
Sussex Dr Blackburn BB1 ... 101 A4
Garstang PR3 ... 178 B7
Haslingden BB4 ... 67 B8
Sussex Rd Blackpool FY3 ... 129 E6
Rishton BB1 ... 101 F8
Southport PR8, PR9 ... 34 D6
Sussex St
21 Barnoldswick BB18 ... 200 B2
Burnley BB11 ... 127 B4
1 Nelson BB9 ... 168 E1
Preston PR1 ... 117 A1
Sussex Wlk 10 BB1 ... 101 A4
Sutch La L40 ... 25 B5
Sutcliffe St Bacup OL13 ... 70 C8
Brierfield BB10 ... 147 F3
18 Burnley BB11 ... 126 F6
7 Chorley PR7 ... 42 D7
Sutcliffe Terr BB1 ... 81 F6
Sutherland Cl BB1 ... 122 A7
Sutherland Rd
Blackpool FY1 ... 129 C8
Heywood OL10 ... 32 F1
Sutherland St BB8 ... 169 C4
Sutherland View 2 FY1 ... 129 C7
Sutton Ave Brierfield BB10 ... 147 D2
Tarleton PR4 ... 56 A8
Sutton Cres BB5 ... 124 F1
Sutton Dr PR2 ... 94 D8
Sutton Gr PR6 ... 60 F4
Sutton La Adlington PR6 ... 30 B8

Sutton La *continued*
Tarleton PR4 55 F5
Sutton Pl FY1 129 C4
Sutton Rd L37 11 E1
Sutton St Blackburn BB2 79 D8
Weeton Camp PR4 131 E6
Sutton's La L37 12 E3
Sutton's Yd FY6 151 E4
Swain St OL12 51 E1
Swainbank St BB11 127 B5
Swaine St BB9 147 C8
Swainson St FY8 89 F3
Swainstead Raike BD24 230 E8
Swaledale LA2 207 B4
Swaledale Ave BB10 147 B4
Swalegate L31 5 C2
Swallow Ave 1 PR1 95 E4
Swallow Cl FY5 173 A4
Swallow Ct PR6 77 C1
Swallow Dr Blackburn BB1 100 E6
Bury BL9 32 B4
Swallow Field PR4 73 E3
Swallow Pk 8 BB11 126 C5
Swallow Wharf 7 LA1 214 A1
Swallowfields
Blackburn BB1 100 E8
Cottam PR4 115 E5
Swallowfold PR2 138 D1
Swan Alley 2 L39 15 E5
Swan Delph L39 15 C2
Swan Dr FY5 172 F1
Swan Farm Cl BB3 80 F7
Swan La L39 5 F6
Swan Mdw BB7 186 D1
Swan Rd BL8 48 F2
Swan St Blackburn BB2 100 E3
Darwen BB3 64 B6
Preston PR1 96 C8
Swan Yd 1 LA1 211 A7
Swanage Ave FY4 109 B6
Swanage Rd BB10 147 C1
Swanfield Ct BB8 170 A5
Swanpool La L39 15 C2
Swansea St PR2 95 C8
Swansey La PR6 77 C1
Swanson St 11 FY1 129 C6
Swarbrick Cl FY1 129 D7
Swarbrick Ct PR3 139 B7
Swarbrick St PR4 113 A4
Sweet Briar Cl OL12 51 E2
Sweet Briar La OL12 51 E2
Sweetclough Dr BB12 125 F6
Swift Cl BB1 100 F5
Swilkin La FY6 174 E6
Swill Brook La 1 PR1 96 C6
Swinate Rd LA5 237 C1
Swinburn Gr WN5 10 D1
Swinburne Cl BB5 103 E2
Swinden Hall Rd BB9 168 E2
Swinden La BB8 169 A2
Swindon Ave 6 FY4 109 D8
Swindon St BB11 126 D5
Swinless St BB10 127 B8
Swinshaw Cl BB4 105 A2
Swiss St BB5 102 F6
Swithemby St BL6 31 A4
Sword Meanygate PR4 55 C6
Sycamore Ave
Blackpool FY4 109 F5
Burnley BB12 126 B7
Euxton PR7 59 D3
Garstang PR3 178 B8
Sycamore Bglws BB7 225 C3
Sycamore Cl
Blackburn BB1 100 F8
Burnley BB12 126 C6
Fulwood PR2 117 C6
Mawdesley L40 39 C2
Rishton BB1 102 B8
Sycamore Cres Caton LA2 231 C3
Clayton-le-M BB5 124 A5
1 Rawtenstall BB4 84 F1
Sycamore Ct PR7 42 B5
Sycamore Dr Kirkham PR4 112 D4
Penwortham PR1 95 E3
1 Skelmersdale WN8 17 E2
Sycamore Gdns
Foulridge BB8 191 D1
Heysham LA3 208 E6
Sycamore Gr
Accrington BB5 103 E3
Darwen BB3 81 B2
Formby L37 11 C1
Lancaster LA1 210 D8
Sycamore Rd
Bilsborrow PR3 157 A5
Blackburn BB1 100 F8
Caton LA2 231 C3
Chorley PR6 60 D2
Fulwood PR2 117 E2
Sycamore Rise BB8 191 D1
Sycamore Trad Est FY4 109 F5
Sycamore Way BB18 200 A1
Sycamore Wlk 1 BL6 31 E1
Syd Brook La PR5,L40 39 E7
Sydenham Terr OL12 51 D3
Sydney Ave BB7 143 D5
Sydney St Accrington BB5 103 C6
1 Burnley BB11 126 F6
Darwen BB3 64 B7
Enfield BB5 124 A1
Hoddlesden BB3 81 F1
Lytham St Anne's FY8 88 F6
Sydney Terr BB8 170 C3
Syke Hill 14 PR1 96 A7
Syke House La PR3 158 E4
Syke La OL12 51 F4
Syke Rd OL12 51 F4
Syke Side Dr BB5 124 E6
Syke St Haslingden BB4 84 C1
Preston PR1 96 A7
Sykefield BB9 147 A5
Sykelands Ave LA2 214 F7
Sykelands Gr LA2 214 F7
Sykes St BL9 32 A3
Sylvan Dr BB11 126 B4
Sylvan Gr PR5 97 A2
Sylvan Pl LA3 208 E6
Sylvancroft PR2 116 A5
Sylvester St LA1 210 E7
Symonds Rd PR2 116 E3

T

Tabby Nook PR4 54 F2
Tabby's Nook
Newburgh WN8 26 A1
Skelmersdale WN8 18 A8
Taberner Cl WN6 28 F1
Tabley La PR2,PR4 115 E7
Tabor St BB12 126 D6
Tadema Gr BB11 126 F2
Tadlow Cl L37 11 C1
Tag Croft PR2 115 F5
Tag Farm Ct PR2 115 F5
Tag La PR2 116 A4
Talaton Cl PR9 53 A5
Talbot Ave 3 BB5 123 F2
Talbot Cl Clitheroe BB7 164 F7
Rawtenstall BB4 67 E8
Talbot Ct 11 Blackpool FY4 129 B1
3 Lytham St Anne's FY8 89 A8
Talbot Dr Brierfield BB10 147 F2
Euxton PR7 59 D2
Southport PR8 34 B6
Talbot Gr BL9 32 A6
Talbot House PR7 60 C2
Talbot Liby PR1 95 D8
Talbot Mkt FY1 129 B1
Talbot Rd Accrington BB5 103 A8
Blackpool FY1,FY3 129 C6
Leyland PR5 75 E2
Lytham St Anne's FY8 90 C4
Penwortham PR1 95 E5
Preston PR1 95 D7
Talbot Row PR7 59 D1
Talbot Sq FY1 129 B5
Talbot St Brierfield BB10 147 F2
Burnley BB11 127 B6
Chipping PR3 182 E3
Chorley PR6 60 E1
Colne BB8 169 D6
Fulwood PR2 116 D4
Rishton BB1 123 C1
Southport PR8 34 A6
Talbot Terr 1 FY8 90 B3
Tamar Cl PR5 59 B7
Tamar St PR1 96 E8
Tamneys The WN8 17 F1
Tan Hill Dr LA1 213 F3
Tan House Cl WN8 26 C3
Tan House La WN8 26 C2
Tan Pit Cotts WN8 19 C4
Tancaster WN8 17 E1
Tanfield Nook WN8 26 C2
Tanfields WN8 17 F1
Tanglewood PR2 117 B5
Tanhouse 6 LA2 207 A4
Tanhouse La PR6 60 F6
Tanhouse Rd WN8 9 E7
Tanner Barn BB5 84 B7
Tanner St 15 BB11 126 F6
Tanners Croft 5 BL0 49 B6
Tanners St BL0 49 B6
Tannersmith La L40 39 F5
Tanpits La LA6 234 B7
Tanpits Rd BB5 102 F6
Tansley Ave PR7 41 D1
Tansley Cl BL6 31 C2
Tansy La PR3 203 F4
Tanterton Hall Rd PR2 116 A6
Tanyard Cl PR7 41 D1
Tape St 2 BL0 49 B6
Taper St BL0 49 B6
Tapestry St BB2 100 D1
Tarbert Cres BB1 101 D4
Tarbet St LA1 211 A7
Tardy Gate Trad Ctr PR5 76 A8
Tarleton Ave BB11 127 B4
Tarleton CE Prim Sch PR4 56 A5
Tarleton Cty High
Sch PR4 56 A7
Tarleton Cty Prim
Sch PR4 55 F8
Tarleton Mere Brow CE
Prim Sch PR4 54 F2
Tarleton Rd PR9 35 A8
Tarleton St BB11 127 B4
Tarlscough La L40 37 D1
Tarlswood WN8 17 F1
Tarn Ave BB5 123 F4
Tarn Brook Cl BB5 124 F1
Tarn Brow L39 15 C3
Tarn Cl Penwortham PR1 94 F4
Storth LA7 237 F5
Tarn Ct FY7 193 D1
Tarn Hows Cl 1 PR7 42 B5
Tarn La LA6 234 B6
Tarn Rd Formby L37 11 D3
Thornton FY5 151 D7
Tarnacre La PR3 177 E2
Tarnacre View PR3 178 C6
Tarnbeck Dr L40 39 D2
Tarnbrick Ave PR4 92 C7
Tarnbrook Cl
Carnforth LA5 217 C1
Hest Bank LA5 215 F2
Tarnbrook Cotts PR3 196 E5
Tarnbrook Dr FY3 130 A7
Tarnbrook Rd
5 Heysham LA3 208 F8
2 Lancaster LA1 213 D2
Tarnside FY4 130 B1
Tarnside Rd WN5 10 E6
Tarnsyke Rd LA1 213 D2
Tarnwater La LA2 206 E7
Tarnway Ave FY5 151 D8
Tarradale PR4 93 F1
Tarragon Dr FY2 150 F4
Tarry Barn La BB7 165 A3
Tarvin Cl Brierfield BB10 147 F3
Southport PR9 53 D5
Tasker St 14 BB5 103 C6
Taskers Croft BB7 143 F8
Tatham Ct FY7 193 C1
Tatham Fells CE (VC)
Prim Sch LA2 233 C4
Tattersall Sq BB4 85 F3
Tattersall St
5 Blackburn BB2 100 E4
Haslingden BB4 84 B6
Oswaldtwistle BB5 102 D4
2 Padiham BB12 125 D8
Tatton St BB8 169 B3
Tauheedul Islam Girls
High Sch BB1 100 E6
Taunton Rd BB2 100 B5
Taunton St
8 Blackpool FY4 129 D1
Preston PR1 117 D1
Tavistock Dr PR8 20 B6
Tavistock St BB9 168 F1
Tawd Rd WN8 9 C8
Tay St Burnley BB11 126 D5
3 Preston PR1 95 D6
Taybank Ave FY4 109 D7
Taydale Cotts BB10 147 E3
Taylor Ave Newchurch BB4 85 F2
Ormskirk L39 16 A5
Taylor Cl BB2 100 C3
Taylor Ct BB4 84 A3
Taylor Gr LA4 213 B6
Taylor Holme Ind
Est OL13 69 B8
Taylor St
Barnoldswick BB18 200 A2
Blackburn BB2 100 D3
Brierfield BB9 147 B6
Burnley BB10 127 A8
Bury BL9 32 A3
Chorley PR7 42 B5
Clitheroe BB7 164 F8
Darwen BB3 64 A8
Haslingden BB4 84 B6
Horwich BL6 31 B3
Preston PR1 95 D6
6 Rawtenstall BB4 85 A3
Rochdale OL12 51 F1
Skelmersdale WN8 17 C1
Whitworth OL12 51 D8
Taylor St W BB5 103 B6
Taylor's Bldgs BB6 142 D1
Taylor's La
Fisher's Row PR3 196 D6
Holmes PR4 55 D3
Taylor's Meanygate PR4 55 A7
Taylors Cl FY6 151 C5
Taylors Pl 18 OL12 51 F1
Taymouth Rd 5 FY4 110 A6
Taywood Cl FY6 151 F4
Taywood Rd FY5 173 A4
Teak St BL9 32 B2
Teal Cl Blackburn BB1 100 D8
Ormskirk L39 15 C2
Thornton FY5 173 A4
Teal Ct FY3 130 B6
Teal Pl PR5 58 D7
Teanlowe Ctr FY6 151 D3
Tears La WN8 17 F8
Teasel Wlk LA3 212 E2
Tebay Ave Cleveleys FY5 172 D4
Kirkham PR4 113 C5
Tebay Cl L31 5 F2
Tebay Ct LA1 213 E4
Tedder Ave Burnley BB12 126 B6
Southport PR9 35 A7
Teenadore Ave 1 FY4 109 E7
Tees Ct FY7 193 D2
Tees St PR1 117 C2
Teesdale 8 LA2 207 A4
Teesdale Ave FY2 129 D8
Teil Gn PR2 117 E6
Telford St Burnley BB12 126 C7
Horwich BL6 31 D2
Temperance St 8 PR6 42 E8
Temperance Terr OL13 86 F1
Temple Cl 2 BB1 101 B4
Temple Ct 10 PR1 95 F7
Temple Dr BB1 101 B4
Temple St
10 Blackpool FY1 129 B5
Burnley BB11 127 B5
Colne BB8 169 E6
Nelson BB9 147 F8
Temple Way PR6 60 D3
Templegate Cl WN6 28 F2
Templemartin 2 WN8 17 F2
Templeton Cl BB3 81 A2
Ten Row LA2 205 E5
Tenby 2 WN8 17 E2
Tenby Cl BB1 100 E7
Tenby Gr 6 OL12 51 C1
Tenby Rd 7 PR1 96 A6
Tenby St OL12 51 C1
Tennis St BB10 127 A8
Tennyson Ave Chorley PR7 42 C6
Lytham St Anne's FY8 90 D4
Oswaldtwistle BB5 102 C4
Padiham BB12 125 E7
Read BB12 144 D2
Thornton FY5 173 A3
Warton PR4 91 E6
Tennyson Cl LA5 216 A5
Tennyson Dr
Longshaw WN5 10 D1
Ormskirk L39 15 D6
Tennyson Pl
Bamber Bridge PR5 96 D2
Great Harwood BB6 123 B4
Tennyson Rd
Blackpool FY3 129 F7
Colne BB8 169 D5
Fleetwood FY7 194 A4
Preston PR1 117 D1
Tennyson St
Brierfield BB10 147 F3
Burnley BB11 126 D5
6 Hapton BB12 125 C4
Tensing Ave FY2 150 D5
Tensing Rd L31 5 D1
Tenterfield St
20 Preston PR1 95 F8
6 Rawtenstall BB4 68 F8
Tenterheads BB4 68 F7
Terance Rd 2 FY4 109 E8
Terra Cotta Bldgs BB4 106 A1
Terrace Row BB7 143 C4
Terrace St PR1 117 C1
Terrace The 7 LA2 233 B8
Terry St BB9 169 A2
Tetbury Cl BB2 79 E8
Teven St 5 PR5 96 E1
Teversham WN8 17 F2
Teviot 4 WN8 17 E2
Teviot Ave FY7 193 D3
Tewkesbury 3 WN8 17 E2
Tewkesbury Ave FY4 109 D5
Tewkesbury Cl BB5 103 E3
Tewkesbury Dr FY8 90 D5
Tewksbury St BB2 100 B1
Thames Ave BB10 147 C3
Thames Dr WN5 10 F7
Thames Ho 8 PR1 96 D8
Thames Prim Sch FY4 109 B7
Thames Rd FY4 109 B7
Thames St PR4 113 F2
Thane Row BB11 106 D7
Thanet WN8 17 F2
Thanet Lee Cl BB10 127 E1
Thealby Cl WN8 17 E2
Theatre St PR1 95 F7
Thelma St BL0 49 B6
Thermdale Cl PR3 178 B7
Thetis Rd LA1 210 C8
Thickrash Brow LA2 233 D7
Third Ave Blackpool FY4 109 C7
Bury BL9 32 D4
Thirlemere Ave FY7 193 C1
Thirlemere Ct LA1 214 B1
Thirlmere Ave
Burnley BB10 147 A2
Carleton FY6 151 C4
Colne BB8 169 F6
Formby L37 12 A2
Haslingden BB4 67 C8
Horwich BL6 31 C2
1 Orrell WN5 10 F7
Orrell, Hall Green WN8 10 B7
Padiham BB12 145 C2
Thirlmere Cl
2 Accrington BB5 124 D1
Adlington PR6 30 B8
6 Blackburn BB1 100 F6
Knott End-on-S FY6 194 F6
Longton PR4 74 B8
Maghull L31 5 E2
Thirlmere Dr Darwen BB3 81 C2
Longridge PR3 138 F5
Morecambe LA4 212 D4
Southport PR8 20 B3
Withnell Fold PR6 78 D2
Thirlmere Gdns LA4 212 E4
Thirlmere Rd
Blackpool FY4 109 C7
Blackrod BL6 30 C3
Burnley BB10 127 E5
Chorley PR7 42 B6
Hightown L38 3 A4
Lancaster LA1 214 B2
Preston PR1 117 F1
Thirlmere Way BB4 105 A1
Thirnby Ct LA6 238 C2
Thirsk WN8 17 E2
Thirsk Ave FY8 89 B7
Thirsk Gr FY1 129 D2
Thirsk Rd LA1 211 B4
Thistle Break LA3 209 A7
Thistle Cl Chorley PR6 42 E8
Cleveleys FY5 172 F5
Hesketh Bank PR4 72 E4
Thistle St 15 OL13 86 F2
Thistlecroft PR2 116 A5
Thistlemount Ave BB4 85 F1
Thistleton Mews 3 PR9 34 C8
Thistleton Rd Preston PR2 94 E8
Thistleton PR4 153 C1
Thomas Gr LA4 212 E5
Thomas St Blackburn BB2 100 D4
Thomas St *continued*
Brierfield BB9 147 A5
Burnley BB11 127 A5
Colne BB8 169 C4
2 Cornholme OL14 108 C1
5 Haslingden BB4 84 A3
Nelson BB9 147 E7
6 Oswaldtwistle BB5 102 D3
4 Preston PR1 96 B7
Whitworth OL12 70 D2
Thomason Fold BL7 47 D6
Thompson Ave L39 16 B5
Thompson Dr BL9 32 C3
Thompson St
Blackburn BB2 100 C4
Darwen BB3 64 B7
Horwich BL6 31 A3
8 Kirkham PR4 112 F6
Padiham BB12 125 D7
Preston PR1 117 D1
Thonock Rd LA4 212 G3
Thorburn Dr OL12 51 B7
Thorn Bank OL13 87 A2
Thorn Cres OL13 87 A2
Thorn Cty Prim Sch OL13 86 F3
Thorn Dr OL13 87 A2
Thorn Gdns OL13 87 A2
Thorn Gr Blackpool FY1 129 E2
Colne BB8 169 F6
Thorn Hill Cl BB1 101 A5
Thorn La PR3 139 B2
Thorn St Bacup OL13 87 A2
Burnley BB10 127 A8
Clitheroe BB7 164 D8
Great Harwood BB6 123 D6
Preston PR1 117 C1
Ramsbottom BL0 49 C3
Rawtenstall BB4 84 F5
Sabden BB7 145 A7
Thorn View BL9 32 C3
Thornbank FY3 130 B7
Thornbank Dr PR3 178 D2
Thornbeck Ave L38 2 F3
Thornber 1 WN8 17 F2
Thornber Ct BB10 147 C1
Thornber Gr FY1 129 D3
Thornber St BB2 100 C3
Thornbridge Ave L40 24 E3
Thornbury WN8 17 F2
Thornby 3 WN8 17 F2
Thorncliffe Dr BB3 64 D8
Thorndale 4 WN8 17 F2
Thorne St BB9 169 A2
Thorney Bank St 7 BB11 126 F5
Thorneybank Ind Est
BB11 125 C2
Thorneycroft Cl FY6 151 B5
Thorneyholme RC
Sch BB7 222 C5
Thorneyholme Rd BB5 103 C8
Thorneyholme Sq BB12 167 E5
Thorneylea OL12 70 D1
Thornfield Lancaster LA1 210 F5
Much Hoole PR4 73 E4
Thornfield Ave
Fulwood PR2 117 F3
Longridge PR3 139 A8
Newchurch BB4 85 E1
8 Rawtenstall BB4 68 F8
Thornton FY5 151 D8
Thorngate PR1 95 B4
Thorngate Cl PR1 95 B4
Thornham Ct FY3 129 E5
Thornhill L39 6 B8
Thornhill Ave
Knott End-on-S FY6 195 A5
Rishton BB1 102 A8
Thornhill Cl Blackpool FY4 109 F5
Ormskirk L39 6 B8
Thornhill Rd Chorley PR6 60 E2
Leyland PR5 58 D8
Ramsbottom BL0 49 A1
Thornhill St BB12 126 A6
Thornlea Dr OL12 51 B2
Thornleigh Cl 10 FY5 173 A2
Thornleigh Dr LA6 234 C7
Thornley Ave BB1 101 C6
Thornley Pl PR2 118 A3
Thornley Rd PR2 118 A3
Thornpark Dr 3 PR2 115 D1
Thorns Ave LA2 215 D1
Thorns The L31 5 B2
Thornton WN8 17 F2
Thornton Ave
Fulwood PR2 116 B4
Lytham St Anne's FY8 89 B8
Morecambe LA4 212 F6
Thornton Cl
Accrington BB5 103 A8
Blackburn BB2 80 F8
Rufford L40 38 C4
Thornton Cres
Burnley BB10 127 E5
Morecambe LA4 212 F5
Thornton Ctr 7 FY5 173 C1
Thornton Dr
Gregson Lane PR5 97 D4
Leyland PR5 75 E4
Thornton Gate FY5 172 D4
Thornton Gr LA4 212 F5
Thornton La
Morecambe LA4 212 F6
Thornton in L LA6 236 F5
Thornton Manor Ct BD23 201 A5
Thornton Pl FY5 173 A4
Thornton Rd Burnley BB10 127 E5
Morecambe LA4 212 F6
Southport PR9 34 F7

Thornton-in-Craven
Cty Prim Sch BD23 201 B6
Thorntrees Ave
Newsham PR3 136 B5
Preston PR2 115 D1
Thornway Ave FY5 151 D8
Thornwood WN8 17 F2
Thornwood Cl
Blackburn BB1 121 E1
Lytham St Anne's FY8 89 E4
Thornylea BB2 80 D7
Thorough Way PR3 198 E7
Thoroughfare The LA5 217 D5
Thoroughgood Cl L40 24 D2
Thorpe WN8 17 F2
Thorpe Ave LA4 213 B4
Thorpe Cl PR1 116 F1
Thorpe St BL0 49 B5
Thrang Brow La LA5 219 C6
Threagill La LA5 217 F5
Three Lane Ends PR6 61 C4
Three Nooks PR5 77 C5
Three Oaks Cl L40 25 B2
Three Pools PR9 53 C3
Three Tuns La L37 11 F3
Three Turns PR3 141 A8
Threefields PR2 116 A5
Threlfall PR7 59 F2
Threlfall Rd FY1 129 D1
Threlfall St 1 PR2 116 C1
Threlfall's La PR9 52 F2
Threlfalls Cl PR9 52 F3
Threshers Ct PR3 204 C2
Threshfield Ave LA3 208 F8
Thrimby Ct LA4 212 E4
Thrimby Pl LA4 212 E4
Thropps La PR4 74 D6
Throstle Cl BB12 127 A7
Throstle Gr LA2 213 F8
Throstle Nest La PR3 198 C4
Throstle St Blackburn BB2 100 C4
7 Nelson BB9 168 E1
Throstle Way 1 FY5 172 F1
Throstle Wlk LA2 213 F8
Throughs La LA7 237 F5
Throup Pl BB9 168 E2
Thrum Fold OL12 51 D3
Thrum Hall La
Rochdale OL12 51 D3
Rochdale OL12 51 E3
Thrush Dr BL9 32 B4
Thrush St OL12 51 C1
Thrushgill Dr LA2 214 F7
Thurcroft Dr WN8 17 E2
Thurland Ct LA4 212 D3
Thurnham Rd PR2 94 E8
Thurnham St LA1 210 F7
Thursby Ave FY4 109 D6
Thursby Cl PR8 20 B3
Thursby Pl 11 BB9 168 F2
Thursby Rd Burnley BB10 147 C1
Nelson BB9 168 F2
Thursby Sq BB10 127 A8
Thursden Ave BB10 147 F3
Thursden Pl BB9 169 B1
Thursfield Ave FY4 109 E8
Thursfield Rd BB10 127 B5
Thursford Gr BL6 30 D1
Thursgill Ave LA4 212 F3
Thurston WN8 17 E2
Thurston Rd PR5 76 A1
Thurston St BB11 127 B6
Thwaite Brow La LA5 216 B6
Thwaite La LA2 233 C5
Thwaites Ave BB2 120 E2
Thwaites Rd BB5 102 C4
Thwaites St BB5 102 C3
Tib St 18 BL0 49 B5
Tiber Ave BB11 126 C4
Tiber St PR1 96 B7
Tibicar Dr E LA3 212 A1
Tibicar Dr W LA3 212 A1
Tilbury Gr WN6 19 D7
Tilcroft WN8 17 E2
Timber Brook PR7 60 A2
Timber St Accrington BB5 103 C5
Bacup OL13 86 F1
Brierfield BB9 147 B6
Timberhurst BL9 32 D2
Timbrills Ave BB7 144 F8
Timms Cl L37 11 F5
Timms La L37 11 F5
Tincklers La PR7 40 A6
Tinedale View BB12 145 D1
Tinker's La LA2 220 B7
Tinkerfield PR2 116 E7
Tinklers La BB7 223 E7
Tinline St BL9 32 A2
Tinniswood PR2 116 B1
Tinsley Ave PR8 34 E3
Tinsley's La
Out Rawcliffe PR3 175 D4
Southport PR8 35 A1
Tintagel WN8 17 E2
Tintagell Cl BB2 79 C7
Tintern Ave Chorley PR7 42 D5
Rochdale OL12 51 E2
Tintern Cl Accrington BB5 103 E2
Read BB12 144 D1
Tintern Cres BB1 101 B8
Tintern Dr L37 12 B2
Tippet Cl BB2 101 A1
Titan Way PR5 75 B2
Tithe Barn La Knowley PR6 61 A4
Runshaw Moor PR5,PR7 58 F5
Scorton PR3 199 E5
Tithebarn Gate FY6 151 D4
Tithebarn Hill LA2 205 E5
Tithebarn Pl FY6 151 D4
Tithebarn Rd PR8 34 E6
Tithebarn St Orrell WN8 10 B7
6 Preston PR1 96 A7
Preston PR1 96 A8
Thornton FY6 151 D4
Tittrington Brow BB7 223 C2
Tiverton Ave WN8 17 E2
Tiverton Cl PR2 116 F8
Tiverton Dr Blackburn BB2 80 C8
Brierfield BB10 147 F3
Tockholes CE Prim Sch
BB3 80 A3
Tockholes Rd Darwen BB3 80 F2
Darwen, Tockholes BB3,PR7 80 A3
Tod Holes La BD23 230 E4
Todd Carr Rd BB4 85 F1
Todd Hall Rd BB4 83 F4
Todd La N PR5 96 C2
Todd La S PR5 76 C8
Todd's La PR9 54 A6
Todmorden Old Rd OL13 87 B5
Todmorden Rd Bacup OL13 87 B4
Burnley BB11 127 B3
Cockden BB10 148 B1
Lytham St Anne's FY8 88 C8
Todmorden Road Prim Sch
BB10 127 B5
Toll Bar Bsns Pk OL13 69 C8
Toll Bar Cres LA1 210 F3
Tollgate PR1 95 E4
Tollgate Rd L40 24 B3
Tolsey Dr PR4 94 D2
Tom Benson Way
PR2,PR4 115 F4
Tom La BB4 85 F2
Tomlinson Rd
Heysham LA3 208 F6
Leyland PR5 75 F2
Preston PR2 116 C2
Tomlinson St BL6 31 B3
Tonacliffe Cty Prim Sch
OL12 51 C6
Tonacliffe Rd OL12 51 C6
Tonacliffe Terr OL12 51 C7
Tonacliffe Way OL12 51 C6
Tong End OL12 70 C2
Tong Ho 19 OL13 87 A3
Tong La Bacup OL13 87 B2
Whitworth OL12 70 D1
Tongbarn WN8 17 E2
Tongues La FY6 195 C6
Tontine WN5 10 C5
Tontine Rd WN5,WN8 10 C6
Tontine St BB1 100 E5
Toogood La WN6 27 D6
Tootell St PR7 42 B6
Tootle La L40 38 A3
Tootle Rd PR3 139 B8
Top Acre PR4 94 C1
Top Acre Rd WN8 9 C7
Top Barn La BB4 85 E1
Top Locks L40 25 A4
Top o' th' Croft BB2 80 D8
Top of Fawna Rd PR3 161 D1
Top of Heap OL10 32 F2
Top of Wallsuches BL6 31 F4
Top Row BB7 144 F8
Topaz St BB1 121 F2
Topham St BL9 32 A1
Topping Fold Rd BL9 32 C3
Topping St Blackpool FY1 129 B5
Bury BL9 32 A3
Toppings The PR3 178 C6
Tor Ave BL8 48 F2
Tor End Rd BB4 66 F6
Tor Scar Rd LA6 236 F6
Tor View Haslingden BB4 84 C1
Rawtenstall BB4 85 A1
Tor View Rd BB4 84 C1
Tor View Sch Valley Site
BB4 67 D8
Torcross Cl PR9 53 A5
Tormore Cl PR6 61 A3
Torn Cotts LA5 216 C6
Toronto Ave Blackpool FY2 150 E3
Fleetwood FY7 193 E2
Toronto Rd BB2 100 C8
Torquay Ave
Blackpool FY3 130 A2
Brierfield BB10 147 D2
Torra Barn Cl BL7 46 E3
Torrentum Ct FY5 173 C1
Torridon Cl BB2 99 F1
Torrisholme Cty Prim Sch
LA4 213 B5
Torrisholme Rd LA1 213 D3
Torrisholme Sq LA4 213 B4
Torside Gr FY6 151 B3
Torsway Ave FY3 129 F6
Torver Cl BB12 126 B8
Totnes Cl FY6 151 C5
Totnes Dr PR9 53 A5
Tottenham Rd BB3 80 F6
Tottington Rd BL7,BL8 47 F2
Tottleworth BB6 123 C3
Tottleworth Rd BB1 123 C2
Toulmin Cl PR3 178 D2
Tower Ave BL0 49 A5
Tower Bldgs 10 PR9 34 C8
Tower Cl FY5 173 A4
Tower Cotts 3 LA3 208 E7
Tower Ct Chapeltown BL7 47 C4
Lancaster LA1 210 F7
Tower End L37 11 C5
Tower Gn PR2 116 F7
Tower Hill Clitheroe BB7 186 F1
Ormskirk L39 16 A5
Tower Hill Rd WN8 10 B6
Tower La PR2 116 F7
Tower Nook WN8 10 A5
Tower Rd Blackburn BB2 99 E2
Darwen BB3 64 B8
Tower St 13 Bacup OL13 86 F2
Blackpool FY1 129 B5
Cornholme OL14 108 A1
Edgworth BL7 47 C4
Oswaldtwistle BB5 102 C5
Tower View Belthorn BB1 82 A5
Blackrod BL6 30 C3
Darwen BB3 81 C1
Penwortham PR1 95 C7
Towers Ave L31 5 C2
Town Brook Ho 5 PR1 116 E1
Town Brow PR5 76 F2
Town End Bolton-le-S LA5 216 A3
Kirkham PR4 113 A5
Slaidburn BB7 223 C7
3 Thornton FY5 173 A2
Town Gate BB6 123 C5
Town Green Ct L39 6 C8
Town Green Cty Sch L39 6 C8
Town Green La L39 6 C8
Town Green Sta L39 6 C8
Town Hall Sq 8 BB6 123 C5
Town Hall St
16 Blackburn BB2 100 E5
9 Great Harwood BB6 123 C5
Town Head BB18 200 A1
Town Hill Bank BB12 145 D1
Town House Rd BB9 148 B8
Town La Coppull PR7 41 C1
Heskin Green PR7 40 C2
Much Hoole PR4 73 D1
Southport PR8 34 E3
Whittle-le-W PR6 60 D6
Town Lane (Kew) PR8 34 E3
Town Rd PR5 57 B2
Town View BB1 100 F4
Town Wlk BB1 100 F4
Towneley High Sch BB11 127 C4
Towneley Rd PR3 139 A7
Towneley Rd W PR3 139 A7
Towneley St BB10 147 B1
Townely Ave BB5 124 F2
Townfield Ave BB10 127 F6
Townfield Cl PR4 73 F7
Townfield La LA2 213 E7
Towngate Eccleston PR7 40 B7
Foulridge BB8 191 D1
Leyland PR5 58 F7
Leyland PR5 59 A8
Townhouse Sch BB9 169 C1
Townley Ave FY4 109 E8
Townley Cl LA1 210 D7
Townley La PR1 94 D4
Townley Par PR3 139 A7
Townley St Brierfield BB9 147 B5
Brierfield, Harle Syke BB10 147 F3
Chorley PR6 42 D7
Colne BB8 169 E6
Morecambe LA4 212 E6
Townsend St
Haslingden BB4 84 A3
Rawtenstall BB4 68 F8
Townsfield LA5 218 C4
Townshill Wlk PR4 113 A6
Townsley St BB9 147 E6
Townsway PR5 76 C8
Towpath Wlk 2 LA5 217 D1
Toxhead Cl BL6 31 A3
Toy & Teddy Bear Mus of
Childhood FY8 88 D7
Tracks La WN5 10 D3
Trafalgar Cl PR2 116 D3
Trafalgar Rd
Blackpool FY1 129 B2
Lancaster LA1 211 A6
Southport PR8 33 E3
Trafalgar St Burnley BB11 126 F5
Chorley PR6 60 D1
Lytham St Anne's FY8 88 F7
Trafford St PR1 116 E2
Tram La LA6 238 C2
Tramway La PR5 77 B6
Tranmere Ave LA3 212 A1
Tranmere Cres LA3 212 A1
Tranmere Rd FY4 129 E1
Tranmoor PR4 73 F6
Trans Brittania Ent Est
BB11 126 A3
Trap Hill L37 11 C2
Trapp La Sabden BB12 144 F4
Simonstone BB12 144 F2
Trash La Darwen BB3 80 B2
Rimington BB7 225 B1
Travellers Ct BB7 225 C3
Travera Lodge 8 PR2 117 F4
Travers Pl PR2 95 C8
Travers St BL6 31 D1
Travis St BB10 127 A8
Trawden Cl BB5 103 C4
Trawden Cres PR2 117 E4
Trawden Forest Prim Sch
BB8 170 C2
Trawden Rd BB8 170 B5
Traylen Way OL12 51 A1
Treales CE Prim Sch PR4 133 E2
Treales Rd PR4 114 B6
Trecastle Rd L33 1 A4
Tredgold St BL6 31 C2
Treen Cl PR9 53 B6
Treesdale Cl PR8 33 F4
Treetop Villas PR9 52 F4
Treetops Ave BL0 49 A3
Trefoil Cl FY5 173 A5
Tremellen St BB5 103 A6
Trengrove St 7 OL12 51 C1
Trent Ave L31 5 F2
Trent Cl
Burscough Bridge L40 24 F5
Lancaster LA3 213 B2
Trent Rd Blackpool FY4 109 B7
Nelson BB9 148 A8
Trent St Longridge PR3 138 F7
Lytham St Anne's FY8 90 D3
Tresco Cl BB2 100 B1
Tretower Way FY5 173 D2
Trevarrick Ct BL6 31 E2
Trevelyan Dr WN5 10 D1
Trevor Cl BB1 100 F7
Trevor Rd Burscough L40 24 E4
Southport PR8 20 C4
Triangle The
Accrington BB5 103 E8
Fulwood PR2 116 E4
Trigg La PR6,PR7 61 D5
Trigge Ho PR7 60 C2
Trinity & St Michael's
CE Prim Sch Croston PR5 57 B1
Croston PR5 57 C2
Trinity Cl Freckleton PR4 92 B7
Padiham BB12 125 D6
Trinity Ct 3 BB1 100 F6
Trinity Fold 23 PR1 95 F8
Trinity Gdns Southport PR8 34 A6
Thornton FY5 173 A3
Trinity Gn BL0 49 B2
Trinity Mews PR9 34 C7
Trinity Pl 27 PR1 95 F8
Trinity Prim Sch WN8 17 F1
Trinity Rd PR7 42 B7
Trinity St 15 Bacup OL13 69 C8
Blackburn BB1 100 F6
Oswaldtwistle BB5 102 D3
Trinity Twrs 6 BB11 126 E6
Trinity Wlks PR4 56 A5
Trinket La LA2 232 E6
Tristan Ave PR4 74 A5
Troon Ave Blackburn BB1 101 C3
Thornton FY5 151 D8
Troon Ct PR1 95 A6
Trough Rd BB7 222 B5
Troughton Cres FY4 109 E8
Trout Beck BB5 123 F4
Trout St 8 Burnley BB10 127 A8
Preston PR1 96 C7
Troutbeck Ave
Fleetwood FY7 193 D2
Forton PR3 204 B3
Maghull L31 5 E2
Troutbeck Cl
Burnley BB12 126 B8
Hawkshaw BL8 48 B2
Troutbeck Cres FY4 110 D8
Troutbeck Dr BL0 49 C7
Troutbeck Pl PR2 117 E5
Troutbeck Rd Chorley PR7 42 B5
Lancaster LA1 214 A1
Lytham St Anne's FY8 109 D1
Trowbarrow Cotts LA5 218 F5
Trower St PR1 96 B6
Troy St BB1 100 F7
Trumacar Com Prim Sch
LA3 208 E5
Trumacar La LA3 208 E5
Truman Ave LA1 210 C7
Trumley Ct LA3 212 D2
Trunnah Gdns FY5 173 B3
Trunnah Rd FY5 173 B3
Truro Ave PR9 53 B5
Truro Pl 8 PR1 117 D1
Truro St 7 FY4 129 D1
Truscott Rd L40 24 D4
Tucker Hill BB7 186 E1
Tucker's Hill Brow WN2 30 B1
Tudor Ave Preston PR1 117 F1
Preston, Lea PR2 115 D1
Tudor Cl Blackpool FY6 151 A4
1 Cleveleys FY5 172 F1
Darwen BB3 81 A2
Langho BB6 142 D1
Preston PR2 115 D1
Tudor Croft PR5 76 C7
Tudor Ct L39 15 F6
Tudor Dr PR4 113 B2
Tudor Gr 2 LA4 213 A6
Tudor Mans PR8 33 F6
Tudor Pl FY4 109 B6
Tudor Rd
Lytham St Anne's FY8 88 D8
Southport PR8 20 B6
Tuer St PR5 75 F2
Tulip Gr OL12 51 E3
Tulketh Ave PR2 116 B1
Tulketh Brow PR2 116 C1
Tulketh Cres PR2 116 C1
Tulketh High Sch PR2 116 B4
Tulketh Rd PR2 116 B1
Tulketh St PR8 34 B7
Tullyallen Sch BB3 80 E3
Tunbridge Pl 7 PR1 117 D1
Tunbridge St 4 PR1 117 D1
Tunbrook Ave PR2 138 E1
Tunley Holme PR5 77 C5
Tunley La WN6 27 E5
Tunley Moss WN6 27 E4
Tunnel St Burnley BB12 126 D6
5 Darwen BB3 64 C7
Tunstall Dr BB5 124 B1
Tunstall Ho 10 LA1 211 A3
Tunstall St LA4 212 D5
Tunstead Ave BB12 124 F8
Tunstead Cres OL13 86 C1
Tunstead La Bacup OL13 69 B8
Rawtenstall BB4,OL13 86 B1
Tunstead Mill Terr 3
OL13 69 B8
Tunstead Rd OL13 86 C1
Tunstill Fold BB12 167 F1
Tunstill St BB10 147 B1
Turbary Rd LA6 236 E7
Turbary The PR2 116 C3
Turf Moor Football Gd
(Burnley AFC) BB10 127 B6
Turf St BB11 127 B6
Turflands PR5 57 B1
Turkey St Accrington BB5 103 D7
Out Rawcliffe PR3 175 A1
Turks Head Yd 23 PR1 96 A7
Turn La BB3 63 F8
Turn Rd BL0 49 E8
Turnacre L37 12 B6
Turnberry WN8 17 D2
Turnberry Ave FY5 151 D8
Turnberry Cl Kirkham PR4 113 A4
Morecambe LA4 212 G6
Turnberry Way PR9 53 D5
Turnbridge Rd L31 5 C3
Turnbury Cl PR7 59 D4
Turncroft Rd BB3 64 B8
Turner Ave PR5 76 A7
Turner Rd BB9 147 B8
Turner St 3 Bacup OL13 69 C8
4 Barnoldswick BB18 200 C2
Clitheroe BB7 164 E7
2 Preston PR1 117 A1
Rochdale OL12 51 E1
Turner's Pl OL12 51 E3
Turnerford Cl BL7 46 E1
Turnfield PR2 115 F6
Turning La PR8 35 A1
Turnpike BB4 85 F1
Turnpike Fold LA2 213 F5
Turnpike Rd L39 15 A2
Turnpike The PR2 116 D6
Turnpike Way BB5 102 C5
Turnstone FY3 130 B6
Turpin Green La PR5 76 B1
Turton Dr PR6 60 E1
Turton Gr BB10 127 D6
Turton Hollow Rd BB4 85 A8
Turton Rd BL8 48 B1
Turton Twr BL7 47 C3
Tuscan Ave BB11 126 C5
Tuson Croft PR4 73 F8
Tuson Dr PR2 95 E8
Tuson Ho 2 PR1 95 E2
Tuxbury Dr FY5 151 D8
Tuxford Ct 1 FY8 89 D6
Tuxford Rd FY8 89 C6
Tweed St Blackburn BB2 80 D8
4 High Bentham LA2 233 D8
Nelson BB9 148 A8
Tweed Street Ct 3 LA2 233 D8
Tweedys Ct PR3 182 C4
Twemlow Par
Heysham LA3 208 F8
Morecambe LA3 212 A1
Twenty Acre La PR4 74 B1
Twickenham Pl 4 FY8 89 D6
Twig La L31 5 E1
Twin Lakes Ind Est PR5 57 A3
Twine Wlk LA6 236 C3
Twinegate OL12 51 E3
Twist Moor La PR6 62 B8
Twistfield Cl PR8 33 F5
Twiston La BB7 188 D5
Twitter La BB7 186 A3
Two Acre La PR1 95 C1
Two Brooks La BL8 48 B2
Two Gates Dr BB3 81 B2
Two Gates Wlk BB3 81 B2
Two Saints Pl 8 L39 15 E5
Twyford Cl L31 5 E1
Tyldesley Rd FY1 129 B3
Tyne Ave 4 FY3 129 D4
Tyne Cl FY5 172 E5
Tyne St
1 Bamber Bridge PR5 96 F1
4 Preston PR1 95 D6
Tynedale Pl FY3 151 A1
Tynedale Rd FY3 151 B1
Tynwald Rd BB2 100 E1
Tyrer Rd L39 15 F7
Tyrer's Ave L31 5 B5
Tyrers Cl L37 11 F2
Tyrone Ave FY2 150 D2
Tyseley Gr BB18 201 A1
Tythebarn St BB3 81 B1

U

Udale Pl 1 LA1 213 E2
Uggle La LA1 210 F3
Uldale Cl Nelson BB9 147 E6
Southport PR8 20 B3
Ulleswater Rd LA1 211 A8
Ullswater Ave
Accrington BB5 124 D1
Fleetwood FY7 172 D8
Morecambe LA4 212 G4
Orrell WN5 10 F7
Rochdale OL12 51 C1
Thornton FY5 173 B1
Ullswater Cl
Blackburn BB1 100 F6
Hambleton FY6 174 C2

Ullswater Cl *continued*
3 Rishton BB1 123 A1
Ullswater Cres
Carnforth LA5 216 E8
Thornton FY5 173 B1
Ullswater Rd
Blackpool FY4 109 C7
Burnley BB10 127 F5
Chorley PR7 42 B6
Fulwood PR2 117 C4
Ullswater Way BB4 105 A1
Ulnes Walton La PR5 58 A6
Ulpha Cl BB12 126 B8
Ulster Rd LA1 211 B5
Ulster St BB11 126 D5
Ulverston Cl
Blackburn BB2 101 A1
Maghull L31 5 E2
Ulverston Cres FY8 89 C7
Ulverston Dr BB1 123 A1
Under Billinge La BB2 99 F4
Underbank Cl 3 OL13 86 F3
Underbank Ho 1 OL13 86 F3
Underbank Rd
Haslingden BB4 83 F3
Rising Bridge BB5 84 A7
Thornton FY5 173 F1
Underbank Way 2 BB4 84 A3
Underley Hall Sch LA6 238 C5
Underley St BB10 147 C3
Underwood PR2 116 C3
Unicon Pk BB4 83 F3
Union Ct 13 OL13 69 C8
Union La PR3 175 C7
Union Pas 6 PR4 113 A5
Union Rd
Oswaldtwistle BB5 102 D3
Rawtenstall BB4 84 D2
Union St Accrington BB5 103 B6
Bacup OL13 86 F2
Bacup, Stacksteads OL13 69 C8
Blackburn BB2 100 E3
Brierfield BB9 147 B5
Chorley PR7 42 C8
Clitheroe BB7 164 C8
Colne BB8 169 E5
Darwen BB3 81 A1
Egerton BL7 46 D2
Haslingden BB4 84 A3
Morecambe LA4 212 D5
11 Preston PR1 95 F8
Ramsbottom BL0 49 C6
Rawtenstall BB4 85 A3
Southport PR9 34 C8
Whittle-le-W PR6 60 C8
Whitworth OL12 51 C8
Union Terr BB4 85 B2
Unit Rd PR8 20 D5
Unity St
3 Barnoldswick BB18 200 C2
Blackburn BB2 100 E2
Kelbrook BB18 192 A6
Unity Trad Est BB2 100 D4
Unity Way BB4 84 F3
Univ of Central Lancashire PR1 95 E8
Univ of Central Lancashire Avenham Annexe PR1 96 A6
Univ of Lancaster LA1 207 B7
Unsworth Ave FY6 195 A4
Unsworth St OL13 69 D7
Up Holland High Sch WN5 10 C4
Up-Brooks BB7 187 A1
Up-brooks Ind Est BB7 187 A1
Upholland Rd WN5 10 D2
Upholland Sta WN8 9 F4
Uplands Chase PR2 116 B6
Uplands Dr BB12 146 D7
Upper Ashmount BB4 85 C1
Upper Aughton Rd PR8 34 B4
Upper Cliffe BB6 123 C6
Upper George St 23 OL12 51 F1
Upper Hill Way BB18 191 B7
Upper Lune St FY7 194 B5
Upper Mead BL7 46 F1
Upper Westby St FY8 90 A3
Upphall La LA6 234 C4
Uppingham WN8 17 D1
Uppingham Dr BL0 49 B7
Upton Ave PR8 20 B6
Upton Barn L31 5 C2
Upwood Cl FY2 150 E5
Urban View PR6 61 F8
Ushers Mdw LA1 210 E7

V

Vale Ave BL6 31 A3
Vale Cl WN6 19 E8
Vale Coppice Horwich BL6 31 A3
Ramsbottom BL0 49 C3
Vale Cotts BL6 30 F2
Vale Cres PR8 20 C2
Vale Ct BB5 124 F1
Vale Gr L32 1 A1
Vale House Cl BB7 143 C5
Vale La L40 17 F5
Vale Rd LA1 213 E3
Vale Royal PR4 113 C5
Vale St Bacup OL13 87 A3
Blackburn BB2 100 E2
Darwen BB3 80 F2
Vale St *continued*
Haslingden BB4 84 B4
Vale Terr Calder Vale PR3 179 E8
Rawtenstall BB4 85 F3
Vale The Appley Bridge WN6 19 D8
Fulwood PR2 116 F5
Valentia Rd FY2 150 D3
Valentines La PR2,PR4 115 E4
Valentines Mdw PR4 115 E4
Valeway Ave FY5 150 D8
Valiants Shireworld Equestrian Ctr PR3 176 A2
Valley Cl BB9 169 A1
Valley Ctr The 4 BB4 85 A2
Valley Dr
Barnoldswick BB18 200 D4
Padiham BB12 125 D8
Valley Gdns
2 Earby BB18 201 B2
Padiham BB11 125 F4
Valley Rd
Barnoldswick BB18 200 C2
Earby BB18 201 B2
Hoghton PR5 98 F3
Longridge PR3 139 C7
Penwortham PR1 95 D5
Wilpshire BB1 121 F5
Valley St BB11 126 B4
Valley Terr BB12 144 E1
Valley View Chorley PR6 42 E7
Fulwood PR2 117 A4
Whitworth OL12 70 D4
Valley View Rd PR1 96 A3
Valligates BB1 101 B7
Vance Rd FY1 129 B4
Vancouver Cres BB2 100 C8
Vandyck Ave BB11 126 E2
Vardon Rd BB2 100 B2
Varley St Colne BB8 169 F6
2 Darwen BB3 81 A1
Preston PR1 117 A2
Varlian Cl L40 16 C3
Vaughan Cl L37 11 D4
Vaughan Rd PR8 34 B4
Vaughan St BB9 147 F7
Vauxhall St BB2 100 B3
Vauze Ave BL6 30 D1
Vauze House Cl BL6 30 D2
Veevers St Brierfield BB9 147 A6
7 Burnley BB11 126 F6
Padiham BB12 125 D8
Velvet St BB2 80 D8
Venables Ave BB8 169 F6
Venice Ave BB11 126 C4
Venice St BB11 126 D5
Ventnor Pl PR2 116 A4
Ventnor Rd Blackpool FY4 109 B6
1 Chorley PR7 42 B6
Haslingden BB4 84 C1
Venture Ct BB5 124 D5
Venture Rd FY7 173 A6
Venture St 18 OL13 87 A3
Verax St OL13 86 F1
Vermont Gr FY5 150 E8
Vernon Ave Blackpool FY3 129 E3
Warton PR4 91 E6
Vernon Cres LA2 207 A3
Vernon Ct 4 Galgate LA2 207 A4
Southport PR8 34 D5
Vernon Lodge FY8 88 F5
Vernon Pk 3 LA2 207 A4
Vernon Rd
Laneshaw Bridge BB8 170 D6
Lytham St Anne's FY8 109 E1
Ramsbottom BL8 49 A1
Southport PR9 35 A8
Vernon St Blackburn BB2 100 E4
Darwen BB3 81 B1
Nelson BB9 147 E7
Preston PR1 116 F1
Verona Ave BB11 126 C5
Verona Ct 6 FY5 173 A2
Veronica St BB3 80 E4
Verulam Rd PR9 53 B3
Vesta St 6 BL0 49 B6
Vevey St PR5 76 A1
Viaduct Rd PR5 98 F2
Vicar St Blackburn BB1 100 F5
Great Harwood BB6 123 C4
Vicarage Ave Caton LA2 231 C3
Cleveleys FY5 172 D3
5 Padiham BB12 125 B8
Vicarage Cl Adlington PR6 30 A8
Burton-in-K LA6 234 C7
Euxton PR7 59 D3
Formby L37 11 D4
Fulwood PR2 116 F4
Lytham St Anne's FY8 88 F7
Morecambe LA3 212 F2
Ormskirk L40 16 B3
Wrea Green PR4 112 B4
Vicarage Dr BB3 64 C8
Vicarage Fold BB7 143 F7
Vicarage Gdns L40 24 D4
Vicarage La
Accrington BB5 103 E1
Banks PR9 53 F7
Blackpool FY4 129 E1
Burton-in-K LA6 234 C7
Churchtown PR3 178 A2
Fulwood PR2 116 F4
Kirkby Lonsdale LA6 238 C2
Newton-with-S PR4 114 A3
Ormskirk L40 16 C3
Samlesbury PR5 118 E1
Wilpshire BB1 121 F6
Rawtenstall BB4 84 F2
Vicarage Rd
Barnoldswick BB18 200 C3
Blackrod BL6 30 D2
Formby L37 11 D4
Kelbrook BB18 192 A6
Nelson BB9 147 D7
Orrell WN5 10 D4
Poulton-le-F FY6 151 E3
Vicarage Rd W BL6 30 C2
Vicarage St 2 PR6 60 D1
Vicarage Wlk L39 15 E5
Vicarsfields Rd PR5 59 A7
Viceroy Ct 3 PR8 34 A6
Victor Ave LA4 213 A6
Victor Mews 6 BB7 164 D7
Victoria Apartments 20 BB12 145 C1
Victoria Ave
Accrington BB5 103 D2
Blackburn BB2 79 E8
Brierfield BB9 147 B6
Chatburn BB7 187 E5
Lancaster LA1 210 F5
Victoria Bldgs Darwen BB3 81 E3
8 Low Bentham LA2 233 B8
Victoria Bridge Rd PR8 34 C6
Victoria Bsns & Ind Ctr BB5 103 B4
Victoria Cross 4 BB1 100 E6
Victoria Ct 6
Blackburn BB1 100 E5
Broughton PR3 136 C2
Chatburn BB7 187 D5
Fulwood PR2 116 E3
Horwich BL6 31 C3
Padiham BB12 125 E7
Southport PR8 33 F4
Victoria Dr BB4 84 B2
Victoria Gdns BB9 168 C2
Victoria Ho BB1 101 B3
Victoria Lodge BB12 144 D2
Victoria Mans PR2 95 A7
Victoria Mews LA4 212 F6
Victoria Par
Morecambe LA4 212 F6
Preston PR2 116 B1
Rawtenstall BB4 68 E8
Victoria Park Ave
Leyland PR5 58 D7
Preston PR2 115 D1
Victoria Park Dr PR2 115 D1
Victoria Pk WN8 17 C1
Victoria Pl Halton LA2 214 E6
6 Lancaster LA1 210 F7
Victoria Quay PR2 95 A7
Victoria Rd
Barnoldswick BB18 200 C2
Blackburn BB2 99 C1
Earby BB18 201 B2
Formby L37 11 D5
Fulwood PR2 117 A4
Horwich BL6 31 C2
Ince Blundell L38 3 E3
Kirkham PR4 112 F5
Lytham St Anne's FY8 88 F5
Ormskirk L39 15 C2
Padiham BB12 125 E7
Poulton-le-F FY6 151 E4
Preston PR1,PR5 96 D5
Victoria Rd E FY5 173 B1
Victoria Rd W FY5 172 E2
Victoria Sq FY5 172 D2
Victoria St Accrington BB5 103 B5
Bacup OL13 69 D8
Bamber Bridge PR5 76 B8
Barrowford BB9 168 D3
25 Blackburn BB1 100 E5
Blackpool FY1 129 B5
Blackrod BL6 30 D2
1 Burnley BB11 126 F5
Burscough Bridge L40 24 E5
Carnforth LA5 217 D1
Chorley PR7 42 D7
Church BB5 102 E6
Clayton-le-M BB5 123 F2
Clayton-le-M BB5 123 F3
Clitheroe BB7 164 D7
9 Cornholme OL14 108 C1
21 Darwen BB3 81 A1
7 Earby BB18 201 B2
Fleetwood FY7 194 B5
Great Harwood BB6 123 D5
Haslingden BB4 84 A3
Longridge PR3 139 A7
Lytham St Anne's FY8 90 C3
Morecambe LA4 212 D5
Nelson BB9 147 D8
Oswaldtwistle BB5 102 D3
Preston PR1 116 E1
Ramsbottom BL0 49 B6
Rawtenstall BB4 85 C1
Rawtenstall, Waterfoot BB4 68 E8
Rishton BB1 123 B1
22 Rochdale OL12 51 F1
Southport PR8 34 B8
Wheelton PR6 61 A7
Whitworth OL12 51 C8
Victoria Terr
Abbey Village PR6 79 B2
12 Bamber Bridge PR5 76 A8
Billington BB7 143 A4
Calder Vale PR3 179 E8
1 Chorley PR6 60 D1
Garstang PR3 178 C7
Glasson LA2 205 F5
6 Leyland PR5 59 A8
Mellor Brook BB2 120 C3
Tockholes BB3 79 F2
Victoria Terr *continued*
Wheelton PR6 61 A7
Victoria Way Formby L37 11 D5
Rawtenstall BB4 85 C2
Southport PR8 33 F7
Victoria Wharf 4 LA1 213 E1
Victory Ave PR9 35 A7
Victory Cl BB9 147 E8
Victory Ctr The 1 BB9 147 E8
Victory Rd FY1 129 C6
Victory Wharf PR2 95 B8
View Rd BB3 80 E5
View St PR7 40 C7
Vihiers Cl BB7 143 C6
Villa Way PR3 178 C6
Village Cl WN8 8 D8
Village Croft PR7 59 D3
Village Dr PR2 117 F2
Village Green La PR2 115 F6
Village Way Blackpool FY2 150 D5
Hightown L38 2 F4
Skelmersdale WN8 8 D8
Villas Rd L31 6 B2
Villas The PR4 115 E5
Villiers Ct PR1 116 E2
Villiers St Burnley BB11 126 C5
Bury BL9 32 A3
Padiham BB12 125 D7
Preston PR1 116 D2
Preston PR1 116 E2
Vincent Ct BB2 80 D8
Vincent Rd BB9 147 F8
Vincent St Blackburn BB2 80 D8
Colne BB8 169 F6
8 Lancaster LA1 211 A7
Vincit St BB10 127 C8
Vine Ct FY2 150 C1
Vine St Accrington BB5 103 A6
Brierfield BB9 147 B5
Chorley PR7 60 C1
Lancaster LA1 210 F6
Oswaldtwistle BB5 102 C3
Preston PR1 95 D8
Ramsbottom BL0 49 A4
Vinery The PR4 74 F8
Viola Cl WN6 28 D2
Violet St BB10 147 A1
Virginia Ave L31 5 D3
Virginia Gr L31 5 C3
Virginia St PR8 34 C6
Vivary Way BB8 169 B5
Vivian Dr PR8 34 A2
Vulcan Rd PR4 113 B1
Vulcan St Burnley BB11 126 F6
4 Nelson BB9 168 F1
Southport PR9 34 C7

W

Wackersall Rd BB8 169 B3
Waddington & West Bradford CE Prim Sch BB7 186 C5
Waddington Ave BB10 127 D6
Waddington Ct FY8 89 C6
Waddington Hospl (Almshouses) BB7 186 B5
Waddington Rd
Accrington BB5 103 D6
Clitheroe BB7 186 E1
Fulwood PR2 118 A2
Lytham St Anne's FY8 89 C7
West Bradford BB7 186 D5
Waddington St
Earby BB18 201 B2
3 Padiham BB12 125 D8
Waddow Gn BB7 164 C8
Waddow Gr BB7 186 C4
Waddow View BB7 186 B4
Wade Brook Rd PR5 57 F6
Wade St BB12 145 D1
Wades Croft PR4 92 C6
Wades Ct FY3 150 F1
Wadham Rd PR1 96 B6
Wagon Rd LA2,PR3 220 B8
Waidshouse Cl BB9 147 E6
Waidshouse Rd BB9 147 E6
Wain Ct BB2 100 B4
Waingap Cres OL12 51 D8
Waingap Rise
Rochdale OL12 51 F4
Whitworth OL12 51 D7
Waingate Grimsargh PR2 138 C1
Rawtenstall BB4 85 B3
Waingate Cl BB4 85 B3
Waingate Ct PR2 138 C1
Waingate La BB4 85 B3
Waingate Rd BB4 85 B3
Waitholme La LA5 234 A7
Wakefield Ave LA4 212 G6
Wakefield Dr LA1 211 A4
Wakefield Rd FY2 150 E4
Walden Rd BB1 121 F4
Waldon St PR1 96 E8
Waldron WN8 8 D8
Wales Rd BB4 85 F1
Walesby Pl FY8 89 D5
Walgarth Dr PR7 42 B7
Walk Mill Pl BB10 127 E1
Walk The Hesketh Bank PR4 72 C4
Southport PR8 34 A5
Walkdale PR4 94 D2
Walker Ave BB5 103 A4
Walker Cl L37 11 F2
Walker Gr LA3 208 F7
Walker La PR2 116 B6
Walker Park Ind Est BB1 81 C7
Walker Pl PR1 96 B7
Walker Rd BB1 81 C7
Walker St Blackburn BB1 100 F4
Blackpool FY1 129 B6
Clitheroe BB7 164 F8
Preston PR1 95 F8
Walker Way FY5 173 B4
Walkers Hill FY4 110 A7
Walkers Ind Est LA3 208 F3
Wall La PR3 153 E5
Wall St Blackpool FY1 129 C7
Newchurch BB4 85 E2
Wallace La PR3 204 C4
Wallbank Dr OL12 51 C7
Wallbrook Ave WN5 10 D1
Wallcroft St WN8 8 E8
Walled Garden The PR6 60 B6
Wallend Rd PR2 94 D7
Waller Ave FY2 150 C5
Waller Hill BB8 191 D1
Walletts Rd PR7 42 B6
Wallhurst Cl BB10 128 B5
Walling's La LA5 218 B4
Wallstreams Ct BB10 128 B5
Wallstreams La BB10 128 B5
Wallsuches BL6 31 F4
Walmer Ct PR8 33 F4
Walmer Gn PR4 73 F5
Walmer Rd
Lytham St Anne's FY8 88 F8
Southport PR8 34 A3
Walmersley Golf Course BL9 32 B8
Walmersley Old Rd BL9 49 F2
Walmesley Ave BB1 102 B8
Walmsgate BB18 200 B2
Walmsley Bridge La
Bilsborrow PR3 157 E8
Claughton PR3 179 E1
Walmsley Brow BB7 143 B4
Walmsley CE Prim Sch BL7 46 E1
Walmsley Cl Church BB5 102 E6
Garstang PR3 178 C7
Walmsley Ct BB5 123 F1
Walmsley St Darwen BB3 81 B2
Fleetwood FY7 194 A4
16 Great Harwood BB6 123 C5
Rishton BB1 123 B1
Walney Pl FY3 130 A7
Walnut Ave Bury BL9 32 C3
Haslingden BB4 84 C3
Walnut Cl PR1 95 B3
Walnut St Bacup OL13 86 F3
Blackburn BB1 100 F7
3 Blackburn BB1 101 A7
Southport PR8 34 C4
Walpole Ave FY4 109 B5
Walpole St Blackburn BB1 100 F4
10 Burnley BB10 147 B1
Walro Mews PR9 53 A3
Walsden Gr BB10 127 C6
Walsh Fold BL7 47 D2
Walsh St Blackburn BB2 100 E2
Horwich BL6 31 B4
Walshaw High Sch BB10 147 D1
Walshaw La BB10 147 D2
Walshaw St BB10 127 B8
Walter Ave FY8 110 A2
Walter Pl FY8 110 A2
Walter Robinson Ct FY3 129 D6
Walter St Accrington BB5 103 B6
Blackburn BB1 101 A4
Blackburn BB1 101 B4
Brierfield BB10,BB9 147 B5
Darwen BB3 64 B5
Huncoat BB5 124 E2
Oswaldtwistle BB5 102 D3
Walter Street Prim Sch BB9 147 B5
Waltham Ave FY4 109 D5
Waltham Cl BB5 103 E3
Waltham Ct LA2 214 E7
Waltho Ave L31 5 E1
Walton Ave
Morecambe LA4 213 B5
Penwortham PR1 95 B3
Walton Cl OL13 87 A1
Walton Cottage Homes BB9 169 A1
Walton Cres BB2 101 A1
Walton Gn PR5 96 C4
Walton Gr LA4 213 B5
Walton High Sch BB9 169 A2
Walton La BB9 169 A1
Walton St Accrington BB5 124 A1
Adlington PR7 30 A6
Barrowford BB9 168 E4
Colne BB8 169 D4
8 Nelson BB9 168 E1
Southport PR9 34 C8
Walton Summit Rd PR5 77 A7
Walton View PR1 96 D8
Walton's Par PR1 95 E7
Walton-le-Dale Cty Prim Sch PR5 96 D2
Walton-le-Dale High Sch PR5 96 F2
Walverden Ave 4 FY4 109 D8
Walverden Cres 3 BB9 147 F8
Walverden Prim Sch BB9 147 F8
Walverden Rd
Brierfield BB9 147 D5
Lane Bottom BB10 148 B4
Walverden Terr BB9 147 F7
Wandales La LA6 238 F2
Wanes Blades Rd L40 25 E5
Wanishar La L39 14 A5

Wansbeck Ave FY7 ....193 D2
Wansbeck Ho FY7 ....193 D2
Wansfell Rd BB7 ....164 C7
Wanstead Cres FY4 ....129 E1
Wanstead St PR1 ....96 E8
Warbreck Ct FY2 ....150 B1
Warbreck Dr FY2 ....150 B2
Warbreck High Sch FY2 ..150 D1
Warbreck Hill Rd FY2 ....150 D1
Warburton Bldgs BB4 ....83 F1
Warburton St BB4 ....83 F1
Warbury St PR1 ....117 E1
Warcock La OL13 ....87 B3
Ward Ave Cleveleys FY5 ....172 D3
Formby L37 ....11 D2
Oswaldtwistle BB5 ....102 C3
Ward Green Cross PR3 ....140 A7
Ward Green La PR3 ....140 A7
Ward St Bamber Bridge PR5 ..76 B7
Belmont BL7 ....45 C5
5 Blackpool FY1 ....129 B1
Burnley BB11 ....126 E6
Chorley PR6 ....42 E7
Great Harwood BB6 ....123 C5
Kirkham PR4 ....113 A4
Ward's End PR1 ....96 A7
Warde St 8 BB9 ....147 E8
Wardle Ct PR6 ....60 C6
Wardle Dr FY5 ....172 F3
Wardle St OL13 ....69 D8
Wardley's La FY6 ....174 A3
Wareham Cl BB5 ....124 B1
Wareham Rd FY3 ....150 F1
Wareham St BB1 ....101 A7
Warehouse La BB8 ....191 D1
Waring Dr FY5 ....173 A2
Warings The
Heskin Green PR7 ....40 E4
Nelson BB9 ....147 E6
Warkworth Terr 17 OL13 ....87 A3
Warley Ave LA3 ....213 A4
Warley Dr LA3 ....213 A4
Warley Rd FY1 ....129 C8
Warley Wise La BB8 ....192 F3
Warmden Ave BB5 ....103 E3
Warne Pl LA1 ....213 D1
Warner Rd PR1 ....117 D1
Warner St Accrington BB5 ..103 C5
Haslingden BB4 ....84 B3
Warpers Moss Cl L40 ....24 F5
Warpers Moss La L40 ....25 A5
Warren Ave N FY7 ....193 F4
Warren Ave S FY7 ....193 F4
Warren Cl LA2 ....213 E8
Warren Ct PR8 ....33 E5
Warren Dr Bacup OL13 ....70 C8
Barrowford BB9 ....168 C3
Blackpool FY5 ....150 E7
Hest Bank LA2 ....213 E8
Warren Fold BB7 ....141 F8
Warren Gn L37 ....11 D3
Warren Gr Blackpool FY5 ....150 E8
Heysham LA3 ....208 E5
Warren Rd Heysham LA3 ...208 E5
Southport PR9 ....35 A8
Warren St FY7 ....194 B4
Warren The
Blackburn BB2 ....100 A7
Preston PR2 ....117 E6
Warrenhouse Rd L33 ....1 B4
Warrenhurst Ho 1 FY7 ...193 F3
Warrenhurst Rd FY7 ....194 A4
Warrenside Cl BB1 ....122 A4
Warrington St BB1 ....101 A8
Warrington Terr BB6 ....143 D8
Warsicks Cotts FY6 ....152 E1
Warth La Barnoldswick LA6 ..236 F2
Rawtenstall BB4 ....68 D8
Warton Ave LA3 ....208 E6
Warton Crag (Nature Reserve) LA5 ....217 C6
Warton Pl PR7 ....42 A8
Warton Rd LA5 ....217 D2
Warton St
Lytham St Anne's FY8 ....90 C3
2 Preston PR1 ....95 E6
Wartonwood View 1 LA5 ....217 D1
Warwick Ave
Accrington BB5 ....103 B7
Clayton-le-M BB5 ....123 F3
Cleveleys FY5 ....172 F4
Darwen BB3 ....80 E3
Lancaster LA1 ....211 A5
Morecambe LA4 ....213 B6
Warwick Cl Church BB5 ....102 F7
Fulwood PR2 ....116 E4
Ramsbottom BL8 ....49 A1
Southport PR8 ....34 B4
Warwick Dr
Barnoldswick BB18 ....200 F1
Brierfield BB9 ....147 D5
Clitheroe BB7 ....186 F2
Padiham BB12 ....125 D7
Warwick Ho 10 PR1 ....96 A6
Warwick Pl Fleetwood FY7 ..194 A5
Normoss FY3 ....130 B8
Warwick Rd
Bamber Bridge PR5 ....96 D4
Blackpool FY3 ....129 D7
Eccleston PR7 ....40 C7
Leyland PR5 ....58 E7
Lytham St Anne's FY8 ....88 F6
Warwick St Adlington PR7 ....29 F6
Church BB5 ....102 F7
Haslingden BB4 ....84 B3
Longridge PR3 ....139 A8
Nelson BB9 ....147 E7
Warwick St *continued*
Preston PR1 ....95 F8
Southport PR8 ....34 B4
Wasdale Ave
Blackburn BB1 ....101 C3
Maghull L31 ....5 F2
Wasdale Cl Leyland PR5 ....59 B6
Padiham BB12 ....145 C1
Wasdale Gr PR3 ....138 F5
Wasdale Rd FY4 ....110 A8
Wash La BL9 ....32 B2
Washbrook Cl BB7 ....164 D1
Washbrook Way L39 ....15 E4
Washburn Ct LA3 ....213 B2
Washington Ave
Blackpool FY2 ....150 E2
3 Morecambe LA4 ....212 E5
Washington Cl LA1 ....210 D7
Washington Ct FY2 ....150 E2
Washington Dr LA5 ....217 E6
Washington Hall Fire Brigade Training Ctr
PR7 ....59 F2
Washington La PR7 ....59 F2
Washington St BB5 ....103 C6
Waste La LA2 ....220 C7
Wastwater Dr 4 LA4 ....213 A4
Watchyard La L37 ....12 A4
Water Fold BB4 ....86 A8
Water La Edenfield BL0 ....67 D2
Preston PR2 ....116 D1
Southport PR9 ....53 D5
Water Mdws BB2 ....80 D7
Water Prim Sch BB4 ....86 A8
Water Ski Ctr OL12 ....70 C2
Water St
10 Accrington BB5 ....103 C6
Adlington PR7 ....30 A6
1 Bamber Bridge PR5 ....96 F2
Brindle PR6 ....77 F5
Chorley PR7 ....60 C1
Clayton-le-M BB5 ....123 F5
1 Colne BB8 ....169 E5
Earby BB18 ....201 B2
Egerton BL7 ....46 D2
Great Harwood BB6 ....123 C5
Hapton BB12 ....125 C4
Lancaster LA1 ....213 F1
Nelson BB9 ....147 E8
8 Ramsbottom BL0 ....49 B5
Rawtenstall BB4 ....85 A8
Ribchester PR3 ....140 E3
Whitworth OL12 ....51 C8
Worsthorne BB10 ....128 B5
Water's Edge PR2 ....115 F3
Waterbarn La OL13 ....69 B8
Waterbarn St 3 BB10 ....147 B1
Waterdale FY2 ....150 E5
Waterfall Terr BL7 ....45 C5
Waterfield Ave BB3 ....64 B6
Waterfold La BL9 ....32 C1
Waterfoot Ave
Blackpool FY3 ....129 E6
Southport PR8 ....20 B3
Waterfoot Bsns Ctr BB4 ....85 F2
Waterfoot Cty Prim Sch
BB4 ....68 F8
Waterford Cl Fairview PR6 ...43 A1
Preston PR2 ....117 C5
Waterford St BB9 ....168 F1
Waterfront 2 BB1 ....100 F3
Waterfront Marine & Ind Est FY8 ....90 E3
Waterhead Cres FY5 ....150 C6
Watering Pool La PR1,PR5 ..96 B1
Waterloo Cl BB2 ....80 B8
Waterloo Rd
Blackpool FY4 ....129 D1
Burnley BB11 ....127 B4
Burnley BB11 ....127 B5
Clitheroe BB7 ....164 F8
Kelbrook BB18 ....192 A6
Preston PR2 ....116 C1
Southport PR8 ....33 E2
Waterloo Sch (Prim & Inf)
FY1 ....129 D1
Waterloo St Chorley PR7 ....60 D1
Enfield BB5 ....124 A1
Waterloo Terr PR2 ....116 C1
Watermans Cl BL6 ....31 C4
Watermede WN5 ....10 E3
Waters Edge BB1 ....100 F4
Waters Reach
Cleveleys FY5 ....172 C3
Lytham St Anne's FY8 ....89 D3
Waterside Cl PR3 ....178 B7
Waterside Ind Est BB8 ....169 E4
Waterside Mews BB12 ....125 D8
Waterside Pl LA4 ....212 E3
Waterside Rd Colne BB8 ...169 D4
Haslingden BB4 ....84 A2
Ramsbottom BL0,BL8,BL9 ....49 C3
Waterside Terr
11 Bacup OL13 ....86 F3
Waterside BB3 ....81 E3
Waterslack Rd LA5 ....218 E6
Waterworks Rd L39 ....16 A6
Watery Gate La PR3,PR4 ...154 D3
Watery La Darwen BB3 ....64 B6
Garstang PR3 ....199 E1
Lancaster LA1 ....213 D3
Preston PR2 ....95 B8
Preston, Fishwick PR1 ....96 E7
Watery Lane Ind Est 2
BB3 ....64 B6
Watford St 5 BB1 ....100 E6
Watkin La PR5 ....76 B7
Watkin Rd PR6 ....60 B8
Watkins Cl BB10 ....147 C4
Watling Cl LA3 ....213 A3
Watling Gate BB6 ....142 C6
Watling St BL8 ....48 A1
Watling Street Rd
Fulwood PR2 ....117 B3
Fulwood, Brookfield PR2 ....117 E5
Watson Ct FY4 ....109 D7
Watson Gdns OL12 ....51 D2
Watson Rd FY4 ....109 C7
Watson St Blackburn BB2 ...100 B2
8 Oswaldtwistle BB5 ....102 E4
Watt St Burnley BB12 ....126 C7
Sabden BB7 ....144 F7
Watton Beck Cl L31 ....5 F2
Watts Cl L33 ....1 A4
Watts St BL6 ....31 C2
Wavell Ave PR9 ....35 B7
Wavell Cl Accrington BB5 ...103 F2
Southport PR9 ....35 B7
Wavell St BB12 ....126 C6
Waverledge Rd BB6 ....123 B4
Waverledge St BB6 ....123 C4
Waverley WN8 ....17 D1
Waverley Ave
Blackpool FY1 ....129 C8
Fleetwood FY7 ....193 D3
Waverley Cl Brierfield BB9 ..147 D4
Read BB12 ....144 D1
Waverley Dr
New Longton PR4 ....74 F7
Tarleton PR4 ....56 A6
Waverley Gdns PR2 ....117 E2
Waverley Pl BB2 ....100 B5
Waverley Rd
Accrington BB5 ....103 E3
Blackburn BB1 ....101 F4
Preston PR1 ....117 D1
Wilpshire BB1 ....121 E4
Waverley St
1 Burnley BB11 ....126 E6
Southport PR8 ....34 A7
Waxy La PR4 ....92 C7
Way Gate FY5 ....172 D5
Way The LA3 ....213 B3
Wayfarers Arc PR8 ....34 B7
Wayman Rd FY3 ....129 D6
Wayoh Croft BL7 ....47 D6
Wayside FY6 ....194 D5
Weald The PR4 ....115 D5
Weasel La BB3 ....80 B2
Weatherhill Cres BB9 ....147 E5
Weaver Ave L40 ....24 F5
Weaver's Brow PR6 ....42 F5
Webb St BL6 ....31 C3
Webber Ct BB11 ....126 A3
Webber Rd L33 ....1 C1
Weber St BB4 ....85 D1
Webster Ave FY4 ....109 E7
Webster Gr LA4 ....213 C6
Webster St PR2 ....116 C1
Wedgewood Rd BB5 ....124 F1
Weeton Ave Blackpool FY4 ..109 E5
Cleveleys FY5 ....172 D3
Lytham St Anne's FY8 ....89 A8
Weeton CE Prim Sch
PR4 ....131 E1
Weeton Cty Prim Sch
PR4 ....131 E6
Weeton Pl 4 PR2 ....115 E1
Weeton Rd
Great Plumpton PR4 ....111 F7
Kirkham PR4 ....112 F7
Kirkham, Weeton PR4 ....112 C8
Weeton PR4 ....131 F2
Weeton Camp FY6,PR4 ....131 E7
Weets View BB18 ....200 C3
Weind The PR3 ....154 B5
Weir La OL13 ....87 A7
Weir St BB2 ....100 E4
Weirden Cl PR1 ....95 C1
Welbeck Ave
Blackburn BB1 ....101 B8
Blackpool FY4 ....129 E1
Fleetwood FY7 ....193 F3
Welbeck Gdns FY7 ....193 F3
Welbeck Rd PR8 ....34 A4
Welbeck Terr PR8 ....34 A4
Welbourne WN8 ....17 D1
Welbury Cl 5 BB18 ....201 B2
Weld Ave PR7 ....42 C5
Weld Blundell Ave L31 ....5 B5
Weld Dr L37 ....11 D4
Weld Par PR8 ....33 F4
Weld Rd PR8 ....33 F5
Weldale PR8 ....33 F4
Weldbank La PR7 ....42 C5
Weldbank St PR7 ....42 C5
Weldon Dr L39 ....15 F4
Weldon St BB11 ....126 E5
Well Ct WN6 ....28 E1
Well Field BB5 ....124 A2
Well Fold BB7 ....164 F8
Well Head BB8 ....170 B4
Well Head Rd BB12 ....167 A3
Well La Brinscall PR7 ....61 F7
Haskayne L39 ....13 E6
High Casterton LA6 ....238 F2
Little Eccleston PR3 ....153 D6
Warton, Carnforth LA5 ....217 E5
Yealand Redmayne LA5 ....219 E3
Well Orch PR5 ....77 B5
Well St Newchurch BB4 ....85 F3
Padiham BB12 ....125 B8
Rishton BB1 ....123 B2
Well St N BL0 ....67 C2
Well St W 6 BL0 ....49 B5
Well Terr BB7 ....186 F1
Welland Cl FY2 ....150 E4
Wellbrow Dr PR3 ....139 B8
Wellbrow Terr OL12 ....51 D2
Wellcross Rd WN8 ....10 B6
Wellesley St BB12 ....125 F6
Wellfield PR4 ....93 F1
Wellfield Ave PR5 ....75 F1
Wellfield Bsns Pk PR1 ....95 D8
Wellfield CE/Meth Sch
BB12 ....126 D8
Wellfield Dr BB12 ....126 D7
Wellfield High Sch PR5 ....75 F1
Wellfield La L40 ....16 C3
Wellfield Rd
Bamber Bridge PR5 ....76 A7
Blackburn BB2 ....100 C6
Preston PR1 ....95 D8
Wellgate BB7 ....164 F8
Wellhouse Rd BB18 ....200 B2
Wellhouse Sq 17 BB18 ....200 B2
Wellhouse St BB18 ....200 B2
Wellington Ave PR5 ....59 B8
Wellington Ct
7 Accrington BB5 ....103 C5
Burnley BB10 ....127 B5
Wellington Fold 3 BB3 ....81 A1
Wellington Pl PR5 ....96 D2
Wellington Rd
Blackburn BB2 ....100 C3
Blackpool FY1 ....129 B2
Edgworth BL7 ....47 D4
Lancaster LA1 ....211 A5
Preston PR2 ....116 C1
Wellington St
Accrington BB5 ....103 C5
Barnoldswick BB18 ....200 B1
Chorley PR7 ....60 C1
Clayton-le-M BB5 ....123 F2
Great Harwood BB6 ....123 C4
Kirkham PR4 ....112 F5
Lytham St Anne's FY8 ....90 D3
16 Nelson BB9 ....168 D1
Preston PR1 ....95 D8
19 Rochdale OL12 ....51 F1
1 Southport PR8 ....34 A6
Wellington Street St Johns
BB1 ....100 D6
Wellington Terr LA4 ....212 E5
Wellogate Gdns FY4 ....109 D6
Wellow Pl FY8 ....89 C5
Wells Cl Morecambe LA3 ....212 E2
Thornton FY5 ....173 A2
Wells Fold Cl PR6 ....77 C1
Wells St Haslingden BB4 ....84 B3
9 Preston PR1 ....117 D1
Welsby Rd PR5 ....58 D8
Welwyn Ave PR8 ....20 E6
Welwyn Pl FY5 ....172 E1
Wembley Ave
Blackpool FY3 ....129 E8
Penwortham PR1 ....95 B5
Poulton-le-F FY6 ....151 E3
Wembley Rd FY5 ....173 B4
Wemyss Cl 1 LA3 ....208 E7
Wendover Rd FY6 ....151 A6
Wenlock Cl BL6 ....31 C6
Wenning Ave
High Bentham LA2 ....233 D7
Maghull L31 ....5 E2
Wenning Ct LA3 ....213 B2
Wenning Pl LA1 ....213 E2
Wenning St BB9 ....147 F7
Wennington Hall Sch
LA2 ....235 E1
Wennington Rd
Southport PR9 ....34 F7
Wray LA2 ....232 D6
Wennington Sta LA2 ....232 E8
Wensley Ave FY7 ....193 E1
Wensley Cl BB11 ....126 E3
Wensley Dr
Accrington BB5 ....103 D5
Lancaster LA1 ....213 F3
Wensley Fold CE Prim Sch
BB2 ....100 B5
Wensley Pl PR2 ....117 D4
Wensley Rd BB2 ....100 B4
Wensleydale Ave FY3 ....130 A7
Wensleydale Cl Maghull L31 ..5 B2
Thornton FY5 ....151 D8
Wentcliffe Dr BB18 ....201 B1
Wentworth Ave
Fleetwood FY7 ....172 D7
Inskip PR4 ....134 C8
Wentworth Cl
Penwortham PR1 ....95 A6
Southport PR8 ....20 C4
Wentworth Cres LA3 ....212 E2
Wentworth Ct PR4 ....113 B4
Wentworth Dr
Broughton PR3 ....136 C3
Euxton PR7 ....59 D4
Thornton FY5 ....151 D8
Wentworth Mews FY8 ....89 A6
Wentworth Pl PR3 ....136 C3
Wenetheh Cl PR1 ....95 F1
Wescoe Cl WN5 ....10 E5
Wesham CE Sch PR4 ....112 F6
Wesham Cross PR4 ....112 F7
Wesham Hall Cl PR4 ....113 A6
Wesham Hall Rd PR4 ....113 A6
Wesham Park Hospl PR4 ..112 F7
Wesley Cl LA2 ....233 D8
Wesley Ct 3 FY7 ....194 B5
Wesley Dr LA3 ....208 F7
Wesley Gr BB12 ....126 D7
Wesley Mews FY4 ....110 A7
Wesley Pl Bacup OL13 ....86 E1
Wesley Pl *continued*
Higham BB12 ....145 F6
Wesley St Accrington BB5 ...102 F6
Bamber Bridge PR5 ....76 F8
Blackburn BB1 ....100 F7
Brierfield BB9 ....147 B6
Oswaldtwistle BB5 ....102 E5
8 Padiham BB12 ....125 D8
Sabden BB7 ....144 F8
Southport PR8 ....34 B7
Wesley Terr OL13 ....87 A7
Wesleyan Row BB7 ....164 E8
Wessex Cl Huncoat BB5 ....103 F8
Standish WN1 ....29 B1
West Ave
Barnoldswick BB18 ....200 B2
Fulwood PR2 ....116 A6
West Bank PR7 ....42 C8
West Bank Ave FY8 ....89 E3
West Beach FY8 ....90 A2
West Bradford Rd
Grindleton BB7 ....187 A6
Waddington BB7 ....186 C5
West Bradford BB7 ....186 F4
West Bridge L31 ....5 C1
West Cliff PR1 ....95 E6
West Cliff Terr PR1 ....95 E6
West Cliffe FY8 ....90 C3
West Close Ave BB12 ....145 F5
West Close Rd BB18 ....200 B3
West Craven High Sch
BB18 ....200 C1
West Cres Accrington BB5 ..103 B8
Broughton PR3 ....136 C3
West Ct FY5 ....172 C5
West Dene WN8 ....26 B2
West Dr Clayton-le-W PR5 ....76 D3
Cleveleys FY5 ....172 E3
Inskip PR4 ....134 C8
Kirkham PR4 ....112 E7
Lancaster LA1 ....213 D2
Whalley BB7 ....143 A7
West Dr W FY5 ....172 D3
West End
Great Eccleston PR3 ....154 A5
Penwortham PR1 ....95 B6
West End Bsns Pk BB5 ....102 B5
West End Cty Prim Sch
Morecambe LA4 ....212 C4
Ormskirk L39 ....15 E7
Oswaldtwistle BB5 ....102 C5
West End La PR4 ....91 B5
West End Rd LA4 ....212 D4
West End Terr PR8 ....34 A7
West Exchange St 7
BB8 ....169 D4
West Field Rd BB18 ....200 A4
West Gate FY7 ....193 D4
West Gdns 1 OL13 ....69 B8
West Gillibrands Ind Est
WN8 ....8 E8
West Hall La LA6 ....235 C6
West Hill BB9 ....168 D4
West Ing La BD23 ....225 D5
West La Downham BB7 ....188 A4
Formby L37 ....11 F6
West Lancashire Light Rly
PR4 ....72 F2
West Leigh Rd BB1 ....100 C8
West Lodge FY6 ....174 C1
West Mdw PR2 ....115 E3
West Meade L31 ....5 B2
West Moss La FY8 ....110 E1
West Mount WN5 ....10 F6
West Paddock PR5 ....58 E8
West Park Ave PR2 ....115 F2
West Park Dr FY3 ....129 E4
West Park La PR2 ....116 A2
West Park Rd BB2 ....100 C6
West Rd Fulwood PR2 ....116 F3
Lancaster LA1 ....210 E8
West Sq PR4 ....74 A8
West St 9 Blackpool FY1 ....129 B5
Burnley BB10 ....127 C8
Chorley PR7 ....42 C7
Colne BB8 ....169 E4
Great Harwood BB6 ....123 C4
Lancaster LA1 ....210 F5
Morecambe LA3 ....212 B4
7 Nelson BB9 ....168 D1
Padiham BB12 ....125 B8
7 Ramsbottom BL0 ....49 B5
Rawtenstall BB4 ....68 E8
Southport PR8 ....34 A7
West Strand PR1 ....95 D8
West Street Cty Prim Sch
BB8 ....169 E4
West View Bacup OL13 ....69 B8
Bamber Bridge PR5 ....76 E7
Blackburn BB2 ....100 B4
Blackpool FY1 ....129 C3
Clitheroe BB7 ....164 D7
Garstang PR3 ....178 C7
Glasson LA2 ....205 E5
Grindleton BB7 ....187 B8
Haslingden BB4 ....84 B4
Haslingden, Bridge End BB4 ...67 A7
Hollins Lane PR3 ....204 D2
Kirkham PR4 ....112 F7
Little Eccleston PR4 ....153 F1
Longton PR4 ....74 A8
4 Newchurch BB4 ....85 F1
1 Ormskirk L39 ....15 F5
Oswaldtwistle BB5 ....102 E4
Over Town BB10 ....107 A8

West View *continued*
Parbold WN8 26 C2
Preston PR1 117 C2
Ramsbottom BL0 67 C2
Waddington BB7 186 B4
Wheelton PR6 61 A7
West View Ave 8 FY1 129 B2
West View Pl BB2 100 B6
West View Rd
Morecambe LA4 212 D5
Whitewell Bottom BB4 85 F5
West View Terr
Darwen BB3 80 A2
Padiham BB12 125 C7
1 Preston PR1 95 D8
West Way Chorley PR7 60 A2
Fleetwood FY7 172 D8
West Wlk BL7 46 D2
Westbank Ave FY4 110 A7
Westboro Cl LA3 212 A1
Westbourne BB4 67 A8
Westbourne Ave
Blackpool FY1 129 C1
Burnley BB11 126 D3
Wrea Green PR4 112 B3
Westbourne Ave S BB11 126 E3
Westbourne Ct FY6 194 D5
Westbourne Dr LA1 210 D7
Westbourne Gdns PR8 33 D4
Westbourne Pl LA1 210 D8
Westbourne Rd
Chorley PR7 42 B6
Cleveleys FY5 172 D5
Heysham LA3 209 A2
Knott End-on-S FY6 194 D5
Lancaster LA1 210 D7
Southport PR8 33 D4
Warton, Carnforth LA5 217 C4
Westbrook Cres PR2 116 A3
Westbury Cl Blackpool FY5 150 C7
Brierfield BB10 147 E2
Westbury Gdns BB1 101 C4
Westby Ave FY4 109 E5
Westby Ct FY6 151 D2
Westby Gr FY7 194 B5
Westby Pl PR2 115 F1
Westby Rd
Lytham St Anne's FY8 88 E8
Westby PR4 111 E5
Westby St FY8 90 B3
Westby Way FY6 151 D2
Westcliff Inf Sch FY5 150 C5
Westcliffe BB6 123 B6
Westcliffe Dr
Blackpool FY3 129 E8
Morecambe LA3 212 D2
Westcliffe Rd PR8 33 F5
Westcliffe Wlk BB9 147 E7
Westcote St 8 BB3 64 B6
Westcroft PR4 73 E3
Westend Ave PR7 41 D1
Westerdale Dr PR9 54 B5
Westerlong PR2 115 D1
Western Ave BB11 126 E4
Western Ct OL13 69 B8
Western Dr PR5 75 D2
Western Rd OL13 69 C8
Westfield
Bamber Bridge PR5 76 A8
1 Nelson BB9 168 D1
Westfield Ave
Blackpool FY3 151 A1
Fleetwood FY7 193 E2
Normoss FY3 130 B7
Read BB12 144 D1
Westfield Ct FY5 173 B4
Westfield Dr
Bolton-le-S LA5 216 A6
Fulwood PR2 117 E4
Gregson Lane PR5 97 D1
Leyland PR5 75 E1
Warton PR4 91 F5
West Bradford BB7 186 E6
Westfield Gr LA4 212 D4
Westfield Rd FY1 129 D1
Westfields PR5 57 A2
Westgate
Barnoldswick BB18 200 A1
Burnley BB11 126 E6
Fulwood PR2 116 D5
Leyland PR5 58 F8
Morecambe LA3,LA4 212 F3
Read BB12 144 C1
Skelmersdale WN8 8 D8
Whitworth OL12 51 B7
Westgate Ave
Morecambe LA3 212 E2
Ramsbottom BL0 49 A2
Westgate Cl OL12 51 B7
Westgate Cty Prim Sch
LA4 212 E3
Westgate Dr WN5 10 D5
Westgate La LA6 236 E5
Westgate Park Rd LA4 212 F3
Westgate Rd FY8 109 C4
Westgate Trad Ctr 2
BB11 126 F6
Westham St LA1 211 A7
Westhaven PR9 34 D8
Westhaven Cres L39 15 C1
Westhead Ave L33 1 A1
Westhead Cl L33 1 A1
Westhead Rd PR5 57 B2
Westhead Wlk
1 Fleetwood FY7 193 F2
Westhead Wlk *continued*
Kirkby L33 1 A1
Westholme Lower Sch
BB2 100 B6
Westholme Sch
Blackburn BB2 100 A6
Blackburn BB2 99 E6
Westhoughton Rd PR6,PR7 42 F1
Westland Ave BB3 63 F8
Westlands PR5 58 C7
Westlands Ct FY5 151 B8
Westleigh Rd PR2 115 F1
Westminster Ave LA4 212 C4
Westminster Cl
Accrington BB5 103 E3
Darwen BB3 80 E3
Morecambe LA3 212 E2
Read BB12 144 D1
Westminster Dr PR8 20 A4
Westminster Pl
Eccleston PR7 40 A8
Hutton PR4 94 D1
Westminster Rd
Blackpool FY1 129 C8
Chorley PR7 42 C7
Darwen BB3 80 E3
Morecambe LA3,LA4 212 B3
Westmoor Gr LA3 208 E5
Westmoreland Rd PR8 34 D5
Westmoreland St BB9 147 C8
Westmorland Ave
Blackpool FY1 129 D3
Cleveleys FY5 172 D4
Westmorland Cl
Leyland PR5 58 E7
Penwortham PR1 95 B4
Preston PR1 95 B4
Westmorland Ho 15
PR1 95 F8
Westmorland St BB11 126 D5
Weston La Heads PR4 131 F1
Weston Pl 4 FY1 129 D1
Weston St 9 PR2 95 D8
Westover Ave LA5 217 E5
Westover Cl L31 5 C1
Westover Gr LA5 217 E5
Westover Rd Maghull L31 5 C1
Warton, Carnforth LA5 217 E5
Westover St LA4 212 E5
Westside FY4 109 F8
Westway Burnley BB11 126 D6
Freckleton PR4 92 A6
Fulwood PR2 117 A4
Hightown L38 2 F4
Maghull L31 5 C2
Westway Ct PR2 117 B4
Westway Sch BB12 126 F8
Westwell Gr 2 FY1 129 C4
Westwell Rd 3 PR6 60 D1
Westwell St Darwen BB3 80 E4
13 Great Harwood BB6 123 C5
Westwood Ave
Blackpool FY3 129 E4
2 Fleetwood FY7 193 E3
Poulton-le-F FY6 151 E3
Rishton BB1 123 A1
Westwood Cl PR8 34 E3
Westwood Ct BB1 101 A6
Westwood Mews FY8 90 A3
Westwood Rd
Blackburn BB1 101 B4
Burnley BB12 126 C8
Clayton Brook PR5,PR6 77 C4
Leyland PR5 76 A2
Lytham St Anne's FY8 90 A3
Westwood St BB5 103 B7
Wetherall St PR2 116 D1
Wetherby Ave FY4 109 B5
Wetherfield Cl LA1 214 A4
Weymouth Rd FY3 129 F3
Weythorne Dr BL9 32 F4
Whalley Abbey BB7 143 B5
Whalley Banks BB2 100 D4
Whalley CE Prim Sch
BB7 143 C5
Whalley Cres Darwen BB3 81 B1
Staining FY3 130 E5
Whalley Dr Formby L37 12 A2
Ormskirk L39 6 D8
Rawtenstall BB4 85 A4
Whalley Gdns OL12 51 B1
Whalley Ind Pk BB7 143 D8
Whalley La FY4 110 A8
Whalley New Rd BB1 121 F1
Whalley Old Rd
Billington BB6,BB7 143 B3
Blackburn BB1 101 A7
Sunny Bower BB1 122 B1
Whalley Pl FY8 89 B6
Whalley Range BB1 100 F6
Whalley Rd
Accrington BB5 103 B7
Bank Lane BL0 49 E7
Barrow BB7 164 D2
Billington BB6,BB7 142 F3
Clayton-le-M BB5,BB6 123 F5
Clitheroe BB7 164 D5
Heskin Green PR7 40 D4
Hurst Green BB7 163 B1
Lancaster LA1 213 F4
Langho BB6 142 D1
Langho BB6 142 D2
Mellor Brook BB2 120 C3
Padiham BB12 125 B8
Read BB12 144 C1
Rochdale OL12 51 B1
Sabden BB7 144 D6
Turner Green BB2,PR5 119 C2
Whalley Rd *continued*
Wilpshire BB1 122 B7
Whalley St
2 Bamber Bridge PR5 96 F2
Blackburn BB1 100 E6
Burnley BB10 147 A1
5 Chorley PR7 42 C7
5 Clitheroe BB7 164 D8
Whalley Sta BB7 143 B6
Whalley Terr BB3 80 B6
Whalleys Rd WN8 18 B5
Wham Bottom La OL12 51 D4
Wham Brook Cl BB5 102 B5
Wham Hey PR4 75 A7
Wham La New Longton PR4 75 A7
Walmer Bridge PR4 74 D4
Whams La LA2 204 D7
Wharf Ho BB2 100 B1
Wharf St Blackburn BB1 100 F5
Lytham St Anne's FY8 90 C3
Rishton BB1 123 C1
Wharfdale LA2 207 B4
Wharfdale Ave BB10 147 B4
Wharfdale Ct FY6 151 C3
Wharfe Ct LA3 213 B3
Wharfedale FY4 109 F7
Wharfedale Ave
Fulwood PR2 117 E5
Thornton FY5 173 B3
Wharfedale Cl
Blackburn BB2 79 D7
Leyland PR5 59 A7
Wharfedale Rd LA1 210 D8
Wharton Ave FY5 173 D1
Whave's La PR6 78 D4
Wheat La L40 25 A4
Wheat St Accrington BB5 103 A6
Padiham BB12 125 D7
Wheatacre WN8 8 E8
Wheatcroft Ave BB12 146 D8
Wheatfield PR5 58 A8
Wheatfield Cl 1 FY5 150 F7
Wheatfield Ct 8 LA1 210 E8
Wheatfield St
Lancaster LA1 210 E8
Rishton BB1 123 B2
Wheathead La BB9 168 B8
Wheatholme St BB4 85 B2
Wheatlands Cres FY3 130 C2
Wheatley Cl Burnley BB12 126 D7
Fence BB12 146 D7
Wheatley Dr PR3 139 B8
Wheatley Gr BB9 168 C3
Wheatley Lane Prim Sch
BB12 146 E8
Wheatley Lane Rd
Barrowford BB9 168 B2
Fence BB12 146 E8
Wheatsheaf Ave PR3 139 A7
Wheatsheaf Wlk
4 Ormskirk L39 15 E5
Standish WN6 28 D1
Wheel La PR3 196 A6
Wheelton La PR5 76 A3
Wheelwrights Cl BB7 225 C3
Wheelwrights Wharf L40 22 F4
Whernside FY4 109 F7
Whernside Cl BB18 200 A2
Whernside Cres PR2 117 D5
Whernside Gr LA5 217 F2
Whernside Rd LA1 213 D3
Whernside Way PR5 76 C1
Whimberry Cl 1 PR6 42 E8
Whimbrel Dr FY5 173 A4
Whin Ave LA5 216 B6
Whin Dr LA5 216 B6
Whin Gr LA5 216 B6
Whin La PR3 153 B8
Whinberry Ave BB4 85 A1
Whinbrick Cotts PR4 112 B6
Whinbrick Terr PR4 112 C5
Whincroft BB11 126 E2
Whinfell Dr LA1 211 A3
Whinfield Ave
6 Chorley PR6 60 D1
Fleetwood FY7 193 E2
Whinfield La PR2 95 A8
Whinfield Pl
Blackburn BB2 100 A6
Preston PR2 95 A8
Whinfield St 8 BB5 124 A1
Whinney Brow PR3 204 C3
Whinney Heys Rd FY3 130 A6
Whinney Hill Rd BB5 124 C1
Whinney La Blackburn BB2 100 C8
Langho BB6 142 D1
Mellor BB2 121 B2
Whinneyfield La PR4 135 D2
Whinny La Euxton PR7 59 E3
Knott End-on-S FY6 194 E4
Waddington BB7 185 E6
Whinnysty La LA3 212 A1
Whinpark Ave FY3 130 A6
Whins Ave BB7 144 E7
Whins La Read BB12 144 E3
Wheelton PR6 61 A8
Whins The BB7 144 E7
Whinsands Cl PR2 117 D5
Whinsfell View LA4 212 E5
Whipp Ave BB7 164 D7
Whitaker St BB5 103 B7
Whitbarrow Sq 8 LA1 211 A8
Whitburn WN8 17 D1
Whitburn Rd L33 1 A4
Whitby Ave Fulwood PR2 115 F5
Southport PR9 53 D6
Whitby Dr BB2 101 A1
Whitby Pl PR2 115 F5
Whitby Rd
Lytham St Anne's FY8 110 A1
Morecambe LA4 212 F5
White Acre Rd BB5 103 E2
White Ash Est BB5 102 D4
White Ash La BB5 102 D3
White Birk Cl BL8 48 F2
White Bull St 4 BB12 126 C6
White Carr La Bury BL9 50 A1
Cleveleys FY5 151 A8
Hollins Lane PR3 204 E4
Moor Side PR4 133 C2
White Cross St LA1 210 F7
White Gate Fold PR7 41 E3
White Gr BB8 169 C6
White Hill Cl OL12 51 D4
White Horse Cl BL6 31 C5
White Horse La PR3 156 E1
White Hough Outdoor
Ed Ctr BB12 167 E5
White House La
Drummersdale L40 36 C1
Lane Heads PR3 154 E4
White Lea PR3 199 C1
White Lee Ave BB8 170 C2
White Lee La PR3 180 C2
White Lund Ave LA3 212 F2
White Lund Rd LA3 212 F2
White Lund Trad Est LA3 212 G2
White Mdw PR2 115 E3
White Moss La FY6 174 E4
White Moss Rd WN8 8 C7
White Moss Rd S WN8 8 D7
White Rd BB2 100 B6
White St Burnley BB12 126 B6
Colne BB8 169 B4
White Walls Cl BB8 169 A3
Whiteacre WN6 28 A2
Whiteacre La BB6 143 E8
Whitebeam Cl
Cleveleys FY5 172 F5
Penwortham PR1 95 B3
Whitebeck La LA6 234 B4
Whitebirk Dr BB1 101 C8
Whitebirk Ind Est BB1 122 C1
Whitebirk Rd BB1 101 D5
Whitechapel Cty Prim Sch
PR3 158 D7
Whitecotes Dr FY8 90 D4
Whitecrest Ave 3 FY5 172 F4
Whitecroft Ave 8 BB4 84 B2
Whitecroft Cl BB4 84 B2
Whitecroft La BB2 120 E2
Whitecroft Mdws BB4 84 B2
Whitecroft View BB5 103 E2
Whitefield Cl L38 2 F2
Whitefield Cty Prim Sch
BB9 147 C8
Whitefield La L40 38 C3
Whitefield Mdws 5 PR5 96 F1
Whitefield Pl LA3 212 F2
Whitefield Prim Sch PR1 95 A4
Whitefield Rd PR1 95 A4
Whitefield Rd E PR1 95 B4
Whitefield Rd W PR1 95 A4
Whitefield St BB12 125 C4
Whitefriar Cl PR2 116 A5
Whitegate LA3 212 G3
Whitegate Cl BB12 125 E7
Whitegate Dr FY3 129 E3
Whitegate Gdns BB12 125 E7
Whitegate Lodge 4 FY1 129 E3
Whitehalgh La BB6 142 C1
Whitehall Ave WN6 19 E8
Whitehall La Blackrod BL6 30 D3
Grindleton BB7 224 A1
Whitehall Rd
Blackburn BB2 100 B7
Darwen BB3 64 A5
Whitehall St Darwen BB3 64 B5
Nelson BB9 168 F1
Rochdale OL12 51 F1
Whitehaven Cl
Blackburn BB2 101 A1
Southport PR8 20 B3
Whitehaven St 7 BB11 126 E5
Whitehead Cl FY3 130 D5
Whitehead St
Blackburn BB2 100 C5
10 Rawtenstall BB4 85 A3
Whitehey WN8 8 E8
Whitehey Rd WN8 8 E8
Whitehill Rd FY4 110 E6
Whiteholme Dr FY6 151 B6
Whiteholme Pl 3 PR2 115 E1
Whiteholme Rd FY5 150 E7
Whitehough Pl BB9 169 B1
Whitehouse Ave L37 12 A3
Whitehouse La L37 12 A3
Whiteledge Rd WN8 9 B6
Whitelees Way FY6 151 D3
Whitelens Ave 4 PR2 115 C1
Whiteley Ave BB2 100 A1
Whiteley St BB4 84 C1
Whiteleys La L40 16 D2
Whitelow Rd BL0 49 E5
Whitely Gr L33 1 A6
Whitemoor Rd BB8 191 C2
Whitemoss OL12 51 B2
Whitemoss Ave FY3 130 B7
Whitendale 8 LA1 213 C2
Whitendale Cres BB1 101 A3
Whitendale Dr
Bamber Bridge PR5 76 F8
Hest Bank LA5 215 F2
Whitendale Hall PR1 116 F1
Whitendale Wlk BB1 101 A3
Whitepits La LA2 233 D5
Whiterails Dr L39 15 D6
Whiterails Mews L39 15 D6
Whiteray Rd 9 LA1 213 D2
Whiteside Fold OL12 51 A1
Whiteside St 7 FY1 129 C6
Whiteside Way FY5 172 E3
Whitestock WN8 8 E8
Whitethorn Cl PR6 77 A2
Whitethorn Mews FY8 110 A2
Whitethorn Sq 4 PR2 115 D1
Whitethorne Mews FY5 151 C8
Whitewalls Dr BB8 169 A4
Whitewalls Ind Est BB8 169 A3
Whitewell Cl PR3 178 D3
Whitewell Dr BB7 164 C7
Whitewell Pl 11 BB1 100 F6
Whitewell Rd BB5 103 D8
Whitewell Vale BB4 85 F2
Whitewood Cl FY8 89 E4
Whitley Ave
4 Blackpool FY3 129 D5
Cleveleys FY5 172 E5
Whitley Rd WN8 19 D3
Whitmoor Cl 7 LA4 212 E5
Whitmore Dr PR2 118 A2
Whitmore Gr PR2 118 A2
Whitmore Pl PR2 118 A2
Whitstone Dr WN8 9 D7
Whittaker Ave FY3 129 E7
Whittaker Cl BB12 126 B8
Whittaker St BB2 100 C5
Whittakers La BB7 186 F8
Whittam Ave FY4 129 E1
Whittam Cres BB7 143 B6
Whittam Rd Chorley PR7 42 B5
Whalley BB7 143 B6
Whittam St BB11 126 F5
Whitters La PR3 198 D2
Whittingham Dr BL0 49 C3
Whittingham La
Goosnargh PR3 137 C5
Grimsargh PR2 138 B2
Whittingham Rd PR3 138 F7
Whittle Brow PR7 41 C1
Whittle Cl BB7 186 F1
Whittle Dr L39 15 E7
Whittle Gn PR4 135 E3
Whittle Hill Egerton BL7 46 E3
Woodplumpton PR4 135 E3
Whittle La WN6,WN8 26 F4
Whittle Pk PR6 77 B2
Whittle St Haslingden BB4 84 A2
Rawtenstall BB4 85 A3
Whittle-le-Woods CE Sch
PR6 60 B8
Whittlefield Cty Prim Sch
BB12 126 D7
Whittles St OL13 70 B8
Whittlewood Dr BB5 124 B1
Whitton Mews 5 BL6 31 B4
Whittycroft Ave BB9 168 E6
Whittycroft Dr BB9 168 E6
Whitwell Ave 4 FY4 109 C5
Whitwell Cl WN6 28 D2
Whitwell Gdns BL6 31 B5
Whitworth Dr PR7 42 A7
Whitworth High Sch OL12 51 C8
Whitworth Rake OL12 51 D8
Whitworth Rd OL12 51 F2
Whitworth Sq OL12 51 D8
Whitworth St Horwich BL6 31 C2
Kirkham PR4 112 F6
Whitworth Way BB18 200 C4
Wholesome La
Drummersdale PR9 36 E3
New Longton PR4 74 E5
Whytha Rd BB7 189 D6
Wicken Tree Row BB12 144 F3
Wickentree Holt OL12 51 A1
Wickliffe St 9 BB9 168 F1
Wicklow Ave FY8 90 E5
Wicks Cres L37 11 C4
Wicks Gdns L37 11 D3
Wicks Gn L37 11 C3
Wicks Green Cl L37 11 C3
Wicks La L37 11 D3
Wickworth St BB9 148 A7
Widford Wlk BL6 30 E1
Widgeon Cl 8 FY5 172 F4
Widow Hill Rd BB10 147 D1
Wigan La
Adlington PR7,WN1 29 D7
Chorley PR7 42 E2
Wigan Rd
Bamber Bridge PR5 76 E7
Euxton PR6,PR7 59 C5
Ormskirk L39 16 A5
Skelmersdale WN8 8 F8
Westhead L40 16 E4
Wiggins La L40 37 B6
Wight Moss Way PR8 34 D3
Wignall St 8 PR1 117 C1
Wignalls Mdw L38 2 F3
Wigston Cl PR8 20 B4
Wigton Ave PR5 58 D7
Wilbraham St PR1 117 C1
Wilcove WN8 17 F1
Wild La FY4 110 D4
Wilderswood Ave BL6 31 C4
Wilderswood Cl PR6 77 C2
Wilderswood Ct BL6 31 D4
Wilding's La FY8 89 B8
Wildman St
3 Blackpool FY3 129 D7
Preston PR1 116 E2
Wildoaks Dr FY5 151 D8
Wilds Pl BL0 49 B5
Wildwood Cl BL0 49 A4

Wilfield St 7 BB11 126 E6
Wilford St FY3 129 E7
Wilfred Dr BL9 32 B4
Wilfred St BB5 103 C4
Wilfrid's Pl WN6 28 F1
Wilkie Ave BB11 126 E2
Wilkin Sq 6 BB7 164 E8
Wilkinson Ave FY3 129 E4
Wilkinson Mount 6
BB18 201 B2
Wilkinson St
Bamber Bridge PR5 76 B8
Barrowford BB9 168 C2
Haslingden BB4 84 B4
Higham BB12 145 F5
Nelson BB9 147 E7
Rawtenstall BB11 105 B4
Wilkinson Way FY6 194 F5
Willacy La PR4 134 E3
Willacy Par LA3 212 B2
Willard Ave WN5 10 D3
Willaston Ave BB9 168 E8
William Henry St 6 PR1 96 C8
William Herbert St 13
BB1 100 F6
William Hopwood St 8
BB1 101 A4
William St Accrington BB5 103 C7
Bacup OL13 70 C8
Blackburn BB2 100 E2
3 Blackpool FY3 129 E7
Brierfield BB9 147 B6
Carnforth LA5 217 D3
Colne BB8 169 E4
11 Darwen BB3 81 A1
5 Earby BB18 201 B1
Enfield BB5 124 A1
Horwich BL6 31 A3
17 Nelson BB9 168 E1
Ramsbottom BL0 67 C1
11 Tardy Gate PR5 76 A8
Whitworth OL12 70 C1
William Thompson
Rec Ctr BB11 127 A5
William Young Cl PR1 117 C2
Williams Ave LA4 213 C6
Williams La PR2 117 C7
Williams Pl 2 BB9 147 F8
Williams Rd BB10 127 B8
Williamson Rd LA1 211 A8
Willing Dr BB2 101 A1
Willis Rd BB2 100 A2
Willis St 6 BB11 126 E5
Willoughby Ave FY5 172 D2
Willoughby St 6 BB1 100 E6
Willow Ave BB4 85 A4
Willow Bank
Bilsborrow PR3 157 A5
Darwen BB3 64 A6
Willow Bank Ct FY6 151 B5
Willow Bank La BB3 80 F1
Willow Brook
Accrington BB5 103 B6
Shirdley Hill L39 22 A6
Willow Chase PR4 112 D4
Willow Cl Adlington PR6 30 B8
Bamber Bridge PR5 76 A8
Barrowford BB9 168 B1
Clayton-le-M BB5 123 E3
Forton PR3 204 B3
Freckleton PR4 92 A5
Gregson Lane PR5 97 E1
Penwortham PR1 95 A4
Thornton FY5 173 D1
Willow Coppice PR2 115 E3
Willow Cres
Burscough Bridge L40 24 F6
Clayton-le-W PR5 76 D3
Fulwood PR2 117 E2
Willow Ct FY6 152 A3
Willow Dr Barrow BB6 143 D8
Charnock Richard PR7 41 D3
Freckleton PR4 92 A5
Garstang PR3 199 C1
Poulton-le-F FY6 130 D8
Skelmersdale WN8 17 E1
Wrea Green PR4 112 C4
Willow End L40 24 F4
Willow Field PR6 77 C3
Willow Field Chase PR5 98 B2
Willow Gn 2 Ormskirk L39 15 F5
Preston PR2 95 A8
Willow Gr Blackpool FY3 151 A1
Formby L37 11 F4
Goosnargh PR3 137 D6
Hambleton FY6 174 B2
Morecambe LA4 213 B6
Rufford L40 38 A3
Southport PR9 34 E7
West Bradford BB7 186 D7
Willow Hey
Skelmersdale WN8 17 F1
Tarleton PR4 56 A7
Willow La LA1 210 C7
Willow Lodge FY8 89 C7
Willow Mill LA2 231 C3
Willow Mount BB1 121 F3
Willow Pk BB5 102 C2
Willow Pl PR4 153 F1
Willow Rd Chorley PR6 60 E2
Wymott PR5 57 F6
Willow St Accrington BB5 103 B6
Blackburn BB1 101 A7
Burnley BB12 126 E6
Bury BL9 32 B3
Clayton-le-M BB5 123 E3
Darwen BB3 80 F1
Fleetwood FY7 194 A4
Willow St continued
Great Harwood BB6 123 C4
Haslingden BB4 84 B3
Rawtenstall BB4 68 E8
Willow Terr FY3 130 C6
Willow Tree Ave
Broughton PR3 136 D3
Rawtenstall BB4 84 E2
Willow Tree Cres PR5 75 D1
Willow Tree Gdns 3 FY5 173 D1
Willow Trees Dr BB1 121 C1
Willow Way PR4 74 F7
Willow Wlk WN8 18 B4
Willow-Dale FY5 173 D1
Willowbank Ave FY4 109 E6
Willowbank Cotts PR5 57 B2
Willowcroft Dr FY6 174 B1
Willowdene FY5 172 E1
Willowfield Rd LA3 209 A7
Willowhey PR9 52 F4
Willowmead Pk FY8 111 F2
Willowmead Way OL12 51 A2
Willows Ave Cleveleys FY5 172 E1
Lytham St Anne's FY8 89 E3
Willows La Accrington BB5 103 A3
Kirkham PR4 112 F5
Willows Park La PR3 139 B8
Willows RC Prim Sch The
PR4 112 F5
Willows The Coppull PR7 28 E8
Lytham St Anne's FY8 89 E3
Mawdesley L40 39 C2
Mellor Brook BB2 120 C3
Southport PR8 33 F6
Whitworth OL12 51 C5
Wills Ave L31 5 C2
Willshaw Rd FY2 150 B1
Willy La LA2 203 D6
Wilmar Rd PR5 76 C2
Wilmcote Gr PR8 20 B4
Wilmore Cl BB8 169 C5
Wilmot Rd PR2 117 E3
Wilpshire Banks BB1 121 F4
Wilpshire Golf Course
BB1 122 A6
Wilpshire Rd BB1 122 E4
Wilson Cl PR4 56 A7
Wilson Dr PR4 153 F1
Wilson Fold BB12 126 B6
Wilson Gr LA3 208 E8
Wilson Sq FY5 150 D7
Wilson St Blackburn BB2 100 D2
Bury BL9 32 A1
Clitheroe BB7 164 E7
Foulridge BB8 191 D1
Horwich BL6 31 A4
Wilson's Endowed
CE Prim Sch LA6 231 B8
Wilton Cl LA1 214 A4
Wilton Gr PR1 95 A4
Wilton Par FY1 129 B7
Wilton Pl 3 PR5 76 B1
Wilton St Barrowford BB9 168 D3
Brierfield BB9 147 B5
Burnley BB10 147 B1
Wiltshire Ave BB12 126 B7
Wiltshire Dr BB4 67 B8
Wiltshire Mews PR4 115 D5
Wilvere Ct FY5 150 C7
Wilvere Dr FY5 150 C8
Wilworth Cres BB1 121 E2
Wimberley Banks BB1 100 F7
Wimberley Gdns 7 BB1 100 E6
Wimberley Pl 8 BB1 100 E6
Wimberley St BB1 100 E7
Wimbledon Ave FY5 150 D7
Wimbledon Ct FY5 150 D6
Wimborne Cl BL6 31 F1
Wimbourne Pl FY4 109 B6
Wimbrick Cl L39 15 D4
Wimbrick Cres L39 15 D3
Winchcombe Rd FY5 150 E7
Winchester Ave
Accrington BB5 103 C7
5 Blackpool FY4 129 D1
Chorley PR7 42 E4
Lancaster LA1 211 B5
Morecambe LA4 212 G6
Winchester Cl
Morecambe LA3 212 E2
4 Orrell WN5 10 F7
Winchester Dr FY6 151 B6
Winchester Rd
Longshaw WN5 10 D2
Padiham BB12 125 D6
Winchester St BB1 101 A3
Winchester Way PR3 178 B7
Winckley Ct 11 PR1 95 F7
Winckley Rd
Clayton-le-M BB5 123 F2
Preston PR1 95 E6
Winckley Sq PR1 95 F7
Winckley St 9 PR1 95 F7
Winder Garth LA6 234 B1
Winder La PR3 204 B2
Windermere Ave
Accrington BB5 124 D1
Burnley BB10 147 A2
Clitheroe BB7 164 C7
Colne BB8 169 F6
Fleetwood FY7 172 D8
Leyland PR5 76 A3
Morecambe LA4 212 G4
Windermere Cl 4 BB1 100 F6
Windermere Cres PR8 20 C3
Windermere Ct 4 LA4 212 G4
Windermere Dr
Adlington PR6 43 B1
Windermere Dr continued
Darwen BB3 81 C3
Maghull L31 5 E2
Rainford Junction WA11 8 F2
Ramsbottom BL0 49 C7
Rishton BB1 123 A1
Windermere Ho PR1 95 B4
Windermere Rd
Bacup OL13 87 A3
Blackpool FY4 109 C8
Bolton-le-S LA5 216 A4
Carnforth LA5 216 E8
5 Chorley PR6 42 E7
Fulwood PR2 117 C4
Hightown L38 3 A4
Lancaster LA1 211 B8
Orrell WN5 10 F8
Padiham BB12 145 C2
Preston PR1 118 A1
Windermere Sq FY8 109 F2
Windfield Cl L33 1 A6
Windflower Dr PR5 76 E2
Windgate Much Hoole PR4 73 E2
Skelmersdale WN8 17 F1
Tarleton PR4 56 A5
Windham Pl LA1 213 C3
Windholme 6 LA1 213 C2
Windle Ash L31 5 C2
Windmill Ave
Kirkham PR4 113 C4
Ormskirk L39 15 F5
Windmill Cl FY3 130 E5
Windmill Ct 9 LA1 211 A3
Windmill Farm L40 37 B4
Windmill Hts WN8 10 A8
Windmill La PR6 78 B7
Windmill Pl FY4 109 F6
Windmill Rd WN8 9 F7
Windmill St LA1 210 D8
Windmill View PR4 113 A6
Windrows WN8 17 F1
Windrush Ave BL0 49 A2
Windrush The OL12 51 C4
Windsor Ave Adlington PR7 29 F6
Blackpool FY4 109 B8
Church BB5 103 A8
Clitheroe BB7 164 C7
Fulwood PR2 116 B2
Haslingden BB4 84 A1
Lancaster LA1 211 B5
Longridge PR3 138 F7
Morecambe LA4 212 D3
New Longton PR4 95 A1
Newchurch BB4 85 E1
Penwortham PR1 95 C3
Thornton FY5 173 B2
Windsor Cl Blackburn BB1 101 B3
Burscough L40 24 E3
Chorley PR7 42 B7
Ramsbottom BL8 49 A1
Read BB12 144 D2
Windsor Ct
Poulton-le-F FY6 151 E3
Southport PR8 33 E4
Windsor Dr Brinscall PR6 61 E8
Fulwood PR2 116 D6
Horwich BL6 31 E2
Windsor Gdns PR3 178 B7
Windsor Gr LA4 212 D4
Windsor Lodge 3 FY8 89 D4
Windsor Pl
Barnoldswick BB18 200 D3
1 Fleetwood FY7 194 B5
Windsor Rd
Bamber Bridge PR5 96 D3
Blackburn, Beardwood BB2 100 B6
Blackburn, Knuzden
Brook BB1 101 E4
Chorley PR7 42 B7
Darwen BB3 80 F3
Eccleston PR7 40 C7
Formby L37 11 F1
Garstang PR3 178 B7
Great Harwood BB6 123 D5
Lytham St Anne's FY8 89 A5
Lytham St Anne's,
Ansdell FY8 89 D4
Morecambe LA3 212 C3
Normoss FY3 130 B7
Orrell WN8 10 A8
Southport PR9 34 D7
Windsor St Accrington BB5 103 C6
Burnley BB12 126 C6
Colne BB8 169 E5
Nelson BB9 148 A7
Windsor Terr FY7 194 B5
Windy Bank BB8 169 E5
Windy Harbour Rd
Singleton FY6 153 A4
Southport PR8 20 E7
Windy Hill LA2 233 E8
Windy St PR3 182 E3
Windyhill 35 LA1 210 F8
Winery La PR1,PR5 96 C5
Winewall La BB8 170 C5
Winewall Rd BB8 170 B5
Wingate Ave
Cleveleys FY5 150 D7
Morecambe LA4 212 F4
Wingate Pl FY5 150 D8
Wingate Wlk L33 1 A3
Wingate-Saul Rd LA1 210 E7
Wingates 2 PR1 95 C3
Wingrove Rd FY7 193 F2
Winifred Ave BL9 32 F4
Winifred La L39 6 B8
Winifred St Blackpool FY1 129 B4
Ramsbottom BL0 49 B5
Winifred St continued
Rochdale OL12 51 B1
Winmarleigh CE Prim Sch
PR3 198 E5
Winmarleigh Rd
Lancaster LA1 211 A2
Preston PR2 116 B1
Winmarleigh St 3 BB1 101 C5
Winmarleigh Wlk BB1 101 C4
Winmoss Dr L33 1 A5
Winnipeg Cl BB2 100 B8
Winnipeg Pl FY2 150 E3
Winscar Wlk FY6 151 B3
Winsford Cres FY5 150 C8
Winsford Wlk BB11 126 B5
Winslow Ave FY6 151 B5
Winslow Cl 7 PR1 95 E2
Winsor Ave PR5 59 B8
Winstanley Coll WN5 10 F3
Winstanley Gr 1 FY1 129 C5
Winstanley Rd Orrell WN5 10 F3
Skelmersdale WN8 8 F8
Winster Cl PR5 97 E4
Winster Ct BB5 123 E2
Winster Pk LA1 213 C2
Winster Pl FY4 130 D1
Winster Wlk LA1 213 C2
Winsters The WN8 17 F1
Winston Ave Cleveleys FY5 172 F2
Lytham St Anne's FY8 89 B6
Winston Cres PR8 34 E2
Winston Rd BB1 100 D7
Winter Hey La BL6 31 B3
Winter Hill Cl PR2 118 C7
Winterburn Rd BB2 80 C7
Winterley Dr BB5 124 E1
Winterton Rd BB3 81 A2
Winthorpe Ave LA4 212 G3
Winton Ave Blackpool FY4 130 A1
Fulwood PR2 116 F6
Winton Gn BL6 31 F1
Winton Rd FY4 130 A2
Winward Cl BB3 80 F6
Wiseman Cl LA4 212 F4
Wiseman St BB11 126 F6
Wisp Hill Gr LA2 214 F6
Wisteria Dr BB3 81 B7
Wiswell Cl Brierfield BB10 147 E2
Rawtenstall BB4 85 A4
Wiswell La BB7 143 D6
Wiswell Shay BB7 143 E7
Witham Cl WN6 28 D1
Witham Rd WN8 17 D1
Withens Rd L31 5 D3
Withers St BB1 100 F4
Witherslack Cl LA4 212 E3
Withgill Piggety Cotts
BB7 163 E6
Within Gr BB5 103 D8
Withington La PR7 40 E2
Withins Field L38 2 F3
Withins La L37 4 A7
Withnell Fold Old Rd PR6 78 E1
Withnell Fold Prim Sch
PR6 78 C3
Withnell Gr PR6 60 E1
Withnell Rd FY4 109 B8
Withy Ct PR2 116 E3
Withy Grove Cl PR5 96 F1
Withy Grove Cres PR5 96 F1
Withy Grove Rd PR5 96 F1
Withy Par PR2 116 E4
Withy Trees Ave PR5 96 F1
Withy Trees Cl PR5 96 F1
Witney Ave BB2 79 E8
Witton Ave FY7 193 E1
Witton Gr FY7 193 E1
Witton Par BB2 100 C3
Witton Park Ctry Pk BB2 99 F4
Witton Park High Sch
BB2 100 A4
Witton St PR1 96 B8
Woborrow Rd LA3 208 E8
Woburn Cl BB5 103 E3
Woburn Gn PR5 76 B2
Woburn Rd FY1 129 C7
Woburn Rise PR3 178 D2
Wold The PR6 61 A3
Wolfenden Gn BB4 68 F8
Wollaton Dr PR8 34 F3
Wolseley Cl PR5 59 A8
Wolseley Pl 21 PR1 96 A7
Wolseley Rd PR1 95 E5
Wolseley St
Blackburn BB2 100 D1
Lancaster LA1 211 A8
Wolsey Cl FY5 172 E3
Wolsley Rd Blackpool FY1 129 B1
Fleetwood FY7 193 F4
Wolverton WN8 8 F8
Wolverton Ave FY2 150 B2
Wood Bank Haslingden BB4 66 F6
Penwortham PR1 95 C3
Wood Cl BB9 168 A5
Wood Close Gdns LA5 237 B2
Wood Clough Platts BB9 147 A5
Wood End Brierfield BB12 146 F3
Kingsfold PR1 95 C1
Wood End Rd PR6 77 B2
Wood Gn Kirkham PR4 113 B7
Leyland PR5 75 E2
Wood Green Dr FY5 150 F8
Wood Hey Gr OL12 51 F4
Wood House La BB7 223 A8
Wood La Haskayne L37, L39 13 D1
Heskin Green PR7 40 E3
Hoscar L40 25 E5
Mawdesley L40 39 D5
Wood La continued
Parbold WN8 26 D2
Wrightington Bar WN6 27 E8
Wood Lea Bank 9 BB4 68 F8
Wood Lea Rd BB4 68 F8
Wood Nook 1 BB4 85 A7
Wood Park Rd FY1 129 E1
Wood Road La BL8,BL9 49 C1
Wood St Blackpool FY1 129 B5
Brierfield BB9 147 B5
Burnley BB10 127 A8
Church BB5 102 E5
Colne BB8 169 E4
Darwen BB3 80 F1
Fleetwood FY7 172 E8
Great Harwood BB6 123 E5
Hapton BB12 125 C4
Horwich BL6 31 C3
1 Lancaster LA1 210 F8
Lytham St Anne's FY8 88 E6
Poulton-le-F FY6 152 A3
Ramsbottom BL0 49 B5
Wood Street Livesey Fold
BB3 80 F2
Wood Terr BB7 187 E5
Wood View Blackburn BB2 99 F1
Burton in L LA6 236 C3
Wood View La FY6 174 C7
Wood's Brow PR3 140 B6
Wood's La PR3 177 A6
Woodacre Rd PR2 118 A2
Woodale Laithe BB9 168 C3
Woodale Rd PR6 77 B3
Woodbank Ave BB3 80 E2
Woodbine Gdns BB12 126 C7
Woodbine Rd
Blackburn BB2 100 B6
Burnley BB12 126 C6
Woodbine Terr OL14 108 B1
Woodbridge Gdns OL12 51 C2
Woodburn Cl BB2 100 A8
Woodbury Ave
Blackburn BB2 100 D2
Fence BB12 146 D7
Woodcock Cl FY5 173 A5
Woodcock Est PR5 76 B6
Woodcock Fold PR7 40 C7
Woodcock Hill Rd BB2 99 B3
Woodcote Cl L33 1 A4
Woodcourt Ave BB11 126 D3
Woodcrest BB1 121 F5
Woodcroft
Appley Bridge WN6 19 E6
Skelmersdale WN8 8 F8
Woodcroft Ave BB4 84 F5
Woodcroft Cl PR1 95 C2
Woodcroft St BB4 84 F5
Woodfall PR7 60 B2
Woodfield PR5 77 C6
Woodfield Ave
Accrington BB5 103 D3
3 Blackpool FY1 129 B2
Rochdale OL12 51 E2
Woodfield Ct FY5 173 B1
Woodfield Rd
Blackpool FY1 129 B2
Chorley PR7 60 C1
Ormskirk L39 15 D3
Thornton FY5 173 D1
Woodfield Terr BB9 147 C5
Woodfield View BB7 143 C5
Woodfields BB7 163 B3
Woodfold PR1 95 B3
Woodfold Cl BB2 120 C3
Woodfold La PR3 199 C5
Woodfold Pl BB2 100 B5
Woodford Copse PR7 42 A7
Woodgate LA3 213 B2
Woodgate Ave BL9 32 D4
Woodgate Hill Rd
Bury BL9 32 C4
Bury,Woodgate Hill BL9 32 D4
Woodgates Rd BB2 99 F5
Woodgrove Rd BB11 127 B3
Woodhall Cres PR5 97 E4
Woodhall Gdns FY6 174 C2
Woodhart La PR7 40 C5
Woodhead Cl
Ramsbottom BL0 49 C4
Rawtenstall BB4 86 A2
Woodhead Rd BB12 144 D2
Woodhey High Sch BL0 49 A3
Woodhey Rd BL0 49 A3
Woodhill Ave LA4 212 D3
Woodhill Cl LA4 212 D3
Woodhill La LA4 212 D4
Woodhouse Rd FY5 151 E8
Woodhouse St 1 BB11 127 B4
Woodhurst Dr WN6 28 D1
Woodland Ave Bacup OL13 86 F5
Bescar L40 22 F7
Thornton FY5 173 B2
Woodland Cl
Hambleton FY6 174 D1
Wrea Green PR4 112 B3
Woodland Cres FY6 195 A6
Woodland Dr
Clayton-le-M BB5 123 F5
Poulton-le-F FY6 151 E1
Standish WN6 28 E2
Woodland Gr
Blackpool FY3 129 E4
Egerton BL7 46 D2
Penwortham PR1 95 B5
Woodland Pk BB7 143 C5

Woodland Pl BB3 80 F7
Woodland Rd OL12 51 C2
Woodland Terr OL13 86 F4
Woodland View
Bacup OL13 86 F4
Brinscall PR7 61 F7
Great Harwood BB6 123 C6
Woodlands Ave
Bamber Bridge PR5 97 A2
Blackburn BB2 99 E1
Fulwood PR2 117 E2
7 Kirkham PR4 112 F5
Penwortham PR1 95 E2
Woodlands Cl Formby L37 11 D2
Newton-with-S PR4 113 F3
Ormskirk L39 16 A4
Southport PR9 34 D8
Storth LA7 237 F4
Woodlands Cres PR3 136 B5
Woodlands Ct 5 FY8 89 D4
Woodlands Dr
Fulwood PR2 116 E8
Kirkham PR4 113 B7
Leyland PR5 75 F1
Morecambe LA3 212 B2
Shevington WN6 19 F4
Silverdale LA5 218 C4
Warton PR4 91 C5
West Bradford BB7 186 D7
Whalley BB7 143 C5
Woodlands Gr
Darwen BB3 80 D2
Grimsargh PR2 138 E1
Morecambe LA3 212 B2
Padiham BB12 145 B1
Woodlands Meadow PR7 42 C3
Woodlands Prim Sch L37 11 D3
Woodlands Rd
Edenfield BL0 67 D2
Formby L37 11 D3
Lancaster LA1 214 A4
Lytham St Anne's FY8 89 D4
Nelson BB9 147 F8
Woodlands Sch PR2 117 E2
Woodlands Specl Sch FY3 129 E4
Woodlands The
Brockhall Village BB6 142 C6
Garstang PR3 178 B8
6 Preston PR2 115 E1
Southport PR8 20 C5
Woodlands View
Over Kellet LA6 231 B8
12 Ramsbottom BL0 49 C6
Woodlands Way
Longton PR4 73 F8
Newsham PR3 136 B5
Woodlea Chase BB3 64 C3
Woodlea Cl PR9 53 D5
Woodlea Gdns BB9 147 D5
Woodlea Jun Sch PR5 58 F8
Woodlea Rd
Blackburn BB1 101 B4
Leyland PR5 58 F8
Woodlee Rd PR4 72 F2
Woodleigh Cl L31 5 B5
Woodley Ave
Accrington BB5 103 C4
Thornton FY5 173 D1
Woodley Park Rd WN8 18 B4
Woodman La LA6 235 F6
Woodmancote PR7 60 B2
Woodmoss La PR8, L40 35 E2
Woodnook Cty Prim Sch BB5 103 C4
Woodnook Rd WN6 19 E8
Woodpecker Hill 3 BB11 126 C5
Woodplumpton La PR3 136 C2
Woodplumpton Rd
Burnley BB11 126 F1
Fulwood PR2 116 C3
Woodplumpton PR4 135 E2
Woodplumpton, Moor Side PR4 135 D4
Woodridge Ave FY5 150 C8
Woodrow WN8 8 E8
Woodrow Dr WN8 26 A1
Woodroyd Dr BL9 32 C3
Woodruff Cl FY5 172 F5
Woodrush LA4 213 B6
Woods Brow BB2 119 D5
Woods Cl L39 14 A4
Woods Gn PR1 95 E6
Woods La PR4,PR3 134 E8
Woodsend Cl BB2 81 A8
Woodside Chorley PR7 42 E4
Euxton PR7 59 C3
Haslingden BB4 84 C1
Leyland PR5 76 C4
Woodside Ave
Clayton Green PR6 77 B1
Fulwood PR2 116 E4
New Longton PR4 74 F7
Preston PR2 117 E3
Rishton BB1 101 F8
Southport PR8 20 B3
Woodside Cl
Accrington BB5 124 F1
Orrell WN8 10 C8
Woodside Cres BB4 85 D1
Woodside Dr
Blackpool FY3 130 A5
Ramsbottom BL0 49 A5
Woodside Gr BB2 80 A8
Woodside Rd
Accrington BB5 124 F1
Huncoat BB5 103 E8
Simonstone BB12 144 E2
Woodside Terr BB9 147 C8
Woodsley St BB12 126 B5
Woodstock Ave FY5 151 C8
Woodstock Cl 8 PR5 76 C8
Woodstock Cres BB2 79 E8
Woodstock Dr PR8 20 F8
Woodstock Gdns FY4 109 B7
Woodstock St 12 OL12 51 C1
Woodtop CE Inf Sch BB11 126 D5
Woodvale Darwen BB3 80 F1
Leyland PR5 58 A8
Woodvale Ct PR9 54 A5
Woodvale Prim Sch PR8 20 D3
Woodvale Rd PR8 20 E2
Woodville Rd
Adlington PR6 42 F1
Blackburn BB1 101 A7
Brierfield BB9 147 C6
2 Chorley PR7 42 C8
Penwortham PR1 95 D2
Woodville Rd W 5 PR1 95 C2
Woodville St
Lancaster LA1 211 A8
Leyland PR5 76 B2
Woodville Terr
Darwen BB3 64 B6
Lytham St Anne's FY8 89 F3
Woodward Rd L33 1 D4
Woodway PR2 116 C4
Woodwell La LA5 218 C1
Wookey Cl PR2 117 D6
Wooley La BB5 103 F2
Woolman Rd FY1 129 C4
Woolpack BB8 169 E3
Woolwich St BB1 101 B5
Woone La BB7 164 D7
Worcester Ave
4 Accrington BB5 103 A7
Garstang PR3 178 B8
Lancaster LA1 211 B5
Leyland PR5 59 B8
Worcester Pl PR7 42 E3
Worcester Rd
Blackburn BB1 101 C5
Blackpool FY3 130 A3
Worchester Gdns PR4 115 D5
Worden Cl PR5 58 F7
Worden La Leyland PR5 59 A7
Withnell Fold PR6 78 E3
Worden Rd PR2 116 D3
Wordsworth Ave
Blackpool FY3 130 B2
Bolton-le-S LA5 216 A5
Longshaw WN5 10 D1
5 Lytham St Anne's FY8 90 D4
Orrell WN5 10 F6
Padiham BB12 125 E7
Thornton FY5 173 A2
Warton PR4 91 E6
Wordsworth Cl
Ormskirk L39 15 D6
Oswaldtwistle BB5 102 C4
Wordsworth Ct 1 FY8 89 C4
Wordsworth Dr BB6 123 B4
Wordsworth Gdns BB3 81 B1
Wordsworth Ho LA1 213 E4
Wordsworth Pl PR5 96 D2
Wordsworth Rd
Accrington BB5 103 A4
Colne BB8 169 D5
Wordsworth St
Brierfield BB10 147 F2
Burnley BB12 126 C6
5 Hapton BB12 125 C4
Wordsworth Terr PR6 60 D2
Workshop Rd LA3 208 F2
Worrall St 1 OL12 51 D2
Worsley Ave FY4 109 C7
Worsley Cl FY6 194 E5
Worsley Ct 13 BB5 102 E4
Worsley Rd FY8 89 C5
Worsley St Accrington BB5 103 D4
Haslingden BB5 84 A8
Worsthorne Prim Sch BB10 128 A6
Worston Cl
Accrington BB5 102 F4
Rawtenstall BB4 85 A4
Worston La BB6 123 F6
Worston Pl BB2 100 C5
Worswick Cres 3 BB4 85 A2
Worthing Cl PR8 33 F3
Worthing Rd PR2 116 A4
Worthington Rd FY4 110 B4
Worthy St PR6 42 E7
Wraith St BB3 64 A8
Wray Cres
Wrea Green PR4 112 C4
Wymott PR5 57 F6
Wray Ct LA1 213 E4
Wray Gr FY5 150 D8
Wray-with-Botton Endowed Prim Sch LA2 232 D6
Wraywood Ct FY7 193 C1
Wren Ave PR1 95 E5
Wren Cl Blackpool FY6 151 A4
Thornton FY5 151 D8
Wren Dr BL9 32 B4
Wren Gr FY3 129 E2
Wren St Burnley BB12 126 C6
Nelson BB9 147 F8
Preston PR1 117 B2
Wrennalls La PR7 40 B5
Wright St Chorley PR6 42 E8
Horwich BL6 31 B4
6 Kirkham PR4 112 F6
Southport PR9 34 C7
Weir OL13 87 A7
Wright St W 3 BL6 31 B4
Wrightington Hospl WN6 27 D2
Wrightington Mossy Lea Prim Sch WN6 27 F6
Wrights Fold PR5 59 C8
Wrights Terr PR8 34 B3
Wrigleys Cl L37 11 F5
Wrigleys La L37 11 F5
Written Stone La PR3 160 E1
Wroxham Cl BB10 147 D2
Wroxton Cl FY5 150 F7
Wycherley Rd OL12 51 B2
Wychnor PR2 116 B7
Wycollar Cl BB5 103 C4
Wycollar Dr BB2 100 A6
Wycollar Rd BB2 100 B6
Wycoller Ave BB10 127 D5
Wycombe Ave FY4 109 B6
Wyfordby Ave BB2 100 A7
Wyke Cop Rd PR8, PR9 35 D2
Wyke La PR8, PR9 35 E6
Wyke Wood La PR9 35 F7
Wykeham Gr OL12 51 B1
Wykeham Rd FY8 90 B4
Wyllin Rd L33 1 A2
Wymundsley PR7 60 A2
Wyndene Cl PR3 139 C8
Wyndene Gr PR4 92 B6
Wyndham Gdns FY4 109 D6
Wyndham Pl LA4 213 B6
Wynfield PR5 96 F2
Wynnstay Ave L31 5 D3
Wynnwood Ave 1 FY1 129 D8
Wynotham St BB10 147 C1
Wyre Ave PR4 113 B5
Wyre Bank PR3 155 B6
Wyre Cl
Great Eccleston PR3 154 C5
Lancaster LA3 213 B2
Wyre Cres BB3 80 D4
Wyre Ct Fleetwood FY7 193 E3
Poulton-le-F FY6 152 A3
Wyre Estuary Ctry Pk FY5 173 E3
Wyre Gr FY1 129 C3
Wyre Ho LA1 210 F7
Wyre La PR3 199 D1
Wyre Rd FY5 151 F6
Wyre Side Cl PR3 178 C8
Wyre St Fleetwood FY7 193 F3
Kirkham PR4 112 F6
Lytham St Anne's FY8 89 A7
Padiham BB12 125 D8
Preston PR2 116 C1
Wyre View FY6 194 E5
Wyredale Ct FY7 193 F3
Wyredale Rd FY8 88 C8
Wyrefields FY6 152 A3
Wyresdale Ave
Accrington BB5 103 A8
Blackpool FY2 150 D4
Morecambe LA3 212 B1
Poulton-le-F FY6 151 C3
Southport PR8 34 D4
Wyresdale Cres
Fulwood PR2 117 D4
Glasson LA2 205 E4
Scorton PR3 199 E7
Wyresdale Ct LA1 211 B7
Wyresdale Dr PR5 59 B6
Wyresdale Gdns LA1 211 B7
Wyresdale Rd
Knott End-on-S FY6 194 D5
Lancaster LA1 211 B6
Quernmore LA2 226 A6
Wyreside Dr FY6 174 B2
Wyreside Ecology Ctr FY5 173 E3
Wyreside Hall LA2 220 B7
Wytham St 6 BB12 125 D7
Wythburn Ave BB2 79 E8
Wythburn Cl BB12 126 B8
Wythorpe Croft LA4 212 E4
Wyvern Way FY6 151 C5

Y

Yale St BL7 47 D4
Yans La LA7 237 F5
Yardley Ctr L33 1 C1
Yardley Rd L33 1 C1
Yare St 7 BB4 68 F8
Yarlside La BD23 225 E4
Yarm Pl BB11 127 A6
Yarmouth Ave BB4 84 C2
Yarraville St BB4 85 A2
Yarrow Ave L31 5 F2
Yarrow Cl Croston PR5 57 B2
Withnell PR6 79 A1
Yarrow Gate PR7 42 E6
Yarrow Gr BL6 31 B4
Yarrow Pl PR5 58 D8
Yarrow Rd Chorley PR6 42 E6
Leyland PR5 58 D8
Yarrow Valley Pk PR7 42 A2
Yarrow Wlk LA3 212 E2
Yarwood St BL9 32 A2
Yates Fold BB2 100 F2
Yates Rd PR7 42 B5
Yates St FY1 129 B6
Yeadon WN8 18 B1
Yeadon Gr PR7 42 A7
Yeadon Way FY4 109 D7
Yealand Ave LA3 208 F6
Yealand Conyers CE Prim Sch LA5 219 E3
Yealand Dr LA1 211 A4
Yealand Gr LA5 217 E2
Yealand Rd LA5 219 E2
Yeargate Ind Est BL9 32 D2
Yellow Hall BB18 192 A5
Yellow House La PR8 34 B6
Yenham La LA3 209 E1
Yeomanry & Cty Mus PR5 96 B8
Yerburgh Rd BB2 120 E2
Yew Ct FY7 193 C1
Yew Gn PR4 113 B7
Yew St 10 Blackburn BB1 101 A7
2 Bury BL9 32 C3
Yew Tree Ave Euxton PR7 59 C4
Grimsargh PR2 138 C2
Yew Tree Cl Garstang PR3 178 B8
Newton-with-S PR4 113 F3
Wilpshire BB1 121 E6
Yew Tree Dr
Blackburn BB2 121 B1
Oswaldtwistle BB5 102 F3
Yew Tree Gr BB4 67 F8
Yew Tree Rd
Blackpool FY3 151 A1
Ormskirk L39 15 E7
Yewbarrow Cl BB12 146 C1
Yewdale WN8 18 A1
Yewdale Ave LA3 208 F6
Yewlands Ave
4 Bamber Bridge PR5 96 F1
Fulwood PR2 116 E6
Heskin Green PR7 40 F3
3 Leyland PR5 76 A1
Yewlands Cres PR2 116 E6
Yewlands Dr
Brierfield BB10 147 B3
Fulwood PR2 116 E6
Garstang PR3 199 C1
2 Leyland PR5 76 A1
Yewtree Ave PR2 118 A4
Yewtree Cl PR7 42 C3
Yewtree Dr LA2 233 C8
Yewtree Gr PR5 76 A7
York Ave Cleveleys FY5 172 D2
Fleetwood FY7 193 E3
Fulwood PR2 116 E4
Haslingden BB4 67 B8
Southport PR8 34 A5
York Cl
4 Bamber Bridge PR5 96 D3
Clayton-le-M BB5 123 F3
Formby L37 11 F6
Leyland PR5 58 E7
York Cres BB1 121 F3
York Dr
Great Eccleston PR3 154 C5
Kirkham PR4 113 B2
Ramsbottom BL0 49 A4
York Fields BB18 200 B1
York Gdns PR8 34 A5
York Gr PR3 178 B7
York Ho 28 PR1 96 A7
York La BB6 122 D8
York Pl Accrington BB5 103 B7
Adlington PR6 30 A8
Morecambe LA4 212 F5
York Rd Blackpool FY2 150 B4
Formby L37 12 A3
Lancaster LA1 211 A5
Langho BB1,BB6 122 D6
Lytham St Anne's FY8 88 F5
Southport PR8 33 F4
York St Accrington BB5 103 B7
Bacup OL13 86 F5
Barnoldswick BB18 200 B2
Blackburn BB2 100 E3
Blackpool FY1 129 B3
Bury BL9 32 A2
Chorley PR7 42 D7
Church BB5 102 E6
Clitheroe BB7 186 F1
Colne BB8 169 F5
Great Harwood BB6 123 D5
Nelson BB9 147 F8
Oswaldtwistle BB5 102 C3
Rawtenstall BB4 85 A7
Rishton BB1 123 A1
York Terr Blackburn BB2 79 D8
4 Southport PR9 34 C8
Yorke St 2 BB11 126 F5
Yorkshire St
Accrington BB5 103 C4
17 Bacup OL13 86 F3
Blackpool FY1 129 B3
Burnley BB11 127 B6
Huncoat BB5 124 E2
12 Nelson BB9 147 E8
Yorkshire St E LA4 212 C4
Yorkshire St W LA3 212 B4
Young Ave PR5 76 C1
Young St Blackburn BB2 100 B2
Ramsbottom BL0 49 B6

Z

Zama St 9 BL0 49 A4
Zebudah St BB2 100 C2
Zetland St Preston PR1 96 C7
Southport PR9 34 D7
Zion Rd BB1 101 A8
Zion St Bacup OL13 87 A3
Colne BB8 169 D4